Electronic Commerce 2006

A Managerial Perspective

Electronic Commerce 2006

A Managerial Perspective

Efraim Turban
University of Hawaii

David King
JDA Software Group, Inc.

Dennis Viehland
Massey University, New Zealand

Jae Lee
Singapore Management University and
Korea Advanced Institute of Science and Technology

with contributions by

Rajiv Kohli
College of William and Mary

Christy Cheung
City University of Hong Kong

Linda Lai
City University of Hong Kong

Upper Saddle River, NJ 07458

Library of Congress Cataloging-in-Publication Data

Electronic commerce 2006 : a managerial perspective / Efraim Turban . . . [et al.].
p. cm.
Includes bibliographical references and index.
ISBN 0-13-185461-5
1. Electronic commerce. 2. Electronic commerce—Management.
I. Turban, Efraim.

HF5548.32.E339 2006
658.8'72—dc22

2005048692

Executive Editor: Bob Horan
VP/Publisher: Jeff Shelstad
Development Editor: Judy Lang
Project Manager: Jeannine Ciliotta
Editorial Assistant: Ana Cordero
Media Project Development Manager: Nancy Welcher
AVP/Executive Marketing Manager: Debbie Clare
Marketing Assistant: Joanna Sabella
Managing Editor: John Roberts
Production Editor: Renata Butera
Permission Supervisor: Charles Morris
Manufacturing Buyer: Michelle Klein
Design Manager: Maria Lange
Interior Design: Jill Little
Art Director: Pat Smythe
Cover Designer: Pat Smythe
Cover Illustrator: John Bleck
Manager Print Production: Christy Mahon
Composition/Full Service Project Management: BookMasters, Inc./Sharon Anderson
Printer/Binder: R.R. Donnelley–Willard

Credits and acknowledgements borrowed from other sources and reproduced, with permission, in this textbook appear on appropriate pages within the text.

Pearson Education LTD.
Pearson Education Singapore, Pte. Ltd.
Pearson Education, Canada, Ltd
Pearson Education–Japan
Pearson Education of Australia PTY, Limited
Pearson Education North Asia Ltd
Pearson Educación de Mexico, S.A. de C.V.
Pearson Education Malaysia, Pte. Ltd

10 9 8 7 6 5 4 3 2
ISBN 0-13-185461-5

Dedicated to all those who are interested in learning about electronic commerce.

Contents in Brief

Contents

Part 5 EC Support Services 424

www.prenhall.com/turban

Online Chapter

Online Appendix

Online Technical Appendices

Online Tutorials

Preface

As we enter the third millennium, we are experiencing one of the most important changes to our daily lives—the move to an Internet-based society. According to Marc Andreessen, a pioneer of the commercial Internet, there were 800 million Internet users worldwide by the end of 2004 (Maney 2004), and that number is expected to reach 3 billion in the next decade. Internet World Stats (*internetworldstats.com*) reported in March 2005 that almost 68 percent of the U.S. population (over 2 million) surf the Internet. More interesting is the fact that over 90 percent of people between the ages of 5 and 17 surf the Internet on a regular basis. It is clear that these percentages will continue to increase, and similar trends exist in most other countries. As a result, much has changed at home, school, work, and in the government—and even in our leisure activities. Some of these changes are spreading around the globe. Others are just beginning in some countries. One of the most significant changes is in how we conduct business, especially in how we manage marketplaces and trading. For example, the senior author of this book pays all his bills online, trades stock online, buys airline and event tickets online, buys books online, and purchased his computer, printer, and memory sticks online, to cite just a few examples.

Electronic commerce (EC) describes the manner in which transactions take place over networks, mostly the Internet. It is the process of electronically buying and selling goods, services, and information. Certain EC applications, such as buying and selling stocks on the Internet, are growing very rapidly. For example, on its busiest day of 2004, Amazon.com received 2.8 million orders, versus 2.1 million on the same day in 2003. But EC is not just about buying and selling; it also is about electronically communicating, collaborating, and discovering information (sometimes referred to as *e-business*). It is about e-learning, e-government, and much more. Electronic commerce will have an impact on a significant portion of the world, affecting businesses, professions, and, of course, people.

The impact of EC is not just in the creation of Web-based businesses. It is the building of a new industrial order. Such a revolution brings a myriad of opportunities, as well as risks. Bill Gates is aware of this, and the company he founded, Microsoft, is continually developing new Internet and EC products and services. Yet Gates has stated that Microsoft is always 2 years away from failure—that somewhere out there is an unknown competitor who could render its business model obsolete (Heller 2005). Bill Gates knows that competition today is not among products or services, but among business models. What is true for Microsoft is true for just about every other company. The hottest and most dangerous new business models out there are on the Web.

The purpose of this book is to describe what EC is—how it is being conducted and managed—as well as to assess its major opportunities, limitations, issues, and risks. It is written from a managerial perspective. Because electronic commerce is an interdisciplinary topic, it should be of interest to managers and professional people in any functional area of business. People in government, education, health services, and other areas also will benefit from learning about EC.

Today, EC and e-business are going through a period of consolidation in which enthusiasm for new technologies and ideas is accompanied by careful attention to strategy, implementation, and profitability. Most of all, people recognize that e-business has two parts; it is not just about technology, it is also about commerce.

This book is written by experienced authors who share academic as well as real-world practices. It is a comprehensive text that can be used in one-semester or two-semester courses. It also can be used to supplement a text on Internet fundamentals, MIS, or marketing.

FEATURES OF THIS BOOK

Several features are unique to this book.

MANAGERIAL ORIENTATION

Electronic commerce can be approached from two major aspects: technological and managerial. This text uses the second approach. Most of the presentations are about EC applications and implementation. However, we do recognize the importance of the technology; therefore, we present the essentials of security in Chapter 12 and the essentials of infrastructure and system development in Chapter 18, which is located on the book's Web site (*prenhall.com/turban*). We also provide some detailed technology material in the appendices and tutorials on the book's Web site. Managerial issues are provided at the end of each chapter.

REAL-WORLD ORIENTATION

Extensive, vivid examples from large corporations, small businesses, and government and not-for-profit agencies from all over the world make concepts come alive. These examples show students the capabilities of EC, its cost and justification, and the innovative ways real corporations are using EC in their operations.

SOLID THEORETICAL BACKGROUND AND RESEARCH SUGGESTIONS

Throughout the book, we present the theoretical foundations necessary for understanding EC, ranging from consumer behavior to the economic theory of competition. Furthermore, we provide Web site resources, many exercises, and extensive references to supplement the theoretical presentations. At the end of each chapter, we provide suggested research topics. Online, we provide a research appendix with an extensive topic-by-topic bibliography.

MOST CURRENT TOPICS

The book presents the most current topics relating to EC, as evidenced by the many 2003 to 2005 citations. Topics such as e-learning, e-government, e-strategy, Web-based supply chain systems, collaborative commerce, mobile commerce, and EC economics are presented from the theoretical point of view as well as from the application side.

INTEGRATED SYSTEMS

In contrast to other books that highlight isolated Internet-based systems, we emphasize those systems that support the enterprise and supply chain management. Intra- and interorganizational systems are highlighted as are the latest innovations in global EC and in Web-based applications.

GLOBAL PERSPECTIVE

The importance of global competition, partnerships, and trade is increasing rapidly. EC facilitates export and import, the management of multinational companies, and electronic trading around the globe. International examples are provided throughout the book.

INTERDISCIPLINARY APPROACH

E-commerce is interdisciplinary, and we illustrate this throughout the book. Major EC-related disciplines include accounting, finance, information systems, marketing, management, and human resources management. In addition, some nonbusiness disciplines are related, especially public administration, computer science, engineering, psychology, political science, and law. Finally, economics plays a major role in the understanding of EC.

EC FAILURES AND LESSONS LEARNED

In addition to EC success stories, we also present EC failures, and, where possible, analyze the causes of those failures.

ONLINE SUPPORT

Over 100 files are available online to supplement text material. These include files on generic topics, such as data mining and intranets; cases; technically oriented text; and much more.

USER-FRIENDLINESS

While covering all major EC topics, this book is clear, simple, and well organized. It provides all the basic definitions of terms as well as logical conceptual support. Furthermore, the book is easy to understand and is full of interesting real-world examples and "war stories" that keep readers' interest at a high level. Relevant review questions are provided at the end of each section so the reader can pause to review and digest the new material.

ORGANIZATION OF THE BOOK

The book is divided into 17 chapters grouped into 6 parts. One additional chapter, a research appendix, four technology appendices, and two tutorials are available as online supplements.

PART 1—INTRODUCTION TO EC

In Part 1, we provide an overview of today's business environment as well as the fundamentals of EC and some of its terminology (Chapter 1) and a discussion of electronic markets and their mechanisms and impacts (Chapter 2).

PART 2—INTERNET CONSUMER RETAILING

In Part 2, we describe EC B2C applications in two chapters. Chapter 3 addresses e-tailing and electronic service industries. Chapter 4 deals with consumer behavior online, market research, and online advertising.

PART 3—BUSINESS-TO-BUSINESS E-COMMERCE

In Part 3, we examine the one-to-many B2B models (Chapter 5), including auctions, and the many-to-many models (Chapter 6), including exchanges. Chapter 7 describes the e-supply chain, intrabusiness EC, and collaborative commerce. An online appendix to Chapter 5 provides a discussion of the transition from traditional EDI to Internet-based EDI and Appendix 6A provides additional material on extranets.

PART 4—OTHER EC MODELS AND APPLICATIONS

Part 4 begins with several interesting applications such as e-government, e-learning, and consumer-to-consumer EC, as presented in Chapter 8. Chapter 9 explores the developing applications in the world of wireless EC (m-commerce, l-commerce, and pervasive computing).

PART 5—EC SUPPORT SERVICES

Chapter 10, the first chapter of Part 5, provides an overview of electronic auctions and bartering. Chapter 11 begins with a discussion of the need to protect privacy and intellectual property. It also describes various types of computer fraud and crime, and discusses how to minimize these risks through appropriate security programs. Chapter 12 describes a major EC support service—electronic payments. Chapter 13 concentrates on order fulfillment and CRM as support services.

PART 6—EC STRATEGY AND IMPLEMENTATION

Chapter 14 discusses strategic issues in implementing and deploying EC. The chapter also presents global EC and EC for small businesses. Chapter 15 deals with the economics of EC including balanced scorecards, metrics, and calculators. Chapter 16 is unique; it describes how to build an *Internet company* from scratch, as well as how to build a storefront. It takes the reader through all the necessary steps and provides guidelines for success. Chapter 17 deals with legal, ethical, and societal issues, and it closes the hard copy of the book with an overview of future EC directions. Finally, Online Chapter 18 deals with EC applications development, including the upcoming wave of Web services.

LEARNING AIDS

The text offers a number of learning aids to the student:

- **Chapter Outlines.** A listing of the main headings ("Content") at the beginning of each chapter provides a quick overview of the major topics covered.
- **Learning Objectives.** Learning objectives at the beginning of each chapter help students focus their efforts and alert them to the important concepts to be discussed.
- **Opening Vignettes.** Each chapter opens with a real-world example that illustrates the importance of EC to modern corporations. These cases were carefully chosen to call attention to the major topics covered in the chapters. Following each vignette, a short section titled "What We Can Learn . . ." links the important issues in the vignette to the subject matter of the chapter.
- **EC Application Cases.** In-chapter cases highlight real-world problems encountered by organizations as they develop and implement EC. Questions follow each case to help direct student attention to the implications of the case material.
- **Insights and Additions.** Topics sometimes require additional elaboration or demonstration. Insights and Additions boxes provide an eye-catching repository for such content.

- **Exhibits.** Numerous attractive exhibits (both illustrations and tables) extend and supplement the text discussion. Many are available online.
- **Review Questions.** Each section ends with a series of review questions about that section. These questions are intended to help students summarize the concepts introduced and to digest the essentials of each section before moving on to another topic.
- **Marginal Glossary and Key Terms.** Each green Key Term is defined in the margin when it first appears. In addition, an alphabetical list of Key Terms appears at the end of each chapter with a page reference to the location in the chapter where the term is discussed.
- **Managerial Issues.** At the end of every chapter, we explore some of the special concerns managers face as they adapt to doing business in cyberspace. These issues are framed as questions to maximize readers' active engagement with them.
- **Research Topics.** At the end of each chapter, we provide suggested research topics, divided into several categories.
- **Chapter Summary.** The chapter summary is linked one-to-one with the learning objectives introduced at the beginning of each chapter.
- **End-of-Chapter Exercises.** Different types of questions measure students' comprehension and their ability to apply knowledge. Questions for Discussion are intended to promote class discussion and develop critical-thinking skills. Internet Exercises are challenging assignments that require students to surf the Internet and apply what they have learned. Over 250 hands-on exercises send students to interesting Web sites to conduct research, investigate an application, download demos, or learn about state-of-the-art technology. The Team Assignment and Role Playing exercises are challenging group projects designed to foster teamwork.
- **Real-World Cases.** Each chapter ends with a real-world case, which is presented in somewhat more depth than the in-chapter EC Application Cases. Questions follow each case.

SUPPLEMENTARY MATERIALS

The following support materials are also available.

ONLINE INSTRUCTOR'S RESOURCE CENTER: www.prenhall.com

This convenient online *Instructor's Resource Center* includes all of the supplements: Instructor's Manual, Test Item File, TestGen, PowerPoint Lecture Notes, and Image Library (text art).

The **Instructor's Manual**, written by Jon Outland, includes answers to all review and discussion questions, exercises, and case questions. The **Test Item File**, written by Jim Steele, is an extensive set of multiple-choice, true-false, and essay questions for each chapter. It is available in Microsoft Word, **TestGen**, and WebCT- and BlackBoard-ready test banks.

The **PowerPoint Lecture Notes**, by Judy Lang, are oriented toward text learning objectives.

Linda Lai of the City University of Hong Kong revised Online Chapter 18.

COMPANION WEBSITE: www.prenhall.com/turban

The book is supported by a Companion Web site that includes:

- An online chapter (Chapter 18 on EC applications and infrastructure).
- Appendices for Chapters 4, 5, and 7 that cover business intelligence, EDI, and intranets.
- Bonus EC Application Cases and Insights and Additions features.
- Four technology appendices.

- Three interactive tutorials, two on storefront development (*store.yahoo.com* and *bigstep.com*) and one on preparing an EC business plan.
- PowerPoint Lecture Notes.
- Self-Study Quizzes, by Jon Outland, include multiple-choice, true-false, and essay questions for each chapter. Each question includes a hint and coaching tip for students' reference. Students receive automatic feedback after submitting each quiz.
- All of the Internet Exercises from the end of each chapter in the text are provided on the Web site for convenient student use.

MATERIALS FOR YOUR ONLINE COURSE

Prentice Hall supports adopters using online courses by providing files ready for upload into both WebCT and BlackBoard course management systems for our testing, quizzing, and other supplements. Please contact your local PH representative or mis_service@prenhall.com for further information on your particular course.

ACKNOWLEDGMENTS

Many individuals helped us create this text. Faculty feedback was solicited via reviews and through a focus group. We are grateful to the following faculty for their contributions.

CONTENT CONTRIBUTORS

The following individuals contributed material for this edition.

- Rajiv Kohli of the University of Notre Dame created the new chapter (Chapter 15) on the economics of EC.
- Christy Cheung of the City University of Hong Kong contributed material to Chapter 4 and helped in updating most of the other chapters. She also conducted much of the online research for this edition.
- Merrill Warkentin of Mississippi State University contributed to Chapter 3. Merrill is a co-author of our *Electronic Commerce 2002*.

REVIEWERS

We wish to thank the faculty who participated in reviews of this text and our other EC titles.

David Ambrosini, Cabrillo College
Deborah Ballou, University of Notre Dame
Martin Barriff, Illinois Institute of Technology
Stefan Brandle, Taylor University
Joseph Brooks, University of Hawaii
Bruce Brorson, University of Minnesota
Clifford Brozo, Monroe College-New Rochelle
Stanley Buchin, Boston University
John Bugado, National University
Ernest Capozzolli, Troy State University
Mark Cecchini, University of Florida
Jack Cook, State University of New York at Geneseo

Larry Corman, Fort Lewis College
Mary Culnan, Georgetown University
Ted Ferretti, Northeastern University
Vickie Fullmer, Webster University
Dennis Galletta, University of Pittsburgh
Ken Griggs, California Polytechnic University
Varun Grover, University of South Carolina
James Henson, Barry University
Brian Howland, Boston University
Paul Hu, University of Utah
Jin H. Im, Sacred Heart University
Jeffrey Johnson, Utah State University
Kenneth H. Johnson, Illinois Institute of Technology
Morgan Jones, University of North Carolina
Douglas Kline, Sam Houston State University
Mary Beth Klinger, College of Southern Maryland
Chunlei Liu, Troy State University
Byungtae Lee, University of Illinois at Chicago
Lakshmi Lyer, University of North Carolina
Michael McLeod, East Carolina University
Susan McNamara, Northeastern University
Mohon Menon, University of South Alabama
Ajay Mishra, State University of New York at Binghamton
Bud Mishra, New York University
William Nance, San Jose State University
Lewis Neisner, University of Maryland
Katherine A. Olson, Northern Virginia Community College
Somendra Pant, Clarkson University
Craig Peterson, Utah State University
Dien D. Phan, University of Vermont
H.R. Rao, State University of New York at Buffalo
Catherine M. Roche, Rockland Community College
Greg Rose, California State University at Chico
Linda Salchenberger, Loyola University of Chicago
George Schell, University of North Carolina at Wilmington
Sri Sharma, Oakland University
Sumit Sircar, University of Texas at Arlington
Kan Sugandh, DeVry Institute of Technology
Linda Volonino, Canisius College
Ken Williamson, James Madison University
Gregory Wood, Canisius College
Walter Wymer, Christopher Newport University
James Zemanek, East Carolina University

Several individuals helped us with the administrative work. Special mention goes to Christy Cheung of City University of Hong Kong who helped with editing, typing, URL verification, and more. We also thank the many students of City University of Hong Kong and KAIST in South Korea for their help in library searches, typing, and diagramming. We thank Daphne Turban, Sarah Miller, and all these people for their dedication and superb performance shown throughout the project.

We also recognize the various organizations and corporations that provided us with permissions to reproduce material.

Thanks also to the Prentice Hall team that helped us from the inception of the project to its completion under the leadership of Executive Editor Bob Horan and Publisher and VP/Editorial Director Jeff Shelstad. The dedicated staff includes Editorial Project Managers Lori Cerreto and Jeannine Ciliotta, Production Managers John Roberts and Renata Butera, Art Directors Maria Lange and Pat Smythe, Editorial Assistant Ana Cordero, Executive Marketing Manager Debbie Clare, Marketing Assistant Joanna Sabella, and Media Project Manager Nancy Welcher.

Last, but not least, we thank Judy Lang, the book's development editor, who spent long hours contributing innovative ideas and providing the necessary editing.

REFERENCE

Heller, R. "Strengths And Weaknesses: Assess The Strengths and Weaknesses of Your Business, as Well as the Opportunities and Threats, with SWOT Analysis." *Thinking Managers*, 2005. *thinkingmanagers.com/management/strengths-weaknesses.php* (accessed June 2005).

Internet World Stats. "Internal Usage Statistics for the Americas." March 2005. *internetworldstats.com* (accessed June 2005).

Maney, K. "Next Big Thing." *USA Today,* October 1, 2004. *usatoday.com/tech/webguide/internetlife/2004-10-01-cover-web_x.htm* (accessed March 2005).

Electronic Commerce 2006

A Managerial Perspective

OVERVIEW OF ELECTRONIC COMMERCE

Content

Learning Objectives

Upon completion of this chapter, you will be able to:

1. Define electronic commerce (EC) and describe its various categories.
2. Describe and discuss the content and framework of EC.
3. Describe the major types of EC transactions.
4. Describe the digital revolution as a driver of EC.
5. Describe the business environment as a driver of EC.
6. Describe some EC business models.
7. Describe the benefits of EC to organizations, consumers, and society.
8. Describe the limitations of EC.
9. Describe the contribution of EC to organizations responding to environmental pressures.

DELL—USING E-COMMERCE FOR SUCCESS

The Problem/Opportunity

Founded in 1985 by Michael Dell, Dell Computer Corp. (now known as Dell) was the first company to offer personal computers (PCs) via mail order. Dell designed its own PC system (with an Intel 8088 processor running at 8 MHz) and allowed customers to configure their own customized systems using the build-to-order concept (see Chapter 2, Appendix 2A). This concept was, and is still, Dell's cornerstone *business model*. By 1993, Dell had become one of the top-five computer makers worldwide, threatening Compaq, which started a price war. At that time, Dell was taking orders by fax and snail mail and losing money. Losses reached over $100 million by 1994. The company was in trouble.

The Solution

DIRECT MARKETING ONLINE

The commercialization of the Internet in the early 1990s and the introduction of the Web in 1993 provided Dell with an opportunity to expand rapidly. Dell implemented aggressive online order-taking and opened subsidiaries in Europe and Asia. Dell also started to offer additional products on its Web site. This enabled Dell to batter Compaq, and in 2000 Dell became number one in worldwide PC shipments. At that time, Internet sales topped $50 million per day (about $18 billion per year). Today, Dell (*dell.com*) sells about $50 billion a year in computer-related products online, from network switches to printers.

Direct online marketing is Dell's major EC activity. Dell sells to the following groups:

- Individuals for their homes and home offices
- Small businesses (up to 200 employees)
- Medium and large businesses (over 200 employees)
- Government, education, and health-care organizations

Sales to the first group are classified as *business-to-consumer (B2C)*. Sales to the other three groups are classified as *business-to-business (B2B)*. Consumers shop at *dell.com* using online electronic catalogs. The sales are completed using mechanisms described in Chapter 3.

In addition, Dell sells refurbished Dell computers and other products in electronic auctions at (*dellauction.com*). As we will see in Chapters 2 and 10, online auctions are an important sales channel.

Business-to-Business EC. Most of Dell's sales are to businesses. Whereas B2C sales are facilitated by standard shopping aids (e.g., catalogs, shopping carts, credit-card payments; see Chapters 2 and 3), B2B customers obtain additional help from Dell. Dell provides each of its nearly 100,000 business customers with Premier Dell service.

For example, British Airways (BA) considers Dell to be a strategic supplier. Dell provides notebooks and desktops to 25,000 BA users. Dell offers two e-procurement services to BA purchasing agents. The more basic service, Premier Dell, allows BA (and other businesses) to browse, buy, and track orders on a Dell Web site customized for the user's requirements. The site enables authorized users to select preconfigured PCs for their business unit or department. A more advanced version, Premier B2B, supports e-procurement systems such as Ariba and Commerce One. This provides automatic requisition and order fulfillment once an authorized user has chosen to buy a PC from Dell. BA has placed the e-procurement tools on their E-Working intranet. This allows authorized staff to purchase PCs through a portal that connects directly into Dell's systems.

In addition to supporting its business customers with e-procurement tools, Dell also is using EC in its own procurement. Actually, Dell developed an e-procurement model that it shares with its business partners, such as BA. One aspect of this model is the use of electronic tendering to conduct bids (see Chapter 5). Dell uses electronic tendering when it buys the components for its products.

In 2000, Dell created a B2B exchange at dell.b2b.com. This venture was a failure, like most other exchanges (see Chapter 6). As a result, Dell's B2B activities (in addition to direct sales and e-procurement) were shifted to collaborative commerce.

E-Collaboration. Dell has many business partners with whom it needs to communicate and collaborate. For example, Dell uses shippers such as UPS and FedEx to deliver its computers to individuals. It also uses third-party logistics companies to collect, maintain, and deliver components from its suppliers, and it has many other partners. As we will see in Chapter 7, Dell is using Web Services, an EC technology, to facilitate communication and reduce inventories. Web Services facilitate B2B integration. Integration efforts began in 2000 with other technologies when Dell encouraged its customers to buy online. The B2B integration offer combines Dell PowerEdge servers based on Intel architecture and webMethods B2B integration software to link customers' existing ERP (enterprise resource planning) or procurement systems directly with Dell and other trading partners. In addition, Dell can provide e-procurement applications and consulting services. Dell also educates customers in its technologies and offers suggestions on how to use them. This is particularly true for emerging technologies such as wireless.

Finally, Dell has a superb communication system with its over 15,000 service providers around the globe.

E-Customer Service. Dell uses a number of different tools to provide superb customer service around the clock. To leverage customer relationship management (CRM)—a customer service approach that is customer centered for lasting relationships, Dell provides a virtual help desk for self-diagnosis and service as well as direct access to technical support data. In addition, a phone-based help desk is open 24/7. Product support includes troubleshooting, user guides, upgrades, downloads, news and press releases, FAQs, order status information, a "my account" page, a community forum (to exchange ideas, information, and experiences), bulletin boards and other customer-to-customer interaction features, training books (at a discount), and much more. Dell keeps a large database of its customers. Using data mining tools, it learns a great deal about its customers and attempts to make them happy. The database is used to improve marketing as well.

Intrabusiness EC. To support its build-to-order capabilities, significantly improve its demand-planning and factory-execution accuracy, reduce order-to-delivery time, and enhance customer service, Dell partnered with Accenture to create a new, high-performance supply chain planning solution. Now in place in Dell's plants around the world, the program, which paid for itself five times over during the first 12 months of operation, enables Dell to adapt more quickly to rapidly changing technologies and the business environment and maintain its position as a high-performance business.

Dell also has automated its factory scheduling, demand-planning capabilities, and inventory management using information technology and e-supply chain models.

The Results

Dell has been one of *Fortune*'s top five "Most Admired" companies since 1999, and it continuously advances in the rankings of the *Fortune* 500 and the *Fortune* Global 500. Dell has over 100 country-oriented Web sites, and profits are nearing $3 billion a year. If you had invested $10,000 in Dell's initial public offering (IPO) in 1987, you would be a millionaire just from that investment. Dell actively supports EC research at the University of Texas in Austin (Dell's headquarters also are in Austin). It also contributes heavily to charity. Dell has partnered with the National Cristina Foundation to provide computer technology to people with disabilities, students at risk, and economically disadvantaged persons. Paired with the company's recycling program, used computers are refurbished and then distributed through NCF (Dell Recycling 2005 and National Cristina Foundation 2005). Through Dell's TechKnow Program, the company donates computers to urban middle schools. The students learn about computers by taking them apart and reassembling them, loading software, setting up and running printers, upgrading hardware, diagnosing and correcting basic hardware problems, and using the Internet. Upon completion of the program, students take home the computer they build and receive one year of free Internet access (Wolfson 2005). Dell also awards grants each year to governmental and educational institutions to organize, promote, stage, and recycle computer equipment in a free "No Computer Should Go to Waste" collection event in their communities. Refurbished machines are dispersed through local charities (Electronic Industry Alliance 2004).

Dell is expanding its business not only in the computer industry, but also in consumer electronics. It is clearly an example of EC success.

Sources: Compiled from *dell.com* and *dellauction.com* (accessed October 12, 2004).

WHAT WE CAN LEARN . . .

Dell exemplifies the major EC business models. First, it pioneered the direct-marketing model for PCs, and then it moved online. Furthermore, Dell supplemented its direct marketing with the build-to-order model on a large scale (mass customization). In doing so, Dell benefited from the elimination of intermediation with the first model and from extremely low inventories and superb cash flow from the second model. To meet the large demand for its quality products, Dell introduced other EC models, notably e-procurement for improving the purchasing of components, collaborative commerce with its partners, and intrabusiness EC for improving its internal operations. Finally, Dell uses e-CRM (CRM done online; see Chapter 13 for details) with its customers. By successfully using e-commerce models, Dell became a world-class company, winning over all of its competitors. Dell's EC business models have become classics and best practices and are followed today by many other manufacturers, notably car makers.

This chapter defines EC and lists the types of transactions that are executed in it. Various EC models and the benefits and limitations of EC also will be examined. Finally, a visual preview of the book's chapters will be provided.

1.1 ELECTRONIC COMMERCE: DEFINITIONS AND CONCEPTS

Let's begin by looking at what the management guru Peter Drucker has to say about EC:

> *The truly revolutionary impact of the Internet Revolution is just beginning to be felt. But it is not "information" that fuels this impact. It is not "artificial intelligence." It is not the effect of computers and data processing on decision making, policymaking, or strategy. It is something that practically no one foresaw or, indeed even talked about 10 or 15 years ago; e-commerce—that is, the explosive emergence of the Internet as a major, perhaps eventually the major, worldwide distribution channel for goods, for services, and, surprisingly, for managerial and professional jobs. This is profoundly changing economics, markets and industry structure, products and services and their flow; consumer segmentation, consumer values and consumer behavior; jobs and labor markets. But the impact may be even greater on societies and politics, and above all, on the way we see the world and ourselves in it. (Drucker 2002, pp. 3–4)*

DEFINING ELECTRONIC COMMERCE

electronic commerce (EC)
The process of buying, selling, or exchanging products, services, or information via computer networks.

Electronic commerce (EC) is the process of buying, selling, transferring, or exchanging products, services, and/or information via computer networks, including the Internet. EC can be defined from the following perspectives:

- **Communications.** From a communications perspective, EC is the delivery of goods, services, information, or payments over computer networks or by any other electronic means.
- **Commercial (trading).** From a commercial perspective, EC provides the capability of buying and selling products, services, and information over the Internet and via other online services.
- **Business process.** From a business process perspective, EC is doing business electronically by completing business processes over electronic networks, thereby substituting information for physical business processes (Weill and Vitale 2001, p. 13).
- **Service.** From a service perspective, EC is a tool that addresses the desire of governments, firms, consumers, and management to cut service costs while improving the quality of customer service and increasing the speed of service delivery.
- **Learning.** From a learning perspective, EC is an enabler of online training and education in schools, universities, and other organizations, including businesses.
- **Collaborative.** From a collaborative perspective, EC is the framework for inter- and intraorganizational collaboration.
- **Community.** From a community perspective, EC provides a gathering place for community members to learn, transact, and collaborate.

EC is often confused with e-business.

DEFINING E-BUSINESS

e-business
A broader definition of EC that includes not just the buying and selling of goods and services, but also servicing customers, collaborating with business partners, and conducting electronic transactions within an organization.

Some people view the term *commerce* only as describing transactions conducted between business partners. If this definition of commerce is used, the term *electronic commerce* would be fairly narrow. Thus, many use the term *e-business* instead. **E-business** refers to a broader definition of EC, not just the buying and selling of goods and services, but also servicing customers, collaborating with business partners, conducting e-learning, and conducting electronic transactions *within* an organization. According to McKay and Marshall (2004), e-business is the use of the Internet and other information technologies to support commerce and improve business performance. However, some view e-business as comprising those activities that do not involve buying or selling over the Internet, such as collaboration and intrabusiness activities (online activities between and within businesses). In this book, we use the broadest meaning of electronic commerce, which is basically equivalent to e-business. The two terms will be used interchangeably throughout the text.

PURE VERSUS PARTIAL EC

EC can take several forms depending on the *degree of digitization* (the transformation from physical to digital) of (1) the *product* (service) sold, (2) the *process*, and (3) the *delivery agent* (or intermediary). Choi et al. (1997) created a framework, shown in Exhibit 1.1, that explains the possible configurations of these three dimensions. A product may be physical or digital, the process may be physical or digital, and the delivery agent may be physical or digital. These alternatives create eight cubes, each of which has three dimensions. In traditional commerce, all three dimensions of the cube are physical (lower-left cube); in pure EC, all dimensions are digital (upper-right cube). All other cubes include a mix of digital and physical dimensions.

If there is at least one digital dimension, we consider the situation EC, but only *partial EC*. For example, purchasing a computer from Dell's Web site or a book from Amazon.com is partial EC, because the merchandise is physically delivered. However, buying an e-book from Amazon.com or a software product from Buy.com is *pure EC*, because the product, delivery, payment, and transfer to the buyer are all digital.

EXHIBIT 1.1 The Dimensions of Electronic Commerce

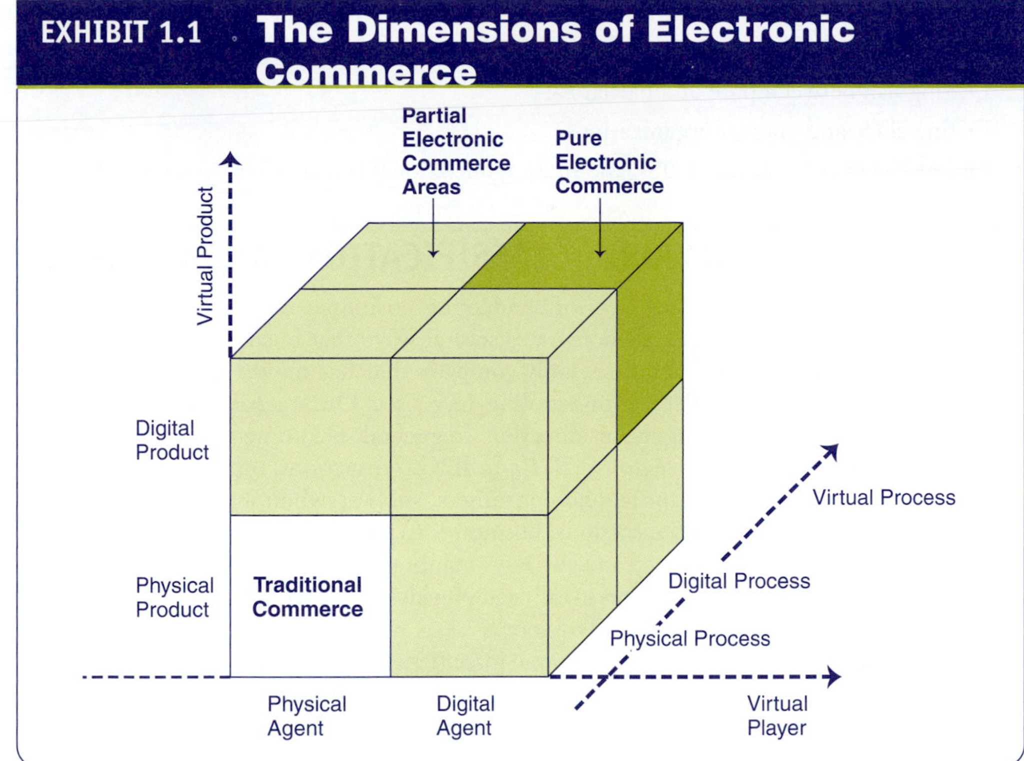

Source: Whinston, A. B., Stahl, D. O., and Choi, S. *The Economics of Electronic Commerce*. Indianapolis, IN: Macmillan Technical Publishing, 1997. Used with permission of the authors.

EC Organizations. Purely physical organizations (companies) are referred to as **brick-and-mortar (or old-economy) organizations**, whereas companies that are engaged only in EC are considered **virtual** or **pure-play organizations**. **Click-and-mortar** (or ***click-and-brick***) **organizations** are those that conduct some EC activities, but conduct their primary business in the physical world. Gradually, many brick-and-mortar companies are changing to click-and-mortar ones (e.g., Marks & Spencer in Online File W1.1).

brick-and-mortar organizations
Old-economy organizations (corporations) that perform most of their business off-line, selling physical products by means of physical agents.

virtual (pure-play) organizations
Organizations that conduct their business activities solely online.

click-and-mortar (click-and-brick) organizations
Organizations that conduct some e-commerce activities, but do their primary business in the physical world.

INTERNET VERSUS NON-INTERNET EC

Most EC is done over the Internet, but EC also can be conducted on private networks, such as *value-added networks* (VANs; networks that add communications services to existing common carriers), on *local area networks* (LANs), or even on a single computerized machine. For example, buying food from a vending machine where you pay with a smart card or a cell phone can be viewed as EC activity.

An example of non-Internet EC would be field employees (such as sales reps) who are equipped with mobile handwriting-recognition computers so they can write their notes in the field, for instance, immediately after a sales call. (For a more in-depth example, see the Maybelline Real-World Case at the end of this chapter.)

ELECTRONIC MARKETS AND INTERORGANIZATIONAL AND INTRAORGANIZATIONAL INFORMATION SYSTEMS

EC can be conducted in an **electronic market** where buyers and sellers meet online to exchange goods, services, money, or information. Electronic markets may be supplemented by interorganizational or intraorganizational information systems. **Interorganizational information systems (IOSs)** are those where only routine transaction processing and information flow take place between two or more organizations. EC activities that take place *within* individual organizations are facilitated by **intraorganizational information systems**. These systems also are known as *intrabusiness EC.*

electronic market (e-marketplace)
An online marketplace where buyers and sellers meet to exchange goods, services, money, or information.

interorganizational information systems (IOSs)
Communications systems that allows routine transaction processing and information flow between two or more organizations.

intraorganizational information systems
Communication systems that enable e-commerce activities to go on within individual organizations.

Section 1.1 ▸ REVIEW QUESTIONS

1. Define EC and e-business.
2. Distinguish between pure and partial EC.
3. Define click-and-mortar organizations.
4. Define electronic markets, IOSs, and intraorganizational information systems.

1.2 THE EC FRAMEWORK, CLASSIFICATION, AND CONTENT

The opening case illustrates a new way of conducting business—electronically, using networks and the Internet. The case demonstrates several ways that businesses can use EC to improve the bottom line. Dell is not the only company that has moved its business online. Thousands of other companies, from retailing (e.g., see Online File W1.1, Marks & Spencer) to hospitals, are moving in this direction. In general, e-commerce is either *business-to-consumer (B2C)* or *business-to-business (B2B)*. In B2C transactions, online transactions are made between businesses and individual consumers, such as when a person purchases a computer at dell.com. In B2B transactions, businesses make online transactions with other businesses, such as when Dell electronically buys components from its suppliers. Dell also collaborates electronically with its partners (EC) and provides customer service online (e-CRM). Several other types of EC will be described soon.

EC is not yet a significant global economic force (less than 5 percent of all transactions). However, some predict that it could become globally significant within 10 to 20 years (Drucker 2002). Networked computing is the infrastructure for EC, and it is rapidly emerging as the standard computing environment for business, home, and government applications. *Networked computing* connects multiple computers and other electronic devices that are located in several different locations by telecommunications networks, including *wireless* ones. This connection allows users to access information stored in several different physical locations and to communicate and collaborate with people separated by great geographic distances.

intranet
An internal corporate or government network that uses Internet tools, such as Web browsers, and Internet protocols.

extranet
A network that uses the Internet to link multiple intranets.

Although some people still use a stand-alone computer exclusively, the vast majority of people use computers connected to a global networked environment known as the *Internet* or to its counterpart within organizations, an intranet. An **intranet** is a corporate or government network that uses Internet tools, such as Web browsers, and Internet protocols. Another computer environment is an **extranet**, a network that uses the Internet to link multiple intranets (see Fingar et al. 2000).

AN EC FRAMEWORK

The EC field is a diverse one, involving many activities, organizational units, and technologies (e.g., see Shaw et al. 2000). Therefore, a framework that describes its content is useful. Exhibit 1.2 introduces one such framework.

As can be seen in the exhibit, there are many EC applications (top of exhibit), some of which were illustrated in the opening case about Dell; others will be shown throughout the book (see also Laudon and Traver 2005; Jelassi and Enders 2005; and Farhoomand and Lovelock 2001). To execute these applications, companies need the right information, infrastructure, and support services. Exhibit 1.2 shows that EC applications are supported by infrastructure and by the five policymaking support areas. These pillars are:

- **People.** Sellers, buyers, intermediaries, information systems specialists, other employees, and any other participants comprise an important support area.
- **Public policy.** Legal and other policy and regulating issues, such as privacy protection and taxation, which are determined by governments. Included as part of public policy is the issue of technical standards, which are established by government or industry-mandated policymaking groups.
- **Marketing and advertisement.** Like any other business, EC usually requires the support of marketing and advertising. This is especially important in B2C online transactions in which the buyers and sellers usually do not know each other.

EXHIBIT 1.2 A Framework for Electronic Commerce

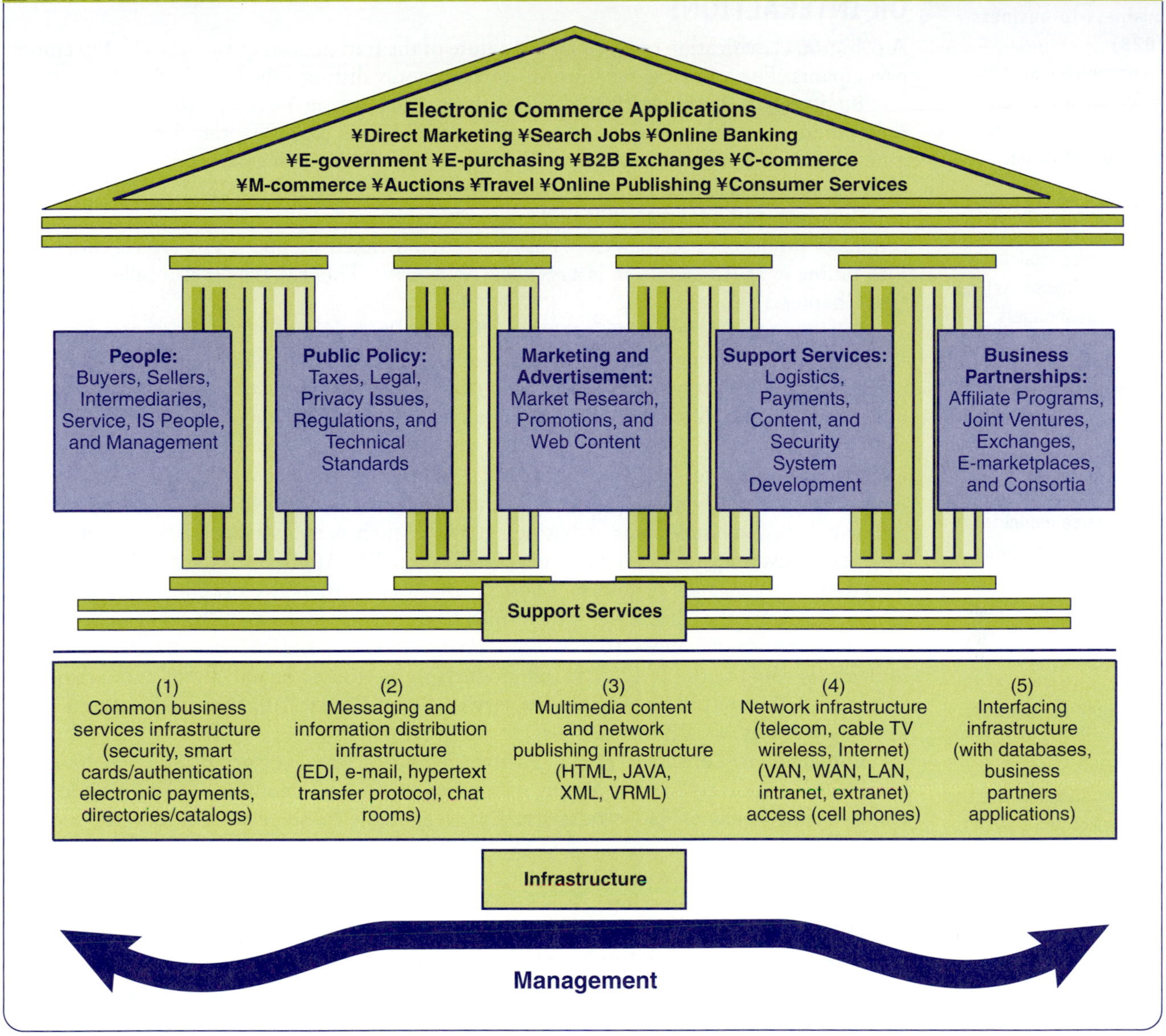

Electronic Commerce Applications
¥Direct Marketing ¥Search Jobs ¥Online Banking
¥E-government ¥E-purchasing ¥B2B Exchanges ¥C-commerce
¥M-commerce ¥Auctions ¥Travel ¥Online Publishing ¥Consumer Services

People: Buyers, Sellers, Intermediaries, Service, IS People, and Management

Public Policy: Taxes, Legal, Privacy Issues, Regulations, and Technical Standards

Marketing and Advertisement: Market Research, Promotions, and Web Content

Support Services: Logistics, Payments, Content, and Security System Development

Business Partnerships: Affiliate Programs, Joint Ventures, Exchanges, E-marketplaces, and Consortia

Support Services

(1) Common business services infrastructure (security, smart cards/authentication electronic payments, directories/catalogs)

(2) Messaging and information distribution infrastructure (EDI, e-mail, hypertext transfer protocol, chat rooms)

(3) Multimedia content and network publishing infrastructure (HTML, JAVA, XML, VRML)

(4) Network infrastructure (telecom, cable TV wireless, Internet) (VAN, WAN, LAN, intranet, extranet) access (cell phones)

(5) Interfacing infrastructure (with databases, business partners applications)

Infrastructure

Management

- **Support services.** Many services are needed to support EC. These range from content creation to payments to order delivery.
- **Business partnerships.** Joint ventures, exchanges, and business partnerships of various types are common in EC. These occur frequently throughout the *supply chain* (i.e., the interactions between a company and its suppliers, customers, and other partners).

At the bottom of Exhibit 1.2 is the infrastructure for EC. Infrastructure describes the hardware, software, and networks used in EC. All of these components require good *management practices*. This means that companies need to plan, organize, motivate, devise strategy, and reengineer processes as needed to optimize their business using EC models and strategies. Management also deals with strategic and operational decisions (see Chapter 14 and examples throughout the book).

Exhibit 1.2 can be viewed as a framework for understanding the relationships among the EC applications and other EC components and for conducting research in the EC field. This text provides details on most of the components of the framework. The infrastructure of EC is described in online Technical Appendices A through D on the book's Web site and in online Chapter 18.

CLASSIFICATION OF EC BY THE NATURE OF THE TRANSACTIONS OR INTERACTIONS

business-to-business (B2B)
E-commerce model in which all of the participants are businesses or other organizations.

business-to-consumer (B2C)
E-commerce model in which businesses sell to individual shoppers.

e-tailing
Online retailing, usually B2C.

business-to-business-to-consumer (B2B2C)
E-commerce model in which a business provides some product or service to a client business that maintains its own customers.

consumer-to-business (C2B)
E-commerce model in which individuals use the Internet to sell products or services to organizations or individuals seek sellers to bid on products or services they need.

consumer-to-consumer (C2C)
E-commerce model in which consumers sell directly to other consumers.

peer-to-peer
Technology that enables networked peer computers to share data and processing with each other directly; can be used in C2C, B2B, and B2C e-commerce.

mobile commerce (m-commerce)
E-commerce transactions and activities conducted in a wireless environment.

A common classification of EC is by the nature of the transactions or the relationship among participants. The following types of EC are commonly distinguished.

Business-to-Business (B2B). All of the participants in **business-to-business (B2B)** e-commerce are either businesses or other organizations (see Chapters 5 through 7). For example, several of Dell's and Marks & Spencer's applications involve B2B with their suppliers. Today, over 85 percent of EC volume is B2B (Cunningham 2001).

Business-to-Consumer (B2C). **Business-to-consumer (B2C)** EC includes retail transactions of products or services from businesses to individual shoppers. The typical shopper at Dell online or at Amazon.com is a *consumer* or *customer*. This EC type is also called **e-tailing** (see Chapter 3).

Business-to-Business-to-Consumer (B2B2C). In **business-to-business-to-consumer (B2B2C)** EC, a business provides some product or service to a client business. The client business maintains its own customers, who may be its own employees, to whom the product or service is provided without adding any value to it. One example of B2B2C is a company that pays AOL to provide its employees with Internet access rather than having each employee pay an access fee directly to AOL. Another example is wholesaler-to-retailer-to-consumer merchandising, such as airlines and travel units that provide travel services, such as airline tickets and hotel rooms, to business partners, such as travel agencies, who then sell the services to customers. As a final example, Godiva (see EC Application Case 1.1) sells chocolates directly to business customers. Those businesses may then give the chocolates as gifts to employees or to other businesses. The term B2B frequently includes B2B2C as well.

Consumer-to-Business (C2B). The **consumer-to-business (C2B)** category includes individuals who use the Internet to sell products or services to organizations and individuals who seek sellers to bid on products or services (see Chapter 10). Priceline.com is a well-known organizer of C2B transactions.

Consumer-to-Consumer (C2C). In the **consumer-to-consumer (C2C)** category (see Chapter 8), consumers transact directly with other consumers. Examples of C2C include individuals selling residential property, cars, and so on in online classified ads. The advertisement of personal services over the Internet and the selling of knowledge and expertise online are other examples of C2C. In addition, many auction sites allow individuals to place items up for auction.

Peer-to-Peer Applications. **Peer-to-peer** technology can be used in C2C, B2B, and B2C (see Chapter 8). This technology enables networked peer computers to share data files and processing with each other directly. For example, in a C2C peer application, people can exchange (swap) music, videos, software, and other digitizable goods electronically.

Mobile Commerce. EC transactions and activities conducted in full or in part in a *wireless environment* are referred to as **mobile commerce**, or **m-commerce** (see Chapter 9). For example, people can use Internet-enabled cell phones to do their banking or order a book from Amazon.com. Many m-commerce applications involve mobile devices. If such transactions are targeted to individuals in specific locations, at specific times, they are referred to as **location-based commerce**, or **l-commerce**. Some people define m-commerce as those transactions conducted when people are away from their home or office; such transactions can be done both on wireless or wireline systems. (See the Maybelline case at the end of this chapter.)

Intrabusiness EC. The **intrabusiness EC** category includes all internal organizational activities that involve the exchange of goods, services, or information among various units and individuals in that organization. Activities can range from selling corporate products to one's employees to online training and collaborative design efforts (see Chapter 7). Intrabusiness EC is usually performed over intranets or *corporate portals* (gateways to the Web).

Business-to-Employees (B2E). The **business-to-employees (B2E)** category is a subset of the intrabusiness category in which the organization delivers services, information, or products to individual employees, as Maybelline is doing (see the Real-World Case at the end of this chapter). A major category of employees is *mobile employees*, such as field representatives. EC support to such employees is called *B2ME (business-to-mobile employees)*.

Collaborative Commerce. When individuals or groups communicate or collaborate online, they may be engaged in **collaborative commerce**, or **c-commerce** (see Chapter 7).

CASE 1.1

EC Application

BUY CHOCOLATE ONLINE? TRY GODIVA.COM

The Business Opportunity

The demand for high-quality chocolate has been increasing rapidly since the early 1990s. Several local and global companies are competing in this market. Godiva Chocolatier is a well-known international company based in New York whose stores can be found in hundreds of malls worldwide. The company was looking for ways to increase its sales, and after rejecting the use of a CD-ROM catalog, it had the courage to try online sales, as early as 1994. The company was a pioneering click-and-mortar e-business that exploited an opportunity years before its competitors.

The Project

Teaming with Fry Multimedia (an e-commerce pioneer), Godiva.com was created as a division of Godiva Chocolatier. The objective was to sell online both to individuals and to businesses. Since its online beginnings in 1994, the Godiva.com story parallels the dynamic growth of e-commerce (see Reda 2004). Godiva.com went through difficult times—testing e-commerce technologies as they appeared; failing at times, but maintaining its commitment to online selling; and, finally, becoming the fastest-growing division of Godiva, outpacing projections. Godiva.com embodies a true success story. Here we present some of the milestones encountered.

The major driving factors in 1994 were Internet *user groups* of chocolate lovers, who were talking about Godiva and to whom the company hoped to sell its product online. Like other pioneers, Godiva had to build its Web site from scratch without EC-building tools. A partnership was made with *Chocolatier Magazine*, allowing Godiva.com to showcase articles and recipes from the magazine on its site in exchange for providing an online magazine subscription form for e-shoppers. The recognition of the importance of relevant content was correct, as was the need for fresh content. The delivery of games and puzzles, which was considered necessary to attract people to EC sites, was found to be a failure. People were coming to learn about chocolate and Godiva and to buy—not to play games. Another concept that failed was the attempt to make the Web site look like the physical store. It was found that different marketing channels should look different.

Godiva.com is a user-friendly place to shop. Its major features include electronic catalogs, some of which are constructed for special occasions (e.g., Mother's Day and Father's Day); a store locator (how to find the nearest physical store); a shopping cart to make it easy to collect items to buy; a gift selector and a gift finder; custom photographs of the products; a search engine by product, price, and other criteria; instructions of how to shop online (take the tour); a chocolate guide that shows you exactly what is inside each box; a place to click for live assistance or for a paper catalog; and the ability to create an address list for shipping gifts to friends or employees. The site also features "My Godiva," a personalized place where customers can access their order history, account, order status, and so on; general content about chocolate (and recipes); and tools for making shipping and payment arrangements.

Godiva.com sells both to individuals and to corporations. For corporations, incentive programs are offered, including address lists of employees or customers to whom the chocolate is to be sent—an example of the B2B2C EC model.

Godiva.com continues to add features to stay ahead of the competition. The site is now accessible using wireless technologies. For example, the store locator is available to wireless phone users, and Palm Pilot users can download mailing lists.

The Results

Godiva.com's online sales have been growing at a double-digit rate every year, outpacing the company's "old economy" divisions as well as the online stores of competitors.

Sources: Compiled from Reda (2004) and from *godiva.com* (accessed October 2004).

Questions

1. Identify the B2B and B2C transactions in this case.
2. Why did Godiva decide to sell online?
3. List the EC drivers in this case.
4. Visit *godiva.com*. How user-friendly is the site?

For example, business partners in different locations may design a product together, using screen sharing; manage inventory online, as in the Dell case; or jointly forecast product demand, as Marks & Spencer does with its suppliers (Online File W1.1).

location-based commerce (l-commerce) M-commerce transactions targeted to individuals in specific locations, at specific times.

Nonbusiness EC. An increased number of nonbusiness institutions such as academic institutions, nonprofit organizations, religious organizations, social organizations, and government agencies are using EC to reduce their expenses or to improve their general operations and customer service. (Note that in the previous categories one can usually replace the word *business* with *organization*.)

E-Learning. In **e-learning**, training or formal education is provided online (see Chapter 8). E-learning is used heavily by organizations for training and retraining employees (called *e-training*). It is also practiced at virtual universities.

intrabusiness EC
E-commerce category that includes all internal organizational activities that involve the exchange of goods, services, or information among various units and individuals in an organization.

business-to-employees (B2E)
E-commerce model in which an organization delivers services, information, or products to its individual employees.

Exchange-to-Exchange (E2E). An **exchange** describes a *public electronic market* with many buyers and sellers (see Chapter 6). As B2B exchanges proliferate, it is logical for exchanges to connect to one another. **Exchange-to-exchange (E2E)** EC is a formal system that connects two or more exchanges.

E-Government. In **e-government** EC, a government entity buys or provides goods, services, or information from or to businesses (G2B) or from or to individual citizens (G2C). An example of an e-government initiative is provided in EC Application Case 1.2.

Many examples of the various types of EC transactions will be presented throughout this book.

THE INTERDISCIPLINARY NATURE OF EC

Because EC is a new field, it is just now developing its theoretical and scientific foundations. From just a brief overview of the EC framework and classification, you can probably see that EC is related to several different disciplines. The major EC disciplines include the following: *computer science, marketing, consumer behavior, finance, economics, management information systems, accounting, management, business law, robotics, public administration,* and *engineering.*

A BRIEF HISTORY OF EC

EC applications were first developed in the early 1970s with innovations such as *electronic funds transfer* (EFT) (see Chapter 12), whereby funds could be routed electronically from one organization to another. However, the use of these applications was limited to large corpora-

CASE 1.2
EC Application

VOICE-BASED 511 TRAVELER INFORMATION LINE

Tellme Networks, Inc. (*tellme.com*) developed the first voice-activated 511 traveler information line in Utah, setting a national example for future 511 services to be launched by Department of Transportation (DOT) agencies on a state-by-state basis in the United States. The 511 service debuted on December 18, 2001. Simply by using their voices, callers on regular or cell phones within the state of Utah are now able to request and get real-time information on traffic, road conditions, public transportation, and so on. The answers are generated from the Internet and participating databases.

In July 2000, the U.S. Federal Communications Commission (FCC) officially allocated 511 as the single nationwide number for traveler information, in the same way callers can dial 411 for directory assistance and 911 for emergency services. Previously, state governments and local transportation agencies used more than 300 local telephone numbers nationwide to provide traffic and traveler information. This marks the first time people can use one number to access travel information whether they are touring the country or simply driving home from work. The Utah 511 travel information line is provided as a free service by the Utah DOT.

During the February 2002 Olympic Winter Games, callers were able to request event schedules, driving directions, up-to-the-minute news and announcements, and tips for avoiding traffic congestion. "The phone is the ideal medium to make government services available and accessible to the general public," said Greg O'Connell, Director of Public Sector Operations at Tellme, "511 is a new wave in public information access" (quoted at *tellme.com*).

The 511 application is a special use of voice portals (see Chapter 9), which enable users to access the Web from any telephone by voice. Martin Knopp, Director of Intelligent Transportation Systems, Utah DOT, said, "As the national 511 working group has stipulated, voice recognition is the way for callers to access information on 511. . . . In addition, there was no up-front capital cost and we were able to leverage the same information and investment we had made in our regular Web infrastructure" (quoted by Singer 2001).

Tellme Networks is revolutionizing how people and businesses use the telephone by fundamentally improving the caller's experience with Internet and voice technologies. Tellme enables businesses and governments to empower their callers while slashing costs and complexity.

Source: Adapted with permission.

Questions

1. Is this G2B or G2C, why?
2. Visit *tellme.com* and find more information about this case. Summarize the benefits of 511 to the users. (Note: If the case is not there anymore, read the 511 Deployment Coalition's brochure, "The Value of Deploying 511," at *deploy511.org/docs/511_Value.pdf*.)
3. What is the role of Tellme? What Internet technology is used?

tions, financial institutions, and a few other daring businesses. Then came *electronic data interchange* (EDI), a technology used to electronically transfer routine documents, which expanded electronic transfers from financial transactions to other types of transaction processing (see Chapter 5 for more on EDI). EDI enlarged the pool of participating companies from financial institutions to manufacturers, retailers, services, and many other types of businesses. More new EC applications followed, ranging from travel reservation systems to stock trading. Such systems were called *interorganizational system* (IOS) applications, and their strategic value to businesses has been widely recognized.

The Internet began life as an experiment by the U.S. government in 1969, and its initial users were a largely technical audience of government agencies and academic researchers and scientists. When the Internet became commercialized and users began flocking to participate in the World Wide Web in the early 1990s, the term *electronic commerce* was coined. EC applications rapidly expanded. A large number of so-called *dot-coms*, or *Internet start-ups,* also appeared (see Cassidy 2002). One reason for this rapid expansion was the development of new networks, protocols, and EC software. The other reason was the increase in competition and other business pressures (see discussion in Section 1.4).

Since 1995, Internet users have witnessed the development of many innovative applications, ranging from online direct sales to e-learning experiences. Almost every medium- and large-sized organization in the world now has a Web site, and most large U.S. corporations have comprehensive portals through which employees, business partners, and the public can access corporate information. Many of these sites contain tens of thousand of pages and links. In 1999, the emphasis of EC shifted from B2C to B2B, and in 2001 from B2B to B2E, c-commerce, e-government, e-learning, and m-commerce. Given the nature of technology and the Internet, EC will undoubtedly continue to shift and change. More and more EC successes are emerging (see Athitakis 2003 and Mullaney 2004).

collaborative commerce (c-commerce)
E-commerce model in which individuals or groups communicate or collaborate online.

e-learning
The online delivery of information for purposes of training or education.

exchange (electronic)
A public electronic market with many buyers and sellers.

exchange-to-exchange (E2E)
E-commerce model in which electronic exchanges formally connect to one another for the purpose of exchanging information.

e-government
E-commerce model in which a government entity buys or provides goods, services, or information to businesses or individual citizens.

EC Successes

The last few years have seen the rise of extremely successful virtual EC companies such as eBay, Google, Yahoo!, VeriSign, AOL, and Checkpoint. Click-and-mortar companies such as Cisco, General Electric, IBM, Intel, and Schwab also have seen great success (see Carton 2002; Farhoomand and Lovelock 2001; Mullaney 2004; and Jelassi and Enders 2005). Additional success stories include start-ups such as Alloy.com (a young-adults-oriented portal), Drugstore.com, FTD.com, PTSweb.com, and Campusfood.com (see EC Application Case 1.3).

EC Failures

Starting in 1999, a large number of EC companies, especially e-tailing ones, began to fail (see disobey.com/ghostsites; Useem 2000; Carton 2002; Perkins and Perkins 2001; and Kaplan 2002). Well-known B2C failures include eToys, Xpeditor, MarchFirst, Drkoop.com, Webvan.com, and Boo.com. Well-known B2B failures include Chemdex.com, Ventro.com, and Verticalnet.com. (Incidentally, the history of these pioneering companies is documented in The Business Plan Archive [businessplanarchive.org/] by David Kirch at the Business School, University of Maryland; see Mark 2004.) The reasons for these and other EC failures are discussed in detail in Chapters 3, 6, and 14.

Does the large number of failures mean that EC's days are numbered? Absolutely not! First, the dot-com failure rate is declining sharply. Second, the EC field is basically experiencing consolidation as companies test different business models and organizational structures. Third, most pure EC companies, including giants such as Amazon.com, are not yet making a profit or are making only small profits, but they *are* expanding operations and generating increasing sales. Some analysts predict that by 2005 many of the major pure EC companies will begin to generate profits.

THE FUTURE OF EC

In 1996, Forrester Research (forrester.com), a major EC-industry analyst, predicted that B2C would be a $6.6 billion business by 2000, up from $518 million in 1996. In 1998, B2C sales in the United States were about $43 billion, or 1 percent of total retail sales (Greenberg

CASE 1.3

EC Application

THE SUCCESS STORY OF CAMPUSFOOD.COM

Campusfood.com's recipe for success was a simple one: Provide interactive menus to college students, using the power of the Internet to replace and/or facilitate the traditional telephone ordering of meals. Launched at the University of Pennsylvania (Penn), the company takes thousands of orders each month for local restaurants, bringing pizzas, hoagies, and wings to the Penn community and to dozens of other universities.

Founder Michael Saunders began developing the site (*campusfood.com*) in 1997 while he was a junior at Penn. With the help of some classmates, Saunders launched the site in 1998. After graduation, he began building the company's customer base. This involved expanding to other universities, attracting students, and generating a list of restaurants from which students could order food for delivery. Currently, some of these activities are outsourced to a marketing firm, enabling the addition of dozens of schools nationwide. In 2004, the company served 200 schools linked to over 1,000 restaurants.

Financed through private investors, friends, and family members, the site was built on an investment of less than $1 million. (For comparison, another company with services also reaching the college-student market invested $100 million.) Campusfood.com's revenue is generated through *transaction fees*—the site takes a 5 percent commission on each order from the sellers (the restaurants).

When you visit *campusfood.com*, you can:

- Navigate through a list of local restaurants, their hours of operation, addresses, phone numbers, and other information.
- Browse an interactive menu. The company takes a restaurant's standard print menu and converts it to an electronic menu that lists every topping, every special, and every drink offered, along with the latest prices.
- Bypass "busy" telephone signals to place an order online, and in so doing, avoid miscommunications.
- Get access to special foods, promotions, and restaurant giveaways. The company is working to set up meal deals that are available online exclusively for Campusfood.com customers.
- Arrange for electronic payment of an order.

Sources: Compiled from Prince (2000) and *campusfood.com* (accessed August 2004).

Questions

1. Classify this application by EC transaction type.
2. Explain the benefits of Campusfood.com for its student customers and for the restaurants it represents.
3. Trace the flow of digitized information in this venture.
4. How does the outsourcing of the marketing activities contribute to the business?

2004). Today's predictions about the future size of EC, provided by respected analysts such as AMR Research, Emarketer.com, and Forrester, vary (see also Plunkett 2001). For example, 2006 total online shopping and B2B transactions in the United States are estimated to be in the range of $3 to $7 trillion. The number of Internet users worldwide is predicted to reach 750 to 999 million by 2008. Experts predict that as many as 50 percent of all Internet users will shop online by that time. EC growth will come not only from B2C, but also from B2B and from newer applications such as e-government, e-learning, B2E, and c-commerce. Overall, the growth of the field will continue to be strong into the foreseeable future. Despite the failures of individual companies and initiatives, the total volume of EC is growing by 15 to 25 percent every year.

Section 1.2 ▶ REVIEW QUESTIONS

1. List the major components of the EC framework.
2. List the major transactional types of EC.
3. Describe the major landmarks in EC history.
4. List some EC successes and failures.

Now that you are familiar with the concepts of EC, let's see what drives it (Sections 1.3 and 1.4).

1.3 THE DIGITAL REVOLUTION DRIVES E-COMMERCE

The major driver of EC is the digital revolution.

THE DIGITAL REVOLUTION

The digital revolution is upon us. We see it every day at home and work, in businesses, schools, and hospitals, on roads, and even in wars. One of its major aspects is the digital economy.

The **digital economy** refers to an economy that is based on digital technologies, including digital communication networks (the Internet, intranets, extranets, and VANs), computers, software, and other related information technologies. The digital economy is sometimes called the *Internet economy*, the *new economy*, or the *Web economy*. In this new economy, digital networking and communications infrastructures provide a global platform over which people and organizations interact, communicate, collaborate, and search for information. According to Choi and Whinston (2000), this platform includes the following characteristics:

digital economy
An economy that is based on digital technologies, including digital communication networks, computers, software, and other related information technologies; also called the Internet economy, the new economy, or the Web economy.

- A vast array of digitizable products—databases, news and information, books, magazines, TV and radio programming, movies, electronic games, musical CDs, and software—are delivered over a digital infrastructure anytime, anywhere in the world.
- Consumers and firms conduct financial transactions digitally through digital currencies or financial tokens that are carried via networked computers and mobile devices.
- Microprocessors and networking capabilities are embedded in physical goods such as home appliances and automobiles.

The term *digital economy* also refers to the convergence of computing and communications technologies on the Internet and other networks and the resulting flow of information and technology that is stimulating EC and vast organizational changes. This convergence enables all types of information (data, audio, video, etc.) to be stored, processed, and transmitted over networks to many destinations worldwide (see also Head 2003; Kehal and Singh 2004; and Turban et al. 2006).

The digital economy is creating an economic revolution (see Chapter 15 and Chen 2004), which, according to the *Emerging Digital Economy II* (U.S. Department of Commerce 1999), is evidenced by unprecedented economic performance and the longest period of uninterrupted economic expansion in U.S. history (1991–2000), combined with low inflation.

The digital revolution accelerates EC mainly by providing competitive advantage to organizations. In a study conducted by Lederer et al. (1998), "enhancing competitiveness or creating strategic advantage" was ranked as the number-one benefit of Web-based systems.

The digital revolution enables many innovations, some of which are listed in Insights and Additions 1.1. Many, many other innovations characterize the digital revolution, and more appear daily.

Exhibit 1.3 describes the major characteristics of digital economy.

Section 1.3 ▶ REVIEW QUESTIONS

1. Define the digital economy.
2. List the characteristics of the digital economy (per Choi and Whinston 2000 and Exhibit 1.3).

1.4 THE BUSINESS ENVIRONMENT DRIVES EC

Whereas the digital revolution drives EC mainly by providing the necessary technologies, the major driver for organizations to *use* EC is today's business environment.

Economic, legal, societal, and technological factors have created a highly competitive *business environment* in which customers are becoming more powerful. These environmental factors can change quickly, sometimes in an unpredictable manner. For example, James Strong, the CEO of Qantas Airways, once said, "The lesson we have learned is how quickly things can change. You have to be prepared to move fast when the situation demands" (*Business Review Weekly of Australia*, August 25, 2000). Companies need to react quickly to both the problems and the opportunities resulting from this new business environment. Because the pace of change and the level of uncertainty are expected to accelerate, organizations are operating under increasing pressures to produce more products, faster, and with fewer resources.

Insights and Additions 1.1 Interesting and Unique Applications of EC

- According to Farivar (2004), VIP patrons of the Baja Beach Club in Barcelona, Spain, can have radio frequency identification (RFID) chips, which are the size of a grain of rice, implanted into their upper arms, allowing them to charge drinks to a bar tab when they raise their arm toward the RFID reader. An RFID is a tiny tag that contains a processor and antenna and can communicate wirelessly with a detecting unit in a reader over a short distance (see Chapters 7 and 9). "You don't call someone crazy for getting a tattoo," says Conrad Chase, director of Baja Beach Clubs international, "Why would they be crazy for getting this?"
- Pearson Education, Inc., the publisher of this book, in collaboration with O'Reilly & Associates, offers professors reasonably priced, customized textbooks for their classes by compiling material from thousands of Pearson's publications and the instructors' own materials. The customized books are either electronic (Chapter 8) or more expensive hard copies.
- In Japan, a person can wave a Casio watch over a scanner to purchase products from a vending machine, pay for food in a cafeteria, or pay for gasoline.
- Dryers and washers in college dorms are hooked to the Web. Students can punch a code into their cell phones or sign in at *esuds.net* and check on the availability of laundry machines. Furthermore, they can pay with their student ID or with a credit card and receive e-mail alerts when their wash and dry cycles are complete. Once in the laundry room, a student activates the system by swiping a student ID card or keying in a PIN number. The system automatically injects premeasured amounts of detergent and fabric softener, at the right cycle time.
- More than 50 percent of all airline tickets sold in the United States are electronic tickets. It costs more to purchase a paper ticket from a local travel agent. In some airports, travelers can get their boarding passes from a machine.
- In January 2004, NASA's Web site received more than 6.5 billion hits in a few days—the biggest Internet government event to date—because people were interested in viewing the rover's landing on Mars.
- Several banks in Japan issue smart cards that can be used only by their owners. When using the cards, the palm vein of the owner's hand is compared with a prestored template of the vein stored on the smart card. When the owner inserts the card into ATM or vendors' card readers that are equipped with the system, it will dispense the person's money. The police are alerted if anyone other than the card's owner tries to use it.
- Jacobi Medical Center in New York tracks the whereabouts of patients in the hospital. Each patient has an RFID in a plastic band strapped to his or her wrist. Each time a patient passes an RFID reader, its location is transmitted in real time to the responsible staff. The RFID is linked to the hospital's computer network, connecting the patient's records to labs, billing, and the pharmacy.
- To find adoptive parents for himself and a baby sister after both parents died of cancer, a Chinese boy in Zhengzhou, China, created a special Web site that described the children and showed photos. Within a short time, dozens of people from many countries expressed an interest (*Zhengzhou Evening News* (in Chinese), September 27, 2004).
- CompUSA offers an ATM-like service that dispenses software like candy from a vending machine. An ATM-like device with a touch screen lets CompUSA consumers shop for software by choosing an operating system and selecting from categories such as business, education, and games. The consumer is presented with a list of titles and descriptions and prices. Once the consumer picks a title, an order ticket is printed. The consumer then presents the order ticket to a sales rep and pays for the software. The rep then enters information into a second machine called an order-fulfillment station. It burns the software onto a CD. The sales rep packages the CD and instructions in a box.

According to Huber (2004), the new business environment is a result of advances in science occurring at an accelerated rate. These advances create scientific knowledge that feeds on itself, resulting in more and more technology. The rapid growth in technology results in a large variety of more complex systems. As a result, the business environment has the following characteristics: a more turbulent environment, with more business problems and opportunities; stronger competition; the need for organizations to make decisions more frequently, either by expediting the decision process or by having more decision makers; a larger scope for decisions because more factors (market, competition, political issues, and global environment) need to be considered; and more information and/or knowledge is needed for making decisions.

THE ENVIRONMENT–RESPONSE–SUPPORT MODEL

In order to succeed—and frequently, even to survive—in the face of these dramatic changes and environmental pressures, companies must not only take traditional actions such as lowering costs and closing unprofitable facilities, but also introduce innovative actions such as cus-

EXHIBIT 1.3 Some Characteristics of the Digital Revolution

Area	Description
Globalization	Global communication and collaboration; global electronic marketplaces.
Digital system	From TV to telephones and instrumentation, analog systems are being converted to digital ones.
Speed	A move to real-time transactions, thanks to digitized documents, products, and services. Many business processes are expedited by 90 percent or more.
Information overload	Although the amount of information generated is accelerating, intelligent search tools can help users find what they need.
Markets	Markets are moving online. Physical marketplaces are being replaced by electronic markets; new markets are being created, increasing competition.
Digitization	Music, books, pictures, and more (see Chapter 2) are digitized for fast and inexpensive distribution.
Business models and processes	New and improved business models and processes provide opportunities to new companies and industries. Cyberintermediation and no intermediation are on the rise.
Innovation	Digital and Internet-based innovations continue at a rapid pace. More patents are being granted than ever before.
Obsolescence	The fast pace of innovation creates a high rate of obsolescence.
Opportunities	Opportunities abound in almost all aspects of life and operations.
Fraud	Criminals employ a slew of innovative schemes on the Internet. Cybercons are everywhere.
Wars	Conventional wars are changing to cyberwars.

tomizing, creating new products, or providing superb customer service (Carr 2001). We refer to both activities as *critical response activities.*

Critical response activities can take place in some or all organizational processes, from the daily processing of payroll and order entry to strategic activities such as the acquisition of a company. Responses can also occur in the supply chain, as demonstrated by the cases of Dell and Marks & Spencer. A response activity can be a reaction to a specific pressure already in existence or it can be an initiative that will defend an organization against future pressures. It can also be an activity that exploits an opportunity created by changing conditions.

Many response activities can be greatly facilitated by EC. In some cases, EC is the *only* solution to these business pressures (Tapscott et al. 1998; Callon 1996; Turban et al. 2006). The relationships among business pressures, organizational responses, and EC are shown in Exhibit 1.4. The pressures are shown as the arrows pointing from the three business environments areas toward organizations (arrows pointing inward). The organizational responses are shown as the arrows pointing from organizations toward the business environment (arrows pointing outward). The organizational responses are supported by information technology (IT) and by EC. In other words, EC is driven by necessity to compete or even survive. Now, let's examine the three components of this model in more detail.

Business Pressures

In this text, business pressures are divided into the following categories: market (economic), societal, and technological. The main types of business pressures in each category are listed in Exhibit 1.5.

Organizational Response Strategies

How can organizations operate in such an environment? How can they deal with the threats and the opportunities? To begin with, many traditional strategies are still useful in today's environment. However, because some traditional response activities may not work in today's turbulent and competitive business environment, many of the old solutions need to be modified, supplemented, or discarded. Alternatively, new responses can be devised. Here we present some examples from among the many EC-supported response activities.

Strategic Systems. *Strategic systems* provide organizations with strategic advantages, enabling them to increase their market share, better negotiate with their suppliers, or prevent competitors

EXHIBIT 1.4 Major Business Pressures and the Role of EC

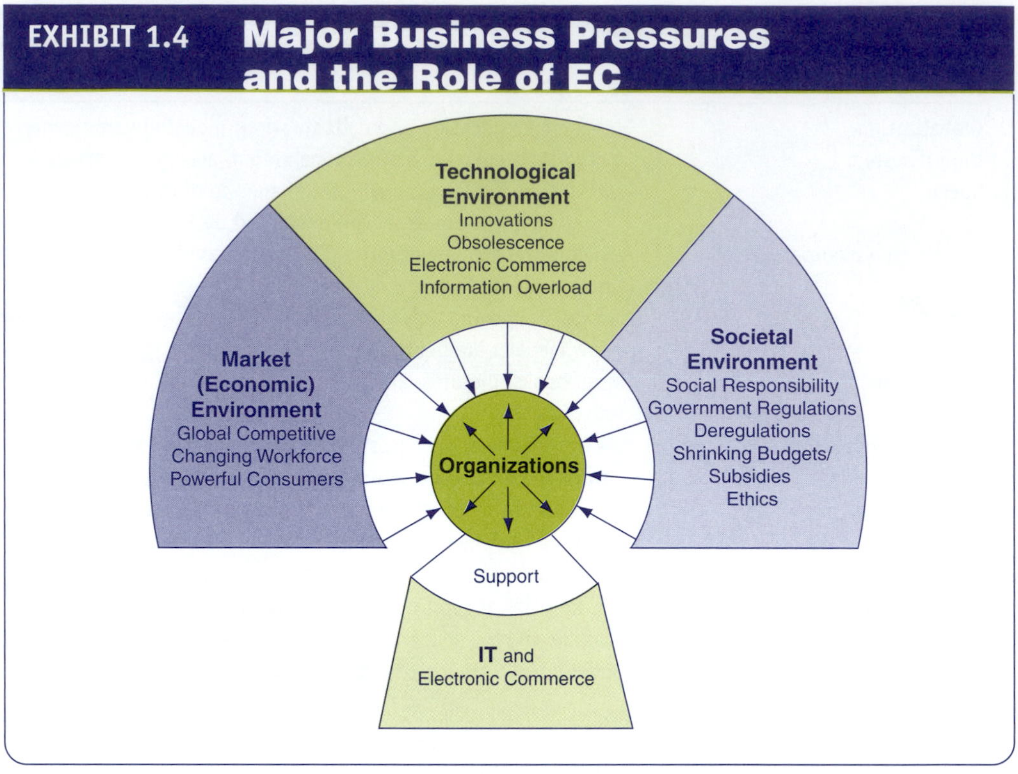

from entering into their territory (Callon 1996). There are a variety of EC-supported strategic systems. One example is FedEx's tracking system, which allows FedEx to identify the status of every individual package, anywhere in the system. Most of FedEx's competitors have already copied the FedEx system. In response, FedEx has introduced new Web-based initiatives (see Online File W1.2).

Agile Systems. Agile organizations have the ability to consistently improve productivity—especially during periods of change. To create business agility, organizations use IT in general and EC in particular. The solution provided by EC enables capitalizing on changing industry, government, and business requirements; assimilating required resources and business processes quickly to meet demand; promptly adapting technology to fit new or modified business processes; leveraging existing resources to do the above; and doing it all economically (see PeopleSoft 2004).

Continuous Improvement Efforts and Business Process Restructuring. Many companies continuously conduct programs to improve their productivity, quality, and customer service. Two examples of how EC can help are Dell and Intel. Dell takes its orders electronically

EXHIBIT 1.5 Major Business Pressures

Market and Economic Pressures	Societal Pressures	Technological Pressures
Strong competition	Changing nature of workforce	Increasing innovations and new technologies
Global economy	Government deregulation, leading to more competition	Rapid technological obsolescence
Regional trade agreements (e.g., NAFTA)	Compliance (e.g., Sarbanes-Oxley Act)	Increases in information overload
Extremely low labor cost in some countries	Shrinking government subsidies	Rapid decline in technology cost versus performance ratio
Frequent and significant changes in markets	Increased importance of ethical and legal issues	
Increased power of consumers	Increased social responsibility of organizations	
	Rapid political changes	

and immediately moves them via *enterprise resource planning* (ERP) software (see Online Tutorial T2) into the just-in-time assembly operation. Using an almost real-time extranet-based monitoring system, Intel tracks the consumption of its products by a dozen of its largest customers in order to plan production schedules and deliveries.

WWW

However, continuous improvement programs may not be a sufficient solution for some business problems. Strong business pressures may require a radical structural change. Such an effort is referred to as *business process restructuring* or *reengineering* (BPR). E-commerce is frequently interrelated with process restructuring that may be needed for implementation of EC initiatives such as e-procurement.

Customer Relationship Management. One of the major symptoms of the digital revolution is that the bargaining power of customers is stronger than ever, and that power is growing. The availability of information and the ability to make quick comparisons online increases this trend. Customers are called "kings" and "queens," and organizations must make their customers happy in order to keep them. As discussed in Chapter 13 and in Insights and Additions 1.2, this may be accomplished through *customer relationship management* (CRM).

As indicated earlier, EC is not just about buying and selling. Supporting CRM, as we will see throughout the book, and especially in Chapter 13, is a major function of EC. Such support is done by multiple technologies, ranging from computerized call centers to intelligent agents. Some of the e-CRM topics highlighted in this book are sales force automation; call center tools and operations; personalization; empowerment of customers and frontline employees; support of mobile employees; and partner relationship management.

Business Alliances. Many companies realize that alliances with other companies, *even competitors*, can be beneficial. For example, General Motors, Ford, and others in the automotive industry created a huge B2B e-marketplace called Covisint (see Chapter 6). Other types of business alliances include resource-sharing partnerships, permanent supplier–company relationships, and joint research efforts. For additional details, see Chapter 14.

Electronic Markets. Electronic markets, private or public, can optimize trading efficiency, enabling their members to compete globally. Most electronic markets require the collaboration of different companies, sometimes even competitors, as will be shown in Chapters 6 and 7.

Reductions in Cycle Time and Time-to-Market. **Cycle time reduction**—shortening the time it takes for a business to complete a productive activity from its beginning to end—is

cycle time reduction
Shortening the time it takes for a business to complete a productive activity from its beginning to end.

Insights and Additions 1.2 E-Commerce and CRM

The topic of *customer relationship management* (CRM) has been closely related to EC since 1997, when EC and CRM were put together for the first time as e-CRM. CRM has many definitions (Greenberg 2004). A panel of CRM experts, working with CRMGuru.com, defined CRM as follows:

> CRM is a business strategy to select and manage customers to optimize long-term value. CRM requires a customer-centric business philosophy and culture to support effective marketing, sales, and service processes. CRM applications can enable effective Customer Relationship Management, provided that an enterprise has the right leadership, strategy, and culture. (*greaterchinacrm.org* 2003)

CRM is a diversified field that can be divided into the following areas (Greenberg 2004; Peppers and Rogers 2004; and Stauss and Seidel 2004):

- **Operational CRM.** Operational CRM is used for typical business functions involving customer services, order management, invoice/billing, or sales and marketing automation and management. It involves integration with all the functional areas, frequently via ERP. EC transactions are closely related to operational CRM.
- **Analytical CRM.** Analytical CRM involves the capture, storage, extraction, processing, interpretation, and reporting of customer data to a user. Then, these data can be analyzed as needed. E-commerce can be closely related to analytical CRM. For example, personalization of data required for one-to-one advertisement, a part of CRM, is done with EC tools.
- **Collaborative CRM.** Collaborative CRM deals with all the necessary communication, coordination, and collaboration between vendors and customers. E-commerce tools, such as corporate portals, are very useful in supporting this type of CRM.

extremely important for increasing productivity and competitiveness (Davis 2001). Similarly, reducing the time from the inception of an idea to its implementation (*time-to-market*) is important, because those who are first on the market with a product, or who can provide customers with a service faster than their competitors, enjoy a distinct competitive advantage. Extranet-based applications can expedite the various steps in the process of product or service development, testing, and implementation. An example of EC-supported cycle time reduction in bringing new drugs to the market is described in EC Application Case 1.4. (Also see the EC Application Case on Procter & Gamble in Chapter 4.)

Empowerment of Employees. Giving employees the authority to act and make decisions on their own is a strategy used by many organizations as part of productivity improvement programs. Management delegates authority to individuals or teams (see Lipnack and Stamps 2000) who can then execute the work faster and with fewer delays. Empowerment of

CASE 1.4

EC Application

THE INTERNET AND THE INTRANET SHORTEN TIME-TO-MARKET FOR NEW PRODUCTS AND SERVICES

The Federal Drug Administration (FDA) must be extremely careful in approving new drugs. However, the FDA is under public pressure to approve new drugs quickly, especially those for cancer and HIV. The problem is that to ensure quality, the FDA requires companies to conduct extensive research and clinical testing. The development programs for such research and testing require 300,000 to 500,000 pages of documentation for each new drug. The subsequent results and analyses are reported on 100,000 to 200,000 additional pages. These pages are then reviewed by the FDA prior to approval of a new drug. Manual processing of this information significantly slows the work of the FDA, so that the total approval process takes 6 to 10 years.

A software program offered a computerized solution. The software used a network-distributed document-processing system that enabled the pharmaceutical company to scan all related documents into a database. The documents were indexed, and full-text search and retrieval software was attached to the system. Using keywords, corporate employees could search the database via their company's intranet. The database was also accessible, via the Internet, to FDA employees, who no longer had to spend hours looking for a specific piece of data. Information could be processed or printed at the user's desktop computer. These functions enabled the U.S. government to offer an electronic submission and online review process for approval of new drugs (*fda.gov/cder*).

This system helped not only the FDA, but also the companies' researchers, who suddenly had every piece of required information at their fingertips. Remote corporate and business partners also could access the system. The overall result was that the time-to-market of a new drug could be reduced by up to a year. Each week saved translates into the saving of many lives and also yields up to $1 million in profits. The system also reduced the time it took to patent a new drug.

An example of an interesting use of this technology is the case of ISIS Pharmaceuticals, Inc. (*isispharm.com*), which developed an extranet-based system similar to the one described here. The company uses CD-ROMs to submit reports to the FDA and opens its intranet to FDA personnel. This step alone could save 6 to 12 months from the average 15-month review time. Simply by submitting an FDA report electronically, the company can save one month of review time. To cut time even further, SmithKline Beecham Corporation is using electronic publishing and hypertext links to enable FDA reviewers to quickly navigate its submissions.

Entelos (*entelos.com*), a biotechnology firm, uses computer software to simulate the behavior of the human body and predict its response to various drugs. Pharmaceutical companies approach Entelos with ideas for new drugs, and Entelos simulates the drug's effect on hundreds of "patients" who take the medication in hundreds of different circumstances. Each trial can involve up to 13,000 simulations. To handle this processing load, Entelos uses grid computing to use processing power from 145 different machines spread across its offices. Simulations that used to take two years on a mainframe now take one month on the grid (Metz 2003).

Caterpiller Inc. connects its engineering and manufacturing divisions with its suppliers, customers, and overseas factories via an extranet-based global collaboration system (Chapters 6 and 7). Requests for improved design flow are available electronically to engineering and other related departments. Cycle time is 70 percent shorter, and there are fewer delays. General Motors and other car manufacturers are using EC tools to cut time-to-market by more than 65 percent.

Finally, the Denver Museum of Nature and Science reduced delivery time of requested information and images from days to minutes using several EC tools.

Sources: Compiled from Folio (2004), Macht (1997), and Metz (2003).

Questions

1. How does the computerized drug application system facilitate collaboration?
2. How is cycle time reduced?

employees may also be part of e-CRM. Empowered salespeople and customer service employees are given the authority to make customers happy and do it quickly, helping to increase customer loyalty. EC allows the decentralization of decision making and authority via empowerment and distributed systems, but simultaneously supports a centralized control.

Supply Chain Improvements. EC, as will be shown throughout the book, and especially in Chapters 7 and 13 and Online Tutorial T2, can help reduce supply chain delays, reduce inventories, and eliminate other inefficiencies. The use of e-supply chain models to automate factory scheduling, which reduces response time and inventory management, was shown in the Dell opening case.

Mass Customization: Make-to-Order in Large Quantities. Today's customers demand customized products and services; the business problem is how to provide customization and do it efficiently. This can be done, in part, by changing manufacturing processes from mass production to mass customization (Anderson 2002; Pine and Gilmore 1997). In mass production, a company produces a large quantity of identical items. In **mass customization**, items are produced in a large quantity but are customized to fit the desires of each customer. EC is an ideal facilitator of mass customization, for example, by enabling interactive communication between buyers and designers so customers can quickly and correctly configure the products they want. Also, orders placed online can reach production facilities in minutes. Note that mass customization is not easy to achieve (e.g., see Zipkin 2001); however, EC can help. Mass customization requires a build-to-order process, as described in Appendix 2A in Chapter 2.

mass customization
Production of large quantities of customized items.

Intrabusiness: From Sales Force Automation to Inventory Control. One area where EC has made major progress in supporting organizational responses is applications inside the business. As seen in Online File W1.1 on Marks & Spencer and in the Real-World Case at the end of this chapter, support can be provided to field representatives, warehouse employees, designers, researchers, and office workers. The improvements in productivity for these kinds of employees were fairly slow until the introduction of EC.

Knowledge Management. **Knowledge management (KM)** refers to the process of creating or capturing knowledge, storing and protecting it, updating and maintaining it, and using it whenever necessary. Knowledge management programs and software are frequently associated with EC. For example, knowledge is delivered via corporate portals to assist users or to teach employees. Also, EC implementation requires knowledge, and EC activities such as market research create knowledge. For more on the EC–KM connection, see Chapter 8.

knowledge management (KM)
The process of creating or capturing knowledge, storing and protecting it, updating and maintaining it, and using it.

Section 1.4 ▶ REVIEW QUESTIONS

1. List the major business pressures faced by organizations today.
2. List the major organizational responses to business pressures.
3. Describe how EC supports organizational responses to business pressures.
4. Describe an agile organization.

1.5 EC BUSINESS MODELS

One of the major characteristics of EC is that it enables the creation of new business models. A **business model** is a method of doing business by which a company can generate revenue to sustain itself. The model also spells out where the company is positioned in the value chain—that is, by what activities the company adds value to the product or service it supplies. (The *value chain* is the series of value-adding activities that an organization performs to achieve its goals at various stages of the production process.) Some models are very simple. For example, Wal-Mart buys merchandise, sells it, and generates a profit. In contrast, a TV station provides free broadcasting to its viewers. The station's survival depends on a complex model involving advertisers and content providers. Public Internet portals, such as Yahoo!, also use a complex business model. One company may have several business models.

business model
A method of doing business by which a company can generate revenue to sustain itself.

Business models are a subset of a business plan or a business case. These concepts frequently are mixed up. (In other words, some equate a *business model* with a *business plan.*) However, as Chapters 14 and 16 and Online Tutorial T1 explain, business plans and cases differ from business models. Also see Boyd (2004) and Currie (2004).

THE STRUCTURE OF BUSINESS MODELS

There are several different EC business models, depending on the company, the industry, and so on. Weill and Vitale (2001) developed a framework for evaluating the viability of e-business initiatives. According to this methodology, there are eight elementary, or "atomic," e-business models that can be combined in different ways to create operational e-business initiatives. The eight atomic business models are *direct marketing, intermediary, content provider, full-service provider, shared infrastructure, value net integrator, virtual community,* and *consolidator of services* for large organizations. For example, the Amazon.com business model combines direct marketing, the intermediary role, virtual community, and content provider. Each atomic model can be described by four characteristics: strategic objectives, sources of revenue, critical success factors, and core competencies required. However, all business models share common elements.

According to McKay and Marshall (2004), a comprehensive business model is composed of the following six elements:

- A description of the *customers* to be served and the company's relationships with these customers, including what constitutes value from the perspective of the customers (*customers' value proposition*).
- A description of all *products* and *services* the business will offer.
- A description of the *business process* required to make and deliver the products and services.
- A list of the *resources* required and the identification of which ones are available, which will be developed in house, and which will need to be acquired.
- A description of the organization *supply chain*, including *suppliers* and other *business partners.*
- A description of the revenues expected (*revenue model*), anticipated costs, sources of financing, and estimated profitability (*financial viability*).

Models also include a *value proposition,* which is an analysis of the benefits of using the specific model (tangible and intangible), including the customers' value proposition cited earlier.

A detailed discussion of and examples of business models and their relationship to business plans is presented in Chapter 16 and Online Tutorial T1.

This chapter presents two of the elements that are needed to understand the material in Chapters 2 through 15: revenue models and value proposition.

Revenue Models

revenue model
Description of how the company or an EC project will earn revenue.

A **revenue model** outlines how the organization or the EC project will generate revenue. For example, the revenue model for Godiva's online EC initiative shows revenue from online sales. The major revenue models are:

- **Sales.** Companies generate revenue from selling merchandise or services over their Web sites. An example is when Wal-Mart or Godiva sells a product online.
- **Transaction fees.** A company receives a commission based on the volume of transactions made. For example, when a homeowner sells a house, he or she typically pays a transaction fee to the broker. The higher the value of the sale, the higher the total transaction fee. Alternatively, transaction fees can be levied *per transaction.* With online stock trades, for example, there is usually a fixed fee per trade, regardless of the volume.
- **Subscription fees.** Customers pay a fixed amount, usually monthly, to get some type of service. An example would be the access fee for AOL. Thus, AOL's primary revenue model is subscription (fixed monthly payments).
- **Advertising fees.** Companies charge others for allowing them to place a banner on their sites (see Chapter 4).
- **Affiliate fees.** Companies receive commissions for referring customers to others' Web sites.
- **Other revenue sources.** Some companies allow people to play games for a fee or watch a sports competition in real time for a fee (e.g., see espn.go.com). Another revenue source is licensing fees (e.g., datadirect-technologies.com). Licensing fees can be assessed as an annual fee or a per usage fee. Microsoft takes fees from each workstation that uses Windows NT, for example.

A company uses its revenue model to describe how it will generate revenue and its business model to describe the *process* it will use to do so. Exhibit 1.6 summarizes five common revenue models. For example, Godiva's revenue model shows that customers can order products online or at a Godiva store, where they can pay the cashier. The customers can pick up the merchandise at a Godiva store or, for an extra charge, have it shipped to their homes. The revenue comes from sales, which take place both off-line and online.

The revenue model can be part of the value proposition or it may complement it.

Value Proposition

Business models also include a value proposition statement. A **value proposition** refers to the benefits, including the intangible, nonquantitative ones, that a company can derive from using the model. In B2C EC, for example, a value proposition defines how a company's product or service fulfills the needs of customers. The value proposition is an important part of the marketing plan of any product or service.

value proposition
The benefits a company can derive from using EC.

Specifically, how do e-marketplaces create value? Amit and Zott (2001) identify four sets of values that are created by e-business: search and transaction cost efficiency, complementarities, lock-in, and novelty. *Search and transaction cost efficiency* enables faster and more informed decision making, wider product and service selection, and greater economies of scale—cost savings per unit as greater quantities are produced and sold (e.g., through demand and supply aggregation for small buyers and sellers). *Complementarities* involve bundling some goods and services together to provide more value than from offering them separately. *Lock-in* is attributable to the high switching cost that ties customers to particular suppliers. *Novelty* creates value through innovative ways for structuring transactions, connecting partners, and fostering new markets.

EXHIBIT 1.6 Common Revenue Models

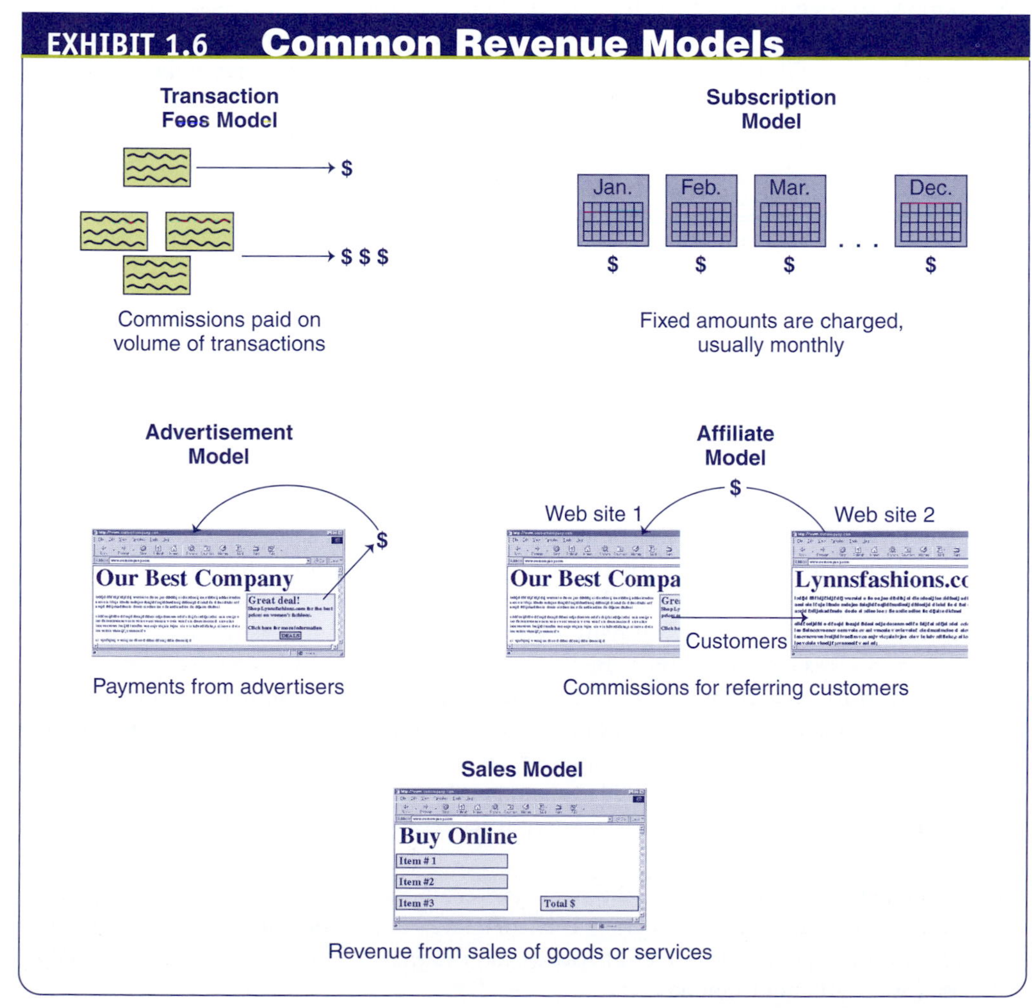

Bakos (1991) identifies similar values: reduced search cost, significant switching cost, economies of scale and scope, and network externality (i.e., the tendency for consumers to place more value on a good or service as more of the market uses that good or service). Bakos regards *search cost reduction* as the attribute most specific to e-marketplaces. It is the subject of analysis in many studies on e-marketplaces.

TYPICAL EC BUSINESS MODELS

There are many types of EC business models. Examples and details can be found throughout this text (and also in Weill and Vitale 2001; Currie 2004; Rossi et al. 2003; and Afuah and Tucci 2003). The following list describes some of the most common or visible models. Details are provided throughout the text.

1. **Online direct marketing.** The most obvious model is that of selling products or services online. Sales may be from a manufacturer to a customer, eliminating intermediaries or physical stores (e.g., Godiva), or from retailers to consumers, making distribution more efficient (e.g., Wal-Mart). This model is especially efficient for digitizable products and services (those that can be delivered electronically). This model has several variations (see Chapters 3 and 5). It is practiced in B2C (where it is called *e-tailing*) and in some B2B types of EC.

tendering (reverse auction)
Model in which a buyer requests would-be sellers to submit bids; the lowest bidder wins.

2. **Electronic tendering systems.** Large organizational buyers, private or public, usually make large-volume or large-value purchases through a **tendering** (bidding) system, also known as a *reverse auction*. Such tendering can be done online, saving time and money. Pioneered by General Electric Corp., e-tendering systems are gaining popularity. Indeed, several government agencies mandate that most of their procurement must be done through e-tendering (see Chapter 5).

name-your-own-price model
Model in which a buyer sets the price he or she is willing to pay and invites sellers to supply the good or service at that price.

3. **Name your own price.** Pioneered by Priceline.com, the **name-your-own-price model** allows a buyer to set the price he or she is willing to pay for a specific product or service. Priceline.com will try to match the customer's request with a supplier willing to sell the product or service at that price. This model is also known as a *demand-collection model* (see Chapter 10).
4. **Find the best price.** According to this model, also known as a *search engine model* (see Bandyopadhyay 2001), a customer specifies his or her need and then an intermediate company, such as Hotwire.com, matches the customer's need against a database, locates the lowest price, and submits it to the consumer. The potential buyer then has 30 to 60 minutes to accept or reject the offer. A variation of this model is available for purchasing insurance: A consumer can submit a request for insurance to Insweb.com and receive several quotes. Many companies employ similar models to find the lowest price. For example, consumers can go to eloan.com to find the best interest rate for auto or home loans. A well-known company in this area is Shopping.com, which is described with similar companies in Chapter 3.

affiliate marketing
An arrangement whereby a marketing partner (a business, an organization, or even an individual) refers consumers to the selling company's Web site.

5. **Affiliate marketing.** **Affiliate marketing** is an arrangement whereby a marketing partner (a business, an organization, or even an individual) refers consumers to a selling company's Web site (see Chapter 4). The referral is done by placing a banner ad or the logo of the selling company on the affiliated company's Web site. Whenever a customer who was referred to the selling company's Web site makes a purchase there, the affiliated partner receives a commission (which may range from 3 to 15 percent) of the purchase price. In other words, by using affiliate marketing, a selling company creates a *virtual commissioned sales force*. Pioneered by CDNow (see Hoffman and Novak 2000), the concept is now employed by thousands of retailers and manufacturers. For example, Amazon.com has close to 500,000 affiliates, and even tiny Cattoys.com offers individuals and organizations the opportunity to put its logo and link on their Web sites to generate commissions.

viral marketing
Word-of-mouth marketing in which customers promote a product or service to friends or other people.

6. **Viral marketing.** According to the **viral marketing** model (see Chapter 4), an organization can increase brand awareness or even generate sales by inducing people to send messages to other people or to recruit friends to join certain programs. It is basically Web-based word-of-mouth marketing.

7. **Group purchasing.** In the off-line world of commerce, discounts are usually available for purchasing large quantities. So, too, EC has spawned the concept of *demand aggregation*, wherein a third party finds individuals or **SMEs** (small-to-medium enterprises), aggregates their small orders to attain a large quantity, and then negotiates (or conducts a tender) for the best deal. Thus, using the concept of **group purchasing**, a small business or even an individual can get a discount. This model, also known as the *volume-buying model,* is described in Chapter 5. One leading aggregator is Letsbuyit.com (see also Rugullis 2000.) Online purchasing groups are also called **e-co-ops**.
8. **Online auctions.** Almost everyone has heard of eBay, the world's largest online auction site. Several hundred other companies, including Amazon.com and Yahoo!, also conduct online auctions. In the most popular type of auction, online shoppers make consecutive bids for various goods and services, and the highest bidders get the items auctioned. E-auctions come in different shapes (Chapters 2 and 10) and use different models. For example, eBay is using about 40,000 "assistants" in a model where the assistants perform the order fulfillments (see Chapter 2).
9. **Product and service customization.** **Customization** of products or services means creating a product or service according to the buyer's specifications. Customization is not a new model, but what *is* new is the ability to quickly customize products online for consumers at costs not much higher than their noncustomized counterparts (see Chapters 3 and 5). Dell is a good example of a company that customizes PCs for its customers.

   Many other companies are following Dell's lead: The automobile industry is customizing its products and expects to save billions of dollars in inventory reduction alone every year by producing made-to-order cars (see Wiegram and Koth 2000; and Li and Du 2004). Mattel's My Design lets fashion-doll fans custom-build a friend for Barbie at Mattel's Web site; the doll's image is displayed on the screen before the person places an order. Nike allows customers to customize shoes, which can be delivered in a week. De Beers allows customers to design their own engagement rings.

   Configuring the details of the customized products, including the final design, ordering, and paying for the products, is done online. Also known as *build-to-order,* customization can be done on a large scale, in which case it is called *mass customization*. For a historical discussion of the development of the idea of mass customization, see Appendix 2A at the end of Chapter 2.
10. **Electronic marketplaces and exchanges.** Electronic marketplaces existed in isolated applications for decades (e.g., stock and commodities exchanges). But as of 1999, hundreds of e-marketplaces have introduced new efficiencies to the trading process. If they are well organized and managed, e-marketplaces can provide significant benefits to both buyers and sellers. Of special interest are *vertical* marketplaces, which concentrate on one industry (e.g., GNX.com for the retail industry and Chemconnect.com for the chemical industry).
11. **Information brokers.** Information brokers (see Chapters 3 through 8) provide privacy, trust, matching, search, content, and other services (e.g., Bizrate.com, Google.com).
12. **Bartering.** Companies use bartering (see Chapters 2 and 10) to exchange surpluses they do not need for things that they do need. A market maker (e.g., Web-barter.com or Tradeaway.com) arranges such exchanges.
13. **Deep discounting.** Companies such as Half.com offer products and services at deep discounts, as much as 50 percent off the retail price (see Chapter 3).
14. **Membership.** A popular off-line model, in which only members get a discount, also is being offered online (e.g., Netmarket.com and NYTimes.com) (for details, see Bandyopadhyay 2001).
15. **Value-chain integrators.** This model offers services that aggregate information-rich products into a more complete package for customers, thus adding value. For example, Carpoint.com provides several car-buying–related services, such as financing and insurance.
16. **Value-chain service providers.** These providers specialize in a supply chain function such as logistics (UPS.com) or payments (PayPal.com, now part of eBay) (see Chapters 7, 12, and 13).

SMEs
Small-to-medium enterprises.

group purchasing
Quantity purchasing that enables groups of purchasers to obtain a discount price on the products purchased.

e-co-ops
Another name for online group purchasing organizations.

customization
Creation of a product or service according to the buyer's specifications.

17. **Supply chain improvers.** One of the major contributions of EC is in the creation of new models that change or improve supply chain management, as shown in the opening case about Dell. Most interesting is the conversion of a *linear* supply chain, which can be slow, expensive, and error prone, into a *hub*. An example of such an improvement is provided in EC Application Case 1.5.

CASE 1.5

EC Application

ORBIS GROUP CHANGES A LINEAR PHYSICAL SUPPLY CHAIN TO AN ELECTRONIC HUB

Orbis (*orbisglobal.com*) is a small, Australian company that provides Internet and EC services. One of its services, ProductBank (*productbank.com.au*), revolutionized the flow of information and products in the B2B advertising field. To put together a retail catalog or brochure, someone must gather pictures of the many products to be advertised and consult with an ad agency on how to present them. These pictures are obtained from each manufacturer, such as Sony or Nokia. The traditional process is linear, as shown in the following figure.

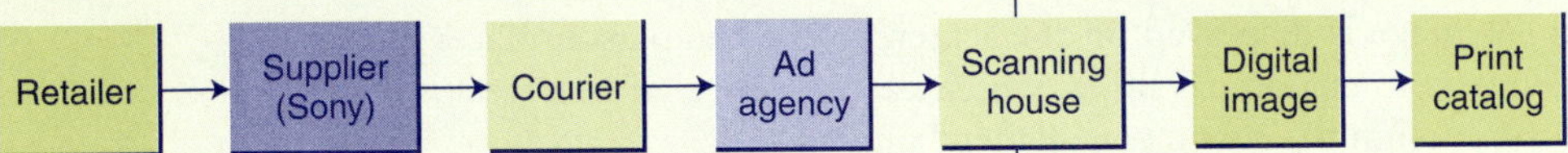

The traditional process works like this: When retailers need a photo of a product for a new brochure, they contact the manufacturers, who send the photos via a courier to a designated ad agency. The agency selects photos and sends them to the retailer for approval. If the photos are not approved, they are sent back to the agency for redesign, then back to the retailer for approval. When the final design is approved, the ad agency sends out the photos to be scanned and converted into digital images, which are transferred to a print house, where the brochures are printed. The cycle time for each photo is 4 to 6 weeks, and the total transaction cost of preparing one picture for a brochure is about $150 AU.

ProductBank simplifies this lengthy process. It has changed the linear flow of products and information to a digitized hub, as shown in the next figure.

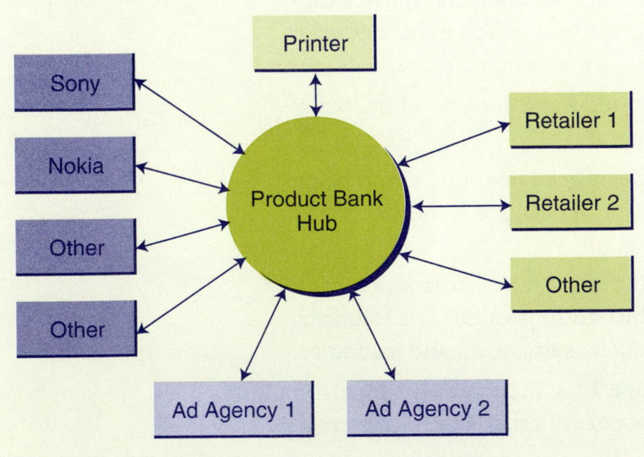

With the new process, manufacturers send digitized photos to Orbis, and Orbis enters and organizes the photos in a database. When retailers need pictures, they can view the digitized images in the database, decide which ones they want to include in their catalog, and communicate that information electronically to their ad agency, which views the photos in the Orbis database. When the ad agency completes its design, the retailer can see it online, and the pictures can be downloaded by the printer into the printing press. The transaction cost per picture (usually paid by the manufacturer) is 30 to 40 percent lower, and the cycle time is 50 to 70 percent shorter than in the traditional catalog production method.

The Orbis case provides some tips for succeeding in the digital economy:

- Digitize as much as you can; eliminate paper and other physical transactions.
- Digitize as early as possible, at the beginning of the transaction process.
- Change the supply chain from a linear model to a hub-based model.
- Aggregate many business partners into one place, such as an information hub or an electronic marketplace.

Sources: Author's attendance at public lecture by Orbis, July 2001; *productbank.com.au* (accessed February 2005); and *orbisglobal.com* (accessed September 2004).

Questions

1. Identify the benefits of the ProductBank system to the supply chain participants.
2. Where does the cost reduction in the ProductBank process come from?
3. Where does the cycle time reduction come from?
4. Explain the benefits of electronic collaboration between the catalog owner and the ad agency.

In order to succeed in the fast-moving marketplace, business and revenue models must change with changing market conditions. A good example is Amazon.com, which moved from selling only books to becoming a huge online store for products and services. Amazon.com also added auctions as a marketing channel. In addition, it provides order-fulfillment services as a subcontractor to others, and much more.

Another example is AOL, which is now part of Time Warner. According to Pruitt (2002), AOL struggled with its business and revenue model strategy in 2002 and considered reviving a revenue model that it had abandoned in 1997, one that is now related to broadband. According to this 1997 model, AOL creates original, exclusive content, such as chats with celebrities or video footage of vacation spots, with the purpose of selling goods and services to AOL subscribers. In 1997, AOL virtually ceased creating content in favor of selling and leasing the space on its Web site to others, who wooed AOL's members.

However, this revenue source (advertising), which was booming until 2000, has plummeted, leaving AOL looking for new sources of revenue. Some question the viability of content creation, which may be too expensive. It would be much cheaper to use content syndicators (see Chapter 16), but then AOL would not be able to distinguish itself from its competitors. Furthermore, content should also be adapted to take advantage of high-speed broadband connections. Of course, AOL is making money from its low-speed, modem-based Internet access services. But the question being asked at the corporate level at Time Warner is whether AOL should concentrate on this source or focus its energies on high-speed broadband connections (a competitive market in which AOL charges more than its competitors, struggling to justify that price to consumers). Choosing the right revenue model at this point in its life may well determine AOL's future existence.

Any of the business models presented in this section can be used alone or in combination with each other or with traditional business models. One company may use several different business models. The models can be used for B2C, B2B, and other forms of EC. Although some of the models are limited to B2C or B2B, others can be used in several types of transactions, as will be illustrated throughout the text.

Section 1.5 ▶ REVIEW QUESTIONS

1. Define the following: business plan, business case, and business model.
2. Describe a revenue model and a value proposition.
3. Describe the following business models: name your own price, affiliate marketing, viral marketing, and product customization.
4. Identify business models related to buying and those related to selling.
5. Describe how a linear supply chain can be changed to a hub.

1.6 BENEFITS AND LIMITATIONS OF EC

Few innovations in human history encompass as many benefits as EC does. The global nature of the technology, the opportunity to reach hundreds of millions of people, its interactive nature, the variety of possibilities for its use, and the resourcefulness and rapid growth of its supporting infrastructures, especially the Web, result in many potential benefits to organizations, individuals, and society. These benefits are just starting to materialize, but they will increase significantly as EC expands. It is not surprising that some maintain that the EC revolution is as profound as the change that accompanied the Industrial Revolution (Clinton and Gore 1997).

THE BENEFITS OF EC

EC provides benefits to organizations, individual customers, and society.

Benefits to Organizations

EC's benefits to organizations are as follows.

Global Reach. EC expands the marketplace to national and international markets. With minimal capital outlay, a company can easily and quickly locate the best suppliers, more cus-

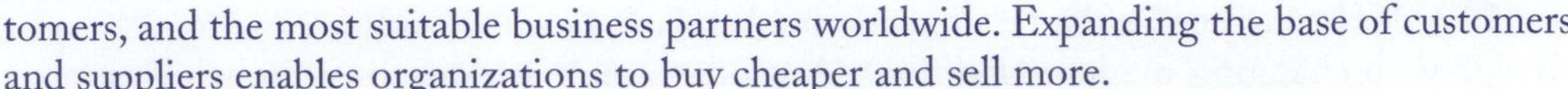

tomers, and the most suitable business partners worldwide. Expanding the base of customers and suppliers enables organizations to buy cheaper and sell more.

Cost Reduction. EC decreases the cost of creating, processing, distributing, storing, and retrieving paper-based information. High printing and mailing costs are lowered or eliminated. Examples of potential cost reductions are provided in Exhibit W1.1 on the book's Web site.

Supply Chain Improvements. Supply chain inefficiencies, such as excessive inventories and delivery delays, can be minimized with EC. For example, by building autos to order instead of for dealers' showrooms, the automotive industry is expecting to save tens of billions of dollars annually just from inventory reduction.

Extended Hours: 24/7/365. The business is always open on the Web, with no overtime or other extra costs.

Customization. Pull-type production (build-to-order) allows for inexpensive customization of products and services and provides a competitive advantage for companies that implement this strategy. A well-known example of pull-type production is that used by Dell.

New Business Models. EC allows for many innovative business models that provide strategic advantages and/or increase profits. Combining group purchasing (Chapter 5) with reverse auctions is one example of an innovative business model.

Vendors' Specialization. EC allows for a high degree of specialization that is not economically feasible in the physical world. For example, a store that sells only dog toys (Dogtoys.com) can operate in cyberspace, but in the physical world such a store would not have enough customers.

Rapid Time-to-Market. EC reduces the time between the inception of an idea and its commercialization due to improved communication and collaboration.

Lower Communication Costs. EC lowers telecommunication costs—the Internet is much cheaper than VANs.

Efficient Procurement. EC enables efficient e-procurement that can reduce administrative costs by 80 percent or more, reduce purchase prices by 5 to 15 percent, and reduce cycle time by more than 50 percent.

Improved Customer Relations. EC enables companies to interact more closely with customers, even if through intermediaries. This allows for personalization of communication, products, and services, which promotes better CRM and increases customer loyalty.

Up-to-Date Company Material. Any material on the Web, such as prices in catalogs, can be correct up to the minute. Company information can always be current.

No City Business Permits and Fees. Online companies that are not registered businesses with employees do not need any permits to operate nor do they pay license fees. If the business is registered, city fees and licenses apply.

Other Benefits. Other benefits include improved corporate image, improved customer service, ease in finding new business partners, simplified processes, increased productivity, reduced paperwork, increased access to information, reduced transportation costs, and increased operation and trading flexibility.

Benefits to Consumers

The benefits of EC to consumers are as follows.

Ubiquity. EC allows consumers to shop or perform other transactions year round, 24 hours a day, from almost any location.

More Products and Services. EC provides consumers with more choices; they can select from many vendors and from more products.

Customized Products and Services. Dell customizes computers and sells them at competitive prices. Customers can get an increased number of products (from shoes to dolls to cars) and services just the way they want them.

Cheaper Products and Services. EC frequently provides consumers with less-expensive products and services by allowing them to shop in many places and conduct quick comparisons.

Instant Delivery. In the cases of digitized products, EC allows for fast delivery.

Information Availability. Consumers can locate relevant and detailed product information in seconds, rather than days or weeks. Also, multimedia support is cheaper and better.

Participation in Auctions. EC makes it possible for consumers to participate in virtual auctions. These allow sellers to sell things quickly and buyers can locate collectors' items and bargains.

Electronic Communities. EC allows customers to interact with other customers in electronic communities (Chapter 17) and exchange ideas as well as compare experiences.

No Sales Tax. In many countries, online business is exempt from sales taxes.

Benefits to Society

The benefits of EC to society are as follows.

Telecommuting. More individuals can work at home and do less traveling for work or shopping, resulting in less traffic on the roads and reduced air pollution.

Higher Standard of Living. Some merchandise can be sold at lower prices, allowing less-affluent people to buy more and increase their standard of living.

Homeland Security. EC technologies facilitate homeland security by improving communication, coordination, information interpretation, and more, as demonstrated in Insights and Additions 1.3.

Hope for the Poor. Because of EC, people in Third World countries and rural areas are now able to enjoy products and services that were unavailable in the past. These include opportunities to learn a skilled profession or earn a college degree.

Availability of Public Services. Public services, such as health care, education, and distribution of government social services, can be done at a reduced cost and/or improved quality. For example, EC provides rural doctors and nurses access to information and technologies with which they can better treat their patients.

THE LIMITATIONS AND BARRIERS OF EC

The limitations of EC can be classified as technological or nontechnological. The major limitations are summarized in Exhibit 1.7.

According to a 2000 study conducted by CommerceNet (commerce.net), the top 10 barriers to EC in the United States, in declining order of importance, are security, trust and risk, lack of qualified personnel, lack of business models, culture, user authentication and lack of public key infrastructure, organization, fraud, slow navigation on the Internet, and legal issues. In global EC, culture, organization, B2B interfaces, international trade barriers, and lack of standards were placed at the top of the barriers list.

Insights and Additions 1.3 Enhancing Homeland Security Electronically

The U.S. Department of Homeland Security (DHS) is responsible for determining which existing applications and data can help the organization meet its goals; migrating data into a secure, usable, state-of-the-art framework; and integrating the disparate networks and data standards of 22 federal agencies, with 170,000 employees, that merged to form the DHS. The real problem is that federal agencies have historically operated autonomously, and their IT systems were not designed to interoperate with one another. Essentially, the DHS needs to link large and complex silos of data together.

Major problems have occurred because each agency has its own set of business rules that dictate how data are described, collected, and accessed. Some of the data are unstructured and not organized in relational databases, and they cannot be easily manipulated and analyzed. Commercial applications, mostly data warehouse and data-mart technologies, are being used for the major integration activities. Informatica, one of several software vendors working with the DHS, has developed data integration solutions that will enable DHS to combine disparate systems to make information more widely accessible throughout the organization (see *informatica.com*).

The DHS system will have information-analysis and infrastructure-protection components. The DHS not only has to make sense of a huge mountain of intelligence gathered from disparate sources, but then it must get that information to the people who can most effectively act on it. Many of these people are outside the federal government.

Sources: Compiled from Foley (2003), Peters (2003), and Thibodeau (2003).

EXHIBIT 1.7 Limitations of Electronic Commerce

Technological Limitations	Nontechnological Limitations
Lack of universal standards for quality, security, and reliability. The telecommunications bandwidth is insufficient, especially for m-commerce. Software development tools are still evolving. It is difficult to integrate Internet and EC software with some existing (especially legacy) applications and databases. Special Web servers are needed in addition to the network servers, which add to the cost of EC. Internet accessibility is still expensive and/or inconvenient. Order fulfillment of large-scale B2C requires special automated warehouses.	Security and privacy concerns deter customers from buying. Lack of trust in EC and in unknown sellers hinders buying. Many legal and public policy issues, including taxation, have not yet been resolved. National and international government regulations sometimes get in the way. It is difficult to measure some of the benefits of EC, such as advertising. Mature measurement methodologies are not yet available. Some customers like to feel and touch products. Also, customers are resistant to the change from shopping at a brick-and-mortar store to a virtual store. People do not yet sufficiently trust paperless, faceless transactions. In many cases, the number of sellers and buyers that are needed for profitable EC operations is insufficient. Online fraud is increasing. It is difficult to obtain venture capital due to the failure of many dot-coms.

Despite these limitations, EC is expanding rapidly. For example, the number of people in the United States who buy and sell stocks electronically increased from 300,000 at the beginning of 1996 to over 25 million by the spring of 2002 (emarketer.com June 2002). In Korea, about 60 percent of all stock market transactions took place over the Internet in the summer of 2004 (versus 2 percent in 1998) (*Korean Times*, September 17, 2004). According to IDC Research (2000), the number of online brokerage customers worldwide will reach 122.3 million in 2004, compared with 76.7 million in 2002 (as reported by Plunkett Research 2004). As experience accumulates and technology improves, the cost-benefit ratio of EC will increase, resulting in greater rates of EC adoption.

The benefits presented here may not be convincing enough reasons for a business to implement EC. Much more compelling, perhaps, are the omnipresence of the digital revolution and the influence of EC on the business environment, as described in Sections 1.3 and 1.4.

Let's conclude now by seeing how one company is networked for EC.

Section 1.6 ▶ REVIEW QUESTIONS

1. Describe some EC benefits to organizations, individuals, and society.
2. List the major technological and nontechnological limitations of EC.
3. Describe some contributions of EC to homeland security.

1.7 NETWORKS FOR EC

The task facing each organization is how to put together the components that will enable the organization to transform itself within the digital economy and gain competitive advantage by using EC (e.g., see Dutta and Biren 2001; Weill and Vitale 2001). The first step is to put in the right infrastructure—connective networks—upon which applications can be structured, as shown in the Marks & Spencer case. The vast majority of EC is done on computers connected to the Internet or to its counterpart within organizations, an intranet. Many companies employ a **corporate portal**, which is a gateway for customers, employees, and partners to reach corporate information and to communicate with the company. (For more details, see Fingar et al. 2000 and Chapter 7.)

corporate portal
A major gateway through which employees, business partners, and the public can enter a corporate Web site.

The major concern of many companies today is how to transform themselves to take part in the digital economy, where e-business is the norm. If the transformation is successful,

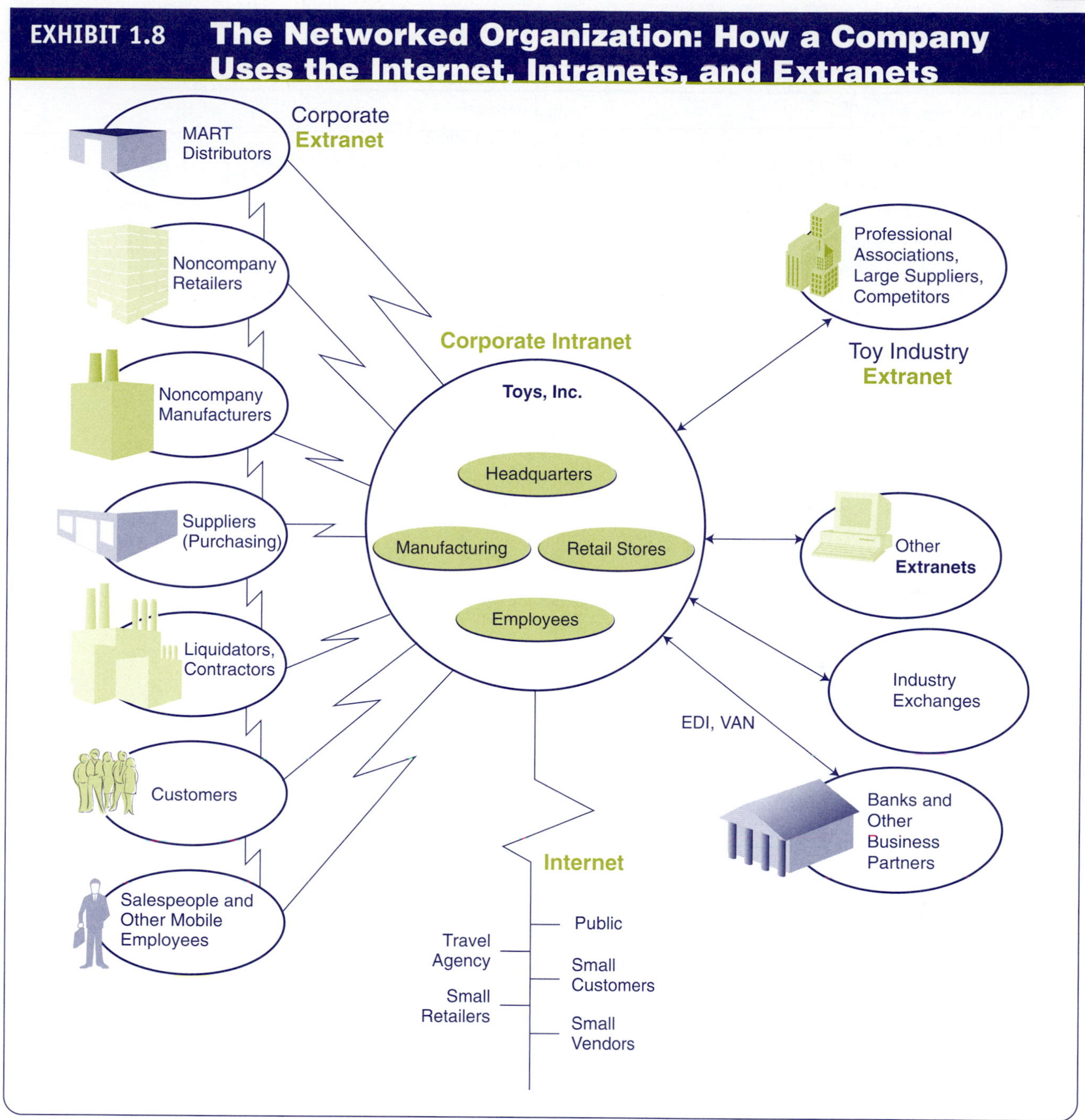

EXHIBIT 1.8 The Networked Organization: How a Company Uses the Internet, Intranets, and Extranets

many companies will reach the status of our hypothetical company, Toys, Inc., shown in Exhibit 1.8, which uses the Internet, intranets, and extranets in an integrated manner to conduct various EC activities.

It may take 5 to 10 years for companies to become fully digitized like the hypothetical Toys, Inc. Major companies, such as Schwab, IBM, Intel, and General Electric, are moving rapidly toward such a state (Slywotzky and Morrison 2001; Weill and Vitale 2001). The major characteristics of such a company are shown in Exhibit 1.9, where they are compared with those of a brick-and-mortar business.

Section 1.7 ▶ REVIEW QUESTIONS

1. Define intranets and extranets.
2. What is a corporate portal?
3. Identify EC transaction models (e.g., B2B) in Exhibit 1.9.

EXHIBIT 1.9 The Digital Versus Brick-and-Mortar Company

Brick-and-Mortar Organizations	Digital Organizations
Selling in physical stores	Selling online
Selling tangible goods	Selling digital goods
Internal inventory/production planning	Online collaborative inventory forecasting
Paper catalogs	Smart electronic catalogs
Physical marketplace	Marketspace (electronic)
Use of VANs and traditional EDI	Use of the Internet and extranets
Physical and limited auctions	Online auctions, everywhere, any time
Broker-based services, transaction	Electronic infomediaries, value-added services
Paper-based billing	Electronic billing
Paper-based tendering	Electronic tendering (reverse auctions)
Push production, starting with demand forecast	Pull production, starting with an order
Mass production (standard products)	Mass customization, build-to-order
Physical-based commission marketing	Affiliated, virtual marketing
Word-of-mouth, slow and limited advertisement	Explosive viral marketing
Linear supply chains	Hub-based supply chains
Large amount of capital needed for mass production	Less capital needed for build-to-order; payments can flow in before production starts
Large fixed cost required for plant operation	Small fixed cost required for plant operation
Customers' value proposition is frequently a mismatch (cost > value)	Perfect match of customers' value proposition (cost = value)

1.8 TEXT OVERVIEW

This book is composed of 17 chapters, divided into six parts, as shown in Exhibit 1.10. Additional content is available online at the book's Web site. On the Web site, you will find a seventh part, one additional chapter, two tutorials, an appendix on EC research, four technical appendices, and online supplemental material for each chapter.

The specific parts and chapters of this textbook are as follows.

PART 1: INTRODUCTION TO E-COMMERCE AND E-MARKETPLACES

This section of the book includes an overview of EC and its content, benefits, limitations, and drivers, which are presented in Chapter 1. Chapter 2 presents electronic markets and their mechanisms, such as electronic catalogs and auctions. Chapter 2 also includes a discussion of the impacts of EC on companies.

PART 2: INTERNET CONSUMER RETAILING

This section includes two chapters. Chapter 3 describes e-tailing (B2C), including some of its most innovative applications for selling products online. It also describes the delivery of services, such as online banking, travel, and insurance. Chapter 4 explains consumer behavior in cyberspace, online market research, and Internet advertising.

PART 3: BUSINESS-TO-BUSINESS E-COMMERCE

Part 3 is composed of three chapters. In Chapter 5, we introduce B2B EC and describe primarily company-centric models (one buyer-many sellers, one seller-many buyers). Electronic exchanges (many buyers and many sellers) are described in Chapter 6. Chapter 7 deals with e-supply chain topics, c-commerce, and corporate portals.

PART 4: OTHER EC MODELS AND APPLICATIONS

Several other EC models and applications are presented in Part 4. E-government, e-learning, C2C, and knowledge management are the major subjects of Chapter 8. In Chapter 9, we introduce the topics of m-commerce and pervasive computing.

EXHIBIT 1.10 Plan of the Book

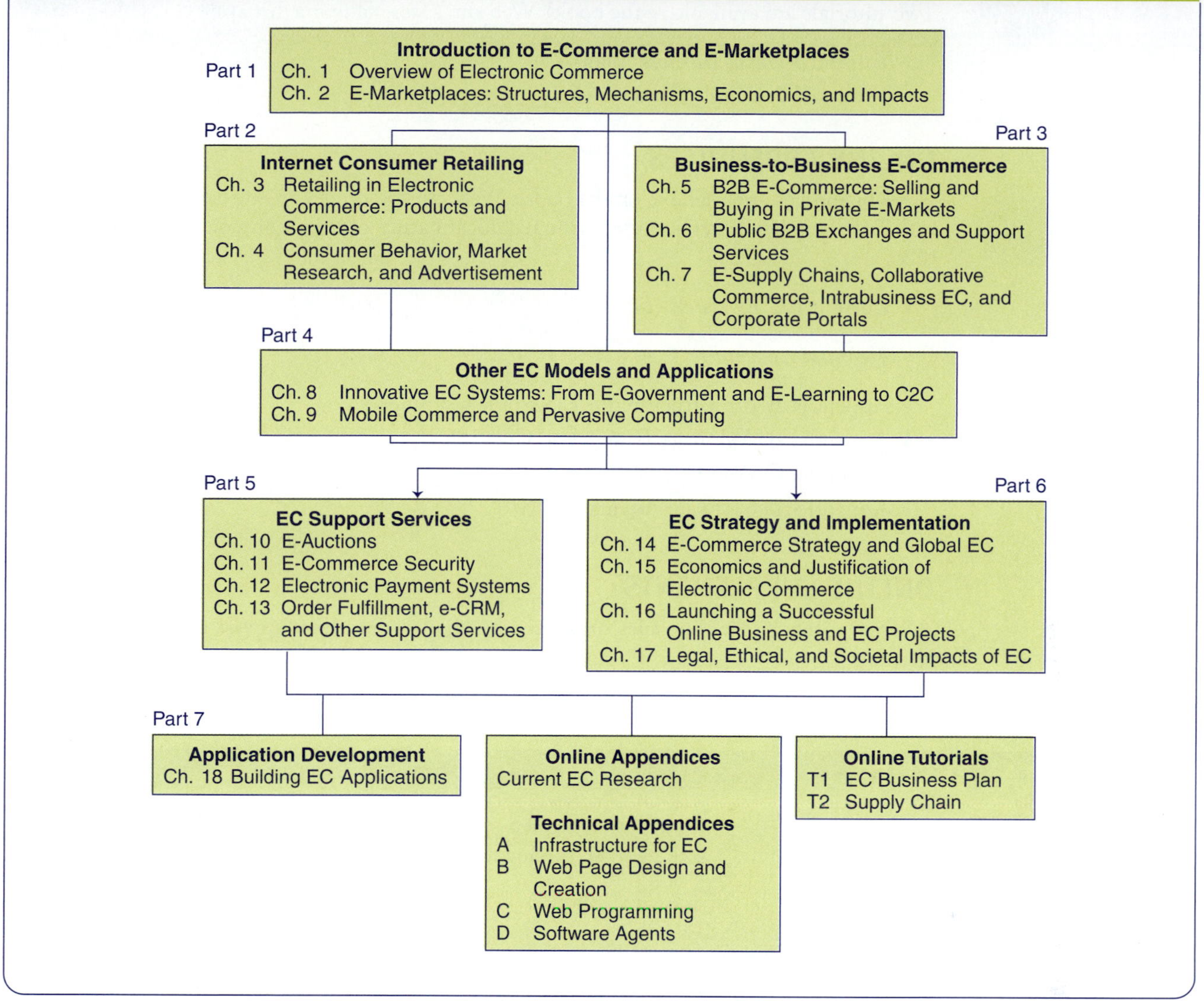

Part 1
Introduction to E-Commerce and E-Marketplaces
Ch. 1 Overview of Electronic Commerce
Ch. 2 E-Marketplaces: Structures, Mechanisms, Economics, and Impacts

Part 2
Internet Consumer Retailing
Ch. 3 Retailing in Electronic Commerce: Products and Services
Ch. 4 Consumer Behavior, Market Research, and Advertisement

Part 3
Business-to-Business E-Commerce
Ch. 5 B2B E-Commerce: Selling and Buying in Private E-Markets
Ch. 6 Public B2B Exchanges and Support Services
Ch. 7 E-Supply Chains, Collaborative Commerce, Intrabusiness EC, and Corporate Portals

Part 4
Other EC Models and Applications
Ch. 8 Innovative EC Systems: From E-Government and E-Learning to C2C
Ch. 9 Mobile Commerce and Pervasive Computing

Part 5
EC Support Services
Ch. 10 E-Auctions
Ch. 11 E-Commerce Security
Ch. 12 Electronic Payment Systems
Ch. 13 Order Fulfillment, e-CRM, and Other Support Services

Part 6
EC Strategy and Implementation
Ch. 14 E-Commerce Strategy and Global EC
Ch. 15 Economics and Justification of Electronic Commerce
Ch. 16 Launching a Successful Online Business and EC Projects
Ch. 17 Legal, Ethical, and Societal Impacts of EC

Part 7
Application Development
Ch. 18 Building EC Applications

Online Appendices
Current EC Research

Technical Appendices
A Infrastructure for EC
B Web Page Design and Creation
C Web Programming
D Software Agents

Online Tutorials
T1 EC Business Plan
T2 Supply Chain

PART 5: EC SUPPORT SERVICES

Part 5 examines issues involving the support services needed for EC applications. Chapter 10 describes the use of e-auctions to conduct EC. Chapter 11 delves into EC security. Of the many diverse Web support activities, we concentrate on three: payments (Chapter 12), order fulfillment (Chapter 13), and CRM (Chapter 13).

PART 6: EC STRATEGY AND IMPLEMENTATION

Part 6 includes four chapters on EC strategy and implementation. Chapter 14 deals with e-strategy and planning, including going global and the impact of EC on small businesses. Chapter 15 deals with the economics of EC. Chapter 16 deals with creating, operating, and maintaining an Internet company. It also deals with initiating EC initiatives and creating EC content. Chapter 17 concludes the book with an examination of legal and societal issues in EC.

ONLINE PART 7: APPLICATION DEVELOPMENT

One additional complete chapter is available online at the book's Web site (prenhall.com/turban). Chapter 18 addresses EC application development processes and methods.

ONLINE TUTORIALS

Two tutorials are available at the book's Web site (prenhall.com/turban):

- Tutorial T1: EC Business Plan
- Tutorial T2: Supply Chain

ONLINE APPENDICES

Five appendices are available on the book's Web site (prenhall.com/turban). Four of these we call *Technical Appendices* because of the technical nature of their content. The online appendices are:

- Current EC Research

Technical Appendices:

- Appendix A Infrastructure for Electronic Commerce
- Appendix B Web Page Design and Creation
- Appendix C Web Programming
- Appendix D Software Agents

ONLINE SUPPLEMENTS

A large number of online files organized by chapter number support the content of each chapter.

MANAGERIAL ISSUES

Many managerial issues are related to EC. These issues are discussed throughout the book and also are summarized in a separate section (like this one) near the end of each chapter. Some managerial issues related to this introductory chapter are as follows.

1. **Is it real?** For those not involved in EC, the first question that comes to mind is, "Is it real?" We believe that the answer is an emphatic "yes." Just ask anyone who has banked from home, purchased company stocks online, or bought a book from Amazon.com. Randy Mott, Wal-Mart's Chief Information Officer (CIO) gives an interesting tip for organizations and managers: "Start EC as soon as possible; it is too dangerous to wait." Jack Welch, former Chief Executive Officer (CEO) of General Electric, has commented, "Any company, old or new, that doesn't see this technology literally as important as breathing could be on its last breath" (McGee 2000).
2. **Why is B2B e-commerce so attractive?** Several reasons: First, some B2B models are easier to implement than traditional off-line models. In contrast, B2C has several major problems, ranging from channel conflict with existing distributors to lack of a critical mass of buyers. Also, the value of transactions is larger in B2B, and the potential savings are larger and easier to justify. Rather than waiting for B2C problems to be worked out, many companies can start B2B by simply buying from existing online stores or selling electronically by joining existing marketplaces or an auction house. The problem is determining where to buy or sell.
3. **There are so many EC failures—how can one avoid them?** Beginning in early 2000, the news was awash with stories about the failure of many EC projects within companies as well as the failure of many dotcoms. Industry consolidation often occurs after a "gold rush." About 100 years ago, hundreds of companies tried to manufacture cars, following Ford's success in the United States; only three survived. The important thing is to learn from the successes and failures of others. For lessons that can be learned from EC successes and failures, see Chapters 3, 6, and 16.
4. **How do we transform our organization into a digital one?** Once a company determines its strategy and decides to move to EC, it is necessary to plan how to implement the strategy. This process is shown in Chapters 14, 16, and 18 (online). (It is also discussed at length by Slywotzky and Morrison 2001; Weill and Vitale 2001; Willcocks and Plant 2001; and Dutta and Biren 2001.)

5. **How should we evaluate the magnitude of business pressures and technological advancement?** A good approach is to solicit the expertise of research institutions, such as Gartner or Forrester Research, which specialize in EC. Otherwise, by the time you determine what is going on, it may be too late. The consulting arms of big certified public accounting companies may be of help too. (PricewaterhouseCoopers, Accenture, and others provide considerable EC information on their Web sites.) It is especially important for management to know what is going on in its own industry.
6. **What should be my company's strategy toward EC?** A company can choose one of three basic strategies: lead, wait, or experiment. This issue is revisited in Chapter 14, together with related issues such as the cost-benefit trade-offs of EC, integrating EC into the business, outsourcing, going global, and how SMEs can use EC. Another strategic issue is the prioritization of the many initiatives and applications available to a company (see Rosen 1999).
7. **What are the top challenges of EC?** The top 10 *technical* issues for EC (in order of their importance) are security, adequate infrastructure, data access, back-end systems integration, sufficient bandwidth, network connectivity, up time, data warehousing and mining, scalability, and content distribution. The top ten *managerial* issues for EC are budgets, project deadlines, keeping up with technology, privacy issues, the high cost of capital expenditures, unrealistic management expectations, training, reaching new customers, improving customer ordering services, and finding qualified EC employees. Most of these issues are discussed throughout this book.

RESEARCH TOPICS

Here are some suggested research topics related to this chapter. For details, references, and additional topics, refer to the appendix entitled "Current EC Research" on the book's Web site.

1. **The EC Life Cycle**
   - Examine the evolution of EC with the view of stage theory.
   - Conduct an empirical study of the EC stages of an industry in a given country and compare it with EC stages in other countries.
   - Research the impact of EC adoption on the market value of firms.
   - Examine the benefits of e-marketplaces by industry and by product type.
   - Study the role of e-marketplaces as coordinator among partners and as an unbiased open-to-all third-party platform.
   - Determine if traditional internal roles can be moved to e-marketplaces.
2. **The Potential and the Limitations of EC Penetration at the Macro Level**
   - Does the nature of an industry impact the potential for EC penetration?
   - Examine the level of EC penetration in different countries.
   - Conduct a cross-country and cross-product/service comparative study to explore differences in EC penetration.
   - Identify generic factors that deter EC penetration and develop a strategy to eliminate such hurdles.
3. **Synergy of EC with Traditional Commerce**
   - Study the optimal and synergetic design of EC including both online activities and the physical process.
   - Examine synergies between electronic retailing and traditional retailing.
   - Examine synergies between traditional logistic services and electronic services.
4. **E-Business Models**
   - What is the relationship between a model's success and the characteristics of organizations using it?
   - How can the best models for a specific situation be identified?
   - Why do some models fail?

SUMMARY

In this chapter, you learned about the following EC issues as they relate to the learning objectives.

1. **Definition of EC and description of its various categories.** EC involves conducting transactions electronically. Its major categories are pure versus partial EC, Internet based versus non-Internet based, and electronic markets versus interorganizational systems.
2. **The content and framework of EC.** The applications of EC, and there are many, are based on infrastructures and are supported by people; public policy and technical standards; marketing and advertising; support services, such as logistics, security, and payment services; and business partners—all tied together by management.
3. **The major types of EC transactions.** The major types of EC transactions are B2B, B2C, C2C, m-commerce, intrabusiness commerce, B2E, c-commerce, e-government, and e-learning.
4. **The role of the digital revolution.** EC is a major product of the digital and technological revolution, which enables companies to simultaneously increase both growth and profits. This revolution enables digitization of products, services, and information.
5. **The role of the business environment as an EC driver.** The business environment is changing rapidly due to technological breakthroughs, globalization, societal changes, deregulations, and more. The changing business environment forces organizations to respond. Traditional responses may not be sufficient because of the magnitude of the pressures and the pace of the changes involved. Therefore, organizations must frequently innovate and reengineer their operations. In many cases, EC is the major facilitator of such organizational responses.
6. **The major EC business models.** The major EC business models include: online direct marketing, electronic tendering systems, name your own price, affiliate marketing, viral marketing, group purchasing, online auctions, mass customization (make-to-order), electronic exchanges, supply chain improvers, finding the best price, value-chain integration, value-chain providers, information brokers, bartering, deep discounting, and membership.
7. **Benefits of EC to organizations, consumers, and society.** EC offers numerous benefits. Because these benefits are substantial, it looks as though EC is here to stay and cannot be ignored.
8. **Limitations of EC.** The limitations of EC can be categorized as technological and nontechnological. As time passes, and network capacity, security, and accessibility continue to improve through technological innovations, the barriers posed by technological limitations will continue to diminish. Nontechnological limitations also will diminish over time, but some, especially the behavioral ones, may persist for many years in some organizations, cultures, or countries.
9. **Contribution to organizations responding to environmental changes.** EC provides strategic advantage so organizations can compete better. Also, organizations can go into remote and global markets for both selling and buying at better prices. Organizations can speed time-to-market to gain competitive advantage. They can improve the internal and external supply chain as well as increase collaboration. Finally, they can better comply to government regulations.

KEY TERMS

Term	Page
Affiliate marketing	22
Brick-and-mortar organizations	5
Business model	19
Business-to-business (B2B)	8
Business-to-business-to-consumer (B2B2C)	8
Business-to-consumer (B2C)	8
Business-to-employees (B2E)	8
Click-and-mortar (click-and-brick) organizations	5
Collaborative commerce (c-commerce)	8
Consumer-to-business (C2B)	8
Consumer-to-consumer (C2C)	8
Corporate portal	28
Customization	23
Cycle time reduction	17
Digital economy	13
E-business	4
E-co-ops	23
E-government	10
E-learning	9
E-tailing	8
Electronic commerce (EC)	4
Electronic market (e-marketplace)	5
Exchange (electronic)	10
Exchange-to-exchange (E2E)	10
Extranet	6
Group purchasing	23
Interorganizational information systems (IOSs)	5
Intrabusiness EC	8
Intranet	6
Intraorganizational information systems	5
Knowledge management (KM)	19
Location-based commerce (l-commerce)	8
Mass customization	19
Mobile commerce (m-commerce)	8
Name-your-own-price model	22
Peer-to-peer	8
Revenue model	20
SMEs	23
Tenering (reverse auction)	22
Value proposition	21
Viral marketing	22
Virtual (pure-play) organizations	5

QUESTIONS FOR DISCUSSION

1. Compare brick-and-mortar and click-and-mortar organizations.
2. Why is buying with a smart card from a vending machine considered EC?
3. Why is e-learning considered EC?
4. Why is it said that EC is a catalyst for fundamental changes in organizations?
5. How does EC facilitate customization of products and services?
6. Discuss the relationships among the various components of a business model.
7. Explain how EC can reduce cycle time, improve employees' empowerment, and facilitate customer support.
8. Compare and contrast viral marketing with affiliate marketing.
9. Explain how EC is related to supply chain management.
10. Discuss the contribution of EC technologies to homeland security.
11. Carefully examine the nontechnological limitations of EC. Which are company dependent and which are generic?
12. Which of the EC limitations do you think will be more easily overcome—the technological or the nontechnological limitations? Why?

INTERNET EXERCISES

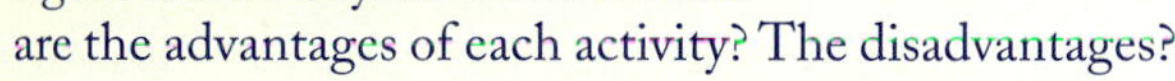

1. Visit bigboxx.com and identify the services the company provides to its customers. What type of EC is this? What business model(s) does Bigboxx use?
2. Visit Amazon.com's site (amazon.com) and locate recent information in the following areas:
   a. Find the five top-selling books on EC.
   b. Find a review of one of these books.
   c. Review the customer services you can get from Amazon.com and describe the benefits you receive from shopping there.
   d. Review the products directory.
3. Visit priceline.com and identify the various business models used by Priceline.com.
4. Go to ups.com and find information about recent EC projects that are related to logistics and supply chain management. How is UPS using wireless services?
5. Go to nike.com and design your own shoes. Next visit iprint.com and create your own business card. Finally, enter jaguar.com and configure the car of your dreams. What are the advantages of each activity? The disadvantages?
6. Visit chemconnect.com. What kind of EC does this site represent? What benefits can it provide to buyers? To sellers?
7. It is time to sell or buy on an online auction. You can try ebay.com, auction.yahoo.com, or an auction site of your choice. You can participate in an auction in almost any country. Prepare a short report describing your experiences.
8. Try to save on your next purchase. Visit letsbuyit.com and buyerzone.com. Which site do you prefer? Why?
9. Enter espn.com and identify and list all of the revenue sources on the site.

TEAM ASSIGNMENTS AND ROLE PLAYING

1. Enter smallbusiness.yahoo.com and google.com and find 15 EC success stories. For each, identify the types of EC transactions and the business model used.
2. Each team will research two EC success stories. Members of the group should examine companies that operate solely online and some that extensively utilize a click-and-mortar strategy. Each team should identify the critical success factors for their companies and present a report to the other teams.
3. View Kaplan (2002) and also search google.com, scholar.google.com, and other sources for stories on EC failures. Based on your research try to identify the reasons for the failures. Determine which EC business model seems to have the most difficulties.

Real-World Case

E-COMMERCE SUPPORTS FIELD EMPLOYEES AT MAYBELLINE

The Problem

Maybelline is a leader in color cosmetic products (eye shadow, mascara, etc.), selling them in more than 70 countries worldwide. The company uses hundreds of salespeople (field merchandising representatives, or "reps"), who visit drugstores, discount stores, supermarkets, and cosmetics specialty stores to close business deals. This method of selling has proven to be fairly effective, and it is used by hundreds of other manufacturers in various industries (e.g., Kodak, Nabisco, and Procter & Gamble). In all cases of field selling, it is necessary for the selling company to know, as quickly as possible, when a deal has been closed or if there is any problem with the customer.

Information technology has been used extensively to support field reps. Until 2000, Maybelline, as well as many other large consumer product manufacturers such as Kodak, equipped their reps with *interactive voice response* (IVR) systems that enabled reps to enter information about their daily activities every evening.

With the IVR system, the Maybelline reps completed paper-based surveys for each store they visited. The reps noted how each product was displayed, how much stock was available, how items were promoted, and so on. In addition to their own company's products, the reps surveyed the competitors' products. In the evening, the reps translated the data from the forms into answers that were then entered into the IVR. The IVR asked the reps routine questions, and the reps answered by pressing the appropriate telephone keys. The system had problems: Frequently, reps were late in reporting. Even if they were on time, information was inflexible, because the reports were all menu driven. The system also consolidated information, bundling and delivering it to top management as hard copy. Unfortunately, these reports sometimes reached top management days or weeks too late, missing important changes in trends and the opportunities to act on them in time.

Another problem was the inflexibility of the system. The reps answered only the specific questions that applied to a situation. To do so, they had to wade through more than 50 questions, skipping the irrelevant ones. This was a waste of time. In addition, some of the material that needed to be reported had no matching menu questions. Considered a success in the 1990s, the IVR system was unable to meet the needs of the twenty-first century. It was too cumbersome to set up and operate and was also prone to input errors.

The Solution

Maybelline equipped its reps with a mobile system from the MEI Group (formerly Thinque Corp.) (*meicpg.com*), called Merchandising Sales Portfolio (MSP). It runs on handheld, pen-based PDAs (from NEC) that are powered by Microsoft's CE operating system. The MSP system enables the reps to enter their reports in handwriting directly from the clients' sites. From the handheld device, data can automatically be uploaded to a Microsoft SQL Server database at corporate headquarters every evening by accessing the corporate intranet via a secure Internet connection (a synchronization process). It also enables district managers to send daily schedules and other important information electronically to each rep.

The system also replaced some of the function of Maybelline's EDI system, a source of pride of the 1990s. For example, the reps' reports now include inventory-scanned data from retail stores. These are processed quickly by an *order management system* and passed whenever needed to the shipment department for inventory replenishment.

In addition to routine information, the new system is used for decision support. It is not enough to speed information along the supply chain; managers need to know the *reasons* why certain products are selling well, or not so well, in every location. They need to know the conditions at retail stores that affect the sales of each product, and they need to know it in a timely manner. The new system offers that capability.

The Results

The MSP system provided Maybelline with an interactive link to the mobile field force. Corporate planners and decision makers can now respond much more quickly to situations that need attention. The solution is helping the company forge stronger ties with its retailers. It also considerably reduces the amount of after-hours time that the reps spend on data transfer to headquarters—from 30 to 50 minutes per day to mere seconds.

The new system also performs market analyses that enable managers to optimize merchandising and customer-service efforts. It also enables Maybelline to use a more sophisticated IVR unit to capture data for special situations. Moreover, it provides browser-based reporting tools that enable managers, regardless of where they are, to view retail information within hours of its capture. Thanks to the error-checking and validation feature in the MSP system, there are significantly fewer data-entry errors (because no rekeying is needed).

Finally, the quality of life of Maybelline reps has been greatly improved. Not only do they save 30 to 40 minutes per day, but their stress level and anxiety due to the possibility of making errors has been significantly reduced. As a result, employee turnover has declined appreciably, saving money for the company.

Source: Microsoft Corp. Case "Industry Solutions—Maybelline" at *microsoft.com/resources/casestudies/*, May 15, 2002. Adapted with permission.

Questions

1. IVR systems are still popular. What advantages do they have over systems that require reps to mail or fax reports?
2. Explain why the MSP application is an e-commerce application. Compare it with the definitions and classifications in the chapter.
3. The existing technology enables transmission of data any time an employee can access the Internet with a PC. Technically, the system can be enhanced so that the data can be sent *wirelessly* from any location as soon as it is entered. Would you recommend such a wireless system to Maybelline? Why or why not?
4. Summarize the advantages of the new MSP system over the IVR.

REFERENCES

Afuah, A., and C. L. Tucci. *Internet Business Models and Strategies,* 2d ed. New York: McGraw-Hill, 2003.

Amit, R., and C. Zott. "Value Creation in E-Business." *Strategic Management Journal* 22, no. 6 (2001).

Anderson, D. *Build-to-Order and Mass Customization.* Los Angeles: CIM Press, 2002.

Athitakis, M. "How to Make Money on the Net." *Business 2.0,* May 2003.

Bakos, J. J. "A Strategic Analysis of Electronic Marketplaces." *MIS Quarterly* 15, no. 3 (1991).

Bandyopadhyay, S. "A Critical Review of Pricing Strategies for Online Business Model." *Quarterly Journal of Electronic Commerce* 2, no. 1 (2001).

Boyd, S. "They Exist. But You'll Only Find Them by Asking the Right Questions: Who's Paying and Who's Invited?" *Darwin,* March 1, 2004.

Callon, J. D. *Competitive Advantage Through Information Technology.* New York: McGraw-Hill, 1996.

Campusfood.com (accessed August 2004).

Carr, N. G. (ed.). *The Digital Enterprise.* Boston: Harvard Business School Press, 2001.

Carton, S. *The Dot.Bomb Survival Guide.* New York: McGraw-Hill, 2002.

Cassidy, J. *Dot.com: The Greatest Story Ever Sold.* New York: Harper Collins Publication, 2002.

Chen, S. *Strategic Management of E-Business,* 2d ed. Chichester, England: John Wiley & Sons, 2004.

Choi, S. Y., and A. B. Whinston. *The Internet Economy, Technology, and Practice.* Austin, TX: Smartecon.com, 2000.

Choi, S. Y., A. B. Whinston, and D. O. Stahl. *The Economics of Electronic Commerce.* Indianapolis, IN: Macmillan Technical Pub, 1997.

Clinton, W. J., and A. Gore, Jr. "A Framework for Global Electronic Commerce." **people.hofstra.edu/faculty/peter_j_spiro/cyberlaw/framework.htm**, 1997 (accessed February 2005).

CommerceNet. "Barriers to Electronic Commerce: 2000 Study." *CommerceNet,* 2000.

Cunningham, M. S. *B2B: How to Build a Profitable E-Commerce Strategy.* Cambridge: Perseus, 2001.

Currie, W. *Value Creation from E-Business Models.* Burlington, MA: Butterworth-Heinemann, 2004.

Davis, B. *Speed Is Life.* New York: Doubleday/Currency, 2001.

Dell Recycling. **www1.us.dell.com/content/topics/segtopic.aspx/dell_recycling?c=us&cs=19&l=en&s=dhs** (accessed February 2005).

Drucker, P. *Managing in the Next Society.* New York: Truman Talley Books, 2002.

Dutta, S., and B. Biren. "Business Transformation on the Internet." *European Management Journal* 19, no. 5 (2001).

Electronic Industry Alliance. "Dell Recycling Grant Program Names 20 Recipients for Fall 2004." Eiae.org, August 31, 2004. **eiae.org/whatsnew/news.cfm?ID=110** (accessed February 2005).

Emarketer.com. "Online Purchases in the U.S., by Category, 2002." **emarketer.com**, June 26, 2002 (accessed April 2004).

Farhoomand, A., and P. Lovelock. *Global E-Commerce.* Singapore: Prentice Hall, 2001.

Farivar, C. "New Ways to Pay." *Business 2.0.* July 1, 2004.

Fingar, P., et al. *Enterprise E-Commerce.* Tampa, FL: Meghan Kiffer Press, 2000.

Foley, J. "Data Debate." *Information Week,* May 19, 2003.

Folio. "SmithKline Beecham Streamlines Its Drug Approval Process." **folio.de/aktuell/IN300797.htm** (accessed August 2004).

GreaterchinaCRM.org. "Definitions of CRM: Perspectives of CRMguru.com's Contributors." **greaterchinacrm.org/eng/content_details.jsp?contentid=413&subjectid=9** (accessed August 2004).

Greenberg, P. *CRM at the Speed of Light: Capturing and Keeping Customers in Internet Real Time,* 3d ed. New York: McGraw-Hill, 2004.

Head, S. *The New Ruthless Economy: Work and Power in the Digital Age.* New York: Oxford University Press, 2003.

Hoffman, K. L., and T. P. Novak. "How to Acquire Customers on the Web." *Harvard Business Review* (May/June 2000).

Huber, G. *The Necessary Nature of Future Firms.* San Francisco, CA: Sage Publications, 2004.

Jelassi, T., and A. Enders. Strategies for e-Business. Harlow, England: FT, Prentice Hall, 2005.

Kaplan, P. J. *F'd Companies: Spectacular Dot.com Flameouts.* New York: Simon and Schuster, 2002.

Kehal, H. S., and V. P. Singh. *Digital Economy: Impacts, Influences, and Challenges.* Hershey, PA: Idea Group Publishing, 2004.

Korean Times, news item, September 17, 2004.

Laudon, K. C., and C. G. Traver. *E-Commerce: Business, Technology, Society, Case Book Update,* 2d ed. Boston: Addison-Wesley, 2005.

Lederer, A. L., G. Erwin, and U. Averweg. "Using Web-based Information Systems to Enhance Competitiveness." *Communication of the ACM* (July 1998).

Li, E. Y., and T. C. Du. *Advances in Electronic Business, Volume 1.* Hershey, PA: Idea Group Publishing, 2004.

Lipnack, J., and J. Stamps. *Virtual Teams—Reaching Across Space, Time, and Organizations with Technology,* 2d ed. New York: John Wiley & Sons, 2000.

Macht, J. D. "The Two Hundred Million Dollar Dash." *Inc.com,* September 15, 1997. **inc.com/magazine/19970915/1432.htm/** (accessed February 2005).

Mark, K. "Wanted: Digital History." *Internetnews.com,* October 2004. **internetnews.com/bus-news/article.php/3425681** (accessed February 2005).

McGee, M. K. "Chiefs of the Year: Internet Call to Arms." *InformationWeek,* November 27, 2000.

McKay, J., and P. Marshall. *Strategic Management of E-Business.* Milton, Qld., Australia: John Wiley and Sons, 2004.

Metz, C. "Grid Computing: Case Study—Entelos." *PC Magazine,* January 1, 2003.

Microsoft Corp. "Maybelline." May 2002. **mcrosoft.com/resources/casestudies/ShowFile.asp?FileResourceID=625** (accessed February 2005).

Mullaney, T. J. " E-Biz Strikes Again!" *Business Week,* May 10, 2004.

National Cristina Foundation. **cristina.org/dsf/dell.ncf** (accessed February 2005).

PeopleSoft, Inc. "Creating Business Agility." *People Talk,* April–June 2004.

Peppers, D., and M. Rogers. "The One-to-One Future Revisited." *CRM white papers,* March 8, 2004. **sarchcrm.techtarget.com/searchCRM/downloads/futurerevisited.pdj** (accessed November 2004).

Perkins, A. B., and M. C. Perkins. *The Internet Bubble: Inside the Overvalued World of High-Tech Stocks—And What You Need to Know to Avoid the Coming Shakeout,* rev. ed. New York: Harper Business, 2001.

Peters, K. M. "Homeland Security Hurdles." *Government Executive,* February 2003.

Pine, B. J., and J. Gilmore. "The Four Faces of Mass Customization." *Harvard Business Review* (January/February 1997).

Plunkett, J. W. *Plunkett's E-Commerce Business Trends and Statistics.* Aylesbury, UK: Plunkett Research Ltd., 2001.

Plunkett Research. "State of Online Financial Services." **plunkettresearch.com/finance/financial_overview.htm#6** (accessed August 2004).

Prince, M. "Easy Doesn't Do It." *Wall Street Journal,* July 17, 2000.

Pruitt, S. "AOL Set to Lay Out New Broadband, Content Strategy." *Infoworld,* November 25, 2002.

"Qantas: Turbulence Ahead." *Business Review Weekly of Australia* 23, no. 33 (August 25, 2000).

Reda, S. "Godiva.com's Story Parallels Dynamic Growth of E-Commerce." *Stores,* February 2004. **stores.org/archives/2004/02/edit.asp** (accessed October 2004).

Rosen, A. *The E-Commerce Q and A Book: A Survival Guide for Business Managers.* New York: AMACOM, 1999.

Rossi, M., T. Saarinen, and V. K. Tuunainen. "New Business Models for Electronic Commerce." *Data Base* (Spring 2003).

Rugullis, E. "Power to the Buyer with Group Buying Sites." *e-Business Advisor* (February 2000).

Shaw, M. J., et al. *Handbook on Electronic Commerce.* Berlin: Springer-Verlag, 2000.

Singer, M. "Tell Me: The 511 in Utah." *Silicon Valley Internet.com,* December 18, 2001. **siliconvalley.internet.com/news/article.php/3531_942671** (accessed August 2004).

Slywotzky, A. J., and D. J. Morrison. *How Digital Is Your Business?* London: Nicholas Brealy Pub., 2001.

Stauss, B., and W. Seidel. *Complaint Management: The Heart of CRM.* Cincinnati, OH: South-Western, 2004.

Tapscott, D., A. Lowy, and D. Ticoll., eds. *Blueprint to the Digital Economy: Wealth Creation in the Era of E-Business.* New York: McGraw-Hill, 1998.

Thibodeau, P. "DHS Sets Timeline for IT Integration." *Computer World,* June 16, 2003.

Turban, E., et al. *Information Technology for Management*, 5th ed. New York: John Wiley & Sons, 2006.

U.S. Department of Commerce. "The Emerging Digital Economy II." June 1999. **esa.doc.gov/reports/EDE2report.pdf** (accessed August 2004).

Useem, J. "Dot-coms: What Have We Learned?" *Fortune*, October 30, 2000.

Weill, P., and M. R. Vitale. *Place to Space: Migrating to eBusiness Models*. Boston: Harvard Business School Press, 2001.

Wiegram, G., and H. Koth. *Custom Enterprise.com*. Upper Saddle River, NJ: Financial Times/Prentice Hall, 2000.

Willcocks, L. P., and R. Plant. "Getting from Bricks to Clicks." *MIT Sloan Management Review* (Spring 2001).

Wolfson, H. "Dell Provides Computers for Students to Take Apart." Al.com, January 26, 2005. **al.com/news/birminghamnews/east.ssf?/base/community/1106735278260730.xml** (accessed February 2005).

Zhengzhou Evening News (in Chinese), September 27, 2004.

Zipkin, P. "The Limits of Mass Customization." *MIT Sloan Management Review* (February 2001).

CHAPTER 2

E-MARKETPLACES: STRUCTURES, MECHANISMS, ECONOMICS, AND IMPACTS

Learning Objectives

Upon completion of this chapter, you will be able to:

1. Define e-marketplaces and list their components.
2. List the major types of e-marketplaces and describe their features.
3. Describe the various types of EC intermediaries and their roles.
4. Describe electronic catalogs, shopping carts, and search engines.
5. Describe the various types of auctions and list their characteristics.
6. Discuss the benefits, limitations, and impacts of auctions.
7. Describe bartering and negotiating online.
8. Define m-commerce and explain its role as a market mechanism.
9. Discuss liquidity, quality, and success factors in e-marketplaces.
10. Describe the economic impact of EC.
11. Discuss competition in the digital economy.
12. Describe the impact of e-marketplaces on organizations.

Content

HOW BLUE NILE INC. IS CHANGING THE JEWELRY INDUSTRY

Blue Nile Inc. (*bluenile.com*), a pure online e-tailer that specializes in diamonds, capitalized on online diamond sales as a dot.com start-up in 1999. The company provides a textbook case of how EC fundamentally undercuts the traditional way of doing business.

The Opportunity

Using the basic EC model—knocking out expensive stores and intermediaries and then slashing prices (up to 35 percent less than rivals to gain market share), Blue Nile captured a high market share in a short time, inducing more and more people to buy online.

How did the start-up defy conventional wisdom that diamonds couldn't be sold online? Basically, Blue Nile offers more information on diamonds than a jewelry expert offers in a physical store. It features educational guides in plain English and provides independent (and trusted) quality ratings for every stone. A customer can look over a rating scale for cut, clarity, color, and so on and then conduct a price comparison with Diamond.com (*diamond.com*) and other online stores. Most important is the 30-day money-back guarantee (now an online industry standard policy). This provides not only a comfort level against fraud, but also a competitive edge against stores that take the stones back but charge a fee to do so. The ability to use rating scales makes diamonds a commodity.

The Results

Blue Nile sales reached $129 million in 2003 (a 79 percent increase over 2002), with a net income of $27 million. In 2004, sales exceeded $175 million. The company became the eighth-largest specialty jewelry company in the United States and went public in 2004 (one of the most successful IPOs of 2004).

To sell $129 million in jewelry, a traditional retail chain needs 116 stores and close to 1,000 employees. Blue Nile does it with one 10,000-square-foot warehouse and 115 staffers. The company also bypasses the industry's tangled supply chain, in which a diamond can pass through five or more middlemen before reaching a retailer. Blue Nile deals directly with original suppliers, such as Thaigem.com (*thaigem.com*; see EC Application Case 2.2).

This is one reason why in the United States some 465 small jewelry stores closed in 2003 alone. The survivors specialize in custom-crafted pieces. Large rivals try to fight back, streamlining the supply chain, emphasizing customer service, and even trying to sell some products online.

The future seems to be clear, as summarized by Roger Thompson, a small jeweler in Lambertville, New Jersey, who said, "Anyone with half a brain, who wants a diamond engagement ring will go to the Internet." So, he stopped selling diamonds. In the meantime, grooms make proposals with Blue Nile rings, saving $3,000 to $5,000.

Source: Adapted with permission from Mullaney T. J. "E-Biz Strikes Again!" *BusinessWeek*, May 10, 2004.

WHAT CAN WE LEARN . . .

Blue Nile is a pure online store (a *storefront*) that uses electronic catalogs, virtual shopping carts, and superb customer service to sell diamonds and jewelry. Storefronts, carts, and catalogs are the major mechanisms for selling online, and they are described here and in Chapter 16. This case also shows the impact of online sales on an industry. Because of low operating costs and global reach, Blue Nile and other online jewelers quickly conquered an impressive market share, driving hundreds of small retailers out of business. This competitive impact and other impacts of EC are discussed in this chapter.

2.1 E-MARKETPLACES

According to Bakos (1998), markets play a central role in the economy, facilitating the exchange of information, goods, services, and payments. In the process, they create economic value for buyers, sellers, market intermediaries, and for society at large.

Markets (electronic or otherwise) have three main functions: (1) matching buyers and sellers; (2) facilitating the exchange of information, goods, services, and payments associated with market transactions; and (3) providing an institutional infrastructure, such as a legal and regulatory framework, which enables the efficient functioning of the market (see Zwass 2003 for details).

In recent years, markets have seen a dramatic increase in the use of IT and EC (Turban et al. 2006). EC has increased market efficiencies by expediting or improving the functions listed in Exhibit 2.1. Furthermore, EC has been able to significantly decrease the cost of executing these functions.

The emergence of *electronic marketplaces* (also called *e-marketplaces* or *marketspaces*), especially Internet-based ones, changed several of the processes used in trading and supply chains. These changes, driven by IT, resulted in:

- Greater information richness of the transactional and relational environment
- Lower information search costs for buyers
- Diminished information asymmetry between sellers and buyers
- Greater temporal separation between time of purchase and time of possession of physical products purchased in the e-marketplace
- Greater temporal proximity between time of purchase and time of possession of digital products purchased in the e-marketplace
- The ability of buyers and sellers to be in different locations

EC leverages IT with increased effectiveness and lower transaction and distribution costs, leading to more efficient, "friction-free" markets. An example of such efficiency is the Blue Nile case. For more on e-marketplaces, see Norris and West (2001) and Varadarajan and Yadav (2002).

MARKETSPACE COMPONENTS

marketspace
A marketplace in which sellers and buyers exchange goods and services for money (or for other goods and services), but do so electronically.

Similar to a physical marketplace, in a **marketspace** sellers and buyers exchange goods and services for money (or for other goods and services if bartering is used), but they do so electronically. A marketspace includes electronic transactions that bring about a new distribution of goods and services. The major components and players in a marketspace are customers, sellers, goods and services (physical or digital), infrastructure, a front end, a back end, intermediaries and other business partners, and support services. A brief description of each follows.

- **Customers.** The tens of millions of people worldwide who surf the Web are potential buyers of the goods and services offered or advertised on the Internet. These consumers are looking for bargains, customized items, collectors' items, entertainment, and more. They are in the driver's seat. They can search for detailed information, compare, bid, and sometimes negotiate. Organizations are the largest consumers, accounting for more than 85 percent of EC activities.
- **Sellers.** Millions of storefronts are on the Web, advertising and offering a huge variety of items. Every day it is possible to find new offerings of products and services. Sellers can sell direct from their Web sites or from e-marketplaces.

digital products
Goods that can be transformed to digital format and delivered over the Internet.

- **Products and services.** One of the major differences between the marketplace and the marketspace is the possible digitization of products and services in a marketspace. Although both types of markets can sell physical products, the marketspace also can sell **digital products**, which are goods that can be transformed to digital format and delivered over the Internet. In addition to digitization of software and music, it is possible to

EXHIBIT 2.1 Functions of a Market

Matching of Buyers and Sellers	Facilitation of Transactions	Institutional Infrastructure
• Determination of product offerings Product features offered by sellers Aggregation of different products • Search (of buyers for sellers and of sellers for buyers) Price and product information Organizing bids and bartering Matching seller offerings with buyer preferences • Price discovery Process and outcome in determination of prices Enabling price comparisons	• Logistics Delivery of information, goods, or services to buyers • Settlement Transfer of payments to sellers • Trust Credit system, reputations, rating agencies like *Consumers Reports* and BBB, special escrow and online trust agencies	• Legal Commercial code, contract law, dispute resolution, intellectual property protection Export and import law • Regulatory Rules and regulations, monitoring, enforcement

Source: "The Emerging Role of Electronic Marketplaces on the Internet," by Y. Bakos, in *Communications of the ACM*, ©1998 by ACM Inc. Used with permission.

digitize dozens of other products and services, as shown in Online Exhibit W2.1. Digital products have different cost curves than those of regular products. In digitization, most of the costs are fixed and variable costs are very low. Thus, profit will increase very rapidly as volume increases, once the fixed costs are paid for.

- **Infrastructure.** The marketspace infrastructure includes electronic networks, hardware, software, and more. (EC infrastructure is presented in Chapter 1 and Exhibit 1.2; see also online Chapter 18.)
- **Front end.** Customers interact with a marketspace via a **front end**. The components of the front end can include the *seller's portal*, electronic catalogs, a shopping cart, a search engine, an auction engine, and a payment gateway. (For details, see Beynon-Davies 2004.)
- **Back end.** All the activities that are related to order aggregation and fulfillment, inventory management, purchasing from suppliers, accounting and finance, payment processing, packaging, and delivery are done in what is termed the **back end** of the business. (For details, see Beynon-Davies 2004.)
- **Intermediaries.** In marketing, an **intermediary** is typically a third party that operates between sellers and buyers. Intermediaries of all kinds offer their services on the Web. The role of these electronic intermediaries (as will be seen throughout the text and especially in Chapters 3, 5, and 10) is frequently different from that of regular intermediaries (such as wholesalers). Online intermediaries create and manage the online markets. They help match buyers and sellers, provide some infrastructure services, and help customers and/or sellers to institute and complete transactions. They also support the vast amount of transactions that exist in providing services, as demonstrated in the WebMD case (EC Application Case 2.1). Most of these online intermediaries operate as computerized systems.
- **Other business partners.** In addition to intermediaries, several types of partners, such as shippers, use the Internet to collaborate, mostly along the supply chain.
- **Support services.** Many different support services are available, ranging from certification and escrow services (to ensure security) to content providers. The essential components and their interactions are shown in Exhibit 2.2.

front end
The portion of an e-seller's business processes through which customers interact, including the seller's portal, electronic catalogs, a shopping cart, a search engine, and a payment gateway.

back end
The activities that support online order-taking, including fulfillment, inventory management, purchasing from suppliers, payment processing, packaging, and delivery.

intermediary
A third party that operates between sellers and buyers.

Section 2.1 ▶ REVIEW QUESTIONS

1. What is the difference between a physical marketplace and an e-marketplace (marketspace)?
2. List the components of a marketspace.
3. Define a digital product and provide five examples.

CASE 2.1

EC Application

WEBMD

WebMD is the largest medical services company in the United States. Although the company is known mainly for its consumer portal *webmd.com*, the most visited medical-related Web site, its core business is being an e-intermediary.

The health-care industry is huge (close to $2 trillion per year, the largest in terms of GNP). Almost $600 billion is spent just on administrative expenses. The government (federal and state) provides large amounts of money to health-care providers (e.g., physicians, hospitals, drug companies), and it attempts to control costs. A major instrument for cost control is the Health Insurance Portability and Accountability Act of 1996 (HIPAA), which requires digital medical records and standardized documents for the health-care industry. WebMD is attempting to capitalize on this act by providing computer-related services to both the providers of services and to the purchasers (government, insurance companies, HMOs), mainly in terms of standardized electronic transactions.

WebMD's major objective is to reduce costs for the participants by facilitating electronic communication and collaboration, because paper-based transactions are 20 to 30 times more expensive than electronic ones. It also seeks to speed cycle time.

WebMD operates via four separate, but electronically linked, divisions:

- **WebMD Envoy.** This division is the leading clearinghouse for real-time transactions (over $2 billion a year) among over 300,000 medical and dental providers, 500 hospitals, 600 software vendors, 36,000 pharmacies and laboratories, and 1,200 government and commercial health agencies. Transactions are secure; large customers use EDI (Chapter 5), and others use the Internet. The system handles all types of transactions, from clinical data to billing.
- **WebMD Practice Services.** This division provides software and programs that help physicians and other providers manage their businesses. Hundreds of different applications are available (this service is referred to as Intergy EHR). Some provide access to patient information whereas others retrieve medical knowledge.
- **WebMD Health.** This information gateway has portals for both consumers and professionals. For consumers, information is provided about wellness, diseases, and treatments. For professionals (physicians, nurses, medical technicians, etc.), the Medscape portal provides medical news, medical education, research-related information, and more.
- **Portex.** The medical product unit manufactures and sells specialty medical products.

WebMD's future as an intermediary is not clear. On one hand, disintermediation is possible due to the fact that the largest customers may develop their own B2B connections. On the other hand, the need to comply with HIPAA may facilitate the role of WebMD, especially for small- and medium-sized health-care participants.

Questions

1. Visit *webmd.com* to learn more about the types of intermediation it provides. Write a report based on your findings.
2. What kind of reintermediation do you foresee for the company?
3. WebMD Health does not bring in much revenue. Should the company close it?
4. What impact can WebMD have on the health-care industry? (Use the chapter's framework in your answer.)

2.2 TYPES OF E-MARKETPLACES: FROM STOREFRONTS TO PORTALS

There are several types of e-marketplaces. The major B2C e-marketplaces are *storefronts* and *Internet malls*. B2B e-marketplaces include private *sell-side* e-marketplaces, *buy-side* e-marketplaces, and *exchanges*. Let's elaborate on these as well as on the gateways to e-marketplaces—portals.

ELECTRONIC STOREFRONTS

storefront
A single company's Web site where products or services are sold.

An electronic or Web **storefront** refers to a single company's Web site where products and services are sold. It is an electronic store. The storefront may belong to a manufacturer (e.g., geappliances.com and dell.com), to a retailer (e.g., walmart.com), to individuals selling from home, or to another type of business.

A storefront includes several mechanisms that are necessary for conducting the sale (see also Chapter 16). The most common mechanisms are an *electronic catalog*, a *search engine* that helps the consumer find products in the catalog; an *electronic cart* for holding items until checkout; *e-auction facilities;* a *payment gateway* where payment arrangements can be made; a *shipment court* where shipping arrangements are made; and *customer services*, including

EXHIBIT 2.2 **The Essential Elements and Mechanisms of an Electronic Market**

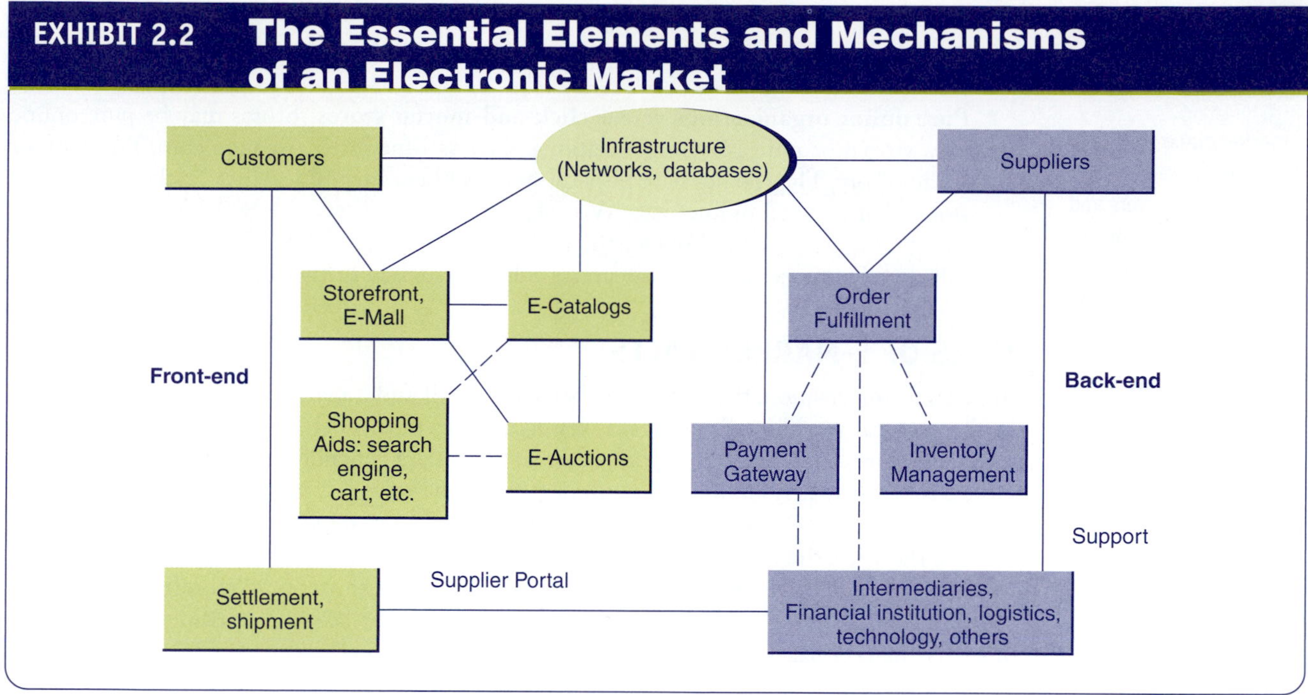

product and warranty information. The first three mechanisms are described in Section 2.4; e-auctions are described in Section 2.5 and in Chapter 10; payment mechanisms are described in Chapter 12; and shipments are discussed in Chapter 13. Customer services, which can be fairly elaborate, are covered throughout the book and especially in Chapter 13 (see CRM). Note: Companies that sell services (such as insurance) may refer to their storefronts as portals. An example of a service-related portal is a hotel reservation system, as shown in Online File W2.1.

ELECTRONIC MALLS

In addition to shopping at individual storefronts, consumers can shop in electronic malls (e-malls). Similar to malls in the physical world, an **e-mall** (online mall) is an online shopping location where many stores are located. For example, Hawaii.com (hawaii.com) is an e-mall that aggregates Hawaiian products and stores. It contains a directory of product categories and the stores in each category. When a consumer indicates the category he or she is interested in, the consumer is transferred to the appropriate independent *storefront*. This kind of a mall does not provide any shared services. It is merely a directory. Other malls do provide shared services (e.g., choicemall.com). Some malls are actually large click-and-mortar retailers; others are virtual retailers (e.g., buy.com).

e-mall (online mall)
An online shopping center where many online stores are located.

TYPES OF STORES AND MALLS

There are several types of stores and malls:

- **General stores/malls.** These are large marketspaces that sell all types of products. Examples are amazon.com, choicemall.com, shop4.vcomshop.com, spree.com, and the major public portals (yahoo.com, aol.com, and lycos.com). All major department and discount stores fall into this category.
- **Specialized stores/malls.** These sell only one or a few types of products, such as books, flowers, wine, cars, or pet toys. Amazon.com started as a specialized e-bookstore, but today is a generalized store. 1800flowers.com sells flowers and related gifts; fashionmall.com/beautyjungle specializes in beauty products, tips, and trends; cattoys.com sells cat toys; and uvine.com sells wine.
- **Regional versus global stores.** Some stores, such as e-grocers or sellers of heavy furniture, serve customers that live nearby. For example, parknshop.com serves the Hong

Kong community; it will not deliver groceries to New York. However, some local stores will sell to customers in other countries if the customer will pay the shipping, insurance, and other costs (e.g., see hothothot.com).

- **Pure online organizations versus click-and-mortar stores.** Stores may be pure online (i.e., virtual or pure-play) organizations, such as Blue Nile, Amazon.com, Buy.com, or Cattoys.com. They do not have physical stores. Others are physical (i.e., brick-and-mortar) stores that also sell online (e.g., Wal-Mart with walmart.com, 1-800-Flowers.com with 1800flowers.com, and Woolworths with woolworths.com.au). This second category is called *click-and-mortar*. Both categories will be described further in Chapter 3.

e-marketplace
An online market, usually B2B, in which buyers and sellers exchange goods or services; the three types of e-marketplaces are private, public, and consortia.

private e-marketplaces
Online markets owned by a single company; may be either sell-side or buy-side e-marketplaces.

sell-side e-marketplace
A private e-marketplace in which a company sells either standard or customized products to qualified companies.

TYPES OF E-MARKETPLACES

In general conversation, the distinction between a mall and a marketplace is not always clear. In the physical world, malls are often viewed as collections of stores (i.e., shopping centers) where the stores are isolated from each other and prices are generally fixed. In contrast, marketplaces, some of which are located outdoors, are often viewed as places where many vendors compete and shoppers look for bargains and are expected to negotiate prices.

On the Web, the term *marketplace* has a different and distinct meaning. If individual customers want to negotiate prices, they may be able to do so in some storefronts or malls. However, the term **e-marketplace** usually implies B2B, not B2C. We distinguish two types of such e-marketplaces: private and public.

Private E-Marketplaces

Private e-marketplaces are those owned by a single company (see Chapter 5). As can be seen in the Raffles Hotel case (Online File W2.1), private markets are either sell-side or buy-side. In a **sell-side e-marketplace**, a company such as Cisco will sell either standard or customized products to qualified companies; this type of selling is considered to be *one-to-many*. It is similar to a B2C storefront. In a **buy-side e-marketplace**, a company purchases from many suppliers; this type of purchasing is considered to be *many-to-one*. For example, Raffles Hotel buys its supplies from approved vendors that come to its market. Private marketplaces are frequently open only to selected members and are not publicly regulated. We will return to the topic of private e-marketplaces in Chapter 5.

buy-side e-marketplace
A private e-marketplace in which a company makes purchases from invited suppliers.

public e-marketplaces
B2B marketplaces, usually owned and/or managed by an independent third party, that include many sellers and many buyers; also known as *exchanges*.

Public E-Marketplaces

Public e-marketplaces are B2B markets. They often are owned by a third party (not a seller or a buyer) or by a group of buying or selling companies (a consortium), and they serve many sellers and many buyers. These markets also are known as *exchanges* (e.g., a stock exchange). They are open to the public and are regulated by the government or the exchange's owners. An example of a public marketplace, NTE.net, is provided in Online File W2.2. Public e-marketplaces are presented in detail in Chapter 6.

INFORMATION PORTALS

A portal is a mechanism that is used in e-marketplaces, e-stores, and other types of EC (e.g., in intrabusiness, e-learning etc.). With the growing use of intranets and the Internet, many organizations encounter information overload at a number of different levels. Information is scattered across numerous documents, e-mail messages, and databases at different locations and in disparate systems. Finding relevant and accurate information is often time-consuming and requires access to multiple systems.

As a consequence, organizations lose a lot of productive employee time. One solution to this problem is the use of *portals*. A portal is an information gateway. It attempts to address information overload by enabling people to search and access relevant information from disparate IT systems and the Internet, using advanced search and indexing techniques, in an intranet-based environment. An **information portal** is a single point of access through a Web browser to critical business information located inside and outside of an organization. Many information portals can be personalized by the user.

information portal
A single point of access through a Web browser to business information inside and/or outside an organization.

Portals appear under many descriptions and shapes. One way to distinguish among them is to look at their content, which can vary from narrow to broad, and their community or audience, which also can vary. The following are the six major types of portals:

- **Commercial (public) portals.** These portals offer content for diverse communities and are the most popular portals on the Internet. Although they can be customized by the user, they are still intended for broad audiences and offer fairly routine content, some in real time (e.g., a stock ticker and news about a few preselected items). Examples of such sites are yahoo.com, aol.com, and msn.com.
- **Corporate portals.** Corporate portals provide organized access to rich content within relatively narrow corporate and partners' communities. They also are known as *enterprise portals* or *enterprise information portals*. Corporate portals appear in different forms and are described in detail in Chapter 7.
- **Publishing portals.** These portals are intended for communities with specific interests. These portals involve relatively little customization of content, but they provide extensive online search features and some interactive capabilities. Examples of such sites are techweb.com and zdnet.com.
- **Personal portals.** These target specific filtered information for individuals. They offer relatively narrow content and are typically very personalized, effectively having an audience of one.
- **Mobile portals.** **Mobile portals** are portals that are accessible from mobile devices (see Chapter 9 for details). Although most of the other portals mentioned here are PC based, increasing numbers of portals are accessible via mobile devices. One example of such a mobile portal is i-mode, which is described in Section 2.7.
- **Voice portals.** **Voice portals** are Web sites, usually portals, with audio interfaces. This means that they can be accessed by a standard telephone or a cell phone. AOLbyPhone is an example of a service that allows users to retrieve e-mail, news, and other content from AOL via telephone. It uses both speech recognition and text-to-speech technologies. Companies such as Tellme.com (see EC Application Case 1.2, page 10) and BeVocal (bevocal.com) offer access to the Internet from telephones and tools to build voice portals. Voice portals are especially popular for 1-800 numbers (Enterprise 800 numbers) that provide self-service to customers with information available in Internet databases (e.g., find flight status at delta.com).

mobile portal
A portal accessible via a mobile device.

voice portal
A portal accessed by telephone or cell phone.

Section 2.2 ▶ REVIEW QUESTIONS

1. Describe electronic storefronts and e-malls.
2. List the various types of stores and e-malls.
3. Differentiate between private and public e-marketplaces.
4. What are information portals? List the six types.

2.3 INTERMEDIATION IN E-COMMERCE

Intermediaries (brokers) play an important role in commerce by providing value-added activities and services to buyers and sellers. There are many types of intermediaries. The most well-known intermediaries in the physical world are wholesalers and retailers. In cyberspace, there are, in addition, intermediaries that control information flow. These electronic intermediaries are known as **infomediaries**. The information flows to and from buyers and sellers via infomediaries, as shown in Exhibit 2.3. Frequently, they aggregate information and sell it to others (see "syndication" in Chapter 16).

infomediaries
Electronic intermediaries that control information flow in cyberspace, often aggregating information and selling it to others.

THE ROLES AND VALUE OF INTERMEDIARIES IN E-MARKETPLACES

Producers and consumers may interact directly in an e-marketplace: Producers provide information to customers, who then select from among the available products. In general, producers set prices; sometimes prices are negotiated. However, direct interactions are

EXHIBIT 2.3 Infomediaries and the Information Flow Model

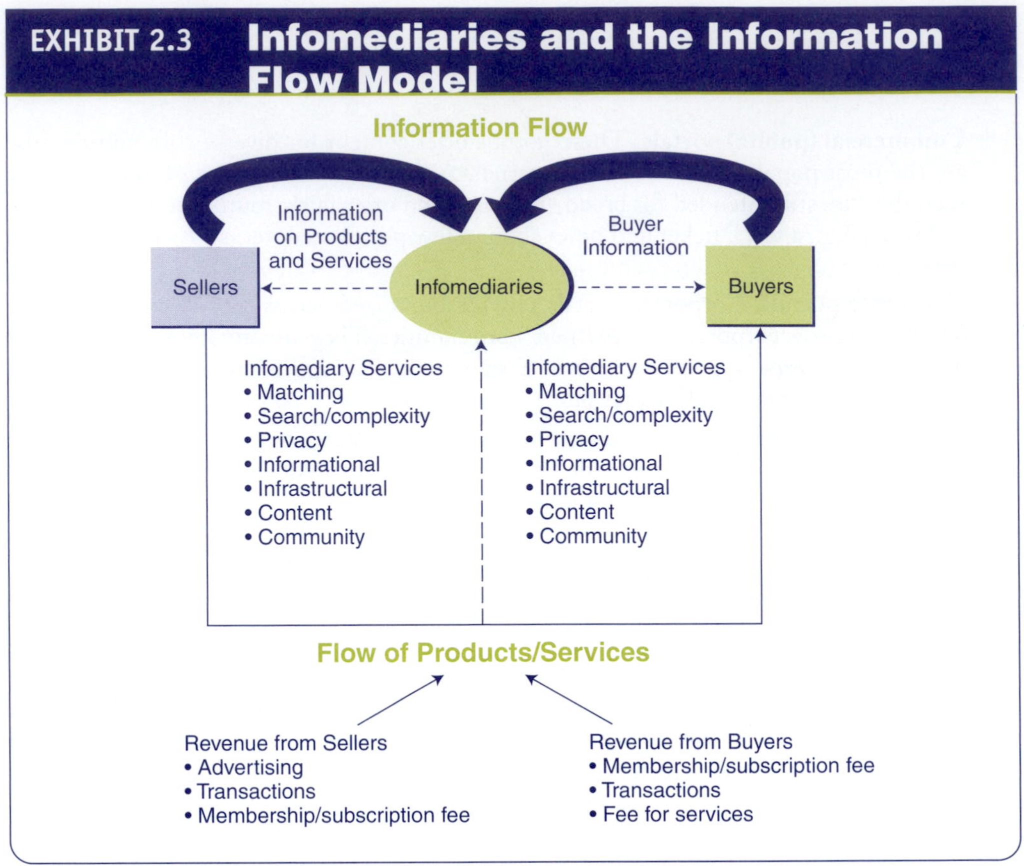

Source: Grover, V., and J. Teng, "E-Commerce and the Information Market." *Communications of the ACM,* © 2001 by ACM Inc. Used with permission.

sometimes undesirable or unfeasible. In that case, intermediation is needed. Intermediaries, whether human or electronic, can address the following five important *limitations* of direct interaction.

1. **Search costs.** It may be expensive for providers and consumers to find each other. In electronic marketplaces, thousands of products are exchanged among thousands of vendors and millions of consumers. Producers may have trouble accurately gauging consumer demand for new products; many desirable items may never be produced simply because no one recognizes the demand for them. Some intermediaries maintain databases of customer preferences, and they can predict demand and *reduce search costs* by selectively routing information from providers to consumers and by *matching* customers with products and/or services.
2. **Lack of privacy.** Either the buyer or seller may wish to remain anonymous or at least protect some information relevant to a trade. Intermediaries can relay messages and make pricing and allocation decisions without revealing the identity of one or both parties.
3. **Incomplete information.** The buyer may need more information than the seller is able or willing to provide, such as information about product quality, competing products, or customer satisfaction. An intermediary can gather product information from sources other than the product provider, including independent evaluators and other customers. Many third-party Web sites provide such information (e.g., bizrate.com, mysimon.com, and consumerguide.com).
4. **Contract risk.** A consumer may refuse to pay after receiving a product or a producer may provide inferior products or give inadequate postpurchase service. Intermediaries have a number of tools to reduce such risks. First, the broker can disseminate information about

the behavior of providers and consumers. The threat of publicizing bad behavior or removing a seal of approval may encourage both producers and consumers to meet the broker's standard for fair dealing. Or, the broker may accept responsibility for the behavior of parties in transactions it arranges and act as a policeman on its own. Third, the broker can provide insurance against bad behavior. The credit card industry uses all three approaches to reduce providers' and consumers' exposure to risk.

In the online auction arena, some companies act as *escrow agencies*, accepting and holding payment from the buyer while the seller completes delivery of the product or service to the escrow agency. Then, if the product is satisfactory, the agency releases payment to the seller and the product to the buyer.

5. **Pricing inefficiencies.** By jockeying to secure a desirable price for a product, providers and consumers may miss opportunities for mutually desirable trades. This is particularly likely in negotiations over unique or custom products, such as houses, and in markets for information products and other public goods where freeloading is a problem. Intermediaries can use pricing mechanisms that induce just the appropriate trades; for example, dealing with an imbalance of buy and sell orders in stock markets.

For a study on how different strategies of intermediation affect the efficiency of electronic markets, see Yarom et al. (2003).

E-Distributors in B2B

A special type of intermediary in e-commerce is the B2B **e-distributor**. These intermediaries connect manufacturers (suppliers) with business buyers, such as retailers (or resellers in the computer industry). E-distributors basically aggregate the catalogs or the product information from many suppliers, sometimes thousands of them, in one place—the intermediary's Web site (see Chapters 5 and 6 for details).

e-distributor
An e-commerce intermediary that connects manufacturers (suppliers) with business buyers by aggregating the catalogs of many suppliers in one place—the intermediary's Web site.

DISINTERMEDIATION AND REINTERMEDIATION

Intermediaries are agents that mediate between sellers and buyers. Usually, they provide two types of services: (1) They provide relevant information about demand, supply, prices, and requirements, and in doing so, help match sellers and buyers. (2) They offer value-added services such as transfer of products, escrow, payment arrangements, consulting, or assistance in finding a business partner. In general, the first type of service can be fully automated, and thus is likely to be assumed by e-marketplaces, infomediaries, and portals that provide free or low-commission services. The second type requires expertise, such as knowledge of the industry, the products, and technological trends, and it can only be partially automated.

Intermediaries who provide only (or mainly) the first type of service may be eliminated, a phenomena called **disintermediation**. An example is the airline industry and its push for electronic ticketing. As of 2004, most airlines require customers to pay $5 per ticket or more if they buy a ticket from an agent, which is equivalent to the agent's commission. This is resulting in the disintermediation of travel agents from the purchasing process. In another example, discount stockbrokers that only execute trades manually are disappearing. However, brokers who manage electronic intermediation are not only surviving, but may actually be prospering. This phenomenon, in which disintermediated entities take on new intermediary roles, is called **reintermediation** (see Chapters 3, 6, and 14).

disintermediation
Elimination of intermediaries between sellers and buyers.

reintermediation
Establishment of new intermediary roles for traditional intermediaries that have been disintermediated.

Disintermediation is more likely to occur in supply chains involving several intermediaries, as illustrated in EC Application Case 2.2. The case also illustrates an intermediary that does both B2C and B2B.

Section 2.3 ▶ REVIEW QUESTIONS

1. List the roles of intermediaries in e-markets.
2. Describe e-distributors.
3. What are disintermediation and reintermediation?

CASE 2.2

EC Application

DIAMONDS FOREVER—ONLINE

The gem market is a global one with hundreds of thousands of traders buying about $50 billion in gems each year. The age-old business is very inefficient: Several layers of intermediaries can jack up the price of a gem 1,000 percent between its wholesale and final retail price.

Chanthaburi (Thailand) is one of the world's leading centers for processing gems. That is where an American, Don Kogen, landed at the age of 15 to search for his fortune. He found it in about 10 years. After failing to become a gem cutter, Kogen moved into gem sorting, and soon he learned to speak Thai. For 3 years, he observed how gem traders haggled over stones, and then he decided to try the business himself. He started by purchasing low-grade gems from sellers who arrived early in the morning and then selling them for a small profit to dealers from India and Pakistan who arrived late in the day. This quick turnover of inventory helped him build up his capital resources.

Using advertising, he reached the U.S. gem market and soon had 800 potential overseas customers. Using faxes, he shortened the order time, which resulted in decreasing the entire time from order to delivery. These various business methods enabled Kogen to grow his mail-order business to $250,000 a year by 1997.

In 1998, Kogen decided to use the Internet. Within a month, he established a Web site (*thaigem.com*) and sold his first gem online. By 2001, the revenue from his online business reached $4.3 million, and it more than doubled (to $9.8 million) in 2002. Online sales account for 85 percent of revenues. The buyers are mostly dealers or retailers such as Wal-Mart or QVC, although he also sells to small buyers. Kogen buys raw or refined gems from all over the world, some online, trying to cater to the demands of his customers. Payments are made safely, securely, and conveniently using either PayPal (*paypal.com*), Escrow.com (*escrow.com*), or Payzip (*payzip.com*).

Thaigem's competitive edge is low prices. The proximity to gem-processing factories and low-cost labor enables Kogen to offer prices significantly lower than his online competitors (such as Tiffany's at *tiffany.com*). Kogen makes only 20 to 25 percent profit, about half the profit that other gem dealers make. Unsatisfied customers can return merchandise within 30 days, no questions asked. Delivery to any place in the world is made via FedEx, at about $15 per shipment. To make his business even more competitive, Kogen is trying to reduce Thaigem's huge gems inventory, which in 2002 he turned over once in a year (his goal is to reduce it to 6 months).

Thaigem's name is trusted by over 68,000 potential customers worldwide. Kogen himself enjoys a solid reputation on the Web. For example, he uses eBay to auction gems as an additional selling channel. Customers' comments on eBay are 99 percent positive. By 2004, Thaigem had become the EC arm of Thaigem Global Marketing Ltd. and its sister company, NCS group (a gemstone wholesaler). Thaigem sells both B2B and B2C on the Web.

Sources: Compiled from *thaigem.com* (accessed February 2005) and from Meredith (2002).

Questions

1. Describe Thaigem's business model, including its revenue model. How are logistics and payments organized? (Visit *thaigem.com* for details.)
2. During the 2000–2002 shakeout of dot-coms, Thaigem prospered. Why do you think it was not affected by the dot-com downturn?
3. Of the $45 billion annual sales in the gem industry, only about 3 percent are done online. Do you think that selling gems online will grow to more than 3 percent? Why or why not?
4. Go to *bluenile.com* and *diamonds.com*. Compare them with *thaigem.com*. How do they differ?

2.4 ELECTRONIC CATALOGS AND OTHER MARKET MECHANISMS

To enable selling online, a Web site usually needs *EC merchant server software* (see Chapters 16 and 18). The basic functionality offered by such software includes electronic catalogs, search engines, and shopping carts.

ELECTRONIC CATALOGS

electronic catalogs
The presentation of product information in an electronic form; the backbone of most e-selling sites.

Catalogs have been printed on paper for generations. Recently, electronic catalogs on CD-ROM and the Internet have gained popularity. **Electronic catalogs** consist of a product database, directory and search capabilities, and a presentation function. They are the backbone of most e-commerce sales sites. For merchants, the objective of electronic catalogs is to advertise and promote products and services. For the customer, the purpose of such catalogs is to locate information on products and services. Electronic catalogs can be searched quickly with the help of search engines, and they can be interactive (Cox and Koelzer 2004). For example, go to hairstyler.com and see how you can insert your photo and then change the hairstyle and color. Electronic catalogs can be very large; for example, the Library of Congress Web catalog (catalog.loc.gov) contains about 15 million records.

The majority of early online catalogs were replications of text and pictures from printed catalogs. However, online catalogs have evolved to become more dynamic, customized, and integrated with selling and buying procedures. As online catalogs have become more integrated with shopping carts, order taking, and payment, the tools for building them are being integrated with merchant suites and Web hosting (e.g., see smallbusiness.yahoo.com/merchant).

Electronic catalogs can be classified according to three dimensions:

1. **The dynamics of the information presentation.** Catalogs may be static or dynamic. In *static catalogs*, information is presented in text and static pictures. In *dynamic catalogs*, information is presented in motion pictures or animation, possibly with supplemental sound.
2. **The degree of customization.** Catalogs may be standard or customized. In *standard catalogs,* merchants offer the same catalog to any customer. In *customized catalogs,* content, pricing, and display are tailored to the characteristics of specific customers.
3. **Integration with business processes.** Catalogs can be classified according to the degree of integration with the following business processes or features: order taking and fulfillment; electronic payment systems; intranet workflow software and systems; inventory and accounting systems; suppliers' or customers' extranets; and paper catalogs. For example, when a customer places an order at amazon.com, the order is transferred automatically to a computerized inventory-availability check.

Although used occasionally in B2C commerce, *customized catalogs* are especially useful in B2B e-commerce. For example, e-catalogs can show only the items that the employees in a specific organization are allowed to purchase and can exclude items the buying company's managers do not want their employees to see or to buy. E-catalogs can be customized to show the same item to different customers at different prices, reflecting discounts or purchase-contract agreements. They can even show the buyer's ID number for the item, model, or *stock-keeping unit* (SKU) number, rather than the seller's ID numbers. Extranets, in particular, can deliver customized catalogs to different business customers.

For a comprehensive discussion of online catalogs, see Norris and West (2001), jcmax.com/advantages.html, and purchasing.about.com.

Online Catalogs Versus Paper Catalogs

The advantages and disadvantages of online catalogs are contrasted with those of paper catalogs in Exhibit 2.4. Although online catalogs have significant advantages, such as ease of updating; the ability to be integrated with the purchasing process; coverage of a wide spectrum of products, interactivity, customization; and strong search capabilities, they do have disadvantages and limitations. To begin with, customers need computers and Internet access in order to view online catalogs. However, as computers and Internet access are spreading rapidly, a large number of paper catalogs will be supplemented by, if not actually replaced by, electronic ones. However, considering the fact that printed newspapers and magazines have not diminished due to online ones, paper catalogs probably will not disappear. There seems to be room for both media, at least in the near future. However, in B2B paper catalogs may disappear more quickly.

A representative tool for building online catalogs is Microsoft's Commerce Server 2002. Radioshack.ca builds and maintains electronic catalogs based on their customers' paper catalogs. The service includes search capabilities, the ability to feature large numbers of products, enhanced viewing capabilities, and ongoing support (Microsoft Corp. 2002).

Customized Catalogs

A *customized catalog* is a catalog assembled specifically for a company, usually a customer of the catalog owner. It also can be tailored to loyal individual shoppers or to a segment of shoppers (e.g., frequent buyers). There are two approaches to creating customized catalogs.

EXHIBIT 2.4 Comparison of Online Catalogs with Paper Catalogs

Type	Advantages	Disadvantages
Paper Catalogs	• Easy to create without high technology • Reader is able to look at the catalog without computer system • More portable than electronic	• Difficult to update changed product information promptly • Only a limited number of products can be catalog displayed • Limited information through photographs and textual description is available • No possibility for advanced multimedia such as animation and voice
Online Catalogs	• Easy to update product information • Able to integrate with the purchasing process • Good search and comparison capabilities • Able to provide timely, up-to-date product information • Provision for globally broad range of product information • Possibility of adding on voice and animated pictures • Long-term cost savings • Easy to customize • More comparative shopping • Ease of connecting order processing, inventory processing, and payment processing to the system	• Difficult to develop catalogs, large fixed cost • There is a need for customer skill to deal with computers and browsers

The first approach is to let the customers identify the parts of interest to them from the total catalog, as is done by software products such as One-to-One from Broadvision (broadvision.com). Then customers do not have to deal with topics that are irrelevant to them. Such software allows the creation of catalogs with branded value-added capabilities that make it easy for customers to find the products they want to purchase, locate the information they need, and quickly configure their order.

The second approach is to let the system automatically identify customer characteristics based on the customer's transaction records. However, to generalize the relationship between the customer and items of interest, data-mining technology (Chapter 4) may be needed. This second approach can be effectively combined with the first one.

As an example of the second approach, consider the following scenario, which uses Oracle's 9i server: Joe Smith logs on to the Acme Shopping site, where he has the option to register as an account customer and record his preferences in terms of address details, interest areas, and preferred method of payment. Acme Shopping offers a wide range of products, including electronics, clothing, books, and sporting goods. Joe is interested only in clothing and electronics. He is neither a sportsman nor a great book lover. Joe also has some very distinct hobby areas—one is photography.

After Joe has recorded his preferences, each time he returns to Acme's electronic store, the first page will show him only the clothing and electronics departments. Furthermore, when Joe goes into the electronics department, he sees only products related to photography—cameras and accessories. Some of the products are out of Joe's price range, so Joe can refine his preferences further to indicate that he is interested only in electronics that relate to photography and cost $300 or less. Such personalization gives consumers a value-added experience and adds to their reasons for revisiting the site, thus building brand loyalty to that Internet store.

Against the backdrop of intense competition for Web time, personalization provides a valuable way to match consumers with the products and information in which they are most interested as quickly and painlessly as possible. An example of how corporations customize their catalogs for corporate clients is provided in EC Application Case 2.3.

CASE 2.3
EC Application
ELECTRONIC CATALOGS AT BOISE CASCADE

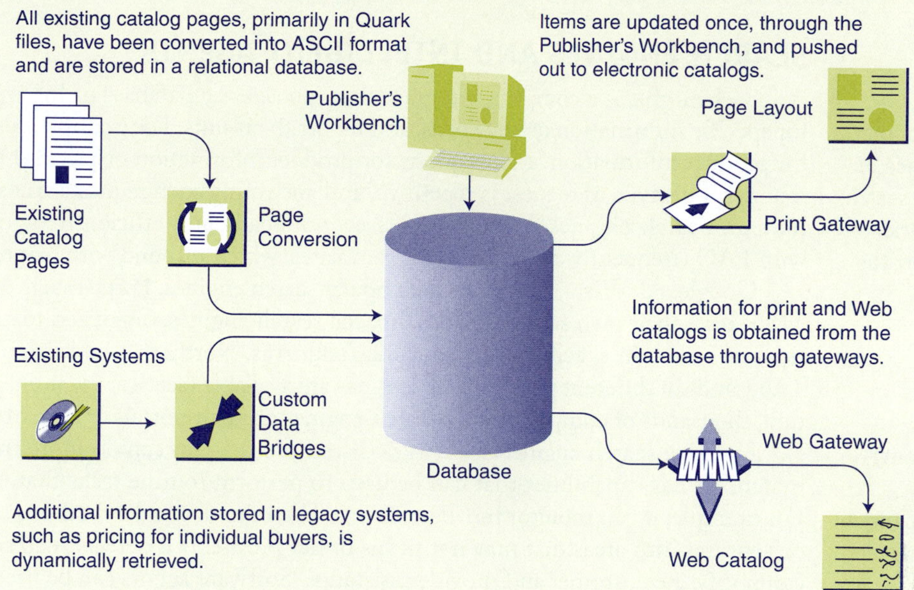

Source: Netscape Diagram © 2005 Netscape Communications Corporation. Diagram used with permission.

Boise Cascade Office Products, now a part of Office Max (*officemaxsolutions.com*), is a $5-billion office products wholesaler and retailer. Its B2B customer base includes over 100,000 large corporate customers and 1 million small ones as well as individuals. The company's 900-page paper catalog used to be mailed to customers once each year. Throughout the year, Boise also sent mini-catalogs tailored to customers' individual needs based on past buying habits and purchase patterns. The company sells over 200,000 different items and has a global reach, allowing it to serve multinational companies.

In 1996, the company placed its catalogs online. Now customers view the catalog at *officemaxsolutions.com* and can order straight from the site or submit orders by e-mail. The orders are shipped the next day. Customers are then billed. In 1997, the company generated 20 percent of its sales through the Web site. In early 1999, the figure was over 30 percent. The company acknowledges that its Internet business is the fastest-growing segment of its business. By 2004, the majority of sales were made via the Internet.

Boise prepares thousands of individualized catalogs for its largest customers. As of 2002, the company has been sending paper catalogs only when specifically requested. As indicated earlier, the vast majority of customers use the online catalogs. It used to take about 6 weeks to produce a single paper customer catalog, primarily because of the time involved in pulling together all the data. Now the process of producing a Web catalog that is searchable, rich in content, and available in a variety of formats takes only 1 week.

One major advantage of B2B customized catalogs is pricing. If everyone has the same catalog, you cannot show the customized price for each buyer, which is based on the contract the customer signed and on the volume of goods being purchased.

Boise estimates that electronic orders cost approximately 55 percent less to process than paper-based ones. The figure shows the process of working with the electronic catalogs. Some catalogs on Web sites provide text and pictures without linking them to order taking. For instance, Coca-Cola's Web site (*cocacola.com*) is not set up to take Coke's orders online; it just reminds people about the taste of Coca-Cola. However, you can buy Coca-Cola collectors items and more at the online store.

As of 2005, Boise sells to small companies and individuals under the OfficeMax brand (OfficeMax is a Boise company).

Sources: *boiseoffice.com/about/ecommerce.shtm* (accessed April 2003); Netscape Customer Profiles, *wp.netscape.com/solutions/business/profiles/boisecascade.html* (accessed April 2003); and *officemaxsolutions.com* (accessed February 2005).

Questions

1. What are the advantages of the electronic catalog to Boise Cascade? To its customers?
2. What are the advantages of customized catalogs?

Implementing E-Catalogs

Implementing e-catalogs on a small scale is fairly simple (see Chapter 16). However, transforming a large-scale catalog to an e-catalog is not an easy task, because it is necessary to create a matching customer support system. See Kapp (2001) for a discussion of the topic, examples of successes and failures, and suggestions for implementation.

SEARCH ENGINES AND INTELLIGENT AGENTS

search engine
A computer program that can access a database of Internet resources, search for specific information or keywords, and report the results.

A **search engine** is a computer program that can access a database of Internet resources, search for specific information or keywords, and report the results. For example, customers tend to ask for product information (e.g., requests for product information or pricing) in the same general manner. This type of request is repetitive, and answering such requests is costly when done by a human. Search engines deliver answers economically and efficiently by matching questions with FAQ (frequently asked question) templates, which respond with "canned" answers.

Google, AltaVista, and Lycos are popular search engines. Portals such as AOL, Yahoo!, and MSN have their own search engines. Special search engines, organized to answer certain questions or search in specified areas, include AskJeeves, Northern Light, Mama, and Looksmart. Thousands of different public search engines are available (see searchengineguide.com). In addition, thousands of companies have search engines on their portals or storefronts.

software (intelligent) agent
Software that can perform routine tasks that require intelligence.

Unlike a search engine, a **software (intelligent) agent** can do more than just "search and match." It has capabilities that can be used to perform routine tasks that require intelligence. For example, it can monitor movements on a Web site to check whether a customer seems lost or ventures into areas that may not fit his or her profile. If it detects such confusion, the agent can notify the customer and provide assistance. Software agents can be used in e-commerce to support tasks such as comparing prices, interpreting information, monitoring activities, and working as an assistant. Users can even chat or collaborate with agents.

Users use both search engines and intelligent agents in e-commerce. If customers are inside a storefront or an e-mall, they can use the search engine to find a product or a service. They can also use Web search engines, such as google.com, to find general information about a product or service. Finally, they can use software agents that make comparisons (e.g., mysimon.com) and conduct other tasks. The essentials of software agents are provided in Online Technical Appendix D. Applications of software agents are described in several chapters, especially in Chapters 3 through 7.

SHOPPING CARTS

electronic shopping cart
An order-processing technology that allows customers to accumulate items they wish to buy while they continue to shop.

An **electronic shopping cart** is an order-processing technology that allows customers to accumulate items they wish to buy while they continue to shop. In this respect, it is similar to a shopping cart in the physical world. The software program of an electronic shopping cart allows customers to select items, review what has been selected, make changes, and then finalize the list. Clicking on "buy" will trigger the actual purchase.

Shopping carts for B2C are fairly simple (visit amazon.com to see an example), but for B2B, a shopping cart may be more complex. A B2B shopping cart could enable a business customer to shop at several sites while keeping the cart on the buyer's Web site to integrate it with the buyer's e-procurement system. A special B2B cart was proposed for this purpose by Lim and Lee (2003) where, in addition to the cart offered at the seller's site, there is a buyers' cart ("b-cart") that resides on the buyers' sites and is sponsored by the participating sellers.

Shopping-cart software is sold or provided for free as an independent component (e.g., monstercommerce.com, easycart.com, edubiz.bizhosting.com, and e-shopping-cart-software.com). It also is embedded in merchants' servers, such as smallbusiness.yahoo.com/merchant. Free online shopping carts (trials and demos) are available at volusion.com and gomerchant.com.

For more on shopping carts, see Chapters 16 and 18.

Section 2.4 ▶ REVIEW QUESTIONS

1. List the dimensions by which electronic catalogs can be classified.
2. List the benefits of electronic catalogs.

3. Explain how customized catalogs are created and used.
4. Compare search engines with software agents.
5. Describe an electronic shopping cart.

2.5 AUCTIONS AS EC MARKET MECHANISMS

One of the most interesting market mechanisms in e-commerce is electronic auctions. They are used in B2C, B2B, C2C, G2B, G2C, and more.

DEFINITION AND CHARACTERISTICS

An **auction** is a market mechanism that uses a competitive process by which a seller solicits consecutive bids from buyers (forward auctions) or a buyer solicits bids from sellers (reverse auctions). Prices are determined dynamically by the bids. A wide variety of online markets qualify as auctions using this definition. Auctions, an established method of commerce for generations, deal with products and services for which conventional marketing channels are ineffective or inefficient, and they ensure prudent execution of sales. For example, auctions can expedite the disposal of items that need to be liquidated or sold quickly.

auction
A competitive process in which a seller solicits consecutive bids from buyers (forward auctions) or a buyer solicits bids from sellers (backward auctions). Prices are determined dynamically by the bids.

There are several types of auctions, each with its own motives and procedures. (For details, see Chapter 10.) Auctions can be done *online* or *off-line*. They can be conducted in *public* auction sites, such as at eBay. They also can be done by invitation to *private* auctions.

This section presents the essential information about auctions that is necessary for understanding Chapters 3 and 4. An even fuller treatment of auctions is available in Chapter 10. See also Kambil and van Heck (2002) and Bajari and Hortacsu (2004).

TRADITIONAL VERSUS E-AUCTIONS

Traditional, physical auctions are still very popular. However, the volume traded on e-auctions is significantly larger and continues to increase.

Limitations of Traditional Off-line Auctions

Traditional off-line auctions, regardless of their type, have the following limitations: They generally last only a few minutes, or even seconds, for each item sold. This rapid process may give potential buyers little time to make a decision, so they may decide not to bid. Therefore, sellers may not get the highest possible price; bidders may not get what they really want, or they may pay too much for the item. Also, in many cases, the bidders do not have much time to examine the goods. Bidders have difficulty learning about auctions and cannot compare what is offered at each location. Bidders must usually be physically present at auctions; thus many potential bidders are excluded.

Similarly, it may be difficult for sellers to move goods to an auction site. Commissions are fairly high, because a location must be rented, the auction needs to be advertised, and an auctioneer and other employees need to be paid. Electronic auctioning removes these deficiencies.

Electronic Auctions

The Internet provides an infrastructure for executing auctions electronically at lower cost, with a wide array of support services, and with many more sellers and buyers. Individual consumers and corporations both can participate in this rapidly growing and very convenient form of e-commerce. Forrester Research projects that the Internet auction industry will reach $54.3 billion in sales by 2007 (Johnson et al. 2002).

Electronic auctions (e-auctions) are similar to off-line auctions except that they are done online. E-auctions have been in existence since the 1980s over local area networks (e.g., flowers; see Kambil and van Heck 2002), and were started on the Internet in 1995. Host sites on the Internet serve as brokers, offering services for sellers to post their goods for sale and allowing buyers to bid on those items.

electronic auction (e-auction)
Auctions conducted online.

Major online auctions, such as eBay, offer consumer products, electronic parts, artwork, vacation packages, airline tickets, and collectibles, as well as excess supplies and inventories being auctioned off by B2B marketers. Another type of B2B online auction is increasingly used to trade special types of commodities, such as electricity transmission capacities and gas and energy options. Furthermore, conventional business practices that traditionally have relied on contracts and fixed prices are increasingly being converted into auctions with bidding for online procurements (e.g., Raffles Hotel, Online File W2.1).

Of course, many consumer goods are not suitable for auctions, and for these items, conventional selling—such as posted-price retailing—is more than adequate. Yet the flexibility offered by online auction trading offers innovative market processes for many other goods. For example, instead of searching for products and vendors by visiting sellers' Web sites, a buyer may solicit offers from all potential sellers. Such a buying mechanism is so innovative that it has the potential to be used in almost all types of consumer goods auctions (as will be shown later when reverse auctions and "name-your-own-price" auctions are discussed). Some examples of innovative auctions are provided in EC Application Case 2.4.

DYNAMIC PRICING AND TYPES OF AUCTIONS

dynamic pricing
Prices that change based on supply and demand relationships at any given time.

A major characteristic of auctions is that they are based on dynamic pricing. **Dynamic pricing** refers to prices that are not fixed, but are allowed to fluctuate as supply and demand in a market change. In contrast, catalog prices are fixed, as are prices in department stores, supermarkets, and many electronic storefronts.

Dynamic pricing appears in several forms. Perhaps the oldest ones are negotiation and bargaining, which have been practiced for many generations in open-air markets. It is customary to classify dynamic pricing into four major categories, depending on how many buyers and sellers are involved. These four categories are outlined in the following text and are discussed more fully in Chapter 10.

CASE 2.4

EC Application

INNOVATIVE AUCTIONS

Here are some examples of innovative implementations of e-auctions.

- Every year, Warren Buffett, the famous U.S. stock investor and investment guru, invites a group of eight people to lunch with him. The eight pay big money for the pleasure. The money is donated to the needy in San Francisco. In the past, Buffett charged $30,000 per group. As of July 2003, Buffett places the invitation on an online auction (eBay). In 2003, bidders pushed the bid from $30,000 to $250,100. The winning bid in 2004 was $202,000. One of the winners commented that he was willing to pay whatever was needed so that he could express to Buffett his appreciation for investment guidance. Before the auction, he had no chance to be invited.
- Initial public offerings (IPOs) of equity securities (stocks) can make their buyers rich. On the first day of trading, prices can go up considerably, frequently over 100 percent. Initial stock allocations typically have been offered for sale to stockbrokers and to some interest groups (e.g., mutual funds and pension funds). In September 2004, Google went public with its IPO by conducting a Dutch auction on the Internet (see Chapter 10). By offering its stocks in this way, the company collected much more money, and the shares were distributed in a fair manner.
- Richard Dan operates an eBay store in Maui, Hawaii, called Safedeal (see trading assistants list on *ebay.com*). Initially he was selling unclaimed items from his pawnbrokership business. Now he is also one of eBay's 40,000 "trading assistants." Web Auction Hawaii and other trading assistants handle advertisements, auction listings, appraisals, descriptions, authentication, payments, shipments, insurance, and more. Dan also advises sellers as to which eBay category is the best for their particular item. Dan is helping nonprofit organizations, estate administrators, and others to sell just about anything, including the four mules he helped sell in September 2004. Dan's basic charge is $25 per item plus a 25 percent commission. (Dan only handles items with an expected price of over $200.)

Questions

1. Explain the logic of using an auction mechanism for an IPO.
2. Why was Buffett so successful with the auctions?
3. You can place your item for sale on eBay without a trading assistant and save on the commission. Why do people use Dan's services?

One Buyer, One Seller

In this configuration, one can use negotiation, bargaining, or bartering. The resulting price will be determined by each party's bargaining power, supply and demand in the item's market, and (possibly) business environment factors.

One Seller, Many Potential Buyers

In this configuration, the seller uses a **forward auction**, an auction in which a seller entertains bids from multiple buyers. (Because forward auctions are the most common and traditional form, they are often simply called *auctions*.) There are four major types of forward auctions: *English* and *Yankee* auctions, in which bidding prices increase as the auction progresses, and *Dutch* and *free-fall* auctions, in which bidding prices decline as the auction progresses. Each of these can be used for either liquidation or for market efficiency (see Chapter 10 and Gallaugher 2002).

forward auction
An auction in which a seller entertains bids from buyers.

One Buyer, Many Potential Sellers

Two popular types of auctions in which there is one buyer and many potential sellers are reverse auctions (tendering) and "name-your-own-price" auctions.

Reverse Auctions. When there is one buyer and many potential sellers, a **reverse auction** (also called a **bidding** or **tendering system**) is effective. In a reverse auction, the buyer places an item he or she wants to buy for bid (or *tender*) on a *request for quote* (RFQ) system. Potential suppliers bid on the item, reducing the price sequentially (see Exhibit 2.5). In electronic bidding in a reverse auction, several rounds of bidding may take place until the bidders do not reduce the price further. The winner is the one with the lowest bid (assuming that only price is considered). Reverse auctions are primarily a B2B or G2B mechanism. (For further discussion and examples, see Chapter 5.)

reverse auction (bidding or tendering system)
Auction in which the buyer places an item for bid (*tender*) on a request for quote (RFQ) system, potential suppliers bid on the job, with the price reducing sequentially, and the lowest bid wins; primarily a B2B or G2B mechanism.

The Name-Your-Own-Price Model. Priceline.com pioneered the **"name-your-own-price" model**. In this model, a would-be buyer specifies the price (and other terms) that he or she is willing to pay to any willing and able seller. For example, Priceline.com presents consumers' requests to sellers, who fill as much of the guaranteed demand as they wish at prices and terms requested by buyers. Alternately, Priceline.com searches its own database that contains vendors' lowest prices and tries to match supply against requests. Priceline.com asks customers to guarantee acceptance of the offer if it is at or below the requested price by giving

"name-your-own-price" model
Auction model in which a would-be buyer specifies the price (and other terms) he or she is willing to pay to any willing and able seller. It is a C2B model that was pioneered by Priceline.com.

EXHIBIT 2.5 **The Reverse Auction Process**

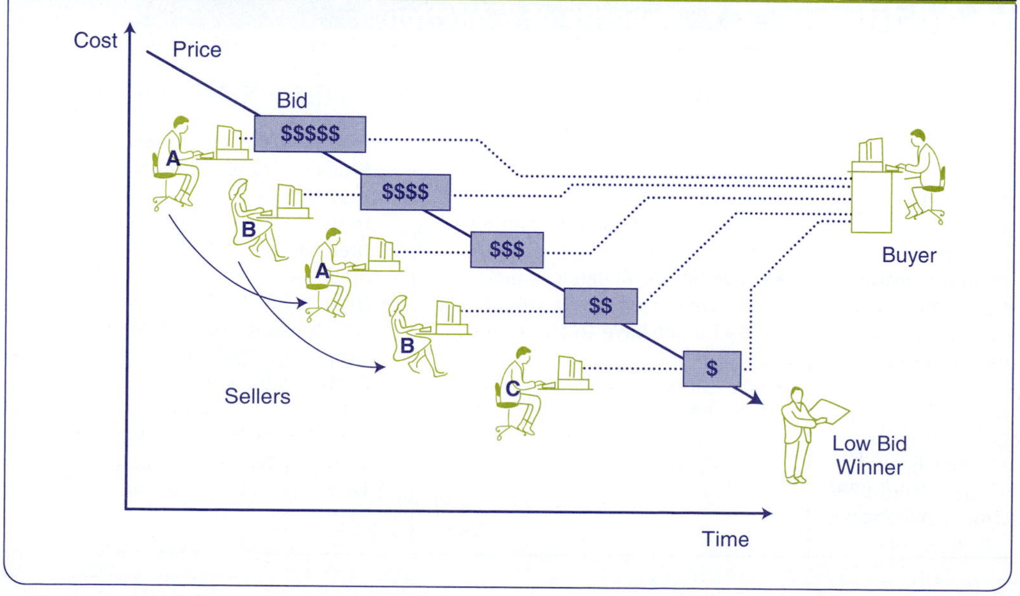

a credit card number. This is basically a C2B model, although some businesses use it too (see Chapter 10 for details.)

Many Sellers, Many Buyers

When there are many sellers and many buyers, buyers and their bidding prices are matched with sellers and their asking prices based on the quantities on both sides. Stocks and commodities markets are typical examples of this configuration. Buyers and sellers may be individuals or businesses. Such an auction is called a **double auction** (see Chapter 10 for details).

double auction
Auctions in which multiple buyers and their bidding prices are matched with multiple sellers and their asking prices, considering the quantities on both sides.

BENEFITS, LIMITATIONS, AND IMPACTS OF E-AUCTIONS

E-auctions are becoming important selling and buying channels for many companies and individuals. E-auctions enable buyers to access goods and services anywhere auctions are conducted. Moreover, almost perfect market information is available about prices, products, current supply and demand, and so on. These characteristics provide benefits to all.

Benefits of E-Auctions

A listing of the benefits of e-auctions to sellers, buyers, and e-auctioneers is provided in Insights and Additions 2.1.

Limitations of E-Auctions

E-auctions have several limitations. The most significant limitations are minimal security, the possibility of fraud, and limited participation.

Minimal Security. Some of the C2C auctions conducted on the Internet are not secure because they are done in an unencrypted environment and credit card numbers could be stolen during the payment process. Payment methods such as PayPal (paypal.com) can be used to solve the payment problem (see Chapter 12). In addition, some B2B auctions are conducted over highly secure private lines.

Possibility of Fraud. Auction items are in many cases unique, used, or antique. Because the buyer cannot see the items, the buyer may get defective products. Also, buyers can commit fraud by receiving goods or services without paying for them. Thus, the fraud rate on e-auctions is very high. For a discussion of e-auction fraud and fraud prevention, see Chapter 10.

Insights and Additions 2.1 Benefits of E-Auctions

Benefits to Sellers	Benefits to Buyers	Benefits to E-Auctioneers
• Increased revenues from broadening bidder base and shortening cycle time. • Opportunity to bargain instead of selling at a fixed price. • Optimal price setting determined by the market (more buyers, more information). • Sellers can gain more customer dollars by offering items directly (saves on the commission to intermediaries; also, physical auctions are very expensive compared with e-auctions). • Can liquidate large quantities quickly. • Improved customer relationship and loyalty (in the case of specialized B2B auction sites and electronic exchanges).	• Opportunities to find unique items and collectibles. • Entertainment. Participation in e-auctions can be entertaining and exciting. • Convenience. Buyers can bid from anywhere, even with a cell phone; they do not have to travel to an auction place. • Anonymity. With the help of a third party, buyers can remain anonymous.	• Higher repeat purchases. Jupiter Research (*jupiterresearch.com*) found that auction sites, such as eBay, tend to garner higher repeat-purchase rates than the top B2C sites, such as Amazon.com. • High "stickiness" to the Web site (the tendency of customers to stay at sites longer and come back more often). Auction sites are frequently "stickier" than fixed-priced sites. Stickier sites generate more ad revenue for the e-auctioneer. • Easy expansion of the auction business.

Limited Participation. Some auctions are by invitation only; others are open to dealers only. Limited participation may be a disadvantage to sellers, who usually benefit from as large a pool of buyers as possible.

Impacts of Auctions

Because the trade objects and contexts for auctions are very diverse, the rationale behind auctions and the motives of the different participants for setting up auctions are quite different. Representative impacts of e-auctions include the following.

Auctions as a Coordination Mechanism. Auctions are used increasingly as an efficient coordination mechanism for establishing an equilibrium in price. An example is auctions for the allocation of telecommunications bandwidth.

Auctions as a Social Mechanism to Determine a Price. For objects that are not traded in traditional markets, such as unique or rare items, or for items that may be offered randomly or at long intervals, an auction creates a marketplace that attracts potential buyers, and often experts. By offering many of these special items at a single place and time, and by attracting considerable attention, auctions provide the requisite exposure of purchase and sale orders, and hence liquidity of the market in which an optimal price can be determined. Typical examples are auctions of fine arts or rare items, as well as auctions of communications frequencies, Web banners, and advertising space. For example, wine collectors can find a global wine auction at winebid.com.

Auctions as a Highly Visible Distribution Mechanism. Some auctions deal with special offers. In this case, a supplier typically auctions off a limited number of items, using the auction primarily as a mechanism to gain attention and to attract those customers who are bargain hunters or who have a preference for the gambling dimension of the auction process. The airline-seat auctions by Cathay Pacific, American Airlines, and Lufthansa fall into this category (see Kambil and van Heck 2002).

Auctions as an EC Component. Auctions can stand alone or they may be combined with other e-commerce activities. An example of the latter is the combination of *group purchasing* with reverse auctions, as described in Online File W2.3.

Section 2.5 ▶ REVIEW QUESTIONS

1. Define auctions and describe how they work.
2. Describe the benefits of electronic auctions over traditional (off-line) auctions.
3. List the four types of auctions.
4. Distinguish between forward and reverse auctions.
5. Describe the "name-your-own-price" auction model.
6. List the major benefits of auctions to buyers, sellers, and auctioneers.
7. What are the major limitations of auctions?
8. List the major impacts of auctions on markets.

2.6 BARTERING AND NEGOTIATING ONLINE

Two emerging mechanisms are gaining popularity (as can be seen in Chapter 10) in EC: e-bartering and e-negotiation.

ONLINE BARTERING

Bartering, the exchange of goods and services, is the oldest method of trade. Today, it is done primarily between organizations. The problem with bartering is that it is difficult to find trading partners. Businesses and individuals may use classified ads to advertise what they need and what they offer, but they still may not be able to find what they want. Intermediaries may be helpful, but they are expensive (20 to 30 percent commission) and very slow.

E-bartering (electronic bartering)—bartering conducted online—can improve the matching process by attracting more partners to the barter. In addition, matching can be done faster, and as a result, better matches can be found. Items that are frequently bartered

bartering
The exchange of goods or services.

e-bartering (electronic bartering)
Bartering conducted online, usually by a bartering exchange.

online include office space, storage, and factory space; idle facilities; and labor, products, and banner ads. (Note that e-bartering may have tax implications that need to be considered.)

bartering exchange
A marketplace in which an intermediary arranges barter transactions.

E-bartering is usually done in a **bartering exchange**, a marketplace in which an intermediary arranges the transactions. These exchanges can be very effective. Representative bartering Web sites include allbusiness.com, intagio.com, and whosbartering.com. The process works like this: First, the company tells the bartering exchange what it wants to offer. The exchange then assesses the value of the company's products or services and offers it certain "points" or "bartering dollars." The company can use the "points" to buy the things it needs from a participating member in the exchange.

Bartering sites must be financially secure. Otherwise users may not have a chance to use the points they accumulate. (For further details, see "virtual bartering 101" at fortune.com/smallbusiness and Lorek 2000).

ONLINE NEGOTIATING

Dynamic prices also can be determined by *negotiation*. Negotiated pricing commonly is used for expensive or specialized products. Negotiated prices also are popular when large quantities are purchased. Much like auctions, negotiated prices result from interactions and bargaining among sellers and buyers. However, in contrast with auctions, negotiation also deals with nonpricing terms, such as the payment method and credit. Negotiation is a well-known process in the off-line world (e.g., in real estate, automobile purchases, and contract work). In addition, in cases where there is no standard service or product to speak of, some digital products and services can be personalized and "bundled" at a standard price. Preferences for these bundled services differ among consumers, and thus they are frequently negotiated. More discussions on electronic negotiations can be found in Bichler et al. (2003).

According to Choi and Whinston (2000), *online (electronic) negotiation* is easier than off-line negotiation. Due to customization and bundling of products and services, it often is necessary to negotiate both prices and terms for online sales. E-markets allow such online negotiations to be conducted virtually for all products and services. Three factors may facilitate online negotiation: (1) the products and services that are bundled and customized, (2) the computer technology that facilitates the negotiation process, and (3) the software (intelligent) agents that perform searches and comparisons, thereby providing quality customer service and a base from which prices can be negotiated.

Section 2.6 ▶ REVIEW QUESTIONS

1. Define bartering and describe the advantages of e-bartering.
2. Explain the role of online negotiation in EC.

2.7 E-COMMERCE IN THE WIRELESS ENVIRONMENT: M-COMMERCE

mobile computing
Permits real-time access to information, applications, and tools that, until recently, were accessible only from a desktop computer.

mobile commerce (m-commerce)
E-commerce conducted via wireless devices.

m-business
The broadest definition of m-commerce, in which e-business is conducted in a wireless environment.

The widespread adoption of wireless and mobile networks, devices (handsets, PDAs, etc.), and *middleware* (software that links application modules from different computer languages and platforms) is creating exciting new opportunities. These new technologies are making **mobile computing** possible. These technologies permit *real-time* access to information, applications, and tools that, until recently, were accessible only from a desktop computer. **Mobile commerce** refers to the conduct of e-commerce via wireless devices or from portable devices (see the Maybelline case at the end of Chapter 1), including smart cards. It is also sometimes called **m-business**, when reference is made to its broadest definition, in which the e-business environment is wireless (Kalakota and Robinson 2001; Sadeh 2002).

There is a reason for the strong interest in the topic of mobile commerce. According to a recent study conducted by Telecom Trends International (2004), the number of m-commerce users was 94.9 million in 2003 and will grow to 1.67 billion in 2008. In addition, the revenues from m-commerce will grow globally from $6.86 billion in 2003 to over $554.37 billion in 2008.

Mobile devices can be connected to the Internet, allowing users to conduct transactions from anywhere. The Gartner Group estimates that at least 40 percent of all B2C transactions, totaling over $200 billion by 2005, will be initiated from smart wireless devices

(Telus Mobility 2002). Others predict much higher figures, because they believe that mobile devices will soon overtake PCs as the predominant Internet access device, creating a global market of over 500 million subscribers. However, others predict a much slower adoption rate (see Chapter 9).

THE PROMISE OF M-COMMERCE

Since 1999, m-commerce has become one of the hottest topics in IT in general and in EC in particular. Mobility significantly changes the manner in which people and trading partners interact, communicate, and collaborate. Mobile applications are expected to change the way we live, play, and do business. Much of the Internet culture, which is currently PC based, may change to be based on mobile devices. As a result, m-commerce creates new business models for EC, notably location-based applications (see Chapter 9).

An emerging area in m-commerce is *pervasive computing* (see Chapter 9). One of its promising applications is the use of RFID to improve the supply chain (see the Real-World Case on Wal-Mart at the end of this chapter).

Although there are currently many hurdles to the widespread adoption of m-commerce, it is clear that many of these will be reduced or eliminated in the future. Many companies are already shifting their strategy to the mobile world. Many large corporations with huge marketing presence—Microsoft, IBM, Intel, Sony, AT&T, TimeWarner, to name a few—are transforming their businesses to include m-commerce-based products and services. Nokia emerged as a world-class company not just because it sells more cell phones than anyone else, but also because it has become the major player in the mobile economy. Similarly, major telecommunications companies, from Verizon to Vodafone, are shifting their strategies to wireless products and services. In the United States, General Motors produced 1.4 million vehicles equipped with in-vehicle safety and communications systems in 2004, and will so equip 2.2 million 2005 models. The company plans to double production of OnStar-equipped vehicles for the model year 2006 (onstar.com 2004). DoCoMo, the world's largest mobile portal (nttdocomo.com; see Vision 2010), is investing billions of dollars to expand its services to other countries via its i-mode Global. Finally, in Europe alone, over 200 companies offer mobile portal services.

I-MODE: A SUCCESSFUL MOBILE PORTAL

To illustrate the potential spread of m-commerce, let's examine DoCoMo's (nttdocomo.com) i-mode, the pioneering wireless service that took Japan by storm in 1999 and 2000. With a few clicks on a handset, i-mode users can conduct a large variety of m-commerce activities, ranging from online stock trading and banking to purchasing travel tickets and booking karaoke rooms. Users can also use i-mode to send and receive color images. Launched in February 1999, i-mode went international in 2000 and had over 15 million users by the end of that year and 44.7 million by June 2004 (nttdocomo.com, accessed February 2005). Here are some interesting applications of i-mode:

- **Shopping guides.** The addresses and telephone numbers of shops in the major shopping malls in Tokyo and other Japanese cities are provided with a supporting search engine. Consumers can locate information about best-selling books and then buy them. Users can purchase music online to enjoy anywhere.
- **Maps and transportation.** Digital maps show detailed guides of local routes and stops of the major public transportation systems in all major Japanese cities. Users can access train and bus timetables, guides to shopping areas, and automatic notification of train delays.
- **Ticketing.** Airline tickets, events, and entertainment tickets can be purchased online.
- **News and reports.** Fast access to global news, local updated traffic conditions, the air pollution index, and weather reports are provided continuously.
- **Personalized movie service.** Updates on the latest movies with related information, such as casting and show times, are provided. Also, subscribers can search for their own favorite movies by entering the name of the movie or the name of the movie theater.
- **Entertainment.** Up-to-date personalized entertainment, such as favorite games, can be searched for and accessed easily. Online "chatting" also is provided, and users can send or receive photos. Also, users can subscribe to receive Tamagotchi's characters each day for

CASE 2.5

EC Application

WIRELESS PEPSI INCREASES PRODUCTIVITY

The Pepsi Bottling Group (PBG; *pbg.com*), the largest manufacturer, seller, and distributor of Pepsi-Cola, has the mountainous job of stocking and maintaining its Pepsi vending machines as well as completing huge amounts of paperwork and searching for parts and equipment to fix the machines. Any time one of the tens of thousands of machines is out of stock or not functioning, the company loses revenue and profits.

In 2002, the company began to equip its service technicians with handheld devices hooked into a wireless wide area network (WWAN). The handheld is the Melard Sidearm (from Melard Technologies of *microslate.com*), and it is designed to work with many wireless platforms. iAnywhere (from Sybase, Inc., *sybase.com*) provides the mobile database application that allows wireless communications around the United States in real time. The database includes the repair parts inventory available on each service truck, so dispatchers know who to send for maintenance and where the truck is at any given moment. It also has a back-office system that maintains the overall inventory. In the near future, the company will be able to locate the whereabouts of each truck in real time, using global positioning systems (GPS). This will make scheduling and dispatching more effective.

In the summer of 2002, only about 700 technicians used the wireless system, but already the company was saving $7 million per year. Each of these technicians has been able to handle one more call each day than previously. PBG provided the wireless capability to about 300 more technicians in 20 more locations in late 2002 and to several thousand by 2005.

Sources: Compiled from Rhey (2002) and from *pbg.com* (accessed February 2005).

Questions

1. What are the capabilities of the handheld devices used by the PBG technicians?
2. How do the handhelds relate to databases and dispatching?
3. This case deals with vending machine maintenance. In what ways, if any, could wireless technologies help with stocking the machines?

only $1 a month. These virtual pets (the translation of their Japanese name means "cute little eggs") exhibit intelligent behavior; for example, a Tamagotchi cat will purr if you pet it, but "bite" if it is hungry.

- **Dining and reservations.** The exact location of a selected participating restaurant is shown on a digital map. Subscribers also can find restaurants that offer meals in a particular price range. Reservations can be made online. Discount coupons also are available online.
- **Additional services.** Additional services, such as banking, stock trading, telephone directory searches, dictionary services, and horoscopes, are available.

These applications are for individual users and are provided via a mobile portal. An even greater number of applications are available in the B2B area and in the intrabusiness area, as illustrated in EC Application Case 2.5. For more complete coverage of m-business applications, see Chapter 9, Kalakota and Robinson (2001), Sadeh (2002), and Dekleva (2004).

Section 2.7 ▶ REVIEW QUESTIONS

1. Define mobile computing and m-commerce.
2. How does m-commerce differ from EC?
3. What are some of the major services provided by i-mode?

2.8 COMPETITION IN THE DIGITAL ECONOMY

One of the major economic impacts of EC is its contribution to competitive advantage, as will be shown next.

THE INTERNET ECOSYSTEM

The prevailing model of competition in the Internet economy is more like a web of interrelationships than the hierarchical, command-and-control model of the industrial economy. Because of these interrelationships, the business model of the Internet economy has been called the **Internet ecosystem**. Just like an ecosystem in nature, activity in the Internet economy is self-organizing: The process of *natural selection* takes place around company profits and value to customers.

Internet ecosystem
The business model of the Internet economy.

The Internet economy has low barriers to entry, and so it is expanding rapidly. As the Internet ecosystem evolves, both technologically and in population, it will be even easier and likelier for countries, companies, and individuals to participate in the Internet economy. Already, there is a $1 trillion technical infrastructure in place, ready and available for anyone to use at any time—free of charge. New ideas and ways of doing things can come from anywhere at any time in the Internet economy. Some of the old rules of competition no longer apply (see discussions at meansbusiness.com/learntdig.asp).

Competitive Factors

EC competition is very intense because online transactions enable the following.

Lower Search Costs for Buyers. E-markets reduce the cost of searching for product information, frequently to zero. This can significantly impact competition, enabling customers to find cheaper (or better) products and forcing sellers, in turn, to reduce prices and/or improve customer service. Sellers that provide information to buyers can exploit the Internet to gain a considerably larger market share. For example, according to Tsai (2004), Wal-Mart and Walgreens are developing intelligent search tools that are expected to increase online sales by 25 to 50 percent.

Speedy Comparisons. Not only can customers find inexpensive products online, but they also can find them quickly. For example, a customer does not have to go to several bookstores to find the best price for a particular book. Using shopping search engines such as allbookstores.com, or bestwebbuys.com/books, or shopping.com for consumer products, customers can find what they want and compare prices. Companies that sell online and provide information to search engines will gain a competitive advantage.

Differentiation and Personalization. **Differentiation** involves providing a product or service that is not available elsewhere. For example, Amazon.com differentiates itself from other book retailers by providing customers with information that is not available in a physical bookstore, such as communication with authors, almost real-time book reviews, and book recommendations. An example of personalization is the Bombay Sapphire case (Online File W2.4).

differentiation
Providing a product or service that is unique.

In addition, EC provides for personalization or customization of products and services. **Personalization** refers to the ability to tailor a product, service, or Web content to specific user preferences. For example, Amazon.com notifies customers by e-mail when new books on their favorite subjects or by their favorite authors are published. Several sites will track news or stock prices based on the consumer's preferences.

personalization
The ability to tailor a product, service, or Web content to specific user preferences.

Consumers like differentiation and personalization and are frequently willing to pay more for them. Differentiation reduces the substitutability between products, thus benefiting sellers who use this strategy. Also, price cutting in differentiated markets does not impact market share very much: Many customers are willing to pay a bit more for the personalized products or services.

Lower Prices. Buy.com, Half.com, Blue Nile, and other companies can offer low prices due to their low costs of operation (no physical facilities, minimum inventories, etc.). If volume is large enough, prices can be reduced by 40 percent or more.

Customer Service. Amazon.com and Dell, for example, provide superior customer service. As will be shown in Chapters 3 and 13, such service is an extremely important competitive factor.

Barriers to Entry Are Reduced. Setting up a Web site is relatively easy and inexpensive, and doing so reduces the need for a sales force and brick-and-mortar stores. Companies have to view this as both a threat (e.g., Where will our next competitor come from?) and as an opportunity (e.g., Can we use our core competencies in new areas of business?).

Virtual Partnerships Multiply. With access to a World Wide Web of expertise and the ability to share production and sales information easily, the ability of a firm to create a virtual team to exploit an EC opportunity increases dramatically. The Internet is especially good at reducing interaction costs, the time and money expended when people and companies exchange goods, services, and ideas (e.g., meetings, sales presentations, telephone calls).

Market Niches Abound. The market-niche strategy is as old as the study of competitive advantage. What has changed is that without the limits imposed by physical storefronts, the number of business opportunities is as large as the Web. The challenge strategists face is to discover and reap the benefits from profitable niches before the competition does so.

Certain other competitive factors have become less important as a result of EC. For example, the size of a company may no longer be a significant competitive advantage (as will be shown later). Similarly, location (geographical distance from the consumer) now plays a less significant role, and language is becoming less important as translation programs remove some language barriers (see Chapters 14 and 16). Finally, digital products are not subject to normal wear and tear, although some become obsolete (see discussion in Choi and Whinston 2000).

All in all, EC supports efficient markets and could result in almost perfect competition. In such markets, a *commodity* (an undifferentiated product) is produced when the consumer's willingness to pay equals the marginal cost of producing the commodity and neither sellers nor buyers can influence supply or demand conditions individually. The following are necessary for *perfect competition*:

- Many buyers and sellers must be able to enter the market at little or no entry cost (no barriers to entry).
- Large buyers or sellers are not able to individually influence the market.
- The products must be homogeneous (commodities). (For customized products, therefore, there is no perfect competition.)
- Buyers and sellers must have comprehensive information about the products and about the market participants' demands, supplies, and conditions.

EC could provide, or come close to providing, these conditions. It is interesting to note that the ease of finding information benefits both buyers (finding information about products, vendors, prices, etc.) and sellers (finding information about customer demands, competitors, etc.).

It can be said that competition between companies is being replaced by competition between *networks*. The company with better communication networks, online advertising capabilities, and relationships with other Web companies (e.g., having an affiliation with Amazon.com) has a strategic advantage. It can also be said that competition is now mostly between *business models*. The company with the better business model will win.

Porter's Competitive Analysis in an Industry

competitive forces model
Model, devised by Porter, that says that five major forces of competition determine industry structure and how economic value is divided among the industry players in an industry; analysis of these forces helps companies develop their competitive strategy.

Porter's (2001b) **competitive forces model** views five major forces of competition that determine an industry's structural attractiveness. These forces, in combination, determine how the economic value created in an industry is divided among the players in the industry. Such an industry analysis helps companies develop their competitive strategy.

Because the five forces are affected by both the Internet and e-commerce, it is interesting to examine how the Internet influences the industry structure portrayed by Porter's model. Porter divided the impacts of the Internet into either positive or negative for the industry. As shown in Exhibit 2.6, most of the impacts are negative (marked by a minus sign). Of course, there are variations and exceptions to the impacts shown in the illustration, depending on the industry, its location, and its size. A negative impact means that competition will intensify in most industries as the Internet is introduced, causing difficulties to a competing company. Thus, the Internet means stronger competition. This competition, which is especially strong for commodity-type products (e.g., toys, books, CDs), was a major contributor to the collapse of many dot-com companies in 2000 to 2001. To survive and prosper in such an environment, a company needs to use innovative strategies.

Section 2.8 ▸ REVIEW QUESTIONS

1. Why is competition so intense online?
2. Describe Porter's competitive forces model as it applies to the Internet and EC.

EXHIBIT 2.6 Porter's Competitive Forces Model: How the Internet Influences Industry Structure

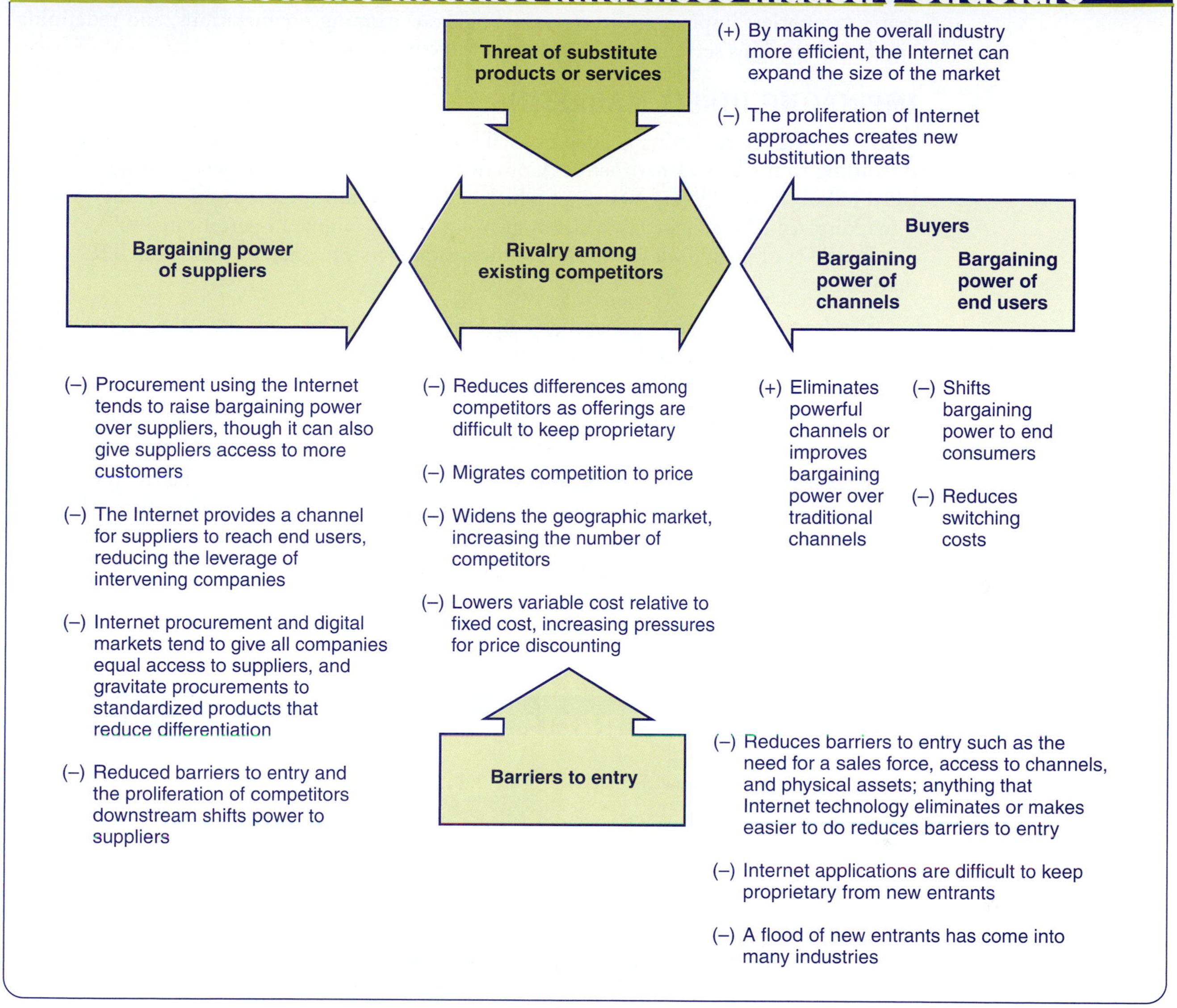

Threat of substitute products or services

(+) By making the overall industry more efficient, the Internet can expand the size of the market

(–) The proliferation of Internet approaches creates new substitution threats

Bargaining power of suppliers

Rivalry among existing competitors

Buyers

Bargaining power of channels | **Bargaining power of end users**

Bargaining power of suppliers:

(–) Procurement using the Internet tends to raise bargaining power over suppliers, though it can also give suppliers access to more customers

(–) The Internet provides a channel for suppliers to reach end users, reducing the leverage of intervening companies

(–) Internet procurement and digital markets tend to give all companies equal access to suppliers, and gravitate procurements to standardized products that reduce differentiation

(–) Reduced barriers to entry and the proliferation of competitors downstream shifts power to suppliers

Rivalry among existing competitors:

(–) Reduces differences among competitors as offerings are difficult to keep proprietary

(–) Migrates competition to price

(–) Widens the geographic market, increasing the number of competitors

(–) Lowers variable cost relative to fixed cost, increasing pressures for price discounting

Bargaining power of channels:

(+) Eliminates powerful channels or improves bargaining power over traditional channels

Bargaining power of end users:

(–) Shifts bargaining power to end consumers

(–) Reduces switching costs

Barriers to entry

(–) Reduces barriers to entry such as the need for a sales force, access to channels, and physical assets; anything that Internet technology eliminates or makes easier to do reduces barriers to entry

(–) Internet applications are difficult to keep proprietary from new entrants

(–) A flood of new entrants has come into many industries

Source: Reprinted by permission of *Harvard Business Review.* From "Strategy and the Internet" by Michael E. Porter, *Harvard Business Review,* March 2001.

2.9 IMPACTS OF EC ON BUSINESS PROCESSES AND ORGANIZATIONS

Little statistical data or empirical research on the full impact of EC is available because of the relative newness of the field. Therefore, the discussion in this section is based primarily on experts' opinions, logic, and some actual data.

New Web technologies are offering organizations unprecedented opportunities to rethink strategic business models, processes, and relationships. Feeny (2001) called these *e-opportunities*, dividing them into three categories: e-marketing (Web-based initiatives that improve the marketing of existing products), e-operations (Web-based initiatives that improve the creation of existing products), and e-services (Web-based initiatives that improve customer services). Zwass (2003) also addressed the opportunities of e-marketplaces: creation of virtual marketplaces with desired rules, flexible pricing (including price discovery), multichannel marketplaces (including bricks-and-clicks), customization, and new business models.

The discussion here is also based in part on the work of Bloch et al. (1996), who approached the impact of e-marketplaces on organizations from a value-added point of view. Their model, which is shown in Exhibit 2.7, divides the impact of e-marketplaces into three major categories: improving direct marketing, transforming organizations, and redefining organizations. This section examines each of these impacts.

IMPROVING DIRECT MARKETING

Traditional direct marketing is done by mail order (catalogs) and telephone (telemarketing). According to the U.S. Department of Commerce, in 2001 direct mail generated sales of over $110 billion in the United States, of which only $5 billion (or about 4.5 percent) was via e-marketplaces. This figure is small, but growing rapidly (about 15 percent in 2005).

Bloch et al. (1996) describe the following impacts of e-marketplaces on B2C direct marketing:

- **Product promotion.** The existence of e-marketplaces has increased the promotion of products and services through direct marketing. Contact with customers has become more information rich and interactive.
- **New sales channel.** Because of the direct reach to customers and the bidirectional nature of communications in EC, a new distribution channel for existing products has been created.
- **Direct savings.** The cost of delivering information to customers over the Internet results in substantial savings to senders of messages. Major savings are realized in delivering digitized products (such as music and software) rather than physical ones.
- **Reduced cycle time.** The delivery time of digitized products and services can be reduced to seconds. Also, the administrative work related to physical delivery, especially across international borders, can be reduced significantly, cutting the cycle time by more than

EXHIBIT 2.7 The Analysis-of-Impacts Framework

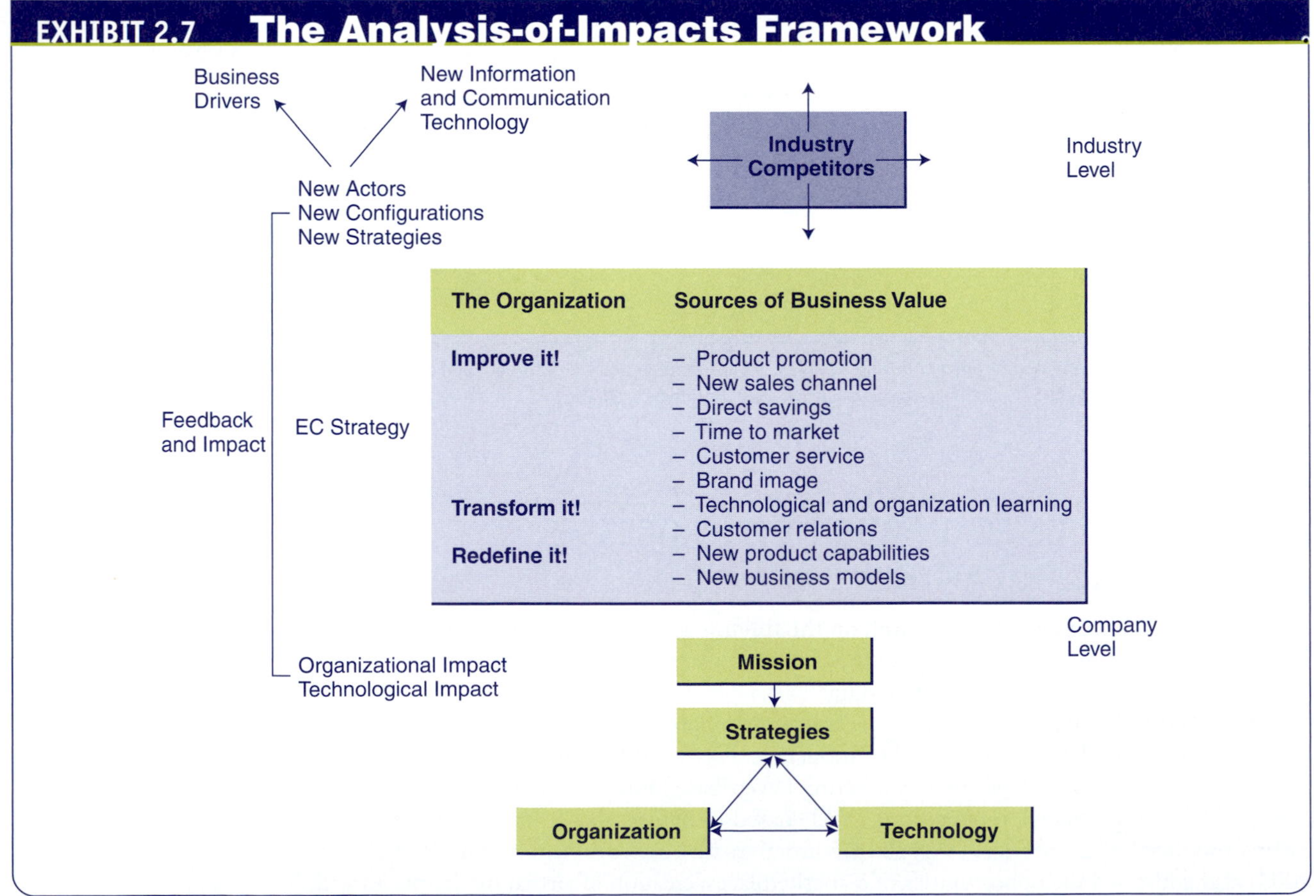

Source: From M. Bloch, Y. Pigneur, and A. Segev. "Leveraging Electronic Commerce for Competitive Advantage: A Business Value Framework." *Proceedings of the Ninth International Conference on EDI-IOS*, Bled, Slovenia, June 1996.

90 percent. One example of this is TradeNet in Singapore, which reduced the administrative time of port-related transactions from days to minutes. Cycle time can be reduced through improvements along the supply chain (e.g., by using RFID).

- **Improved customer service.** Customer service can be greatly enhanced by enabling customers to find detailed information online. For example, FedEx and other shippers allow customers to trace the status of their packages. Also, autoresponders (see Chapter 13) can answer standard e-mail questions in seconds. Finally, human experts' services can be expedited using help-desk software.
- **Brand or corporate image.** On the Web, newcomers can establish corporate images very quickly. What Amazon.com did in just 3 years took traditional companies generations to achieve. A good corporate image facilitates trust, which is necessary for direct sales. Traditional companies such as Intel, Disney, Wal-Mart, Dell, and Cisco use their Web activities to affirm their corporate identity and brand image. Online File W2.4 demonstrates how one company uses personalization to bolster its image.

In addition to the impacts suggested by Bloch et al. (1996), additional impacts of e-marketplaces on direct marketing include the following:

- **Customization.** EC enables customization of products and services. Buying in a store or ordering from a television advertisement usually limits customers to a supply of standard products. Dell is the classic example of customization success. Today, customers can configure not only computers, but also cars, jewelry, shoes, clothes, gifts, and hundreds of other products and services. If done properly, a company can achieve mass customization that provides a competitive advantage and increases the overall demand for certain products and services. Customization is changing marketing and sales activities both in B2C and in B2B.
- **Advertising.** With direct marketing and customization comes one-to-one, or direct, advertising, which can be much more effective than mass advertising. Direct advertising creates a fundamental change in the manner in which advertising is conducted, not only for online transactions, but also for products and services that are ordered and shipped in traditional ways. As will be shown in Chapter 4, the entire concept of advertising is going through a fundamental change due to EC.
- **Ordering systems.** Taking orders from customers can be drastically improved if it is done online, reducing both processing time and mistakes. Electronic orders can be quickly routed to the appropriate order-processing site. This process reduces expenses and also saves time, freeing salespeople to develop marketing plans.
- **Market operations.** Direct e-marketing is changing traditional markets. Some physical markets may disappear, as will the need to make deliveries of goods to intermediaries in the marketplace. In an e-marketspace, goods are delivered directly to buyers upon completion of the purchase, making markets much more efficient and saving the cost of the shipment into and from the brick-and-mortar store.

For digitally based products—software, music, and information—the changes brought by e-markets will be dramatic. Already, small but powerful software packages are delivered over the Internet. The ability to deliver digitized products electronically affects (eliminates) packaging and greatly reduces the need for specialized distribution models.

New sales models such as shareware, freeware, and pay-as-you-use are emerging. Although these models currently exist only within particular sectors, such as the software and publishing industries, they will eventually pervade other sectors.

Another way to view the impact of e-marketplaces on marketing is provided by Wind (2001), who summarized the changes in marketing. These changes are listed in Exhibit 2.8.

All of these impacts of e-markets on direct marketing provide companies with a competitive advantage over those that use traditional direct-sales methods, as vividly illustrated in the Blue Nile case. Furthermore, because the competitive advantage is so large, e-markets are likely to replace many nondirect marketing channels. Some people predict the "fall of the shopping mall," and many retail stores and brokers of services (e.g., stocks, real estate, and insurance) are labeled by some as soon-to-be-endangered species.

EXHIBIT 2.8 The Changing Face of Marketing

	Old Model—Mass and Segmented Marketing	New Model—Customization
Relationships with customers	Customer is a passive participant in the exchange	Customer is an active coproducer
Customer needs	Articulated	Articulated and unarticulated
Segmentation	Mass market and target segments	Segments looking for customized solutions and segmented targets
Product and service offerings	Line extensions and modification	Customized products, services, and marketing
New product development	Marketing and R&D drive new product development	R&D focuses on developing the platforms that allow consumers to customize
Pricing	Fixed prices and discounting	Customer determined pricing (e.g., Priceline.com; auctions); value-based pricing models
Communication	Advertising and PR	Integrated, interactive, and customized marketing communication, education, and entertainment
Distribution	Traditional retailing and direct marketing	Direct (online) distribution and rise of third-party logistics services
Branding	Traditional branding and cobranding	The customer's name as the brand (e.g., My Brand or Brand 4 ME)
Basis of competitive advantage	Marketing power	Marketing finesse and "capturing" the customer as "partner" while integrating marketing, operations, R&D, and information

Source: Wind, Y., "The Challenge of Customization in Financial Services." *The Communications of the ACM.* ©2001 AMC, Inc. Used with permission.

TRANSFORMING ORGANIZATIONS

The second impact of e-marketplaces suggested by Bloch et al. (1996) is the transformation of organizations. Here, we look at two key organizational transformations: organizational learning and the nature of work.

Technology and Organizational Learning

Rapid progress in EC will force a Darwinian struggle: To survive, companies will have to learn and adapt quickly to the new technologies. This struggle will offer them an opportunity to experiment with new products, services, and business models, which may lead to strategic and structural changes. These changes may transform the way in which business is done. We believe that as EC progresses, it will have a large and durable impact on the strategies of many organizations (see the Rosenbluth [now part of American Express] case, Online File W2.6).

Thus, new technologies will require new organizational structures and approaches. For instance, the structure of the organizational unit dealing with e-marketspaces might be different from the conventional sales and marketing departments. Specifically, a company's e-commerce unit might report directly to the chief information officer (CIO) rather than to the sales and marketing vice president. To be more flexible and responsive to the market, new processes must be put in place. For a while, new measurements of success may be needed. For example, the measures—called *metrics*—used to gauge success of an EC project in its early stages might need to be different from the traditional revenue–expenses framework (see Chapters 14 and 15). However, in the long run, as many dot-coms have found out, no business can escape the traditional revenue–expenses framework.

In summary, corporate change must be planned and managed. Before getting it right, organizations may have to struggle with different experiments and learn from their mistakes.

The Changing Nature of Work

The nature of some work and employment will be restructured in the Digital Age; it is already happening before our eyes. For example, driven by increased competition in the global marketplace, firms are reducing the number of employees down to a core of essential staff and outsourcing whatever work they can to countries where wages are significantly lower. The upheaval brought on by these changes is creating new opportunities and new risks and is forcing people to think in new ways about jobs, careers, and salaries.

Digital Age workers will have to be very flexible. Few will have truly secure jobs in the traditional sense, and many will have to be willing and able to constantly learn, adapt, make decisions, and stand by them. Many will work from home.

The Digital Age company will have to view its core of essential workers as its most valuable asset. It will have to constantly nurture and empower them and provide them with every means possible to expand their knowledge and skill base (see Drucker 2002).

REDEFINING ORGANIZATIONS

The following are some of the ways in which e-markets will redefine organizations.

New and Improved Product Capabilities

E-markets allow for new products to be created and for existing products to be customized in innovative ways. Such changes may redefine organizations' missions and the manner in which they operate. Customer profiles, as well as data on customer preferences, can be used as a source of information for improving products or designing new ones.

Mass customization, as described earlier, enables manufacturers to create specific products for each customer, based on the customer's exact needs (see Appendix 2A on build-to-order at the end of this chapter). For example, Motorola gathers customer needs for a pager or a cellular phone, transmits the customer's specifications electronically to the manufacturing plant where the device is manufactured, and then sends the finished product to the customer within a day. Dell and General Motors use the same approach in building their products. Customers can use the Web to design or configure products for themselves. For example, customers can use the Web to design T-shirts, furniture, cars, jewelry, Nike shoes, and even a Swatch watch. With the use of mass-customization methods, the cost of customized products is at or slightly above the comparable retail price of standard products. Exhibit 2.9 shows how customers can order customized Nike shoes.

EXHIBIT 2.9 How Customization Is Done Online: The Case of Nike Shoes

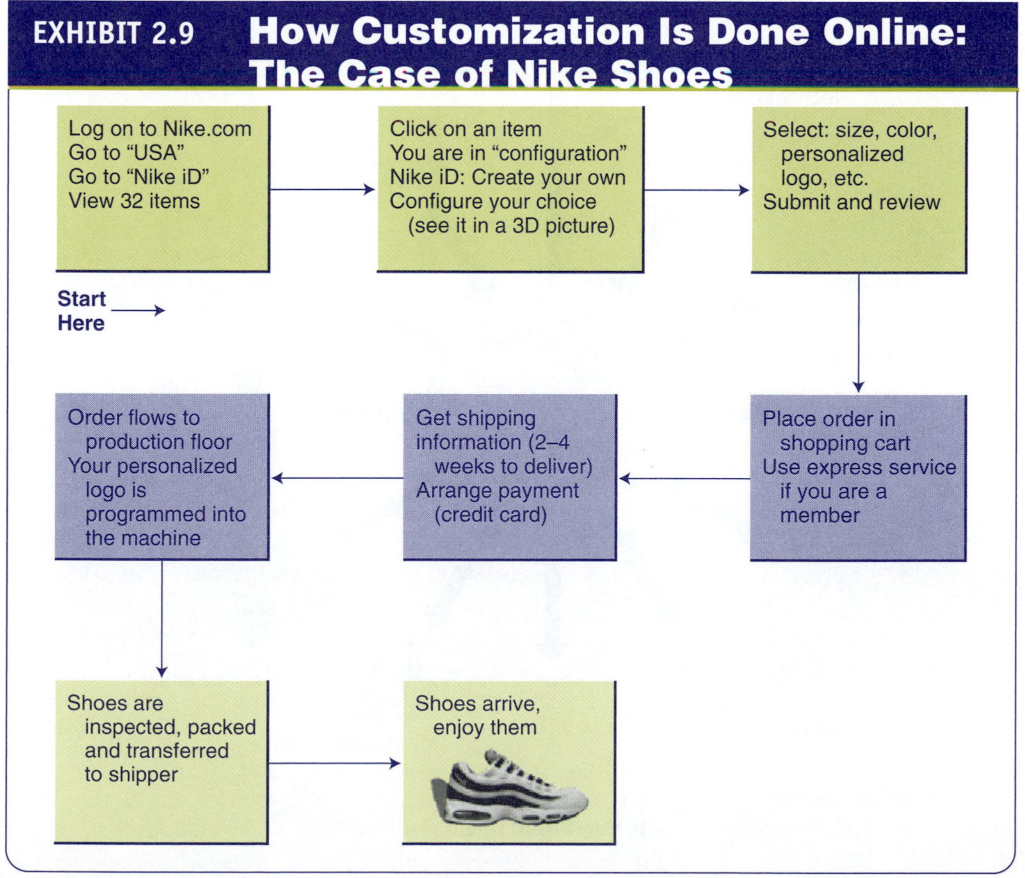

New Business Models

E-markets affect not only individual companies and their products, but also entire industries. The wide availability of information and its direct distribution to consumers will lead to the use of new business models (e.g., the name-your-own-price model of Priceline.com).

Improving the Supply Chain

One of the major benefits of e-markets is the potential improvement in supply chains. A major change is the creation of a hub-based chain, as shown in Exhibit 2.10, the Real-World Case at the end of this chapter, and in Chapter 7.

Impacts on Manufacturing

EC is changing manufacturing systems from mass production lines to demand-driven, just-in-time manufacturing (see Peoplesoft 2004). These new production systems are integrated with finance, marketing, and other functional systems, as well as with business partners and customers. Using Web-based ERP systems (supported by software such as SAP R/3), companies

EXHIBIT 2.10 Changes in the Supply Chain

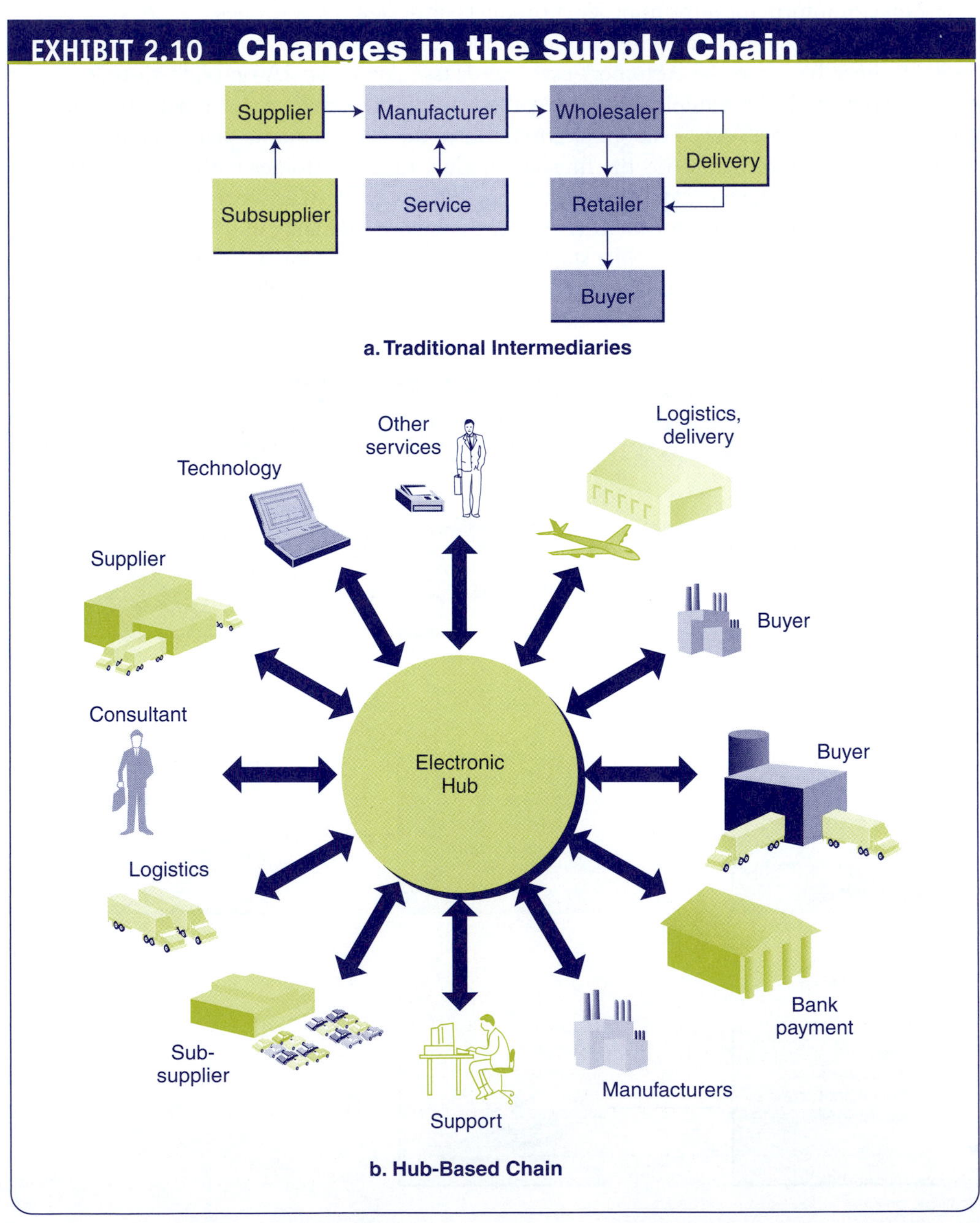

can direct customer orders to designers and/or to the production floor within seconds (see Norris et al. 2000). Production cycle time is cut by 50 percent or more in many cases, especially if production is done in a different country from where the designers and engineers are located.

Build-to-Order Manufacturing. Build-to-order (pull system) is a manufacturing process that starts with an order (usually customized). Once the order is paid for, the vendor starts to fulfill it. This changes not only production planning and control, but also the entire supply chain and payment cycle. For example, manufacturing or assembly starts only after an order is received. For more on build-to-order production, see Appendix 2A at the end of this chapter. One implementation of build-to-order is presented next.

build-to-order (pull system)
A manufacturing process that starts with an order (usually customized). Once the order is paid for, the vendor starts to fulfill it.

Real-Time Demand-Driven Manufacturing. Successful manufacturing organizations must respond quickly and efficiently to demand. Strategies and techniques of the past no longer work, and it's a challenge to transform from the traditional, inventory-centric model to a more profitable and flexible demand-driven enterprise. *Demand-driven manufacturing* (DDM) provides customers with exactly what they want, when and where they want it. Effective communication between the supply chain and the factory floor is needed to make it happen. Partnerships must be focused on reducing costs through shared quality goals, shared design responsibility, on-time deliveries, and continuous performance reviews. The DDM process is shown in Exhibit 2.11. An explanation of the headings in the figure is provided in Online File W2.2.

Virtual Manufacturing. An interesting organizational concept is that of *virtual manufacturing*—the ability to run multiple manufacturing plants as though they were at one location. A single company controls the entire manufacturing process, from the supply of components to shipment, while making it completely transparent to customers and employees. For example, Cisco works with 34 plants globally, 32 of which are owned by other companies. Each of Cisco's products will look exactly alike, regardless of where it was manufactured. Up-to-the-minute information sharing is critical for the success of this mass-customization approach (Pine 1999).

Assembly Lines. Companies such as IBM, General Motors, General Electric, and Boeing assemble products from components that are manufactured in many different locations, even different countries. Subassemblers gather materials and parts from their vendors, and they may use one or more tiers of manufacturers. Communication, collaboration, and coordination are critical in such multitier systems. Using electronic bidding, assemblers acquire subassemblies 15 to 20 percent cheaper than before and 80 percent faster. Furthermore, such systems are flexible and adaptable, allowing for fast changes with minimum cost. Also, costly inventories that are part of mass-production systems can be minimized.

EXHIBIT 2.11 Real-Time Demand-Driven Manufacturing

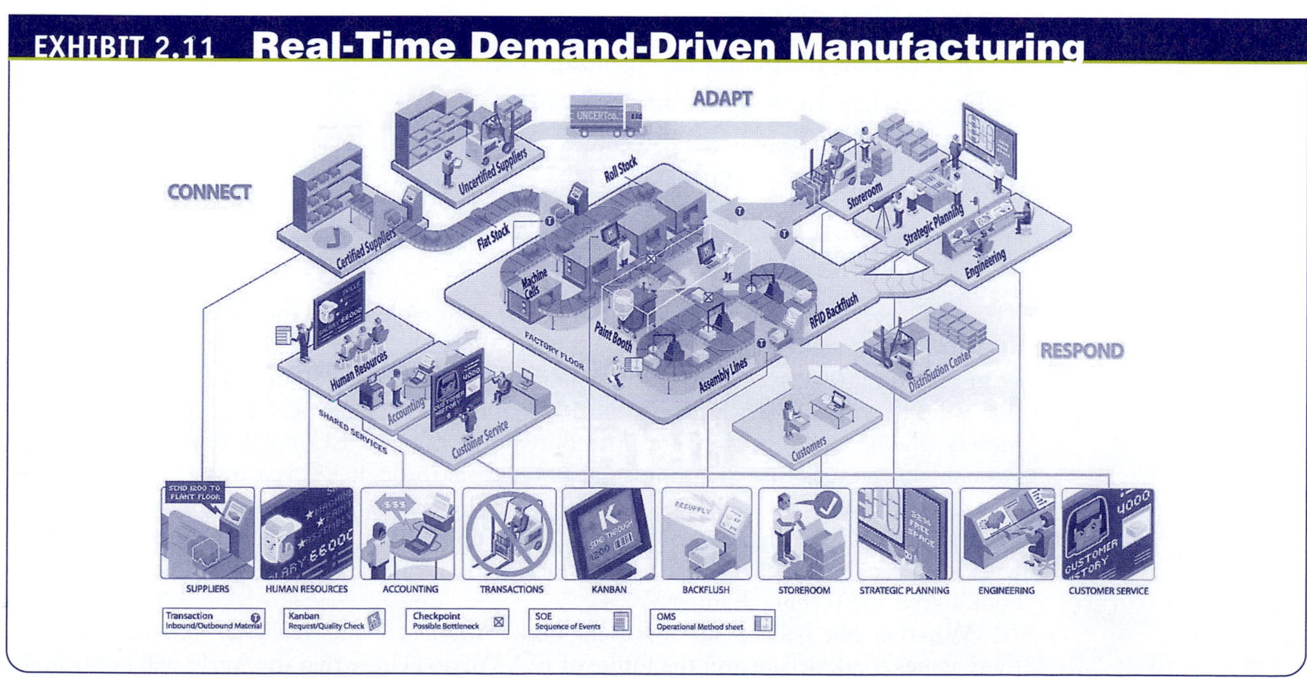

Source: PeopleTalk. "Real Time Demand Driven Manufacturing." Vol. 15, No. 3, July–Sept. 2004, pp. 14–15. XPLANATIONS® by XPLANE®, © 2005, *XPLANE.com*. Courtesy of Oracle.

Impacts on Finance and Accounting

E-markets require special finance and accounting systems. Most notable of these are electronic payment systems. Traditional payment systems are ineffective or inefficient for electronic trade. The use of new payment systems such as electronic cash is complicated because legal issues and agreements on international standards are involved. Nevertheless, electronic cash is certain to come soon, and it will change how payments are made. It could also change consumers' financial lives and shake the foundations of financial systems.

Executing an electronic order triggers an action in what is called the *back office*. Back-office transactions include buyers' credit checks, product availability checks, order confirmation, changes in accounts payable, receivables, billing, and much more. These activities must be efficient, synchronized, and fast so that the electronic trade will not be slowed down. An example of this is online stock trading. In most cases, orders are executed in less than 1 second, and the trader can find an online confirmation of the trade immediately.

One of the most innovative concepts in accounting and finance is the "virtual close," which would allow companies to close their accounting records, or "books," within a day. This Cisco Systems project is described in Online File W2.5.

Impact on Human Resources Management and Training

EC is changing how people are recruited (see Chapter 3), evaluated, promoted, and developed. EC also is changing the way training and education are offered to employees. Online distance learning is exploding, providing opportunities that never existed in the past. Companies are cutting training costs by 50 percent or more, and virtual courses and programs are mushrooming (see Chapter 8).

New e-learning systems offer two-way video, on-the-fly interaction, and application sharing. Such systems provide for interactive remote instruction systems, which link sites over a high-speed intranet. At the same time, corporations are finding that e-learning may be their ticket to survival as changing environments, new technologies, and continuously changing procedures make it necessary for employees to be trained and retrained constantly, a process known as e-Human Resources (Ensher et al. 2002). EC systems are revolutionizing human resources (HR) operations (see Online File W2.3).

Section 2.9 ▶ REVIEW QUESTIONS

1. List the major parts of Bloch et al.'s model.
2. Describe how EC improves direct marketing.
3. Describe how EC transforms organizations.
4. Describe how EC redefines organizations.
5. Describe the concept of build-to-order (customization).
6. Describe the concept of the virtual close.

2.10 E-REALITY

The overexpectations of what EC would accomplish ended with the failure of hundreds of dot-com companies. In place of the hype came the realization that the adoption of EC will be much slower than anticipated. Rosenbloom (2002) identified 10 myths about e-commerce that were heavily publicized during the 1998–2000 period of hype; he argues that these are merely *myths,* and that they are not contributing to the EC revolution. For example, Rosenbloom argues that the promise of lower costs through EC is a myth. The reality, he says, is that lower costs are not occurring, due to the costs of order fulfillment and customer acquisition, both of which are very high. Rosenbloom's argument is debatable; some agree with it, others disagree. A list of Rosenbloom's myths and the realities is presented on the book's Web site (Online Exhibit W2.4).

Whether one believes all of Rosenbloom's "myths" or the "realities," or some of each, these issues spark debate over the future of EC. We do believe that the world will be strongly impacted by the Web and by EC. The successful implementation of EC is only a matter of time and of learning. Over time, organizations, individuals, and society will reap the full benefits of EC, including those that at present are myths. Also, as pointed out by Porter (2001b), the real value of EC is in exploiting the characteristics that by themselves may only be myths in such a way that one can use EC to complement the conventional ways of doing business. To reap the economic advantages of EC, a company needs an EC strategy (see Chapter 14 and Porter 2001a and 2001b). According to Mullaney (2004) and the U.S. Department of Commerce News (2004), EC started to accelerate again in 2004.

Section 2.10 ▶ REVIEW QUESTION

1. List the myths that, in your opinion, will become realities first.

MANAGERIAL ISSUES

Some managerial issues related to this chapter are as follows.

1. **What about intermediaries?** Many EC applications will change the role of intermediaries. This may create a conflict between a company and its distributors. It may also create opportunities. In many cases, distributors will need to change their roles. This is a sensitive issue that needs to be planned for during the transformation to the e-business plan.
2. **Should we auction?** A major strategic issue is whether to use auctions as a sales channel. Auctions do have some limitations, and forward auctions may create conflicts with other distribution channels. If a company decides to auction, it needs to select an auction mechanism and determine a pricing strategy. These decisions determine the success of the auction and the ability to attract and retain visitors on the site. Auctions also require support services. Decisions about how to provide these services and to what extent to use business partners are critical to the success of high-volume auctions.
3. **Should we barter?** Bartering can be an interesting strategy, especially for companies that lack cash, need inventory or machinery, and have some surplus inventory. However, the valuation of what is bought or sold may be hard to determine, and the tax implications in some countries are not clear.
4. **What m-commerce opportunities are available?** A company should develop an m-commerce strategy if it is likely to be impacted by m-commerce. The opportunities presented by m-commerce are enormous, but so are the risks. However, doing nothing may be even riskier. For further discussion, see Kalakota and Robinson (2001) and Sadeh (2002).
5. **How do we compete in the digital economy?** Although the basic theories of competition are unchanged, the rules are different. Of special interest are digital products and services, whose variable costs are very low. Competition involves both old-economy and new-economy companies. The speed of changes in competitive forces can be rapid, and the impact of new business models can be devastating. As Bill Gates once said, "Competition is not among companies, but among business models" (Financial Analysts Meeting, 1998).
6. **What organizational changes will be needed?** Companies should expect organizational changes in all functional areas once e-commerce reaches momentum. At a minimum, purchasing will be done differently in many organizations; introducing models such as forward auctions and affiliate programs may also have a major impact on business operations.

RESEARCH TOPICS

Some EC research issues related to this chapter follow. For details, references, resources, and more, refer to the "Current EC Research" appendix on the book's Web site.

1. **Benefits of E-marketplaces**
   - Analyze the benefits of e-marketplaces by industry and by product.
   - What is the role of e-marketplaces in facilitating coordination with partners and third parties?
   - What traditional internal roles can be moved to e-marketplaces?
   - Summarize and compare empirical EC studies and outline potential EC studies.

2. **The Roles of Intermediaries in E-marketplaces**
   - Examine the traditional roles of intermediaries and their roles in e-marketplaces.
   - Investigate how intermediation affects competition and customer service.
   - Analyze disintermediation and reintermediation in e-marketplaces.
3. **Electronic Catalogs**
   - What are the benefits of intelligent catalog-search tools to buyers?
   - From the buyer's point of view, what are the benefits of customized, aggregated catalogs?
   - Devise a framework for a personalization procedure and how decision makers use it.
   - How can companies balance personalization and flexible selectivity?
   - How accurate is dynamic customer profiling?
4. **Auctions and Negotiation as B2B EC Mechanisms**
   - Investigate the reasons for the success of online auctions.
   - Examine how businesses use auctions, especially reverse ones, as a business strategy.
   - Research different aspects of online negotiation (e.g., the role of intelligent agents).
5. **The Impact of EC**
   - Research the impact of EC on organizations, functional departments, competition, market structures, and business processes.
   - Use surveys and statistics to research the impact of EC on different countries and industries.
6. **Mobile Computing and Commerce**
   - Use general models, frameworks, and surveys to compare and contrast m-commerce and e-commerce.
   - Examine how wireline and wireless technologies are related (complementation, substitution, facilitation).
   - Investigate new m-commerce technologies, such as RFID.
7. **Build-to-Order Manufacturing and Assembly**
   - Investigate the implementation strategy of EC and its relationship to mass customization from different angles (e.g., by industry, by product type).
   - Examine the design of information systems used to facilitate build-to-order.
8. **Agent-Based E-marketplaces**
   - Discuss creation of protocols of agent-based EC.
   - Will people use intelligent agents? Is there a limit to what autonomous agents can do?
   - Research the integration of Agent Communication Language (ACL), EDI, and B2B protocols.
   - How are agents incorporated into Web Services?
   - How do agents extract knowledge from Web pages?
   - Describe Semantic Web with eXtensible Rule Markup Language (XRML) frameworks.
   - Describe design of market mechanisms and experimental simulation of their performances.
   - Examine agents in context-aware ubiquitous environments: architectures and applications.
9. **The Effect of EC on Organizational Structures**
   - How has EC changed the organizational structure of firms?
   - How has EC affected procurement and sales departments?
   - What kinds of internal processes can be outsourced?
   - Examine trends in online outsourcing.

SUMMARY

In this chapter you learned about the following EC issues as they relate to the learning objectives.

1. **E-marketplaces and their components.** A marketspace or e-marketplace is a virtual market that does not suffer from limitations of space, time, or borders. As such, it can be very effective. Its major components include customers, sellers, products (some digital), infrastructure, front-end processes, back-end activities, electronic intermediaries, other business partners, and support services.
2. **The role of intermediaries.** The role of intermediaries will change as e-markets develop; some will be eliminated (disintermediation), others will change their roles and prosper (reintermediation). In the B2B area, for example, e-distributors connect manufacturers with buyers by aggregating electronic catalogs of many suppliers. New value-added services that range from content creation to syndication are mushrooming.
3. **The major types of e-marketplaces.** In the B2C area, there are storefronts and e-malls. In the B2B area, there are private and public e-marketplaces, which may be vertical (within one industry) or horizontal (across different industries). Different types of portals provide access to e-marketplaces.

4. **Electronic catalogs, search engines, and shopping carts.** The major mechanisms in e-markets are electronic catalogs, search engines, software (intelligent) agents, and electronic shopping carts. These mechanisms facilitate EC by providing a user-friendly shopping environment.
5. **Types of auctions and their characteristics.** In forward auctions, bids from buyers are placed sequentially, either in increasing (English and Yankee) mode or in decreasing (Dutch and free-fall) mode. In reverse auctions, buyers place an RFQ and suppliers submit offers in one or several rounds. In "name-your-own-price" auctions, buyers specify how much they are willing to pay for a product or service, and an intermediary tries to find a supplier to fulfill the request.
6. **The benefits and limitations of auctions.** The major benefits for sellers are the ability to reach many buyers, to sell quickly, and to save on commissions to intermediaries. Buyers have a chance to obtain bargains and collectibles while shopping from their homes. The major limitation is the possibility of fraud.
7. **Bartering and negotiating.** Electronic bartering can greatly facilitate the swapping of goods and services among organizations, thanks to improved search and matching capabilities, which is done in bartering exchanges. Software agents can facilitate online negotiation.
8. **The role of m-commerce.** Mobile commerce is emerging as a phenomenon that can provide Internet access to millions of people. It also creates new location-related applications.
9. **Competition in the digital economy.** Competition in online markets is very intense due to the increased power of buyers, the ability to find the lowest price, and the ease of switching to another vendor. There is more global competition as well.
10. **The impact of e-markets on organizations.** All functional areas of an organization are affected by e-markets. Broadly, e-markets improve direct marketing and transform and redefine organizations. Direct marketing (manufacturers to customers) and one-to-one marketing and advertising are becoming the norm, and mass customization and personalization are taking off. Production is moving to a build-to-order model, changing supply chain relationships and reducing cycle time. Virtual manufacturing is also on the rise. Financial systems are becoming more efficient as they become networked with other business functions, and the human resources activities of recruiting, evaluation, and training are being managed more efficiently due to employees' interactions with machines.

KEY TERMS

Term	Page
Auction	55
Back end	43
Bartering	59
Bartering exchange	60
Build-to-order (pull system)	71
Buy-side e-marketplace	46
Competitive forces model	64
Differentiation	63
Digital products	42
Disintermediation	49
Double auction	58
Dynamic pricing	56
E-bartering (electronic bartering)	59
E-distributor	49
E-mall (online mall)	45
E-marketplace	46
Electronic auction (e-auction)	55
Electronic catalog	50
Electronic shopping cart	54
Forward auction	57
Front end	43
Infomediary	47
Information portal	46
Intermediary	43
Internet ecosystem	63
M-business	60
Marketspace	42
Mobile commerce (m-commerce)	60
Mobile computing	60
Mobile portal	47
"Name-your-own-price" model	57
Personalization	63
Private e-marketplace	46
Public e-marketplace	46
Reintermediation	49
Reverse auction (bidding or tendering system)	57
Search engine	54
Sell-side e-marketplace	46
Software (intelligent) agent	54
Storefront	44
Voice portal	47

QUESTIONS FOR DISCUSSION

1. Compare marketplaces with marketspaces. What are the advantages and limitations of each?
2. Compare and contrast competition in traditional markets with that in digital markets.
3. Why are sell-side and buy-side marketplaces in the same company usually separated, whereas in an exchange they are combined?
4. Discuss the need for portals in EC.

5. Discuss the advantages of dynamic pricing over fixed pricing. What are the potential disadvantages of dynamic pricing?
6. The "name-your-own-price" model is considered a reverse auction. However, this model does not include RFQs or consecutive bidding. Why is it called a reverse auction?
7. Discuss the advantages of m-commerce over e-commerce.
8. Discuss the relationship of DDM with build-to-order.

INTERNET EXERCISES

1. Visit **bluenile.com** and **thaigem.com**. Compare the sites. Comment on the similarities and the differences.
2. Go to **cisco.com**, **google.com**, and **cio.com** and locate information about the status of the "virtual close." Write a report based on your findings.
3. Visit **ticketmaster.com**, **ticketonline.com**, and other sites that sell event tickets online. Assess the competition in online ticket sales. What services do the different sites provide?
4. Examine how bartering is conducted online at **tradeaway.com**, **buyersbag.com**, **u-exchange.com**, and **intagio.com**. Compare the functionalities and ease of use of these sites.
5. Enter **ebay.com/anywhere** and investigate the use of "anywhere wireless." Review the wireless devices and find out how they work.
6. Enter **mfgquote.com** and review the process by which buyers can send RFQs to merchants of their choice. Evaluate all of the online services provided by the company. Write a report based on your findings.
7. Enter **bloomsburgcarpet.com**. Explain how the site solves the problem of sending carpet sample books to representatives all over the country. What are the special features of the electronic catalogs here? (*Hint:* It might be useful to read Kapp 2001.)
8. Enter **respond.com** and send a request for a product or a service. Once you receive replies, select the best deal. You have no obligation to buy. Write a short report based on your experience.
9. Enter **onstar.com** and review its services. Comment on the usability of each service.
10. Compare the search engines at **invisibleweb.com** and at **northernlight.com**. Report on the unique capabilities of each.

TEAM ASSIGNMENTS AND ROLE PLAYING

1. Have several teams each review Porter's (2001b) and Bako's (1998) articles. Each team member will research one of the issues raised in the papers (e.g., competition, disintermediation, and Internet impacts) in light of recent developments in the economy and the e-commerce field.
2. Reread the opening case and discuss the following.
   a. Discuss the key success factors for Blue Nile.
   b. Amazon.com makes only a 15 percent margin on the products it sells. This enables Amazon.com to sell diamond earrings for $1,000 (traditional jewelers charge $1,700 for the same). Do you think that Amazon.com will succeed in selling this type of jewelry as Blue Nile did in selling expensive engagement rings?
   c. Competition between Blue Nile and Amazon.com will continue to increase. In your opinion, which one will win (visit their Web sites and see how they sell jewelry).
   d. Why is "commoditization" so important in the diamond business?
   e. Compare the following three sites: diamond.com, ice.com, and bluenile.com.
   f. Follow the performance of Blue Nile's IPO (symbol: Nile).

Real-World Case

WAL-MART LEADS RFID ADOPTION

In the first week of April 2004, Wal-Mart (*walmart.com*) launched its first live test of RFID tracing technology. Using one distribution center and seven stores, 21 products from participating vendors were used in the pilot test.

In the pilot application, passive RFID chips with small antennae were attached to cases and pallets. When passed near an RFID "reader," the chip activated, and its unique product identifier code was transmitted back to an inventory control system. Cases and pallets containing the 21 products featuring RFID tags were delivered to the distribution center in Sanger, Texas, where RFID readers installed at the dock doors notified both shippers and Wal-Mart what products had entered the Wal-Mart distribution center and where the products were stored. RFID readers were also installed in other places, such as conveyor belts, so that each marked case could be tracked. The readers used by Wal-Mart have an average range of 15 feet. (See Chapter 7 for more on how RFID works.)

Wal-Mart has set a January 2005 target for its top 100 suppliers to place RFID tags on cases and pallets destined for Wal-Mart stores. Wal-Mart believes that the implementation of the pilot scheme will pave the way for achieving this goal. The system is expected to improve flows along the supply chain, reduce theft, increase sales, reduce inventory costs (by eliminating both overstocking and understocking), and provide visibility and accuracy throughout Wal-Mart's supply chain.

Although some of Wal-Mart's suppliers are late in implementing the system, it is clear that if the pilot is successful (and so far it is), RFID will become an industry standard. After all, nearly $70 billion is lost in the retail sector in the United States every year due to products getting lost in the supply chain or being stored in wrong places.

The next step in Wal-Mart's pilot is to mark each individual item with a tag. This plan raises a possible privacy issue: What if the tags are not removed from the products? People fear that they will be tracked after leaving the store. Wal-Mart also can use RFIDs for many other applications. For example, it could attach tags to shoppers' children, so if they are lost in the megastore, they could be tracked in seconds.

Retailers such as Wal-Mart believe that the widespread implementation of RFID technology marks a revolutionary change in supply chain management, much as the introduction of bar codes was as seen as revolutionary two decades ago.

Sources: Condensed from Lundquist (2003); Business Week Online (2004); and Kaiser (2004).

Questions

1. Assuming the cost of RFID is low (less than $0.05 per item), what advantages can you see for tagging individual items in each store? Is it necessary to do so?
2. Find some information regarding the advantages of RFIDs over regular bar codes.
3. Is this an e-business application? Why or why not? If it is, what business model is being used?
4. What are some of the business pressures driving the use of RFID in retailing?

REFERENCES

Bajari, P., and A. Hortacsu. "Economic Insights from Internet Auctions." *Journal of Economic Literature* (June 2004).

Bakos, Y. "The Emerging Role of Electronic Marketplaces on the Internet." *Communications of the ACM* (August 1998).

Beynon-Davies, P. *@-business*. New York: Palgrave-Macmillan, 2004.

Bichler, M., G. Kersten, and C. Weinhardt. "Electronic Negotiations: Foundations, Systems and Experiments—Introduction to the Special Issue of." *Group Decision and Negotiation*, 12 (May-December 2003).

Bloch, M., Y. Pigneur, and A. Segev. "Leveraging Electronic Commerce for Competitive Advantage: A Business Value Framework." *Proceedings of the Ninth International Conference on EDI-IOS*, June 1996, Bled, Slovenia.

Boise Office. **boiseoffice.com/about/ecommerce.shtm** (accessed April 2003). *Note: No longer active.*

Business Week. "A Slow Climb from Wireless' Dark Ages: Cell Phones at the Crossroads." *Business Week*, February 15, 2002. **businessweek.com/technology/content/feb2002/tc20020215_3636.htm** (accessed February 2005).

Business Week Online. "Like It or Not, RFID Is Coming." Business Week Online, March 18, 2004. **businessweek.com/technology/content/mar2004/tc20040318_7698_tc121.htm** (accessed February 2005).

Business Week Online. "Talking RFID with Wal-Mart's CIO." Business Week Online, February 4, 2004. **businessweek.com/technology/content/feb2004/tc2004024_3168_tc165.htm** (accessed February 2005).

Choi, S. Y., and A. B. Whinston. *The Internet Economy: Technology and Practice*. Austin, TX: Smartecon.com, 2000.

Cox, B. G., and W. Koelzer. *Internet Marketing*. Upper Saddle River, NJ: Prentice Hall, 2004.

Dekleva, S. "M-Business: Economy Driver or a Mess?" *Communications of the AIS* (February 2004).

Drucker, P. *Managing in the Next Society*. New York: Truman Talley Books, 2002.

Ensher E. A., E. Grant-Vallone, and T. R. Nielson. "Tales from the Hiring Line." *Organizational Dynamics* (October–December 2002).

Feeny, D. "Making Business Sense of the E-Opportunity." *MIT Sloan Management Review* (Winter 2001).

Financial Analysts Meeting, Seattle, Washington, July 23, 1998.

Gallaugher, J. M. "E-Commerce and the Undulating Distribution Channel." *Communications of the ACM* (July 2002).

Grover, V., and J. Teng. "E-Commerce and the Information Market." *Communications of the ACM*, 44, no. 4 (April 2001).

Johnson, C., A. Dash, and K. Delhagen. "Online Auctions Will Boom Through 2007." Forester Research, October 2002. **forrester.com/ER/Research/Brief/Excerpt/0,1317,15776,00.html** (accessed April 2003).

Kaiser, E. "Wal-Mart Starts RFID Test." *Forbes.com*, April 30, 2004. **forbes.com/home/newswire/2004/04/30/rtr1355059.html** (accessed February 2005).

Kalakota, R., and M. Robinson. *M-Business: The Race to Mobility*. New York: McGraw-Hill, 2001.

Kambil, A., and E. van Heck. *Making Markets*. Boston: Harvard Business School Press, 2002.

Kapp, K. "A Framework for Successful E-technology Implementation: Understand, Simplify, Automate." *Journal of Organizational Excellence* (Winter 2001).

Lim, G. G., and J. K. Lee. "Buyer Carts for B2B EC: The B-cart Approach." *Organizational Computing and Electronic Commerce* (July–September 2003).

Lorek, L. "Trade Ya? E-barter Thrives." *InteractiveWeek*, August 14, 2000.

Lundquist, E. "Wal-Mart Gets It Right." *E-Week*, July 14, 2003.

Meredith, R. "From Rocks to Riches." *Forbes Magazine*, August 8, 2002.

Microsoft Corp. "RadioShack.ca Increases Customer Satisfaction While Decreasing Management Time and Cost with Commerce Server 2002." *Microsoft.com*, July 1, 2002. **microsoft.com/resources/casestudies/CaseStudy.asp?CaseStudyID=13381** (accessed February 2005).

Mullaney, T. J. "E-Biz Strikes Again!" *Business Week*, May 10, 2004.

Netscape Customer Profiles. "Boise Cascade Saves $1 Million in First Year of Web Catalog." **wp.netscape.com/solutions/business/profiles/boisecascade.html** (accessed April 2003).

Norris, G., et al. *E-Business and ERP*. New York: John Wiley and Sons, 2000.

Norris M., and S. West. *eBusiness Essentials*, 2d ed. Chichester U.K.: John Wiley & Sons, Ltd., 2001.

NTE. **nte.com** (accessed 2003).

nttdocomo.com (accessed February 2005).

Office Max. **officemax.comsolutions** (accessed February 2005).

OnStar. "GM to Double Production of OnStar-equipped Vehicles: Customer Demand Prompts GM Decision." September 21, 2004. **onstar.internetpressroom.com/prr_releases_detail.cfm?id=297** (accessed February 2005).

Peoplesoft. "Demand-Driven Manufacturing." *PeopleTalk*, July–Sept 2004.

Pepsi Bottling Group. **pbg.com** (accessed November 2004).

Pine, J., II. *Mass Customization*. Boston: Harvard Business School Press, 1999.

Porter, M. E. *Competitive Advantage: Creating and Sustaining Superior Performance*, rev. ed. New York: The Free Press, 2001a.

Porter, M. E. "Strategy and the Internet." *Harvard Business Review* (March 2001b).

Rhey, E. "Pepsi Refreshes, Wirelessly." *PC Magazine*, September 17, 2002.

Rosenbloom, B. "The 10 Deadly Myths of E-commerce." *Business Horizons*, March–April 2002.

Sadeh, N. *Mobile Commerce: New Technologies, Services and Business Models*. New York: John Wiley & Sons, April 2002.

Telecom Trends International. "Mobile Commerce Takes-Off: Market Trends and Forecasts." **telecomtrends.net/pr_MIIS-1.htm** (accessed November 2004).

Telus Mobility. "Wireless Security Primer." *Telus Mobility*, August 2002. **telusmobility.com/pdf/business_solutions/security_primer.pdf** (accessed November 2004).

Thaigem. **thaigem.com/wel_about.php** (accessed August 2004).

Tsai, M. "Online Retailers See Improved Site Search as Sales Tools." *Dow Jones Newswires*, August 20, 2004.

Turban, E., et al. *Information Technology for Management*, 5th ed. New Jersey: Wiley, 2006.

U.S. Department of Commerce News. "Retail Indicators Branch Report." *U.S. Census Bureau*, August 20, 2004. **census.gov/mrts/www/current.html** (accessed November 2004).

Varadarajan, P. R., and M. S. Yadav. "Marketing Strategy and the Internet: An Organizing Framework." *Academy of Marketing Science*, 30, no. 4 (Fall 2002).

Wind, Y. "The Challenge of Customization in Financial Services." *Communications of the ACM* (2001).

Yarom, I., C. V. Goldman, and J. S. Rosenschein. "The Role of Middle-Agents in Electronic Commerce." *IEEE Intelligent Systems* (November–December 2003).

Zwass, V. "Electronic Commerce and Organizational Innovation: Aspects and Opportunities." *International Journal of Electronic Commerce*, 7, no. 3 (2003).

BUILD-TO-ORDER PRODUCTION

The concept of *build-to-order* means that a firm starts to make a product or service only after an order for it is placed. This concept is as old as commerce itself and was the only method of production until the Industrial Revolution. According to this concept, if a person needs a pair of shoes, he or she goes to a shoemaker, who takes the person's measurements. The person negotiates quality, style, and price and pays a down payment. The shoemaker buys the materials and makes a customized product for the customer. Customized products are expensive, and it takes a long time to finish them. The Industrial Revolution introduced a new way of thinking about production.

The Industrial Revolution started with the concept of dividing work into small parts. Such *division of labor* makes the work simpler, requiring less training for employees. It also allows for *specialization*. Different employees become experts in executing certain tasks. Because the work segments are simpler, it is easier to *automate* them. As machines were invented to make products, the concept of *build-to-market* developed. To implement build-to-market, it was necessary to design standard products, produce them, store them, and then sell them.

The creation of standard products by automation drove prices down, and demand accelerated. The solution to the problem of increased demand was *mass production*. In mass production, a company produces large amounts of standard products at a very low cost and then "pushes" them to consumers. Thus began the need for sales and marketing organizations. Specialized sales forces resulted in increased competition and the desire to sell in wider, and more remote, markets. This model also required the creation of large factories and specialized departments such as accounting and personnel to manage the activities in the factories. With mass production, factory workers personally did not know the customers and frequently did not care about customers' needs or product quality. However, the products were inexpensive and good enough to fuel demand, and thus the concept became a dominant one. Mass production also required inventory systems at various places in the supply chain, which were based on forecasted demand. If the forecasted demand was wrong, the inventories were incorrect. Thus, companies were always trying to achieve the right balance between not having enough inventory to meet demand and having too much inventory on hand.

As society became more affluent, the demand for customized products increased. Manufacturers had to meet the demand for customized products to satisfy customers. As long as the demand for customized product was small, it could be met. Cars, for example, have long been produced using this model. Customers were asked to pay a premium for customization and wait a long time to receive the customized product, and they were willing to do so.

Slowly, the demand for customized products and services increased. Burger King introduced the concept of "making it your way," and manufacturers sought ways to provide customized products in large quantities, which is the essence of *mass customization*. Such solutions were usually enhanced by some kind of information technology (Pine and Gilmore 1997). The introduction of customized personal computers (PCs) by Dell was so successful that many other industries wanted to try mass customization. However, they found that it is not so easy to do (Zipkin 2001; Agrawal et al. 2001).

EC can facilitate customization and even mass customization (Holweg and Pil 2001). To understand how companies can use EC for customization, let's first compare mass production, also known as a *push system*, and mass customization, also known as a *pull system*, as shown in Exhibit 2A.1.

Notice that one important area in the supply chain is order taking. Using EC, a customer can self-configure the desired product online. The order is received in seconds. Once the order is verified and payment arranged, the order is sent electronically to the production floor. This saves time and money. For complex products, customers may collaborate in real time with the manufacturer's designers, as is done at Cisco Systems. Again, time and money are saved and errors are reduced due to better communication and collaboration. Other contributions of EC are that the customers' needs are visible to all partners in the order fulfillment chain (fewer delays, faster response time), inventories are reduced due to rapid communication, and digitizable products and services can be delivered electronically.

A key issue in mass customization is understanding what the customers want. EC is very helpful in this area due to the use of online market research methods such as collaborative filtering (see Chapter 4 and Holweg and Pil 2001). Using collaborative filtering, a company can discover what each customer wants without asking the customer directly. Such market research is accomplished more cheaply by a machine than by human researchers.

From the production point of view, EC also can enable mass customization. In the factory, for example, IT in general and e-commerce in particular can help in expediting the production changeover from one item to another. Also, because most mass production is based on the assembly of standard components, EC can help a company create the production process for a product in minutes and identify needed

EXHIBIT 2A.1 **Push Versus Pull Production Systems**

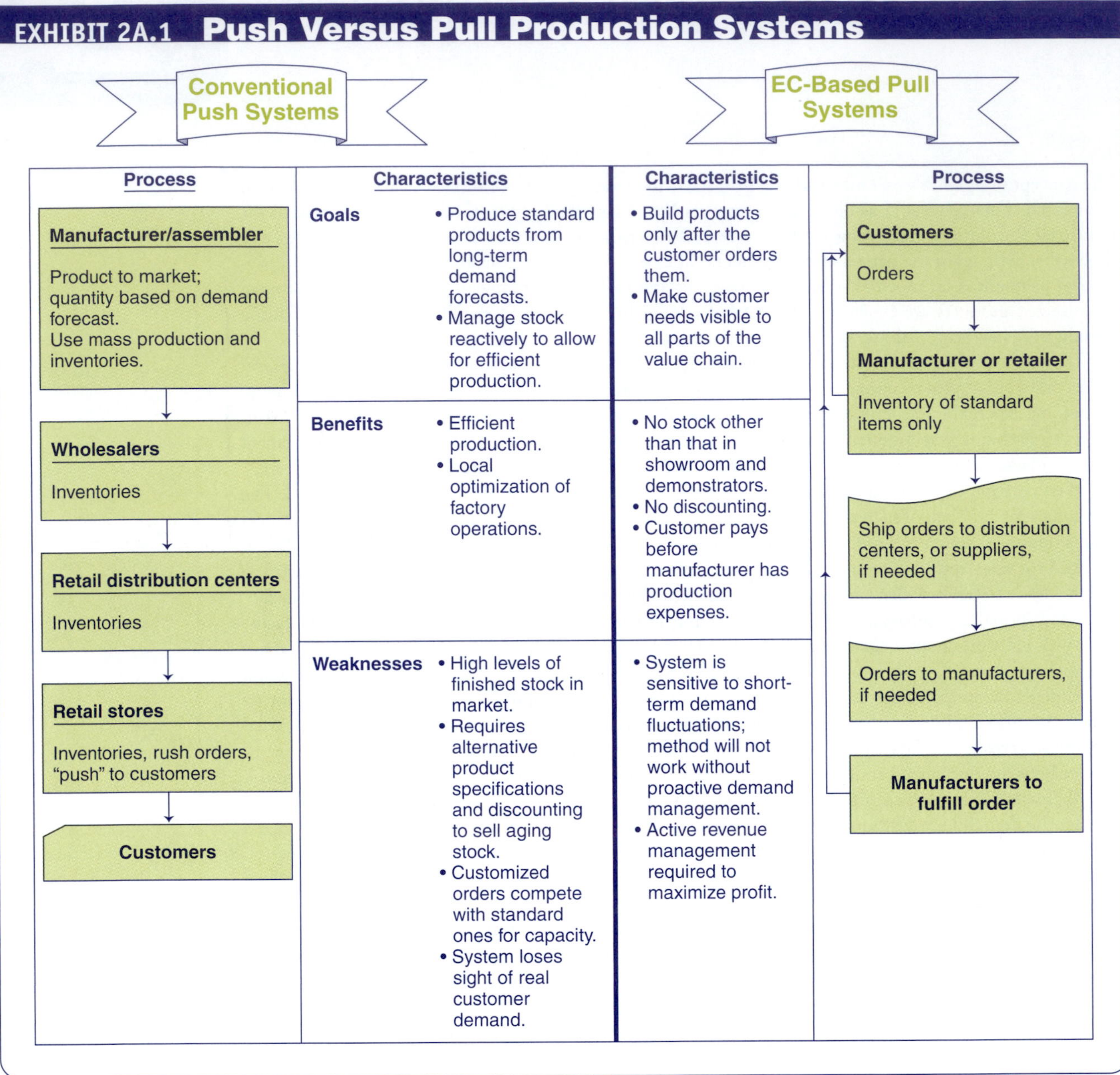

components and their location. Furthermore, a production schedule can be generated automatically and needed resources can be deployed, including money. This is why many industries, and particularly the auto manufacturers, are planning to move to build-to-order using EC. By doing so, they are expecting huge cost reductions, shorter order-to-delivery times, and lower inventory costs (see Agrawal et al. 2001, Exhibit 1; Holweg and Pil 2001).

Mass customization on a large scale is not easy to attain (Zipkin 2001; Agrawal et al. 2001), but if properly performed, it may become the dominant model in many industries.

REFERENCES

Agrawal, M., T. V. Kumaresh, and G. A. Mercer. "The False Promise of Mass Customization." *The McKinsey Quarterly* no. 3 (2001).

Holweg, M., and F. Pil. "Successful Build-to-Order Strategies Start with the Customer." *MIT Sloan Management Journal* 43, no. 1 (2001): 74–83.

Pine, B. J., and J. Gilmore. "The Four Faces of Mass Customization." *Harvard Business Review* 75, no. 1 (January–February 1997): 91–101.

Zipkin, P. "The Limits of Mass Customization," *MIT Sloan Management Review* (Spring 2001).

RETAILING IN ELECTRONIC COMMERCE: PRODUCTS AND SERVICES

Content

Learning Objectives

Upon completion of this chapter, you will be able to:

1. Describe electronic retailing (e-tailing) and its characteristics.
2. Define and describe the primary e-tailing business models.
3. Describe how online travel and tourism services operate and their impact on the industry.
4. Discuss the online employment market, including its participants, benefits, and limitations.
5. Describe online real estate services.
6. Discuss online stock-trading services.
7. Discuss cyberbanking and online personal finance.
8. Describe on-demand delivery by e-grocers.
9. Describe the delivery of digital products and online entertainment.
10. Discuss various e-tail consumer aids, including comparison-shopping aids.
11. Identify the critical success factors and failure avoidance tactics for direct online marketing and e-tailing.
12. Describe reintermediation, channel conflict, and personalization in e-tailing.

AMAZON.COM: THE KING OF E-TAILING

The Opportunity

It was not a business problem but an opportunity that faced entrepreneur Jeff Bezos: He saw the huge potential for retail sales over the Internet and selected books as the most logical product for e-tailing. In July 1995, Bezos started Amazon.com, an e-tailing pioneer, offering books via an electronic catalog from its Web site (*amazon.com*).

Over the years, the company has recognized that it must continually enhance its business models and electronic store by expanding product selection, improving the customer's experience, and adding services and alliances. Also, the company recognized the importance of order fulfillment and warehousing. It invested hundreds of millions of dollars in building physical warehouses designed for shipping small packages to hundreds of thousands of customers. Amazon.com's challenge was, and remains, how to succeed where many have failed—namely, how to compete in selling consumer products online, showing profit and a reasonable rate of return on the huge investment it has made.

The Technology Used

In addition to its initial electronic bookstore, Amazon.com has expanded in a variety of directions: It now offers specialty stores, such as its professional and technical store. It has expanded its editorial content through partnerships with experts in certain fields. It has increased product selection by adding millions of used and out-of-print titles. It also is expanding its offerings beyond books. For example, in June 2002 it became an authorized dealer of Sony Corp., selling Sony products online. Key features of the Amazon.com superstore are easy browsing, searching, and ordering; useful product information, reviews, recommendations, and personalization; broad selection; low prices; secure payment systems; and efficient order fulfillment.

The Amazon.com Web site has a number of features that make the online shopping experience more enjoyable. Its "Gift Ideas" section features seasonally appropriate gift ideas and services. Its "Community" section provides product information and recommendations shared by customers. Through its "E-Cards" section, customers can send free animated electronic greeting cards to friends and family. And the site offers consumers much, much more.

Amazon.com also offers various marketplace services. Amazon Auctions hosts and operates auctions on behalf of individuals and small businesses throughout the world. The zShops service hosts electronic storefronts for a monthly fee, offering small businesses the opportunity to have customized storefronts supported by the richness of Amazon.com's order-fulfillment processing. People can access Amazon.com and shop anywhere, anytime, by using Web-enabled cell phones, PDAs, or Pocket PCs. Amazon.com also can be accessed via AT&T's #121 voice service.

Amazon.com is recognized as an online leader in creating sales through customer intimacy and CRM, which are cultivated by informative marketing front ends and one-to-one advertisements. For example, to support CRM, in May 2002 Amazon started posting—at no cost—restaurant menus from thousands of restaurants. In addition, sales are supported by highly automated, efficient back-end systems. When a customer makes a return visit to Amazon.com, a cookie file (see Chapter 4) identifies the user and says, for example, "Welcome back, Sarah Shopper," and then proceeds to recommend new books from the same genre of previous customer purchases. The company tracks customer purchase histories and sends purchase recommendations via e-mail to cultivate repeat buyers. It also provides detailed product descriptions and ratings to help consumers make informed purchase decisions. These efforts usually result in satisfactory shopping experiences and encourage customers to return. The site has an efficient search engine and other shopping aids. Amazon.com has a superb warehousing system. This system, which is described in Chapter 13, gives the company an advantage over the competition.

Customers can personalize their accounts and manage orders online with the patented "1-Click" order feature. This personalized service includes an *electronic wallet* (see Chapter 12), which enables shoppers to place an order in a secure manner without the need to enter their address, credit card number, and other information each time they shop. 1-Click also allows customers to view their order status, cancel or combine orders that have not yet entered the shipping process, edit the shipping options and addresses on unshipped orders, modify the payment method for unshipped orders, and more.

In 1997, Amazon.com started an extensive affiliates program. By 2002, the company had more than 500,000 partners that refer customers to Amazon.com. Amazon.com pays a 3 to 5 percent commission on any resulting sale. Starting in 2000, Amazon.com has undertaken alliances with major "trusted partners" that provide knowledgeable entry into new markets. For example, Amazon.com's alliance with Carsdirect.com allows it to sell cars online. Clicking "Health and Beauty" on the Amazon.com Web site takes the visitor to a site Amazon.com operates jointly with Drugstore.com; clicking on "Wireless Phones" will suggest a service plan from an Amazon.com partner in that market. (Later in this chapter, we discuss the rocky alliance between Amazon.com and Toys"R"Us.) In yet another extension of its services, in September 2001 Amazon signed an agreement with Borders Group Inc., providing Amazon.com's users with the option of picking up books, CDs, and other merchandise at Borders' physical bookstores. Amazon.com also is becoming a Web fulfillment contractor for national chains such as Target and Circuit City. Amazon.com also has its own search engine, called A9.com (*a9.com*).

The Results

According to a study by Retail Forward, *Top E-Retail 2003* (Retail Forward 2002), Amazon.com was the number one e-tailer in 2003, generating $5.3 billion in sales. This level of sales represented 25 percent of the total online sales for all 50 companies in the study. According to Bayers (2002), Amazon.com is becoming very successful in reducing its costs and increasing profitability.

Annual sales for Amazon.com have trended upward, from $15.7 million in 1996 to $600 million in 1998 to about $5.3 billion by 2003. This pioneer e-tailer now offers over 17 million book, music, and DVD/video titles to some 20 million customers. Amazon.com also offers several features for international customers, including over 1 million Japanese-language titles.

In January 2002, Amazon.com declared its *first* profit—for the 2001 fourth quarter. In 2003, net profit topped $35 million. However, the company's financial success is by no means assured. Like all businesses—and especially e-tailing ones—Amazon.com, the king of e-tailers, will continue to walk the fine line of profitability, at least in the short run.

Sources: Compiled from Bayers (2002), Daisey (2002), Sandoval (2002), and press releases from Amazon.com (2001–2004).

WHAT WE CAN LEARN . . .

The case of Amazon.com, the most recognized e-tailer in the world, demonstrates some of the features and managerial issues related to e-tailing. It demonstrates the evolution of e-tailing, some of the problems encountered by e-tailers, and the solutions employed by Amazon.com to expand its business. In this chapter, we will look at the delivery of both products and services online to individual customers. We also will discuss e-tailing successes and failures.

3.1 INTERNET MARKETING AND ELECTRONIC RETAILING

The Amazon.com case illustrates how marketing can be done on the Internet. Indeed, the amount and percentage of goods and services sold on the Internet is increasing rapidly, despite the failure of many dot-com companies. According to marketwatch.com (reported by Cox and Koelzer 2004), the number of online shoppers in 2003 in the United States was 101 million, and the number is predicted to reach 121 million in 2005. As discussed in Chapters 1 and 2, companies have many reasons to market online. Although initially companies used the Internet to post cyberbrochures, there is evidence of the increasing use of innovative marketing strategies online.

This chapter presents an overview of Internet retailing, its diversity, prospects, and limitations. (For more detailed analysis, see Wang et al. 2002 and Cox and Koelzer 2004.) Retailing, especially when done in a new frontier, must be supported by an understanding of consumer buying behavior, market research, and advertising, topics that will be presented in Chapter 4. Let's begin our discussion of EC products and services with an overview of electronic retailing.

OVERVIEW OF ELECTRONIC RETAILING

A retailer is a sales *intermediary*, a seller that operates between manufacturers and customers. Even though many manufacturers sell directly to consumers, they supplement their sales through wholesalers and retailers (a *multichannel approach*). In the physical world, retailing is done in stores (or factory outlets) that customers must visit in order to make a purchase. Companies that produce a large number of products, such as Procter & Gamble, must use retailers for efficient distribution. However, even if a company sells only a relatively few products (e.g., Kodak), it still may need retailers to reach a large number of customers.

Catalog sales offer companies and customers a relief from the constraints of space and time: Catalogs free a retailer from the need for a physical store from which to distribute products, and customers can browse catalogs on their own time. With the ubiquity of the Internet, the next logical step was for retailing to move online. Retailing conducted over the Internet is called **electronic retailing**, or **e-tailing**, and those who conduct retail business online are called **e-tailers**. E-tailing also can be conducted through auctions. E-tailing makes

electronic retailing (e-tailing)
Retailing conducted online, over the Internet.

e-tailers
Retailers who sell over the Internet.

it easier for a manufacturer to sell directly to the customer, cutting out the intermediary (e.g., Dell and Godiva in Chapter 1). This chapter examines the various types of e-tailing and related issues.

The concept of retailing and e-tailing implies sales of goods and/or services to *individual customers*—that is, B2C EC. However, the distinction between B2C and B2B EC is not always clear. For example, Amazon.com sells books mostly to individuals (B2C), but it also sells to corporations (B2B). Amazon.com's chief rival in selling books online, Barnes & Noble (barnesandnoble.com), has a special division that caters only to business customers. Wal-Mart (walmart.com) sells to both individuals and businesses (via Sam's Club). Dell sells its computers to both consumers and businesses from dell.com, Staples sells to both markets at staples.com, and insurance sites sell to both individuals and corporations.

SIZE AND GROWTH OF THE B2C MARKET

The statistics for the volume of B2C EC sales, including forecasts for future sales, come from many sources. The sites listed in Exhibit 3.1 provide statistics on e-tailing as well as on other Internet and EC activities. Typical statistics used in describing e-tailing and consumer behavior include Internet usage by demographics (online sales by age, gender, country, etc.); online sales by item; online sales by vendor; and buying patterns online.

The following are some general statistics about online sales. According to Shop.org (shop.org), a May 2004 survey by Forrester Research showed that online sales in 2003 were $73 billion (excluding travel and other services), which is 5.4 percent of total retail sales (versus 3.6 percent in 2002, and a projected 6.6 percent in 2004). In January 2004, Jupiter Research predicted that annual growth in online sales will be at least 17 percent (reported by ePaynews.com 2004). Reda (2004) reports that Forrester Research indicates that B2C sales are growing 30 to 50 percent each year, reaching $145 billion in 2004 (including services), with a projection to top $200 billion in 2005. Also, profitability is up, and marketing costs per order are declining.

The Economics and Statistics Administration, a division of the U.S. Census Bureau, publishes periodic reports on retail e-commerce sales at census.gov/mrts/www/mrtshist.html. For example, in May 2004 the Census Bureau reported sales of $15.5 billion in the first quarter of 2004 (up 28 percent from the first quarter of 2003). The Census Bureau also estimates

EXHIBIT 3.1 Representative Sources of EC Statistics

AM Research (*amresearch.com*)
BizRate (*bizrate.com*)
Business 2.0 (*business2.com*)
ClickZ Network (*clickz.com*)
ClickZ Nua Archives (*nua.ie/surveys*)
Fulcrum Analytics (*cyberdialogue.com*)
DoubleClick (*doubleclick.com*)
Ecommerce Info Center (*ecominfocenter.com*)
Forrester Research (*forrester.com*)
Gartner (*gartner.com*)
Gomez (*gomez.com*)
IDe (*ide.com*)
JupiterResearch (*jup.com*)
Lionbridge (*lionbridge.com*)
Nielsen//Netratings (*nielsen-netratings.com*)
Shop.org (*shop.org*)
StatMarket (*statmarket.com*)
Yankee Group (*yankeegroup.com*)
U.S. Department of Commerce (*commerce.gov*)

e-commerce sales each quarter. The annual 2004 sales were estimated to be over $70 billion (census.gov/mrts/www/current.html), and the average online shopper spent over $350 per quarter. Finally, Forrester Research (see Johnson et al. 2004) estimates that e-tailing will reach $316 billion by 2010.

Reported amounts of online sales *deviate substantially* based on how the numbers are derived. Some of the variation stems from the use of different definitions and classifications of EC. For example, when tallying financial data, some analysts include the investment costs in Internet infrastructure, whereas others include only the value of the actual transactions conducted via the Internet. Another issue is how the items for sale are categorized. Some sources combine certain products and services, others do not.

WHAT SELLS WELL ON THE INTERNET

Hundreds of thousands of items are available on the Web from numerous vendors. The most recognizable categories are the following.

Computer Hardware and Software. Dell and Gateway are the major online vendors of computer hardware and software, with more than $20 billion in sales in 2004. People buy lots of hardware and software online—it is the largest category of products sold online. For example, the computer used in preparing this book, together with Microsoft Office and other software, was purchased at Dell.

Consumer Electronics. According to the Consumer Electronics Association 10 to 15 percent of consumer electronics are sold online (Lacy 2004). Digital cameras, printers, scanners, and wireless devices (including PDAs and cell phones) are just some of the consumer electronics bought online.

Office Supplies. Sales of office supplies at OfficeDepot.com, up 10 percent in 2004, grew to $13.6 billion compared to 2003 (Internetretailer.com 2005). Both B2C and B2B sales of office supplies are increasing rapidly, all over the world.

Sporting Goods. Sporting goods sell very well on the Internet. However, it is difficult to measure the exact amount of sales, because only a few e-tailers sell sporting goods exclusively online (e.g., fogdog.com).

Books and Music. Amazon.com and Barnesandnoble.com are the major sellers of books (around $6.4 billion in 2003). However, hundreds of other e-tailers sell books on the Internet, especially specialized books (e.g., technical books, children's books).

Toys. After two rocky Christmas seasons in which toy e-tailers had problems delivering ordered toys, toy sales are now moving successfully to the click-and-mortar mode. Toys"R"Us and Amazon.com lead the pack, followed by Kbtoys.com. Consumers also can buy their favorite toys online at discount stores (e.g., Target and Wal-Mart), department stores, or direct from some manufacturers (e.g., mattel.com, lego.com).

Health and Beauty. A large variety of health and beauty products, from vitamins to cosmetics to jewelry, are sold online by most large retailers and by specialty stores.

Entertainment. This is another area where dozens of products, ranging from tickets to events (e.g., ticketmaster.com) to paid fantasy games (see Section 3.8), are embraced by millions of shoppers worldwide.

Apparel and Clothing. With the possibility of buying customized shirts, pants, and even shoes, the online sale of apparel also is growing.

Jewelry. Following the success of selling on TV channels, several companies now sell jewelry online. Of the industry's $45 billion annual sales, over $2 billion were sold online in 2004 (Mullaney 2004), with online jewelers Blue Nile Inc. (Chapter 2), Diamond.com, and Ice.com being in the lead, followed by Amazon and eBay. Mullaney (2004) predicts that jewelry sales will be one of the next six future successful e-tailers, as evidenced from the success of Blue Nile (see Chapter 2).

Cars. The sale of cars over the Internet is just beginning (people still like to "kick the tires"), but cars could be one of the top sellers on the Internet by 2007. Already, car manufacturers, retailers, and intermediaries that provide related services, both click-and-mortar and pure-play companies, are participating. The business is a multibillion dollar one, involving new and used cars, fleets or rental car companies, and auto parts; the market includes B2B, B2C, C2C, and G2B. Customers like the build-to-order capabilities, but even selling used cars online has advantages and is increasing rapidly. Auctions of antique, used, or new cars are very popular, too. Support services such as financing, warranties, and insurance also are selling well online. Yamada (2004) studies how automobile dealer portals help vehicle makers cut costs and boost profits.

Services. Sales in service industries, especially travel, stock trading, electronic banking, real estate, and insurance, are increasing—more than doubling every year in some cases. According to Bonne (2004), one popular EC activity is online banking and bill paying, which is used by 44 percent of all U.S. Internet users. Eighty-seven percent buy tickets online. Services online are covered in Sections 3.3 through 3.6.

Others. Many other products, ranging from prescription drugs to custom shoes (see Insights and Additions 3.1), are offered on the Internet. As more and more retailers sell online, virtually every item that is available in a physical store may be sold online as well. Many of these items are specialized or niche products. The Internet offers an open and global market to shops that are trying to sell specialized products they would not be able to market in any other way (e.g., antique Coca-Cola bottles at antiquebottles.com and tea tree oil at teatree.co.uk).

CHARACTERISTICS OF SUCCESSFUL E-TAILING

Retail and e-tail success comes from offering quality merchandise at good prices, coupled with excellent service. In that sense, the online and traditional channels are not very different. However, e-tailers can offer expanded consumer services not offered by traditional retailers. For a comparison of e-tailing and retailing, see Exhibit 3.2.

With all else being equal in the online environment, goods with the following characteristics are expected to facilitate higher sales volumes:

- High brand recognition (e.g., Lands' End, Dell, Sony)
- A guarantee provided by highly reliable or well-known vendors (e.g., Dell, L.L. Bean)

Insights and Additions 3.1 Selling Prescription Drugs Online

The price consumers are asked to pay for prescription drugs in the United States is very high. In an effort to reduce costs, e-pharmacies are trying to sell prescription drugs online. Only four percent of Americans have purchased prescription drugs online, because most Americans do not fully trust the online prescription drug marketplace (Pew Internet reported by Shop.org 2004).

Those buying online tend to come from higher income households and have at least six years' of online experience. Drugs purchased online were mostly for chronic disorders (e.g., arthritis). Pew Research suggests that although Americans may be cautious now, they will likely grow more comfortable as friends and neighbors order without trouble (CNN.com 2004), despite incentives offered by HMOs. Some of the more established sites offering this service are *drugstore.com* (partner of Rite Aid), *cvs.com*, *more.com*, *cranespharmacy.com*, and *longs.com*. These and other companies are experimenting with different strategies to capture a share in a market of over $140 billion (in 2004).

The importance of online pharmacies is growing rapidly with the trend to buy prescription drugs from Canada. Legislation (Safe Importing of Medical Products and Rx Therapies Act) may be signed into law soon. The Act will allow drug importation, and it would require the federal government to set up a Web site to help consumers purchase drugs in approved overseas places, where they are 30 to 70 percent cheaper.

Many U.S. states (e.g., Minnesota, Florida) help people buy online drugs safely in Canada. Florida requires sellers to apply for an Internet pharmacy permit from the state's health department.

E-prescriptions include not only the distribution of drugs, but also the entering of prescriptions by physicians by voice, handwriting, or typing directly into a special wireless PDAs that can recognize any entry and have it confirmed by the prescriber (e.g., PocketScript from Zix Corp.). Approximately 7,000 people die per year due to unforeseen drug interactions. According to Callaghan (2004), more than 150 million calls are made from pharmacies to prescribers in order to verify handwritten prescriptions. It is easy to see the advantage of e-prescriptions that usually perform drug interaction searches as well. According to AIS Health Care (2004), one of the largest HMOs in the United States, WellPoint Health Networks, invested $40 million in electronic prescriptions. The system is managed by Microsoft's health-care group.

Café Rx is an alliance of organizations (including Microsoft, Cisco, and HP) whose objective is to accelerate the adoption of e-prescription. Also, several national prescribing communication networks have been created (e.g., RxHub and SureScripts Messenger Services).

EXHIBIT 3.2 Retailing Versus E-Tailing

	Retailers	E-Tailers
Physical expansion (when revenue increases as the number of visitors grows)	• Expansion of retailing platform to include more locations and space	• Expansion of e-commerce platform to include increased server capacity and distribution facilities
Physical expansion (when revenue does not increase as the number of visitors grows)	• May not need physical expansion • Expand marketing effort to turn "window shoppers" into effective shoppers	• May still need physical expansion to provide sustainable services • Expand marketing to turn "pane shoppers" into effective shoppers
Technology	• Sales automation technologies such as POS systems	• Front-end technologies • Back-end technologies • "Information" technologies
Customer relations	• More stable due to nonanonymous contacts • More tolerable of disputes due to visibility • "Physical" relationships	• Less stable due to anonymous contacts • More intolerant of disputes due to invisibility • "Logical" relationships
Cognitive shopping overhead	• Lower cognitive shopping overhead due to easy-to-establish mutual trust	• Higher cognitive shopping overhead due to hard-to-establish mutual trust
Competition	• Local competition • Fewer competitors	• Global competition • More competitors
Customer base	• Local area customers • No anonymity • Fewer resources needed to increase customer loyalty	• Wide area customers • Anonymity • More resources needed to increase customer loyalty

Source: Lee, S. C., and Brandyberry, A. A., "The E-tailer's Dilemma." ACM SIGMIS Database, June 2003. © 2003 by ACM Inc. Used with permission.

- Digitized format (e.g., software, music, or videos)
- Relatively inexpensive items (e.g., office supplies, vitamins)
- Frequently purchased items (e.g., groceries, prescription drugs)
- Commodities with standard specifications (e.g., books, CDs, airline tickets), making physical inspection unimportant
- Well-known packaged items that cannot be opened even in a traditional store (e.g., foods, chocolates, vitamins)

The next section examines business models that have proved successful in e-tailing.

Section 3.1 ▶ REVIEW QUESTIONS

1. Describe the nature of B2C EC.
2. What sells well in B2C?
3. What are the characteristics of high-volume products and services?

3.2 E-TAILING BUSINESS MODELS

In order to better understand e-tailing, let's look at it from the point of view of a retailer or a manufacturer that sells to individual consumers. The seller has its own organization and must also buy goods and services from others, usually businesses (B2B in Exhibit 3.3). As also shown in Exhibit 3.3, e-tailing, which is basically B2C (right side of the exhibit), is done between the seller (a retailer or a manufacturer) and the buyer. The exhibit shows other EC transactions and related activities, because they may impact e-tailing. In this section, we will look at the various B2C models and their classifications.

EXHIBIT 3.3 **E-Tailing as an Enterprise EC System**

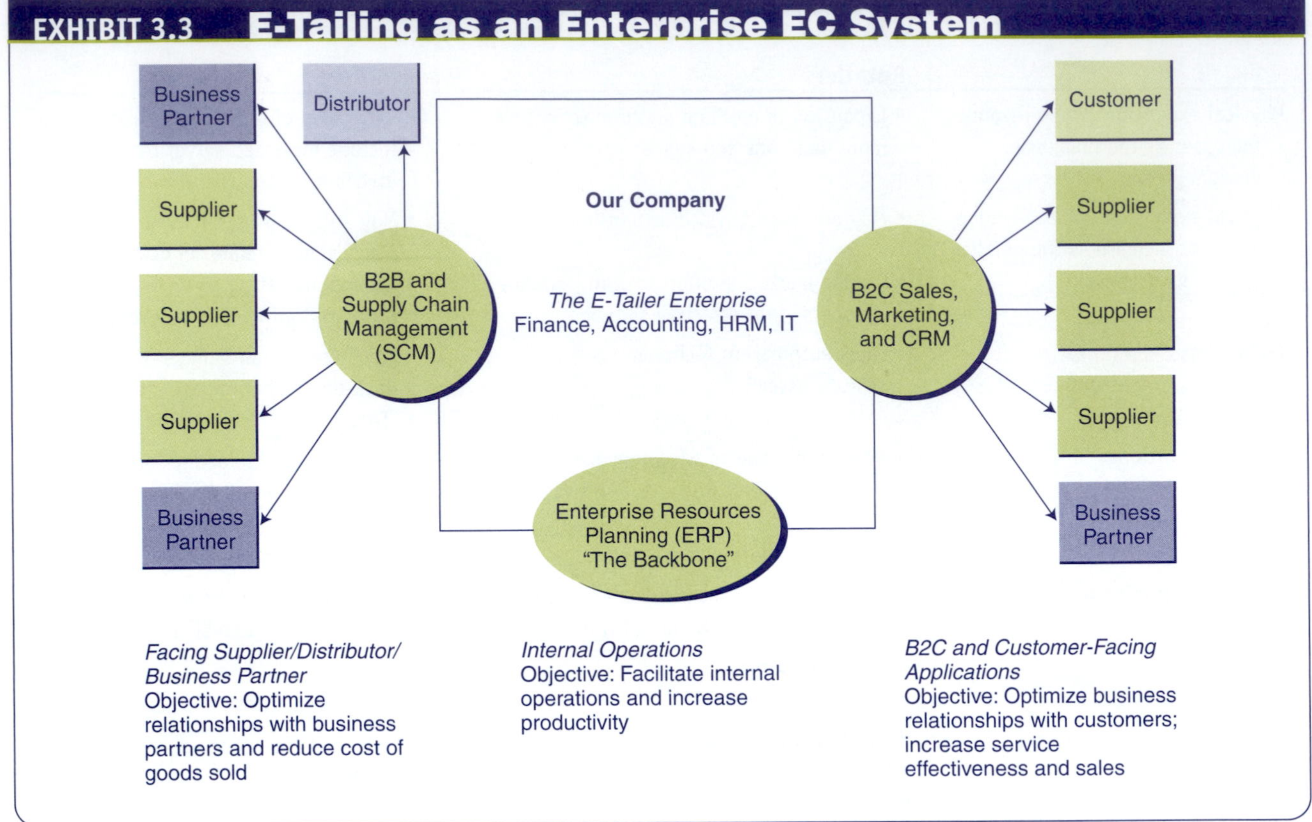

CLASSIFICATION BY DISTRIBUTION CHANNEL

E-tailing business models can be classified in several ways. For example, some classify e-tailers by the scope of items handled (general purpose versus specialty e-tailing) or by the scope of the sales region covered (global versus regional), whereas others use classification by revenue models (see Chapter 1). Here we will classify the models by the distribution channel used, distinguishing five categories.

1. **Mail-order retailers that go online.** Most traditional mail-order retailers, such as QVC, Sharper Image, and Lands' End, simply added another distribution channel—the Internet. Several of these retailers also operate physical stores, but their main distribution channel is direct marketing.
2. **Direct marketing from manufacturers**. Manufacturers, such as Dell, Nike, Lego, Godiva (Chapter 1), and Sony, market directly online from company sites to individual customers. Most of these manufacturers are click-and-mortar, also selling in their own physical stores or via retailers. However, the manufacturer may be a pure-play company (e.g., Dell).
3. **Pure-play e-tailers.** These e-tailers do not have physical stores, only an online sales presence. Amazon.com is an example of a pure-play e-tailer.
4. **Click-and-mortar retailers.** These are traditional retailers with a supplementary Web site (e.g., walmart.com, homedepot.com, and sharperimage.com).
5. **Internet (online) malls.** As described in Chapter 2, these malls include large numbers of independent storefronts.

We'll look at each of these categories of distribution channels in the pages that follow.

direct marketing
Broadly, marketing that takes place without intermediaries between manufacturers and buyers; in the context of this book, marketing done online between any seller and buyer.

Direct Marketing by Mail-Order Companies

In a broad sense, **direct marketing** describes marketing that takes place without intermediaries. Direct marketers take orders directly from consumers, bypassing traditional wholesale or retail distribution.

An Example of a Successful Mail-Order Company. Firms with established, mature mail-order businesses have a distinct advantage in online sales, given their existing payment processing, inventory management, and order-fulfillment operations, as shown in EC Application Case 3.1.

Direct Sales by Manufacturers

The parties in direct marketing have a great opportunity to influence each other. Sellers can understand their markets better because of the direct connection to consumers, and consumers gain greater information about the products through their direct connection to the manufacturers. Dell is primarily using direct marketing combined with a build-to-order approach (see Appendix 2A for more on build-to-order), customizing its products. Insights and Additions 3.2 describes the process by which customers can configure and order cars online.

CASE 3.1

EC Application

LANDS' END: HOW A MAIL-ORDER COMPANY MOVED ONLINE

Some of the most successful B2C e-tailers are mail-order companies that were once based solely on paper catalogs. One reason for their success is the logistics system such companies already had in place. Here we look at Lands' End, now a subsidiary of Sears, Roebuck and Company.

Lands' End is a successful direct-marketing company. The company is well-known for its quality products, casual-styled clothing, and customer service. Internet sales in 2000 (before it became a subsidiary of Sears) were 10 percent of the company's $1.3 billion total, doubling the 5 percent in Internet sales of 1999. Projected Internet sales are over 20 percent in 2004. Lands' End's Web site (*landsend.com*) offers all of the company's catalog products. (To show how far the company has come with e-tailing, in 1995 it offered only 100 products online; as of 2002, all of its products are online.)

Besides the product offerings, the Web site allows women customers to build and store a three-dimensional model of their body (called the Personal Model; see Internet Exercise number 7). The Web site then recommends outfits that flatter certain body profiles and suggests sizes based upon the customer's measurements. Male customers can use a feature called "Oxford Express" to sort through hundreds of fabrics, styles, collar and cuff options, and sizes within seconds. Personal shopping accounts also are available on the Web site. It is very easy to order and customize clothes. Reda (2002c) reports that 40 percent of all chinos and jeans sales on the Web-site are custom ordered.

In addition, customers can use the Web site to track their order status and request catalogs. The company has an affiliate's program that pays a 5 percent commission for every sale that comes from a referral. It also maintains a B2B "store" at *landsend.com/corpsales*, where companies can customize clothing such as polo shirts with their logo for use as company uniforms, incentives, or gifts. Lands' End Live allows online customers to shop with the assistance of a "real" personal shopper. Lands' End extends its presence globally by having localized sites for Japan, Germany, and the United Kingdom.

Lands' End operates 16 physical distribution outlets in the United States and 3 in the United Kingdom. Orders made online are shipped from these distribution outlets. Because of their order-fulfillment capabilities, U.S. customers usually receive their orders two days after they are placed.

Lands' End became a subsidiary of Sears in 2002, and it continues to offer its products through its catalogs and on its Web site. Beginning in fall 2002, an assortment of Lands' End clothing for men, women, and children, as well as products for the home, became available at a select group of Sears stores around the country; in 2003 Lands' End products became featured items in all Sears stores.

Because 88 percent of the company's customers are college graduates, most having computers, the company expects its online business to continue to grow rapidly during the next few years.

Sources: Compiled from *landsend.com* (accessed October 2002 and October 2004) and Reda (2002c).

Questions

1. Discuss the advantages of Lands' End over other online stores such as the Gap (*gap.com*).
2. Identify the factors that are critical to the company's success. (In business jargon, these are called critical success factors [CSFs].)
3. Enter *landsend.com* and configure your ideal outfit. Report on your experience.

Insights and Additions 3.2 Buying Cars Online: Build to Order

The world's automobile manufacturers are complex enterprises with thousands of suppliers and millions of customers. Their traditional channel for distributing cars has been the automobile dealer, who orders cars and then sells them from the lot. When a customer wants a particular feature or color ("options"), the customer may have to wait weeks or months until the "pipeline" of vehicles has that particular car on the production line.

In the traditional system, the manufacturers conduct market research in order to estimate which features and options will sell well, and then they make the cars they wish to sell. In some cases, certain cars are ultimately sold from stock at a loss when the market exhibits insufficient demand for a particular vehicle. The carmakers have long operated under this "build-to-stock" environment, building cars that are carried as inventory during the outbound logistics process (ships, trucks, trains, and dealers' lots). General Motors (GM) estimates that it holds as much as $40-billion worth of unsold vehicles in its distribution channels. Other automakers hold large amounts as well.

Ford and GM, along with other carmakers around the world, have announced plans to implement a build-to-order program, much like the Dell approach to building computers. These auto giants intend to transform themselves from build-to-stock companies to build-to-order companies, thereby cutting inventory requirements in half (Simison 2000; Gapper 2004), while at the same time giving customers the vehicle they want, in a short period (e.g., one to two weeks).

As an example of this trend toward build-to-order mass customization in the new car market, Jaguar car buyers can build a dream car online. On Jaguar's Web site (*jaguar.com*), consumers are able to custom configure their car's features and components, see it online, price it, and have it delivered to a nearby dealer. Using a virtual car on the Web site, customers can view in real time more than 1,250 possible exterior combinations out of several million, rotate the image 360 degrees, and see the price updated automatically with each selection of trim or accessories. After storing the car in a virtual garage, the customer can decide on the purchase and select a dealer at which to pick up the completed car. (Thus conflicts with the established dealer network channel are avoided.) The Web site helps primarily with the research process—it is not a fully transactional site. The configuration, however, can be transmitted to the production floor, thereby reducing delivery time and contributing to increased customer satisfaction. Similar configuration systems are available from all the major car manufacturers. Customers can electronically track the progress of the car, including visualization of the production process in the factory.

Sources: Compiled from Simison (2000); Agrawal et al. (2001); Gapper (2004); and *jaguar.com* (accessed October 2004).

Pure-Play E-Tailers

virtual (pure-play) e-tailers
Firms that sell directly to consumers over the Internet without maintaining a physical sales channel.

Virtual (pure-play) e-tailers are firms that sell directly to consumers over the Internet without maintaining a physical sales channel. Amazon.com is a prime example of this type of e-tailer. Virtual e-tailers have the advantage of low overhead costs and streamlined processes. Virtual e-tailers may be *general purpose* or *specialized*.

General e-tailers, such as LaYoYo (layoyo.com) selling DVD, VCD, and music CD titles, capitalize on the Internet to offer a wide range of titles to a very diverse group of customers geographically without the need to maintain a large physical retail network (Lee and Cheung 2004).

Specialty e-tailers can operate in a very narrow market, as does Cattoys.com, described in Online File W3.1. Such a specialized business could not survive in the physical world because it would not have enough customers.

Click-and-Mortar Retailers

click-and-mortar retailers
Brick-and-mortar retailers that offer a transactional Web site from which to conduct business.

The fourth type of online retailer is a **click-and-mortar retailer**, a brick-and-mortar retailer with an added-on transactional Web site. **Brick-and-mortar retailers** are retailers that conduct business in the physical world, in traditional brick-and-mortar stores. Traditional retailing frequently involves a single distribution channel, the physical store. In some cases, traditional sellers also may operate a mail-order business. In today's digital economy, click-and-mortar retailers sell via stores, through voice phone calls to human operators, over the Internet through interactive Web sites, and by mobile devices. A firm that operates both physical stores and an online e-tail site is said to be a click-and-mortar business selling in a **multichannel business model** (see Reda 2002a). Examples would be department stores such as Macy's (macys.com) or Sears (sears.com), as well as discount stores such as Wal-Mart (walmart.com). It also includes supermarkets and all other types of retailing (e.g., see the Godiva case in Chapter 1).

Although there may be practical advantages to being a virtual seller, such as lower overhead costs, it has many drawbacks and barriers, which are described later. Therefore, many experts suggest that the ultimate winners in many market segments will be the companies that are able to leverage the best of both worlds using the click-and-mortar approach.

brick-and-mortar retailers
Retailers who do business in the non-Internet, physical world in traditional brick-and-mortar stores.

multichannel business model
A business model where a company sells in multiple marketing channels simultaneously (e.g., both physical and online stores).

Retailing in Online Malls

Online malls, as described in Chapter 2, are of two types: referring directories and malls with shared services (see Cox and Koelzer 2004).

Referring Directories. This type of mall is basically a directory organized by product type. Catalog listings or banner ads at the mall site advertise the products or stores. When users click on the product and/or a specific store, they are transferred to the storefront of the seller, where they then complete the transaction. An example of a directory is hawaii.com/marketplace. The stores listed in a directory either collectively own the site or they pay a subscription fee or a commission to the third party (e.g., a portal) that advertises their logos. This type of e-tailing is basically a kind of affiliate marketing. An interesting directory is available at delamez.com.

Malls with Shared Services. In online malls with shared services, a consumer can find a product, order and pay for it, and arrange for shipment. The hosting mall provides these services, but they usually are executed by each store independently. (To see the variety of services provided, consult smallbusiness.yahoo.com.) The buyer must repeat the process in each store visited in the mall, but it is basically the same process. The storefront owners pay rent and/or transaction fees to the owner. ChoiceMall (choicemall.com) is an example of such a mall. Both manufacturers and retailers sell in such malls. As described in the online Cattoys.com case, Yahoo! hosts cattoys.com. When a user goes to Yahoo! and clicks "toys" and then "cattoys," the user will be directed to the Cattoys.com store. Alternatively, a user can go directly to cattoys.com; in this case, the user will not know that he or she is in the Yahoo! environment until the check-out process. Other malls with shared services are firststopshops.com and shopping.msn.com.

Ideally, the customer would like to go to different stores in the same mall, use one shopping cart, and pay only once. This arrangement is possible in Yahoo! store, (smallbusiness.yahoo.com/merchant) for example.

OTHER B2C MODELS AND SPECIAL RETAILING

Several other business models are used in B2C. They are discussed in various places throughout the book. Some of these models also are used in B2B, B2B2C, G2B, and other types of EC. A summary of these other models is provided in Exhibit 3.4.

Representative Special B2C Services

Of the many other B2C services, four of interest are those that deliver physical products, digital products, and services.

Postal Services. One of the early applications of EC was online postal services with pioneering sites such as estamp.com (now stamps.com). Today, Internet postage services are available in dozens of countries and on a variety of sites. For example, in China, customers can go to the post office and use computers that offer online services to make remittances to sellers. (In China, the use of credit cards is very limited.) Another example of postal services is Postage by Phone (pb.com), offered by Pitney Bowes. It offers highly secure and reliable functions such as printing postage, as well as flexibility and convenience. The entire mailing process is done online or via a telephone.

The U.S. Postal Service offers an integrated online postage meter, scale, and printer. The service allows (1) the downloading of postage via the Internet; (2) the weighing of a letter or package, calculating postage instantly; and (3) the printing of postage. With PC postage software, users can purchase postage over the Internet and use standard desktop printers to print the PC postage indicia directly onto envelopes or onto labels for packages (see usps.com/postagesolutions for details).

EXHIBIT 3.4 Other B2C Business Models

Model Name	Description	Location in Book
Transaction brokers	Electronically mediate between buyers and sellers. Popular in services, the travel industry, the job market, stock trading, and insurance.	Chapters 3, 9
Information portals	Besides information, most portals provide links to merchants, for which they are paid a commission (affiliate marketing). Some provide hosting and software (e.g., *store.yahoo.com*), some also sell.	Chapters 3, 6
Community portal	Combines community services with selling or affiliate marketing (e.g., *virtualcommunities.start4all.com*).	Chapter 17
Content creators or disseminators	Provide content to the masses (news, stock data). Also participate in the syndication chain (e.g., *espn.com, reuters.com, cnn.com*).	Chapters 2, 16
Viral marketing	Use e-mail or SMS to advertise. Also can sell direct or via affiliates (e.g., *blueskyfrog.com*).	Chapters 4, 9
Market makers	Create and manage many-to-many markets (e.g., *chemconnect.com*); also auction sites (e.g., *ebay.com, dellauction.com*). Aggregate buyers and/or sellers (e.g., *ingrammicro.com*).	Chapters 6, 7
Make (build)-to-order	Manufacturers that customize their products and services via online orders (e.g., *dell.com, nike.com, jaguar.com*).	Chapters 2, 3, 4
B2B2C	Manufacturer sells to a business, but delivers to individual customers (*godiva.com*).	Chapters 2, 3
Service providers	Offer online payments, order fulfillment (delivery), and security (e.g., *paypal.com, escrow.com*).	Chapters 3, 12, 13

For $14.95 per month (in 2003), the U.S. Postal Service offers a system that enables customers to purchase and print postage around the clock, weigh packages up to 4.4 pounds, and prepare first class, priority, express, and international mail. Meters can be leased from commercial manufacturers in cooperation with the postal service that allow customers to download postage directly into their machines and then print it as they need it. Customers can store frequent mailing addresses, print exact postage, track postage use, and more. The hardware is small enough to fit in the palm of a hand.

Services and Products for Adults. Selling virtual sex on the Internet is probably the most profitable B2C model. There is nothing new about online pornography. According to a 1994 study conducted by Carnegie Mellon University (see McNeill 2002), 83.5 percent of all images posted on Usenet newsgroups were pornographic in nature. Today, over 100,000 pornographic Web sites are in operation worldwide. With little or no advertising effort to attract viewers, many of these sites are making good money. According to reports by market research firms that monitor the industry, such as Forrester, IDC, DataMonitor, Jupiter, and NetRating, viewers eagerly pay substantial subscription fees to view adult sites. One reason is that many customers may be hesitant to make a purchase at a local physical store but are comfortable making such purchases online because of the privacy afforded by such sites.

The sites also use innovative streaming video to attract customers. Adult entertainment sites also are well versed in the art of up-selling and cross-selling (e.g., adultshop.com). Many sites also collect fees from advertisers. Finally, adult entertainment sites cut costs by using banner exchanges, joint ventures, and affiliate programs.

A major problem for these sites is their ability to work within the regulatory framework of the local environment. Also, competition is strong; as with any other successful business model, newcomers are continuously trying their luck. Increased competition drives down prices, and many porn sites may go out of business.

Wedding Channels. Each year, almost 500,000 brides-to-be use The Knot to plan their weddings. A "Knot Box" with insert folders is sent to users by regular mail. Each insert is linked to a corresponding page on theknot.com. Advertisers underwrite the mail campaign. The Web site provides brides with information and help in planning the wedding and selecting vendors. Orders can be placed by phone or online (although not all products can be ordered online). WeddingChannel (weddingchannel.com) is a similar service, but it operates primarily online.

Gift Registries. The U.S. bridal industry is estimated to have annual revenues of $30 to $50 billion. The gift-registry part of the industry—where the lucky couple lists what presents they hope their guests will buy for them—is estimated to be about $17 billion (von Hoffman 2001). Gift registries also are used by people buying gifts for other occasions (anniversaries, birthdays, graduations, etc.).

From an IT point of view, a gift registry is a relatively complex set of database and supply chain interactions. Usually the gift registry is done jointly between the gift registry company and a department store (e.g., macys.com). The database has to present a secure environment to the person who is registering. That information is then displayed to those who are buying the gifts. When a specific gift is selected, it is removed from the list before anyone else orders the same thing. Meanwhile, the database has to interact with the selling company's inventory lists, showing what's in stock and, in the best of all possible worlds, alerting buyers and registrants when items are backordered.

Selling physical products online requires their physical delivery. In contrast, selling services online usually involves online delivery. Therefore, the potential savings are very large, and online services are very popular. The following sections describe the delivery of services online.

Section 3.2 ▶ REVIEW QUESTIONS

1. List the B2C distribution channel models.
2. Describe how mail-order houses are going online.
3. Describe the direct marketing model used by manufacturers.
4. Describe virtual e-tailing.
5. Describe the click-and-mortar approach.
6. Describe e-malls.

3.3 TRAVEL AND TOURISM SERVICES ONLINE

Online travel is probably the most successful e-commerce implementation. According to the *eMarketer Daily* (2004), online travel comprises about 25 percent of all travel booking, and it is growing by 30 to 40 percent a year and is projected to reach 33 percent of all travel by 2006.

Some major travel-related Web sites are expedia.com, orbitz.com, travelocity.com, travelzoo.com, asiatravel.com, hotwire.com, travelweb.com, ebookers.com, eurovacations.com, and priceline.com. Online travel services also are provided by all major airlines, vacation services, large conventional travel agencies, trains (e.g., amtrak.com), car rental agencies, hotels, commercial portals, and tour companies. Publishers of travel guides such as Fodors and Lonely Planet provide considerable amounts of travel-related information on their Web sites (fodors.com and lonelyplanet.com), as well as selling travel services there. Online ticket consolidator ebookers.com and travel information broker tiscover.com are linking up to create a comprehensive Web-travel resource.

The revenue models of online travel services include direct revenues (commissions), revenue from advertising, consultancy fees, subscription or membership fees, revenue-sharing fees, and more. Other important considerations for the growth of online travel services are the value propositions, such as increased customer trust, loyalty, and brand image (see Joo 2002).

SERVICES PROVIDED

Virtual travel agencies offer almost all of the services delivered by conventional travel agencies, from providing general information to reserving and purchasing tickets, accommodations, and entertainment. In addition, they often provide services that most conventional travel agencies do not offer, such as travel tips provided by people who have experienced certain situations (e.g., a visa problem), electronic travel magazines, fare comparisons, city guides, currency conversion calculators, fare tracking (free e-mail alerts on low fares to and from a city and favorite destinations), worldwide business and place locators, an outlet for travel accessories and books, experts' opinions, major international and travel news, detailed driving maps and directions within the United States and several other countries (see biztravel.com), chat rooms and bulletin boards, and frequent-flier deals. In addition, some offer several other innovative services, such as online travel auctions.

SPECIAL SERVICES

Many online travel services offer travel bargains. Consumers can go to special sites, such as those offering stand-by tickets, to find bargain fares. Lastminute.com offers very low airfares and discounted accommodations prices to fill otherwise-empty seats and hotel rooms. Last-minute trips also can be booked on americanexpress.com, sometimes at a steep discount. Travelzoo.com and hotwire.com offer deep travel discounts. Special vacation destinations can be found at priceline.com, tictactravel.com, stayfinder.com, and greatrentals.com. Flights.com offers cheap tickets and also Eurail passes. Travelers can access cybercaptive.com for a list of thousands of Internet cafes around the world. Similar information is available via many portals, such as Yahoo! and MSN.

Also of interest are sites that offer medical advice and services for travelers. This type of information is available from the World Health Organization (who.int), governments (e.g., cdc.gov/travel), and private organizations (e.g., tripprep.com, medicalert.org, webmd.com).

Wireless Services

Several airlines (e.g., Cathay Pacific, Delta, and Qantas) allow customers with cell phones with Internet access to check their flight status, update frequent flyer miles, and book flights. As of the summer of 2001, Singapore Airlines offers customers global flight alerts via short message service (SMS). Users register the flight for which they want to receive an alert at singaporeair.com and specify when they wish to receive the alert and provide their phone number. British Air offers a broadband Internet connection for passengers on board (initially for first and business classes). As of 2003, Lufthansa offers Wi-Fi Internet connections for laptops (for a fee).

Direct Marketing

Airlines sell electronic tickets over the Internet. When a person purchases electronic tickets online (or by phone), all the traveler has to do is print his/her boarding pass from their computer's printer or upon arrival at the airport is enter his or her credit card at an *electronic kiosk* to get a boarding pass. Alternatively, the traveler can get the boarding pass at the ticket counter.

Using direct marketing techniques, airlines are able to build customer profiles and target specific customers with tailored offers. Many airlines offer "specials" or "cyber offers" on their Web sites (e.g., cathaypacific.com). Airlines such as Scandinavian Airlines offer booking, seat selection, Web check-in, automated flight status service, frequent-flyer programs, personalized services, and more (see sas.se).

Alliances and Consortia

Airlines and other travel companies are creating alliances to increase sales or reduce purchasing costs. For example, some consortia aggregate only fares purchased over the Internet. Several alliances exist in Europe, the United States, and Asia. For example, zuji.com is a travel portal dedicated to Asia-Pacific travelers. It is a consortium of regional airlines, Travelocity, some hotel chains, and car-rental providers. It specializes in tour packages in the region. The company also has a booking engine for travel agents, enabling them to store their customers e-mail addresses (a B2B2C service).

BENEFITS AND LIMITATIONS OF ONLINE TRAVEL SERVICES

The benefits of online travel services to travelers are enormous. The amount of free information is tremendous, and it is accessible at any time from any place. Substantial discounts can be found, especially for those who have time and patience to search for them. Providers of travel services also benefit: Airlines, hotels, and cruise lines are selling otherwise-empty spaces. Also, direct selling saves the provider's commission and its processing.

Online travel services do have some limitations. First, many people do not use the Internet. Second, the amount of time and the difficulty of using virtual travel agencies may be significant, especially for complex trips and for inexperienced Internet surfers. Finally, complex trips or those that require stopovers may not be available online because they require specialized knowledge and arrangements, which may be better done by a knowledgeable, human travel agent. Therefore, the need for travel agents as intermediaries remains, at least for the immediate future. However, as will be discussed later, intelligent agents may lessen some of these limitations, further reducing the reliance on travel agents.

CORPORATE TRAVEL

The corporate travel market is huge and has been growing rapidly in recent years. Corporations can use all of the travel services mentioned earlier. However, many large corporations receive additional services from large travel agencies. To reduce corporate travel costs, companies can make arrangements that enable employees to plan and book their own trips. Using online optimization tools provided by travel companies, such as those offered by Rosenbluth International (rosenbluth.com, now an American Express company; see Online File W2.6), companies can try to reduce travel costs even further. Travel authorization software that checks availability of funds and compliance with corporate guidelines is usually provided by travel companies such as Rosenbluth International. Another vendor in the corporate travel market is Amadeus Global Travel Distribution (amadeus.com), via e-Travel (e-travel.com), which provides marketing, distribution, and IT services to automate and manage online booking. Expedia Inc. (expedia.com), Travelocity (travelocity.com), and Orbitz (orbitz.com) also offer software tools for corporate planning and booking.

An example of how a major corporation uses online corporate travel services is described in Online File W3.2.

IMPACT OF EC ON THE TRAVEL INDUSTRY

Bloch and Segev (1997) predicted that travel agencies as we know them today will disappear. Only the value-added activities of travel agencies will not be automated, and these activities will be performed by travel organizations that will serve certain targeted markets and customers (also see Van der Heijden 1996). Travel superstores, which will provide many products, services, and entertainment, may enter the industry, as will innovative individuals operating as travel agents from their homes. A more recent analysis of the impact of online travel services on the travel industry is provided by Standing and Vasudavan (2001). The *Economist* (2004) analyzed the travel industry and predicted that most travel bookings are likely to move online within a decade.

With the increased popularity of online reservations, several service providers, such as the large hotel chains, have found that an additional intermediary has appeared between them and the consumers: Consumers who used to order accommodations directly from a hotel are now using the Internet to compare prices and frequently are buying from an intermediary (such as Hotwire.com) that provides them with the lowest price. The large hotel chains now offer similar services (e.g., see hilton.com). (For a comprehensive discussion, see Rich 2002.) By late 2004, so many companies were selling travel online, including all major portals, that the accelerated rate of growth of Expedia and other pure-play vendors slowed.

INTELLIGENT AGENTS IN TRAVEL SERVICES

There is no doubt that EC will play an even greater role in the travel industry in the future. One area that is very promising is the use of software (intelligent) agents. The agents emulate the work and behavior of human agents in executing organizational processes, such as travel authorization, planning (Camacho et al. 2001), or decision making (Milidiu et al. 2003). Each agent is capable of acting autonomously, cooperatively, or collectively to achieve the stated goal (see Online Technical Appendix D). The system increases organizational productivity by carrying out several tedious watchdog activities, thereby freeing humans to work on more challenging and creative tasks.

Intelligent agents could also be involved in buyer–seller negotiations, as shown in the following scenario: You want to take a vacation in Hawaii. First you called a regular travel agent who gave you the impression he was too busy to help you. Finally, he gave you a travel plan and a price that you do not like. A friend suggested that you use a software agent instead. Here is how the process works: First you enter your desired travel destination, dates, available budget, special requirements, and desired entertainment to your online agent residing on your computer. The software agent then "shops around," entering the Internet and communicating electronically with the databases of airlines, hotels, and other vendors. The agent attempts to match your requirements against what is available, sometimes negotiating with the vendors' agents. These agents may activate other agents to make special arrangements, cooperate with each other, activate multimedia presentations, or make special inquiries. Within minutes the software agent returns to you with suitable alternatives. You have a few questions and you want modifications. No problem. Within a few minutes, the agent will provide replies. Then it is a done deal. No waiting for busy telephone operators and no human errors. Once you approve the deal, the intelligent agent will make the reservations, arrange for payments, and even report to you about any unforeseen delays in your departure. How do you communicate with your software agent? By voice, of course. This scenario is not as far off as it may seem. Such a scenario may be possible by 2008.

Section 3.3 ▶ REVIEW QUESTIONS

1. What travel services are available online that are not available off-line?
2. List the benefits of online travel services to travelers and to service providers.
3. What role do software (intelligent) agents have in online travel services? What future applications may be possible?

3.4 EMPLOYMENT PLACEMENT AND THE JOB MARKET ONLINE

The job market is very volatile, and supply and demand are frequently unbalanced. Traditionally, job matching has been done in several ways, ranging from ads in classified sections of newspapers to the use of corporate recruiters, commercial employment agencies, and headhunting companies. The job market has now also moved online. The online job market connects individuals who are looking for a job with employers who are looking for employees with specific skills. It is a very popular approach. For example, one study found that 50 million Americans have used the online job market (Pew Internet and American Life Project 2002). Advantages of the online job market over the traditional one are listed in Exhibit 3.5.

EXHIBIT 3.5 Traditional Versus Online Job Markets

Characteristic	Traditional Job Market	Online Job Market
Cost	Expensive, especially in prime space	Can be very inexpensive
Life cycle	Short	Long
Place	Usually local and limited if global	Global
Context updating	Can be complex, expensive	Fast, simple, inexpensive
Space for details	Limited	Large
Ease of search by applicant	Difficult, especially for out-of-town applicants	Quick and easy
Ability of employers to find applicants	May be very difficult, especially for out-of-town applicants	Easy
Matching of supply and demand	Difficult	Easy
Reliability	Material can be lost in mail	High
Communication speed between employees and employers	Can be slow	Fast
Ability of employees to compare jobs	Limited	Easy, fast

THE INTERNET JOB MARKET

The Internet offers a rich environment for job seekers and for companies searching for hard-to-find employees. According to *eMarketer* (2003), 74 percent of U.S. job seekers rely on the Internet, and 57 percent have had success. The job market is especially effective for technology-oriented companies and jobs because these companies and workers use the Internet regularly. However, thousands of other types of companies advertise available positions, accept resumes, and take applications over the Internet (e.g., see Brice and Waung 2002). The following parties use the Internet job market:

- **Job seekers.** Job seekers can reply to employment ads. Or, they can take the initiative and place their resumes on their own homepages or on others' Web sites, send messages to members of newsgroups asking for referrals, and use the sites of recruiting firms, such as careerbuilder.com, hotjobs.com, and monster.com (see Harrington 2002). For entry-level jobs and internships for newly minted graduates, job seekers can go to company.monster.com/jobd. Job seekers can also assess their market value at different U.S. cities at wageweb.com.
- **Employers seeking employees.** Many organizations, including public institutions, advertise openings on their Web sites. Others advertise job openings on popular public portals, online newspapers, bulletin boards, and with recruiting firms. Employers can conduct interviews and administer tests on the Web. Some employers, such as Home Depot, have kiosks in some of their stores on which they post job openings and allow applicants to complete an application electronically.
- **Job agencies.** Hundreds of job agencies are active on the Web. They use their own Web pages to post available job descriptions and advertise their services in e-mails and at other Web sites. Job agencies and/or employers use newsgroups, online forums, bulletin boards, Internet commercial resume services, and portals such as Yahoo! and AOL. Most portals are free; others, such as mktgladder.com, charge membership fees but offer many services.

  An unsuccessful dot-com employment agency was Refer.com. The company listed vacancies for hard-to-fill positions. People and agencies were asked to find candidates. The finders received $1,000 or more for a successful match. The company folded in 2001, because employers were flooded with hundreds of unqualified candidates. Employers preferred to continue to work with their regular off-line agencies, who did better screening of potential employees (see Dixon 2001).
- **Government agencies and institutions.** Many government agencies advertise openings for government positions on their Web sites and on other sites; some are required by law to do so. In addition, some government agencies use the Internet to help job seekers find jobs elsewhere, as is done in Hong Kong and the Philippines (see Online File W3.3).

A Consortium of Large Employers

Large employers such as GE, IBM, and Xerox spend hundreds of thousands of dollars annually on commissions to online job companies. To save money, those companies and others have joined a nonprofit consortium that created a career portal called directemployers.com. The site is used primarily to catalog job postings from the sites of the member employers. Having the job postings of a number of large employers in one place makes it easy for job searchers to explore available openings.

Global Online Portals

The Internet is very helpful for anyone looking for a job in another country. An interesting global portal for Europe is described in Online File W3.4.

BENEFITS AND LIMITATIONS OF THE ELECTRONIC JOB MARKET

As indicated earlier, the electronic job market offers a variety of benefits for both job seekers and employers. These major advantages are shown in Exhibit 3.6.

Probably the biggest limitation of the online job market is the fact that many people do not use the Internet. This limitation is even more serious with non-technology-oriented jobs.

EXHIBIT 3.6 Advantages of the Electronic Job Market for Job Seekers and Employers

Advantages for Job Seekers	Advantages for Employers
• Can find information on a large number of jobs worldwide • Can communicate quickly with potential employers • Can market themselves directly to potential employers (e.g., *quintcareers.com*) • Can write and post resumes for large-volume distribution (e.g., Personal Search Agent at *careerbuilder.com, brassring.com*) • Can search for jobs quickly from any location • Can obtain several support services at no cost (e.g., *hotjobs.com* and *monster.com* provide free career-planning services) • Can assess their market value (e.g., *wageweb.com* and *rileyguide.org*; look for salary surveys) • Can learn how to use their voice effectively in an interview (*greatvoice.com*) • Can access newsgroups that are dedicated to finding jobs (and keeping them)	• Can advertise to a large numbers of job seekers • Can save on advertisement costs • Can reduce application-processing costs by using electronic application forms • Can provide greater equal opportunity for job seekers • Increased chance of finding highly skilled employees • Can describe positions in great detail • Can conduct interviews online (using video teleconferencing) • Can arrange for testing online • Can view salary surveys for recruiting strategies

To overcome this problem, companies may use both traditional advertising approaches and the Internet. However, the trend is clear: Over time, more and more of the job market will be on the Internet. One solution to the problem of limited access is the use of Internet kiosks, as described in Online File W3.3 and as used by companies such as Home Depot.

Security and privacy may be another limitation (see Bergstein 2003). For one thing, resumes and other online communications are usually not encrypted, so one's job-seeking activities may not be secure. For another, it is possible that someone at a job seeker's current place of employment (possibly even his or her boss) may find out that that person is job hunting. The electronic job market may also create high turnover costs for employers by accelerating employees' movement to better jobs. Finally, finding candidates online is more complicated than most people think, mostly due to the large number of resumes available online. Some sites offer prescreening of candidates (e.g., monstertrack.monster.com), which may alleviate this problem.

INTELLIGENT AGENTS IN THE ELECTRONIC JOB MARKET

The large number of available jobs and resumes online makes it difficult both for employers and employees to search the Internet for useful information. Intelligent agents can solve this problem by matching resumes with open positions. Exhibit 3.7 shows how three intelligent agents in the online job market work for both job seekers and recruiters.

Intelligent Agents for Job Seekers

A free service that uses intelligent agents to search the Internet's top job sites and databases for job postings based on users' profiles is offered at careershop.com. Users can create as many as five different profiles based on more than 100 different job categories, geographic regions, and keywords. Users receive a daily e-mail containing job opportunities from over a dozen top job sites around the Internet (e.g., Personal Search Agentt at careerbuilder.com), that match their career interests. This saves the users a tremendous amount of time. For technology jobs, try dice.com.

Intelligent Agents for Employers

Employers may be flooded by hundreds of thousands of applications. To find which ones are worthless, one can use software tools, as Southern Co. is doing (see EC Application Case 3.2).

EXHIBIT 3.7 **Intelligent Agents Match Resumes with Available Jobs**

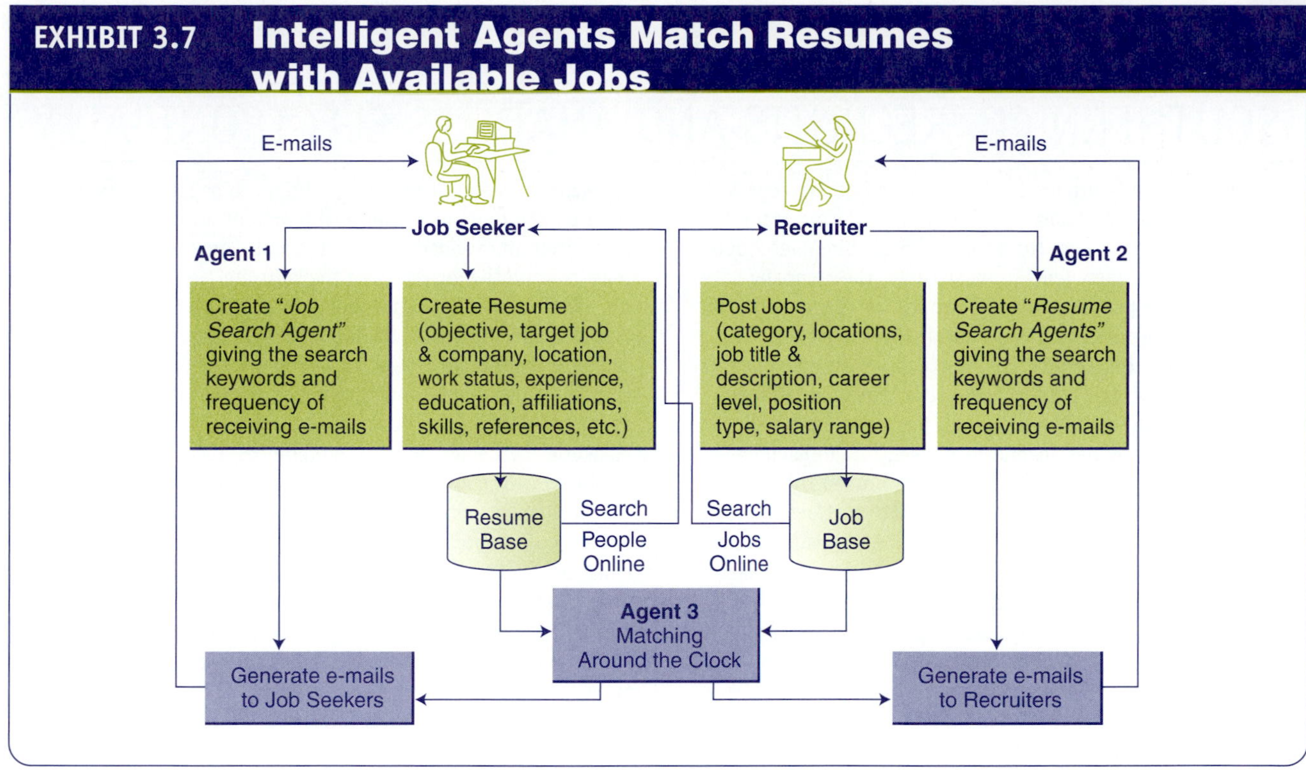

A special search engine powered by an intelligent agent can help employers find resumes that match specific job descriptions. For example, here is how the search engine Resumix at resumix.yahoo.com works: Hiring managers can view job applications; operators can scan resumes; and a recruiter can search for a candidate or identify existing employees for training programs, redeployment opportunities, or new initiatives. The core of this powerful system is Resumix's Knowledge Base, a computerized intelligent system. The Knowledge Base interprets a candidate's resume, determining skills based on context and matching those skills with the position criteria. For example, a potential employer might be looking for a product manager. Being a member of the AMA (American Marketing Association) might be one of the desirable properties for the job. However, if the potential employer used only a basic keyword search, they might get candidates who have listed AMA, but are really members of the American Medical Association or the American Meatpackers Association. Those are not relevant to their search. Resumix Knowledge Base would select only the candidates who are members of the American Marketing Association and who possess whatever other relevant skills the potential employer specifies. For an assessment of software tools (e.g., workforce-planning tools) see Agrawal et al. (2003).

Section 3.4 ▶ REVIEW QUESTIONS

1. What are the driving forces of the electronic job market?
2. What are the major advantages of the electronic job market to the candidate? To employers?
3. Describe the role of intelligent agents in the electronic job market.

3.5 REAL ESTATE, INSURANCE, AND STOCK TRADING ONLINE

Online financial services are exploding on the Internet and are being embraced by customers (Verma 2004). According to Dandapani (2004), financial services essentially altered the industry landscape. Sainsbury's Bank estimates that around 3 million people will take out a financial product, such as a credit card or insurance, online during 2004, 31 percent more than during 2003. The major financial services are presented in this and the following section.

CASE 3.2

EC Application

SOUTHERN CO. RECRUITS AND ANALYZES ELECTRONICALLY

The energy firm Southern Co. has over 26,000 employees in Georgia, Florida, Alabama, and Mississippi. To maintain its required staffing levels, the company must hire over 2,000 new employees each year. In most cases, the company advertises available positions mainly online. The response is over 100,000 applicants every year, all of whom must be evaluated carefully. The company must comply with government regulations, and it wants to make sure that no qualified employee is turned down before all positions are filled.

The company has several recruiters, one in each geographical region. In the past, recruiters posted their open positions on the company's Web site, with instructions for candidates to send an e-mail with the job requisition code in the subject line. However, the system wasn't very workable. If the correct code was not in the subject line, the e-mail would go into a wrong place. But even when the e-mails wound up with the right recruiter, there were major problems. To begin with, some candidates would apply to every open job on the Web site, some of which they were legitimately qualified for, and some for which they were not. Then, the resumes wouldn't necessarily list the key information the recruiter needed, such as whether the applicant had worked on a particular piece of equipment. This meant that the recruiters would have to follow up with the candidates to chase down the missing information. The situation became unacceptable. The company solicited proposals from all major vendors to install appropriate HR information systems.

Southern Co. selected Hire.com, a privately owned recruitment application service provider (ASP; see Online Chapter 18) headquartered in Austin, Texas. Its HireEnterprise suite contains three modules: electronic recruiting, applicant tracking, and staffing analytics. Southern Co. uses just the recruitment software.

Hire.com started with a focus on candidate relationships and candidate screening so that companies do not have to deal with high volumes of unqualified candidates. Hire.com hosts its software in its data centers in Austin, Texas, and Dublin, Ireland. Users access the software through a browser interface. Because Southern Co. didn't have to install and configure the software at its end, it took only 35 days to get the initial functions up and running. (Additional functions and more in-depth integration were added later.) After that, Hire.com sent in a team to train the recruiters on the software.

When someone goes to apply for a job on Southern Co.'s Web site and clicks the jobs link, it takes them to the Hire.com server, though there is nothing to indicate to the applicant that he or she is accessing a different site. On the site, applicants can establish accounts and search for open positions based on their education, job preferences, location, and so on. Applicants also can sign up to receive e-mail alerts when jobs that meet their criteria become available in the future. Southern Co. reports that 60 percent of its job candidates come through this push feature.

The biggest advantage, however, is not in finding applicants, but in narrowing down which ones the company should pursue. Southern Co. uses the software's testing functions to prescreen candidates. Screening is done online, and it can take several different forms. Based on the screening, the software assesses each applicant.

By using online prescreening, the recruiter can spend time phone screening or following up on the best 10 applicants rather than having to sort through 100. At first, the system was used for about 65 percent of the applications, whereas today it handles 90 to 95 percent of applications to Southern Co.

Sources: Compiled from Hire.com (2005) and Robb (2004).

Questions

1. What drove Southern Co. to automate the evaluation process?
2. Resumix uses a different method that does not require testing. Comment on the potential value of testing.
3. What are the advantages and risks of conducting the recruiting and testing on the Hire.com Web site?

REAL ESTATE ONLINE

Real estate transactions are an ideal area for EC for a number of reasons. First, potential homebuyers can view many properties online, at any time, from anywhere, saving time for both the buyer and the broker. For example, the online real estate market in London is very active; in addition to the locals, buyers from Hong Kong, Singapore, India, and many other countries are buying and selling there. To optimize their business with such international buyers, a number of developers that have real estate properties in London actively advertise on the Internet: galliard-homes.co.uk, berkeleyhomes.co.uk, weston-homes.com, and fpdsavills.com. (For details, see Dymond 2002.)

A second reason for using the Internet for real estate transactions is that potential buyers can sort and organize properties according to specific criteria and preview the exterior and interior design of the properties, shortening the search process. Finally, potential homebuyers can find *detailed information* about the properties and frequently get larger real estate listings than brokers provide.

In some locations, real estate databases are only available to realtors over private networks in their offices, but in many cities, this information is available to potential buyers from their personal Internet connections. For example, realtor.com allows Web surfers to search a database of over 1.5 million homes located all over the United States. The database is composed of local multiple listings of all available properties and of properties just sold in hundreds of locations. In addition, other realtors, such as Cushman and Wakefield of New York (cushwake.com), are using the Internet to sell commercial property (e.g., office buildings).

Builders, too, now use virtual reality technology on their Web sites to demonstrate three-dimensional floor plans to homebuyers. "Virtual models" enable buyers to "walk through" three-dimensional mock-ups of homes.

REAL ESTATE APPLICATIONS

The real estate industry is projected as one of the six industries to be changed by EC soon (Mullaney 2004). Some real estate applications and services, with their representative Web addresses, are shown in the following list. More applications and services are sure to proliferate in the coming years.

- Advice to consumers on buying or selling a home is available at assist2sell.com.
- The International Real Estate Directory and News (ired.com) is a comprehensive real estate Web site.
- Commercial real estate listings can be found at starboardnet.com.
- Listings of residential real estate in multiple databases can be viewed at homescout.com, justlisted.com, and realestate.yahoo.com.
- The National Association of Realtors (realtor.com) has links to house listings in all major cities. Also see homestore.com and homes.com.
- Maps are available on mapquest.com and realestate.yahoo.com.
- Information on current mortgage rates is available at bankrate.com, eloan.com, and quickenloans.quicken.com.
- Mortgage brokers can pass loan applications over the Internet and receive bids from lenders who want to issue mortgages (e.g., eloan.com).
- Online lenders, such as arcsystems.com, can tentatively approve loans online.
- To automate the closing of real estate transactions, which are notorious for the paperwork involved, see Broker Backoffice from realtystar.com (realtystar.com/brokerbackoffice.htm, accessed February 2005).
- Property management companies (residential, commercial, and industrial) are using the Internet for many applications ranging from security to communication with tenants. For an example, see superhome.net in Hong Kong.
- Sites for home sellers such as owners.com provide a place for persons who want to sell their homes privately, without using a real estate agent.
- Decided not to buy? Rental properties are listed on homestore.net. Several services are available, including a virtual walk-through of some listings.

In general, online real estate is supporting rather than replacing existing agents. Due to the complexity of the process, real estate agents are still charging high commissions. However, several Web sites have started to offer services at lower commissions (e.g., see assist2sell.com), some at 1 percent instead of 6 percent (see discounted brokers at ziprealty.com and foxtons.com).

Real Estate Mortgages

Large numbers of companies compete in the residential mortgage market. Several online companies are active in this area (e.g., see lendingtree.com and eloan.com). Many sites offer loan calculators (e.g., eloan.com and quickenloans.quicken.com). Mortgage brokers can pass loan applications over the Internet and receive bids from lenders who want to issue mortgages.

Priceline.com (priceline.com) offers its "name your own price" model for obtaining residential loans. In another case, a Singaporean company aggregates loan seekers and then places the package for bid on the Internet. Some institutions approve loans online in 10 minutes and settle in 5 days (e.g., homeside.com.au). Large numbers of independent brokers are active on the Internet, sending unsolicited e-mails to millions of people in the United States, promising low rates for refinancing and new home loans (an activity that some recipients see as *spamming*).

INSURANCE ONLINE

Although the uptake of EC in the insurance industry is relatively slow in some countries, such as New Zealand (Yao 2004), an increasing number of companies use the Internet to offer standard insurance policies, such as auto, home, life, or health, at a substantial discount. Furthermore, third-party aggregators offer free comparisons of available policies. Several large insurance and risk-management companies offer comprehensive insurance contracts online. Although many people do not trust the faceless insurance agent, others are eager to take advantage of the reduced premiums. For example, a visit to insurance.com will show a variety of different policies. At order.com customers and businesses can compare car insurance offerings and then make a purchase online. At travel-insurance-online.com, customers can book travel insurance. Some other popular insurance sites include insweb.com, insurance.com, ebix.com, and quicken.com. Many insurance companies use a dual strategy (MacSweeney 2000), keeping human agents, but also selling online. Like the real estate brokers, insurance brokers send unsolicited e-mails to millions of people.

ONLINE STOCK TRADING

Although U.S. stock traders were among the first to embrace the Internet, traders in Korea really love it. By 2003, more than 55 percent of all stock trades in Korea were transacted online (versus about 30 percent in the United States). The majority of the stock trading is carried out via the Internet; 12 brokerage firms handle 75 percent of all online trades (Cropper 2004). Why trade securities (stocks and bonds) online? Because it makes a lot of "dollars and sense."

The commission for an online trade is between $4 and $19, compared with an average fee of $100 from a full-service broker and $25 from a discount broker. With online trading, there are no busy telephone lines, and the chance for error is small, because there is no oral communication in a frequently noisy environment. Orders can be placed from anywhere, at any time, day or night, and there is no biased broker to push a sale. Furthermore, investors can find a considerable amount of free information about specific companies or mutual funds.

Several discount brokerage houses initiated extensive online stock trading, notably Charles Schwab in 1995. Full-service brokerage companies such as Merrill Lynch followed in 1998–1999. By 2002, most brokerage firms in the United States offered online trading, and the volume of trading has increased significantly in the last 5 years. In 2002, Charles Schwab opened cybertrader.com, charging only $9.95 per trade.

How does online trading work? Let's say an investor has an account with Schwab. The investor accesses Schwab's Web site (schwab.com), enters his or her account number and password, and clicks stock trading. Using a menu, the investor enters the details of the order (buy, sell, margin or cash, price limit, or market order). The computer tells the investor the current (real-time) "ask" and "bid" prices, much as a broker would do over the telephone, and the investor can approve or reject the transaction. The flow chart of this process is shown in Exhibit 3.8. However, companies such as Schwab are now also licensed as exchanges. This allows them to match the selling and buying orders of their own customers for many securities in 1 to 2 seconds.

Some well-known companies that offer online trading are E*TRADE, Ameritrade, TD Waterhouse, Suretrade, Discover, and Brownco. E*TRADE offers many finance-related services using multimedia software (e.g., see Adams 2004). It also challenges investors to participate in a simulated investment game.

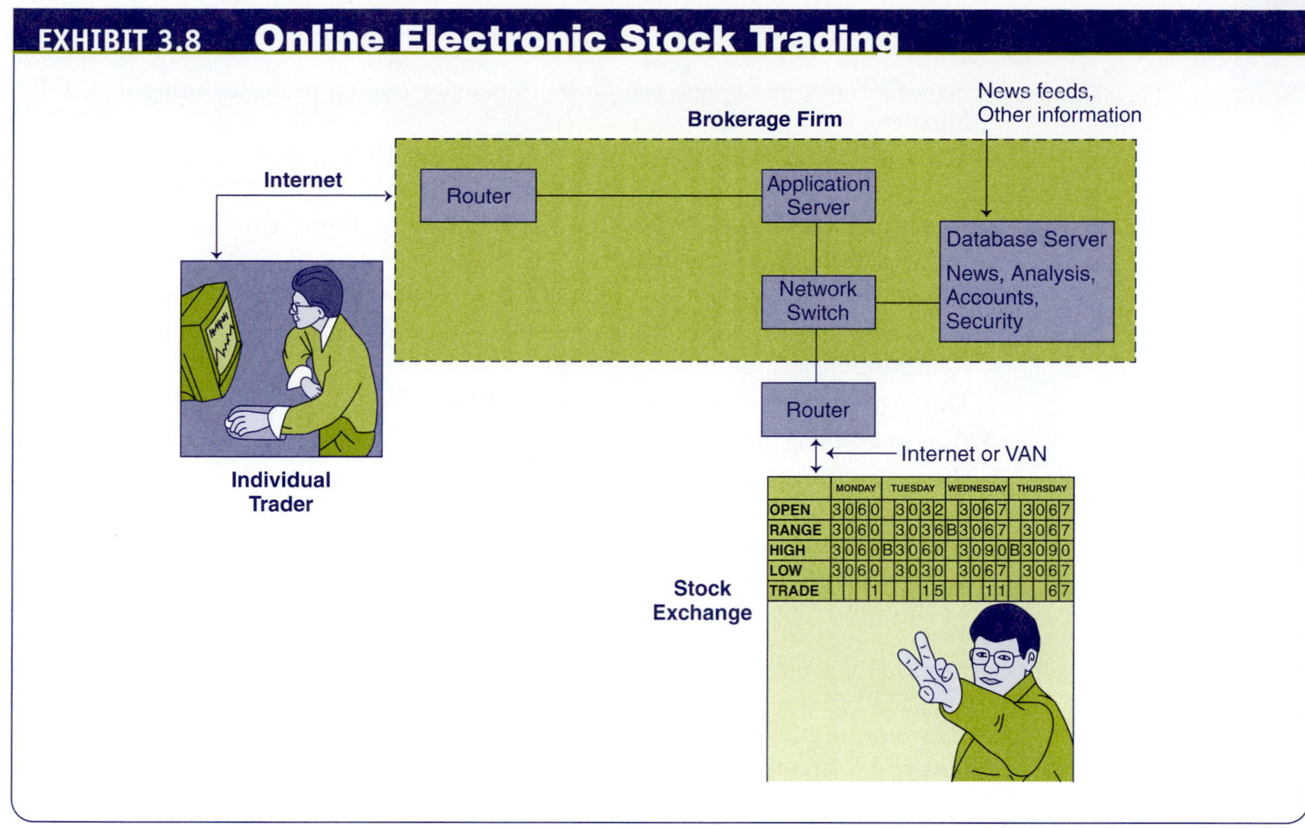

EXHIBIT 3.8 Online Electronic Stock Trading

Of the many brokers online, of special interest are ameritrade.com and datek.com. These two brokers have now combined as one company and offer customers extremely fast executions or their commission money back. The most innovative collection of online brokerage services is that of E*TRADE. In 1999, E*TRADE broadened its services by starting its own portfolio of mutual funds. E*TRADE is expanding rapidly into several countries, enabling global stock trading. For more on brokerage services provided online, see Gilbert et al. (2000), Adams (2004), and Cropper (2004).

With the rapid pace of adoption of mobile handsets, mobile banking will become more and more popular. Mobile banking services enable users to receive information on their account balances via SMS and to settle payments for bills and purchase stocks (Mallat et al. 2004).

Investment Information

An almost unlimited amount of investment-related information is available online, mostly for free (usually in exchange for a registration or for customers only). Here are some examples:

- Current financial news is available at CNN Financial (money.cnn.com). This portal also has large amounts of company information, all free. Similar information is available at Hoover's (hoovers.com) and Bloomberg (bloomberg.com).
- Municipal bond prices are available at bloomberg.com.
- Many tools are available to help investors in the bond market. For example, "how to invest manuals," free research reports, and charts and tables of foreign currencies all are available at bloomberg.com.
- A good source of overall market information, with many links to other financial sites, is investorguide.com.
- Free "guru" (expert) advice is available from thestreet.com.
- Stock screening and evaluation tools are available at MultexInvestor (marketguide.com) and money.cnn.com.

- Articles from the *Journal of the American Association of Individual Investors* can be read at aaii.org.
- Schwab Trader encourages consumers to practice trading strategies, using its CT Pro Simulator (schwabtrader.com/pro/simulator).
- The latest on funding and pricing of IPOs is available at hoovers.com/global/ipoc/index.xhtml and at ipodata.com.
- People can learn about investing at edgarscan.pwcglobal.com; it covers everything from financial ratios to stock analyses.
- Chart lovers will enjoy bigcharts.com. Charts also are available on many other sites.
- Mutual fund evaluation tools and other interesting investment information are available from Morningstar (morningstar.com).
- Earnings estimates and much more are available at thomson.com.
- Almost anything that anyone would need to know about finance and stocks can be found at finance.yahoo.com.
- A comprehensive site that tries to educate, amuse, and enrich is The Motley Fool (fool.com). A portal for individual investors, the site has gained considerable popularity. It acts as a community and is managed by two brothers who also author books and write a nationally syndicated newspaper column.

Most of these services are free. Many other services relating to global investing, portfolio tracking, and investor education also are available. For example, a number of free Web sites allow investors to scan mutual-fund offerings to find a suitable investment sector, country to invest in, and risk profile. For instance, Morningstar (morningstar.com) not only rates mutual funds, but also provides a search engine to help users narrow their search. An investor can use the "Fund selector" option and go to "Morningstar category." If the investor wants to invest in, say, Southeast Asia, he or she can find funds operating not only in the United States, but also in Hong Kong, Singapore, or Malaysia. Once the investor has picked a market, it can be segmented further by the size of the fund, by return on investment during the last 5 or 10 years, and by other criteria. The investor also can consider the fund's risk level and even the fund manager's tenure. The site has news and chat rooms for each fund. It also lets investors look at the top-10 holdings of most funds. Other evaluation sites similar to Morningstar, such as lipperweb.com, also rank funds by volatility. Investors can get their fund details and charts showing past performance against a relevant index for each fund.

Related Financial Markets

In addition to stocks, online trading is expanding to include commodities, financial derivatives, and more. Futures exchanges around the world are moving to electronic trading. For example, the Chicago Board of Trade, the world's largest futures exchange, is offering full-range electronic trading. Of special interest is *mortgage banking online* (see Stanford 2002 and mbaa.org).

The Risk of Having an Online Stock Account

The major risk of online trading is security. Although all trading sites require users to have an ID and password, problems may still occur, as illustrated in EC Application Case 3.3.

In 2004, it was discovered that hackers can steal users' ID numbers and passwords when they use the Windows operating system. The problem has been corrected. Problems of this nature also may occur when conducting online trading or online banking, our next topic.

Section 3.5 ◗ REVIEW QUESTIONS

1. List the major online real estate applications.
2. What are the advantages of online stock tracking?
3. What investment information is available online?
4. What are some of the risks of trading stocks online?

CASE 3.3

EC Application

THE DANGERS OF ONLINE TRADING

The South Koreans hold several Internet usage records, including the fact that almost 55 percent of stock trading in South Korea is done online. However, on Friday, August 23, 2002, Koreans were shocked to learn how easy it was to conduct a $20.7 million (25 billion in South Korean *won*) fraudulent online stock trade.

A criminal used a PC in an Internet cafe to place a buy order at a fairly high price for 5 million shares of Delta Information and Communication in the name of a well-known buyer, Hyundai Investment Trust Management, using the trust company's correct account number and password, which he had stolen. Over 100 people sold more than 10,000 shares each for a total of 2.7 million shares in 90 seconds, pushing the price of the shares way up. Then, the hacker stopped buying and disappeared. Because there were no more buyers, the price of Delta's shares started to decline, and by the time the fraud was announced publicly the following Monday, the shares had lost 12 percent (the daily limit on Korea's stock exchange) on each of two trading days, August 23 and 26. The Hyundai account is managed by a large brokerage firm, Daewoo Securities, which suffered $5 million in paper losses in 2 days.

The police speculated that some of Delta's shareholders, who sold shares on August 23, may have been involved in the scheme, but stated that it would be difficult to prove who conspired with the unknown hacker. Daewoo Securities suffered the losses because they had to take the 2.7 million shares into their account. Besides the $5 million in paper losses in the 2 days, shares of Daewoo Securities dropped considerably.

Sources: Compiled from television and newspaper stories in South Korea, August 24–27, 2002, and BBC News, August 24, 2002.

Questions

1. Most online trading systems accept an account number and a password as sufficient to conduct a trade. Therefore, a similar incident could have occurred elsewhere. How can this type of fraud be prevented? (See Chapters 11 and 12 for some ideas).
2. In this case, the buyer's account was managed by Daewoo, therefore Daewoo will pay for the damage. If the hacker had selected a "buyer" whose account was not managed by a brokerage firm, who would pay the damage? How would you feel if someone bought shares into your account, and then they plunged 12 percent in a day?

3.6 BANKING AND PERSONAL FINANCE ONLINE

Electronic banking (e-banking), also known as *cyberbanking, virtual banking, online banking,* or *home banking,* includes various banking activities conducted from home, business, or on the road rather than at a physical bank location. Consumers can use e-banking to check their accounts, pay bills online, secure a loan electronically, and much more.

electronic banking (e-banking)
Various banking activities conducted from home or the road using an Internet connection; also known as cyberbanking, virtual banking, online banking, and home banking.

E-banking saves users time and money. For banks, it offers an inexpensive alternative to branch banking and a chance to enlist remote customers. Many physical banks now offer home banking services, and some use EC as a major competitive strategy. One such U.S. bank is Wells Fargo (wellsfargo.com). In Hong Kong, a leading bank is the Bank of East Asia (hkbea-cyberbanking.com). Overall, 24 million online bank accounts were active in 2004 in the United States and 50 million worldwide (Dandapani 2004). According to Fox (2005), 54 million Americans (44 percent of all adult Internet users) use online banking in 2005. This is a 47 percent increase in two years, making it the fastest growing EC area on the Internet. Also, many traditional banks around the world offer diversified e-banking services (e.g., see main.hangseng.com). Many banks offer wireless services (see Chapter 9). According to itfacts.biz banking online is becoming popular even with small businesses, two thirds of which expect to source most of their financial services online over the next five years (itfacts.biz 2005).

In 2004, about 16 percent of small businesses banked online, versus 3.3 percent in 2001 (Celent 2004).

HOME BANKING CAPABILITIES

Southard and Siau (2004) divide banking applications into the following categories: informational, administrative, transactional, portal, and others (see Exhibit 3.9). They also found that the larger the bank, the more services offered. A description of some of the major e-banking capabilities is provided in Online Exhibit W3.1.

EXHIBIT 3.9 Online Banking Capabilities

Informational	General bank information and history Financial education information Employment information Interest rate quotes Financial calculators Current bank and local news
Administrative	Account information access Applications for services Personal finance software applications
Transactional	Account transfer capabilities Bill-pay services Corporate services (e.g., cash management, treasury) Online insurance services Online brokerage services Online trust services
Portal	Links to financial information Links to community information Links to local business Links to nonlocal businesses (and/or advertisers)
Others	Wireless capabilities Search function

Source: Peter B. Southard, Keng Siau: A Survey of Online e-Banking Retail Initiatives. *Communications of the ACM* 47(10): 99–102 (2004). © 2004 by ACM Inc. Used with permission.

Electronic banking offers several of the EC benefits listed in Chapter 1, both to the bank and to its customers, such as expanding the bank's customer base and saving on the cost of paper transactions (Gosling 2000; Pascoe 2004; and Anderson 2004).

VIRTUAL BANKS

In addition to regular banks adding online services, *virtual banks* have emerged; these have no physical location, but only conduct online transactions. Security First Network Bank (SFNB) was the first such bank to offer secure banking transactions on the Web. Amidst the consolidation that has taken place in the banking industry, SFNB has since been purchased and now is a part of RBC Centura (centura.com). Other representative virtual banks in the United States, from about 30 in total (see Rickards 2004), are NetBank (netbank.com) and First Internet Bank (firstib.com). Virtual banks exist in many other countries (e.g., bankdirect.co.nz). In some countries, virtual banks are involved in stock trading (e.g., see Bank One at oneinvest.com), and some stockbrokers are doing online banking (e.g., see etrade.com). According to Dandapani (2004), 97 percent of the hundreds of pure-play virtual banks failed by 2003 due to lack of financial viability.

A word of caution about virtual banking: Before sending money to any cyberbank, especially those that promise high interest rates for your deposits, make sure that the bank is a legitimate one. Several cases of fraud already have occurred.

INTERNATIONAL AND MULTIPLE-CURRENCY BANKING

International banking and the ability to handle trades in multiple currencies are critical for international trading. Although some international retail purchasing can be done by providing a credit card number, other transactions may require international banking support. Examples of such cross-border support include the following:

- Hongkong and Shanghai Banking Corporation (hsbc.com.hk) developed a special system called HEXAGON to provide electronic banking in Asia. Using this system, the bank has leveraged its reputation and infrastructure in the developing economies of Asia to become a major international bank rapidly, without developing an extensive new branch network (Peffers and Tunnainen 1998).
- Tradecard and MasterCard have developed a multiple-currency system for global transactions (see tradecard.com). This system is described in Chapter 12.
- Bank of America and most other major banks offer international capital funds, cash management, trades and services, foreign exchange, risk management investments, merchant services, and special services for international traders.
- Fxall.com is a multidealer foreign exchange service that enables faster and cheaper foreign exchange transactions (e.g., see Sales 2002). Special services are being established for stock market traders who need to pay for foreign stocks (e.g., at Charles Schwab). See Global Finance (2004) for more information about foreign exchange banks.

IMPLEMENTATION ISSUES IN ONLINE FINANCIAL TRANSACTIONS

As one would expect, the implementation of online banking and online stock trading can be interrelated. In many instances, one financial institution offers both services. The following are some implementation issues for online financial transactions. For an in-depth analysis, see Dewan and Seidmann (2001), e-Consultancy (2003), Bughin (2004), and Dandapani (2004).

Securing Financial Transactions

Financial transactions for home banking and online trading must be very secure. In Chapter 12, we discuss the details of secure EC payment systems. In EC Application Case 3.4, we give an example of how a bank provides security and privacy to its customers.

Access to Banks' Intranets by Outsiders

Many banks provide their large business customers with personalized service by allowing them access to the bank's intranet. For example, Bank of America allows its business customers access to accounts, historical transactions, and other data, including intranet-based decision-support applications, which may be of interest to large business customers. Bank of America also allows its small business customers to apply for loans through its Web site.

Using Imaging Systems

Several financial institutions (e.g., Bank of America and Citibank) allow customers to view images of all of their incoming checks, invoices, and other related online correspondence. Image access can be simplified with the help of a search engine.

Pricing Online Versus Off-Line Services

Computer-based banking services are offered free by some banks, whereas others charge \$5 to \$10 a month. Also, some banks charge fees for individual transactions (e.g., fee per check, per transfer, and so on). Financial institutions must carefully think through the pricing of online and off-line services. Pricing issues must take into account the costs of providing the different types of services, the organization's desire to attract new customers, and the prices offered by competitors. For further discussion, see Baker et al. (2001) and Ericson (2004).

Risks

Online banks, as well as click-and-mortar banks, may carry some risks and problems, especially in international banking. The first risk that most people think of is the risk of hackers getting into their account. In addition, some believe that virtual banks carry *liquidity* risk (the risk of not having sufficient funds to pay obligations as they come due) and could be more

CASE 3.4

EC Application

ONLINE SECURITY AT A BANK

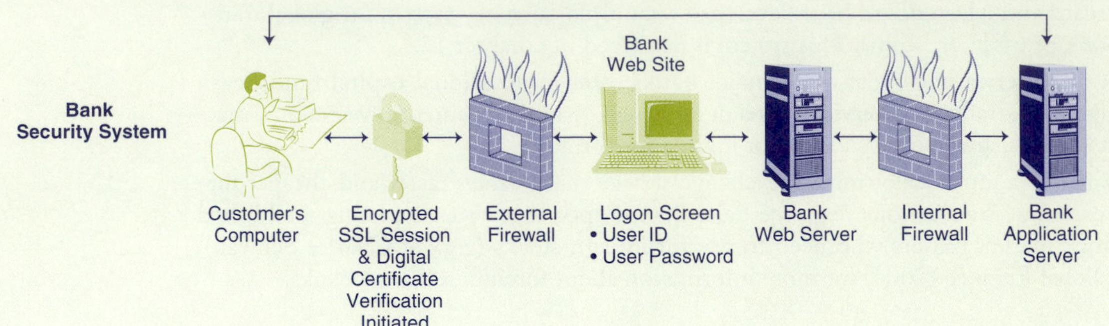

Banks provide extensive security to their customers. The following describes some of the safeguards provided.

Customers accessing the bank system from the outside must go through encryption provided by SSL (Secure Socket Layer) and digital certification verification (see Chapters 11 and 12). The certification process assures users each time they sign on that they are indeed connected to their specific bank. The customer inquiry message then goes through an external firewall. Once the log-on screen is reached, a user ID and a password are required. This information flows through a direct Web server and then goes through an internal firewall to the application server.

The bank maintains accurate information. Corrections are made quickly.

Information is shared among the company's family of partners only for legitimate business purposes. Sharing information with outside companies is done with extreme care.

The bank does not capture information provided by customers when they conduct "what-if" scenarios using the bank's planning tools (to assure privacy). The company does use cookies to learn about its customers; however, customers can control both the collection and use of the information. In addition, the bank provides suggestions on how users can increase security (e.g., "Use a browser with 128-bit encryption.")

Sources: Compiled from various security statements of online bank Web sites including *co-operativebank.co.uk/servlet/Satellite?cid=1077177611507&pagename=CoopBank%*, *prosperitybanktx.com/Internet_Banking/internet_banking.html*, and *thestatebank.com/securitystatement.htm* (accessed March 2005).

Questions

1. Why is security so important for a bank?
2. Why is there a need for two firewalls?
3. Who is protected by the bank's security system—the customer, the bank, or both? Elaborate.
4. What might be the limitations of such a system?

susceptible to panic withdrawals. Regulators are grappling with the safeguards that need to be imposed on e-banking.

PERSONAL FINANCE ONLINE

Individuals often combine electronic banking with personal finance and portfolio management. Also, brokerage firms such as Schwab offer personal finance services such as retirement planning. However, vendors of specialized personal finance software offer more diversified services (Tyson 2003). For example, both Intuit's Quicken (Tessler 2004) and Microsoft's Money offer the following capabilities: bill paying and electronic check writing; tracking of bank accounts, expenditures, and credit cards; portfolio management, including reports and capital gains (losses) computations; investment tracking and monitoring of securities; stock quotes and past and current prices of stocks; personal budget organization; record keeping of cash flow and profit and loss computations; tax computations and preparations; and retirement goals, planning, and budgeting.

Although Quicken is the most popular personal finance software, more sophisticated packages such as Prosper (from Ernst & Young) and Captool (captools.com) are available. All of these products are available as independent software programs for use with the Internet or coupled with other services, such as those offered by AOL.

Online Billing and Bill Paying

The era of e-payment is around the corner. The number of checks the U.S. Federal Reserve System processed in 2003 decreased for the fourth consecutive year, dropping 4.7 percent to 15.81 billion checks, while commercial automated clearinghouse (ACH) volume increased 12.1 percent to $95.96 billion payments (Dernovsek 2004). Many people prefer to pay monthly bills, such as telephone, utilities, rent, credit cards, cable, and so on, online. The recipients of such payments are equally eager to receive money online, because online payments are received much more regularly and quickly and have lower processing costs.

The following are representative payment systems:

- **Automatic transfer of mortgage payments.** This method has existed since the late 1980s. Payers authorize their bank to pay the mortgage directly from their bank account.
- **Automatic transfer of funds to pay monthly utility bills.** Since fall 1998, the city of Long Beach has allowed its customers to pay their gas and water bills automatically from their bank accounts. Many other utilities worldwide provide such an option today.
- **Paying bills from online banking accounts.** Payments from one bank account can be made into any other bank account. Many people pay their monthly rent and other bills directly into the payees' bank account.
- **Merchant-to-customer direct billing.** Under this model, a merchant such as American Express posts bills on its Web site, where customers can then view and pay them. (This approach is called presentment and payment; see Chapter 12.) Utilities in many cities allow customers to pay bills on the utilities' Web sites, charging customers up to 20 cents per transaction, which is less than the price of a stamp. However, this means that customers have to go to many different Web sites to pay all of their bills.
- **Using an intermediary for bill consolidation.** In this model, a third party such as Transpoint (from Microsoft, Citibank, and First Data Corporation) consolidates all of a customer's bills at one site and in a standard format. Collecting a commission on each transaction, the intermediary makes it convenient both for the payee and payer to complete transactions. This latest model is of interest to many vendors, including E*TRADE and Intuit.
- **Person-to-person direct payment.** An example of this service is PayPal (paypal.com), which enables a person to send funds to another individual over the Internet. A person opens an account with PayPal (now part of eBay.com) and charges the amount he or she wants to send on a credit card or bank account. PayPal alerts the person to whom the user wants to send the funds by e-mail, and the recipient accesses the account and transfers the funds to his or her credit card or bank account (see Chapter 12). PayPal is being followed in the market by a number of competitors.
- **Pay bills at bank kiosks.** As described in Chapter 12, some banks allow customers to pay bills from their account using electronic kiosks outside the bank (usually combined with regular ATMs).

Online billing and bill paying can be classified into B2C, B2B, or C2C. This section has focused largely on B2C services, which help consumers save time and payees save on processing costs. However, large opportunities also exist in B2B services, which can save businesses about 50 percent of billing costs. In Hong Kong, for example, CitiCorp enables automatic payments by linking suppliers, buyers, and banks on one platform.

Taxes

One important area in personal finance is advice about and computation of taxes. Dozens of sites are available to help people in their federal tax preparations. Many sites will help people legally cut their taxes. The following list offers some sites worth checking:

- irs.gov: The official Web site of the Internal Revenue Service.
- webtax.com: A massive directory of tax-related information, research, and services.
- fairmark.com: A tax guide for investors.
- moneycentral.msn.com/tax/home.asp: A useful reference and educational site.

- quicken.com/taxes: Emphasizes tax planning.
- taxcut.com/taxtips/hrblock_tips.html: Offers advice on minimizing taxes.
- taxaudit.com: Offers advice on minimizing taxes.
- taxprophet.com: Provides tax advice in an entertaining manner.
- bankrate.com/brm/itax: Contains informative articles about taxation.
- 1040.com: Information about deduction rules.
- unclefed.com: Offers advice on audits.

Section 3.6 ▶ REVIEW QUESTIONS

1. List the capabilities of online banking. Which of these capabilities would be most beneficial to you?
2. Discuss some implementation issues of financial services.
3. List the major personal finance services available online.
4. Explain online bill paying.

3.7 ON-DEMAND DELIVERY SERVICES AND E-GROCERS

Most e-tailers use common carriers to deliver products to customers. They may use the postal system within their country or they may use private shippers such as UPS, FedEx, or DHL. Delivery can be made within days or overnight if the customer is willing to pay for the expedited shipment.

Some e-tailers and direct marketing manufacturers own a fleet of delivery vehicles and incorporate the delivery function into their business plan in order to provide greater value to the consumer. These firms will either provide regular deliveries on a daily or other regular schedule or they will deliver items within very short periods of time, usually 1 hour. They may also provide additional services to increase the value proposition for the buyers. An example is Bigboxx.com (bigboxx.com), presented in Chapter 5 (page 202). An online grocer, or **e-grocer**, is a typical example of businesses in this category. Home delivery of food from restaurants is another example. In addition, another class of firms (groceries, office supplies, repair parts, and pharmaceutical products) promise virtually instantaneous or at least same-day delivery of goods to consumers.

e-grocer
A grocer that takes orders online and provides deliveries on a daily or other regular schedule or within a very short period of time.

Whether the delivery is made by company-owned vehicles or is outsourced to a carrier, an express delivery model is referred to as an **on-demand delivery service** (see Warkentin and Bajaj 2001). In such a model, the delivery must be done fairly quickly after an order is received. (For more on this topic, see Chapter 13.) A variation of this model is *same-day delivery*. According to this model, delivery is done faster than "overnight," but slower than the 30 to 60 minutes expected in on-demand delivery. E-grocers often deliver using the same-day delivery model.

on-demand delivery service
Express delivery made fairly quickly after an online order is received.

THE CASE OF E-GROCERS

The U.S. grocery market is valued at over $300 billion annually. It is a very competitive market, and therefore margins are very thin. Online grocery sales exceeded $2.4 billion in 2004, doubling 2003 sales (Freedman 2004). Many e-grocers are click-and-mortar retailers that operate in the countries where they have physical stores, such as Woolworths in Australia (woolworths.com.au) and Albertsons (albertsons.com) in the United States. (For statistics on the grocery industry, see retailindustry.about.com/library.)

All e-grocers offer consumers the ability to order items online and have them delivered to their houses. Some e-grocers offer free regular "unattended" weekly delivery (e.g., to the customer's garage), based on a monthly subscription model. Others offer on-demand deliveries (if the customer is at home), with a surcharge added to the grocery bill, and sometimes an additional delivery charge. One e-grocer sells only nonperishable items shipped via common carrier. Many offer additional services, such as dry-cleaning pickup and delivery. Other add-on features include "don't run out" automatic reordering of routine foods or home office supplies, as well as fresh flower delivery, movie rentals, meal planning, recipe tips, multimedia features, and nutritional information.

Today, it is possible to shop for groceries from cell phones and PDAs (see Chapter 9 and Lawrence et al. 2001).

Implementing E-Grocery

An extensive survey conducted by the Consumer Direct Cooperative in 2000 (Cude and Morganosky 2000) pointed to the following groups of potential online grocery shoppers: *Shopping avoiders* are willing to shop online because they dislike going to the grocery store; *necessity users* would do so because they are limited in their ability to shop (e.g., disabled and elderly people, shoppers without cars). *New technologists,* those who are young and comfortable with technology, represent another group of online grocery shoppers. Extremely busy, *time-starved consumers* may be willing to shop online in order to free up time in their schedules. Finally, some consumers gain a sense of self-worth from online shopping and being on the *leading edge* of what may be a new trend.

Online grocery customers are generally repeat customers who order week after week in a tight ongoing relationship with the grocer. The user interaction with the Web site is much more substantial than with other B2C Web sites, and user feedback is more prevalent. Shopping for groceries online is a very sophisticated purchase compared to most EC shopping transactions. As an example, in a typical online shopping experience at amazon.com a person might buy one to four items; in an e-grocery purchase, the average order has 54 different items in different food categories (Kruger 2000).

Around the world, many e-grocers are targeting the busy consumer with the promise of rapid home delivery of groceries. For example, Parknshop (parknshop.com), the largest supermarket chain in Hong Kong, offers a "personal shopping list" that helps customers easily order repetitive items on each visit. (The Web site also uses advertising as an additional source of revenue to make the business model a bit more solid.) The Tesco chain in the United Kingdom (tesco.com) is another successful e-grocer. (For a discussion of the success factors of e-grocers, see Keh and Shieh 2001 and Punakivi and Saranen 2001.) So far, online sales are usually not as profitable as sales in physical grocery stores due to the delivery costs and low volume of online sales. However, this additional channel allows grocers to increase their sales volume and serve customers who are unable to visit their physical stores. In addition, they can increase their brand recognition by maintaining an Internet presence.

However, despite the promise that on-demand delivery seems to hold, virtual e-grocers have not been successful in this competitive market. (For an analysis, see Keh and Shieh 2001.) For example, StreamLine.com and ShopLink.com folded in 2000. HomeGrocer.com and Kozmo.com folded in 2001 (see Chapter 13). Other virtual e-grocers, such as Peapod.com (peapod.com) and NetGrocer.com (netgrocer.com), were still struggling in 2005. Data from the fourth quarter of 2002 of e-grocer performance found that leading firms continuing to improve in areas that make most sense in the e-grocery market—such as ease of use of Web sites, convenience, personal interface between buyer and seller, and service after the sale (Ernst and Hooker 2003). Successful pure e-grocers include FreshDirect (freshdirect.com) and Simon Delivers (simondelivers.com).

One of the most interesting stories of e-grocers that failed is that of Webvan.com, a company that raised many expectations and was founded in 1999 with a goal of delivering anything (particularly groceries), anytime and anywhere in an efficient manner. Webvan designed and started to build sophisticated automated warehouses—each the size of seven football fields and equipped with more than four miles of conveyor belts (see Steinert-Therlkeld 2000). In 2001, Webvan purchased Homegrocer.com, a smaller rival, but was unable to merge the two companies properly. Furthermore, the company was unable to secure more funds due to the accumulating failures of dot-com companies, which led to a loss of investor confidence, and declining demands due to economic conditions contributed to staggering losses. Finally, in 2001, Webvan folded. Overall, it lost more than $1 billion, the largest of any dot-com failure. (For more details, see Helft 2001 and Online File W3.5.)

A similar company, Groceryworks.com, was purchased by Safeway, a successful click-and-mortar grocer. The results have been quite different from those of Webvan, as detailed in Online File W3.6.

Section 3.7 ▶ REVIEW QUESTIONS

1. Explain on-demand delivery service.
2. Describe e-grocers and how they operate.
3. Who are the typical e-grocery shoppers? (Would you shop online for groceries?)

3.8 ONLINE DELIVERY OF DIGITAL PRODUCTS, ENTERTAINMENT, AND MEDIA

Certain goods, such as software, music, or news stories, may be distributed in a physical form (such as hard-copy, CD-ROM, DVD, and newsprint) or they may be digitized and delivered over the Internet. For example, a consumer may purchase a shrink-wrapped CD-ROM containing software (along with the owner's manual and a warranty card) or pay for the software at a Web site and immediately download it onto his or her computer (usually through File Transfer Protocol [FTP], a fast way to download large files).

As described in Chapter 2, products that can be transformed to digital format and delivered over the Internet are called *digital products*. Exhibit 3.10 provides some digital products that may be distributed either physically or digitally. Each delivery method has advantages and disadvantages for both sellers and buyers. Customers, for example, may prefer the formats available through physical distribution. They perceive value in holding a physical CD-ROM or music CD as opposed to a downloaded file. In addition, the related packaging of a physical product may be significant. In some cases, customers enjoy the "liner notes" that accompany a music CD. Paper-based software user manuals and other materials also have value, and may be preferred over online help features. On the other hand, customers may have to wait days for physical products to be delivered.

For sellers, the costs associated with the manufacture, storage, and distribution of physical products (DVDs, CD-ROMs, paper magazines, etc.) can be enormous. Inventory management also becomes a critical cost issue, and so does delivery and distribution. The need for retail intermediaries requires the establishment of relationships with channel partners and revenue-sharing plans. Direct sales of digital content through digital download, however, allow a producer of digital content to bypass the traditional retail channel, thereby reducing overall costs and capturing greater profits. However, retailers are often crucial in creating demand for a product through in-store displays, advertising, and human sales efforts, all of which are lost when the producer "disintermediates" the traditional channel.

THE NAPSTER EXPERIENCE: ITS RISE, COLLAPSE, AND REVIVAL

With improvements in Internet technologies, the possibility exists for widespread distribution of digital content from businesses to consumers and from consumers to consumers. The rise in importance of Napster and similar Web sites that allow individuals to find and share music files, movies, and even photos and private documents coincided with the near universality of computer availability on college campuses and the widespread adoption of MP3 as a music file compression standard. MP3 files are much smaller than earlier file alternatives and

EXHIBIT 3.10 Distribution of Digital Versus Physical Products

Type of Product	Physical Distribution	Digital Distribution
Software	Boxed, shrink-wrapped	FTP, direct download, e-mail
Newspapers, magazines	Home delivery, postal mail	Display on Web, "e-zines"
Greeting cards	Retail stores	E-mail, URL link to recipient
Images (e.g., clip-art, graphics)	CD-ROM, magazines	Web site display, downloadable
Movies	DVD, VHS, NTSB, PAL	MPEG3, streaming video, RealNetwork, AVI, QuickTime, etc.
Music	CD, cassette tape	MP3, WAV, RealAudio downloads, wireless devices, iTunes

allow individuals to download a standard song in far less time. The Napster network does not require the use of a standard Web browser such as Internet Explorer. Nor does the user's client machine actually download the MP3 files from Napster's servers. Rather, Napster only shares "libraries," or lists of songs, and then enables a *peer-to-peer* file-sharing environment (see Chapter 8) in which the individual users literally download the music from each others' machines (called *peers*). The growth of the "Napster community"—with over 60 million registered users by the end of 2002 and as many as 1.3 million using the service at the same time—was nothing short of phenomenal (Borland 2002). It is said to have grown faster than any other community in history.

Because of the potential challenge to their revenue sources, the Recording Industry Association of America (RIAA) and five major record labels engaged in a legal battle with Napster, suing it for *copyright infringement* (see Chapter 17). Napster argued that its file sharing never actually published music that could be "pirated" or copied illegally in violation of internationally recognized copyright and licensing laws. However, the court ruled that as a manager of file exchanges, Napster must observe copyright. Thus, free file sharing is no longer allowed; Napster was forced to charge customers for use of its file-sharing service. The users of the free services were not happy with the charge and abandoned the service, driving Napster into bankruptcy.

Napster's assets have been acquired by Roxio Inc. which revived Napster as a for-fee service. In 2004, Napster introduced its for-fee file sharing, making agreements with several universities for deep discounts to students. (For additional information, see napster.com.)

The future of this consumer environment is clearly in doubt, though it is clear that technological developments will probably continue to outpace the ability of the market and legal structures to react and adapt. Other peer-to-peer tools, including Kazaa, Edonkey.com, Freenet, and Gnutella, continued to offer variations of file sharing (see Chapter 8 for details) and are involved in their own legal battles.

ONLINE ENTERTAINMENT

Online entertainment is growing rapidly. A survey by Knowledge Networks/Statistical Research Inc. (Castex 2002) shows that online entertainment is already the most popular medium in the United States among young people between the ages of 8 and 17. Thirty-three percent of these respondents prefer to be entertained online, whereas only 26 percent prefer to watch television. There are many kinds of Internet entertainment. Basically, Internet entertainment can be broadly categorized into two types: interactive and noninteractive.

Interactive Entertainment

Interactive entertainment is online entertainment in which the user is involved by making decisions or suggestions or by exchanging information. The major forms of interactive entertainment are the following.

- **Web browsing.** This category includes Web sites that require more than the usual user input as part of the process of using the Web site. It is likely in the future that the Web itself will transform into an environment where the user can move through the Web in a virtual reality world.
- **Internet gaming.** This includes all forms of gaming, including arcade type, lotteries, casino gaming, promotional incentives, and so on. Some individuals can make big money from such games (see Fong 2004). Some of the games are quite violent (*eMarketer Daily* 2003).
- **Fantasy sport games.** According to *eMarketer Daily*, the number of unique visitors to fantasy sports sites exceeds 7.4 million a month (reported by realSEO.com 2004). The major sites are sportline.com and Espn.com.
- **Single and multiplayer games.** These include online games in which multiple users log on to a Web site to participate in a game as well as games that require downloading from the Web site and installation on a PC. Examples of such sites include battle.net, zone.msn.com, chess.net, and casesladder.com.

- **Adult entertainment.** Adult entertainment has exploded onto the Internet. This is one industry that seems certain to find a lucrative home on the Internet. Indeed, adult entertainment has been called the Net's most profitable business model (see Chapter 8).
- **Card games.** These are very popular and some involve gambling. For a discussion, see Chapter 8.
- **Participatory Web sites.** Participatory Web sites include clubs, user groups, and "infotainment" sites (a site that provides information on all aspects of a topic and provides mechanisms for the user to interact with other people interested in the topic, for example, a Web site about sports).
- **Reading.** E-books are now published on the Web (see Chapter 8). Web versions of print media, including magazines and newspapers, are now available.

Noninteractive Entertainment

Noninteractive entertainment refers to Internet activities that are related to entertainment but in which users are not being entertained. The major forms of noninteractive entertainment are the following.

- **Event ticketing.** The click-and-mortar giant TicketMaster (ticketmaster.com) is the most popular place for getting tickets to many types of off-line entertainment. However, tickets also can be obtained from the vendors directly. An example of ticketing in Asia is cityline.com.hk, which offers tickets to events and movie theaters. Tickets also are being sold via cell phone (see Chapter 9).
- **Restaurants.** Many restaurants allow online reservations. Some offer deliveries as well. Examples are pizza places and Chinese restaurants. This kind of service is frequently accomplished via cell phones, telephones, or the Internet (e.g., geoexpat.com).
- **Information retrieval.** Many portals offer entertainment-related information for retrieval by users. The Internet has quickly become the largest source of information on many topics.
- **Retrieval of audio and video entertainment.** Users can download audio, music, video, and movies from Internet servers for non-real-time playback. In 2003, Apple introduced iPod and iTunes, a service that allows songs to be sold online (100 million were sold the first year). In July 2004, Duke University gave all of its incoming freshmen free iPods. Other companies offer similar services. The university arranged a Web site, modeled on iTunes, that allows the downloading of lectures, music, audio, books, and so on.
- **Live events.** Sports fans can listen to live sporting events on the Internet, sometimes for free.

Both interactive and noninteractive entertainment are available in many countries via cell phone (e.g., i-mode in Japan).

DEVELOPMENTS IN THE DELIVERY OF DIGITAL PRODUCTS

An interesting development in music distribution is the availability of CD customization sites (e.g., see angelfire.com and grabware.com). These sites enable consumers to collect their favorite songs from various artists and then create a "personal favorites" compilation CD, which is shipped to the consumer. The CD mastering sites pay royalties to the various artists through established channels.

Another trend is the disintermediation of traditional print media. Several journals and magazines ceased publishing "dead paper" versions and have become strictly online distributors of digital content (e.g., pcai.com), generating revenues through advertising or by online subscriptions. (Some of these transformations were subsequently reversed due to lack of financial success of the online version.) Other prominent publications, including the *Wall Street Journal*, now offer either a paper-only subscription, an online-only subscription (at a lower subscription price), or a dual-mode subscription for consumers who want to access their business news through both methods so that they can use search engines to find archived information or read information not available in the paper version.

Similarly, Egghead Software closed all of its brick-and-mortar stores and became a pure-play software store. In doing so, the company dramatically cut operating costs and streamlined its inventory requirements but lost certain advantages offered by a physical presence. Unfortunately, Egghead.com went out of business due to strong online competition in 2001; its assets were picked up by Amazon.com. As you may recall from Chapter 1, CompUSA is now selling software from kiosks. Hundreds of software companies are selling their products as downloads (e.g., Norton Security from Symantec). Time will tell if digital delivery replaces or enhances traditional delivery methods for various types of digital content.

Section 3.8 ▶ REVIEW QUESTIONS

1. Describe digital goods and their delivery.
2. Explain the Napster business model.
3. What are the benefits and the limitations of digital delivery?

3.9 ONLINE PURCHASE-DECISION AIDS

Many sites and tools are available to help consumers with online purchasing decisions. Wal-Mart, for example, equipped its online store with an intelligent search engine. Consumers must decide which product or service to purchase, which site to use for the purchase (a manufacturer site, a general-purpose e-tailer, a niche intermediary, or some other site), and what other services to employ. Some sites offer price comparisons as their primary tool, others evaluate services, trust, quality, and other factors. Shopping portals, shopping robots ("shopbots"), business ratings sites, trust verification sites, and other shopping aids also are available.

SHOPPING PORTALS

Shopping portals are gateways to storefronts and e-malls. Like any other portal, they may be comprehensive or niche oriented. Comprehensive or general-purpose portals have links to many different sellers and present and evaluate a broad range of products. Comprehensive portals include Gomez Advisors (ecost.com) and activebuyersguide.com. Several public portals also offer shopping opportunities and comparison aids. Examples are shopping.com, shopping.yahoo.com, eshop.msn.com, and in-store.com. These all have clear shopping links from the main page of the portal, and they generate revenues by directing consumers to their affiliates' sites. Some of these portals even offer comparison tools to help identify the best price for a particular item. Several of these evaluation companies have purchased shopbots (see the following discussion) or other, smaller shopping aids and incorporated them into their portals.

shopping portals
Gateways to e-storefronts and e-malls; may be comprehensive or niche oriented.

Shopping portals may also offer specialized niche aids, with information and links for purchasers of automobiles, toys, computers, travel, or some other narrow area. Such portals also help customers conduct research. Examples include bsilly.com for kid's products and zdnetshopper.cnet.com and shopper.cnet.com for computer equipment. The advantage of niche shopping portals is their ability to specialize in a certain line of products and carefully track consumer tastes within a specific and relevant market segment. Some of these portals seek only to collect the referral fee from their affiliation with sites they recommend. Others have no formal relationship with the sellers; instead, they sell banner ad space to advertisers who wish to reach the communities who regularly visit these specialized sites. In other cases, shopping portals act as intermediaries by selling directly to consumers, though this may harm their reputation for independence and objectivity.

SHOPBOTS SOFTWARE AGENTS

Savvy Internet shoppers may bookmark their favorite shopping sites, but what if they want to find other stores with good service and policies that sell similar items at lower prices? **Shopping robots** (also called **shopping agents** or **shopbots**) are tools that scout the Web for consumers who specify search criteria. Different shopbots use different search methods. For example, MySimon (mysimon.com) searches the Web to find the best prices and availability for thousands of popular items. This is not a simple task. The shopbot may have to evaluate different SKU (stock-keeping unit) numbers for the same item, because each e-tailer may have a different SKU rather than a standardized data-representation code.

shopping robots (shopping agents or shopbots)
Tools that scout the Web on behalf of consumers who specify search criteria.

Some agents specialize in certain product categories or niches. For example, consumers can get help shopping for cars at autobytel.com, autovantage.com, and autos.msn.com. Zdnet.com searches for information on computers, software, and peripherals. A shopping agent at office.com helps consumers find the best price for office supplies. A shopping agent for books is isbn.nu. In addition, agents such as pricegrabber.com are able to identify customers' preferences. Shopping.com allows consumers to compare over 1,000 different merchant sites and seeks lower prices on their behalf. There are even negotiation agents and agents that assist auction bidders (e.g., auctionbid.com) by automating the bid process using the bidder's instructions. For a comparison of shopping bots, see Mulrean (2003).

"Spy" Services

"Spy" services in this context are not the CIA or MI5 (mi5.gov.uk). Rather, they are services that visit Web sites for customers, at their direction, and notify them of their findings. Web surfers and shoppers constantly monitor sites for new information, special sales, ending time of auctions, stock updates, and so on, but visiting the sites to monitor them is time consuming. Several sites will track stock prices or airline special sales and send e-mails accordingly. For example, cnn.com, pcworld.com, and expedia.com will send people personalized alerts. spectorsoft.com enables users to create a list of "spies" that visit Web sites and send an e-mail when they find something of interest. Users can choose predesigned spies or create their own (see Internet Exercise 15). Special searches are provided by web2mail.com, which responds to e-mail queries. Of special interest is Yahoo! Alerts (alerts.yahoo.com), an index of e-mail alerts for many different things, including job listings, real estate, travel specials, and auctions. Users set up alerts so that they hit their in-boxes periodically or whenever new information is available. The alerts are sent via e-mailed and come with commercial ads.

Of course, one of the most effective ways to spy on Internet users is to introduce cookies and spyware in their computers. (See Chapters 4 and 17 for details.)

Wireless Shopping Comparisons

Users of Mysimon.com (all regular services) and AT&T Digital PocketNet service have access to wireless shopping comparisons. Users who are equipped with an AT&T Internet-ready telephone can find the service appearing on the main menu of AT&T; it enables shoppers to compare prices any time from anywhere, including from any physical store.

BUSINESS RATINGS SITES

Many Web sites rate various e-tailers and online products based on multiple criteria. Bizrate.com, Consumer Reports Online (consumerreports.org), Forrester Research (forrester.com), and Gomez Advisors (gomez.com) are such well-known sites. At gomez.com, the consumer can actually specify the relative importance of different criteria when comparing online banks, toy sellers, e-grocers, or others. Bizrate.com organized a network of shoppers that report on various sellers and uses the compiled results in its evaluations. Note that different raters may provide different rankings.

TRUST VERIFICATION SITES

With so many sellers online, many consumers are not sure whom they should trust. A number of companies purport to evaluate and verify the trustworthiness of various e-tailers. The TRUSTe seal appears at the bottom of each TRUSTe-approved e-tailer's Web site. E-tailers pay TRUSTe for use of the seal (which they call a "trustmark"). TRUSTe's 1,300-plus members hope that consumers will use the seal as an assurance and as a proxy for actual research into their conduct of business, privacy policy, and personal information protection. However, even TRUSTe is not foolproof. It has been criticized for its lax verification processes, and a number of high-profile privacy violations and other problems with TRUSTe members have led to publication of a study that investigated a TRUSTe "Hall of Shame" (Rafter 2000). Most of these problems were corrected in 2001.

The most comprehensive trust verification sites are VeriSign, BBBOnline, and WebTrust (cpawebtrust.org). VeriSign (verisign.com) tends to be the most widely used.

Other sources of trust verification include Secure Assure (secureassure.com), which charges yearly license fees based on a company's annual revenue. In addition, Ernst and Young, the global public accounting firm, has created its own service for auditing e-tailers in order to offer some guarantee of the integrity of their business practices.

OTHER SHOPPER TOOLS

Other digital intermediaries assist buyers or sellers, or both, with the research and purchase processes. For example, escrow services (e.g., escrow.com and fortis-escrow.com) assist buyers and sellers in the exchange of items and money. Because buyers and sellers do not see or know each other, a trusted third party frequently is needed to facilitate the proper exchange of money and goods. Escrow sites may also provide payment-processing support, as well as letters of credit (see Chapter 12).

Other decision aids include communities of consumers who offer advice and opinions on products and e-tailers. One such site is epinions.com, which has searchable recommendations on thousands of products. Pricescan.com is a price comparison engine, and pricegrabber.com is a comparison shopping tool that covers over 1 million products. onlineshoes.com specializes in all types of shoes, and iwon.com specializes in apparel, health and beauty, and other categories. Other software agents and comparison sites are presented in Exhibit 3.11.

Another shopping tool is a *wallet*—in this case, an *electronic wallet*, which is a program that contains the shopper's information. To expedite online shopping, consumers can use electronic wallets so that they do not need to reenter the information each time they shop. Although sites such as Amazon.com offer their own specialized wallets, Microsoft has a universal wallet in its Passport program (see Chapters 12 and 17 for details).

Amazon.com's A9 Search Engine

Amazon.com offers a special search tool known as A9.com. A9.com is a powerful search engine; it uses Web search and image search results enhanced by Google, Search Inside the Book® results from Amazon.com, reference results from GuruNet, movie results from IMDb, and more.

A9.com remembers information so the user doesn't have to. A user can make notes about any Web page and search them. It offers a new way to store and organize bookmarks. It even recommends new sites and favorite old sites specifically for the user to visit. With the A9 Toolbar installed, the user's Web browsing history will be saved, allowing the user to search through his or her whole history (and clear items the user doesn't want kept). A9.com uses the user's history to recommend new sites, to alert the user of new search results, and to let the user know the last time he or she visited a particular page.

GuruNet

According to Nielsen//NetRating (reported by Berkowitz 2004), finding relevant information is the most important feature of a search tool, followed by getting credible results and doing it quickly. GuruNet is a start-up that provides what customers want. See details at Berkowitz (2004) and gurunet.com.

An example of another tool that speeds up the search process is provided in the EC Application Case 3.5.

Section 3.9 ▶ REVIEW QUESTIONS

1. Define shopping portals and provide two examples.
2. What are shopbots?
3. Explain the role of business and Web site rating and site verification tools in the purchase-decision process.
4. Why are escrow services and electronic wallets useful for online purchases?
5. Describe the role of search engines to support shopping.

EXHIBIT 3.11 Representative Shopping Software Agents and Comparison Sites

Agent Classification	Product (URL)	Description
Learning agents	Empirical (*vignette.com*)	Surveys user's reading interests and uses machine learning to find Web pages using neural-network-based collaborative filtering technology.
	Blinkx (*blinkx.com*)	Searches intelligently and constantly for topics of the user's choice.
Comparison shopping agents	MySimon (*mysimon.com*)	Using VLA (virtual learning agent) technology, shops for the best price from merchants in hundreds of product categories with a real-time interface.
	CompareNet (*compare.net*)	Interactive buyer's guide that educates shoppers and allows them to make direct comparisons between brands and products.
	Kelkoo (*kelkoo.co.uk*)	Price comparison on UK Web sites.
AI/Logic-supported approaches	Cnetshopper (*shopper.cnet.com*)	Makes price comparisons.
Computer-related shopping guide	Netbuyer (*shopping.zdnet.co.uk/shopping*)	Supplies sales and marketing solutions to technology companies, by delivering information about computer and communications industry trends, product developments, and buyer activity.
Car-related shopping guides	Auto-by-Tel (*autobytel.com*)	A low-cost, no-haggle car-buying system used by leading search engines and online programs such as Excite, NetCenter, Lycos, and AT&T WorldNet Services.
	Trilegiant Corp. (*trilegiant.com*)	The Web's premier savings site for great deals on autos. (Also offers travel, shopping, dining, and other services.)
	CarPoint (*carpoint.msn.com*)	A one-stop shopping place for searching and purchasing automobiles.
Find lowest prices	PriceScan (*pricescan.com*)	Searches for lowest price for a given product.
	PriceGrabber (*pricegrabber.com*)	Looks for the best deals.
Aggregator portal	Pricing Central (*pricingcentral.com*)	Aggregates information from other shopping agents and search engines. Comparison shopping is done in real time (latest pricing information).
Personalized information	Newsbot (*newsbot.msnbc.msn.com*)	Automatic personalization of business and industry news.
Real-time agents	Kanndu (*kanndu.com*)	Allows users to surf over to a single mobile Internet portal and click around to multiple e-shopping sites to make purchases with only a few keystrokes.
Comparison shopping agents	Shopping.com (*shopping.com*)	Compares prices; saving the consumer time and money by giving key information as the consumer is shopping online.
Evaluation and comparisons	BizRate (*bizrate.com*)	Rates merchants based on real consumer feedback, per product. Comparison of similar products.

CASE 3.5

EC Application

COMPUSA INCREASES ONLINE SALES WITH SHOPPING AIDS

CompUSA, like many companies that are selling online, suffered from a low online *conversion rate* (Chapter 4). Specifically, potential customers would log onto the Web site, initiate a search, and then abruptly abandon the site without buying. CompUSA found that the major reason for this was that the customers couldn't find what they needed fast enough. The reason was that customers had to navigate 500 categories in which about 15,000 out of 120,000 products are displayed on any given day.

To increase the **conversion rate**, namely the percentage of the site visitors that stay there and buy, CompUSA installed a shopping aid called Endeca InFront. It is an index-based navigational/merchandising/reporting tool.

conversion rate
The percentage of Web site visitors who stay and buy.

Endeca (*endeca.com*) provides a powerful search engine for information retrieval from catalogs, information portals, intranets, knowledge bases, and other data sources. Users can navigate such sources very rapidly. The tool allows interactive dialog between users and data. The product, which is customized for each company, including CompUSA, helps maximize sales opportunities by ensuring that customers are always presented with relevant product information and even suggestions during their interactive session. This way, customers can find what they are looking for very rapidly.

The software helps both B2C and B2B EC. Search time has been reduced by up to 97 percent. The program is used by store employees as well. In addition, CompUSA's Web merchants are able to automatically identify products that deserve maximum exposure based on sales-performance criteria preselected by CompUSA. For example, on its opening category page for notebook computers, CompUSA prominently displays top sellers.

While the default is set for popularity defined by sales velocity, CompUSA also gives customers the ability to sort by criteria such as low-to-high prices, product name, or alphabetically sorted brand name. "That's something we couldn't do before," says Will Pendegast, director of e-commerce at CompUSA. "It was an expensive query for us to perform, but that's a function that Endeca provided to us right out of the box."

Pendergast has a long list of merchandising rules CompUSA wants to implement on the Web site, including "new releases" and "coming soon." Realizing that many customers are brand centric, Pendegast says that CompUSA will "eventually start to drive deeper into the brand showcases."

Eventually, CompUSA's merchants will only have to focus on merchandising at the top level of the navigation tree. InFront will automatically merchandise the sublevels, basing its allocations of blocks and positioning on the criteria set by Comp USA. Not having to worry about merchandising at three levels will "definitely give our merchants more time to determine the better products and the better cross-selling items that go along with them," says Pendergast.

As part of the implementation, the two companies analyzed CompUSA.com's metrics, measuring factors such as the products and categories people were searching for and clicking most often. "We looked at it from every angle," says Pendergast, "and determined that a majority of the people . . . are doing research on the Web site before they go into our stores. So we definitely knew that a fast and effective searching feature was a must."

CompUSA also began to comprehend how customers were behaving as they visited the front page of the Web site, as well as what they were doing as they navigated the site.

A basic search engine can take a customer to all product descriptions that include the word(s) that they enter. For example, if a customer types "iPod," the search engine will bring up an inventory of all products with that word in their names or on their package labels. Many peripherals, however, do not include iPod in their product name or packaging.

Within less than a year, CompUSA's customers increased their conversion rate by over 30 percent, so online sales jumped 30 percent, covering the investment in the system.

Sources: Compiled from Parks (2004) and *endeca.com* (accessed October 25, 2004).

Questions

1. From your own experience, relate search time to frustration level.
2. Explain how the Endeca's software can help reorganize catalogs.
3. Enter *compusa.com* and search for a product. Comment on your experience.
4. Enter *endeca.com* and look at its customer list. How do customers use its product? What is the common thread?

3.10 SUCCESSFUL CLICK-AND-MORTAR STRATEGIES

Although thousands of companies have evolved their online strategies into mature Web sites with extensive interactive features that add value to the consumer purchase process, many sites remain simple "brochureware" sites with limited interactivity. Many traditional companies are in a transitional stage. Today, about 35 percent of all companies that sell products or services do it online as well. Mature transactional systems include features for payment processing, order fulfillment, logistics, inventory management, and a host of other services. In most cases, a company must replicate each of its physical business processes and design many more that can only be performed online. Today's environment includes sophisticated access to order information, shipping information, product information, and more through Web pages, touchtone phones, Web-enabled cellular phones, and PDAs over wireless networks. Faced with all of these variables, the challenges to implementing EC can be daunting.

The real gains for traditional retailers come from leveraging the benefits of their physical presence and the benefits of their online presence. Web sites frequently offer better prices and selection, whereas physical stores offer a trustworthy staff and opportunities for customers to examine items before purchasing. (Physical examination often is critical for clothing and ergonomic devices, for example, but not for commodities, music, or software.) Large, efficient established retailers, such as Wal-Mart (walmart.com), Marks & Spencer (marksandspencer.com), Takashimaya (takashimaya.co.jp), and Nordstrom (nordstrom.com) are able to create the optimum value proposition for their customers by providing a complete offering of services.

A traditional brick-and-mortar store with a mature Web site uses a click-and-mortar strategy to do the following:

- **Speak with one voice.** A firm can link all of its back-end systems to create an integrated customer experience. Regardless of how a customer interfaces with a company, the information received and service provided should be the same.
- **Leverage the multichannels.** The innovative retailer will offer the advantages of each marketing channel to customers from all channels. Whether the purchase is made online or at the store, the customer should benefit from the presence of both channels. For example, customers who purchase from the Web site should be allowed to return items to the physical store (Eddie Bauer's policy). In addition, many physical stores, such as BestBuy, now have terminals in the store for ordering items from the Web site if they are not available in the store. Needless to say, prices should be consistent in both channels to avoid "channel conflict" (discussed in Section 3.12).
- **Empower the customer.** The seller needs to create a powerful 24/7 channel for service and information. Through various information technologies, sellers can give customers the opportunity to perform various functions interactively, at any time. Such functions include the ability to find store locations, product information, and inventory availability online. Circuit City's Web site (circuitcity.com), for example, allows customers to receive rich product comparisons between various models of consumer electronics products, as we will explain in the following section.

Here we provide examples of two click-and-mortar strategies as used by some well-known companies: the successful transformation to click-and-mortar accomplished by retailer Circuit City and the failure of the alliance between a virtual and a traditional retailer (Amazon.com and Toys"R"Us).

TRANSFORMATION TO CLICK-AND-MORTAR OPERATIONS: CIRCUIT CITY

Circuit City is the second-largest U.S. retailer of consumer electronics (behind BestBuy), operating about 650 stores located across the United States. Prior to the summer of 1999, Circuit City's Web site was largely a brochureware site, capable only of selling gift certificates. When Circuit City launched the new circuitcity.com in 1999, it already had some of the needed EC systems in place—the credit card authorization and inventory-management systems at its brick-and-mortar stores. However, linking the company's brick-and-mortar systems with the EC system was neither cheap nor easy. "It's safe to say that millions of dollars need to be spent to have a *Fortune* 500 kind of presence on the Web in a transactional way," indicated George Barr, Circuit City's director of Web development. "It's just not something you could do for $100,000" (Calem 2000).

A few features of the circuitcity.com site (click "services") deserve special attention. First, the site educates customers about the various features and capabilities of different products, cutting through the jargon to help the customer understand why these features may be desirable and what the trade-offs are. In this personal and non-threatening way, customers can gain valuable knowledge to assist them in the purchase decision. (Some consumers find shopping in the traditional brick-and-mortar Circuit City store to be intimidating because they do not understand the terms and product features discussed by store personnel.) Second, at the Web site, customers can perform powerful searches on a product database to help find the appropriate models to consider. Third, the site offers an extensive amount of generic information about electronics and other products, organized in a very flexible way. This assists buyers as they gather information before a purchase is made, whether or not they eventually buy from circuitcity.com. Visitors can select several product models and compare them by viewing a dynamically created table of purchase criteria, displayed side-by-side, with drill-down details if necessary.

Circuit City has engineered the online purchase to be smooth, secure, and seamless. Poor process design will scare off many customers. It has been reported that in other stores only 17 percent of all online purchase processes are completed, versus over 50 percent for Circuit City. Customers who abandon the purchase typically do so because of confusion and complexity, surprises (such as shipping costs), concerns about security and privacy of personal information, system errors, slow transmission speeds, and other factors.

Finally, the site's order fulfillment method is flexible. The customer is given three choices: (1) receive the purchase via common carrier with no sales tax but with a small shipping charge for 3-day delivery, (2) pay a larger shipping charge for overnight delivery, or (3) pick up the item at the nearby brick-and-mortar store and pay sales tax but no shipping, and thus have the item almost immediately. If the customer chooses the self-pickup, the customer prints a confirmation page and takes it to the service desk of the store, along with a picture ID. The customer can pick up a new purchase, such as a DVD player, in under 2 minutes.

ALLIANCE OF VIRTUAL AND TRADITIONAL RETAILERS: AMAZON.COM AND TOYS"R"US

In online toy retailing, eToys was the pioneer. However, as electronic orders increased, particularly during the peak holiday season, eToys was unable to meet its delivery requirements due to its limited logistics capability and poor demand forecasting. Price wars and high customer acquisition costs also caused problems for this e-tailer. Eventually, eToys closed, and its assets were sold to KB Toys (kbtoys.com).

Meanwhile, giant toy retailer Toys"R"Us, a competitor of KB Toys, had been unsuccessful in creating an independent e-tailing business. One solution seemed promising: an alliance between Toys"R"Us and Amazon.com. Amazon.com is known as a premier site for creating customer loyalty and for driving sales through its execution of CRM with efficient back-office order fulfillment systems. Toys"R"Us, backed by 40 years of toy-industry experience, is known for its broad product offerings and a deep understanding of the toys market, customer tastes, and suppliers. It has strong B2B supplier relationships and a well-developed inventory system.

Before the alliance with Toys"R"Us, Amazon.com had failed in the toy business because it lacked the strong B2B supplier relationships with toy manufacturers. It could not get the best toys and prices from manufacturers and did not know how to manage inventory against product demand (Karpinski 2000). Toys"R"Us also had problems. It could not figure out how to effectively manage a direct-to-consumer distribution center or how to balance its retail-store business with its online business (Karpinski 2000).

After bad press, lost business, and rebates to customers during the 1999 Christmas season, these two companies decided to combine their efforts for 10 years, commencing with the 2000 Christmas season. They have pooled their expertise to form a single online toy store.

The alliance allows the partners to leverage each other's core strengths (Schwartz 2000). Under the 10-year agreement, Toys"R"Us identifies, purchases, and manages inventory, using the parent company's clout to get the best lineup of toys. Because Amazon.com has a distribution network with plenty of excess capacity and a solid infrastructure, it is responsible for order fulfillment and customer service. Amazon.com applies its expertise in front-end site design, offering a powerful customer-support environment. Revenues are split between the two companies; the risks also are equally shared. This arrangement worked for only four years. Then the partners sued each other (June 2004).

One reason for the difficulties was that the two companies had to coordinate disparate systems—operational, technological, and financial—as they merged their corporate cultures. For example, Toys"R"Us wanted Amazon.com to sell only Toys"R"Us toys, and it paid $250 million a year for this exclusivity. Amazon.com interpreted the agreement to allow them to sell toys from any company. Despite the failure of this alliance, there is much evidence of successful ones. For one story of a successful alliance, see Reda (2002b).

Section 3.10 ▶ REVIEW QUESTIONS

1. What motivates a brick-and-mortar company to sell online?
2. What customer services are provided by Circuit City on its Web site?
3. Describe the logic of the alliance between Amazon.com and Toys"R"Us and explore the reasons for its failure.

3.11 PROBLEMS WITH E-TAILING AND LESSONS LEARNED

As the experiences of eToys and others indicate, e-tailing is no panacea. Some companies do not even try e-tailing. Reasons that retailers give for not going online include: product is not appropriate for Web sales, 47 percent; lack of significant opportunity, 24 percent; too expensive, 17 percent; technology not ready, 9 percent; online sales conflict with core business, 3 percent (Diorio 2002). Others try e-tailing but do not succeed. E-tailing offers some serious challenges and tremendous risks for those who fail to provide value to the consumer, who fail to establish a profitable business model, or who fail to properly execute the model they establish. The road to e-tail success is littered with dead companies that could not deliver on their promises. The shakeout from mid-2000 to late-2002 caused many companies to fail; others learned and adapted. For more on problems and issues in e-tailing, see Lee and Brandyberry (2003).

Insights and Additions 3.3 provides a sample of failed B2C companies. Some enduring principles can be distilled from the failures, and these "lessons learned" are discussed next. (See Chapter 14 for further discussion.)

WHAT LESSONS CAN BE LEARNED FROM THESE FAILURES?

Painful as failures are, at least they can point out some valuable lessons. The following lessons can be drawn from the B2C dot-com failures in Insights and Additions 3.3 and other cases.

Don't Ignore Profitability

One fundamental lesson is that each marginal sale should lead to a marginal profit. It has been said that in business, "If it doesn't make cents, it doesn't make sense." The trouble with most virtual e-tailers is that they lose money on every sale as they try to grow to a profitable size and scale.

Many pure-play e-tailers were initially funded by venture capital firms that provided enough financing to get the e-tailers started and growing. However, in many cases, the funding ran out before the e-tailer achieved sufficient size and maturity to break even and become self-sufficient. In some cases, the underlying cost and revenue models were not sound—the firms would never be profitable without major changes in their funding sources, revenue model and pricing, and controlled costs. Long-run success requires financial viability.

Insights and Additions 3.3 B2C Dot-Com Failures

During 2000–2001, more than 600 dot-coms folded in the United States, and more than 1,000 folded worldwide. Here are some examples.

Kozmo.com. Kozmo.com initiated a creative idea for on-demand deliveries of movie rentals (and related items) to customer's doors. The first problem was how to return the movies. Drop boxes for the returns were vandalized, volume was insufficient, competitors entered the market, and even an alliance with Starbucks (to host the drop boxes) and a large porn selection did not help. In addition, the company was sued for refusal to deliver to low-income neighborhoods that had high crime rates. The company failed in 2001 after "burning" $250 million. (See Chapter 13 for the full story.)

Furniture.com. Selling furniture on the Internet may sound like a great idea. Furniture.com even paid $2.5 million for its domain name. Delivering the furniture was the problem. A number of manufacturers were not able to meet the delivery dates for the most popular items. In addition, many pieces of furniture cannot be delivered by UPS because of their size and weight. The cost of special deliveries was $200 to $300 per shipment, resulting in a loss. The company folded in 2001 after "burning" $75 million.

eRegister.com. Registering online for classes via an intermediary may sound interesting to investors, but not to customers. If a person wants to register to take a class at the YMCA or Weight Watchers, why not do it directly? The business model simply did not work, and the company folded in 2001.

Go.com. Go.com was a Disney portal site that was formed to manage Disney's Web sites and generate revenue from advertising. The business model did not work. To cover the salaries of its 400 employees, it was necessary for Go.com to sell 2 *billion* paid ad impressions per year. The company was able to sell only 1.6 million impressions. After losing $790 million in write-offs and $50 million in expenses, the site closed in February 2000. No amount of Disney magic helped.

Pets.com. Pets.com, a Web site devoted to selling pet food, pet toys, and pet supplies, operated in a very competitive market. This market competition forced Pets.com to advertise extensively and to sell goods below cost. The cost of acquiring customers mounted to $240 per new customer. Yet, being one of the early dot-com companies, it was able to buy a rival, Petstore.com, in 2000. After spending $147 million in less than 2 years, Pets.com had a lot of brand recognition, but not a real brand. After collapsing, its assets were sold to Petsmart.com, a click-and-mortar pet supplies retailer. At the same time, click-and-mortar Petco.com purchased Petopia.com, another B2C failure in the pet area.

Source: Compiled from Kaplan (2002).

Manage New Risk Exposure

The Internet creates new connectivity with customers and offers the opportunity to expand markets. However, it also has the potential to expose a retailer to more sources of risk. Local companies have to contend only with local customers and local regulations, whereas national firms have more constituents with which to interact. Global firms have to contend with numerous cultural, financial, and other perspectives: Will they offend potential customers because of a lack of awareness of other cultures? Global Internet firms also have to manage their exposure to risk from the mosaic of international legal structures, laws, and regulations. For example, they can be sued in other countries for their business practices. (For additional details, see Chapter 14.)

Groups of disgruntled employees or customers can band together to contact the news media, file a class action lawsuit, or launch their own Web site to publicize their concerns. One example of this was Walmartsucks.com, which was created by a customer who felt that he was mistreated at one Wal-Mart store. He created a repository of all the negative news stories he could find about Wal-Mart and anecdotal accounts from fired employees and unhappy customers. Similar information about other corporations and government agencies is available at sucks500.com. When each disgruntled individual tells 50 friends and co-workers about his or her frustration, it may result in a few lost sales; with the Internet, these people can now reach thousands or even millions of potential customers.

Watch the Cost of Branding

Branding has always been considered a key to retail success. Consumers are thought to be more willing to search out products with strong brand recognition, as well as pay a bit more for them. According to Dayal et al. (2000), Internet sites such as Amazon.com are putting established brands (e.g., traditional brick-and-mortar booksellers) at risk by creating quick brand recognition. However, in e-tailing, the drive to establish brand recognition quickly often leads to excessive spending. In one case, an upstart e-tailer (Epidemic.com) spent over 25 percent of its venture capital funding on one 30-second television advertisement during the Super Bowl! The company folded a few months later (Carton and Locke 2001). In other cases, e-tailers offered extravagant promotions and loss-leading offers to drive traffic to their sites, and then lost money on every sale. The huge volume of site traffic merely served to increase their losses. The lesson from success stories is that most customers, especially long-term loyal customers, come to a Web site from affiliate links, search engines, or personal recommendations—not from Super Bowl ads.

Do Not Start with Insufficient Funds

It may seem obvious that a venture will not succeed if it lacks enough funds at the start, but many people are so excited about their business idea that they decide to try anyway. An example of this is the failure of Garden.com. Garden.com was a Web site that provided rich, dynamic gardening content (how to plant bulbs, tips on gardening, an "ask the expert" feature, etc.) and a powerful landscape design tool, which allowed a visitor to lay out an entire garden and then purchase all the necessary materials with one click. Garden.com also hosted various "community" features with discussions about various gardening-related topics. Gardeners are often passionate about their hobby and like to learn more about new plants and gardening techniques. The business idea sounded good. However, the site failed due to the company's inability to raise sufficient venture capital necessary to cover losses until enough business volume was reached.

The Web Site Must Be Effective

Today's savvy Internet shoppers expect Web sites to offer superior technical performance—fast page loads, quick database searches, streamlined graphics, and so forth. Web sites that delay or frustrate consumers will not experience a high sales volume because of a high percentage of abandoned purchases. Online Chapter 18 describes the functionalities that are needed for effective sites.

Keep It Interesting

Web sites without dynamic content will bore returning visitors. Static design is a turnoff. Today, most e-tailers offer valuable tips and information for consumers, who often come back just for that content and may purchase something in the process. L.L. Bean, for example, offers a rich database of information about parks and recreational facilities as well as its buying guides. Visitors who enter the site to find a campground or a weekend event may also purchase a tent or a raincoat.

Although there have been many e-tailing failures (mostly pure-play e-tailers, but some click-and-mortar companies or EC initiatives, too), there are many success stories. Many are described throughout this book and in Taylor and Terhune (2002). The successful case of a floral business is presented in Online File W3.7. In general, whereas pure-play online retailing is risky and its future is not clear, online retailing is growing very rapidly as a complementary distribution channel to physical stores and mail-order catalogs. In other words, the click-and-mortar model appears to be winning.

Section 3.11 ▶ REVIEW QUESTIONS

1. Why are virtual e-tailers usually not profitable?
2. Relate branding to profitability.
3. Why are technical performance and dynamic site content important?

3.12 ISSUES IN E-TAILING

The following are representative issues that need to be addressed when conducting B2C.

DISINTERMEDIATION AND REINTERMEDIATION

In the traditional distribution channel, intermediating layers exist between the manufacturer and consumer, such as wholesalers, distributors, and retailers, as shown in part a of Exhibit 3.12. In some countries, such as Japan, one may find inefficient distribution networks with as many as 10 layers of intermediaries. These extra layers can add as much as a 500 percent markup to a manufacturer's prices.

Intermediaries traditionally have provided trading infrastructure (such as a sales network), and they manage the complexity of matching buyers' and sellers' needs. However, the introduction of EC has resulted in the automation of many tasks provided by intermediaries. Does this mean that travel agents, real estate brokers (e.g., see Grant and Rich 2000), job agency employees, insurance agents, and other such jobs will disappear?

Manufacturers can use the Internet to sell directly to customers and provide customer support online. In this sense, the traditional intermediaries are eliminated, or *disintermediated.* **Disintermediation** refers to the removal of organizations or business process layers responsible for certain intermediary steps in a given supply chain. As shown in parts b and c of Exhibit 3.12, the manufacturer can bypass the wholesalers and retailers, selling directly to consumers. Also, e-tailers may drive regular retailers out of business. For a vivid case of such disintermediation, see the Blue Nile case in Chapter 2.

disintermediation
The removal of organizations or business process layers responsible for certain intermediary steps in a given supply chain.

However, consumers may have problems selecting an online vendor, vendors may have problems delivering to customers, and both may need an escrow service to ensure the transaction. Thus, new online assistance may be needed, and it may be provided by new or by

EXHIBIT 3.12 Disintermediation and Reintermediation in the B2C Supply Chain

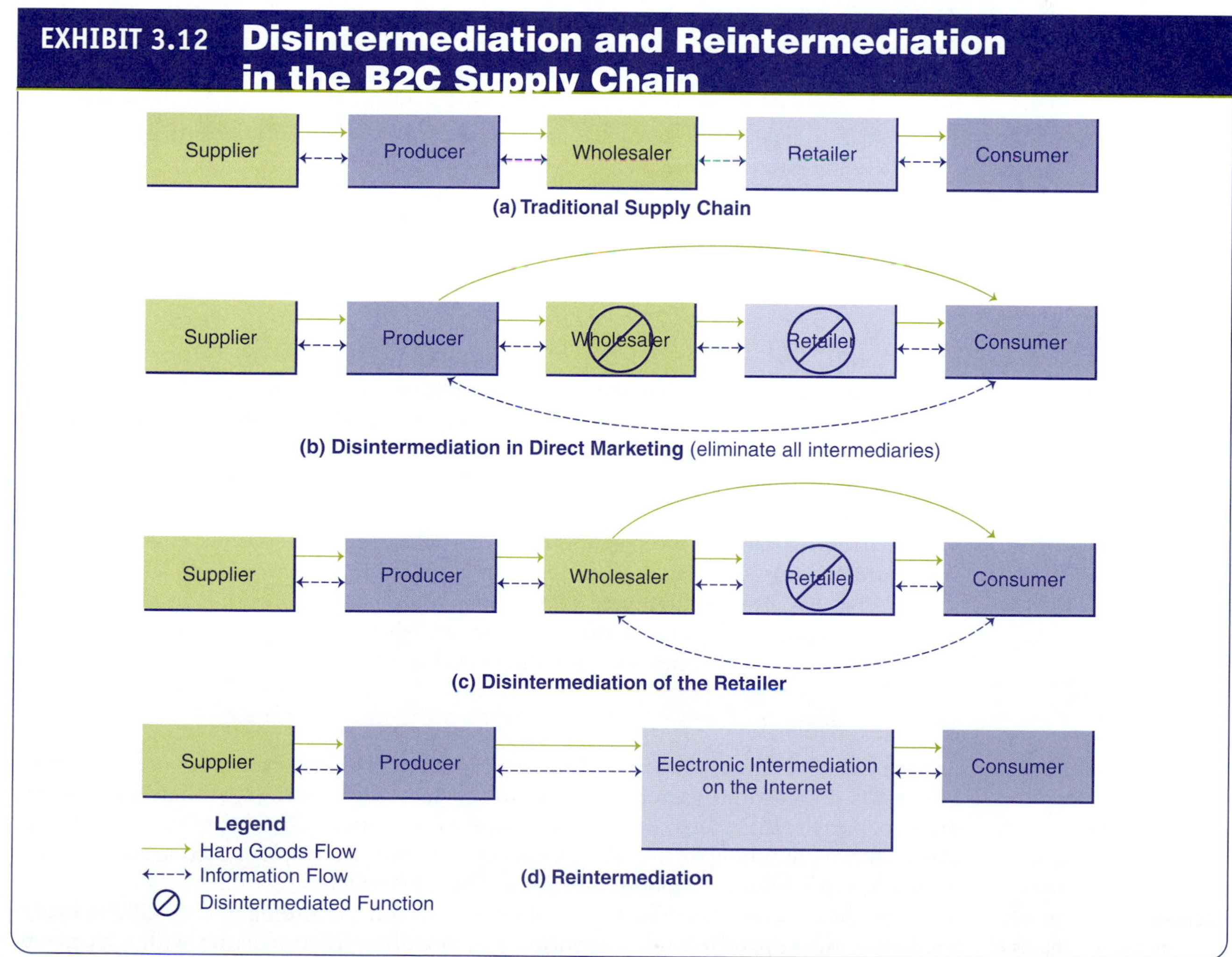

Source: Modified from Warkentin, M., et al. "The Role of Mass Customization in Enhancing Supply Chain Relationships in B2C E-Commerce Markets." *Journal of Electronic Commerce Research* 1, no. 2 (2000): 1–17. Used with permission.

traditional intermediaries. In such cases, the traditional intermediaries fill new roles, providing *added value* and assistance. This process is referred to as **reintermediation**. It is pictured in part d of Exhibit 3.12. Thus, for the intermediary, the Internet offers new ways to reach new customers, new ways to bring value to customers, and perhaps new ways to generate revenues.

reintermediation
The process whereby intermediaries (either new ones or those that had been disintermediated) take on new intermediary roles.

An example of reintermediation is that of Rosenbluth International (now an American Express company; see the Online File W2.6). This travel company completely changed its business model by providing value-added services to its business customers. At a time when many travel agencies were losing their role as intermediaries, Rosenbluth was able to survive, and even prosper, by using EC-based reintermediation business models.

The intermediary's role is shifting to one that emphasizes value-added services such as assisting customers in comparison shopping from multiple sources, providing total solutions by combining services from several vendors, and providing certifications and trusted third-party control and evaluation systems. For instance, in the world of online new and used car sales, electronic intermediaries assist buyers and/or sellers. These are new *reintermediaries*; intermediaries that have restructured their role in the purchase process.

Example of the new roles of intermediaries are Kelly Blue Book (kbb.com), which offers pricing information for consumers; Edmunds (edmunds.com), which gives consumers information about the dealer's true costs; CARFAX (carfax.com), which can research a specific used car and tells the consumer if it has ever been in an accident or had an odometer rollback; and iMotors (imotors.com), which offers members discounts on insurance, gas, and repairs. Additionally, "lead services" direct buyers to member dealers and, in some cases, also offer direct sales of new cars. The leading site in this category is autobytel.com, others include Amazon.com's partner CarsDirect (carsdirect.com), Autoweb (autoweb.com), and Cars.com (cars.com).

Some reintermediaries are newcomers, rivaling the traditional retail stores (e.g., Blue Nile), whereas others are additional operations established by the traditional retailers or intermediaries, such as Edmunds that use both the old and the new intermediation methods (like click-and-mortar). Some reintermediaries cooperate with manufacturers or retailers to provide a needed service to the seller or distributor in the online environment. Other reintermediaries are virtual e-tailers that fill a unique niche. Intermediaries such as online retailers and shopping portals can also act as reintermediaries. The evolution and operation of these companies is critical to the success of e-commerce.

Cybermediation

cybermediation (electronic intermediation)
The use of software (intelligent) agents to facilitate intermediation.

In addition to reintermediation, there is a completely new role in EC called **cybermediation**, or **electronic intermediation**. These terms describe special Web sites that use intelligent agents to facilitate intermediation. Cybermediators can perform many roles in EC. To illustrate the diversity of such roles, Giaglis et al. (1999) examined the market functions listed in Exhibit 3.13 and found that cybermediation can affect most market functions. For example, intelligent agents can find when and where an item that a consumer wants will be auctioned. The matching services described in this chapter are done by *cybermediator agents*. Cybermediator agents also conduct price comparisons of insurance policies, long-distance calls, and other services. Cybermediation services are spreading rapidly around the globe (Vandermerwe 1999; Berghel 2000; Kauffman et al. 2000).

Hypermediation

In some cases, EC transactions require extensive human and electronic intermediation. Many EC applications require content providers, security services, affiliate sites, search engines, portals, ISPs, software makers, escrow services, and more. A large e-tailer, such as Amazon.com, for example, uses all of these services, and also employs auction services, payments services, logistics support, and more. This phenomenon is called **hypermediation**, meaning the extensive use of new types of intermediation. According to Carr (2000), hypermediation runs opposite to disintermediation, providing intermediaries with a chance to profit from EC.

hypermediation
Extensive use of both human and electronic intermediation to provide assistance in all phases of an e-commerce venture.

EXHIBIT 3.13 Opportunities and Threats to Intermediaries in Electronic Markets

Market Function	Electronic Market Influence	Likely Effects on Intermediation
Determination of product offerings	Personalization of products	Disintermediation (especially in digital products)
	Aggregation	Cybermediation (aggregators)
	Disaggregation	Disintermediation (pay-per-use)
Searching	Lower search costs	Disintermediation
	More complex search requirements	Cybermediation
	Lower barriers to entry	Cybermediation/Reintermediation
Price discovery	Redistribution of mechanisms	Cybermediation/Reintermediation
	New markets	Cybermediation
Logistics	Lower logistical costs	Disintermediation
	Economics of scale	Reintermediation
Settlement	New cost structures	Reintermediation
	New payment mechanisms	Cybermediation/Reintermediation
Trust	Increased protection requirements	Cybermediation/Reintermediation
Legal and regulatory	Institutional support for electronic markets	Reintermediation

Source: Compiled from Giaglis, G. M., S. Klein, and R. M. O'Keefe, "The Role of Intermediaries in Electronic Marketplaces: Developing a Contingency Model," *Information Systems Journal* 12:3, (2002): 231–246. Courtesy of Blackwell Publishing.

Unbundling

An EC application may have another impact that is related to disintermediation and reintermediation. Bauer and Colgan (2002) call this impact *unbundling*. According to this concept, old economy processes will be broken into specialized segments that can be delivered by specialized intermediaries. For example, in the financial services industry, buying a stock may be done in five separate segments: information gathering, trade ordering, execution, settlement, and account keeping. As a result of unbundling the processes, the specialized services that are offered can be executed in small segments better, faster, and more efficiently.

CHANNEL CONFLICT

Many traditional retailers establish a new marketing channel when they start selling online. Similarly, some manufacturers have instituted direct marketing initiatives in parallel with their established channels of distribution, such as retailers or dealers. In such cases, channel conflict may occur. **Channel conflict** refers to any situation in which the online marketing channel upsets the traditional channels due to real or perceived damage from competition.

channel conflict
Situation in which an online marketing channel upsets the traditional channels due to real or perceived damage from competition.

Another type of marketing conflict may occur between the online and off-line departments of the same company. For example, the online department may want to offer lower prices and have more online advertising than the off-line department offers. The off-line department wants the opposite. Because the two departments are competing in different markets, they need different strategies. The conflict occurs when corporate resources are limited and an action by one department may be at the expense of another. *Staff conflict* also may occur, as staff members want to join the new, future-oriented, online department, and those in the off-line department feel left behind. Finally, a price conflict may occur.

DETERMINING THE RIGHT PRICE

Pricing a product or service on the Internet, especially by a click-and-mortar company, is complicated. On one hand, prices need to be competitive on the Internet. Today's comparison engines will show the consumer the prices at many stores, for almost all commodity products. On the other hand, prices should be in line with the corporate policy on profitability, and in a click-and-mortar company, in line with the off-line channel's pricing strategy. To avoid price conflict, some companies have created independent online subsidiaries.

Baker et al. (2001) maintain that EC offers companies new opportunities to test prices, segment customers, and adjust to changes in supply and demand. The authors argue that companies are not taking advantage of these opportunities. Companies can make prices more precise (optimal prices), they can be more adaptable to changes in the environment, and they can be more creative and accurate regarding different prices to different segments. In addition, in one-to-one marketing (Chapter 4), a company can have personalized prices. (For more on pricing strategies as they relate to different business models, see Bandyopadhyay et al. 2001; for use of price optimization tools in retailing, see Parks 2004.)

PERSONALIZATION

One significant characteristic of many online marketing business models is the ability of the seller to create an element of *personalization* for each individual consumer. For example, an e-tailer can use cookie files and other technologies to track the specific browsing and buying behavior of each consumer. With that information, the e-tailer can create a marketing plan tailored to that consumer's pattern by showing items of interest, offering incentives that appeal to that consumer's sense of value, or providing certain services that will attract that consumer back to the Web site. The Internet also allows for easy self-configuration ("design it your way"). This creates a large demand for personalized products and services. Manufacturers can meet that demand by using a *mass customization* strategy. As indicated earlier, many companies offer customized products from their Web sites.

Although pure-play e-tailing is risky, and its future is unclear, e-tailing is growing rapidly as a complementary distribution channel to traditional stores and catalogs (see Lee and Brandyberry 2003). In other words, the *click-and-mortar model is winning currently*. (See the Real-World Case at the end of the chapter and Online File W3.7.)

WWW

FRAUD AND OTHER ILLEGAL ACTIVITIES

A major problem in B2C is the increasing rate of online fraud. This can cause losses to both buyers and sellers. See the discussion of online fraud in Chapter 17.

HOW TO MAKE CUSTOMERS HAPPY

A critical success factor for B2C is to find what customers want, so the vendor can make them happy. In addition to price, customers want convenience, service, quality, and more. Merchants can find out what customers want through *market research*, the topic of our next chapter.

Section 3.12 ▶ REVIEW QUESTIONS

1. Define disintermediation.
2. Describe mediation issues, including disintermediation, reintermediation, cybermediation, hypermediation, and unbundling.
3. Describe channel conflict and other conflicts that may appear in e-tailing.
4. Describe price determination in e-tailing.
5. Explain personalization and mass customization opportunities in e-tailing.

MANAGERIAL ISSUES

Some managerial issues related to this chapter are as follows.

1. **What should our strategic position be?** The most important decision for retailers and e-tailers is the overall *strategic position* they establish within their industry. What niche will they fill? What business functions will they execute internally, and which functions will be outsourced? What partners will they use? How will they integrate brick-and-mortar facilities with their online presence? What are their revenue sources in the short and long run, and what are their fixed and marginal costs? An e-business is still a business and must establish solid business practices in the long run in order to ensure profitability and viability. We discuss such issues in Chapters 14 and 16.
2. **Are we financially viable?** The collapse of the dot-com bubble that started in early 2000 provided a

wake-up call to many e-tailers. Some returned to business fundamentals, whereas others sought to redefine their business plan in terms of click-and-mortar strategies or alliances with traditional retailers. Because most easy sources of funding have dried up and revenue models are being scrutinized, many e-tailers also are pursuing new partners, and consolidation will continue until there is greater stability within the e-tail segment. Ultimately, there will likely be a smaller number of larger sellers with comprehensive sites and many smaller, specialized niche sites.

3. **Should we recruit out of town?** Online out-of-town recruitment can be an important source of skilled workers. Using e-mails and video teleconferencing, recruiters can interview potential employees from a distance. Aptitude tests also can be taken from a distance. Furthermore, for many jobs, companies can use telecommuters. This could be a major strategy in the twenty-first century.
4. **Are there international legal issues regarding online recruiting?** Various legal issues must be considered with international online recruiting. For example, online recruitment of people from other countries may involve immigration and legal constraints. For example, the validity of contracts signed in different countries must be checked by legal experts.
5. **Do we have ethics and privacy guidelines?** Ethical issues are extremely important in an agentless system. In traditional systems, human agents play an important role in assuring the ethical behavior of buyers and sellers. Will online ethics and the rules of etiquette be sufficient to guide behavior on the Internet? Only time will tell. For example, as job-applicant information travels over the Internet, security and privacy become even more important. It is management's job to make sure that information from applicants is secure. Also, e-tailers need to establish guidelines for protecting the privacy of customers who visit their Web sites.
6. **How will intermediaries act in cyberspace?** It will take a few years before the new roles of Internet intermediaries will be stabilized, as well as their fees. Also, the emergence of support services, such as escrow services in global EC, will have an impact on intermediaries and their role.
7. **Should we set up alliances?** Alliances for online initiatives are spreading rapidly. For example, in Hong Kong, four banks created a joint online e-bank (to save on capital costs and share the risk). Some online trading brokers are teaming up with banks. Banks are teaming up with telecommunications companies, software companies, and even airlines. Finally, six of the largest music retailers created a joint company (named Echo) to sell music that can be downloaded from the Web (Patsuris 2003). Alliances involving retailers are very popular (see Reda 2002b). However, the collapse of the Amazon.com–Toy"R"Us alliance indicates that careful analysis must be done. See Chapters 14 and 16 for more information.

RESEARCH TOPICS

Here are some suggested topics related to this chapter. For details, references, and additional topics, refer to the book's "Current EC Research," in the Online Appendix.

1. **Performance Evaluation of Electronic Retailers**
   - Compare the performance of e-tailers with traditional retailer by time, industry, and country
   - Contrast popular merchandise for e-tailing and physical retailing (what sells well on the Internet and why)
   - Impact of e-tailing on digital contents such as music and electronic books
2. **Pricing Issues in Electronic Channels**
   - Risk versus advantages of differential prices on the Internet
   - Empirical study of how companies are currently treating differential pricing online
   - Customers' behavior and their perception of online pricing
   - Evolution of pricing strategies in electronic markets
   - Diffusion of price comparison and lowest price matching services
   - Effect of group purchasing on price discounts (Chapter 5)
   - Effect of using intelligent agents in price reduction
3. **Channel Conflict and Its Resolution**
   - Resolution strategies of conflicting channels between online and off-line channels
   - Theory of power and coalition in conflict resolution
4. **Online Services and Their Strategies**
   - Consumer's preference of using online service in comparison with other service delivery mode
   - Consumer search behavior in online services

- Effect of bundling digitized products and its pricing strategy
- Security protection strategies for online software distribution

5. **Software Agents for Customer Purchase Decision Aids**
   - Design of agents to use for several of the most time-consuming stages of the buying process
   - Buyer behavior framework for development of software agents
   - Human-computer collaboration for purchase decisions
   - Next generation multimedia call center equipped with software agents (also related to material in Chapter 13)
6. **Internet Banking**
   - Strategy of reengineering the traditional branches after the penetration of electronic channels
   - Analyze revenue structure of Internet banking services
   - Evaluate the risks of Internet banking and consumer attitudes toward Internet banking
7. **Online Stock Trading**
   - Application of intelligent agents in online stock trading
   - Restructuring the traditional branch offices after large penetration of electronic channel
   - Analyzing the revenue structure of online brokerage services versus brick-and-mortar ones
8. **Customer's Information Processing Provisions and Cost for Online Stock Trading**
   - Disintermediation: Where it is really happening, to what extent
   - What companies can do about disintermediation

SUMMARY

In this chapter, you learned about the following EC issues as they relate to the learning objectives.

1. **The scope of e-tailing.** E-tailing, the online selling of products and services, is growing rapidly. Computers, software, and electronics are the major items sold online. Books, CDs, toys, office supplies, and other standard commodities also sell well. More successful are services sold online, such as airline tickets and travel services, stocks, and insurance.
2. **E-tailing business models.** The major e-tailing business models can be classified by distribution channel—a manufacturer or mail-order company selling direct to consumers, pure-play (virtual) e-tailing, a click-and-mortar strategy with both online and traditional channels, and online malls that provide either referring directories or shared services.
3. **How online travel/tourism services operate.** Most services available through a physical travel agency also are available online. In addition, customers get much more information, much more quickly through online resources. Customers can even receive bids from travel providers. Finally, travelers can compare prices, participate in auctions and chat rooms, and view videos and maps.
4. **The online job market and its benefits.** The online job market is growing rapidly, with thousands and thousands of jobs matched with job seekers each year. The major benefits of online job markets are the ability to reach a large number of job seekers at low cost, to provide detailed information online, to take applications, and even to conduct tests. Also, using intelligent agents, resumes can be checked and matches made more quickly. Millions of job offers posted on the Internet help job seekers, who also can post their resumes for recruiters.
5. **The electronic real estate market.** The online real estate market is basically supporting rather than replacing existing agents. However, both buyers and sellers can save time and effort in the electronic market. Buyers can purchase distant properties much more easily and in some places have access to less expensive services. Eventually, commissions on regular transactions are expected to decline as a result of the electronic market for real estate, and more sales "by owner" will materialize.
6. **Online trading of stocks and bonds.** One of the fastest growing online businesses is the online trading of securities. It is inexpensive, convenient, and supported by a tremendous amount of financial and advisory information. Trading is very fast and efficient, almost fully automated, and moving toward 24/7 global trading. However, security breaches may occur, so tight protection is a must.
7. **Cyberbanking and personal finance.** Branch banking is on the decline due to less expensive, more convenient online banking. The world is moving toward online banking; today, most routine banking services can be done from home. Banks can reach customers in remote places, and customers can bank with faraway institutions. This makes the financial markets more

efficient. Online personal finance applications, such as bill paying, tracking of accounts, and tax preparation, also are very popular.

8. **On-demand delivery service.** On-demand delivery service is needed when items are perishable or when delivering medicine, express documents, or urgently needed supplies. One example of on-demand delivery is e-groceries; these may be ordered online and are shipped or ready for store pickup within 24 hours or less.
9. **Delivery of digital products.** Anything that can be digitized can be successfully delivered online. Delivery of digital products such as music, software, movies, and other entertainment online has been a success. Some print media, such as electronic versions of magazines or electronic books (see Chapter 8), also are having success when digitized and delivered electronically.
10. **Aiding consumer purchase decisions.** Purchase decision aids include shopping portals, shopbots and comparison agents, business rating sites, trust verification sites, and other tools.
11. **Critical success factors.** Critical success factors for direct online sales to consumers and e-tailing are managing risk properly; using correct business models; creating a profitable, effective, and interesting site; and watching operating costs. Also, sufficient cash flow is critical, as is appropriate customer acquisition.
12. **Disintermediation and reintermediation.** Direct electronic marketing by manufacturers results in disintermediation by removing wholesalers and retailers. However, online reintermediaries provide additional value, such as helping consumers make selections among multiple products and vendors. Traditional retailers may feel threatened or pressured when manufacturers decide to sell online; such direct selling can cause channel conflict. Pricing of online and off-line products and services is one issue that always needs to be addressed.

KEY TERMS

Brick-and-mortar retailers	90	**Disintermediation**	125	**Multichannel business model**	90
Channel conflict	127	**E-grocer**	110	**On-demand delivery service**	110
Click-and-mortar retailers	90	**E-tailers**	83	**Reintermediation**	126
Conversion rate	119	**Electronic banking (e-banking)**	105	**Shopping robots (shopbots shopping agents)**	115
Cybermediation (electronic intermediation)	126	**Electronic retailing (e-tailing)**	83	**Shopping portals**	115
Direct marketing	88	**Hypermediation**	126	**Virtual (pure-play) e-tailers**	90

QUESTIONS FOR DISCUSSION

1. What are Amazon.com's critical success factors? Is its decision not to limit its sales to books, music, and movies, but to offer a much broader selection of items, a good marketing strategy? With the broader selection, do you think the company will dilute its brand or extend the value proposition to its customers? (Read Bayers 2002.)
2. Compare the major e-tail business models.
3. Will direct marketing of automobiles be a successful strategy? How should the dealers' inventory and the automakers' inventory and manufacturing scheduling be coordinated to meet a specific order with a quick due date?
4. Discuss the advantages of established click-and-mortar companies such as Wal-Mart over pure-play e-tailers such as Amazon.com. What are the disadvantages of click-and-brick retailers as compared with pure-play e-tailers?
5. Discuss the advantages of an online partnership such as that between Amazon.com and Toys"R"Us. Are there any disadvantages?
6. Discuss the advantages of shopping aids to the consumer. Should a vendor provide a comparison tool on its site that will show that a competitor is cheaper? Why or why not?
7. Discuss the advantages of a specialized e-tailer, such as dogtoys.com. Can such a store survive in the physical world? Why or why not?
8. Discuss the benefits of build-to-order to buyers and sellers. Are there any disadvantages?
9. Why are online travel services a popular Internet application? Why do so many Web sites provide free travel information?
10. Compare the advantages and disadvantages of online stock trading with off-line trading.

11. It is said that the service Zuji.com provides to travel agents will lead to their reintermediation. Discuss.
12. Intelligent agents read resumes that are posted online and forward them to potential employers without the knowledge of the candidates. What are the benefits of this use of intelligent agents? Do they violate the privacy of job seekers?
13. Online employment services make it easy to change jobs; therefore, turnover rates may increase. This could result in total higher costs for employers because of increased costs for recruiting and training new employees and the need to pay higher salaries and wages to attract or keep employees. What can companies do to ease this problem?
14. How can brokerage houses offer very low commissions for online stock purchases (as low as $4 per trade, with some even offering no commission for certain trades)? Why would they choose to offer such low commissions? Over the long run, do you expect commissions to increase, stay the same, or continue to decrease? Why?
15. Explain what is meant by the statement, "Intermediaries will become knowledge providers rather than transaction providers."
16. Compare the advantages and disadvantages of distributing digitizable products electronically versus physically.
17. How can a sports-related merchant target fantasy game players?

INTERNET EXERCISES

1. Visit the following e-grocers: **stopandshop.com**, **freshdirect.com**, **albertson.com**, and **netgrocer.com**. Compare the products and services offered by the online companies and evaluate their chances for success. Why do you think "unattended delivery" e-grocers such as Shoplink.com failed?
2. Many consumer portals offer advice and ratings of products or e-tailers. Identify and examine two separate general-consumer portals that look at other sites and compare prices or other purchase criteria. Try to find and compare prices for a digital camera, a microwave oven, and an MP3 player. Visit **clusty.com**. How can this site help you in your shopping? Summarize your experience. Comment on the strong and weak points of such shopping tools.
3. Design a trip to Kerala, India (use **stayfinder.com** to start). Find accommodations, restaurants, health clubs, festival information, and art. Arrange a tour for two people for seven days. How much will it cost?
4. Almost all car manufacturers allow consumers to configure their cars online. Visit a major automaker's Web site and configure a car of your choice (e.g., **jaguar.com**). Also visit one electronic intermediary (e.g., **autobytel.com**). After you decide what car you want, examine the payment options and figure your monthly payments. Print your results. How does this process compare with visiting an auto dealer? Do you think you found a better price online? Would you consider buying a car this way?
5. Visit **amazon.com** and identify at least three specific elements of its personalization and customization features. Browse specific books on one particular subject, leave the site, and then go back and revisit the site. What do you see? Are these features likely to encourage you to purchase more books in the future from Amazon.com? Check the 1-Click feature and other shopping aids provided. List the features and discuss how they may lead to increased sales.
6. Use a statistics source (e.g., **shop.org**, **emarketer.com**, or **clickz.com/stats/**) and look for recent statistics about the growth of Internet-based consumer-oriented EC in your country and in three other countries. Where is the greatest growth occurring? Which countries have the largest total e-tail sales? Which countries have the highest per-capita participation (i.e., "penetration rate")? What are the forecasts for continued growth in the coming years?
7. Visit **landsend.com** and prepare a customized order for a piece of clothing. Describe the process. Do you think this will result in better-fitting clothing? Do you think this personalization feature will lead to greater sales volume for Lands' End?
8. Make your resume accessible to millions of people. Consult **asktheheadhunter.com** or **careerbuilder.com** for help in rewriting your resume. See **jobweb.com** for ideas about planning your career. Get prepared for a job interview. Also, use the Web to determine what salary you can get in the city of your choice in the United States.
9. Visit **homeowner.com**, **decisionaide.com**, or a similar site and compute the monthly mortgage payment on a 30-year loan at 7.5 percent fixed interest. Also check current interest rates. Estimate your closing costs on a $200,000 loan. Compare the monthly payments of the fixed rate with that of an adjustable rate for the first year. Finally, compute your total payments if you take the loan for 15 years at the going rate. Compare it with a 30-year mortgage. Comment on the difference.

10. Access the Virtual Trader game at **virtualtrader.co.uk** and register for the Internet stock game. You will be bankrolled with £100,000 in a trading account every month. You also can play investment games at **investorsleague.com**, **fantasystockmarket.com**, and **etrade.com**.
11. Enter **etrade.com** and **boom.com** and find out how you can trade stocks in countries other than the one you live in. Prepare a report based on your findings.
12. Enter **google.com** and **yahoo.com**. Find information about the virus Download.Ject. What does it endanger home banking and stock trading?
13. Examine the consolidated billing process. Start with **e-billingonline.com** and **intuit.com**. Identify other consolidators in the field. What standard capabilities do they all offer? What capabilities are unique to certain sites?
14. Compare the price of a Sony digital camera at **shopping.com**, **mysimon.com**, **bottomdollar.com**, **bizrate.com**, and **pricescan.com**. Which site locates the best deal? Where do you get the best information?
15. Enter **dice.com** and see how it can assist technically oriented job seekers and employers. Compare the services offered with those at **monster.com**.

TEAM ASSIGNMENTS AND ROLE PLAYING

1. Each team will investigate the services of two online car selling sites from the following list (or other sites). When teams have finished, they should bring their research together and discuss their findings.
   a. Buying new cars through an intermediary (**autobytel.com**, **carsdirect.com**, **autoweb.com**, or **amazon.com**)
   b. Buying used cars (**autotrader.com**)
   c. Buying used cars by auto dealers (**manheim.com**)
   d. Automobile ratings sites (**carsdirect.com**, and **fueleconomy.gov**)
   e. Car-buying portals (**thecarportal.com** and **cars.com**)
   f. Buying antique cars (**classiccars.com** and **antiquecars.com**)
2. Each team will represent a broker-based area (e.g., real estate, insurance, stocks, job finding). Each team will find a new development that has occurred in the assigned area over the most recent three months. Look for the site vendor's announcement and search for more information on the development with **google.com** or another search engine. Examine the business news at **bloomberg.com**. After completing your research, as a team, prepare a report on disintermediation in your assigned area.
3. You can buy books from hundreds of book stores. Have each team examine the prices of the same books at **amazon.com**, **buy.com**, **overstock.com**, or another site. Compare the sites' customer support services. Also look at technical book stores, textbook stores, or other specialty stores (each team should look at one type).
4. Each team will examine fantasy games at various sites. Each team should examine the type of game, the rules, and the cost. Play at least one time. Each team should write a report based on its experiences.
5. Team members should examine online and off-line record stores. Assess the competition between the two and assess the impact of online music sources on traditional record stores.

Real-World Case

WAL-MART GOES ONLINE

Wal-Mart is the largest retailer in the world with over 2,971 stores in the United States, about 1,355 stores in other countries, and 538 SAM'S Clubs. Altogether, Wal-Mart employs 1.5 million people. Its standard company cheer ends with, "Who's number one? The customer." Wal-Mart has established itself as a master of the retail process by streamlining its supply chain process and undercutting competitors with low prices. However, one problem with its strategy for growing online sales is the demographics of its primary customer base. Wal-Mart's target demographic is households with $25,000 in annual income, whereas the median income of online consumers is perhaps $60,000.

Despite these demographics, online sales (primarily in music, travel, and electronics) through *walmart.com* already account for about 10 percent of Wal-Mart's U.S. sales. Its long-time chief rival, Kmart, Inc., tried to attract its demographic audience to its Web site (*kmart.com*) by offering free Internet access. This appealed to its cost-conscious, lower-income constituency, and also provided the opportunity for those customers to access the site to conduct purchases. However, this move decreased company profits in the short run and was one of the factors that led Kmart to file for bankruptcy in 2002.

Wal-Mart also has concerns about cannibalizing its in-store sales. Its 2001 alliance with AOL is designed to provide cobranded $9.94/month Internet access to dwellers in both very rural and very urban areas, where there are no Wal-Mart stores nearby. The intent is to lure new market segments and thus cancel the effect of cannibalization. Ultimately, a hybrid e-tailer that can offer a combination of huge selection with the click-and-mortar advantages of nearby stores (e.g., merchandise pickup or returns) may prove to be the 800-pound gorilla of online consumer sales.

In 2002, *walmart.com* matured, offering order status and tracking, a help desk, a clear return policy and mechanisms, a store locator, and information on special sales and liquidations. Also, community services such as photo sharing are provided.

Wal-Mart only offers some of its merchandise online, but the selection is increasing, including items not available in some or all stores (e.g., spas, mattresses). In 2004, Wal-Mart started selling songs online for 88 cents each, competing with Apple's iTune. Inexpensive items (e.g., those that sell for less than $5) are not available online. Also in 2004, during a four-day Thanksgiving special, Wal-Mart began to court more affluent shoppers with new and more expensive items available only online. Products included cashmere sweaters and shiatsu massage chairs. The Web site averaged 8 million visitors each week prior to the promotion. In November 2004, the number of visitors to the Web site increased by approximately 11 percent over the 2003 holiday traffic (McGann 2004).

As of 2005, Wal-Mart has added many new products to its online catalog. International customers can buy Wal-Mart products directly from Wal-Mart (if shipping is available) or from affiliate sites. For example, see ASDA (*asda.co.uk*), a Wal-Mart owned U.K. company.

Sources: Maguire (2002), Bhatnagar (2004), and *walmart.com* (2002–2004).

Questions

1. Compare *walmart.com* with *amazon.com*. What features do the sites have in common? Which are unique to Wal-Mart.com? To Amazon.com?
2. Will Wal-Mart become the dominant e-tailer in the world, replacing Amazon.com, or will Amazon.com dominate Wal-Mart online? What factors would contribute to Wal-Mart's success in the online marketplace? What factors would detract from its ability to dominate online sales the way it has been able to dominate physical retail sales in many markets?
3. Check the shopping aids offered at *walmart.com*. Compare them with those at *amazon.com*.
4. What online services can be purchased on *walmart.com*?
5. Compare buying a song from *walmart.com* versus buying it from Apple.
6. *Walmart.com* sells movies online for a monthly fee. How do similar sellers compare?
7. Visit *walmart.com*, *target.com*, *marksandspencer.com*, and *sears.com*. Identify the common features of their online marketing and at least one unique feature evident at each site. Do these sites have to distinguish themselves primarily in terms of price, product selection, or Web site features?
8. Investigate the options for international customers on the Wal-Mart Web site.

REFERENCES

Adams, J. "Trading: New Tools for CyberTraders." *Bank Technology News*, March 1, 2004.

Agrawal, M., T. V. Kumaresh, and G. A. Mercer. "The False Promise of Mass Customization." *The McKinsey Quarterly* no. 3 (2001).

Agrawal, V., J. M. Manyika, and J. E. Richards "Matching People and Jobs." *The McKinsey Quarterly*, Special Edition: Organization (2003).

AIS Healthcare. "More E-Prescribing Programs Begin, Partly in Response to Medicare Law." March 12, 2004. **aishealth.com/DrugCosts/DCMREPrescribingBegins.html** (accessed November 2004).

Anderson, M. "Banking-on-the-Net." *Sacramento Business Journal* 21, no. 21, July 30, 2004.

Baker, W. L., et al. "Getting Prices Right on the Web." *The McKinsey Quarterly* no. 2 (2001).

Bandyopadhyay, S., et al. "A Critical Review of Pricing Strategies for Online Business Models." *Quarterly Journal of Electronic Commerce* 2, no. 1 (2001).

Bank of America. **bankofamerica.com** (accessed November 2004).

Bauer, C., and J. Colgan. "The Internet as a Driver for Unbundling: A Transaction Perspective from the Stockbroking Industry." *Electronic Markets* 12, no. 2 (2002).

Bayers, C. "The Last Laugh (of Amazon's CEO)." *Business 2.0*, September 2002.

BBC News. "South Korea Probes Online Dealing Fraud." August 26, 2002. news.bbc.co.uk/2/hi/business/2217584.stm (accessed April 2003).

Berghel, H. "Predatory Disintermediation." *Communications of the ACM* 43, no. 5 (2000).

Bergstein, B. "Study Find Major Privacy Holes in Job-Search Web Sites." *The Maui News*, November 12, 2003.

Berkowitz, D. "GuruNet Turns Paid Search on its Noggin." *eMarketer*, March 23, 2004.

Bhatnagar, P. "Walmart.com's Going Upscale." CNNMoney, November 18, 2004. money.cnn.com/2004/11/18/news/fortune500/walmart_online/ (accessed November 2004).

Bloch, M., and A. Segev. "The Impact of Electronic Commerce on the Travel Industry." *Proceedings 30th Annual HICSS*, Maui, Hawaii, January 1997.

Bonne, J. "Life's Not the Same without the Net." MSNBC News, August 11, 2004. msnbc.msn.com/id/5664826/ (accessed November 2004).

Borland, J. "Napster CEO Touts New Swapping Service." *News.com*, January 9, 2002. news.com.com/2100-1023-806886.html (accessed April 2003).

Brice, T., and M. Waung. "Web Site Recruitment Characteristics: America's Best Versus America's Biggest." *SAM Advanced Management Journal* 67, no. 1 (2002).

Bughin, J. "'Attack or Convert?': Early Evidence from European On-line Banking." *Omega*, February 2004.

Calem, R. E. "Deal Clinchers: How to Get from Brochureware to Online Business." *Industry Standard,* February 14, 2000.

Callaghan, D. "Pharmacists Tap Net." *eWeek*, September 20, 2004.

Camacho, D., D. Borrajo, and J. M. Molina. "Intelligent Travel Planning: A MultiAgent Planning System to Solve Web Problems in the e-Tourism Domain." *Autonomous Agents and Multi-Agent Systems* no. 4 (2001).

Carr, N. G. "Hypermediation: Commerce as Clickstream." *Harvard Business Review* (January–February 2000).

Carton, W., and C. Locke. *Dot.Bomb*. New York: McGraw-Hill, 2001.

Castex, S. "Trends and News." *Promotional Products Business*, July 2002. ppai.org/Publications/PPB/Article.asp?NewsID=1436 (accessed September 2004).

Celent. "Banks Increase Their Focus on Small Businesses." Celent.com, November 3, 2004. celent.com/PressReleases/20041103/SmallBusVendors.htm (accessed November 2004).

CNN. "Study: Few Buy Drugs Online." CNN.com, October 11, 2004. cnn.com/2004/HEALTH/10/11/internet.drugs.ap/ (no longer available online).

Cox, B., and W. Koelzer. *Internet Marketing*, Upper Saddle River, NJ: Prentice Hall, 2004.

Cropper, C. M. "Choosing An Online Broker; Most—But Not All—Brokerage Web Sites Now Slap on a Slew of Fees." *Business Week*, May 17, 2004.

Cude, B. J., and M. A. Morganosky. "Online Grocery Shopping: An Analysis of Current Opportunities and Future Potential." *Consumer Interests* 46 (2000). consumerinterests.org/files/public/online.PDF (accessed February 2005).

Daisey, M. *21 Dog Years: Doing Time @ Amazon.com*. New York: Free Press, 2002.

Dandapani, K. "Success and Failures in Web-Based Financial Services." *Communications of the ACM* (May 2004).

Dayal, S., H. Landesberg, and M. Zeisser. "Building Digital Brands." *The McKinsey Quarterly* no. 2 (2000).

Dernovsek, D. "The Move to E-payments." *Credit Union Magazine*, August 2004.

Dewan, R., and A. Seidmann (Eds.). "Current Issues in E-Banking." *Communications of the ACM* (June 2001).

Diorio, S. *Beyond "e."* New York: McGraw-Hill, 2002.

Dixon, P. *Job Searching Online for Dummies*. Foster City, CA: IDG Books, 2001.

Dymond, C. "High-Tech Spin on Sales." *Financial Times*, June 29–30, 2002.

e-Consultancy. "Retail Financial Services Online—Top Issues, Trends, Resources." White paper, 2003.

The Economist. "Click to Fly." *The Economist*, May 13, 2004.

ePaynews.com. "Online Retail to See CAGR of 17 Per Cent to 2008." Baltimore Sun, Feb 19 2004 cardinalcommerce.com/articles/March_2004/Online%20Retail%20To%20See%20CAGR%20Of%2017%20Per%20Cent%20To%202008.htm (accessed February 2005).

Ericson, J. "Name Your Price." *Line56*, January 19, 2004.

Ernst, S., and N. H. Hooker. "E-Grocery: Emerging Trend or Just Another Case Study?" The Ohio State University Outlook Policy Program, 2003. www-agecon.ag.ohio-state.edu/programs/e-agbiz/pagepapersandpres/papers_presentations/2003outlookegrocery.pdf (accessed August 2004).

Fong, M. "Don't Tell the Kids: Computer Games Can Make You Rich." *The Wall Street Journal*, May 21, 2004.

Fox, S. "Online Banking 2005." *PEW/Internet*, February 9, 2005. pewinternet.org/PPF/12/149/report_display.asp (accessed February 2005).

Freedman, J. "Groceries with a Click." *Money*, July 2004.

Gapper, J. "Why Nobody Sells the Car We Really Want." *Financial Times*, June 29, 2004.

Giaglis, G. M., S. Klein, and R. M. O'Keefe. "Disintermediation, Reintermediation, or Cybermediation." *Proceedings of the 12th International EC Conference,* Bled, Slovenia, June 1999.

Gilbert, J., et al. *Online Investment Bible*. Berkeley, CA: Hungry Minds, Inc., 2000.

Global Finance. "World's Best Foreign Exchange Banks 2004." *Global Finance*, March 2004.

Gosling, P. *Changing Money: How the Digital Age Is Transforming Financial Services*. Dulles, VA: Capital Books, Inc., 2000.

Grant, P., and M. Rich. "Goldman's Real-Estate Web Site Bypasses Traditional Brokers." *The Asia Wall Street Journal*, April 14–15, 2000.

Harrington, A. "Can Anyone Build a Better Monster?" *Fortune*, May 13, 2002.

Helft, M. "What a Long, Strange Trip It's Been for Webvan." *The Industry Standard*, July 23, 2001.

Hire.com. "Southern Company." *Hire.com Case Study*, 2005. **hire.com/clients/casestudies/southern.shtml** (accessed February 2005).

Internetretailer.com. "Office Depot's web sales grew 19.2% in 2004." *Internetretailer.com*, February 10, 2005. **internetretailer.com/dailyNews.asp?id=14109** (accessed February 2005).

ITfacts.biz. "Two-Thirds of Small Business Prefer Online Banking to Offline." **itfacts.biz/index.php?id=P1372** (accessed February 2005).

jaguar.com (accessed October 2004).

Johnson, C. A., et al. *U.S. eCommerce Overview: 2004 to 2010*. Cambridge, MA: Forrester Research, August 2, 2004.

Joo, J. "A Business Model and Its Development Strategies for Electronic Tourism Markets." *Information System Management* (Summer 2002).

Jupiter Research. "Jupiter Consumer Survey." September 30, 2002. **jupiterresearch.com/jupres_onlineshopper. html** (accessed April 2003). Note: No longer available online.

Kaplan, P. J. *The F'd Companies: Spectacular Dot.Com Flameouts*. New York: Simon & Schuster, 2002.

Karpinski, R. "E-Business Risk Worth Taking on Path to Success." *BtoBonline*, August 28, 2000.

Kauffman, R., M. Subramani, and C. A. Wood. "Analyzing Information Intermediaries in Electronic Brokerage." *Proceedings of the Thirty-Third HICSS*, Maui, Hawaii, January 2000.

Keh, H., and E. Shieh. "Online Grocery Retailing: Success Factors and Potential Pitfalls." *Business Horizons*, July–August 2001.

Kruger, J. Interview by Merrill Warkentin, September 13, 2000.

Lacy, S. "Will Electronics Burn Out PC Makers?" *Businessweek.com*, September 2004. **businessweek.com/technology/content/sep2004/tc20040923_9691_tc024.htm** (accessed February 2005).

Lands' End. *landsend.com* (accessed October 2002 and October 2004).

Lawrence, R. B., B. Zank, G. M. Jennings, and D. F. Stading, "Alternative Channels of Distribution E-Commerce Strategies for Industrial Manufacturers." *Production and Inventory Management Journal* (Third/ Fourth Quarter 2001).

Lee, M. K. O., and C. M. K. Cheung. "Internet Retailing Adoption by Small-to-Medium Sized Enterprises (SMEs): A Multiple-Case Study." *Information Systems Frontiers* (2004).

Lee, S. C., and Brandyberry, A. A. "The E-tailer's Dilemma." *ACM SIGMIS Database* (June 2003).

MacSweeney, G. "Dual Strategy." *Insurance and Technology*, July 2000.

Maguire, J. "Case Study: Walmart.com." *Internet.com*, November 15, 2002. **ecommerce.internet.com/news/insights/trends/article/0,,10417_1501651,00.html** (no longer available online).

Mallat, N., M. Rossi, and V. K. Tuunainen. "Mobile banking services." *Communications of the ACM* (May 2004).

McGann, R. "Online Retail Traffic Surges on Thanksgiving Day and Black Friday." Clickz.com, November 29, 2004. **clickz.com/stats/sectors/retailing/article.php/3441171** (accessed February 2005).

McNeill, L. "The Net's Most Profitable B2C Business Model?" *e-strategy online newsletter*, November–December, 2002.

Milidiu, R. L., T. Melcop, F. dos S. Liporace, and C. J. Pereira de Lucena. "SIMPLE—a Multi-Agent System for Simultaneous and Related Auctions." *Proceedings of the IEEE/WIC International Conference on Intelligent Agent Technology 2003*, Beijing, China, October 13–16, 2003.

Mullaney, T. J. "E-Biz Strikes Again." *Business Week*, May 10, 2004.

Mulrean, J. "How Shopping Bots Really Work." *MSN Money*. **moneycentral.msn.com/content/Savinganddebt/Finddealsonline/P36484.asp** (accessed August 2004).

Parks, L. "Making Sure the Price Is Right." *Stores*, August 2004.

Pascoe, J. "Put Your Money Where Your Mouse Is." *Smart Computing in Plain English*, March 2004.

Patsuris, P. "Music Chains Raise the Volume on Downloads." *Forbes.com*, January 27, 2003. **forbes.com/2003/01/27/cx_pp_0127music.html** (accessed February 2005).

Peffers, K., and V. K. Tunnainen. "Expectations and Impacts of a Global Information System: The Case of a Global Bank from Hong Kong." *Journal of Global Information Technology Management* 1, no. 4 (1998).

Pew Internet and American Life Project. "Online Job Hunting: A Pew Internet Project Data Memo." July 17, 2002. **pewinternet.org/releases/release.asp?id=46** (accessed April 2003).

Punakivi, M., and T. Saranen. "Identifying the Success Factors in e-Grocery Home Delivery." *International Journal of Retail and Distribution Management* 20, no. 4 (2001).

Rafter, M. V. "Trust or Bust?" *Industry Standard*, March 6, 2000.

RealSEO.com. "Sports Can Attract Sales to a Website." *RealSEO.com*, July 29, 2004. **realseo.com/archives/000473.html** (accessed February 2005).

Reda, S. "Online Retail Grows Up." *Stores*, February 2002a.

Reda, S. "1-800-Flowers.com and AT&T Cultivate Relationship Rooted in Common Business Objectives." *Stores*, October 2002b.

Reda, S. "At Lands' End, E-Commerce Pioneer Aim to Humanize Online Shopping." *Stores*, November 2002c.

Reda, S. "It Clicks! Sales and Profitability Up for Online Retailers." *Stores*, July 2004.

Retail Forward. "Multichannel Retailers Gain Ground Among Top 50 e-Retailers, Retail Forward Study Reports." Retailforward.com, July 2002. retailforward.com/freecontent/pressreleases/press48.asp (accessed September 2004).

Rich, M. "Your Reservation Has Been Cancelled." *Wall Street Journal Europe*, June 14–16, 2002.

Rickards, G. "What's All This About Online Banking?" *MsMoney.com*. msmoney.com/mm/banking/articles/about_online_banking.htm (accessed November 2004).

Robb, D. "Career Portals Boost Online Recruiting." SHRM Online, April 2004. shrm.org/hrmagazine/articles/0404/0404robb.asp#rg (accessed February 2005).

Sales, R. "Electronic FX: Reality or Just a Smoke Screen?" *Wall Street and Technology*, April 2002, 16–17.

Sandoval, G. "Amazon: How Big Can It Get?" *CNET News.com*, June 25, 2002. news.com.com/2100-1017-823319.html (accessed September 2004).

Schwartz, E. "Amazon, Toys R Us in E-Commerce Tie-Up." *InfoWorld* 22 (August 14, 2000).

Shop.org. "Statistics: US Online Shoppers." Pew Internet, October 2004. shop.org/learn/stats_usshop_general.asp (accessed February 2005).

Simison, R. L. "GM Retools to Sell Custom Cars Online." *Wall Street Journal*, February 22, 2000.

Southard, P., and K. Siau. "A Survey of Online E-Banking Retail Initiatives." *Communications of the ACM* (October 2004).

Stanford, M. "Mortgage Banking: Internet and Integration Are Key." *IEEE IT Professional* 4, no. 2 (2002).

Standing, C., and T. Vasudavan. "The Impact of Electronic Commerce on the Travel Agency Sector." *Journal of Information Technology Cases and Applications* 3, no. 1 (2001).

Steinert-Therlkeld, T. "GroceryWorks: The Low Touch Alternative." *Interactive Week*, January 31, 2000.

Taylor, D., and A. D. Terhune. *Doing E-Business*. New York: John Wiley & Sons, 2002.

Tessler, F. N. "Online Banking Made Easy." *Macworld* 21, no. 8 (August 2004).

Tyson, E. *Personal Finance for Dummies*, 4th ed. New York: John Wiley and Sons, 2003.

U.S. Census Bureau, Economics and Statistics Administration. "U.S. Department of Commerce News." Revised February 24, 2003. census.gov/mrts/www/current.html (accessed April 2003).

Van der Heijden, J. G. M. "The Changing Value of Travel Agents in Tourism Networks: Towards a Network Design Perspective." In Stefan Klein, et al. (Eds.), *Information and Communication Technologies in Tourism*, pages 151–159. New York: Springer-Verlag, 1996.

Vandermerwe, S. "The Electronic 'Go-Between Service Provider': A New Middle Role Taking Center." *European Management Journal* (December 1999).

Verma, R., Z. Iqbal, and G. Plaschka. "Understanding Choices in E-Financial Services." *California Management Review* (Summer 2004).

Von Hoffman, C. "For Better or for Worse." *CIO Magazine*, April 6, 2001. cio.com/archive/060101/better.htm (accessed February 2005).

Wal-Mart. walmart.com (accessed 2002–2003).

Wang, F., N. Archer, and M. Head. "E-Tailing: An Analysis of Web Impacts on the Retail Market." *Journal of Business Strategies* 19, no. 1 (2002).

Warkentin, M., and A. Bajaj. "The On-Demand Delivery Services Model for E-Commerce." In A. Gangopadhyay (Ed.), *Managing Business with Electronic Commerce: Issues and Trends*. Hershey, PA: Idea Group Publishing, 2001.

Yahoo! Directory. dir.yahoo.com (accessed February 2005).

Yamada, K. "Let's Make a Deal." *Line56.com*, June 01, 2004. line56.com/articles/default.asp?ArticleID=5761 (accessed August 2004).

Yao, J. T. "Ecommerce Adoption of Insurance Companies in New Zealand." *Journal of Electronic Commerce Research* 5, no. 1 (2004).

CHAPTER 4

CONSUMER BEHAVIOR, MARKET RESEARCH, AND ADVERTISEMENT

Learning Objectives

Upon completion of this chapter, you will be able to:

1. Describe the factors that influence consumer behavior online.
2. Understand the decision-making process of consumer purchasing online.
3. Describe how companies are building one-to-one relationships with customers.
4. Explain how personalization is accomplished online.
5. Discuss the issues of e-loyalty and e-trust in EC.
6. Describe consumer market research in EC.
7. Describe Internet marketing in B2B, including organizational buyer behavior.
8. Describe the objectives of Web advertising and its characteristics.
9. Describe the major advertising methods used on the Web.
10. Describe various online advertising strategies and types of promotions.
11. Describe permission marketing, ad management, localization, and other advertising-related issues.
12. Understand the role of intelligent agents in consumer issues and advertising applications.

Content

RITCHEY DESIGN LEARNS ABOUT CUSTOMERS

The Problem

Ritchey Design, Inc., of Redwood City, California, is a relatively small designer and manufacturer of mountain-bike components. The company sells its products to distributors and/or retailers, who then sell them to individual consumers. The company opened a Web site in 1995 (*ritcheylogic.com*), but like so many companies' Web sites, Ritchey's was more a status symbol than a business tool. Most of the site's visitors came to get information on Team Ritchey (now Ritchey Yahoo! Team), the company's world-class mountain-bike team, or to find out where Ritchey products were sold, but that was where the site's usefulness ended. It did not give customers all the information they wanted nor did it enable the company to gain insight into its customers' wants and needs.

The Solution

In late 1995, Philip Ellinwood, Ritchey's chief operating officer and IS director, decided to rework the Web site so that the company could hear from its customers directly. First, Ellinwood set up customer surveys on the site. To induce visitors to participate, the company offers visitors who answer the surveys a chance to win free Ritchey products. Visitors are asked to enter their names and addresses and then to answer questions about the company's products.

A special software program, Web Trader, automatically organizes and saves the answers in a database. The information is later used to help make marketing and advertising decisions. Ellinwood can easily change the questions to learn customers' opinions about any of about 15 new products Ritchey develops each year. In the past, the company knew little about how consumers might react to a new product until it was in the stores. Ellinwood says, "The process could save us as much as $100,000 a year on product development."

To educate retailers and consumers about the technological advantages of Ritchey's high-end components over competitors' parts, Ellinwood created an electronic catalog, accessible through the Web site. Visitors can browse through the product catalog, which includes detailed descriptions and graphics of Ritchey's products.

The Results

As of this writing, consumers can purchase bikes, parts, accessories, and team items such as T-shirts, bags, water bottles, and other gear directly from the Ritchey Web site (*ritcheylogic.com*). In addition, dealers can place orders on the site, and they can learn about new products quickly, so they no longer push only those products with which they are most familiar. The site is basically used in B2C EC for communicating with customers, conducting market research (offering incentives to customers for responding to surveys from time to time), and delivering advertising, which are basic activities in Internet marketing (Catalano and Smith 2001).

Source: Compiled from *ritcheylogic.com* (accessed 2000–2004). Adapted with permission.

WHAT WE CAN LEARN . . .

This case illustrates the benefits a company can derive from changing its Web site from a passive one (just having a *presence* on the Web) to one with interactivity. Ritchey can now hear from its customers directly, even though it also uses intermediaries for its sales. The new interactive Web site allows the company to learn more about its customers, educate customers, and conduct market research. The company also uses the site for customer service. In addition, the company uses the site for advertising (Sections 4.6 through 4.9), and it is a companion site for collaboration with its business partners (Chapter 7). These topics are the subjects of this chapter.

4.1 LEARNING ABOUT CONSUMER BEHAVIOR ONLINE

Companies today operate in an increasingly competitive environment. Therefore, they treat customers like royalty as they try to lure them to buy their goods and services. Finding and retaining customers is a major critical success factor for most businesses both off-line and online. One of the keys to building effective customer relationships is an understanding of consumer behavior online.

A MODEL OF CONSUMER BEHAVIOR ONLINE

For decades, market researchers have tried to understand consumer behavior, and they have summarized their findings in various models. The purpose of a consumer behavior model is to help vendors understand how a consumer makes a purchasing decision. If a firm understands the decision process, it may be able to influence the buyer's decision, for example, through advertising or special promotions.

Exhibit 4.1 shows the basics of a consumer behavior model in the EC environment. The model is composed of the following parts:

- *Independent* (or uncontrollable) *variables,* which are shown at the top of Exhibit 4.1, can be categorized as *personal characteristics* and *environmental characteristics.*
- *Intervening* or *moderating variables* are variables within the vendors' control. They are divided into *market stimuli* (on the left) and *EC systems* (at the bottom) in Exhibit 4.1.
- The *decision-making process,* which is shown in the center of the exhibit, is influenced by the independent and intervening variables. This process ends with the buyers' decisions (shown on the right) resulting from the decision-making process.
- The *dependent variables* describe types of decisions made by buyers (in the box at the right).

Exhibit 4.1 identifies some of the variables in each category. This chapter examines the following model-related issues: the decision process, seller–customer relationship building, and customer service. Discussions of other issues can be found in Internet marketing books, such as Cox and Koelzer (2004).

Before examining the consumer behavior model's variables, let's examine who the EC consumers are. Online consumers can be divided into two types: *individual consumers*, who get much of the media attention, and *organizational buyers*, who do most of the actual shopping in cyberspace in terms of dollar volume of sales. Organizational buyers include governments, private corporations, resellers, and public organizations. Purchases by organizational buyers are generally used to create other products (services) by adding value to the products. Also, organizational buyers may purchase products for resale without any further modifications. We will briefly discuss organizational purchasing in Section 4.5 and describe it in detail in Chapter 5 (e-procurement).

The Independent Variables

Two types of independent variables are distinguished: personal characteristics and environmental variables.

Personal Characteristics. Personal characteristics, which are shown in the top-left portion of Exhibit 4.1, refer to demographic factors, internal individual factors, and behavioral characteristics (Cheung et al. 2005). Several Web sites provide information on customer buying habits online (e.g., emarketer.com and comscore.com). The major demographics that such sites track are gender, age, marital status, educational level, ethnicity, occupation, and household income, which can be correlated with Internet usage and EC data. For example, higher education and/or income levels are associated with more online shopping. Exhibit 3.1 (page 84) provides the major sources and types of these and other Internet and EC statistics.

It is interesting to note that the more experience people have with Internet shopping, the more likely they are to spend more money online. We can learn from Internet statistics not only what people buy, but also why they *do not* buy. The two most-cited reasons for *not* making purchases are shipping charges (51 percent) and the difficulty in judging the quality of the product (44 percent). About 32 percent of users do not make purchases because they can-

EXHIBIT 4.1 **EC Consumer Behavior Model**

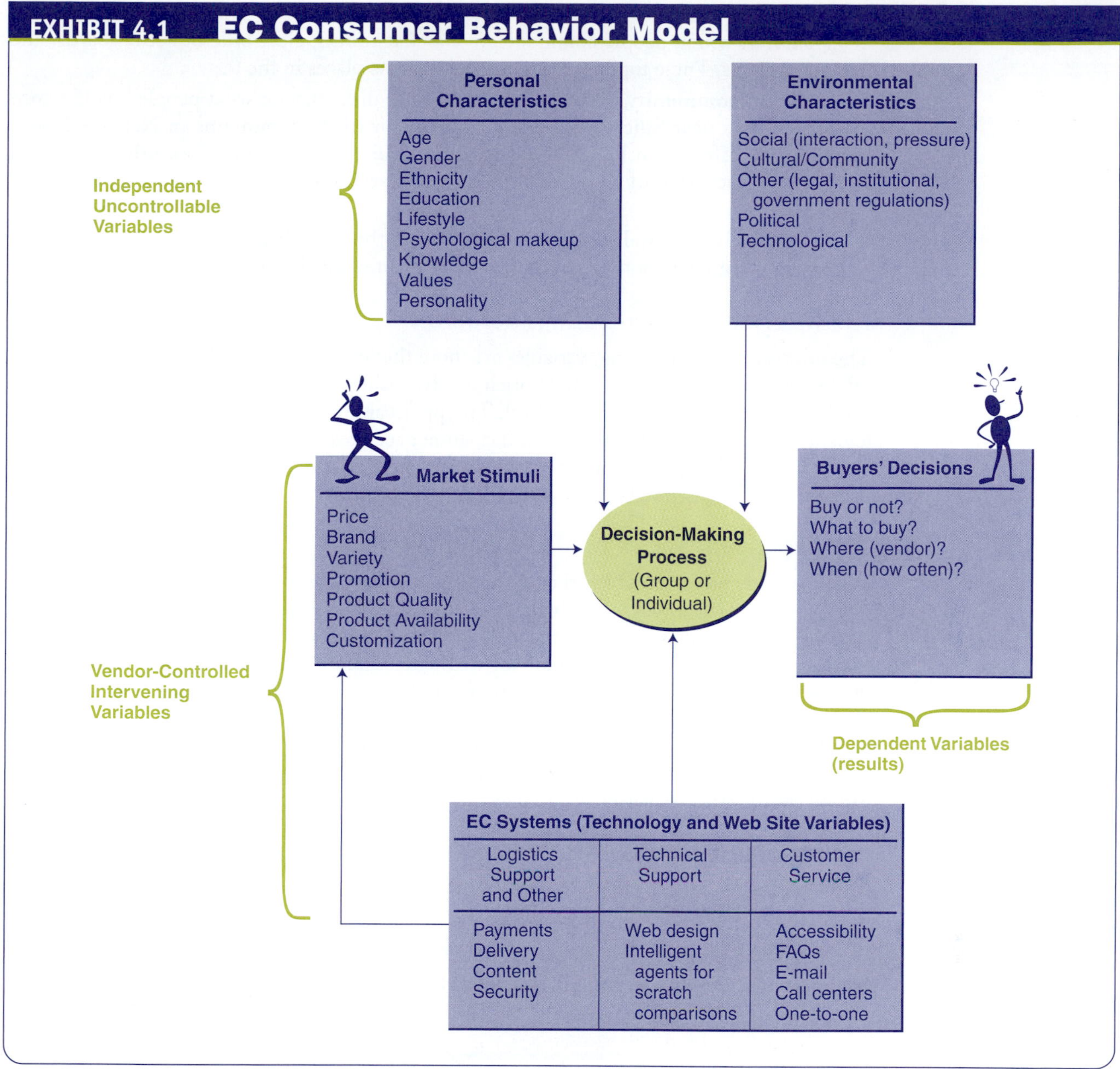

not return items easily. Twenty-four percent are worried about credit card safety. An additional 23 percent of users do not purchase online because they cannot ask questions; 16 percent say they do not buy when it takes too long to download the screen; 15 percent are concerned about delivery time; and 10 percent enjoy shopping off-line. However, only 1.9 percent of online consumers have actually had an unfavorable experience (the least-cited reason for not making more purchases on the Web). (Note: People were asked to cite the three most important reasons; thus, the answers total to more than 100 percent.) According to Forrester Research (Temkin 2002), psychological variables are another personal characteristic studied by marketers. Such variables include personality and lifestyle characteristics. These variables are briefly mentioned in several places throughout the text. The reader who is interested in the details of psychological variables in e-marketing should see Cheung et al. (2005) and Solomon (2004).

Environmental Variables. As shown in the box in the top-right portion of the figure, the *environmental variables* can be grouped into the following categories:

- **Social variables.** These variables play an important role in EC purchasing. People are influenced by family members, friends, coworkers, and "what's in fashion this year." Of special importance in EC are *Internet communities* (covered in Chapter 17) and *discussion groups*, in which people communicate via chat rooms, electronic bulletin boards, and newsgroups. These topics are discussed in various places in the text.

- **Cultural/community variables.** It makes a big difference in what people buy if a consumer lives near Silicon Valley in California or in the mountains in Nepal. Chinese shoppers differ from French shoppers, and rural shoppers differ from urban ones. For further discussion of the impact of cultural variables, see Nicholls et al. (2003) and Witkowski (2005).
- **Other environmental variables.** These include things such as the available information, government regulations, legal constraints, and situational factors.

The Intervening (Moderating) Variables

The intervening (moderating) variables are those that can be controlled by vendors. As in the off-line environment, these include pricing, advertising and promotions, and branding (the products themselves and their quality). The physical environment (e.g., display in stores), logistics support, technical support, and customer services also are important. Customer service is described in this chapter; the other intervening variables (e.g., logistics and technical support) will be described in various chapters of the book.

The Dependent Variables: The Buying Decisions

With the dependent variables, the customer is making several decisions, such as "to buy or not to buy?" "what to buy?" and "where, when, and how much to buy?" (see Bhatnagar et al. 2000). These decisions *depend* on the independent and intervening variables. The objective of learning about customers and conducting market research is to know enough so that the vendors who provide some of the market stimuli and/or control the EC systems can make decisions on the intervening variables.

The structure of the consumer behavior model in Exhibit 4.1 is a simplified version of what actually goes on in the decision-making process. In reality, consumer decision making can be complicated, especially when new products or procedures need to be purchased.

Section 4.1 ▶ REVIEW QUESTIONS

1. Describe the major components and structure of the consumer online purchasing behavior model.
2. List some major personal characteristics that influence consumer behavior.
3. List the major environmental variables of the purchasing environment.
4. List and describe the major vendor-controlled variables.

4.2 THE CONSUMER DECISION-MAKING PROCESS

Returning to the central part of Exhibit 4.1, where consumers make purchasing decisions, let's clarify the roles people play in the decision-making process. The major roles are as follows (Kotler and Armstrong 2004; Armstrong and Kotler 2005):

- **Initiator.** The person who first suggests or thinks of the idea of buying a particular product or service.
- **Influencer.** A person whose advice or view carries some weight in making a final purchasing decision.
- **Decider.** The person who ultimately makes a buying decision or any part of it—whether to buy, what to buy, how to buy, or where to buy.
- **Buyer.** The person who makes an actual purchase.
- **User.** The person who consumes or uses a product or service.

If one individual plays all of these roles, the marketer needs to understand and target that individual. When more than one individual plays these different roles, it becomes more difficult to properly target advertising and marketing efforts. How marketers deal with the issue of multiple people in decision-making roles is beyond the scope of this book.

Several models have been developed in an effort to describe the details of the decision-making process that lead up to and culminate in a purchase. These models provide a framework for learning about the process in order to predict, improve, or influence consumer decisions. Here we introduce three relevant models.

A GENERIC PURCHASING-DECISION MODEL

A general purchasing-decision model consists of five major phases (Kotler 2003). In each phase, we can distinguish several activities and, in some, one or more decisions. The five phases are (1) need identification, (2) information search, (3) evaluation of alternatives, (4) purchase and delivery, and (5) after-purchase evaluation. In addition, one should look at repurchase (see Cheung et al. 2003). Although these phases offer a general guide to the consumer decision-making process, one should not assume that every consumer's decision-making process will necessarily proceed in this order. In fact, some consumers may proceed to a point and then revert back to a previous phase or they may skip a phase altogether.

The first phase, *need identification*, occurs when a consumer is faced with an imbalance between the actual and the desired states of a need. A marketer's goal is to get the consumer to recognize such imbalance and then convince them that the product or service the seller offers will fill this gap.

After identifying the need, the consumer *searches for information* (phase 2) on the various alternatives available to satisfy the need. Here, we differentiate between two decisions: what product to buy (**product brokering**) and from whom to buy it (**merchant brokering**). These two decisions can be separate or combined. In the consumer's search for information, catalogs, advertising, promotions, and reference groups influence decision making. During this phase, online product search and comparison engines, such as can be found at shopping.com, buyersindex.com, and mysimon.com, can be very helpful.

product brokering
Deciding what product to buy.

merchant brokering
Deciding from whom (from what merchant) to buy a product.

The consumer's information search will eventually generate a smaller set of preferred alternatives. From this set, the would-be buyer will further *evaluate the alternatives* (phase 3) and, if possible, negotiate terms. In this phase, a consumer will use the collected information to develop a set of criteria. These criteria will help the consumer evaluate and compare alternatives. In phase 4, the consumer will make the *purchasing decision*, arrange payment and delivery, purchase warranties, and so on.

The final phase is a *postpurchase* phase (phase 5), which consists of customer service and evaluation of the usefulness of the product (e.g., "This product is really great!" or "We really received good service when we had problems").

In addition, repeat site visits and repeat purchases can be included in the model as decision activities.

A CUSTOMER DECISION MODEL IN WEB PURCHASING

The preceding generic purchasing-decision model was widely used in research on consumer-based EC (Cheung et al. 2003). O'Keefe and McEachern (1998) built a framework for a Web purchasing model. As shown in Exhibit 4.2, each of the phases of the purchasing model can be supported by both Consumer Decision Support System (CDSS) facilities and Internet and Web facilities. The CDSS facilities support the specific decisions in the process. Generic EC technologies provide the necessary mechanisms as well as enhance communication and collaboration. Specific implementation of this framework and explanation of some of the terms are provided throughout this chapter and the entire text.

Others have developed similar models. The point here is that the planner of B2C marketing needs to consider the Web purchasing models in order to better influence the customer's decision making (e.g., by effective one-to-one advertising and marketing).

ONLINE BUYER DECISION SUPPORT MODEL

Silverman et al. (2001) developed a model for a Web site that supports buyer decision making and searching. This model revises the generic model by describing the purchasing framework that is shown in Online Exhibit W4.1. The model is divided into three parts. The first is based on Miles et al. (2000), and it includes three stages of buyer behavior (see top of

EXHIBIT 4.2 Purchase Decision-Making Process and Support System

Steps in the Decision-Making Process	CDSS Support Facilities	Generic Internet and Web Support Facilities
Need recognition ↓	Agents and event notification	Banner advertising on Web sites URL on physical material Discussions in newsgroups
Information search ↓	Virtual catalogs Structured interaction and question/answer sessions Links to (and guidance on) external sources	Web directories and classifiers Internal search on Web site External search engines Focused directories and information brokers
Evaluation, negotiation, selection ↓	FAQs and other summaries Samples and trials Models that evaluate consumer behavior Pointers to and information about existing customers	Discussions in newsgroups Cross-site comparisons Generic models
Purchase, payment, and delivery ↓	Ordering of product or service Arrangement of delivery	Electronic cash and virtual banking Logistics providers and package tracking
After-purchase service and evaluation ↓	Customer support via e-mail and newsgroups	Discussions in newsgroups

Source: O'Keefe, R. M., and T. McEachern. "Web-Based Customer Decision Support System." *The Communications of the ACM*, March 1998. © 1998 ACM, Inc. Used with permission.

exhibit): identify and manage buying criteria, search for products and merchants, and compare alternatives. Below these activities are seven boxes with decision support system (DSS) design options (such as product representation), the options to support searching, and the options to compare alternatives.

The second part (on the right), which is based on Guttman et al. (1998), has three boxes: price, shipping, and finance. These become relevant when alternatives are compared. The third part, at the bottom of the exhibit, is composed of three boxes. The model demonstrates the flow of data and the decisions that support EC.

OTHER MODELS

Several other purchasing-decision models have been proposed. Some are referenced in the Online Research Appendix "Current EC Research." Of special interest is a model proposed by Chaudhury et al. (2001). In this model, the buying decision is influenced by how much time is available and the locale (space) where the purchasing is done. In this context, *space* is the equivalent to shelf space in a physical store—namely how well a product is presented online and where it is presented on the Web site. Space also can refer to whether products are sold via wireline or wireless devices. The model distinguishes four scenarios: "less time and more space," "more time and less space," "more time and more space," and "less time and less space." For example, the space on a small banner ad is more limited than the space on a large pop-up ad. For each scenario, the vendors can develop different Web sites.

Section 4.2 ▶ REVIEW QUESTIONS

1. List the roles people play in purchasing.
2. List the five stages in the generic purchasing-decision model.
3. Describe the Web-based purchasing-decision model.
4. Describe the structure of the online buyer decision support model.

4.3 ONE-TO-ONE MARKETING, LOYALTY, AND TRUST IN EC

One of the greatest benefits of EC is its ability to match products and services with individual consumers. Such a match is a part of **one-to-one marketing**, which treats each customer in a unique way to fit marketing and advertising with the customer's profile and needs. The ability of EC to match individuals with products/services and/or with advertising includes *personalization* or *customization* of products/services ("make it your way"). Let's first look at the one-to-one relationship in EC in general.

one-to-one marketing
Marketing that treats each customer in a unique way.

HOW ONE-TO-ONE RELATIONSHIPS ARE PRACTICED

Although some companies have had one-to-one marketing programs for years, it may be much more beneficial to institute a corporate-wide policy of building one-to-one relationships around the Web. This can be done in several ways. For example, Gartner Inc., an IT consulting company, proposed what it calls "the new marketing cycle of relationship building" (see Marcus 2001). This proposal, illustrated in Exhibit 4.3, views relationships as a two-way street: The process can start at any place in the cycle. Usually, though, it starts with "Customer receives marketing exposure" (at the top of the figure). The customer then decides how to respond to the marketing exposure (e.g., whether to buy the product online or off-line; if online, whether to buy as individual or to use group purchasing). When a sale is made, customer information is collected (lower-right corner) and then is placed in a database. Then, a customer's profile is developed, and the so-called *four P's* of marketing (product, place, price, and promotion) are generated on a one-to-one basis. Based on this individualized profile, appropriate advertisements are prepared that will hopefully lead to another purchase by the customer. Once a purchase is made, the detailed transaction is added to the database, and the cycle is repeated. All of this can, and should, be done in the Web environment.

One of the benefits of doing business over the Internet is that it enables companies to better communicate with customers and better understand customers' needs and buying habits. These improvements, in turn, enable companies to enhance and frequently customize their future marketing efforts. For example, Amazon.com can e-mail customers announcements of the availability of books in their areas of interest as soon as they are published; Expedia.com will ask consumers where they like to fly and then e-mail them information about special discounts to their desired destination.

Here we will address several key issues related to one-to-one marketing: personalization, collaborative filtering, customer loyalty, and trust. For details on these and other issues related

EXHIBIT 4.3 The New Marketing Model

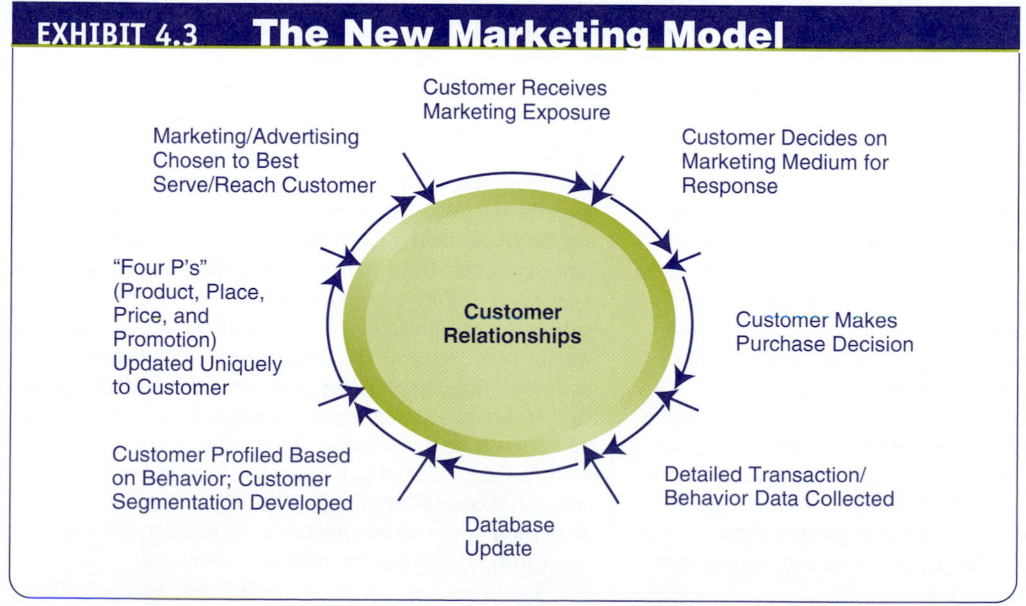

Source: Nelson, S. "The New Marketing Relationship Model," Gartner, Inc., July 22, 1996. © Gartner, Inc. Used with permission.

to implementing EC-based one-to-one marketing, see Berkley (2003) and Todor and Todor (2001). For discussion of how one-to-one marketing is related to CRM, see Chapter 13.

PERSONALIZATION

personalization
The matching of services, products, and advertising content with individual consumers.

user profile
The requirements, preferences, behaviors, and demographic traits of a particular customer.

cookie
A data file that is placed on a user's hard drive by a Web server, frequently without disclosure or the user's consent, that collects information about the user's activities at a site.

Personalization refers to the matching of services, products, and advertising content to individuals. According to a 2004 ChoiceStream survey (Greenspan 2004), surfers are willing to provide personal information in order to get personalized content and service. The matching process is based on what a company knows about the individual user. This knowledge is usually referred to as a **user profile**. The user profile defines customer preferences, behaviors, and demographics.

Profiles can be generated in several ways. The major strategies used to compile user profiles include the following:

- **Solicit information directly from the user.** This is usually done by asking the user to fill in a questionnaire or by conducting an interview with the user.
- **Observe what people are doing online.** A common way to observe what people are doing online is through use of a **cookie**—a data file that is stored on the user's hard drive, frequently without disclosure or the user's consent. Sent by a Web server over the Internet, the information stored will surface when the user's browser again accesses the specific Web server, and the cookie will collect information about the user's activities at the site (see cookiecentral.com). The use of cookies is one of the most controversial issues in EC, as discussed in Insights and Additions 4.1. Other tools such as spyware and Webbugs are described in Section 4.4. For an overview of personalization in EC, see Chan (2005).
- **Build from previous purchase patterns.** For example, Amazon.com builds customer profiles to recommend books, CDs, and other products, based on what customers have purchased before, rather than asking customers, using cookies, or doing market research.
- **Perform marketing research.** Firms can research the market using tools such as data mining, as is described in Online Appendix W4A.
- **Make inferences.** Infer from information provided by customers on other issues or by analyzing similar customers. (See collaborative filtering later in this section.)

Once a customer profile is constructed, a company matches the profile with a database of products, services, or contents. Manual matching is time-consuming and expensive; therefore, the matching process is usually done by software agents.

Insights and Additions 4.1 Cookies in E-Commerce

Are cookies bad or good? The answer is "both." When users revisit Amazon.com or other sites, they are greeted by their first name. How does Amazon.com know a user's identity? Through the use of cookies! Vendors can provide consumers with considerable personalized information if they use cookies that signal a consumer's return to a site. A variation of cookies is known as *e-sugging* ("SUG-ing," which means selling under the guise of research). For example, if a consumer visits several travel sites, he or she may get more and more unsolicited travel-related e-mails and pop-up ads.

Cookies can provide a wealth of information to marketers, which then can be used to target ads to consumers. Thus, marketers get higher rates of "click-throughs," and customers can view the most relevant information. Cookies can also prevent repetitive ads because vendors can arrange for a consumer not to see the same ad twice. Finally, advanced data mining companies, such as NCR and Sift, can analyze information in cookie files and better meet the customers' needs.

However, some people object to cookies because they do not like the idea that "someone" is watching their activity on the Internet. If a consumer does not like cookies, he or she can *disable* them in many cases. However, some consumers may want to keep the friendly cookies. For example, many sites recognize a person as a subscriber, so that they do not need to reregister. Netscape 6 and higher allows users to block third-party cookies. Internet Explorer (IE) 6.09 and higher also gives users control over third-party cookies. (Go to "Internet Options" under "Tools" and select "Private tab," click "Advanced," and put a check mark next to "Override automatic cookie handling." Then, direct the IE to accept first-party cookies.) See *pcworld.com/resource/browse/0,cat,1384,sortIdx,1,00.asp* for more on cookies.

One-to-one matching can be applied through several different methods. One well-known method is *collaborative filtering*.

COLLABORATIVE FILTERING

Once a company knows a consumer's preferences (e.g., music preferences), it would be useful if the company could predict, without asking, what other products or services this consumer might enjoy. One way to do this is through **collaborative filtering**, which uses customer data to infer customer interest in other products or services. This prediction is based on special formulas derived from behavioral sciences. For more on the methods and formulas used to execute collaborative filtering, see Vezina and Militaru (2004) and Zeng et al. (2004). The prediction also can be based on what marketers know about other customers with similar profiles. One of the pioneering filtering systems was Firefly (now embedded in Microsoft's Passport System). Many personalization systems are based on collaborative filtering (e.g., backflip.com and choicestream.com).

collaborative filtering
A personalization method that uses customer data to predict, based on formulas derived from behavioral sciences, what other products or services a customer may enjoy; predictions can be extended to other customers with similar profiles.

The following are some variations of collaborative filtering:

- **Rule-based filtering.** A company asks consumers a series of yes/no or multiple-choice questions. The questions may range from personal information to the specific information the customer is looking for on a specific Web site. Certain behavioral patterns are predicted using the collected information. From this information, the collaborative filtering system derives behavioral and demographic rules such as, "If customer age is greater than 35, and customer income is above $100,000, show Jeep Cherokee ad. Otherwise, show Mazda Protégé ad."
- **Content-based filtering.** With this technique, vendors ask users to specify certain favorite products. Based on these user preferences, the vendor's system will recommend additional products to the user. This technique is fairly complex because mapping among different product categories must be completed in advance.
- **Activity-based filtering.** Filtering rules can also be built by watching the user's activities on the Web.

For more about personalization and filtering, see knowledgestorm.com and cio.com.

Legal and Ethical Issues in Collaborative Filtering

Information is frequently collected from users without their knowledge or permission. This raises several ethical and legal questions, including invasion-of-privacy issues. Several vendors offer *permission-based* personalization tools. With these, companies request the customer's permission to receive questionnaires and ads (e.g., see knowledgestorm.com). See Chapter 17 for more on privacy issues and Section 4.8 for information on permission marketing.

CUSTOMER LOYALTY

One of the major objectives of one-to-one B2C marketing, as well as B2B marketing, is to increase customer loyalty. *Customer loyalty* is the degree to which a customer will stay with a specific vendor or brand for repeat purchasing. Customer loyalty is expected to produce more sales and increased profits over time. A 2004 Gartner survey found that "attracting and retaining loyal customers" was the most important issue for any selling company, including e-tailers. Also, it costs a company between five to eight times more to *acquire* a new customer than to *keep* an existing one. Increased customer loyalty can bring cost savings to a company in various ways: lower marketing costs, lower transaction costs, lower customer turnover expenses, lower failure costs such as warranty claims, and so on. Customer loyalty also strengthens a company's market position because loyal customers are kept away from the competition.

Loyalty is a multidimensional concept. Coyles and Gokey (2002) distinguish six levels of loyalty. Three of the levels identify customers as loyalists; that is, the customers are maintaining or increasing their expenditures with the company. These customers are loyal because they are emotionally attached to their current provider, have rationally chosen it as their best option, or do not regard switching as worth the trouble. The remaining levels—the downward migrators in terms of loyalty—have one of three reasons for spending less: their lifestyle has changed (as a result, say, of moving or having a child), so they have developed new needs that the company is not meeting; they continually reassess their options and have found a better one; or they are actively dissatisfied, often because of a single bad experience (e.g., a rude salesperson). Understanding customers' feelings and logic in these six levels enables sellers to solidify loyalty.

The introduction of EC decreases loyalty in general because customers' ability to shop, compare, and switch to different vendors becomes easier, faster, and less expensive given the aid of search engines and other technologies. However, companies have found that loyal customers end up buying more when they have a Web site to shop from. For example, W.W. Grainger, a large industrial-supply company, found that loyal B2B customers increased their purchases substantially when they began using Grainger's Web site (grainger.com). (See Grainger, Inc. [1998] for more information.) Also, loyal customers may refer other customers to a site. Every company's goal is to increase customer loyalty. The Web offers ample opportunities to increase loyalty.

E-Loyalty

e-loyalty
Customer loyalty to an e-tailer.

E-loyalty refers to customers' loyalty to an e-tailer or a manufacturer that sells directly online. Customer acquisition and retention is a critical success factor in e-tailing. The expense of acquiring a new customer can be over $100; even for Amazon.com, which has a huge reach, it is more than $15. In contrast, the cost of maintaining an existing customer at Amazon.com is $2 to $4.

Companies can foster e-loyalty by learning about their customers' needs; interacting with customers, as Ritchey Design did (see opening case); and providing superb customer service. A major source of information about e-loyalty is e-loyaltyresource.com. One of its major services is an online journal, the *e-Loyalty Resource Newsletter*, which offers numerous articles describing the relationships among e-loyalty, customer service, personalization, CRM, and Web-based tools. Another source of information is colloquy.com, which concentrates on loyalty marketing. Comprehensive reviews of the use of the Web and the Internet to foster e-loyalty are provided by Harris and Goode (2004).

In addition, e-loyalty is a major barrier that customers must cross when deciding to exit to a competitor. See Online File W4.1 at the book's Web site for more on customer exit barriers.

SATISFACTION IN EC

Satisfaction has long been the major factor associated with loyalty and retention in traditional marketing. Given the changing dynamics of the global marketplace and the increasingly intense competition, delivering world-class customer online experience becomes a differentiating strategy. Satisfaction is one of the most important consumer reactions in B2C online environment. Recent statistics show that 80 percent of highly satisfied online consumers would shop again within 2 months, and 90 percent would recommend the Internet retailers to others. However, 87 percent of dissatisfied consumers would permanently leave their Internet retailers without any complaints (Cheung and Lee 2005).

Satisfaction has been receiving enormous attention in studies of consumer-based EC. ForeSee Results, an online customer satisfaction measurement company, partnered with the University of Michigan and developed the American Customer Satisfaction Index (ACSI) for measuring customer satisfaction with e-retail. In 2003, the ACSI for e-commerce grew healthily to 80.8 on a 100-point scale (*Ecommerce in Action,* September 15, 2004). Researchers have proposed several research models to explain the formation of satisfaction. For example, Cheung and Lee (2005) proposed a framework for consumer satisfaction with Internet shopping by correlating the end-user satisfaction perspective with the service quality viewpoint. As shown in Exhibit 4.4, the framework suggests that consumer satisfaction with Internet shopping is impacted by beliefs about information quality, system quality, and service quality. Shop.org and BizRate.com conduct periodic shopping satisfaction surveys. Survey results indicate that customer satisfaction is increasing (see *eMarketer* 2004). Customers shop online in order to save time, to shop when off-line stores are closed, to avoid the crowd, and to get better prices. Customers also enjoy online benefits such as finding in-stock products and learning about free promotions, gift ideas, and special sales.

EXHIBIT 4.4 **Research Framework of Consumer Satisfaction with Internet Shopping**

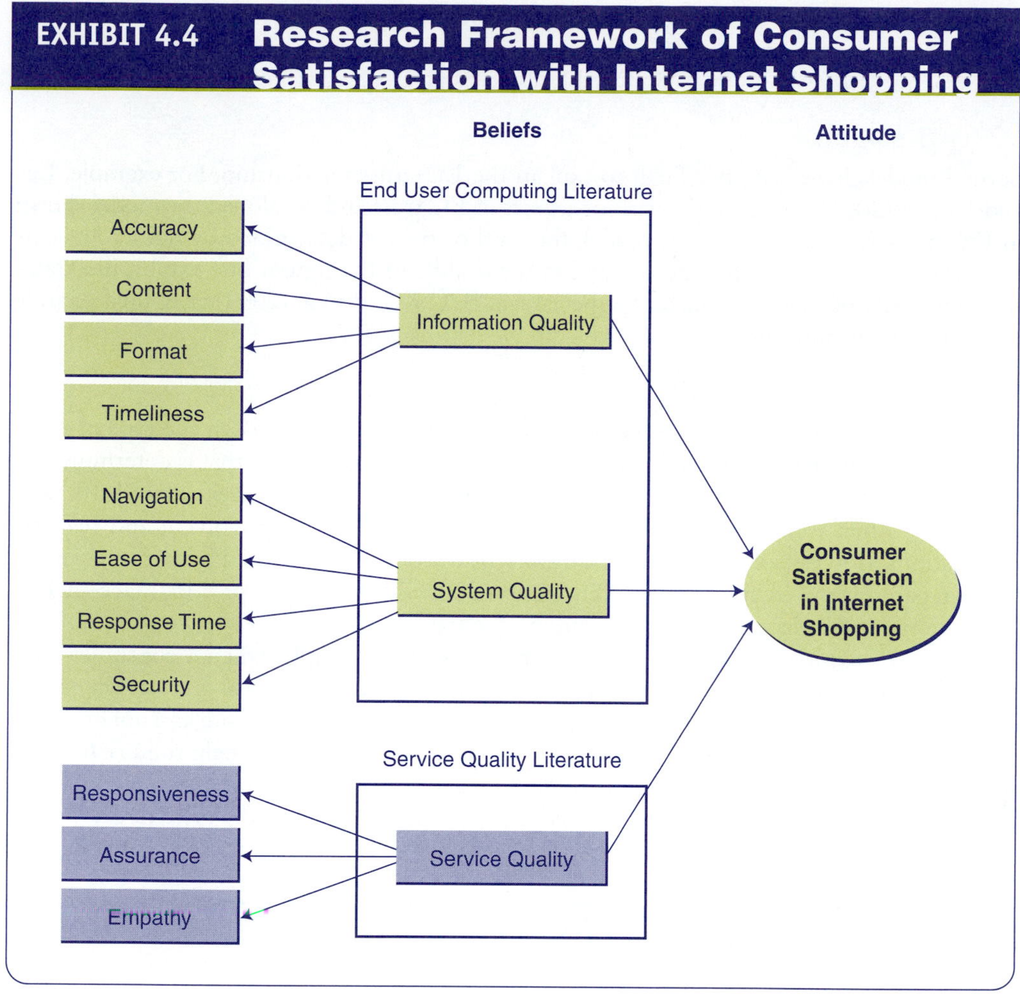

Source: Cheung, C. M. K., and M. K. O. Lee. "Research Framework for Consumer Satisfaction with Internet Shopping." Working Paper 2005, City University of Hong Kong.

The 2005 ASCI Annual Report shows that satisfaction is dropping with the large players such as Amazon and eBay. These companies expanded their business models to include more products (Amazon), or focus on aggregation for small businesses instead of individuals (eBay). In the online world, it is much easier to move from one site to another than in the physical world, so customer loyalty depends upon customer service (ForeseeResults 2005a and 2005b).

Why do customers abandon online purchases? A 2004 survey by NetIQ showed shipping costs and lengthy delivery times to be major factors (San Jose and Silicon Valley Business Journals 2004). Also, sellers request too much information from buyers, but do not provide enough product information. Further discussion on EC satisfaction can be found in Bansal et al. (2004) and Kohli et al. (2004).

TRUST IN EC

Trust is the psychological status of involved parties who are willing to pursue further interactions to achieve a planned goal. When people trust each other, they have confidence that as transaction partners they will keep their promises. However, both parties in a transaction assume some risk. In the marketspace, sellers and buyers do not meet face to face. The buyer can see a picture of the product but not the product itself. Promises of quality and delivery can be easily made—but will they be kept? To deal with these issues, EC vendors need to establish high levels of trust with current and potential customers. Trust is particularly important in global EC transactions due to the difficulty in taking legal action in cases of a dispute or fraud and the potential for conflicts caused by differences in culture and business environments.

trust
The psychological status of involved parties who are willing to pursue further interaction to achieve a planned goal.

In addition to sellers and buyers trusting each other, both must have trust in the EC computing environment and in the EC infrastructure. If people do not trust the security of the EC infrastructure, they will not feel comfortable about using credit cards to make EC purchases.

EC Trust Models

Several models have been put forth to explain the EC–trust relationship. For example, Lee and Turban (2001) examined the various aspects of EC trust and developed the model shown in Exhibit 4.5. According to this model, the level of trust is determined by numerous variables (factors) shown on the left side and in the middle of the figure. The exhibit illustrates the complexity of trust relationships, especially in B2C EC. Pavlou (2003) examined the role of perceived risk and trust.

How to Increase Trust in EC

How does one establish the necessary level of trust for EC? It depends on the type of trust. For example, with trust between buyers and sellers, the desired level of trust is determined by the following factors: the degree of initial success that each party experienced with EC and with each other, well-defined roles and procedures for all parties involved, and realistic expectations as to outcomes from EC. Conversely, trust can be decreased by any user uncertainty regarding the technology (see Pennington 2003–2004), by lack of initial face-to-face interactions, and by lack of enthusiasm among the trading parties.

Brand recognition is very important in EC trust. For example, when a consumer buys online from Dell or Wal-Mart, the consumer probably will have a great deal of trust. Obviously, the consumer needs to be assured that he or she is on the actual Dell Web site and not on a fake site that looks similar to Dell's. Therefore, EC security mechanisms can help solidify trust. In addition, it is necessary for EC vendors to disclose and update their latest business status and practices to potential customers and to build transaction integrity into the system. They must also guarantee information and protect privacy through various communication channels.

EXHIBIT 4.5 The EC Trust Model

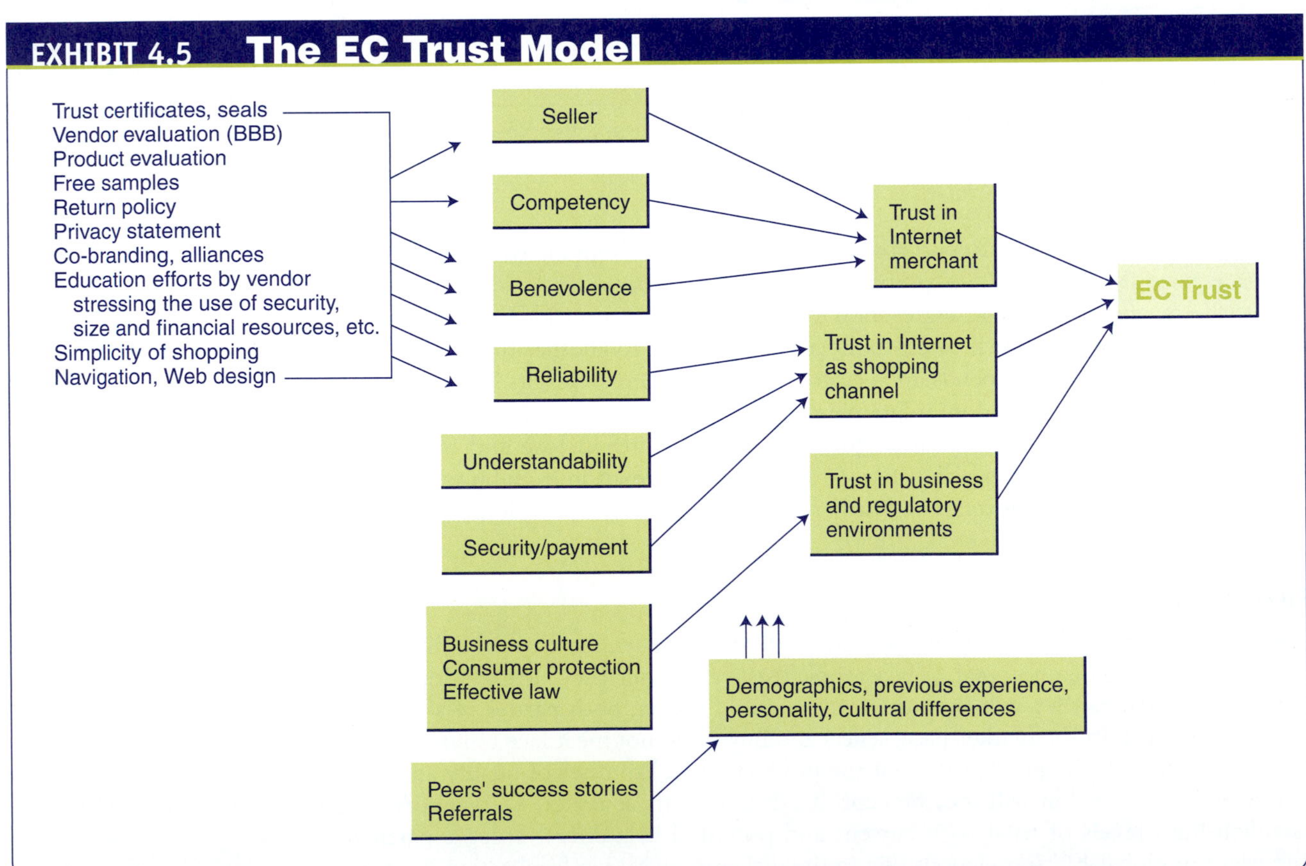

Source: From Lee, Matthew K. O., and Efraim Turban. "A Trust Model for Consumer Internet Shopping." *International Journal of Electronic Commerce*, vol. 6, no. 1 (Fall 2001).

Several third-party vendors operate services that aim to increase trust (Cook and Luo 2003). Notable are companies such as TRUSTe (truste.com) and BBBOnLine (bbbonline.org) (the online version of the Better Business Bureau). Also useful are escrow providers and reputation finders (see Wagner 2002 and sites such as cyberalert.com and cymfony.com), which provide business-critical intelligence on how brands are being used on the Internet as well as research about spying on businesses. Working against EC trust are stories of a considerable amount of fraud on the Internet, especially when unknown parties are involved. In Chapters 11 and 17, we describe measures that are being taken to reduce fraud and increase trust. For a more comprehensive treatment of EC trust, see Cheung and Lee (2003) and Koufaris and Hampton-Sosa (2004).

Section 4.3 ▶ REVIEW QUESTIONS

1. Describe one-to-one marketing.
2. Explain how personalization (matching people with goods/services) is done.
3. Define loyalty and describe e-loyalty.
4. Describe the issue of trust in EC and how to increase it.
5. What influences consumer satisfaction online? Why do companies need to monitor it?

4.4 MARKET RESEARCH FOR EC

The goal of market research is to find information and knowledge that describes the relationships among consumers, products, marketing methods, and marketers. Its aim is to discover marketing opportunities and issues, to establish marketing plans, to better understand the purchasing process, and to evaluate marketing performance. On the Web, the objective is to turn browsers into buyers. Market research includes gathering information about topics such as the economy, industry, firms, products, pricing, distribution, competition, promotion, and consumer purchasing behavior. Here we focus on the latter. In Chapter 14, we will look at some other market research topics: the need to research the market, the competition (e.g., see rivalwatch.com), the technology, the business environment, and much more.

Businesses, educational institutions, and governments use various tools to conduct consumer market research both *off-line* and *online*. For example, business representatives with questionnaires in shopping malls collect information from people about clothing, consumer products, or Internet usage. Surveyors may appear just about anywhere there is high traffic, such as supermarkets, theaters, and airport terminals. They are replicating surveys in various cities that can yield fairly generalized results. Another conventional way of conducting market research is by telephone surveys, where an interviewer calls current or prospective customers or a randomly selected sample of customers and asks questions regarding a specific product or service. Questionnaires also may be sent to specific individuals in a company or household.

In addition, *focus groups* can be useful. In these, groups of selected individuals are asked to discuss products or services so that marketers can identify differences in attributes, benefits, and values of various potential markets. Analyzing these differences among groups of consumers is important in identifying new target markets.

Because EC also has to identify an appropriate customer group for specific products and services, it is important first to understand how groups of consumers are classified. This classification is called *segmentation*.

MARKET SEGMENTATION

For years, companies used direct mail to contact customers. However, they frequently did so regardless of whether the products or services were appropriate for the specific individuals on the company's mailing list. For example, ABC Company sends out four mailings of 1,000,000 pieces each year. The cost of the direct mailings is $1.25 per customer, and only 1 percent respond. This means the cost per responding customer is $125. Obviously, this type of direct marketing usually is not cost-effective (techmorrow.com 2003).

Markets can be segmented to increase the percentage of responses and formulate effective marketing strategies that appeal to specific consumer groups. **Market segmentation** is

market segmentation
The process of dividing a consumer market into logical groups for conducting marketing research, advertising, and sales.

the process of dividing a consumer market into logical groups for conducting marketing research, advertising, and sales. A consumer market can be segmented in several ways, for example, by geography, demographics, psychographics, and benefits sought, as shown in Exhibit 4.6. For a description, see Chan (2005).

A company can separate even millions of customers into smaller segments and tailor its campaigns to each of those segments. Brengman et al. (2005) segmented Internet shoppers based on their Web usage–related lifestyle, themes of Internet usage, Internet attitude, and psychographic and demographic characteristics. They identified four online shopping segments (tentative shoppers, suspicious learners, shopping lovers, and business users) and four online nonshopping segments (fearful browsers, positive technology muddlers, negative technology muddlers, and adventurous browsers). By isolating and identifying combinations of attributes that make markets, prospects, and customers unique, marketers use strategies developed to appeal to targeted segments.

Segmentation is done with the aid of tools such as data modeling (Oh et al. 2003) and data warehousing. Using data mining (Berry and Linoff 2002) and Web mining (see Online Appendix W4A), businesses can look at consumer buying patterns to slice segments even finer. This is not an easy process, and it requires considerable resources and computer support. Most of the segmentation success stories involve large companies. For example, Royal Bank of Canada segments its 10 million customers at least once a month to determine credit risk, profitability, and so on. This segmentation has been very successful: The response to Royal Bank of Canada advertising campaigns has increased from 3 to 30 percent (Gold 2001). Segmentation can be very effective in the Web environment, especially when used with appropriate statistical tools (see Parks 2004).

CONDUCTING MARKET RESEARCH ONLINE

EC market research can be conducted through conventional methods, such as those described earlier, or it can be done with the assistance of the Internet. Although telephone or shopping mall surveys will continue, interest in Internet research methods is on the rise. Market research that uses the Internet frequently is faster and more efficient and allows the researcher to access a more geographically diverse audience than those found in off-line surveys (see FAQs at casro.org and accutips.com). Also, on the Web, market researchers can conduct a very large study much more cheaply than with other methods. The larger the sample size, the larger the accuracy and the predictive capabilities of the results. Telephone surveys can cost as much as $50 per respondent. This may be too expensive for a small company that needs several hundred respondents. An online survey will cost a fraction of a similarly sized telephone survey and can expedite research considerably, as shown in EC Application Case 4.1. Hewson et al. (2003) provide a comprehensive review of online market research technologies, methods, tools, and issues, including ethical ones.

EXHIBIT 4.6 Consumer Market Segmentation in the United States (a partial list)

Segmentation	Bases/Descriptors
Geographic	Region; size of city, county, or Standard Metropolitan Statistical Area (SMSA); population density; climate; language
Demographic	Age, occupation, gender, education, family size, religion, race, income, nationality, urban (or suburban or rural)
Psychographic (lifestyle)	Social class, lifestyle, personality, activities, VALS typology (see *sric-bi.com/VALS/presurvey.shtml*)
Cognitive, affective, behavioral	Attitudes, benefits sought, loyalty status, readiness stage, usage rate, perceived risk, user status, innovativeness, usage situation, involvement, Internet shopping experience

CASE 4.1

EC Application

INTERNET MARKET RESEARCH EXPEDITES TIME-TO-MARKET AT PROCTER & GAMBLE

For decades, Procter & Gamble (P&G) and Colgate-Palmolive have been competitors in the market for personal care products. Developing a major new product, from concept to market launch, used to take over 5 years. First, a concept test was conducted: The companies sent product photos and descriptions to potential customers, asking whether they might buy the product. If the feedback was negative, they tried to improve the product concept and then repeated previous tasks. Once positive response was achieved, sample products were mailed out, and the customers were asked to fill out detailed questionnaires. When customers' responses met the companies' internal hurdles, the companies would start with mass TV advertising.

However, thanks to the Internet, it took P&G only 3 and one-half years to get Whitestrips, the teeth-brightening product, onto the market and to a sales level of $200 million a year—considerably quicker than other oral care products. In September 2000, P&G threw out the old marketing test model and instead introduced Whitestrips on the Internet, offering the product for sale on P&G's Web site. The company spent several months studying who was coming to the site and buying the product and collecting responses to online questionnaires, which was much faster than the old mail-outs.

The online research, which was facilitated by data mining conducted on P&G's huge historical data (stored in a data warehouse) and the new Internet data, revealed the most enthusiastic groups. These included teenage girls, brides-to-be, and young Hispanic Americans. Immediately, the company started to target these segments with appropriate advertising. The Internet created a product awareness of 35 percent, even before any shipments were made to stores. This buzz created a huge demand for the product by the time it hit the shelves.

From this experience, P&G learned important lessons about flexible and creative ways to approach product innovation and marketing. The whole process of studying the product concept, segmenting the market, and expediting product development has been revolutionized.

Sources: Compiled from Buckley (2002) and from *pg.com* (accessed February–December 2002).

What Are Marketers Looking for in EC Market Research?

By looking at a personal profile that includes observed behaviors on the Web, it is possible for marketers to explain and predict online buying behavior. For example, companies want to know why some customers are online shoppers whereas others are not (see Limayem et al. 2004). Major factors that are used for prediction are (in descending order of importance): product information requested, number of related e-mails, number of orders made, products/services ordered, and gender.

Typical questions that online market research attempts to answer are: What are the purchase patterns for individuals and groups (segmentation)? What factors encourage online purchasing? How can we identify those who are real buyers from those who are just browsing? How does an individual navigate—does the consumer check information first or do they go directly to ordering? What is the optimal Web page design? Knowing the answers to questions such as these helps a vendor to advertise properly, to price items, to design the Web site, and to provide appropriate customer service. Online market research can provide such data about individuals, about groups, and even about the entire Internet.

An example of what market research looks at is provided by Ranganathan and Grandon (2002), who explored the factors affecting online sales. They looked at content, design, security, and privacy factors. Using a survey, they found that the most significant factors affecting online sales are frequent update of content, information on a company, provision for having individual accounts and passwords, tight site security, and availability of good privacy statements. This study targeted the general Internet population, but a similar study could be conducted on a segment population regarding a specific product.

Internet-based market research is often done in an interactive manner, allowing personal contact with customers, and it provides marketing organizations with a greater ability to understand the customer, the market, and the competition. For example, it can identify early shifts in product and customer trends, enabling marketers to identify products and marketing opportunities and to develop those products that customers really want to buy. It also tells management when a product or a service is no longer popular. To learn more about market research on the Web, see the tutorials at webmonkey.com.

The following discussion describes some online market research methods.

Online Market Research Methods

Online research methods range from one-to-one communication with specific customers, usually by e-mail, to moderated focus groups conducted in chat rooms to questionnaires placed on Web sites to tracking of customers' movements on the Web. Professional pollsters and marketing research companies frequently conduct online voting polls (e.g., see cnn.com and acnielsen.com). For an overview of online market research methods, see Hewson et al. (2003). A typical Internet-based market research process is shown in Exhibit 4.7.

Companies offer incentives such as games, prizes, or free software to draw customers. Then, using questionnaires, the companies collect information from customers before they are allowed to play the games, win prizes (see opening case study), or download the free software. However, according to surveys conducted by the Georgia Institute of Technology (1998), more than 40 percent of the information people place on such questionnaires is incorrect. Appropriate design of Web questionnaires and incentives for true completion are critical for the validity of the results (Birnbaum 2004).

Online market researchers have to address numerous issues. For example, customers may refuse to answer certain questions. Also, the analysis of questionnaires can be lengthy and costly. Furthermore, researchers risk losing respondents to online questionnaires because respondents may not have the latest computers or the fastest Internet connections.

Implementing Web-Based Surveys. Web-based surveys are becoming popular with companies and researchers. For example, Mazda North America used a Web-based survey to help design its Miata line. Web surveys may be passive (a fill-in questionnaire) or interactive (respondents download the questionnaires, add comments, ask questions, and discuss issues).

EXHIBIT 4.7 Online Market Research Process

Steps in Collecting Market Research Data

1. Define the research issue and the target market.
2. Identify newsgroups and Internet communities to study.
3. Identify specific topics for discussion.
4. Subscribe to the pertinent groups; register in communities.
5. Search discussion group topic and content lists to find the target market.
6. Search e-mail discussion group lists.
7. Subscribe to filtering services that monitor groups.
8. Read FAQs and other instructions.
9. Visit chat rooms.

Content of the Research Instrument

1. Post strategic queries to groups.
2. Post surveys on a Web site.
3. Offer rewards for participation.
4. Post strategic queries on a Web site.
5. Post relevant content to groups, with a pointer to a Web site survey.
6. Post a detailed survey in special e-mail questionnaires.
7. Create a chat room and try to build a community of consumers.

Target Audience of the Study

1. Compare audience with the target population.
2. Determine editorial focus.
3. Determine content.
4. Determine what Web services to create for each type of audience.

Source: Based on Vassos (1996), pp. 66–68.

For more information and additional software tools, see supersurvey.com, surveymonkey.com, websurveyor.com, and clearlearning.com. For an introduction on how to conduct Web-based surveys, see Faught et al. (2004) and Wharton et al. (2003).

A major provider of online surveys is Zoomerang (zoomerang.com). At Zoomerang, users can select survey templates, edit them, and send them to preselected recipients. The basic service is free. For an evaluation of leading Web survey software, see Chen (2004).

The limitations of Web surveys are difficulties in getting a representative sample, the quality of the collected data, the lack of experience of those conducting the research, and the fact that people need to sit at a computer to answer the questions.

Online Focus Groups. Several research firms create panels of qualified Web regulars to participate in online focus groups. For example, NPD's panel (npd.com) consists of 15,000 consumers recruited online and verified by telephone; Greenfield Online (greenfieldonline.com) picks users from its own database, then calls them periodically to verify that they are who they say they are. Another online research firm, Research Connections (researchconnections.com), recruits participants in advance by telephone and takes the time to help them connect to the Internet, if necessary. Use of preselected focus group participants helps to overcome some of the problems (e.g., small sample size and partial responses) that sometimes limit the effectiveness of Web-based surveys.

Hearing Directly from Customers. Instead of using focus groups, which are costly and possibly slow, one can ask customers directly what they think about a product or service. Nikitas (2002), who advocates such an approach, cites an example of toy maker Lego, who used a market-research vendor to establish a survey on an electronic bulletin board where millions of visitors read each other's comments and shared opinions about Lego toys. The research vendor analyzed the responses daily and submitted the information to Lego. In addition, companies can use chat rooms, newsgroups, and electronic consumer forums to interact with consumers.

Software tools that can be used to hear directly from customers include C-Feedback Suite (used by Lego) from Informative, Inc. (informative.com), Betasphere (betasphere.com), InsightExpress (insightexpress.com), and Survey.com (survey.com).

Customer Scenarios. According to Seybold (2001), companies often concentrate on their own offerings, failing to see how those products and services fit into the real lives of their customers. To correct this deficiency, Seybold suggests the use of *customer scenarios*, situations that describe the customer's needs and the manner in which the product fulfills those needs. For example, one customer may buy a refrigerator because they need an "emergency replacement," whereas another customer may buy a similar refrigerator because they are "furnishing a home." The information gathered is used to design products and advertising. Seybold describes the case of National Semiconductor's customer scenario, in which they offer Web tools to help engineers design electronic devices. Another user of this approach is Tesco (tesco.co.uk).

Tracking Customer Movements. To avoid some of the problems of online surveys, especially the giving of false information, some marketers choose to learn about customers by observing their behavior rather than by asking them questions. Many marketers keep track of consumers' Web movements using methods such as transaction logs (log files) or cookie files.

Transaction Logs. A **transaction log** records user activities at a company's Web site. A transaction log is created by a *log file*, which is a file that lists actions that have occurred. With log file analysis tools, it is possible to get a good idea of where visitors are coming from, how often they return, and how they navigate through a site (Nicholas and Huntington 2003). The transaction log approach is especially useful if the visitors' names are known (e.g., when they have registered with the site). In addition, data from the shopping-cart database can be combined with information in the transaction log.

transaction log
A record of user activities at a company's Web site.

Note that as customers move from site to site, they establish their **clickstream behavior**, a pattern of their movements on the Internet, which can be seen in their transaction logs. Both ISPs and individual Web sites are capable of tracking a user's clickstream.

clickstream behavior
Customer movements on the Internet.

An example of the use of transaction logs is Internet Profile Corporation (IPC) (ipro.com), which collects data from a company's client/server logs and provides the company with periodic reports that include demographic data such as where customers come from or how many customers have gone straight from the homepage to placing an order. IPC also translates the Internet domain names of visitors into real company names. This way, a company knows where its customers are coming from.

Cookies, Web Bugs, and Spyware. Cookies and Web bugs can be used to supplement transaction-log methods. As discussed earlier, cookies allow a Web site to store data on the user's PC; when the customer returns to the site, the cookies can be used to find what the customer did in the past. Cookies are frequently combined with **Web bugs**, tiny graphics files embedded in e-mail messages and on Web sites. Web bugs transmit information about the user and his or her movements to a monitoring site.

Web bugs
Tiny graphics files embedded on e-mail messages and in Web sites that transmit information about users and their movements to a Web server.

Spyware is software that gathers user information through an Internet connection without the user's knowledge (Stafford and Urbaczewski 2004). Originally designed to allow freeware authors to make money on their products, spyware applications are typically bundled together with freeware for download onto users' machines. Many users do not realize that they are downloading spyware with the freeware. Sometimes the freeware provider may indicate that other programs will be loaded onto the user's computer in the licensing agreement (e.g., "may include software that occasionally notifies users of important news"). Spyware stays on the user's hard drive and continually tracks the user's actions, periodically sending information on the user's activities to the owner of the spyware. It typically is used to gather information for advertising purposes. Users cannot control what data are sent via the spyware, and unless they use special tools, they often cannot uninstall the spyware, even if the software it was bundled with is removed from the system. Effective tools for fighting spyware include: Ad-aware (lavasoftusa.com/software/adaware), Spykiller (spykiller.com), and Webwasher Spyware from cyberguard.com. For more on spyware and banners, see Online File W4.2.

spyware
Software that gathers user information over an Internet connection without the user's knowledge.

Representative vendors that provide tools for tracking customers' movements are Tealeaf Technology, Inc. (tealeaf.com, log files), Acxiom Corp. (acxiom.com, data warehousing), and Net IQ (netiq.com/webtrends, real-time tracking).

The use of cookies and Web bugs is controversial. Many believe that they invade the customer's privacy (see privacyfoundation.org). Tracking customers' activities *without their knowledge or permission* may be unethical or even illegal.

Analysis of B2C Clickstream Data. Large and ever-increasing amounts of B2C data can be collected on consumers, products, and so on. Such data come from several sources: internal data (e.g., sales data, payroll data, etc.), external data (e.g., government and industry reports), and clickstream data. **Clickstream data** are data generated in the Web environment; they provide a trail of a user's activities (the user's clickstream behavior) in a Web site (Park and Fader 2004). These data include a record of the user's browsing patterns: every Web site and every page of every Web site the user visits, how long the user remains on a page or site, in what order the pages were visited, and even the e-mail addresses of mail that the user sends and receives. By analyzing clickstream data, a firm can find out, for example, which promotions are effective and which population segments are interested in specific products.

clickstream data
Data that occur inside the Web environment; they provide a trail of the user's activities (the user's clickstream behavior) in the Web site

According to Inmon (2001), B2C clickstream data can reveal information such as the following:

- What goods the customer has looked at
- What goods the customer has purchased
- What goods the customer examined but did not purchase
- What items the customer bought in conjunction with other items
- What items the customer looked at in conjunction with other items but did not purchase
- Which ads and promotions were effective and which were not
- Which ads generate a lot of attention but few sales
- Whether certain products are too hard to find and/or too expensive
- Whether there is a substitute product that the customer finds first
- Whether there are too many products for the customer to wade through
- Whether certain products are not being promoted
- Whether the products have adequate descriptions

Several companies offer tools that enable such an analysis. For example, WebTrends 7 features several advanced tools for analyzing clickstream data (e.g., see webtrends.com).

In addition, clickstream data can be maintained in a clickstream data warehouse for further analysis (see Sweiger et al. 2002). However, it is fairly difficult to analyze transaction logs or clickstream data.

Web Analytics

Web analytics services and software have grown beyond simply reporting which page was clicked and how long a visitor stayed there. They now offer more advanced functions that retailers are finding indispensable. For example, options from Coremetrics Inc. (coremetrics.com) and others are enabling retailers to make site adjustments on the fly, manage online marketing campaigns and e-commerce initiatives, and track customer satisfaction. Also, if a company redesigns its Web site, it can gain almost-instant feedback on how the new site is performing. Web analytics can be done on a customer-by-customer or prospect-by-prospect basis, helping marketers decide which products to promote and merchandisers achieve a better understanding of the nature of demand.

LIMITATIONS OF ONLINE MARKET RESEARCH

One problem with online market research is that too much data may be available. To use data properly, one needs to organize, edit, condense, and summarize it. However, such a task may be expensive and time-consuming. The solution to this problem is to automate the process by using data warehousing and data mining. The essentials of this process, known as *business intelligence*, are provided in Online Appendix W4A.

Some of the limitations of online research methods are accuracy of responses, loss of respondents because of equipment problems, and the ethics and legality of Web tracking. In addition, focus group responses can lose something in the translation from an in-person group to an online group. A researcher may get people online to talk to each other and play off of each other's comments, but eye contact and body language are two interactions of traditional focus group research that are lost in the online world. However, just as it hinders the two-way assessment of visual cues, Web research can actually offer some participants the anonymity necessary to elicit an unguarded response. Finally, a major limitation of online market research is the difficulty in obtaining truly representative samples.

Concerns have been expressed over the potential lack of representativeness in samples of online users. Online shoppers tend to be wealthy, employed, and well educated. Although this may be a desirable audience for some products and services, the research results may not be extendable to other markets. Although the Web-user demographic is rapidly diversifying, it is still skewed toward certain population groups, such as those with Internet access. Another important issue concerns the lack of clear understanding of the online communication process and how online respondents think and interact in cyberspace.

It is important for a company to identify the intended target audience or demographic so that the right kind of sampling can be performed. Web-based surveys typically have a lower response rate than e-mail surveys, and there is no respondent control for public surveys. If target respondents are allowed to be anonymous, it may encourage them to be more truthful in their opinions. However, anonymity may result in the loss of valuable information about the demographics and characteristics of the respondents. Finally, there are still concerns about the security of the information transmitted, which also may have an impact on the truthfulness of the respondents.

To overcome some of the limitations of online market research, companies can outsource their market research needs. Only large companies have specialized market research departments. Most other companies use third-party research companies, such as AC Nielsen.

Some researchers are wildly optimistic about the prospects for market research on the Internet; others are more cautious (Wharton et al. 2003). The American Statistical Association (2000) predicted that in the next few years, 50 percent of all market research will be done on the Internet and that 5 years from now national telephone surveys will be the subject of research methodology folklore. Others predict that such changes will take place in 20 years.

Section 4.4 ▶ REVIEW QUESTIONS

1. Describe the objectives of market research.
2. Define and describe segmentation.
3. Describe how market research is done online and the major market research methods.
4. Describe the role of Web logs and clickstream data.

5. Relate cookies, Web bugs, and spyware to market research.
6. Describe the limitations of online market research.

4.5 INTERNET MARKETING IN B2B

B2B marketing is completely different from B2C marketing, which was introduced in Chapter 3 and in Sections 4.1 through 4.4. Major differences also exist between B2B and B2C with respect to the nature of demand and supply and the trading process. Here we discuss the corporate purchaser's buying behavior and the marketing and advertising methods used in B2B. More discussion is provided in Chapters 5 through 7.

ORGANIZATIONAL BUYER BEHAVIOR

Organizations buy large quantities of *direct materials* that they consume or use in the production of goods and services and in the company's operations. They also buy *indirect materials*, such as PCs, delivery trucks, and office supplies, to support their production and operations processes.

Although the number of organizational buyers is much smaller than the number of individual consumers, their transaction volumes are far larger, and the terms of negotiations and purchasing are more complex. In addition, the purchasing process itself, as will be seen in Chapter 5, usually is more complex than the purchasing process of an individual customer. Also, the organization's buyer may be a group. In fact, decisions to purchase expensive items are usually decided by a group. Therefore, factors that affect individual consumer behavior and organizational buying behavior are quite different.

A Behavioral Model of Organizational Buyers

The behavior of an organizational buyer can be described by a model similar to that of an individual buyer, which was shown in Exhibit 4.1. A behavioral model for organizational buyers is shown in Exhibit 4.8. Compare the two models. Note that some independent variables differ; for example, in the organizational model, the family and Internet communities may have no influence. Also, an *organizational influences module* is added to the B2B model. This module includes the organization's purchasing guidelines and constraints (e.g., contracts with certain suppliers) and the purchasing system used. Also, interpersonal influences, such as authority, are added. Finally, the possibility of group decision making must be considered. For a detailed discussion of organizational buyers, see Kotler and Armstrong (2004) and Armstrong and Kotler (2005). For information on Internet procurement by purchasing agents, see Martin and Hafer (2002).

THE MARKETING AND ADVERTISING PROCESSES IN B2B

The marketing and advertising processes for businesses differ considerably from those used for selling to individual consumers. For example, traditional (off-line) B2B marketers use methods such as trade shows, advertisements in industry magazines, e-mail and paper catalogs, and salespeople who call on existing customers and potential buyers.

In the digital world, these approaches may not be effective, feasible, or economical. Therefore, organizations use a variety of online methods to reach business customers. Popular methods include online directory services, matching services, the marketing and advertising services of exchanges (Chapter 6), co-branding or alliances, affiliate programs, online marketing services (e.g., see digitalcement.com), or e-communities (see Chapter 17 and b2bcommunities.com). Several of these methods are discussed next.

METHODS FOR B2B ONLINE MARKETING

When a B2C niche e-tailer seeks to attract its audience of skiers, musicians, or cosmetic customers, it may advertise in traditional media targeted to those audiences, such as magazines or television shows. The same is true in B2B when trade magazines and directories are used. But when a B2B vendor wants to grow by adding new customers or products, it may not have a reliable, known advertising channel. How can it reach new customers?

EXHIBIT 4.8 A Model of Organizational Buyer Behavior

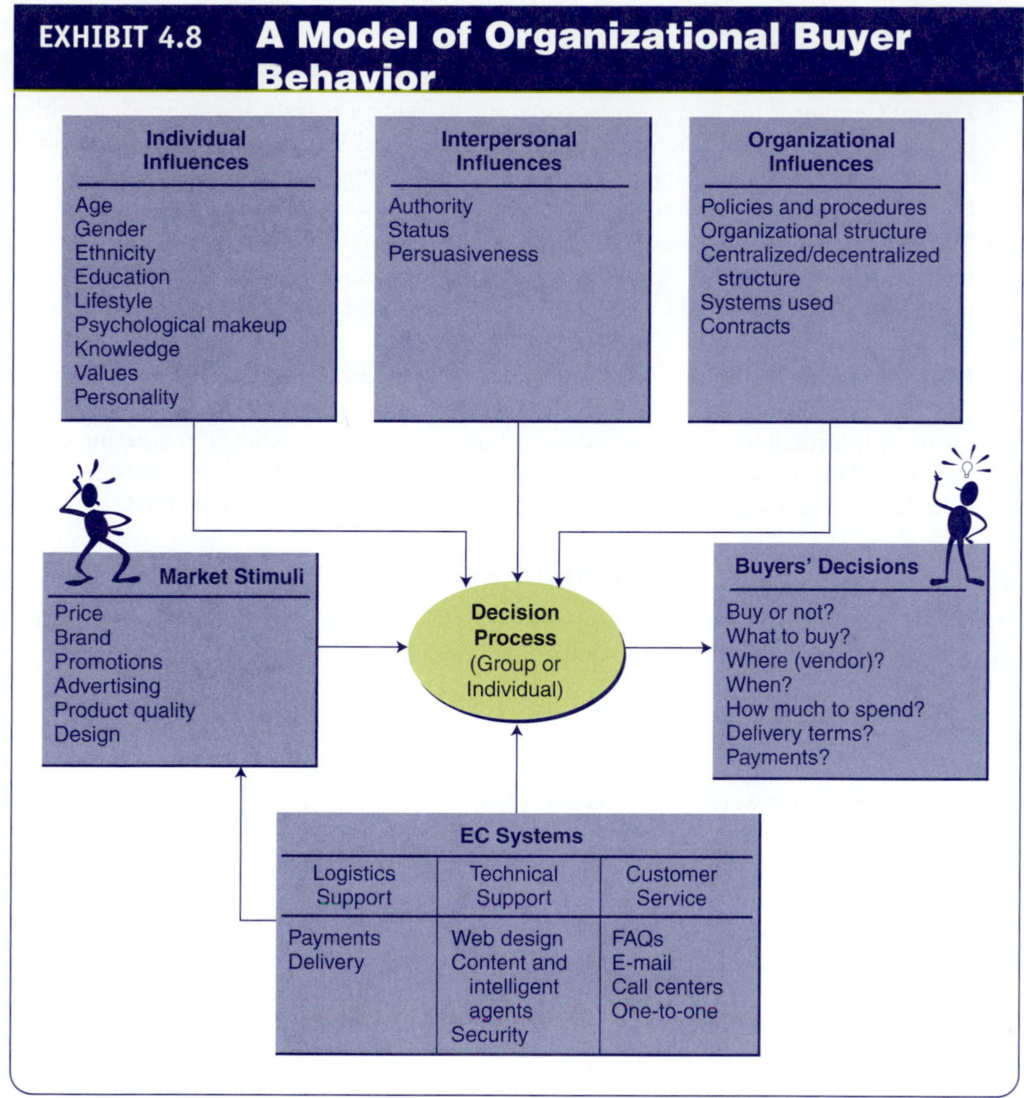

Targeting Customers

A B2B company, whether a provider of goods or services, an operator of a trading exchange, or a provider of digital real-time services, can contact all of its targeted customers individually when they are part of a well-defined group. For example, to attract companies to an exchange for auto supplies, one might use information from industry trade association records or industry magazines to identify potential customers.

Another method of bringing new customers to a B2B site is through an affiliation service, which operates just as a B2C affiliate program does. A company pays a small commission every time the affiliate company "drives traffic" to its site. For more on online B2B marketing, see Harrison-Walker and Neeley (2004) and b2business.net.

An important part of any marketing effort is advertising. Several of the advertising methods that will be presented later in this chapter are applicable both to B2C and B2B. For example, an *ad server network provider*, such as DoubleClick (doubleclick.com), can be used to target customers in B2B2C EC.

Electronic Wholesalers

One of the interesting B2B ventures is the e-wholesaler. Like click-and-mortar e-tailer Sam's Club, this kind of intermediary sells directly to businesses, but does so exclusively online. An example is Bigboxx.com, described in Chapter 5 (page 202).

Other B2B Marketing Services

Several other B2B marketing services exist. Here are several examples:

- **Digital Cement.** This firm provides corporate marketing portals. In essence, it provides content tailored to the client's customer base. Digital Cement (digitalcement.com) advocates a private-label content approach versus partnering with a branded dot-com that will give a company content for free, but may also take away its customers.
- **National Systems.** This company (nationalsystems.com) will track what is going on in a particular industry. It then generates competitive intelligence on pricing, product mix, promotions, and ad content and provides the client company with tailored marketing and advertising services.
- **BusinessTown.** This firm (businesstown.com) provides information and services to small businesses, including start-ups. It includes a directory of businesses in over 20 industries, information on functional areas (accounting, finance, legal, marketing), and business-planning advice. Although much of its offerings deal with intrabusiness and B2C EC, it offers several directories and information sources relevant to B2B.

AFFILIATE PROGRAMS, INFOMEDIARIES, AND DATA MINING

Many more methods and approaches can be used in B2B marketing and advertising (e.g., see Oliva 2004). Here we examine three popular methods: affiliate programs, infomediaries, and online data mining services.

Affiliate Programs

B2C affiliation services were introduced in Chapter 1. There are several types of affiliate programs. With the simplest type, which is used extensively in B2C EC, an affiliate puts a banner of another vendor, such as Amazon.com, on its site. When a consumer clicks the vendor's banner, the consumer is taken to that vendor's Web site, and a commission is paid to the affiliate if the customer makes a purchase. The same method works for B2B.

With B2B, additional types of affiliate programs are possible. Schaeffer Research (schaeffersresearch.com), for example, offers financial institutions a *content* alliance program in which content is exchanged so that all obtain some free content. For more on B2B affiliate programs, see Gary and Gary (2000).

Infomediaries and Online Data Mining Services

Marketing managers must understand current shopping behaviors in order to effectively advertise to customers in the future. Traditional B2C retailers evaluate point-of-sale (POS) data (e.g., grocery scanner data) and other available data to generate valuable marketing information. In today's online environment, more relevant information is available than ever before. However, the potential of the information can only be realized if the clickstream data can be analyzed and mined to produce constructive knowledge that can be used to improve services and marketing efforts. A new intermediary is emerging to provide such services to Web site owners who do not have the specialized knowledge and systems to perform such data mining on their own. As described in Chapter 2, these B2C and B2B intermediaries are called *infomediaries*.

Infomediaries start by processing existing information until new, useful information is extracted from it. This new information is sold to B2B customers or exchanged for more information, which is manipulated yet again, until even more valuable information can be extracted. B2B vendors use the information from infomediaries to identify likely buyers with much greater precision than ever before—leading to increased sales and drastically reduced marketing expenses. Representative infomediaries and data mining specialists are SAS Institute (sas.com), NetTracker (sane.com), WebTrends (webtrends.com), NetIntellect (available from Bizdesign.com), HitList (hitlist.com), and SurfReport from netrics.com. For a discussion of data mining and an example of its use in B2B, see Online Appendix W4A.

One of the major objectives of market research is to provide tactics and strategies for EC advertisement, the topic of Section 4.6.

Section 4.5 ▶ REVIEW QUESTIONS

1. Distinguish between organizational buyers and individual consumers.
2. Describe B2B marketing and advertising methods.
3. Explain how affiliate programs and data mining work in B2B.

4.6 WEB ADVERTISING

Advertising on the Web by all types of organizations plays an extremely important role in e-commerce (Dreze and Hussherr 2003). Blacharski (2005) reports that Internet advertisers are growing very rapidly and companies are changing their advertisement strategies, which gives them a competitive edge.

OVERVIEW OF WEB ADVERTISING

Advertising is an attempt to disseminate information in order to affect buyer–seller transactions. In *traditional* marketing, advertising was impersonal, one-way mass communication that was paid for by sponsors. Telemarketing and direct mail ads were attempts to personalize advertising to make it more effective. These *direct marketing* approaches worked fairly well but were expensive and slow and seldom truly one-to-one interactive. For example, say a direct mail campaign costs about $1 per person and has a response rate of only 1 to 3 percent. This makes the cost per responding person in the range of $33 to $100. Such an expense can be justified only for high-ticket items (e.g., cars).

One of the problems with direct mail advertising was that the advertisers knew very little about the recipients. Segmentation of markets by various characteristics (e.g., age, income, gender) helped a bit, but did not solve the problem. The Internet introduces the concept of **interactive marketing**, which has enabled advertisers to interact directly with customers. In interactive marketing, a consumer can click an ad to obtain more information or send an e-mail to ask a question. Besides the two-way communication and e-mail capabilities provided by the Internet, vendors also can target specific groups and individuals on which they want to spend their advertising dollars. Finally, the Internet enables truly one-to-one advertising (Stewart and Pavlou 2002).

interactive marketing
Online marketing, enabled by the Internet, in which advertisers can interact directly with customers and consumers can interact with advertisers/vendors.

Companies use Internet advertising as *one* of their advertising channels. At the same time, they also may use TV, newspapers, or other channels. In this respect, the Web competes with the other channels. A comparison of mass advertising, direct mail advertising, and interactive online advertising is shown in Exhibit 4.9. There are two major business models for

EXHIBIT 4.9 From Mass Advertising to Interactive Advertising

	Mass Advertising	Direct Mail Advertising	Interactive Advertising
Desired outcomes	Volume sales	Targeted reach, more sales, customer data	Volume sales, CRM, customer feedback
Consumer activities	Passive	Passive	Active
Leading products	Food, personal care products, beer, autos, cameras, computers, appliances	Credit cards, travel, autos, some appliances	Upscale apparel, banking, books, travel, insurance, computers, autos, jewelry, office supplies
Market strategy	High-volume products	Targeted goods to segments	Targeted individual or groups
Nerve centers (command centers)	Madison Avenue (advertisers)	Postal distribution centers, warehouses	Cyberspace, logistics companies
Preferred media vehicle	Television, newspapers, magazines	Mailing lists	Online services, e-commerce, banners
Preferred technology	Storyboards, TV	Databases	Servers, on-screen navigators, the Web
Worst outcome	Channel surfing	Recycling bins	Log off

Source: Based on "From Mass Advertising to Interactive Advertising." *InformationWeek,* October 3, 1994, p. 26. Adapted with permission.

advertising online: (1) using the Web as a channel to advertise a firm's own products and services and (2) making a firm's site a public portal site and using captive audiences to advertise products offered by other firms. For example, the audience might come to a P&G Web site to learn about Tide, but they might also get additional ads for products made by companies other than P&G.

This chapter deals with Internet advertising in general. For additional resources on Internet advertising, see adage.com and webmonkey.wired.com.

ad views
The number of times users call up a page that has a banner on it during a specific time period; known as *impressions* or *page views.*

click (click-through or ad click)
A count made each time a visitor clicks on an advertising banner to access the advertiser 's Web site.

CPM (cost per thousand impressions)
The fee an advertiser pays for each 1,000 times a page with a banner ad is shown.

conversion rate
The percentage of visitors who actually make a purchase.

click-through rate (or ratio)
The percentage of visitors who are exposed to a banner ad and click on it.

click-through ratio
The ratio between the number of clicks on a banner ad and the number of times it is seen by viewers; measures the success of a banner in attracting visitors to click on the ad.

hit
A request for data from a Web page or file.

visit
A series of requests during one navigation of a Web site; a pause of a certain length of time ends a visit.

SOME INTERNET ADVERTISING TERMINOLOGY

The following glossary of terms will be of use as you read about Web advertising.

- **Ad views.** Ad views are the number of times users call up a Web page that has a banner on it during a specific time period (e.g., "ad views per day"). They are also known as *impressions* or *page views.*
- **Button.** A *button* is a small banner that is linked to a Web site. It may contain downloadable software.
- **Page.** A *page* is an HTML (Hypertext Markup Language) document that may contain text, images, and other online elements, such as Java applets and multimedia files. It may be generated statically or dynamically.
- **Click.** A click (click-through or ad click) is counted each time a visitor clicks on an advertising banner to access the advertiser's Web site.
- **CPM.** The CPM is the cost per thousand impressions. This is the fee the advertiser pays for each 1,000 times a page with a banner ad is accessed by a viewer.
- **Conversion rate.** The conversion rate is the percentage of visitors who actually make a purchase.
- **Click-through rate (or ratio).** The click-through rate is the percentage of visitors who are exposed to a banner ad and click on it.
- **Hit.** A hit refers to any request for data from a Web page or file. Hits are often used to determine the popularity/traffic of a site in the context of getting so many "hits" during a given period.
- **Visit.** A user may make a sequence of requests during one navigation, or visit, to a site. Once the visitor stops making requests from a site for a given period of time, called a *time-out* (usually 15 or 30 minutes), the next hit by this visitor is considered a new visit.
- **Unique visit.** A unique visit is a count of the number of visitors to a site, regardless of how many pages they view per visit.
- **Stickiness.** The characteristic that influences the average length of time a visitor stays in a site is termed stickiness. The longer visitors stay at a site, the stickier it is considered to be.

WHY INTERNET ADVERTISING?

The major traditional advertising media are television (about 36 percent), newspapers (about 35 percent), magazines (about 14 percent), and radio (about 10 percent) (Boswell 2002). Although Internet advertising is a small percentage of the $120-billion-a-year advertising industry (about 8 percent in 2004), it is growing rapidly and will reach 17 percent by 2007 (Lewin 2004). For example, according to ZenithOptimedia (2004), Internet advertising expenditures in North America will grow from $156 million in 2002 to $184 million in 2006. Interactive Advertising Bureau (2004) also found that online advertising spending in the United States totaled $2.37 billion in the second quarter of 2004, representing an increase of 42.7 percent over spending in the second quarter of 2003. *eMarketer Daily* (2004) projects $9.1 billion in online ads in 2004 and $11.2 billion in 2005.

Companies advertise on the Internet for several reasons. To begin with, television viewers are migrating to the Internet. The UCLA Center for Communication Policy (2004) found that Internet users are spending time online that they previously spent viewing television. Worldwide, Internet users are spending significantly less time watching television and more time using the Internet at home. This trend will continue, especially as Internet-enabled cell phones become commonplace. In addition, many Internet users are well educated and have high incomes. These Internet surfers are a desired target for advertisers.

unique visit
A count of the number of visitors to a site, regardless of how many pages are viewed per visit.

stickiness
Characteristic that influences the average length of time a visitor stays in a site.

Advertisers are limited in the amount of information they can gather about the television and print ads they place. Advertisers are not able to track the number of people who actually view an ad in a print publication or on TV. Print ads cannot be rotated when a person opens the same page multiple times. Print and television ads cannot be filtered only to female readers who earn over $50,000, own a home, and work in a university. Of the people who do look at the ad, the advertiser cannot even record the amount of time they spent looking at it. The only piece of hard data available for traditional advertising is the total number of print copies sold or the estimated viewing audience of the TV program. Everything else is guesswork.

Much more information and feedback is possible with Internet advertising. Special tracking and ad management programs enable online advertisers to do all of the things mentioned here and more (see Sections 4.7 and 4.8).

Meeker (1997) examined the length of time it took for each ad medium to reach the first 50 million U.S. users. Meeker found that it took radio 38 years, television 13 years, and cable television 10 years to reach 50 million viewers. Remarkably, it took only about 5 years for the Internet to reach 50 million users! It is estimated that more than 700 million people will use the Internet in 2008 (Pyramid Research 2003). According to these statistics, the Internet is the fastest-growing communication medium by far. See Online Exhibit W4.2 for adoption rates for various media. Of course, advertisers are interested in a medium with such potential reach, both locally and globally.

Other reasons why Web advertising is growing rapidly include:

- **Cost.** Online ads are sometimes cheaper than those in other media. In addition, ads can be updated at any time with minimal cost.
- **Richness of format.** Web ads can effectively use the convergence of text, audio, graphics, and animation. In addition, games, entertainment, and promotions can be easily combined in online advertisements. Also, services such as MySimon.com enable customers to compare prices, and using PDA or cell phone, do it at any time from anywhere.
- **Personalization.** Web ads can be interactive and targeted to specific interest groups and/or individuals. That is, the Web is a much more focused medium.
- **Timeliness.** Internet ads can be fresh and up-to-the-minute.
- **Location-basis.** Using wireless technology and GPS, Web advertising can be location based; Internet ads can be sent to consumers whenever they are in a specific time and location (e.g., near a restaurant or a theater).
- **Digital branding.** Even the most price-conscious online shoppers are willing to pay premiums for brands they trust. These brands may be click-and-mortar brands (e.g., P&G), or dot-coms such as Amazon.com. British Airways places many Internet banner ads. However, these ads are not for clicking on to buy; they are all about branding, that is, establishing British Airways as a brand.

As of 1998, these factors began to convince large, consumer-products companies, such as P&G, to shift an increasing share of their advertising dollars away from traditional media to Web advertising.

Of course, each advertising medium, including the Internet, has its advantages and limitations. Online Exhibit W4.3 compares the advantages and limitations of Internet advertising against traditional advertising media. For a comprehensive comparison of the effectiveness of Internet ads versus traditional methods, see Yoon and Kim (2001). Moreover, Chang and Thorson (2004) found that television–Web synergy can help attract more attention than each media on its own. New Media Age (2003) showed that a TV campaign increases brand awareness by 27 percent, whereas a combined TV and online campaign increases it by 45 percent. A TV campaign increases intent to purchase by 2 percent, whereas a combined TV and online campaign increases it by 12 percent.

ADVERTISING NETWORKS

advertising networks
Specialized firms that offer customized Web advertising, such as brokering ads and targeting ads to select groups of consumers.

One of the major advantages of Internet advertising is the ability to customize ads to fit individual viewers. Specialized firms have sprung up to offer this service to companies that wish to locate customers through targeted advertising. Called **advertising networks** (or *ad server networks),* these firms offer special services such as brokering banner ads for sale, bringing together online advertisers and providers of online ad space, and helping target ads to consumers who are presumed to be interested in categories of advertisements based on technology-based consumer profiling. DoubleClick is a premier company in this area. DoubleClick created an advertising network for several hundred companies. It prepares thousands of ads for its clients every week, following the process shown in EC Application Case 4.2.

One-to-one targeted advertising and marketing may be expensive, but it can be very rewarding. According to Taylor (1997), for example, successful targeted online ads proved very effective for selling Lexus cars, at a cost of $169 per car sold. Targeting ads to groups based on segmentation rather than to individuals also can be very cost-effective depending on the advertising method used.

Section 4.6 ◗ REVIEW QUESTIONS

1. Define Web advertising and the major terms associated with it.
2. Describe the reasons for the growth in Web advertising.
3. List the major characteristics of Web advertising.
4. Explain the role of ad networks in Web advertising.

4.7 ADVERTISING METHODS

Several methods can be used for online advertising. Most notable are banners, pop-ups (and pop-unders), and e-mails.

BANNERS

banner
On a Web page, a graphic advertising display linked to the advertiser's Web page.

keyword banners
Banner ads that appear when a predetermined word is queried from a search engine.

random banners
Banner ads that appear at random, not as the result of the user's action.

A **banner** is a graphic display that is used for advertising on a Web page. The size of the banner is usually 5 to 6.25 inches in length, 0.5 to 1 inch in width, and is measured in pixels. A banner ad is linked to an advertiser's Web page. When users "click" the banner, they are transferred to the advertiser's site. Advertisers go to great lengths to design a banner that catches consumers' attention. Banners often include video clips and sound. Banner advertising including pop-up banners is the most commonly used form of advertising on the Internet.

There are several types of banners. **Keyword banners** appear when a predetermined word is queried from a search engine. They are effective for companies that want to narrow their target audience. **Random banners** appear randomly, not as a result of some action by the viewer. Companies that want to introduce new products (e.g., a new movie or CD) or promote their brand use random banners. *Static banners* are always on the Web page. Finally, *pop-up banners* appear when least expected, as will be described later.

If an advertiser knows something about a visitor, such as the visitor's user profile, it is possible to *match* a specific banner with that visitor. Obviously, such targeted, personalized banners are usually most effective.

In the near future, banner ads will greet people by name and offer travel deals to their favorite destinations. Such personalized banners are being developed by dotomi.com. It delivers ads to consumers who opt in to its system. Initial results show a 14 percent click-through rate versus 3 to 5 percent with nonpersonalized ads.

Benefits and Limitations of Banner Ads

The major benefit of banner ads is that by clicking on them users are transferred to an advertiser's site, and frequently directly to the shopping page of that site. Another advantage of using banners is the ability to customize them for individual surfers or a market segment of surfers. Also, viewing of banners is fairly high because, in many cases, customers are forced to see banner ads while waiting for a page to load or before they can get the free information or

CASE 4.2

EC Application

TARGETED ADVERTISING: THE DOUBLECLICK APPROACH

One-to-one targeted advertising can take many forms. Assume that 3M Corp. wants to advertise its multimedia projectors that cost $10,000. It knows that potential buyers are people who work in advertising agencies, in information systems departments of large corporations, or in companies that use the UNIX operating system. 3M approaches DoubleClick and asks the firm to identify such potential customers. How does DoubleClick find them? The answer is both clever and simple.

As of 1997, DoubleClick (*doubleclick.com/us*) monitors people browsing the Web sites of several hundred cooperating companies such as Quicken (*quicken.com*) and Travelocity (*travelocity.com*). By inspecting the Internet addresses of the visitors to these companies' Web sites and matching them against a database with about 100,000 Internet domain names that include a line-of-business code (code that tells the classification of each industry), DoubleClick can find those people working for advertising agencies. By checking the users' browsers, it also can find out which visitors are using UNIX. Although DoubleClick cannot find out a visitor's name, it can build a dossier on the visitor that is attached to an ID number that was assigned during the visitor's first visit to any of the cooperating sites. As the visitor continues to visit the sites, an intelligent (software) agent builds a relatively complete dossier on the visitor that includes the sites they visit, the pages they looked at, the Internet address from which they came, and so on. This process is done with a cookie, so the Web site can "remember" a visitor's past behavior on the Internet.

DoubleClick then prepares an ad about 3M projectors. The ad is targeted to people whose profiles match the criteria listed earlier. If a visitor is a UNIX user or an employee of an advertising agency, on the visitor's next browsing trip to *any* of the participating Web sites, he or she will be greeted with an ad that 3M hopes will be of interest—an ad for a multimedia projector.

How is this activity financed? DoubleClick charges 3M for the ad. The fee is then split with the participating Web sites that carry the 3M ads based on how many times the ad is matched with visitors.

In 1998, DoubleClick expanded the service, called Dynamic Advertising Reporting and Targeting (DART), from pinpoint target and ad design to advertising control, ad frequency determination, and providing verifiable measures of success. DoubleClick brings the right advertisement to the right person at the right time. DART works with 22 criteria that it tries to find on each consumer (e.g., location, time of day, etc.). A schematic view of the process is shown in the following figure.

(*continued*)

How DoubleClick Matches Ads to Customers

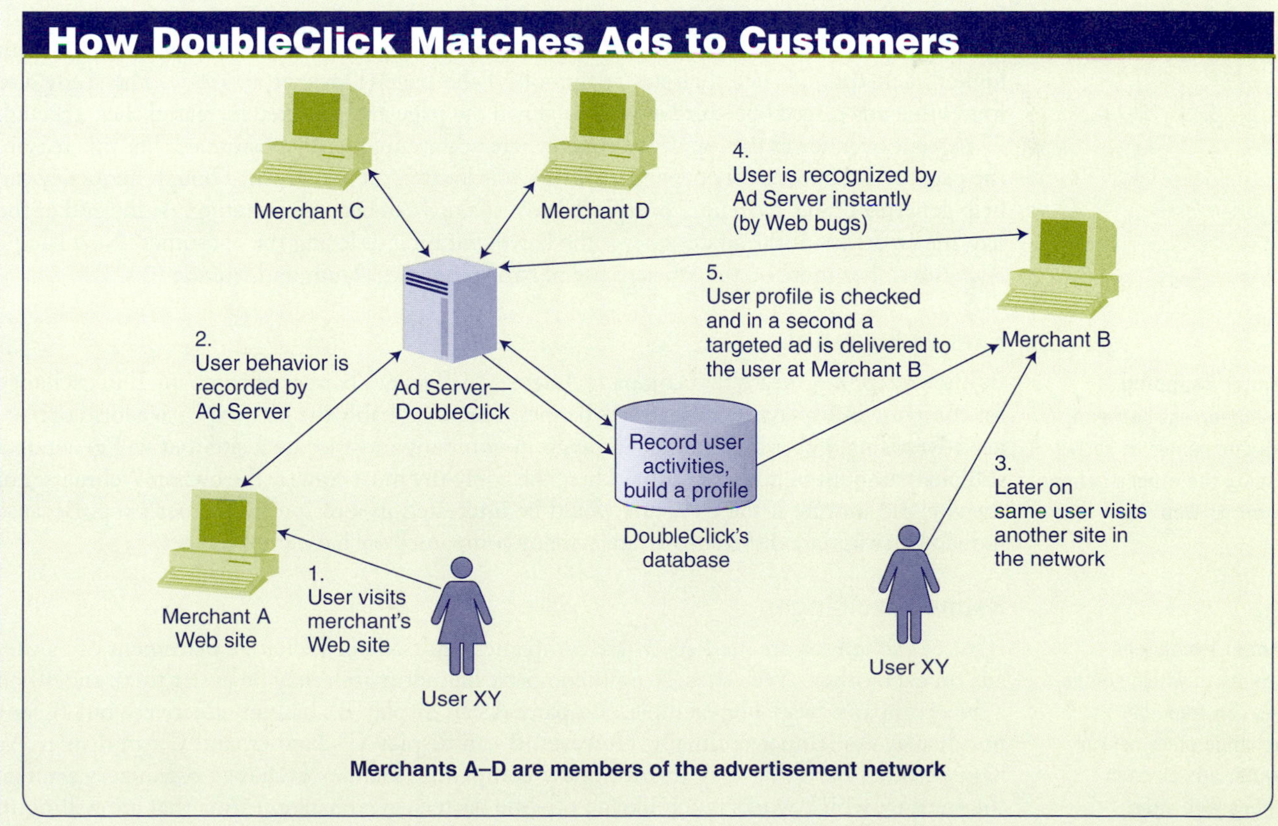

Merchants A–D are members of the advertisement network

CASE 4.2 (continued)

In June 1999, DoubleClick announced the purchase of Abacus Direct, whose database contains the buying habits of 88 million U.S. households. DoubleClick wanted to tie its online consumer data with that of Abacus to collect personal information online. This way, names and addresses would be in DoubleClick's database. Privacy-protection groups opposed the merger, asking the FTC to open an investigation. Under pressure, DoubleClick agreed to limit the connection.

Sources: Compiled from Rothenberg (1999), *doubleclick.com* (accessed 2001–2003), and Brown (2002).

Questions

1. How does DoubleClick build dossiers on people?
2. How are ads matched with individual viewers?
3. Why is an advertising network needed?
4. What role do the "participating sites" play in the DART system?

entertainment that they want to see (a strategy called "forced advertising"). Finally, banners may include attention-grabbing multimedia.

The major disadvantage of banners is their cost. If a company demands a successful marketing campaign, it will need to allocate a large percentage of the advertising budget to place banners on high-volume Web sites. Another drawback is that a limited amount of information can be placed on the banner. Hence, advertisers need to think of a creative but short message to attract viewers.

However, it seems that viewers have become somewhat immune to banners and simply do not notice them as they once did. The click-through rate, which measures the success of a banner in attracting visitors to click it, has been declining over time. For example, if a page receives 1,000 views and the banner is clicked on 30 times, the click ratio is 3 percent. The University of Michigan found the average click ratio, which was 3 percent in the mid-1990s, to be less than 1 percent today, and it is declining (Doyle et al. 1997; Meskauskas 2001). According to *eMarketer* (2004), it was less than 0.8 percent in late 2004, but is slowly increasing again.

Because of these drawbacks, it is important to decide where on the screen to place banners. For example, a study of Web ads conducted by the University of Michigan found that ads placed in the lower-right-hand corner of the screen, next to the scrollbar, generate a 228 percent higher click-through rate than ads at the top of the page (Doyle et al. 1997). The study also found that ads placed one-third of the way down the page and centered increased click-through 77 percent over ads at the top of the page, where ads are frequently positioned. For this reason, the price of the banner may depend on where it is located on the screen. Though frequency can help generate brand awareness, overplayed advertisings can become irritating. At the end of the day, the creativity of the ad designer is the key to winning or losing the consumer (New Media Age 2004). For more on the efficient use of banner ads, see Amiri and Menon (2003).

Banner Swapping

banner swapping
An agreement between two companies to each display the other's banner ad on its Web site.

Banner swapping means that company A agrees to display a banner of company B in exchange for company B displaying company A's banner. This is probably the least expensive form of banner advertising, but it is difficult to arrange. A company must locate a site that will generate a sufficient amount of relevant traffic. Then, the company must contact the owner/Webmaster of the site and inquire if the company would be interested in a reciprocal banner swap. Because individual swaps are difficult to arrange, many companies use banner exchanges.

Banner Exchanges

banner exchanges
Markets in which companies can trade or exchange placement of banner ads on each other's Web sites.

Banner exchanges are markets where companies can trade or exchange placement of banner ads on each other's Web sites. A multicompany banner match may be easier to arrange than a two-company swap. For example, company A can display B's banner effectively, but B cannot display A's banner optimally. However, B can display C's banner, and C can display A's banner. Such bartering may involve many companies. Banner exchange organizers arrange the trading, which works much like an off-line bartering exchange. Firms that are willing to display others' banners join the exchange. Each time a participant displays a banner for one of the exchange's other members, it receives a credit. After a participant has "earned" enough credits, its own banner is displayed on a suitable member's site. Most exchanges offer members the opportunity to purchase additional display credits.

Examples of exchanges are express-marketing.com, linkswap.co.uk, click4click.com, and microsoft.com/smallbusiness.

Banner exchanges are not without their disadvantages. To begin with, some charge fees, charging members either money or ad space, or both. Second, some banner exchanges will not allow certain types of banners. In addition, there are tax implications for companies that barter their banners.

Overall, banner advertising was very valuable in the 1990s. However, its share of the market is declining, because Web users are increasingly ignoring banner ads.

POP-UP AND SIMILAR ADS

One of the most annoying phenomena in Web surfing is the increased use of pop-up, pop-under, and similar ads. A **pop-up ad**, also known as *ad spawning*, is the automatic launching of new browser windows with an ad when a visitor enters or exits a site, on a delay, or on other triggers. A pop-up ad appears in front of the active window. A **pop-under ad** is an ad that appears underneath (in back of) the current browser window; when users close the active window, they see the ad. (There also are pop-under exchanges that function much like banner exchanges.) Pop-ups cover the user's current screen and may be difficult to close. Pop-up and pop-under ads are controversial: Many users strongly object to this advertising method, which they consider intrusive (see Chapter 17, Section 17.4).

pop-up ad
An ad that appears in a separate window before, after, or during Internet surfing or when reading e-mail.

pop-under ad
An ad that appears underneath the current browser window, so when the user closes the active window, he or she sees the ad.

Several related tactics, some of which are very aggressive, are used by advertisers, and their use is increasing. Here are a few examples from cyveillance.com (2003).

- **Mouse-trapping.** Disables the user's ability to go back, exit, or close while viewing the page.
- **Typo-piracy and cyber-squatting.** Uses misspellings and derivations of a popular brand name to divert traffic to an unintended site.
- **Unauthorized software downloads.** Leaves behind software that contains embedded advertising or tracking capabilities. Sometimes coupled with mislabeling of buttons so that the download occurs regardless of whether "yes" or "no" is selected.
- **Visible seeding.** Visibly places popular brands, slogans, and proprietary content into a site to optimize search-engine rankings.
- **Invisible seeding.** Hides content to optimize search service rankings.
- **Changing homepage or favorites.** Substitutes a new homepage setting or makes changes to the user's "favorites" list.
- **Framing.** Keeps customer on the original site while the customer views content of another site through the original site's window; the site can then use higher visit time statistics to attract advertisers.
- **Spoof or magnet pages.** Seeds site content with select words, brands, slogans, and personalities to draw traffic.
- **Mislabeling links.** Falsely labels hyperlinks that send the shopper to an unintended destination.

Some of these tactics are accompanied by music, voice, and other rich multimedia. Protection against pop-ups is offered by ISPs (e.g., AOL), by software security vendors (e.g., STOPzilla at stopzilla.com, and Pop-up Stopper from panicware.com), and by portals. In summer 2004, Microsoft introduced a built-in blocker in Internet Explorer. Also, legal attempts have been made to control pop ups, because they are basically a form of spam (see Chapter 17, Section 17.4).

Interstitials

An **interstitial**, a type of pop-up ad, is a page or box that appears after a user clicks a link. These ads remain while content is loading. (The word *interstitial* comes from *interstice*, which means a small space between things.) An interstitial may be an initial Web page or a

interstitial
An initial Web page or a portion of it that is used to capture the user's attention for a short time while other content is loading.

portion of one that is used to capture the user's attention for a short time, either as a promotion or a lead-in to the site's homepage or to advertise a product or a service. They pop onto the PC screen much like a TV commercial.

How to Deal with Unsolicited Pop-Ups, Pop-Unders, and Interstitials

If viewers do not want to see these ads, they can remove them by simply closing them or by installing software to block them. Several software packages are available on the market to assist users in blocking these types of ads.

E-MAIL ADVERTISING

A popular way to advertise on the Internet is to send company or product information to people or companies listed in mailing lists via e-mail. According to Berkowitz (2004), online e-mail expenditures were between $1.2 and $2.1 billion in 2003, and they are projected to reach between $1.67 and $6 billion in 2008. The Direct Marketing Association (2003) found that e-mail marketing has the highest ROI index when compared with 11 other types of media for direct response marketing in the United States. DoubleClick (2004) also found that e-mail continued to enjoy popularity among consumers and that there is an increasing acknowledgment of e-mail as a legitimate and relied-upon marketing channel. E-mail messages may be combined with brief audio or video clips promoting a product and with on-screen links that users can click to make a purchase. E-mail also is exploding because it is now available in a wireless environment as well as on interactive TV (e.g., in France).

The advantages of the e-mail advertising approach are its low cost and the ability to reach a wide variety of targeted audiences. Also, e-mail is an *interactive* medium, and it can combine advertising and customer service. It can include a direct link to any URL, so it acts like a banner. A 2004 study by Interactive Prospect Targeting (IPT) found that 32 percent of consumers picked e-mail as the most effective marketing communication channel. IPT also found that consumers are more likely to respond to e-mail messages related to discounts or special sales. Most companies have a database of customers to whom they can send e-mail messages. However, using e-mail to send ads (sometimes floods of ads) without the receivers' permission is considered *spamming*.

Undoubtedly, the quantity of e-mail that consumers receive is exploding. In light of this, marketers employing e-mail must take a long-term view and work toward motivating consumers to continue to read the messages they receive. As the volume of e-mail increases, consumers' tendency to screen and block messages will rise as well. Many e-mail services (e.g., see hotmail.com) permit users to block messages from specific sources.

A list of e-mail addresses can be a very powerful tool with which a company can target a group of people it knows something about. For information on how to create a mailing list, consult groups.yahoo.com (the service is free), or topica.com. E-mail also can be sent to PDA devices and to mobile phones. Mobile phones offer advertisers a real chance to advertise interactively and on a one-to-one basis with consumers, anytime, any place. In the future, e-mail ads will be targeted to individuals based not only on their user profiles, but also on their physical location at any point in time. See Chapter 9 for a description of this concept, known as *l-commerce*.

E-Mail Advertising Management

Although sending e-mail ads sounds simple, it really is not. Preparing mailing lists, deciding on content, and measuring the results are some of the activities that are part of e-mail advertising management. One important area is getting reliable mailing lists. Companies such as Worldata.com can help supply lists for both B2C and B2B EC. Worldata.com also provides ad management services. (See the demo of the e-mail tracking system at worldata.com.)

Given the new e-marketing technologies, consumer frustration over spam, and new regulations, marketers should reevaluate how their e-mail advertisements are created, deployed, and measured. The Peppers and Rogers Group (2004) suggests four guidelines that marketers should consider to leverage customer insights throughout the e-mail marketing campaign lifecycle: (1) thinking about customer experience, (2) making privacy protection a part of their brand promise, (3) ensuring their recipients know about their privacy protection, and

(4) measuring impact. By applying these guidelines, companies can enhance customer experiences and create long-term and loyal relationships.

E-mail Hoaxes. E-mail hoaxes are very popular; some of them have been going on for years (e.g., Neiman Marcus' cookie recipe, the Nigerian treasure). Some of these are scams. For details, see ftc.gov and Fleita (2003).

E-Mail Advertising Methods and Successes

E-mail advertising can be done in a number of different ways (see Gordon-Lewis 2002 and Chase 2004), as shown in the following examples.

E-Mail Promotions. E-Greetings Network (egreetings.com) produces digital postcards and animations to its customers, who are both individuals and corporations. For a modest membership fee ($13.95 annually), members have access to over 5,000 e-greeting cards, plus designs for flyers, fax covers, and envelopes. Through its free membership trial and its members list, E-Greetings Network has compiled a database of millions of recipients. E-Greetings Network's goals for its e-mail promotion campaign include bringing value to its customers, driving traffic and transactions at the customer's site, stimulating involvement with the site, expanding customer relationships, offering added means of sponsorship, and supporting brand affinity. E-Greetings' main relationship-building tool is its newsletter "What's Up @ E-greetings!" Key factors in its success are the fact that the mailing list is totally voluntarily (opt-in); newsletters are distributed on a regular, biweekly schedule; the content is relevant; and it handles unsubscribe difficulties and customer service in a timely manner.

Discussion Lists. Internet Security Systems (ISS), with $1 billion in sales per year, provides software that detects weaknesses in systems and gives detailed corrective measures for fixing security holes. Its success began when its founder, Chris Klaus, posted a notice about his security software on a newsgroup. He then offered a shareware version of the program to the newsgroup members and received 200 e-mail responses the following day. His company's discussion list program includes approximately 80 specialized e-mail lists reaching over 100,000 people through discussions, partner lists, customer lists, and product announcement lists (Kinnard 2002). Sponsorship of discussion groups, communities, and newsletters is becoming quite popular on the Web (see sponsorship.com).

E-Mail List Management. L-Soft's Listserv (lsoft.com), the leader in software for e-mail list management and marketing, is known for its electronic newsletters, discussion groups, and direct e-mail messaging. According to Kinnard (2002), the company understands that 9 out of 10 customer interactions are not transactions, so it offers database integration, mail merges, and customizable Web interfaces that allow companies to send pertinent information, such as product details or advertising, to specific customers. Listserv delivers 30 million messages each weekday and 1 million messages per hour from a single server. For e-mail challenges, see Berkowitz (2004).

NEWSPAPER-LIKE STANDARDIZED ADS

In 2001, the Internet Advertising Bureau, an industry trade group, adopted five standard ad sizes for the Internet. These standardized ads are larger and more noticeable than banner ads. They look like the ads in a newspaper or magazine, so advertisers like them. Tests found that users read these ads four times more frequently than banners (Tedeschi 2001). The ads appear on Web sites in columns or boxes. One of the most popular of the standardized ads is a full-column-deep ad called a *skyscraper ad.* Publishers, such as the *New York Times* (nytimes.com), publish these standardized ads, sometimes as many as four on one Web page. Some of these ads are interactive; users can click on a link inside the ad for more information about a product or service. These sizes also are used in pop-up ads, in fixed banners, or in classified ads. (To find out how much an Internet ad currently costs, see webconnect.com/wise.)

Classified Ads

Another newspaper-like ad is the *classified* ad. These ads can be found on special sites (e.g., infospace.com), as well as on online newspapers, exchanges, portals, and so on. In many cases, posting regular-size classified ads is free, but placing them in a larger size or with some noticeable features is done for a fee. For examples, see traderonline.com and advertising.msn.com.

SEARCH ENGINE ADVERTISEMENT

Most search engines allow companies to submit their Internet addresses, called URLs (Universal Resource Locators), for free so that these URLs can be searched electronically. Search engine spiders crawl through the submitted site, indexing its content and links. The site is then included in future searches. Because there are several thousand search engines, advertisers who use this method should register URLs with as many search engines as possible.

The major advantage of using URLs as an advertising tool is that it is *free*. Anyone can submit a URL to a search engine and be listed. By using URLs, it is likely that searchers for a company's products will receive a list of sites that mention the products, including the company's own site.

However, the URL method has several drawbacks. The major one has to do with location: The chance that a specific site will be placed at the top of a search engine's display list (say, in the first 10 sites) is very slim. Furthermore, even if a company's URL makes it to the top, others can quickly displace the URL from the top slot. Second, different search engines index their listings differently; therefore, it is difficult to make the top of several lists. The searcher may have the correct keywords, but if the search engine indexed the site listing using the "title" or "content description" in the meta tag, then the effort could be fruitless. A meta tag is a coding statement (in HTML) that describes the content of a Web page and is used by search engines to index content so it can be found.

Improving a Company's Search-Engine Ranking (Optimization)

By simply adding, removing, or changing a few sentences, a Web designer may alter the way a search engine's spider ranks its findings (see Seda 2004) and therefore improve a company's ranking on the search engine's list. Several companies have services that *optimize* Web content so that a site has a better chance of being discovered by a search engine (e.g., keywordcount.com or webpositiongold.com). More tips for improving a site's listing in various search engines can be found at searchenginewatch.com.

Another way to improve the search-engine ranking is via link partnerships. For example, tucsonproperties.net, a real estate company, contacts other real estate companies and proposes placing links on each other's Web sites. The more links made, the higher the ranking may be.

Paid Search-Engine Inclusion

Several search engines charge fees for including URLs at or near the top of the search results. For example, google.com and overture.com charge firms for "sponsor matching." The more the company pays, the closer it will be to the top of the sponsor's list. Overture works with several search engines.

ADVERTISING IN CHAT ROOMS

A chat room can be used to build a community, promote a political or environmental cause, support people with medical problems, or allow hobbyists to share their interest. It can be used for advertising as well (e.g., see Gelb and Sundaram 2002).

Vendors frequently sponsor chat rooms. The sponsoring vendor places a chat link on its site, and the chat vendor does the rest (e.g., talkcity.com), including placing the advertising that pays for the session. The advertising in a chat room merges with the activity in the room, and the user is conscious of what is being presented.

The main difference between an advertisement that appears on a static Web page and one that comes through a chat room is that the latter allows advertisers to cycle through messages and target the chatters again and again. Also, advertising can become more thematic in a chat room. An advertiser can start with one message and build upon it to a climax, just as an author does with a good story. For example, a toy maker may have a chat room dedicated to electronic toys. The advertiser can use the chat room to post a query such as, "Can anyone tell me about the new Electoy R3D3?" In addition, a company can go to competitors' chat rooms and observe the conversations there.

Chat rooms also are used as one-to-one connections between a company and its customers. For example, Mattel (mattel.com) sells about one-third of its Barbie dolls to collectors. These collectors use the chat room to make comments or ask questions that are then answered by Mattel's staff.

ADVERTISING IN NEWSLETTERS

Free newsletters are abundant; in e-commerce there are many. An example is *Ecommerce Times*. This informative newsletter (ecommercetimes.com) solicits ads from companies (see "How to Advertise"). Ads are usually short, and they have a link to details. They are properly marked as "Advertisement."

OTHER FORMS OF ADVERTISING

Online advertising can be done in several other ways, ranging from ads in newsgroups to ads in computer kiosks. Advertising on *Internet radio* is just beginning, and soon advertising on *Internet television* will commence. In November 2004, Amazon.com launched a series of short films for the holiday season that promoted items that customers could purchase. (BMW promotes its cars with short films as well.) According to Wang (2004), marketers are beginning to use online videos in B2B. *eMarketer* (2004) reports that video ads are increasing more than 50 percent each year, topping $120 million in revenue in 2004.

Some marketers use **advertorials**. An advertorial is material that looks like editorial content or general information, but is really an advertisement.

advertorial
An advertisement "disguised" to look like editorial content or general information.

Others advertise to members of Internet communities (Chapter 17). Community sites, such as geocities.com, offer targeted advertising opportunities and vendors usually offer discounts to members on the advertised products. There also are ads that, when clicked on, link users to other sites that might be of interest to community members. Advertisers also use online fantasy sports to send ads to the specific sport fans (e.g., National Football League [NFL] and Major League Baseball [MLB]).

In addition, a site's *domain name* may be used for brand recognition. This is why some companies pay millions of dollars to keep certain domain names under their control (see alldomains.com) or to buy popular names.

Finally, as will be shown in Chapter 9, advertising on cell phones and other mobile devices is expected to increase rapidly, especially after 2007.

Section 4.7 ▶ REVIEW QUESTIONS

1. Define banner ads and describe their benefits and limitations.
2. Describe banner swapping and banner exchanges.
3. Describe the issues surrounding pop ups and similar ads.
4. Explain how e-mail is used for advertising.
5. Describe advertising via standardized and newspaper-like ads.
6. Discuss advertising via URLs and in chat rooms.

4.8 ADVERTISING STRATEGIES AND PROMOTIONS ONLINE

Several advertising strategies can be used over the Internet. In this section, we will present the major strategies used.

ASSOCIATED AD DISPLAY

Sometimes it is possible to associate the content of a Web page with a related ad. Suppose a person is interested in finding material on e-loyalty. If she uses Yahoo! to search for e-loyalty, she will receive a list of sources and a banner ad with "sponsor results." Banner ads may appear when she clicks on the top sites that deal with e-loyalty. This strategy of displaying a banner ad related to a term entered in a search engine is called **associated ad display** or **text links**. For example, when using MapQuest (mapquest.com), which provides maps and driving directions, the user will receive the results and related sponsored links.

associated ad display (text links)
An advertising strategy that displays a banner ad related to a term entered in a search engine.

Another example of associated ad display can be found at amazon.com. When a customer reads about a book, a list of books is displayed under the heading "Customers who bought this book also bought. . . ." To support this kind of service, Amazon.com uses data mining capabilities. The associated ads appear only as a reaction to user actions.

Companies usually implement the associated ad display strategy through their *affiliate programs* (e.g., see Helmstetter and Metivier 2000), as is done by Yahoo!

Posting Press Releases Online

Millions of people visit popular portals such as Yahoo!, MSN, AOL, or Google every day looking for news. Thus, it makes sense to try to reach an audience through such sites. And indeed, Southwest Airlines was successful in selling $1.5 million in tickets by posting four press releases online. However, it is not as simple as it sounds. For a discussion of how to place online press releases, see the case study at Marketingsherpa (2004).

Google Targeting

When Google initiated its IPO in fall 2004, asking over $100 per share, most analysts were skeptical. After an initial price decline, the share price almost doubled in a few weeks, making Google's capitalization one of the world's largest (see case in Chapter 14). What drove the price of the share was the expectation that Google will generate billions of dollars in advertisement revenue, as discussed in Online File W4.3.

AFFILIATE MARKETING AND ADVERTISING

affiliate marketing
A marketing arrangement by which an organization refers consumers to the selling company's Web site.

In Chapters 1 through 3, we introduced the concept of **affiliate marketing**, the revenue model by which an organization refers consumers to the selling company's Web site. Affiliate marketing is used mainly as a revenue source for the referring organization and as a marketing tool for sellers. However, the fact that the selling company's logo is placed on many other Web sites is free advertising as well. Consider Amazon.com, whose logo can be seen on about 500,000 affiliate sites! For a comprehensive directory of affiliate programs, see cashpile.com. In addition, Hoffman and Novak (2000) provide an example of how CDNow (a subsidiary of Amazon.com) and Amazon.com both use affiliate marketing.

ADS AS A COMMODITY

With the *ads-as-a-commodity* approach, people are paid for time spent viewing an ad. This approach is used at mypoints.com, clickrewards.com, and others. At mypoints.com, interested consumers read ads in exchange for payment from the advertisers. Consumers fill out data on personal interests, and then they receive targeted banners based on their personal profiles. Each banner is labeled with the amount of payment that will be paid if the consumer reads the ad. If interested, the consumer clicks the banner to read it, and after passing some tests as to its content, is paid for the effort. Readers can sort and choose what they read, and the advertisers can vary the payments to reflect the frequency and desirability of the readers. Payments may be cash (e.g., $0.50 per banner) or product discounts.

VIRAL MARKETING

viral marketing
Word-of-mouth marketing by which customers promote a product or service by telling others about it.

Viral marketing or advertising refers to word-of-mouth marketing in which customers promote a product or service by telling others about it. This can be done by e-mails, in conversations facilitated in chat rooms, by posting messages in newsgroups, and in electronic consumer forums. Having people forward messages to friends, asking them, for example, to "check out this product," is an example of viral marketing. This marketing approach has been used for generations, but now its speed and reach are multiplied by the Internet. This ad model can be used to build brand awareness at a minimal cost (*MarketingWeek* 2004), because the people who pass on the messages are paid very little or nothing for their efforts.

Viral marketing has long been a favorite strategy of online advertisers pushing youth-oriented products. For example, advertisers might distribute, embedded within a sponsor's e-mail, a small game program that is easy to forward. By releasing a few thousand copies of the game to some consumers, vendors hope to reach hundreds of thousands of others. Viral marketing also was used by the founder of Hotmail, a free e-mail service, which grew from zero to 12 million subscribers in its 18 initial months and to over 50 million in about 4 years. Each e-mail sent via Hotmail carries an invitation for free Hotmail service. Also known as *advocacy marketing*, this innovative approach, if properly used, can be effective, efficient, and relatively inexpensive.

One of the downsides of this strategy is that several e-mail hoaxes have been spread this way (see Fleitas 2003). Another danger of viral advertising is that a destructive virus can be added to an innocent advertisement-related game or message. Fraud also is a danger. For example, a person may get an e-mail stating that his or her credit card number is invalid or that the his or her AOL service or newspaper delivery will be terminated unless another credit card number is sent as a reply to the e-mail. For protection against such hoaxes, see scambusters.org.

CUSTOMIZING ADS

The Internet has too much information for customers to view. Filtering irrelevant information by providing consumers with customized ads can reduce this information overload. BroadVision (broadvision.com) provides a customized ad service platform called One-to-One. The heart of One-to-One is a customer database, which includes registration data and information gleaned from site visits. The companies that advertise via One-to-One use the database to send customized ads to consumers. Using this feature, a marketing manager can customize display ads based on users' profiles.

Another model of personalization can be found in **Webcasting**, a free Internet news service that broadcasts personalized news and information as well as e-seminars (Chapter 8). Users sign into the Webcasting system and select the information they would like to receive, such as sports, news, headlines, stock quotes, or desired product promotions. The users receive the requested information along with personalized ads based on their expressed interests and general ads based on their profile.

Webcasting
A free Internet news service that broadcasts personalized news and information, including seminars, in categories selected by the user.

ONLINE EVENTS, PROMOTIONS, AND ATTRACTIONS

In the winter of 1994, the term *EC* was hardly known, and people were just starting to discover the Internet. One company, DealerNet, which was selling new and used cars from physical lots, demonstrated a new way of doing business: It started a virtual car showroom on the Internet. It let people "visit" dozens of dealerships and compare prices and features. At the time, this was a revolutionary way of selling cars. To get people's attention, DealerNet gave away a car over the Internet.

This promotion, unique at the time, received a lot of off-line media attention and was a total success. Today, such promotions are regular events on thousands of Web sites. Contests, quizzes, coupons (see coolsavings.com), and giveaways designed to attract visitors are as much a part of online marketing as they are of off-line commerce (see Clow and Baack 2004; O'Keefe 2002). Some innovative ideas used to encourage people to pay attention to online advertising are provided in Online File W4.4.

Live Web Events

Live Web events (concerts, shows, interviews, debates, videos), if properly done, can generate tremendous public excitement and bring huge crowds to a Web site. According to Akamai Technologies, Inc. (2000a), the best practices for successful live Web events are:

- Careful planning of content, audience, interactivity level, preproduction, and schedule
- Executing the production with rich media if possible
- Conducting appropriate promotion via e-mails, affinity sites, and streaming media directories, as well as conducting proper off-line and online advertisement
- Preparing for quality delivery
- Capturing data and analyzing audience response so that improvements can be made

Admediation

Conducting promotions, especially large-scale ones, may require the help of vendors who specialize in promotions such as those listed in Online File W4.5. Gopal and Walter (2001) researched this area and developed a model that shows the role of third-party vendors (such as mypoints.com), which they call **admediaries**. Their model is shown in Exhibit 4.10. The

admediaries
Third-party vendors that conduct promotions, especially large-scale ones.

EXHIBIT 4.10 Framework for Admediation

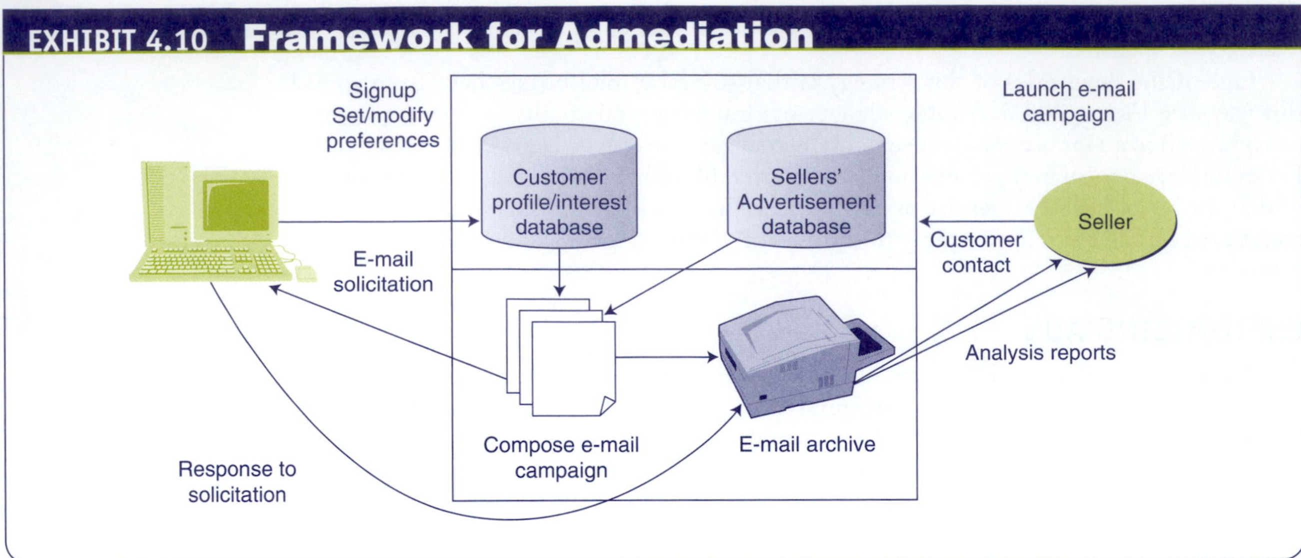

Source: Gopal, R. D., et al. "Admediation: New Horizons in Effective Email Advertising." *The Communications of the ACM.* ©2001 ACM Inc. Used with permission.

exhibit concentrates on e-mail and shows the role of the admediaries (in the box between the customers and sellers).

Running promotions on the Internet is similar to running off-line promotions. According to Thomton and Lin (2003) and Clow and Baack (2004), some of the major considerations when implementing an online ad campaign include the following:

- The target audience needs to be clearly understood and should be online surfers.
- The traffic to the site should be estimated, and a powerful enough server must be prepared to handle the expected traffic volume.
- Assuming that the promotion is successful, what will the result be? This assessment is needed to evaluate the budget and promotion strategy.
- Consider cobranding; many promotions succeed because they bring together two or more powerful partners.

For more information about promotions and ad strategies, see Clow and Baack (2004).

Section 4.8 ▶ REVIEW QUESTIONS

1. Describe the associated ad (text links) strategy.
2. Discuss the process and value of affiliate marketing.
3. How does the ads-as-a-commodity strategy work?
4. Describe viral marketing.
5. How are ads customized?
6. List some typical Internet promotions.
7. Define admediaries and describe their roles.

4.9 SPECIAL ADVERTISING TOPICS

The following are major representative topics related to Internet advertisement.

PERMISSION ADVERTISING

One of the major issues of one-to-one advertising is the flooding of users with unwanted (junk) e-mail, banners, pop ups, and so on. One of the authors of this book experienced a flood of X-rated ads. Each time such an ad arrived, he blocked receipt of further ads from this source. That helped for a day or two, but then the same ads arrived from another e-mail address. His e-mail service provider, Hotmail (hotmail.com), was very helpful in providing several options to minimize this problem. Hotmail can place software agents to identify and block such junk mail. This problem, the flooding of users with unsolicited e-mails, is called **spamming** (see Chapter 17). Spamming typically upsets consumers, which may keep useful advertising from reaching them in the future.

One solution used by advertisers is **permission advertising** (**permission marketing** or the *opt-in approach*), in which users register with advertisers and *agree* to accept advertising (see netcreations.com). For example, the authors of this book agreed to receive large numbers of e-commerce newsletters, knowing that some would include ads. This way we can keep abreast of what is happening in the field. We also agree to accept e-mail from research companies, newspapers, travel agencies, and more. These vendors push, for free, very valuable information to us. The accompanying ads pay for such services. One way to conduct permission advertisement is to provide incentives, as discussed in Section 4.8.

spamming
Using e-mail to send unwanted ads (sometimes floods of ads).

permission advertising (permission marketing)
Advertising (marketing) strategy in which customers agree to accept advertising and marketing materials.

ADVERTISEMENT AS A REVENUE MODEL

Many of the dot-com failures in 2000 to 2002 were caused by a revenue model that contained advertising income as the major, or only, revenue source (e.g., see the story of Go.com in Chapter 3, p. 123). Many small portals failed, but several large ones are dominating the field: AOL, Yahoo!, Google, and MSN. However, even these heavy-traffic sites reported only small revenue growth in 2001–2002, and only in 2003 and 2004 have they showed significant improvement. There are simply too many Web sites competing for advertising money. For these reasons, almost all portals are adding other sources of revenue.

However, if careful, a small site can survive by concentrating on a niche area. For example, playfootball.com is doing well. It pulls millions of dollars in advertising and sponsorship by concentrating on NFL fans. The site provides comprehensive and interactive content, attracting millions of visitors.

MEASURING ONLINE ADVERTISING'S EFFECTIVENESS

One managerial issue is how to measure the effectiveness of online advertisement. A related topic is how to charge for ads. These two topics are presented as a complete section in Online File W4.5. For a special report on the topic, see Blanford (2004).

AD MANAGEMENT

The activities involved in Web advertising, which range from tracking viewers to rotating ads, require a special methodology and software known as **ad management**. Ad management software lets an advertiser send very specific ads on a schedule and target ads to certain population segments, which can be very small. For example, an advertiser can send an ad to all male residents of Los Angeles County between the ages of 26 and 39 whose income level is above $30,000. The advertiser can even refine the segment further by using ethnic origin, type of employment, or whether they own their home.

ad management
Methodology and software that enable organizations to perform a variety of activities involved in Web advertising (e.g., tracking viewers, rotating ads).

When selecting ad management software, a company should look for the following features, which will optimize their ability to advertise online:

- **The ability to match ads with specific content.** Being able to match ads with Web content would allow an advertiser, for example, to run an ad from a car company in an article about the Indy 500.
- **Tracking.** Of course, the advertiser will need to deliver detailed metrics (performance measures) to its customers, showing impression rates, click-through rates, and other metrics. Tracking of viewing activity is essential in providing such metrics.
- **Rotation.** Advertisers may want to rotate different ads in the same space.
- **Spacing impressions.** If an advertiser buys a given number of impressions over a period of time, the software should be able to adjust the delivery schedule so that they are spread out evenly.

A variety of ad management software packages are available, including some from application service providers (ASPs) and some freeware. A comprehensive package is AdManager from accipiter.com, which delivers all of the features just discussed.

One topic in ad management is *campaign management*; that is, management of an entire marketing and advertising campaign. Campaign management tools fall into two categories: those that are folded into CRM, which consist mainly of marketing automation, and those that are targeted, stand-alone campaign management products. Companies such as DoubleClick provide partial management. More comprehensive management is provided by Atlas DMT's Digital Marketing suite.

Another topic in ad management is measuring the effectiveness of Web advertising, which was discussed earlier. Yet another is localization.

LOCALIZATION

localization
The process of converting media products developed in one environment (e.g., country) to a form culturally and linguistically acceptable in countries outside the original target market.

Localization is the process of converting media products developed in one environment (e.g., a country) to a form culturally and linguistically acceptable outside the original target market. It is usually done by a set of *internationalization* guidelines. Web-page translation (Chapters 15 and 17) is just one aspect of internationalization. However, several other aspects also are important. For example, a U.S. jewelry manufacturer that displayed its products on a white background was astonished to find that this display might not appeal to customers in some countries where a blue background is preferred.

If a company aims at the global market (and there are millions of potential customers out there), it must make an effort to localize its Web pages. This may not be a simple task because of the following factors:

- Many countries use English, but the English used may differ in terminology, spelling, and culture (e.g., United States versus United Kingdom versus Australia).
- Some languages use accented characters. If text includes an accented character, the accent will disappear when converted into English, which may result in an incorrect translation.
- Hard-coded text and fonts cannot be changed, so they remain in their original format in the translated material.
- Graphics and icons look different to viewers in different countries. For example, a U.S. mailbox resembles a European trashcan.
- When translating into Asian languages, significant cultural issues must be addressed, for example, how to address older adults in a culturally correct manner.
- Dates that are written mm/dd/yy (e.g., June 8, 2002) in the United States are written dd/mm/yy (e.g., 8 June 2002) in many other countries. Therefore, "6/8" would have two meanings (June 8 or August 6), depending on the location of the writer.
- Consistent translation over several documents can be very difficult to achieve. (For free translation in six languages, see freetranslation.com.)

Automatic Versus Manual Web Page Translation

Certain localization difficulties result in a need for experienced human translators, who are rare, expensive, and slow. Therefore, companies are using automatic translation software, at least as an initial step to expedite the work of human translators. (See Chapter 14 for further discussion and references.)

Using Internet Radio for Localization

Internet radio
A Web site that provides music, talk, and other entertainment, both live and stored, from a variety of radio stations.

Internet radio Web sites provide music, talk, and other entertainment, both live and stored, from a variety of radio stations. The big advantage of Internet radio is that there are few limits on the type or number of programs it can offer, as compared with traditional radio stations. It is especially useful in presenting programming for local communities. For example, kiisfm.com is a Los Angeles site that features music from up-and-coming L.A. bands, live concerts, interviews with movie stars, and so forth. About 40 percent of the site's traffic comes from listeners in California, and the rest from listeners around the world. The company that powers kiisfm.com also operates sites focused on country music, Latin music, and so forth. Advertisers can reach fairly narrow audience segments by advertising on a particular Internet radio site.

VERT Intelligent Displays: Advertising Used Atop Taxi Cabs

Source: Courtesy of Vert Incorporated.

WIRELESS ADVERTISING

As will be seen in Chapter 9, the number of applications of m-commerce in marketing and advertising is growing quickly. One area is that of *pervasive computing*—the idea that computer chips can be embedded in almost any device (clothing, tools, appliances, homes, and so on) and then a device can be connected to a network of other devices. An interesting application of this is digital ads atop 12,000 taxis in various U.S. cities. The ads also include public service announcements. The technology comes from VERT Inc. (vert.net).

The VERT system is linked to the Internet via a wireless modem, as well as to databases and a global positioning system (GPS) that uses satellites to identify a taxi's location. For example, two ads were created specifically to take advantage of VERT's real-time capabilities. One is "Top 10" stock quotes from NASDAQ and the other is a weather report. Leonid Fridman, president of VERT, based in Somerville, Massachusetts, says that the technology could eventually be used to vary the ads based on the neighborhood the taxi is driving through, the weather, or any other changing condition.

AD CONTENT

The content of ads is extremely important, and companies use ad agencies to help in content creation for the Web just as they do for other advertising media. A major player in this area is Akamai Technologies, Inc. (akamai.com). In a white paper (Akamai Technologies, Inc. 2000b), the company points out how the right content can drive traffic to a site. The paper also suggests how to evaluate third-party vendors and determine what content-related services are important.

Content is especially important to increase *stickiness*. Customers are expensive to acquire, therefore it is important that they remain at a site, read its content carefully, and eventually make a purchase. The writing of the advertising content itself is of course important (see adcopywriting.com and Chapter 16.) Finding a good ad agency to write content and shape the advertising message is one of the key factors in any advertising campaign, online or off-line. Yet, matching ad agencies and advertising clients can be complex. Agencyfinder.com maintains a huge database that can be tapped for a perfect match.

Section 4.9 ▶ REVIEW QUESTIONS

1. Describe permission advertising.
2. What is localization? What are the major issues in localizing Web pages?
3. How is wireless advertising practiced?
4. What is the importance of ad content?

4.10 SOFTWARE AGENTS IN MARKETING AND ADVERTISING APPLICATIONS

As the volume of customers, products, vendors, and information increases, it becomes uneconomical, or even impossible, for customers to consider all relevant information and to manually match their interests with available products and services. The practical solution to handling such information overload is to use software (intelligent) agents. In Chapter 3, we demonstrated how intelligent agents help online shoppers find and compare products, resulting in significant time savings.

In this section, we will concentrate on how software agents can assist customers in the online purchasing decision-making process as well as in advertisement. Depending on their level of intelligence, agents can do many things (see Kang and Han 2003; Greenwald et al. 2003; and Online Technical Appendix D).

WWW

A FRAMEWORK FOR CLASSIFYING EC AGENTS

Exhibit 4.2 detailed the customer's purchase decision-making process. A logical way to classify EC agents is by relating them to this decision-making process (in a slightly expanded form), as shown in Exhibit 4.11. In the decision-making model in Exhibit 4.2, the second step was information search. Because of the vast quantity of information that software (intelligent) agents can supply, the step has been split into two types of agents: those that first answer the question, "What to buy?" and those that answer the next question, "From whom?" Let's see how agents support each of the phases of the decision-making process.

EXHIBIT 4.11 The Purchase Decision-Making Process: Agent Classification

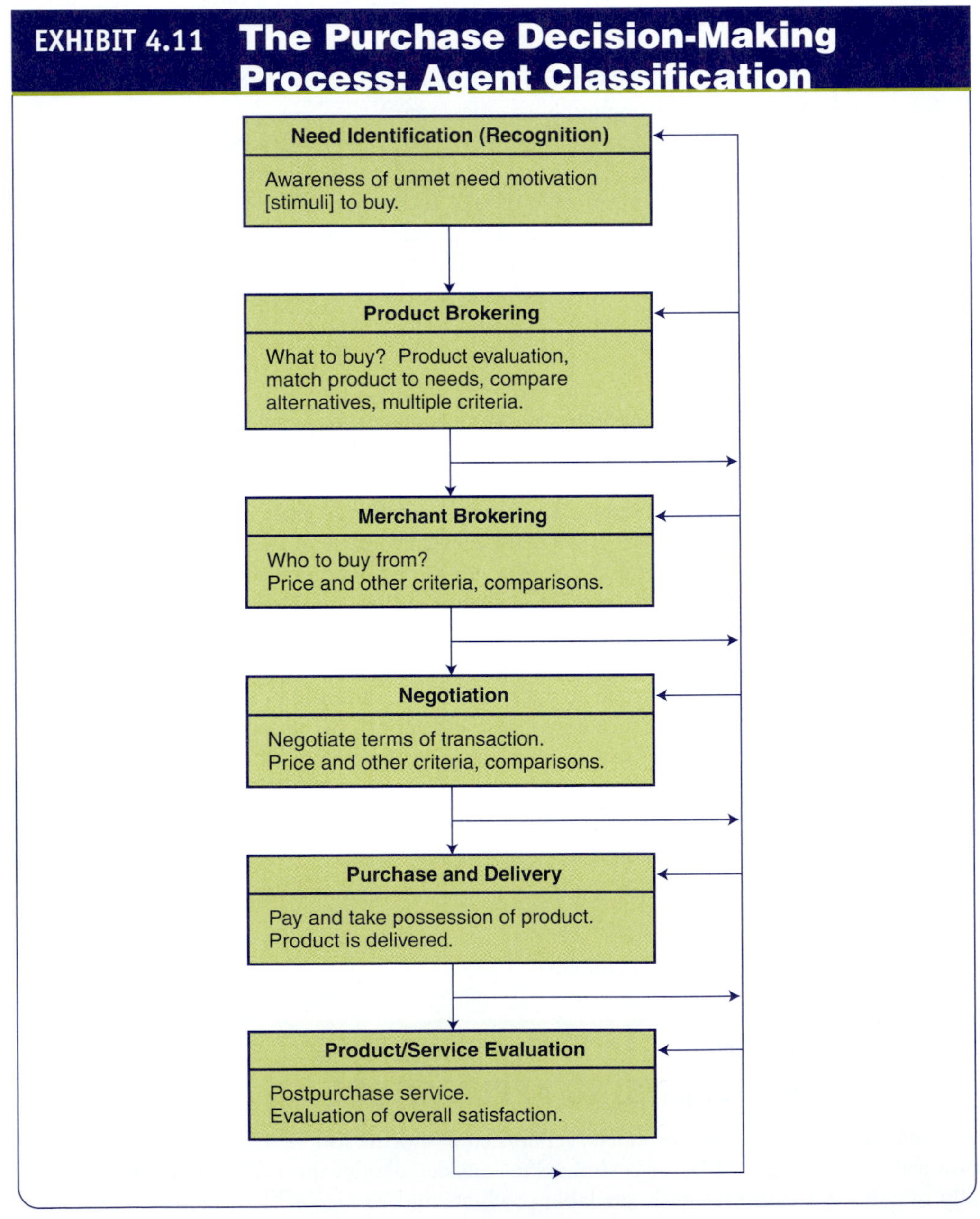

Agents That Support Need Identification (What to Buy)

Agents can help buyers recognize their need for products or services by providing product information and stimuli. For example, expedia.com notifies customers about low airfares to a customer's desired destination whenever they become available.

Several commercial agents can facilitate need recognition directly or indirectly. For example, salesmountain.com helps people find certain items when they are put "on sale." If customers specify what they want, salesmountain.com will send notification when the item is discounted. Similarly, findgift.com asks customers questions about the person they are buying a gift for and helps them hunt down the perfect gift.

Agents That Support Product Brokering (From Whom to Buy)

Once a need is established, customers search for a product (or service) that will satisfy the need. Several agents are available to assist customers with this task. The comparison agents cited in Chapter 3 belong to this category. An example of how these agents are used in advertising is provided in EC Application Case 4.3.

Some agents can match people that have similar interest profiles. Even more ambitious agents try to predict which brands of computers, cars, and other goods will appeal to customers based on market segmentation preferences in a variety of different product categories such as wine, music, or breakfast cereal. (See the earlier discussion on *collaborative filtering.*) For a discussion on agents that do both product and merchant brokering, see He and Leung (2002).

Agents That Support Merchant Brokering and Comparisons

Once a customer has a specific product in mind, he or she needs to find a place to buy it. BargainFinder (from Accenture) was the pioneering agent in this category. When used for online CD shopping, for example, this agent queried the price of a specific CD from a number of online vendors and returned a list of prices. However, this system encountered problems because vendors who did not want to compete on price managed to block out the agent's requests. (Today's version is at cdrom-guide.com, "Bargain finder") The blocking problem has been solved by agents such as Inktomi Shopping Agent, My Simon (mysimon.com), and Junglee (of amazon.com). These agents originate the requests from whatever computer the user is accessing at the time. This way, vendors have no way of determining whether the request comes direct from a real customer or from the comparison agent.

CASE 4.3

EC Application

FUJITSU USES AGENTS FOR TARGETED ADVERTISING IN JAPAN

Fujitsu (*fujitsu.com*) is a Japanese-based global provider of Internet-focused information technology solutions. Since the end of 1996, Fujitsu has been using an agent-based technology called the Interactive Marketing Interface (iMi). The system allows advertisers to interact directly with specific segments of the consumer market through the use of software agents, while ensuring that consumers remain anonymous to advertisers. Consumers submit a personal profile to iMi, indicating such characteristics as product categories of interests, hobbies, travel habits, and the maximum number of e-mail messages per week that they are willing to receive. In turn, customers receive product announcements, advertisements, and marketing surveys by e-mail from advertisers based on their personal profile information. By answering the marketing surveys or acknowledging receipt of advertisements, consumers earn iMi points, redeemable for gift certificates and phone cards. Many other companies in Japan (e.g., *nifty.com* and *lifemedia.co.jp*) also use this technology.

Source: Compiled from *fujitsu.com* (accessed 2001).

Questions

1. Why would customers agree to have a personal profile built on them?
2. What is the role of the software agent in this case?

Fraud is of major concern to buyers, because buyers cannot see the products or the sellers (see Chapter 17). Several vendors offer agent-based fraud detection systems. One such system is Risk Suite (fairisaac.com). It is based on pattern recognition driven by neural computing.

Comparison Agents. Part of the merchant-brokering process is determining price and other purchase criteria. Large numbers of agents enable consumers to perform all kinds of comparisons, as was shown in Chapter 3. Here are some additional examples:

- Allbookstores.com and bestbookbuys.com are two of several agents that help consumers find the lowest prices of books available online.
- Bottomdollar.com, compare.net, pricewonders.com, shopper.com, roboshopper.com, and bargainvillage.com are examples of agents (out of several dozen) that suggest brands and compare prices once consumers specify what they want to buy.
- Pricescan.com guides consumers to the best prices on thousands of computer hardware and software products.
- Buyerzone.com is a B2B portal at which businesses can find the best prices on many products and services.

Agents That Support Buyer–Seller Negotiation

The traditional concept of "market" implies negotiation, mostly about price. Whereas many large retail stores engage in fixed-price selling, many small retail stores and most markets use negotiation extensively. In several cultures (e.g., Chinese), negotiation is very common. In many B2B transactions, negotiation is common, too. The benefit of dynamically negotiating a price is that the pricing decision is shifted from the seller to the marketplace. In a fixed-price situation, if the seller fixes a price that is too high, sales volume will suffer. If the price is set too low, profits will be lower.

Negotiations, however, are time-consuming and often disliked by individual customers who cannot negotiate properly because they lack information about the marketplace and prices or because they have not learned to negotiate. Many vendors do not like to negotiate either. Therefore, electronic support of negotiation can be extremely useful.

Agents can negotiate in pairs or one agent can negotiate for a buyer with several sellers' agents. In the latter case, the contact is done with each seller's agent individually, and the buyer's agent can conduct comparisons. Also, customers can negotiate with sellers' agents. One system automates the bargaining on a seller's side. The system can bargain with customers based on their bargaining behavior. For example, if the customer starts very low, the system helps the seller know how to respond. For details, see Zhu (2004), Greenwald et al. (2003), and Chapter 5 (for B2B).

Agents That Support Purchase and Delivery

Agents are used extensively during the actual purchase, often arranging payment and delivery. For example, if a customer makes a mistake when completing an electronic order form, an agent will point it out immediately. When a customer buys stocks, for example, the pricing agent will tell the customer when a stock they want to buy on margin is not marginable or when the customer does not have sufficient funds. Similarly, delivery options are posted by agents at amazon.com, and the total cost of the transaction is calculated in real time.

Agents That Support After-Sale Service and Evaluation

Agents also can be used to facilitate after-sale service. For example, the automatic e-mail answering agents described in Chapter 13 usually are effective in answering customer queries. A non-Internet agent can monitor automobile usage and notify owners when it is time to take their car in for periodic maintenance. Agents that facilitate feedback from customers also are useful.

CHARACTER-BASED ANIMATED INTERACTIVE AGENTS

Several agents enhance customer service by interacting with customers via animated characters. Other agents are used to facilitate advertising. Animated characters are software agents with personalities. They are versatile and employ friendly front ends to communicate with users.

They are not necessarily intelligent. These animated agents also are called *avatars*. **Avatars** are animated computer representations of humanlike movements and behaviors in a computer-generated three-dimensional world. Advanced avatars can "speak" and exhibit behaviors such as gestures and facial expressions. They can be fully automated to act like robots. The purpose of avatars is to introduce believable emotions so that the agents gain credibility with users. Insights and Additions 4.2 describes the use of avatars at a virtual mall in Korea.

avatars
Animated computer characters that exhibit humanlike movements and behaviors.

Avatars are considered a part of **social computing**, an approach aimed at making the human–computer interface more natural (Castronova 2004). Studies conducted by Extempo Systems (extempo.com 1999) showed that interactive characters can improve customer satisfaction and retention by offering personalized, one-to-one service. They also can help companies get to know their customers and support advertising.

social computing
An approach aimed at making the human–computer interface more natural.

Chatterbots

A special category of animated characters is characters that can chat, known as **chatterbots**. A chatterbot is a program that attempts to simulate a conversation, with the aim of at least temporarily fooling a customer into thinking they are conversing with a human. The concept started with Eliza, created by Joseph Weizenbaum at MIT in 1957. In his program, users conversed with a psychoanalyst. Today's version is very powerful (try www14.brinkster.com/ecceliza1; the program can be downloaded for free). The major differences are that today the programs are on the Web and they include a static or moving character. The technology is

chatterbots
Animation characters that can talk (chat).

Insights and Additions 4.2 Brand Names at a Korean Virtual Mall

Avatars are big business in South Korea. Internet users express themselves by putting clothes, shoes, and accessories on their avatars. The clothes are really pixels on the computer screen designed for avatars that represent the users and are moved around a virtual chat room. Clothing the avatars in attire bought in virtual malls is part of the fun. Sayclub, operated by NeoWiz, was the first to introduce avatar services there in 2000. The company had more than 15 million members in 2002 who spent a total of $1.6 million a month on their avatars, dressing them in the over 30,000 outfits from the virtual shopping mall (*saymall.sayclub.com*).

"It is an unusual strategy, but avatars can be very effective marketing tools," says Chung Jae Hyung, chief executive officer at DKIMS Communications, an online marketing agency. "They are so popular with young people these days that they can get you a lot of exposure very quickly. An avatar is a given; just like everyone has a cell phone, everyone has an avatar," says Chung. Samsung Economic Research Institute estimates that the avatar industry generated $16 million in revenue in 2001 (Yoon 2002). By 2004, according to private communications with Samsung researchers, the estimate grew to $25 million.

As competition grew from the top portals, such as Yahoo!, Sayclub responded by offering more items, including hair dyes, accessories, and brands. "We needed something to differentiate ourselves and improve our brand image," says Chang Hyun Guk, manager of the business-planning team at Sayclub. "The best way to do that was to bring real-life brands to our virtual mall." Therefore, to improve its own brand image, Sayclub sought to offer well-known consumer brands as products one could buy for one's avatar from the Sayclub site. In addition to improving the Sayclub brand, these products would generate money from additional sales.

However, convincing top brands to go virtual was not easy. For example, because Mattel, the maker of Barbie, did not have any idea what the avatar market was all about, it needed to be educated before it would sign a licensing agreement allowing outfits from the Barbie Fashion Avenue line of doll dresses to be "avatarized" for a percentage of total sales. Numerous Barbie outfits have gone on sale at prices ranging from $4 to $5.35. That may not sound like much, but as of June 2002, avatar outfits made up almost 15 percent of Barbie's licensing business in Korea. By exposing Sayclub's users (mostly people in their teens and 20s) to Barbie paraphernalia, Mattel has been able to extend her popularity beyond children the ages of 8 or 9. Jisun Lee, a 23-year-old student, had not owned anything "Barbie" in over a decade, but spent more than $85 in 2002 dressing her avatar.

During the Korean World Cup games in June 2002, Sayclub formed a partnership with Nike Korea and introduced avatars based on real images of Korean soccer players. They provided various soccer-related avatar items, including uniforms and Nike products. Sayclub granted uniform numbers of national soccer players to all users who bought Nike soccer items, including soccer player avatars or national team uniforms. They also gave away gifts to users with uniform numbers (selected by lottery) if the players their avatars represented scored during the games.

Sources: Compiled from Yoon (2002), *sayclub.com* (accessed 2004), and *neowiz.com* (accessed 2004).

based on *natural language programming* (NLP), an applied artificial intelligence program that can recognize typed or spoken key words and short sentences.

A major use of character-based interactive agents is in customer service and CRM. The following sites offer demos and the opportunity to converse with virtual representatives:

- Artificial-life.com. This site offers CRM and other agents. The site can be accessed by cell phones as well as traditional Web connections. (In Chapter 13, we illustrate the CRM agents of this company; see Exhibit 13.9.) This company offers e-learning applications, too.
- verity.com. This site offers "Virtual Response" that acts as a "v-rep" (virtual representative) that can answer customer questions and provide potential solutions.
- Zabaware.com. This site provides desktop assistance for answering customers' queries.

For an inventory of chatterbots and other resources, visit Simon Laven's site (simonlaven.com).

Chatterbots can do many things to enhance customer service, such as greeting a consumer when they enter a site or giving the consumer a guided tour of the site. For example, consider the following chatterbot agents: Mr. Clean (mrclean.com) guides consumers to cleaning-related Procter & Gamble products. The Personal Job Search Agent at monster.com helps users find a job. "Ed, Harmony, and Nina" are virtual guides that help visitors who wish to learn more about products and tools available at extempo.com (which specializes in avatars). For additional information on interactive characters, see Rice (2001), microsoft.com/msagent/, and artificial-life.com.

OTHER EC AGENTS

Other agents support consumer behavior, customer service, and advertising activities. For example, Resumix (see Chapter 3) is an application that wanders the Web looking for Web pages containing resume information. If it identifies a page as being a resume, it tries to extract pertinent information from the page, such as the person's e-mail address, phone number, skill description, and location. The resulting database is used to connect job seekers with recruiters. For current lists of various EC agents, see botspot.com and agents.umbc.edu (see the "Agents 101" tutorial). For a comprehensive guide to EC agents, see Iyer and Pazgal (2003).

Section 4.10 ▸ REVIEW QUESTIONS

1. List the major types of software (intelligent) agents used in customer-related and advertising applications.
2. What role do software agents play in *need identification*?
3. How do software agents support *product brokering* and *merchant brokering*?
4. What are avatars and chatterbots? Why are they used on Web sites?

MANAGERIAL ISSUES

Some managerial issues related to this chapter are as follows.

1. **Do we understand our customers?** Understanding customers, specifically what they need and how to respond to those needs, is the most critical part of consumer-centered marketing. To excel, companies need to satisfy and retain customers, and management must monitor the entire process of marketing, sales, maintenance, and follow-up service.
2. **Should we use intelligent agents?** Any company engaged in EC must examine the possibility of using intelligent agents to enhance customer service, and possibly to support market research and match ads with consumers. Commercial agents are available on the market at a reasonable cost. For heavy usage, companies may develop customized agents.
3. **Who will conduct the market research?** B2C requires extensive market research. This research is not easy to do, nor is it inexpensive. Deciding whether to outsource to a market research firm or maintain an in-house market research staff is a major management issue.
4. **Are customers satisfied with our Web site?** This is a key question, and it can be answered in several ways.

Many vendors are available to assist you; some provide free software. For discussion on how to improve customer satisfaction, see webhelp.com and e-satisfy.co.uk. For Web site improvements, see futurenowinc.com.

5. **Can we use B2C marketing methods and research in B2B?** Some methods can be used with adjustments; others cannot. B2B marketing and marketing research require special methods.
6. **How do we decide where to advertise?** Web advertising is a complex undertaking, and outsourcing should seriously be considered for large-scale ads. Some outsourcers specialize in certain industries (e.g., ebizautos.com for auto dealers). Companies should examine the adage.com site, which contains an index of Web sites, their advertising rates, and reported traffic counts, before selecting a site on which to advertise. Companies also should consult third-party audits.
7. **What is our commitment to Web advertising, and how will we coordinate Web and traditional advertising?** Once a company has committed to advertising on the Web, it must remember that a successful program is multifaceted. It requires input and vision from marketing, cooperation from the legal department, and strong technical leadership from the corporate information systems (IS) department. A successful Web advertising program also requires coordination with non-Internet advertising and top management support.
8. **Should we integrate our Internet and non-Internet marketing campaigns?** Many companies are integrating their TV and Internet marketing campaigns. For example, a company's TV or newspaper ads direct the viewers/readers to the Web site, where short videos and sound ads, known as *rich media*, are used. With click-through ratios of banner ads down to less than 0.5 percent at many sites, innovations such as the integration of off-line and online marketing are certainly needed to increase click-throughs.
9. **What ethical issues should we consider?** Several ethical issues relate to online advertising. One issue that receives a great deal of attention is spamming, which is now subject to pending legislation. Another issue is the selling of mailing lists and customer information. Some people believe not only that a company needs the consent of the customers before selling a list, but also that the company should share with customers the profits derived from the sale of such lists. Using cookies without an individual's consent is another ethical issue.
10. **Are any metrics available to guide advertisers?** A large amount of information has been developed to guide advertisers as to where to advertise, how to design ads, and so on. Specific metrics may be used to assess the effectiveness of advertising and to calculate the ROI from an organization's online advertising campaign.

RESEARCH TOPICS

Here are some suggested topics related to this chapter. For details, references, and additional topics, refer to the book's "Current EC Research" in the Online Appendix.

1. **Online Consumer Behavior Models**
   - Key drivers and behavioral factors of online purchasing
   - Consumers' attitude toward Internet shopping in comparison with other channels
   - Potential and status of penetration in online purchasing by product (service) types
   - Stage theory of online purchasing by country
   - Impact of broadband penetration of consumer purchasing online
2. **Factors Influencing the Online Purchases**
   - Product and service types
   - Price and quality level of products
   - Consumer attitudes about shopping online
   - Shoppers' online experience
   - Gender, age, and occupation
   - Online services and privacy concerns
   - Behavior related to the acceptance of new technology
   - Country and cultural differences
   - Behavior regarding time to delivery
   - Brand effect and trust
3. **Online Customers Trust**
   - Role and importance of trust on EC
   - Trust requirement and previous experiences regarding trust in e-business
   - Impact of trust on relationship building and acceptance of EC
   - Ways to build consumer trust in online purchasing
   - Role of certifications to ensure the trust

4. **Factors Used to Measure Online Customer Satisfaction with Metrics**
   - Technology acceptance behavior
   - Transaction cost
   - Service quality
   - Perceived importance of online services
   - Expectations toward online services including both the desire for and the lack of confidence in the ability of those services
5. **Customer Relationship Management for EC Using Personalized Services**
   - Status and maturity of CRM in e-commerce
   - Factors that determine customer retention in EC
   - Design of EC to enhance the stickiness for customer retention
   - Design of personalized services based on CRM
   - Data mining techniques and decision support systems for CRM
   - Impact of customer participation on brand loyalty
   - Integration of multiple channels and database design for CRM
6. **Internet Market Research**
   - Techniques and methods of online market research
   - Existing practices of Internet research
   - Consumer opportunity, ability, and motivation to participate in market research online
   - Cost and benefit of Internet market research method in comparison with traditional research methods
7. **Impact of Internet Advertising**
   - Customer attitudes about online advertisement in comparison with other advertising channels
   - Design of Internet advertising methods
   - Impact of Internet advertising on firm value
   - How to attract customers to Internet advertising
   - Selection of Web sites for online advertisement
   - Comparison challenge as an advertising model
8. **Comparing Internet Advertising Methods**
   - Algorithms for customized advertisement method
   - Business models for effective e-mail advertising
   - Effectiveness of banner advertising
   - Optimal ad placement method

SUMMARY

In this chapter, you learned about the following EC issues as they relate to the learning objectives.

1. **Essentials of online consumer behavior.** Consumer behavior in EC is similar to that of any consumer behavior, but it has some unique features. It is described in a stimuli-based decision model that is influenced by independent variables (personal characteristics and environmental characteristics). The model also contains a significant vendor-controlled component that includes both market stimuli and EC systems (logistics, technology, and customer service). All of these characteristics and systems interact to influence the decision-making process and produce an eventual buyer decision.
2. **The online consumer decision-making process.** The goal of marketing research efforts is to *understand* the consumers' online decision-making process and formulate an appropriate strategy to *influence* their behavior. For each step in the process, sellers can develop appropriate strategies.
3. **Building one-to-one relationships with customers.** EC offers companies the opportunity to build one-to-one relationships with customers that are not possible in other marketing systems. Product customization, personalized service, and getting the customer involved interactively (e.g., in feedback, order tracking, and so on) are all practical in cyberspace. In addition, advertising can be matched with customer profiles so that ads can be presented on a one-to-one basis.
4. **Online personalization.** Using personal Web pages, customers can interact with a company, learn about products or services in real time, or get customized products or services. Companies can allow customers to self-configure the products or services they want. Customization also can be done by matching products with customers' profiles.
5. **Increasing loyalty and trust.** Customers can switch loyalty online easily and quickly. Therefore, enhancing e-loyalty (e.g., through e-loyalty programs) is a must. Similarly, trust is a critical success factor that must be nourished.
6. **EC customer market research.** Several fast and economical methods of online market research are avail-

able. The two major approaches to data collection are: (1) soliciting voluntary information from the customers and (2) using cookies, transaction logs, or clicksteam data to track customers' movements on the Internet. Understanding market segmentation by grouping consumers into categories also is an effective EC market research method. However, online market research has several limitations, including data accuracy and representation of the statistical population by a sample.

7. **B2B Internet marketing and organizational buyers.** Marketing methods and marketing research in B2B differ from those of B2C. A major reason for this is that the buyers must observe organizational buying policies and frequently conduct buying activities as a committee. Organizations use modified B2C methods such as affiliate marketing.
8. **Objectives and characteristics of Web advertising.** Web advertising attempts to attract surfers to an advertiser's site. Once at the advertiser's site, consumers can receive information, interact with the seller, and in many cases, immediately place an order. With Web advertising, ads can be customized to fit groups of people with similar interests or even individuals. In addition, Web advertising can be interactive, is easily updated, can reach millions at a reasonable cost, and offers dynamic presentation by rich multimedia.
9. **Major online advertising methods.** Banners are the most popular online advertising method. Other frequently used methods are pop-ups and similar ads (including interstitials), e-mail (including e-mail to mobile devices), classified ads, registration of URLs with search engines, and advertising in chat rooms.
10. **Various advertising strategies and types of promotions.** The major advertising strategies are ads associated with search results (text links), affiliate marketing, pay incentives for customers to view ads, viral marketing, ads customized on a one-to-one basis, and online events and promotions. Web promotions are similar to off-line promotions. They include giveaways, contests, quizzes, entertainment, coupons, and so on. Customization and interactivity distinguish Internet promotions from conventional ones.
11. **Permission marketing, ad management, and localization.** In permission marketing, customers are willing to accept ads in exchange for special (personalized) information or monetary incentives. Ad management deals with planning, organizing, and controlling ad campaigns and ad use. Finally, in localization, attempts are made to fit ads to a local environment.
12. **Intelligent agents.** Intelligent agents can gather and interpret data about consumer-purchasing behavior. Advanced agents can even learn about customer behavior and needs by observing their Web movements. Agents can facilitate or support all aspects of the purchasing process, including product brokering, merchant brokering, product comparison, buyer–seller negotiation, purchase and delivery, and after-sale customer service. Character-based interactive agents such as avatars and chatterbots "put a face" on the computing experience, making it more natural.

KEY TERMS

Ad management 175
Ad views 162
Admediaries 173
Advertising networks 164
Advertorial 171
Affiliate marketing 172
Associated ad display (text links) 171
Avatars 181
Banner 164
Banner exchanges 166
Banner swapping 166
Chatterbots 181
Click (click-through or ad click) 162
Click-through rate (or ratio) 162
Clickstream behavior 155
Clickstream data 156
Collaborative filtering 147
Conversion rate 162
Cookie 146
CPM (cost per thousand impressions) 162
E-loyalty 148
Hit 162
Interactive marketing 161
Internet radio 176
Interstitial 167
Keyword banners 164
Localization 176
Market segmentation 151
Merchant brokering 143
One-to-one marketing 145
Permission advertising (permission marketing) 175
Personalization 146
Pop-under ads 167
Pop-up ads 167
Product brokering 143
Random banners 164
Social computing 181
Spamming 175
Spyware 156
Stickiness 162
Transaction log 155
Trust 149
Unique visit 162
User profile 146
Viral marketing 172
Visit 162
Web bugs 156
Webcasting 173

QUESTIONS FOR DISCUSSION

1. What would you tell an executive officer of a bank about the critical success factors for increasing loyalty of banking customers by using the Internet?
2. Why is data mining becoming an important element in EC? How is it used to learn about consumer behavior? How can it be used to facilitate customer service?
3. Explain why online trust is more difficult to achieve than off-line trust.
4. Discuss the similarities and differences between data mining and Web mining. (*Hint:* To answer this question, you will need to read Online Appendix W4A.)

5. How can research on satisfaction and dissatisfaction help online sellers?
6. Discuss why B2C marketing and advertising methods may not fit B2B.
7. Compare banner swapping with a banner exchange.
8. Discuss why banners are popular in Internet advertising.
9. Discuss the relationship between market research and advertisement (see Atlas DMT at **atlasdmt.com** for a start).
10. Discuss the advantages and limitations of listing a company's URL with various search engines.
11. How might a chat room be used for advertising?
12. Is it ethical for a vendor to enter a chat room operated by a competitor and pose queries?
13. Relate Web ads to market research.
14. Explain why online ad management is critical.
15. Examine some Web avatars and try to interact with them. Discuss the potential benefits and drawbacks of using avatars as an advertising media.
16. Explain the advantages of using chatterbots. Are there any disadvantages?
17. Discuss the benefits of using software agents in marketing and advertising.

INTERNET EXERCISES

1. Surf the Home Depot Web site (**homedepot.com**) and check whether (and how) the company provides service to customers with different skill levels. Particularly, check the "kitchen and bath design center" and other self-configuration assistance. Relate this to market research.
2. Examine a market research Web site (e.g., **acnielsen.com** and **claritas. com**). Discuss what might motivate a consumer to provide answers to market research questions.
3. Enter **mysimon.com** and share your experiences about how the information you provide might be used by the company for marketing in a specific industry (e.g., the clothing market).
4. Enter **marketingterms.com** and conduct a search by keywords as well as by category. Check the definitions of 10 key terms in this chapter.
5. Enter **2020research.com**, **infosurv.com**, and **marketingsherpa.com**, and identify areas for market research about consumers.
6. Enter **nielsenmedia.com** and view the demos on e-market research. Then go to **clickz.com** and find its offerings. Summarize your findings.
7. Enter **selfpromotion.com** and find some interesting promotion ideas for the Web.
8. Enter the Web sites of **ipro.com** and **selfpromotion.com**. What Internet traffic management, Web results, and auditing services are provided? What are the benefits of each service? Find at least one competitor in each category (e.g., **netratings.com**). Compare the services provided and the prices.

9. Enter **hotwired.com** and **espn.com**. Identify all of the advertising methods used on each site. Can you find those that are targeted advertisements? What revenue sources can you find on the ESPN site? (Try to find at least seven.)
10. Compare the advertisements and promotions at **thestreet.com** and **marketwatch.com**. Write a report.
11. Enter **adweek.com**, **newroads.com**, **wdfm.com**, **ad-tech.com**, **iab.com**, and **adage.com** and find new developments in Internet advertisement. Write a report based on your findings.
12. Enter **clairol.com** to determine your best hair color. You can upload your own photo to the studio and see how different shades look on you. You can also try different hairstyles. It also is for men. How can these activities increase branding? How can they increase sales?
13. Enter **positionagent.com** (part of Microsoft's "bCentral") and ask the Position Agent to rank your Web site or a site with which you are familiar. Assess the benefits versus the costs.
14. What resources do you find to be most useful at **targetonline.com**, **clickz.com**, **admedia.org**, **marketresearch.com**, and **wdfm.com**?
15. Enter **doubleclick.com** and examine all of the company's products. Prepare a report.

TEAM ASSIGNMENTS AND ROLE PLAYING

1. Enter **harrisinteractive.com**, **infosurv.com**, and similar sites. Have each team member examine the free marketing tools and related tutorials and demos. Each team will try to find a similar site and compare the two. Write a report discussing the team's findings.
2. Each team will choose one advertising method and conduct an in-depth investigation of the major players in that part of the ad industry. For example, direct e-mail is relatively inexpensive. Visit **the-dma.org** to learn about direct mail. Then visit **ezinedirector.com**, **permissiondirect.com**, and **venturedirect.com**. Each team will prepare and present an argument as to why its method is superior.
3. In this exercise, each team member will enter **uproar.com** to play games and win prizes. What could be better? This site is the destination of choice for game and sweepstakes junkies and for those who wish to reach a mass audience of fun-loving people. Relate the games to advertising and marketing.
4. Let the team try the services of **constantcontact.com**. Constant Contact offers a turnkey e-mail marketing package solution. In less than 5 minutes, you can set up an e-mail sign-up box on your Web site. As visitors fill in their names and e-mail addresses, they can be asked to check off topics of interest (as defined by you) to create targeted groups.

   Constant Contact provides a system for creating custom e-mail newsletters that can be sent to your target users on a predetermined schedule. The site manages your mailings and provides reports that help you assess the success of your efforts. Pricing is based on the number of subscribers; less than 50 and the service is free. Write a report summarizing your experiences.

Real-World Case

WEB ADVERTISING STRATEGY HELPS P&G COMPETE

The Problem

The consumer goods market is a global one and extremely competitive. Giant corporations such as Procter & Gamble, Colgate Palmolive, Unilever, Nestlé, and The Coca-Cola Company are competing on hundreds of products, ranging from toothpaste to baby diapers to beverages. To survive, these companies must constantly research the markets, develop new products, and advertise, advertise, advertise. Market research and advertising budgets can amount to as much as 20 percent of sales, thus reducing profits. However, failure to advertise sufficiently and properly results in smaller revenue, loss of market share, and possibly going out of business. Thus, the proper advertising strategy, including Web advertising, is critical to the welfare of any company in the consumer goods industry.

Procter & Gamble (P&G) is the largest packaged-goods company in the United States, with over 300 brands (ranging from Crest to Tide to Pampers) and annual sales of over $55 billion. P&G spends more money on advertising than any other company, about $5 billion a year. P&G's business problem is how to best use its advertising budget to get the most marketing "bang for its bucks."

The Solution

P&G started to advertise on the Internet in the late 1990s, both on major portals (using pop-up and banner ads for Scope and Tide) and on its own Web sites. By 2000, it had 72 active sites, mostly one site for each product (e.g., *pampers.com*, *tide.com*, and *crest.com*). Several of the sites were general (e.g., *beinggirl.com*, where teens find answers to questions about their bodies as well as advice about boys; *pantene.com*, where consumers can get personalized hair consultations; and *reflect.com*, where consumers can get customized beauty products). Today, P&G is considered by many (e.g., Bulik 2000) to be "pushing the envelope on the Web" by experimenting with many Web projects, mostly related to market research online and online advertising.

P&G's major objective is to build around each major product a community of users on the Web. The company has the following objectives in building and maintaining these sites: developing brand awareness and recognition (brand equity); collecting valuable data from consumers; cutting down on advertising costs; conducting one-to-one advertisement; experimenting with direct sales of commodity-type products; and selling customized beauty products to individuals (through *reflect.com*).

P&G's off-line approach has always included research, development, and investment in hundreds of products simultaneously. Thus, the company's broad online approach is no surprise. Other aspects of its online advertising strategy include developing marketing partnerships (e.g., with iVillage.com), investing in promising start-ups (e.g., Plumtree Software), and joining Transora.com, a B2B marketplace consortium (other partners include

Unilever, Coca-Cola, and Hershey Foods). P&G's advertising approach is in itself experimental in nature: The company believes that its Internet strategy could lead to a comprehensive e-commerce position in the market. However, P&G also recognizes that the strategy could be just branding and result in a waste of money.

P&G's key reason for branching out from the laundry-tip types of sites (e.g., *tide.com*) to the more interactive sites (e.g., *being-me.com*) is so that it can conduct data mining on Web data. Interactive sites not only build brand equity and test the waters for direct sales to customers; they also collect valuable data from consumers. This information helps curtail marketing and advertising expenses by enabling the company to target consumers more precisely and economically. It lets the company gather more information about both the customers and the products and permits more one-to-one advertising. Examples of sites developed for research purposes are:

- *Being-me.com*. Users take a quiz to determine what feminine products best fit their individual needs and then can purchase the products.
- *Reflect.com*. Beauty products are customized based on the user's preferences.
- *Physique.com*. A site for a hair-styling product registered 600,000 consumers in its "club" before the brand was even launched.

The Results

As Robert Rubin of Netquity (a joint venture between Forrester Research and Information Resources) says, "P&G is the leading consumer packaged-goods company on the Net because they're willing to try everything" (Bulik 2000). Although most of the improvements achieved by its Web advertising strategy were qualitative, P&G also was doing extremely well during the economic downturn of 2000–2003. As an indication of its success, its stock price climbed about 50 percent, whereas the average stock price on the New York Stock Exchange dropped over 30 percent in the same period.

Sources: Compiled from Bulik (2000) and from *tide.com*, *crest.com*, *pantene.com*, *beinggirl.com*, *being-me.com*, *reflect.com*, and *physique.com*.

Questions

1. Why was the online approach more effective than the traditional one?
2. Discuss the logic of multiple Web sites for one company.
3. What are the benefits of marketing partnerships?
4. What kind of marketing research can be conducted online by P&G?

REFERENCES

Akamai Technologies, Inc. "Best Practices for Successful Live Web Event." Akamai Technologies, Inc., report, 2000a.

Akamai Technologies, Inc. "Delivering the Profits: How the Right Content Delivery Provider Can Drive Traffic, Sales, and Profits Through Your Web Site." Akamai Technologies, Inc., white paper, 2000b.

American Statistical Association. "ASA Series: What is a Survey?" American Statistical Survey. August 2000. **isixsigma.com/offsite.asp?A=Fr&Url=http://www.amstat.org/sections/srms/brochures/telephone.pdf** (accessed February 2005).

Amiri, A., and S. Menon. "Effectiveness Scheduling of Internet Banner Advertisements." *ACM Transactions on Internet Technology*, November 2003.

Armstrong, G., and P. Kotler. *Marketing: An Introduction*, 7th ed. Upper Saddle River, NJ: Prentice Hall, 2005.

Bansal, H. S., S. Dikolli, G. McDougall, and K. Sedatole. "Relating E-satisfaction to Behavioral Outcomes: An Empirical Study." *The Journal of Services Marketing* 18, no. 4/5 (2004).

Beinggirl.com. **beinggirl.com** (accessed September 2002).

Being-me.com. **being-me.com** (accessed September 2002).

Bell, D. "The Power of Viral Marketing." *Evrsoft.com*, October 2004. **developers.evrsoft.com/article/internet-marketing/affiliate-marketing/the-power-of-viral-marketing.shtml** (accessed February 2005).

Berkley, H. *Low-Budget Online Marketing*. Toronto, Canada: Self-Counsel Press, 2003.

Berkowitz, D. "Responsys Responds to E-mail Challenges." *eMarketer*, April 9, 2004.

Berry, M. J. A., and G. S. Linoff. *Mining the Web: Transforming Customer Data*. New York: John Wiley & Sons, 2002.

Bhatnagar, A., S. Misra, and H. R. Rao. "On Risk, Convenience, and Internet Shopping Behavior." *Communications of the ACM* 43, no. 11 (2000).

Birnbaum, M. H. "Human Research and Data Collection via the Internet." *Annual Review of Psychology* 55 (2004).

Blacharski, D. "Advertising as Lifeblood of the Internet." ITWorld.com (IT Insights), February 23, 2005. **itworld.com/Tech/2421/nls_itinsights050223/** (accessed February 2005).

Blanford, R. "Measuring Online Advertising's Effectiveness." *eMarketer Special Report*, July 2004.

Boswell, K. "Digital Marketing vs. Online Advertising Breaking Waves for Marketers to Catch." *The Marketleap*

Report 2, no. 5 (2002). marketleap.com/report/ml_report_24.htm (accessed April 2003).

Brengman, M., M. Geuens, S. M. Smith, W. R. Swinyard and B. Weijters. "Segmenting Internet Shoppers Based on Their Web-Usage-Related Lifestyle: A Cross-Cultural Validation." *Journal of Business Research* 58 (2005).

Broadvision. broadvision.com (accessed October 2002).

Brown, J. "Click, Two." *Business Week*, February 18, 2002.

Buckley, N. "E-Route to Whiter Smile." *Financial Times*, August 26, 2002.

Bulik, B. S. "Procter & Gamble's Great Web Experiment." *Business 2.0*, November 28, 2000.

Castronova, E. "The Price of Bodies: A Hedonic Pricing Model of Avatar Attributes in a Synthetic World." *Kyklos* 57, no. 2 (2004).

Catalano, F., and B. Smith. *Internet Marketing for Dummies*. Foster City, CA: IDG Books, 2001.

Chan, S. *Strategic Management of e-Business*, 2d ed. Chichester, UK: John Wiley & Sons, 2005.

Chang. Y., and E. Thorson. "Television and Web Advertising Synergies." *Journal of Advertising* 33, no. 2 (2004).

Chase, L. "Top Ten Tips Effective E-mail Marketing." Web Digest for Marketers wdfm.com/e-mailmarketing1.hton (accessed April 2004). Note: no longer available online.

Chaudhury, A., D. Mallick, and H. R. Rao. "Web Channels in E-Commerce." *Communications of the ACM*, January 2001.

Chen, A. "Surveys Boost Satisfaction." *eWeek*, October 4, 2004.

Cheung, C. M. K., and M. K. O. Lee. "An Integrative Model of Consumer Trust in Internet Shopping." *Proceedings of European Conference on Information Systems*, Naples, Italy, June 2003.

Cheung, C. M. K., and M. K. O. Lee. "The Asymmetric Impact of Website Attribute Performance on User Satisfaction: An Empirical Study." *Proceedings of Hawaii International Conference on System Sciences*, Big Island, Hawaii, January 2005.

Cheung, C. M. K., L. Zhu, T. C. H. Kwong, G. W. W. Chan, and M. Limayem. "Online Consumer Behavior: A Review and Agenda for Future Research." *Proceedings of Bled eCommerce Conference*, Bled, Slovenia, June 2003.

Cheung, C. M. K., et al. "A Critical Review of Consumer Behavior and Electronic Commerce." *Journal of Electronic Commerce in Organizations*, forthcoming, 2005.

Clow, K., and D. Baack. *Integrated Advertising, Promotion, and Marketing Communication*. Upper Saddle River, NJ: Prentice Hall, 2004.

Cook, D. P., and Luo, W. "The Role of Third-Party Seals in Building Trust Online." *E-Service Journal* 2, no. 3 (2003).

Cox, B., and W. Koelzer. *Internet Marketing*. Upper Saddle River, NJ: Prentice Hall, 2004.

Coyles, S., and T. C. Gokey. "Customer Retention Is Not Enough." *The McKinsey Quarterly* no. 2 (2002).

Crest.com. crest.com (accessed November 2004).

Cyveillance. cyveillance.com (accessed January 2003).

Diorio, S. *Beyond "e."* New York: McGraw Hill, 2002.

Direct Marketing Association. "http://www.the-dma.org/cgi/wpviews?storyid=91." October 2003. the-dma.org/cgi/whitepapersarchive (accessed February 2005).

DoubleClick. doubleclick.com (accessed November 2004).

DoubleClick. "Fifth Annual Consumer E-mail Study." DoubleClick, 2004. www3.doubleclick.com/market/2004/10/dc/email.htm?c=0410_smrid_lead=newsletterid_source=newsletter_0410 (accessed December 2004).

Doyle, K., A. Minor, and C. Weyrich. "Banner Ad Placement Study." University of Michigan, 1997. webreference.com/dev/banners (accessed November 2004).

Dreze, X., and F. X. Hussherr. "Internet Advertising: Is Anybody Watching?" *Journal of Interactive Marketing* 17, no. 4 (2003).

eMarketer. "Measuring Online Advertising's Effectiveness." *eMarketer Daily Special Research Report*, July 28, 2004. emarketer.com/Report.aspx?on_ad_eff_jul04 (accessed March 2005).

eMarketer. "The E-Mail Marketing Report." eMarketer, June 2004. emarketer.com/Report.aspx?e-mail.jun04 (accessed October 2004).

Extempo Systems, Inc. "Smart Interactive Characters: Automating One-to-One Customer Service." 1999. extempo.com/company_info/press/webtechniques.shtml (accessed September 2002). Note: no longer available online.

Faught, K. S., K. W. Green Jr., and D. Whitten. "Doing Survey Research on the Internet." *Journal of Computer Information Systems* 44, no. 3 (2004).

Fleita, A. "The top nine e-mail hoaxes." *MSN Money*, news item, November 15, 2003. moneycentral.msn.com.

ForeseeResults. "ASCI Annual E-Commerce Report 2005." foreseeresults.com/Form_ACSIFeb2005. html (accessed March 2005a).

ForeseeResults. "Satisfaction with E-Commerce is Waning, According to American Customer Satisfaction Index." foreseeresults.com/Press_WaningSatisfaction.html (accessed March 2005b).

Fujitsu. fujitsu.com (accessed October 1999).

Gartner Inc. "Gartner G2 Key Business Issues Study." *Web Casting, Gartner Inc.*, February 2004 (with *Forbes Magazine*).

Gary, D., and D. Gary. *The Complete Guide to Associate and Affiliate Programs on the Net*. New York: McGraw-Hill, 2000.

Gelb, B. D., and S. Sundaram. "Adapting to 'Word of Mouse.'" *Business Horizons*, July–August 2002.

Georgia Institute of Technology, Graphics, Visualization, and Usability (GVU) Center. *Tenth WWW User Survey*. Georgia Institute of Technology, 1998. cc.gatech.edu/gvu/user_surveys/survey-1998-10/ (accessed February 2005).

Gold, R. Y. "Segmenting Strategically: Building Customer Piece of Mind." RBC Royal Bank, March 5, 2001. royalbank.com/sme/articles/segmenting.html (accessed April 2003).

Gopal, R. D., and Z. D. Walter. "Admediation: New Horizons in Effective E-mail Advertising." *Communications of the ACM* 44, no. 12 (2001).

Gordon-Lewis, H. *Effective E-Mail Marketing*. New York: Amacom, 2002.

Grainger, Inc. "E-Commerce Gaining Loyalty among Businesses Buying Operating Supplies Online." PRNewswire, December 10, 1998. prnewswire.com/cgi-bin/stories.pl?ACCT=105&STORY=/www/story/12-10-1998/0000822471 (accessed March 2005).

Greenspan, R. "Surfers Prefer Personalization." ClickzStats, August 3, 2004. clickz.com/stats/sectors/retailing/article.php/3389141 (accessed December 2004).

Greenwald, A., N. R. Jennings, and P. Stone. "Agents and Markets." *IEEE Intelligent Systems* 18, no. 6 (2003).

Guttman, R., A. G. Moukas, and P. Maes. "Agent-Mediated Electronic Commerce: A Survey." *Knowledge Engineering Review* 13, no. 3 (1998).

Harris, L. C., and M. M. H. Goode. "The Four Levels of Loyalty and the Pivotal Role of Trust: A Study of Online Service Dynamics." *Journal of Retailing* 80, no. 2 (2004).

Harrison-Walker, L. S., and S. E. Neeley. "Customer Relationship Building on the Internet in B2B Marketing: A Proposed Typology." *Journal of Marketing Theory and Practice* 12, no. 1 (2004).

He, M. H., and H. F. Leung. "Agents in E-Commerce: State of the Art." *Knowledge and Information Systems* 4, no. 3 (2002).

Helmstetter, G., and P. Metivier. *Affiliate Selling: Building Revenue on the Web*. New York: Wiley, 2000.

Hewson, C., et al. *Internet Research Methods*. London: Sage, 2003.

Hoffman, D. L., and T. P. Novak. "How to Acquire Customers on the Web." *Harvard Business Review*, May–June 2000.

Inmon, B. "Why Clickstream Data Counts." *e-Business Advisor*, April 2001.

Interactive Advertising Bureau. "Q3 2004 Interactive Advertising Revenues Total Over $2.4" Billion Fourth Record-Setting Quarter" IAB Press Release, November 15, 2004. iab.net/news/pr_2004_11_15.asp (accessed December 2004).

IPT. "Consumers Respond Favorably to E-mail Marketing." *eMarketer*, 2004. emarketer.com/Article.aspx?1003093 (accessed October 2004).

Iyer, G., and A. Pazgal. "Erratum: Internet Shopping Agents: Virtual Co-location and Competition." *Marketing Science* 22, no. 2 (2003).

Kang, N., and S. Y. Han. "Agent-based E-Marketplace System for More Fair and Efficient Transaction." *Decision Support Systems* 34, no. 2 (2003).

Kinnard, S. *Marketing with E-Mail*, 3d ed. Gulf Breeze, FL: Maximum Press, 2002.

Kohli, R., S. Devaraj, and M.A. Mahmood. "Understanding Determinants of Online Consumer Satisfaction: A Decision Process Perspective." *Journal of Management Information Systems* 21, no. 1 (2004).

Kotler, P. *Marketing Management*, 11th ed. Upper Saddle River, NJ: Prentice Hall, 2003.

Kotler, P., and G. Armstrong. *Principles of Marketing*, 10th ed. Upper Saddle River, NJ: Prentice Hall, 2004.

Koufaris, M., and W. Hampton-Sosa. "The Development of Initial Trust in an Online Company by New Customers." *Information and Management* 41, no. 3 (2004).

Lee, M., and E. Turban. "Trust in B2C Electronic Commerce: A Proposed Research Model and its Application." *International Journal of Electronic Commerce* 6, no. 1 (2001).

Lewin, J. "Advertisers Confident in Online Ads." ITWorld.com, November 10, 2004. itworld.com/Man/3827/nls_ecommercead041110/ (accessed December 2004).

Limayem, M., C. Cheung, and G. Chan. "Online Consumer Behavior: What We Know and What We Need to Know." *Proceedings of the European and Mediterranean Conference on Information Systems*, Tunis, Tunisia, July 2004.

Linden, A. "Management Update: Data Mining Trends Enterprises Should Know About." *Gartner Inc.*, October 9, 2002.

Marcus, C. "Loyal Customers Can't Be Strangers." *Microsoft Executive Circle* 1, no. 2 (May 2001).

Marketingsherpa. "How Southwest Airlines Sold $1.5 Million in Tickets by Posting Four Press Releases." Marketing sherpa.com, October 27, 2004. library.marketingsherpa.com/barrier.cfm?ContentID=2845 (accessed February 2005).

Martin, T. N., and J. C. Hafer. "Internet Procurement by Corporate Purchasing Agents: Is It All Hype?" *SAM Advanced Management Journal*, Winter 2002.

Meeker, N. *The Internet Advertising Report*. New York: Morgan Stanley Corporation, 1997.

Meskauskas, J. "Are Click-through Rates Really Declining?" Clickz.com, January 16, 2001. clickz.com/media/plan_buy/article.php/835391 (accessed April 2003).

Microsoft. microsoft.com/misc/external/executivecircle/2001_q2/loyal_customers.asp (accessed April 2003). Note: File no longer available.

Miles, G. E., A. Davies, and A. Howes. "A Framework for Understanding Human Factors in Web-Based E-Commerce." *International Journal of Human Computer Studies* 52, no. 1 (2000).

NeoWiz.com. neowiz.com (accessed October 2002).

New Media Age. "Research Reveals Positive Effect of Web Advertising." *New Media Age*, March 2003.

New Media Age. "How to Get Users to like Online Ads." *New Media Age*, April 2004.

Nicholas, D., and P. Huntington. "Mico-mining and Segmented Log File Analysis: A Method for Enriching the Data Yield from Internet Log Files." *Journal of Information Science* 29, no. 5 (2003).

Nicholls, J. A. F., F. Li, C. Kranendonk, and T. Mandokovic. "Structural or Cultural: An Exploration into Influences on Consumers' Shopping Behavior of Country Specific Factors Versus Retailing Formats." *Journal of Global Marketing* 16, no. 4 (2003).

Nikitas, T. "Your Customers Are Talking. Are You Listening?" *Smart Business*, February 1, 2002.

O'Keefe, R. M., and T. McEachern. "Web-Based Customer Decision Support System." *Communications of the ACM*, March 1998.

O'Keefe, S. *Complete Guide to Internet Publicity*. New York: Wiley, 2002.

Oh, M. S., J. W. Choi, and D.-G. Kim. "Bayesian Inference and Model Selection in Latent Class Logit Models with Parameter Constraints: An Application to Market Segmentation." *Journal of Applied Statistics* 30, no. 2 (2003).

Oliva, R. A. "Playing the Search." *Marketing Management* 13, no. 2 (2004).

Pantene. pantene.com (accessed September 2002).

Park, Y. H., and P. S. Fader. "Modeling Browsing Behavior at Multiple Websites." *Marketing Science* 23, no. 3 (2004).

Parks, L. "Nectar Finds Loyalty's Sweet Spot." *Stores*, July 2004.

Pavlou, P. A. "Consumer Acceptance of Electronic Commerce: Integrating Trust and Risk with the Technology Acceptance Model." *International Journal of Electronic Commerce* 7, no. 3 (2003).

Pennington R., V. Grover, and H. D. Wilcox. "The Role of Systems Trust in B2C Transactions." *Journal of MIS*, Winter 2003–2004.

Peppers and Rogers Group. "E-mail Marketing as a Relationship Strategy: The Four Steps to High Impact E-mail Marketing." Peppers and Rogers, white paper, 2004.

Proctor & Gamble. pg.com (accessed February–December 2002).

Physique.com. physique.com (accessed November 2004).

Pyramid Research. "Pyramid Predicts 709 Million Wi-Fi Users by 2008." Pyramidresearch.com, July 21, 2003. pyramidresearch.com/info/press/release_030721.asp (accessed February 2005).

Ranganathan, C., and E. Grandon. "An Exploratory Examination of Factors Affecting Online Sales." *Journal of Computer Information Systems* 42, no. 3 (2002).

Reflect.com. reflect.com (accessed November 2004).

Rice, V. "Service Bots Are Hot," *eWeek*, April 24, 2001.

Ritchey Design. ritcheylogic.com (accessed 2000–2003).

Rothenberg, R. "An Advertising Power, but Just What Does DoubleClick Do?" *New York Times*, September 22, 1999.

San Jose/Silicon Valley Business Journals. "Study Reveals Why Online Shoppers Don't Buy." January 13, 2004. sanjose.bizjournals.com/sanjose/stories/2004/01/12/daily19.html (accessed February 2005).

Sayclub.com. sayclub.com (accessed September 2004).

Seda, C. *Search Engine Advertising: Buying Your Way to the Top to Increase Sales*, 2d ed. Upper Saddle River, NJ: Prentice Hall, 2004.

Seybold, P. B. "Get Inside the Lives of Your Customers." *Harvard Business Review*, May 2001.

Silverman, B. G., M. Bachann, and K. Al-Akharas. "Implications of Buyer Decision Theory for Design of E-Commerce Web Sites." *International Journal of Human Computer Studies* 55, no. 5 (2001).

Solomon, M. R. *Consumer Behavior*. Upper Saddle River, NJ: Prentice Hall, 2004.

Stafford, T. F., and A. Urbaczewski. "Spyware: The Ghost in the Machine." *Communications of the Association for Information Systems* 14, no. 15 (2004).

Stewart, D. W., and P. A. Pavlou. "From Consumer Response to Active Consumer: Measuring the Effectiveness of Interactive Media." *Academy of Marketing Science* 30, no. 4 (2002).

Sweiger, M., J. Langston, H. Lombard, and M. Madsen. *Clickstream Data Warehousing*. New York: Wiley, 2002.

Taylor, C. P. "Is One-to-One the Way to Market?" *Interactive Week*, May 12, 1997.

Techmorrow.com. "Increased Profits Via Customer Relationship Marketing (CRM/ECRM)." *techmorrow.com*, techmorrow.com/article_3.htm (accessed April 2003). Note: no longer available online.

Tedeschi, B. "E-Commerce Report: New Alternatives to Banner Ads." *New York Times*, February 20, 2001.

Temkin, B. C. "Focus on Customer Experience, Not CRM." Forrester Research, September 2002. forrester.com/ER/Research/Report/Summary/0,1338,14798,FF.html (accessed April 2003).

Thomton, R. H., and B. Lin. "Electronic Advertising: Examination and Implications." *Journal of Promotion Management* 9, nos. 1 and 2, 2003.

Tide. tide.com (accessed September 2002).

Todor, J. I., and W. D. Todor. *Winning Mindshare: The Psychology of Personalization and One-to-One Marketing*. Marion, IA: Whetstone Group, 2001.

UCLA Center for Communication Policy. "UCLA Internet Report 2004: Surveying the Digital Future. Year 4." UCLA Center for Communication Policy, 2004. ccp.ucla.edu/pages/NewsTopics.asp?Id=45 (accessed December 2004).

Vassos, T. *Strategic Internet Marketing*. Indianapolis, IN: Que Publishing, 1996.

VERT. vert.net (accessed January 2003).

Vezina, R., and D. Militaru. "Collaborative Filtering: Theoretical Positions and a Research Agenda in Marketing." *International Journal of Technology Management* 28, no. 1 (2004).

Wagner, M. "Standing Watch over Corporate Reputations." *B to B*, June 10, 2002.

Wang, N. "Marketers Connect with Online Video." *B2B Online*, August 9, 2004. btobonline.com/article.cms?articleId=13042 (accessed February 2005).

Wharton, C. M., R. Hall, J. S. Hampl, and D. M. Winham. "PCs or Paper-and-Pencil: Online Surveys for Data

Collection." *Journal of the American Dietetic Association,* November 2003.

Witkowski, T. H. "Cross-cultural Consumer and Business Research: An Introduction to the Special Section." *Journal of Business Research* 58, no. 1 (2005).

Yoon, S. "Brand Names Are at the Virtual Mall." *Wall Street Journal Europe*, June 13, 2002.

Yoon, S. J., and J. H. Kim. "Is the Internet More Effective Than Traditional Media? Factors Affecting the Choice of Media." *Journal of Advertising Research,* November–December 2001.

Zeng, C., C. X. Xing, L. Z. Zhou, and X. H. Zheng. "Similarity Measure and Instance Selection for Collaborative Filtering." *International Journal of Electronic Commerce* 8, no. 4 (2004).

ZenithOptimedia. "Ad Spending Rising Around the World." *eMarketer.com,* October 13, 2004. **emarketer.com/Article.aspx?1006088** (accessed October 2004).

Zhu, J. "A Buyer–Seller Game Model for Selection and Negotiation of Purchasing Bids: Extensions and New Models." *European Journal of Operational Research* 154, no. 1 (2004).

B2B E-COMMERCE: SELLING AND BUYING IN PRIVATE E-MARKETS

Content

Learning Objectives

Upon completion of this chapter, you will be able to:

1. Describe the B2B field.
2. Describe the major types of B2B models.
3. Discuss the characteristics of the sell-side marketplace, including auctions.
4. Describe the sell-side intermediary models.
5. Describe the characteristics of the buy-side marketplace and e-procurement.
6. Explain how reverse auctions work in B2B.
7. Describe B2B aggregation and group purchasing models.
8. Describe other procurement methods.
9. Explain how B2B administrative tasks can be automated.
10. Describe infrastructure and standards requirements for B2B.
11. Describe Web EDI, XML, and Web Services.

GENERAL MOTORS' B2B INITIATIVES

The Problem

General Motors (GM) is the world's largest vehicle manufacturer. The company sells cars in 190 countries and has manufacturing plants in about 50. Because the automotive industry is very competitive, GM is always looking for ways to improve its effectiveness. Its most publicized new initiative is a futuristic project with which GM expects to custom build the majority of its cars in a few years. The company hopes to use the system to save billions of dollars by reducing its inventory of finished cars.

In the meantime, GM sells custom-designed cars online through its dealers' sites. Because such online sales are not considered direct marketing to the final consumers, GM is able to avoid *channel conflict* with the non-company-owned dealers. This collaboration requires sharing information with dealers for online marketing and service on cars and on warranties. Both GM and its many dealers also need to collaborate with GM's suppliers. These suppliers work with other automakers as well. Therefore, a good communications system is needed.

Besides the need for effective communication, GM faces many operational problems that are typical of large companies. One of these is an ongoing financial challenge of what to do with manufacturing machines that are no longer sufficiently productive. These capital assets depreciate (lose value) over time and eventually must be replaced. GM traditionally has sold these assets through intermediaries at physical auctions. The problem was that these auctions took weeks, even months to conclude. Furthermore, the prices obtained at the auctions seemed to be too low, and a 20 percent commission had to be paid to the third-party auctioneers.

Another operational problem for GM relates to procurement of commodity products, which can be either *direct* materials that go into the vehicles or *indirect* materials, such as light bulbs or office supplies. GM buys about 200,000 different products from 20,000 suppliers, spending over $100 billion annually. The company was using a manual bidding process to negotiate contracts with potential suppliers. Specifications of the needed materials were sent by mail to the potential suppliers, the suppliers would then submit a bid, and GM would select a winner if a supplier offered a low enough price. If all the bids were too high, second and third rounds of bidding were conducted. In some cases, the process took weeks, even months, before GM was confident that the best deal, from both price and quality standpoints, had been achieved. The submission preparation costs involved in this process kept some bidders from submitting bids, so a less than optimal number of suppliers participated, resulting in higher prices paid by GM.

The Solution

To solve the problem of *connecting dealers and suppliers*, GM established an extranet infrastructure called *ANX* (Automotive Network eXchange). ANX, which was supported by other automakers, has evolved into a B2B exchange, Covisint (*covisint.com*), which is described in more detail in EC Application Case 6.2 on page 249). To address the *capital assets problem*, in early 2000 GM implemented its own electronic market on *covisint.com* from which *forward auctions* are conducted. The first items put up for bid were eight 75-ton stamping presses. GM invited 140 certified bidders to view the pictures and service records of the presses online. After only 1 week of preparation, the auction went live online, and the presses were sold in less than 2 hours.

For the *resource procurement problem*, GM automated the bidding process using *reverse auctions* on its e-procurement site. Qualified suppliers use the Internet to bid on each item GM needs to purchase. Bids are "open," meaning that all bidders can see the bids of their competitors. GM is able to accept bids from many suppliers concurrently, and using predetermined criteria, such as price, delivery date, and payment terms, can award jobs quickly to the most suitable bidder.

The Results

Within just 89 minutes of the opening of the first *forward auction*, eight stamping presses were sold for $1.8 million. With the old off-line method, a similar item would have sold for less than half of its online price, and the process would have taken 4 to 6 weeks. Since 2001, GM conducted hundreds of other electronic auctions. Other sellers were encouraged to put their items up for sale at the site as well, paying GM a commission on the final sales price.

In the first online *reverse auction*, GM purchased a large volume of rubber sealing packages for vehicle production. The price GM paid was significantly lower than the price the company had been paying for the same items previously negotiated by manual tendering. Now, many similar bids are conducted on the site every week. The administrative costs per order have been reduced by 40 percent or more.

Sources: Miscellaneous press releases at *gm.com* (accessed August 2002).

WHAT WE CAN LEARN . . .

The GM case demonstrates the involvement of a large company in two EC activities: (1) electronically auctioning used equipment to buyers and (2) conducting purchasing via electronic bidding. The auctioning and purchasing activities were conducted from GM's *private e-marketplace*, and the transactions were B2B. In B2B transactions, the company may be a seller, offering goods or services to many corporate buyers, or it may be a buyer, seeking goods or services from many corporate sellers (suppliers). When conducting such trades, a company can employ auctions, as GM did, or it can use electronic catalogs or other market mechanisms. These mechanisms and methods are the subject of this chapter.

5.1 CONCEPTS, CHARACTERISTICS, AND MODELS OF B2B EC

B2B EC has some special characteristics as well as models and concepts. The major ones are described next.

BASIC B2B CONCEPTS

Business-to-business e-commerce (B2B EC), also known as *eB2B* (*electronic B2B*) or just *B2B*, refers to transactions between businesses conducted electronically over the Internet, extranets, intranets, or private networks (see Mahadevan 2003 and Haig 2003). Such transactions may take place between a business and its supply chain members, as well as between a business and any other business. In this context, a business refers to any organization, private or public, for profit or nonprofit. The major characteristic of B2B is that companies attempt to electronically automate trading or communication processes in order to improve them. Note that B2B commerce can also be done without the Internet, but in this book we use the term B2B to mean B2B EC.

business-to-business e-commerce (B2B EC)
Transactions between businesses conducted electronically over the Internet, extranets, intranets, or private networks; also known as *eB2B* (*electronic B2B*) or just *B2B*.

Key business drivers for B2B are the availability of a secure broadband Internet platform and private and public B2B e-marketplaces; the need for collaborations between suppliers and buyers; the ability to save money, reduce delays, and improve collaboration; and the emergence of effective technologies for intra- and interorganizational integration. (For details, see Warkentin 2002.)

MARKET SIZE AND CONTENT OF B2B

First let's look at the B2B market. *eMarketer* (2003) and International Data Corporation (IDC) idc.com (2004) estimate worldwide B2B transaction volume at $1.4 trillion in 2003 and $2.4 trillion in 2004. Market forecasters estimate that by 2008 the global B2B market may reach $7 to $10 trillion, continuing to be the major component of the EC market (Mehrotra 2001). The percentage of Internet-based B2B as a proportion of total non-Internet B2B commerce increased from 0.2 percent in 1997 to 2.1 percent in 2000 and is expected to grow to 10 percent by 2005 (Goldman Sachs Group 2001). Chemicals, computer electronics, utilities, agriculture, shipping and warehousing, motor vehicles, petrochemicals, paper and office products, and food are the leading items in B2B. According to *eMarketer* (2003), the dollar value of B2B comprises at least 85 percent of the total transaction value of e-commerce.

The B2B market, which went through major consolidation in 2000–2001, is growing rapidly. Different B2B market forecasters use different definitions and methodologies. Because of this, predictions frequently change and statistical data often differ. Therefore, we will not provide any more data here. Data sources that can be checked for the latest information on the B2B market are provided in Chapter 3 (Exhibit 3.1).

B2B EC is now in its fifth generation, as shown in Exhibit 5.1 (page 196). This generation includes collaboration with suppliers, buyers, and other business partners (see Chapter 7), internal and external supply chain improvements (Chapter 7), and expert (intelligent) sales systems. Note that older generations co-exist with new ones. Also, some companies are still using only EC from early generations. In this chapter, we mainly describe topics from the second and third generation.

THE BASIC B2B TRANSACTION TYPES

The number of sellers and buyers and the form of participation used in B2B determine the basic B2B transaction types:

- **Sell-side.** One seller to many buyers (covered in Chapter 5).
- **Buy-side.** One buyer from many sellers (covered in Chapter 5).
- **Exchanges.** Many sellers to many buyers (covered in Chapter 6).
- **Collaborative commerce.** Activities other than buying or selling among business partners, for example, communicating, collaborating, and sharing of information for joint design, planning, and so on (covered in Chapter 7).

Exhibit 5.2 illustrates these four B2B types.

EXHIBIT 5.1 Key Drivers for B2B E-Commerce

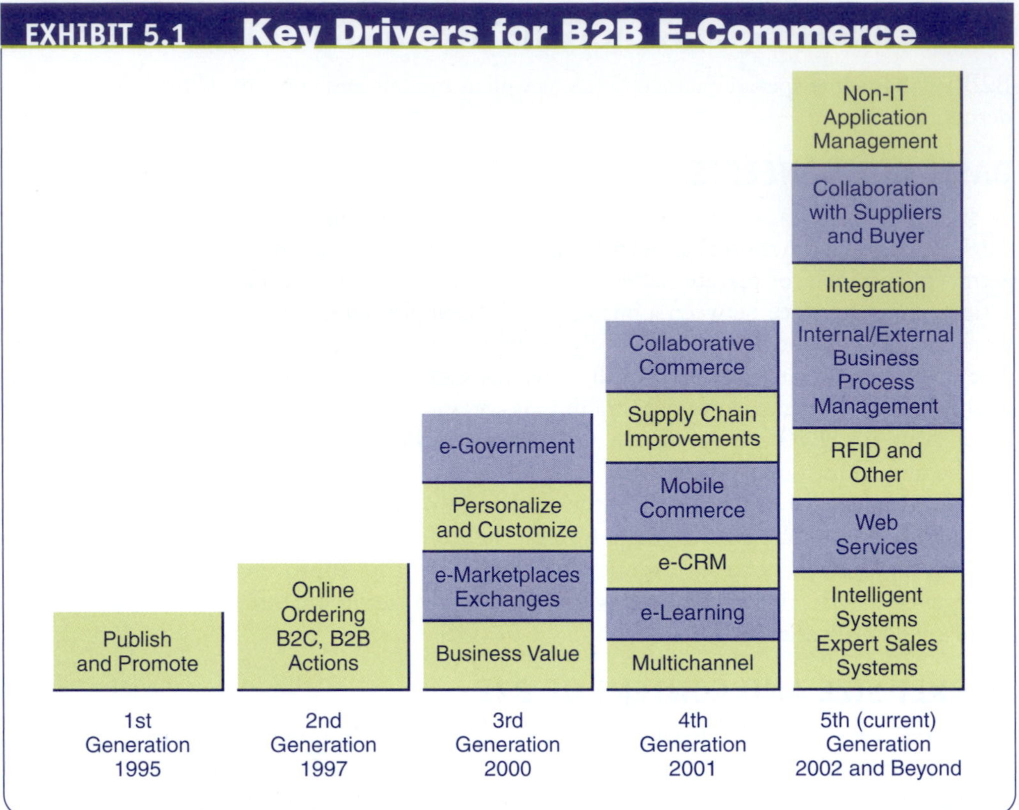

Source: Based on Gartner Inc. (2000).

EXHIBIT 5.2 Types of B2B E-Commerce

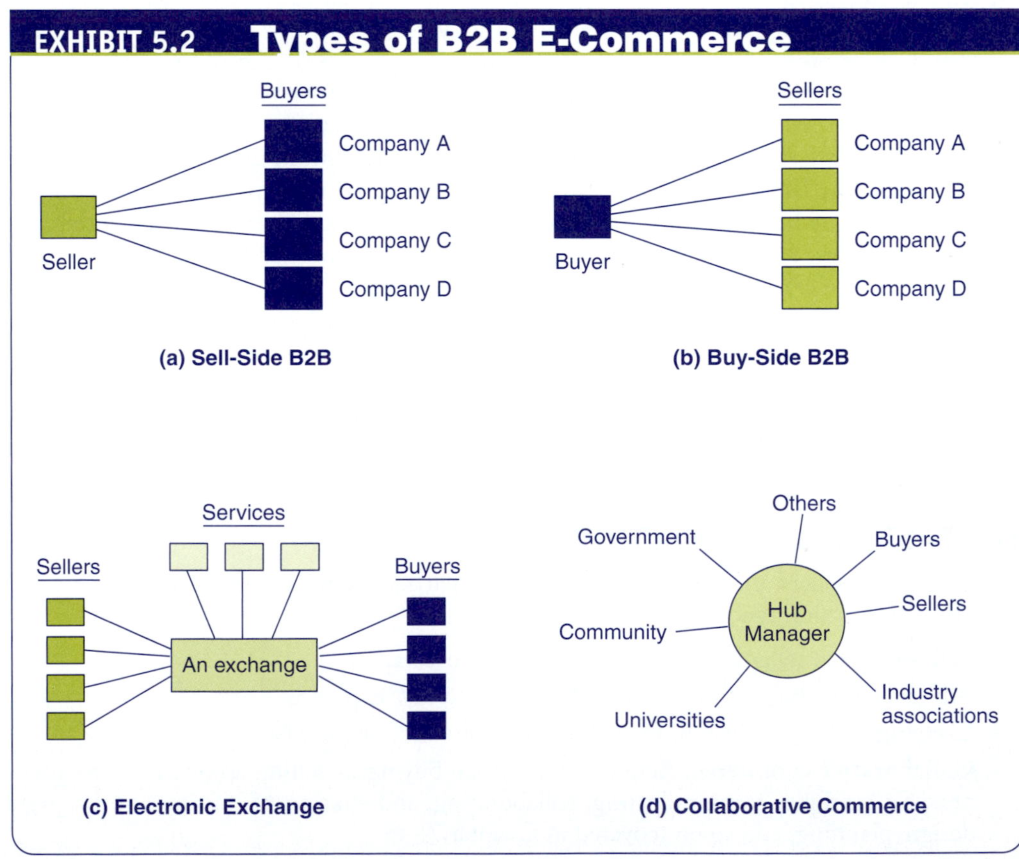

THE BASIC TYPES OF B2B E-MARKETPLACES

The following are the basic types of B2B e-marketplaces.

One-to-Many and Many-to-One: Private E-Marketplaces

In one-to-many and many-to-one markets, one company does either all of the selling (*sell-side market*) or all of the buying (*buy-side market*). Because EC is focused on a single company's buying or selling needs in these transactions, this type of EC is referred to as **company-centric EC**. Company-centric marketplaces—both sell-side and buy-side—are the topic of this chapter.

company-centric EC
E-commerce that focuses on a single company's buying needs (many-to-one, or buy-side) or selling needs (one-to-many, or sell-side).

In company-centric marketplaces, the individual sell-side or buy-side company has complete control over who participates in the selling or buying transaction and the supporting information systems. Thus, these transactions are essentially private. Therefore, sell-side and buy-side markets are considered **private e-marketplaces**.

private e-marketplaces
Markets in which the individual sell-side or buy-side company has complete control over participation in the selling or buying transaction.

Intermediaries

Many one-to-many or many-to-one EC activities are conducted without the help of intermediaries. However, when it comes to auctions, aggregating buyers, or complex transactions, an intermediary frequently is used. (Even when an intermediary is used, the market is still considered private, because the single buyer or seller that hires the intermediary may maintain control of who is invited to participate in the market.)

Many-to-Many: Exchanges

In many-to-many e-marketplaces, many buyers and many sellers meet electronically for the purpose of trading with one another. There are different types of such e-marketplaces, which are also known as **exchanges**, **trading communities**, or **trading exchanges**. We will use the term *exchanges* in this book. Exchanges are usually owned and run by a third party or by a consortium. They are described in more detail in Chapter 6. Exchanges are open to all interested parties (sellers and buyers), and thus are considered **public e-marketplaces**.

exchanges (trading communities or trading exchanges)
Many-to-many e-marketplaces, usually owned and run by a third party or a consortium, in which many buyers and many sellers meet electronically to trade with each other; also called *trading communities* or *trading exchanges*.

public e-marketplaces
Third-party exchanges that are open to all interested parties (sellers and buyers).

Collaborative Commerce

Businesses deal with other businesses for purposes beyond just selling or buying. One example is that of *collaborative commerce*, which is communication, design, planning, and information sharing among business partners. To qualify as collaborative commerce, the activities that are shared must represent far more than just financial transactions. For example, they may include activities related to design, manufacture, or management. Collaborative commerce is described in Chapter 7.

B2B2C

A special case of B2B is B2B2C (see the Godiva case in Chapter 1). With B2B2C, a business sells to a business, but delivers small quantities to individuals or business customers.

B2B CHARACTERISTICS

Similar to the classic story of the blind men trying to describe an elephant, B2B can be described in a variety of ways depending on which characteristic is the focus. Here we examine various qualities by which B2B transactions can be characterized.

Parties to the Transaction

B2B commerce can be conducted *directly* between a *buyer* and a *seller* or it can be conducted via an **online intermediary**. The intermediary is an online third party that brokers the transaction between the buyer and seller; it may be a virtual intermediary or a click-and-mortar intermediary. See Davis and Benamati (2003) for details. Some of the electronic intermediaries for consumers mentioned in Chapter 3 also can be referenced for B2B by replacing the individual consumers with business customers. Consolidators of buyers or sellers are typical B2B intermediaries (Section 5.3).

online intermediary
An online third party that brokers a transaction online between a buyer and a seller; may be virtual or click-and-mortar.

Types of Transactions

spot buying
The purchase of goods and services as they are needed, usually at prevailing market prices.

strategic (systematic) sourcing
Purchases involving long-term contracts that usually are based on private negotiations between sellers and buyers.

B2B transactions are of two basic types: spot buying and strategic sourcing. **Spot buying** refers to the purchasing of goods and services as they are needed, usually at prevailing market prices, which are determined dynamically by supply and demand. The buyers and the sellers may not even know each other. Stock exchanges and commodity exchanges (oil, sugar, corn, etc.) are examples of spot buying. In contrast, **strategic (systematic) sourcing** involves purchases based on *long-term contracts*.

Spot buying may be conducted most economically on the public exchanges. Strategic purchases can be supported more effectively and efficiently through direct buyer–seller online negotiations, which can be done in private exchanges or private trading rooms in public exchanges.

Types of Materials Traded

direct materials
Materials used in the production of a product (e.g., steel in a car or paper in a book).

indirect materials
Materials used to support production (e.g., office supplies or light bulbs).

MRO (maintenance, repair, and operation)
Indirect materials used in activities that support production.

Two types of materials and supplies are traded in B2B: direct and indirect. **Direct materials** are materials used in making the products, such as steel in a car or paper in a book. The characteristics of direct materials are that their use is scheduled and planned for. They are usually not shelf items, and they are frequently purchased in large quantities after extensive negotiation and contracting.

Indirect materials are items, such as office supplies or light bulbs, that support production. They are usually used in **maintenance, repair, and operation (MRO)** activities. Collectively, they are known as nonproduction materials.

Direction of Trade

vertical marketplaces
Markets that deal with one industry or industry segment (e.g., steel, chemicals).

horizontal marketplaces
Markets that concentrate on a service, materials, or a product that is used in all types of industries (e.g., office supplies, PCs).

B2B marketplaces may be classified as vertical or horizontal. **Vertical marketplaces** are those that deal with one industry or industry segment. Examples include marketplaces specializing in electronics, cars, steel, or chemicals. **Horizontal marketplaces** are those that concentrate on a service or a product that is used in all types of industries. Examples are office supplies, PCs, or travel services.

The various characteristics of B2B transactions are presented in summary form in Insights and Additions 5.1.

SUPPLY CHAIN RELATIONSHIPS IN B2B

In the various B2B transaction types, business activities are usually conducted along the supply chain of a company. The supply chain process consists of a number of interrelated subprocesses and roles. These extend from the acquisition of materials from suppliers, to the processing of a product or service, to packaging it and moving it to distributors and retailers. The process ends with the eventual purchase of a product by the end consumer. B2B can make supply chains more efficient and effective or it can change the supply chain completely, eliminating one or more intermediaries.

Historically, many of the segments and processes in the supply chain have been managed through paper transactions (e.g., purchase orders, invoices, and so forth). B2B applications are offered online so they can serve as supply chain enablers that offer distinct competitive advantages. Supply chain management also encompasses the coordination of order generation, order taking, and order fulfillment and distribution (see Chapters 7, 13, and Online Tutorial T2 for more discussion of supply chain management).

Hoffman et al. (2002) looked at the effect of various B2B types on supply chain relationships. They found, for example, that a B2B private e-marketplace provides a company with high supply chain power and high capabilities for online interactions. This is basically how much bargaining and control power a company has. Joining a public e-marketplace, on the other hand, provides a business with high buying and selling capabilities, but will result in low supply chain power. Companies that choose an intermediary to do their buying and selling will be low on both supply chain power and buying/selling capabilities. Hoffman et al. (2002) recommend private e-marketplaces as most likely to result in effective supply chain relationships. A major reason for companies to collaborate is to improve their joint supply chain. In Chapter 7, we illustrate how Cisco lost a large amount of money due to lack of col-

Insights and Additions 5.1 Summary of B2B Characteristics

Parties to Transactions	Types of Transactions
Direct, seller to buyer or buyer to seller	Spot buying
Via intermediaries	Strategic sourcing
B2B2C: A business sells to a business, but delivers to individual consumers	
Types of Materials Sold	**Direction of Trade**
Direct	Vertical
Indirect (MROs)	Horizontal
Number and Form of Participation	**Degree of Openness**
One-to-many: Sell-side (e-storefront)	Private exchanges
Many-to-one: Buy-side	Public exchanges
Many-to-many: Exchanges	
Many, connected: Collaborative	

laboration along the supply chain. An example of a promising future collaboration is Wal-Mart's RFID initiative (see Chapter 2).

VIRTUAL SERVICE INDUSTRIES IN B2B

In addition to trading products between businesses, services also can be provided electronically in B2B. Just as service industries such as banking, insurance, real estate, and stock trading can be conducted electronically for individuals, as described in Chapter 3, so they can be conducted electronically for businesses. The major B2B services are:

- **Travel and entertainment services.** Many large corporations arrange their travel electronically through corporate travel agents. To further reduce costs, companies can make special arrangements that enable employees to plan and book their own trips online. For instance, Rosenbluth International, now a subsidiary of American Express (americanexpress.com), provides an agentless service to corporate clients (see Online File W2.6, Chapter 2). Expedia, Travelocity, Orbitz, and other online travel services provide B2B services as well.
- **Real estate.** Commercial real estate transactions can be large and complex. Therefore, the Web may not be able to completely replace existing human agents. Instead, the Web can help businesses find the right properties, compare properties, and assist in negotiations. Some government-run foreclosed real estate auctions are open only to corporate real estate dealers and are conducted online.
- **Financial services.** Internet banking is an economical way of making business payments, transferring funds, or performing other financial transactions. For example, electronic funds transfer (EFT) is popular with businesses. Transaction fees over the Internet are less costly than any other alternative method. To see how payments work in

B2B, see Chapter 12. Businesses can also purchase insurance online, both from pure online insurance companies and from click-and-mortar ones.

- **Online stock trading.** Some corporations are large stock investors. Online trading services are very attractive to institutional investors because fees for online trading are very low and flat, regardless of the trading amount. Most institutional investment is facilitated by electronic trading.
- **Online financing.** Business loans can be solicited online from lenders. Bank of America, for example, offers its commercial customers a matching service on IntraLoan, which uses an extranet to match business loan applicants with potential lending corporations. Several sites, such as garage.com, provide information about venture capital.
- **Other online services.** Consulting services, law firms, health organizations, and others sell knowledge and special services online. Many other online services, such as the purchase of electronic stamps (similar to metered postage, but generated on a computer), are available online (see stamps.com).

THE BENEFITS AND LIMITATIONS OF B2B

The benefits of B2B depend on which model is used. In general, though, the major benefits of B2B are that it:

- Creates new sales (purchase) opportunities
- Eliminates paper and reduces administrative costs
- Expedites processing and reduces cycle time
- Lowers search costs and time for buyers to find products and vendors
- Increases productivity of employees dealing with buying and/or selling
- Reduces errors and improves quality of services
- Makes product configuration easier
- Reduces marketing and sales costs (for sellers)
- Reduces inventory levels and costs
- Enables customized online catalogs with different prices for different customers
- Increases production flexibility, permitting just-in-time delivery
- Reduces procurement costs (for buyers)
- Facilitates mass customization
- Provides for efficient customer service
- Increases opportunities for collaboration

B2B EC has limitations as well, especially regarding channel conflict and the operation of public exchanges. These will be discussed later in this chapter and in Chapter 6.

The introduction of B2B may eliminate the distributor or the retailer, which could be a benefit to the seller and the buyer (though not a benefit to the distributor or retailer). In previous chapters, such a phenomenon is referred to as *disintermediation* (Chapters 2 and 3).

In the remainder of the chapter, we will look at the company-centric B2B models and topics introduced in this opening section in more depth.

Section 5.1 ▶ REVIEW QUESTIONS

1. Define B2B.
2. Discuss the following: spot buying versus strategic sourcing, direct materials versus indirect materials, and vertical markets versus horizontal markets.
3. What are company-centric marketplaces? Are they public or private?
4. Define B2B exchanges.
5. Relate the supply chain to B2B transactions.
6. List the B2B online services.
7. Summarize the benefits and limitations of B2B.

5.2 ONE-TO-MANY: SELL-SIDE E-MARKETPLACES

Most B2B activities involve direct selling.

SELL-SIDE MODELS AND ACTIVITIES

In Chapter 3, we introduced the direct-selling model in which a manufacturer or a retailer sells electronically directly to consumers from a *storefront*. In a **sell-side e-marketplace** a business sells products and services to business customers, frequently over an extranet. The seller can be a manufacturer selling to a wholesaler, to a retailer, or to an individual business. Intel, Cisco, and Dell are examples of such sellers. Or, the seller can be a distributor selling to wholesalers, to retailers, or to businesses (e.g., W.W. Grainger). In either case, sell-side e-marketplaces involve one seller and many potential buyers. In this model, both individual consumers and business buyers may use the same sell-side marketplace (e.g., dell.com) or they may use different marketplaces. Exhibit 5.3 shows the architecture of sell-side B2B marketplaces.

sell-side e-marketplace
A Web-based marketplace in which one company sells to many business buyers from e-catalogs or auctions, frequently over an extranet.

The architecture of this B2B model is similar to that of B2C EC. The major differences are in the process (see Jakovijeric 2004). For example, in B2B, large customers may be provided with customized catalogs and prices. Usually, companies will separate B2C orders from B2B orders. One reason for this is that B2C and B2B orders have different *order-fulfillment processes* (see Chapter 13).

The one-to-many model has three major pricing methods: (1) selling from *electronic catalogs*; (2) selling via *forward auctions* (as GM does with its old equipment); and (3) *one-to-one* selling, usually under a *negotiated* long-term contract. Such one-to-one negotiating is familiar: The buying company negotiates price, quantity, payments, delivery, and quality terms with the selling company (see Section 5.8). We describe the first method in this section and the second in Section 5.3.

B2B Sellers

Sellers in the sell-side marketplace may be click-and-mortar manufacturers or intermediaries (e.g., distributors or wholesalers). The intermediaries may even be online pure companies (virtual), as in the case of Bigboxx.com, described in EC Application Case 5.1.

EXHIBIT 5.3 Sell-Side B2B Marketplace Architecture

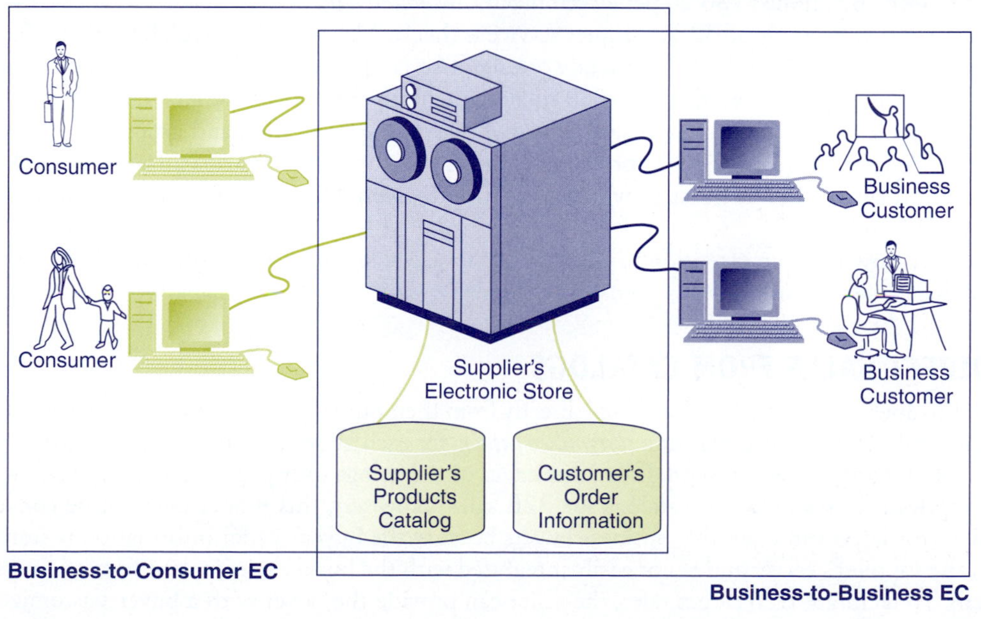

CASE 5.1

EC Application

BUYING FROM VIRTUAL SELLER BIGBOXX.COM

Bigboxx.com (*bigboxx.com*), based in Hong Kong, is a B2B retailer of office supplies. It has no physical stores and sells products through its online catalog; thus, Bigboxx.com is an online intermediary. The company has three types of customers: large corporate clients, medium-sized corporate clients, and small office/home offices (SOHO). It offers more than 10,000 items from 300 suppliers. Bigboxx.com's goal is to sell its products in various countries in Southeast Asia.

The company's portal is attractive and easy to use and includes tutorials that instruct users on how to use the Web site. Once registered, the user can start shopping using the online shopping cart. Users can look for items by browsing through the online catalog or by searching the site with a search engine. The ordering system is integrated with an SAP-based back-office system.

Users can pay by cash or by check (upon delivery), via automatic bank drafts, by credit card, or by purchasing card. Soon users will be able to pay through Internet-based direct debit, by electronic bill presentation and payment, or by Internet banking.

Using its own trucks and warehouses, deliveries scheduled online are made within 24 hours or even on the same day.

Bigboxx.com provides numerous value-added services for customers. Among these are the ability to check item availability in real time; the ability to track the status of each item in an order; promotions and suggested items based on customers' user profiles; customized prices for every product, for every customer; control and central-approval features; automatic activation at desired time intervals of standing orders for repeat purchasing; and a large number of Excel reports and data, including comparative management reports.

Bigboxx.com began operations in spring 2000. By the end of 2004, it had over 8,000 registered customers.

Sources: Compiled from Chan et al. (2001) and *bigboxx.com* (accessed 2004).

Questions

1. Enter *bigboxx.com* and *staples.com* and compare their B2B offerings and purchase processes. (Take the tutorial at *bigboxx.com*.) What support services are provided?
2. Someday customers may become accustomed to buying office supplies online. Then, they may try to buy directly from the manufacturers. Will Bigboxx.com then be disintermediated?

Customer Service

Online sellers can provide sophisticated customer services. For example, General Electric receives 20 million calls a year regarding appliances. Although most of these calls come from individuals, many come from businesses. By using the Internet and automatic-response software agents (autoresponders), GE has reduced the cost of handling calls from $5 per call when done by phone to $0.20 per electronically answered call.

Another example of B2B customer service is that of Milacron, Inc., which produces consumable industrial products for metalworking. The company launched an award-winning EC site aimed at its more than 100,000 small to medium enterprises (SMEs) customers. The site provides an easy-to-use and secure way of selecting, purchasing, and arranging delivery (if needed) of Milacron's 55,000 products. From this site, the SMEs also can access a level of technical service beyond that provided previously to even Milacron's largest customers (see milacron.com).

We now turn our attention to the first of the sell-side methods—selling from electronic catalogs.

DIRECT SALES FROM CATALOGS

Companies can use the Internet to sell directly from their online catalogs. A company may offer one catalog for all customers or a *customized catalog* for each large customer (usually both).

In Chapter 2, we presented the advantages of e-catalogs over paper catalogs and showed how Boise Cascade uses e-catalogs for B2B sales. However, this model may not be convenient for large and repetitive business buyers because the buyer's order information is stored in the supplier's server and is not easily integrated with the buyer's corporate information system. To facilitate B2B direct sales, the seller can provide the buyer with a buyer-customized shopping cart (such as Bigboxx.com offers), which can store order information that can be integrated with the buyer's information system. This is particularly important when buyers have to visit several sites in one shopping mall (see Lim and Lee 2003).

Many sellers provide separate pages and catalogs to their major buyers. For example, Staples.com, an office supply vendor, offers its business customers personalized catalogs of 80,000 products and pricing at stapleslink.com.

Another example of B2B direct sales from catalogs is Microsoft, which uses an extranet to sell over $6 billion of software annually to its channel partners. Using Microsoft's extranet-based order-entry tool (MOET), customer partners can check inventory, make transactions, and look up the status of orders. The online orders are automatically fed into the customer's SAP applications. MOET was started in Europe in 1997 and has since been rolled out worldwide. The extranet handles about 650,000 transactions per year. The system significantly reduces the number of phone calls, e-mails, and incorrect product shipments (Wagner 2000).

Configuration and Customization

As with B2C EC, B2B direct sales offer an opportunity for efficient customization. As we will see in the case of Cisco (described in detail later in the chapter), manufacturers can provide online tools for self-configuration, pricing, ordering, and so on. Business customers can customize products, get price quotes, and submit orders, all online.

Many click-and-mortar companies today use a *multichannel distribution system,* in which the Internet is a new, but supplemental, channel that enables greater efficiency in the ordering process, as shown in the case of Whirlpool in EC Application Case 5.2.

Benefits and Limitations of Direct Sales from Catalogs

Successful examples of the B2B direct sales model include manufacturers, such as Dell, Intel, IBM, and Cisco, and distributors, such as Ingram Micro (which sells to value-added retailers; the retailer adds some service along with the product). Sellers that use this model may be successful as long as they have a superb reputation in the market and a large enough group of loyal customers.

CASE 5.2

EC Application

WHIRLPOOL B2B TRADING PORTAL

Whirlpool (*whirlpool.com*) is a $13-billion corporation based in Benton Harbor, Michigan. It is in the company's best interest to operate efficiently and to offer as much customer service for the members of its selling chain as possible. However, the middle-tier partners, who comprise 25 percent of the total partner base and 10 percent of Whirlpool's annual revenue, were submitting their orders by phone or fax because they were not large enough to have system-to-system computer connections direct to Whirlpool.

To improve customer service for these dealers, Whirlpool developed a B2B trading partner portal (Whirlpool Web World), using IBM e-business solutions. The technologies enable fast, easy Web self-service ordering processes. Using these self-service processes, Whirlpool was able to cut the cost per order to under $5—a savings of 80 percent.

The company tested ordering via the Web by developing a portal for low-level products. It was so successful (resulting in a 100 percent ROI during the first 8 months of use) that Whirlpool went to a second-generation portal, which services the middle-tier partners. The Whirlpool Web World allows middle-tier trade partners to place orders and track their status through a password-protected site.

Simultaneously, the company implemented SAP R/3 for order entry, which is utilized by the middle-tier partners on the second-generation portal. The company also is using IBM's Application Framework for e-business, taking advantage of its rapid development cycles and associated cost reductions.

Using the same IBM platform, Whirlpool launched a B2C site for U.S. customers for ordering small appliances and accessories. The site was so successful that the company realized a 100 percent ROI in just 5 months.

Sources: Compiled from IBM (2000) and *whirlpool.com* (accessed 2004).

Questions

1. How do Whirlpool's customers benefit from the portal?
2. What are the benefits of the trading portal for Whirlpool?
3. Relate the B2B sell-side to a B2C storefront.

Although the benefits of direct sales are similar to that of B2C and to the generic B2B benefits described earlier, there also are limitations. One of the major issues facing direct sellers is how to find buyers. Many companies know how to advertise in traditional channels but are still learning how to contact would-be buyers online. Also, B2B sellers may experience channel conflicts with their existing distribution systems. Another limitation is that if traditional EDI (the computer-to-computer direct transfer of business documents) is used, the cost to the customers can be high, and they will be reluctant to go online. The solution to this problem is the transfer of documents over the extranets (see Appendix 6A). Finally, the number of business partners online must be large enough to justify the system infrastructure and operation and maintenance expenses.

DIRECT SALES: THE EXAMPLE OF CISCO SYSTEMS

Cisco Systems (cisco.com) is the world's leading producer of routers, switches, and network interconnection services. Cisco's portal has evolved over several years, beginning with technical support for customers and developing into one of the world's largest direct sales EC sites. Today, Cisco offers about a dozen Internet-based applications to both end-user businesses and reseller partners (see Slater 2003).

Customer Service

Cisco began providing electronic support in 1991 using value-added networks (VANs). The first applications offered were software downloads, defects tracking, and technical advice. In spring 1994, Cisco moved its system to the Web and named it Cisco Connection Online (CCO). By 2004, Cisco's customers and reseller partners were logging onto Cisco's Web site over 2 million times a month to receive technical assistance, place and check orders, or download software. The online service has been so well received that nearly 85 percent of all customer service inquiries and 95 percent of software updates are delivered online. The service is delivered globally in 16 languages. The CCO is considered a model for B2B success, and several books have been written about it (e.g., Bunnel and Brate 2000; Slater 2003; Waters 2002).

Online Ordering by Customers

Virtually all of Cisco's products are made-to-order. Before CCO, ordering a product was a lengthy, complicated, and error-prone process because it was done by fax or by "snail mail." Cisco began deploying Web-based commerce tools in July 1995, and within a year, its Internet Product Center allowed users to configure and purchase any Cisco product over the Web. Today, a business customer's engineer can sit down at a PC, configure a product, and find out immediately if there are any errors in the configuration (some feedback is given by intelligent agents).

By providing online pricing and configuration tools to customers, 99 percent of orders are now placed through CCO, saving time for both Cisco and its customers. In the first 5 months of online ordering operations in 1996, Cisco booked over $100 million in online sales. This figure grew to $4 billion in 1998, to over $8 billion in 2002, and to about $10 billion in 2004 (Cisco Annual Report 2003).

Order Status

Each month Cisco used to receive over 150,000 order-status inquiries such as, "When will my order be ready?" "How should the order be classified for customs?" "Is the product eligible for NAFTA agreement?" "What export control issues apply?" Cisco provides self-tracking and FAQ tools so that customers can find the answers to many of their questions by themselves. In addition, the company's primary domestic and international freight forwarders update Cisco's database electronically about the status of each shipment. CCO can record the shipping date, the method of shipment, and the current location of each product. All new information is made available to customers immediately. As soon as an order ships, Cisco notifies the customer via e-mail (see Waters 2002).

Benefits

Cisco reaps many benefits from the CCO system. The most important benefits include the following (Interwoven 2001):

- **Reduced operating costs for order taking.** By automating its order process online in 1998, Cisco has saved $363 million per year, or approximately 17.5 percent of its total operating costs. This is due primarily to increased productivity of the employees who take and process orders.
- **Improved quality.** The system facilitates the Six Sigma mission of Cisco.
- **Enhanced technical support and customer service.** With more than 85 percent of its technical support and customer service calls handled online, Cisco's technical support productivity has increased by 250 percent per year.
- **Reduced technical support staff cost.** Online technical support has reduced technical support staff costs by roughly $125 million each year.
- **Reduced software distribution costs.** Customers download new software releases directly from Cisco's site, saving the company $180 million in distribution, packaging, and duplicating costs each year. Having product and pricing information on the Web and Web-based CD-ROMs saves Cisco an additional $50 million annually in printing and distributing catalogs and marketing materials to customers.
- **Faster service.** Lead times were reduced from 4 to 10 days to 2 to 3 days.

The CCO system also benefits customers. Cisco customers can configure orders more quickly, immediately determine costs, and collaborate much more rapidly and effectively with Cisco's staff. Also, customer service and technical support are faster.

Section 5.2 ▶ REVIEW QUESTIONS

1. List the types of sell-side B2B transaction models.
2. Distinguish between the use and nonuse of intermediaries in B2B sell-side transactions.
3. What are buy-side and sell-side transactions? How do they differ?
4. Describe customer service in B2B systems.
5. Describe direct B2B sales from catalogs.
6. Discuss the benefits and limitations of direct B2B sales from catalogs.
7. Describe Cisco's B2B activities and list their benefits to Cisco and to its customers.

5.3 SELLING VIA INTERMEDIARIES

Manufacturers frequently use intermediaries to distribute their products to a large number of buyers. Known as *distributors*, the intermediaries buy products from many vendors and aggregate them into one catalog from which they sell. Now, many of these distributors are selling online.

As in B2C, many distributors (including retailers) also offer their products online via storefronts. Some well-known online distributors for businesses are SAM's Club (of Wal-Mart), Amazon.com, and W. W. Grainger. Most e-distributors sell in horizontal markets, meaning that they sell to businesses in a variety of industries. However, some specialize in one industry (vertical market), such as Boeing PART (see Online File W5.1). A well-known intermediary of electrical parts is Marshall Industries. Its story is provided in Online File W5.2. Most intermediaries sell at fixed prices; however, some offer quantity discounts.

The case of W. W. Grainger is provided in EC Application Case 5.3.

Section 5.3 ▶ REVIEW QUESTIONS

1. What are the advantages of using intermediaries in B2B sales?
2. What special services are provided to buyers by Boeing Parts? (Online File W5.1)
3. Compare Grainger's case with Marshall (Online File W5.2). What are the common elements? What are the differences?
4. Compare an e-distributor in B2B to Amazon.com. What are the similarities? What are the differences?

CASE 5.3

EC Application

W. W. GRAINGER AND GOODRICH CORPORATION

W. W. Grainger has a number of Web sites, but its flagship is *grainger.com*. In 2004, of Grainger's over $6 billion in annual sales, more than $600 million was done over the Web, with the majority of those sales placed through *grainger.com*.

More than 600,000 brand-name MRO supplies are offered at *grainger.com*, and a growing number of Grainger's 2.2 million customers are ordering online. The Web site continues the same kind of customer service and wide range of industrial products provided by Grainger's traditional off-line business with the additional convenience of 24/7 ordering, use of search engines, and additional services.

This convenience is what first attracted BFGoodrich Aerospace (now called Goodrich Corporation) in Pueblo, Colorado. They found *grainger.com* to be one of the most convenient and easy purchasing sites to use. The purchasing agent of this small Goodrich plant of approximately 250 employees used to call in an order to a supplier, give the salesperson a part number, and wait until the price could be pulled up. Goodrich's purchaser now can place orders online in a matter of minutes, and the purchaser's display has Goodrich's negotiated pricing built in.

Goodrich can get just about anything it needs from *grainger.com*. Grainger interfaces with other suppliers, so if Goodrich needs something specific that Grainger does not normally carry, Grainger will research and find the items through its *findmro.com* site. With Grainger's buying power, Goodrich can get better prices.

Goodrich has achieved additional savings from the tremendous decrease in paperwork that has resulted from buying through *grainger.com*. Individuals in each department now have access to purchasing cards, which allow them to do some of their own ordering. Before, the central purchasing department had to issue purchase orders for every single item. Now, employees with P-cards and passwords can place orders according to the spending limits that have been set up based on their positions.

In 2002, the Goodrich Pueblo operation spent $200,000 for purchases from *grainger.com*, which reflected a 10 to 15 percent savings on its purchases. Goodrich has now signed a companywide enterprise agreement that allows every Goodrich facility in the country to order through *grainger.com*, with an expected savings of at least 10 percent.

Sources: Compiled from *Fortune* (2000), *grainger.com* (accessed 2004), and Lucas (2005).

Questions

1. Enter *grainger.com* and review all of the services offered to buyers. Prepare a list of these services.
2. Explain how Goodrich's buyers save time and money.
3. What other benefits does Goodrich enjoy by using *grainger.com*?
4. How is desktop purchasing implemented at Goodrich Corporation?

5.4 SELLING VIA AUCTIONS

Auctions are gaining popularity as a B2B sales channel. Some major B2B auction issues are discussed in this section.

USING AUCTIONS ON THE SELL SIDE

As you read in the opening case study, GM uses *forward auctions* to sell its unneeded capital assets. In such a situation, items are displayed on an auction site (private or public) for quick disposal. Forward auctions offer a number of benefits to B2B sellers:

- **Revenue generation.** Forward auctions support and expand online and overall sales. For example, Weirton Steel Corp. doubled its customer base when it started forward auctions (Fickel 1999). Forward auctions also offer businesses a new venue for quickly and easily disposing of excess, obsolete, and returned products.
- **Cost savings.** In addition to generating new revenue, conducting auctions electronically reduces the costs of selling the auctioned items. These savings also help increase the seller's profits.
- **Increased page views.** Forward auctions give Web sites "stickiness." As discussed in Chapter 4, *stickiness* is a characteristic describing customer loyalty to a site, demonstrated by the number and length of visits to a site. Stickiness at an auction site, for example,

means that auction users spend more time on a site, generate more page views than other users, and trade more.

- **Member acquisition and retention.** All bidding transactions result in additional registered members, who are future business contacts. In addition, auction software aids enable sellers to search and report on virtually every relevant auction activity for future analysis and use.

Forward auctions can be conducted in two ways. A company may conduct its forward auctions from its own Web site or it can sell from an intermediary auction site, such as ebay.com or asset-auctions.com. Let's examine these options.

SELLING FROM THE COMPANY'S OWN SITE

For large and well-known companies that frequently conduct auctions, such as GM, it makes sense to build an auction mechanism on the company's own site. Why should a company pay a commission to an intermediary if the intermediary cannot provide the company with added value? Of course, if a company decides to auction from its own site, it will have to pay for infrastructure and operate and maintain the auction site. However, if the company already has an electronic marketplace for selling from e-catalogs, the additional cost for conducting auctions may not be too high. On the other hand, a significant added value that could be provided by intermediaries is the attraction of many potential buyers to the auction site.

USING INTERMEDIARIES

Large numbers of intermediaries offer B2B auction sites (e.g., see asset-auctions.com; others are discussed in Chapter 10). An intermediary may conduct private auctions for a seller, either from the intermediary's or the seller's site. Or, a company may choose to conduct auctions in a public marketplace, using a third-party hosting company (e.g., eBay, which has a special "business exchange" for small companies).

Using a third-party hosting company for conducting auctions has many benefits. The first is that no additional resources (e.g., hardware, bandwidth, engineering resources, or IT personnel) are required. Nor are there any hiring costs or opportunity costs associated with the redeployment of corporate resources. B2B auctions also offer fast time-to-market: They enable a company to have a robust, customized auction up and running immediately. Without the intermediary, it may take a company weeks to prepare an auction site in-house.

Another benefit of using an intermediary relates to who owns and controls the auction information. In the case of an intermediary-conducted private auction, the intermediary sets up the auction to show the branding (company name) of the merchant rather than the intermediary's name. (For example, if an intermediary prepares a private auction for Blue Devils Company, customers see the Blue Devils name and logo.) Yet, the intermediary does the work of collecting data on Web traffic, page views, and member registration; setting all the auction parameters (transaction fee structure, user interface, and reports); and integrating the information flow and logistics. Of course, if a company wants to dispose of unwanted assets without advertising to the public that it is doing so, an intermediary-conducted public auction would be the logical choice. If a manufacturer is selling off products, buyers may become suspicious of the quality of the items. If an intermediary does the auction, it doesn't have to provide answers regarding the quality of the product.

Another benefit of using intermediaries relates to billing and collection efforts, which are handled by the intermediary rather than the company. For example, intermediaries calculate merchant-specific shipping weights and charge customers for shipping of auctioned items. All credit card data are encrypted for secure transmission and storage, and all billing information easily can be downloaded by the merchant company for integration with existing systems. These services are not free, of course. They are provided as part of the merchant's commission to the intermediary, a cost often deemed worth paying in exchange for the ease of the service.

EXAMPLES OF B2B FORWARD AUCTION

The GM opening case provides an example of a company using a forward auction to sell surplus materials, which is a major objective of B2B EC auctions. Surpluses are sold online by intermediaries (e.g., asset-auctions.com) or by large manufacturers (e.g., Dell). The following are examples of B2B auctions:

- Whirlpool Corp. sold $20 million in scrap metal in 2003, increasing the price received by 15 percent (asset-auctions.com 2004).
- SAM's Club (samsclub.com) auctions thousands of items (especially electronics) at auctions.samsclub.com. Featured auctions include the current bid, the number of bids, and the end date.
- ResortQuest, a large vacation rental company, uses auctionanything.com to auction rental space.
- At GovernmentAuctions.org (governmentauctions.org), businesses can bid on foreclosures, seized items, abandoned property, and more.
- Yahoo! conducts both B2C and B2B auctions of many items.

Section 5.4 ▶ REVIEW QUESTIONS

1. List the benefits of using B2B auctions for selling.
2. List the benefits of using auction intermediaries.

5.5 ONE-FROM-MANY: BUY-SIDE E-MARKETPLACES AND E-PROCUREMENT

buy-side e-marketplace
A corporate-based acquisition site that uses reverse auctions, negotiations, group purchasing, or any other e-procurement method.

When a buyer goes to a sell-side marketplace such as Cisco's, the buyer's purchasing department sometimes has to manually enter the order information into its own corporate information system. Furthermore, manually searching e-stores and e-malls to find and compare suppliers and products can be very slow and costly. As a solution, large buyers can open their own marketplaces, as GM did, called **buy-side e-marketplaces**, and invite sellers to browse and fulfill orders. The term *procurement* is used to refer to the purchase of goods and services for organizations. It is usually done by *purchasing agents,* also known as *corporate buyers* (see Martin et al. 2001).

PROCUREMENT METHODS

Companies use different methods to procure goods and services depending on what and where they buy, the quantities needed, how much money is involved, and more. The major procurement methods include the following:

- Conduct bidding or tendering (a reverse auction) in a system in which suppliers compete against each other. This method is used for large-ticket items or large quantities (Section 5.6).
- Buy directly from manufacturers, wholesalers, or retailers from their catalogs and possibly by negotiation. Frequently, a contract implements such a purchase (Section 5.8).
- Buy from the catalog of an intermediary (e-distributor) that aggregates sellers' catalogs, (Section 5.7).
- Buy from an internal buyer's catalog, in which company-approved vendors' catalogs, including agreed upon prices, are aggregated. This approach is used for the implementation of *desktop purchasing,* which allows the requisitioners to order directly from vendors, bypassing the procurement department (Section 5.7).
- Buy at private or public auction sites in which the organization participates as one of the buyers (Section 5.6).
- Join a group-purchasing system that aggregates participants' demand, creating a large volume. Then the group may negotiate prices or initiate a tendering process (Section 5.7).
- Buy at an exchange or industrial mall (Chapter 6).

- Collaborate with suppliers to share information about sales and inventory, so as to reduce inventory and stock-outs and enhance just-in-time delivery. (See Chapter 7 on collaborative commerce.)

Some of these activities are done in private marketplaces, others in public exchanges.

INEFFICIENCIES IN TRADITIONAL PROCUREMENT MANAGEMENT

Procurement management refers to the coordination of all the activities pertaining to the purchasing of the goods and services necessary to accomplish the mission of an enterprise. Approximately 80 percent of an organization's purchased items, mostly MROs, constitute 20 to 25 percent of the total purchase value. Furthermore, a large portion of corporate buyers' time is spent on non-value-added activities such as data entry, correcting errors in paperwork, expediting delivery, or solving quality problems.

procurement management
The coordination of all the activities relating to purchasing goods and services needed to accomplish the mission of an organization.

For high-value items, purchasing personnel spend a great deal of time and effort on procurement activities. These activities include qualifying suppliers, negotiating prices and terms, building rapport with strategic suppliers, and carrying out supplier evaluation and certification. If buyers are busy with the details of the smaller items (usually the MROs), they do not have enough time to properly deal with the purchase of the high-value items.

Other inefficiencies also may occur in conventional procurement. These range from delays to paying too much for rush orders. One procurement inefficiency is **maverick buying**. This is when a buyer makes unplanned purchases of items needed quickly, which results in buying at non-pre-negotiated, usually higher prices. The traditional procurement process, shown in Exhibit 5.4, often is inefficient. To correct the situation, companies reengineer their procurement systems, implement new purchasing models, and, in particular, introduce e-procurement.

maverick buying
Unplanned purchases of items needed quickly, often at non-pre-negotiated higher prices.

THE GOALS AND BENEFITS OF E-PROCUREMENT

Improvements to procurement have been attempted for decades, usually by using information technologies. The real opportunity for improvement lies in the use of **e-procurement**, the electronic acquisition of goods and services for organizations. The general e-procurement process (with the exception of tendering) is shown in Exhibit 5.5.

e-procurement
The electronic acquisition of goods and services for organizations.

By automating and streamlining the laborious routines of the purchasing function, purchasing professionals can focus on more strategic purchases, achieving the following goals:

- Increasing the productivity of purchasing agents (providing them with more time and reducing job pressure)
- Lowering purchase prices through product standardization, reverse auctions, volume discounts, and consolidation of purchases
- Improving information flow and management (e.g., supplier's information and pricing information)

EXHIBIT 5.4 A Traditional Procurement Process

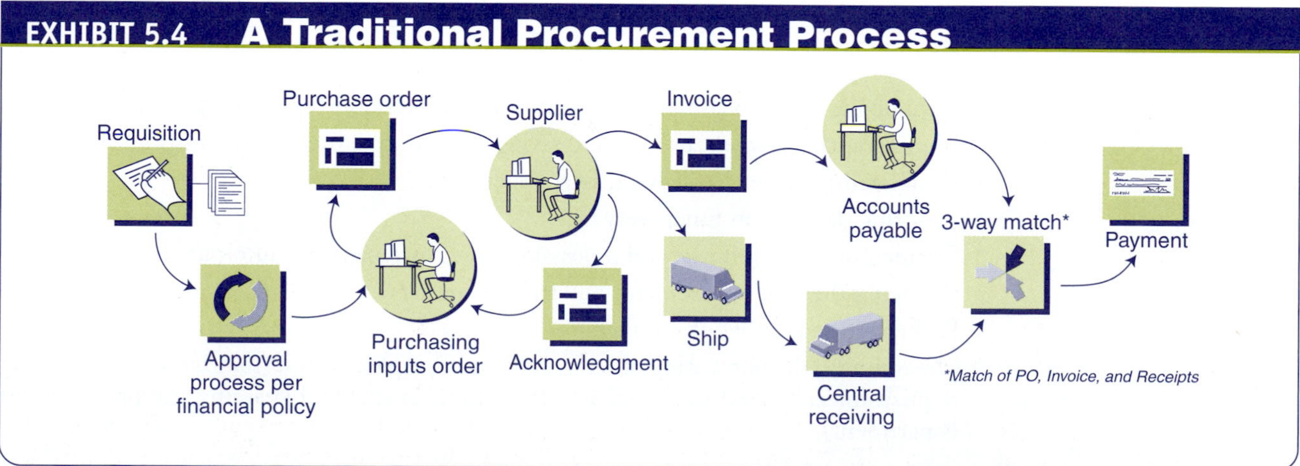

Source: Ariba.com, February 2001. Courtesy of Ariba Inc.

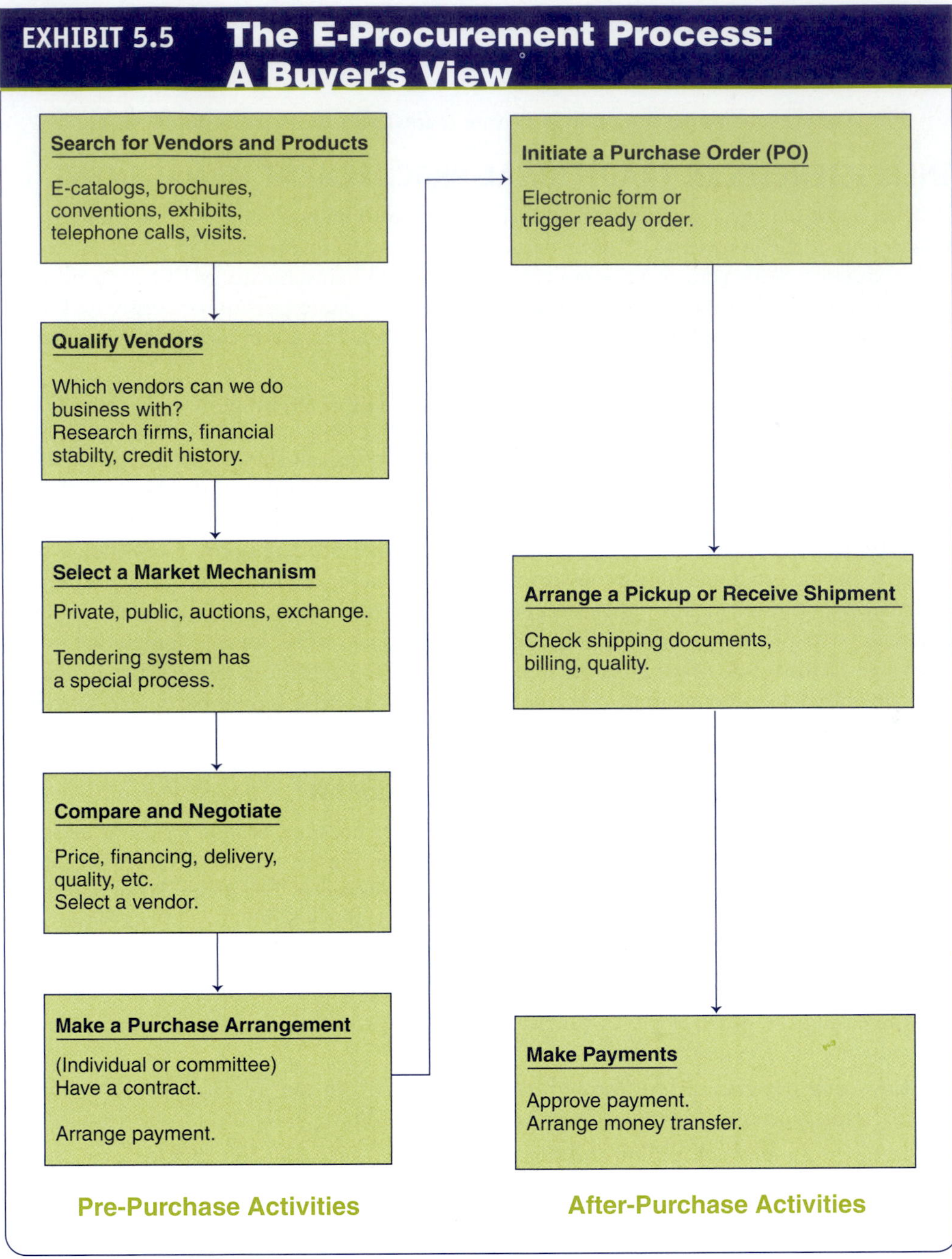

- Minimizing the purchases made from noncontract vendors (eliminating maverick buying)
- Improving the payment process and savings due to expedited payments (for sellers)
- Establishing efficient, collaborative supplier relations
- Ensuring delivery on time, every time
- Slashing order-fulfillment and processing times by leveraging automation
- Reducing the skill requirements and training needs of purchasing agents
- Reducing the number of suppliers
- Streamlining the purchasing process, making it simple and fast (may involve authorizing requisitioners to perform purchases from their desktops, bypassing the procurement department)

- Streamlining invoice reconciliation and dispute resolution
- Reducing the administrative processing cost per order by as much as 90 percent (e.g., GM achieved a reduction from $100 to $10)
- Finding new suppliers and vendors that can provide goods and services faster and/or cheaper (improved sourcing)
- Integrating budgetary controls into the procurement process
- Minimizing human errors in the buying or shipping process
- Monitoring and regulating buying behavior.

E-procurement is relatively easy to implement (see Metz 2002). Channel conflict usually does not occur, and resistance to change is minimal. Also, a wide selection of e-procurement software packages and other infrastructure are available at a reasonable cost.

MROs often are the initial target for e-procurement. However, improvements can be made in the purchasing of direct materials as well. All existing manual processes of requisition creation, requests for quotation, invitation to tender, purchase order issuance, receiving goods, and making payments can be streamlined and automated. However, to most effectively implement such automated support, the people involved in procurement must collaborate with the suppliers along the supply chain, as described in Chapter 7.

IMPLEMENTING E-PROCUREMENT

Putting the buying department on the Internet is the easy part of e-procurement. The more difficult part is implementing it. The components of e-procurement systems are shown in Online Exhibit W5.1.

The following are some of the major implementation issues that companies must consider when planning e-procurement initiatives:

- **Fitting e-procurement into the company EC strategy.** For example, suppose the strategy is outsourcing. In this case e-procurement can be done in an exchange, or the customer can buy at the sellers' Web sites.
- **Reviewing and changing the procurement process itself.** E-procurement may affect the number of purchasing agents, where they are located, and how purchases are approved. The degree of purchasing centralization also may be affected.
- **Providing interfaces between e-procurement and integrated enterprisewide information systems, such as ERP or supply chain management.** If the company does not have such systems, it may be necessary to do some restructuring before moving to e-procurement.
- **Coordinating the buyer's information system with that of the sellers.** Sellers have many potential buyers. For this reason, some major suppliers, such as SKF (a Swedish automotive parts maker; see skf.com), developed an integration-oriented procurement system for its buyers. The SKF information system is designed to make it easier for the procurement systems of others (notably the distributors in other countries) that buy the company's bearings and seals to interface with the SKF system. The SKF system allows distributors to gain real-time technical information on the products, as well as details on product availability, delivery times, and commercial terms and conditions.
- **Consolidating the number of regular suppliers and integrating with their information systems, and if possible, with their business processes.** Having fewer suppliers minimizes the number of connectivity issues that need to be resolved and will lower expenses. Also, with fewer suppliers, the company will buy more from each supplier, allowing the company to get a quantity discount. Collaboration with each supplier also will be enhanced.

Many companies that have implemented e-procurement have been extremely satisfied with the payoffs. One such example is described in EC Application Case 5.4.

CASE 5.4

EC Application

E-PROCUREMENT AT SCHLUMBERGER

Schlumberger is the world's largest oil service company, with over 50,000 employees in 100 countries and annual sales of over $10 billion (*schlumberger.com;* accessed November 15, 2004). In 2000, the company installed a Web-based automated procurement system in Oilfield Services, its largest division. With this system, employees can buy office supplies and equipment, as well as computers, straight from their desktops.

The system replaced a number of older systems, including automated and paper-based ones. The single system streamlines and speeds up the purchasing operation, reducing costs as well as the number of people involved in the process. It also enables the company to consolidate purchases for volume discounts from vendors.

The new system had two parts:

1. The internal portion uses Commerce One's Buy procurement software and runs on the company's intranet. Using it is like shopping at an online store: Once the employee selects an item, the system generates the requisition, routes it electronically to the proper people for approval, and turns it into a purchase order.
2. Commerce One's Conductor is used to transmit purchase orders to suppliers. The B2B Internet marketplace connects Schlumberger with hundreds of suppliers with a single, low-cost system.

Prices are negotiated with individual vendors before their items are put into Schlumberger's system. For example, Office Depot's entire catalog is posted on the MarketSite (now part of Conductor from Commerce One), but Schlumberger employees only see negotiated products and prices. In 2005, the company plans to negotiate prices in real time through auctions and other bidding systems.

The benefits of the procurement system are clear. The cost of goods has been reduced; transaction costs also have fallen. Employees spend much less time in the ordering process, thus giving them more time for their core work. The system also is more cost-efficient for the suppliers, who can then pass along savings to Schlumberger. By using one system worldwide, employees who are transferred do not have to learn a new system at their new location. Procurement effectiveness has been increased because it is now possible to track all procurement activities.

Getting the system up and running was easy because it was implemented in stages and ran at the same time as existing systems. Employees did not have to deal with implementation issues—once the system was in place, the old system was disabled, and there were no complaints with regard to the old system being shut down, because it was no longer in use.

By 2004, the system was used by over 6,000 users in 83 countries procuring over $2 billion in goods and services each year. The system delivers significant cost savings, improved productivity, and error reduction. A 2004/2005 initiative is automating the RFQ process and its special request purchases, using the Commerce One Conductor platform, which is designed to connect and compose business processes between systems and partners (see *commerceone.com/solutions/products/SRM.html*).

Sources: Compiled from Ovans (2000), *schlumberger.com* (accessed 2002–2004), and *commerceone.com* (accessed March 2005).

Questions

1. Describe the benefits of the new system over the old system.
2. Describe how the e-procurement system operates.
3. Summarize the benefits of e-procurement to the company and its employees.
4. Explain the benefits of automating the RFQ (see the Schlumberger case at *commerceone.com*).

E-Sourcing

e-sourcing
The process and tools that electronically enable any activity in the sourcing process, such as quotation/tender submittance and response, e-auctions, online negotiations, and spending analyses.

When implementing e-procurement, companies also should evaluate **e-sourcing**, the processes and tools that electronically enable any activity in the procurement process, such as quotation/tender requests and responses, e-auctions, online negotiations, and spending analyses (see ariba.com and commerceone.com). E-Sourcing is the automation of strategic sourcing.

Strategic sourcing is the process of identifying opportunities, evaluating potential sources, negotiating contracts, and managing supplier relationships to achieve corporate goals, such as cost reductions and increased quality and service. In an e-sourcing study by AMR (Murphree 2003), the companies surveyed reported savings of 10 to 15 percent in the cost of direct goods and 20 to 25 percent in the cost of indirect goods and services. Companies also reported reductions in sourcing cycle times.

Strategic sourcing requires a holistic process that automates the entire sourcing process, including order planning, RFQ creation, bid evaluation, negotiation, settlement, and order execution. The promise of strategic sourcing is in reducing total acquisition costs while increasing value. A fundamental shortcoming of sourcing tools today is their inability to allow the creation of complex RFQs that allow for a variety of bid structures that exploit complementarities and economies of scale in suppliers' cost structures.

E-sourcing attempts to improve strategic sourcing by making it more effective and efficient. For example, Moai Technologies (moai.com) provides the following e-sourcing solutions:

- **Just-in-Time Sourcing (JITS).** Moai's JITS integrates strategic consulting services with licensed software products. The software directs customers through the e-sourcing process including negotiating with vendors and securing reliable suppliers, thereby lowering sourcing costs.
- **Strategic Consulting Services.** *RapidSource*, Moai's strategic consulting program, promotes testing and validation of e-sourcing to those new to the concept. With this guidance, users are guaranteed a return on investment in the program.
- **Hosted Sourcing Software.** Delays, IT complexities, and costs associated with in-house deployments are eliminated with Moai's hosted services.

Section 5.5 ▶ REVIEW QUESTIONS

1. Define procurement and list the major procurement methods.
2. Describe the inefficiencies of traditional procurement.
3. Define e-procurement and its goals.
4. How do direct materials and MROs differ? Why are MROs good candidates for e-procurement?
5. Describe the implementation of e-procurement.
6. Describe e-sourcing and its benefits.

5.6 BUY-SIDE E-MARKETPLACES: REVERSE AUCTIONS

One of the major methods of e-procurement is through reverse auctions. Recall from our discussions in Chapters 1 and 2 that a *reverse auction* is a tendering system in which suppliers are invited to bid on the fulfillment of an order and the lowest bid wins. In B2B usage of a reverse auction, a buyer may open an electronic market on its own server and invite potential suppliers to bid on the items the buyer needs. The "invitation" to such reverse auctions is a form or document called an **RFQ (request for quote)**. The reverse auction is referred to as the *tendering* or *bidding model.* Traditional tendering usually implied sealed bidding (see Chapter 10), whereas the reverse auction opens the auction to competing bidders. See Smeltzer and Carr (2002) for a comprehensive overview of reverse auctions.

request for quote (RFQ)
The "invitation" to participate in a tendering (bidding) system.

Governments and large corporations frequently mandate reverse auctions, which may provide considerable savings. To understand why this is so, see Insights and Additions 5.2, which compares the pre-Internet tendering process with the Web-based reverse auction process. The electronic process is faster and administratively much less expensive. It also can result in locating the cheapest possible products or services.

CONDUCTING REVERSE AUCTIONS

As the number of reverse auction sites increases, suppliers will not be able to manually monitor all relevant tendering sites. This problem has been addressed with the introduction of *online directories* that list open RFQs. Another way to solve this problem is through the use of monitoring software agents (see Chapter 10). Software agents also can aid in the bidding process itself. Examples of agents that support the bidding process are auctionsniper.com and auctionflex.com.

Alternatively, a third-party intermediary may run the electronic bidding, as they do for forward auctions. General Electric's GXS (now an independent company, described in detail in Online File W5.3) is open to any buyer. Auction sites such as A-Z Used Computers (a-zuc.com), FreeMarkets (now a part of ariba.com), and (asset-auctions.com) also belong to this category. Conducting reverse auctions in B2B can be a fairly complex process (see the United Technologies

Insights and Additions 5.2 Comparison of Pre-Internet and Web-Based Reverse Auction Processes

The Pre-Internet Tendering System Process	The Web-Based Reverse Auction Process
The buyer prepares a paper-based description of the product (project) that needs to be acquired. The description includes specifications, blueprints, quality standards, delivery date, and required payment method.	The buyer gathers product information automatically from online sources and posts it on its secured corporate portal.
The buyer announces the RFQ via newspaper ads, direct mail, fax, or telephone.	The buyer sends e-mail alerts to selected vendors, inviting them to view the projects available for bid. Many suppliers constantly monitor buyers' sites.
Bidders (suppliers) that express interest receive detailed information (sometimes for a fee), usually by postal mail or a courier.	The buyer identifies potential suppliers from among those who responded to the online RFQ and invites suppliers to bid on the project. Bidders download the project information from the Web.
Bidders prepare proposals. They may call the company for additional information. Sometimes changes in the specs (specifications) are made, which must be disseminated to all interested bidders.	Bidders conduct real-time or delayed reverse auctions. Requests for more information can be made online. Changes in specs can be disseminated electronically.
Bidders submit paper proposals, usually several copies of the same documents, by a preestablished deadline.	Bidders submit proposals in electronic format.
Proposals are evaluated, usually by several departments, sequentially, at the buyer's organization. Communication and clarification may take place via letters or phone/fax.	The buyer evaluates the suppliers' bids (by several departments, simultaneously). Communications, clarifications, and negotiations to achieve the "best deal" take place electronically.
Buyer awards a contract to the bidder(s) that best meets its requirements. Notification is usually done via postal mail.	Buyer awards a contract to the bidder(s) that best meets its requirements. Notification is done online.

case in Online File W5.4). This is why an intermediary may be essential, as demonstrated in the case of the State of Pennsylvania in EC Application Case 5.5. (Other examples of bidding managed by an intermediary are shown in Chapter 10.)

The reverse auction process is demonstrated in Exhibit 5.6. As the exhibit shows, the first step is for the would-be buyer to post bid invitations. When bids arrive, contract and purchasing personnel for the buyer evaluate the bids and decides which one(s) to accept. The details of this process are explained in the General Electric case in Online File W5.3.

GROUP REVERSE AUCTIONS

B2B reverse auctions are done in a private exchange or at an aggregator's site for a group of buying companies. Such *group reverse auctions* are popular in South Korea and usually involve large conglomerates. For example, the LG Group operates the LG MRO auction for its members, and the Samsung Group operates iMarketKorea, as described in Online File W5.5.

Section 5.6 ▶ REVIEW QUESTIONS

1. Describe the manual tendering system.
2. How do online reverse auctions work?
3. List the benefits of Web-based reverse auctions.
4. Describe the business drivers of GE's TPN now (GXS) and its evolution over time. (See Online File W5.3.)
5. What was a primary challenge to GE in implementing its e-procurement system? (See Online File W5.3.)

CASE 5.5

EC Application

HOW THE STATE OF PENNSYLVANIA SELLS SURPLUS EQUIPMENT

The Pennsylvania Department of Transportation (DOT) for years used a traditional off-line auction process. In a radio address on December 6, 2003, Governor Ed Rendell announced that the state would begin holding online auctions to sell its surplus heavy equipment. The old, live-in-person auction system generated about $5 million a year. Using the Internet, the DOT expected at least a 20 percent increase in revenue.

The State of Pennsylvania conducted its initial online sale of surplus DOT items in October 2003. The sale consisted of 77 items (including 37 dump trucks). Onsite inspection was available twice during the two-week bidding period. The online sale allowed the Commonwealth of Pennsylvania to obtain an average price increase of 20 percent while reducing labor costs related to holding a traditional on-site sale. On high-value specialty items (i.e., a bridge inspection crane and a satellite van) results exceeded the estimated sale prices by over 200 percent.

The auction was conducted by *asset-auctions.com*. The results of the auction are shown below:

- Total Sales: $635,416.03
- Half of the bidding activity occurred in the final 2 days
- Every lot received multiple bids
- Overtime bidding occurred in 39 lots
- Over 200 bidders registered for the sale
- 174 bidders from 19 states and Mexico made about 1,500 bids in 5 days
- 47 different buyers participated

Source: Material compiled from *asset-auctions.com*. Used with permission.

Questions

1. Why is heavy equipment amenable to such auctions?
2. Why did the state generate 20 percent more in revenues with the online auction?
3. Why do you need an intermediary to conduct such an auction?
4. Comment on the number of bidders and bids as compared with off-line auctions.

5.7 OTHER E-PROCUREMENT METHODS

Companies also have implemented other innovative e-procurement methods. Some common ones are described in this section.

AN INTERNAL PURCHASING MARKETPLACE: AGGREGATING SUPPLIERS' CATALOGS

Large organizations have many corporate buyers or purchasing agents that are usually located in different places. For example, Bristol-Myers Squibb Corporation has more than 3,000 corporate buyers that are located all over the world. These agents buy from a large number of suppliers. The problem is that even if all purchases are made from approved suppliers, it is difficult to plan and control procurement. In many cases, to save time, buyers engage in *maverick buying*. In addition, an organization needs to control the purchasing budget. This situation is especially serious in government agencies and multinational entities where many buyers and large numbers of purchases are involved.

One effective solution to the procurement problem in large organizations is to aggregate the catalogs of all approved suppliers, combining them into a single *internal* electronic catalog. Prices can be negotiated in advance or determined by a tendering, so that the buyers do not have to negotiate each time they place an order. By aggregating the suppliers' catalogs on the buyer's server, it also is easier to centralize and control all procurement. Such an aggregation of catalogs is called an **internal procurement marketplace**.

internal procurement marketplace
The aggregated catalogs of all approved suppliers combined into a single *internal* electronic catalog.

Benefits of Internal Marketplaces

Corporate buyers can use search engines to look through internal aggregated catalogs to quickly find what they want, check availability and delivery times, and complete electronic requisition forms. Another advantage of such aggregation is that a company can reduce the number of suppliers it uses. For example, Caltex, a multinational oil company, reduced the

EXHIBIT 5.6 The Reverse Auction Process

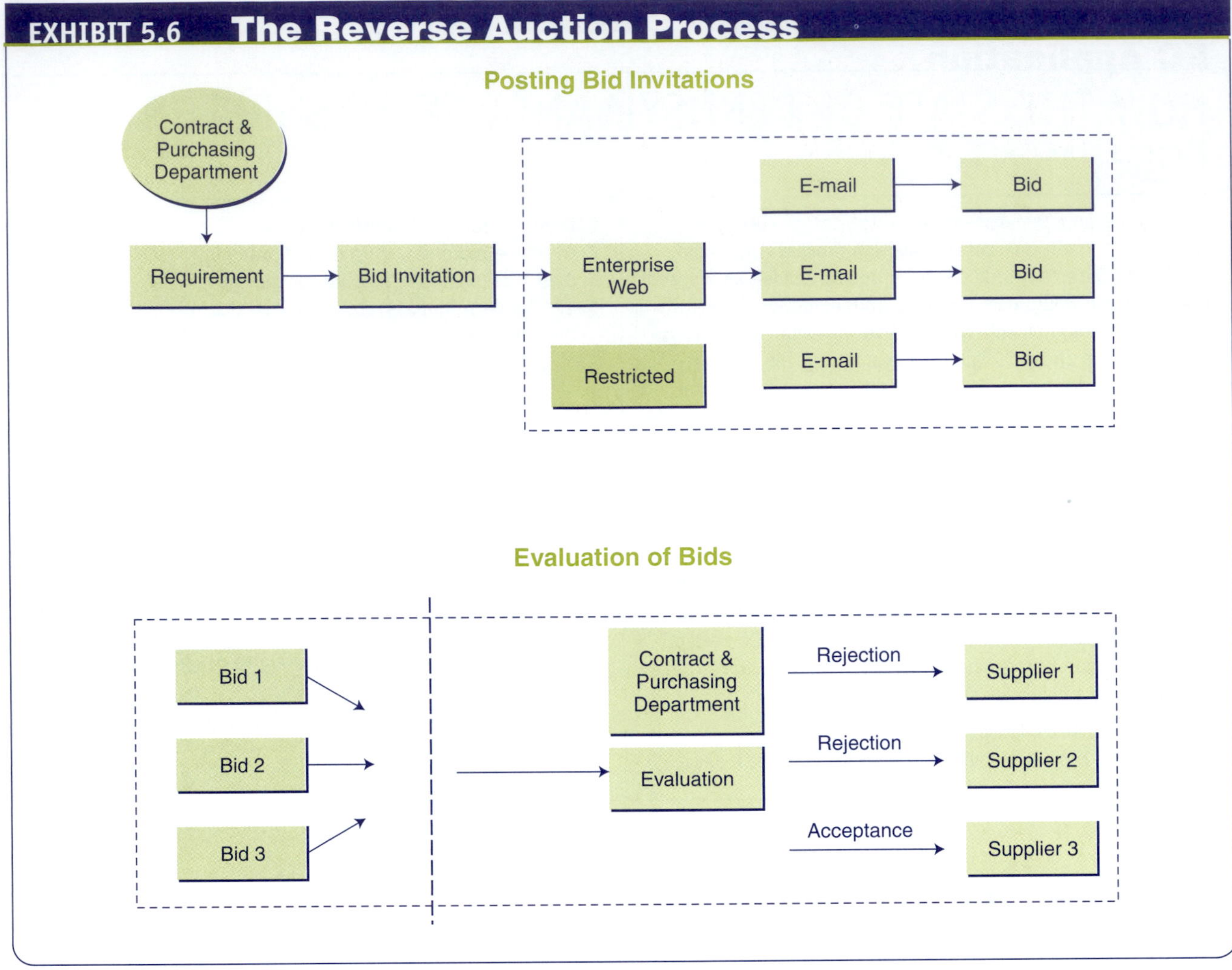

number of its suppliers from over 3,000 to 800. Such reduction is possible because the central catalog enables buyers at multiple corporate locations to buy from remote but fewer sellers. Buying from fewer sellers typically increases the quantities bought from each, lowering the per unit price.

Another example of a successful aggregation of suppliers' catalogs is that of MasterCard International, which aggregates more than 10,000 items from the catalogs of approved suppliers into an internal electronic catalog. The goal of this project is to consolidate buying activities from multiple corporate sites, improve processing costs, and reduce the supplier base. Payments are made with MasterCard's corporate procurement card. By 2004, the system was used by more than 2,500 buyers. MasterCard is continually adding suppliers and catalog content to the system.

Finally, internal marketplaces allow for easy financial controls. As buyers make purchases, their account balances are displayed. Once the budget is depleted, the system will not allow new purchase orders to go through. Therefore, this model is especially popular in public institutions and government entities.

Desktop Purchasing

desktop purchasing
Direct purchasing from internal marketplaces without the approval of supervisors and without the intervention of a procurement department.

The implementation of internal purchasing marketplaces is frequently done via desktop purchasing. **Desktop purchasing** implies purchasing directly from internal marketplaces without the approval of supervisors and without the intervention of a procurement department. This is usually done by using a *purchasing card* (*P-card*) (see Chapter 12). Desktop purchasing reduces the administrative cost and cycle time involved in purchasing urgently needed or frequently purchased items of small dollar value. This approach is especially effective for MRO purchases.

Microsoft built its internal marketplace, named MS Market, for the procurement of small items. The aggregated catalog that is part of MS Market is used by Microsoft employees worldwide, whose purchasing totals over $3.5 billion annually. The system has drastically reduced the role and size of the procurement department. For more on desktop purchasing at Microsoft, see EC Application Case 5.6.

The desktop purchasing approach also can be implemented by partnering with external private exchanges. For instance, Samsung Electronics of South Korea, a huge global manufacturer and its subsidiaries, has tightly integrated its iMarketKorea exchange (see Online File W5.5) with the e-procurement systems of its buying agents. This platform can be easily linked with *group purchasing*, which is described later in this section.

Desktop purchasing automates and supports purchasing operations such as product and supplier selection, requisitions, catalog searches, approval processes, purchase order processing, catalog updates and content management, and report generation. These systems are designed to support the nonpurchasing professional (employees whose job is other than purchasing agent) and casual end users. A schematic overview of such a system is shown in Exhibit 5.7. In addition to end-user support, the system features administrative modules to support the central purchasing group and the IT features and activities (e.g., connectivity, integration, communication, security). For details, see Segev and Gebauer (2001). A major vendor of such systems is Oracle (Loney and Koch 2002).

CASE 5.6

EC Application

MS MARKET FOR MICROSOFT: DESKTOP PURCHASING

Purchasing agents and employees of Microsoft are scattered worldwide. They need to procure MROs such as PCs, servers, and office supplies. They also arrange for travel and purchase services. Before 1996, the company's corporate procurement process relied on a multitude of paper forms and multiple custom applications for purchasing goods and services. Every week, thousands of purchase requests of less than $1,000 represented about 70 percent of total purchasing volume, but only 3 percent of accounts payable. For such purchases, employees were wasting time turning requisitions into purchase orders and trying to follow business rules and processes. Microsoft wanted to find a way to reduce administrative costs and wasted time. Cutting prices of requisitioned items was a secondary concern.

In summer of 1996, the Microsoft Corporate Procurement Group implemented an online internal marketplace (an aggregated catalog), called MS Market, which works on Microsoft's intranet. Employees can order directly online, bypassing the manager's approval and the procurement department and avoiding cumbersome paperwork and bureaucratic processes. If an employee is not approved to make the requested purchase, workflow software automatically e-mails the order to that employee's manager for approval. On the back end of the system, the order is sent electronically to the appropriate vendor, such as Boise Cascade, Marriott, HP, Toshiba, or Dell.

In its first year, MS Market was used to purchase more than $1 billion in supplies. MS Market reduced the administrative cost of each purchase order from $60 to about $5, and reduced the purchase cycle time from 8 to 3 days. Some 6,000 employees worldwide have used the system, in which the company invested $1.1 million. This investment paid for itself in less than 2 months, for an annual savings of $7.3 million. The number of purchasing employees was reduced from 19 to 2, and procurement department overhead was reduced accordingly. By 2000, some 11,000 employees purchased 99.8 percent of their orders (valued at over $5 billion), from servers to employee birthday cakes, via MS Market.

By making it easier for employees to purchase from approved vendors at contractually approved prices, the company eliminated maverick purchasing. Overall, Microsoft saves 10 to 20 percent on the cost of supplies by purchasing them through a common channel. The way employees manage business requisitions and distribute company resources also has changed significantly. An order is now placed online in less than 3 minutes, without administrative paperwork and bureaucratic processes.

The success of MS Market has spawned a new innovation at Microsoft—a technical template for MS Market with Site Server, Commerce Edition, which includes sample sites that can be used to set up custom e-commerce intranet-based solutions.

Sources: Compiled from Wagner (2000), Kalakota and Robinson (2001), Neef (2001), and Microsoft (2004).

Questions

1. What is the role of MS Market at Microsoft?
2. What is the primary benefit of using MS Market?
3. Did the overhead of the procurement department change after the introduction of MS Market?

EXHIBIT 5.7 **Desktop Purchasing: Key Functionality and Connectivity**

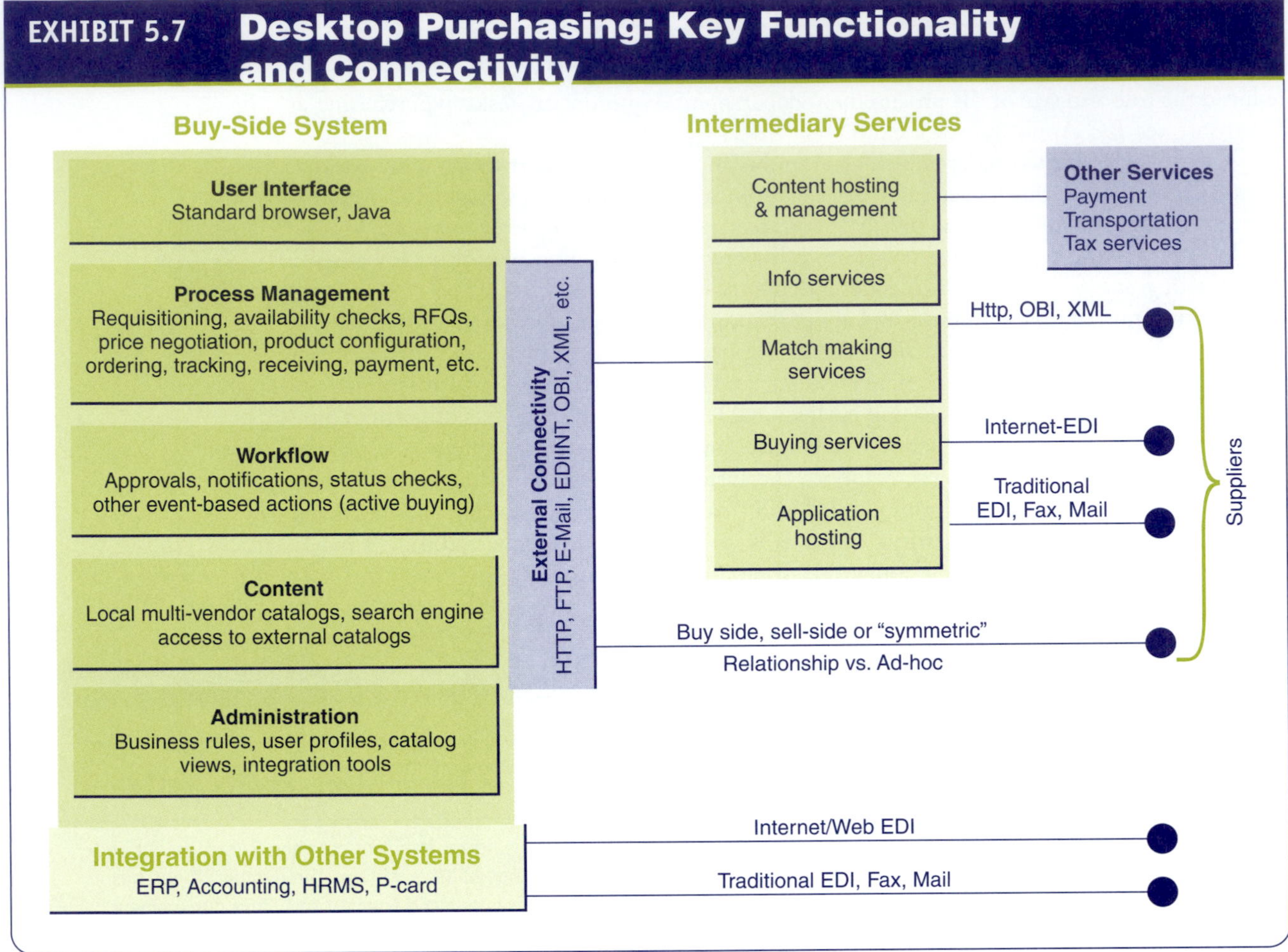

Source: *Information and Technology Management*, 2001, p. 246, "B2B Procurement and Marketplace Transformation," Segev, A., and J. Gebauer, fig. 4. Used with kind permission of Springer Science and the authors.

BUYING AT E-AUCTIONS

Another popular approach to procurement is e-auctions. As described in Section 5.4, sellers are increasingly motivated to sell surpluses and even regular products via auctions. In some cases, e-auctions provide an opportunity for buyers to find inexpensive or unique items fairly quickly. A prudent corporate buyer should certainly look at both those manufacturers and distributors that conduct auctions periodically (e.g., GM or Dell) and at third-party auctioneers (e.g., eBay, or auctions.yahoo.com). As will be shown in Chapter 10, auction aggregators can help purchasers find where and when auctions of needed items are being conducted.

GROUP PURCHASING

group purchasing
The aggregation of orders from several buyers into volume purchases so that better prices can be negotiated.

Many companies, especially small ones, are moving to group purchasing. With **group purchasing**, orders from several buyers are aggregated into volume purchases so that better prices can be negotiated. Two models are in use: *internal aggregation* and *external* (third-party) *aggregation*.

Internal Aggregation

Large companies, such as GE, buy billions of dollars of MROs every year. Companywide orders, from several plants, for identical items are aggregated using the Web and are replenished automatically. Besides economies of scale (lower prices for large purchases) on many items, GE saves on the administrative cost of the transactions, reducing transaction costs from $50 to $100 per transaction to $5 to $10 (Rudnitsky 2000). With 5 million transactions annually at GE, this is a substantial savings.

External Aggregation

Many SMEs would like to enjoy quantity discounts but have difficulty finding others to join group purchasing to increase the procurement volume. Finding partners can be accomplished by an external third party such as BuyerZone.com (buyerzone.com), HIGPA (higpa.org), or United Sourcing Alliance (usa-llc.com). The idea is to provide SMEs with better prices, selection, and services by aggregating demand online and then either negotiating with suppliers or conducting reverse auctions (see Mudambi et al. 2004). The external aggregation group purchasing process is shown in Exhibit 5.8.

One can appreciate the importance of this market by taking into consideration some data about small businesses: In the United States, according to the U.S. Department of Commerce, 90 percent of all businesses have fewer than 100 employees, yet they account for over 35 percent of all MRO business volume (Small Business Administration 2002). Therefore, the potential for external aggregators is huge.

Several large companies, including large CPA firms, EDS, and Ariba, are providing similar aggregation services, mainly to their regular customers. Yahoo! and AOL offer such services, too. A key to the success of these companies is a critical mass of buyers. An interesting strategy is for a company to outsource aggregation to a third party. For example, energy-solutions.com provides group buying for community site partners in the energy industry.

Group purchasing, which started with commodity items such as MROs and consumer electronic devices, has now moved to services ranging from travel to payroll processing and Web hosting. Some aggregators use Priceline's "name-your-own-price" approach. Others try to find the lowest possible price. Similar approaches are used in B2C, and several vendors serve both markets.

BUYING FROM E-DISTRIBUTORS

Section 5.3 described how companies use e-distributors as a sales channel (recall the case of W. W. Grainger). When buying small quantities, purchasers often buy from an e-distributor. If they buy online, it is considered e-procurement.

EXHIBIT 5.8 The Group Purchasing Process

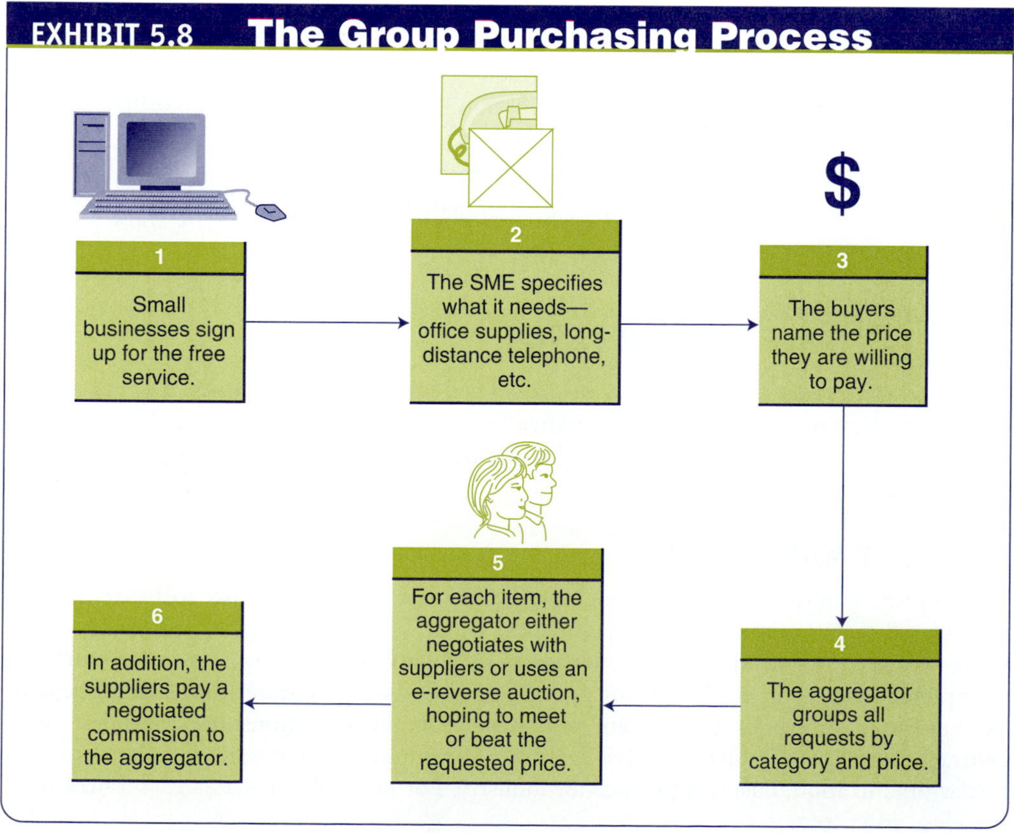

PURCHASING DIRECT GOODS

Until 2001, most B2B e-procurement implementations took place in the sell-side of large vendors (Cisco, Intel, IBM) and in the procurement of MROs. In general, MROs comprise 20 to 50 percent of a company's purchasing budget. The remaining 50 to 80 percent of corporate purchases are for *direct materials* and *services*. Therefore, most companies would reap great benefits in using e-purchasing to acquire direct goods: Buyers would be able to purchase direct goods more quickly, reduce unit costs, reduce inventories, avoid shortages, and expedite their own production processes. Sourcing direct materials typically involves more complex transactions requiring negotiation (Section 5.8) and *collaboration* between the seller and buyer and greater information exchange. This leads us to collaborative commerce, which will be discussed in Chapter 7.

ELECTRONIC BARTERING

Bartering is the exchange of goods or services without the use of money. As described Chapters 2 and 10, the basic idea is for a company to exchange its surplus for something that it needs. Companies can advertise their surpluses in classified ads and may find a partner to make an exchange, but in most cases a company will have little success in finding an exact match. Therefore, companies usually ask an intermediary to help.

A bartering intermediary can use a manual search-and-match approach or it can create an electronic bartering exchange. With a **bartering exchange**, a company submits its surplus to the exchange and receives points of credit, which the company can then use to buy items that it needs. Popular bartering items are office space, idle facilities and labor, products, and even banner ads.

bartering exchange
An intermediary that links parties in a barter; a company submits its surplus to the exchange and receives points of credit, which can be used to buy the items that the company needs from other exchange participants.

BUYING IN EXCHANGES AND INDUSTRIAL MALLS

Another option for the e-procurer is to buy at a B2B exchange or shop at an industrial e-mall. These options are described in Chapter 6.

Section 5.7 ▶ REVIEW QUESTIONS

1. Describe an internal procurement marketplace and list its benefits.
2. Describe the benefits of desktop purchasing.
3. Discuss the relationship of desktop purchasing with internal procurement marketplaces and with group purchasing.
4. Explain the logic of group purchasing and how it is organized.
5. Describe how e-distributors operate and discuss their appeal to buyers.
6. How does B2B bartering work?

5.8 AUTOMATING B2B TASKS

The previous section described how businesses sell and buy electronically. These activities involve many managerial and administrative tasks. Some of these tasks can be fully automated; others are done manually, but can be supported by software. Let's look at some representative tasks.

CONTRACT MANAGEMENT

To simplify, standardize, and better manage contracts, one can use software such as CompleteSource Contract Management from Moai Technologies (moai.com). This software provides advanced contract management capabilities and is integrated with the CompleteSource Sourcing Management and Spend Analysis solutions from Moai. The software provides companies with the ability to manage supplier relationships and the resultant contracts, terms, conditions, nested obligations and complex pricing that are unique to a particular organization, business practice, or industry. For more about managed services solutions, see ariba.com.

In general, contract-management software can:

- Reduce contract negotiation time and efforts
- Facilitate inter- and intracompany contract analysis and development
- Provide for proactive contract compliance management
- Enable enterprisewide standardization of contracts
- Improve understanding of contract-related risks
- Provide a more efficient approval process

SPEND MANAGEMENT

Companies spend a considerable amount of money on goods and services. Companies can use spend management software (e.g., from Ariba or Moai) to see their purchasing behavior in real time. Such software is designed to meet the needs of companies that require advanced spend analysis capabilities. Spend analysis software provides companies with the ability to view and analyze purchasing spend data across complex, multilocation, and multipurchasing organizations.

The following tools and features may be found in spend management software:

- A data warehouse repository designed to manage data from multiple data sources
- Data management of contracts, supplier catalogs, and product content
- Data management of pricing
- Detailed standard and ad-hoc purchasing activity analysis and report tools
- Updates, notifications, and alerts regarding purchasing

SOURCING MANAGEMENT AND NEGOTIATION

Companies that want to implement an e-sourcing solution in-house can use sourcing management software. Designed to meet the needs of customers that require advanced e-sourcing capabilities and integrated with spend analysis and contract management solutions, the software provides companies with the flexibility to create online negotiation scenarios that are unique to a particular organization, business practice, or industry.

Sourcing management software includes tools and features such as:

- Bid comparison, including exports of detailed bid data
- User management functions that eliminate data redundancy, simplify data management, and reduce risk to data integrity
- Weighted scoring of parameters to calculate the total value offered by suppliers
- Total merchandise purchased cost model with winner selection and ranking
- Reverse auctions and sealed bids, with a full set of features such as proxy bids and bid-time extensions (see Chapter 10)
- Negotiation support tools

Negotiation Support Tools

Companies are spending considerable amounts of time on price negotiations, payment schedules, delivery options, quality assurance, insurance, and more.

Ideally, the negotiation process would be automated. And indeed, studies of e-negotiation both in B2C and B2B are fairly popular in the academic environment, where a special journal is dedicated to the topic (*Group Decision and Negotiation*). Representative efforts in e-negotiation are provided in Online File W5.6 and in Veit (2004).

In the real world, negotiations primarily are done manually. However, vendors do provide software tools to streamline the manual negotiation process. One such tool is Ozro Negotiate, which is described in EC Application Case 5.7.

E-PROCUREMENT MANAGEMENT

If properly implemented, not only can an e-procurement system be used for making online purchases, but also to connect companies and their business processes directly with suppliers, all the while managing the interactions between them. This includes management of

CASE 5.7
EC Application

OZRO NEGOTIATE

Ozro Negotiate is a patented negotiation engine at the center of the Ozro Agreements application suite from Eyedeas (*eyedeas.net*). The technology is designed to facilitate people-centric, iterative, and multi-attribute negations by providing competitive advantage by prompting, capturing and synchronizing communications and data, and producing supporting documentation. Basically, it fosters comprehensive agreements in any context.

Ozro Negotiate approaches comprehensive agreement management in the following areas:

- **RFx Management.** Buyers can create and manage their requests for information, such as proposals and quotes, which are known as RFx, online. Previous requests can be used as templates or new information about products, delivery schedules, payment terms, etc. can be entered or imported.
- **Offer Management.** Sellers can also create and manage their offers, such as proposals and quotes, online. Starting with a buyer's request, information about price lists, products, availability, terms and conditions, etc. is entered or imported into Ozro's system.
- **Negotiation.** Requests are exchanged between buyers and sellers in a structured manner. Well-established negotiation techniques are used to iteratively bring their exchanges to a conclusion and create detailed commercial agreements.
- **Agreement Templates.** Although similar to current manual processes, existing agreements may be used as templates to start the development of new agreements between buyers and sellers.
- **Workflow.** In order to streamline the highly collaborative process of creating a request or an offer in an organization, the software tracks current status and ownership in real-time as users contribute and approve content.
- **Security.** Ozro utilizes leading-edge security mechanisms to safeguard the highly confidential and critical information contained in requests, offers, and agreements during exchanges between involved parties.
- **Notifications/Alerts.** Ozro Negotiate notifies negotiation teams about changes by tracking the status of all requests, offers and agreements. Alerts are sent to end-users and other systems regarding any status changes to accelerate the development and advancement of commercial agreements.
- **Change and Update Management.** Commercial agreements are rarely constant, and relationships evolve to continue to meet the needs of the marketplace. Ozro Negotiate technology supplies end-users with the ability to re-open and re-establish agreements to ensure they consistently reflect the ever-shifting aspects of the relationship.
- **Audit Trail.** The concept of non-repudiation (Chapter 11) is fundamental to the development and application of commercial agreements by preventing future disputes over the commitments that were made in support of each party's intent. Ozro Negotiate technology tracks all changes, including the identity of the user that makes the changes, which allows for complete non-repudiation and ensures the validity of agreements reached through the Ozro solution.
- **Archives.** Creating and managing the volumes of approved terms and conditions for an enterprise is a complex procedure. Ozro Negotiate technology provides a "clause library" to store approved boilerplate text for standard terms that a company typically uses. The clauses are easily stored, updated, and retrieved for use across agreements.

Source: Material compiled from *eyedeas.net*. Used with permission.

Questions

1. Identify the direct support that Ozro Negotiate provides to negotiators.
2. Visit *eyedeas.net* and find the Ozro demo. View the demo. Which features are most important? Why?
3. Which companies, in your opinion, would benefit the most from the product? Why?

correspondence, bids, questions and answers, previous pricing, and e-mails sent to multiple participants.

A good e-procurement system helps a firm organize its interaction with its most important suppliers. It provides users a set of built-in monitoring tools to help control costs and ensure maximum supplier performance. In addition, it provides an organized system to help keep lines of communication open with potential suppliers during the business process. The system also allows managers to confirm previous pricing and leverage agreements to make certain that each new price quote is more competitive than the previous one.

The decision-making process is enhanced by e-procurement since relevant information is neatly organized and time-stamped. Template driven e-procurement solutions guarantee that all transactions are standardized and traceable. This improves a company's ability to keep track of all bids, thereby allowing it to leverage its knowledge to obtain better pricing and to focus on its most lucrative trading partners and contracts. E-procurement systems that allow multiple access levels and permissions help managers organize administrative users by roles, groups, or tasks. Thus, procurement managers do not need extensive training or increased wages because software systems are standardized and easy to learn. For details on e-procurement, see epiqtech.com/e-procurement.htm.

Section 5.8 ▶ REVIEW QUESTIONS

1. How is contract management being automated?
2. Describe spend management programs.
3. How is negotiation supported electronically?
4. Describe e-procurement management tools.

5.9 INFRASTRUCTURE, INTEGRATION, AND SOFTWARE AGENTS IN B2B EC

In implementing B2B EC, issues that need to be examined include: what infrastructure to use, how to integrate the applications, and which software agents should be employed.

INFRASTRUCTURE FOR B2B

Large numbers of vendors, including Ariba, Oracle, Microsoft, and IBM, offer all of the necessary B2B tools. The major infrastructures needed for B2B marketplaces include the following:

- Software to support various B2B activities, for example, software for electronic catalogs, direct sales and auctions, e-procurement, reverse auctions, call centers, and Web storefronts.
- Telecommunications networks and protocols (including EDI, extranets, and XML)
- Server(s) for hosting databases and the applications
- Security for hardware and software

B2B software products are sold independently as components or integrated as suites. Most companies use vendors to build their B2B applications, as shown in the Real-World Case at the end of this chapter. The vendor sells or leases the company all of the necessary software to create the e-marketplace. The major B2B software vendors are IBM, Microsoft, Ariba, Oracle, and HP (see Online Chapter 18 for a description of vendors' offerings).

Extranets and EDI

For business partners to effectively communicate online, companies must implement some type of secure interorganizational network, such as a VAN or an extranet, and a common protocol, such as EDI or XML. Briefly, *extranets* ("extended intranets") are secured networks, usually Internet based, that allow business partners to access portions of each other's intranets. Extranets and their core technology are explained more fully in Appendix 6A.

Electronic data interchange (EDI) is the electronic transfer of specially formatted standard business documents, such as bills, orders, and confirmations, sent between business partners. Traditional EDI systems, which have been around for about 30 years, were implemented in **value-added networks (VANs)**, which are private, third-party-managed common carriers that also provide communications services and security. However, VANs are relatively expensive and inflexible, and so many SMEs found EDI over VANs to be unaffordable.

However, many companies have found **Internet-based (Web) EDI** to be more affordable. It can be used to replace or supplement traditional EDI. Downing (2002) discovered that companies using Web-based EDI experience superior performance, both internally and externally. Web-based EDI easily can be implemented on the Internet. The sending company posts its files on its Web site. The sending company then informs the receiving company by e-mail that the file has been posted on its Web site. The receiving company can then download the EDI files from the sending company's Web site without special software. Thus, Web-based EDI can be implemented among a small group of users without severe arguments about which standards to use. However, a potential limitation is that the received file may not be compatible with the input format of the receiver's system (though standards such as AS2 for data transmission may solve this problem). For example, the file received may be in a European standard, while the receiving company uses the U.S. EDI standards that are

electronic data interchange (EDI)
The electronic transfer of specially formatted standard business documents, such as bills, orders, and confirmations, sent between business partners.

value-added networks (VANs)
Private, third-party-managed networks that add communications services and security to existing common carriers; used to implement traditional EDI systems.

Internet-based (Web) EDI
EDI that runs on the Internet and is widely accessible to most companies, including SMEs.

different. See Online Appendix W5A for more on the evolution of traditional EDI to Internet-based EDI.

According to Boucher-Ferguson (2002), all major retailers, from Home Depot to Wal-Mart, and many manufacturers, such as Sara Lee Corp., are *requiring* their suppliers to conduct business via regular or Web-based EDI. EDI services are provided by companies such as GXS (gxs.com) and Sterling Commerce (sterlingcommerce.com) (see Chapter 6).

INTEGRATION

A critical success factor for many B2B initiatives is the proper integration of the systems involved. Two major cases are distinguished: (1) integration with the existing internal infrastructure and applications and (2) integration with business partners.

Integration with the Existing Internal Infrastructure and Applications

EC applications of any kind need to be connected with the company's existing internal information systems. For example, an ordering system in sell-side B2B is usually connected with a payment verification system and an inventory management application. Representative systems that must be integrated with EC applications include marketing databases and databases from other departments; legacy systems and their applications; ERP software, which may include procurement functions; catalog (product) information; the payment system; CRM software; logistics and inventory systems; workflow systems; sales statistics; SCM systems; and DSS applications. All major EC software vendors, including Ariba, IBM, Microsoft, Oracle, and SAP, provide for such integration.

Integration with Business Partners

EC can be integrated more easily with internal systems than with external ones. For instance, in the sell-side e-marketplace, it is not easy for the many buying companies to connect with each seller. Similarly, a buy-side e-marketplace needs to be connected with hundreds or even thousands of suppliers for each buyer. One solution is to go to exchanges, where each buyer or seller is connected only once. Another solution is a buyer-owned shopping cart (Lim and Lee 2003). The interface with back-end information systems allows the customer to put items from different sellers in a single cart. This makes shopping much more convenient because the customer pays only one time even though purchases are made from multiple sites.

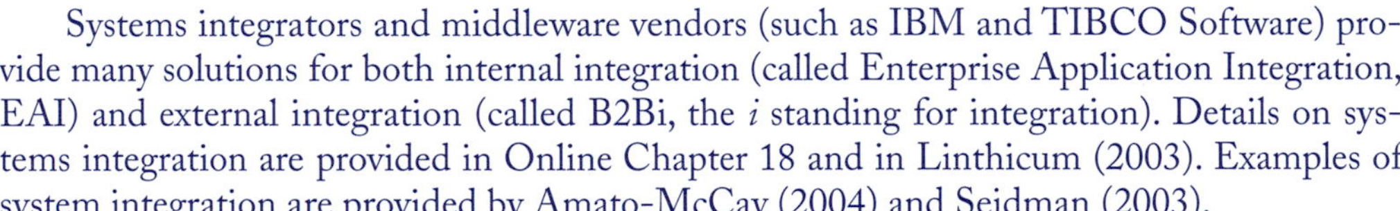

Systems integrators and middleware vendors (such as IBM and TIBCO Software) provide many solutions for both internal integration (called Enterprise Application Integration, EAI) and external integration (called B2Bi, the *i* standing for integration). Details on systems integration are provided in Online Chapter 18 and in Linthicum (2003). Examples of system integration are provided by Amato-McCay (2004) and Seidman (2003).

Two competing approaches are used to integrate B2B with exchanges. The first is ERP II (or Extended ERP) solutions. ERP II is provided by traditional ERP solution providers by adding B2B functions (such as SCM, SRM, and CRM) to ERP (see Online Tutorial T2). The other is the ECM (Electronic Commerce Management) approach, which provides a multivendor open architecture for the integration of B2B and ERP. ERP integrates all the back-office operations (accounting, inventory, finance, etc.). Back-office operations must be integrated with EC because when an order is received in the front office, fulfillment starts by checking payment credibility, inventory, and so on. Later in the purchase process, billing and insurance need to be arranged. Finally, both Web Services (Online Chapter 18) and XML (Online Technical Appendix B) are playing an increasing role in integration support.

THE ROLE OF STANDARDS, ESPECIALLY XML, IN B2B INTEGRATION

For B2B companies to interact with each other easily and effectively, they must be able to connect their servers, applications, and databases. For this to happen, standard protocols and data representation schemes are needed. EDI is one such standard, but it has several limitations and is not structured for the Internet (see Online Appendix W5A).

The Web is based on the standard communication protocols of *TCP/IP* (Transmission Control Protocol/Internet Protocol) and *HTTP* (Hypertext Transfer Protocol). Further, Web pages are written in the universally recognized standard notation of *HTML* (Hypertext Markup Language and its variants). However, this standard environment is useful only for displaying static, visual Web pages. To further extend the functionality of EC sites, one can use JavaScript and other Java and ActiveX programs. These tools allow for human interaction, but they still do not address the need of interconnecting back-end database systems and applications. For that purpose, the industry is pursuing several alternatives for standardized data representation, such as XML.

XML

One of the most promising standards is **XML (eXtensible Markup Language)** and its variants (see Raisinghani 2001; Linthicum 2000). XML is a simplified version of a general data description language known as SGML (Standard Generalized Markup Language). XML is promoted as a new platform for B2B and sometimes as a replacement for EDI systems. It is used to improve compatibility between the disparate systems of business partners by defining the meaning of data in business documents.

XML (eXtensible Markup Language)
Standard (and its variants) used to improve compatibility between the disparate systems of business partners by defining the meaning of data in business documents.

XML was created in an attempt at overcoming barriers to EDI implementation, which are discussed in Online Appendix W5A. XML can overcome EDI barriers for three reasons:

1. XML is a flexible language, therefore new requirements and changes can be incorporated into messages. This expands the rigid ranges of EDI.
2. Message content can be easily read and understood by people using standard browsers. Thus, receivers do not need EDI translators. This enables SMEs to receive, understand, and act on XML-based messages.
3. EDI implementation requires highly specialized knowledge of EDI methodology. Implementation of XML-based technologies requires less-specialized skills.

XML and other related standards require national and international agreements and cooperation. Several organizations are devoted to these topics. For example, ebXML, developed by UN/EDIFACT (EDI for Administration Commerce and Transport), is a popular standard, and most B2B XML protocols support it. See Online Technical Appendix B for the basics of XML and a list of some important standards organizations and links to their Web sites. XML is combined frequently with Web Services in a Service-Oriented Architecture (Erl 2004). One XML variant is voice XML, which is used to increase interactivity and accessibility with speech-recognition systems.

For an example of how XML works, see Online File W5.7. See Online Chapter 18, Online Technical Appendix B, and xml.org for more details on XML.

Web Services

Web Services is a general-purpose architecture that enables distributed applications to be assembled from a web of software services in the same way that Web sites are assembled from a web of HTML pages. It currently is one of the most talked about topics in e-commerce and IT (see Erl 2004 and Glass 2002). The major technologies behind Web Services include XML, SOAP, UDDI, and WDSL (see Online Chapter 18). Using these standards, Web Services allows different applications from different organizations to communicate data without custom coding. Because all communication is in XML, Web Services is not tied to any one operating system or programming language.

Web Services
An architecture enabling assembly of distributed applications from software services and tying them together.

Web Services are viewed as building blocks for distributed systems. Many believe that Web Services will trigger a fundamental shift in the way that most distributed systems are created. Thus, Web Services will play a major role in facilitating B2B because it makes it easier to meet the demands of business customers and channel partners.

THE ROLE OF SOFTWARE AGENTS IN B2B EC

Software (intelligent) agents play multiple roles in B2B (see Chapter 6, Section 6.8). Chapter 3 discussed how software agents are used to aid customers in the comparison-shopping process in B2C. The major role of software agents in B2C is collecting data from multiple sellers' sites. Similarly, in B2B, software agents collect information from business sellers' sites for the benefit of business buyers.

Software agents play a similar role in the B2B buy-side marketplace. Suppose that a large number of buyers need to request quotes from multiple potential suppliers. Doing so manually would be slow, physically difficult, and uneconomical. Therefore, software agents are needed to assist both buyers and sellers. Also, agents are very useful in reverse auctions (see Chapter 10).

Section 5.9 ▶ REVIEW QUESTIONS

1. List the major infrastructures required for B2B EC.
2. Describe the difficulties of integration with business partners.
3. Describe the roles of extranets and EDI in interorganizational networks.
4. Distinguish traditional EDI from Web-based EDI.
5. Describe the purpose of XML.
6. Describe Web Services and its role in integration.
7. What role do software agents play in B2B?

MANAGERIAL ISSUES

Some managerial issues related to this chapter are as follows.

1. **Can we justify the cost of B2B applications?** Because there are several B2B models, each of which can be implemented in different ways, it is critical to conduct a cost-benefit analysis of the proposed applications (projects). Such an analysis should include organizational impacts such as possible channel conflicts and how to deal with resistance to change within the organization. Also, implementation difficulties may increase costs (see Jap and Mohr 2002 and Langelier and Lapierre 2003). One way to justify B2B is to look at the experiences of successful companies, best practices, and guidelines for success (see Cronin 2001).
2. **Which vendor(s) should we select?** Vendors normally develop the B2B applications, even for large organizations. Two basic approaches to vendor selection exist: (1) Select a primary vendor such as IBM, Ariba, or Oracle. This vendor will use its software and procedures and add partners as needed. (2) Use an integrator that will mix and match existing products and vendors to create "the best of breed" for your needs. See Online Chapter 18 for details. WWW
3. **Which B2B model(s) should we use?** The availability of so many B2B models, especially in e-procurement, means that companies need to develop selection strategies based on preferred criteria. In addition to the company-centric models, several types of exchanges should be considered.
4. **Should we restructure our procurement system?** If volume is heavy enough to attract the attention of major vendors, the company that is doing the purchasing might decide to restructure the procurement process by establishing a buy-side marketplace on its server.

   For example, IBM completely restructured its procurement processes prior to moving them online. Many organizations fail to understand that a fundamental change in their internal processes must be implemented to realize the full benefits of e-procurement. The two critical success factors that many organizations overlook are the need to cut down the number of routine tasks and the reduction of the overall procurement cycle through the use of appropriate information technologies such as workflow, groupware, and ERP software.
5. **What are the ethical issues in B2B?** Because B2B EC requires the sharing of proprietary information, business ethics are a must. Employees should not be able to access unauthorized areas in the trading system, and the privacy of trading partners should be protected both technically and legally.
6. **Will there be *massive* disintermediation?** With the increased use of private e-marketplaces, disintermediation and channel conflicts are bound to occur. However, reintermediation may occur with those vendors that can adapt to EC (see Dai and Kauffman 2002 and Zeng et al. 2003).
7. **How can trust and loyalty be cultivated in B2B?** As discussed in Chapter 4, trust and loyalty are important in any type of EC in which the partners do not know each other. For a discussion and a case study, see Ratnasingam and Phan (2003).

RESEARCH TOPICS

Some research issues related to this chapter are provided next. For others, see the Current Research Appendix on the book's Web site. We recommend topics such as:

1. **Issues in Adopting B2B**
   - Surveys on factors that facilitate or hinder the adoption of B2B
   - Who makes adoption decisions and how
   - Related to this is identification of critical success factors (assuming success increases adoption)
   - Surveys can be done by industry, B2B business model, etc.
2. **B2B Relationship Management**
   - How important relationships are and how to find the optimal level of investment in such relationships
   - Interactive buyer-seller relationships are of interest too
3. **Issues in E-Procurement**
   - Investigation of the selection model and the implementation processes of e-procurement
   - Investigation of the cost/benefit and impacts of e-procurement
   - The need for restructuring the procurement processes
   - Issues relating to implementing reverse auctions (design, communication, process, security)
4. **Intelligent Agents in B2B**
   - Agent already used for research, comparisons, evaluation and control (e.g., in auctions)
   - Multi-agent systems can play a major role in B2B processes
   - One promising area is in B2B negotiations
5. **Issues in B2B Integration.** This is one of the most difficult issues in B2B. In addition to the various options available (all with some advantages and limitations) one needs to investigate:
   - Issues such as information sharing, security and cost/benefit
   - When integrating systems with those of business partners, a slew of additional issues surfaces
   - Surveys of best practices and role of intermediaries can be useful
6. **Electronic Data Interchange**
   - The direction of EDI and the role of Internet-based and XHL-based EDI
   - In addition to adoption, cost-benefit of various EDI configurations needs to be analyzed
7. **B2B Mechanisms and Models**
   - Investigation of the various B2B models
   - Examination of the B2B mechanisms such as customized catalogs, auctions and negotiations
8. **Conflict Resolutions in B2B**
   - How changing selling channels creates conflicts with existing distribution channels
   - A close examination of how to handle such conflicts
9. **B2B Intermediation.** A large number of intermediaries may be needed for proper B2B EC
   - What roles intermediaries play, how best to select an intermediary, and how to assess their contribution
   - Which services will suffer from disintermediation and what types of intermediation would be most useful

SUMMARY

In this chapter, you learned about the following EC issues as they relate to the learning objectives.

1. **The B2B field.** The B2B field comprises e-commerce activities between businesses. B2B activities account for 77 to 85 percent of all EC. B2B e-commerce can be done using different models.
2. **The major B2B models.** The B2B field is very diversified. It can be divided into the following segments: sell-side marketplaces (one seller to many buyers), buy-side marketplaces (one buyer from many sellers), and trading exchanges (many sellers to many buyers). Intermediaries play an important role in some B2B models.
3. **The characteristics of sell-side marketplaces.** Sell-side B2B EC is the online direct sale by one seller (a

manufacturer or an intermediary) to many buyers. The major technology used is electronic catalogs, which allow for efficient customization, configuration, and purchase by customers. In addition, forward auctions are becoming popular, especially for selling surplus inventory. Sell-side auctions can be conducted from the seller's own site or from an intermediary's auction site. Sell-side activities can include extensive customer service.

4. **Sell-side intermediaries.** The role of intermediaries in B2B primarily is to provide value-added services to manufacturers and business customers. They also can aggregate buyers and conduct auctions.
5. **The characteristics of buy-side marketplaces and e-procurement.** Today, companies are moving to e-procurement to expedite purchasing, save on item and administrative costs, and gain better control over the purchasing process. Major procurement methods are reverse auctions (bidding system); buying from storefronts and catalogs; negotiation; buying from an intermediary that aggregates sellers' catalogs; internal marketplaces and group purchasing; desktop purchasing; buying in exchanges or industrial malls; and e-bartering. E-procurement offers the opportunity to achieve significant cost and time savings.
6. **B2B reverse auctions.** A reverse auction is a tendering system used by buyers to collect bids electronically from suppliers. Auctions can be done on a company's Web site or on a third-party auction site. Reverse auctions can dramatically lower buyer's costs, both product costs and the time and cost of the tendering process.
7. **B2B aggregation and group purchasing.** Increasing the exposure and the bargaining power of companies can be done by aggregating either the buyers or the sellers. Aggregating suppliers' catalogs into an internal marketplace gives buying companies better control of purchasing costs. In desktop purchasing, buyers are empowered to buy from their desktops up to a set limit without the need for additional approval. They accomplish this by viewing internal catalogs with pre-agreed-upon prices with the suppliers. Industrial malls specialize in one industry (e.g., computers) or in industrial MROs. They aggregate the catalogs of thousands of suppliers. A purchasing agent can place an order at an industrial mall, and shipping is arranged by the supplier or the mall owner. Buyer aggregation through group purchasing is very popular because it allows SMEs to get better prices on their purchases. In addition to direct purchasing, items can be acquired via bartering.
8. **Other purchasing methods.** Desktop purchasing by end users expedites and simplifies the process of buying inexpensive products or services. Buying from e-distributors and at exchanges also is popular, as are auctions and bartering.
9. **Administrative tasks.** The major administrative tasks that can be automated are contract management, spend management, e-sourcing management, and negotiation.
10. **Infrastructure and standards in B2B.** To implement B2B, an organization will need a comprehensive set of hardware and software that includes networks and protocols, multiple servers, application software, and security. Of special utility are extranets and EDI (both traditional and Web based).
11. **Web-based EDI, XML, and Web Services.** Traditional EDI systems were implemented over VANs, making EDI inaccessible to most small companies. Web-based EDI can replace traditional EDI or supplement it. To improve connectivity between business partners' systems, standards organizations are pursuing XML, a standard for defining data elements. The connectivity of B2B also can be facilitated by Web Services.

KEY TERMS

QUESTIONS FOR DISCUSSION

1. Explain how a catalog-based sell-side e-marketplace works and describe its benefits.
2. Discuss the advantages of selling through online auctions over selling from catalogs. What are the disadvantages?
3. Discuss the role of intermediaries in B2B. Distinguish between buy-side and sell-side intermediaries.
4. Discuss and compare all of the mechanisms that group-purchasing aggregators can use.
5. Should desktop purchasing only be implemented through an internal marketplace?
6. How do companies eliminate the potential limitations and risks associated with Web-based EDI? (See Online Appendix W5A.)
7. How can software agents work for multiple sellers and buyers?
8. Discuss the role of XML in B2B. Why is it so important?
9. Discuss the importance of Web Services to B2B integration.

INTERNET EXERCISES

1. Enter gxs.com and review GSX Express's bidding process. Describe the preparations your company would make in order to bid on a job. Also, check how some of the customers are using the company (e.g., Rohm & Haas).
2. Enter commerceone.com and review the capabilities of Conductor and Commerce One Buy. Find out how Commerce One supports global trades.
3. Visit allsystem.com to learn about All-System Aerospace International, Inc., a company that handles aircraft parts from several vendors. From an aircraft repair technician's point of view, evaluate whether this site can compete with Boeing's PART system (see Online File W5.1).
4. Examine the following sites: ariba.com, trilogy.com, electricnet.com, and icc.net. Match a B2B business model with each site.
5. Visit supplyworks.com and examine how the company streamlines the purchase process. How does this company differ from ariba.com?
6. Enter soho.org and locate EC applications for SOHOs. Also, check the business services for small businesses provided by officedepot.com.
7. Visit ebay.com and identify all of the activities related to its small business auctions. What services are provided by eBay?
8. Review the Cisco Connection Online (CCO) case.
   a. What is the CCO business model?
   b. What are the success factors of CCO?
   c. What kinds of inquiries are supported when customers check their order status?
   d. What are the major benefits of CCO to Cisco and its customers?
9. Enter ondemandsourcing.com and view the demo. Prepare a list of benefits to small and mid-tier organizations.
10. Enter bitpipe.com and find recent B2B vendor reports related to e-procurement. Identify topics not covered in this chapter.
11. Visit iasta.com and examine the tools they sell for conducting various types of e-procurement. List and analyze each tool.
12. Enter bambooweb.com and find information about EDI. Prepare a report.

TEAM ASSIGNMENTS AND ROLE PLAYING

1. Predictions about the future magnitude of B2B and statistics on its actual volume in various countries keep changing. In this activity, each team will locate current B2B predictions and statistics for different world regions (e.g., Asia, Europe, North America). Using at least five sources, each team will find the predicted B2B volume (in dollars) for the next 5 years in their assigned region. Possible statistics sources are listed in Exhibit 3.1 (page 84).
2. Your goal in this assignment is to investigate the major B2B vendors. Each team should investigate a major vendor (e.g., Ariba, Microsoft, HP, Oracle, or IBM) or an application type (buy-side, sell-side, or auction).

Find the major products and services offered. Examine customer success stories. Write a report based on your findings. Convince the class that your vendor is the best.

3. Each team should explore a different e-procurement method and prepare a paper for a class presentation. The paper should include the following about the e-procurement method:
   a. The mechanisms and technologies used
   b. The benefits to buyers, suppliers, and others (if appropriate)
   c. The limitations
   d. The situations for which each method is recommended
4. Each team will research digital music wholesale by B2B. Enter any music wholesalers sites and find the B2B activities. Describe them. How do digital music wholesalers deal with intellectual property rights? What DRM-protected digital music does it deal with? Find its major competitors. Relate to Roxio's Napster and Apple's iTunes.

Real-World Case

EASTMAN CHEMICAL MAKES PROCUREMENT A STRATEGIC ADVANTAGE

Eastman Chemical (ECM), a multibillion-dollar, multinational corporation, operates in an extremely competitive environment (*eastman.com*). In response to competitive pressures, management decided to improve on the procurement of MRO items. In its effort to do so, the company embarked on two interrelated activities: integrating the supply chain and introducing e-procurement. The objectives of the project, which was implemented in 2001, were:

- To increase compliance with purchasing policies (reduce maverick buying)
- To support frontline employees while maintaining existing rules
- To reduce procurement transaction costs via elimination of non-value-added and redundant processes
- To leverage corporate spending to negotiate favorable trading terms with channel supply partners

Before the system was installed, the company purchased over $900 million in MROs from over 3,500 suppliers. The company used an SAP R/3 ERP system, part of the legacy system that interfaced with the e-procurement application. The system provided good control, but at a cost of $115 per order when a purchasing card (see Chapter 12) was used. The ERP system helped to reduce the workload on accounts payable and procurement personnel; however, purchasing from noncontracted suppliers increased (the card made such purchasing easy). This maverick buying reduced purchase volumes with primary suppliers, thus reducing the company's negotiating power and increasing costs.

As part of its initiative to improve the MRO procurement process, Eastman Chemical established channel partnership relationships with its largest MRO suppliers. This increased the company's buying leverage and reduced costs and delays. Inventories and service levels were improved. In addition, the company introduced two new EC applications to its procurement system: Commerce One Buy e-procurement software for dealing with the suppliers and Commerce One Conductor for transaction management, Partner Relationship Management (PRM), and value-added services.

Using the Buy software, Eastman Chemical has created an *internal catalog* of all MRO products located in Eastman's storerooms. The software checks availability and prevents redundant purchases. The software also supplies catalog-management features that ensure that all vendors' changes and updates are entered into the internal catalog.

The Conductor application supported the creation of a portal that enables:

- Use of a common Web browser by all of Eastman Chemical's 16,000 employees
- Different types of employees to use the system without need for additional training
- The ability to integrate the SAP R/3 with EC and the procurement card
- An effective and efficient catalog management strategy
- Maintenance of the existing systems infrastructure
- Simplification of business processes
- Flexibility and empowerment of frontline employees

The overall effect of the new portal is to reduce costs and to increase profitability and competitiveness.

By 2004, the system was used by over 6,000 users in 83 countries in procuring over $2 billion worth of goods. The system delivers significant cost savings, improved productivity, and error reduction. A 2004/2005 initiative is automating the RFQ process and special request purchases, using the Commerce One Conductor platform that is designed to connect and compose business processes between systems and partners (see *commerceone.com/download/*).

Eastman Chemical has a large sell-side marketplace as well. Customers order plastics, resins, and fibers online and track their purchases and transaction history, even down to the level of a part of a shipment. Eastman Chemical also auctions its surplus materials in the marketplace.

Overall, Eastman Chemical's e-business logged 11 percent of the company's revenue in 2001 (*Forbes* 2002).

Sources: Compiled from *eastman.com* (accessed 2002), *aberdeen.com* (accessed 2002), *Forbes* (2002), King (2001), and *commerceone.com/news/printer_template.html?keyyear=1998&keyid=22* (accessed March 2005).

Questions

1. Enter *commerceone.com* and find information about the capabilities of Buy and Conductor. How do they differ?
2. Why did Eastman Chemical start first with e-procurement rather than with the sell-side? You may want to visit *eastman.com* to learn more about the company.
3. In July 2000, Eastman Chemical introduced an EC project that enables buyers to participate in its private online price negotiations using LiveExchange from Moai (*moai.com*). Explain how the software works and why it is referred to as "dynamic commerce."
4. Which of the problems cited in this case can be solved by other EC applications? Relate your answer to Commerce One and Ariba products.

REFERENCES

Aberdeen Group. **aberdeen.com** (accessed December 2002).

Amato-McCay, D. "Michael Foods Dishes out Superior Service with Business Integration Solution." *Stores*, February 2004.

Ariba. "Real-World Decision Support: Applying Next-Generation Optimization Technology to Online Sourcing." Ariba, white paper, November 1, 2002. **learningcenter.ariba.com/wp_resource.cfm** (accessed November 2004).

ariba.com (accessed October 2001).

Asset Auctions. **asset-auctions.com/casestudy_whirlpool.html** (accessed October 2004).

Bigboxx.com. **bigboxx.com** (accessed February 2005).

Boucher-Ferguson, R. "Writing the Playbook for B2B." *Wilson Internet*, January 29, 2002.

Bunnell, D., and A. Brate. *Making the Cisco Connection*. New York: John Wiley & Sons, 2000.

Chan, W. C., T. C. Chu, A. R. Gold, and G. Leibowitz. "Thinking Out of the Box." *The McKinsey Quarterly* no. 2 (2001).

Cisco Systems. "Cisco Annual Report 2003." **cisco.com/warp/public/749/ar2002/online/financial_review/mda.html** (accessed April 2003).

Commerce One. "Eastman Chemical Company Selects Commerce One to Drive Electronic Commerce Initiative." News release, September 28, 1998. **commerceone.com/news/printer_template.html?keyyear=1998&keyid=22** (accessed March 2005).

Commerce One. "Schlumberger: Customer Profile." **commerceone.com/customers/profiles/schlumberger.pdf** (accessed November 2004). Note: no longer available online.

Cronin, C. "Five Success Factors for Private Trading Exchanges." *e-Business Advisor*, July–August 2001. **e-businessadvisor.com/doc/08240** (accessed March 2005).

Dai, Q., and R. J. Kauffman. "Business Models for Internet-based E-procurement Systems and B2B Electronic Markets: An Exploratory Assessment." *International Journal of Electronic Commerce* 6, no. 4 (2002).

Davis, W. S., and J. Benamati. *E-Commerce Basics*. Boston: Addison Wesley, 2003.

Downing, C. E. "Performance of Traditional and Web-Based EDI." *Information Systems Management* 19, no. 1 (2002).

Eastman. **eastman.com** (accessed December 2002).

eMarketer. "Has B2B E-commerce Stagnated?" *Emarketer.com*, February 3, 2003. **emarketer.com/products/database.php?f_arg_0=B2B+85+percent+of+e-commerce+2002&f_arg_0_b=B2B+85+percent+of+e-commerce+2002&f_num_args_changed=1&f_num_articles_found=2&f_num_charts_found=2&f_num_reports_found=0&f_reports_found=&f_request=&f_search_type=Basic&Image81.x=0&Image81.y=0** (accessed April 2003). Note: no longer available online.

Erl, T. *Service-Oriented Architecture*. Upper Saddle River, NJ: Prentice Hall, 2004.

"Estimates of the B2B Market." Forrester Research, March 7, 2001. forrester.com (accessed January 2003).

Eyedeas.net. "Ozro Agreement™ for Procurement." eyedeas.net/clients/ozro/oursolutions/eprocurement.cfm (accessed March 2005).

Fickel, L. "Online Auctions: Bid Business." *CIO Web Business Magazine*, June 1, 1999.

Forbes. October 8, 2002. forbes.com (accessed December 2002).

Fortune. "E-Procurement: Unleashing Corporate Purchasing Power." *Fortune,* 2000. fortune.com/sections/eprocurement2000 (accessed April 2003). Note: no longer available online.

General Motors. gm.com (accessed August 2002).

Glass, G. *Web Services*. Upper Saddle River, NJ: Prentice Hall, 2002.

Goldman Sachs Group. "Goldman Sachs Reports on Worldwide B2B Commerce." Goldman Sachs report, February 15, 2001. gs.com (accessed July 2001). Note: no longer available online.

Grainger. grainger.com (accessed January 2003).

Haig, M. *The B2B E-Commerce Handbook*. UK: Kogan Page Ltd., 2003.

Hoffman, W., J. Keedy, and K. Roberts. "The Unexpected Return of B2B." *The McKinsey Quarterly* no. 3 (2002).

IBM. *Whirlpool's B2B Trading Portal Cuts per Order Cost Significantly*. White Plains, NY: IBM Corporation Software Group, Pub. # G325-6693-00, 2000.

IDC. "Worldwide Dynamic Pricing B2B eCommerce Sales Volume 2003-2008 Forecast." March 2004. idc.com/getdoc.jsp?containerId=30892 (accessed March 2005).

Interwoven, Inc. "Interwoven Solutions Power Cisco Connection Online." Interwoven case study, 2001. interwoven.com/documents/casestudies/cisco_august.pdf (accessed April 2003).

Jakovijeric, P. J. "Differences in Complexity between B2C and B2B E-Commerce." *TechnologyEvaluation.Com*, March 4, 2004. technologyevaluation.com/Registration/TEC.asp?url=/Research/ResearchHighlights/eCommerce/2004/03/research_notes/TU_EC_PJ_03_04_04_1.asp (accessed March 2005).

Jap, S. D., and J. J. Mohr. "Leveraging Internet Technologies in B2B Relationships." *California Management Review* (July 1, 2002).

Kalakota, R., and M. Robinson. *E-Business 2.0*. Reading, MA: Addison-Wesley, 2001.

King, J. "Chemical Weapon." ComputerWorld.com, July 16, 2001. computerworld.com/industrytopics/manufacturing/story/0,10801,61471,00.html (accessed March 2005).

Langelier, P., and V. Lapierre. "Winning Strategies for B2B E-Commerce." *IQ Collectif*, February 2003.

Lim, G., and J. K. Lee. "Buyer-Carts for B2B EC: The B-Cart Approach." *Organizational Computing and Electronic Commerce* (July–September 2003).

Linthicum, D. S. *Next Generation Application Integration: From Simple Information to Web Services*. Boston: Addison-Wesley, 2003.

Linthicum, D. S. "Applications with XML." *e-Business Advisor*, May 2000.

Loney, K., and G. Koch. *Oracle 9i: The Complete Reference*. New York: McGraw-Hill, 2002.

Lucas, H. C. *Information Technology: Strategic Decision Making for Managers*. Hoboken, NJ: John Wiley and Sons, 2005.

Mahadevan, B. "Making Sense of the Emerging Market Structure in B2B E-Commerce." *California Management Review* (Fall 2003).

Martin, T. N., et al. "Purchasing Agents: Use of the Internet as a Procurement Tool." *Quarterly Journal of Electronic Commerce* 2, no. 1 (2001).

Mehrotra. P. "Dotcoms Back with a Bang." Cyberzest.com, March 2001. cyberzest.com/ecommerce/Dotcoms%20back%20with%20a%20bang.html (accessed March 2005).

Metz, C. "Purchasing Power." *PC Magazine*, November 21, 2002.

Microsoft. "Case Study: MS Market." microsoft.com/business/~howmicrosoftworks/casestudies/msmarket.asp (accessed November 2004). Note: no longer available online.

Mudambi, R., C. P. Schründer, and A. Monger. "How Co-Operative is Co-Operative Purchasing in Smaller Firms." *Long-Range Planning*, February 2004.

Murphree, J. "Global Enabled Supply and Demand Chain Series: Sourcing." *iSource*, February–March 2003. parnold.com/articles/mindflow/mfisource4.htm (accessed December 2004).

Neef, D. *E-Procurement: From Strategy to Implementation*. Upper Saddle River, NJ: Prentice Hall, 2001.

Ovans, A. "E-Procurement at Schlumberger." *Harvard Business Review* (May–June 2000).

Raisinghani, M. S. "Extensible Markup Language: Synthesis of Key Ideas and Perspectives for Management." *Information Management* 14, no. 3, 4 (2001).

Ratnasingam, P., and D. D. Phan. "Trading Partner Trust in B2B E-Commerce: A Case Study." *Information Systems Management* (Summer 2003).

Rudnitsky, H. "Changing the Corporate DNA." *Forbes,* July 24, 2000. forbes.com/global/2000/0724/0314099a.html (accessed August 2000).

Schlumberger. schlumberger.com (accessed 2002–2004).

Segev, A., and J. Gebauer. "B2B Procurement and Marketplace Transformation." *Information Technology and Management* (July 2001).

Seidman, T. "QVC.com and Costco.com Talk to Business Partners in the Same Language." *Stores*, January 2003.

Slater, R. *The Eye of the Storm: How John Chambers Steered Cisco Through the Technology Collapse*. New York: HarperCollins, 2003.

Small Business Administration. **sba.gov/advo/stats** (accessed February 2002). Note: no longer available online.

Smeltzer, L. R., and A. Carr. "Reverse Auctions in Industrial Marketing and Buying." *Business Horizons*, March–April 2002.

Veit, D. J. *Matchmaking in Electronic Markets*. New York: Springer-Verlag, 2004.

Wagner, M. "Web Helps Microsoft Automate Its Business." *Internet Week*, 2000. **internetweek.com/100/tech.htm** (accessed April 2003).

Warkentin, M. (ed.). *Business to Business Electronic Commerce: Challenges and Solutions*. Hershey, PA: Idea Group Publishing, 2002.

Waters, J. K. *John Chambers and the Cisco Way*. New York: Wiley, 2002.

Whirlpool. **whirlpool.com** (accessed September 2004).

Zeng, Y. E., H. J. Wen, and D. C. Yen. "Customer Relationship Management (CRM) in Business-to-Business (B2B) E-Commerce." *Information Management and Computer Security* 11 (2003).

CHAPTER 6

PUBLIC B2B EXCHANGES AND SUPPORT SERVICES

Learning Objectives

Upon completion of this chapter, you will be able to:

1. Define exchanges and describe their major types.
2. Describe the various ownership and revenue models of exchanges.
3. Describe B2B portals.
4. Describe third-party exchanges.
5. Distinguish between purchasing (procurement) and selling consortia.
6. Define dynamic trading and describe B2B auctions.
7. Discuss integration issues of e-marketplaces and exchanges.
8. Describe the major support services of B2B.
9. Discuss B2B networks.
10. Discuss issues in managing exchanges.
11. Describe the critical success factors of exchanges.

Content

CHEMCONNECT: THE WORLD CHEMICAL EXCHANGE

The Problem

The trading of raw and partially processed chemicals, plastics, and related materials is done daily by thousands of companies in almost every country in the world. Before the Internet, the trading process was slow, fragmented, ineffective, and costly. As a result, buyers paid too much, sellers had high expenses, and intermediaries were needed to smooth the trading process.

The Solution

Today, buyers and sellers of chemicals and plastics can meet electronically in a large Internet public marketplace (founded in 1995) called ChemConnect (*chemconnect.com*). Global chemical industry leaders, such as British Petroleum, Dow Chemical, BASF, Hyundai, Sumitomo, and many more, make transactions over ChemConnect every day in real time. They save on transaction costs, reduce cycle time, and find new markets and trading partners around the globe. It was the first mover B2B e-market in the chemical industry.

ChemConnect provides a trading marketplace and an information portal to over 9,000 members in 135 countries. Members are producers, consumers, distributors, traders, and intermediaries involved in the chemical industry.

ChemConnect offers its members a Trading Center with three trading places:

1. **Marketplace for buyers.** In this marketplace, buyers can find suppliers all over the world. They can post RFQs with reverse auctions, negotiate, and more.
2. **Marketplace for sellers.** This marketplace provides sellers with exposure to many potential new customers. It provides automated tools for quick liquidation. More than 1,000 products are negotiated in auctions.
3. **Commodity markets platform.** This platform provides a powerful connection to the global spot marketplaces for chemicals, plastics, and other materials. Members can trade at market prices, access real-time market intelligence, and effectively manage risk. Traders can exchange bids and offers quickly, confidently, and anonymously, until the deal is complete.

ChemConnect members can use the Trading Center to streamline sales and sourcing processes by automating requests for quotes, proposals, and new suppliers. The center enables a member to negotiate more efficiently with existing business partners as well as with new companies the member may invite to the table—all in complete privacy. With over 9,000 companies, the Trading Center is a highly effective way to get the best prices and terms available on the worldwide market. In addition, members can access a database containing more than 63,000 chemicals and plastics—virtually any product members are ever likely to look for.

ChemConnect is an independent, third-party intermediary; thus it works within certain rules and guidelines that ensure an unbiased approach to trades. All legal requirements, payments, trading rules, and other guidelines are fully disclosed. (Click "Policies, Fees, and Legal Information" on the site for more information on ChemConnect's disclosure policies.) The revenue model includes members' annual transaction fees, subscription fees (for trading and for auctions), and fulfillment transaction fees. Members pay transaction fees only for successfully completed transactions.

All three trading locations provide up-to-the-minute market information (via *bloomberg.com*) that can be translated into 30 different languages. Business partners provide several support services. For example, Citigroup and ChemConnect jointly offer several financial services for exchange members. ChemConnect also offers systems for connecting companies' back-end systems with their business partners and with ChemConnect itself.

ChemConnect is linked to GXS (see Insights and Additions 6.1, page 260), which manages a network of tens of thousands companies.

The Results

The overall benefits of ChemConnect to its members are more efficient business processes, lower overall transaction costs, and time saved during negotiation and bidding. For example, conducting a reverse auction in a trading room enables buyers to save up to 15 percent of a product's cost in just 30 minutes. The same process using manual bidding methods would take several weeks or months. One company that placed an RFQ for 100 metric tons of a certain acid to be delivered in Uruguay with a starting price of $1.10 per kilogram reduced the price to $0.95 in only six consecutive bids offered in 30 minutes. In addition, sellers can reach more buyers and liquidate surpluses rapidly.

ChemConnect continues to grow, adding members and increasing its trading volume each year. (Transaction volume in 2004 was over $10 billion.) The company hopes to become profitable in 2004. One of the company's success factors is that 40 large chemical companies hold about one-third of the company's stock. Another factor is the fact that about 44 percent of the industry uses the exchange on a regular basis. Finally, ChemConnect market data are distributed by Bloomberg (*bloomberg.com*), a major financial information services company

Sources: Based on information from *chemconnect.com* (accessed September 2004) and Angwin (2004).

WHAT WE CAN LEARN . . .

The ChemConnect story demonstrates an e-marketplace with many buyers and many sellers, all in one industry (a vertical e-marketplace). These buyers and sellers, as well as other business partners, congregate electronically to conduct business. This type of a marketplace is an *electronic exchange* that is owned and operated by a third-party intermediary. As will be seen later in the chapter, ownership of an exchange has some major implications for B2B marketplaces.

In contrast with the company-centric models that were the focus of Chapter 5, the models in this chapter include *many buyers* and *many sellers*. They usually are *public* e-marketplaces, which are known by a variety of names and have a variety of functions. For now, we will simply call them *exchanges*.

6.1 B2B ELECTRONIC EXCHANGES—AN OVERVIEW

public e-marketplaces (public exchanges)
Trading venues open to all interested parties (sellers and buyers); usually run by third parties.

exchange
A many-to-many e-marketplace. Also known as an *e-marketplaces,* an *e-markets,* and a *trading exchanges.*

market maker
The third party that operates an exchange (and in many cases, also owns the exchange).

As defined in Chapter 2, **public e-marketplaces**, or **public exchanges**, are trading venues open to all interested parties (many sellers and many buyers) that use a common technology platform and that are usually run by third parties or industry consortia (see Kambil and van Heck 2002). The term **exchange** is often used to describe many-to-many e-marketplaces. In the context of e-commerce, exchanges are *virtual* (online) trading venues, not physical locales, and they are electronically operated. Many exchanges support community activities, such as distributing industry news, sponsoring online discussion groups, and providing research. They also provide support services such as payments and logistics (see *Darwin Magazine* 2001 and Gebauer and Shaw 2002).

Exchanges are known by a variety of names: *e-marketplaces, e-markets,* and *trading exchanges.* Other terms include *trading communities, exchange hubs, Internet exchanges, Net marketplaces,* and *B2B portals.* We will use the term *exchange* in this book to describe the general many-to-many e-marketplaces, but we will use some of the other terms in more specific contexts (e.g., see Sharma 2002).

As discussed in the next section ("Classification of Exchanges"), exchanges may be vertical (industry oriented) or horizontal, and they can be used for long-term buying relationships or for fulfilling a short-term need. Auctions may be part of any of these types of exchanges. Despite their variety, all exchanges share one major characteristic: Exchanges are electronic trading-community meeting places for many sellers and many buyers, and possibly for other business partners, as shown in Exhibit 6.1. At the center of every exchange is a **market maker**, the third party that operates the exchange and, in many cases, may also own it.

In an exchange, just as in a traditional open-air marketplace, buyers and sellers can interact and negotiate prices and quantities. Generally, free-market economics rule the exchange trade community, as demonstrated by ChemConnect.

According to Forrester Research (as reported by Shetty 2001), 2,500 exchanges worldwide, at several stages of operation, were in operation in the spring of 2001. Since then, more than 70 percent have folded due to a lack of customers, cash, or both (e.g., Chemdex and MetalSite). However, the companies that use exchanges, both as sellers and buyers, are generally pleased with them and plan to increase the number of exchanges they are participating in (from 1.7 to 4.1, on average), within 2 years (Dolinoy et al. 2001). Traders usually more than double the value of transactions that they do through an exchange after the first two years of participation.

CLASSIFICATION OF EXCHANGES

Exchanges can be classified in several ways. We will use the approach suggested by Kaplan and Sawhney (2000) and by Durlacher Research (2000). According to this classification, an exchange can be classified into one of four cells of a matrix, as shown in Exhibit 6.2. The matrix has two dimensions. Across the top, two types of materials are traded, either *direct* or *indirect* (MRO), as defined in Section 5.1. Down the left side are two possible sourcing strategies: *strategic* and *spot* (see Section 5.1). The intersection of these characteristics results in four exchange classifications (the four cells of Exhibit 6.2).

EXHIBIT 6.1 **Trading Communities: Information Flow and Access to Information**

EXHIBIT 6.2 **Classification of B2B Exchanges**

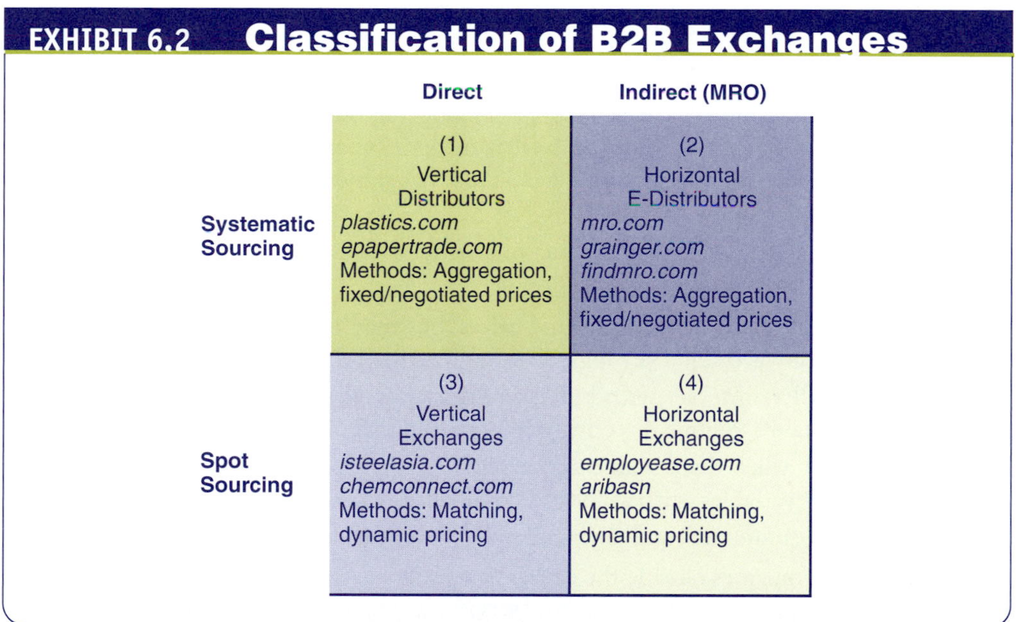

If strategic sourcing is used for direct materials, the market maker aggregates the buyers, the sellers, or both, and provides the platform for *negotiated* prices and contracted terms (first cell). Strategic sourcing of direct materials, which are usually traded in large quantities, is frequently done with the aid of intermediaries. An example of this type of exchange can be found at plastics.com, an exchange for the plastics industry. Using the speed, access, and ease of the Internet, the exchange simplifies and streamlines the process of buying and selling at substantially reduced administrative costs, and sometimes reduced product costs as well.

In strategic sourcing of indirect materials (MROs) (second cell), the market maker basically aggregates sellers' catalogs, as MRO.com (mro.com) does. MRO.com provides tools and technology in a hosted environment that enables manufacturers and distributors of industrial parts—the "supply" of the industrial supply chain—to participate in EC quickly and affordably. MRO.com creates one catalog containing products from multiple suppliers, connects the catalog to an order-processing system, and offers different types of industrial buyers a single source from which to buy their MROs.

vertical exchange
An exchange whose members are in one industry or industry segment.

Spot sourcing of *direct materials* (third cell) takes place in **vertical exchanges**, which are considered vertical because sales take place in one industry or industry segment. Examples of vertical exchanges are ChemConnect and an exchange called ISteelAsia (isteelasia.com), which conducts online auctions and bids for steel.

horizontal exchange
An exchange that handles materials used by companies in different industries.

Spot sourcing of indirect materials (fourth cell) takes places in **horizontal exchanges**. These exchanges are considered horizontal because they handle materials traded for use by companies from different industries. For example, light bulbs and office supplies might be purchased in a horizontal exchange by both an automaker and a steelmaker. (In these horizontal exchanges, MROs can include both products, such as office supplies, and services, such as temporary labor.) Horizontal exchanges offer a variety of mechanisms, as shown in Online Exhibit W6.1.

DYNAMIC PRICING

dynamic pricing
A rapid movement of prices over time, and possibly across customers, as a result of supply and demand.

The market makers in both vertical and horizontal exchanges match supply and demand in their exchanges, and this matching determines prices. In spot sourcing, the prices are *dynamic* and are based on changes in supply and demand. (In strategic sourcing, they are negotiated or fixed.) **Dynamic pricing** refers to a rapid movement of prices over time, and possibly across customers, as a result of supply and demand at any given time. Stock exchanges are the prime example of dynamic pricing. Prices on stock exchanges sometimes change by the second, depending at any moment on how much buyers are willing to pay for a stock and how many sellers of that stock are willing to sell at various prices. Another good example of dynamic pricing occurs in *auctions*, where prices vary all the time. The result of dynamic pricing may be that the exact same product or service is sold to different customers at different prices.

Dynamic pricing is based on market information being available to buyers and sellers. One of the reasons the U.S. stock exchanges are thought to work as well as they do is the amount of financial information generally available to the traders. The Internet and certain market mechanisms (such as auctions) provide a large amount of product information, sometimes in real time. Therefore, the Internet facilitates many of the dynamic pricing models for both B2B and B2C.

The typical process that results in dynamic pricing in most exchanges includes the following steps:

1. A company posts a bid to buy a product or an offer to sell one.
2. An auction (forward or reverse) is activated.
3. Buyers and sellers can see the bids and offers, but may not always see who is making them. Anonymity is often a key ingredient of dynamic pricing.
4. Buyers and sellers interact with bids and offers in real time. Sometimes buyers join together to obtain a volume discount price (group purchasing).
5. A deal is struck when there is an exact match between a buyer and a seller on price, volume, and other variables, such as location or quality.
6. The deal is consummated, and payment and delivery are arranged.

Third-party companies outside the exchange usually provide supporting services such as credit verification, quality assurance, escrow service, insurance, and order fulfillment. They ensure that the buyer has the money and that the product is in good condition. They also may coordinate product delivery (see Chapter 13).

In Chapter 5, we described group purchasing, negotiating, and forward auctions, which also employ dynamic pricing. When dynamic pricing is used with methods such as auctions, the process is referred to as *dynamic trading*. For example, IBM's WebSphere Commerce suite (see Online Chapter 18) includes a dynamic trading module that enables reverse auctions, exchanges, and contract negotiations.

WWW

FUNCTIONS OF EXCHANGES

According to Tumolo (2001), exchanges have three major functions:

1. **Matching buyers and sellers.** The matching of buyers and sellers includes such activities as establishing product offerings; aggregating and posting different products for sale;

providing price and product information; organizing bids, bartering, and auctions; matching supplier offerings with buyer preferences; enabling price and product comparisons; supporting negotiations and agreements between buyers and suppliers; and providing directories of buyers and sellers.

2. **Facilitating transactions.** Facilitating transactions includes the following activities: arranging logistics of delivering information, goods, or services to buyers; providing billing and payment information, including addresses; defining terms and other transaction values; inputting searchable information; granting exchange access to users and identifying company users eligible to use the exchange; settling transaction payments to suppliers, collecting transaction fees and providing other escrow services; registering and qualifying buyers and suppliers; maintaining appropriate security over information and transactions; and arranging for group (volume) purchasing.
3. **Maintaining exchange policies and infrastructure.** Maintaining institutional infrastructure involves the following activities: ascertaining compliance with commercial code, contract law, export and import laws, and intellectual property law for transactions made within the exchange; maintaining technological infrastructure to support volume and complexity of transactions; providing interface capability to standard systems of buyers and suppliers; and obtaining appropriate site advertisers and collecting advertising and other fees.

To execute these various functions, exchanges go through a process similar to that shown in Exhibit 6.3. The top of the exhibit shows the conventional process. The bottom shows the EC process. As can be seen, the EC process is simpler (and quicker).

OWNERSHIP, GOVERNANCE, AND ORGANIZATION OF EXCHANGES

Before we conclude our overview of exchanges and move on to detailed discussions of each type of exchange, let's look at issues related to the ownership and organization of exchanges.

Ownership of Exchanges

Ownership models for Internet exchanges are of three basic types: industry giant, neutral entrepreneur, and a consortium.

- **An industry giant.** In this model, one manufacturer, distributor, or broker sets up the exchange and runs it. An example is IBM, which established an exchange for the purpose of selling patents (delphion.com). In 1999, IBM placed 25,000 of its own patents up for sale and invited others to sell their patents as well. This model is an extension of the sell-side model described in Chapter 5. General Electric's TPN (see Online File W5.3) is another classic example of a buy-side exchange that was initially controlled by an industry giant. It led to the creation of the GXS exchange, which is now owned by a group of investors. In the past, Samsung of South Korea manually brokered various commodities; as of 2002 it had several online exchanges, including one for fish. The major potential problem for this type of exchange is whether the giant's large competitors will be willing to use it.

- **A neutral entrepreneur.** Under this model, a *third-party* intermediary sets up an exchange and promises to run an efficient and unbiased exchange. ChemConnect, for example, is a neutral exchange. (This type of exchange is discussed in Section 6.3.) The potential problem for such exchanges is whether buyers and sellers will use the exchange.
- **The consortium (or co-op).** With this type of exchange, several industry players get together and decide to set up an exchange so that all can benefit. Covisint is an example of such as exchange. (Consortia are discussed in Section 6.4.) A major potential problem with this model is determining who is in charge of the exchange.

Revenue Models

Exchanges, like all organizations, require revenue to survive. Therefore, an exchange's owners, whoever they are, must decide how they will earn revenue. The following are potential sources of revenue for exchanges.

- **Transaction fees.** Transaction fees are basically a commission paid *by sellers* for each transaction they make (see Chapter 1). However, sellers may object to transaction fees,

EXHIBIT 6.3 **Conventional Versus Exchange Processes**

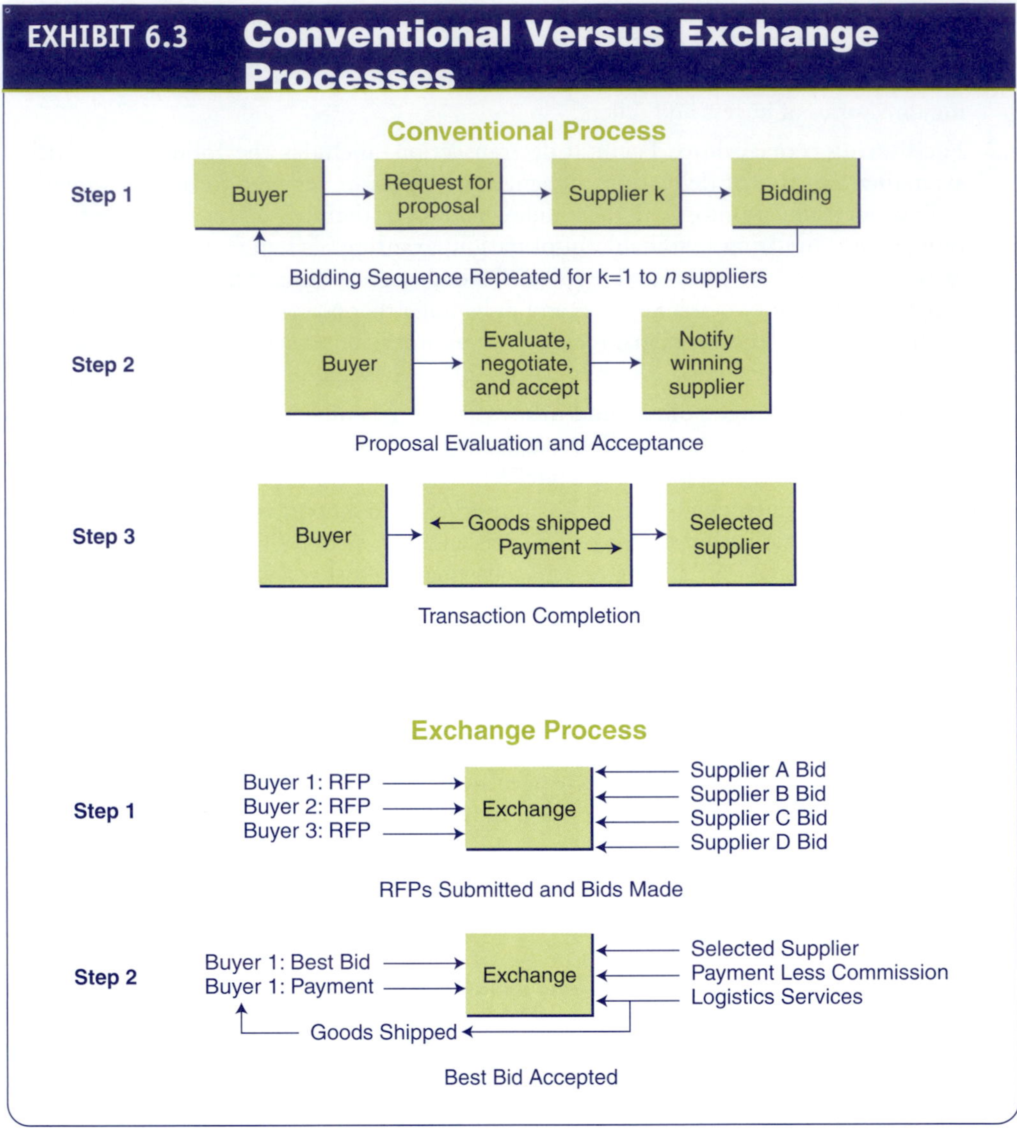

Source: Based on Brint.com.

especially when their regular customers are involved. Exchanges charge relatively low transaction fees per order in order to attract sellers. Therefore, to cover its expenses, the exchange must generate sufficient volume, find other revenue sources, or be forced to raise its transaction fees.

- **Fee for service.** Some exchanges have successfully changed their revenue model from commission (transaction fee) to "fee for service." Sellers are more willing to pay for value-added services than for commissions. Sometimes buyers also pay service charges.
- **Membership fees.** A membership fee is a fixed annual or monthly fee. It usually entitles the exchange member to get some services free or at a discount. In some countries, such as China, the government may ask members to pay annual membership fees and then provide the participating sellers with free services and no transaction fees. This encourages members to use the exchange. The problem is that low membership fees may result in insufficient revenue to the exchange. However, high membership fees discourage participants from joining.
- **Advertising fees.** Exchanges also can derive income from fees for advertising on the information-portal part of the exchange. For example, some sellers may want to increase their exposure and will pay for special advertisements on the portal (like boxed ads in the yellow pages of telephone books).

- **Other revenue sources.** If an exchange is doing auctions, it can charge auction fees. License fees can be collected on patented information or software. Finally, market makers can collect fees for their services.

Governance and Organization

Exchanges have their own board of directors and are governed by guidelines and rules, some of which are required by law. These rules and guidelines must be very specific regarding how the exchange operates, what the requirements are to join the exchange, what fees are involved, and what rules need to be followed. Furthermore, the governance document needs to specify security and privacy arrangements, what will happen in case of disputes, and so forth. The contract terms between an exchange and buyers and sellers also are critical, as are assurances that the exchange is fair.

Regardless of their ownership, revenue model, and governance structure, exchanges may include the following organizational elements.

Membership. Membership refers to the community's relationship to the exchange, to the fees charged, and to the class type of the member. Members can have full privileges, partial privileges (associate members), or partial privileges. Also, there are different types of fees. For example, exchanges that do not charge members a fee to join (e.g., alibaba.com) may collect transaction or service fees. For exchanges that charge registration fees and annual membership fees (e.g., chemconnect.com), varying levels of membership may be offered. For example, members may be either *observing members*, who can only view what is going on but not trade, or *trading members*, who can make offers and bid, pay, and arrange deliveries. Trading members usually need to go through a qualification process with the market maker. In some cases, a cash deposit is required. There may be other categories of members (e.g., associate members). Some exchanges set limits on how much each member can trade.

Site Access and Security. Exchanges must be secure. Because members' activities may be strategic and competitors frequently congregate in the same exchange, information must be carefully protected. In addition to regular EC security measures, special attention should be made to prevent illegal offers and bids. Several exchanges have a list of individuals who are authorized to represent the participating companies.

Services Provided by Exchanges. Exchanges provide many services to buyers and sellers. The types of services offered depend on the nature of the exchange. For example, the services provided by a stock exchange are completely different from those provided by a steel or food exchange or by an intellectual property or patent exchange. However, most exchanges provide the services shown in Exhibit 6.4.

ADVANTAGES AND LIMITATIONS OF EXCHANGES

Exchanges have several benefits, including making markets more efficient, providing opportunities for sellers and buyers to find new business partners, cutting the administrative costs of ordering MROs, and expediting trading processes. They also facilitate global trade and create communities of informed buyers and sellers.

Despite these benefits, beginning in 2001, exchanges started to collapse, and both buyers and sellers realized that they faced the risk of exchange failure or deterioration. In the case of exchange failure, the risk is primarily a financial one—of suddenly losing the market in which one has been buying and selling, and therefore having to scramble to find a new exchange or to find buyers and sellers on one's own. In addition, finding a new place to trade is an operational risk. Buyers also risk potentially poor product performance and receipt of incomplete information from degraded exchanges, which is a risk the sellers may face too.

The potential gains and risks of B2B exchanges for buyers and for sellers are summarized in Exhibit 6.5. As the exhibit shows, the gains outnumber the risks.

Section 6.1 ▶ REVIEW QUESTIONS

1. Define B2B exchanges and list the various types of public exchanges.
2. Describe strategic sourcing and spot sourcing.
3. Differentiate between a vertical exchange and a horizontal exchange.

EXHIBIT 6.4 Services in Exchanges

4. What is dynamic pricing? How does it work?
5. Describe the types of ownership and the possible revenue models of exchanges.
6. List the potential advantages, gains, limitations, and risks of exchanges.

6.2 B2B PORTALS

B2C sometimes can be conducted in *information portals* (often called just *portals*), such as MSN or Yahoo!, where information (such as Yahoo!'s shopping directory) is targeted at individual customers or businesses. Buyers can place orders on some portals, but in many cases buyers are transferred to sellers' storefronts to complete their transactions.

B2B portals
Information portals for businesses.

Similar situations exist in B2B. **B2B portals** are information portals for businesses. Some e-marketplaces act as pure information portals. They usually include *directories* of products offered by each seller, lists of buyers and what they want, and other industry or general information. Buyers then visit sellers' sites to conduct their transactions. The portal may get commissions for referrals or only derive revenue from advertisements. Thus, information

EXHIBIT 6.5 Potential Gains and Risks in B2B Exchanges

	For Buyers	For Sellers
Potential gains	• One-stop shopping, huge variety • Search and comparison shopping • Volume discounts • 24/7 ordering from any location • Make one order from several suppliers • Unlimited, detailed information • Access to new suppliers • Status review and easy reordering • Fast delivery • Less maverick buying	• New sales channel • No physical store is needed • Reduced ordering errors • Sell 24/7 • Reach new customers at little extra cost • Promote the business via the exchange • An outlet for surplus inventory • Can go global more easily
Potential risks	• Unknown vendors; may not be reliable • Loss of customer service quality (inability to compare all services)	• Loss of direct CRM and PRM • More price wars • Competition for value-added services • Must pay transaction fees (including on seller's existing customers) • Possible loss of customers to competitors

portals may have a difficult time generating sufficient revenues. Because of this, many information portals are beginning to offer, for a fee, additional services that support trading, such as escrow and shipments. An example B2B portal is MyBoeingFleet.com (myboeingfleet.com), which is a Web portal for airplane owners, operators, and MRO operators. Developed by Boeing Commercial Aviation Services, MyBoeingFleet.com provides customers (primarily businesses) direct and personalized access to information essential to the operation of Boeing aircraft.

Like exchanges, information portals may be horizontal (e.g., Alibaba.com, described later), offering a wide range of products to different industries. Or, they may be vertical, focusing on a single industry or industry segment. Vertical portals are often referred to as **vortals**.

vortals
B2B portals that focus on a single industry or industry segment; "vertical portals."

Some use the word *portal* when referring to an exchange. The reason for this is that many B2B portals are adding capabilities that make them look like exchanges. Also, many exchanges include information portals.

The two examples that follow illustrate some of the differences between *portals* and *exchanges*.

THOMAS REGISTER

Thomas Register of America (thomasnet.com), an information portal, publishes a directory of millions of manufacturing companies. In 1998, it teamed up with General Electric to create the TPN Register (now embedded in GXS; gxs.com), a portal that facilitates business transactions for MROs. TPN Register worked with buyers and sellers to build electronic trading communities. Sellers can distribute information on what they have to sell; buyers can find what they need and purchase over a comprehensive and secure procurement channel that helps them reduce costs, shrink cycle times, and improve productivity. For-fee services also are available. However, the Thomas Register is basically an information portal, because it does not offer any opportunity for transactions on its site. For example, it does not offer a list of products with quantities needed (requests to buy) or offer what is available from sellers. A similar information-only service is provided by Manufacturing.Net (manufacturing.net).

ALIBABA.COM

Another intermediary that started as a pure information portal but is moving toward becoming a trading exchange is Alibaba.com (alibaba.com). Launched in 1999, Alibaba.com initially concentrated on China; in November 2004, it had over 4.8 million registered traders in 240 countries. It includes a large, robust community of international buyers and sellers who are interested in direct trade without an intermediary. Initially, the site was a huge posting place for classified ads. Alibaba.com is a portal in transition, showing some characteristics of an information portal plus some services of an exchange. To understand the capabilities of Alibaba.com, we need to explore its marketplace capabilities and offerings (take the multimedia tour!).

The Database

The center of Alibaba.com is its huge database, which is basically a horizontal information portal with offerings in a wide variety of product categories. The portal is organized into 27 major product categories (as of 2004), including agriculture, apparel and fashion, automobiles, and toys. Each product category is further divided into subcategories (over 700 in total). For example, the toy category includes items such as dolls, electrical pets, and wooden toys. Each subcategory includes classified ads organized into four groups: sellers, buyers, agents, and cooperation. Each group may include many companies. The ads are fairly short. Note that in all cases a user can click an ad for details. In 2004, all postings were still free. Some categories have thousands of postings; therefore, a search engine is provided. The search engine works by country, type of advertiser, and age of the postings.

Reverse Auctions

Alibaba.com also allows buyers to post RFQs. Would-be sellers can then send bids to the buyer, conduct negotiations, and accept a purchase order when one is agreed upon. As of

March 2003, the process was not fully automated. (To see how the process works, go to "My trade activity" and take the tour, initiate a negotiation, and issue a purchase order.)

Features and Services

In fall 2004, the following features were provided: free e-mail, Trust Service, FAQs, tutorials for traders, free e-mail alerts, a China club membership, news (basically related to importing and exporting), trade show information, legal information, arbitration, and forums and discussion groups. In addition, a member can create a personalized company Web page as well as a "sample house" (for showing their products); members also can post their own marketing leads (where to buy and sell). As of 2003, the site offers its services in English, Chinese, and Korean. Also, the site is doing e-tailing.

Certain other services are available for a fee. For-fee services include, for example, business credit reports, export/import reports, and a quote center for shipping services. In the future, additional services will be added to increase the company's revenue stream.

Alibaba.com also has subsidiaries: china.alibaba.com, a marketplace for China's domestic trade, and japan.alibaba.com. It also had a major stake in taobao.com, a Chinese C2C auction site.

Revenue Model

In fall 2004, the site's revenue stream was expanded from advertisements to fees for special services. For example, income is generated through paid memberships, online booths, priority listings, and so on. Alibaba.com competes with several global exchanges that provide similar services (e.g., see asia-links.com and globalsources.com). The advantage of Alibaba.com is its low operational costs. Therefore, it probably will be able to sustain losses much longer than its competitors. Someday in the future, Alibaba.com may be in a position that will enable it to make a great deal of money. Alibaba.com was strong enough to sustain losses until 2003 when it made $12 million profit.

Section 6.2 ▶ REVIEW QUESTIONS

1. Define B2B portals.
2. Distinguish a vortal from a horizontal portal.
3. List the major services provided by Alibaba.com.
4. Compare Alibaba with its competitors such as asia-links.com and globalsources.com.

6.3 THIRD-PARTY (TRADING) EXCHANGES

The opening vignette introduced ChemConnect, a neutral, public, third-party vertical market maker. ChemConnect's initial success was well publicized, and dozens of similar third-party exchanges, mostly in specific industries, have been developed since. A thriving example of a third-party exchange is Rawmart.com, described in EC Application Case 6.1.

Some other successful exchanges are RetailExchange (retailexchange.com), which links manufacturers and retailers to buy and sell excess inventory (5,000 members and $306 billion in goods in 2003); Neoforma Inc. (neoforma.com), which sells medical supplies; Globalnetxchange (gnx.com), which serves the global retail industry; Global Healthcare Exchange (ghx.com), which specializes in hospital supplies; i-MARK (imark.com), which sells surpluses; Winery Exchange (wineryexchange.com), which specializes in wines; ChemConnect (chemconnect.com), which offers chemicals and plastics; and farms.com for agriculture-related business.

Third-party exchanges are characterized by two contradicting properties. On one hand, they are *neutral*, because they do not favor either sellers or buyers. On the other hand, because they do not have a built-in constituency of sellers or buyers, they sometimes have a problem attracting enough buyers and sellers to attain financial viability. Therefore, to increase their financial viability, these exchanges try to team up with partners, such as large sellers or buyers, financial institutions that provide payment schemes (as ChemConnect did with Citigroup), and logistics companies that fulfill orders. The goal of such partnerships and

CASE 6.1

EC Application

WORLDWIDE RETAIL EXCHANGE

In March 2000, 17 international retailers founded the WorldWide Retail Exchange (WWRE) to enable participating retailers and manufacturers to simplify, rationalize, and automate supply chain processes, thereby eliminating inefficiencies in the supply chain. Today, the WWRE is the premier Internet-based business-to-business (B2B) exchange in the retail e-marketplace. Utilizing the most sophisticated Internet technology available, the WWRE enables retailers and manufacturers in the food, general merchandise, textile/home, and drugstore sectors to substantially reduce costs across product development, e-procurement, and supply chain processes. Membership in 2005 consists of 64 retailers from around the world. The Exchange is used by more than 100,000 suppliers, partners, and distributors worldwide.

The Exchange operates as an open, independently managed company that generates benefits for its members (retailers and manufacturers), and ultimately the consumer. The WWRE is run as a private company with no plans of going public. Rather, the WWRE concentrates on bringing value to its members and customers.

Founding Principles

The following six principles guide the WWRE's development and growth: openness, commitment to utilizing the best available technology, focus on improving efficiency and lowering costs for the retail industry, operation as a neutral company, equivalent fee structures for all participants, and confidentiality of transaction information.

Value Proposition

Members realize value through seven key ways:

- Low-cost product offerings that are robust, scaleable, integrated, and fully supported
- Shared technology investments and outsourced assets
- Ability to access a global membership community and network with other retailers/manufacturers
- Value-added services from a trusted source, at competitive costs
- Participation in collaborative activities
- Complex transactions and interactions made easy through automation
- Standard setting benefits for all B2B activities

The Exchange includes members such as J. C. Penney, Target, BestBuy, Marks and Spenser, Tesco, and Lotte. It became profitable in 2004 (press release December 15, 2004). In 2005, the exchange merged with GNX (press release February 26, 2005). GNX is described later in this chapter.

An example of one of WWRE's current projects is its Global Item Synchronization. Inaccurate product and item information costs the consumer goods industry more than $40 billion each year. WWRE developed a solution that enables retailers and suppliers to accurately maintain item information using industry standards and achieve a single point of entry into the Global Data Synchronization Network. The project is supported by webMethods Corporation, which provides the necessary integration (*webMethods.com* 2005).

Sources: Compiled from *WWRE.com* (accessed 2005) and *webMethods.com* (accessed 2005).

Questions

1. Enter *WWRE.com* and find information about services offered, including auctions and negotiations. Write a report.
2. Enter the FAQs and identify the benefits to retailers and to suppliers. Write a summary.
3. Enter *webMethods.com* and find information about the item synchronization project. Summarize the benefits to retailers and to suppliers.

alliances is to cut costs, save cash, and possibly increase liquidity. **Market liquidity** is the degree to which something can be bought or sold in a marketplace without affecting its price (e.g., without having to discount the price). To achieve market liquidity, there must be a sufficient number of participants in a marketplace as well as a sufficient volume of transactions (see Section 6.7).

market liquidity
The degree to which something can be bought or sold in a marketplace without affecting its price. It is measured by the number of buyers and sellers in the market and the transaction volume.

However, not all partnerships bring the desired results. In a partnership that did not work, Chemdex, a pioneering exchange that closed in late 2000, allied itself with VWR Scientific Products, a large brick-and-mortar intermediary. In the case of Chemdex, its liquidity was not large enough, despite the alliance.

Third-party exchanges are electronic intermediaries. In contrast with a portal, such as Alibaba.com, the intermediary not only presents catalogs (which the portal does), but also tries to *match* buyers and sellers and encourage them to make transactions by providing electronic trading floors and rooms (which portals, in general, do not). Let's see how this is done by looking at two models of third-party exchanges: supplier aggregation and buyer aggregation.

THE SUPPLIER AGGREGATION MODEL

In the *supplier aggregation model*, virtual distributors standardize, index, and aggregate suppliers' catalogs or content and make this content available to buyers in a centralized location.

An example is Commerce One's catalog of MRO suppliers at commerceone.com. As shown in Exhibit 6.6, a market aggregation, such as Commerce One, aggregates suppliers' catalogs and presents them to potential buyers. (This model is similar to the sell-side e-marketplace described in Chapter 5, but with *many* sellers. But, supplier aggregation is more difficult to manage.)

Notice that Exhibit 6.6 shows two types of buyers: large and small (SMEs). Large buyers need software to support the purchase-approval process (e.g., workflow software, see Chapter 7), budgeting, and the tracking of purchases across the buying organization. This requires system integration with existing company regulations, contracts, pricing, and so forth. Such integration may be provided by an ERP architecture. As you may recall from Chapter 5, Bigboxx.com provided such a service to its large buyers using SAP software (see EC Application Case 5.1, on page 202). For more on ERP integration, see Sandoe et al. (2003) and Online Tutorial T2. For smaller buyers, hosted workflow software and other applications are available from ASPs.

The major problems encountered in the supplier aggregation model are in recruiting suppliers and introducing the system to buyers. Solving these problems requires a strategic plan (see Cunningham 2000).

THE BUYER AGGREGATION MODEL

In the *buyer aggregation model*, buyers' RFQs are aggregated and then linked to a pool of suppliers that are automatically notified of the RFQs. The suppliers can then make bids. (This is similar to the buy-side e-marketplace described in Chapter 5, but with several buyers.) The buyers (usually small businesses) can benefit from volume discounts, especially if they use a group-purchasing approach. The sellers benefit from the new source of pooled buyers. Exhibit 6.7 shows the buyer aggregation model.

SUITABILITY OF THIRD-PARTY EXCHANGES

The aggregation models work best with MROs and services that are well defined, that have stable prices, and where the supplier or buyer base is fragmented. Buyers save on search and transaction costs and are exposed to more sellers. Sellers benefit from lower transaction costs as well as from an increase in their customer base.

As in other types of e-marketplaces, the most important key to the success of any third-party exchange is the critical mass of buyers and sellers. Fram (2002) believes that third-party exchanges, if properly planned and built, will be one of the prominent EC pillars of the future. In 2004, third-party exchanges were still struggling, but on the whole performing better.

EXHIBIT 6.6 **Supplier Aggregation Model**

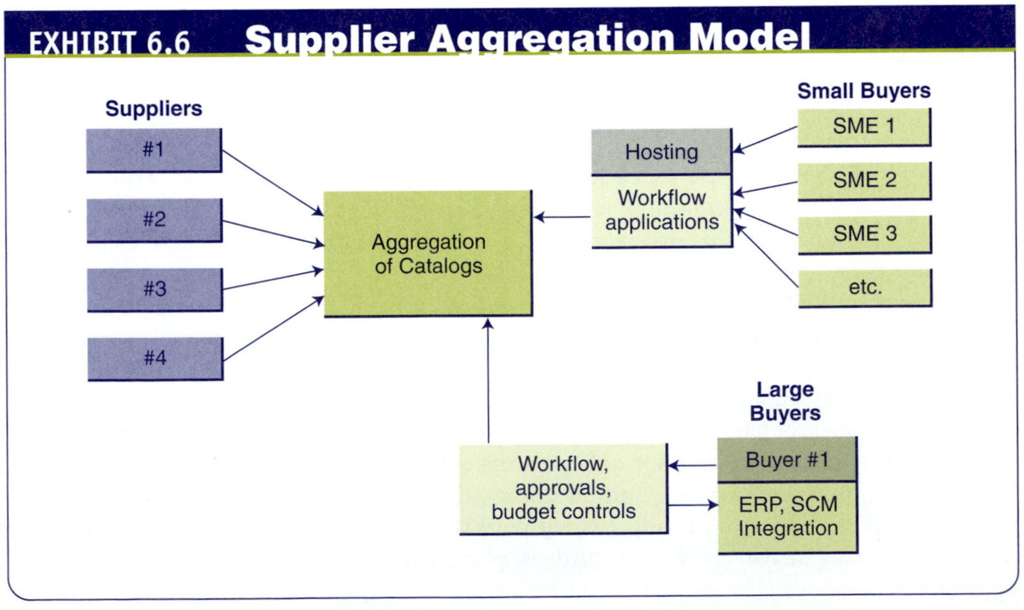

EXHIBIT 6.7 **Buyer Aggregation Model**

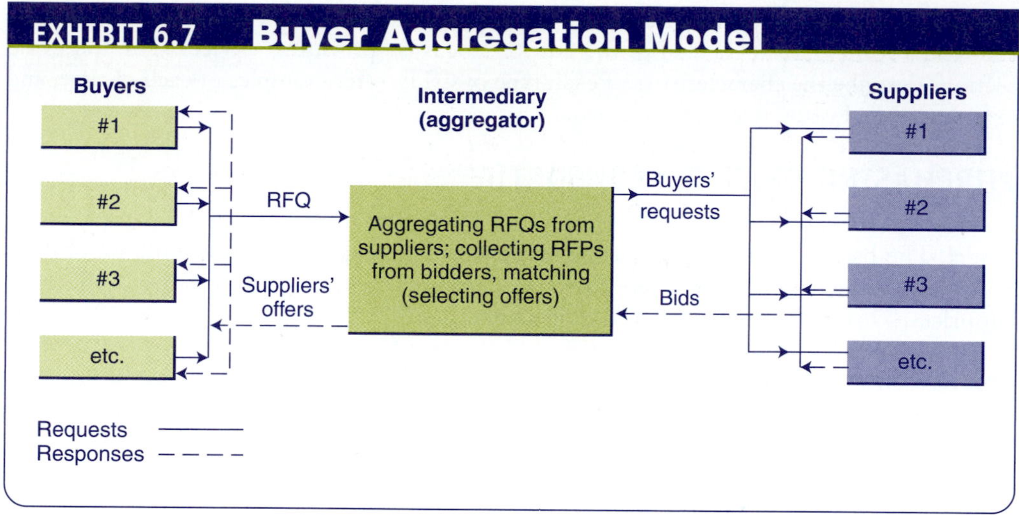

Section 6.3 REVIEW QUESTIONS

1. What is a third-party exchange?
2. Define liquidity.
3. Describe the supplier aggregation exchange.
4. Describe the buyer aggregation exchange.
5. List the market characteristics that are most suitable for third-party exchanges.

6.4 CONSORTIUM TRADING EXCHANGES

A subset of third-party exchanges is a **consortium trading exchange (CTE)**, an exchange formed and operated by a group of major companies. The major declared goal of CTEs (also called *consortia*) is to provide industrywide transaction services that support buying and selling. These services include links to the participants' back-end processing systems as well as collaborative planning and design services.

consortium trading exchange (CTE)
An exchange formed and operated by a group of major companies to provide industrywide transaction services.

Markets operate in three basic types of environments, shown in the following list. The type of environment indicates which third-party exchange is most appropriate.

1. **Fragmented markets.** These markets have large numbers of both buyers and sellers. Examples include the life sciences and food industries. When a large percentage of the market is fragmented, third-party managed exchanges are most appropriate.
2. **Seller-concentrated markets.** In this type of market, several large companies sell to a very large number of buyers. Examples are the plastics and transportation industries. In this type of market, consortia may be most appropriate.
3. **Buyer-concentrated markets.** In this type of market, several large companies do most of the buying from a large number of suppliers. Examples are the automotive, airline, and electronics industries. Here, again, consortia may be most appropriate.

According to Karpinski (2001), CTEs fared much better than independent third-party exchanges during the dot-com shakeout that took place in 2000–2002. Yet, of the hundreds of CTEs that existed all over the world in 2000, by 2002 many had folded or were inactive. By 2004, CTEs had achieved stability and some new exchanges arrived on the business scene.

There are four types of CTEs, classified by two main criteria: (1) whether they focus on buying or selling and (2) whether they are vertical or horizontal. The four types of consortia are:

1. Purchasing oriented, vertical
2. Purchasing oriented, horizontal
3. Selling oriented, vertical
4. Selling oriented, horizontal

In addition to these categories, some CTEs, such as GTN's Ocean Portal, described in the Real-World Case at the end of the chapter, focus on providing services. The following sections describe the characteristics of each type of CTE, offer examples of each of type, and examine several issues related to consortia.

PURCHASING-ORIENTED CONSORTIA

Purchasing-oriented (procurement) consortia are by far the most popular B2B consortium model. The basic idea is that a group of companies join together to streamline purchasing processes. Some claim that another goal of procurement consortia is to pressure suppliers to cut prices. This model may be vertical or horizontal.

Vertical Purchasing-Oriented CTEs

Most CTEs are *vertical*, meaning that all the players are in the same industry. One example is Covisint, discussed in EC Application Case 6.2 (also see Baker and Baker 2000).

Although the declared objective of vertical procurement CTEs is to support buying *and* selling, it is obvious that in a market owned and operated by large buyers the orientation is toward purchasing. Many of the consortia listed in Exhibit 6.8 (page 250) are vertical exchanges (e.g., aerospace, airlines, hospitality, mining, retailers). Each exchange may have thousands of participating suppliers.

Horizontal Purchasing-Oriented CTEs

In a *horizontal* purchasing-oriented CTE, the owner–operators are large companies from different industries that unite for the purpose of improving the supply chain of MROs used by most industries. An example of this kind of CTE is CorProcure in Australia (corprocure.com.au). Fourteen of the largest companies in Australia (Qantas, Telstra Communications, the Post Office, ANZ Banking Group, Coles Myer, Coca-Cola, etc.) created the Corprocure exchange in 2001 to buy MROs.

SELLING-ORIENTED CONSORTIA

Selling-oriented consortia are less common than buying-oriented ones. Most selling-oriented consortia are vertical. Participating sellers have thousands of potential buyers within a particular industry. Here are some examples of selling-oriented consortia:

- Cargill Foods, a producer and marketer of basic food ingredients, has a wide range of buyers and has major ownership in a food exchange (cargillfoods.com).
- The major retailers are served by gnx.com, which helps retailers in both selling and buying.
- Several international airline consortia act like large travel agencies, selling tickets or travel packages to business buyers (e.g., staralliance.com) and both to businesses and individuals (orbitz.com).
- Several consortia act as suppliers and distributors of health-care products (e.g., ghx.com).
- TRPlastics.com (trplastics.com) is a consortia that serves the plastics industry.

OTHER ISSUES FOR CONSORTIA

Consortia face a variety of other issues, including legal challenges. This section presents these challenges and also looks at the critical success factors for consortia-based exchanges and the issue of combining consortia and third-party exchanges.

Legal Challenges for B2B Consortia

B2B exchanges and other e-marketplaces typically introduce some level of collaboration among both competitors and business partners. In both cases, antitrust and other competition laws must be considered. The concept of consortia itself may lead to antitrust scrutiny by governments, especially for industries in which either a few firms produce most or all of the output (oligopolies or duopolies) or in which there are only a few buyers (monopsonies). This could happen in many countries, especially in European countries, the United States, Australia, Japan, South Korea, Hong Kong, and Canada.

CASE 6.2

EC Application

COVISINT: THE E-MARKET OF THE AUTOMOTIVE INDUSTRY

There are only several automakers, but they buy parts, materials, and supplies from thousands of suppliers, who frequently buy parts and materials from thousands of subsuppliers. At times, the procurement process is slow, costly, and ineffective.

On February 25, 2000, General Motors Corporation, Ford Motor Company, and DaimlerChrysler launched a B2B integrated buy-side marketplace called Covisint. The goal was to eliminate redundancies from suppliers through integration and collaboration, with promises of lower costs, easier business practices, and marked increases in efficiencies for the entire industry.

The name Covisint (pronounced KO-vis-int) is a combination of the primary concepts of why the exchange was formed: The letters "Co" represent *connectivity, collaboration*, and *communication;* "vis" represents the *visibility* that the Internet provides and the *vision* of the future of supply chain management; and "int" represents the *integrated* solutions the venture offers as well as the *international* scope of the exchange.

The purpose of the marketplace's connectivity is to integrate buyers and sellers into a single network. Visibility would provide real-time information presented in a way that speeds decision making and enables communication through every level of a company's supply chain, anywhere in the world. By using the Web, a manufacturer's production schedule and any subsequent changes can be sent simultaneously and instantly throughout its entire supply chain. The result is less need for costly inventory at all levels of the supply chain and an increased ability to respond quickly to market changes.

To better understand the Covisint concept, examine the attached exhibit. The left side shows an automaker's traditional supply chain. Typically, an automaker would buy parts from one supplier, who in turn would buy from its suppliers (subsuppliers), who would then buy from other suppliers (sub-sub-suppliers). In this traditional linear supply chain, the automaker communicates only with its top-tier (tier 1) suppliers.

Imagine that the auto manufacturer has hundreds of similar supply chains, one for each supplier, and that many of the suppliers, in all tiers, produce for several manufacturers. The flow of information (as shown by the connecting lines in the drawing) will be very complex. This complexity introduces inefficiencies in communication as well as difficulties for the suppliers in planning their production schedules to meet demand, resulting in supply chain problems.

The Covisint process greatly changed supply chain communication in the automobile industry. Rather than being at the top point of a pyramid, as in the industry's traditional supply chain, the auto manufacturers now are at the center of a spoke-and-wheel arrangement. By 2004, there were 19 automakers in the Covisint marketplace. Covisint has created a trading hub whereby any one of the automakers and the various suppliers and subsuppliers can communicate directly with anyone else. Instead of an array of unorganized communication lines, it is all organized in one place.

One of the major objectives of the exchange is to facilitate product design. Covisint offers its customers best-of-breed functionality; customers take the best aspects from multiple technical providers. The ability to integrate providers across the supply chain creates a unique environment for collaborative design and development (collaborative commerce), enables e-procurement, and provides a broad marketplace of buyers and suppliers. It makes accessible a wealth of supply chain expertise and experience, ranging from procurement to product development. Covisint's potential membership is about 30,000 suppliers.

(*continued*)

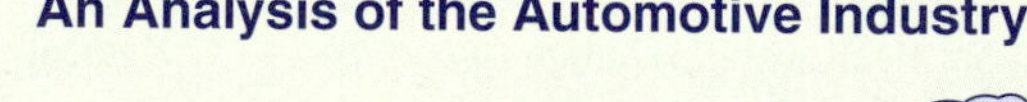

An Analysis of the Automotive Industry

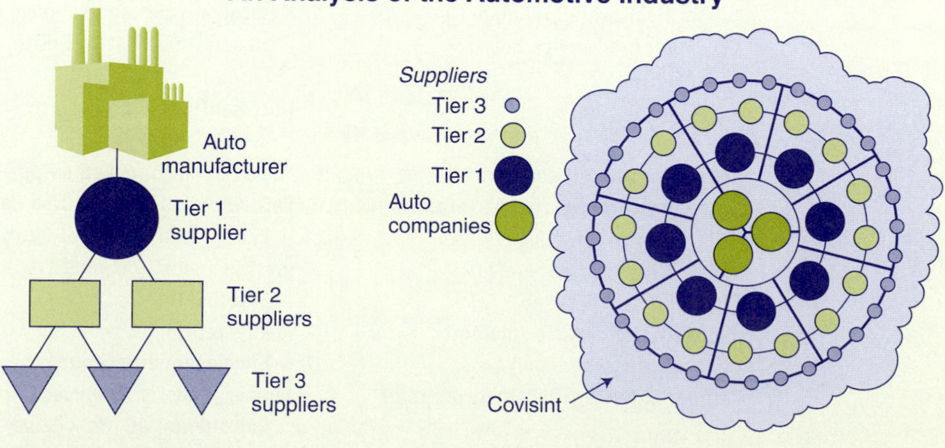

a. Before Covisint: a linear supply chain

b. Covisint's hub concept

CASE 6.2 (continued)

Because of its large size, the exchange is developing slowly. Nevertheless, Cleary (2001) reports that on May 8, 2001, DaimlerChrysler used Covisint to successfully conduct a $3-billion reverse auction for auto parts that lasted four days. By early 2003, a new CEO was trying to accelerate the progress of Covisint. In July 2002, the founders of Covisint ceased to provide funding. They remain shareholders, but Covisint is now run by an independent board and an advisory council made up of 21 of the largest suppliers and OEMs (Original Equipment Manufacturers) to the automotive industry. In summer 2004, Covisint was acquired by Compuware Corp. By September 2004, the exchange was still struggling financially, even though it provides services to 20,000 companies in 96 countries.

Sources: Compiled from *covisint.com* (accessed October 2004), Covisint press releases (2001a and 2001b), and Cleary (2001).

Questions

1. Describe the concepts upon which Covisint is structured.
2. Describe how Covisint changed the supply chain in the automobile industry.
3. Investigate the current ownership and management of Covisint.

EXHIBIT 6.8 Representative Vertical Consortia

Consortium (CTE)	Industry Participants
Exostar (*exostar.com*)	Aerospace industry (Boeing, Lockheed Martin)
E-Markets (*e-markets.com*)	Agricultural commodities (Dow AgriSciences, Croplan Genetics)
Star Alliance (*staralliance.com*)	Airlines industry (Air Canada, Lufthansa)
Covisint (*covisint.com*)	Automotive industry (GM, Ford, DaimlerChrysler)
corProcure (*corprocure.com*)	MRO procurement
GlobalNetXchange (*gnx.com*)	Packaged consumer products (Sears, Roebuck Co.; Karstadt Quelle; IBM Business Consulting)
Trade-Ranger (*trade-ranger.com*)	Energy industry (Royal/Dutch Shell, BP Amoco, Conoco)
Forest Express (*forestexpress.com*)	Paper and forest products (International Paper, Georgia-Pacific)
Transora (data collection) (*transora.com*)	Major consumer packaged goods manufacturers (57 members)
E2Open (*e2open.com*)	Personal computer manufacturers (Ariba, Hitachi, IBM, Netegrity, Oracle)
Amtrex Global Logistics (*amtrex.com*)	Global transport exchange (Bayer AG, Toshiba America, Newport Corp.)
World Wide Retail Exchange (*worldwideretailexchange.org*)	Major global retailers (Best Buy, Campbell's, J.C. Penney's)
Global Healthcare Exchange (*ghx.com*)	Medical services and supplies (AmeriNet, Neoforma)
ElectronicFoodservice Network (*efsnetwork.com*)	Food service industry (BiRite, McDonald's Company, Nestle)
Avendra (*avendra.com*)	Hospitality industry (Hyatt, Fairmont Hotels & Resorts, others)
Ocean Connect (*oceanconnect.com*)	Fuel trading for ocean shippers
Intercontinental Exchange (*intcx.com*)	Petroleum industry (British Petroleum, PG&E Energy Trading, Royal Bank of Canada)
PlasticsNet (*plasticsnet.com*)	Plastics industry (Grand Effect Plastics, Strategic Systems International)
Constellation Real Technologies (*constellationllc.com*)	Real estate industry (Equity Office Properties Trust, Simon Property Group)
Rubber Network (*rubbernetwork.com*)	Rubber industry (Goodyear Tire & Rubber, Continental AG, Yokohama)
Transplace (*transplace.com*)	Transportation (air and land) industry (J.B. Hunt, U.S. Xpress, Werner)

GE Silicones (gesilicones.com) is an exchange for industrial sealants. GE Toshiba Silicone initiated this exchange and started discussions with other leading industrial sealant makers, such as Dow Corning, Wacker Chemical, and Shin-Etsu Chemical, about joining the marketplace. The initial group of participants controls over 80 percent of the world market of industrial sealants. The potential exists for the participants to deal with some sensitive business issues, such as industry pricing policies, price levels, price changes, and price differentiations, in ways that may violate antitrust laws. Similarly, many fear that buyers' consortia will "squeeze" the small suppliers in an unfair manner. Antitrust issues and investigations may slow the creation of CTEs, especially global ones. For example, the Covisint venture required government approval in the United Kingdom, the United States, and Germany. The German antitrust investigation was very slow and delayed the project by several months.

Critical Success Factors for Consortia

The critical success factors for consortia, according to Goldman Sachs (2000), include the following.

Appropriate Business and Revenue Models. B2B exchanges exhibit a variety of business and revenue models. As discussed earlier in the chapter, revenue can come from *transaction fees* (platform fees, per unit fees), *auction fees* (advertisement fees and fees for services provided), *license revenue, market-maker fees*, and *subscription fees* (content and license fees). The strategy of which revenue model to use and how much to charge can make or break the exchange.

Size of the Industry. The larger the industry, the larger the addressable market, which in turn means a greater volume of transactions on the site. This leads to greater potential cost savings to the exchange participants and ultimately more profitability for the exchange itself. The danger is that industry size may spawn several competing consortia, which has happened in the banking, mining, and airline industries.

Ability to Drive User Adoption. Consortia must have the ability to provide quick liquidity to an exchange. The more oligopolistic the consortium is (the more it is controlled by a few players), the more accelerated the adoption can be.

Elasticity. A critical factor for any exchange is the degree of elasticity the exchange fosters. **Elasticity** is a measure of the incremental spending by buyers as a result of the savings generated. The consortium has the potential to reduce prices of individual products, thus enabling and encouraging consortium members to buy more.

elasticity
The measure of the incremental spending by buyers as a result of the savings generated.

Standardization of Commodity-Like Products. The breadth of the suppliers brought in to transact with the buyers will help standardize near-commodity products due to content management and product-attribute description needs of online marketplaces. The more commodity-like the products are, the greater the market competition, and the lower the prices.

Management of Intensive Information Flow. A consortium has the ability to be a repository for the huge amounts of data that flow through supply chains in a given industry. It can also enable information-intensive collaboration between participants, including product collaboration, planning, scheduling, and forecasting. The more information the exchange has, the more added value the exchange provides the participants, and the more buyers will come to the exchange.

Smoothing of Supply Chain Inefficiencies. It is important for the consortium-led exchange to help smooth inefficiencies in the supply chain, such as those in order fulfillment, logistics, and credit-related services.

Harmonized Shared Objectives. If the consortium cannot agree on shared objectives, the individual interests will be greater than the collective interests, and the exchange may fold.

Section 6.10 discusses critical success factors for exchanges in general, many of which also apply to consortia.

Combining Consortia and Third-Party Exchanges

Goldman Sachs (2000) suggested merging large consortia with a third-party owner (usually a dot-com) into what they call *dot-consortia*. Such a combination may bring about the advantages of ownership and minimize third-party limitations, such as low liquidity. Indeed, in a number of exchanges, several industry leaders are shareholders, but the exchange is managed by a third party, as with Covisint.

According to Coia (2002a), consortia arrangements are common in the transportation industry. There, groups of shippers within an industry use a public exchange as a "semiprivate exchange" to leverage the amount of freight that they ship, allowing greater opportunities for competitive rates.

Section 6.4 ▶ REVIEW QUESTIONS

1. Define CTEs.
2. Describe purchasing-oriented consortia and selling-oriented consortia.
3. Describe potential legal issues for consortia.
4. List the major critical success factors of consortia.

6.5 DYNAMIC TRADING: MATCHING AND AUCTIONS

dynamic trading
Exchange trading that occurs in situations when prices are being determined by supply and demand (e.g., in auctions).

Dynamic pricing, the rapid change in prices based on supply and demand, was discussed earlier. One of the major features of exchanges is dynamic trading. **Dynamic trading** is exchange trading that occurs in situations in which prices are determined by supply and demand, therefore changing continuously. Two major mechanisms are used in dynamic trading in exchanges: matching and auctions.

MATCHING

An example of *matching* supply and demand is the stock market. When buyers place their bids and sellers list their asking prices, the market makers conduct the matching, sometimes by buying or selling stocks from their own accounts. The matching process may be more complex than buying and selling in regular auctions (discussed next) due to the need to match both prices and quantities. In other cases, quantity, delivery times, and locations also need to be matched. Today, matching in stock exchanges is fully computerized. Most commodity exchanges (e.g., wheat, oil, silver) are B2B, as are some financial markets, and they are fully computerized.

AUCTIONS

As seen in the ChemConnect case, exchanges offer members the ability to conduct auctions or reverse auctions in *private trading rooms*. When this takes place, the one-to-many model is activated, as described in Chapter 5, with the hosting done by the exchange. The advantage of running an auction in an exchange is the ability to attract many buyers to a forward auction and many suppliers to a reverse auction. For SMEs that wish to buy or sell via auctions, finding auction participants can be a major problem. By going to an exchange, this problem may be solved.

Auctions can be arranged in several ways. Two options are as follows:

- An exchange offers auction services as one of its many activities, as ChemConnect does. Most vertical exchanges offer this option.
- An exchange is fully dedicated to auctions. Examples of this auctions-only arrangement are eBay for Businesses, Ariba's Dynamic Trading, FirstAuction.com, and QXL.com.

An exchange also can conduct many-to-many public auctions. These auctions may be vertical or horizontal and can run on the Internet or over private lines. Examples of auctions conducted over private lines are Aucnet in Japan, through which used cars are sold to dealers, and TFA, the Dutch flower market auction, described in Online File W6.1.

Exhibit 6.9 summarizes the major B2B, many-to-many models discussed thus far in the chapter.

Section 6.5 ▶ REVIEW QUESTIONS

1. Explain how matches are made in exchanges.
2. Explain how private and public auctions are conducted in public exchanges.
3. Compare fully dedicated and partially dedicated auction exchanges.

EXHIBIT 6.9 Comparing the Major B2B Many-to-Many Models

Name	Major Characteristics	Types
B2B catalog-based exchanges	• A place for selling and buying • Fixed prices (updated as needed)	• Vertical, horizontal • Shopping directory, usually with hyperlinks (only) • Shopping carts with services (payment, etc.)
B2B portals	• Community services • Communication tools • Classified ads • Employment markets • May sell, buy • Fixed prices • May do auctions	• Vertical (vortals), horizontal • Shopping directory, usually with hyperlinks
B2B dynamic exchanges	• Matches buyer/seller orders at dynamic prices, auctions • Provides trading-related information and services (payment, logistics) • Highly regulated • May provide general information, news, etc. • May provide for negotiations	• Vertical, horizontal • Forward auctions • Reverse auctions • Bid/ask exchanges

6.6 BUILDING AND INTEGRATING E-MARKETPLACES AND EXCHANGES

Building large marketplaces, especially those that accommodate many sellers, buyers, and services, can be very complex. Also, consideration of how companies will be connected to the exchanges, as well as how the exchanges will be tied together, is necessary.

BUILDING E-MARKETPLACES

Building e-marketplaces and exchanges is a complex process. It is usually performed by a major B2B software company, such as Commerce One, Ariba, Oracle, or IBM. In large exchanges, a management consulting company such as PriceWaterhouseCoopers, Gartner Group, or McKinsey usually participates. Also, technology companies such as IBM, Oracle, EDS, i2, Intel, Microsoft, and SAP have major roles in building large exchanges. Most exchanges are built jointly by several vendors.

Most large B2B software vendors have specially designed e-marketplace packages. For example, IBM, Oracle, Microsoft, and Commerce One each has a set of e-marketplace solutions. A typical process for building a vertical e-marketplace is shown in Online Exhibit W6.2.

THE INTEGRATION ISSUE

So far we have cited several value-added services that exchanges may offer, such as payments, matching of buyers and sellers, and order fulfillment. These services need to interact with each other. In exchanges, the integration of such services becomes very important. Seamless integration is needed between the third-party exchange and the participants' front- and back-office systems. Communication among trading partners is necessary. Also, in private exchanges, one needs to integrate the seller's computing system with that of the customers (in a sell-side case) or integrate the buyer's system with that of the suppliers (in a buy-side case). This takes place through interfacing with applications and protocols. In addition, integration across multiple, frequently incompatible exchanges—each with its own XML scheme—is required. TIBCO (tibco.com) is the major infrastructure service provider for vertical exchanges. Some exchanges take care of the connectivity, others do not. For example,

ChemConnect provides a central connectivity hub where members' communications needs are met no matter what message formats they use. This eliminates the need to maintain multiple connections with supply chain partners.

The four most common elements of B2B integration solutions, which are discussed in the following sections, are external communications, process and information coordination, Web Services, and system and information management.

External Communications

External communications require the following:

- **Web/client access.** Businesses can use a Web browser, such as Internet Explorer, to interact with Web server applications hosted by other businesses.
- **Data exchange.** Information is extracted from an application, converted into a neutral data format, and sent to other businesses. Examples of data exchange include EDI over VANs and Internet-based EDI.
- **Direct application integration.** Application integration often requires middleware technologies, such as distributed object technologies, message queuing, and publish/subscribe brokers, to coordinate information exchange between applications (see ibm.com and peregrine.com).
- **Shared procedures.** Businesses can agree to use the same procedures for certain processes. For example, a supplier and a buyer may agree to use the same order-management process.

Process and Information Coordination in Integration

Process and information coordination involves the coordination of *external communications* and *internal information systems*. This coordination includes external processes, internal processes, data transformation, and exception handling. For example, an online sales transaction must be processed directly to an internal accounting system.

Use of Web Services in Integration

Web Services essentially enable different Web-based systems to communicate with each other using Internet-based protocols such as XML (see Online Chapter 18 and Online Appendix B), SOAP (Simple Object Access Protocol), and UDDI (Universal Description Discovery and Integration). WSDL (Web Services Description Language) makes it expedient to use Web Services to connect different systems. For example, many companies still use legacy systems that are expensive to maintain and provide poor customer service. Also, large companies such as AT&T may have a mishmash of networks patched together over the years, some of which use proprietary languages and custom codes. Every time a change is made in one application, a Herculean effort is required to rewrite code in every connected application. It is very difficult to work under these kinds of conditions in B2B in general and in exchanges in particular.

By using Web Services, the time it takes to connect complex systems can be reduced by about 75 percent. Also, development costs can be reduced by 10 percent (Ferris and Farrel 2003).

System and Information Management in Integration

System and information management involves the management of software, hardware, and several information components, including partner-profile information, data and process definitions, communications and security settings, and users' information. Furthermore, because hardware and software change rapidly (i.e., upgrades or releases of new versions), the management of these changes is an essential element of B2B integration.

Section 6.6 ▶ REVIEW QUESTIONS

1. List the steps in building a vertical exchange.
2. Describe the integration issues for third-party exchanges.

6.7 SUPPORT SERVICES FOR E-MARKETPLACES AND PRM

In order to succeed in B2B, and particularly in exchanges, it is necessary to have support services. The Delphi Group (2001; delphigroup.com) suggests that B2B services be organized into six major categories: e-infrastructure, e-processes, e-markets, e-content, e-communities, and e-services. E-processes (e.g., e-payments, order fulfillment, and content provision) will be addressed in their generic form (B2B, B2C, etc.) in Chapters 12, 13, and 16. The topic of e-infrastructure is presented in Online Chapter 18 and in the Online Technical Appendices. E-services are described in Chapter 13 for B2C; this section examines a few other support services that are related directly to B2B.

DIRECTORY SERVICES AND SEARCH ENGINES

The B2B landscape is huge, with hundreds of thousands of companies online. Directory services can help buyers and sellers manage the task of finding potential partners. Some popular directories are listed and described in Exhibit 6.10. Note that the last three entries in the exhibit are specialized search engines, which can be used to find information about B2B. Some of these are embedded in the directories.

PARTNER AND SUPPLIER RELATIONSHIP MANAGEMENT

Successful e-businesses carefully manage partners, prospects, and customers across the entire value chain, most often in a 24/7 environment. Therefore, one should examine the role of e-service solutions and technology, such as call centers and collaboration tools, in creating an integrated online environment for engaging e-business customers and partners. The use of such solutions and technology appears under two names: CRM and PRM.

In Chapter 13, we will introduce the concept of CRM in the B2C environment. Here our interest is with the situation in which the customer is a business, shifting offerings to business partners, such as suppliers. Many of the customer service features of B2C also are used in B2B. For example, it may be beneficial to provide corporate customers with a chat room and a discussion board. A Web-based call center also may be useful for companies with many partners.

Corporate customers may require additional services. For example, customers need to have access to the supplier's inventory status report so they know what items a supplier can deliver quickly. Customers also may want to see their historical purchasing records, and they may need private showrooms and trade rooms. Large numbers of vendors are available for designing and building appropriate B2B CRM solutions. The strategy of providing such comprehensive, quality e-service for business partners is sometimes called **partner relationship management (PRM)**.

partner relationship management (PRM)
Business strategy that focuses on providing comprehensive quality service to business partners.

In the context of PRM, customers are only one category of business partners. Suppliers, partners in joint ventures, service providers, and others also are part of the B2B community in an exchange or company-centric B2B initiative. PRM is particularly important to companies that conduct outsourcing (Hagel 2004; Ross and Westerman 2004). Companies with many suppliers, such as the automobile companies, may create special programs for them. Such programs are called *supplier relationship management (SRM).*

Supplier Relationship Management

supplier relationship management (SRM)
A comprehensive approach to managing an enterprise's interactions with the organizations that supply the goods and services it uses.

One of the major categories of PRM is **supplier relationship management (SRM)**, in which the partners are the suppliers. For many companies (e.g., retailers and manufacturers), the ability to work properly with suppliers is a major critical success factor. PeopleSoft, Inc. (peoplesoft.com), developed a model for managing relationships with suppliers in real time.

PeopleSoft's SRM Model. PeopleSoft's SRM model (see Schecterle 2003) is generic and could be considered by any large company. It includes 12 steps, illustrated in Exhibit 6.11. The details of the steps are shown in Online Exhibit W6.3. The core idea of this model is that an e-supply chain is based on integration and collaboration. The supply chain processes are connected, decisions are made collectively, performance metrics are based on common understanding, information flows in real time (whenever possible), and the only thing a new partner needs in order to join the SRM system is a Web browser.

EXHIBIT 6.10 B2B Directory Services and Search Engines

Directory	Description
b2business.net	A major resource for B2B professionals that provides listings of business resources in about 30 functional areas, company research resources (e.g., credit checks, customs research, financial reviews), and information on start-ups.
b2btoday.com	Contains listings of B2B services organized by type of service (e.g., Web site creation, B2B marketing, and B2B software) and product category (e.g., automotive, books).
communityb2b.com	Offers many B2B community services, such as news, a library, events calendar, job market, and resource directory.
a2zofb2b.com	Company directory organized in alphabetical order or industry order. Specifies the type and nature of the company, the venture capital (VC) sponsor, and the stock market ticker (if it is an IPO).
i-stores.co.uk	A UK-based directory of online stores; provides validation of secure Web sites.
dmoz.org/business	A large business directory organized by location and by product or service. Also provides listings by industry and subindustry (according to SIC code).
thomasnet.com	Directory of more than 150,000 manufacturers of industrial products and services.
jupiterdirect.com	A comprehensive B2B guide for marketers that provides directories, news, auctions, and much more.
b2b.yahoo.com	Provides business directories that cover over 250,000 companies (as of 2003).
line56.com/directory	Provides information about B2B software, services, and marketplaces.
bocat.com	Bocat provides a B2B portal for marketplaces, directories, news, and resources supported by powerful search engines.
business.com	A comprehensive directory of B2B markets and services.
Search Engines	
moreover.com	In addition to locating information, also aggregates B2B (and other business) news.
google.com	In addition to its search tools, offers a directory of components for B2B and B2C Web sites (e.g., currency exchange calculators, server performance monitors, etc.).
Ientry.com	Provides B2B search engines, targeted "niche engines," and several industry-focused newsletters. Operates a network of Web sites and e-mail newsletters that reaches over 2,000,000 unique opt-in subscribers.

Implementing PRM and SRM is different from implementing CRM with individual customers. For example, behavioral and psychological aspects of the relationships are less important in B2B than in CRM. However, trust, commitment, quality of services, and continuity are more important in B2B. For details, see Pavlou and Ratnasingam (2003).

E-COMMUNITIES AND PRM

B2B applications involve many participants: buyers and sellers, service providers, industry associations, and others. Thus, in many cases, the B2B implementation creates a *community*. In such cases, the B2B market maker needs to provide community services such as chat rooms, bulletin boards, and possibly personalized Web pages. A detailed list of such services is provided in Online Chapter 18.

According to the Delphi Group (2000), e-communities are connecting personnel, partners, customers, and any combination of the three. E-communities offer a powerful resource

EXHIBIT 6.11 SRM from PeopleSoft

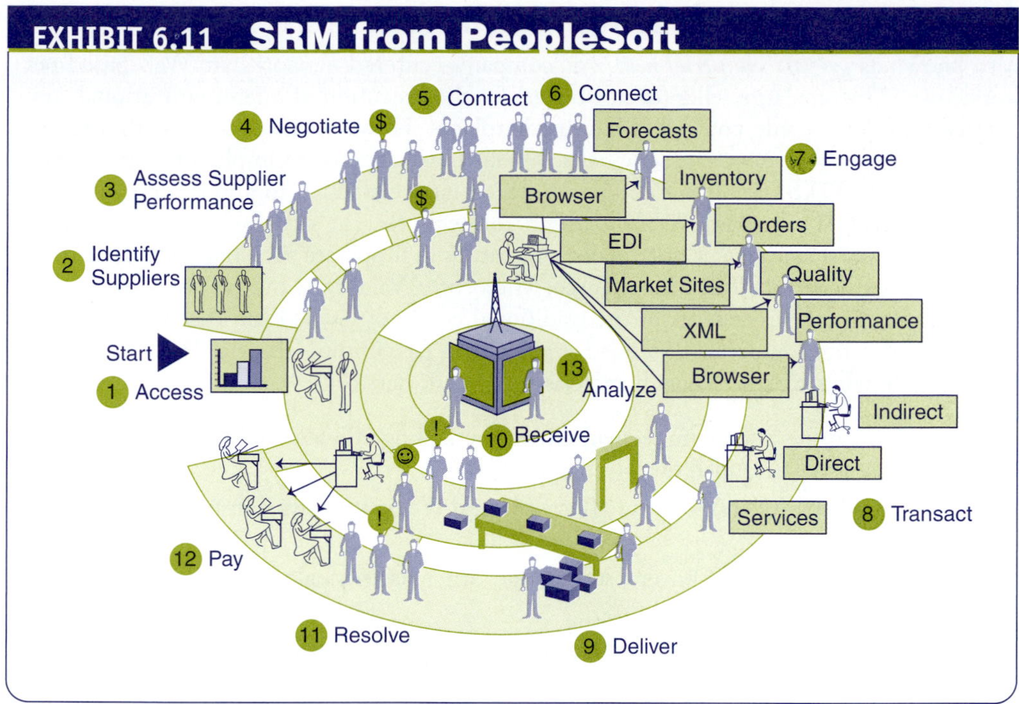

Source: Based on B. Schecterle, "Management and Extending Supplier Relationships," *People Talk*, April–June 2003. XPLANATIONS® by XPLANE®, ©2005 XPLANE.com. Courtesy of Oracle. Used with permission.

for e-businesses to leverage online discussions and interaction in order to maximize innovation and responsiveness. It is therefore beneficial to study the tools, methods, and best practices of building and managing e-communities. Although the technological support of B2B e-communities is basically the same as for any other online community (see Chapter 17), the nature of the community itself, and the information provided by the community, is different.

B2B e-communities are mostly communities of transactions, and as such, the major interest of the members is trading. Most of the communities are associated with vertical exchanges; therefore, their needs may be fairly specific. However, it is common to find generic services such as classified ads, job vacancies, announcements, industry news, and so on. Service providers are also available for the design of exchange portals and their community services.

Section 6.7 ▶ REVIEW QUESTIONS

1. What type of information is provided by B2B directory services and search engines?
2. How does PRM differ from SRM?
3. List five other services for B2B.
4. Describe e-communities in B2B.

6.8 B2B NETWORKS

To implement any B2B system, one needs to think about appropriate networks and their infrastructure. In Chapter 5, we mentioned the potential for the use of EDI between a company and its suppliers (Online Appendix W5.A); in this chapter, we describe the use of extranets (Appendix 6A). Consider the case of Covisint: It is not sufficient to have an electronic trading platform for the automotive industry and its suppliers, it also is necessary to have a secure network for buyers, sellers, and other participants to communicate, collaborate, and trade. Covisint operates on the auto industry extranet known as the Automotive Network Exchange (ANX), which provides all the necessary connecting devices for the participants (e.g., EDI, e-mail, CAD/CAM file transfer). This is an example of a private industry-wide network, or a *vertical network*. Two other types of networks (also referred to as *industrial networks*) exist: company centered and global. Networks can be made up of suppliers (Dyer and Hatch 2004), buyers, or both.

COMPANY-CENTERED (PRIVATE) NETWORKS

Also known as *private industrial networks*, company-centered networks are Web-based networks owned by one large seller (or one buyer) for the execution of interorganizational communications in buy-side and sell-side e-marketplaces. However, in contrast with a regular EDI, such a network extends its activities to all business partners. Examples of such networks are GE's TPN (GXS) (Online File W5.3), which later expanded to a global network, and Boeing's PART (Online File W5.1), which connects Boeing's customers to Boeing and Boeing to its parts suppliers. Other major companies that operate such networks are Procter and Gamble, Coca-Cola, Dell, IBM, Cisco, Microsoft, Wal-Mart, and Nokia. Most of these networks are direct descendents of the traditional company-owned (or leased) EDI. These networks cover the companies' extended supply chain (see Online Tutorial T2).

The following are the major characteristics of such networks:

- Provide the infrastructure for e-marketplaces, enabling efficient and effective buying and selling along the extended supply chain.
- Allow suppliers to communicate effectively and efficiently with subsuppliers along several tiers.
- Increase the visibility of buyers, sellers, and other partners along the supply chain and around the globe (see Dubie 2003).
- Operate on a large scale, from one company with its thousands of suppliers, to tens of thousands of firms globally.
- Foster collaboration and closer relationships among business partners.
- Enable industrywide resource planning (Chapter 7).
- Provide support services, especially financial ones (e.g., settlements), for the benefit of trading partners.
- Provide insurance, financial derivatives, and so on to reduce risks in certain markets.

INDUSTRYWIDE (VERTICAL) NETWORKS

Company-centered networks may be a waste of money because they are used by only one buyer (buyer's industrial network) or only by one seller (seller's industrial network), and they may not be open to all. In contrast, private industry networks are usually open to many sellers and buyers in the industry. As such, they support exchanges, especially CTEs.

TRANSINDUSTRY AND GLOBAL NETWORKS

Companies sometimes need to collaborate with companies in other industries or with companies in other countries. In such situations, they can use horizontal exchanges or networks that cover several industries. An example is Nistevo Network (nistevo.com), a collaborative logistics network. It manages the entire shipment life cycle, from load planning to invoice auditing to performance management (see the demo on the Web site). Over 4,000 participants, including major companies such as International Paper, General Mills, Land O' Lakes (see Chapter 7), and Coca-Cola, participate. Nistevo coordinates, for example, excess shipping capacity of members in order to improve utilization. The participants manage over 4 million shipments a year (in 2004), saving 5 to 25 percent of their logistics expenses.

A special network model that enables transindustry collaboration was proposed by the Keenan Report (2002). According to this model, business-to-exchange (B2X) hubs connect all Internet business services, e-merchant services, exchange infrastructures, buying and selling, member enterprises, and other B2X exchanges, as shown in Online Exhibit W6.4.

Networks of Exchanges (E2E)

With the increasing number of vertical and horizontal exchanges, some in different countries, it is logical to think about connecting them. Large corporations may work with several exchanges, and they would like these exchanges to be connected in a seamless fashion. Today, most exchanges have different log-on procedures, separate sets of rules for fulfilling orders,

EXHIBIT 6.12 How Several Exchanges Work in One Supply Chain

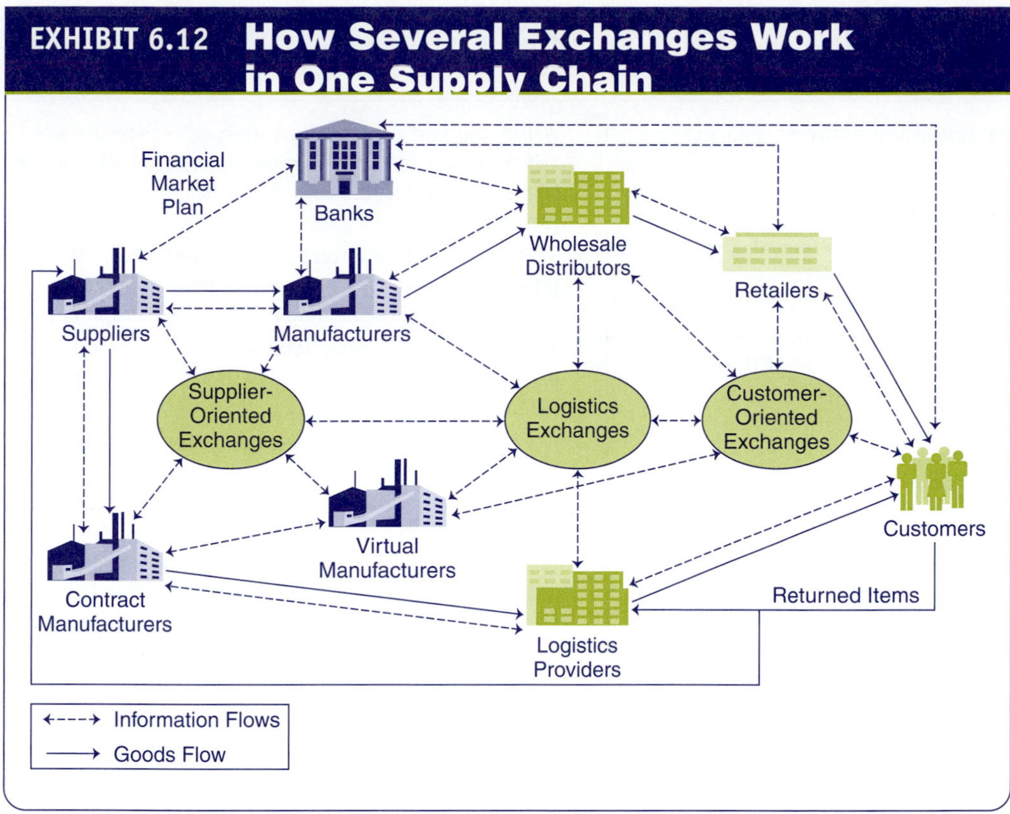

and different business models for charging for their services. Exchanges also can be connected in an industry's supply chain, as shown in Exhibit 6.12. Each exchange serves different participants, but some are members of two or more exchanges. Exchanges also may be connected via global networks.

Global Networks

Global networks serve multiple industries and countries. They provide international trade gateways. Notable vendors of such networks are GXS and Ariba (see Insights and Additions 6.1). Other vendors are Commerce One and its supplier network Perfect Commerce (perfect.com) and Sterling Commerce, which runs EDI networks for businesses.

Section 6.8 ▶ REVIEW QUESTIONS

1. Describe private B2B networks and list their characteristics.
2. Compare vertical and horizontal networks.
3. Describe the GXS network and its Trading Grid.
4. Describe Ariba's SN network.

6.9 B2B IMPLEMENTATION ISSUES

Large exchanges are supposed to bring together entire industry sectors, creating supply chain efficiencies and reduced costs for buyers and sellers alike. However, despite the fact that thousands of exchanges were created between January 1999 and December 2000, only a few hundred were active by the end of 2001, and less than half of these were conducting a high volume of transactions (AMR Research 2001). By 2003, signs of improvement appeared. Existing exchanges solidified, and a few new exchanges appeared. However, due to the worldwide economic slowdown, these exchanges were not doing so well. Let's look at some of the implementation issues that might explain why.

Insights and Additions 6.1 B2B Public Networks

Here are two examples of well-known networks: GXS and Ariba SN.

Global eXchange Services (GXS)

Global eXchange Services (GXS) is a global provider of business-to-business integration, synchronization, and collaboration solutions. The company operates a highly reliable, secure *global network services platform*, enabling more than 100,000 trading partners, including over half of the *Fortune* 500, to actively conduct business together in real time.

GXS offers an extensive range of solutions to help companies, both large and small, connect worldwide with their business partners, synchronize product and price information, optimize inventory levels and demand forecasts, and speed the overall execution of their global supply chains.

GXS is providing traditional EDI services as well as other e-business services, which enable customers to:

- Accelerate the reliable exchange of information.
- Provide all of the information needed along supply chains.
- Serve large and small customers jointly and distinctly.
- Streamline cross-enterprise business processes.

In order to achieve the above, GXS created the Extended Value Chain, shown below.

GXS provides its services via its Trading Grid, a global integration platform that enables and streamlines enterprise business processes.

Trading Grid has five major, integrated components, which are described below and shown in the following figure:

- **Trading Grid Infrastructure Services** provide the foundation to Trading Grid and include an online, centralized, Web-based portal that allows users to register for services, self-provision, and self-service. A powerful data aggregation store also locates data that other Trading Grid services can utilize.
- **SMB Enablers and Enterprise Adapters** allow all users to effortlessly integrate with Trading Grid to conduct electronic commerce without changing existing business processes.
- **Trading Grid Messaging Services** assist in the event-driven exchange of data between business partners securely and reliably.
- A suite of **Trading Grid Intelligence Services** provides data and event processing according to each company's profile and business rules. Since purely moving data is not enough to give customers a competitive edge, Trading Grid Intelligence Services provide a superior level of responsiveness, which reduces the potential impact of unexpected changes in supply or demand. Analytics also provides real business insight.
- **Trading Grid Application Services** power the other services to automate industry-specific business processes. Customers' internal systems are complemented and additional software purchases are not required. Unlike with large software installations, businesses easily obtain a level of visibility, collaboration, and analytics. Small and medium-sized businesses can utilize these services to be more competitive with much larger businesses.

Ariba Supplier Network (SN)

Ariba Supplier Network (Ariba SN) connects and transacts with a broad range of suppliers, partners, and distribution channels using Ariba's global eCommerce network. Ariba SN provides access to a global supplier community through a single

(*continued*)

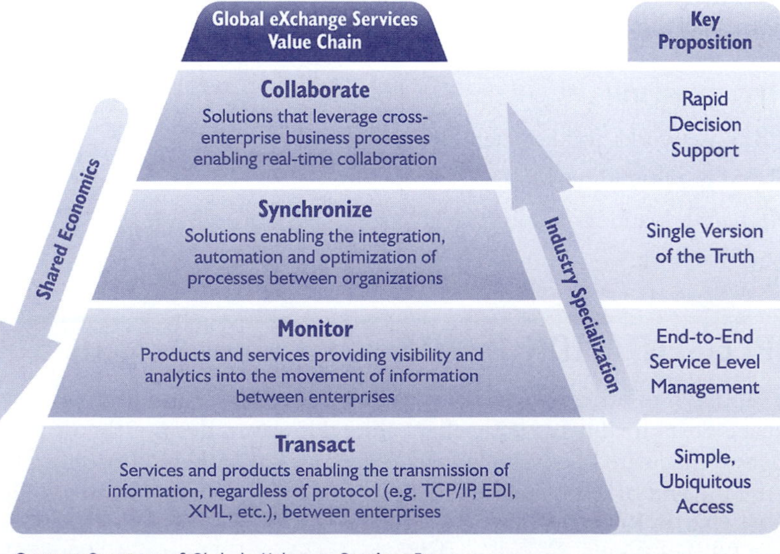

Source: Courtesy of Global eXchange Services Inc.

Insights and Additions 6.1 *(continued)*

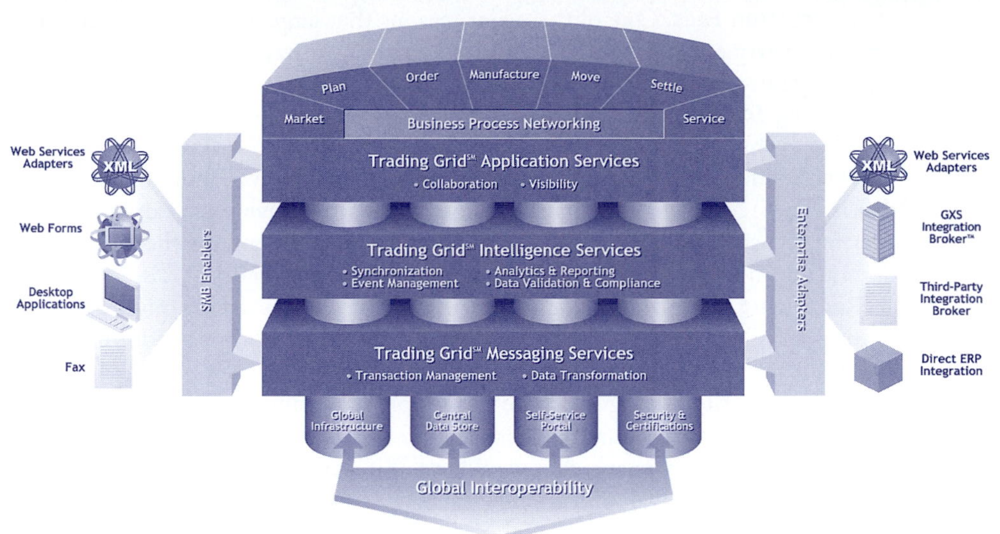

Source: Courtesy of Global eXchange Services Inc.

connection. Buyers can leverage Ariba SN to access global public supplier directories of thousand of enabled suppliers while benefiting from negotiated visibility, security, and privacy. SN provides support for multiple content models, from static catalogs to robust, dynamic content, and reliable exchange of business documents, including invoice management.

Bringing suppliers online enables organizations to collaborate with each other as well as to better manage their expenditures by transacting business and exchanging documents electronically through a single, integrated supplier network. Because supplier participation is important for a business's success, SN provides software solutions—from zero-cost online tools to complete system-to-system XML integration—that help bring suppliers of all sizes in all industries online. In addition, Ariba SN enables suppliers to register and transact business free of charge.

The extensive resources and functionality of SN meet the needs of suppliers as well as buyers, giving companies the following advantages:

- Immediate network participation and robust connectivity to tens of thousands of trading partners worldwide.
- Support for secure electronic transactions and routing of information and documents to achieve full-cycle process integration quickly and efficiently.
- Lower operation costs using a single, consistent infrastructure.
- Reduced process and content management costs through flexible, easy-to-use supplier enablement capabilities and efficient content management tools.
- Instant access to robust, up-to-date business, product, and category information on suppliers.
- Faster implementation and more rapid supplier adoption through seamless integration of all business processes and support for various messaging types.
- Systematic deployment of best practices helps ensure highly profitable, long-term relationships with important suppliers.

Sources: Compiled from *gxs.com* (accessed November 2004), *gxs.com/TradingGrid* (accessed November 2004), and *ariba.com/solutions/ariba_product.cfm?solutionid=24* (accessed August 2004).

PRIVATE MARKETPLACES VERSUS PUBLIC EXCHANGES

As described earlier, exchanges owned by a third party are referred to as *public exchanges*. In contrast, **private marketplaces** are owned and operated by one company. In October 2001, the Gartner Group (as reported by Konicki 2000) estimated that there were 30,000 active private marketplaces and 600 public exchanges in the United States, and the numbers have not changed much since then. Both have implementation and viability problems (e.g., see Varon 2001).

private marketplaces E-marketplaces that are owned and operated by one company. Also known as *company-centric marketplaces*.

Problems with Public Exchanges

Exchanges need to attract sellers and buyers. Attracting sellers, especially large businesses, to public exchanges is difficult for the following reasons.

Transaction Fees. One of the major reasons that large and successful suppliers refuse to join third-party exchanges is that they are required to pay transaction fees even when they engage in transactions with their existing customers.

Sharing Information. Many companies do not join public exchanges because they do not want to share key business data with their competitors.

Cost Savings. Many of the first-generation exchanges were horizontal, concentrating on MROs. These are low-value items. Although administrative costs can be reduced by online ordering, the cost of the products to the buyers remains essentially the same. Thus, the monetary savings may not be attractive enough to buyers, especially SMEs.

Recruiting Suppliers. One of the major difficulties facing public exchanges is the recruitment of large suppliers. For example, GE Plastics, a major vendor of plastic materials, said that it had been asked to join a public exchange, PlasticsNet (plasticsnet.com), but it did not see any benefit in doing so. There was simply no business case for it. Instead, GE Plastics decided to develop e-purchasing capabilities for its customers. The company likes the *direct contact* with its customers, which it would lose if it were part of a public exchange. Also, some suppliers just want to wait and see how exchanges will fare before they make a commitment to join.

Too Many Exchanges. When an exchange receives the publicity of being the *first mover*, as Chemdex did, or when it becomes a success, it is sure to attract some competition. Competitors believe that they can do a better job than the first mover or that they have "deeper pockets" to sustain losses and survive. Two chemical exchanges started a year after Chemdex. Because of the competition, Chemdex was forced to close in 2000.

Supply Chain Improvers

Public exchanges prepare the entire necessary infrastructure and ask suppliers to just "plug in" and start selling. However, companies also are interested in streamlining their internal supply chains, which requires integration with internal operations, not just plugging in. This is why companies such as i2 and Aspect, leaders in SCM, are partnering with some exchanges. According to *Business Review Weekly* of Australia (*BRW* Staff 2000), focusing on supply chain savings rather than on buy/sell savings can be very beneficial to exchanges. An example of an exchange that emphasizes supply chain improvement is Asite, as described in EC Application Case 6.3.

A private exchange is a many-to-many marketplace owned by one company. In contrast, a private marketplace (company-centered) has one seller and many buyers or one buyer and many sellers.

Problems with Private Exchanges

Some (e.g., Young 2002) believe that public exchanges will not do as well as private exchanges. However, private exchanges have their problems, too. The primary problem is that they may not be trusted because they are run by one company, usually a large one. Such distrust can lead to liquidity issues.

SOFTWARE AGENTS IN B2B EXCHANGES

The use of B2B exchanges has fostered a need within the B2B community for an efficient infrastructure to provide real-time, tighter integration between buyers and sellers and to facilitate management of multiple trading partners and their transactions across multiple virtual industry exchanges. Such capabilities can be provided by software agents.

One software agent, Dotcom-Monitor (dotcom-monitor.com), monitors traffic on a B2B exchange and takes appropriate actions when needed, such as sending an alert to management when traffic is too heavy or routing traffic to other places. Some of the types of shopping agents cited in Chapters 3 and 4 (e.g., comparison and search agents) also can be used for B2B purposes.

CASE 6.3

EC Application

ASITE'S B2B E-MARKETPLACE FOR THE CONSTRUCTION INDUSTRY

Asite (*asite.com*) is a B2B e-marketplace for the construction industry in the United Kingdom that focuses on procurement and project management. The construction industry is typified by a high degree of physical separation and fragmentation, and communication among the members of the supply chain (e.g., contractors, subcontractors, architects, supply stores, building inspectors) has long been a primary problem. Founded in February 2000 by leading players in the construction industry, the company understands two of the major advantages of the Internet: The ability it provides to communicate more effectively and the increase in processing power that Internet technologies make possible. Taking advantage of the functions of an online portal as information broker and gateway to the services of technology partners, Asite developed a comprehensive portal for the construction industry.

Asite drew on employees from partner organizations with profound industry knowledge and expertise and has benefited from having an anchor group of buyers participating at an early stage of its development. This combination has enabled Asite to rapidly build up the liquidity that online portals require. The company's goal is to be the leading information and transaction hub in the European construction industry.

Asite made the decision not to build its own technology, but to establish partnerships with technology vendors that have highly specialized products. It formed core partnerships with Commerce One (which provides the business solution for the portal), Microsoft (which provides the technology platform and core applications), and Attenda (the designer and manager of the Internet infrastructure).

Asite set up seven interconnected marketplaces within its portal to serve all the needs of the participants in the construction industry—building owners, developers, trade contractors, general contractors, engineers, architects, and materials suppliers—from design through procurement to materials delivery (see below). It began by addressing business problems, such as ineffective procurement processes and hit-or-miss information flows.

(continued)

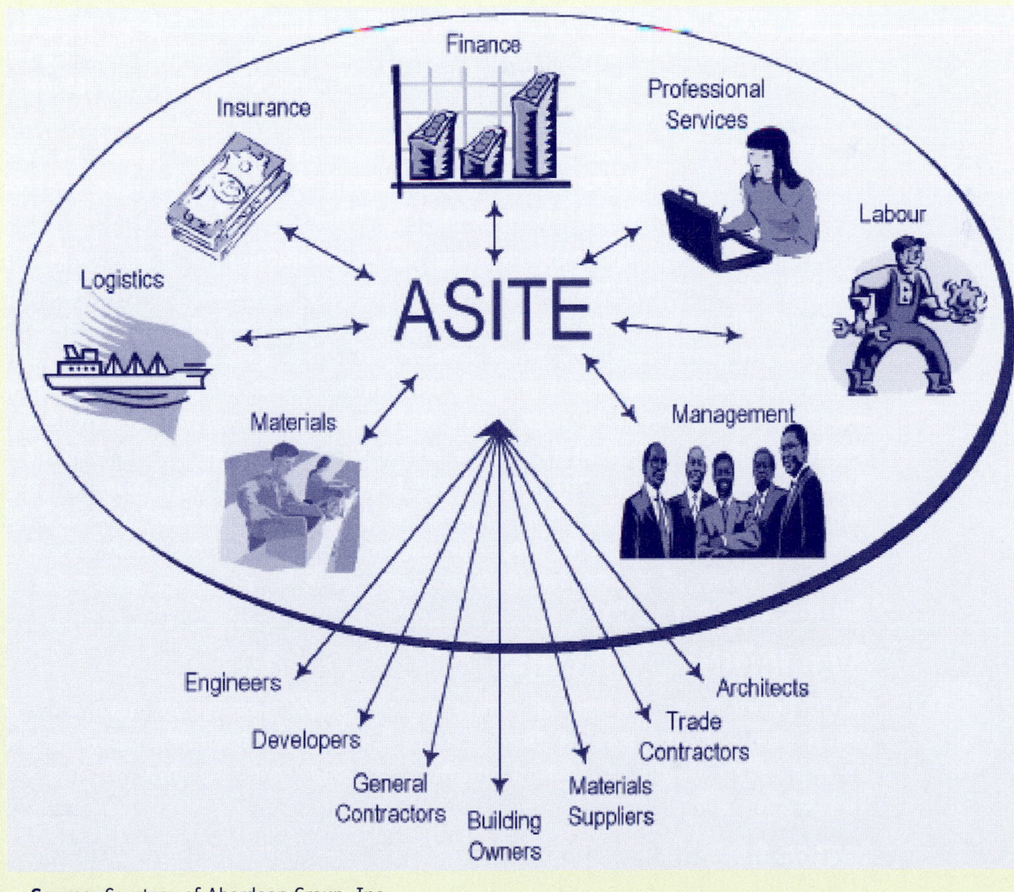

Source: Courtesy of Aberdeen Group, Inc.

CASE 6.3 (continued)

Asite is committed to strong partnerships that allow it to seamlessly interact with other e-marketplaces. The open standards espoused by these vendors also mean that the technology can be incorporated easily with participating firms' back-end technologies, allowing full visibility of the supply and demand chains. Participating firms need nothing more sophisticated than a browser to connect to Asite's portal. This ease of access makes it particularly well suited to an industry such as construction, which is distinguished by a high proportion of small, and even single-person, firms.

The combination of strong backing from industry participants, experienced management from the construction industry, and the commitment to working with best-of-breed technology infrastructure providers is helping construction firms streamline their supply chains.

Sources: Compiled from Aberdeen Group (2001) and *asite.com* (accessed 2004).

Questions

1. Identify the success factors of this company (see the list of success factors in Section 6.9).
2. How would you classify the ownership of this e-marketplace?
3. Examine the Webcor EC Application Case in Chapter 7. How does Webcor differ from Asite? How is it similar?
4. Enter *asite.com* and read about any new developments (those within the last 6 months).
5. What is the exchange's revenue model?
6. Using the classification scheme presented in this chapter, is *asite.com* a portal or an exchange?
7. Examine the site's tendering, procurement, and project management tools.

DISINTERMEDIATION AND REINTERMEDIATION

Exchanges, especially consortia-like ones, could replace traditional B2B intermediaries (i.e., cause disintermediation). Let's look at some examples of exchanges that might replace (i.e., reintermediate) traditional B2B intermediaries in certain industries.

- Sun Microsystems, after publicly announcing that there was no need for third-party exchanges because they waste time, joined a consortium, headed by IBM, which develops and smooths lines in the computer maker's supply chain. This exchange competes with a similar exchange created by HP, AMD, and NEC. Such exchanges may eliminate some distributors of computer components.
- Marriott, Hyatt, and several other competing hoteliers created an MRO exchange (avendra.com) concentrating on procurement that could eliminate wholesalers in hotel industry due to its purchasing power ($2 billion annually).

The Web offers new opportunities for reintermediation. First, brokers are especially valuable when the number of market participants is enormous, as with the stock market, or when complex information products are exchanged. Second, many brokering services require information processing. Electronic versions of these services can offer more sophisticated features at a lower cost than is possible with human labor. Finally, for delicate negotiations, a computer mediator may be more predictable, and hence more trustworthy than a human. For example, suppose a mediator's roles is to inform a buyer and a seller whether a deal can be made without revealing either side's initial price to the other, because such a revelation would influence subsequent price negotiations. A software-based mediator will reveal only the information it is supposed to; a human mediator's fairness is less easily ensured.

An analysis of reintermediation strategies in B2B, including exchanges, is provided by Dai and Kauffman (2002b).

EVALUATING EXCHANGES

With the increased number of competing exchanges, companies need to evaluate carefully which ones will work best for them. Online File W6.2 offers some useful questions that buyers and sellers should ask when evaluating exchanges and deciding whether to join (also see Ranganatan 2003).

Section 6.9 ▶ REVIEW QUESTIONS

1. List the problems of public exchanges.
2. List the problems of private exchanges.

3. How can exchanges cause disintermediation?
4. What role do software agents play in B2B?
5. What are some of the questions one should ask when evaluating exchanges? (Hint: see Online File W6.2.)

6.10 MANAGING EXCHANGES

The topic of managing exchanges is very broad. This section will describe a couple of major management issues. For more on exchange management, see Schully and Woods (2000). This section concludes with an examination of the critical success factors for exchanges (see also Diorio 2002 and Woods 2003).

CENTRALIZED MANAGEMENT

Managing exchanges and providing services to participants on an individual basis can be expensive (see Schully and Woods 2000). Therefore, it makes sense to have "families" of jointly managed exchanges. This way, one market maker can build and operate several exchanges from a unified, centralized location. The market maker manages all of the exchanges' catalogs, auction places, discussion forums, and so on, thus centralizing accounting, finance, human resources, and IT services. Furthermore, dealings with third-party vendors that provide logistic services and payment systems may be more efficient if a vendor is supplying services for many exchanges instead of just one.

Two such "families" of exchanges were those of VerticalNet and Ventro. They managed the administrative aspects involved for a large number of exchanges. However, due to the large number of exchange failures in 2001, Ventro (now nexprise.com) changed its business model and became a software provider. VerticalNet (verticalnet.com) is now a supply chain management software provider and consultant. In general, this model is very difficult to implement; thus it has not yet been successful.

CRITICAL SUCCESS FACTORS FOR EXCHANGES

By early 2001, there were thousands of B2B exchanges. Since that time, as in the B2C area, many exchanges (perhaps 90 percent) have folded or are failing, including Chemdex. In certain areas or countries, there are too many competing exchanges. For example, Hong Kong probably did not have enough room for three toy exchanges (two failed by summer 2002). Therefore, B2B exchanges will continue to fail and consolidate. The question is what determines whether an exchange will survive.

Diorio (2002) and Woods (2003) offer a number of suggestions on how B2B exchanges can succeed (see Online Exhibit W6.5). According to Ramsdell (2000) of McKinsey & Company, a major management consulting firm, the following five factors are influencing the outcome of the B2B exchange shakeout.

1. **Early liquidity.** Recall that liquidity requires having a sufficient number of participants and amount of transaction volume. The *earlier* a business achieves the necessary liquidity level, the better its chances for survival. The more buyers that trade on an exchange, the more suppliers will come, which will lead to lower transaction fees, which in turn will increase volume and liquidity even more.
2. **The right owners.** One way to increase liquidity is to partner with companies that can bring transactions to the exchange. For example, Covisint was founded by the big automakers, and they are committed to buying via the exchange. The desire to have suitable partners is why many vertical exchanges are of the consortia type. In a situation where both the sellers and buyers are fragmented, such as in the bioscience industry, the best owner may be an intermediary who can increase liquidity by pushing both the sellers and the buyers to use the exchange.
3. **The right governance.** Good management and effective operations and rules are critical to success. The governance provides the rules for the exchange, minimizes conflicts, and supports decision making. Furthermore, good management will try to induce the necessary liquidity. Also, good governance will minimize conflicts among the owners and the

participants. Owners may try to favor some of their trading partners, a situation that may hurt the exchange if not checked by effective management. To succeed, good exchanges must be unbiased. In addition, good management of operations, resources, and people is mandatory for success. Finally, privacy must be protected.

4. **Openness.** Exchanges must be open to all, from both organizational and technological perspectives. Commitment to open standards is required, but there should be universal agreement on these standards. Using the wrong standards may hurt the exchange.
5. **A full range of services.** Although prices are important, buyers and sellers are interested in cutting their total costs. Therefore, exchanges that help cut inventory costs, spoilage, maverick buying, and so on, will attract participants. Many exchanges team up with banks, logistics services, and IT companies to provide support services. Furthermore, exchanges must be integrated with the information systems of their members—not a simple task (see the Real-World Case at the end of this chapter).

In addition to Ramsdell's five factors, a number of other factors are critical to the success of an exchange. These are presented and discussed in Insights and Additions 6.2. In order to achieve these critical success factors, market makers must carefully select the vendors that design and build the exchanges.

For further discussion of critical success factors for exchanges, see Bryant (2002) and Koulopoulos and Champy (2004).

NEW DIRECTIONS FOR B2B MARKETPLACES

The difficulties encountered by both third-party marketplaces and consortia have resulted in a search for new directions (such as the merger of the two). Berryman and Heck (2001) edited a special section of *The McKinsey Quarterly* in which they, with others, presented the *third wave of B2B exchanges.* (The first wave is dot-com-owned B2B exchanges; the second wave is consortia-owned exchanges.) After analyzing the problems of the first and second waves, they concurred with the view of Agrawal and Pak (2001) that many of the failures in the former waves mainly were due to the failure of these marketplaces to foster a broad-based sharing of information. The third wave contains both proven and potential success factors

In the past, information flowed only between pairs of parties in a supply chain. The result was a multibillion-dollar version of the game of "telephone," in which small errors, magnified up and down the chain, led to incorrect forecasts and to either excessive or insufficient inventories. In contrast, marketplaces that became *information hubs* for distinct segments of the supply chain could instantaneously share data and insights gathered from each corporate participant. Such a hub-and-spoke model may be the way not only to save these B2Bs, but also to realize their value-creating potential.

Devine et al. (2001) explained why many consortia did not fare much better than third-party exchanges. In many cases, members of the consortium did not shift as much of their trading volume to the exchange as had been expected (*The Economist* 2004), thus the liquidity that their participation was supposed to guarantee did not materialize. Such consortia must recognize the more fundamental asset provided by their member base—its unique knowledge of the industry. Such recognition should enable consortia to become arenas for *sharing this knowledge,* and thereby make it possible to standardize products and processes, to spread risk, to uncover new opportunities, to do joint forecasting and demand planning, as well as to participate in the order–ship–settle process electronically (Brooks 2004). Marketplaces that offer their members such benefits will have no shortage of liquidity.

Hansen et al. (2001) believe that one hallmark of third-wave B2B approaches is the idea of choosing a different model for each kind of transaction. Companies purchasing a commodity, for example, might value the liquidity, the transparency, and the price orientation of an online exchange (much like the benefits offered by commodity contracts already traded at the Chicago Mercantile Exchange and elsewhere). In contrast, companies making highly specialized purchases might value the possibilities for customization offered by the traditional bilateral relationship between buyers and sellers.

According to Baumgartner et al. (2001), sellers' reaction to B2B has ranged from skepticism to horror. Such negative reaction is based on the idea that these marketplaces serve a

Insights and Additions 6.2 Some Critical Success Factors for Exchanges

- **Importance of domain expertise.** To meaningfully aggregate buyers and sellers in a community and subsequently enable transactions among them, operators should have knowledge of a given industry's structure and business processes, the nature of buyer and seller behavior in the industry and government, and policy stipulations that impact the sector.
- **Targeting inefficient industry processes.** The traditional business processes in most industries have many inefficiencies. These contribute to increased costs and delays for businesses transacting with one another. Addressing these inefficiencies may create significant opportunities for vertical exchanges to add value.
- **Targeting the right industries.** The most attractive characteristics suitable for vertical exchanges are: (1) a large base of transactions; (2) many fragmented buyers and sellers; (3) difficulties in bringing buyers and sellers together; (4) high vendor and product search/comparison costs, which may be caused by information-intensive products with complex configurations and nonstandard specifications; (5) high process costs associated with manual processes based on paper catalogs, manual requisitioning, telephone- or fax-based ordering, the need for credit verification, and order tracking; (6) strong pressure to cut expenses; (7) a complex value chain, such as in the automotive industry; and (8) a climate of technological innovation. Targeting industries with some of these characteristics is desirable.
- **Brand building.** The low switching costs inherent in exchanges will make branding of exchanges of paramount importance to their long-term viability. Exchange operators must first invest in gaining brand awareness and getting businesses to use their exchange. For example, in Hong Kong, Bigboxx.com even advertises on buses. Exchange operators must then focus on customer retention. Adding valuable features and functionality is one way to increase switching costs (in this case, the services the customer would lose by switching).
- **Exploiting economies of scope.** Once a critical mass is reached, exchange operators must expand the services they provide to users. Value-added services, such as industry news, expert advice, or detailed product specification sheets, can make an exchange even more compelling. Expanding the range of services may also increase switching costs. Better-developed exchanges are now offering services such as systems integration, hosting, financial services (e.g., payment processing, receivables management, credit analysis), and logistics services (e.g., shipping, warehousing, and inspection), as well as risk-mitigation services.
- **Choice of business/revenue models.** To optimize the chances for success, exchange operators should generate multiple revenue streams, including software licensing, advertising, and sponsorship, and recurring revenues from transaction fees, subscription fees, and software subscription revenues. Other value-added services and applications, such as auctions, financial services, business reporting, and data mining services, may provide other sources of revenue.
- **Blending content, community, and commerce.** Exchanges differ in their approaches; some originate from a content/community perspective, whereas others have a focus on conducting EC transactions. Though content and community features have the advantage of stimulating traffic, the ability to conduct EC transactions is thought to create a higher level of customer "stickiness" and greater value for the exchanges. A successful exchange should combine rich content and community with the ability to conduct EC transactions.
- **Managing channel conflict.** The movement of buyers to interact directly with sellers and the consequent disintermediation of some portion of the supply chain intermediaries may be viewed as a hostile activity by existing fulfillment channels. The result sometimes is price erosion, which may affect a company's medium-term profitability. Exchanges are trying to minimize the conflict by using existing services of the major buyers and sellers.
- **Other factors.** Diorio (2002) added the following critical success factors for exchanges: value-added content, expertise, trust relationships, appropriate financing, first-mover advantage, and availability of resources. For more on these factors, see Online Exhibit W6.5.

WWW

single overriding purpose—the promotion of price transparency—that entails a race to the profitless bottom. Of course, the authors note, certain buyers really are extremely price sensitive when they make certain purchases, and those buyers will naturally migrate to low-cost producers. However, many other purchases will continue to involve information-rich bilateral relationships. In fact, Ordanini et al. (2004) found in their survey that large private exchanges have a superior capability to generate turnover compared with vertical niche operators due to specific choices of content, structure, and governance.

A third model (Berryman and Heck 2001), is the *e-distributor* (see Chapter 5), which lies between the two extremes of the stand-alone third-party exchange and the consortium. In this model, e-distributors, like distributors in the off-line world, take title to the goods they sell, aggregate those goods for the convenience of buyers, and, because they only carry certain products, in effect advise buyers as to which products to purchase. In addition, e-distributors perform a critical service for sellers by reaching hard-to-find buyers, such as small ones. The result, in many cases, is significant *extra value* for buyers and decent profits for sellers. For evaluation of models, see Ranganatan (2003).

Murtaza et al. (2004) review the opportunities and challenges in different types of e-marketplaces. Another set of new directions is presented by Dai and Kauffman (2002a) in a special section of the journal *Electronic Markets* in which six research papers were presented. Of special interest are interviews with leading scholars in the field. This special presentation deals with many of the topics presented in Chapters 5 through 7.

Section 6.10 ▶ REVIEW QUESTIONS

1. Describe the concept of centrally managed exchanges.
2. List the five critical success factors for exchanges cited by Ramsdell.
3. Discuss other critical success factors for exchanges.
4. Describe the new directions of B2B exchanges.

MANAGERIAL ISSUES

Some managerial issues related to this chapter are as follows.

1. **Have we done our homework?** Study the options and select the most secure and economical choice for exchange implementation. Consult the technical staff inside and outside of each partnering company. Planning is essential. This is true for exchange creators, operators, and users.
2. **Can we use the Internet?** Review the current proprietary or leased networks and determine if they can be replaced by intranets and extranets (see Appendix 6A). Replacing them may reduce costs and widen connectivity for customers and suppliers. In making this decision, also consider whether it is safe enough to switch to the extranet.
3. **Which exchange to join?** One of the major concerns of management is selecting exchanges in which to participate. At the moment, exchanges are not integrated, so there may be a substantial start-up effort and cost for joining an exchange. This is a multicriteria decision that should be analyzed carefully. A related issue is whether to join a third-party public exchange or a consortium or to create a private exchange.
4. **Will joining an exchange force restructuring?** Joining an exchange may require a restructuring of the internal supply chain, which may be expensive and time-consuming. Therefore, this possibility must be taken into consideration when deciding whether to join an exchange.
5. **Will we face channel conflicts?** Channel conflicts may arise when a company joins an exchange. You may anger your existing suppliers if you buy via an exchange. This issue must be considered, and an examination of its impact must be carried out.
6. **What are the benefits and risks of joining an exchange?** Companies must take very seriously the issues listed in Exhibit 6.5. The risks of joining an exchange must be carefully weighed against the expected benefits.
7. **Can we trust new trading partners?** Typical to the Internet, new partners are easy to find. But can they be trusted? As in B2C, intermediaries may provide services to increase trust. Also, trust involves a learning process (see Ratnasingam and Phan 2003).

RESEARCH TOPICS

Here are some suggested topics related to this chapter. For details, references, and additional topics, refer to the Online Appendix "Current EC Research."

1. **Ownership Composition of B2B Marketplaces**
   - Evolution of B2B ownership structure
   - Effect of existing corporate power in the market ownership structure
   - Why the buyer-centric marketplace is used most frequently
   - Why the third party exchanges suffer in obtaining transactions

- Competitive roles of public marketplaces in comparison with private marketplaces
- Dynamic restructuring of B2B marketplaces
- Pros and cons of consortia for B2B marketplaces

2. **CSF of B2B Marketplaces**
   - Revenue models of successful B2B marketplaces
   - Metrics of CSFs of B2B marketplaces
   - Evolution of CSFs
   - Survival strategies of B2B marketplaces
   - Evolution of service scopes
3. **Matching Buyers and Sellers**
   - Representation of buyer's needs
   - Representation of seller's specifications for e-catalogs
   - Matching buyer's needs and seller's specifications
   - Combinatorial auctions as matching services
   - Configuration as a matching process
   - Standardizations for representation
   - Role of agents to discover the matched counterpart
   - Protocol of discovering matched counterparts
   - Web services as a platform of matching services
4. **Case Studies of B2B Marketplaces: Successes and Failures**
   - Case studies of buyer-centric marketplaces
   - Case studies of seller-centric marketplaces
   - Case studies of the evolution of third party marketplaces such as Covisint and GXS
   - Comparative study between industries
   - Comparative study between countries
5. **Integration of Exchanges with External Components**
   - Architectures of business-to-exchange integration
   - Business models of exchange-to-exchange integration
   - Integrated services of marketplaces with ASP and collaboration hubs
   - International integration of exchanges
   - Architectures of successful extranets

SUMMARY

In this chapter, you learned about the following EC issues as they relate to the learning objectives.

1. **E-marketplaces and exchanges defined and the major types of exchanges.** Exchanges are e-marketplaces that provide a trading platform for conducting business among many buyers, many sellers, and other business partners. Other names used are *trading portals* or *Net marketplaces.* Types of public e-marketplaces include B2B portals, third-party trading exchanges, consortium trading exchanges, and dynamic trading floors for matching supply and demand and for auctions. Exchanges may be vertical (industry oriented) or horizontal. They may target systematic buying (long-term relationships) or spot buying (for fulfilling an immediate need).
2. **Ownership and revenue models.** Exchanges may be owned by one large buyer or seller, an intermediary (a neutral third party), or a large group of buyers or sellers (a consortium). The major revenue models are transaction fees (flat or percentage), fees for value-added services, annual membership fees, and advertisement income.
3. **B2B portals.** These portals are similar to B2C portals such as Yahoo! B2B portals are gateways to B2B community-related information. They are usually of a vertical structure, in which case they are referred to as *vortals.* Some B2B portals offer product and vendor information and even tools for conducting trades, sometimes making it difficult to distinguish between B2B portals and trading exchanges.
4. **Third-party exchanges.** Third-party exchanges are owned by an independent company and usually operate in highly fragmented markets. They are open to anyone and therefore are considered public exchanges. They try to maintain neutral relations with both buyers and sellers. Their major problem is acquiring enough participants to ensure liquidity. Two models of third-party exchanges are those that aggregate suppliers' catalogs and those that aggregate buyers' RFQs.
5. **Consortia and e-procurement.** A consortium trading exchange (CTE) is an exchange formed and operated by a group of major involved companies. Buying-oriented consortia are established by several large buyers (e.g., automakers). Their major objective is to smooth the procurement (purchasing) process. Selling-oriented consortia are owned and operated by several large sellers, usually in the same industry (e.g., plastics, airlines). Their major objective is to increase sales and smooth the supply chain to their customers. CTEs sometimes face antitrust scrutiny by governments.
6. **Dynamic pricing and trading.** Dynamic pricing occurs when prices are determined by supply and demand at any given moment. Dynamic trading refers to trading in which prices are continuously changing. The two major dynamic pricing mechanisms are matching of supply and demand (such as in stock markets) and auctions (forward and reverse).

7. **Integrating marketplaces and exchanges.** One of the major problems in building e-marketplaces is systems integration, especially between business partners. In addition to application integration, there may also be problems of data and database integration as well as process integration. In the future, Web Services will provide a universal open environment that will ease the integration problem.
8. **Major B2B support services.** Six categories of support services exist: e-infrastructure, e-processes, e-markets, e-content, e-communities, and e-services. Directory services and B2B search engines are examples of e-services. Partnership relationship management (PRM) is important in B2B, and it may be facilitated by various B2B support services.
9. **B2B networks.** B2B requires networks that enable efficient and effective trade and communication. They may be company centered, for one industry, or global. Well-known examples are GXS and Ariba's Supplier Network.
10. **Exchange networks and management of exchanges.** Customers will benefit if exchanges are connected to one another. Such integration is complex and may take years to complete. Managing individual exchanges can be expensive; therefore, "families" of exchanges may be managed centrally. The major implementation issues for exchanges are choosing between private and public exchanges (or their combination), evaluating exchanges, identifying problem areas, and using software agents as a support mechanism.
11. **Critical success factors for exchanges.** Some of the major critical success factors for exchanges are early liquidity, proper ownership, proper governance and management, openness (technological and organizational), and a full range of services.

KEY TERMS

Term	Page
B2B portals	243
Consortium trading exchange (CTE)	247
Dynamic pricing	238
Dynamic trading	252
Elasticity	251
Exchange	236
Horizontal exchange	238
Market liquidity	245
Market maker	236
Partner relationship management (PRM)	255
Private marketplaces	261
Public e-marketplaces (public exchanges)	236
Supplier relationship management (SRM)	255
Vertical exchange	238
Vortals	243

QUESTIONS FOR DISCUSSION

1. How does dynamic pricing differ from fixed pricing?
2. Suppose a manufacturer uses an outside shipping company. How can the manufacturer use an exchange to arrange for the best possible shipping? How can a shipment's status be tracked?
3. Discuss the legal concerns regarding consortia.
4. Which types of exchanges are most suitable for third-party ownership and why?
5. Compare and contrast the supplier aggregation model with the buyer aggregation model in an industry of your choice.
6. Describe the various issues of integration related to B2B exchanges.
7. Explain the logic for networks of exchanges.
8. Discuss the need for auctions in exchanges and the types of auctions used.
9. Explain the importance of early liquidity and describe methods to achieve it.
10. How do exchanges affect disintermediation?
11. What questions should buyers and sellers ask when evaluating exchanges?
12. Compare the operation and viability of private exchanges versus public exchanges.

INTERNET EXERCISES

1. Visit **ariba.com** and **microsoft.com**. Find the software tools they have for building e-markets. Check the capabilities provided by each and comment on their differences.
2. Go to **alibaba.com** and sign up as a member (membership is free). Go to the site map and find the "sample house." Create a product

and place it in the sample house. Tell your instructor how to view this product.

3. Compare the services offered by **globalsources.com** with those offered by **alibaba.com** and **asia-links.com**. Assuming you are a toy seller, with which one would you register? Why? If you are a buyer of auto parts, which one would you join and why?
4. Enter **chemconnect.com** and view the demos for different trading alternatives. Examine the revenue model. Evaluate the services from both the buyer's and seller's points of view. Also, examine the site policies and legal guidelines. Are they fair? Compare **chemconnect.com** with **chemicalonline.com** and **trade-ranger.com**. Which of these do you think will survive? Explain your reasoning.
5. Most of the major exchanges use an ERP/SCM partner. Enter **i2.com** and view its solutions. What are the benefits of these solutions?
6. Enter eBay's Business Industrial area (**business.ebay.com** or **ebay.com**, select "wholesale"). What kind of e-marketplace is this? What are its major capabilities?
7. Visit **converge.com**. What kind of exchange is this? What services does it provide? How do its auctions work?
8. Enter **bigyellow.com** and **netb2b.com**. What services do they provide that are relevant to exchanges?
9. Enter **communityb2b.com** and find recent material on B2B exchanges (within the last 6 months). Prepare a report on developments not covered in this chapter.

TEAM ASSIGNMENTS AND ROLE PLAYING

1. Form two teams (A and B) of five or more members. On each team, person 1 plays the role of an assembly company that produces television monitors. Persons 2 and 3 are domestic parts suppliers to the assembling company, and persons 4 and 5 play foreign parts suppliers. Assume that the TV monitor company wants to sell televisions directly to business customers. Each team is to design an environment composed of membership in exchanges they can use and present its results. A graphical display is recommended.
2. Investigate the status of Covisint, both in the United States and in Europe. What are the relationships between Covisint and the company-centered marketplaces of the large automakers? Have another team find similar industrywide exchanges and compare them with Covisint. Research how Compuware is changing Covisint. Will Covisint survive as a profitable unit? Why or why not?
3. Enter **isteelasia.com**, **metalworld.com**, and **lme.co.uk**. Compare their operations and services. These exchanges compete in global markets. Examine the trading platforms, portal capabilities, and support services (e.g., logistics, payments, etc.) offered by each. In what areas do these companies compete? In what areas do they not compete? What are the advantages of **isteelasia.com** in dealing with Asian companies? Are regional exchanges needed? If it is good for Asia to have a regional exchange, why not have a Western European exchange, an Eastern European exchange, a Central American exchange, and so on? If regional exchanges are needed, can they work together? How? If there are too many exchanges, which are likely to survive? Research this topic and prepare a report.

Real-World Case

GLOBAL TRANSPORTATION NETWORK OCEAN PORTAL

Although much publicity is given to public exchanges that deal with materials and products, such as ChemConnect and Covisint, several service-oriented exchanges have been created, and some of them are growing rapidly. One such exchange is a global transportation exchange for ocean transportation named Global Transportation Network (GTN).

GTN was formed in 2001 by a consortium of 13 ocean carriers (lines) that collectively represent more than 40 percent of worldwide capacity, and a software company, GT Nexus (*gtnexus.com*), that specializes in global logistics and supply chain products.

The objective of the exchange, which is primarily a *portal* type, is to serve the ocean-shipping industry. The industry is composed of carriers, shippers (such as Wal-Mart and others who import many goods from abroad), and service providers (such as banks, insurance brokers, freight forwarders, and logistics providers). The mission of the exchange is to fundamentally change the process of getting goods around the world by using the Internet to provide superior service that maintains complete security for customers and the carriers. GT Nexus and its CEO are the exchange managers.

To develop the portal, the management team worked with many customers to identify customer needs and determine how the portal could help meet them. Customers wanted a multi-EC model that could meet their diversified needs in a unified way. Existing B2B software products were too narrow; a custom portal had to be built.

The GTN e-commerce platform is much more than a portal. It supports core transactional capabilities such as booking, invoicing, payment, tracking and tracing, rate negotiation, container management, and scheduling. GTN offers standardized booking, documentation, and tracking systems and provides better and more efficient customer support. In addition, it provides customized capabilities tailored for specific customers and carriers, including rate and contract management, cargo forecasting, and resource allocation. The benefits of the system to the ocean-shipping industry include:

- **Significant efficiencies and cost savings.** A 2002 study conducted by Accenture estimated that cost savings from these process improvements and efficiencies alone resulted in savings of 5 to 10 percent for carriers and customers across a range of industries (Coia 2002b). GTN frees individual carriers from the huge capital costs associated with the advanced technologies and resources required to create proprietary technology methods.
- **Standardization and ease of use.** GTN automates core transactions and makes it easier for customers to conduct business with multiple providers using common standards.
- **Secure and confidential access.** GTN provides a secure and confidential environment for customers and carriers to conduct business over the Internet.

Industry experts have observed various improvements for the participants of the exchange (Goodman 2002). A single carrier cannot afford to offer as many EC applications as the exchange offers; therefore, the exchange has greatly expanded the number of applications available to carriers. The system also has enabled customers to do business electronically throughout every process in the shipment cycle. For example, contract negotiation, a very time-consuming process, has been speeded up by the exchange. In addition, because carriers now have access to many more shippers than they could have found on their own, the number of electronic transactions for carriers has doubled, even in the first year of operation in the exchange. Carriers have also been able to improve customer service, one of the major motivators for using the exchange.

The shipping industry is deregulated and very competitive. However, lots of cooperation, such as vessel sharing, still goes on. The GTN system helps to facilitate such collaboration. Several alliances among carriers also exist, and they are supported by the system. Information sharing via open standards and Web-enabled systems is a primary objective of the portal.

The technology of the exchange has contributed to its effectiveness. Data fit the internal IT systems of all users. Standardized processes allow carriers to present their services to shippers in the same way. Clients are able to use one interface to retrieve any information, regardless of the carrier with which the booking was made. The system uses a secured Internet connection (with a VPN) and has an optional EDI for some transactions. It also allows for competitive tendering through *reverse auctions*. The exchange was recognized by *InfoWorld Magazine* (Sanborn 2002) as one of top three technology projects.

Sources: Compiled from Goodman (2002), *gtnexus.com/gtn/en/company* (accessed 2004), Angwin (2004), and Coia (2002b).

Questions

1. Identify the critical success factors of this exchange.
2. Is a consortium the best type of ownership for this kind of exchange?
3. Although there are thousands of shippers, some of them are very large (e.g., Wal-Mart). Does it make sense to have them create a shippers' exchange? Why or why not?
4. What motivates a carrier to participate in the exchange?
5. What motivates a shipper to participate in the exchange?
6. How was customer service improved by the exchange?
7. Research GT Nexus' on-demand model and list its capabilities.

REFERENCES

Aberdeen Group, Inc. "Asite Builds E-Marketplace Using Combined Strength of Commerce One, Microsoft, and Attenda." *Aberdeen Group Profile*, May 2001, p. 5. **aberdeen.com/abpercent5Fabstracts/2001/05/05012573.htm** (accessed September 2002). Note: No longer available online.

Agrawal, M. K., and M. H. Pak. "Getting Smart about Supply Chain Management." *The McKinsey Quarterly* no. 2 (2001).

Alibaba.com. **alibaba.com** (accessed September 2004).

AMR Research Staff. "B2B Marketplaces Report, 2000–2005." AMR Research, August 1, 2001. **amrresearch.com/Content/view.asp?pmillid=14510&docid=600** (accessed January 2003).

Angwin, J. "Top Online Chemical Exchange Is an Unlikely Success Story." *The Wall Street Journal Online*, January 8, 2004. **webreprints.djreprints.com/90766007 2246.html** (accessed March 2005).

Asite.com. **asite.com** (accessed September 2004).

"B2B: 2B or Not 2B." goldmansachs.com, January 5, 2000. **goldmansachs.com/hightech/research/b2b/** (accessed May 8, 2000). Note: No longer available online.

Baker, S., and K. Baker. "Going Up! Vertical Marketing on the Web." *Journal of Business Strategy*, May–June 2000.

Baumgartner, T., et al. "A Seller's Guide to B2B Markets." *The McKinsey Quarterly* no. 2 (2001).

Berryman, K., and S. Heck. "Is the Third Time the Charm for B2B?" *The McKinsey Quarterly* no. 2 (2001).

Brooks, A. "Exchange Values." *Purchasing B2B* 46, no. 3 (2004).

BRW Staff. "B2B: The Rocky Road to Profits for Exchanges." *Business Review Weekly of Australia*, November 10, 2000.

Bryant, G. "E-Markets Hit the Mark." *Businessonline*, February 2002. **businessonline.org** (accessed June 2003). Note: No longer available online.

ChemConnect. **chemconnect.com** (accessed September 2004).

Cleary, M. "Covisint Talks Trash." *Interactive Week*, May 21, 2001.

Coia, A. "Going Online Brought Smooth Sailing to World of Ocean Shipping." **supplychainbrain.com** (accessed June 2002a).

Coia, A. "Evolving Transportation Exchanges." *World Trade*, July 2002b.

Covisint. "Mercator Software Selected by Covisint to Integrate Best-of-Breed Applications." Covisint press release, February 7, 2001. **covisint.com/about/pressroom/pr/2001/2001.FEB.07.shtml** (accessed April 2001a).

Covisint. "Supply Chain Management: Supplyconnect." **covisint.com/downloads/print/supplier_conn.pdf** (accessed February 2001b). Note: No longer available online.

Cunningham, M. J. *B2B: How to Build a Profitable E-Commerce Strategy*. Cambridge, MA: Perseus Book Group, 2000.

Dai, Q., and R. J. Kauffman. "B2B E-Commerce Revisited: Revolution or Evolution." *Electronic Markets* 12, no. 2 (2002a).

Dai, Q., and R. J. Kauffman. "Business Models for Internet-based E-procurement Systems and B2B Electronic Markets." *International Journal of Electronic Commerce* 6, no. 4 (Summer 2002b).

Darwin Magazine. "Commerce Leads the Evolution of the E-Marketplace." White paper. **darwinmag.com/read/whitepapers/041501_co.html** (accessed August 2001).

Delphi Group. "Industry's Most Focused B2B e-Business Conference Now Accepting Case Study Submissions." Delphi Group press release, January 13, 2000. **delphigroup.com/about/pressreleases/2000-PR/20000113-summitpapercall.htm** (accessed July 2001).

Devine, D. A., et al. "Building Enduring Consortia." *The McKinsey Quarterly* no. 1 (2001).

Diorio, S. *Beyond "e": 12 Ways Technology Is Transforming Sales and Marketing Strategy*. New York: McGraw-Hill, 2002.

Dolinoy, M., et al. "Customer Defined Networks." **forrester.com/ER/Research/Report/Summary/0,1338,11071,FF.html** (accessed April 2001). Note: No longer available online.

Dubie, D. "Going Global." Ebusinessiq.com, March 13, 2003. **publish.com/article2/0,,1762086,00.asp** (accessed March 2005).

Durlacher Research, Ltd. "Business to Business E-Commerce Report: An Investment Perspective." **durlacher.com/downloads/b2breports.pdf** (accessed May 6, 2000). Note: No longer available online.

Dyer, J. H., and N. W. Hatch. "Using Supplier Networks to Learn Faster." *MIT Sloan Management Review*, Spring 2004.

The Economist. "Survey: A Market Too Far." *The Economist* 371, no. 8375 (2004).

Ferris, C., and J. Farrell. "E-Services: What Are Web Services?" *Communications of the ACM*, June 2003.

Fram, E. "E-Commerce Survivors: Finding Value Amid Broken Dreams." *Business Horizons*, July–August 2002, pp. 15–20.

Gebauer, J., and M. J. Shaw (Eds.) "Business-to-Business Electronic Commerce." *International Journal of Electronic Commerce*, Special Section (Summer 2002).

Global eXchange Services, Inc. "Global eXchange Service Mission." 2004. **gxs.com/pdfs/DS_GXS_Mission_GXS_71604.pdf** (accessed December 2004).

Goodman, R. "Going Online Brought Smooth Sailing to World of Ocean Shipping." Supplychainbrain.com, June 2002. **supplychainbrain.com/archives/6.02.ocean.htm?adcode=90** (accessed January 2003).

GT Nexus. "GT Nexus Names Jeff Lynch Vice President of Sales." GT Nexus press release, October 2002. **gtnexus.com/cgi-perl/press_releases.cgi?releaseID=45&lang=en** (accessed April 2004). Note: No longer available online.

Hagel, J. "Offshoring Goes on the Offensive." *The McKinsey Quarterly* no. 2 (2004).

Hansen, M. A., et al. "A Buyer's Guide to B2B Markets." *The McKinsey Quarterly* no. 2 (2001).

Kambil, A., and E. van Heck. *Making Markets.* Boston: Harvard Business School Press, 2002.

Kaplan, S., and M. Sawhney. "E-Hubs: The New B2B Market Places." *Harvard Business Review*, May–June 2000.

Karpinski, R. "Special Report: E-Marketplaces Come Full Circle." *BtoBOnline.com*, January 8, 2001.

Keenan Report. "Internet Exchange 2000." **http://www.eyefortransport.com/archive/keenanvision17.pdf#search='Keenan%20Report.%20Internet%20Exchange%202000'** (accessed March 2005).

Konicki, S. "Exchanges Go Private," *InformationWeek*, June 12, 2000. **informationweek.com/790/private.htm** (accessed September 2001).

Koulopoulos, T., and J. Champy. "The Invisible Hand of Commerce." *Optimizemag.com*, July 2004. **optimizemag.com/article/showArticle.jhtml?articleId=22101761** (accessed December 2004).

Murtaza, M. B., et al. "E-marketplaces and the Future of Supply Chain Management: Opportunities and Challenges." *Business Process Management Journal* 10, no. 3 (2004).

Murtaza, M. B., and J. R. Shah. "Managing Information for Effective Business Partner Relationships." *Information Systems Management* (Spring 2004).

Norris, G., et al. *E-Business and ERP*. New York: John Wiley & Sons, 2000.

Ordanini, A. S., et al. "Failure and Success of B-to-B Exchange Business Models: A Contingent Analysis of Their Performance." *European Management Journal* 22, no. 3 (2004).

Pavlou, P. A., and P. Ratnasingam, "Technology Trust in B2B EC: Conceptual Foundation." In Kangas, K. (ed.), *Business Strategies for IT Management*. Hershey, PA: The Idea Group, 2003.

Ramsdell, G. "The Real Business of B2B: Five Factors for Success." White paper, *McKinsey & Company*, October 2, 2000. **techupdate.zdnet.com/techupdate/stories/main/0,14179,2635155-1,00.html** (accessed March 2005).

Ranganatan, C. "Evaluating the Options for B2B E-Exchanges." *Information Systems Management*, Summer 2003.

Ratnasingam, P., and D. D. Phan. "Trading Partner Trust in B2B E-Commerce: A Case Study." *Information Systems Management*, Summer 2003.

Rawmart.com. **rawmart.com** (accessed September 2004).

Ross, J. W., and G. Westerman. "Preparing for Utility Computing: The Role of IT Architecture and Relationship Management." *IBM Systems Journal*, 2004.

Sanborn, S. "Sailing Online." *Infoworld Magazine*, October 18, 2002. **archive.infoworld.com/articles/fe/xml/02/11/04/021104fegtn.xml** (accessed December 2002). Note: No longer available online.

Sandoe K., et al. *Enterprise Integration with E-Business ERP.* New York: Wiley, 2003.

Schecterle, B. "Managing and Extending Supplier Relationships." *People Talk*, April–June 2003.

Schully, A. B., and W. W. Woods. *B2B Exchanges*. New York: ISI Publications, 2000.

Sharma, A. "Trends in Internet B2B Marketing." *Industrial Marketing Management* 31, no. 1 (2002).

Shetty, B. "Forecast Online Sales by Exchange Type." *Forrester Research*, August 2001. **forrester.com/search/1,6260,,00.html?squery=2percent2C500+exchanges+worldwide** (accessed September 2002). Note: No longer available online.

Tumolo, M. "Business to Business Exchanges." Brint.com, February 2001. **brint.com/members/01040530/b2bexchanges** (accessed February 2005).

Varon, E. "What You Need to Know About Public and Private Exchanges." *CIO Magazine*, September 1, 2001.

webMethods. "Powering WWRE's Global Item Synchronization Solution." WWRE Success Story, 2005. **webmethods.com/meta/default/folder/0000006269?successstoriesdetails_param0=3352** (accessed May 2005).

Woods, W. A. *B2B Exchange 2.0: Not All Are Dot-bomb*. New York: ISI Publications, 2003.

WWRE. "WWRE Overview." 2005. **worldwideretailexchange.org/cs/en_US/about/wr0100.html** (accessed May 2005).

Young, E. "Web Marketplaces that Really Work." *Fortune/CNET Tech Review*, Winter 2002.

COMMUNICATION NETWORKS AND EXTRANETS FOR B2B

Chapter 5 pointed out the need for networks to support communication and collaboration among B2B business partners. It also described EDI and its supporting role in facilitating B2B communication and collaboration. This appendix looks at the networks needed for private e-marketplaces and public exchanges.

The major network structure used in e-marketplaces and exchanges is an *extranet*, or "extended intranet." An extranet uses the Internet to connect individual companies' intranets. Because the Internet is free, extranets are much less expensive than VANs. An extranet adds value to the Internet by increasing its security and expanding the available bandwidth. To better understand how an extranet interfaces with the Internet and intranets, we will first consider the basic concepts of the Internet and intranets and then turn our attention back to extranets.

THE INTERNET

The **Internet** is a public, global communications network that provides direct connectivity to anyone over a local area network (LAN), usually via an Internet service provider (ISP) (for details see Online Appendix C). Because access to the Internet is open to all, control and security are at a minimum.

Internet
A public, global communications network that provides direct connectivity to anyone over a LAN via an ISP or directly via an ISP.

INTRANETS

An **intranet** is a corporate LAN or wide area network (WAN) that uses Internet technology and is secured behind a company's firewalls. (Firewalls are discussed in Chapter 11.) An intranet links various servers, clients, databases, and application programs, such as ERP, within a company. Although intranets are based on the same TCP/IP protocol as the Internet, they operate as a private network with limited access. Only authorized employees are able to use them.

Intranets are limited to information pertinent to the company, and they contain exclusive, often proprietary, sensitive information. The intranet can be used to enhance communication and collaboration among authorized employees, customers, suppliers, and other business partners. Because an intranet allows access through the Internet, it does not require any additional implementation of leased networks. This open and flexible connectivity is a major capability and advantage of intranets. More on intranets can be found in Online Appendix W7A.

intranet
A corporate LAN or WAN that uses Internet technology and is secured behind a company's firewalls.

EXTRANETS

An **extranet** uses the TCP/IP protocol to link intranets in different locations (as shown in Exhibit 6A.1). Extranet transmissions are usually conducted over the Internet, which offers little privacy or transmission security. Therefore, it is necessary to add security features. This is done by creating tunnels of secured data flows, using cryptography and authorization algorithms, to provide secure transport of private communications. An Internet with tunneling technology is known as a **virtual private network (VPN)** (see Chapter 11 for details).

extranet
A network that uses a virtual private network (VPN) to link intranets in different locations over the Internet; an "extended intranet."

virtual private network (VPN)
A network that creates tunnels of secured data flows, using cryptography and authorization algorithms, to provide secure transport of private communications over the public Internet.

Extranets provide secured connectivity between a corporation's intranets and the intranets of its business partners, materials suppliers, financial services, government, and customers. Access to an extranet is usually limited by agreements of the collaborating parties, is strictly controlled, and is available only to authorized personnel. The protected environment of an extranet allows partners to collaborate and share information and to perform these activities securely.

Because an extranet allows connectivity between businesses through the Internet, it is an open and flexible platform suitable for B2B. To increase security, many companies replicate the portions of their databases that they are willing to share with their business partners and separate them physically from their regular intranets. However, even separated data need to be secured. (See Chapter 11 for more on EC network security.)

According to Szuprowicz (1998), extranet benefits fall into five categories:

1. **Enhanced communications.** The extranet enables improved internal communications; improved business partnership channels; effective marketing, sales, and customer support; and facilitated collaborative activities support.
2. **Productivity enhancements.** The extranet enables just-in-time information delivery, reduction of information overload, productive collaboration between workgroups, and training on demand.

EXHIBIT 6A.1 The Structure of an Extranet

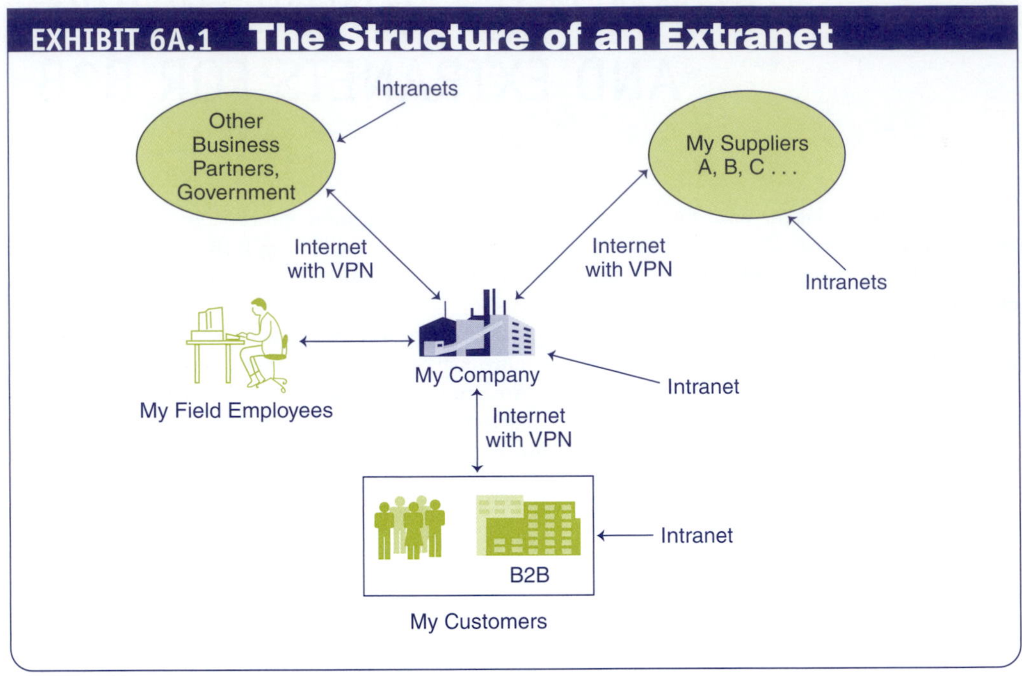

3. **Business enhancements.** The extranet enables faster time-to-market, potential for simultaneous engineering and collaboration, lower design and production costs, improved client relationships, and creation of new business opportunities.
4. **Cost reduction.** The extranet results in fewer errors, improved comparison shopping, reduced travel and meeting time and cost, reduced administrative and operational costs, and elimination of paper-publishing costs.
5. **Information delivery.** The extranet enables low-cost publishing, leveraging of legacy systems, standard delivery systems, ease of maintenance and implementation, and elimination of paper-based publishing and mailing costs.

Rihao-Ling and Yen (2001) reported additional advantages of extranets, such as ready access to information, ease of use, freedom of choice, moderate setup cost, simplified workflow, lower training cost, and better group dynamics. They also listed disadvantages, such as difficulty in justifying the investment (measuring benefits and costs), high user expectations, and drain on resources. Finally, Chow (2004) describes success factors of using extranets in e-supply chains.

KEY TERMS

Extranet	275	**Intranet**	275	**Virtual private network (VPN)**	275
Internet	275				

REFERENCES

Chow, W. S. "An Exploratory Study of the Success Factors for Extranet Adoption in E-Supply Chain." *Journal of Global Information Management*, January–March 2004.

Rihao-Ling, R., and D. C. Yen. "Extranet: A New Wave of Internet." *SAM Advanced Management Journal*, Spring 2001.

Szuprowicz, B. *Extranet and Intranet: E-Commerce Business Strategies for the Future*. Charleston, SC: Computer Technology Research Corp., 1998.

CHAPTER 7

E-SUPPLY CHAINS, COLLABORATIVE COMMERCE, INTRABUSINESS EC, AND CORPORATE PORTALS

Content

Learning Objectives

Upon completion of this chapter, you will be able to:

1. Define the e-supply chain and describe its characteristics and components.
2. List supply chain problems and their causes.
3. List solutions to supply chain problems provided by EC.
4. Define c-commerce and list the major types.
5. Describe collaborative planning and Collaboration, Planning, Forecasting, and Replenishing (CPFR) and list the benefits of each.
6. Define intrabusiness EC and describe its major activities.
7. Discuss integration along the supply chain.
8. Understand corporate portals and their types and roles.
9. Describe e-collaboration tools such as workflow software and groupware.

HOW GENERAL MOTORS IS COLLABORATING ONLINE

The Problem

Designing a car is a complex and lengthy process. Take, for example, just a small part of the process at General Motors (GM). Each model created needs to go through a frontal crash test. GM builds prototypes that cost about $1 million each and tests how they react to a frontal crash. GM crashes these cars, makes improvements, and then crashes them again. Even as late as the 1990s, GM crashed as many as 70 prototype versions of each new model.

The information regarding a new design collected from these crashes and other tests has to be shared among approximately 11,000 designers and engineers in hundreds of divisions and departments at 16 GM design labs, some of which are located in different countries. In addition, GM must communicate and collaborate with the design engineers of the more than 1,000 key suppliers. All of this communication and collaboration slowed the design process and increased costs. It took over four years to get a new model to the market, and the new car often looked "stale" on arrival because public tastes had changed during the course of development.

The Solution

GM, like its competitors, has been transforming itself to an e-business. This gradual transformation has been going on since the mid-1990s, when Internet bandwidth increased sufficiently. GM's first task was to examine over 7,000 existing legacy IT systems, reducing that number to about 3,000 and making them Web enabled. GM's new EC system is centered on a computer-aided design (CAD) program from EDS (a large IT company, *eds.com*). This system, known as Unigraphics, allows 3D design documents to be *shared online* by both the designers (internal and external) and engineers; all of whom are connected by the EDS software. In addition, collaborative and Web conferencing software tools, including Microsoft's NetMeeting and EDS's eVis, were added to enhance teamwork. In 2003, the company moved to eVis 4.0, which allows all of the suppliers, from large companies to mom-and-pop operations, to communicate with GM. These tools have radically changed the vehicle-review process.

To understand how GM now collaborates with a supplier, let's take as an example a needed cost reduction in a new seat frame made by Johnson Control. GM electronically sends its specifications for the seat to the vendor's product data system. Johnson Control's collaboration system (eMatrix) is integrated with EDS's Unigraphics. This collaboration enables joint searching, designing, tooling, and testing of the seat frame in real time, expediting the process and cutting costs by more than 10 percent. Finally, use of math-based modeling and a real-time, Web-based review process enables GM to electronically "crash" some of the cars during the design phases rather than doing it physically after each design change. GM supports this collaboration with its Advanced Design Studio and Virtual Realty lab.

The Results

It now takes less than 18 months to bring a new car to market, compared with 4 or more years before, and the design cost is now much lower. For example, during the design phases, 60 cars are now "crashed" electronically, and only 10 prototype cars are crashed physically. The change has produced enormous savings. In addition, the shorter cycle time enables GM to bring out more new car models more quickly, providing the company with a competitive edge.

These changes have translated into profit. Despite the economic slowdown, GM's revenues increased more than 6 percent in 2002, and its earnings in the second quarter of 2002 doubled that of 2001. By 2004, assembly-line defects dropped by 25 percent, cutting inventory costs by 20 percent.

Sources: Compiled from Sullivan (2002), Rifkin (2002), and Ulfelder (2003).

WHAT WE CAN LEARN . . .

The process of designing cars involves many internal and external partners. The design process used to take a long time, and it was done at a very high cost. To improve the process, GM introduced several information systems that enabled electronic collaboration both internally and externally. The company also introduced information technology to expedite design, reduce problems along the supply and value chains of the design process, and drastically reduce costs. This case demonstrates several applications of EC that do not involve buying or selling: collaborative commerce, improvements along the supply chain, and B2E. These and related issues are the topics of Chapter 7.

7.1 E-SUPPLY CHAINS

Many people equate e-commerce with selling and buying on the Internet. However, although a company's success is clearly dependent on finding and retaining customers, its success may be far more dependent on what is *behind* the Web page than on what is *on* the Web page. In other words, the company's internal operations (the back end) and its relationships with suppliers and other business partners are as critical, and frequently much more complex, than customer-facing applications such as taking an order online. This is of course true in the off-line business as well. In many cases, these non-customer-facing applications are related to the company's supply chain.

It has been well known for generations that the success of many organizations—private, public, and military—depends on their ability to manage the flow of materials, information, and money into, within, and out of the organization. Such a flow is referred to as a *supply chain*. Because supply chains may be long and complex and may involve many different business partners, we frequently see problems in the operation of the supply chains. These problems may result in delays, in customer dissatisfaction, in lost sales, and in high expenses that result from fixing the problems once they occur. World-class companies, such as Dell, attribute much of their success to effective supply chain management (SCM), which is largely supported by IT and e-commerce technologies.

This chapter focuses on supply chain issues related to e-commerce. In addition, it covers several related topics such as collaboration and integration along the supply chain. The topic of financial supply chains (payment systems) is covered in Chapter 12, and order fulfillment is covered in Chapter 13. The essentials of supply chains and their management are described in Online Tutorial T2.

DEFINITIONS AND CONCEPTS

To understand e-supply chains, one must first understand nonelectronic supply chains. A **supply chain** is the flow of materials, information, money, and services from raw material suppliers through factories and warehouses to the end customers. A supply chain also includes the *organizations* and *processes* that create and deliver products, information, and services to the end customers. The term *supply chain* comes from the concept of how the partnering organizations are *linked* together.

supply chain
The flow of materials, information, money, and services from raw material suppliers through factories and warehouses to the end customers.

As shown in Exhibit 7.1, a simple linear supply chain links a company that manufactures or assembles a product (middle of the chain) with its suppliers (on the left) and distributors and customers (on the right). The upper part of the figure shows a generic supply chain. The bottom part shows a specific example of the toy-making process. The solid links in the figure show the flow of materials among the various partners. Not shown is the flow of returned goods (e.g., defective products) and money, which are flowing in the reverse direction. The broken links, which are shown only in the upper part of Exhibit 7.1, indicate the bidirectional flow of information.

A supply chain involves activities that take place during the entire product *life cycle*, "from dirt to dust," as some describe it. However, a supply chain is more than that, because it also includes the movement of information and money and the procedures that support the movement of a product or a service. Finally, the organizations and individuals involved are considered part of the supply chain as well. When looked at very broadly, the supply chain actually ends when the product reaches its after-use disposal—presumably back to Mother Earth somewhere.

The supply chain shown in Exhibit 7.1 is fairly simple. As will be shown in Online Tutorial T2, supply chains can be much more complex, and they are of different types.

When a supply chain is managed electronically, usually with Web technologies, it is referred to as an **e-supply chain**. As will be shown throughout this chapter, improvements in e-supply chains are a major target for EC applications. However, before examining how e-supply chains are managed, it is necessary to better understand the composition of supply chains.

e-supply chain
A supply chain that is managed electronically, usually with Web technologies.

EXHIBIT 7.1 A Simple Supply Chain

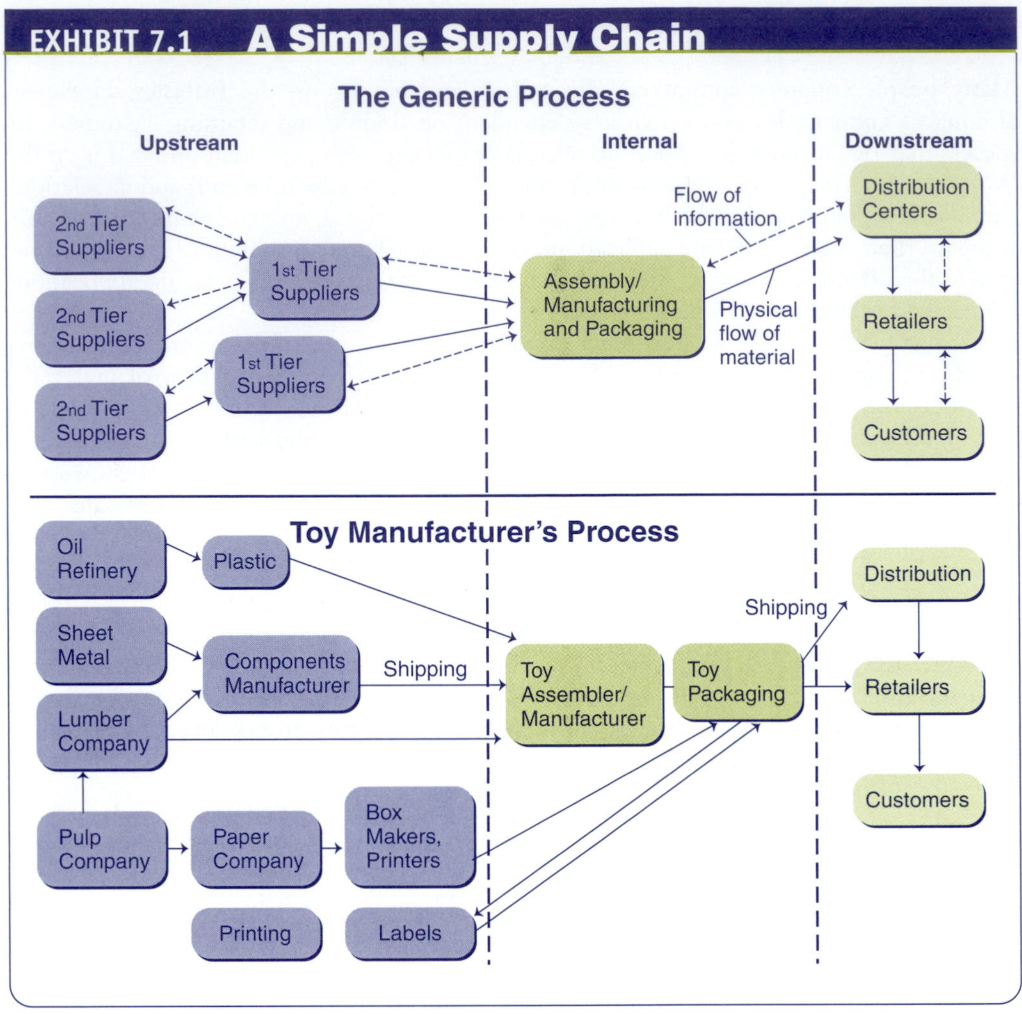

SUPPLY CHAIN PARTS

A supply chain can be broken into three major parts: upstream, internal, and downstream, as was shown in Exhibit 7.1.

- **Upstream supply chain.** The upstream part of the supply chain includes the activities of a manufacturing company with its suppliers (which can be manufacturers, assemblers, or both) and their connections with their suppliers (second-tier suppliers). The supplier relationship can be extended to the left in several tiers, all the way to the origin of the material (e.g., mining ores, growing crops). In the upstream supply chain, the major activity is *procurement*.
- **Internal supply chain.** The internal part of the supply chain includes all of the in-house processes used in transforming the inputs received from the suppliers into the organization's outputs. It extends from the time the inputs enter an organization to the time that the products go to distribution outside of the organization. In this part of the supply chain, the major concerns are production management, manufacturing, and inventory control. The activities along the internal supply chain are referred to as the company's *value chain* (see Online Tutorial T2 and Davenport and Brooks 2004). The value chain also can be seen as an integrator between customers (B2C) and suppliers (B2B). For details, see Davis and Benamati (2003). The primary objective of the value chain is to add value along the internal supply chain in what we describe as *intrabusiness e-commerce* (see Section 7.5 and Chapter 6 in Davis and Benamati 2003).

- **Downstream supply chain.** The downstream part of the supply chain includes all the activities involved in delivering the products to the final customers. In the downstream supply chain, attention is directed at distribution, warehousing, transportation, and after-sale service.

A company's supply chain and its accompanying value chain (see Online Tutorial T2) encompass an array of business processes that create value by delivering goods or services to customers.

MANAGING SUPPLY CHAINS

Managing supply chains can be difficult due to the need to coordinate several business partners, several internal corporate departments, numerous business processes, and possibly many customers. Managing medium to large supply chains manually is almost impossible. Information technology provides two types of software solutions: (1) SCM and (2) ERP and its predecessors MRP and MRP II. (These types of software are defined and described in Online Tutorial T2.) A major requirement for any medium- to large-scale company that is moving to EC implies an integration between the Web and the ERP/MRP/SCM solutions—in other words, creating an e-supply chain and managing it.

E-Supply Chains and Their Management

According to Norris et al. (2000), **e-supply chain management (e-SCM)** is the collaborative use of technology to enhance B2B processes and improve speed, agility, real-time control, and customer satisfaction. It involves the use of information technologies to improve the operations of supply chain activities (e.g., procurement) as well as the management of the supply chains (e.g., planning, coordination, and control). E-SCM is not about technology change alone; it also involves changes in management policies, organizational culture, performance metrics, business processes, and organizational structure across the supply chain.

e-supply chain management (e-SCM)
The collaborative use of technology to improve the operations of supply chain activities as well as the management of supply chains.

The success of an e-supply chain depends on the following:

- **The ability of all supply chain partners to view partner collaboration as a strategic asset.** It is the tight integration and trust among the trading partners that generates speed, agility, and lower cost.
- **Information visibility along the entire supply chain.** Information about inventories at various segments of the chain, demand for products, delivery times, and any other relevant information must be visible to all members of the supply chain at any given time. Therefore, information must be managed properly—with strict policies, discipline, and daily monitoring.
- **Speed, cost, quality, and customer service.** These are the metrics by which supply chains are measured. Consequently, companies must clearly define the measurements for each of these four metrics together with the target levels to be achieved. The target levels should be attractive to the business partners.
- **Integrating the supply chain more tightly.** An e-supply chain will benefit from tighter integration, both within a company and across an extended enterprise made up of suppliers, trading partners, logistics providers, and the distribution channel.

Activities and Infrastructure of E-SCM

E-supply chain activities include the following.

Supply Chain Replenishment. Supply chain replenishment encompasses the integrated production and distribution processes. Companies can use replenishment information to reduce inventories, eliminate stocking points, and increase the velocity of replenishment by synchronizing supply and demand information across the extended enterprise. Real-time supply and demand information facilitates make-to-order and assemble-to-order manufacturing strategies across the extended enterprise. Supply-chain replenishment is a natural companion to Web-enabled customer orders. (For more on this topic, see Stevenson 2004.)

E-Procurement. E-procurement, as described in Chapter 5, is the use of Web-based technology to support the key procurement processes, including requisitioning, sourcing, contracting, ordering, and payment. E-procurement supports the purchase of both direct and indirect materials and employs several Web-based functions such as online catalogs, contracts, purchase orders, and shipping notices. E-procurement can improve the operation of the supply chain in various ways: Online catalogs can be used to eliminate redesign of components in product development; visibility of available parts and their attributes enables quick decision making; online purchase orders expedite the ordering process; and advanced-shipping notifications and acknowledgments streamline delivery.

Supply Chain Monitoring and Control Using RFID. This is one of the most promising applications of RFID. We will return to this topic later in this chapter.

Inventory Management Using Wireless Devices. MemorialCare in Southern California is just one of many hospitals that are using PDAs to enter inventory item counts and then loading the data directly into the mainframe procurement system. This process is not only faster and less prone to error, but the data are processed in real time and orders (if needed) are generated automatically. The system is based on XML architecture. If orders are needed (based on the inventory count), the mainframe automatically transfers the order to a PeopleSoft system. This system creates purchase orders, e-mails them to the appropriate suppliers, generates invoices, and processes payments, all without any additional information (see PeopleSoft 2003).

Collaborative Planning. Collaborative planning requires buyers and sellers to develop shared demand forecasts and supply plans for how to support demand. These forecasts and supply plans should be updated regularly, based on information shared over the Internet. Such collaborative planning requires B2B workflow across multiple enterprises over the Internet, with data exchanged among partners dynamically (see Brenchley 2004). This topic is discussed further in Section 7.4.

Collaborative Design and Product Development. Collaborative product development involves the use of product design and development techniques across multiple companies to improve product launch success and reduce time-to-market (as demonstrated in the GM opening case). During product development, engineering and design drawings can be shared over a secure network among the contract firm, testing facility, marketing firm, and downstream manufacturing and service companies. Other techniques include sharing specifications, test results, and design changes and using online prototyping to obtain customer feedback. Development costs can be reduced by tightly integrating and streamlining communication channels.

E-Logistics. E-logistics is the use of Web-based technologies to support the material acquisition, warehousing, and transportation processes. E-logistics enables distribution to couple routing optimization with inventory tracking information. For example, Internet-based freight auctions allow spot buying of trucking capacity. Third-party logistics providers offer virtual logistics services by integrating and optimizing distribution resources. For example, a company may consider collaboration with its competitors to improve its supply chain. For an example of how Land O'Lakes collaborates with its competitors via an electronic market, see Online File W7.1. This topic will be covered in Chapter 13. For additional discussion of this topic, see Bayles (2001) and Kannan (2004).

Use of B2B Exchanges and Supply Webs. The B2B exchanges introduced in Chapter 6 could play a critical role in e-supply chain management. Norris et al. (2000) view this role in what they call *supply webs*. Supply webs emerge as alternative configurations to the traditional supply chains. Information, transactions, products, and funds all flow to and from *multiple* nodes in a supply web. Supply webs (or vortals) serve industry sectors by integrating the supply chain systems of various buyers and sellers creating *virtual trading communities*.

Infrastructure for e-SCM

The key activities just described use a variety of infrastructure and enabling tools. The following are the major infrastructure elements and tools of e-supply chains.

- **Electronic Data Interchange.** EDI (see Appendix 6A) is the major tool used by large corporations to facilitate supply chain relationships. Many companies are shifting from internal EDI to Internet-based EDI.
- **Extranets.** These are described in Appendix 6A. Their major purpose is to support interorganizational communication and collaboration. For details on success factors for using extranets in eSCM, see Chow (2004).
- **Intranets.** These are the corporate internal networks for communication and collaboration. They are described in the Online Appendix W7A.

- **Corporate portals.** These provide a gateway for external and internal collaboration, communication, and information search. They are described in Section 7.7.

- **Workflow systems and tools.** These are systems that *manage* the flow of information in organizations. They are described in Section 7.8. Also see Kanakamedala et al. (2003).
- **Groupware and other collaborative tools.** A large number of tools facilitate collaboration and communication between two parties and among members of small as well as large groups. Various tools, some of which are collectively known as *groupware,* enable such collaboration, as described in Section 7.8.

Section 7.1 ▶ REVIEW QUESTIONS

1. Define the e-supply chain and list its three major parts.
2. Describe success factors of e-supply chain management.
3. List the eight processes of e-supply chains.
4. List the major e-supply chain management infrastructures and enabling tools.

7.2 SUPPLY CHAIN PROBLEMS AND SOLUTIONS

Supply chains have been plagued with problems, both in military and business operations, for generations. These problems have sometimes caused armies to lose wars and companies to go out of business. The problems are most apparent in complex or long supply chains and in cases where many business partners are involved. As this section will show, some remedies are finally available through the use of IT and EC.

TYPICAL PROBLEMS ALONG THE SUPPLY CHAIN

Supply chains can be very long, involving many internal and external partners located in different places. Both materials and information must flow among several entities, and these transfers, especially when manually handled, can be slow and error prone. (See Cook and Hagey 2003.)

In the off-line world, there are many examples of companies that were unable to meet demand for certain products while having oversized and expensive inventories of other products. Similar situations exist online (see Chapter 13). One of the most publicized problems in EC was the supply-demand mismatch of toys during the holiday season of November–December 1999 (see Chapter 13). In this case, there was a shortage of toys due to incorrect demand forecasting. A demand forecast is influenced by a number of factors, including consumer behavior, economic conditions, competition, prices, weather conditions, technological developments, and more. Companies can improve their demand forecasting by using IT-supported forecasts, which are done in collaboration with business partners.

Another problem in the 1999 toy season was related to shipping. A lack of logistics infrastructure prevented the right toys from reaching their destinations on time. Various uncertainties exist in delivery times, which depend on many factors, ranging from vehicle failures to road conditions.

Quality problems with materials and parts also can contribute to deficiencies in the supply chain. The worst case is when quality problems create production delays, idling factories and workers and crimping inventories. Some companies grapple with quality problems due to general misunderstandings or to shipments of wrong materials and parts. Sometimes, the high cost of expediting operations or shipments is the unfortunate result.

Pure EC companies are likely to have more supply chain problems because they do not have a logistics infrastructure and are forced to use external logistics services. This can be expensive, plus it requires more coordination and dependence on outsiders. For this reason, some large virtual retailers, such as Amazon.com, have developed physical warehouses and logistics systems. Other virtual retailers are creating strategic alliances with logistics companies or with brick-and-mortar companies that have their own logistics systems. Other problems along the EC supply chain mainly stem from the need to coordinate several activities and internal units and business partners. For more on supply chain problems, see Handfield et al. (2002) and Balakrishnan and Geunes (2004).

The Bullwhip Effect

bullwhip effect
Erratic shifts in orders up and down supply chains.

One additional supply chain problem, called the **bullwhip effect**, is worth noting. The bullwhip effect refers to erratic shifts in orders up and down supply chains (see Davies 2004 and Plunkett 2004). This effect was initially observed by P&G with their disposable diapers in off-line retail stores. Although actual sales in stores were fairly stable and predictable, orders from distributors had wild swings, creating production and inventory problems for P&G. An investigation revealed that distributors' orders were fluctuating because of poor demand forecasts, price fluctuations, order batching, and rationing within the supply chain. All of this resulted in unnecessary inventories in various places along the supply chain, fluctuations in P&G orders to its suppliers, and the flow of inaccurate information. Distorted or late information can lead to tremendous inefficiencies, excessive inventories, poor customer service, lost revenues, ineffective shipments, and missed production schedules.

The bullwhip effect is not unique to P&G. Firms from HP in the computer industry to Bristol-Myers Squibb in the pharmaceutical field have experienced a similar phenomenon (Handfield et al. 2002 and Davies 2004). Basically, even slight demand uncertainties and variabilities become magnified when viewed through the eyes of managers at each link in the supply chain. If each distinct entity makes ordering and inventory decisions with an eye to its own interest above those of the chain, stockpiling may be occurring simultaneously at as many as seven or eight places across the supply chain. Such stockpiling can lead to as many as 100 days of inventory waiting "just in case." A 1998 industry study by the American Agricultural Economic Association (aaea.org, reported by Ricks et al. (1999)), projected that $30 billion in savings could materialize in the grocery industry supply chains alone as a result of improved *information sharing*. Thus, companies may avoid the "sting of the bullwhip" if they take steps to share information along the supply chain. Such sharing is facilitated by EDI, extranets, and groupware technologies and is part of interorganizational EC and *collaborative commerce*, topics discussed elsewhere in this chapter.

THE NEED FOR INFORMATION SHARING ALONG THE SUPPLY CHAIN

By definition, a supply chain includes the flow of information to and from all participating entities. The information can be supportive of physical shipments or of shipments of digitized products (or services). It includes product pricing, inventory, shipping status, credit and financial information, and technology news. Many, if not most, of the supply chain problems that occur are the result of poor flow of information, inaccurate information, untimely information, and so on. Information must be managed properly in each supply chain segment.

Information systems are the links that enable communication and collaboration along the supply chain. According to Handfield and Nichols (2002), they represent one of the fundamental elements that link the organizations of the supply chain into a unified and coordinated system. In today's competitive business climate, information and information technology are one of the keys to the success, and perhaps even the survival, of any SCM initiative (Handfield et al. 2002).

Case studies of some world-class companies, such as Wal-Mart, Dell, and FedEx, indicate that these companies have created very sophisticated information systems, exploiting the latest technological developments and creating innovative solutions. However, even world-class companies such as Cisco Systems may suffer from inappropriate information sharing (see EC Application Case 7.1).

EC SOLUTIONS ALONG THE SUPPLY CHAIN

EC as a technology provides solutions along the supply chain, as has been shown throughout this book. Such solutions are beneficial both to brick-and-mortar operations and to online companies (Craighead and Shaw 2003). Here is a representative list of the major solutions provided by an EC approach and technologies.

- *Order taking* can be done over the Internet, EDI, EDI/Internet, or an extranet, and it may be fully automated. For example, in B2B, orders are generated and transmitted automatically to suppliers when inventory levels fall below certain levels. The result is a fast, inexpensive, and more accurate (no need to rekey data) order-taking process. In B2C, Web-based ordering using electronic forms expedites the process, makes it more

CASE 7.1

EC Application

CISCO'S SUPPLY CHAIN: FAILURE AND SUCCESS

Surprising as it may seem, Cisco Systems does not manufacture its own hardware, nor does it program its own software. These activities are outsourced. Cisco basically designs products, doing the necessary research and development (R&D); submits the blueprints to reliable suppliers (who may use subsuppliers for the components); and then concentrates on marketing and sales. Once a customer decides to purchase from Cisco, a sales contract is agreed on and Cisco transfers the customer's order to an appropriate supplier who then ships the item directly to the customer. Cisco's suppliers and subsuppliers also work for Cisco's competitors. Cisco's customers may purchase both from Cisco as well as from Cisco's suppliers. The process is shown in the attached exhibit.

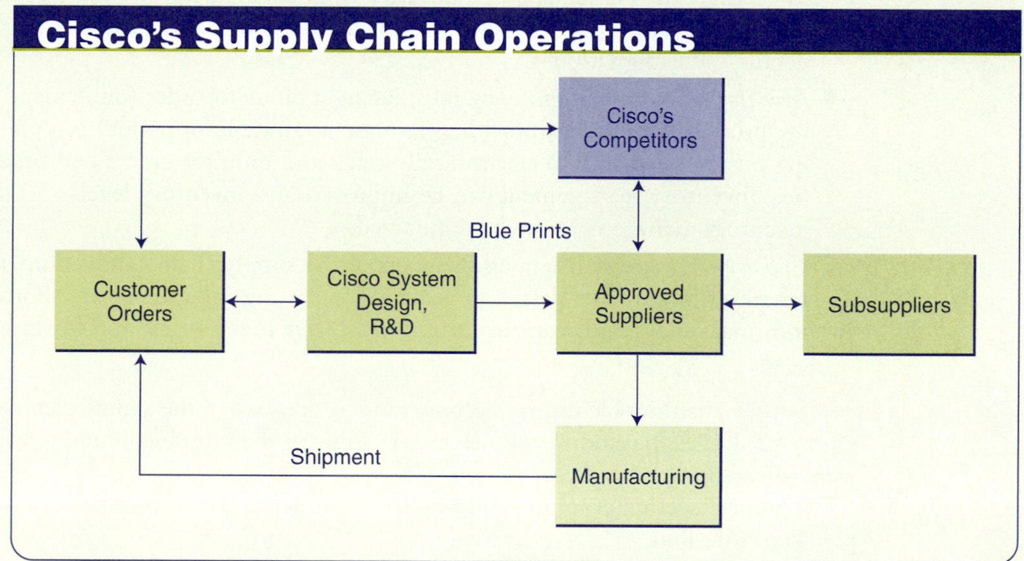

The system appeared to work well; Cisco's profit increased dramatically (as did its share price). However, in May 2001 Cisco announced a one-time $2.2 billion inventory write-off. According to Kaihla (2002), a primary cause of Cisco's inventory write-off was a failure of the supply chain integration system.

The problem started when Cisco's customers, anticipating high demand and possible shortages, placed duplicate orders for routers and switches with both Cisco and Cisco's competitors with the intent of buying from the supplier offering the earliest delivery date and then canceling the other orders. Unaware of the duplicate orders, Cisco's supply chain integration system generated what turned out to be a very large demand forecast. Cisco's manufacturing suppliers, fearing shortages, reacted to that forecast by placing duplicate orders for components and subassemblies with their subtier suppliers. Because those subtier suppliers were unable to see Cisco's initial forecast, they had no knowledge of the duplicate orders and thus developed plans to manufacture components to meet what they thought was the real demand. The result was to take an already too high forecast and further inflate it. When the recession hit in 2000, Cisco was left holding roughly three times as many routers and switches as its customers were willing to buy. Because technology changes quickly, many of the products became obsolete.

Cisco's supply chain failure illustrates the importance of an accurate demand forecast. If the forecast is flawed, subsequent computations and decisions will almost certainly compound the initial error. Cisco responded by improving its supply chain system by implementing *e*Hub, an exchange that makes relevant information visible to all supply chain participants at all levels. Run by Viacore (*viacore.net*), a supply chain intermediary, *e*Hub promises to improve demand forecasts.

Source: Compiled from Kaihla (2002).

Questions

1. Discuss the importance of demand forecast in build-to-order (like Cisco) versus build-to-market.
2. How can the *e*Hub solve the problem of order duplication at various segments of the supply chain? (You will need to do some research.)
3. Is this an example of the bullwhip effect? Why or why not?

accurate (intelligent agents can check the input data and provide instant feedback), and reduces processing costs.

- *Order fulfillment* can become instant if the products can be digitized (e.g., software). In other cases, EC order taking interfaces with the company's back-office systems, including logistics. Such an interface, or even integration, shortens cycle time and eliminates errors. (See Chapter 13 for more on order fulfillment.)
- *Electronic payments* can expedite both the order fulfillment cycle and the payment delivery period. Payment processing can be significantly less expensive and fraud can be better controlled. (See Chapter 12 for more on electronic payments.)
- *Managing risk* to avoid supply-chain breakdown (Chopra and Sodhi 2004) can be done in several ways. Inventories are effective but can be expensive. Also, in certain cases the risk increases because products may become obsolete. To combat terrorism and reduce cargo theft the National Cargo Security Council, a part of the Transportation Security Administration (tsa.gov) provides information about new products (e.g., RFID). For details, see Emigh (2004).
- *Inventories can be minimized* by introducing a build-to-order (on demand) manufacturing process as well as by providing fast and accurate information to suppliers. By allowing business partners to electronically track and monitor orders and production activities, inventory management can be improved and inventory levels and the expense of inventory management can be minimized.
- *Collaborative commerce* among members of the supply chain can be done in many areas, ranging from product design to demand forecasting. The results are shorter cycle times, minimal delays and work interruptions, lower inventories, and lower administrative costs.

Supply chain problems may become more serious when the supply chain involves global segments. EC Application Case 7.2 reviews some of these problems and examines how they were solved by Corning Inc.

The next section examines collaborative commerce, which may be used to provide supply chain solutions.

Section 7.2 ▶ REVIEW QUESTIONS

1. Describe some typical problems along the supply chain.
2. Describe the reasons for supply-chain-related problems.
3. Describe the bullwhip effect.
4. Describe the benefits of information sharing along the supply chain.
5. List some EC solutions to supply chain problems.

7.3 COLLABORATIVE COMMERCE

Previous chapters introduced B2B activities related mainly to selling and buying. E-commerce also can be used to improve collaboration within and among organizations along the supply chain.

ESSENTIALS OF COLLABORATIVE COMMERCE

collaborative commerce (c-commerce)
The use of digital technologies that enable companies to collaboratively plan, design, develop, manage, and research products, services, and innovative EC applications.

Collaborative commerce (c-commerce) refers to the use of digital technologies that enable companies to collaboratively plan, design, develop, manage, and research products, services, and innovative EC applications. These activities differ from selling and buying. An example would be a company that it is collaborating electronically with a vendor that designs a product or a part for the company, as was shown in the GM opening case. C-commerce implies communication, information sharing, and collaborative planning done electronically through tools such as groupware and specially designed EC collaboration tools.

Numerous studies (e.g., line56.com 2002) suggest that collaborative relationships result in significant impacts on organizations' performance. Major benefits cited are cost reduction, increased revenue, and better customer retention. These benefits are the results of fewer stock

CASE 7.2

EC Application

GLOBAL SUPPLY CHAIN SYNCHRONIZATION AT CORNING, INC.

Corning Inc., a glass manufacturer headquartered in upstate New York, makes optical fiber, cables, and photonic components, LCD glass for flat-panel displays and other products, as well as the glassware and cookware that were the company's original products. The company has multiple businesses and research, production, and distribution sites in 34 countries.

Although they share the direction and global focus of the organization, the company's 12 business units have been managing independently, since 1995, their own planning, order management, production, and other supply chain operations. Such decentralization empowers the units, but the company has experienced problems ranging from delivery delays to excessive inventory costs along its long and unsynchronized supply chains.

To ease these problems, Corning looked for solutions that would enable it to create and optimize truly global supply chains within its businesses. The Supply Chain Technology Strategy group, along with the process owners (the Corning managers who are responsible for the various processes), did wide-ranging analyses of each business unit. The group planned improvements in the supply chain process and tried to find the best SCM solutions to help carry out the improvements. Corning chose PeopleSoft as its ERP vendor. Using PeopleSoft technology, Corning was able to integrate the relevant activities of its manufacturers, suppliers, customer service organizations, sales organizations, and technology innovators.

To enable an optimized, real-time "virtual factory" environment, Corning Specialty Materials Group (manufacturer of semiconductors, photonics, and technical materials) combines PeopleSoft manufacturing, customer fulfillment management, and supply chain planning solutions to improve *collaboration* among the 14 factories and sales and research sites worldwide.

Rick Beers, Director of Supply Chain Technology at Corning, explains, "High performance at Corning means agility. We need to react quickly to opportunities or problems in our supply chains—to see snags coming and plan accordingly, or adjust production levels in response to demand. That requires real-time data and interoperability among applications. It all comes down to having the right information at the right place at the right time" (PeopleSoft 2002).

The improved infrastructure, specifically a common database shared throughout Corning's organization, has made possible the flexibility to increase yield, decrease cycle time, and maintain low levels of inventory based on sales forecasts. The new process has transformed the supply chain by increasing or improving collaboration, workflow, planning, strategic analysis, and e-business initiatives. Corning is now experiencing significantly fewer problems along its supply chain.

Sources: Compiled from Springer (2002), *corning.com* (press releases, 2002), and PeopleSoft (June 2002). (Note: PeopleSoft was acquired by Oracle in 2005.)

Questions

1. What were the problems of Corning's old system?
2. What was the logic behind decentralizing operations?
3. How is integration of information done in the decentralized environment?
4. How is flexibility provided by the new system?

outs, less exception processing, reduced inventory throughout the supply chain, lower materials costs, increased sales volume, and increased competitive advantage. For examples, see Brook (2004).

COLLABORATION HUBS

One of the most popular forms of c-commerce is the **collaboration hub**, which is used for the members of a supply chain.

collaboration hub
The central point of control for an e-market. A single c-hub, representing one e-market owner, can host multiple collaboration spaces (c-spaces) in which trading partners use c-enablers to exchange data with the c-hub.

C-commerce activities usually are conducted between and among supply chain partners (Simatupang and Sridharan 2002). Chapter 1 (page 24) provided an example of Orbis, a small Australian company that uses a hub to communicate among all its business partners. A similar model is used by Webcor Builders, as shown in Online File W7.2. Finally, Lowe & Partners use a variation of a hub on a PC, as shown in EC Application Case 7.3.

There are several varieties of c-commerce, ranging from joint design efforts to forecasting. Collaboration can be done both between and within organizations. For example, a collaborative platform can help in communication and collaboration between headquarters and subsidiaries or between franchisers and franchisees. The platform provides, for example, e-mail, message boards and chat rooms, and online corporate data access around the globe, no matter what the time zone. The following sections demonstrate some types and examples of c-commerce.

CASE 7.3

EC Application

COLLABORATION CREATES A SWARM AT LOWE & PARTNERS WORLDWIDE

When an account executive at the Hong Kong branch of Lowe & Partners Worldwide (*loweworldwide.com*), a large advertising agency, receives a request for a proposal from a prospective client, she opens up a *collaboration space* on her PC and invites in subject-area experts, planners, and other creative people from several countries (e.g., the United States, India, or England). Each expert can invite others from his or her personal network, whether inside or outside the company. In minutes, a "swarm" of creative talent is exploiting the opportunity. Artists post relevant images; content experts surf the Web in unison to find useful sites; researchers drop in pertinent files; copywriters type or edit documents together in real time.

Swarming is a type of collaboration in which large numbers of geographically dispersed people quickly self-organize in a peer-to-peer network to deal with a problem or opportunity. It is a fluid network with no central control. A swarm can be as complex as a global business network or as simple as a "cell-phone posse" (a group, or swarm, of people holding an impromptu teleconference on their cell phones). Swarming lets organizations quickly accomplish more, using the same resources, and it enables more agile, rapidly assembled, ad-hoc collaborations of all kinds.

In an attempt to match the agility of smaller competitors, Lowe, a large multinational organization (180 offices in over 80 countries), turned to Groove Networks (*groove.net*) to facilitate the swarming approach. Lowe's prospective clients have asked to see how the team space works, and they have been invited to come in by downloading free trial software from the Web. As a result, the clients have become collaborators.

For Lowe, swarming has saved on expenses such as international couriers, travel, and faxing. The swarming technology saved Lowe a lot of problems and money when the SARS virus brought commerce in Hong Kong to a virtual halt in 2003. Real-time collaboration spaces linked clients in Hong Kong, subcontractors in India and Taiwan, and headquarters executives in London.

Source: Compiled from Melymuka (2003).

Questions

1. Is there any control over the swarm at Lowe? If not, should there be? If needed, how would you implement control over a swarm?
2. Would a lack of control over a swarm cause the swarm to be less effective?
3. What other applications can you think of for swarms?
4. Why is this a collaborative hub?

COLLABORATIVE NETWORKS

Traditionally, collaboration took place among supply chain members, frequently those that were close to each other (e.g., a manufacturer and its distributor or a distributor and a retailer). Even if more partners were involved, the focus was on the optimization of information and product flow between existing nodes in the traditional supply chain. Advanced approaches such as Collaboration, Planning, Forecasting and Replenishing (CPFR), which is described in the next section, do not change the basic structure.

Traditional collaboration results in a vertically integrated supply chain. However, as stated in Chapters 1 and 2, EC and Web technologies can *fundamentally change* the shape of the supply chain, the number of players within it, and their individual roles. The new supply chain can be a hub, as shown in the Orbis case (see Chapter 1), or even a network. A comparison between the traditional supply chain and the new one, which is made possible by Web technologies, is shown in Exhibit 7.2. Notice that the traditional chain in Part A is basically linear. The *collaborative network* in Part B shows that partners at any point in the network can interact with each other, bypassing traditional partners. Interaction may occur among several manufacturers or distributors, as well as with new players such as software agents that act as aggregators, B2B exchanges, or logistics providers.

The collaborative network can take different shapes depending on the industry, the product (or service), the volume of information flow, and more. Examples of collaborative networks are provided by Poirier (2001) and by Szekely (2003).

EXHIBIT 7.2 Comparing the Traditional Collaborative Supply Chain and Collaborative Networks

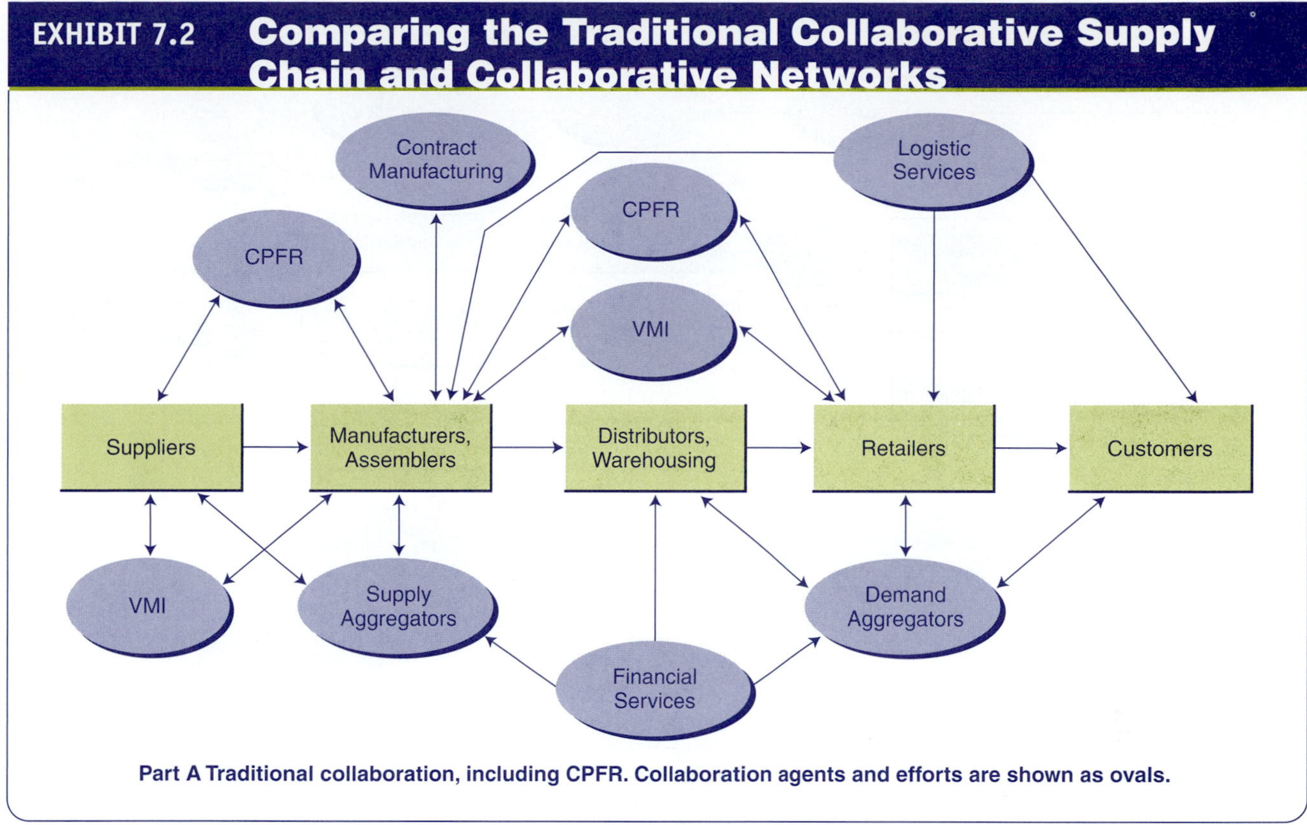

Part A Traditional collaboration, including CPFR. Collaboration agents and efforts are shown as ovals.

Mobile Collaborative Networks and Grid Computing

As mobile technologies become more and more mature, mobile collaborative networks are gradually coming into being. These networks have the ability to share valuable business information in mobile scenarios with those who are co-located or remote and who are not necessarily from the same enterprise. Mobile workers are able to communicate and share information anytime, anywhere (Bartram and Blackstock 2003; Divitini et al. 2004).

The latest and most ambitious type of collaborative network is grid computing. **Grid computing** is a form of distributed computing that involves coordinating and sharing computing, application, data, storage, or network resources across dynamic and geographically dispersed organizations. Grid technologies promise to change the way organizations tackle complex computational problems. However, the vision of large-scale resource sharing is not yet a reality in many areas. Grid computing is an evolving area of computing; standards and technology are still being developed to enable this new paradigm. Perhaps dynamic virtual corporations based on mobile technologies and grid computing will be the most common business model in the future (Vallés et al. 2004). For further information about grid computing, see grid.org, www-1.ibm.com/grid, and oracle.com/grid.

grid computing
A form of distributed computing that involves coordinating and sharing computing, application, data, storage, or network resources across dynamic and geographically dispersed organizations.

REPRESENTATIVE EXAMPLES OF E-COLLABORATION

Leading businesses are moving quickly to realize the benefits of c-commerce. For example, the real estate franchiser RE/MAX uses a c-commerce platform to improve communications and collaboration among its nationwide network of independently owned real estate franchises, sales associates, and suppliers. Similarly, Marriott International, the world's largest hospitality company, started with an online brochure and then developed a c-commerce system that links corporations, franchisees, partners, suppliers, and customers around the world. (See Intel 1999a and 1999b for details.)

Leading companies such as Dell, Cisco, and HP have begun to use collaborative commerce strategically, enabling sophisticated business models while transforming their value

EXHIBIT 7.2 *(continued)*

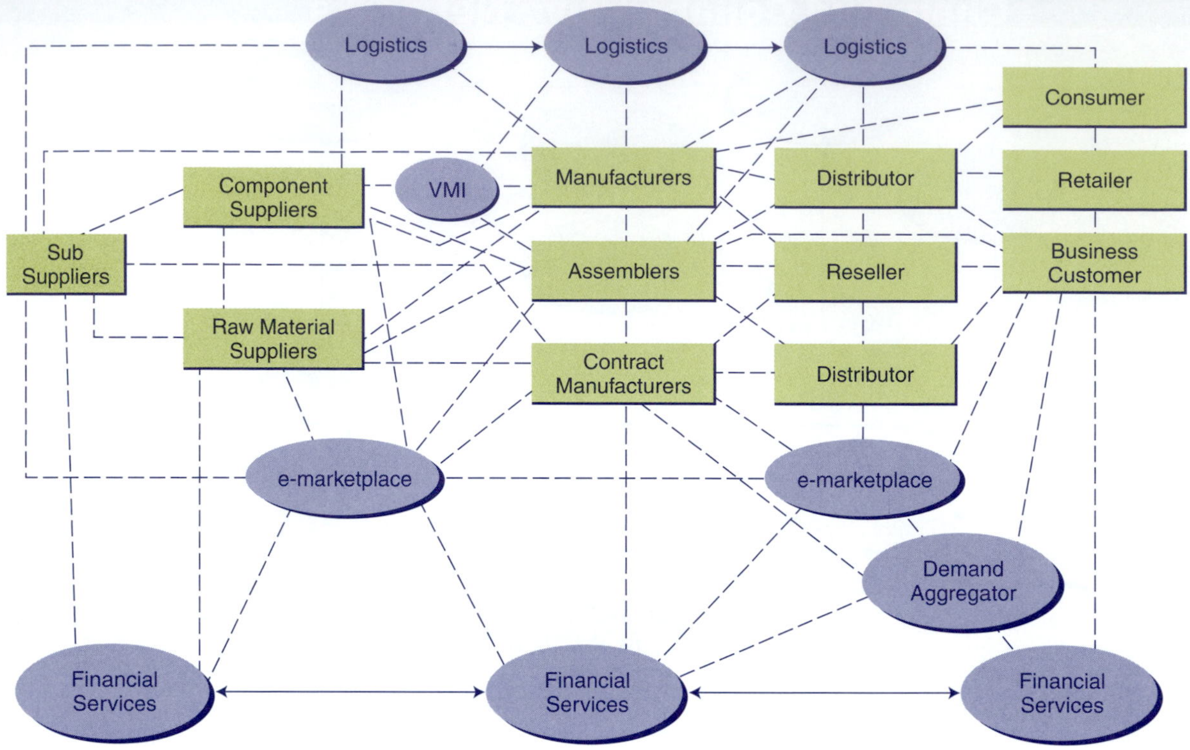

Logistics
Logistics
Logistics
Consumer
Component Suppliers
VMI
Manufacturers
Distributor
Retailer
Sub Suppliers
Assemblers
Reseller
Business Customer
Raw Material Suppliers
Contract Manufacturers
Distributor
e-marketplace
e-marketplace
Demand Aggregator
Financial Services
Financial Services
Financial Services

Part B Supply chains are evolving into collaborative networks. Ovals designate agents and services.

Sources: (b) Poirier, C. "Collaborative Commerce: Wave Two of the Cyber Revolution." *Computer Sciences Corporation Perspectives* (221):8, p. 9-8, fig. 1. Used with permission of Computer Sciences Corporation. All rights reserved.

chains. They also have implemented e-procurement and other mature collaboration techniques to streamline operations, reduce overhead, and maintain or enhance margins in the face of intense competition. For example, Dell implemented end-to-end integrated configuration and ordering, a single enterprise middleware backbone, and multitier collaborative planning. This has enabled Dell to support a make-to-order business model with best-in-class speed and efficiency. Cisco chose to support a virtual business model focusing on time-to-market and customer satisfaction. Cisco has integrated its order process with back-end processes, implemented purchase order automation, and enabled collaborative product development (SupplyChainBrain.com 2001).

In addition, as described in Online File W7.3, Nygard of Canada has developed a collaborative system along its entire supply chain. There are many examples of e-collaboration. Some additional representative examples follow. For more, see Schram (2004), Davison and de Vreede (2001), and Frank (2004).

Vendor Managed Inventory

vendor managed inventory (VMI)
The practice of retailers making suppliers responsible for determining when to order and how much to order.

With **vendor managed inventory (VMI)**, retailers make their suppliers responsible for determining when to order and how much to order. The retailer provides the supplier with real-time information (e.g., point-of-sale data), inventory levels, and a threshold below which orders are replenished. The reorder quantities also are predetermined and usually recommended by the supplier. By using this approach, the retailer is no longer burdened with inventory management, demand forecasting becomes easier, the supplier can see the potential need for an item before the item is ordered, there are no purchase orders, inventories are kept low, and stockouts become infrequent. This method was initiated by Wal-Mart in the 1980s and was supported by EDI. Today, it can be supported by CFPR and special software. VMI software solutions are provided by Sockeye Solutions, Cactus Communications, and JDA Software. For details, see Richardson (2004) and Bury (2004).

Information Sharing Between Retailers and Suppliers: P&G and Wal-Mart

Information sharing among business partners, as well as among the various units inside each organization, is necessary for the success of SCM. Information systems must be designed so that sharing becomes easy. One of the most notable examples of information sharing is between P&G and Wal-Mart. Wal-Mart provides P&G access to sales information on every item P&G makes for Wal-Mart. The information is collected by P&G on a daily basis from every Wal-Mart store, and P&G uses the information to manage inventory replenishment for Wal-Mart. By monitoring the inventory level of each P&G item in every Wal-Mart store, P&G knows when the inventories fall below the threshold that triggers a shipment. All this is done electronically. The benefit for P&G is accurate demand information; the benefit for Wal-Mart is adequate inventory. P&G has similar agreements with other major retailers. For more on Wal-Mart, see Staff (2004a). Another example is that of Target Corp.

Retailer–Supplier Collaboration: Target Corporation

Target Corporation (targetcorp.com) is a large retail conglomerate (owner of Target Stores, Marshall Field's, Mervyn's, and Target Direct). It needs to conduct EC activities with about 20,000 trading partners. In 1998, then operating under the name Dayton-Hudson Corporation, the company established an extranet-based system for those partners that were not connected to its VAN-based EDI. The extranet enabled the company not only to reach many more partners, but also to use many applications not available on the traditional EDI. The system (based on GE's InterBusiness Partner Extranet platform, geis.com) enabled the company to streamline its communications and collaboration with suppliers. It also allowed the company's business customers to create personalized Web pages that were accessible via either the Internet or GE's private VAN, as shown in Exhibit 7.3.

Lower Transportation and Inventory Costs and Reduced Stockouts: Unilever

Unilever's 30 contract carriers deliver 250,000 truckloads of shipments annually. Unilever's Web-based database, the Transportation Business Center (TBC), provides these carriers with site specification requirements when they pick up a shipment at a manufacturing or distribution center or when they deliver goods to retailers. TBC gives carriers all the vital information they need: contact names and phone numbers, operating hours, the number of dock doors at a location, the height of the dock doors, how to make an appointment to deliver or pick up shipments, pallet configuration, and other special requirements. All mission-critical information that Unilever's carriers need to make pickups, shipments, and deliveries is now available electronically 24/7. TBC also helps Unilever organize and automate its carrier selection processes based on contract provisions and commitments. When a primary carrier is unable to accept a shipment, TBC automatically recommends alternative carriers.

Reduction of Design Cycle Time: Adaptec, Inc.

Adaptec, Inc. (adaptec.com) is a large microchip manufacturer that supplies critical components to electronics-equipment makers. The company outsources manufacturing tasks, concentrating on product research and development. Outsourcing production, however, put the company at a disadvantage against competitors that have their own manufacturing facilities and can optimize their delivery schedules. It took Adaptec up to 15 weeks to deliver products to customers; competitors were able to deliver similar chips in only 8 weeks.

The longer delivery time mainly was caused by the need to coordinate design activities between Adaptec headquarters in California and its three principal fabrication factories in Hong Kong, Japan, and Taiwan. To solve this problem, the company introduced extranet-based collaboration and enterprise-level supply chain integration software, which incorporates automated workflow and EC tools.

One initial benefit of the new system was a reduction in the time required to generate, transmit, and confirm purchase orders. Adaptec now uses e-mail to communicate with

EXHIBIT 7.3 **Target's Extranet**

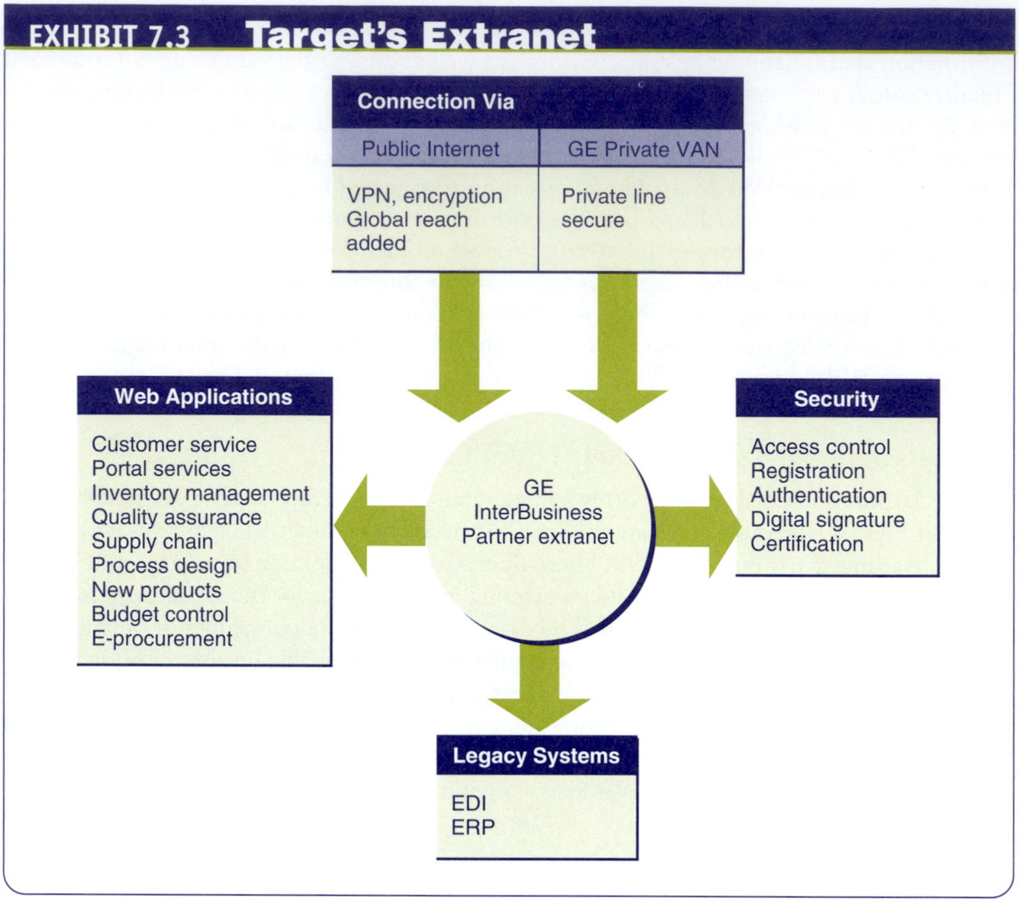

manufacturers across several time zones to automatically start the flow of raw materials, which in turn reduces invoicing and shipping times. In addition to business transaction documents, Adaptec can send chip design diagrams over the extranet, enabling the manufacturers to prepare for product changes and new designs. This faster communication method required Adaptec to adjust its decision-making processes, which were based on the old assumption that at least 2 weeks were needed to put an order into production. The overall result was a reduction in its order-to-product-delivery time from 15 weeks to between 10 and 12 weeks.

See Goldberg (2004) and Manninen (2004) for more on collaborative virtual design environments.

Reduction of Product Development Time: Caterpillar, Inc.

Caterpillar, Inc. (caterpillar.com) is a multinational heavy-machinery manufacturer. In the traditional mode of operation, cycle time along the supply chain was long because the process involved the transfer of paper documents among managers, salespeople, and technical staff. To solve the problem, Caterpillar connected its engineering and manufacturing divisions with its active suppliers, distributors, overseas factories, and customers through an extranet-based global collaboration system. By means of the collaboration system, a request for a customized tractor component, for example, can be transmitted from a customer to a Caterpillar dealer and on to designers and suppliers, all in a very short time. Customers also can use the extranet to retrieve and modify detailed order information while the vehicle is still on the assembly line.

Remote collaboration capabilities between the customer and product developers have decreased cycle time delays caused by rework time. Suppliers also are connected to the system so that they can deliver materials or parts directly to Caterpillar's shops or directly to the customer, if appropriate. The system also is used for expediting maintenance and repairs. Other companies also are using EC technologies to reduce the time needed for product development (e.g., see the chapter's opening case).

USING RFID TO IMPROVE SUPPLY CHAINS

One of the newest and possibly revolutionary solutions to supply chain problems is RFID. We introduced the concept of RFID in Chapter 2 by describing how Wal-Mart is mandating that its largest suppliers attach RFID tags to every pallet or box they ship to Wal-Mart. Eventually, RFIDs will be attached to every item. This can be done due to the tag's tiny size and low cost (less than 5 cents per tag).

What effect will RFID have on supply chains? Let's look at Exhibit 7.4, which shows the relationship between a retailer (Wal-Mart) and a supplier (P&G). P&G's suppliers also are shown. All of the companies in the figure use RFIDs. Basically, automatic alerts are sent within each company and between companies. It is no longer necessary to count inventories, and all business partners are able to view inventory information. This transparency can go several tiers down the supply chain. Additional applications, such as rapid checkout, eliminating the need to scan each item, will be provided by RFID in the future.

Other applications of RFID are shown in Exhibit 7.5. The upper part of the figure shows how the tags are used as merchandise travels from the supplier to the retailer. Note that the RFID transmits real-time information on the location of the merchandise. The lower part shows the use of the RFID at the retailer, mainly to locate merchandise, control inventory, prevent theft, and expedite processing of relevant information. For further discussion, see Reda (2003).

More About RFID

An RFID tag is about the size of a pinhead. The RFID tag includes an antenna and a chip that contains an electronic product code (EPC). The EPC stores much more information than a regular bar code (e.g., when and where the item was made, where the components are from, and when the item might expire).

Unlike bar codes, which need line-of-sight contact to be read, RFID tags also act as passive tracking devices, signaling their presence over a radio frequency when they pass within yards of a special scanner. The tags have long been used in high-cost applications such as automated tolling systems (see Online File W9.11) and security-ID badges, but recent

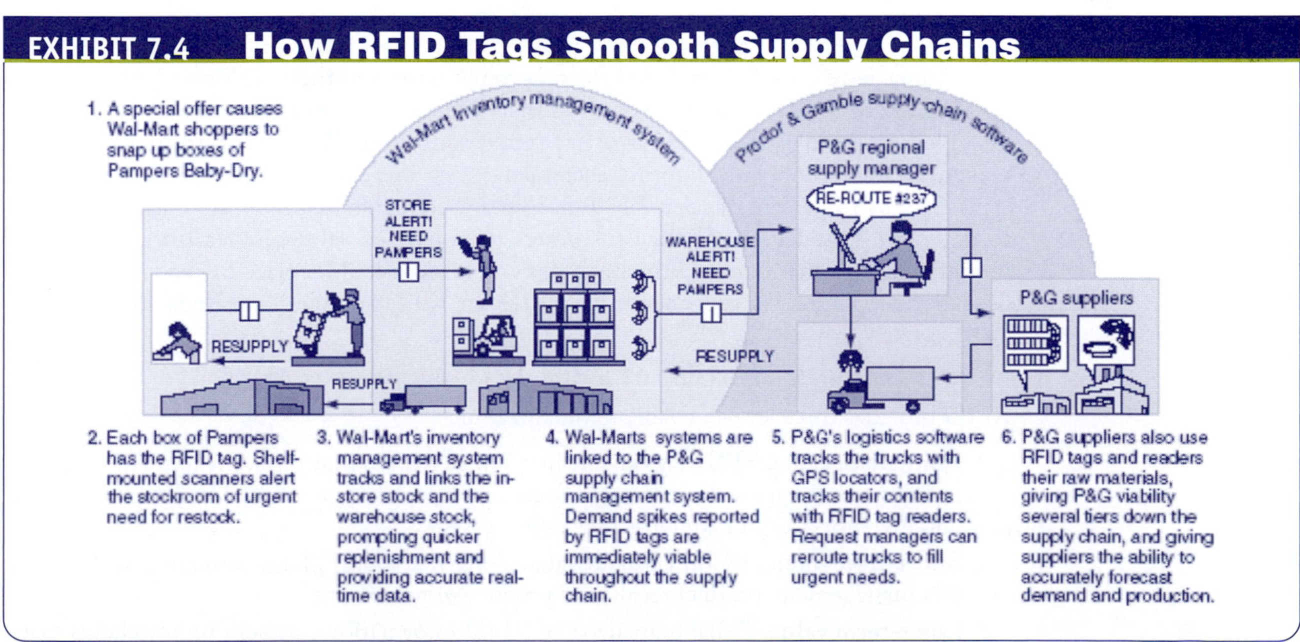

Source: Heizner, J. and B. Render, *Operations Management*, 7th ed. ©2004. Reproduced by permission of Pearson Education, Inc. Upper Saddle River, NJ: Prentice-Hall.

EXHIBIT 7.5 How RFID Works in a Manufacturer–Retailer Supply Chain

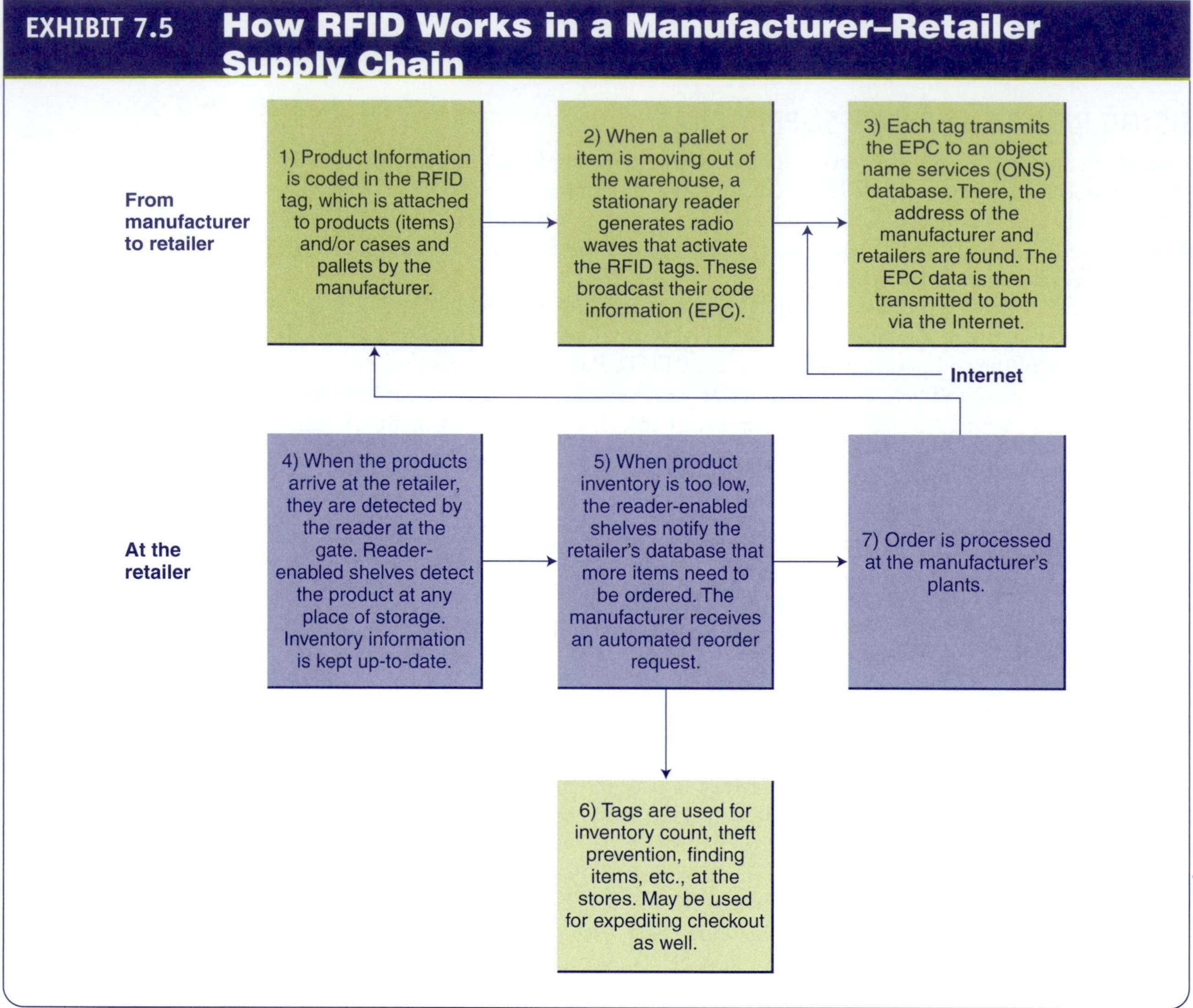

innovations have caused the price of the tags to plummet and their performance to improve. RFID tags are widely expected to cost less than 5 cents apiece in a few years.

The prospect of affordable tags has retailers drooling. If every item in a shop were tagged, retailers could both improve customer service and combat top-line losses, which are typically 2 to 15 percent of sales. RFID technology could be used to locate mislaid products, to deter theft, and even to offer customers personalized sales pitches through displays mounted in dressing rooms. Ultimately, tags and readers could replace bar codes and checkout labor altogether. For more about the RFID, see Kinsella (2003) and Reda (2003).

RFID Technology Contributes Value at Three Levels

RFID provides three levels of value to organizations:

- **Immediate value.** RFID tags enable items to be read in multiples, without requiring line of sight or human involvement, and from a distance of up to 9 feet, which can cut checkout, inventory control, and loss prevention costs.
- **Short-term value.** RFID can add value along the supply chain through asset tracking and management, product recall, and product-origin tracing.
- **Long-term value.** Collaborative use of RFID information can help supply chains manage inventory efficiently. Demand-driven, product fulfillment systems can link consumer behavior back to inventory planning, logistics, and even product design.

Limitations of RFID

RFID does have a number of limitations. For small companies, the cost of the system may be too high (at least for the near future). Radio frequency interference and RFID's limited range (30 to 50 feet) also may be problematic. These limitations should be minimized in the future. Concerns over customer privacy (see Chapter 2, Wal-Mart) are another issue. Agreeing on universal standards, as well as connecting the RFIDs with existing IT systems is yet another issue. For other limitations, see Kinsella (2003).

COLLABORATIVE COMMERCE AND KNOWLEDGE MANAGEMENT

Knowledge management (KM) is the process of capturing or creating knowledge. According to Thuraisingham et al. (2002), collaborative commerce is essentially an integration of KM, EC, and collaboration tools and methodologies that are designed to carry out transactions and other activities within and across organizations. One can use various architectures to combine these ingredients. Therefore, c-commerce will differ in various industries and in B2B and B2C settings.

Knowledge and its management play a strategic role in collaboration. For example, one function of knowledge management often is to gather and make available experts' opinions, and these opinions can be provided by one partner to others. Thus, one model of collaboration includes a knowledge provider with clients who want to acquire knowledge. Learning also is important in c-commerce, and it may be facilitated by KM (see Chapter 8). Creating a knowledge-sharing platform for collaboration can be facilitated by knowledge portals (see Kesner 2003 and Section 7.7). For further discussion of the integration of KM, EC, and collaborative tools, see Thuraisingham et al. (2002). Also, see the Amway case at the end of this chapter.

An interesting collaborative KM is finding experts within a given company online. See *expert location systems* in Chapter 8.

BARRIERS TO C-COMMERCE

Despite the many potential benefits, c-commerce is moving ahead fairly slowly. Reasons cited in various studies include technical reasons involving integration, standards, and networks; security and privacy concerns over who has access to and control of information stored in a partner's database; internal resistance to information sharing and to new approaches; and lack of internal skills to conduct collaborative commerce (Schram 2004).

A big stumbling block to the adoption of c-commerce is the lack of defined and universally agreed-on standards. Even early initiatives such as CPFR (see next section) are still in their infancy. New approaches such as the use of XML and its variants and the use of Web Services could significantly lessen the problem of standards.

Sometimes collaboration is an organizational culture shock—people simply resist sharing. One reason for this is lack of trust. According to Gibson-Paul (2003), companies such as Boeing are grappling with the trust factor. Some techniques she suggests to increase trust include starting small (e.g., synchronizing one type of sales data), picking projects that are likely to provide a quick return on investment for both sides, meeting face-to-face in the beginning of a collaboration, and showing the benefits of collaboration to all parties. Despite an initial lack of trust, if potential collaborators judge the benefits of collaboration to be sufficient, and fairly distributed among collaborators, they will be more eager to join in.

Finally, global collaboration involves all of the above potential barriers, and more. Some of these additional barriers are described in Chapter 13. For more on c-commerce barriers, see Schrage (2004) and Davison and de Vreede (2001).

Specialized c-commerce software tools will break down some of the barriers to c-commerce (see Section 7.8). In addition, as companies learn more about the major benefits of c-commerce—such as smoothing the supply chain, reducing inventories and operating costs, and increasing customer satisfaction and the competitive edge—it is expected that more will rush to jump on the c-commerce bandwagon.

Section 7.3 ▶ REVIEW QUESTIONS

1. Define c-commerce.
2. List the major types of c-commerce.

3. Describe some examples of c-commerce.
4. Define collaborative networks and distinguish them from traditional supply chain collaboration.
5. Describe how RFID can be used to improve supply chains.
6. Explain how RFID works in a supplier–retailer system.
7. Describe KM–collaboration relationships.
8. List some major barriers to c-commerce.

C-commerce is a response to business pressure (Chapter 1). Let's examine the case of a global supply chain in the fashion retailing industry (Insights and Additions 7.1).

7.4 COLLABORATIVE PLANNING, CPFR, AND COLLABORATIVE DESIGN

In *collaborative planning*, business partners—manufacturers, suppliers, distribution partners, and other partners—create initial demand (or sales) forecasts, provide changes as necessary, and share information, such as actual sales, and their own forecasts. Thus, all parties work

Insights and Additions 7.1 Using EC in the Retail Industry to Reduce Time and Cost

Retailers, especially those dealing with fashion clothing (apparel), must deal with difficult environmental pressures (Chapter 1). Specifically, they must deliver products very quickly to their stores while cutting costs at the same time. Cost cutting is done, in many cases, by moving production to Asia. This means creating a global supply chain, because the major retailers are located mostly in Europe and United States.

The fashion retail supply chain can be complex and long, because it includes numerous functions—product design, merchandiser input, procurement of raw materials, manufacturing, and distribution. Therefore, communication and collaboration are critical. If lead time is not compressed, the risk of the product being too late on the shelf or obsolete is increased. All of this is done in an environment in which customer demand changes rapidly. If a retailer is too slow to react, store shelves will be stocked with uninspired fashions—resulting in substantial markdowns and anemic sales growth. As mentioned earlier in this chapter, demand forecasting can be very difficult.

Many retailers have implemented sourcing initiatives such as just-in-time (JIT) manufacturing, quick response (QR), efficient consumer response (ECR), and fast-moving consumer goods (FMCC). However, many retailers are still in trouble. Unfortunately, most solutions involve two contradicting factors: increasing speed and reducing or holding costs. If a company can do both simultaneously, it will be a winner. To do both, a company must use EC tools and possibly change business processes. Changes in business processes may include component-based product design, e-sourcing, and supply chain improvements; all of which are supported electronically.

For example, Web-enabled planning, execution, and optimization tools improve data availability and boost collaborative efforts between retail and brand managers and their suppliers. Product development management (PDM) software allows brand managers to conduct online, "what-if" scenarios relating to product design. To expedite cycle time, tools from companies such as Freeborders (*freeborders.com*), Logility (*logility.com*), SupplyChainge (*supplychainge.com*), and New Generation Computing (*ngcsoftware.com*), can be utilized. Lead time optimization (LTO) tools (e.g., from SupplyChainge) also are useful. These tools relate demand forecast to supply forecast and support planning in an uncertain environment from an enterprisewide perspective. For example, using optimization techniques, the tools allow performance of supply chain activities in parallel.

These solutions usually are limited to one segment of the internal supply chain. Unfortunately, this may not be sufficient, because the supply chain crosses numerous functions—including product design, merchandiser's input, raw material procurement, manufacturing, and distribution. Therefore, collaboration and communication are needed to supplement these tools.

To enhance collaboration and communication, retailers can implement Web-based collaborative product design (CPD) solutions. With CPD tools, different people can work on the same design at the same or different times, from different locations. Yet another set of tools allows brand managers to build an item's design into a system and generate all of the cutting patterns and distribute them to manufacturers in seconds. A major key for all of the above is partnership and collaboration. For details, see Reda (2003).

according to a unified schedule aligned to a common view, and all have access to order and forecast performance that is globally visible through electronic links. Schedule, order, or product changes trigger immediate adjustments to all parties' schedules.

Collaborative planning is designed to synchronize production and distribution plans and product flows, optimize resource utilization over an expanded capacity base, increase customer responsiveness, and reduce inventories. Collaborative planning is a necessity in e-SCM (see Kalakota and Robinson 2001). The planning process is difficult because it involves multiple parties and activities, as shown in Exhibit 7.6.

This section examines several aspects of collaborative planning and collaborative design.

THE CPFR PROJECT

Collaborative planning, forecasting, and replenishment (CPFR) is a project in which suppliers and retailers collaborate in planning and demand forecasting in order to ensure that members of the supply chain will have the right amount of raw materials and finished goods when they need them. When implementing a CPRF project, the collaborators agree on a standard process, shown in Exhibit 7.7. The process ends with an order forecast. CPFR provides a *standard framework* for collaborative planning. Retailers and vendors determine the "rules of engagement," such as how often and at what level information will be provided. Typically, they share greater amounts of more detailed information, such as promotion schedules and item point-of-sale history, and use store-level expectations as the basis for all forecasts.

collaborative planning, forecasting, and replenishment (CPFR)
Project in which suppliers and retailers collaborate in their planning and demand forecasting to optimize flow of materials along the supply chain.

The idea is to improve demand forecasting for all of the partners in the supply chain and then communicate forecasts using information-sharing applications (already developed by

EXHIBIT 7.6 The Collaborative Planning Process

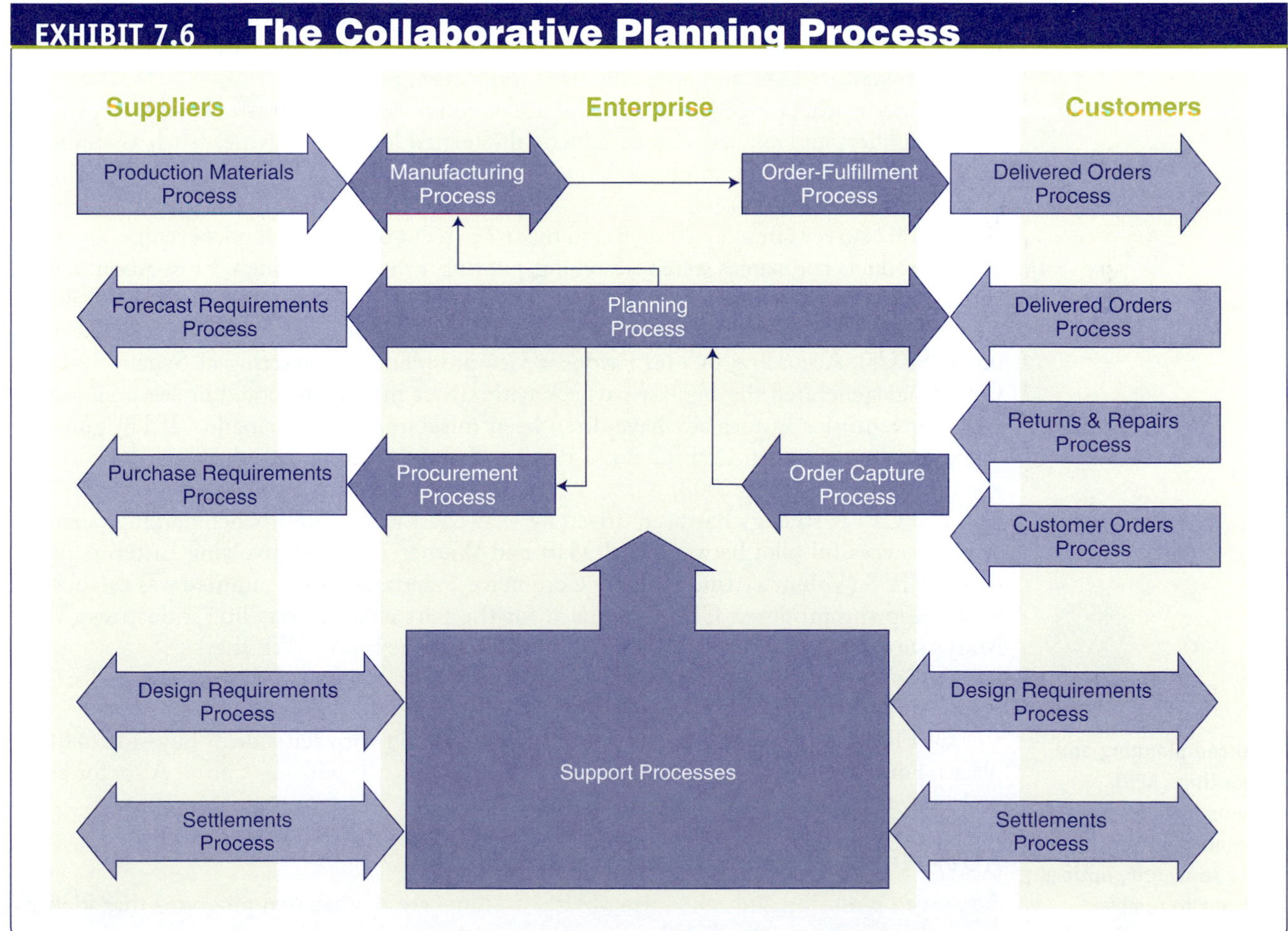

Source: Norris, G., et al., *E-Business and ERP: Transforming the Enterprise,* ©2000, John Wiley & Sons, Inc. This material is used by permission of John Wiley & Sons, Inc.

EXHIBIT 7.7 The CPFR Process

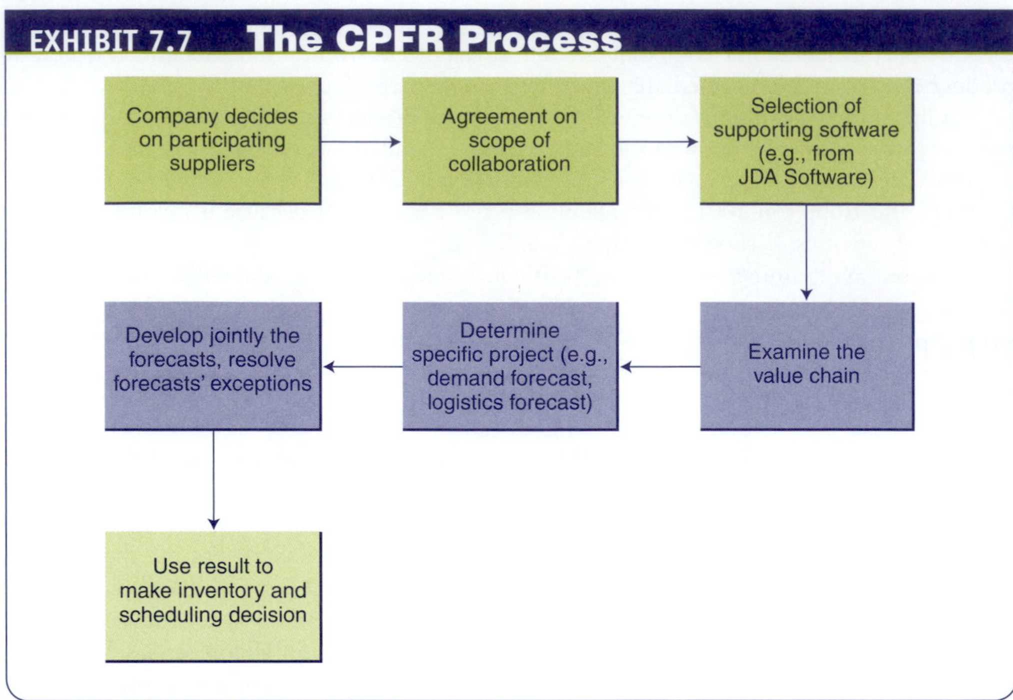

technology companies such as Manugistics, Oracle, PeopleSoft, and i2). For the retailer, collaborative forecasting means fewer out-of-stocks and resultant lost sales and less stored inventory. For the manufacturer, collaborative forecasting means fewer expedited shipments, optimal inventory level, and optimally sized production runs.

Besides working together to develop production plans and forecasts for stock replenishment, suppliers and retailers also coordinate the related logistics activities (such as shipment or warehousing) using a common *language standard* and new information methodologies (Ireland and Bruce 2000).

A 2002 survey (Bradley 2002) found that 67 percent of 43 large food, beverage, and consumer products companies were researching, piloting, or implementing CPFR. About half of the respondents who were looking at CPFR said they planned to go ahead with their initiatives. However, CPFR is not the answer for all trading partners or all types of stock-keeping units (SKUs). According to Tim Paydos, a vice president of marketing at Syncra Systems, CPFR has generated the highest payback with either highly promoted or seasonal goods, whose inventories historically have often been misaligned with demand. "If I'm going to make the investment in CPFR," notes Paydos, "I want to do it with the products with the greatest return" (Bradley 2002).

The CPFR strategy has been driven by Wal-Mart and various benchmarking partners. After a successful pilot between Wal-Mart and Warner-Lambert involving Listerine products, a VICS (Voluntary Interindustry Commerce Standards) subcommittee was established to develop the proposed CPFR standard for the participating retailing industries (Wal-Mart's suppliers). (For more, see Online File W7.4 at the book's Web site.)

An interesting application of CPFR is that of Ace Hardware Corp., presented in EC Application Case 7.4.

CPFR can be used with a company-centric B2B and with sell-side or buy-side marketplaces. For more on the benefits of CPFR, see cpfr.org/cpfr_pdf/index.html. Also, for comprehensive coverage, see Industry Directions (2000).

advanced planning and scheduling (APS) systems
Programs that use algorithms to identify optimal solutions to complex planning problems that are bound by constraints.

ADVANCED PLANNING AND SCHEDULING

Advanced planning and scheduling (APS) systems are math-based programs that identify optimal solutions to complex planning problems that are bound by constraints, such as limited machine capacity or labor. Using algorithms (such as linear programming), these systems

CASE 7.4

EC Application

CPFR INITIATIVES AT ACE HARDWARE AND SEARS

Ace Hardware Corporation (*acehardware.com*), based in Oak Brook, Illinois, is a chain of 5,100 independently owned stores that sell everything from 10-penny nails to toasters. In 1999, Ace implemented a CPFR process, using its buy-side private exchange to achieve more intelligent relationships with its suppliers. This platform creates and executes a single, shared demand forecast, allowing Ace to increase revenue while reducing costs.

Ace began using CPFR with a single supplier, Henkel Consumer Adhesives, a manufacturer of duct tape, adhesives, and other do-it-yourself home and office products. During the first year of implementation, the two companies improved forecast accuracy by 10 percent, lowered distribution costs by 28 percent, lowered freight costs by 18 percent, increased annual sales by 9 percent, and increased employee productivity by more than 20 percent.

Since then, Ace has implemented CPFR initiatives with several dozen suppliers, including Black & Decker, Rust-Oleum, Master Lock, and Sherwin-Williams. More accurate forecasts and seasonal profiles ensure that products are available when consumers want to buy them. Improved service levels, increased sales, and decreased supply chain costs have combined to make Ace Hardware more competitive.

To improve efficiency and effectiveness of inventory management with its major suppliers, Sears is using CPFR software from GNX (*gnx.com*). The system enables total supply chain visibility. The first experiment was with all major tire vendors (Michelin, Goodyear, Sumitomo). Using this software, all partners collaborated weekly about optimal replenishment and inventory plans to minimize stock, maximize customer service level, and optimize transport. Each week's actual and forecast sales information were refreshed for more than 500 SKUs related to tires. The initial results of the pilot project were so successful that Sears is implementing the program with all of its strategic partners.

Sources: Compiled from Buss (2002), Richardson (2004), press releases at *acehardware.com* (accessed 2002, 2004), and *gnx.com* (accessed 2004).

Questions

1. What motivated Ace to try CPFR?
2. Describe how Ace deployed the CPFR system.
3. Can you guess the common characteristics of the suppliers Ace used first?
4. Why did Sears start using CPFR with tires?
5. What are the benefits of CPFR to Sears? To its suppliers?

are able to solve a wide range of problems, from operational (e.g., daily schedule) to strategic (e.g., network optimization). For examples, see Gregory (2004).

The role of APS in EC can be seen in Exhibit 7.8. Basically, it supplements ERP in revolutionizing a manufacturing or distribution firm's supply chain, providing a seamless flow of order fulfillment information from consumers to suppliers. It helps integrate ERP, CRM, SFA, KM, and more, enabling collaborative fulfillment and an integrated EC strategy. For additional details and discussion of ERP, SCM, and APS, see Online Tutorial T2.

PRODUCT LIFECYCLE MANAGEMENT

product lifecycle management (PLM) Business strategy that enables manufacturers to control and share product-related data as part of product design and development efforts.

Product lifecycle management (PLM) is a business strategy that enables manufacturers to control and share product-related data as part of product design and development efforts and in support of supply chain operations (Day 2002; Teresko 2004; IBM 2005). Internet and other new technologies can automate the *collaborative aspects* of product development that even within one company can prove tedious and time-consuming if not automated. For example, by means of concurrent engineering and Web-based tools, companies simultaneously and interactively can design a product, its manufacturing process, and the supply chain that supports it. By overlapping these formerly disparate functions, a dynamic collaboration takes place among them, essentially forming a single, large product team.

PLM can have a significant beneficial impact in engineering change, cycle time, design reuse, and engineering productivity. Studies have shown that electronic-based collaboration can reduce product costs by 20 percent and travel expenses by 80 percent, as well as significantly reduce costs associated with product-change management. Moreover, an explosion of new products that have minimal life cycles, as well as increasing complexity in supply chain management, are driving the need for PLM.

EXHIBIT 7.8 **Components of Collaborative Fulfillment and APS**

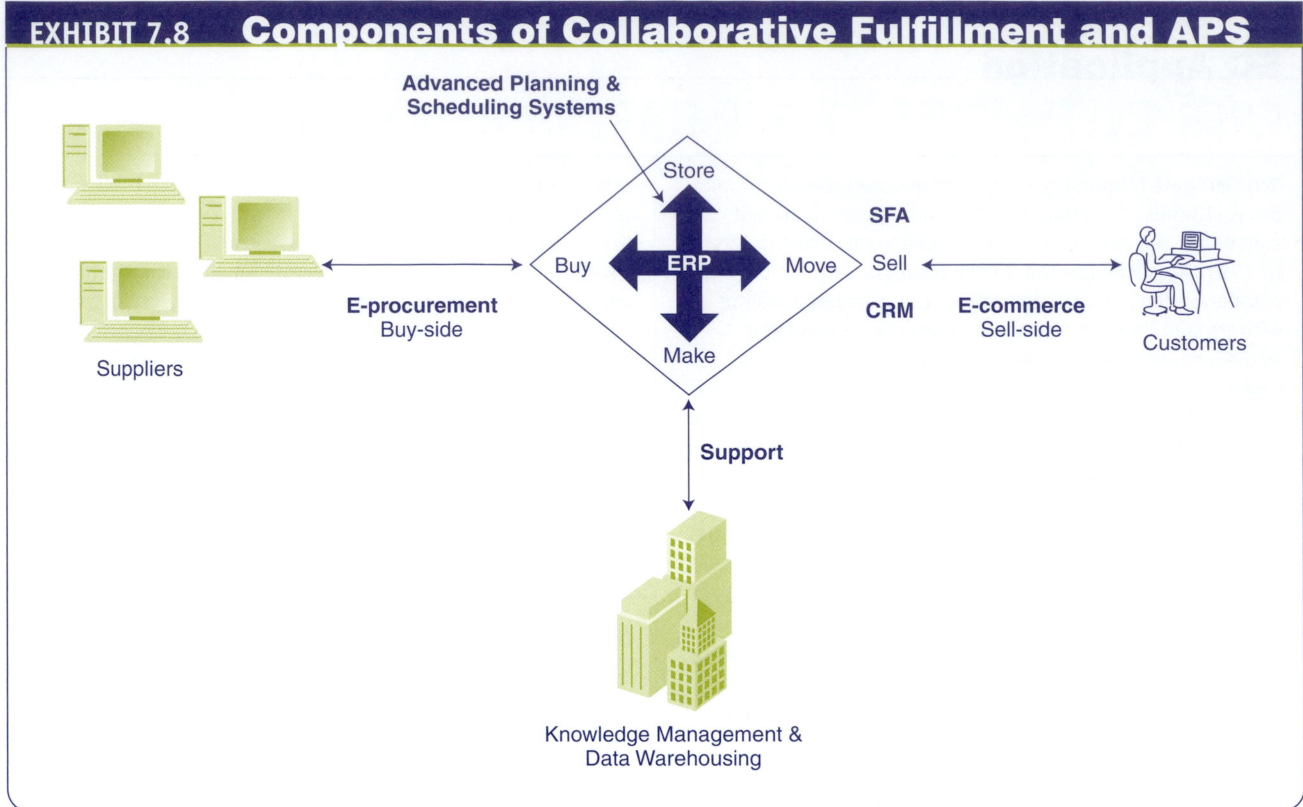

Source: Modified from Neef, D., *E-Procurement: From Strategy to Implementation*, © 2001. Used by permission of Pearson Education, Inc., Upper Saddle River, NJ.

PLM is a big step for an organization, requiring it to integrate a number of different processes and systems. Ultimately, information must be moved through an organization as quickly as possible to reduce cycle time and increase profitability. The faster different groups know that a new component or design change is on its way, the faster they can react and get it manufactured or reengineered and out the door, and the sooner the organization can realize revenue. PLM tools are offered by SAP (MYSAP PLM, see Buxmann 2004), Matrix One, EDS, PTC, Dassault Systems, and IBM (IBM PLM).

SUPPORTING JOINT DESIGN

Collaborative efforts are common in joint design, as illustrated in the GM opening case. This is one of the oldest areas of electronic collaboration, which is becoming even more popular due to EC tools, as discussed in Online File W7.5 on the book's Web site. Another example of joint design is provided in EC Application Case 7.5.

Section 7.4 ▶ REVIEW QUESTIONS

1. Define collaborative planning.
2. Define CPFR and describe its advantages.
3. Describe APS efforts.
4. Describe PLM.

7.5 INTERNAL SUPPLY CHAIN SOLUTIONS: INTRABUSINESS AND B2E

The EC supply chain solutions presented thus far are mostly intended to rectify situations among business partners. This and the next section concentrate on solutions related to the parts of the supply chain that are *internal* to an organization.

CASE 7.5

EC Application

SAFEWAY COLLABORATES IN DESIGNING STORES

The Problem

Safeway Plc, a large food retailer in the UK (now a subsidiary of Morrison Supermarkets), builds about 10 new stores every year and renovates over 100. Being in stiff competition with other supermarkets, the company must manage this construction carefully so it meets its budget and time plans. This is not an easy job given that hundreds of the company's employees must collaborate with hundreds of vendors throughout the lifecycle of a building, including design, construction, and ongoing facility management.

In the past, communications were handled primarily through the postal system and e-mail, an often slow and inefficient process, because stores are scattered throughout England, Scotland, Wales, and Northern Ireland. Finally, in addition to stores, Safeway frequently builds public structures, such as a school or bridge, which it donates to a community in exchange for a parcel of land for a store. The diversity of structures (there are four types of stores plus community structures) adds to the difficulties in managing the construction projects.

The Solution

By using an online project collaboration service called Buzzsaw (from Autodesk, *autodesk.com*), the company can store and share project information in a secure location that can be accessed anytime and anywhere using a Web-based extranet. This enhances communication between internal departments and outside partners (such as developers, planning consultants, architects, structural and mechanical engineers, builders, repair staff, and building enforcement authorities).

Key users can view drawings online, mock up drawings, and make changes and post them for other staff to view, all in real time (e.g., using screen-sharing capabilities). Buzzsaw also automatically tracks and logs what's been changed.

The Results

Communication log time plummeted from 2 to 3 weeks to 5 to 10 minutes. Also, because the design is rapid, it includes cutting-edge features. All supermarkets want to use the latest design. Buzzsaw is helping Safeway to be *first to market* with innovative new formats such as Internet cafés and new departments.

Another benefit is the reduction in travel time of architects and structural and mechanical engineers, who can stay in their offices and collaborate electronically, minimizing travel time and costs by 10 to 15 percent. The cost of printing drawings has been reduced by 30 percent. Also, project turnaround time is shorter. The time for store modifications has been reduced from 6 to 7 months to as little as 3 months. Design changes are now transmitted in 5 to 10 minutes instead of 1 to 2 days.

Collaboration is being taken to a better and more integrated level. Users can monitor crucial information, and the software lets them know when decisions are required. Finally Buzzsaw provides enhanced e-mail that helps users to prioritize the large number of messages generated.

Source: Compiled from Parks, L. "Buzzsaw Keeps Safeway Store Design on the Cutting Edge." *Stores*, February 2004. Adapted with permission.

Questions

1. Who collaborates with whom in this case?
2. What different EC technologies are used? What are they used for?
3. Find out more about Buzzsaw's capabilities. Write a report based on your findings.

The internal parts of the supply chain are related to the value chain and include inbound logistics, production processes, outbound logistics, marketing and sales, and customer services. For details, see Davis and Benamati (2003).

An internal supply chain can exist among the various departments in a manufacturing plant, between a warehouse and manufacturing facility, among several manufacturing plants, between warehouse and retail stores of a retailer, and so on. As in other parts of the supply chain, internal supply chains include flows of material, information, and sometimes funds.

One of the major targets for internal supply chain improvement is intrabusiness and B2E e-commerce. These frequently deal with the integration of isolated "islands" of automation that exist along the components of the value chain. As will be seen later, this is done by using intranets (Online Appendix W7A).

INTRABUSINESS AND B2E EC

As indicated in Chapter 1, e-commerce is conducted not only between business partners, but also *within* organizations, frequently along the internal supply chain. Such within-the-company EC activity is referred to as **intrabusiness EC**, or just *intrabusiness*. Intrabusiness can be done (1) between a business and its employees, (2) between units within the business, and (3) among employees in the same business. This section examines each of these forms of intrabusiness.

intrabusiness EC
E-commerce activities conducted *within* an organization.

B2E EC: Between a Business and Its Employees

business-to-employee (B2E)
Intrabusiness EC in which an organization delivers products or services to its employees.

Intrabusiness in which an organization delivers products or services to its employees is termed **business-to-employee (B2E)**. B2E can be used either to increase employee productivity or for employees' personal use. According to Hansen and Deimler (2001), many companies (e.g., Cisco, Schwab, Coca-Cola, Delta Airlines) are setting up B2E systems that emulate B2B and B2C models; in many of these systems, employees are treated like the customers in B2C. In the process, the companies get a more satisfied, more productive workforce while enjoying major cost reductions. The decision support system described in EC Application Case 7.6 is an example of a B2E tool that increases productivity.

Some representative applications of B2E include the following:

- Providing field representatives and employees in yards, warehouses, and other nonoffice places with electronic communication tools
- Training and education provided over intranets

CASE 7.6

EC Application

EC PROVIDES DECISION SUPPORT TO HI-LIFE

Hi-Life International Corp. owns and operates 720 convenience retail stores in Taiwan in which it sells over 3,000 different products. A major problem is keeping a proper level of inventory in each store. Overstocking is expensive due to storage costs and tying money up to buy and maintain inventory. Understocking reduces sales and could result in unhappy customers who may go to a competitor. To calculate the appropriate level of inventory, it is necessary to know exactly how many units of each product are in stock at any time. This is known as *stock count*. A periodic stock count is needed because the actual amount in stock frequently differs from the theoretical one. The difference is due to "shrinkage" (e.g., theft, spoiled items, misplaced items, etc.).

Until 2002, the stock count was done manually. Employees counted the quantity of each product and recorded it on data collection sheets that were preprinted with the products' names. Then, the data were painstakingly keyed into each store's PC. The process took over 21 person hours in each store and was done on a weekly basis. This process was expensive and frequently delayed, causing problems along the entire supply chain due to delays in count and errors. Suppliers, customers, and employees were unhappy.

The first phase of improvement was introduced in spring 2002. Management provided each store with a Pocket PC (Jornada) from HP that runs on Microsoft Windows (Chinese version). The Pocket PC enables employees to enter inventory tallies directly on on-screen forms by hand, using Chinese characters for additional notes. The Pocket PC has a synchronized cradle called ActiveSync. Once the Pocket PC is placed in the cradle, inventory information can be relayed instantly to Hi-Life's headquarters. The main menu of the Pocket PC contains an order-placing program, product information, and even weather reports in addition to the inventory module.

In the second phase, in 2003, a compact bar code scanner was added to the Pocket PC's expansion slot. Employees scan the products' bar codes and enter the quantity they find on the shelf. This expedites data entry and minimizes errors in product identification. The up-to-the second information enables headquarters to compute appropriate inventory levels, shipment schedules, and purchasing strategies using DSS formulas, all in minutes. The stores use the Internet (with a secured VPN) to upload data to the company's intranet.

The results were astonishing. The inventory process was reduced from 21 hours to less than 4 hours per store. Errors were down by more than 90 percent; order placing now is simple and quick, and administrative paperwork has been eliminated. In addition, quicker and more precise inventory counts resulted in faster response times for changes in demand and in lower inventory levels. The entire product management process became more efficient and improved purchasing, stocking, selling, shelf-price audit and price checks, reticketing, discontinuance, and customer inquiries. The new EC-based system provides a total merchandise solution.

The employees like the solution, too. It is very user friendly, both to learn and to operate, and the Pocket PC battery provides at least 24 hours of power, so charging can be done after hours. Finally, Hi-Life's employees now have more time to plan, manage, and chat with customers. More important, faster and better decisions are made possible at headquarters, contributing to greater competitiveness and profitability for Hi-Life.

Sources: Compiled from *hp.com/jornada* (accessed 2002) and *microsoft.com* (accessed 2004).

Questions

1. How is corporate decision making improved by the new system?
2. Summarize the benefits of the Jornada system to the customers, suppliers, store management, and employees.
3. The data collected at ActiveSync can be uploaded to a PC and transmitted via regular telephone lines (or a DSL) to the corporate intranet via the Internet. It has also been suggested that transmission be done using a wireless system. Comment on the proposal.

- Employee use of electronic catalogs and ordering forms to order supplies and material needed for their work (e.g., desktop purchasing)
- Employee use of the corporate intranet for both corporate and personal use to purchase discounted insurance, travel packages, and tickets to events
- Providing office employees with electronic tools for communication, collaboration, and information discovery
- Offering corporate stores on the intranet that sell the companies' products to their own employees, usually at a discount (payment may be deducted from payroll or paid with the employee's personal credit card)
- Systems that disseminate information or allow employees to manage their fringe benefits via the intranet

Based on a survey they conducted, Hansen and Deimler (2001) found three types of B2E programs: online business processes, online people management, and online services to the workplace (see details in Online Exhibit W7.1). In each of these areas, the B2E program may result in significant cost reductions and productivity improvement.

Activities Between Business Units

Large corporations frequently consist of independent units, called *strategic business units* (SBUs), that "sell" or "buy" materials, products, and services from each other. (An SBU may be either a seller or a buyer.) Transactions of this type can be easily automated and performed over the organization's intranet.

Many large corporations also have a network of dealerships that are usually wholly or partially owned by the corporation. In such cases, a special network is constructed to support communication, collaboration, and execution of transactions between headquarters and the dealerships. For example, such intrabusiness commerce is conducted by auto manufacturers (e.g., Ford; see EC Application Case 7.7), equipment manufacturers (e.g., Caterpillar), oil

CASE 7.7

EC Application

THE DEALERCONNECTION PORTAL AT FORD MOTOR

Ford Motor Co. in Europe serves 18 countries with 7,500 dealers speaking 15 different languages. In order to connect them all, Ford created a portal called DealerConnection.

The portal provides dealers with a single point of real-time access to all of the information and tools they need to manage daily tasks efficiently, such as warranty checks and parts ordering, keeping dealers from having to access separate systems. In addition, prior to the portal, updating dealers on new information often took 5 days due to the time needed to prepare, print, and distribute materials; now all information on pricing, products, servicing, customer services, and marketing is available to the dealers online. The portal is already resulting in real efficiencies for Ford.

With DealerConnection, local country dealers and Ford representatives have control over their own Enterprise Web applications. Unlike traditional applications, Enterprise Web applications built on Plumtree (*plumtree.com*) portal software combine existing data and processes from enterprise systems with new shared services that are managed within one administrative framework at the corporate level, allowing the creation of real online communities. DealerConnection also facilitates self-service among dealers, allowing Ford to implement a more streamlined and centralized back office.

Instead of creating 18 different portals for the countries in which Ford operates, the company has developed one pan-European portal with applications for each respective country and each line of business. By adopting this approach, Ford is empowering each country to create its own environment under the European umbrella of DealerConnection, even though Ford still has central control over its brand, image, and communication. The vendor believes that the portal has delivered real ROI both for Ford and its network of dealers.

Source: Compiled from Plumtree Software Inc. "Ford Connects European Dealer Network with Plumtree Corporate Portal." *plumtree.com/news_events/pressreleases/2003/press101403c.htm*, October 14, 2003. Adapted with permission.

Questions

1. Why does Ford only use one portal?
2. How about the multilanguage, multicultural aspects? (*Hint:* See Enterprise Web at *plumtree.com*.)
3. Who can collaborate with whom in this portal?
4. What are the benefits to the dealers? To Ford Motor Co.?

companies (e.g., ExxonMobil), and many other large manufacturers. Online File W7.6 describes intrabusiness commerce at a consumer-products company, Toshiba America.

Activities Among Corporate Employees

Many large organizations also provide a system by which employees can collaborate on an individual (sometimes nonbusiness) level. For example, some organizations allow employees to place classified ads on the intranet, through which they can buy and sell personal products and services from each other. Also, via classified ads, corporate equipment may be sold to employees for private use. Such ads are especially popular in universities and high-tech companies, where such advertisement was conducted even before the commercialization of the Internet. All of these activities are done on the corporate portal (Section 7.7). Another example of activities among employees from different departments in one organization is collaborating on projects, such as the design of new products/services using an internal hub, as it is done at Amway (see EC Application Case 7.8).

Supply Chain Management Software

During the 1990s, several major vendors created software to improve segments of the internal supply chain, mainly by cutting costs. Although major savings were realized in many cases, much more would have been possible by integrating the information along the supply chain (Davenport and Brooks 2004).

CASE 7.8

EC Application

PORTAL SPEEDS PRODUCT R&D AT AMWAY: INTRABUSINESS COLLABORATION

Through thousands of independent agents all over the world, Amway sells about 500 home, nutrition and wellness, and personal products. To be effective, the research and development (R&D) department at Amway must develop new products in a streamlined and cost-efficient manner. The R&D department consists of 550 engineers, scientists, and quality-assurance staff who have more than 1,000 projects in the works at any one time.

Fast and easy access to information such as product specifications, formulas, design criteria, production schedules, costs, and sales trends is required for supporting the design activity. Access to this information used to be difficult because the data sometimes resided in 15 to 20 disparate repositories. When scientists needed production or financial data, for instance, they had to request paper reports from each department, which could take days to be processed. Also the corporate knowledge and experience were scattered in a disorganized fashion over many different locations.

To meet the need for easier access to corporate knowledge, Amway developed a business intelligence and knowledge management portal called Artemis, which is used with Lotus Notes/Domino. Tailored to the R&D division, Artemis is a browser-based *intranet* application that enables R&D staff to find the information and knowledge they require quickly. It also includes features such as collaboration tools and a database for locating company experts. Using the Lotus Notes/Domino search agent, Artemis enables employees to pull data from disparate corporate sources and generate dynamic reports in response to user queries. This information is highly secured by Domino's superb security capabilities.

Artemis's collaborative features include a time-accounting function used to help the R&D staff calculate R&D tax credits. The Artemis event-reporting database also tracks project content and status.

After a staged rollout of Artemis, all employees now have access to the system. The time required to access information dropped from days to minutes or seconds, enabling fast "what-if" investigations by product developers. Initial user surveys indicated that 60 percent of the users were saving 30 minutes or more per week; that figure increased to 1 hour for most employees after additional links to more information sources were added and users gained comfort with the system. The target for the near future is a savings of 2 hours per employee each week. The system paid for itself ($250,000) in less than 6 months.

Sources: Abbott (2000) and Amway press releases (2002).

Questions

1. Relate this case to the internal supply chain of Amway.
2. Discuss the relationship to collaborative tools.
3. Relate this case to c-commerce.

Section 7.5 ▶ REVIEW QUESTIONS

1. What is an internal supply chain?
2. List the major intrabusiness EC categories.
3. Describe B2E EC.
4. Describe EC activities among business units.
5. Describe EC among corporate employees. Can you think of additional activities among corporate employees that might be of interest?

7.6 INTEGRATION ALONG THE SUPPLY CHAIN

Previous chapters (Chapters 5 and 6) pointed out the need for systems integration in EC. For example, these chapters discussed the need for integrating systems between an exchange and its members, as well as between a company and its customers and suppliers. Such integration is usually done along the supply chain.

HOW INFORMATION SYSTEMS ARE INTEGRATED

The integration issue can be divided into two parts: internal integration and integration with business partners. Internal integration includes connecting applications with databases and with each other and connecting customer-facing applications (front end) with order fulfillment and the functional information systems (back end). Integration with business partners connects an organization's systems with those of its external business partners; for example, a company's ordering system to its suppliers' fulfillment systems. Another example of integration with business partners would be connecting an organization's e-procurement system to the engineering departments of bidding companies.

In large corporations, it is necessary to connect the EC applications to the ERP system (see Siau and Tian 2004). An ERP system automates the flow of routine and repetitive information, such as submission of purchasing orders, billing, and inventory management. An example of the integration of EC applications with an ERP system is provided in EC Application Case 7.9.

ENABLING INTEGRATION AND THE ROLE OF STANDARDS AND WEB SERVICES

Integrating EC systems can be a complex task. As will be described in Online Chapter 18, integration involves connectivity, compatibility, security, and scalability. In addition, applications, data, processes, and interfaces must be integrated. Finally, a major difficulty is the connection of Web-based systems with legacy systems.

To ease the task of integration, vendors have developed integration methodologies and special software called *middleware* (see Online Chapter 18). In addition, major efforts are being undertaken to develop standards and protocols that will facilitate integration, such as XML. The topic of Web Services, one of the major goals of which is to facilitate seamless integration, will be further discussed in Online Chapter 18.

INTEGRATION ALONG THE EXTENDED SUPPLY CHAIN

The discussion in Insights and Additions 7.2 provides an illustration of information integration along the extended supply chain—all the way from raw material to the customer's door. Such integration is possible with second-generation ERP (see Online Tutorial T2). Also, large corporations use EDI (and now Internet-based EDI) to support their collaboration with partners. As an example, one can look at Boeing, which relies on hundreds of internal and external suppliers, in dozens of different countries, for the several million components needed to build a large airplane. Boeing is using EDI and other systems (e.g., PART, see Online File W5.1) to facilitate collaboration with its partners. For more information and examples, see Davenport and Brooks (2004).

CASE 7.9

EC Application

INTEGRATING EC AND ERP AT CYBEX

In the late 1990s, Cybex International (*cybexintl.com*), a global maker of fitness machines, was having trouble meeting the soaring demand for its popular products. To meet demand, the company had to work with rush orders from its almost 1,000 suppliers, at an extremely high cost. This was a result of poor demand forecasting for the machine's components that was caused by using three different legacy systems that Cybex had inherited from merger partners.

After examining existing vendors' supply chain software, Cybex decided to install an ERP system (from PeopleSoft) for its supply chain planning and manufacturing applications. Together with the software installation, the company analyzed its business processes and made the necessary improvements. It also reduced the number of parts suppliers from 1,000 to 550.

Here is how the system works: Customer orders are accepted at the corporate Web site and are instantly forwarded to the appropriate manufacturing plant (the company has two specialized plants). The ERP uses its *planning module* to calculate which parts are needed for each model. Then, the ERP's *product configurator* constructs a component list and a bill-of-materials needed for each specific order. This takes seconds and expedites shipment.

The ERP system helps with other processes as well. For example, Cybex can e-mail a vendor detailed purchase orders with engineering changes clearly outlined. These changes are visible to everyone, so if one engineer leaves the company, his or her knowledge is in the system and is easy to find. Furthermore, dealers now know that they will get deliveries in less than 2 weeks instead of the previous 4 weeks, and they can now track the status of each order. The system also helps Cybex to better manage its 550 suppliers. For example, the *planning engine* looks at price variations across product lines, detecting opportunities to negotiate price reductions by showing suppliers that their competitors offer the same products at lower prices.

The new system gives Cybex's suppliers projected long-term and short-term production schedules. This helps suppliers with their own planning, and it helps Cybex ensure that all parts and materials are available when needed. More timely delivery of parts and materials also reduces the inventory level at Cybex. Furthermore, suppliers that cannot meet the required dates are replaced after quarterly reviews.

Some of the most impressive results included cutting Cybex's bill-of-material counts from 15,200 to 200; reducing the number of vendors from 1,000 to 550; decreasing paperwork by two-thirds; and reducing build-to-order time from 4 to 2 weeks. Despite intense industry price cuts over the last few years, Cybex has remained very profitable, mainly due to its e-supply chain. Introducing the integrated ERP system cost money, of course. In addition to the software, the technology staff has been increased from 3 to 12. However, the company feels that the investment has been more than justified, especially because it provided for much greater harmony between Cybex and its customers and suppliers.

Sources: Compiled from Gustke (2002) and from press releases at *cybexintl.com* (accessed 2002–2004).

Questions

1. Discuss the relationships between the EC applications and the ERP system. (Try to identify as many relationships as possible.)
2. What is the role of the planning module?
3. Summarize all of the activities needed for successful implementation of the ERP system at Cybex.
4. List some of the benefits of the ERP system to Cybex.

Section 7.6 ▶ REVIEW QUESTIONS

1. Describe internal and external integration.
2. Explain the need to connect to an ERP system.
3. Describe the need for integrating standards and methodologies.

7.7 CORPORATE (ENTERPRISE) PORTALS

Portals and corporate portals were defined in Chapter 2. Corporate portals facilitate collaboration with suppliers, customers, employees, and others; like workflow and groupware tools (see Section 7.8). This section provides in-depth coverage of corporate portals, including their support of c-commerce and intrabusiness EC.

Insights and Additions 7.2 Seamless Integration of Business Partners' Systems

In Chapter 6, we raised the issue of B2B integration and some of the methods and standards used (for more details, see Bussler 2003). One also can use these standards and methods, as well as some special tools which we describe here, to facilitate integration.

Retailers, such as Costco, Wal-Mart, QVC, Sears, Target, and Staples need to talk to their business partners in the "same language." They want to do so without learning "foreign" languages that may be used by their partners' systems. Those different languages are "translated" using special integration software and order management services from CommerceHub (*commercehub.com*). The company's translation platform enables retailers to electronically integrate with all of their suppliers, regardless of differing systems and incompatibilities. In addition to connectivity, the software provides real-time visibility and control over transactions. This enables better performance at a reduced cost.

According to Seideman (2004), QVC and its 200 suppliers tap into CommerceHub's universal translator instead of making separate links. The suppliers can be connected to QVC and to other retailers.

Companies that use traditional EDI have problems if their partners use different EDI standards or messages. Also, EDI runs on expensive VANs and is focused strictly on transactions. CommerceHub's service overcomes traditional EDI deficiencies. CommerceHub's software runs on Web EDI (see Online Appendix W5A), which is much cheaper, more flexible, and more capable. The software also enables performance and expense monitoring, finds abnormalities, and solves order fulfillment problems.

WWW

A food distributor, Michael Foods, is using Sterling Commerce's (*sterlingcommerce.com*) Gentran Integration Suite to provide communication and collaboration when it deals with retailers such as Wal-Mart. Michael Foods uses collaboration tools and data synchronization to provide retail partners with assurance that products flow through the supply chain efficiently. The Gentran suite works with EDI that is used by Michael Food and large retailers, but it also can accommodate new integration standards (e.g., ebXML, Web Services). The business partners can maintain their existing business processes and communication languages.

For example, in 2003, Michael Foods had to comply with Wal-Mart's requirement of moving to *AS2 Communication* (a new B2B protocol). Gentran Integration Suite made the transfer easy and inexpensive. Here is how it works: When a retail customer sends a purchase order EDI data file to Michael Foods, Gentran pulls the order and "wraps" it with the proper Internet elements to ensure security. It then translates the data file into the AS2 protocol and routes the order as a B2B file to the appropriate place at Michael Foods. There, the order is processed and fulfilled quickly and with fewer data errors. For further details, see Amato-McCoy (2004).

CORPORATE PORTALS: AN OVERVIEW

A **corporate (enterprise) portal** is a gateway to a corporate Web site that enables communication, collaboration, and access to company information. Kounadis (2000) more formally defines a corporate portal as a personalized, single point of access through a Web browser to critical business information located inside and outside of an organization. In contrast with commercial portals such as Yahoo! and MSN, which are gateways to general information on the Internet, corporate portals provide a single point of access to information and applications available on the Internet, intranets, and extranets of a specific organization. Companies may have separate portals for outsiders and for insiders.

corporate (enterprise) portal
A gateway for entering a corporate Web site, enabling communication, collaboration, and access to company information.

Corporate portals offer employees, business partners, and customers an organized focal point for their interactions with the firm. Through the portal, these people can have structured and personalized access to information across large, multiple, and disparate enterprise information systems, as well as the Internet. A schematic view of a corporate portal is provided in Exhibit 7.9.

Many large organizations are already implementing corporate portals. The reasons for doing so are to cut costs, to free up time for busy executives and managers, and to add to the bottom line. (See ROI white papers and reports at plumtree.com [2001, 2002].) Corporate portals are especially popular in large corporations, as shown in Insights and Additions 7.3.

EXHIBIT 7.9 **Corporate Portal as a Gateway to Information**

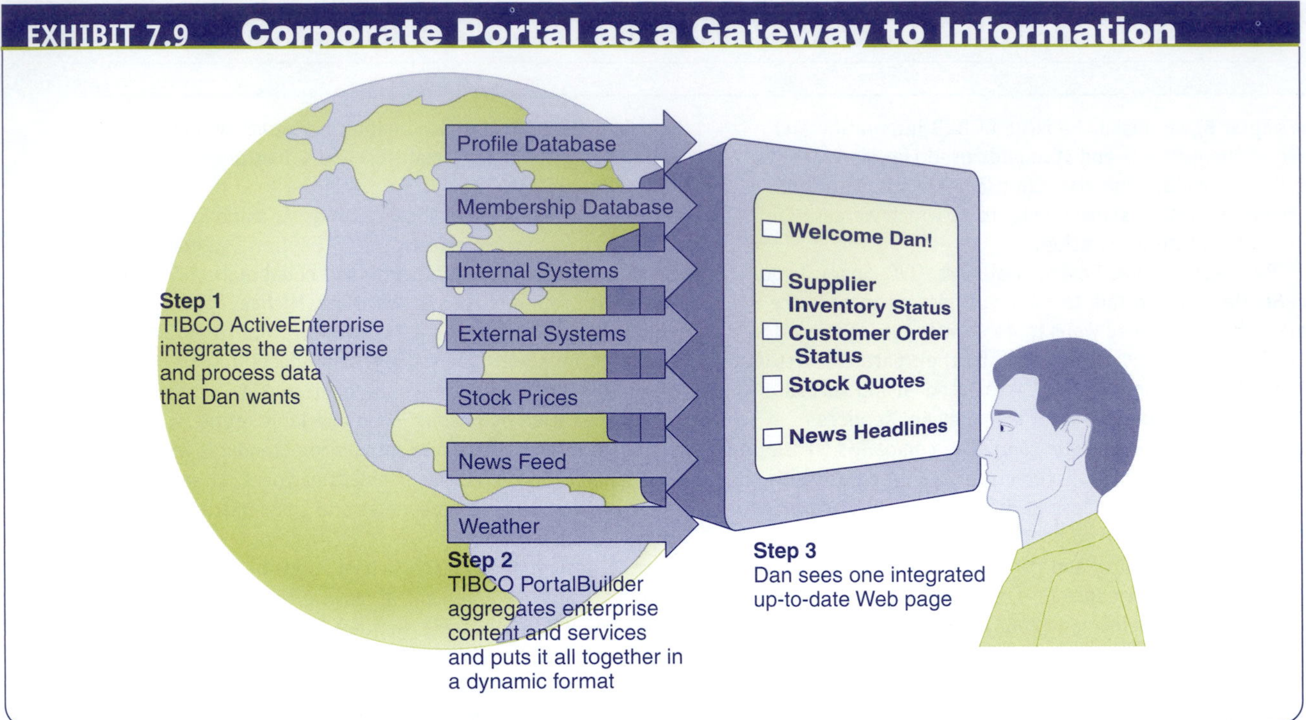

Source: Courtesy of TIBCO Software, Inc. (*tibco.com*).

TYPES OF CORPORATE PORTALS

Corporate portals are either generic or functional. Generic portals are defined by their audience (e.g., suppliers, employees). Functional portals are defined by the functionalities they offer. Portals are popular both in the private as well as the public sectors. For example, on implementation in the City of Calgary, Canada, see WebTrends (2003).

Types of Generic Portals

The following generic types of portals can be found in organizations.

Portals for Suppliers and Other Partners. Using such portals, suppliers can manage their own inventories online. They can view what they sold to the portal owner and for how much. They can see the inventory levels of the portal owner and send material and supplies when they see that a reorder level is reached, and they can collaborate with corporate buyers and other staff.

An example of a partners' portal is that of Samsung Electronic America's Digital IT. The company must keep in touch with 110,000 resellers and distributors. As part of its PRM, Samsung developed a portal that enables it to personalize relationships with each partner (e.g., conduct promotions, special pricing, etc.). The portal helped to increase sales by 30 percent; related expenses dropped by 25 percent. For details, see Schneider (2004).

Customer Portals. Portals for customers can serve both businesses and individual customers. Customers can use these *customer-facing portals* to view products and services and to place orders, which they can later track. They can view their own accounts and see what is going on with their accounts in almost real time. They can pay for products and services and arrange for warranties and deliveries.

At some portals, a repository of trending data enables a marketing manager to forecast whether a particular customer program would be useful based on usage patterns, transactional history, and data from similar customers. This enables marketing managers to push specific value-added programs to targeted customer segments at the customer portal.

In some applications, the relationship between the portal and its customers is completely transparent. A business customer, rather than calling, faxing, e-mailing, or using a catalog and creating a purchase order (PO), can go into its own system and create a PO. Then, the customer's system takes that PO and sends an XML message to the vendor's SCM system,

Insights and Additions 7.3 Some Large-Company Corporate Portals

Three examples of corporate portals—P&G, DuPont, and Staples—are presented here to demonstrate how companies use corporate portals.

P&G

The IT division of P&G developed a system for sharing documents and information over the company's intranet. The scope of this system later expanded into a global knowledge catalogue to support the information needs of all 98,000 P&G employees worldwide. Although the system helped in providing required information, it also led to information overload. To solve this problem, P&G developed a corporate portal that provides personalized information to each employee.

P&G's corporate portal, implemented by Plumtree (*plumtree.com*), provides P&G's employees with marketing, product, and strategic information and with industry-news documents numbering over 1 million Web pages. The corporate portal can be accessed through a Web browser without having to navigate through all of the different divisions' Web sites. Employees can gain access to the required information through customized preset views of various information sources and links to other up-to-date information.

DuPont

DuPont implemented an internal portal to organize millions of pages of scientific information stored in information systems throughout the company. The initial version of the portal was intended for daily use by over 550 employees to record product orders, retrieve progress reports for research products, and access customer-tracking information. Today, DuPont uses the portal for its 55,000 employees in 30 business units in 70 countries.

Staples

The corporate portal for Staples, an office supply company, was launched in February 2000. It was immediately used by the company's 3,000 executives, knowledge workers, and store managers; by 2003 there were over 10,000 users, with the objective to reach 46,000 employees by 2004. The portal serves as the interface to Staples' business processes and applications. It offers e-mail, scheduling, headlines on articles about the competition, new product information, internal news, job postings, and newsletters. The portal is used by top management as well as by managers of contracts, procurement, sales and marketing, human resources, and retail stores and by the company's three B2B Web sites.

Sources: Compiled from Konicki (2001) and from press releases from the companies described (2002–2003).

which accepts the message. In this case, the communication back and forth between a customer and the company using the seller's portal is done largely at a system level. This creates a tighter integration between the seller and the customer. It gives both customers and suppliers more efficiencies, and it facilitates more of a partnership than a typical customer–vendor relationship.

Employee Portals. Such portals are used for training, dissemination of company news and information, discussion groups, and more. Employee portals also are used for self-service activities, mainly in the personnel area (e.g., change of address forms, tax withholding forms, expense reports, class registration, and tuition reimbursement forms). Employees' portals are sometimes bundled with supervisors' portals in what are known as *workforce portals* (e.g., Workbrain Enterprise Workforce Management, workbrain.com).

Executive and Supervisor Portals. These portals enable managers and supervisors to control the entire workforce management process—from budgeting to workforce scheduling. For example, Pharmacia (a Pfizer company) built a portal for its executives and managers worldwide, the Global Field Force Action Planner, which provides a single, worldwide view of the company's finances and performance; business goals and sales figures are readily available on a consistent and transparent basis, allowing corporate management to evaluate and support field offices more effectively. Country managers also can share best practices with their peers and learn from other action plans, helping them to make better decisions.

mobile portals
Portals accessible via mobile devices, especially cell phones and PDAs.

Mobile Portals. Mobile portals are portals accessible via mobile devices, especially cell phones and PDAs. Most mobile portals are noncorporate information portals (i.e., they are commercial portals), such as DoCoMo's i-mode. (See the description of i-mode in Chapter 9 and in Bughin et al. 2001.) Eventually, large corporations will introduce mobile corporate portals. Alternatively, they will allow access to their regular portals from wireless devices, which many already do (e.g., major airlines, banks, and retailers).

The Functionalities of Portals

information portals
Portals that store data and enable users to navigate and query these data.

collaborative portals
Portals that allow collaboration.

Whatever their audience, the functionalities of portals range from simple **information portals** that store data and enable users to navigate and query that data to sophisticated **collaborative portals** that enable collaboration.

Several types of functional portals exist: *Business intelligence portals* are used mostly by middle- and top-level executives and analysts to conduct business analyses and decision support activities (Imhoff 2001; Ferguson 2001). For example, a business intelligence portal might be used to generate ad hoc reports or to conduct a risk analysis. *Intranet portals* are used mostly by employees for managing fringe benefits and for self-training (Ferguson 2001). *Knowledge portals* are used for collecting knowledge from employees and for disseminating collected knowledge. (For an example of a business intelligence and knowledge management portal, see EC Application Case 7.8 on p. 304 and Kesner 2003.)

CORPORATE PORTAL APPLICATIONS

According to a 2002 Delphi Group survey (*DM Review* 2003), the top portal applications, in decreasing order of importance, are as follows: knowledge bases and learning tools; business process support; customer-facing (front-line) sales, marketing, and services; collaboration and project support; access to data from disparate corporate systems; personalized pages for various users; effective search and indexing tools; security applications; best practices and lessons learned; directories and bulletin boards; identification of experts; news; and Internet access.

Exhibit 7.10 depicts a corporate portal framework. This framework illustrates the features and capabilities required to support various organizational applications.

EXHIBIT 7.10 Corporate Portal Framework

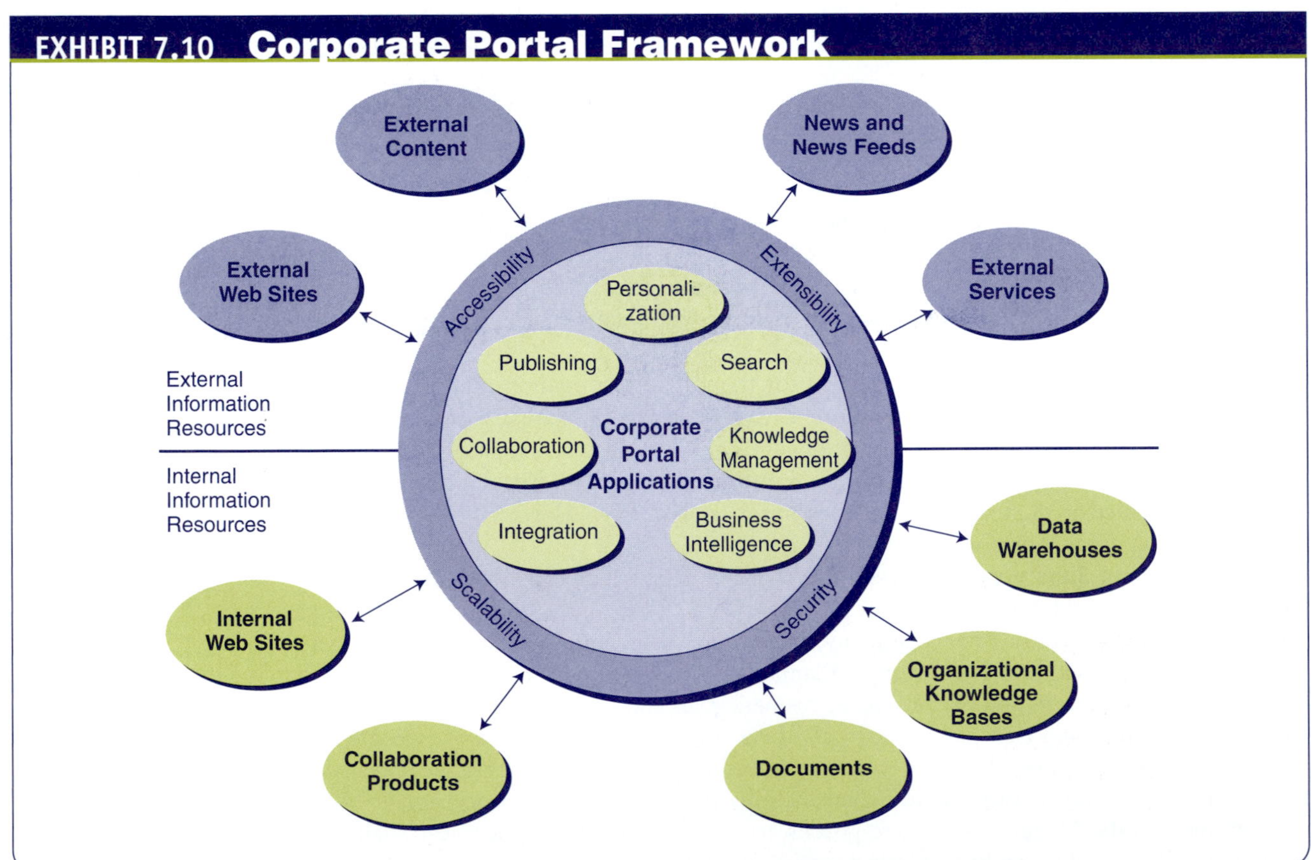

Source: Compiled by N. Bolloju, City University of Hong Kong, from Aneja et al. (2000) and Kounadis (2000).

JUSTIFYING PORTALS

As with any IT project, management needs to be able to justify the development and use of a corporate portal by comparing its cost with its benefits. However, most of the benefits of portals are *intangible*. For example, Reda (2002) claims that employee portals have the potential to fundamentally change and improve employer–employee relationships—a desirable benefit, although somewhat difficult to measure. According to Ferguson (2001), portals offer the following benefits that are difficult to quantify:

- They offer a simple user interface for finding and navigating content via a browser.
- They improve access to business content and increase the number of business users who can access information, applications, and people.
- They offer access to common business applications from anywhere in a geographically distributed enterprise and beyond. Using Web-enabled mobile or wireless devices, content can be accessed from anywhere.
- They offer the opportunity to use platform-independent software (Java) and data (XML).

However, given that portals are relatively low-cost, low-risk devices (Cunningham 2002), it is not surprising that they are being adopted by thousands of organizations worldwide. A formal approach to justifying portals is offered by Plumtree (2002), which devised a framework for assessing the ROI of portals. The company offers several white papers and examples on this topic (e.g., see Plumtree.com 2001) at its Web site (plumtree.com). For methods of justifying intangible benefits, see Chapter 15. For details on strategic supply chain planning, see Sodhi (2003).

DEVELOPING PORTALS

Before a company can develop a corporate portal, it must decide what the purpose and content of the portal will be. For some practical guidelines for determining a corporate portal strategy, see Smith (2004) and Online File W7.7.

Many vendors offer tools for building corporate portals as well as hosting services. Representative vendors are TIBCO (Portal Builder at tibco.com), Computer Associates (Jasmine II Portal at ca.com), Sybase, PeopleSoft, and Plumtree. See Mendoza et al. (2002) for a case study.

Section 7.7 ▸ REVIEW QUESTIONS

1. What is a corporate portal?
2. List the types of corporate portals.
3. List five applications of portals.
4. Discuss the issue of justifying enterprise portals.
5. List the major benefits of corporate portals.

workflow
The movement of information as it flows through the sequence of steps that make up an organization's work procedures.

workflow systems
Business process automation tools that place system controls in the hands of user departments to automate information-processing tasks.

workflow management
The automation of workflows, so that documents, information, and tasks are passed from one participant to the next in the steps of an organization's business process.

7.8 COLLABORATION-ENABLING TOOLS: FROM WORKFLOW TO GROUPWARE

As mentioned earlier, corporate portals facilitate e-collaboration. A large number of tools and methodologies also are available that facilitate e-collaboration. This section presents workflow technologies, groupware, and other collaboration-enabling tools.

WORKFLOW TECHNOLOGIES AND APPLICATIONS

Workflow is the movement of information as it flows through the sequence of steps that make up an organization's work procedures. **Workflow systems** are business process automation tools that place system controls in the hands of user departments. They employ a set of software programs that automate almost any information-processing task.

Workflow management is the automation of workflows so that documents, information, or tasks are passed from one participant to another in a way that is governed by the organization's rules or procedures. Workflow management involves all of the steps in a business process from start to finish, including all exception conditions. The key to workflow management is the tracking of process-related information and the status of each activity of the business process (see van der Aalst 2002). The major activities to be managed are job routing and monitoring, document imaging, document management, supply chain optimization, and control of work.

Types of Workflow Applications

Workflow applications fall into three major categories: collaborative, production, and administrative workflow.

- **Collaborative workflow.** Collaborative workflow refers to those software products that address project-oriented and collaborative types of processes. They are administered centrally, yet are capable of being accessed and used by workers from different departments and even from different physical locations. The goal of collaborative workflow tools is to empower knowledge workers. The focus of an enterprise solution for collaborative workflow is on allowing workers to communicate, negotiate, and collaborate within a unified environment. Some leading vendors of collaborative workflow applications are Lotus, JetForm, FileNet, and Action Technologies.
- **Production workflow.** Production workflow tools address mission-critical, transaction-oriented, high-volume processes. They often are deployed only in a single department or to a certain set of users within a department. These applications often include document imaging and storage and retrieval capabilities. They also may include the use of intelligent forms, database access, and ad hoc capabilities. The goal is to improve productivity and the quality of business processes. The leading vendors of workflow applications are FileNet, Staffware, IBM (MQ3), and Eastman WorkFlow. An example of production workflow that is mixed with collaborative workflow is presented in EC Application Case 7.10. For other applications, see Torode (2004) and Staff (2004b).
- **Administrative workflow.** Administrative workflow can be considered as a cross between the previous two types of workflow. The flow is predefined (such as the steps required to approve an expense report), but it can be changed if needed. The goal of administrative workflow applications is to reduce clerical costs in systems with a low volume of complex transactions. The major vendors are Staffware, InTempo, and Metro.

In conclusion, the benefits of workflow management systems include the following:

- Improved control of business processes, with far less management intervention and fewer chances for delays or misplaced work than in other systems.
- Improved quality of services through quicker response times with the best person available.
- Lower staff training costs because the work can be guided through complex procedures.
- Lower management costs, which enables managers to concentrate on nurturing employees and handling special cases rather than on routine reporting and distribution issues.
- Improved user satisfaction. Users typically have greater confidence that they are doing the best they can, and they enjoy greater satisfaction when completing their work with fewer conflicting requirements.

A major area for EC workflow applications is the aggregation of sellers or buyers, which was described in Chapters 5 and 6. When large suppliers or buyers are involved, a workflow system is needed for both the collaborative efforts and for supply chain and production improvements.

For information on workflow management, see Fischer (2002) and Basu and Kumar (2002). Additional information can be found at wfmc.org, aiim.org, waria.com, and omg.org. For a discussion of the functionalities of workflow management systems, see Online File W7.8.

Because workflow management systems support more than one individual, they are considered by some to be a subset of groupware, which is the next topic.

CASE 7.10

EC Application

USE OF A WORKFLOW SYSTEM TO MANAGE CURRENCY FLOWS AT A GERMAN BANK

Dresdner Bank in Germany has automated the way it handles the trading of currency orders. Whether they originate from within a single branch operation or across its trading rooms worldwide, it routes these orders using a workflow system called Limit Order Application (LORA). This workflow system, built on top of Microsoft Exchange, has replaced telephone and fax-based processes.

One of the main problems that Dresdner Bank sought to solve with the workflow system was the allocation and uptake of orders among different trading rooms around the world. Being able to route orders would allow more efficient trading across the different time zones; for instance, making it easier for traders to execute a Frankfurt customer's order in New York after the close of business in Germany.

Three types of bank staff—traders, controllers, and administrators—use this system, which works as follows: First, when an order is received, it is placed into an electronic folder by the controller. All order folders are held in a "public" file and can be viewed by the relevant staff. Next, when a trader accepts an order, the trader is responsible for that order from that moment on. Although the order can still be canceled or reversed at this stage, the price details and order quantity cannot be changed. The status of the order is displayed, and the order is locked to prevent anyone from altering it. (Even small changes in the details of an order could result in huge profits or losses for the bank or its clients). Finally, when the order is executed, or if it is canceled, reversed, or expires, it is sent to a subfolder to be archived.

The bank dropped an initial plan of implementing global common folders that could be accessed by any of its 1,000 traders from any location. It did so because of resistance from the traders, who did not like the idea of relinquishing local control and allowing other traders to process or execute their orders. Instead, the bank has implemented a system of local folders that reside within the branch of origin; these can be read by, but not processed by, traders elsewhere. Traders can decide whether orders are passed to other locations for processing.

With LORA, users can respond more quickly and accurately to customer queries because they are able to access and view on the computer screen the precise status of orders. Control also has been improved, because every order is assigned to a staff member. The user interface was carefully designed to meet stringent requirements with respect to efficiency and ease of use.

LORA was built mainly with Visual Basic, with provisions to extend the system to allow reuse of existing components. The system was implemented in about 6 months to the bank's 500 dealers in Frankfurt. By 2003, it was implemented in all of the bank's branches.

Sources: Compiled from Microsoft (2002), *microsoft.com/resources/casestudies/CaseStudy.asp?CaseStudyID=13324* (accessed 2000, 2003), and *dresdner-bank.com* (accessed 2003).

Questions

1. Identify the parties in this case that need to collaborate with each other.
2. Create a diagram that shows the flow of information in LORA.
3. How does the workflow system differ from a typical transaction-oriented application?
4. Explain how the system facilitates collaboration.

GROUPWARE: COLLABORATION TOOLS

Groupware refers to software products that support groups of people who share a common task or goal and collaborate on its accomplishment. These products provide a way for groups to share resources and opinions. Groupware implies the use of networks to connect people, even if they are in the same room. Many groupware products are available on the Internet or an intranet, enhancing the collaboration of a large number of people worldwide (e.g., see Henrie 2004). There are many different approaches and technologies for the support of groups on the Internet.

groupware
Software products that use networks to support collaboration among groups of people who share a common task or goal.

Groupware products and features that support collaboration and conferencing are listed in Exhibit 7.11.

Synchronous Versus Asynchronous Products

Notice that the features in Exhibit 7.11 may be *synchronous*, meaning that communication and collaboration are done in real time, or *asynchronous*, meaning that communication and collaboration are done by the participants at different times (e.g., by leaving a message on a bulletin

EXHIBIT 7.11 Major Features in Collaboration and Conferencing Tools

General

- Built-in e-mail, messaging system, instant messaging
- Browser interface
- Joint Web-page creation
- Sharing of active hyperlinks
- File sharing (graphics, video, audio, or other)
- Built-in search functions (by topic or keyword)
- Workflow tools
- Use of corporate portals for communication, collaboration
- Shared screens
- Electronic decision rooms
- Peer-to-peer networks

Synchronous (same-time)

- Videoconferencing, multimedia conferencing
- Audioconferencing
- Shared whiteboard, smart whiteboard
- Text chart
- Brainstorming, polling (voting), and other decision support (consensus builder, scheduler)

Asynchronous (different times)

- Threaded discussions
- Users can receive/send e-mail, SMS
- Users can receive activity notification via e-mail
- Users can collapse/expand threads
- Users can sort messages (by date, author, or read/unread)
- Chat session logs
- Bulletin boards, discussion groups
- Use of blogs
- Collaborative planning and/or design tools

board to be read and answered later). Web conferencing and instant messaging as well as Voice-over-IP (VOIP) are associated with synchronous mode. Associated with asynchronous mode are databases, browsers, and *online workspaces* where participants can collaborate on joint designs or projects but work at different times. Vignette (vignette.com) and Groove Networks (groove.net) allow users to set up online workspaces for sharing and storing documents. According to Henrie (2004), many of the tools offered by vendors are converging. This is done with the help of new technologies such as VOIP.

Groupware products are either stand-alone products that support one task (such as e-mail) or integrated kits that include several tools (such as e-mail and screen sharing). In general, groupware technology products are fairly inexpensive and can be easily incorporated into existing information systems.

The Internet, intranets, extranets, and private communication lines provide the infrastructure needed for groupware. Most of the software products are Web based. The following describes some of the most common collaboration tools.

Electronic Meeting Systems

An important area of virtual collaboration is electronic meetings. For decades, people have attempted to improve face-to-face meetings, which are known to have many potential dysfunctions. Initially, people attempted to better organize group meetings by using a facilitator and established procedures (known as *group dynamics*). Numerous attempts have been made to use information technologies to improve meetings conducted in one room. The advancement of Web-based systems opens the door for improved electronically supported **virtual meetings**, where members are in different locations and even in different countries. For example, online meetings and presentation tools are provided by webex.com and by gotomeetings.com.

virtual meetings
Online meetings whose members are in different locations, even in different countries.

The events of September 11 and the economic slowdown of 2001–2003 have made virtual meetings more popular (e.g., see Powell et al. 2004 and Bray 2004). It is hard for companies to ignore reported cost savings, such as the $4 million a month that IBM reported it saved just from cutting travel-related meeting expenses (Callaghan 2002). In addition, improvements in supporting technology, reductions in the price of the technology, and the acceptance of virtual meetings as a respected way of doing business are fueling their growth (see Vinas 2002).

Virtual meetings are supported by a variety of groupware tools, as will be shown in the remainder of this section. We begin our discussion with the support provided to decision making.

Group Decision Support Systems

A **group decision support system (GDSS)** is an interactive computer-based system that facilitates the solution of semistructured and unstructured problems by a group of decision makers. The goal of GDSSs is to improve the productivity of decision-making meetings, either by speeding up the decision-making process or by improving the quality of the resulting decisions, or both.

group decision support system (GDSS)
An interactive computer-based system that facilitates the solution of semistructured and unstructured problems by a group of decision makers.

The major characteristics of a GDSS are as follows:

- Its goal is to support the process of group decision makers by providing automation of subprocesses using information technology tools.
- It is a specially designed information system, not merely a configuration of already-existing system components. It can be designed to address one type of problem or a variety of group-level organizational decisions.
- It encourages generation of ideas, resolution of conflicts, and freedom of expression. It contains built-in mechanisms that discourage development of negative group behaviors such as destructive conflict miscommunication and "groupthink."

The first generation of GDSSs was designed to support face-to-face meetings in what is called a *decision room*. Today, support is provided over the Web to virtual groups (group members may be in different locations). The group can meet at the same time or at different times by using e-mail, sending documents, and reading transaction logs face-to-face. GDSS is especially useful when controversial decisions have to be made (such as resource allocation or determining which individuals to lay off). GDSS applications require a facilitator when done in one room or a coordinator or leader when done with virtual meetings.

GDSSs can improve the decision-making process in various ways. For one, GDSSs generally provide structure to the planning process, which keeps the group on track, although some permit the group to use unstructured techniques and methods for idea generation. In addition, GDSSs offer rapid and easy access to external information needed for decision making. GDSSs also support parallel processing of information and idea generation by participants and allow asynchronous computer discussion. They make possible larger meetings that would otherwise be unmanageable; a larger group means that more complete information, knowledge, and skills will be represented in the same meeting. Finally, voting can be anonymous, with instant results, and all information that passes through the system can be recorded for future analysis (producing organizational memory).

The major benefit of GDSSs, however, is in conducting virtual meetings. Meetings can be called very quickly and the company can save on travel expenses.

GDSS Products. More general GDSS products such as Microsoft NetMeeting, WebEx, and Lotus Notes/Domino provide for some of the functionalities just discussed. A more specialized GDSS product is GroupSystems, which is a complete suite of electronic meeting software (both for one room and virtual meetings). (Visit groupsystems.com and view the demo there.) Another specialized product is eRoom (now owned by EMC Documentum at documentum.com). This is a comprehensive Web-based suite of tools that can support a

variety of collaboration scenarios (see Online Exhibit W7.2). A third product is Team Expert Choice, which is an add-on product for Expert Choice (expertchoice.com). It has limited decision-support capabilities, mainly supporting one-room meetings.

Real-Time Collaboration Tools

The Internet, intranets, and extranets offer tremendous potential for real-time and synchronous interaction for people working in groups. *Real-time collaboration (RTC) tools* help companies bridge time and space to make decisions and collaborate on projects. RTC tools support synchronous communication of graphical and text-based information. These tools are being used in distance training, product demonstrations, customer support, e-commerce, and sales applications.

RTC tools can be purchased as stand-alone tools or used on a subscription basis (as offered by many vendors). Exhibit 7.12 shows a screen from one vendor of RTC tools, WebEx.

teleconferencing The use of electronic communication that allows two or more people at different locations to have a simultaneous conference.

video teleconference Virtual meeting in which participants in one location can see participants at other locations on a large screen or a desktop computer.

data conferencing Virtual meeting in which geographically dispersed groups work on documents together and exchange computer files during videoconferences.

Electronic Teleconferencing

Teleconferencing is the use of electronic communication that allows two or more people at different locations to have a simultaneous conference. It is the simplest infrastructure for supporting a virtual meeting. Several types of teleconferencing are possible. The oldest and simplest is a telephone conference call, wherein several people talk to each other from three or more locations. The biggest disadvantage of this is that it does not allow for face-to-face communication. Also, participants in one location cannot see graphs, charts, and pictures at other locations. Although the latter disadvantage can be overcome by using a fax, this is a time-consuming, expensive, and frequently poor-quality process. One solution is *video teleconferencing*, in which participants can see each other as well as the documents.

Video Teleconferencing. In a **video teleconference**, participants in one location can see participants at other locations. Dynamic pictures of the participants can appear on a large screen or on a desktop computer. Originally, video teleconferencing was the transmission of live, compressed TV sessions between two or more points. Today, video teleconferencing (or *videoconferencing*) is a digital technology capable of linking various types of computers across networks. Once conferences are digitized and transmitted over networks, they become a computer application.

With videoconferencing, participants can share data, voice, pictures, graphics, and animation. Data can also be sent along with voice and video. Such **data conferencing** makes it

EXHIBIT 7.12 WebEx

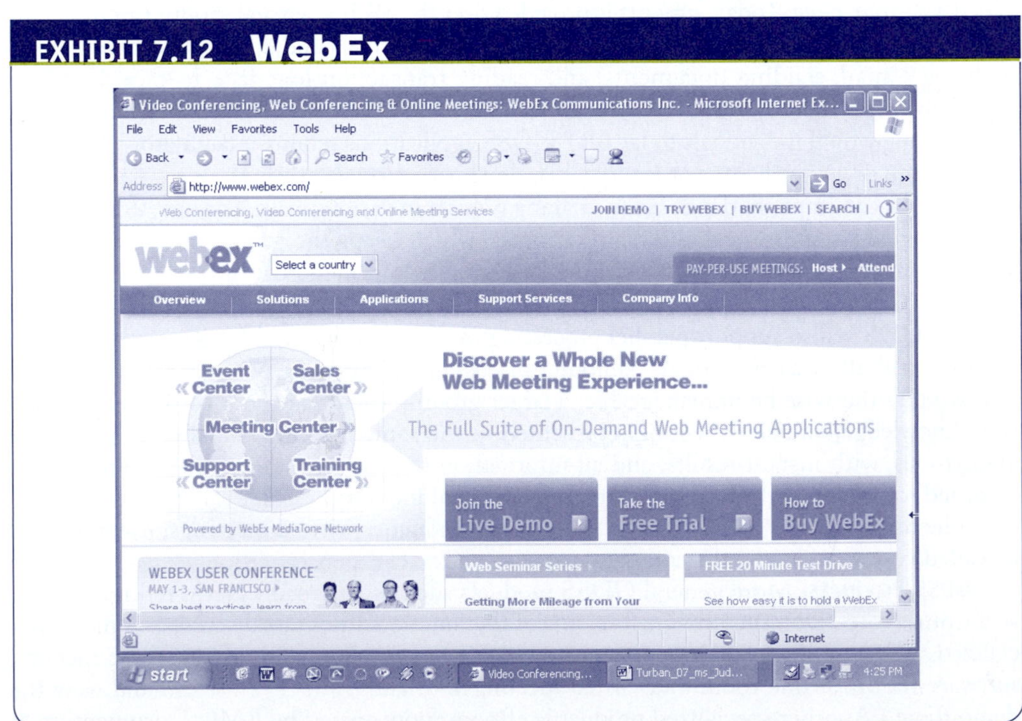

Source: Courtesy of WebEx Communications, Inc.

possible to work on documents and to exchange computer files during videoconferences. This allows several geographically dispersed groups to work on the same project and to communicate by video simultaneously.

Video teleconferencing offers various benefits. Two of them—providing the opportunity for face-to-face communication for individuals in different locations and supporting several types of media during conferencing—have already been discussed. Video teleconferencing also improves employee productivity, cuts travel costs, conserves the time and energy of key employees, and increases the speed of businesses processes (such as product development, contract negotiation, and customer service). It improves the efficiency and frequency of communications and saves an electronic record of a meeting, enabling specific parts of a meeting to be reconstructed for future purposes. Video teleconferencing also makes it possible to hold classes at different locations. Finally, the tool can be used to conduct meetings with business partners as well as to interview candidates for employment.

Web Conferencing. *Web conferencing* is conducted on the Internet for as few as two and for as many as thousands of people. It allows users to simultaneously view something on their computer screens, such as a sales presentation in Microsoft PowerPoint or a product drawing; interaction takes place via messaging or a simultaneous phone teleconference. Web conferencing is much cheaper than videoconferencing because it runs over the Internet.

The latest technological innovations permit both B2B and B2C Web conferencing applications. For example, banks in Alaska use *video kiosks* in sparsely populated areas instead of building branches that will be underutilized. The video kiosks operate on the banks' intranet and provide videoconferencing equipment for face-to-face interactions. A variety of other communication tools, such as online polls, whiteboards, and question-and-answer boards may also be used. Such innovations can be used to educate staff members about a new product line or technology, to amplify a meeting with investors, or to walk a prospective client though an introductory presentation. People can use Web conferencing to view presentations, seminars, and lectures, and to collaborate on documents.

Web conferencing is becoming very popular. Almost all Web conferencing products provide whiteboarding and polling features and allow users to give presentations and demos and share applications. Popular Web conferencing products are Centra EMeeting, Genesys Meeting Center, PlaceWare, and WebEx Meeting Center.

Voice-over-IP

Voice-over-IP (VOIP) refers to communication systems that transmit voice calls over Internet Protocol–based networks. Corporations are moving their phone systems to Internet standards to cut costs and boost efficiency. Strategies for how to do this are described in Sturdevant (2004) and by Blickstein (2004). VOIP also is known as *Internet telephony*. Free Internet telephony software is available from pc-telephone.com. Most browsers provide for VOIP capabilities. The browsers enable you to receive telephone calls initiated on the Internet (with a microphone and special VOIP software, which may be provided with the sender's browser).

Voice-over-IP (VOIP)
Communication systems that transmit voice calls over Internet Protocol–based networks.

Interactive Whiteboards

Whiteboards are another type of groupware. Computer-based whiteboards work like real-world whiteboards with markers and erasers, except for one big difference: Instead of one person standing in front of a meeting room drawing on the whiteboard, all participants can join in. Throughout a meeting, each user can view and draw on a single document "pasted" onto the electronic whiteboard on a computer screen. Users can save digital whiteboarding sessions for future use. Some whiteboarding products let users insert graphics files that can be annotated by the group.

Take, for example, an advertisement that needs to be cleared by a senior manager. Once the proposed ad has been scanned into a PC, both parties can see it on their screens. If the senior manager does not like something, she highlights what needs to be changed using a stylus pen. This tool makes communication between the two parties easier and clearer. The two parties also can share applications. For example, if party A works with Excel, party B does not have to have Excel in order to work with it in the whiteboarding tool.

Besides being used to support people working on the same task, whiteboards also are used for training and learning. The following are two example whiteboarding products: Digital Wall Display and Intelligent Whiteboard.

- Digital Wall Display from 3M Corp. (3m.com) is a multifunction whiteboard. It shows whatever is written on it as well as anything—text, charts, still and moving pictures—that is stored in a computer and loaded onto the whiteboard. With a remote mouse, presenters or teachers can edit and move the material around on the touch-screen board. All of this, including audio, can be transmitted instantaneously to any connected board, anywhere in the world, making it useful for virtual, long-distance teaching or training. The system also is used for sharing research among colleagues.
- Intelligent Whiteboard from Smart Technologies Inc. (smarttech.com) was designed to support teaching. It has a "write" feature in electronic ink, a "touch" feature for controlling applications, and a "save" feature to save work to computer files. A model named Camfire is equipped with digital cameras that photograph what is written on the whiteboard. The images are then transferred to a Web site or e-mailed to students. The system also can connect to devices, such as a microscope, for presentation of hard-to-see information.

Screen Sharing

screen sharing
Software that enables group members, even in different locations, to work on the same document, which is shown on the PC screen of each participant.

In collaborative work, members frequently are in different locations. Using **screen sharing** software, group members can work on the same document, which is shown on the PC screen of each participant. For example, two authors can work on a single manuscript. One may suggest a correction and execute it so that the other author can view the change. Collaborators can work together on the same spreadsheet or on the resultant graphics. Changes can be done by using the keyboard or by touching the screen. This capability can expedite the design of products, the preparation of reports and bids, and the resolution of conflicts.

A special screen-sharing capability is offered by Groove Networks (groove.net). Its product enables the joint creation and editing of documents on a PC (see Team Assignment 1).

Instant Video

The spread of instant messaging and Internet telephony has naturally led to the idea of linking people via both voice and audio. Called *instant video*, the idea is for a kind of video chat room. It allows users to chat in real time and see the person(s) they are communicating with. A simple way to do this is to add video cameras to the participants' computers. A more sophisticated and better-quality approach is to integrate an existing online videoconferencing service with instant messaging software, creating a service that offers the online equivalent of a videophone.

This idea is still in the early stages. One instant video pioneer is CUworld (cuworld.com). Here is how its CUworld software (which was in beta testing in January 2003) works: Users get free software (CUworld 6.0) that can compress and decompress video signals sent over an online connection. To start a conference, a user sends a request to an online buddy (via instant messenger). The CUworld software goes to the directory of the instant messaging service to determine the Internet addresses of the users' connections, and, using the Web addresses, the computers of the video participants are linked directly via the Internet. A video conference can then begin.

Instant video sounds like a good product, but no one yet knows for sure how commercially viable it will be.

Integration and Groupware Suites

Because groupware technologies are computer based, with the same objectives of supporting group work, it makes sense to integrate them among themselves and/or with other computer-based technologies. A *software suite* is created when several products are integrated into one system. Integrating several technologies can save time and money for users. For example, PictureTel Corporation (picturetel.com), in an alliance with software developer Lotus, developed an integrated desktop video teleconferencing product that uses Lotus Notes. Using this integrated system, publisher Reader's Digest has built several applications that have videoconferencing capabilities. A seamless integration also is provided in *groupware suites*. The following are some examples of popular groupware suites.

Lotus Notes/Domino. The Lotus Notes/Domino suite includes a document management system, a distributed client/server database, a basis for intranet and e-commerce systems, and a communication-support tool. It enhances real-time communications with asynchronous electronic connections (e.g., e-mail and other forms of messaging).

Group members using Lotus Notes/Domino may store all of their official memos, formal reports, and informal conversations related to particular projects in a shared database.

Lotus Notes provides online collaboration capabilities, workgroup e-mail, distributed databases, bulletin whiteboards, text editing, (electronic) document management, workflow capabilities, instant virtual meetings, application sharing, instant messaging, consensus building, voting, ranking, and various application development tools. All of these capabilities are integrated into one environment with a graphic-menu-based user interface. By the end of 2003, there were over 90 million Notes users worldwide (Langley 2004). For even more Lotus Notes/Domino capabilities, see Internet Exercise 11 at the end of the chapter.

Microsoft NetMeeting. Microsoft's groupware suite, NetMeeting, is a real-time collaboration package that supports whiteboarding, application sharing (of any Microsoft Windows application document), remote desktop sharing, file transfer, text chat, data conferencing, desktop audio, and videoconferencing. The NetMeeting suite is included in Windows 98 and more recent versions.

Novell GroupWise. Novell's GroupWise offers a wide range of communication and collaboration capabilities integrated with document management capabilities, including e-mail, calendaring, group scheduling, imaging, workflow, electronic discussions, and more.

OTHER COLLABORATIVE TOOLS

Many different collaborative tools are available. A sampler of these tools is provided in Online File W7.9. Consult that resource for information about collaborative tools in addition to those already discussed. Before closing this discussion of collaborative tools, however, we need to mention another tool—virtual reality.

Virtual Reality

In order to facilitate virtual collaboration in product design, one can use the technology of virtual reality. **Virtual reality (VR)** is a system that delivers interactive computer-generated 3D graphics to a user through a head-mounted display. It is an environment that provides artificially generated sensory cues sufficient to engender in the user some willing suspension of disbelief. Kan et al. (2001) proposed the use of Internet-based VR for product design in a collaborative environment. This system, based on Java and VRML (Virtual Reality Modeling Language), also can be used in virtual supermarkets, allowing customers to "pick up" products from shelves and place them in virtual shopping carts. It also can be used to explore new buildings, even before they are constructed, as well as new fashions (Fitzgerald 2004).

virtual reality (VR)
System that delivers interactive computer-generated 3D graphics to a user through a head-mounted display.

IMPLEMENTATION ISSUES FOR ONLINE COLLABORATION

This chapter has presented numerous online collaboration issues of one sort or another. Here are a few implementation issues that must be addressed when planning online collaboration. First, to connect business partners, an organization needs an effective collaborative environment. Such an environment is provided by groupware suites such as Lotus Notes/Domino or Cybozu Share360 (cybozu.com). Another issue is the need to connect collaborative tools with file management products on an organization's intranet. Two products that offer such connection capabilities are WiredRed's server and client (wiredred.com) and eRoom's server (documentum.com).

In addition, to create a truly collaborative environment, one needs protocols. The protocols are needed for easy integration of different applications and for standardizing communication. One such protocol, which is relatively new, is WebDAV (Web Distributed Authoring and Versioning protocol; see webdav.org).

Finally, note that online collaboration is not a panacea for all occasions or all situations. Many times, a face-to-face meeting is a must. People sometimes need the facial cues and the physical closeness that no computer system can currently provide. (A technology called *pervasive computing* attempts to remove some of these limitations by interpreting facial cues.

For more, see Chapter 9.) However, face-to-face meetings may sometimes be improved by collaborative technologies, such as GDSS, described earlier.

Section 7.8 ▶ REVIEW QUESTIONS

1. Define workflow systems and management.
2. Explain the types of workflow systems and the benefits of such systems.
3. List the major groupware tools.
4. Describe GDSSs and electronic meeting systems.
5. Describe the various types of electronic teleconferencing, including Web-based conferencing.
6. Describe whiteboards and screen sharing.
7. Describe integrated suites and their benefits.

MANAGERIAL ISSUES

Some managerial issues related to this chapter are as follows.

1. **How difficult is it to introduce e-collaboration?** Dealing with the technology may be the easy part. Tackling the behavioral changes needed within an organization and its trading partners may be a greater challenge. Change management requires an understanding of the new interdependencies being constructed and the new roles and responsibilities that must be adapted in order for the enterprise and its business partners to collaborate. Finally, e-collaboration costs money and needs to be justified. This may not be an easy task due to the intangible benefits involved.
2. **How much can be shared with business partners? Can they be trusted?** Many companies are sharing forecast data and actual sales data. But when it comes to allowing real-time access to product design, inventory, and ERP systems, there may be some hesitation. It is basically a question of trust. The more information that is shared, the better the collaboration. However, sharing information can lead to the giving away of trade secrets. In some cases, there is a cultural resistance against sharing (some employees do not like to share information even within their own organization). The value of sharing needs to be carefully assessed against its risks.
3. **Who is in charge of our portal and intranet content?** Because content is created by many individuals, two potential risks exist. First, proprietary corporate information may not be secure enough, so unauthorized people may have access to it. Second, appropriate intranet "netiquette" must be maintained; otherwise unethical or even illegal behavior may develop. Therefore, managing content, including frequent updates, is a must (see Chapter 13).
4. **Who will design the corporate portal?** Corporate portals are the gateways to corporate information and knowledge. Appropriate portal design is a must, not only for easy and efficient navigation, but also because portals portray the corporate image to employees and to business partners who are allowed access to it. Design of the corporate portal must be carefully thought out and approved by management.
5. **Should we conduct virtual meetings?** Virtual meetings can save time and money and if properly planned can bring as good or even better results than face-to-face meetings. Although not all meetings can be conducted online, many can. The supporting technology is getting cheaper and better with time.

RESEARCH TOPICS

Here are some suggested topics related to this chapter. For details, references, and additional topics, refer to the book's "Current EC Research" in the Online Appendix.

1. **Development of New Methods for Supply Chain Management**
   - The evolution of methods used to supporting SCM
   - Modeling inter- and intra-organizational coordination for SCM
   - Collaboration methods for planning, forecasting, PLM, and other SCM topics
   - Appropriate methods for the implementation and use of Vendor Managed Inventory
   - Design protocols for continuous replenishment

- Modeling of interorganizational workflow
- Managing flexibility and agility in interorganizational supply chains
- Demand chain management for multiple large customers
- Restructuring the supply chain and related procedures using RFID

2. **Appropriate Design of SCM Systems**
   - Comparative evaluation of SCM solutions
   - Selection of and building a portfolio of SCM solutions
   - Standards for the deployment of CPFR
   - Integration of supply chain components with ERP and other IT systems
   - Using groupware in supply chain coordination and collaboration
   - Using workflow to automate inter- and intra-organizational SCM operations
   - Using multi-agent technology for SCM improvements
   - Using Knowledge Management Systems for SCM improvements
3. **Cost Benefit Analysis of Supply Chain Management**
   - Strategic and tactical issues for analyzing the supply chain in e-business
   - Costs and benefits of supply chain collaboration for both industries and individual companies
   - Real and ideal incentives for firms to share information vertically
   - Risk of information sharing and protective measures to take
   - Empirical studies of the value of electronic replenishment in supply chain
   - Issues and solutions concerning the role of intermediaries in collaborative commerce
   - Empirical studies concerning performance assessment of collaborative planning and forecasting
   - Use of balanced scorecard for performance evaluation of different supply chain types
4. **Managerial Issues Related to SCM**
   - Factors that determine trust building in B2B partnering
   - Managing trust and commitment in collaborative supply chain relationships
   - Relationship attributes in supply chain partnerships
   - How to contract information sharing in demand forecasts
   - Factors that impact the evaluation of suppliers and data collection methods
   - Studying the behavior of suppliers who have adopted SRM systems
   - An analysis of barriers to adoption of SCM
   - How to motivate small suppliers to participate in EC-based SCM systems
5. **Other B2B Service Issues**
   - Quality metrics of intranet-based services
   - Design of corporate portals

SUMMARY

In this chapter, you learned about the following EC issues as they relate to the learning objectives.

1. **The e-supply chain, its characteristics, and its components.** Digitizing and automating the flow of information throughout the supply chain and managing it via the Web results in an entity called the e-supply chain. The major parts of the e-supply chain are upstream (to suppliers), internal (in-house processes), and downstream (to distributors and customers). Activities of e-supply chains include replenishment, procurement, collaborative planning, collaborative design/development, e-logistics, and use of exchanges or supply webs—all of which can be Internet based.
2. **Supply chain problems and their causes.** The major supply chain problems are too large or too small inventories, lack of supplies or products when needed, the need for rush orders, deliveries of wrong materials or to wrong locations, and poor customer service. These problems result from uncertainties in various segments of the chain (e.g., in transportation), from mistrust of partners and a lack of collaboration and information sharing, and from difficulties in forecasting demand (e.g., the bullwhip effect). Also, lack of appropriate logistics infrastructure can result in problems.
3. **Solutions to supply chains problems provided by EC.** EC technologies automate and expedite order taking, speed order fulfillment, provide for e-payments, properly control inventories, provide for correct forecasting and thus better scheduling, and improve collaboration among supply chain partners. Of special interest is the emerging RFID technology that could revolutionize supply chain management.
4. **C-commerce: Definitions and types.** Collaborative commerce refers to a planned use of digital technology

by business partners. It includes planning, designing, researching, managing, and servicing various partners and tasks, frequently along the supply chain. Collaborative commerce can be between different pairs of business partners or among many partners participating in a collaborative network.

5. **Collaborative planning and CPFR.** Collaborative planning concentrates on demand forecasting and on resource and activity planning along the supply chain. Collaborative planning tries to synchronize partners' activities. CPFR is a business strategy that attempts to develop standard protocols and procedures for collaboration. Its goal is to improve demand forecasting by collaborative planning in order to ensure delivery of materials when needed. In addition to forecasting, collaboration in design is facilitated by IT, including groupware. Product lifecycle management (PLM) enables manufacturers to plan and control product-related information.
6. **Intrabusiness EC.** Intrabusiness EC refers to all EC initiatives conducted within an organization. These can be activities between an organization and its employees, between SBUs in the organization, and among the organization's employees.
7. **Integration along the supply chain.** Integration of various applications within companies and between business partners is critical to the success of companies. To simplify integration, one can use special software as well as employ standards such as XML. Web Services is a promising new approach for facilitating integration.
8. **Types and roles of corporate portals.** The major types of corporate portals are those for suppliers, customers, employees, and supervisors. There also are mobile portals (accessed by wireless devices). Functional portals such as knowledge portals and business intelligence portals provide the gateway to specialized knowledge and decision making. Corporate portals provide for easy information access, communication, and collaboration.
9. **Collaborative tools.** Hundreds of different collaboration tools are available. The major groups of tools are workflow and groupware. In addition, specialized tools ranging from group decision support systems (GDSSs) to devices that facilitate product design also are available.

KEY TERMS

Term	Page
Advanced planning and scheduling (APS) systems	298
Bullwhip effect	284
Business-to-employee (B2E)	302
Collaboration hub	287
Collaborative commerce (c-commerce)	286
Collaborative planning, forecasting, and replenishment (CPFR)	297
Collaborative portals	310
Corporate (enterprise) portal	307
Data conferencing	316
E-supply chain	279
E-supply chain management (e-SCM)	281
Grid computing	289
Group decision support system (GDSS)	315
Groupware	313
Information portals	310
Intrabusiness EC	301
Mobile portals	309
Product lifecycle management (PLM)	299
Screen sharing	318
Supply chain	279
Teleconferencing	316
Vendor managed inventory (VMI)	290
Video teleconference	316
Virtual meetings	315
Virtual reality	319
Voice-over-IP (VOIP)	317
Workflow	311
Workflow management	311
Workflow systems	311

QUESTIONS FOR DISCUSSION

1. Discuss the benefits of e-supply chains.
2. Discuss the relationship between c-commerce and corporate portals.
3. Compare and contrast a commercial portal (such as Yahoo!) with a corporate portal.
4. Explain the need for groupware to facilitate collaboration.
5. Discuss the need for workflow systems as a companion to e-commerce.
6. Discuss the relationship between portals and intranets at the same organization.
7. It is said that c-commerce signifies a move from a transaction focus to a relationship focus among supply chain members. Discuss.
8. Discuss the need for virtual meetings.
9. Discuss how CPFR can lead to more accurate forecasting and how it can resolve the bullwhip effect.

10. Discuss the advantage of suites such as Lotus Notes/Domino. Do these tools have any disadvantages?
11. Describe the advantages of RFID over a regular bar code in light of supply chain management.
12. Explain the importance of EPC (electronic product code) in RFID.
13. Compare a collaborative hub and a collaborative network.

INTERNET EXERCISES

1. Enter ca.com/products and register. Then take the Clever Path Portal Test Drive. (Flash Player from Macromedia is required.) Then enter peoplesoft.com and plumtree.com. Prepare a list of the major products available for building corporate portals.
2. Enter plumtree.com. Find the white papers about corporate portals and their justification. Prepare a report based on your findings.
3. Enter doublediamondsoftware.com/product_overview.htm. Identify all potential B2B applications and prepare a report about them.
4. Investigate the status of CPFR. Start at vics.org/committees/cpfr, google.com, and yahoo.com. Also enter supply-chain.org and find information about CPFR. Write a report on the status of CPFR.
5. Enter mysap.com and plumtree.com and find the key capabilities of their enterprise portals. List the benefits of using five of the capabilities of portals
6. Enter nokia.com, mdsi.com, and symbolic.com. Identify the B2E products you find at these sites. Prepare a list of the different products.
7. Enter i2.com and review its products. Explain how some of the products facilitate collaboration.
8. Enter collaborate.com and read about recent issues related to collaboration. Prepare a report.
9. Enter kolabora.com or mindjet.com. Find out how collaboration is done. Summarize the benefits of this site to the participants.
10. Enter vignette.com or cybozu.com and read the company vision for collaborative commerce. Then view the demo. Explain in a report how the company facilitates c-commerce.
11. Enter lotus.com and find the collaboration-support products. How do these products support groups?
12. Enter supplyworks.com and worldchain.com. Examine the functionalities provided for supply chain improvements (the inventory management aspects).
13. Enter 3m.com and smarttech.com. Find information about their whiteboards. Compare the products.
14. Enter electronicssupplychain.org, then click "Resources." Find new material on supply chain automation.
15. Enter nrf.com/rfid and learn about new RFID applications. Write a report.
16. Enter epiqtech.com and find information about products related to this chapter.

TEAM ASSIGNMENTS AND ROLE PLAYING

1. Have each team download a free copy of Groove from groove.net. Install the software on the members' PCs and arrange collaborative sessions. What can the free software do for you? What are its limitations?
2. Each team is assigned to an organization. The team members will attempt to identify several supply chains, their components, and the partners involved. Draw the chains and show which parts can be treated as e-supply chain parts.
3. Each team is assigned to a major vendor of corporate portals, such as Plumtree, Tibco Computer Associates, IBM, or PeopleSoft. Each team will check the capabilities of the corporate portal tools and try to persuade the class that its product is superior.
4. Each team is assigned to one area of collaborative commerce. The mission is to find recent applications and case studies in that area. Present the findings to the class.

Real-World Case

PORTAL AND COLLABORATION AT PIONEER

Pioneer is a large global oil and gas company that needed EC tools to streamline business processes, automate workflows, and improve communication internally and with business partners. The company also needed an EC infrastructure on which to build enterprise Web applications. The employees needed a system that would enable them to work together and also have an up-to-date view of the company's finances and production. The company selected a comprehensive software suite, Enterprise Web, from Plumtree. The suite includes a corporate portal, a content server, and a collaboration server. The suite met Pioneer's requirements, helping it to better manage oil exploration and extraction processes. All of this of resulted in higher productivity and profit.

The portal is fundamentally changing the way Pioneer works, from empowering employees in remote locations to collaborate on data analysis to giving executives and key employees the ability to monitor oil and gas field production volumes in near real time. The new system simplifies access to information, freeing Pioneer employees from the complexity of underlying systems.

To integrate information and functionality from systems running on different application servers and coded in different languages, Pioneer needed the openness provided by Plumtree's Web Services Architecture. In addition, the Enterprise Web technologies offered an integrated solution of portal and collaboration technologies, giving users a unified, interactive environment and project sponsors a low total cost of ownership.

Enterprise Web applications are applications hosted on different application servers but managed within one framework. Enterprise Web applications differ from traditional applications in three ways. First, Enterprise Web applications combine existing data and processes from diverse enterprise systems with new shared services, providing greater return on assets. Second, Enterprise Web applications are assembled dynamically, incorporating new capabilities on-the-fly, allowing for greater agility in solving business problems. Finally, Enterprise Web applications are designed for integration into an enterprisewide environment, providing greater economies of scale. Users can easily navigate between or search across applications, and Web Services developed for one Enterprise Web application can be reused as-is in other applications.

A special functionality is the ability to unlock data hidden in complex systems, provide real-time production monitoring via dashboards, capture knowledge in collaborative communities, and provide balanced-scorecard applications.

Pioneer selected Plumtree both for the functionalities listed above and because of its documented success with other companies in the oil and gas industry. Pioneer leases the software from Plumtree, paying a monthly fee based on the number of users.

Source: Compiled from "Pioneer Deploys Plumtree Enterprise Web Suite to Employees Worldwide, Integrating Over 100 Services in 30 New Enterprise Web Applications" *plumtree.com/news_events/pressreleases/2003/press101403b.htm*. Adapted with permission.

Questions

1. Why was Plumtree selected?
2. Relate the case to the issue of integration.
3. Why did the company need the collaboration server?
4. What is the role of Web Services?
5. Which problems were solved by the use of the software?

REFERENCES

Abbott, C. "At Amway, BI Portal Speeds Product R&D." *DM Review*, October 2000.

Ace Hardware. acehardware.com (accessed September 2002 and January 2003).

Amato-McCoy, D. "Michael Foods Dishes out Superior Service with Business Integration Solution." *Stores*, February 2004.

Amway. amway.com (accessed September 2002).

Aneja, A., et al. "Corporate Portal Framework for Transforming Content Chaos on Intranets." *Intel Technology Journal* Q1 (2000).

Balakrishnan, A., and J. Geunes. "Collaboration and Coordination in Supply Chain Management and E-Commerce." *Production and Operations Management* 13, no. 1 (2004).

Bartram, L., and M. Blackstock, "Designing Portable Collaborative Networks." *Queue* 1, no. 3 (2003): 40–49.

Basu, A., and A. Kumar. "Research Commentary: Workflow Management Issues in e-Business." *Information System Research* (March 2002).

Bayles, D. L. *E-Commerce Logistics and Fulfillment*. Upper Saddle River, NJ: Prentice Hall, 2001.

Blickstein, J. "Internet Telephony: A Sound Move?" *CIO Insight*, July 2004.

Bradley, P. "CPFR Gaining Converts." *Logistics*, April 2002.

Bray, R. "Virtual Meetings: The New Business Travel: Business Travel Briefing." *Financial Times*, 2004.

Brenchley, D. "Collaboration Made Easy." *Supply Management* 9, no. 14 (2004).

Brook, O. "Auto-Tech Display Shows Promise for Future of Collaborative Commerce." *MSI* 22, no. 11 (2004).

Bughin, J. R., et al. "Mobile Portals." *The McKinsey Quarterly* no. 2 (2001).

Bury, S. "Vendor-Managed Inventory." *Purchasing B2B* 46, no. 3 (2004).

Buss, D. "CPFR Initiative Allows Ace to Boost Revenue While Cutting Costs." *Stores*, September 2002.

Bussler, C. *B2B Integration*. Boston: Springer, 2003.

Buxmann, P., et al. *Inter-organizational Cooperation with SAP Solutions*. Boston: Springer, 2004.

Callaghan, D. "IBM: E-Meetings Save $4 Million a Month." *eWeek*, June 26, 2002.

Chopra, S., and M. S. Sodhi. "Managing Risk to Avoid Supply-Chain Breakdown." *MIT Sloan Management Review* 46, no. 1 (2004).

Chow, W. S. "An Exploratory Study of the Success Factors for Extranet Adoption in E-supply Chain." *Journal of Global Information Management*, January–March 2004.

Cook, M., and R. Hagey. "Why Companies Flunk Supply-Chain 101." *Journal of Business Strategy* 24, no. 4 (2003).

Corning, Inc. **corning.com** (accessed September 2002).

Craighead, C. W., and N. G. Shaw. "E-Commerce Value Creation and Destruction: A Resource-Based, Supply Chain Perspective." *Data Base*, Spring 2003.

Cunningham, M. J. "Getting the Portal Payback." *e-Business Advisor*, March 2002.

Cybex International. **cybexintl.com** (accessed 2002 and June 2003).

Davenport, T. H., and J. D. Brooks. "Enterprise Systems and the Supply Chain." *Enterprise Information Management* 17, no. 1 (2004).

Davies, C. "Game Shows It's Professionals Who Cause the Bullwhip Effect." *Supply Chain Europe* 13, no. 4 (2004).

Davis, W. S., and J. Benamati. *E-Commerce Basics*. Boston: Addison Wesley, 2003.

Davison, R., and G. de Vreede. "The Global Application of Collaborative Technologies." *Communications of the ACM* (December 2001).

Day, M. "What Is PLM?" *CADserver*, April 15, 2002.

Delphi Group. "Business Portals: Applications & Architecture." Delphi Group, 1999. **delphigroup.com/research/reports/bus-port-excerpt.htm** (accessed April 2001).

Divitini, M., et al. "Mobile Computing and Applications (MCA): Collaboration Support for Mobile Users." *Proceedings of the 2004 ACM Symposium on Applied Computing*, Nicosia, Cyprus, March 14–17, 2004, pp. 1191–1195.

DM Review. "Top Priorities in Deploying Portal Software: Delphi Group." *DM Direct Special Report*, July 8, 2003. **dmreview.com/editorial/newsletter_article.cfm?nl=bireport&articleId=7068&issue=219** (accessed January 2005).

Dresdner-bank.com (accessed March 2005).

Emigh, J. "Supply Chain Group Goes Global to Combat Terrorism." *eWeek*, December 20, 2004.

Ferguson, M. "Corporate and E-Business Portals." *myITadviser*, April 2001.

Fischer, L. *Workflow Handbook 2002*. Lighthouse Point, FL: Future Strategies, Inc., 2002.

Fitzgerald, M. "Fashion Tech, More Fantasy than Fact." *ExtremeTech.com*, 2004.

Frank, M. "Industry Showcase: LANSA Delivers e-Collaboration On Demand." *LANSA*, February 2004. **lansa.com/casestudies/ecollaboration.htm** (accessed May 2004).

Gibson-Paul, L. "Suspicious Minds." *CIO Magazine*, January 15, 2003.

GNX. "GNX Supply Chain Collaboration." *GNX.com*. **gnx.com/reg/branding.jsp?sec=solutions&sec2=cpfr** (accessed December 2004).

Goldberg, H. E. "Working Together on the Web." *Architecture* 93, no. 11 (2004).

Gregory, A. "How Best to Deal with the Unexpected?" *Works Management* 57, no. 6 (2004).

Gustke, C. "No More Heavy Lifting at Cybex." *Forbes* (supplement), October 7, 2002.

Handfield, R. B., et al. *Supply Chain Redesign: Transforming Supply Chains into Integrated Value Systems*. Upper Saddle River, NJ: Financial Times Management/Prentice Hall, 2002.

Handfield, R. B., and E. L. Nichols, Jr. *Supply Chain Management Redesign*. Upper Saddle River, NJ: Prentice Hall, 2002.

Hansen, U. T., and M. S. Deimler. "Cutting Costs While Improving Morale with B2E Management." *MIT Sloan Management Review*, Fall 2001.

Heizner, J., and B. Render. *Operations Management*, 7th ed. Upper Saddle River, NJ: Prentice Hall, 2004.

Henrie, K. S. "All Together Now." *CIO Insight*, July 2004.

HP. **hp.com/jornada** (accessed May 2002).

IBM. "Product Lifecycle Management." **ibm.com/solutions/plm/** (accessed February 2005).

Imhoff, C. "Power Up Your Enterprise Portal." *e-Business Advisor*, May 2001.

Industry Directions. "The Next Wave of Supply Chain Advantage: CPFR." White paper, April 2000. **industrydirections.com/pdf/CPFRPublicReport.pdf** (accessed March 2002).

Intel Corp. "Franchising Meets the Internet." **intel.com/ebusiness/** (go to Industry Solutions) (accessed March 1999a).

Intel Corp. "Marriott International Checks In." **intel.com/ebusiness/** (go to Industry Solutions) (accessed March 1999b).

Ireland, R., and R. Bruce. "CPFR: Only the Beginning of Collaboration." *Supply Chain Management Review*, September–October 2000.

Kaihla, P. "Inside Cisco's $2 Billion Blunder." *Business 2.0*, March 2002.

Kalakota, R., and M. Robinson. *E-Business 2.0*. Reading, MA: Addison-Wesley, 2001.

Kan, H. Y., et al. "An Internet Virtual Reality Collaborative Environment for Effective Product Design." *Computers in Industry* 45 (2001).

Kanakamedala, K., et al. "Getting Supply Chain Software Right." *The McKinsey Quarterly* no. 1 (2003).

Kannan, S. "e-Logistics' Plans." *The Hindu*, 2004.

Kesner, R. M. "Building a Knowledge Portal: A Case Study in Web-Enabled Collaboration." *Information Strategy: The Executive Journal*, Winter 2003.

Kinsella, B. "Wal-Mart Factor." *Industrial Engineer*, November 2003.

Konicki, S. "The New Desktop: Powerful Portals." *InformationWeek*, May 1, 2001. **informationweek.com/784/portal.htm** (accessed January 2005).

Kounadis, T. "How to Pick the Best Portal." *e-Business Advisor*, August 2000.

Langley, N. "Notes users can spread their skills." *Computerweekly*. March 23, 2004. **computerweekly.com/articles/article.asp?liArticleID=129281&liArticleTypeID=20&liCategoryID=2&liChannelID=30&liFlavourID=1&sSearch=&nPage=1** (accessed March 2005).

Line56.com. "Transportation and Warehousing Improving the Value of Your Supply Chain Through Integrated Logistics." *Line56.com*, May 1, 2002. **elibrary.line56.com/data/detail?id=1043954015_280&type=RES&x=1033897490** (accessed August 2002). Note: No longer available online.

Lotus. **lotus.com** (accessed January 2003).

Manninen, M. *Rich Interaction Model for Game and Virtual Environment Design*. Academic Dissertation, Department of Information Processing Science, University of Oulu, 2004. **herkules.oulu.fi/isbn9514272544/isbn9514272544.pdf** (accessed May 2003).

McCreary, L. "Intranet Winners 1999." *CIO Web Magazine*, July 1, 1999.

Melymuka, K. "Meeting of the Minds." *Computerworld*, July 28, 2003.

Mendoza, L. E., et al. "Evaluation of Environments for Portals Development: A Case Study." *Information Systems Management* (Spring 2002).

Microsoft. "Dresdner Bank." *Microsoft.com*, December 31, 2002. **microsoft.com/resources/casestudies/CaseStudy.asp?CaseStudyID=13645** (accessed March 2005).

Microsoft. "Hi-Life: Retailer Leads Mobile Revolution with Pocket PC." *Microsoft Case Study*. **microsoft.com/resources/casestudies/CaseStudy.asp?CaseStudyID=13683** (accessed December 2004).

Neef, D. *E-Procurement: From Strategy to Implementation*. Upper Saddle River, NJ: Prentice Hall, 2001.

Norris, G., et al. *E-Business and ERP: Transforming the Enterprise*. New York: McGraw-Hill, 2000.

Parks, L. "Buzzsaw Keeps Safeway Store Design on the Cutting Edge." *Stores*, February 2004.

PeopleSoft. **peoplesoft.com** (accessed October 2002).

PeopleSoft. "Corning: Discovering beyond Imagination." *Peoplesoft.com*, June 2002. **peoplesoft.com/media/en/pdf/success/corning_ss_0602.pdf** (accessed December 2004).

PeopleSoft. "PDA Materials Management for MemorialCare." *PeopleTalk*, January–March 2003. **peoplesoft.com/corp/en/peopletalkonline/january_2003/solutionsfocus/memorialcare.jsp** (accessed December 2004.)

Plumtree. "A Framework for Assessing Return on Investment for a Corporate Portal Deployment: The Industry's First Comprehensive Overview of Corporate Portal ROI." *Plumtree.com*, April 2002. **plumtree.com/webforms/MoreInfo_FormActionTemplate.asp** (updated April 2002). Note: No longer available online.

Plumtree. "Ford Connects European Dealer Network." *Plumtree.com*, October 14, 2003a. **www.plumtree.com/news_events/pressreleases/2003/press101403c.htm** (accessed December 2004).

Plumtree. "Pioneer Deploys Plumtree Enterprise Web Suite to Employees Worldwide, Integrating Over 100 Services in 30 New Enterprise Web Applications." *Plumtree.com*, October 14, 2003b. **plumtree.com/news_events/pressreleases/2003/press 101403b.htm** (accessed March 2005).

Plumtree. "Plumtree, META Publish ROI Study of Ketchum myKGN Portal Global Public Relations Firm Projects Four-Year Return of $12.1 Million." *Plumtree.com*, June 19, 2001. **plumtree.com/news_events/pressreleases/2001/press061901.htm** (accessed December 2004).

Plunkett, K. "Supply-Chain Dynamics and Run Strategy." *Logistics and Transport Focus* 6, no. 6 (2004).

Poirier, C. "Collaborative Commerce: Wave Two of the Cyber Revolution." *Computer Sciences Corporation Perspectives* (2001): 8.

Powell, A., et al. "Virtual Teams: A Review of Current Literature and Directions for Future Research." *Data Base* (Winter 2004).

Reda, S. "New Systems Foster Interaction with Store Employees." *Stores*, February 2002.

Reda, S. "The Path to RFID." *Stores*, June 2003.

Richardson, H. L. "The Ins & Outs of VMI." *Logistics Today* 45, no. 3 (2004).

Ricks, D., et al. "Improving Vertical Coordination of Agricultural Industries through Supply Chain Management." *American Agricultural Economic Association*, October 1999. **agecon.lib.umn.edu/cgi-bin/pdf_view.pl?paperid=1780&ftype=.pdf** (accessed July 2002).

Rifkin, G. "GM's Internet Overhaul." *MIT Technology Review* (October 2002).

Schneider, M. "Samsung's Partner Portal Delivers a 30 percent Sales Increase." *CRM Magazine*, May 2004.

Schrage, M. "Now You See It, Now You Don't." *CIO*, March 15, 2004.

Schram, P. *Collaborative Commerce: Going Private to Get Results*. New York: Deloitte Consulting. **dc.com** (accessed June 2004).

Seideman, T. "QVC.com and Costco.com Talk to Business Partners in the Same Language." *Stores*, February 2004.

Siau, K., and Y. Tian. "Supply Chains Integration: Architecture and Enabling Technologies." *Journal of Computer Information Systems*, Spring 2004.

Simatupang, T. M., and R. Sridharan. "The Collaborative Supply Chain." *International Journal of Logistic Management* 13, no. 1 (2002).

Smith, M. A. "Portals: Toward an Application Framework for Interoperability." *Communications of the ACM*, October 2004.

Sodhi, M. "How to do Strategic Supply-Chain Planning." *MIT Sloan Management Review*, Fall 2003.

Springer, A. "Corning Synchronizes its Global Supply Chain." *PeopleTalk* 13, no. 3 (2002).

Staff. "AS2 is A-OK at Wal-Mart." *Chain Store Age* 80, no. 2 (2004a).

Staff. "Canadian Firm to Debut New Workflow Management System." *Operations Management* (2004b).

Stevenson, W. *Operations Management,* 8th ed. New York: McGraw-Hill, 2004.

Sturdevant C. "How to Make the Move to IP Telephony." *CIO Insight*, Special Report, July 2004.

Sullivan, M. "GM Moves into the Passing Lane." *Forbes* (*Best of the Web* supplement), October 7, 2002.

SupplyChainBrain.com. "The Private Side of Collaboration." SupplyChainBrain.com, August 2001. **glscs.com/archives/8.01.collaboration.htm?adcode=75** (accessed January 2005).

Szekely, B. "Build a Life Sciences Collaboration Network with LSID." *IBM DeveloperWorks*, August 15, 2003. **www-106.ibm.com/developerworks/webservices/library/os-lsid2** (accessed May 2004).

Teresko, J. "Small is Beautiful." *IndustryWeek* 253, no. 11 (2004).

Thuraisingham, B., D. Morey, and M. Maybury (eds.). *Knowledge Management: Classic and Contemporary Works.* Cambridge, MA: MIT Press, 2002.

TIBCO. **tibco.com** (accessed 2001).

Torode, C. "Kronos Plans Web-based Workflow Management." *Mass High Tech* 22, no. 35 (2004).

Ulfelder, S. "GM Gears up with Collaboration Based on Web Services." *NetworkWorldFusion,* May 26, 2003. **nwfusion.com/research/2003/0526gm.html?page=1** (accessed December 2004).

Vallés, J., et al. "The Grid for e-Collaboration and Virtual Organisations." *Proceedings of the Second European Across Grids Conference*, Nicosia, Cyprus, January 28–30, 2004.

van der Aalst, W. M. P. *Workflow Management: Models, Methods, and Systems.* Boston: MIT Press, 2002.

Vinas, T. "Meeting Makeover." *IndustryWeek*, February 2002.

Walton, B., and M. Princi. "From Supply Chain to Collaborative Network." White paper, Andersen Consulting, 2000. **ascet.com/documents.asp?d_ID=266** (accessed June 2003).

WebEx. **webex.com/services/online-meeting-svc.html** (accessed October 2002).

WebTrends. *The City of Calgary Enhances Its Web Portal Effectiveness with WebTrends.* San Jose, CA: NetIQ Corp., 2003.

CHAPTER 8

INNOVATIVE EC SYSTEMS: FROM E-GOVERNMENT AND E-LEARNING TO C2C

Learning Objectives

Upon completion of this chapter, you will be able to:

1. Describe e-government to citizens (G2C), to businesses (G2B), and to others.
2. Describe various e-government initiatives.
3. Discuss online publishing, e-books, and blogging.
4. Describe e-learning and virtual universities.
5. Describe knowledge management and dissemination as an e-business.
6. Describe C2C activities.
7. Understand how peer-to-peer technology works in intrabusiness, in B2B, and in C2C.

Content

E-LEARNING AT CISCO SYSTEMS

The Problem

Cisco Systems (*cisco.com*) is one of the fastest growing high-tech companies in the world, selling devices that connect computers to the Internet and to other networks. Cisco's products continuously are being upgraded or replaced, so extensive training of employees and customers is needed. Cisco recognizes that its employees, business partners, and independent students seeking professional certification all require training on a continuous basis. Traditional classroom training was flawed by its inability to scale rapidly enough. Cisco offered in-house classes 6 to 10 times a year, at many locations, but the rapid growth in the number of students, coupled with the fast pace of technological change, made the training both expensive and ineffective.

The Solution

Cisco believes that *e-learning* is a revolutionary way to empower its workforce and its partners with the skills and knowledge needed to turn technological change to an advantage. Therefore, Cisco implemented e-learning programs that enable students to learn new software, hardware, and procedures. Cisco believes that once people experience e-learning, they will recognize that it is the fastest, easiest way to get the information they need to be successful.

To implement e-learning, Cisco created the Delta Force, which was made up of its CEO John Chambers, the IT unit, and the Internet Learning Solution Group. The group's first project was to build two learning portals, one for 40 partner companies that sell Cisco products and one for 4,000 systems engineers who deploy and service the products after the sale.

Cisco also wants to serve as a model of e-learning for its partners and customers, hoping to convince them to use its e-learning programs. To encourage its employees to use e-learning, Cisco:

- Makes e-learning a mandatory part of employees' jobs.
- Offers easy access to e-learning tools via the Web.
- Makes e-learning nonthreatening through the use of an anonymous testing and scoring process that focuses on helping people improve rather than on penalizing those who fail.
- Gives those who fail tests precision learning targets (remedial work, modules, exercises, or written materials) to help them pass and remove the fear associated with testing.
- Enables managers to track, manage, and ensure employee development, competency change, and, ultimately, performance change.
- Offers additional incentives and rewards such as stock grants, promotions, and bonuses to employees who pursue specialization and certification through e-learning.
- Adds e-learning as a strategic top-down metric for Cisco executives, who are measured on their deployment of IT in their departments.

For its employees, partners, and customers, Cisco operates E-Learning Centers for Excellence. These centers offer training at Cisco's office sites as well as at customers' sites via intranets and the Internet. Some of the training requires the use of partnering vendors.

Cisco offers a variety of training programs supported by e-learning. For example, in 2001, Cisco converted a popular four-and-a-half-day, instructor-led training (ILT) course on Cisco's signature IOS (interorganizational information system) technologies into an e-learning program that blends both live and self-paced components. The goal was to teach seasoned systems engineers (SEs) how to sell, install, configure, and maintain those key IOS technologies and to do so in a way that would train more people than the 25 employees the on-site ILT course could hold.

The Results

With the IOS course alone, Cisco calculated its ROI as follows:

- It cost $12,400 to develop the blended course.
- The course saved each SE 1 productivity day and 20 percent of the travel and lodging cost of a 1-week training course in San Jose. Estimating $750 for travel and lodging and $450 for the productivity day, the savings totaled $1,200 per SE.
- Seventeen SEs attended the course the first time it was offered, for a total savings of $20,400. Therefore, in the first offering of the course, Cisco recovered the development costs and saved $8,000 over and above those costs.
- Since March 2001, the IOS Learning Services team has presented two classes of 40 SEs per month. At that rate, Cisco saves $1,152,000 net for just this one course every 12 months.

In 2004, over 12,000 corporate salespeople, 150,000 employees of business partners, and 200,000 independent students were taking courses at Cisco learning centers, many using the e-learning courses. By 2004, Cisco had developed over 100 e-learning courses and was planning to develop many more. According to Galagan (2002), e-learning is a major underpinning of Cisco's economic health.

Sources: Compiled from *cisco.com* (accessed 2001–2004), Galagan (2002), and Delahoussaye and Zemke (2001).

WHAT WE CAN LEARN . . .

This opening case demonstrates the application of e-learning as an efficient training tool, a topic that is gaining increasing attention in e-businesses. E-learning also is becoming popular in all levels and types of schools and universities. This chapter covers the topic of e-learning both in business and academic settings. It also examines e-government, e-publishing, and knowledge management as well as consumer-to-consumer, peer-to-peer, and other EC applications.

8.1 E-GOVERNMENT: AN OVERVIEW

E-government encompasses many topics (see U.S. Government 2003.) This section presents the major e-government topics.

SCOPE AND DEFINITION

e-government
The use of IT and e-commerce to provide access to government information and delivery of public services to citizens and business partners.

As e-commerce matures and its tools and applications improve, greater attention is being given to its use to improve the business of public institutions and governments (country, state, county, city, etc.). **E-government** is the use of information technology in general, and e-commerce in particular, to provide citizens and organizations with more convenient access to government information and services and to provide delivery of public services to citizens, business partners, and those working in the public sector. It also is an efficient and effective way of conducting government business transactions with citizens and businesses and within governments themselves. See Marchioni (2003) and Ciment (2003) for details.

In the United States, the use of e-government by the federal government was driven by the 1998 Government Paperwork Elimination Act and by former President Clinton's December 17, 1999, Memorandum on E-Government, which ordered the top 500 forms used by citizens (such as tax forms) to be placed online by December 2000. The memorandum also directed agencies to construct a secure e-government infrastructure. Other drivers of e-government, according to Miller (2000), are increased computing power, the reduced cost of computing, the increased number of businesses and individuals on the Internet, and the need to make governments more efficient.

Some use the term *e-government* to mean an extension of e-commerce to government procurement. This use of the term views e-government only in the realm of B2G (business-to-government) transactions (International Trade Centre 2000). However, in this book, the term will be used in the broader context described earlier—the bringing together of governments, citizens, and businesses in a network of information, knowledge, and commerce.

In that broader view, e-government is both the advent of a new form of government and the birth of a new marketplace. It offers an opportunity to improve the efficiency and effectiveness of the functions of government and to make governments more transparent to citizens and businesses by providing access to more of the information generated by government.

Several major categories fit within this broad definition of e-government: government-to-citizens (G2C), government-to-business (G2B), government-to-government (G2G), Internal Efficiency and Effectiveness (IEE), and government-to-employees (G2E). The performance objectives of the first four categories are provided in Exhibit 8.1. For a comprehensive listing of e-government resources, tutorials, and more, see egov.gov. For a description of the range of e-government activities in the United States, see Dean (2000), U.S. Government (2003), and whitehouse.gov/egov/index2.html.

GOVERNMENT-TO-CITIZENS

government-to-citizens (G2C)
E-government category that includes all the interactions between a government and its citizens.

The **government-to-citizens (G2C)** category includes all of the interactions between a government and its citizens that can take place electronically. See U.S. Government (2003) or Abramson and Means (2001) for an overview of G2C. As shown in the Real-World Case about Hong Kong at the end of the chapter, G2C can involve dozens of different initiatives. The basic idea is to enable citizens to interact with the government from their homes. G2C

EXHIBIT 8.1 Categories of E-Government Performance Objectives

G2C	G2B
Reduce the average time for citizens to find benefits and determine eligibility Reduce the number of clicks to access relevant loan information Increase the number of citizens who use the Internet to find information on recreational opportunities	Increase the ability for citizens and businesses to find, view, and comment on rules and regulations Reduce burden on business by enabling online tax filing Reduce the time to fill out export forms and locate information Reduce time for businesses to file and comply with regulations
G2G	**IEE**
Decrease response times for jurisdictions and disciplines to respond to emergency incidents Reduce the time to verify birth and death entitlement information Increase the number of grant programs available for electronic application	Increase availability of training programs for government employees Reduce the average time to process clearance forms Increase use of e-travel services within each agency Reduce the time for citizens to search for federal jobs Reduce time and overhead cost to purchase goods and services throughout the federal government

Source: U.S. Government (2003).

applications enable citizens to ask questions of government agencies and receive answers, pay taxes, receive payments and documents, and so forth. For example, citizens can renew driver's licenses, pay traffic tickets, and make appointments for vehicle emission inspections and driving tests. Governments also can disseminate information on the Web, conduct training, help citizens find employment, and more. In California, for example, drivers' education classes are offered online and can be taken anytime, anywhere.

According to emarketer.com (2002b), the major features of government Web sites are phone and address information (96 percent), links to other sites (71 percent), publications (93 percent), and databases (57 percent). The major areas of G2C activities are tourism and recreation (77 percent), research and education (70 percent), downloadable forms (63 percent), discovery of government services (63 percent), information about public policy (62 percent), and advice about health and safety issues (49 percent).

An interesting area of application is the use of the Internet by politicians, especially during election periods. For example, during the 2004 presidential election in the United States, both major-party candidates sent e-mail messages to potential voters and had comprehensive information portals. In South Korea, politicians log onto the Internet to recruit voters, because many people who surf the Internet rarely read newspapers or watch TV. The target audience of these politicians is 20- to 30-year-olds, the vast majority of whom surf the Internet. Pasdaq, the Seoul-based over-the-counter stock exchange, offers an Internet game that simulates the stock market and measures the popularity of some 300 politicians by allowing players to buy "stocks" in a politician. In one year, over 500,000 members signed up. It became a necessity in South Korea for politicians to have a Web site. Involved citizens even make donations over the Internet using credit cards. Some politicians make decisions based on citizens' opinions collected on the Internet.

Another area of G2C activity is in solving constituents' problems. The government (or a politician) can use CRM-type software to assign inquiries and problem cases to the appropriate staff member. Workflow CRM software can then be used to track the problem's progress. For details and other applications, see "CRM for government" at peoplesoft.com/corp/en/products/industry/federal/index.jsp.

Yet another common G2C use is the broadcasting of city council meetings, press conferences, and public addresses. In many municipalities, delivering training and educational courses, both to citizens and to employees, is a very popular Internet activity. For more on G2C, see Aberdeen Group (2004) and nbc.gov/g2c.cfm.

Electronic Voting

Voting processes inherently are subject to error and also are historically subject to manipulation and fraud. In many countries, there are attempts to "rig" the votes; in others, the losers want to recount and recount. Voting may result in major political crises, as happened in the Ukraine in November 2004. The U.S. 2000 presidential election problems accelerated the trend toward electronic voting.

Voting processes require extraordinary integrity (particularly for any computerized systems involved) as well as honesty and experience among the people involved in administering elections. In many countries, elections are observed by experts from other countries. The election process may require considerable sophistication on the part of voters as well.

Voting encompasses a broad spectrum of technological and social problems that must be systematically addressed—from registration and voter authentication to the casting of ballots and subsequent tallying of results. Because of this, **electronic voting** means different things to different people.

electronic voting
Voting process that involves many steps including registering, preparing, voting, and counting (voting and counting all done electronically).

Each of the current voting technologies has its own set of vulnerabilities; none are infallible. However, fully electronic voting systems have raised considerable controversy because of a variety of factors, such as the proprietary nature of the software, the weakness of the certification criteria, the inability of black-box testing to provide full assurances of correctness, the general secrecy of the evaluation process, the vendor-commissioned evaluations, and the lack of any mechanism whereby independent recounting of the ballots and auditing of the vote totals can be performed. Several of these issues are the subject of a special issue of the *Communications of the ACM* (see Neumann 2004).

The first country to use fully computerized balloting, as of 2000, was Brazil. In the United States, electronic systems have been in use since 1980 (mainly for counting the results); large-scale implementation of touch-screen systems will probably occur only in 2008. It is interesting to note that several states (e.g., California, Nevada) require that touch-screen machines be able to produce a printed record. A good voting machine should show the voter what he or she has entered and ask for confirmation, much like when purchasing a book online from Amazon.com, transferring funds, or selling stocks.

From a technology point of view, voting machines make electronic fraud unprecedentedly simple. Election fraud could easily be carried out by changing a program to count votes for X twice or not to count votes for Y at all. (See DiFranco et al. 2004.) Therefore, security and auditing measures are key to the success of e-voting (Coggins 2004; Jones 2004; and Jefferson et al. 2004). However, considering the amount of fraud that occurs with traditional, non-e-voting systems and the fact that e-security is improving, e-voting eventually will be the norm. For more information on e-voting see fcw.com.

Many believe that with the ever-increasing percentage of Net users who get information about governments and politics online, also known as **Netizens**, the manner in which elections are conducted will change drastically in the not-so-distant future. For further discussion of online voting, and why it may take years to *fully* implement it in the United States, see Neumann (2004) and Jefferson et al. (2004).

Netizen
A citizen surfing the Internet.

Electronic Benefits Transfer

One e-government application that is not new is *electronic benefits transfer* (EBT), which has been available since the early 1990s. The U.S. government, for example, transfers more than $800 billion in benefits to its citizens annually. In 1993, the U.S. government launched an initiative to develop a nationwide EBT system to deliver government benefits electronically. Initially, the attempt was made to deliver benefits to recipients' bank accounts. However, more than 20 percent of these transfers go to citizens who do not have bank accounts. To solve this problem, the government is initiating the use of smart cards (see Chapter 12). Benefit recipients will be able to load electronic funds onto the cards and use the cards at automated teller machines (ATMs), point-of-sale locations, and grocery and other stores, just like other bank card users do. When the smart card systems are in place, recipients will either get electronic transfers to their bank accounts or be able to download money to their smart cards. The advantage is not only the reduction in processing costs (from about 50 cents per paper check to 2 cents for electronic payment), but also the reduction of fraud. With biometrics (see Chapter 11) coming to smart cards and PCs, officials expect fraud to be reduced substantially.

The smart card system is part of a nationwide EBT system for miscellaneous payments, such as those for Social Security and welfare. Agencies at the federal, state, and local levels are expanding EBT programs into new areas, including health, nutrition, employment, and education. Also, many states operate EBT systems for state-provided benefits. Governments also use smart cards as purchasing media for G2B procurement. For more information on EBT in government, see fns.usda.gov.

GOVERNMENT-TO-BUSINESS

Governments seek to automate their interactions with businesses. Although we call this category **government-to-business (G2B),** the relationship works two ways: government-to-business and business-to-government. Thus, G2B refers to e-commerce in which government sells products to businesses or provides them with services as well as to businesses selling products and services to government (see Schubert and Hausler 2001). Two key G2B areas are e-procurement and the auctioning of government surpluses. For other U.S. G2B initiatives, see nbc.gov/g2b.cfm.

government-to-business (G2B)
E-government category that includes interactions between governments and businesses (government selling to businesses and providing them with services and businesses selling products and services to government).

Government E-Procurement

Governments buy large amounts of MROs and other materials direct from suppliers. In many cases, RFQ (or tendering) systems are mandated by law. For years, these tenderings were done manually; the systems are now moving online. These systems employ *reverse auctions* (buy-side auction systems), such as those described in Chapter 5. An example of a reverse auction used for G2B procurement in Hong Kong is briefly described in the Real-World Case at the end of the chapter and at info.gov.hk. For additional information about such reverse auctions, see gsa.gov. In the United States, for example, the local housing agencies of HUD (Housing and Urban Development), which provides housing to low-income residents, are moving to e-procurement (see Corbeil 2002 and U.S. Department of Housing and Urban Development 2001). Governments provide all the support for such tendering systems, as shown in EC Application Case 8.1.

Group Purchasing

The concept of online group purchasing, introduced in Chapters 1 and 5, is practiced by the U.S. government as well. For example, the eFAST service conducts reverse auctions for aggregated orders (see gsa.gov). Suppliers post group-purchasing offers, and the prices fall as more orders are placed. Alternatively, government buyers may post product requests, which other buyers may review and join in on. Pooled orders are then forwarded to suppliers for reverse auction bidding. Also, government hospitals and public schools actively purchase in groups online.

Forward E-Auctions

Many governments auction equipment surpluses or other goods, ranging from vehicles to foreclosed real estate. Such auctions used to be done manually and then were done electronically over private networks. These auctions are now moving to the Internet. Governments can auction from a government Web site or they can use third-party auction sites such as eBay.com, bid4assets.com, or governmentauctions.org for this purpose. In January 2001, the U.S. General Services Administration (GSA) launched a property auction site online (auctionrp.com) where real-time auctions for surpluses and seized goods are conducted. Some of these auctions are restricted to dealers; others are open to the public (see governmentauctions.org).

Tax Collection and Management

Every year millions of individuals file tax reports. Similarly, hundreds of thousands of businesses do the same. Businesses in the United States and other countries must file quarterly reports. Electronic filing of taxes is now available in over 100 countries, from Thailand to Finland to the United States. In addition to personal and income taxes, it also is possible to pay online sales taxes and value-added taxes. For a case study of successful online tax implementation in Thailand, see Hopfner (2002).

CASE 8.1

EC Application

CONTRACT MANAGEMENT IN AUSTRALIA

The focus of the Western Australian (WA) government agency Contract and Management Services (CAMS) is to develop online contract management solutions for the public sector. CAMS Online allows government agencies to search existing contracts, to find those that are commonly used. It also assists suppliers that want to sell to the government. Suppliers can view the current tenders (bids) on the Western Australia Government Contracting Information Bulletin Board and can download tender documents from this site.

CAMS Online also provides government departments and agencies with unbiased expert advice on e-commerce, Internet, and satellite services and how-to's on building a bridge between the technological needs of the public sector and the expertise of the private sector. The center offers various types of support for government procurement activities.

Support of E-Commerce Activities

WA's e-commerce activities include electronic markets for government purchasing. Government clients can purchase goods and services on the *CAMS Internet Marketplace,* which provides services ranging from sending a purchase order to receiving an invoice and paying for an item. The *WA Government Electronic Market* provides online supplier catalogs, electronic purchase orders, electronic invoicing, EFT, and check and credit card payments. The Victoria government and the New South Wales government in WA are spending over US $500 million on e-procurement systems under the Government Electronic Market system (2002).

Other WA e-commerce functions are *ProcureLink,* a CAMS service that sends electronic purchase orders to suppliers via EDI, EDI Post (an online hybrid mail service), facsimile, and the Internet; *SalesNet,* by which the government secures credit card payments for the sale of government goods and services across the Internet; and *DataLink,* which enables the transfer of data using a secure environment for message management. DataLink is an ideal solution for government agencies that need to exchange large volumes of operational information.

Training Online

In addition to G2B functions, the site also offers online training to citizens. A service called *Westlink* delivers adult training and educational programs to remote areas and schools, including rural and regional communities. A videoconferencing service offers two-way video and audio links, enabling government employees to meet together electronically from up to eight sites at any one time.

Access to the Online Services Centre is given to government employees and businesses that deal with the government via the CAMS Web site at *doir..wa.gov.au/ business.*

Sources: Compiled from *doir..wa.gov.au/ business* (accessed 2002) and *ecc.online.wa.gov.au/news* (accessed 2002).

Questions

1. How is contract management in WA facilitated by e-commerce tools?
2. What other e-commerce activities does the government perform?
3. Describe the WA online training program.

GOVERNMENT-TO-GOVERNMENT

government-to-government (G2G) E-government category that includes activities within government units and those between governments.

The **government-to-government (G2G)** category consists of EC activities between units of government, including those within one governmental body. Many of these are aimed at improving the effectiveness or the efficiency of the government. Here are a few examples from the United States:

- **Intelink.** Intelink is an intranet that carries classified information shared by the numerous U.S. intelligence agencies.
- **Procurement at GSA.** The GSA's Web site (gsa.gov) uses technologies such as demand aggregation and reverse auctions to buy for various units of the federal government. The agency seeks to apply innovative Web-based procurement methods to government buying. The site offers many, many services (see gsa.gov/Portal/gsa/ep/contentView.do?contentId=9881&contentType=GSA_BASIC).
- **Federal Case Registry (Department of Health and Human Services).** This service helps state governments locate information about child support, including data on paternity and enforcement of child-support obligations. It is available at acf.dhhs.gov/programs/cse/newhire/fcr/fcr.htm.
- **Procurement Marketing and Access Network (Small Business Administration).** This service (pro-net.sba.gov) presents PRO-Net, a searchable database that contracting officers in various government units can use to find products and services sold by small, disadvantaged, or women-owned businesses.

For more examples of G2G services, see the Real-World Case at the end of the chapter, govexec.com, and nbc.gov/g2g.cfm.

GOVERNMENT-TO-EMPLOYEES AND INTERNAL EFFICIENCY AND EFFECTIVENESS

Governments employ large numbers of people. Therefore, governments are just as interested as private-sector organizations are in electronically providing services and information to their employees. Indeed, because employees of federal and state governments often work in a variety of geographic locations, **government-to-employee (G2E)** applications may be especially useful in enabling efficient communication. One example of G2E is the Lifelines service provided by the U.S. government to U.S. Navy employees and their families, described in EC Application Case 8.2.

government-to-employees (G2E)
E-government category that includes activities and services between government units and their employees.

Internal Efficiency and Effectiveness

These internal initiatives provide tools for improving the effectiveness and efficiency of government operations and processes are basically intrabusiness applications (Chapter 7) implemented in government units. The U.S. Office of Management and Budget (2002) provides the following examples:

- *E-payroll.* Consolidate systems at more than 14 processing centers across government.
- *E-records management.* Establish uniform procedures and standards for agencies in converting paper-based records to electronic files.
- *E-training.* Provide a repository of government-owned courseware.
- *Enterprise case management.* Centralize justice litigation case information.
- *Integrated acquisition.* Agencies share common data elements to enable other agencies to make better informed procurement, logistical, payment, and performance assessment decisions.
- *Integrated human resources.* Integrate personnel records across government.
- *Recruitment one-stop.* Automate federal government information on career opportunities, resume submission, routing, and assessment. Streamline the federal hiring process and provide up-to-the-minute application status for job seekers.

For more on implementing IEE in the government, see nbc.gov/iee.cfm.

CASE 8.2
EC Application

G2E IN THE U.S. NAVY

The U.S. Navy uses G2E to improve the flow of information to sailors and their families. Because long shipboard deployments cause strains on navy families, in 1995 the navy began seeking ways to ensure that quality-of-life information reaches navy personnel and their loved ones all over the world. Examples of quality-of-life information include self-help, deployment support, stress management, parenting advice, and relocation assistance.

Lifelines (*lifelines.navy.mil*) uses the Internet, simulcasting, teleconferencing, cable television, and satellite broadcasting to reach overseas personnel. The navy has found that certain media channels are more appropriate for different types of information. Lifelines regularly features live broadcasts, giving forward-deployed sailors and their families welcome information and, in some cases, a taste of home. On the Web, an average of 5,500 people access the Lifelines portal each day. In 2004, the portal covered dozens of topics, ranging from jobs to recreation.

The government provides several other e-services to navy personnel. Notable are online banking, personal finance services, and insurance. Education and training also are provided online. In 2001, the navy started issuing mobile computing devices to sailors while they are deployed at sea. The handheld devices offer both entertainment and information to navy personnel on active duty.

Sources: Compiled from *GovExec.com* (2000), Dean (2000), and *lifelines.navy.mil* (accessed 2004).

Questions

1. Why is the navy using multiple media channels?
2. Compare the G2E services provided by the navy with the B2E services discussed in Section 7.5.

FACILITATING HOMELAND SECURITY

A major responsibility of the government is homeland security. We introduced this topic briefly in Chapter 1. The government is using different electronic and other information technology systems to improve security. For more information on security in e-government, see Wang and Wang (2004). A list of such systems is provided in Online Exhibit W8.1.

Section 8.1 ▶ REVIEW QUESTIONS

1. Define e-government.
2. What are the four major categories of e-government services?
3. Describe G2C.
4. Describe how EBT works.
5. Describe the two main areas of G2B activities.

8.2 IMPLEMENTING E-GOVERNMENT

Like most other organizations, government entities want to move into the digital era and become click-and-mortar organizations. Therefore, one can find a large number of EC applications in government organizations. For information on the difficulties of implementing e-government, see Liu and Hwang (2003). This section examines some of the issues involved in *implementing* e-government.

THE TRANSFORMATION TO E-GOVERNMENT

The transformation from traditional delivery of government services to full implementation of online government services may be a lengthy process. The business consulting firm Deloitte and Touche conducted a study (see Wong 2000) that identified six stages in the transformation to e-government. These stages are shown in Exhibit 8.2 and described in the following list.

- **Stage 1: Information publishing/dissemination.** Individual government departments set up their own Web sites. These provide the public with information about the specific department, the range of services it offers, and contacts for further assistance. In stage 1, governments may establish an electronic brochure, the purpose of which is to reduce the number of phone calls customers need to make to reach the employee who can fulfill their service requests. These online resources also help reduce paperwork and the number of help-line employees needed.
- **Stage 2: "Official" two-way transactions with one department at a time.** With the help of legally valid digital signatures and secure Web sites, customers are able to submit personal information to and conduct monetary transactions with single government departments. For example, the local government of Lewisham in the United Kingdom lets citizens claim income support and housing benefits by filing an electronic form and then receiving benefits online. In Singapore, payments to citizens and from citizens to various government agencies can be performed online. In many countries (e.g., United States, United Kingdom, Hong Kong), tax returns are filed online with attached payments, if needed. At this stage, customers must be convinced of the department's ability to keep their information private and free from piracy.
- **Stage 3: Multipurpose portals.** At this stage, customer-centric governments make a big breakthrough in service delivery. Based on the fact that customer needs can cut across department boundaries, a portal allows customers to use a single point of entry to send and receive information and to process monetary transactions across multiple departments. For example, in addition to acting as a gateway to its agencies and related governments, the government of South Australia's portal (sa.gov.au) features a "business channel" and a link for citizens to pay bills (utilities, automotive), manage bank accounts, and conduct personal stock brokering. The portal described in the Real-World Case at the end of this chapter is such a portal, as are Singapore's portals (ecitizen.gov.sg and

EXHIBIT 8.2 The Stages of E-Government

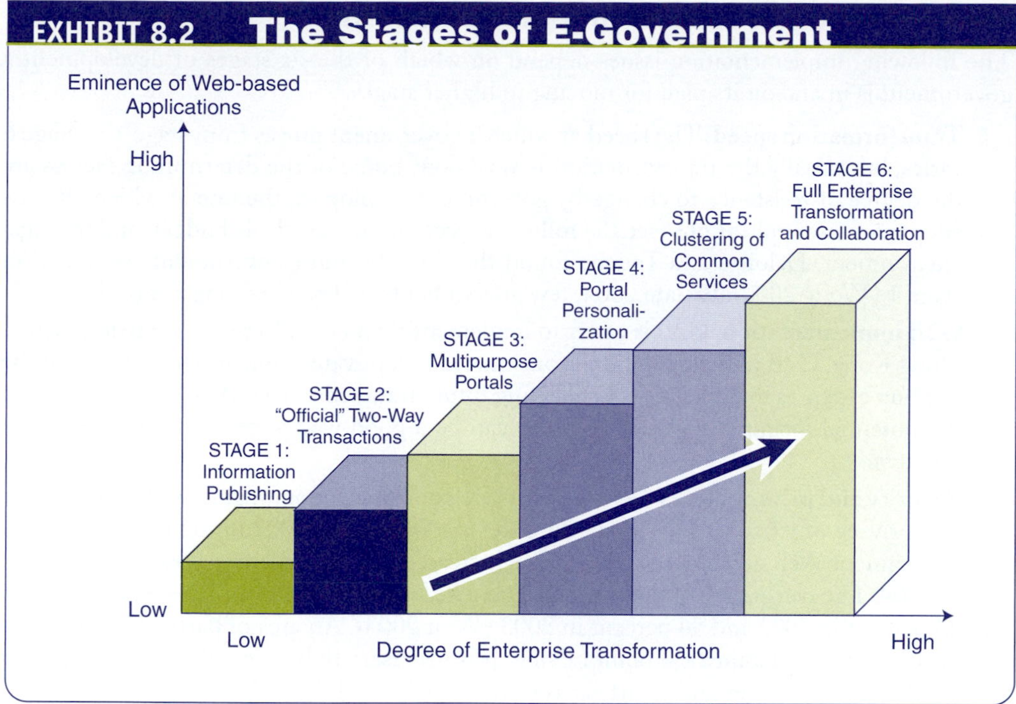

Source: Wong, W. Y., *At the Dawn of E-Government*. New York: Deloitte Research, Deloitte & Touche, 2000.

gov.sg). The design of one-stop e-government sites is explored by Wimmer (2002), who developed a model for integrating multiple services in one location.

- **Stage 4: Portal personalization.** Through stage 3, customers can access a variety of services at a single Web site. In stage 4, government puts even more power into customers' hands by allowing them to customize portals with their desired features. To accomplish this, government sites require much more sophisticated Web programming that permits interfaces to be manipulated by the users. The added benefit of portal personalization is that governments get a more accurate read on customer preferences for electronic versus nonelectronic service options. This allows for true CRM in government. Governmental use of such portals began in spring 2001, and many state and county governments in the United States (e.g., U.S. Department of Education at ed.gov and the Internal Revenue Service at irs.gov), Australia, and several other countries implemented them by 2004.
- **Stage 5: Clustering of common services.** Stage 5 is where real transformation of government structure takes shape. As customers now view once-disparate services as a unified package through the portal, their perception of departments as distinct entities will begin to blur. They will recognize groups of transactions rather than groups of agencies. To make this happen, governments will cluster services along common lines to accelerate the delivery of shared services. In other words, a business restructuring will take place. Initial stage 5 implementations started in Australia, Canada, New Zealand, the United Kingdom, and the United States in late 2004.
- **Stage 6: Full integration and enterprise transformation.** Stage 6 offers a full-service center, personalized to each customer's needs and preferences. At this stage, old walls defining silos of government services have been torn down, and technology is integrated across the new structure to bridge the shortened gap between the front and back offices. In some countries, new departments will be formed from the remains of predecessors. Others will have the same names, but their interiors will look nothing like they did before the e-government implementation. Full electronic collaboration among government agencies and between governments, citizens, and other partners will occur during this phase, which is in its planning stage.

For more on e-transformation in government, see Malkia et al. (2004).

IMPLEMENTATION ISSUES OF E-GOVERNMENT

The following implementation issues depend on which of the six stages of development a government is in and on its plan for moving to higher stages.

- **Transformation speed.** The speed at which a government moves from stage 1 to stage 6 varies, but usually the transformation is very slow. Some of the determining factors are the degree of resistance to change by government employees, the rate at which citizens adopt the new applications (see the following section), the available budget, and the legal environment. Deloitte and Touche found that in 2000 most governments were still in stage 1 (Wong 2000). By late 2004, few governments had reached stages 3 or 4.
- **G2B implementation.** G2B is easier to implement than G2C. In some countries, such as Hong Kong, G2B implementation is outsourced to a private company that pays all of the start-up expenses in exchange for collecting future transaction fees. As G2B services have the potential for rapid cost savings, they can be a good way to begin an e-government initiative.
- **Security and privacy issues.** Governments are concerned about maintaining the security and privacy of citizens' data. According to emarketer.com (2002b), the number of U.S. government Web sites with *security policies* increased from 5 percent in 2000 to 63 percent in 2004. The percentage of those with *privacy policies* increased from 7 percent in 2000 to 43 percent in 2002 and 54 percent in 2003 (West 2004). An area of particular concern is health care. From a medical point of view, it is necessary to have quick access to people's data, and the Internet and smart cards provide such capabilities; however, the protection of such data is very expensive. Deciding on how much security to provide is an important managerial issue. In the United States, the 2002 E-Government Act requires all federal agencies to conduct privacy assessments of all government information systems.
- **Wireless applications.** Several wireless applications suitable for e-government will be presented in Chapter 9. Notable are B2E applications, especially for field employees, and B2C information discovery, such as the 511 system described in Chapter 1. Another example is the city of Bergen, Norway, which provides wireless tourism services. An interesting wireless application in the city of Manchester (United Kingdom) is provided by Davies et al. (2002). Many more applications are expected in the future. Therefore, such applications must be included in any transformation plan. For more information, see Michael (2004).

See Bacon et al. (2001), Hart-Teeter (2001), and Association for Federal Information Resources Management (2002) for additional implementation issues.

CITIZEN ADOPTION OF E-GOVERNMENT

One of the most important issues in implementing e-government is its adoption and usage by citizens. Warkentin et al. (2002) constructed a model that attempts to explore this issue. They believe that the adoption rate depends on many variables, as shown in Exhibit 8.3. One of the major variables is "trust in e-government," which is itself determined by several variables. Other variables, such as perceived ease of use and perceived usefulness, are generic to EC adoption. Moderating variables, such as culture, also are important.

NON-INTERNET E-GOVERNMENT

Today, e-government is associated with the Internet. However, governments have been using other networks, especially internal ones, to improve government operations for over 18 years. For example, on January 17, 1994, a major earthquake shook Southern California. About 114,000 buildings were damaged, and more than 500,000 victims turned to the Federal Emergency Management Agency (FEMA) for help. Initially, tired and dazed citizens stood hours in lines to register and have in-person interviews. To expedite the process, an e-government application was installed to expedite the issuance of checks to citizens. Citizens called an 800 number, and operators entered the information collected directly into online electronic forms. Then the data traveled electronically to the mobile disaster inspectors. Once checked, data went electronically to financial management and finally to check writing. The dataflow never touched paper, and the cycle time was reduced by more

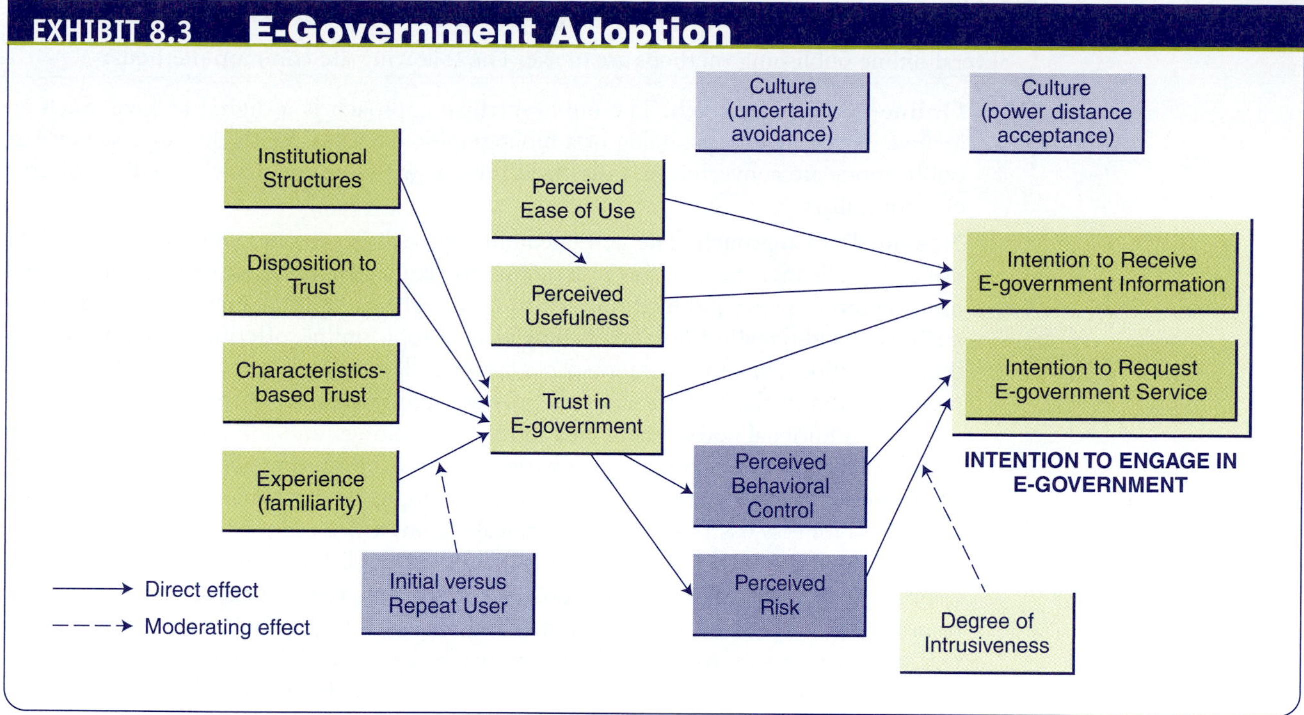

Source: Warkentin, M., et al. "Encouraging Citizen Adoption of E-Government by Building Trust." *Electronic Markets* 12, no. 3 (2002). Courtesy of Taylor & Francis Ltd., *tandf.co.uk.journals*.

than 50 percent. Another example of non-Internet e-government is auctions conducted over private, secured telecommunication lines. Sooner or later, such non-Internet e-government initiatives will probably be converted to Internet-based ones.

Section 8.2 ▶ REVIEW QUESTIONS

1. List and briefly describe the six stages of e-government development.
2. Describe some e-government implementation issues.
3. Provide an example of a non-Internet e-government service.

8.3 ONLINE PUBLISHING, E-BOOKS, AND BLOGGING

Another major area of EC applications is online publishing and associated activities. Moving paper information to electronic form has created a revolution that impacts both the dissemination of information and learning. **Online publishing** is the electronic delivery of newspapers, magazines, books, news, music, videos, and other digitizable information over the Internet (see Zhao and Resh 2001). Initiated in the late 1960s, online publishing was designed to provide online bibliographies and to sell knowledge that was stored in online commercial databases. Publicly funded online publishing was established for the purpose of disseminating medical, educational, and aerospace research information. It initially was conducted over private communication lines.

online publishing
The electronic delivery of newspapers, magazines, books, news, music, videos, and other digitizable information over the Internet.

Today, online publishing has additional purposes. It supports e-learning, provides entertainment, disseminates knowledge, and supports advertising (because it is sometimes provided for free to attract people to sites where advertising is conducted). Publishers of traditional hard-copy media have expanded to add online operations. Magazine and newspaper publishers such as *Ad Week, PC Magazine*, the *Wall Street Journal*, and the *Los Angeles Times* all use online publishing to disseminate information online. Many magazines are offered only online; they are referred to as **e-zines**. Online publishing includes materials supplied for free or by subscription fee; sometimes such material may be customized for the recipient. The potential of new interactive technologies and other Internet applications is expected to aid the growth of online publishing.

e-zines
Electronic magazine or newsletter delivered over the Internet or via e-mail.

ONLINE PUBLISHING APPROACHES AND METHODS

Several online publishing methods are in use. The following are common methods.

- **Online-archive approach.** The online-archive approach is a digital archive. Such an archive may be a library catalog or a bibliographic database. With this approach, paper publications are converted to a digitized format, without any changes, and are offered electronically.
- **New-medium approach.** The new-medium approach is used by publishers that seek to use the publication capabilities of the Web to create new material or add content and multimedia to paper publications. With this approach, publishers may provide extra analysis or additional information on any issue or topic online, offering more information than a traditional magazine or newspaper can offer. For example, chicagotribune.com (the online version of the *Chicago Tribune*) provides information from the paper's hard-copy issue plus additional news details, jobs and housing listings, and community service information. It also has an archive of past issues. One way of offering additional content is to offer integrated hypertext links to related stories, topics, and graphics. The Web medium also allows for easy customization or personalization, which old publishing media do not. Major journal publishers, such as Taylor and Francis Publishing Co., have placed many of their journals online. The publisher provides, at no charge, abstracts, search engines, and more. Users who want the full-version article are asked to pay. Subscribers are provided with research services, hypertext links, summaries, and more. The new-medium approach also offers up-to-date material, including breaking news. Examples of the new-medium approach include HotWired (hotwired.lycos.com), which complements a paper version of *Wired* magazine, and the *Wall Street Journal Online* (wsj.com). The student companion Web site for this book is another example.
- **Publishing-intermediation approach.** The publishing-intermediation approach can be thought of as an online directory for news services. Publishing intermediation is an attempt to help people locate goods, services, and products online. Yahoo!, MSN Network, and other portals provide publishing-intermediation services.
- **Dynamic approach.** The dynamic approach personalizes content *in real time* and transmits it on the fly in the format best suited to the user's location, tastes, and preferences. This approach also is referred to as the *just-in-time* approach, *print-on-demand*, or *point casting*.

Content Providers and Distributors

Content providers and distributors are, as their name implies, those who provide and distribute content online. These services are offered by several specialized companies (e.g., akamai.com, and mirror-image.com), as well as by news services such as the Associated Press and ABC News. Due to the difficulty of presenting multimedia, especially in wireless systems, content providers face major challenges when operating in an environment of less-developed infrastructures. Also, the issue of intellectual property payments is critical to the success of content distribution. If authors do not receive payments for or recognition of their work, content providers may face legal problems. However, if payments *are* made, the providers' costs may be too high.

Many online content providers are starting to charge for content, because advertising is proving insufficient to cover their expenses. In addition, more readers appear willing to pay for online publications. For example, *The New York Times* and *South China Morning Post* started to charge for articles in 2002.

Of special interest in this area is Digimarc (digimarc.com), which provides a tool for linking print publications with the Web.

Publishing of Music, Videos, Games, and Entertainment

The Internet is an ideal medium for publishing music, videos, electronic games, and related entertainment. As with content providers, a major issue here is the payment of intellectual property fees (see Chapter 17).

One of the most interesting new capabilities in this area is peer-to-peer networks over which people swap digital files, such as music or video files (see Section 8.7). When such swapping is managed by a third-party exchange (e.g., Napster or Kazaa), the third party may be in violation of copyright law. (For more on the legal difficulties faced by Napster and its eventual collapse, see Chapters 3 and 17.) For a comprehensive review of online music, see Drummond (2000).

More and more people are willing to pay for digital music, as shown by the success of Apple's iTunes and others. For a survey, examples, and discussion, see Dahl (2003).

Webcasting

One way that new or obscure musicians promote their work on the Web is by using **Webcasting**, or "live Webcasting shows." For example, Onlineevents.com broadcasts on the Web—that is, Webcasts—live transmissions to inform clients about U.S. and international capital markets. Affiliate clubs and artists get royalty payments based on how many people purchase and download a performance. House of Blue's hob.com has been a pioneer, offering pay-per-view Webcasts.

Webcasting
Live shows broadcast on the Web.

Webcasting provides not only music but also public lectures. For example, *DM Review* (dmreview.com) offers Webcast Direct, a series of Webcast seminars, known as **Webinars**, or e-seminars, on topics related to business intelligence, data warehousing and mining, and data quality. Many other sites offer e-seminars.

Webinars
Seminars on the Web (Web-based seminars).

ELECTRONIC BOOKS

An electronic book, or **e-book**, is a book in digital form that can be read on a computer screen, including handheld computers. A major event in electronic publishing occurred on March 24, 2000, when Stephen King's book *Riding the Bullet* was published exclusively online. For $2.50, readers could purchase the e-book at barnesandnoble.com/ebook and other e-book providers. Several hundred thousand copies were sold in a few days. However, the publishing event did not go off without some problems. Hackers breached the security system and distributed free copies of the book.

e-book
A book in digital form that can be read on a computer screen or on a special device.

Publishers of e-books have since become more sophisticated, and the business of e-publishing has become more secure. E-books can be delivered and read in various ways:

- **Via Web access.** Readers can locate a book on the publisher's Web site and read it there. The book cannot be downloaded. It may be interactive, including links and rich multimedia.
- **Via Web download.** Readers can download the book to a PC.
- **Via a dedicated reader.** The book must be downloaded to a special device (an e-book reader).
- **Via a general-purpose reader.** The book can be downloaded to a general-purpose device such as a Palm Pilot.
- **Via a Web server.** The contents of a book are stored on a Web server and downloaded for print-on-demand (see later discussion).

Most e-books require some type of payment. Readers either pay when they download a book from a Web site or they pay when they order the special CD-ROM edition of the book.

Depending on the method by which the book is delivered, software and hardware may be needed to read the book. For example, e-book software such as Adobe Acrobat eBook Reader or Microsoft Reader may be required to read an e-book. These readers can be downloaded *for free* from Amazon.com or from other e-book sites. A portable hardware device such as Softbook or Rocket ebook also may be necessary. E-books also can be loaded to some PDAs (see Boulton 2001). After installing the software, the user downloads the e-book and within minutes can enjoy reading it. The books may be portable (e.g., see Pocket PC store at amazon.com) and convenient to carry; 70 e-books (on average) can be loaded onto one CD-ROM; more can be loaded onto special memory cards that (in 2004) could store up to 20GB (see tigerdirect.com). Books also can be read online, in which case no special hardware is needed.

Several aids are available to help readers who want to read large amounts of material online. For example, ClearType from Microsoft and CoolType from Adobe can be used to improve screen display, colors, and font sizes.

Types of e-Books

Several types of e-books are available.

- **Traditional book format.** This type of e-book is a classic or new book that is presented in traditional linear format, usually without any special features such as hyperlinks or search mechanisms. With the right software (Adobe Portable Document Format), a reader can print the book.
- **Online bookshelf.** This is a *collection* of books (rather than just a single book) that can be read online or downloaded. They are simple in format and do not have hyperlinks.
- **The download.** This is an e-book in simple text files, HTML source documents, or Adobe Acrobat files that *can be downloaded* once the viewer has paid a fee.
- **The Rubics-cube hyperlink book.** This is a truly multimedia, online-only book. It has hyperlinks and provides three-dimensional text and display, employing graphics, audio, and video in a dramatically supportive manner. It supports nonlinear exploration of topics. It is especially useful in supporting learning.
- **The interactive, build-your-own (BYO) decision book.** This kind of book puts the reader "in the driver's seat." Combined with multimedia and VRML (a three-dimensional version of HTML), this e-book leads to dramatic engagement with content, plot, destiny, and responsibility. More information about BYO Decision books can be found at From Now On fno.org. However, not many of these books have yet been developed; they are hard to find.

In addition to regular books, electronic *technical* documents and manuals are available from the eMatter division of Fatbrain (now a Barnesandnoble.com company). An increasing number of publishers produce e-books. In addition to all the major publishers that sell e-books directly from their Web sites, readers also can buy e-books at electronic bookstores. All major textbook publishers (e.g., Pearson Education, the publisher of this text) are creating electronic companion textbooks that feature audio, video, and other interactive elements (see Stellin 2001).

Advantages and Limitations of E-Books

For e-books to make an impact, they must offer advantages to both readers and publishers. Otherwise, there would be little incentive to change from the traditional format.

The major advantage of e-books to readers is portability. As noted earlier, readers can carry as many as 70 books wherever they go (and more when portable memory drives are used). Other advantages are easy search capabilities and links; easy downloading; the ability to quickly and inexpensively copy material, including figures; easy integration of content with other text; no wear and tear on a physical book; ability to find out-of-print books; and books can be published and updated quickly, so they can be up-to-the-minute.

E-books also can reduce some of the physical burdens of traditional books. A number of studies have shown that 6 out of 10 students ages 9 to 20 report chronic back pain related to heavy backpacks filled with book. Some schools have eliminated lockers for safety reasons, causing students to carry heavy backpacks not only to and from school, but all day long. A number of schools are experimenting with eliminating textbooks altogether and using an Internet-based curriculum or school materials on CD-ROMs (Ergonomics Today 2004 and Rosenthal 2004).

The primary advantage that e-books offer publishers is lower production, marketing, and delivery costs, which have a significant impact on the price of books. Other advantages for publishers are lower updating and reproduction costs; the ability to reach many readers; the ease of combining several books, so professors can customize textbooks by using materials from different books by the same publisher; and lower advertising costs.

Of course, e-books have some limitations: They require hardware and software that may be too expensive for some readers; some people have difficulty reading large amounts of material on a screen; batteries may run down; there are multiple, competing standards; and finally, only a few books are available as e-books.

E-Book Issues

The Association of American Publishers reported that sales of e-books grew from $211,000 in net sales in January 2002 to slightly more than $3.3 million in January 2003, an increase of 1,447.4 percent (Gwiazdowski 2003). According to the Association of American Publishers

(2004), e-book sales were up 83.5 percent in July 2004, and 75.8 percent for the year 2004. Despite this growth and their advantages, e-books generally are not selling well in relation to the overall size of the book market. Although e-books are easy to read, are generally platform independent, have high-resolution displays, and can be read using long-lasting batteries, customers are still reluctant to change their habits. However, in Japan, where people ride trains daily for long periods of time, one sees hundreds of people reading e-books.

Nevertheless, the functionality of e-books is increasing rapidly. Software providers are supplying tools that make e-books easier to use—tools that search like search engines and that enable easy annotation and bookmarks that enable readers to expedite research of large volumes of information. Various other issues, when resolved, will contribute to the ease of use and popularity of e-books. These issues include:

- How to protect the publisher's/author's copyright.
- How to secure content (e.g., use encryption, employ Digital Rights Management [DRM]; see Chapters 11 and 17).
- How to distribute and sell e-books.
- How much to charge for an e-book versus a hard copy, and how to collect payment for e-books.
- How to best support navigation in an e-book.
- Which standards to use (e.g., see the Online Information Exchange Standard [ONIX] developed by EDItEUR [editeur.org/onix.html]). Also see Beat et al. (2001).
- How to increase reading speed. On the average screen, reading is 25 percent slower than hard-copy reading.
- How to transform readers from hard-copy books to e-books; how to deal with resistance to change.
- How to design an e-book (e.g., how to deal with fonts, typefaces, colors, etc., online).
- How publishers can justify e-books in terms of profit and market share.

Free e-books and white papers on e-publishing are available from a number of different sites (e.g., free-ebooks.net, fictionwise.com). For more information on e-books, see ebookconnections.com and netlibrary.com.

Digital Libraries

Many organizations are building digital libraries of e-books, journals, periodicals, and other materials. In fact, most universities no longer subscribe to paper periodicals. Electronic periodicals are cheaper, easier to handle, do not require storage space, and are amenable to electronic searches.

The problem, according to Thong et al. (2004), is that millions of potential users are still ignoring these libraries. The search engine giant Google announced plans to digitize millions of printed volumes to add to the Google Print database. Partnering with Google on this project are universities, including Harvard, Stanford, and Oxford, as well as the New York Public Library (Price 2004 and Vise 2004).

PRINT-ON-DEMAND

A new trend in publishing is *print-on-demand,* which refers to customized printing jobs, usually in small quantities, possibly only one document or book. The process is especially attractive for small print jobs because both the total fixed setup cost and the per unit setup cost are very low.

The print-on-demand process has three steps:

1. A publisher creates a digital master, typically in Adobe Systems' Acrobat format, and sends it to a specialized print-on-demand company. The files are stored on the printing company's network.
2. When an order is placed, a print-on-demand machine prints out the text of the document or book and then covers, binds, and trims it. The entire process can take about a minute for a 300-page book.
3. The book is packaged and shipped to the publisher or the consumer.

See Robinson (2001) for additional details on print-on-demand. By 2004, many textbook publishers offered print-on-demand textbooks, including Pearson Education, the publisher of this book. For some issues related to the topic, see Metz (2004).

BLOGGING (WEBLOGGING)

Weblogging/blogging
Technology for personal publishing on the Internet.

blog
A personal Web site that is open to the public to read and to interact with others using the blog; dedicated to specific topics or issues.

The Internet offers an opportunity for individuals to publish on the Web using a technology known as **Weblogging**, or **blogging**. A **blog** is a personal Web site, open to the public, in which the owner expresses his or her feelings or opinions. Blogs deal with many topics. People can write stories, tell news, and provide links to other articles and Web sites. Some blogs offer information that many Web surfers may have overlooked. People can read blogs to get up to speed rapidly on an issue of special interest (Powers 2002). The number of blogs is growing; emarketer.com (2002a) estimates that there were close to 1 million of them on the Internet (as of 2002). According to Pew Internet & American Life Project (pewinternet.org) survey, a new weblog is created every 5.8 seconds. That translates into 15,000 new blogs every day. Of these, only about 1 million are updated on a regular basis (reported by McGann 2004).

Blogs became very popular after the terrorist attacks of September 11, 2001. People were looking for as many sources of information as possible and for personal connections to the tragedy. Blogs comfort people in times of stress. They offer a place where people feel their ideas are noticed, and they can result in two-way communication and collaboration, group discussion, and so on. For sources on blogging, see Powers (2002) and Bausch et al. (2002).

An example blog is Instapundit (instapundit.com), created by Dr. Glenn Reynolds of the University of Tennessee. Reynolds uses his blog to provide commentary on current affairs. Launched in August 2001, the blog initially had about 1,500 hits a day. After September 11, 2001, traffic increased to an average of 4,800 hits, and on certain days it now reaches 80,000 hits. The blog has enabled Reynolds to trade e-mails with leading U.S. newspaper columnists who otherwise would probably never communicate with him. Other interesting blogs are coldfury.com, and samizdata.net.

It is becoming easier and easier to build blogs. Programs from blogger.com, blogspot.com, pitas.com, and others are very user-friendly. Also, some portals offer blog services. For example, in December 2004, Microsoft's MSN Internet division debuted a preliminary version of MSN Spaces, designed to bring blogs to the masses. Spaces are free; the goals is to make it easy for users to create Web journals or blogs. "Bloggers" (the people who create and maintain blogs) are handed a fresh space on their Web site to write in each day. They can easily edit, add entries, and broadcast whatever they want by simply clicking the send key. Bloggers use a special terminology. (For a dictionary of blog terms, see samizdata.net.)

Blogs have been criticized for their tendency to coalesce into self-referential cliques. Bloggers are noted for their mutual backslapping, endlessly praising and linking to one another's sites. Kiely (2003) claims that bloggers are not objective and are trying to rewrite rules of journalism. Some companies are using blogs for commercial purposes.

WikiLog

wikiLog (wikiblog)
A blog that allows everyone to participate as a peer; any one may add, delete, or change content.

A wikilog (or wikiblog) is an extension of a blog. Whereas a blog usually is created by an individual (or maybe a small group) and may have a discussion board, a **wikilog** is essentially a blog that allows everyone to participate as a peer. Anyone may add, delete, or change content. It is like a loose-leaf notebook with a pencil and eraser left in a public place. Anyone can read it, scrawl notes, tear out a page, and so on. Creating a wikilog is a *collaborative* process. For description and details, see usemod.com/cgi-bin/mb.pl?WikiLog.

Commercial Use of Blogs

The idea of blogs has been transferred quickly to the corporate world. According to Weidlich (2003), blogging enables companies and executives to talk informally with customers, vendors, business partners, and employees. Blogging provides the ability to supplement corporate public relations, press releases, and brochures with more personal, "from the heart" talk and offer convenient links to related sources. Blacharski (2004) suggests that a blog can be an especially good business tool for keeping customers apprised of new product developments, business partners up-to-date on availability or new developments, and employees informed on what's happening throughout the company. For an overview on blogging and marketing, see Mucha (2004).

Some people see risks in corporate blogging (e.g., Lewin 2004). Two obvious examples are the risk of revealing trade secrets and of making statements that are or could be construed as libel or defamation. Many companies have corporate policies on blogging. Groove Networks is one such example (see Ozzie 2002); the company even has corporate lawyers review the contents of its blogs.

Bloggers and Politics

Bloggers are getting more and more active in politics. When Senator Tom Daschle (who lost the 2004 Senate election in South Dakota) went to court at the last minute to sue his opponent, several hundred bloggers in South Dakota and elsewhere attacked him, saying that the lawsuit was "pathetic" and showed desperation. One blogger even "live broadcasted" the court hearing on its site.

Online publishing is related to e-learning, the subject of the next section, and to knowledge management (see Zhao and Resh 2001 and Section 8.5).

Section 8.3 ▶ REVIEW QUESTIONS

1. Define online publishing and list some advantages it offers over traditional media.
2. List the major methods of online publishing.
3. What issues are involved in content creation and distribution?
4. Describe e-books and list their advantages.
5. Describe blogging and describe the advantages and risks of blogs.

8.4 E-LEARNING

The topic of e-learning is gaining much attention, especially because world-class universities such as MIT, Harvard, and Stanford in the United States and Oxford in the United Kingdom are implementing it. Exhibit 8.4 shows the forces that are driving the transition from traditional education to online learning in the academic setting. E-learning also is growing as a method for training and information delivery in the business world and is becoming a major e-business activity. The research firm Eduventures predicted that the online distance learning market would grow more than 38 percent in 2004, taking in $5.1 billion in revenue (reported by eMarketer 2003). In this section, we will discuss several topics related to e-learning.

THE BASICS OF E-LEARNING

E-learning is the online delivery of information for purposes of education, training, or knowledge management. (See Garrison and Anderson 2003; Allen 2003; and elearnmag.org.) It is a Web-enabled system that makes knowledge accessible to those who need it, when they need it, anytime, anywhere. E-learning can be useful both as an environment for facilitating learning at schools and as an environment for efficient and effective corporate training, as shown in the Cisco case at the beginning of this chapter.

e-learning
The online delivery of information for purposes of education, training, or knowledge management.

Liaw and Huang (2002) describe how Web technologies can facilitate learning, and Zhang and Nunamaker (2003) expand the discussion to include other information technology tools. For an overview and discussion of research issues related to e-learning, see Piccoli et al. (2001); this resource also compares e-learning with traditional classroom teaching. A comprehensive site about e-learning, including videos and PowerPoint presentations, is available at e-learningcenter.com and e-learningcentre.co.uk.

BENEFITS AND DRAWBACKS OF E-LEARNING

E-learning has many benefits. However, it also has several drawbacks, thus making it a controversial topic.

EXHIBIT 8.4 The Effects of E-Commerce Forces in Education

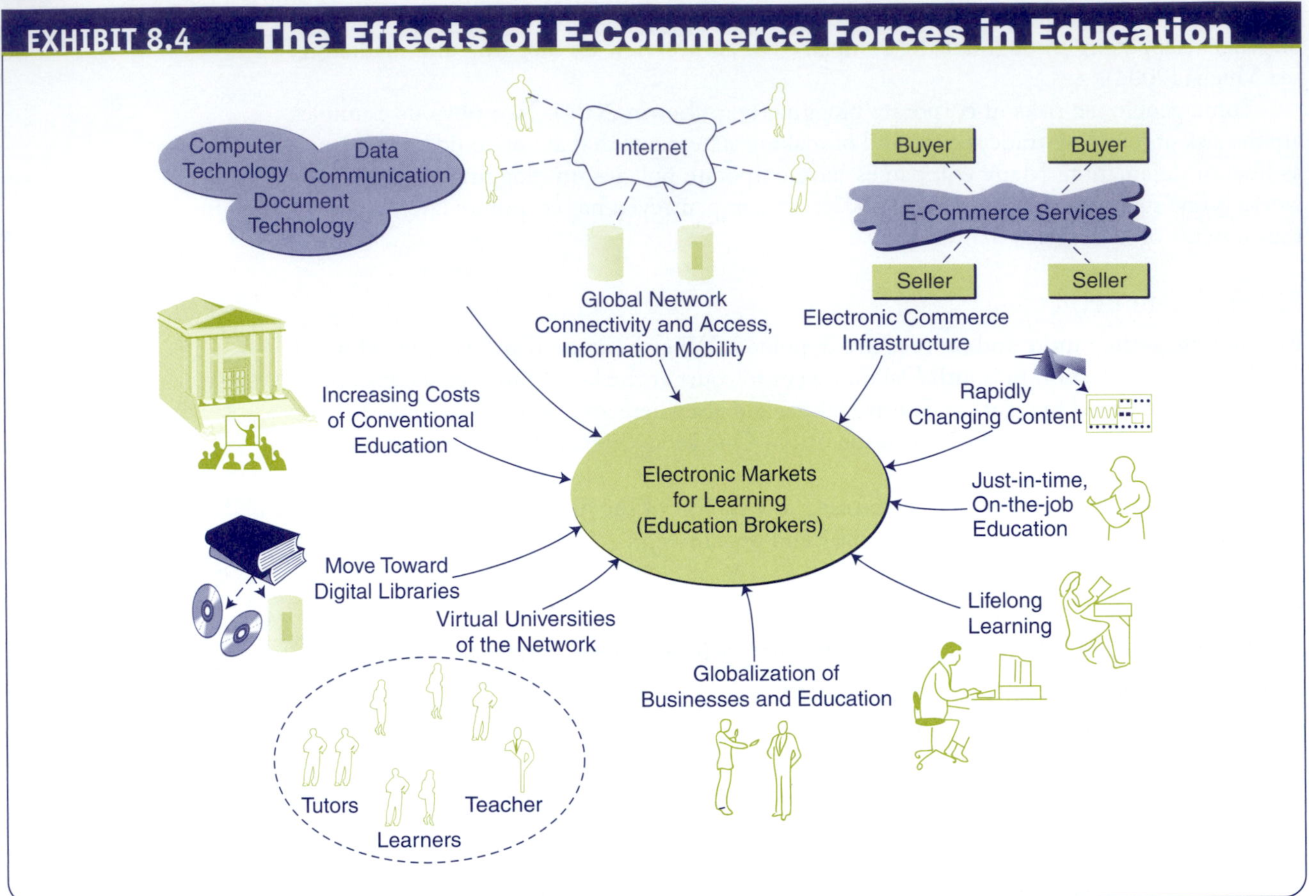

Source: Hamalainen, M. and A. Whinston. "Electronic Marketing for Learning: Education Brokerages on the Internet." *The Communications of the ACM,* ©1996, ACM, Inc. Reprinted with permission.

Benefits of E-Learning

E-learning can be a great equalizer: By eliminating barriers of time, distance, and socioeconomic status, it can enable individuals to take charge of their own lifelong learning. In the information age, skills and knowledge need to be *continually updated* and refreshed to keep up with today's fast-paced business environment. E-learning of new content will help organizations and countries adapt to the demands of the Internet economy by training their workers and educating their citizens. E-learning can save money, reduce travel time, increase access to experts, enable large numbers of students to take classes simultaneously, provide on-demand education, and enable self-paced learning. It also may make learning less frustrating by making it more interactive and engaging (e.g., see Delahoussaye and Zemke 2001 and Liaw and Huang 2002).

More specific benefits of e-learning are as follows:

- **Time reduction.** As shown in the Cisco case, e-learning can reduce training time by 50 percent.
- **Large volume and diversity.** E-learning can provide training to a large number of people from diverse cultural backgrounds and educational levels even though they are at different locations in different time zones.
- **Cost reduction.** One study reported that the cost of providing a learning experience can be reduced by 50 to 70 percent when classroom lectures are replaced by e-learning sessions (see Urdan and Weggen 2000).
- **Higher content retention.** E-learning students usually are self-initiated and self-paced. Their motive for acquiring more knowledge may be to widen their scope of view or to develop career skills. Urdan and Weggen (2000) contend that such self-motivation

results in content retention that could be 25 to 60 percent higher than that of lecturer-led training.

- **Flexibility.** E-learners are able to adjust the time, location, content, and speed of learning according to their own personal schedules. For example, if necessary, they can refer back to previous lectures without affecting the learning pace of other students.
- **Updated and consistent material.** It is almost impossible to economically update the information in textbooks more frequently than every 2 or 3 years; e-learning can offer just-in-time access to timely information. In addition, as Urdan and Weggen (2000) reported, e-learning may be 50 to 60 percent more consistent than material presented than traditional classroom learning because variations between teachers are eliminated.
- **Fear-free environment.** E-learning can facilitate learning for students who may not wish to join a face-to-face group discussion or participate in class. This kind of behavior usually is attributed to their reluctance to expose their lack of knowledge in public. E-learning can provide a fear-free and privacy-protected environment in which students can put forth any idea without fear of looking stupid.

These benefits, according to Zhang et al. (2004), may enable remote learners to outperform traditional classroom students. For more discussion of the benefits of e-learning, see e-learningguru.com/articles/art1_3.htm and elearnmag.com.

E-learning provides a new set of tools that can add value to traditional learning modes. It may not replace the classroom, but it can enhance it, taking advantage of new content and delivery technologies. The better the match of the content and delivery vehicle to an individual's learning style, the greater the content retention, and the better the learning results. Advanced e-learning support environments, such as Blackboard and WebCT, add value to traditional learning. See Insights and Additions 8.1 for descriptions of these e-learning tools.

As the opening vignette about Cisco showed, e-learning also can be used in the business environment. Besides increasing access to learning and reducing costs, e-learning equips employees with the knowledge needed to help increase customer satisfaction, expand sales, and accelerate technology adoption. In short, e-learning enables companies to prepare their workforces for an increasingly competitive world marketplace.

For a classification of the dimensions of e-learning environments, see Piccoli et al. (2001) and Online Exhibit W8.2.

Insights and Additions 8.1 Blackboard and WebCT

There is a good chance that you will use the Blackboard or WebCT framework when using this text. These competing products provide the Internet software needed for e-learning, and thus serve one of the fastest-growing industry segments in the world. The research firm Eduventures predicted the online distance learning market would grow more than 38 percent in 2004, taking in $5.1 billion in revenue (Botelho 2004).

How do these products work? A publisher places a book's content, teaching notes, quizzes, and other materials on Blackboard or WebCT in a standardized format. Instructors can access modules and transfer them into their own specific Blackboard or WebCT sites, which can be accessed by their students.

Blackboard offers a complete suite of enterprise software products and services that power a total "e-education infrastructure" for schools, colleges, universities, and other education providers. Blackboard's two major lines of business are Course & Portal Solutions and Commerce & Access Solutions.

WebCT provides a similar set of tools, but with a different vision and strategy. It uses advanced pedagogical tools to help institutions of higher education make distance-learning courses possible. Such courses enable schools to expand campus boundaries, attract and retain students and faculty, and continually improve course and degree program quality.

Textbook publishers are embracing these tools by making their major textbooks Blackboard and/or WebCT enabled. Thus, a professor can easily incorporate a book's content into the software that is used by thousands of universities worldwide.

As of 2004, both WebCT and Blackboard deliver corporate and government employee training programs that increase productivity and reduce costs.

Sources: Compiled from *webct.com* (accessed 2005) and *blackboard.com* (accessed 2005).

Drawbacks and Challenges of E-Learning

Despite the numerous benefits, e-learning does have some drawbacks. Issues cited as possible drawbacks of e-learning are as follows.

- **Need for instructor retraining.** Some instructors are not competent in teaching by electronic means and may require additional training. It costs money to provide such training.
- **Equipment needs and support services.** Additional funds are needed to purchase multimedia tools to provide support services for e-learning creation, use, and maintenance.
- **Lack of face-to-face interaction and campus life.** Many feel that the intellectual stimulation that takes places through instruction in a classroom with a "live" instructor cannot fully be replicated with e-learning.
- **Assessment.** In the environment of higher education, one criticism is that professors may not be able to adequately assess student work completed through e-learning. There is no guarantee, for example, of who actually completed the assignments or exams.
- **Maintenance and updating.** Although e-learning materials are easier to update than traditionally published materials, there are practical difficulties (e.g., cost, instructors' time) in keeping e-learning materials up-to-date. The content of e-learning material can be difficult to maintain due to the lack of ownership of and accountability for Web site material. In addition, no online course can deliver real-time information and knowledge in the way a "live" instructor can.
- **Protection of intellectual property.** It is difficult and expensive to control the transmission of copyrighted works downloaded from the e-learning platform.
- **Computer literacy.** E-learning cannot be extended to those students who are not computer literate.
- **Student retention.** Without some human feedback, it may be difficult to keep some students mentally engaged and enthusiastic about e-learning over a long period of time.

Some of these drawbacks can be reduced by advanced technologies. For example, some online products have features that help stimulate student thinking. Offsetting the assessment drawback, biometric controls can be used to verify the identity of students who are taking examinations from home. However, these features add to the costs of e-learning.

In addition to these drawbacks, e-learning faces challenges that threaten its acceptance (e.g., see Zhang et al. 2004). From the learner's perspective, the challenge is simply to change the mind-set of how learning typically takes place. Learners must be willing to give up the idea of traditional classroom training, and they must come to understand that continual, lifelong learning will be as much a part of normal work life, past the college years, as voice mail and e-mail. From the teaching perspective, all learning objects must be converted ("tagged") to a digital format. This task can be challenging. Finally, another challenge for e-learning systems is the updating of the knowledge in them—who will do it and how often? Also, how will the cost of the updating be covered?

PREVENTING E-LEARNING FAILURES

Many of those who have tried e-learning have been pleased with it. In many cases, self-selection ensures that those who are likely to benefit from e-learning choose e-learning opportunities. For example, students who live at a great distance from school or who have family responsibilities during traditional school hours will be motivated to put in the time to make e-learning work. Similarly, employees for whom a training course at a distant site is a problem, either because of budget or personal constraints, are likely to be enthusiastic about e-learning programs.

E-learning does not work for everyone, though. Weaver (2002) believes that e-learning failures are due to the following issues:

- *Believing that e-learning is always a cheaper learning or training alternative.* E-learning can be less expensive than traditional instruction, depending on the number of students. However, if only a few students are to be served, e-learning can be very expensive because of the high fixed costs.
- *Overestimating what e-learning can accomplish.* People sometimes do not understand the limitations of e-learning and therefore may expect too much.

- *Overlooking the shortcomings of self-study.* Some people cannot do self-study or do not want to. Others may study incorrectly.
- *Failing to look beyond the course paradigms.* The instructor needs to look at the entire problem in the area of teaching and at material creation and delivery as well.
- *Viewing content as a commodity.* This results in a lack of attention to quality and delivery to individuals.
- *Ignoring technology tools for e-learning or fixating too much on technology as a solution.* A balanced approach is needed.
- *Assuming that learned knowledge will be applied.* This is difficult to accomplish successfully.
- *Believing that because e-learning has been implemented, employees and students will use it.*

To prevent failure, companies and schools need to address these issues carefully and systematically. Balancing the benefits and the drawbacks of e-learning, many people remain enthusiastic about its potential.

DISTANCE LEARNING AND ONLINE UNIVERSITIES

The term **distance learning** refers to formal education that takes place off campus, often from home. The concept is not new. Educational institutions have been offering correspondence courses and degrees for decades. What is new, however, is the application of IT in general and the Web in particular to expand the opportunities for distance learning to the online environment. Hofmann (2002) describes the role of the Internet in distance learning in higher education, surveying implementation issues in terms of technology, course content, and pedagogy.

distance learning
Formal education that takes place off campus, usually, but not always, through online resources.

The concept of **virtual universities**, online universities from which students take classes from home or an off-site location via the Internet, is expanding rapidly. Hundreds of thousands of students in dozens of countries, from the United Kingdom to Israel to Thailand, are studying in such institutions. A large number of existing universities, including Stanford University and other top-tier institutions, offer online education of some form. Some universities, such as University of Phoenix (phoenix.edu), California Virtual Campus (cvc.edu), and the University of Maryland (umuc.edu/distance), offer hundreds of courses and dozens of degrees to students worldwide, all online. Other universities offer limited online courses and degrees but use innovative teaching methods and multimedia support in the traditional classroom, as described in Online File W8.1.

virtual university
An online university from which students take classes from home or other off-site locations, usually via the Internet.

For a list of schools that offer online courses, see distancelearn.about.com.

The virtual university concept allows universities to offer classes worldwide. Moreover, integrated degrees may soon appear, by which students can customize a degree that will best fit their needs and take courses at different universities. Several other virtual schools include eschool-world.com, waldenu.edu, and trainingzone.co.uk.

ONLINE CORPORATE TRAINING

Like educational institutions, a large number of business organizations are using e-learning on a large scale (e.g., see Kapp 2002). Many companies offer online training, as Cisco does. Some, like Barclays Bank, COX Industries, and Qantas Airways, call such learning centers "universities." New employees at IBM Taiwan Corp. are given Web-based "electronic training," and KPMG Peat Marwick offers e-learning to its customers.

Corporate training often is done via intranets and corporate portals. However, in large corporations with multiple sites and for studies from home, the Internet is used to access the online material. For discussion of strategies for implementing corporate e-learning, see Delahoussaye and Zemke (2001). Vendors of online training and educational materials can be found at digitalthink.com and deitel.com.

For examples of successful corporate training, see Insights and Additions 8.2.

The Drivers of E-Training

The business forces that are driving the transition from traditional education to online learning are described next. See elearnmag.org for more information on drivers and justification.

Insights and Additions 8.2 Examples of Corporate Training

Here are a few examples of successful e-training:

- Sheetz operates approximately 300 convenience stores across five states. It uses e-training via a corporate portal to train and certify store associates in the proper procedures for alcohol sales. It uses a compliance-tracking tool from Compliance Solutions of Arlington, Virginia, to monitor employee participation in the classes. The employees must know both government and corporate policies and regulations. The program helped to train about 1,000 employees in 2003, saving the company a considerable amount of money. Compliance Solutions prepares teaching materials for the entire industry. For details, see Korolishin (2004a).
- Tweeter Home Entertainment Group must continuously train its 2,600 sales associates in the new technologies of electronic entertainment products, such as high definition TV or surround sound. To help with its traditional classroom training, the company is using two e-learning products from OutStart (an e-learning software company). E-learning has been especially useful for people who are experts in the field. These people can log into the system from anywhere and do a quick brush-up. Two OutStart products are in use: Evolution (for content) and Evolution Learner Management (for course administration). The course content can be paced to fit the learners' time availability. For details, see Korolishin (2004b).
- Shoney's Restaurant chain (over 400 restaurants) needs to provide training continuously to its thousands of employees, from busboys to managers. A multicasting solution (RemoteWare from XcelleNet) is used to offer computer-based training. With multicasting, files are sent by telephone line or satellite from a server to many remote computers at the same time. The system helps both in communication and information dissemination as well as in training. These capabilities have allowed Shoney's to use PCs located at the chain's sites for computer-based training (CBT). Each restaurant has one computer (with speakers) used exclusively for staff training. Training files containing video clips, animation, and spot quizzes are easily transferred to the restaurants' computers. The solution also offers management and evaluation tools (e.g., which employees have completed which courses and how they scored on tests). Course evaluation also is done online. Test results provide indications that aid in improving content. The cost is much lower than training offered via videotape or CD-ROM. Training material is kept up-to-date and is consistent across the corporation. Good training has helped the company reduce employee attrition, which means people stay longer at their jobs and provide better customer service. For details, see McKinley (2003).

Technological Change. Technological changes and global network connectivity have increased the complexity and velocity of the work environment. Today's workforce has to process more and more information in a shorter amount of time. New products and services are emerging with accelerating speed. As product life cycles and life spans shorten, today's knowledge quickly will become obsolete. In the age of just-in-time (on demand) production, just-in-time training becomes a critical element to organizational success.

Competition and Cost Pressures. Fierce competition in most industries leads to increasing cost pressures. In today's competitive environment, organizations can no longer afford to inflate training budgets with expensive travel and lodging. Time spent away from the job, traveling or sitting in a classroom, tremendously reduces per-employee productivity and revenue.

Globalization. Globalization of business is resulting in many challenges. Today's businesses have more locations in different time zones and employ larger numbers of workers with diverse cultural backgrounds and educational levels than ever before. Corporations worldwide are seeking innovative and efficient ways to deliver training to their geographically dispersed workforces in other countries. E-learning is an effective way to achieve just this. Companies do not need to bring employees to a trainer or training facility (or even send a trainer to the employees); online classes can run anywhere in the world.

Continual Learning. In the new economy, corporations face major challenges in keeping their workforces current and competent. Learning has become a continual process rather than a distinct event. To retain their competitive edge, organizations have started to investigate which training techniques and delivery methods enhance motivation, performance, collaboration, innovation, and a commitment to lifelong learning.

Network Connectivity. The Internet provides an ideal delivery vehicle for education. The emergence of online education relates not only to economic and social change, but also to access. Through its increasing penetration and simplicity of use, the Internet has opened the door to a global market where language and geographic barriers for many training products have been erased. Because of the popularity of the Internet, e-learning is perhaps the most effective way to deliver training electronically.

A study by Roberts and Stevenson (2001) on e-learning in business education identified three trends: (1) Traditional MBA programs are developing e-learning courses and programs, some in partnership with other universities, for a mostly international market. (2) Independent e-learning companies are developing course content on their own or in partnership with existing business schools. (3) The executive education marketplace is flooded with e-learning offerings.

Examples of top traditional MBA programs that are introducing e-learning are MIT, Kellogg (Northwestern), INSEAD, University of Chicago, Duke, Berkeley, Purdue, Wharton (University of Pennsylvania), and Cornell. Examples of joint ventures of MBA programs with industry can be seen at Duke, Darden (University of Virginia), UCLA, and INSEAD (partners with Pensure); Columbia, Stanford, and University of Chicago (partners with UNext); and Wharton (partners with FT Knowledge). Of special interest is the Harvard/Stanford Joint Venture in developing e-learning materials for executives. The materials are delivered in a combination of classroom teaching and e-learning known as Leading Change and Organizational Renewal. A similar venture is that of MIT (Sloan School) and IMD of Switzerland.

IMPLEMENTING E-LEARNING AND E-TRAINING IN LEARNING CENTERS

Most schools and industries use e-learning as a *supplementary* channel to traditional classrooms. One facility that is used in the integration of the two approaches is the learning center. A *learning center* is a focal point for all corporate training and learning activities, including online ones. Some companies have a dedicated online learning center, a learning center dedicated only to online training. However, most companies combine online and off-line activities, as done by W. R. Grace and described in EC Application Case 8.3.

Learning center facilities may be run by a third party rather than connected to any particular corporation; these are referred to as *electronic education malls* (see Langenbach and Bodendorf 1999–2000). For example, Turbolinux (turbolinux.com), in collaboration with Hong Kong University, developed such a mall for primary and secondary schools in Hong Kong. For additional information about e-learning, see trainingmag.com, elearningmag.com, and learningcircuits.org.

EDUTAINMENT

Edutainment is a combination of education and entertainment, often through games. One of the main goals of edutainment is to encourage students to become active rather than passive learners. With active learning, a student is more involved in the learning process, which makes the learning experience richer and the knowledge gained more memorable. Edutainment embeds learning in an entertaining environment to help students learn almost without their being aware of it.

edutainment
The combination of education and entertainment, often through games.

Edutainment covers various subjects, including mathematics, reading, writing, history, and geography. It is targeted at various age groups, ranging from preschoolers to adults, and it is also used in corporate training over intranets. Software Toolworks (toolworks.com, now a part of The Learning Company at broderbund.com) is a major vendor of edutainment products.

For over a decade, educational games have been delivered mostly on CD-ROMs. However, since 1998, increasing numbers of companies now offer online edutainment in a distance-learning format (e.g., Knowledge Adventure products at sunburst.com and education.com). One of the facilitators of edutainment is e-books.

E-LEARNING TOOLS

Many e-learning tools are available (e.g., see Zhang and Nunamaker 2003). WebCT and Blackboard, described earlier, are two such tools. The following are several other examples.

- LearningSpace from Lotus Corporation (lotus.com/products/learnspace.nsf/wdocs/homepage) is a Web-based tool that can be customized to fit a company's training needs.

CASE 8.3

EC Application

ONLINE GLOBAL LEARNING CENTER AT W. R. GRACE

The newest concept for training and development is the *online learning center*. Online learning centers combine the Internet, intranets, and e-delivered courses with conventional learning media such as books, articles, instructor-led courses, and audio and videotapes.

W. R. Grace, a global specialty chemicals company (*grace.com*), initiated its online learning center in 2001. The company's human resources leaders were looking for a solution that would provide fast and easy access to a wide selection of tools for developing employee skills. Surveys indicated a need for self-paced professional and personal training support for employees. Strategic Partners' learning center concept provided the solution. A pilot program was initiated in March 2001. Within 6 months, the center was available 24/7 to 6,000 employees worldwide.

The learning center is organized around the core competencies that characterize the knowledge, skills, and abilities all W. R. Grace employees are expected to achieve. It offers internal classroom training; external courses; CD-ROM courses; self-paced learning tools; streaming video; Internet learning conferences; e-learning courses; coaching tips for managers and mentors; audio and videotapes; books and articles; information about the corporate mission, values, and strategy; strategy guides suggesting specific development actions, on-the-job and in the community; and corporate and industry news. Employees can access resources on a particular topic; they can search a range of appropriate tools and action alternatives specific to their needs, including training sessions, recommended readings, a rental library, and a strategy guide.

The center's Global Steering Committee, made up of representatives from all the functional areas of the business from around the world, keeps the center in tune with the development needs of employees and encourages the use of the center in all regions. The committee also provides human resources management with feedback on how the center is meeting identified needs.

Every 6 weeks, the center's electronic newsletter lands on each employee's desktop. The publication keeps employees up-to-date on the offerings of the center, reports on how employees are using the center, and encourages all employees to use the center as a source for learning and development. Corporate news also is included in the newsletter, keeping the company's initiatives and communications visible to all employees.

Based on its experience, W. R. Grace offers the following suggestions for the successful implementation of a learning center:

- Line up strong senior management support.
- Build gradually—start with a modest center, get it running smoothly, gather feedback from the users, make needed adjustments, and develop a more extensive center over time.
- Invite involvement—people support what they help to create.
- Provide a variety of learning tools, mixing in-house and external resources.
- Keep the learning center visible.
- Ensure the content is fresh and up-to-date.

W. R. Grace's Global Learning Center supports employee growth in a cost-effective manner while relating learning to performance and talent management, strategic communication, and individual development planning. It has proved to be a powerful learning and communications channel for the entire corporation.

Sources: Compiled from Boxer and Johnson (2002) and press releases at *grace.com* (accessed 2002).

Questions

1. List the factors that drive e-learning at W. R. Grace.
2. How is e-learning integrated with other learning methods?
3. List the e-learning offerings of W. R. Grace's learning center.
4. Describe the critical success factors of e-learning offered by W. R. Grace.

The 5.0 and higher releases include self-paced learning and collaboration capabilities—all in real time. The product supports 22 languages.

- ComputerPREP (computerprep.com) offers almost 400 e-learning products, including a comprehensive library of Web-based classroom, distance learning, and self-study curricula. Students can even combine products from different categories to customize learning environments.
- Macromedia offers tools for wireless devices at macromedia.com/software/.
- eCollege (ecollege.com) offers an e-learning platform that includes free collaboration tools.
- Artificial Life, Inc., launched an e-learning portal based on intelligent agents for teaching English and basic sciences in China. This is done in collaboration with Extempo Systems, Inc., which offers an interactive character-based e-learning portal for teaching English as a second language.

For more e-learning tools, see Online File W8.2.

E-learning content can be created with the aid of knowledge management, which is presented in the next section.

Section 8.4 ▶ REVIEW QUESTIONS

1. Define e-learning and describe its benefits.
2. List some of the major drawbacks of e-learning.
3. Describe virtual universities.
4. List some e-learning tools and describe WebCT and Blackboard.
5. Describe learning centers in industry.

8.5 KNOWLEDGE MANAGEMENT AND E-COMMERCE

The term *knowledge management* frequently is mentioned in discussions of e-learning. Why is this? To answer this question, one first needs to understand what knowledge management is.

Knowledge management and e-learning both use the same "coin of the realm"—knowledge. Whereas e-learning uses that "coin" for the sake of *individual* learning, knowledge management uses it to improve the functioning of an *organization.* Knowledge is one of the most important assets in any organization, and thus it is important to capture, store, and apply it. These are the major purposes of knowledge management. Thus, **knowledge management (KM)** refers to the process of capturing or creating knowledge, storing and protecting it, updating it constantly, and using it whenever necessary. For a comprehensive discussion of KM, see Holsapple (2003), Rao (2004), and kmworld.com.

knowledge management (KM)
The process of capturing or creating knowledge, storing it, updating it constantly, interpreting it, and using it whenever necessary.

Knowledge is collected from both external and internal sources. Then it is examined, interpreted, refined, and stored in what is called an **organizational knowledge base**, the repository for the enterprise's knowledge. A major purpose of an organizational knowledge base is to allow for *knowledge sharing*. Knowledge sharing among employees, with customers, and with business partners has a huge potential payoff in improved customer service, the ability to solve difficult organizational problems, shorter delivery cycle times, and increased collaboration within the company and with business partners. Furthermore, some knowledge can be sold to others or traded for other knowledge.

organizational knowledge base
The repository for an enterprise's accumulated knowledge.

KM promotes an *integrated* approach to the process of handling an enterprise's information assets, both those that are documented and the tacit expertise stored in individuals' heads. The integration of information resources is at the heart of KM. EC implementation involves a considerable amount of knowledge—about customers, suppliers, logistics, procurement, markets, and technology. The integration of that knowledge is required for successful EC applications. These applications are aimed at increasing organizational competitiveness (see Tiwana 2001 and Holsapple 2003).

The KM/EC connection will be described in more detail later in this section. First, though, let's examine KM types and activities.

KM TYPES AND ACTIVITIES

According to Lai and Chu (2002), organizational knowledge is embedded in the following resources: (1) *human capital*, which includes employee knowledge, competencies, and creativity; (2) *structured capital (organizational capital)*, which includes organizational structure and culture, processes, patents, and the capability to leverage knowledge through sharing and transferring; and (3) *customer capital*, which includes the relationship between organizations and their customers and other partners.

This organizational knowledge must be properly managed, and this is the purpose of KM. According to Davenport and Prusak (2000), KM has four tasks: (1) creating knowledge repositories where knowledge can be stored and retrieved easily; (2) enhancing a knowledge environment in order to conduct more effective knowledge creation, transfer, and use; (3) managing knowledge as an asset so as to increase the effective use of knowledge assets over time; and (4) improving knowledge access to facilitate its transfer between individuals. The knowledge access and transfer between individuals is part of knowledge usage and sharing. For a comprehensive list of KM activities and tools, see Rao (2004) and kmworld.com.

Knowledge Sharing

Knowledge is of limited value if it is not shared. The ability to share knowledge decreases its cost and increases its effectiveness for greater competitive advantage. Thus, another major purpose of KM is to increase knowledge sharing. Song (2002) demonstrated that through effective knowledge sharing, organizations can reduce uncertainty and risk, improve efficiency, reduce training costs, and more. Roberts-Witt (2002) noted that KM used to be about sharing company databases, but that increasingly it is also about sharing the information stored in people's heads.

Song (2002) proposed a framework for organizing and sharing knowledge gleaned from the Internet. According to this framework, organizations promote knowledge sharing via the use of rewards or incentives, through the use of different sharing mechanisms according to the type of knowledge, and by appropriately codifying knowledge. The proposed framework begins with the listing of strategic goals and objectives and the critical information needed for their attainment. Then, an analysis and storage mechanism is built as part of a business intelligence system (see Online Appendix W4A). The framework also deals with knowledge collection (from internal and external sources) and its dissemination in support of attaining the goals. An example knowledge sharing system at Xerox is provided in EC Application Case 8.4.

The KM discussion thus far has been fairly generic. For additional material regarding major KM activities, see the discussion of KM activities in Online File W8.3. Let's now consider how KM relates to EC.

HOW IS KNOWLEDGE MANAGEMENT RELATED TO E-COMMERCE?

As seen throughout this book, EC has many external as well as internal applications, including both CRM and PRM. To better perform its EC tasks, organizations need knowledge, which is provided by KM. For example, according to Sugumaran (2002), who proposed a

CASE 8.4

EC Application

ONLINE KNOWLEDGE SHARING AT XEROX

In the early 1990s, Xerox Corporation had a nationwide database that contained information that could be used to fix its copiers, fax machines, and high-speed printers. However, the information was not readily available to the 25,000 service and field employees and engineers whose job it is to repair the machines at customer sites. Satisfaction with customer service was low.

The engineers at Xerox's Palo Alto Research Center (PARC) spent 6 months observing repair personnel, watching how they worked, noting what their frustrations were, and identifying what kind of information they needed. They determined that the repair personnel needed to share their knowledge with their peers. PARC engineers developed Eureka, an online knowledge-sharing system created to assist the service people with time-consuming and complicated repair problems.

Ray Everett, program manager for Eureka, describes the powerful impact the program has had on service: "You went from not knowing how to fix something to being able to get the answer instantly. Even better, you could share any solutions you found with your peers around the globe within a day, as opposed to the several weeks it used to take."

Since its inception in 1996, Eureka has been implemented in 71 countries. It has helped solve 350,000 problems and has saved \$3 to \$4 million in parts and labor every year. The system is available to all of Xerox's service engineers via notebook computers and is accessed through the Internet. Product fixes (50,000 of them), documentation updates, and product-update bulletins are delivered over the Web. Individual service employees and engineers can enter possible new solutions to problems into the system. The solution will appear in Eureka, giving credit to the author and noting the service employee's country of origin. An alert about a new solution is sent to validators who test the solution; if it works consistently, it is sent to all engineers via Eureka updates.

The 2004 version is designed to work over wireless Internet connections. Eureka is a constantly evolving and growing system that connects and shares the collective knowledge of Xerox's service force.

Sources: Compiled from Roberts-Witt (2002) and *xerox.com* (accessed 2002).

Questions

1. What knowledge is shared via Eureka? How is it shared?
2. What EC technologies are described in this case? Classify the EC transactions.
3. What were the drivers of the program?
4. What advantages may be provided by the wireless system?

KM framework for EC organizations, strategic planning in traditional organizations needs considerable amounts of knowledge. To mitigate this problem, e-businesses can proactively incorporate KM processes to facilitate quick access to different types of knowledge.

In the EC marketspace, large amounts of data can be gathered easily, and by analyzing these data in a timely manner, organizations can learn about their clients and generate useful knowledge for planning and decision making. For example, in the B2B market, organizations can scan the environment to monitor changes in a vertical industry and can form strategic alliances or partnerships in response to business pressures. For these activities to be successful in both B2B and B2C, appropriate knowledge is needed to interpret information and to execute activities.

Core knowledge management activities for companies doing EC should include the following electronically supported activities: identification, creation, capture and codification, classification, distribution, utilization, and evolution of the knowledge needed to develop products and partnerships. *Knowledge creation* involves using various computer-based tools and techniques to analyze transaction data and generate new ideas. *Knowledge capture and codification* includes gathering new knowledge and storing it in a machine-readable form. *Knowledge classification* organizes knowledge using appropriate dimensions relating it to its use. *Knowledge distribution* is sharing relevant information with suppliers, consumers, and other internal and external stakeholders through electronic networks—both public and private. *Knowledge utilization* involves appropriate application of knowledge to problem solving. *Knowledge evolution* entails updating knowledge as time progresses.

Nah et al. (2002) investigated the specific relationship of KM and EC in B2C and auctions. Chen and Liou (2002) explored the relationship of the two from a theoretical point of view. Shaw et al. (2001) related KM and EC through data mining. Bose (2002) explored the relationship between KM and infrastructure for EC.

Fahey et al. (2001) believe that a major role of KM is linking e-business and operating processes. Specifically, knowledge generated in e-business contributes to the enhancement of three core operating processes: CRM, SCM, and product development management. For more on KM-enabling technologies and how they can be applied to business unit initiatives, see Online Exhibit W8.3, Rao (2004), and kmworld.com.

KNOWLEDGE PORTALS

Knowledge portals are single-point-of-access software systems intended to provide easy and timely access to knowledge and to support communities of knowledge workers who share common goals. Knowledge portals can be used for either external or internal use. A knowledge portal also can be defined as an information portal that will be used by knowledge workers.

knowledge portal
A single point of access software system intended to provide timely access to information and to support communities of knowledge workers.

Knowledge portals support various tasks performed by knowledge workers: gathering, organizing, searching for, and analyzing information; synthesizing solutions with respect to specific task goals; and then sharing and distributing what has been learned with other knowledge workers. These tasks are illustrated in Exhibit 8.5. In this example, Mack et al. (2001) illustrate how a knowledge portal was used to support the work of knowledge-work consultants at IBM and what technologies can be used to support each category of tasks. For further details on how knowledge portals are related to collaborative and intellectual capital management, see Mack et al. (2001) and Raisch (2001).

Information Intelligence

Information intelligence refers to information, data, knowledge, and the semantic infrastructure that enables organizations to create more business applications. It creates a platform that leverages information analytics, patterns, and associations to extract business value from internal and external knowledge. For details, see Delphi Group (2004).

information intelligence
Information, data, knowledge, and semantic infrastructure that enable organizations to create more business applications.

ONLINE ADVICE AND CONSULTING

Finally, another use of knowledge online is offering advice and consulting services. The online advice and consulting field is growing rapidly as tens of thousands of experts of all kinds sell or provide for free their expertise over the Internet. The following are some examples.

- **Medical advice.** Companies such as WebMD (webmd.com) and others (see kasamba.com, and keen.com) provide health-advice consultations with top medical experts. Consumers

EXHIBIT 8.5 Knowledge Work Tasks with Examples of Supporting Technology

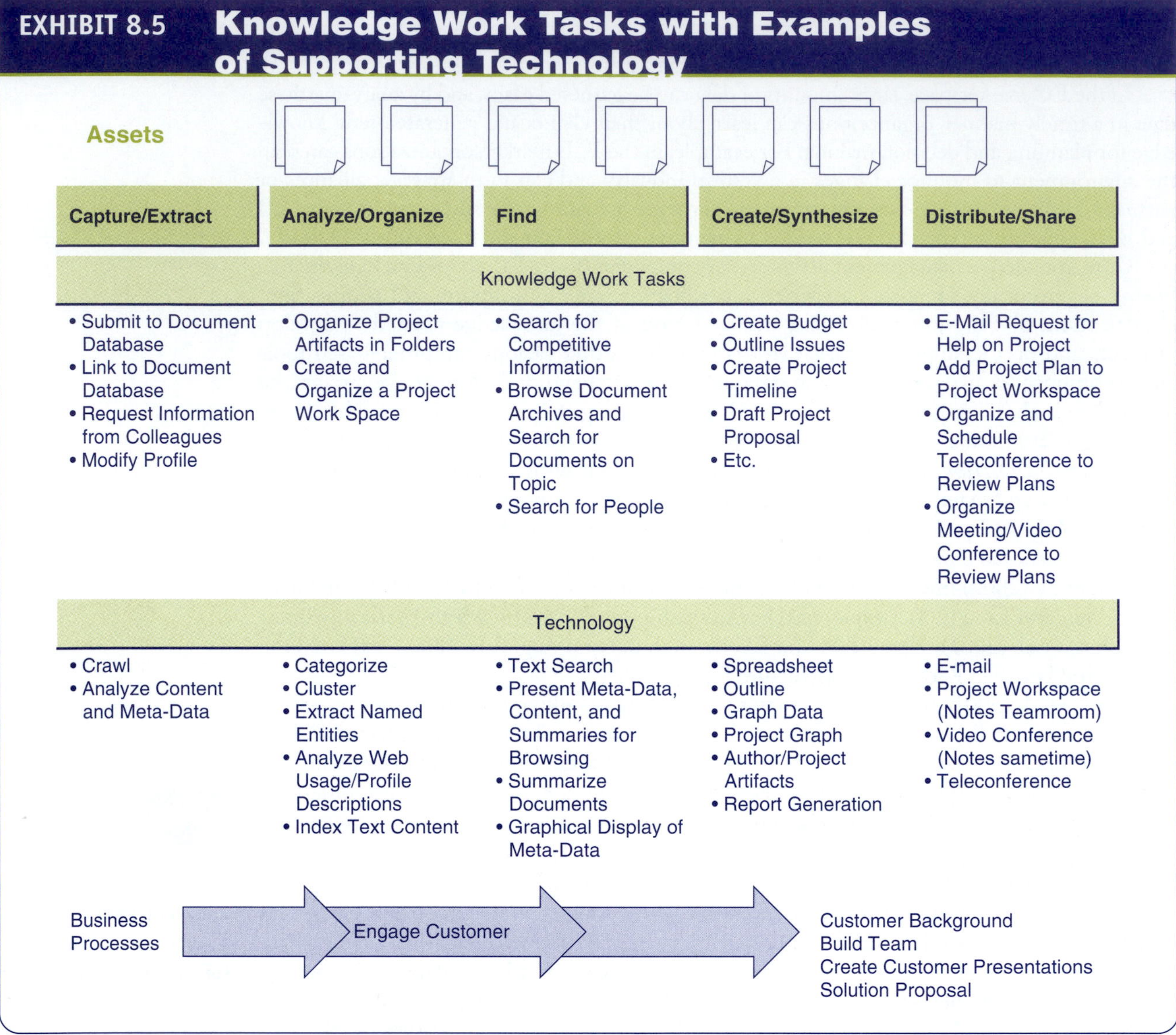

Source: Mark, R., et al. "Knowledge Portals and the Emerging Digital Knowledge Workplace." *IBM Systems Journal* 40, no. 4 (2001).

can ask specific questions and get an answer from a specialist in a few days. Health sites also offer specialized advice and tips for travelers.

- **Management consulting.** Many consultants are selling their accumulated expertise from organizational knowledge bases. A pioneer in this area was Andersen Consulting (now Accenture at accenture.com). Other management consultants that sell knowledge online are Aberdeen (aberdeen.com) and Forrester Research (forresterresearch.com). Because of their high consultation fees, such services mainly are used by corporations.
- **Legal advice.** Delivery of legal advice to individuals and businesses by consultation services has considerable prospects. For example, Atlanta-based law firm Alston & Bird coordinates legal counseling with 12 law firms for a large health-care company and for many other clients. The company created an organizational knowledge base that contains information from some of the best law firms in the country. This information is then made available to all 12 of the law firms in the consultation group. Also, many lawyers offer inexpensive consulting services online. Linklaters, a leading law firm in the United Kingdom, created a separate company (blueflag.com) to sell its legal services online. The company offers several products and also sells support technology to other law firms.

- **Gurus.** Several sites provide diversified expert services, some for free. One example is guru.com, which offers general advice and a job board for experts on legal, financial, tax, technical, lifestyle, and other issues. It aggregates over 200,000 professional "gurus." Expertise is advertised at elance.com, where one can post a required service for experts to bid on. Of special interest is sciam.com, which offers advice from science experts at *Scientific American*.
- **Financial advice.** Many companies offer extensive financial advice. For example, Merrill Lynch Online (askmerrill.ml.com) provides free access to some of the firm's research reports and analyses.
- **Other advisory services.** Many other advisory services are available online—some for free, and others for a fee. For example, guestfinder.com makes it easy for people who work in the media to find guests and interview sources.

One word of caution about advice: It is not wise to risk your health, your money, or your legal status on free or even for-fee online advice. Always seek more than one opinion, and carefully check the credentials of any advice provider.

EXPERT ADVICE WITHIN ORGANIZATIONS

Expert advice can be provided within an organization in a variety of ways. Human expertise is rare; therefore, companies attempt to preserve it electronically in corporate knowledge bases. Alternatively, electronic expert systems may be used. Although such systems are very useful, and they can be used directly by nonexperts, they cannot solve all problems, especially new ones. For such cases, human experts are needed. In large organizations it may be difficult to locate experts quickly.

Finding Experts Electronically

Companies know that information technology can be used to find experts. People who need help may post their problem on the corporate intranet and ask for help. Similarly, companies may ask for advice on how to exploit an opportunity. IBM frequently uses this method. Sometimes it obtains hundreds of useful ideas within a few days. It is a kind of brainstorming. The problem with this approach is that it may take days to get an answer, if an answer is even provided, and the answer may not be from the top experts. Therefore, companies employ expert location systems.

Expert Location Systems

Expert location systems are interactive computerized systems that help employees find and connect with colleagues with expertise required for specific problems—whether they are across the country or across the room—in order to solve specific, critical business problems in seconds. Such software is made by companies such as AskMe and Tacit Knowledge Systems Inc. They work similarly, exploring knowledge bases for either an answer to the problem (if it exists there) or locating qualified experts. The process is shown in Exhibit 8.6.

EC Application Case 8.5 demonstrates how such a system works for the U.S. government.

expert location systems
Interactive computerized systems that help employees find and connect with colleagues who have expertise required for specific problems—whether they are across the country or across the room—in order to solve specific, critical business problems in seconds.

Section 8.5 ▶ REVIEW QUESTIONS

1. Define KM.
2. Discuss the relationship between KM and EC.
3. Describe knowledge portals.
4. Describe online advisory services.
5. Describe expert location systems and their benefits.

8.6 CUSTOMER-TO-CUSTOMER E-COMMERCE

Previous chapters examined transactions between individuals and businesses (B2C, C2B) and among businesses (B2B). Another possible type of EC transaction is that between individual consumers. **Customer-to-customer (C2C)** e-commerce refers to e-commerce in

customer-to-customer (C2C)
E-commerce in which both the buyer and the seller are individuals, not businesses; involves activities such as auctions and classified ads.

EXHIBIT 8.6 How Expert Location Systems (Save) Work

Step 1:
An employee submits a question into the expertise location management system.

Step 2:
The software searches its database to see if an answer to the question already exists. If it does, the info (research reports, spreadsheets, etc.) is returned to the employee. If not, the software searches documents and archived communications for an "expert."

Step 3:
Once a qualified candidate is located, the system asks if he is able to answer a question from a colleague. If so, he submits a response. If the candidate is unable (perhaps he is in a meeting or otherwise indisposed), he can elect to pass on the question. The question is then routed to the next appropriate candidate until one responds.

Step 4:
After the response is sent, it is reviewed for accuracy and sent back to the querist. At the same time, it is added to the knowledge database. This way, if the question comes up again, it will not be necessary to seek real time assistance.

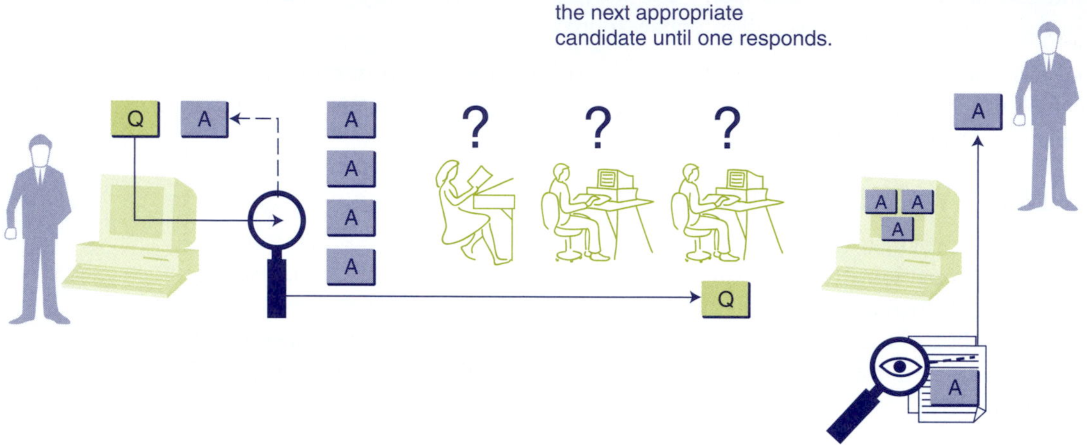

Source: D'Agostino D., "Expertise Management: Who Knows About This?" *CIO Insight*, July 1, 2004. Used with permission of artist David Falherty.

which both the buyer and the seller are individuals, not businesses. C2C is conducted in several ways on the Internet; the best-known C2C activities are auctions. Millions of individuals are buying and selling on eBay and hundreds of other auction sites worldwide. In addition to the major C2C activity of auctions, other C2C activities include classified ads, personal services, exchanges, selling virtual properties, and support services.

C2C AUCTIONS

In dozens of countries, selling and buying on auction sites is exploding. Most auctions are conducted by intermediaries (e.g., eBay). Consumers can select general sites such as ebay.com or auctionanything.com or they can use specialized sites such as uBid.com. In addition, many individuals are conducting their own auctions with the use of special software. For example, greatshop.com provides software to create C2C reverse auction communities online. See Chapter 10 for more on auctions.

CLASSIFIED ADS

People sell to other people every day through classified ads. Internet-based classified ads have several advantages over newspaper classified ads. They offer a national, rather than a local, audience. This greatly increases the supply of goods and services available and the number of potential buyers. For example, classifieds2000.com contains a list of about 500,000 cars, compared with the much smaller number one might find locally. It also includes apartments for rent across the United States (powered by rent.com) and personal ads (powered by match.com). Another example is freeclassified.com. Many newspapers also offer their classified ads online. In many cases, placing an ad on one Web site brings it automatically into the classified sections of numerous partners. This increases ad exposure, at no additional cost. To help narrow the search for a particular item, on some sites shoppers can use search engines. In addition, Internet-based classifieds often can be placed for free by private parties, can be edited or changed easily, and in many cases can display photos of the product offered for sale.

CASE 8.5

EC Application

HOW THE U.S. DEPARTMENT OF COMMERCE USES AN EXPERT LOCATION SYSTEM

The U.S. Commercial Service Division at the Department of Commerce (DOC) conducts approximately 200,000 counseling sessions a year involving close to $40 billion in trade. The division employs many specialists who frequently need to do research or call on experts to answer a question posed by a U.S. corporation.

For example, in May 2004, a U.S.-based software company called Brad Anderson, a DOC specialist, for advice. The software company wanted to close a deal with a customer in Poland, but the buyer wanted to charge the U.S. company a 20 percent withholding tax, a tax it attributed to Poland's recent admission into the European Union. Was the tax legitimate?

To find out, Anderson turned to the DOC Insider, an *expertise location system* (from AskMe). After typing in his question, Anderson first found some documents that were related to his query, but they did not explain the EU tax code completely. Anderson next asked the system to search the 1,700-strong Commercial Service for a real "live" expert, and, within seconds, he was given a list of 80 people in the DOC who might be able to help him. Of those, he chose the six people he felt were most qualified and then forwarded his query.

Before the DOC Insider was in place, Anderson says, it would have taken him about three days to answer the same question. "You have to make many phone calls and deal with time zones," he says. Thanks to the expertise location system, however, he had three responses within minutes, a complete answer within an hour, and the sale went through the following morning. Anderson estimates that he now uses the system for roughly 40 percent of the work he does.

The DOC Insider is an invaluable tool. Anderson thinks the tool is vital enough to provide it to other units at the agency. In the first 9 months the system has been in place, it has saved more than 1,000 man hours.

Source: Compiled from D'Agostino (2004).

Questions

1. What are the benefits of the expertise location system to the DOC? To U.S. companies?
2. Review Exhibit 8.6 and relate it to this case.
3. What in your opinion are the limitations of this system? Can they be overcome? How?

The major categories of classified ads are similar to those found in a newspaper: vehicles, real estate, employment, general merchandise, collectibles, computers, pets, tickets, and travel. Classified ads are available through most ISPs (AOL, MSN, etc.), in some portals (Yahoo!, etc.), and from Internet directories, online newspapers, and more. Once a person finds an ad and gets the details, he or she can e-mail or call the other party to find out additional information or to make a purchase. Most classified ads are provided for free. Some classified ad sites generate revenue from advertisers who pay for larger ads, especially when the sellers are businesses. Classified ad Web sites accept no responsibility for the content of any advertisement.

PERSONAL SERVICES

Numerous personal services are available on the Internet (lawyers, handy helpers, tax preparers, investment clubs, dating services). Some are in the classified ads, but others are listed in specialized Web sites and directories. Some are free, some charge a fee. Be very careful before purchasing any personal services. Fraud or crime could be involved (e.g., a lawyer online may not be an expert in the area professed or may not deliver the service at all). Online advising and consulting, described in Section 8.5, also are examples of personal services.

C2C EXCHANGES

C2C exchanges are of several types. They may be *consumer-to-consumer bartering exchanges* (e.g., targetbarter.com) in which goods and services are exchanged without monetary transactions. Or, they may be *consumer exchanges* that help buyers and sellers find each other and negotiate deals. Another form of C2C exchange is one in which consumers exchange information about products (e.g., consumerdemocracy.com and epinions.com). For a complete list of such exchanges, see business2.com/b2/webguide/0,17811,7909,00.html.

SELLING VIRTUAL PROPERTIES

Believe it or not, millions of online game players in Asia, and especially in China, are selling and buying online virtual properties. Here is how it works: With popular multiplayer online role playing games (MMORPG) such as Jianxia Qingyuan or Legend of MIR, players own virtual properties that are registered under their names. The players can buy or sell these virtual properties via auctions when playing the game. According to Ding (2004), who quoted an IDC report, 26.7 percent of the 13.8 million MMORPG players (or about 3.7 million) have bought or sold virtual a property, for about US $120 million a year. Ding projects this figure will reach US $1.66 billion in 2006.

The trading platform is provided by companies such as Intelligence Dragon Software Technology. People win items in MMORPG games such as rings or shields, and then they can sell them (in e-auctions or classified ads) for as much as 30,000 yuan (about $361) a piece. Of course, there are risks. Hackers may steal items, and even market organizers can sell them. Because the industry is not regulated, the player may have little chance of recovering the virtual property. In addition, there is the risk of the buyer not paying for the item.

SUPPORT SERVICES FOR C2C

When individuals buy products or services from other individuals online, they usually buy from strangers. The issues of assuring quality, receiving payments, and preventing fraud are critical to the success of C2C. One service that helps C2C is payments by intermediary companies such as PayPal (paypal.com) (see Chapter 12). Other innovative services and technologies that support C2C are described in Chapters 12 and 13.

Section 8.6 ▶ REVIEW QUESTIONS

1. List the major C2C applications.
2. Describe how C2C works in classified online ads.
3. Describe C2C personal services, exchanges, and other support services.

8.7 PEER-TO-PEER NETWORKS AND APPLICATIONS

peer-to-peer (P2P)
A network architecture in which workstations (or PCs) share data and processing with each other directly rather than through a central server.

Several C2C applications are based on a computer architecture known as peer-to-peer. **Peer-to-peer (P2P)** computer architecture is a type of network in which each client computer can share files or computer resources (such as processing power) *directly* with others rather than through a central server. This is in contrast with a *client-server* architecture in which some computers serve other computers via a central server. (Note that the acronym P2P also can stand for *people-to-people, person-to-person,* or *point-to-point.* Our discussion here refers to *peer-to-peer networks* over which files and other computing resources are shared.)

P2P technology is really two different things—the direct sharing of digital files and the sharing of different computers' processing power. The main benefit of P2P is that it can expand enormously the universe of information accessible from a personal computer or a mobile device (users are not confined to just Web pages). Additionally, some proponents claim that a well-designed P2P system can offer better security, reliability, and availability of content than the client-server model on which the Web is currently based. Other advantages over the client-server architecture include the following: no need for a network administrator, the network is fast and inexpensive to set up and maintain, and each PC can make a backup copy of its data to other PCs for security. P2P technology is more productive than client-server technology because it enables direct connections between computers. However, P2P has some drawbacks that limit its usability, including bandwidth limitations, privacy violations, and potential security problems.

CHARACTERISTICS OF P2P SYSTEMS

P2P systems have the following key characteristics: They provide for real-time access to other users through techniques such as instant messaging and multichannel collaboration applications. The user computers can act as both clients and servers. The overall system is easy to use and is well integrated, and it includes tools for easy creation of content or for adding functionalities. P2P systems maximize the use of physical attributes such as processor cycles, storage space, bandwidth, and location on the network. They employ user interfaces that load outside of a Web browser. They address the need to reach content resources located on the Internet periphery. They support "cross-networking" protocols such as SOAP or XML-RPC (remote procedure call, a protocol that enables a program on one computer to execute a program on a server computer). Finally, they often do something new or exciting, which creates popular interest.

As these characteristics of P2P computing indicate, devices can join the P2P network from any location with little effort. Instead of dedicated LANs, the Internet itself becomes the network of choice. Easier configuration and control over applications enable people without network savvy to join the user community. In fact, P2P signifies a shift in peer-networking emphasis—from hardware to applications (e.g., see Lethin 2003).

P2P networking connects people directly to other people. It provides an easy system for sharing, publishing, and interacting that does not require knowledge of system administration. The system wraps everything up into a user-friendly interface and lets people share or communicate with each other (for details, see Kwok et al. 2002). P2P networks overcome existing client-server inefficiencies and limitations. They will not replace the client-server architecture, but they can be used to create hybrid P2P/client-server networks that are faster, cheaper, and more powerful. According to Kini (2002), P2P networking improves upon the existing client-server hierarchy to efficiently use the processing power, disk space, and data available in a significant number of information sharing and knowledge management applications.

An example of a P2P network is shown in Exhibit 8.7. The PCs shown in the drawing perform computer-to-computer communication directly through their own operating systems; individual resources such as printers, CD-ROM drives, or disk drives are transformed into shared, collective resources that are accessible from any PC on the P2P network.

Notice that these characteristics—such as expressing themselves, trading, selling—enable more Internet equality. These activities that previously required large amounts of money are now available at low costs, as suggested by Agre (2003).

MODELS OF P2P APPLICATIONS

Kwok et al. (2002) developed a framework of P2P business and service applications (see Online Exhibit W8.4). Four distinct models of P2P applications exist:

- **Collaboration.** This model allows real-time direct interactions between people, including instant messaging and videoconferencing applications.
- **Content distribution.** This model enables file sharing, made famous by Napster, Kazaa, and other music file-sharing services.
- **Business process automation.** This model is used to enhance existing business process applications. For example, users can control the type of data their e-mail client will accept.
- **Distributed search.** This model enables the sending of search requests in real time to multiple information repositories rather than searching a centralized index.

EXHIBIT 8.7 Peer-to-Peer Networks

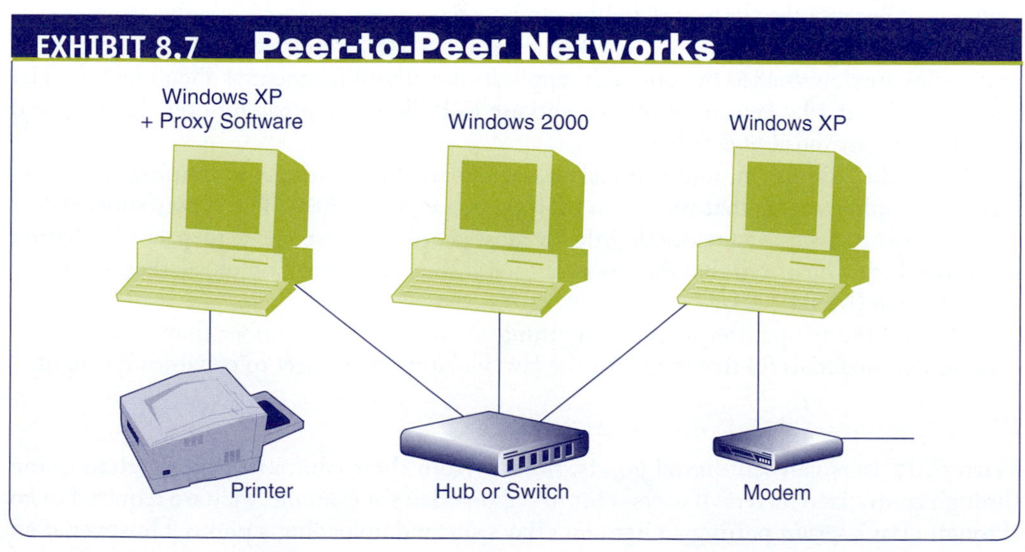

The characteristics and models just described allow for the various applications discussed next.

C2C P2P APPLICATIONS

The most publicized P2P applications are in the area of C2C. The most well known of these applications is the file sharing of music, software, movies, and other digital media.

Napster—The File-Sharing Utility

In Chapter 3, Napster was presented as an example of C2C EC. By logging onto services such as Napster, people could download files that other people were willing to share. The network enabled users to search other members' hard drives for a particular file, including data files created by users or copied from elsewhere. Digital music and games were the most popular files accessed. Napster had more than 60 million members in 2002 before it went out of business.

The Napster server functioned as a directory that listed the files being shared by other users. Once logged into the server, users could search the directory for specific songs and locate the file owner. They could then directly access the owner's computer and download the songs they had chosen. Napster also included chat rooms to connect its millions of users.

However, a U.S. federal court found Napster to be in violation of copyright laws because it enabled people to obtain music files without paying the creators of the music for access to their material. Following this ruling, in March 2002, Napster closed its free services. Napster continued to operate, with users paying a fee for file sharing and Napster passing along part of the fee to copyright owners.

In December 2002, Roxio, a software maker specializing in CD-burning software, bought Napster's intellectual property assets, including its patents and brand name. (Roxio did not assume any of Napster's legal or financial liabilities.) Napster's remaining hardware—servers, routers, and miscellaneous computers—became part of the company's bankruptcy proceedings and were auctioned off December 11, 2002. Roxio relaunched Napster in 2004. (For more on Napster, see Chapter 17.)

Other File-Sharing Programs

A number of free file-sharing programs still exist. For example, an even purer version of P2P is Gnutella (gnutella.com), a P2P program that dispenses with the central database altogether in connecting the peer computers. Similarly, Kazaa (kazaa.com) offers music file sharing, and it is becoming very popular (see Reuters 2003). Attempts are being made to "kill" Kazaa (and others like it), but because Kazaa's servers are located in Denmark and it operates from Australia, and users trade files using anonymous "supernodes," these attempts are facing legal difficulties (see Chapter 17). To access games over P2P networks, try fusiongames.com and battle.net. ICQ (the instant messenger-type chat room) can be considered a hybrid P2P technology because the chatters share the same screen.

A survey conducted by Ipsos-Reid in September 2002 reported that 49.7 percent of music files are downloaded by some P2P application without payment to their creators. The study found that 19.2 percent of people who use P2P file-sharing pay for downloading, and 24.8 percent buy music at e-tailers.

Frost and Sullivan (an international strategic market consulting and training firm) performed an online survey that was taken by 150,000 people in 2004. The survey showed that the purchasing of music increases slightly for most people who used peer-to-peer file-sharing networks. It demonstrated that most people used P2P networks to find music that is actually worth buying (Mello 2004).

Despite the temptation to get "something for nothing," remember that downloading copyrighted materials for free is against the law; violators are subject to penalties if caught.

Other Commercial P2P Applications in C2C

With P2P, users can sell digital goods directly from their computers rather than going through centralized servers. If users want to sell on eBay, for example, they are required to go through eBay's server, putting an item on eBay's site and uploading a photo. However, if an auction site uses *file sharing*, it can direct customers to the seller's Web site, where buyers can find an extensive amount of information, photos, and even videos about the items being sold. In this case, an auction site serves as an intermediary, making the P2P link between the sellers and buyers.

INTRABUSINESS P2P APPLICATIONS

Several companies are using P2P to facilitate internal collaboration. For example, in 1990, Intel wrote a file transfer program called NetBatch, which allows chip designers to use the additional processing power of colleagues' computers across sites in California, Arizona, and even foreign countries such as Israel. Intel saved more than $500 million between 1992 and 2001 (intel.com 2002). Under this arrangement, users were able to solve more complex problems that otherwise would have required the use of supercomputers.

After the Napster debacle, companies have been hesitant to use P2P collaboration tools. But tools such as those developed by Groove Networks (groove.net) are aiding companies to come to an understanding of how the efficiency of P2P technologies can improve the fine art of collaboration and be incorporated into the work environment (Serva 2004).

B2B P2P APPLICATIONS

P2P could be a technology panacea for systems innovators building B2B exchanges. With P2P, people can share information, but they are not required to send it to an unknown server, as they do when using a regular exchange. Some companies fear that exchanges make it possible for unauthorized personnel to gain access to corporate data files. P2P applications enable such companies to store documents in-house instead of on an unknown, and possibly unsecured, server. According to McAffee (2000), P2P networks allow companies to avoid the fees charged by B2B exchanges and reduce the complexity and expense of the networking. Netrana Corporation's (netrana.com) software replaces the model of funneling all buyers and sellers into a central place with the ability of direct connection.

Several companies are using the P2P architecture as a basis for speeding up business transactions, as shown in the following examples.

- Groove Networks enables direct collaboration by small groups (see Kini 2002). Its Groove 2 product, which was introduced in April 2002, has many P2P-based capabilities.
- Hilgraeve of Monroe, Michigan, has a technology called DropChute hilgraeve.com/dropchute that establishes a connection between two computers and allows users to transfer files. The company has won a U.S. patent for its P2P communication process, which touts four levels of encryption and virus-scanning protection. Fort Knox Escrow Service in Atlanta, Georgia, which transmits legal and financial documents that must be highly secure, has leveraged DropChute to enable clients to deliver material electronically. "Instead of having to wait for an overnight package, we can do it all over the Internet," said Jeanna Israel, Fort Knox's director of operations (Lason Company 2000).
- Biz2Peer Technologies offers a trading platform that allows P2P product searches, cataloging, and order entry.
- Blue Tiger Networks offers a platform for P2P trading between businesses.
- Consilient creates "sitelets," which are mobile XML documents designed to manage themselves through built-in workflow rules. (For further explanation of this complex technology, see openp2p.com; search for Consilient.)

Peer networks effectively address some of the Web's B2B deficiencies. The model is a natural fit for the needs of business, because business relationships are intrinsically peer to peer. Peer networks allow businesses to communicate, interact, and transact with each other as never before by making business relationships interactive, dynamic, and balanced—both within and between enterprises.

However, the success of P2P in B2B is not guaranteed. It depends in part on the ability of the technology to address security and scalability issues. For additional information on P2P in B2B, see Gong (2002) and internetnews.com (2001).

B2C P2P APPLICATIONS

P2P has potential applications to marketing, advertising, and B2C payments. For example, Certapay (certapay.com) is a P2P e-mail payment platform that enables e-banking customers to send and receive money using only an e-mail address. Another company, Fandango (fandango.com), combines P2P with collaborative filtering (Chapter 4) for online ticket buying activities. Assuming a user is conducting a search for a ticket using Fandango's product, the user enters a search keyword, and the keyword is sent to 100 peers, which search local indexes of the Web pages they have visited. Those computers relay the query to 100 of their peers, and that group submits it to 100 of theirs, yielding, in theory, up to 1 million queries. The resulting URLs are returned to the user, weighted in favor of the most recently visited pages and peers with similar interests.

P2P is certain to enable new EC applications, but it has both technical and social limitations (see Lethin 2003). Although sensitive information may require special security arrangements and many users may encounter scalability issues, P2P is indeed a very promising technology.

Section 8.7 ▶ REVIEW QUESTIONS

1. Define P2P networks and list their major characteristics.
2. List the major P2P models.
3. Describe P2P applications in C2C.
4. Describe P2P applications in B2B.

MANAGERIAL ISSUES

Some managerial issues related to this chapter are as follows.

1. **What are the e-government opportunities?** If an organization is doing business with the government, eventually some or all of it may be moved online. Organizations may find new online business opportunities with the government, because governments are getting serious about going online. Some even mandate it as the only way to conduct B2G and G2B.
2. **Are there e-learning and e-training opportunities?** Adding an e-learning component to a company's activities is useful when employees need to retrain themselves and keep up with new knowledge. Organizations can cut retraining costs and shorten the learning period. Also, companies can help customers train their employees in new products.
3. **Can we capitalize on C2C?** Businesses cannot capture much C2C activity unless they are providers of some innovative service, such as paypal.com. Businesses may consider using P2P to support C2C.
4. **How well are we managing our knowledge?** Connecting e-commerce initiatives with a KM program, if one exists, is a very viable strategy. The knowledge is needed for the operation and implementation of EC projects as well as for e-training.
5. **Are there P2P applications?** Watch for new developments in P2P tools and applications. Some experts say a major revolution is coming for faster and cheaper online communication and collaboration. As with any new innovation, it will take time to mature. This technology could be very helpful in B2B applications.

RESEARCH TOPICS

Here are some suggested topics related to this chapter. For details, references, and additional topics, refer to the book's "Current EC Research," in the Online Appendix.

1. **Multiple Technologies and Ranges of Expertise on Complex E-Government and IT Policy Issues**
   - Biodiversity
   - Data sharing and integration
   - Data visualization
   - Digital libraries and archives
   - Geographical information systems
   - HCI usability

- Information architecture and management
- Knowledge management
- Metadata
- Modeling and simulation
- Security and privacy
- Semantic web
- Wireless

2. **E-Government Research Relevant to EC Classified by the Government Domain**
   - Communication
   - Data privacy
   - Digital divide
   - Education
   - E-government/service delivery
   - Inter-/intra-government relations
   - Institutional and organizational analysis
   - Law and regulation
   - Natural resource management
   - Political process
   - Public management/administration
   - Statistics and surveying

3. **Managerial and Political Issues Important to the Success of E-Government**

   E-government architectures by applications
   - Metrics of e-government progress and evaluation by countries
   - Integration of governmental internal administrative systems with external e-marketplaces
   - Integration of departments on the Web Services platform
   - Secure Internet voting protocols
   - Citizen adoption of e-government services

4. **The Importance of E-Learning as a Medium for Public and Corporate Education**
   - Potential target market of e-learning
   - Impact and limitation of e-learning as a corporate training program
   - Propagation of e-learning by application and by country
   - Architecture of e-learning systems
   - Business models of e-learning systems
   - Hybrid design of online and off-line learning services
   - Changed role of the virtual professor
   - Asynchronous collaboration in on-demand education
   - Transformation of knowledge process via Internet publishing
   - Comparative performance of blogs in building community

5. **Knowledge Management Used in the Context of EC**
   - When knowledge management succeeds and when it fails
   - Knowledge management for customer relationship management
   - Knowledge management for supplier relationship management
   - Role of knowledge management in the online community
   - Using agents to collect knowledge about buyers and sellers
   - Architecture of knowledge management systems on Semantic Web Services
   - Framework of demand-driven knowledge management
   - Using knowledge management systems for decision support
   - Collaborative tools in building innovative virtual teams for interorganizational knowledge sharing

6. **The Advantages of P2P Computing as a Useful Architecture and a Complement to Client/Server Architecture**
   - Technical and social components of P2P computing
   - Prospects for P2P computing
   - Risks and opportunities of P2P technology
   - Conditions present when P2P is more advantageous than client/server architecture
   - Grid computing in the P2P computing environment

SUMMARY

In this chapter, you learned about the following EC issues as they relate to the learning objectives.

1. **E-government to citizens, businesses, and others.** Governments worldwide are providing a variety of services to citizens over the Internet. Such initiatives increase citizens' satisfaction and decrease government expenses in providing customer service applications including electronic voting. Governments also are active in electronically trading with businesses. Finally, EC is done within and between governments.

2. **Other e-government activities.** Governments, like any other organization, can use EC applications for great savings. Notable applications are e-procurement using reverse auctions, e-payments to and from citizens and businesses, auctioning of surplus goods, and electronic travel and expense management systems. Governments also conduct electronic business with other governments. Finally, governments can facilitate homeland security with EC tools.
3. **Online publishing and e-books.** Online publishing of newspapers, magazines, and books is growing rapidly, as is the online publishing of other digitizable items such as software, music, games, movies, and other entertainment. Of special interest is blogging, the publishing of newsletter-like commentaries by individuals on the Internet.
4. **E-learning and virtual universities.** E-learning is the delivery of educational content via electronic media, including the Internet and intranets. Degree programs, lifelong learning topics, and corporate training are delivered by thousands of organizations worldwide. A growing area is distance learning via online university offerings. Some are virtual; others are delivered both online and off-line. Online corporate training also is increasing and is sometimes conducted at formal corporate learning centers.
5. **Knowledge management and dissemination as an e-business.** Knowledge has been recognized as an important organizational asset. It needs to be properly captured, stored, managed, and shared. Knowledge is critical for many e-commerce tasks. Knowledge can be shared in different ways; expert knowledge can be provided to nonexperts (for fee or free) via a knowledge portal or as a personal service (e.g., via e-mail).
6. **C2C activities.** C2C consists of consumers conducting e-commerce with other consumers, mainly in auctions (such as at eBay). Buying and selling of goods and personal services can also take place through the use of online classified ads, exchanges, and special services.
7. **Peer-to-peer technology and applications.** Peer-to-peer (P2P) technology enables direct communication among client computers. It enables file sharing among individuals and between organizations. The P2P technology has tremendous potential for increased effectiveness and reduced cost of communication, information processing, and collaboration.

KEY TERMS

Term	Page
Blog	344
Customer-to-customer (C2C)	357
Distance learning	349
E-book	341
E-government	330
E-learning	345
E-zines	339
Edutainment	351
Electronic voting	332
Expert location systems	357
Government-to-business (G2B)	333
Government-to-citizens (G2C)	330
Government-to-employees (G2E)	335
Government-to-government (G2G)	334
Information intelligence	355
Knowledge management (KM)	353
Knowledge portal	355
Netizen	332
Online publishing	339
Organizational knowledge base	353
Peer-to-peer (P2P)	360
Virtual university	349
Webcasting	341
Webinars	341
Weblogging (blogging)	344
WikiLog (wikiblog)	344

QUESTIONS FOR DISCUSSION

1. Some say that B2G is simply B2B. Explain.
2. Compare and contrast B2E with G2E.
3. Which e-government EC activities are intrabusiness activities? Explain why they are intrabusiness.
4. Identify the benefits of G2C to citizens and to governments.
5. How can e-government enhance homeland security?
6. Discuss the major issues and problems in homeland security and some of the solutions provided by EC tools.
7. In what way can online publishing support paper-based publications?
8. Discuss the advantages and disadvantages of e-books.
9. Will paper-based books and magazines be eliminated in the long run? Why or why not?
10. Check an online version of a newspaper or magazine you are familiar with and discuss the differences between the print and online versions.
11. Describe the social phenomenon of blogging and speculate on its commercial possibilities.
12. Discuss the advantages of e-learning for an undergraduate student.
13. Discuss the advantages of e-learning in the corporate training environment.
14. Discuss the relationship between KM and a portal.

15. In what ways does KM support e-commerce?
16. Why do you think people trade online virtual properties?
17. Discuss the advantages of expert location systems over corporate knowledge bases that contain experts' knowledge. What are the disadvantages? Can they be combined? How?
18. Discuss the major characteristics of P2P.
19. Discuss some of the potential ethical and legal implications of people using P2P to download (i.e., file sharing) music, games, and so forth.
20. Discuss the relationship between P2P and KM. (Hint: See Kini 2002.)

INTERNET EXERCISES

1. Enter whitehouse.gov/government and review the "Gateway to Government." Based on the stages presented in Exhibit 8.2, what stage does this site represent? Review the available tours. Suggest ways the government could improve this portal.
2. Enter oecd.org and identify the studies conducted by the Organization for Economic Cooperation and Development (OECD) on the topic of e-government. What are the organization's major concerns?
3. Enter fcw.com and read the latest news on e-government. Identify initiatives not covered in this chapter. Check the B2G corner. Then enter gcn.com. Finally, enter estrategy.gov. Compare the information presented on the three Web sites.
4. Enter procurement.com and govexec.com. Identify recent e-procurement initiatives and summarize their unique aspects.
5. Enter doir.wa.gov.au/bus and fcw.com and find the specific G2C information provided. Prepare a list.
6. Enter pcmag.com, fortune.com, or other online versions of popular magazines. How would you compare reading the electronic magazine against the print version?
7. Enter webct.com and blackboard.com. Compare the capabilities of the two products.
8. Enter e-learningcentre.co.uk and evaluate its resources and activities.
9. Enter elearningmag.com and elearningpost.com. Identify current issues and find articles related to the effectiveness of e-training. Write a report.
10. Identify a difficult business problem. Post the problem on elance.com. Summarize the offers to solve the problem.
11. Enter knowledgeleader.com. Sign up for the free service for 30 days. Use it to prepare a report on Service-Oriented Architecture (SOA) and the Committee of Sponsoring Organizations (COSO).
12. Enter openp2p.com, centrata.com, and badblue.com and evaluate some of the solutions offered. Also, enter aberdeen.com to learn more about P2P operations.
13. Enter groove.net, netrana.com, and openp2p.com and explore the latest developments in P2P.

TEAM ASSIGNMENTS AND ROLE PLAYING

1. Assign each team to a different country. Each team will explore the e-government offerings of that country. Have each team make a presentation to convince the class that its country's offerings are the most comprehensive. (Exclude Hong Kong.)
2. Create four teams, each representing one of the following: G2C, G2B, G2E, and G2G. Each team will prepare a plan of its major activities in a small country such as Denmark, Finland, or Singapore. A fifth team will deal with the coordination and collaboration of all e-government activities in each country. Prepare a report based on the activity.
3. Have teams search for virtual universities (e.g., the University of Phoenix, uophx.edu). Write a summary of the schools' e-learning offerings.
4. Have each team represent one of the following sites: netlibrary.com, ebooks.com, and zanderebooks.com. Each team will examine the technology, legal issues, prices, and business alliances associated with its site. Each team will then prepare a report answering the question, "Will e-books succeed?"
5. Have teams investigate various homeland security activities and how they are facilitated electronically. Write a report that expands on the material in Section 8.1. Investigate several countries.

Real-World Case

E-GOVERNMENT INITIATIVES IN HONG KONG

The Hong Kong (HK) Special Administrative Region (SAR) government initiated several e-government projects under the Digital 21 IT strategy (*info.gov.hk/digital21*). The major projects of this initiative were the electronic service delivery scheme (ESD), the interactive government services directory (IGSD), the electronic tendering system (ETS), the HKSAR Government Information Center, and the HK post office certification service (Post e-Cert). The highlights of some of these initiatives are provided here. Further information can be found at the specific URLs presented at *info.gov.hk*.

The Electronic Service Delivery Scheme (ESD)

The ESD project provides a major infrastructure through which the public can transact business electronically with 38 different public services provided by 11 government agencies, as demonstrated by the following examples.

1. **Transport Department.** Applications for driving and vehicle licenses, appointments for vehicle examinations and road tests, change-of-address reports, and so forth.
2. **Immigration.** Applications for birth/death/marriage certificates, appointments for ID card issuance, applications for foreign domestic helpers, communication on any other issue concerning immigration.
3. **HK Tourist Association.** Tourism information, maps, answers to queries.
4. **Labour Department.** List of job openings, job searches for job seekers, searches for applicants by employers, FAQs regarding legal issues, information on employee-compensation plans.
5. **Social Welfare Department.** Applications for senior citizen cards and special program participation, welfare information, registration for volunteer activities, requests for charitable fund-raising permits.
6. **Inland Revenue Department.** Electronic filing of tax returns, electronic payment program, change of address forms, interactive tax Q&A, applications for sole proprietor certificates, applications for business registrations, purchase of tax reserve certificates.
7. **Registration and Electoral Office.** Applications for voter registration, change of address forms, interactive Q&A.
8. **Trade and Industry Department.** Business license information and applications, SME information center.
9. **Treasury Department.** Electronic bill payment.
10. **Rating and Valuation Department.** Changes of rates and/or government rent payers.
11. **Innovation and Technology Commission.** Information on technology funding schemes, electronic applications for funding.

These services are provided in Chinese and English. The project is managed by ESD Services Limited (*esdlife.com*). For additional information, see *esd.gov.hk*.

In addition to these services, the Web site includes eight ESD clubs, or communities. The public can sign up for a club, get information, share experiences, or just chat. The eight clubs are ESDbaby (for new parents, family planning, etc.), ESDkids (how to raise kids), ESDteens (a meeting point for the teens on music, culture, learning, etc.), ESD1822 (lifestyle, education, jobs, and so on for adults aged 18 to 22), ESDcouples (information on getting married and building a family), ESDprime (information on jobs, education, entertainment, investment, travel, for middle-aged adults, etc.), ESDsenior (health care, fitness, education, lifestyle), and ESDhospice (complete services for the end of life).

The Interactive Government Services Directory (IGSD)

IGSD is an interactive service that enables the public to access information and services not included in the ESD. For example, it includes:

- A telephone and Web site directory of public services containing information and links to hundreds of services
- An interactive investment guide offered by the Industry Department (for investing in Hong Kong)
- Interactive employment services
- Interactive road traffic information

The Electronic Tendering System (ETS)

ETS is a G2B Web site that manages the reverse auctions conducted by the government supplies department. It includes supplier registration, notification of tenders, downloading of tendering documents, interactive Q&A, submission of tender offers, and more. The HK government conducts more than 5,000 tenders a year. For more information, see *ets.com.hk*.

The HKSAR Government Information Center

The HKSAR Government Information Center is the official government Web site (*info.gov.hk*). This site enables people to view news, government notices, guides to major government services, information on leisure and cultural activities, and more.

The HK Post E-Cert

HK Post e-Cert is the home of the Hong Kong Public Certification Authority (*hongkongpost.com*). The Hong Kong Post created a PKI system (see Chapter 12) and issues digital certificates (Post e-Certs) to individuals and organizations. It also maintains a certificate repository and directory of all certificates issued, so the public can verify the validity of the certificates. Post e-Cert also issues certificates to servers and to security systems.

Accessibility to the extensive Hong Kong e-government portal is available not only from PCs, but also from hundreds of kiosks placed in many public places in Hong Kong.

For additional government activities, see Online File W8.4.

WWW

Sources: Compiled from *ESDLife.com* and *info.gov.hk/digital21* (all accessed November 2004).

Questions

1. Identify each of the five initiatives as G2C, G2B, C2G, or G2E.
2. Visit *info.gov.hk/digital21* and identify the goals of the five e-government initiatives.
3. How will the role of the HK government change when the initiatives mature and are fully utilized?
4. Compare the services offered by Hong Kong with those offered in Singapore (*ecitizen.gov.sg*). What are the major differences between the two?
5. What applications could the HK government add in the future?

REFERENCES

Aberdeen Group. *"E-Government: Mission Critical for Citizen-Centric Public."* Aberdeen Group Inc., white paper, March 2004.

Abramson, M. A., and G. E. Means (eds.). *E-Government 2001*. Lanham, MD: Rowman and Littlefield, 2001.

Agre, P. E. "P2P and the Promise of Internet Equality." *Communications of the ACM*, February 2003.

Allen, M. W. *Michael Allen's Guide to e-Learning*. Hoboken, NJ: John Wiley & Sons, 2003.

Association of American Publishers. "Year to Date Publishing Sales on Track in July Despite no Net Gains for the Month." AAP press release, September 10, 2004. **advances60.advances.net/publishers/press/releases.cfm?PressReleaseArticleID=219** (accessed December 2004).

Association for Federal Information Resources Management. "A Blueprint for Successful E-Government Implementation: Steps to Accelerate Cultural Change and Overcome Stakeholder Resistance." *Affirm.org*, June 2002. **affirm.org/Pubs/Affirm.pdf** (accessed December 2004).

Bacon, K., et al. *E-Government: The Blue Print*. New York: John Wiley & Sons, 2001.

Bausch, P., et al. *We Blog: Publishing Online with Weblogs*. Indianapolis, IN: Wiley, 2002.

Beat, F., et al. "A Proposal for a Structured Database in the Complex World of Standards: What about a Structured Single Entry Point to the Standardization World?" *Electronic Markets* 11, no. 4 (December 2001).

Blacharski, D. "Blogs as a Business Tool." *Business Insight*, September 2, 2004. **itworld.com/nl/ebus_insights/09022004/pf_index.html** (accessed March 2005).

Blackboard. **blackboard.com** (accessed December 2005).

Bose, R. "Knowledge Management Capabilities and Infrastructure for E-Commerce." *Journal of Computer Information Systems* 42, no. 5 (2002).

Botelho, G. "Online Schools Clicking with Students." CNN News, August 13, 2004. **cnn.com/2004/EDUCATION/08/13/b2s.elearning/** (accessed December 2004).

Boulton, C. "Palm Unit to Dispense E-Books from HarperCollins." *InternetNews*, November 20, 2001. **internetnews.com/ec-news/article.php/926681** (accessed March 2005).

Boxer, K. M., and B. Johnson. "How to Build an Online Center." *Training and Development* (August 2002). **doir.wa.gov.au business /** (accessed October 2002).

Chen, M., and Y. I. Liou. "Building a Knowledge-Enabled EC Environment." *Journal of Computer Information Systems* 42, no. 5 (2002).

Ciment, M. "A Personal History of the NSF Digital Government Program." *Communications of the ACM* (January 2003).

Cisco Systems. "Partner E-Learning Connection—Celebrates One Year." Cisco Partner Summit, Las Vegas, Nevada, April 2001. **cisco.com/warp/public/10/wwtraining/elearning/press/Final_PEC_release3_271.pdf** (accessed August 2002). Note: no longer available online.

Coggins, C. "Independent Testing of Voting Systems." *Communications of the ACM* 47, no. 10 (October 2004).

Corbeil, P. "One-Stop Shopping." *Journal of Housing and Community Development*, March–April 2002.

D'Agostino D. "Expertise Management: Who Knows About This?" (Expert location systems), *CIO Insight*, July 1, 2004.

Dahl, E. "Online Music: New Hits and Misses," *PCWorld*, September 2003.

Davenport, T. H., and L. Prusak. *Working Knowledge: How Organizations Manage What They Know*. Cambridge, MA: Harvard Business School Press, 2000.

Davies, N., et al. "Future Wireless Applications for a Networked City." *IEEE Wireless Communications*, February 2002.

Dean, J. "E-Gov in the Works." *GOVEXEC.com*, November 2000. **govexec.com/features/1100/egov/egovworks.htm** (accessed March 2005).

Delahoussaye, M., and R. Zemke. "About Learning Online." *Training*, September 2001.

Delphi Group. "Information Intelligence: Content Classification and the Enterprise Taxonomy Practice." *Delphi Group Report*, June 2004.

DiFranco, A., et al. "Small Vote Manipulations Can Sway Elections." *Communications of the ACM* 4, no. 10 (October 2004).

Ding, E. "Virtual Property: Treasure or Trash?" *China International Business*, September 2004.

Drummond, M. "Big Music." *Business 2.0*, December 12, 2000.

ecc.online.wa.gov.au/main/site_index.htm (accessed April 2002).

ecc.online.wa.gov.au/news (accessed April 2002).

EMarketer. "E-Learning Gains Momentum." *eMarketer.com*, July 17, 2003. **66.116.100.71/elearning_news.htm** (accessed March 2005).

eMarketer. "Blogging in Web's Footsteps." *eMarketer*, February 8, 2002a.

eMarketer. "U.S. Government Web Sites Concentrate on Security, Privacy." *eMarketer*, October 2, 2002b.

Ergonomics Today. "Study Links Long-Term Back Pain to Backpacks." *Ergonomics Today*, September 8, 2004. **ergoweb.com/news/detail.cfm?id=985** (accessed December 2004).

Fahey, L., et al. "Linking E-Business and Operating Processes: The Role of KM." *IBM Systems Journal* 40, no. 4 (2001).

Galagan, P. A. "Delta Force at Cisco." *Training and Development*, July 2002.

Garrison, D. R., and T. Anderson. *E-Learning in the 21st Century*. London: Routledge-Falmer, 2003.

Gong, L. (ed.). "Peer-to-Peer Networks in Action." *IEEE Internet Computing*, Special Issue (January–February 2002).

GovExec.com. "Digital Government: Government to Employee." *GovExec.com*, November 2000. **govexec.com/features/1100/egov/g2e.htm** (accessed June 2003).

Grace. **grace.com** (accessed December 2002).

Gwiazdowski, A. "E-Book Sales Lead Off 2003." Association of American Publishers press release, March 18, 2003. **publishers.org/press/releases.cfm?PressReleaseArticleID=138** (accessed March 2005).

Hamalainen, M., et al. "Electronic Marketing for Learning: Education Brokerages on the Internet." *Communications of the ACM* (June 1996).

Hart-Teeter, R. *E-Government: The Next American Revolution*. Washington, D.C.: Council for Excellence in Government, 2001.

Hofmann, D. W. "Internet-Based Learning in Higher Education." *Techdirections*, August 2002.

Holsapple, C. W. (ed.) *Handbook on Knowledge Management*. Heidelberg, Germany: Springer Computer Science, 2003.

Hopfner, J. "A Revolution in (Tax) Revenue." *MIS Asia* (May 2002).

info.gov.hk/digital21, student interview, February 2001 and 2002.

Intel. "Peer-to-Peer: Spreading the Computing Power." **intel.com/eBusiness/products/peertopeer/ar011102.htm** (accessed June 2002). Note: no longer available online.

International Trade Centre. "Export Development in the Digital Economy." *Executive Forum 2000*, September 2000. **tradeforum.org/news/fullstory.php/aid/215/ITC_Executive_Forum_-_Export_Development_in_the_Digital_Economy.html** (accessed March 2005).

Internetnews.com. "CommerceNet and Peer Intelligence Research P2P for Business." *SiliconValley.Internet.com*, August 17, 2001. **siliconvalley.internet.com/news/article.php/868511** (accessed July 2002).

Ipsos-Reid. "Digital Music Behavior Continues to Evolve." Ipsos-Reid, February 1, 2002. **ipsos-reid.com/pdf/publicat/docs/TEMPO_DldingPrevalence.pdf** (accessed December 2002).

Jefferson, D. "Analyzing Internet Voting Security." *Communications of the ACM* 47, no. 10 (October 2004).

Jones, D. W. "Auditing Elections." *Communications of the ACM* 47, no. 10 (October 2004).

Kapp, K. "Anytime E-Learning Takes Off in Manufacturing." *APICS* (June 2002).

Kiely, K. "Freewheeling 'Bloggers' are Rewriting Rules of Journalism." *USA Today*, December 30, 2003.

Kini, R. B. "Peer-to-Peer Technology: A Technology Reborn." *Information Systems Management* (2002).

Korolishin, J. "Sheetz Keeps Tabs on Training Compliance via Web Portal." *Stores*, February 2004a.

Korolishin, J. "Tweeter Gives Training a Tweak." *Stores*, August 2004b.

Kwok, S. H., et al. "Peer-to-Peer Technology Business and Service Models: Risks and Opportunities." *Electronic Markets* 12, no. 3 (2002).

Lai, H., and T. H. Chu. "Knowledge Management: A Review of Industrial Cases." *Journal of Computer Information Systems*, special issue 42, no. 5 (2002).

Langenbach, C., and F. Bodendorf. "The Electronic Mall: A Service Center for Distance Learning." *International Journal of Electronic Commerce*, Winter 1999–2000.

Lason Company. "Fort Knox Escrow Services—A Lason Company—Unveils Escrow Direct." Lason Company press release, March 20, 2000. **lason.com** (accessed June 2003).

Lethin, R. (ed.). "Technical and Social Components of Peer-to-Peer Computing." *Communications of the ACM* (February 2003).

Lewin, J. "Blog Risk." *E-Commerce in Action*, September 29, 2004. 66.51.97.137/2367202.txt (accessed March 2005).

Liaw, S., and H. Huang. "How Web Technology Can Facilitate Learning." *Information Systems Management*, Winter 2002.

lifelines.navy.mil (accessed December 2004).

Liu, S., and J. D. Hwang. "Challenge to Transforming IT in the U.S. Government." *IT PRO*, May–June 2003.

Mack, R., et al. "Knowledge Portals and the Emerging Digital Knowledge Workplace." *IBM Systems Journal* 40, no. 4 (2001).

Malkia, M., et al. *E-Transformation in Governance: New Directions in Government*. Hershey, PA: The Idea Group, 2004.

Marchioni, G., et al. (eds.). "Digital Government." *Communications of the ACM*, Special Issue (January 2003).

McAffee, A. "The Napsterization of B2B." *Harvard Business Review*, November–December 2000.

McGann, R. "The Blogosphere by the Numbers." Clickz.com, November 22, 2004. .clickz.com/stats/sectors/traffic_patterns/article.php/3438891 (accessed March 2005).

McKinley, E. "Multitasking Solution Ushers in New Era of Computer-based Training at Shoney's." *Stores*, April 2003.

Mello, J. P. "Survey Finds File-Sharing Networks Boost CD Buys." *TechNewsWorld*, June 17, 2004. technewsworld.com/story/34544.html (accessed January 2005).

Metz, C. "Who Owns Print-on-Demand." *PCMagazine*, March 2004.

Michael, S. "Wireless Net to Test Agencies' Mettle." *Federal Computer Week*, May 3, 2004. fcw.com/fcw/articles/2004/0503/pol-wireless-05-03-04.asp (accessed March 2005).

Miller, J. R. "Technology, Digital Citizen, and E-Government: The E-Invention Revolution." World Markets Research Center, 2000. wmrc.com/businessbriefing/pdf/wued2000/Publication/miller.pdf (accessed June 2002). Note: no longer available online.

Mucha, T. "Have Blog, Will Market." *Business 2.0*, September 30, 2004. business2.com/b2/web/articles/0,17863,703479,00.html (accessed December 2004).

Nah, F., et al. "Knowledge Management Mechanisms in E-Commerce: A Study of Online Retailing and Auction Sites." *Journal of Computer Information Systems* 42, no. 5 (2002).

Neumann, P. (ed.). "The Problems and Potentials of Electronic Voting Systems." *Communications of the ACM* (October 2004).

Ozzie, R. CEO of Groove Networks personal blog, August 24, 2002. ozzie.net/blog/2002/08/24.html.

Piccoli, G., et al. "Web-Based Virtual Learning Environments." *MIS Quarterly*. (December 2001).

Powers, S. (ed.). *Essential Blogging*. San Francisco: O'Reilly Associates, 2002.

Price, G. "Google Partners with Oxford, Harvard, and Others to Digitize Libraries." *SearchEngineWatch*, December 14, 2004. searchenginewatch.com/searchday/article.php/3447411 (accessed December 2004).

Raisch, W. D. *The eMarketplace*. New York: McGraw-Hill, 2001.

Rao, M. *Knowledge Management Tools and Techniques*. Burlington, MA: Elsevier, 2004.

Reuters (TechNews). "Kazaa Nears Download Record." *News.com*, May 22, 2003.

Roberts, M. J., and H. Stevenson. *Background Brief: The Evolving Market for Business Education (A Research Note)*. Boston: Harvard Business School Press, 2001.

Roberts-Witt, S. "A 'Eureka' Moment at Xerox." *PC Magazine*, March 26, 2002. pcmag.com/article2/0,4149,28792,00.asp (accessed August 2002).

Robinson, S. "Print-on-Demand Could Be Publishing's Future." *Interactive Week*, April 2, 2001.

Rosenthal, L. "A Pain in the Back: Backpacks Create Health Problems for Kids." *Greatschools.net*. greatschools.net/cgi-bin/showarticle/pa/256/parent (accessed 2004).

Schubert, P., and U. Hausler. "E-Government Meets E-Business: A Portal Site for Start-up Companies in Switzerland." *Proceedings 34th HICSS*, Maui, Hawaii, January 2001.

Serva, S. "P2P Collaboration Tools at Work." *Econtentmag.com*, June 1, 2004. econtentmag.com/Articles/ArticlePrint.aspx?ArticleID=6599IssueID=208 (accessed January 2005).

Shaw, M. J., et al. "Knowledge Management and Data Mining for Marketing." *Decision Support Systems*, May 2001.

Song, S. "An Internet Knowledge Sharing System." *Journal of Computer Information Systems* (Spring 2002).

Stellin, S. "Textbook Publishers Try Online Education." *The New York Times*, March 7, 2001.

Sugumaran, V. *Intelligent Support Systems Technology: Knowledge Management*. Hershey, PA: Idea Publishing Group, 2002.

Thong, J. Y. L., et al. "What Leads to User Acceptance of Digital Libraries." *Communications of the ACM*, November 2004.

Tiwana, A. *The Essential Guide to Knowledge Management: E-Business and CRM Applications*. Upper Saddle River, NJ: Prentice Hall, 2001.

Urdan, T., and C. Weggen. "Corporate E-Learning: Exploring a New Frontier." W. R. Hambrecht & Co., March 2000. digitalpipe.com/pdf/dp/white_papers/e_learning/corporate_elearning_H_Q.pdf (accessed May 2003). Note: no longer available online.

U.S. Department of Housing and Urban Development. "Electronic Government Strategic Plan: Fiscal Years 2001–2005." February 2001. hud.gov/offices/cio/egov/splan.pdf (accessed June 2003).

U.S. Government. "E-Government Strategy." Office of the President of the United States, Special Report, 2003. whitehouse.gov/omb/egov/2003egov_strat.pdf (accessed March 2005).

U.S. Office of Management and Budget. "E-Government Strategy: Delivery of Services to Citizens." OMB Internal Report, February 27, 2002.

Vise, D. A. "Google to Digitize Some Library Collections." *Washington Post*, December 14, 2004. **washingtonpost.com/wp-dyn/articles/A62251-2004 Dec13.html** (accessed December 2004).

Wang, H., and S. Wang. "Cyber Warfare: Steganography vs. Steganalysis." *Communications of the ACM*, October 2004.

Warkentin, M., et al. "Encouraging Citizen Adoption of E-Government by Building Trust." *Electronic Markets* 12, no. 3 (2002).

Weaver, P. "Preventing E-Learning Failure." *Training and Development* 56, no. 8 (2002): 45–50.

WebCT. **webct.com** (accessed December 2005).

Weidlich, T., "The Corporate Blog Is Catching On." *New York Times*, June 26, 2003.

West, D. "State and Federal E-Government in the United States, 2004." Center for Public Policy Report, September 2004. **insidepolitics.org/egovt04us.html** (accessed December 2004).

Wimmer, M. A. "Integrated Service Modeling for Online One-Stop Government." *Electronic Markets* 12, no. 3 (2002).

Wong, W. Y. *At the Dawn of E-Government*. Report, Deloitte & Touche, New York, 2000.

Xerox. "Eureka." PARC Research. **parc.com/groups/spl/projects/commknowledge/eureka.html** (accessed October 2002).

Xerox. "Knowledge Sharing for the Enterprise." *Xerox.com*, May 2002. **xerox.com/downloads/usa/en/x/xerox_digital_perspective.pdf** (accessed December 2004).

Zhang, D., and J. F. Nunamaker. "Powering E-Learning in the New Millennium: An Overview of E-Learning Enabling Technology." *Information Systems Frontiers*, April 2003.

Zhang, D., et al. "Can E-learning Replace Classroom Learning?" *Communications of the ACM*, May 2004.

Zhao, J. L., and V. H. Resh. "Internet Publishing and Transformation of Knowledge Processes." *Communications of the ACM*, December 2001.

CHAPTER 9

MOBILE COMMERCE AND PERVASIVE COMPUTING

Content

Learning Objectives

Upon completion of this chapter, you will be able to:

1. Define mobile commerce and understand its relationship to e-commerce.
2. Understand the mobile computing environment that supports m-commerce.
3. Describe the four major types of wireless telecommunications networks.
4. Discuss the value-added attributes and fundamental drivers of m-commerce.
5. Discuss m-commerce applications in finance, advertising, and provision of content.
6. Describe the application of m-commerce within organizations.
7. Understand B2B and supply chain management applications of m-commerce.
8. Describe consumer and personal applications of m-commerce.
9. Understand the technologies and potential application of location-based m-commerce.
10. Describe the major inhibitors and barriers of m-commerce.
11. Discuss the key characteristics and current uses of pervasive computing.

7-ELEVEN TRACKS INVENTORY WIRELESSLY

The Problem

Despite the origins of its name—"open from 7 A.M. until 11 P.M."—most of the 27,000 stores in the worldwide chain of 7-Eleven stores operate 24 hours per day in a unique market, one quite different from many other retailers.

One unique feature of this $36-billion retail convenience store giant is its large and varied product mix. A typical 7-Eleven carries about 2,500 different products, from gasoline and sandwiches to prepaid phone cards and money orders.

A large portion of that inventory—sandwiches, fresh food, and dairy products—is perishable, requiring constant monitoring for freshness and strategies to reduce the amount of spoilage, or goods that have to be thrown away. The amount of inventory that goes out the back door, not the front door, can have an immediate and dramatic impact on profits.

Also consider the broad demographic mix of 7-Eleven's 6 million daily customers. The 7-Eleven customer base is one of the most diversified in the retail market, cutting across all ages and income categories.

Because of its diverse customer base and neighborhood locations, 7-Eleven delegates an unusually high proportion of its purchasing decisions to the store-manager level. In some areas, customer demands vary from street to street, and management has to be responsive to this diversity.

Finally, consider the small size of each store. Despite a large and varied product mix, on-site inventory is minimal. At any point, a large proportion of 7-Eleven's inventory is on a truck somewhere on its way to a store.

The small store size also means that often there are only two or three checkout stations, or points-of-sale (POS). Because the customer expects a quick trip in and out of the store, the POS hardware and software must be fast and responsive. An inconvenient convenience store is not long for this world.

The Solution

Sherry Neal is checking the refrigerated shelves of her 7-Eleven store in Rockwall, Texas. She touches the screen of a small handheld computer and gets an instant 4-week sales history on turkey sandwiches. With a couple of keystrokes on the wireless computer, this 7-Eleven store manager places an order for the next day's supply without ever leaving the aisle.

At the same time, a dairy truck driver pulls up to another 7-Eleven store and prepares to deliver crates of milk when the store manager stops him. "Hold on a moment," the manager says, as he looks at his RFID reader. "These crates over here are bad. Sure, they're registering a good temperature now, but it looks like they were warm for 9 hours yesterday. Sorry, I won't take these three, but the others are fine. Bring them in."

The milk-delivery scenario is hypothetical, but Sherry Neal's small handheld computer is real. The technology is not yet commonplace at 7-Eleven stores, but it is possible and is being tested for widespread roll out.

Both scenarios depend on radio frequency identification (RFID) technology. A "passive" RFID tag on each sandwich contains information, such as the manufacture date, sell-by date, origin, and lot number, that was loaded onto a computer chip when the sandwich was packaged for sale. The chip and an attached antenna are sealed in a small piece of plastic about the size of a U.S. 25-cent coin. When activated by a radio wave from an RFID reader, the chip sends its information to the reader. The manager can then compare current inventory, and its freshness, with recent sales and place a new order with increased confidence. The milk-delivery scenario depends on a "smart" RFID tag that can record changing environmental conditions; however, this technology is still too expensive for widespread use.

Keith Morrow, 7-Eleven's CIO, says that his chain is very interested in RFID and that it is item-level tracking that interests him most. He says, "We want that information at a more granular level about products, especially at the food and drink level. In a perfect world, we'd be able to monitor [everything] through the life of fresh products."

But at what cost? Morrow adds that his chief worry is the pricing impact: "What would it do to the cost of a sandwich?" At today's cost per tag and reader, widespread use of RFID technology is not realistic. However, RFID costs are expected to decrease sharply between now and when per-item tracking is ready for wide-scale deployment, about a half-decade from now.

In the meantime, 7-Eleven recently signed a deal to combine its own proprietary POS software with hardware from HP, NCR, and NEC. This technology, in the process of being rolled out to its 5,300 U.S. locations, is the kind of technology that promises to change the way that convenience stores are run. It offers some of the fastest checkout speeds in the business, but it is just the beginning. Soon the company plans to test prepaid radio-frequency payment cards at stores in Texas and Florida. These cards—similar to Exxon Mobil Corp.'s Speedpass—mean even faster checkout for 7-Eleven customers.

The most visible part of 7-Eleven's *mobile commerce* future is the NEC handheld ordering device. 7-Eleven stores in Japan, licensed by 7-Eleven's parent company Ito-Yokado Co., have had a basic version of the small handheld computers for several years. However, the tool is not totally wireless—store employees still must transfer data into a networked computer in the back office before placing an order.

The Results

7-Eleven officials say that the wireless version of the handheld computer being tested by Sherry Neal will help managers do a better job of balancing inventory with demand. The device is designed to help store managers handle one of their most challenging tasks: ordering just the right amount of each item. Empty shelves mean lost sales, and getting stuck with leftovers means costly write-offs due to spoilage.

The device also must meet the special needs of retailers, who often have high employee turnover. The device has a touch screen and pictures of items, not just bar code numbers. According to Morrow, "It's got to be simple to use, reliable and rugged or it won't work in a convenience store."

The NEC handheld was tested in 10 Dallas-area stores beginning in March 2004, but is now in use only at the Rockwall store. NEC plans to make modifications based on store managers' suggestions, including adding a stylus and making the unit lighter.

Sherry Neal gives the mobile technology the big tick. "It brings the computer out here on the floor, and it saves time," Neal said. "I'm not a backroom manager. I'd rather be out front helping the customers."

Sources: Compiled from Koenig (2004) and Schuman (2004).

WHAT WE CAN LEARN . . .

7-Eleven is one of many companies that are exploring the use of mobile computing devices to better manage inventory, increase productivity, improve customer service, and raise profits. For example, Wal-Mart has an even bigger and more advanced RFID trial underway. As described in other cases in this chapter, businesses are equipping their sales forces with tablet PCs, providing mobile field service technicians with wearable computer systems, improving job dispatch for freight companies, offering customers free or low-cost wireless Internet connections, and using remote sensor networks to monitor agricultural field conditions. All of these companies, and many more, are using mobile commerce to accomplish business objectives.

The embedded nature of the RFID technology means that it is pervasive computing, a topic explored in the last section of this chapter. As in the 7-Eleven trials, pervasive computing technology is not quite ready for widespread deployment, but it is coming.

We also can learn from the bold, but cautious, approach 7-Eleven is taking to the mobile commerce future. 7-Eleven's CIO believes the company must lead the way, but not deploy untested technology, and keep a watchful eye on the technology's impact on the customer and the bottom line.

The focus of this chapter is the infrastructure, technologies, limitations, and applications of mobile commerce. We begin our exploration of this exciting topic with an examination of the technology that supports m-commerce—mobile computing.

9.1 MOBILE COMPUTING

After a brief introduction to mobile commerce, this section discusses several aspects of mobile computing: devices, hardware, software, and services. Section 9.2 describes wireless telecommunications networks. These first two sections present the technological foundations of m-commerce, as shown in Exhibit 9.1. In Section 9.3, the value-added attributes and various drivers of mobile commerce are discussed (the middle column in Exhibit 9.1). The various applications of mobile commerce are examined in Sections 9.4 through 9.9, the third column in Exhibit 9.1. Because mobile commerce is, after all, commerce, underpinning this whole discussion are management and financial considerations such as planning, implementation, cost-benefit analysis, risk assessment, profits, and much, much more, which are represented by the horizontal bar in Exhibit 9.1.

OVERVIEW OF MOBILE COMMERCE

Mobile commerce (m-commerce), also known as **m-business**, includes any business activity conducted over a wireless telecommunications network. This includes B2C and B2B commercial transactions as well as the transfer of information and services via wireless mobile devices, especially in intrabusiness. Other authors (e.g., Paavilainen 2002) make a distinction between m-commerce and m-business, defining *m-business* broadly, as we do here, but restricting *m-commerce* activities to financial transactions. However, as used in this chapter, *m-commerce* and *m-business* are any e-commerce or e-business activity conducted in a wireless environment. Like regular EC applications, m-commerce can be done via the Internet, via private communication lines, or over other computing networks.

mobile commerce (m-commerce, m-business)
Any business activity conducted over a wireless telecommunications network.

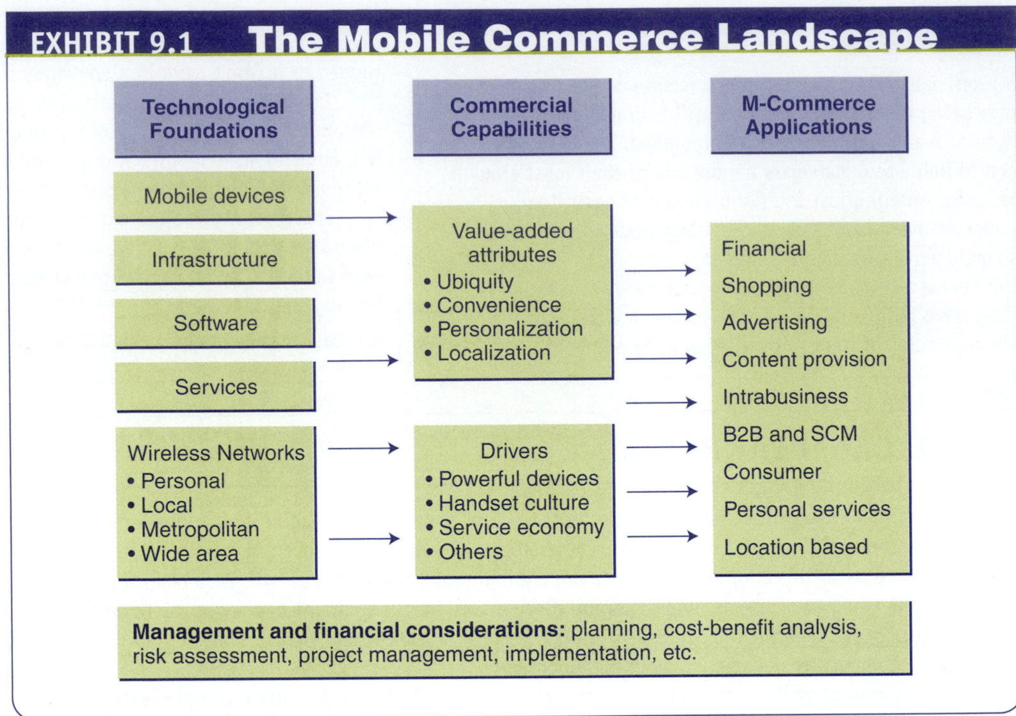

M-commerce is a natural extension of e-commerce. Mobile devices create an opportunity to deliver new services to existing customers and to attract new ones. However, the small screen size and limited bandwidth of most computing devices have limited consumer interest. So even though the mobile computing industry recognizes the potential for B2C m-commerce applications, the number of existing applications is quite small and uptake has been minimal. Instead, it is intrabusiness applications that are receiving most of the attention and that offer the best short-range benefits for businesses. Twelve categories of m-commerce applications are provided in Online Exhibit W9.1 on the book's Web site. Academic journals specializing in mobile commerce include the *International Journal of Mobile Communications* and the *International Journal of Mobile Computing and Commerce.* Online resources for monitoring the development of m-commerce include wireless.ittoolbox.com, mobileinfo.com, mobiforum.org, and mobilemediajapan.com.

An extensive discussion of mobile commerce—its attributes, drivers, applications, trends, barriers—is presented in Sections 9.4 through 9.10. First let's explore mobile computing and then move on to a description of wireless telecommunications networks (Section 9.2).

MOBILE COMPUTING DEVICES

In the traditional computing environment, users require a desktop computer, and networked computers are connected to each other, to networks, to servers, and to peripheral devices, such as printers, via wires in cables. This situation has limited the use of computers and has created difficulties for people who need to be mobile in their work. Specifically, salespeople, field service employees, law enforcement agents, inspectors, utility workers, and executives who travel frequently can be more effective if they can use information technology while at their jobs in the field or in transit. Additionally, most people want to be able to connect to the Internet or use mobile telephone services anyplace, anytime.

personal digital assistant (PDA)
A handheld computer principally used for personal information management.

smartphone
Internet-enabled cell phone that can support mobile applications.

Blackberry
A handheld device principally used for e-mail.

The first solution to meet the needs of these mobile workers was to make computers small enough so that they could be carried around easily—in other words, mobile (as shown on the vertical axis in Exhibit 9.2). The desktop computer was followed by the laptop computer, which was followed by the palmtop computer, most recently exemplified by the OQO (pronounced OH-cue-oh). Portable specialized computing devices also emerged, such as the **personal digital assistant (PDA)**, the **smartphone**, the **Blackberry**, and now the Ogo (pronounced O-Go). These devices are explained in more detail in Exhibit 9.3.

EXHIBIT 9.2 The Wireless Mobile Environment

	Wired	Wireless
Mobile	Laptop computer PDA	Cellular phone Wireless laptop or PDA Blackberry, smartphone, Ogo, etc.
Fixed	Desktop computer Landline phone Cable television	Free-to-air television Amateur radio Commercial radio

The second solution was to replace wires with wireless communication. Radios, televisions, and telephones have been wireless for a long time, so it was natural to adapt this technology to the computing environment. For more information, see *Wired* (2003).

The result is a combination of mobile and wireless solutions (upper-right quadrant in Exhibit 9.2). **Wireless mobile computing** (or just **mobile computing**) enables a real-time connection between a mobile device and computing networks or to another computing device, anytime, anywhere. Mobile computing offers a computing environment suitable for workers who travel outside the boundaries of their workplace or for anyone on the move. Salespeople are able to "close the deal" at a customer's office instead of having to say, "I'll have to check on that at the office," and perhaps lose the sale. A busy executive can receive and send e-mail during normally unproductive "dead" time in an airport lounge. A field service worker can conduct an inventory check for a faulty part, find the closest source, and arrange for delivery time of a replacement. The innovation of mobile computing is creating a revolution in the manner in which people use computers at work, home, and school and in health care, entertainment, security, and much more.

wireless mobile computing (mobile computing)
Computing that connects a mobile device to a network or another computing device, anytime, anywhere.

Other aspects of mobile computing devices include synchronization, docking stations, and attachable keyboards.

Synchronization. **Synchronization**, the exchange of updated information with other computing devices, is a requirement of any mobile computing device that stores data. Some mobile devices use wires (e.g., a USB cable, a docking station) to exchange information with other devices or the network. For example, Millstone Coffee, a U.S. distributor of roasted coffee beans, has equipped its 300 drivers with handheld devices to track inventory, generate invoices, and capture detailed sales and marketing data at each store. The devices are not wireless. Instead, drivers synchronize their handheld computers with the company's main systems at the end of the day, a process that takes only 2 minutes (Cohen 2002). Similarly, changes made to a PDA's calendar during the day need to be synchronized with the centralized office calendar. Even if a mobile device is able to make a wireless connection, it may be inconvenient or temporarily impossible for real-time updates. For example, changes in the electronic product catalog made by the home office need to be exchanged with a salesperson's tablet PC, but it is more convenient to do so when the salesperson is not actively using it.

synchronization
The exchange of updated information with other computing devices.

Docking Stations. At the end of the mobile computing day, most devices need to be plugged into a docking station or docking cradle to recharge their batteries, to connect to attachable keyboards or larger display screens, or to provide for faster synchronization, as illustrated in the Real-World Case at the end of this chapter.

Attachable Keyboards. Because of their small size, mobile devices generally use a miniature keyboard, a keypad, or a stylus-activated touch screen for data entry. These data input

EXHIBIT 9.3 Mobile Computing Devices

Mobile Device	Applications
Wireless portable computer: A laptop or notebook computer can become wireless with the addition of a wireless network card.	Full functionality of a desktop computer, including Microsoft Office, Internet connectivity, and a wide range of business applications.
Tablet PC: A favorite of salespersons and "meeting warriors"; a tablet PC typically includes a stylus, handwriting-recognition software, a virtual on-screen keyboard, and an attachable keyboard for data entry.	Full functionality of a desktop computer, including Microsoft Office, Internet connectivity, and a wide range of business applications. The Microsoft XP Tablet Edition is the most widely used tablet operating system.
Palmtop: Early palmtop computers had limited functionality and poor usability factors. The OQO features a thumb keyboard, miniature joystick mouse, thumb-wheel scroll device, a stylus-sensitive touch screen, microphone, USB port, Wi-Fi antenna, Bluetooth transmitter, and a 2-inch, 20Gb hard drive.	The OQO supports Microsoft Office, other Windows applications, and Internet connectivity. Memory-intensive programs such as desktop publishing, video editing, and 3D highly interactive games will not work well due to limited memory (256 Mb) and the small screen.
Personal digital assistant (PDA): The first handheld computing device has come a long way from its humble beginnings. Modern PDAs feature color screens, tiny keyboards, and many are mobile telephones, too. Indeed, PDAs are converging with smartphones.	Personal information management applications such as calendars, address books, and task lists. Windows Mobile offers Pocket Word and Excel and some PDAs have video and still cameras, audio notebooks, and USB, infrared, Bluetooth, and Wi-Fi connectivity.
Smartphone: All major cell phone manufacturers now make Internet-enabled cell phones. Modern smartphones, such as the Nokia 3510i, feature color screens, cameras, and innovative keyboard designs for ease of text entry.	Of course, a smartphone offers a telephone connection similar to a cell phone. Other applications include SMS (texting), Internet access, games, calendars, address books, alarm clocks, and calculators.
Blackberry: A handheld device for e-mail. A screen, tiny keyboard, and innovative interface keep office workers connected to e-mail while traveling or at leisure.	The primary application of Blackberry is e-mail. However, it also has personal information management applications (contacts, calendars, tasks) and a mobile phone. Blackberry offers an integrated user environment, no ISP is required.
Ogo: Targeted at the "thumb tribe" (younger users who use text messaging), this inexpensive handheld device just sends and receives text. Slightly larger than a cell phone, the Ogo includes a thumb keyboard and special navigation keys for messaging.	Supports instant messaging and e-mail to/from AOL, MSN, and Yahoo! Also supports SMS to/from any SMS-capable mobile phone.

solutions are not satisfactory for significant data entry tasks; many tablet PCs, smartphones, PDAs, and other mobile devices come with small keyboards that can be used at a table or desk. Attachable desktop display screens and CD-ROM drives also are available for some devices.

While the number of new mobile devices continues to expand—for example the Ogo was introduced into the market in late 2004 and is largely untested as this is being written—other devices are declining in widespread use or are converging with other devices. For example, cell phones have largely replaced interactive pagers, except in small niche markets (e.g., hospitals, emergency services). The next casualty may be the stand-alone PDA, because mobile users want portable devices that integrate cell phones, personal information management, wireless Web surfing, and streaming video and audio. Overall, PDA sales were down more than $23 billion for the 12 months ending March 30, 2004. According to Ross Rubin from NPD TechWorld, "Over time, I think the PDA just failed to establish a killer application beyond personal information management" (Diaz 2004). In the future, smartphones and PDAs are likely to converge, offering users a range of voice and data connectivity options and with a variety of software for personal information management, Office applications, and Internet access.

MOBILE COMPUTING INFRASTRUCTURE

Behind every m-commerce transaction or activity is a hardware infrastructure that supports the mobile devices just described. Some of this infrastructure (e.g., network access points, mobile communications server switches, cellular transmitters and receivers) supports the wireless connection. Other parts of this infrastructure (e.g., WAP gateway, GPS locator, GPS satellite) support delivery of services over the wireless connection. Most of these components of the mobile computing infrastructure are discussed elsewhere in this chapter in the context in which they are used.

As one would expect, other infrastructure components support m-commerce activity in the same way that they do typical e-commerce transactions. For example, a Web server, database server, and enterprise application server offer the same services to a wireless device as they do to a wired computer, with one significant exception. Certain characteristics of mobile devices—small screens, reduced memory, limited bandwidth, and restricted input capabilities—means that hardware and software designers need to anticipate special requirements and design the system accordingly. For example, a Web server may need two versions of the same Web page—a "normal" page with full graphics for desktop computers and a "mobile" page for PDAs and smartphones—as well as a way to distinguish between devices requesting the Web page.

The infrastructure to support mobile commerce is not cheap, and it is not simple to put in place. This also is a technological area that is moving very fast, with new announcements almost every week. A more extensive discussion of mobile hardware infrastructure is available in Elliott and Phillips (2004), Hansmann et al. (2003), and other mobile computing textbooks and professional books.

MOBILE COMPUTING SOFTWARE

Developing software for wireless devices is challenging for several reasons. First, there are a number of competing standards for application development on various devices. This means that software applications must be customized for each type of device with which the application may communicate. Second, software applications have to adapt to match the requirements of the device, not the other way around. Specifically, all software must deal with the technological challenges of small display screens, reduced bandwidth, limited input capabilities, and restricted memory that are common on most mobile devices. In the desktop computing world, the inability of a computer to properly load an application due to insufficient memory is solved by adding more memory. In the mobile computing world, the solution is to redesign the application.

The major software components associated with mobile computing are described in the following paragraphs.

Mobile Operating System. Microsoft, Linux, and other, more specialized, operating systems are available for most mobile devices. For example, PDA manufacturers have a choice of operating systems: Palm OS from Palm Computing, Windows CE (PocketPC) from Microsoft, and EPOC from the Symbian consortium.

Mobile Application User Interface. The interface is the application logic in a PDA, smartphone, Wintel notebook, or other device. Small handheld computing devices use a variety of interface approaches including a touch screen, mini-joystick, jog dial, and thumb wheel.

Microbrowsers. Microbrowsers, as their name implies, resemble standard Internet browsers on desktop computers and are used to access the Web. However, they have been adapted to deal with the special requirements of mobile devices, especially small screens, limited bandwidth, and minimal memory.

Wireless Application Protocol. The Wireless Application Protocol (WAP) is a suite of network protocols designed to enable different kinds of wireless devices (e.g., mobile phones, PDAs) to access WAP-readable files on an Internet-connected Web server. The central part of the WAP architecture (see Exhibit 9.4) is a WAP gateway server that sits between the mobile device and the Internet. The gateway server is responsible for translating information requests from the device into an HTTP request the Web server can understand. The server also checks ("parses") the WAP-compatible file from the Web server to ensure it is correct for

microbrowser
Wireless Web browser designed to operate with small screens and limited bandwidth and memory requirements.

Wireless Application Protocol (WAP)
A suite of network protocols designed to enable different kinds of wireless devices to access WAP-readable files on an Internet-connected Web server.

EXHIBIT 9.4 WAP Architecture

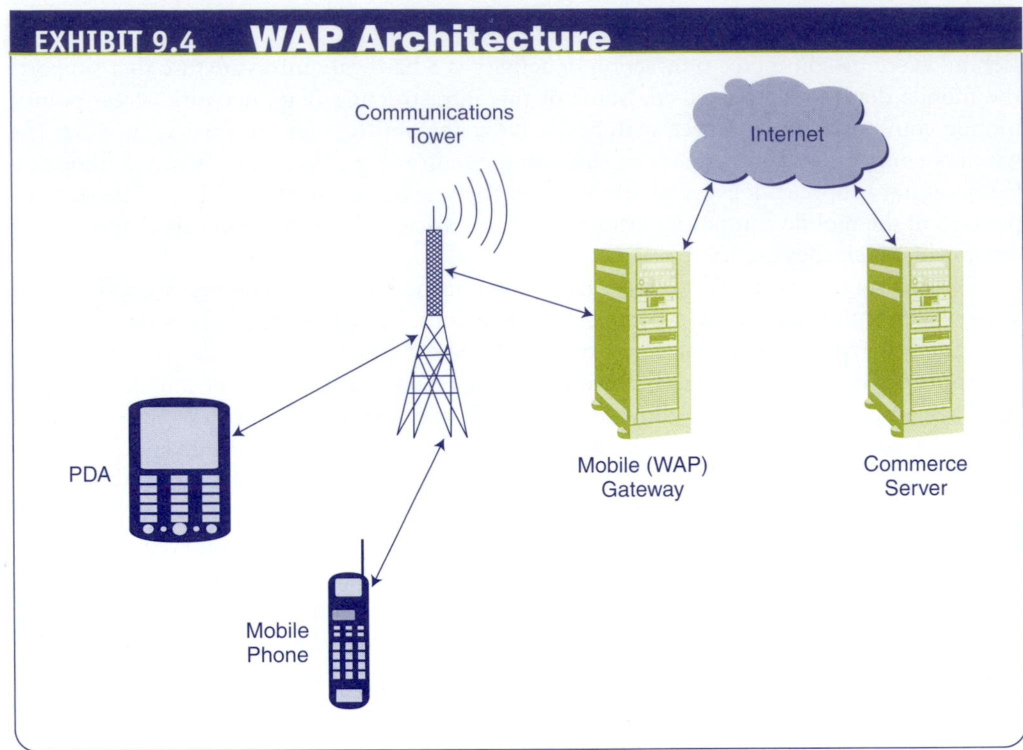

the device and then forwards the file to the device. WAP was the first standard for accessing data from the Internet, but today WAP is being challenged by several other competing standards, including Java-based applications (the J2ME platform), which offer better graphics and security.

Wireless Markup Language (WML)
A scripting language used to create content in the WAP environment; based on XML, minus unnecessary content to increase speed.

Compact Hypertext Markup Language (cHTML)
A scripting language used to create content in i-mode.

Extensible Hypertext Markup Language (xHTML)
A general scripting language; compatible with HTML; a standard set by W3 Consortium.

voice XML (VXML)
An extension of XML designed to accommodate voice.

Short Message Service (SMS)
A service that supports the sending and receiving of short text messages on mobile phones.

Markup Languages. An area of competing standards is the Internet software languages used to write applications for mobile devices. **Wireless Markup Language (WML)** is the scripting language used to create content in the WAP environment. WML is based on XML, and pages written in WML are usually abbreviated versions of their HTML counterparts, sometimes offering only the most relevant text-based content.

Compact Hypertext Markup Language (cHTML) is the scripting language used in i-mode, an extremely popular mobile Internet service that originated in Japan (i-mode is described in more detail in EC Application Case 9.1 later in this chapter).

Extensible Hypertext Markup Language (xHTML) is the most recent software language to be offered to application developers. xHTML has considerable potential, especially to replace WML, for several reasons. First, xHTML is a subset of XML, but it is compatible with HTML. This means that normal Web browsers can view pages developed in xHTML. Second, the xHTML standard has been set by the World Wide Web Consortium, the most widely recognized standards-setting organization for the Web. More than any other scripting language, xHTML represents increased compatibility between the "normal Web" and the "mobile Web." Finally, there is **voice XML (VXML)**, which is an extension of XML designed to accommodate voice.

MOBILE COMPUTING SERVICES

In a separate category all their own—software-enabled but not truly applications—are a range of mobile computing services mostly developed for mobile phones. These services fulfill the needs of mobile device users, but they also provide a foundation for supporting many applications described later in this chapter. For example, SMS is the underlying service that supports most financial applications.

Short Message Service. **Short Message Service (SMS)** is a service that supports the transmittal of short text messages (up to 160 characters) between mobile phones on a cellular telephone network. SMS is frequently referred to as *text messaging* or simply *texting*. The limited message length means users often use acronyms to convey the message in shortened text. Texting has been wildly popular in Asia and Europe for some time, and now it is increasing in popularity in the United States. In China, 550 billion text messages were sent in 2004, a figure expect to rise to 1.4 trillion messages by 2006 (*Designerz.com* 2004).

Enhanced Messaging Service. **Enhanced Messaging Service (EMS)** is an extension of SMS that can send tiny pictures, simple animations, sounds, and formatted text. EMS is sometimes referred to as *picture texting* or *pictxt*.

Enhanced Messaging Service (EMS)
An extension of SMS that can send simple animation, tiny pictures, sounds, and formatted text.

Multimedia Messaging Service. **Multimedia Messaging Service (MMS)** is the next generation of wireless messaging that will deliver rich media, including video and audio, to mobile phones and other devices. MMS enables the convergence of mobile devices and personal computers, because MMS messages can be sent between PCs, PDAs, and mobile phones that are MMS-enabled (Elliott and Phillips 2004).

Multimedia Messaging Service (MMS)
The next generation of wireless messaging; MMS will be able to deliver rich media.

Micropayments. **Micropayments**, which are electronic payments for small-purchase amounts, generally less than $10, have not become widespread in the e-commerce world, at least in part because of the relatively high cost of conducting such transactions (see Chapter 12). However, cellular telephone companies already have mechanisms for billing small amounts (e.g., send a text message for 10 cents) and charging them to the phone owner's account. Accordingly, many mobile commerce transactions may use micropayment services offered by mobile network providers. However, the provision of this service does incur an element of financial risk for the network provider. Unless a subscription revenue model is used, the cellular telephone company incurs the obligation to pay the debt without guarantee of payment from the customer. This means that the mobile telephone company acts as a bank, with much of the risk but few of the benefits or protections of a bank. Some examples of m-commerce applications that use micropayments are provided in the discussion of wireless electronic payment systems in Section 9.4.

micropayments
Electronic payments for small-purchase amounts (generally less than $10).

Location-Based Services. Another support service that can be built into many m-commerce applications, location-based services use the **global positioning system (GPS)**, a worldwide satellite-based tracking system that enables users to determine their position anywhere on the earth. This supports localization of products and services (see Section 9.3) and location-based m-commerce (see Section 9.9).

global positioning system (GPS)
A worldwide satellite-based tracking system that enables users to determine their position anywhere on the earth.

Voice-Support Services. The most natural mode of human communication is voice. Voice recognition and voice synthesization in m-commerce applications offer advantages such as hands- and eyes-free operation, better operation in dirty or moving environments, faster input (people talk about two-and-a-half times faster than they type), and ease-of-use for disabled people. Most significantly, increased use of voice-support services exploits the built-in audio capabilities of many mobile devices and reduces the device's dependence on less-than-satisfactory input solutions such as handwriting recognition, keypads, or virtual touch-screen keyboards.

Voice support applications such as **interactive voice response (IVR)** systems enable users to interact with a computerized system to request and receive information and to enter and change data using a telephone. These systems have been around since the 1980s, but are becoming more functional and widespread as artificial intelligence and voice recognition capabilities continue to improve. The highest level of voice support services is a **voice portal**, a Web site with an audio interface that can be accessed through a telephone call. A visitor requests information by speaking, and the voice portal finds the information, translates it into a computer-generated voice reply, and provides the answer by voice. For example, tellme.com and bevocal.com allow callers to request information about weather, local restaurants, current traffic, and other handy information. IVR and voice portals are likely to become important ways of delivering m-commerce services over audio-enabled computing devices.

interactive voice response (IVR)
A computer voice system that enables users to request and receive information and to enter and change data through a telephone.

voice portal
A Web site with an audio interface that can be accessed through a telephone call.

Mobile services is a rapidly developing area in mobile computing and additional services can be expected to be offered as mobile computing devices become more powerful, as increased bandwidth (e.g., 3G) becomes widespread, and as mobile commerce becomes more commonplace. In other words, "watch this space."

Section 9.1 ▶ REVIEW QUESTIONS

1. Define mobile commerce.
2. What two needs of users have propelled the development of wireless mobile devices?

3. List and describe the mobile devices used in m-commerce.
4. Define synchronization and give a business example of its use.
5. What characteristics of mobile devices influence the development of software?
6. Distinguish between WML, cHTML, and xHTML.
7. Distinguish between SMS, EMS, and MMS.

9.2 WIRELESS TELECOMMUNICATIONS NETWORKS

All mobile devices need to connect with a telecommunications network or another device. How they do this depends on the purpose of the connection, the capabilities and location of the device, and what connection options are available at the time. This section explores four levels of telecommunication networks: (a) personal area networks for device-to-device connections up to 30 feet; (b) wireless local area networks for medium-range connections, typically up to 300 feet; (c) wireless metropolitan area networks for connections up to 31 miles; and (d) wireless wide area networks for connecting to a network from anywhere with cellular phone coverage.

PERSONAL AREA NETWORKS

personal area network (PAN)
A wireless telecommunications network for device-to-device connections within a small range.

Bluetooth
A set of telecommunications standards that enables wireless devices to communicate with each other over short distances.

A good place to begin a discussion of mobile wireless networks is at the personal level. A **personal area network (PAN)** is suitable for mobile users who need to make short-range device-to-device wireless connections within a small space, typically a single room. The most common way to establish a PAN is with Bluetooth.

Bluetooth is a set of telecommunications standards that enables wireless devices to communicate with each other over short distances of up to 10 meters (30 feet). Bluetooth uses low-power radio technology in the 2.4GHz radio spectrum, and up to seven simultaneous connections can be made to link individual devices. Bluetooth operates under the IEEE (Institute of Electrical and Electronic Engineers) 802.15 standard. Bluetooth gets its curious name from the heroic tenth-century Viking king who united Denmark and conquered Norway. More information about Bluetooth technology is available from bluetooth.com.

Why would someone want to create a PAN? Suppose a mobile worker with a cell phone and a wireless laptop needs to connect to the Internet from a rural area. The laptop has a Web browser, but it is unable to connect to the Internet without a wireless network signal, which is unavailable in this remote location. The cell phone can make a dial-up connection to the Internet, but it does not have a Web browser. If both devices are Bluetooth enabled, then the worker can *pair* the devices ("introduce" one device to another through a shared profile) to establish a communication link between them. Now the mobile user can dial up an ISP on the cell phone and wirelessly pass the information to the laptop, where it is displayed on the Web browser.

Another common PAN is Bluetooth-enabled headsets that some people use with their cell phones. Once the Bluetooth-enabled headset is paired with the mobile phone, the wearer can answer a call, speak, listen, and terminate a call through the headset; the wearer can do everything except place an outgoing call (at least not until speech recognition becomes commonplace in mobile phones). The mobile phone can be on the person, in a purse, in a briefcase, in a docking station, or some other location as long as it is within Bluetooth's radio range.

Bluetooth can be used to pair a number of different devices—wireless keyboards with tablet PCs, PDAs with computers for easy data synchronization, digital cameras with printers. Bluetooth also can link more than two devices, as is done in connectBlue's (connectblue.se) operating-room control system. Equipment that monitors a patient's heartbeat, ECG, respiration, and other vital signs all can be linked via Bluetooth, eliminating obstructive and dangerous cables and increasing the portability of the equipment.

Bluetooth does have some limitations, however, other than the obvious one of its short range. First, the communication is very directional, and objects located between paired devices can interrupt the connection. Similarly, because 2.4GHz is a commonly used radio range, interference can arise from microwave ovens, cordless phones, and similar sources. Security can be a problem, too, especially if the default low-level security setting is used. Finally, first-time and infrequent users sometimes have difficulty finding the right profile and doing the necessary set-up procedures to make the initial pairing.

WIRELESS LOCAL AREA NETWORKS

In the past few years, the fastest-growing area of wireless connectivity has been in making medium-range network connections inside a building or a house. As its name implies, a **wireless local area network**, or **WLAN**, is equivalent to a wired LAN, but without the cables.

Most WLANs run on a telecommunications standard known as IEEE 802.11 or, more commonly, as **Wi-Fi** (for **wireless fidelity**). 802.11 comes in three forms:

- **802.11b** is the most widely used standard. WLANs employing this standard have communication speeds of 11 Mbps for ranges up to 100 meters (300 feet) for indoor use and up to 275 meters (900 feet) for open space or outdoor use. The 802.11b standard operates in the 2.4GHz range, and microwave ovens, cordless phones, and other devices using this same range can cause interference.
- **802.11a**, which was issued at the same time as 802.11b, offers faster transfer rates (54 Mbps) but a weaker signal range (maximum of 25 meters or 82 feet).
- **802.11g** is a newer standard that attempts to combine the best of both of the other standards. 802.11g offers the high transfer rate (54 Mbps) of 802.11a, a strong signal range like 802.11b, and is backwards compatible with 802.11b. However, few mobile devices can utilize the higher transfer rate and 802.11g is more expensive.

Increasingly, 802.11g is being used in commercial environments where cost is not a major issue and where laptop computers can take advantage of the 54 Mbps transfer rate. 802.11b remains the Wi-Fi standard of choice for inexpensive installations in most public areas and homes.

A standard currently under development, 802.11n, promises bandwidth transfer rates 10 to 20 times greater than current standards. Although currently not very practical because it exceeds the limits of most broadband connections used by homes and businesses, as Internet connections move from cable or DSL to fiber-optic cables, the need for Wi-Fi connections at these high speeds will grow (Asaravala 2004).

Physically, the heart of a WLAN is a **wireless access point** that connects wireless devices to the desired network (see Exhibit 9.5). The access point is analogous to the network cable plugged into a desktop computer, but without the wires. On the back end, the wireless access point makes a wired connection to the Internet, an intranet, or any other network in the same manner as a wired LAN cable. Mobile devices send and receive signals from the access point via a wireless network card, installed by the user or built into the device by the manufacturer.

WLANs provide fast and easy Internet or intranet broadband access from public **hotspots** located in airports, hotels, restaurants, and conference centers. Eating establishments, including many Starbucks and McDonald's restaurants, offer connectivity for little or no additional cost if a meal is purchased. Hotels from the high-class Marriott chain to the budget-traveler-oriented Red Roof Inns are installing hotspots throughout their premises. WLANs are being used in universities to allow students to make Internet connections from the classroom and the cafeteria. Airports and airlines are providing travelers with wireless connections, usually for a small charge, as explained in Insights and Additions 9.1. Web sites such as wi-fihotspotlist.com and hotspot-locations.com allow travelers to locate free or paid public hotspots from which they can make a wireless Internet connection.

Wi-Fi is becoming a useful business tool, too. Ticket sellers at Universal Studios in Hollywood use Wi-Fi-enabled devices and belt-mounted printers to sell tickets and access information for customers (Scanlon 2003). CVS Corporation, the largest retail pharmacy in the United States, uses Wi-Fi-based devices throughout its 4,100 stores to support direct store delivery, price management, inventory control, and receiving. Benefits include faster transfer rates, increased productivity and performance, reduced costs, and improved customer service (Symbol 2004). A California vineyard is using Wi-Fi to monitor field conditions (see EC Application Case 9.3 later in this chapter).

Wi-Fi has residential applications, too. Many homeowners install a WLAN to enable Internet connectivity throughout their home without the need to retrofit the house with cables. However, security is sometimes lacking in these residential installations. Unprotected

wireless local area network (WLAN)
A telecommunications network that enables users to make medium-range wireless connections to the Internet or another network.

Wi-Fi (wireless fidelity)
The common name used to describe the IEEE 802.11 standard used on most WLANs.

802.11b
The most popular Wi-Fi standard; it is inexpensive and offers sufficient speed for most devices; however, interference can be a problem.

802.11a
This Wi-Fi standard is faster than 802.11b but has a smaller range.

802.11g
This fast but expensive Wi-Fi standard is mostly used in businesses.

wireless access point
An antenna that connects a mobile device to a wired LAN.

hotspot
An area or point where a wireless laptop or PDA can make a connection to a wireless local area network.

EXHIBIT 9.5 How Wi-Fi Works

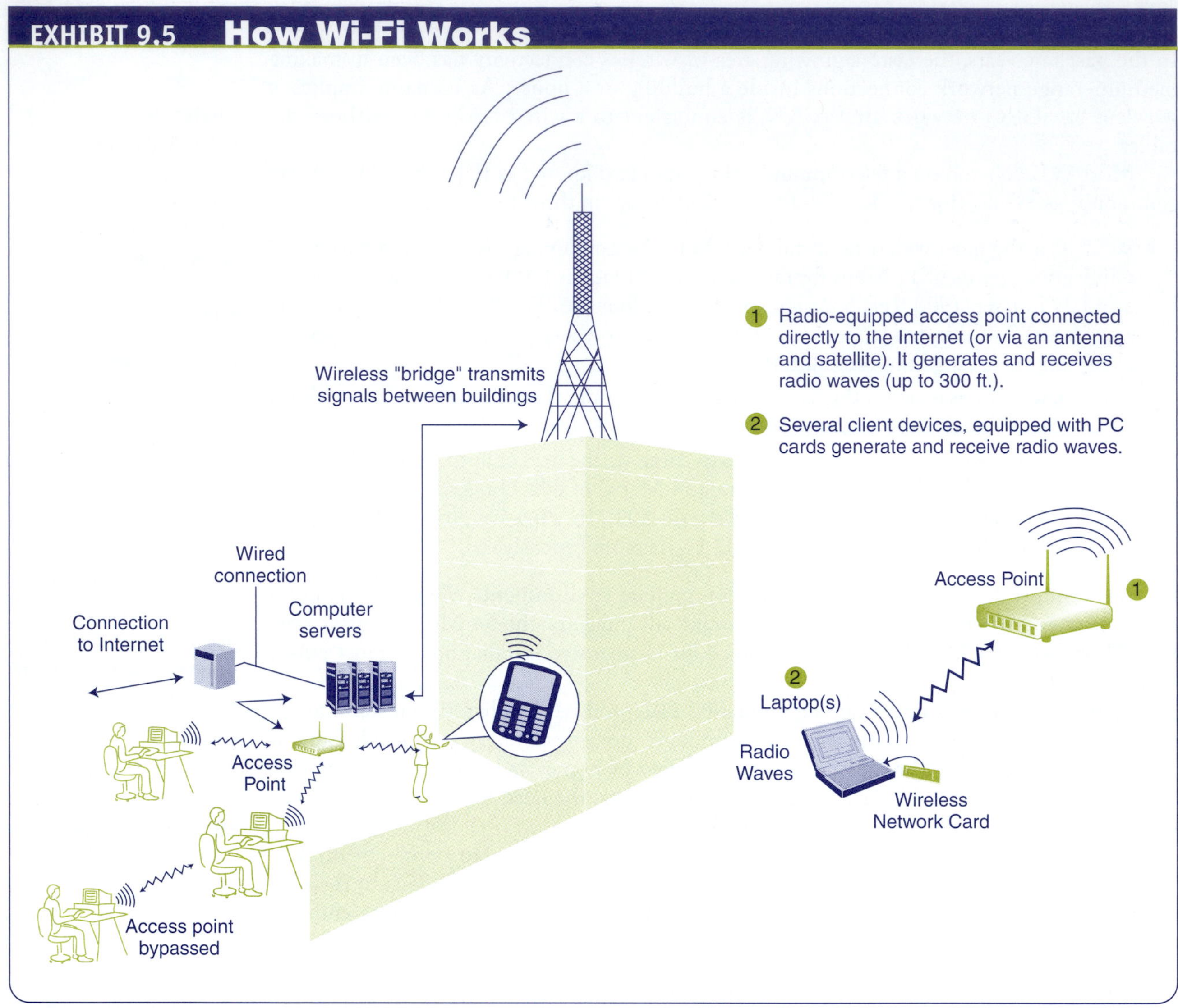

WLANs in homes and small businesses can be discovered via *war driving*, with unanticipated consequences for the homeowner (see Insights and Additions 9.2).

One wireless access point or hotspot can provide service to a number of users within a small geographical area. Several wireless access points can be used to support a larger number of users across a larger geographical area. Multiple hotspots can operate simultaneously in any given area, providing overlapping coverage. The hotspots do not interfere with each other as long as they are operating on different radio channels.

WIRELESS METROPOLITAN AREA NETWORKS

One obvious limitation of wireless local area networks is the word *local*. A nomadic worker traveling around a city will always have to search for another hotspot to make an Internet connection. Municipal governments have recognized this limitation and, wanting to promote an image of being a "wired town" or "connected city," many have encouraged or sponsored widespread distribution of hotspots. For example, in Wellington, New Zealand, CityLink has installed over 90 hotspots in the city's central business district (see cafenet.co.nz). American cities with widespread Wi-Fi initiatives underway include New York City (where wireless access points would be placed on top of 18,000 lampposts), Philadelphia, San Francisco, Cleveland, and Corpus Christi (SiliconValley.com 2004). Chaska, Minnesota, too, has plans to provide inexpensive, widespread Wi-Fi service to its 18,000 residents. However, one industry expert has questioned the initiative. According to

Insights and Additions 9.1 Wi-Fi Takes Off

Perhaps nowhere else in the world is there a more compelling case for Wi-Fi connectivity than in air travel. Airports and airplanes are the places that travelers are most likely to have spare time on their hands. Business travelers are keen to make productive use of this "dead" time by answering e-mail or conducting business research on the Web. Recreational travelers frequently want to send e-mail to or read e-mail from friends and family, catch up with fellow travelers through instant messaging, or investigate activities at their next destination. Both types of travelers may need to book accommodations, alert contacts at their destination of expected arrival times, or reserve taxis or shuttles.

The air transport industry knows this, and Wi-Fi is taking off in airports around the world. According to a report by IT-industry research firm IDC, Wi-Fi hotspots will more than double at American airports in 2004 and will nearly triple again by 2008, exceeding the growth rate at hotels, cafes, and restaurants (Levere 2004).

Not only is the number of airport-based hotspots increasing faster than in other locations, but the number of users using Wi-Fi is expected to grow faster because of the nature of the target audience—travelers need Internet connectivity more than restaurant patrons or hotel visitors.

Airport hotspots are being installed in a number of ways. Terminal-wide access is available at airports in Austin, Texas; Kansas City, Missouri; and San Francisco, California. Access is restricted to certain terminals or gate areas at airports such as Kennedy and La Guardia in New York City and Newark Liberty in Newark, New Jersey. In other airports, airport authorities have left it to restaurants (e.g., McDonald's) or airlines to offer Wi-Fi services to their customers.

Wi-Fi access usually is free in the business-class lounges of all major airlines. However, most airport authorities, restaurants, and airlines view Wi-Fi access as something travelers are willing to pay for and charge for it. Rates usually are set by the Wi-Fi provider (e.g., T-Mobile, Wayport) and tend to be $7 to $10 per day or $20 to $40 per month (Levere 2004).

Of course, another source of unproductive travel time is in the airplane itself, and Wi-Fi is taking off into the skies as well. Lufthansa offers in-flight Wi-Fi service on its long-haul fleet. The hotspots are connected to the Internet via satellites and the user pays $25 or $35 to use the service (Fleishman 2003).

Sources: Levere (2004) and Fleishman (2003).

Derek Kerton, using a series of overlapping Wi-Fi hotspots for broad coverage is like "using a hammer to drive in a screw. You can do it, but wouldn't it be better if you found a better tool?" (Ojeda-Zapata 2004).

That better tool could be WiMax. **WiMax** (Worldwide Interoperability for Microwave Access), is a wireless standard (IEEE 802.16) for making broadband network access widely available over a large area of up to 50 kilometers (31 miles). WiMax, which is a technology for **wireless metropolitan area networks (WMAN)**, is under development as this is being written; it is scheduled for release in 2005.

WiMax
A wireless standard (IEEE 802.16) for making broadband network connections over a large area.

wireless metropolitan area network (WMAN)
A telecommunications network that enables users to make long-range wireless connections to the Internet or another network.

WiMax uses the same technology as Wi-Fi, but its potential is more like the fast data communications services being developed by cell phone companies. WiMax uses a radio-based, ultrawide bandwidth, offering normal data transfer speeds of 70 Mbps and peaks of up to 268 Mbps. The first phase of WiMax, planned for 2005, is the installation and support of fixed rooftop antennas. The second phase, planned for 2006, is the rollout of indoor antennas, greatly reducing installation costs. The third phase, planned for 2007, moves wireless connectivity down to mobile devices such as notebooks, PDAs, and 3G phones, allowing connectivity anywhere within range of an antenna. Intel expects to integrate WiMax into its Centrino wireless chip beginning in late 2006 (Dekleva 2004).

Despite its designation for use in WMANs, WiMax's biggest impact may not be in cities. In large markets with crowded airwaves, a WiMax service would have to use a costly spectrum. Competition from mobile telephone carriers and Wi-Fi also may tend to blunt its impact. Instead, WiMax seems ideal for the delivery of high broadband speeds to rural areas of the United States and other developed countries and to cities and towns in developing countries without a mature communications infrastructure (Davidson 2004).

WiMax is still an evolving telecommunications standard, and its eventual impact on m-commerce is speculative. As with other aspects of rapidly developing wireless technologies, the only sure thing that can be said is "watch this space."

Insights and Additions 9.2 War Driving and War Chalking

Why would anyone pay $8 a day or $30 a month for Wi-Fi access when it is readily available in many locations for free? Because it is relatively inexpensive to set up a wireless access point that is connected to the Internet, a number of businesses offer customers Wi-Fi access without charging them for the service (Richtel 2004). In fact, one organization, FreeNetworks.org (*freenetworks.org*) was founded to support the creation of free community wireless network projects around the globe.

In other cases, spillover signals and poor security measures allow users to surreptitiously make a connection to a WLAN. How? First, to ensure adequate coverage throughout a building or home, a strong signal strength may be set. For example, if a wireless access point is installed in the front of a home, and the signal range is set to reach upper bedrooms and the back yard, the signal will also be detectable from the street. Second, although Wi-Fi does have a built-in security system known as Wireless Encryption Protocol (WEP), many small business owners and homeowners with WLANs never turn it on. Similarly, for their own convenience or via an oversight, many WLAN owners do not employ password protection. As a result, they sponsor an open and free network connection to anyone who happens by with a wireless device that can pick up the signal.

Knowing this, a small number of people have made a hobby out of war driving. *War driving* is the act of locating open (unsecured) WLANs while driving around a city or other geographic area (see *wardriving.com*). To war drive, a person needs a vehicle, a computer or PDA with a wireless card running in promiscuous mode, software that will probe for access points, and an antenna that can be mounted on top of or positioned inside the car. A knowledgeable war driver is able to detect a signal, intrude into the network, obtain a free Internet connection, and possibly gain access to important data and other resources. The term *war driving* is derived from the term *war dialing,* a technique in which a hacker programs his or her computer to call hundreds of phone numbers until a modem answers, which indicates a dial-up connection to a computer. War dialing is demonstrated in the movie *War Games,* which features Matthew Broderick performing the technique.

A related practice is *war chalking.* Once an open Wi-Fi connection is found, it can be identified by symbols on a sidewalk or wall to indicate nearby wireless access. The term war chalking was inspired by the practice of hobos during the Great Depression who used chalk marks to indicate which homes offered food or shelter.

One of the primary aims of people engaged in war driving is to highlight the lax security of Wi-Fi-based networks. This motivation seems warranted. In November 2003, Toronto police investigated a parked car and found that the driver was naked from the waist down with a laptop computer on the front seat, playing a child pornography video that was being streamed from an insecure residential hotspot. An attorney speculated that if homeowners are negligent in setting up proper security, they could be held accountable for activities carried out on their networks, including criminal activities such as launching spam, distributing viruses, stealing data, or downloading child pornography (Shim 2003).

Sources: Richtel (2004) and Shim (2003).

WIRELESS WIDE AREA NETWORKS

The broadest wireless coverage is offered by the world's most well-established wireless communications network—cellular networks operated by telecommunications companies. A **wireless wide area network (WWAN)** offers widespread wireless coverage over a large geographical area. Most WWANs are cellular phone networks.

wireless wide area network (WWAN)
A telecommunications network that offers wireless coverage over a large geographical area, typically over a cellular phone network.

subscriber identification module (SIM) card
An extractable storage card used for identification, customer location information, transaction processing, secure communications, and the like.

Physical Topology of a WWAN

A WWAN achieves its widespread coverage though a set of overlapping cells that collectively form a cell cluster (see Exhibit 9.6). At the center of each cell is a base station transceiver or cell tower that is used to send and receive signals to and from mobile devices operating within the cell. These signals are, in turn, communicated to a base station controller (BSC) that is connected to a mobile switching center (MSC) that is connected to the land-based public switched telephone network.

A unique feature of a WWAN is how the mobile switching station tracks a cellular phone user as the user moves from cell to cell. When a device is turned on, a **subscriber identification module (SIM) card** inside the device identifies itself to the network. This SIM card is an extractable memory storage card that is used for identification, customer location information, transaction processing, secure communications, and the like. A SIM card also makes it possible for a handset owner to change phone numbers.

EXHIBIT 9.6 Cellular Telephone Network

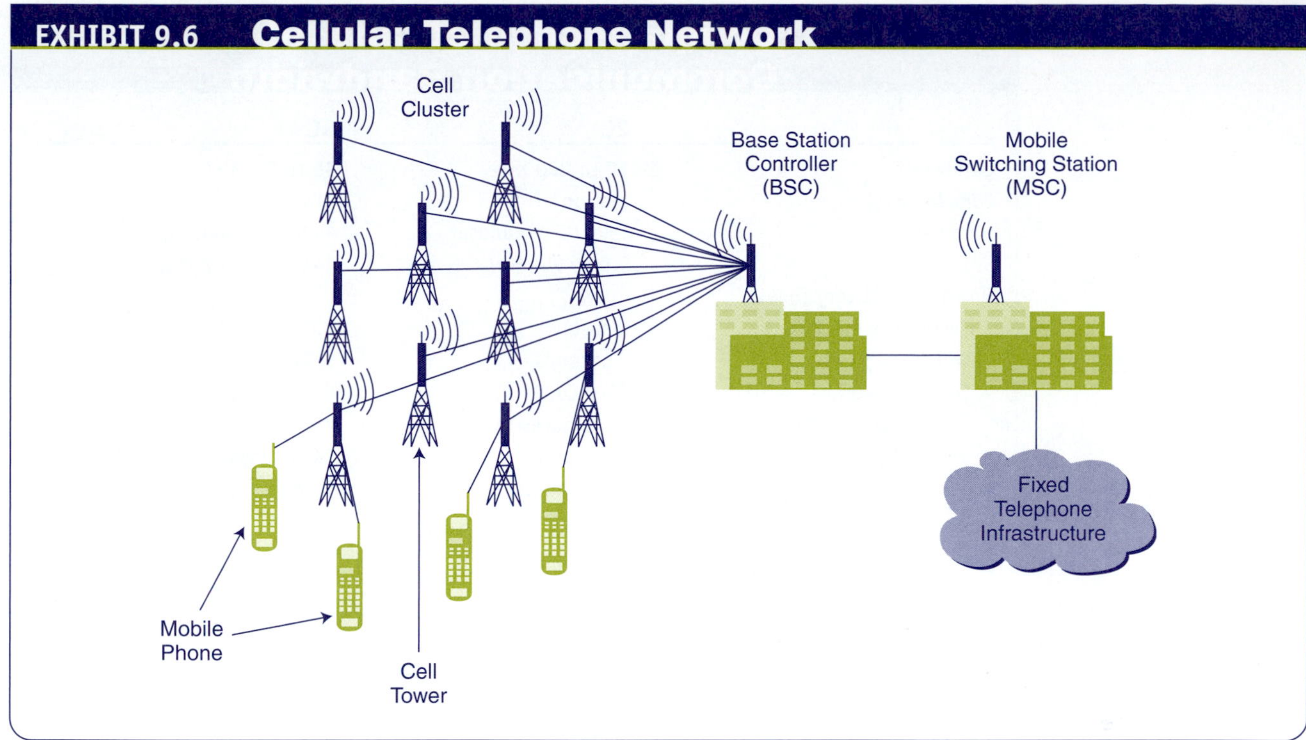

As the mobile phone user changes physical location, the "mobility management protocol" in the mobile switching station directs each base station controller to make the handoff from one transceiver to the next as the user moves from cell to cell and cell cluster to cell cluster.

The size of a cell is determined by the number of objects that may interfere with the signal and the traffic volume. For both of these reasons, a cell in a dense urban area is likely to be small, perhaps a few hundred feet wide, whereas a cell in a rural area may be over 6 miles (10 kilometers) in size.

WWAN Communication Bandwidths

All WWANs are not equal. Currently, four generations of communications technology can be distinguished:

- **1G.** The first generation of wireless technology. It was an analog-based technology in effect from 1979 to 1992 and was used exclusively for voice.
- **2G.** This second generation of digital wireless technology is in widespread existence today. 2G is based on digital radio technology and is able to accommodate text messages (SMS).
- **2.5G.** An interim technology based on new cell phone protocols such as GPRS (General Packet Radio Service) and CDMA2000 (Code Division Multiple Access). This generation can communicate limited graphics, such as in picture text messages (EMS).
- **3G.** The third generation of digital wireless technology, which will support rich media such as video. 3G utilizes packet switching in the high 15 to 20 MHz range. 3G started in Japan in 2001, reached Europe in 2002, and the United States and much of Asia in 2003. As of 2004, the number of 3G-enabled devices was only a tiny fraction of the cell phone market. However, sales are projected to increase gradually as more 3G networks and applications become available. IT research firm IDC projects annual sales of 3G handsets will reach 100 million by 2007 (Sharma 2004).
- **4G.** The expected next generation after 3G. The arrival of 4G, which will provide faster display of multimedia, is expected between 2006 and 2010.

Exhibit 9.7 compares 2G and 3G on a number of important variables. Of most interest for m-commerce are the faster download speeds and the extension of cellular connectivity to mobile devices other than phones.

1G
The first generation of wireless technology, which was analog based.

2G
The second generation of digital wireless technology; accommodates voice and text.

2.5G
An interim wireless technology that can accommodate voice, text, and limited graphics.

3G
The third generation of digital wireless technology; supports rich media such as video.

4G
The expected next generation of wireless technology that will provide faster display of multimedia.

EXHIBIT 9.7 Comparison of 2G and 3G Communication Bandwidth

	2G	3G
Bandwidth	30 to 200 KHz	15 to 20 MHz
Connectivity	Dial up	Always on
Hardware	Telephone handset	Mobile computing device
Speed	9.6 to 384 Kbps	144 Kbps to 2 Mbps
Download delivery times:		
E-mail file (10 Kb)	8 seconds	0.04 second
Web page (9 Kb)	9 seconds	0.04 second
Text file (40 Kb)	33 seconds	0.2 second
Large report (2 Mb)	28 minutes	7 seconds
Video clip (4 Mb)	48 minutes	14 seconds
TV quality movie (6 Gb)	1,100 hours	5 hours (approximately)

Sources: Hansmann et al. (2003), p. 278; Burkhardt et al. (2002), p. 94.

In addition to the high data transmission rates illustrated in Exhibit 9.7, all 3G networks aim to offer efficient spectrum utilization (see communication protocols immediately below) and worldwide connectivity or global roaming (see network systems below). These benefits come at a cost, however. A fairly complete new infrastructure has to be built on top of the existing one, and telecommunications providers have already paid high prices for 3G frequencies in frenzied auctions at the height of the dot-com boom. The rollout of 3G has been slow, and large profits remain uncertain. However, the potential is there for 3G to change the way mobile devices are used and dramatically increase m-commerce applications and activities.

WWAN Communication Protocols

A second way WWANs differ is in the communication protocols they use. These multiplexing communication protocols are used to provide service to large numbers of users with limited communication bandwidth. In today's mobile world, there are three main multiplexing protocols:

- **Frequency Division Multiple Access (FDMA).** This protocol divides the available bandwidth into different frequency channels, and each device is given its own frequency on which to operate. Although easy to implement and necessary in the circuit-switched analog world of 1G, it is terribly wasteful of limited bandwidth.
- **Time Division Multiple Access (TDMA).** Widely used in 2G networks, TDMA assigns different users different time slots on a communications channel (e.g., every one-eighth time slot). TDMA is sometimes used in conjunction with FDMA; the available bandwidth is divided into frequencies and each frequency is divided into time slots.
- **Code Division Multiple Access (CDMA).** Designed for 3G networks, this protocol divides data into small packets that are distributed across the frequency spectrum in a set pattern. CDMA is very reliable and efficient (Hansmann et al. 2003).

Even more advanced communications protocols, such as orthogonal frequency-division multiplexing (OFDM), are under development.

WWAN Network Systems

A third way WWANs differ is in the network standards they use. These competing standards resulted from the simultaneous development of cellular networks in different countries (e.g., Global System for Mobile Communications [GSM] in Europe, Personal Digital Cellular [PDC] in Japan, both IS-95 and IS-136 in the United States). The differences among these systems have been the primary cause for incompatibility of handsets between different countries, and even within countries, in the first decade of cellular networks.

Global System for Mobile Communications (GSM)
An open, nonproprietary standard for mobile voice and data communications.

The **Global System for Mobile Communications (GSM)** has emerged as the most popular standard, currently in use in over 170 countries and with 72 percent of the world's mobile market (Yapp 2004). GSM's popularity is likely to grow further as, according to the GSM Association, 85 percent of the world's mobile network operators have chosen 3GSM for delivery of 3G services (*GSM World* 2004). To learn more about GSM, visit gsmworld.com.

This concludes our overview of the technological foundations upon which mobile commerce is based. Mobile computing—devices, infrastructure, software, and services—and wireless telecommunications networks—personal, local, metropolitan, and wide area—have been presented and discussed. These two sections explored the *mobile* part of mobile commerce. Next we turn our attention to an in-depth exploration of the *commerce* aspect.

Section 9.2 ▶ REVIEW QUESTIONS

1. Describe a scenario in which Bluetooth might be used.
2. List the distinguishing characteristics of each of the three Wi-Fi standards.
3. What is war driving? List at least two reasons why someone would war drive.
4. What distinguishes WiMax from the other telecommunication networks discussed in this section?
5. Define 3G and list some potential uses of 3G technology.

9.3 MOBILE COMMERCE

At the beginning of this chapter, *mobile commerce (m-commerce)* was defined as any business activity conducted over a wireless telecommunications network. This section begins our in-depth examination of mobile commerce by defining value-added attributes and identifying the various drivers of m-commerce. Then the next six sections will describe m-commerce applications in a number of diverse categories.

ATTRIBUTES OF M-COMMERCE

Generally speaking, many of the EC applications described in this book also apply to m-commerce. For example, online shopping, Internet banking, e-stock trading, and online gambling are gaining popularity in wireless B2C. Auction sites are starting to use m-commerce (e.g., sending a text-message alert when an auction is about to close) and wireless collaborative commerce in B2B EC is emerging. The major attributes described here offer the opportunity for development of new applications that are possible only in the mobile environment.

Ubiquity. *Ubiquity* means being available at any location at any time. A wireless mobile device such as a smartphone or tablet PC can deliver information when it is needed, regardless of the user's location. Ubiquity creates easier information access in a real-time environment, which is highly valued in today's business and consumer markets.

Convenience. It is very convenient for users to operate in the wireless computing environment. Mobile computing devices are increasing in functionality and usability while remaining the same size or becoming smaller. Unlike traditional computers, mobile devices are portable, can be set in a variety of monitoring modes, and most feature instant connectivity (i.e., no need to wait for the device to boot up). Mobile devices enable users to connect easily and quickly to the Internet, intranets, other mobile devices, and online databases. Thus, the new wireless devices could become the most convenient, preferred way to access many forms of information.

Interactivity. In comparison with the desktop computing environment, transactions, communications, and service provision are immediate and highly interactive in the mobile computing environment. Businesses in which customer support and delivery of services require a high level of interactivity with the customer are likely to find a high value-added component in mobile computing.

Personalization. Mobile devices are truly personal computing devices. Whereas a computer in a home, library, or Internet café may be used by a number of people, mobile devices are almost always owned and operated by a single individual. This enables consumer personalization—the delivery of information, products, and services designed to meet the needs of individual consumers. For example, a user planning a trip can be sent travel-related information for retrieval when and where they want. Consumer personalization applications on mobile devices are still limited. However, the personal nature of the computing device, the increasing availability of personalized services, and transaction feasibility via mobile portals means that the mobile computing device could become the primary EC tool for delivering personalized information, products, and services.

Localization. Knowing where a user is physically located at any particular moment is key to offering relevant services (Clarke 2001). Such services are known as location-based m-commerce (see Section 9.9). Localization may be general; for example, targeting everyone in a certain location (e.g., all shoppers at a shopping mall). Or, even better, it may be targeted so that users get messages that depend both on where they are and what their preferences are, thus combining personalization and localization. For instance, if it is known that a person likes Italian food and that person is strolling in a mall that has an Italian restaurant, the device owner could receive a text message that displays the restaurant's menu offerings and offers a 10 percent discount.

Vendors and carriers can differentiate themselves in the competitive marketplace by offering new, exciting, and useful services based on these attributes. These value-adding attributes can be the basis for businesses to better deliver the value proposition they offer to customers. The services these attributes represent will help e-businesses attract and keep customers and grow their revenues.

DRIVERS OF M-COMMERCE

In addition to the value-added attributes just discussed, the development of m-commerce is being driven by the following technological, business, social, and economic factors.

Widespread Availability of More Powerful Devices. As of the end of 2004, the number of cell phones throughout the world exceeded 1.5 billion (*CellularOnline* 2004). In 120 countries, the number of mobile phones exceeds the number of landline phones (Yapp 2004), and total worldwide mobile phone ownership may top 2 billion by 2006 (*The Age* 2004b). These devices are increasing in power, functionality, and features (e.g., color screens, GPS locators, Internet access) that support m-commerce. Thus, a potential mass market for conducting m-commerce is emerging.

The Handset Culture. A closely related driver is the widespread use of cell phones among the 15- to 25-year-old age group. These users will constitute a major market of online buyers once they begin to make and spend reasonable amounts of money.

The Service Economy. The transition from a manufacturing to a service-based economy is encouraging the development of mobile-based services, especially when customer service is a differentiator in highly competitive industries. Time-starved but resource-rich individuals will pay for mobile services that perform a range of tasks at their convenience (McKay and Marshall 2004).

Vendor's Push. Both mobile communication network operators and manufacturers of mobile devices are advertising the many potential applications of m-commerce so that they can push new technologies, products, and services to buyers. The advertising expenditure by these companies to encourage businesses to "go mobile" or "mobilize your business" is huge.

The Mobile Workforce. Some workers, such as salespeople and field service employees, have always worked away from an office. Increasingly, other sectors of the workforce also are "going mobile." This is being driven by social work trends such as telecommuting, employers' concerns about security, employees' desires for improved work–life balance, and a general questioning of where knowledge workers need to be located to conduct their work.

Increased Mobility. The most widely recognized benefit of increased mobility is the productive use of travel time. Workers who commute long distances, and especially executives who travel frequently, want to make more productive use of time they spend in public transportation vehicles or in airport lounges. However, there also are spatial, temporal, and contextual aspects of increased mobility that introduce business and personal benefits (Kakihara and Sorensen 2002).

Improved Price/Performance. The price of wireless devices and the per-minute pricing of mobile services continues to decline even as available services and functionality are increasing. This is leading to improvements in the price/performance ratio. This is enticing new owners into the market and encouraging existing owners to increase consumption of services and to upgrade their handsets.

Improvement of Bandwidth. To properly conduct m-commerce, it is necessary to have sufficient bandwidth to transmit the desired information via text, picture, voice, video, or multimedia. The 3G communications technology is expected to provide that at a data rate of up to 2 Mbps.

Section 9.3 ▶ REVIEW QUESTIONS

1. Briefly describe the value-added attributes of m-commerce.
2. List eight major drivers of m-commerce.

9.4 MOBILE FINANCIAL APPLICATIONS

Most mobile financial applications are simply a mobile version of their wireline counterparts, but they have the potential to turn a mobile device into a business tool, replacing banks, ATMs, and credit cards by letting a user conduct financial transactions with a mobile device, anytime, anywhere. In this section, we will look at some of the most popular mobile applications in financial services.

MOBILE BANKING

Throughout Europe, the United States, and Asia, an increasing percentage of banks are offering mobile access to financial and account information. For instance, Merita Bank in Sweden pioneered many services (Sadeh 2002), and Citibank in the United States has a diversified mobile banking service. Customers of such banks can use their mobile handsets to access account balances, pay bills, and transfer funds using SMS. The Royal Bank of Scotland, for example, uses a mobile payment service (Lipset 2002), and Banamex, one of Mexico's largest banks, is a strong provider of wireless services to customers. Many banks in Japan allow for all banking transactions to be done via cell phone (Scornavacca and Barnes 2004). A study of banks in Germany, Switzerland, and Austria found that over 60 percent offered some form of mobile financial service (Hornberger and Kehlenbeck 2002). Of special interest to banking customers are financial-alert applications (e.g., a loan payment is due, a scheduled rental payment has not been made, a bank balance has fallen below a specified amount).

To date, though, the uptake of mobile banking has been minimal. However, surveys indicate a strong latent demand for these offerings; customers may be waiting for the technology and transmission speeds to improve. The same can be said for other mobile financial applications, such as mobile brokering, insurance, and stock market trades.

WIRELESS ELECTRONIC PAYMENT SYSTEMS

Wireless payment systems transform mobile phones into secure, self-contained purchasing tools capable of instantly authorizing payments over the cellular network. In the United States, for example, Cellbucks offers a mobile payment service that enables fans at participating sports stadiums to purchase food, beverages, and merchandise by cell phone and have it delivered to their seats. Any fan who is a member of the Cellbucks Network can dial a toll-free number, enter his or her pass code and seat location, and then select numbered items that correspond to desired menu selections. Once authorized, the purchase request is passed on to stadium personnel who prepare the food and deliver it to the fan's seat. An e-mail detailing the transaction is sent to the fan as further confirmation of the order. In Europe and Japan, using wireless technology to buy tickets to movies and other events is popular (Sadeh 2002).

In Frankfurt, Germany, people can use cell phones to pay for taxi rides. In Japan and Israel, people can purchase drinks from vending machines with their mobile phones. In Italy and New Zealand, cell phones can be used to pay for time on parking meters (DPS-Promatic 2002; Synergy 2004). As discussed earlier in this chapter, these micropayments are likely to become one of the most popular support services for m-commerce applications. An A. T. Kearney study (*ClickZ Stats* 2002) found that more than 40 percent of mobile phone users surveyed would like to use their mobile phone for small cash transactions, such as transit fares or vending machines. The desire for such services was highest in Japan (50 percent) and lowest in the United States (38 percent). The percentage of mobile phone users who had actually used their phones for such purposes was only 2 percent, reflecting the fact that very few vendors were offering micropayments in their applications as of 2002.

Micropayment technology has wide-ranging applications, such as making payments to parking garages, restaurants, grocery stores, and public transportation. The success of micropayment applications, however, ultimately depends on the cost of the transactions (transaction costs will be small only if there is a large volume of transactions) and the willingness of the mobile service provider to accept the risk of potential nonpayments by customers.

Wireless Wallets

An *e-wallet* (see Chapter 12) is a piece of software that stores an online shopper's credit card numbers and other personal information so that the shopper does not have to reenter that information for every online purchase. In the recent past, companies such as SNAZ offered **m-wallet (mobile wallet)** (also known as *wireless wallet*) technologies that enabled cardholders to make purchases with a single click from their mobile devices. Although most of these companies are now defunct, some cell phone providers have incorporated m-wallets into their offerings. A good example is the Nokia wallet. This application provides users with a secure storage space in their phones for information (such as credit card numbers) to be used in mobile payments. The information also can be used to authenticate transactions through the use of digital signatures. Microsoft is offering its e-wallet, Passport, in a wireless environment.

m-wallet (mobile wallet)
Technologies that enable cardholders to make purchases with a single click from their wireless device.

WIRELESS BILL PAYMENTS

In addition to paying bills through wireline banking or from ATMs, a number of companies are now providing their customers with the option of paying their bills directly from a cell phone (Lipset 2003). HDFC Bank of India (hdfcbank.com), for example, allows customers to pay their utility bills using SMS. An example of how bill payments can be made using a mobile device is shown in Exhibit 9.8. This service is offered by Nordea, a pioneering provider of wireless banking services in Scandinavia. According to Poropudas (2003), more and more ATMs and vending machines can communicate with mobile phones, giving consumers the opportunity to access virtual cash, buy goods or services, or pay bills.

Section 9.4 ▶ REVIEW QUESTIONS

1. Describe some of the services provided by mobile banking.
2. Discuss mobile payments, especially the potential for wireless micropayments.
3. Describe the m-wallet and wireless bill payments.

9.5 MOBILE SHOPPING, ADVERTISING, AND CONTENT PROVISION

As in e-commerce, m-commerce B2C applications are concentrated in three major areas—retail shopping for products and services, advertising, and providing content for a fee (see Rupp and Smith 2002).

WIRELESS SHOPPING

An increasing number of online vendors allow customers to shop from wireless devices, especially PDAs (see pilotzone.com for more information how to do this). Shopping from wireless devices enables customers to perform quick searches, compare prices, use a shopping cart, order, and view the status of their order using their cell phones or wireless PDAs. Wireless shoppers are supported by services similar to those available for wireline shoppers. For example, mobile shoppers have access to shopping carts, as well as product search and price comparison tools.

An example of restaurant shopping from wireless devices is the joint venture between Motorola and Food.com. The companies offer restaurant chains an infrastructure that enables consumers to place an order for pickup or delivery virtually anytime, anywhere. Donatos Pizzeria was the first chain to implement the system in 2002.

EXHIBIT 9.8 Nordea's WAP Solo Banks Portal

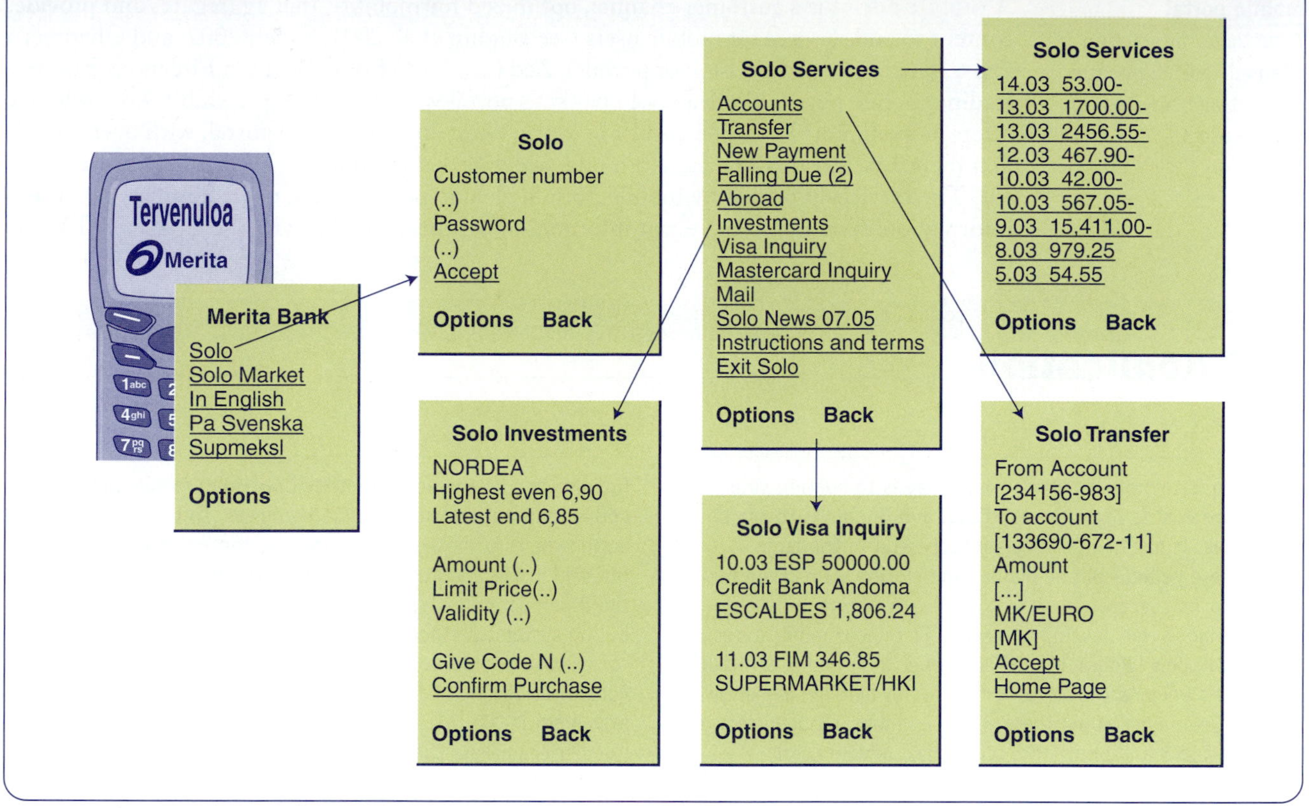

Tervenuloa
Merita

Merita Bank
Solo
Solo Market
In English
Pa Svenska
Supmeksl
Options

Solo
Customer number
(..)
Password
(..)
Accept
Options Back

Solo Investments
NORDEA
Highest even 6,90
Latest end 6,85
Amount (..)
Limit Price(..)
Validity (..)
Give Code N (..)
Confirm Purchase
Options Back

Solo Services
Accounts
Transfer
New Payment
Falling Due (2)
Abroad
Investments
Visa Inquiry
Mastercard Inquiry
Mail
Solo News 07.05
Instructions and terms
Exit Solo
Options Back

Solo Visa Inquiry
10.03 ESP 50000.00
Credit Bank Andoma
ESCALDES 1,806.24
11.03 FIM 346.85
SUPERMARKET/HKI
Options Back

Solo Services
14.03 53.00-
13.03 1700.00-
13.03 2456.55-
12.03 467.90-
10.03 42.00-
10.03 567.05-
9.03 15,411.00-
8.03 979.25
5.03 54.55
Options Back

Solo Transfer
From Account
[234156-983]
To account
[133690-672-11]
Amount
[...]
MK/EURO
[MK]
Accept
Home Page
Options Back

Source: *M-Commrece*, N. Sadeh, © 2002 John Wiley & Sons, reprinted with permission of John Wiley & Sons.

Cell phone users also can participate in online auctions. For example, eBay offers "anywhere wireless" services. Account holders at eBay can access their accounts, browse, search, bid, and rebid on items from any Internet-enabled phone or PDA. The same is true for participants in Amazon.com Auctions.

TARGETED ADVERTISING

Knowing the current location of mobile users and their preferences or surfing habits, marketers can send user-specific advertising messages to wireless devices. Location-sensitive advertising (using GPS) can inform a potential buyer about shops, malls, and restaurants close to where the mobile device owner is. This topic is discussed in more detail in Section 9.9. If the interests and personality type of an individual mobile user are known, the network provider may consider using "push" or "pull" methods of mobile advertising on a per-user basis or to a class of users (market segmentation). Examples of companies capitalizing on targeted advertising, including paying users to listen to advertising, are included in Online File W9.1 at the book's Web site.

Currently SMS is the principal technology used to deliver advertising to cell phones. However, as more wireless bandwidth becomes available, content-rich advertising involving audio, pictures, and video clips will be generated for individual users with specific needs, interests, and inclinations.

A mobile advertising campaign should be done with some caution. The number of ads pushed to an individual customer should be limited, to avoid overwhelming a user with too much information and also to avoid the possibility of congestion over the wireless networks. Wireless network managers may consider ad traffic to be of a lower priority compared with purchases or customer interaction. Finally, because advertisers need to know a user's current location, a third-party vendor may be used to provide location services. This will require the sharing of revenues with a location service provider.

MOBILE PORTALS

mobile portal
A customer interaction channel that aggregates content and services for mobile users.

A **mobile portal** is a customer channel, optimized for mobility, that aggregates and provides content to and services for mobile users (see Bughin et al. 2001; Sadeh 2002; and Chapters 5 and 6 for additional discussion of portals). Zed (zed.com) from Sonera in Finland is Europe's leading mobile portal. Nordea's Solo banking portal was illustrated in Exhibit 9.8. Vodafone offers its customers Vodafone Live! The world's best-known mobile portal, with over 40 million members, mostly in Japan, is i-mode, which is described in EC Application Case 9.1.

The services provided by mobile portals include news, sports, entertainment and travel information; restaurants and event information; leisure-related services (e.g., games, TV and

CASE 9.1

EC Application

I-MODE

i-mode is to mobile portals what eBay is to auction sites, Amazon.com is to online retailing, and Google is to search engines. It has been extremely successful in the large Japanese cellular phone market and closely scrutinized for keys to its success.

i-mode was developed by Japan's telecommunications giant Nippon Telegraph and Telephone (NTT) and is controlled by NTT's DoCoMo (DoCoMo means "everywhere" in Japanese). As of September 2004, there were 42 million i-mode users in Japan and 3 million in other countries, mostly Europe.

i-mode users can send and receive e-mail as well as SMS text messages. i-mode users also have access to the Web and can visit Web sites that offer video games, news and weather reports, train schedules, city maps, ringtone melodies, event ticketing, and much, much more. Entertainment services have proven to be the most popular; downloadable wallpaper images and ringtones for mobile phones have been the most profitable for content providers (Krishnamurthy 2001).

One aspect of i-mode that has drawn considerable interest from other mobile portal operators is the distinction between official and unofficial Web sites. Official Web sites, as approved by DoCoMo, are easily accessible to users; any charges incurred when visiting or using the site appear on the individual's monthly i-mode bill. Unofficial sites can only be accessed if the user hears about it from outside i-mode; the URL must be entered manually, and these sites must establish separate payment arrangements or make money in other ways. The official i-mode Web sites, 83,000 of them as of September 2004, are a large revenue generator for DoCoMo; thus the strong interest of other mobile portal operators.

What are the reasons for i-mode's success? First is its strong connection with NTT. NTT owns an advanced packet-switched network that was made available to DoCoMo. NTT has a strong brand position in Japan, and its NTT connections gave DoCoMo the clout it needed to form partnerships with handset manufacturers. Second is the nature of the wired versus wireless Internet access market in Japan. Japan has a relatively low level of PC penetration and a high level of mobile phone penetration. Also, PC-based Internet access is billed by the minute, making it much more expensive than the one-price-for-unlimited-access model used in most other countries. Both factors favor wireless communications services over wired rivals in the Japanese market. Third, NTT DoCoMo has partnered with official outside providers to deliver content and services to customers. This is a win-win arrangement for both DoCoMo and the content providers. NTT DoCoMo makes its profits from the traffic on its network and the 9 percent commission from transaction charges on its billing system. Partners get privileged access to a large customer base and do not need to build a billing system. Fourth, in addition to a small monthly fee (US $2.70 as of November 2004), users pay for network traffic based on the number of packets they send, not for the amount of time spent online. In addition, i-mode users pay through what is perhaps the world's first successful implementation of a micropayments system. Fifth, the handsets are well designed and easy to use, with special appeal to the Japanese audience. Sixth, cultural factors, such as the Japanese love for gadgets, has contributed to i-mode's success.

In recent years NTT DoCoMo has started to expand the i-mode service model beyond Japan. Investments and partnerships have been arranged with telecommunications providers in Hong Kong (service started in May 2000), Europe, South Korea, Taiwan, and Brazil. In 2002, a partnership between NTT DoCoMo and AT&T Wireless led to the introduction of mMode, a mobile Internet service similar to i-mode, in the United States.

Initial indications are that NTT DoCoMo has not experienced the same degree of success in these markets as i-mode did in Japan. As the list of success factors presented earlier indicate, i-mode owes much of its success to the particular circumstances and nature of the Japanese market. The ability for NTT DoCoMo to replicate a formula for success outside the Japanese market has yet to be determined.

Sources: Krishnamurthy (2001) and *nttdocomo.com* (accessed November 2004).

Questions

1. Why can i-mode be considered a mobile portal?
2. What factors have led to i-mode's success in Japan?
3. What is the win-win situation for NTT DoCoMo and official site content providers?

movie listings); e-mail; community services; and stock trading. A sizeable percentage of the portals also provide downloads and messaging, music-related services, and health, dating, and job information. Mobile portals frequently charge a monthly fee to access basic information services and also charge a per-service fee for premium content, such as location-based weather reports or downloads.

Section 9.5 ▶ REVIEW QUESTIONS

1. Describe how mobile devices can be used to shop.
2. Explain targeted advertising in the wireless environment.
3. Describe mobile portals and the types of information they provide.

9.6 MOBILE INTRABUSINESS APPLICATIONS

Although B2C m-commerce gets considerable publicity in the media and first mention in most discussions of m-commerce, for most organizations the greatest short-term benefit from mobile commerce is likely to come from intrabusiness applications, especially B2E (business-to-employee) ones. This section looks at how mobile devices and technologies can be used within organizations.

SUPPORT OF MOBILE EMPLOYEES

Mobile workers are employees who work outside the corporate premises. Examples of mobile workers are members of sales teams, traveling executives, telecommuters, people working in corporate yards or warehouses, and repair or installation employees who work at customers' sites or in the field. These mobile workers need the same corporate data available to employees working inside the company's offices. However, it may be inconvenient or impossible for these off-site employees to use wireline-based devices, even portable ones.

The solution is smaller, simpler wireless devices such as tablet PCs, PDAs, and smartphones. Increasingly, companies are realizing that equipping their mobile employees with mobile computing devices will cause employee productivity to increase (Estrada 2002; Kakihara and Sorensen 2003), customer service levels to improve, and employee morale and job satisfaction to increase. In short, the company will receive considerable gains from its investment. Perhaps in no area is this more true than in the use of mobile devices in sales force mobilization.

Sales Force Mobilization

Many employees who sell must travel. Whether making a sales pitch to a potential customer, demonstrating a new product to an existing customer, checking inventory in the customer's store, or maintaining a close working relationship with customers, salespeople spend a lot of time away from the office. Mobile computing devices can keep these employees better informed about new product launches, product information, pricing schedules, orders status, manufacturing schedules, inventory levels, and delivery schedules.

The business case for **sales force mobilization**—equipping sales force employees with wireless computing devices—is a compelling one. Sales staff can enter sales meetings with the most current and accurate information, perhaps even checking sales and product information during the meeting itself. When it is time to close the deal, the salesperson can wirelessly check production schedules and inventory levels to confirm product availability and even specify a delivery date. This available-to-promise/capacity-to-promise (ATP/CTP) capability means no more "I will have to check on that" promises that can sometimes delay or cancel a sale. It also can mean more competitive and realistic offers to customers.

sales force mobilization
The process of equipping sales force employees with wireless computing devices.

If taking inventory of existing product on a client's shelf is part of the sales duties, the time devoted to this can be dramatically reduced through RFID tags (explained later in this chapter and illustrated in the case at the beginning of this chapter). Making this task easier and less time consuming can increase employee job satisfaction and make more time available for higher-revenue-generating activities.

Finally, by enabling sales force employees to record orders in real time, the organization benefits through improved manufacturing and delivery scheduling, fewer data entry errors, less clerical and administrative overhead, and better decision making. An example of improved sales productivity through wireless mobile computing is provided in EC Application Case 9.2.

Job Dispatch

Another group of inherently mobile employees are those involved in delivery and dispatch services, including transportation (e.g., delivery of food, oil, newspapers, and cargo; courier services; tow trucks; taxis), utilities (e.g., gas, electricity, phone, water), field services (e.g., computer, office equipment, home repair), health care (e.g., visiting nurses, doctors, social services), and security (e.g., patrols, alarm installation). Mobile devices are becoming an integral part of the groupware and workflow applications that support these employees. Mobile computing can assist in dispatch functions—assigning jobs to mobile employees—and provide workers with detailed information about the task.

A dispatching application for wireless devices allows improved response with reduced resources, real-time tracking of work orders, increased dispatcher efficiency, and a reduction in administrative work. For example, AirIQ's OnLine system (airiq.com) combines Internet, wireless, GPS, digital mapping, and intelligent information technologies. The system collects information about a vehicle's direction, speed, and location from a device housed in each vehicle. Managers can view and access information about the fleet on digital maps, monitor vehicles on the Internet, and monitor the operating condition of their fleet. AirIQ promises savings of about 30 percent in communication costs and increases in workforce efficiency of about 25 percent. Online File W9.2 at the book's Web site provides a detailed description of

CASE 9.2

EC Application

MARKETSOURCE MOBILIZES ITS WORKFORCE

As a provider of outsourced sales and marketing programs, MarketSource knows sales. With approximately 80 percent of its 2,000 employees working away from the office, either calling on customers or working on site, MarketSource also knows from first-hand experience the impact of mobile computing on sales force automation.

The majority of the company's employees work remotely from retailer sites or from home offices, so connectivity and communications are critical to using their time efficiently. MarketSource representatives need to capture sales information, competitive data, and point-of-sale activity in the field through the firm's own Web-based applications and transmit that information back to the corporate office to produce vital sales reports.

One solution MarketSource uses to accomplish this is tablet PCs running the Windows XP Tablet PC Edition operating system. As of May 2003, approximately 5 percent of MarketSource's full-time staff were using tablet PCs, a percentage that is expected to grow.

"We're primarily deploying tablet PCs to people who go to a lot of meetings and travel a lot," says Jim Hibbard, MarketSource Manager of QA and Training. "This group takes advantage of the handwriting recognition and digital ink capabilities built into Windows XP Tablet PC Edition to take notes in meetings and store them electronically so that they can be quickly searched or sent in e-mail."

Using tablet PCs, MarketSource sales representatives do in-store surveys in real time and easily send and receive e-mail throughout the workday. This gives them more "face time" with the customer and helps them get reporting done faster, which reduces the amount of time spent working at home.

The wireless network support in Windows XP Professional also helps make meetings more productive. "People bring their notebook computers or tablet PCs to meetings because they can access things on the network from the conference room rather than run back to their office for something," Hibbard says. "When a question comes up in a meeting, they just connect where they are and immediately get answers. They can send files back and forth to other users in the meeting, which also saves time."

The deployment "has made a significant impact on the organization in terms of productivity and lowered TOC [total cost of ownership]," says Kristin McQuiddy, MarketSource Director of Business Development. "But the real value comes from our ability to deliver better results for our partners."

Source: Microsoft. "Your Mobile Work Force Needs Mobile Solutions" *MSN Tech and Gadgets*, 2003. *tech.msn.com/guides/670780.armx* (accessed October 2004).

Questions

1. Which MarketSource employees use tablet PCs and for what purposes?
2. What benefits are MarketSource and its employees receiving from this deployment of intrabusiness m-commerce?

a job-dispatching system that a truck service company has used to provide benefits to both itself and its customers.

Wearable Devices

Employees who work on buildings, electrical poles, or other "climbable workplaces" may be equipped with special mobile wireless computing devices called **wearable devices**. Workers wear these devices on their arms, clothes, helmets, or other parts of their bodies. Examples of wearable devices include:

wearable devices
Mobile wireless computing devices for employees who work on buildings and other climbable workplaces.

- **Screen.** A computer screen is mounted on a safety hat, in front of the worker's eyes, displaying information to the worker.
- **Camera.** A camera is mounted on a safety hat. Workers can take digital photos and videos and transmit them instantly to a portable computer nearby. Photo transmission is usually made possible by Bluetooth.
- **Keyboard.** A wrist-mounted keyboard can be typed on by the other hand. Wearable keyboards are an alternative to voice recognition systems, which also are wireless.
- **Touch-panel display.** In addition to the wrist-mounted keyboard, mobile employees can use a flat-panel screen attached to a hand that responds to the tap of a finger or stylus.
- **Speech translator.** For those mobile employees who do not have their hands free to use a keyboard, a wearable speech translator is handy (see Smailagic et al. 2001).

For an example of wearable devices used to support mobile employees, see Online File W9.3 at the book's Web site. Other sources of information about wearable wireless devices are xybernaut.com, essworld.net, and media.mit.edu/wearables.

SUPPORTING OTHER TYPES OF WORK

There are many other examples of how wireless devices can support workers. The applications will surely grow as the technology matures and as workers discover new ways to apply the functions of wireless devices to their jobs. Here are four examples.

- Tractors equipped with sensors, onboard computers, and a GPS help farmers save time, effort, and money. GPS determines the precise location of the tractor and can direct its automatic steering. Because the rows of planting resulting from GPS-guiding are more exact, the farmers save both on seeds and on fertilizers, due to minimized overlapping and spillage. Farmers also can work longer hours with the satellite-controlled steering to take advantage of good weather. Another savings is due to the instant notification to the service department of any machine that breaks down. For details, see Scanlon (2003).
- Taco Bell provides its mystery shoppers (shoppers who visit restaurants to conduct a survey unknown to the owners) with handheld computers so that they can communicate more quickly with the company's headquarters (Microsoft 2002). The visitors must answer 35 questions, ranging from the speed of service to food quality. Before the devices, information was provided by filling out paper forms that were mailed overnight and scanned into computers for processing. The information flow using the handheld computers is both faster and more accurate.
- Like e-mail, SMS can be used to bolster collaboration. According to Kontzer (2003), the following are 10 applications of SMS for mobile workers: (1) alerting mobile technicians to system errors; (2) alerting mobile executives to urgent voice messages; (3) confirming with mobile sales personnel that a faxed order was received; (4) informing travelers of delays and changes; (5) enabling contract workers to receive and accept project offers; (6) keeping stock traders up to date on urgent stock activity; (7) reminding data services subscribers about daily updates; (8) alerting doctors to urgent patient situations; (9) enabling mobile sales teams to input daily sales figures into corporate database; and (10) sending mobile sales representatives reminders of appointments and other schedule details.
- To increase national security and safeguard national borders, countries are using facial-recognition and iris-scanning biometrics (see Chapter 11), both of which are supported by wireless systems.

CUSTOMER SUPPORT

Mobile access extends the reach of CRM to both employees and business partners on a 24/7 basis, to any place where recipients are located. In large software suites, such as Siebel's CRM, the two CRM functions that have attracted the most interest are sales force mobilization and field service, both discussed earlier. Two illustrations of the use of mobile technologies for sales support and customer service support are provided in Online File W9.4 at the book's Web site.

Voice portals also can be used to enhance customer service or to improve access to data for employees. For example, customers who are away from the office could use a vendor's voice portal to check on the status of deliveries to a job site. Salespeople could check on inventory status during a meeting to help close a sale. There are a wide variety of CRM applications for voice portal technology. The challenge is in learning how to create the navigation and other aspects of interaction that makes customers feel comfortable with voice-access technology.

NON-INTERNET INTRABUSINESS APPLICATIONS

Wireless applications in the non-Internet environment have been around since the early 1990s. Examples include wireless networking, used to pick items out of storage in warehouses via laptops mounted on forklifts; delivery-status updates, entered on PCs inside distribution trucks; and collection of data, such as competitors' inventories in stores and customer orders, using a handheld (but not wireless) device, from which data are transferred to company information systems each evening. Three more recent examples of such intrabusiness applications are described next.

- Employees at companies such as Telecom Italia Mobile (*Republica.IT* 2001) get their monthly pay slips as SMS messages sent to their mobile phones. The money itself is transferred electronically to a designated bank account. The method is much cheaper for the company and results in less paperwork than the old method of mailing monthly pay slips.
- Kemper Insurance Company has piloted an application that lets property adjusters report from the scene of an accident. Kemper attached a wireless digital imaging system to a camera that lets property adjusters take pictures in the field and transmit them to a processing center (Henning 2001; Nelson 2000). The cameras are linked to Motorola's StarTac data-enabled cellular phone service, which sends the information to a database. These applications eliminate delays in obtaining information and in film processing that exist with conventional methods.
- A medical care organization developed a mobile enterprise application that allows sales representatives to check orders and inventories during their visits with physicians and instantly report on what they can deliver to the physician's office and when (Ellison 2004).

Online Exhibit W9.2 at the book's Web site lists other ways that wireless technologies can be used to improve intrabusiness workflow. The use of RFID to improve productivity in intrabusiness applications will be discussed later in this chapter. Now, however, our examination of m-commerce applications leaves organizational boundaries to look at interbusiness applications in B2B m-commerce and supply chain management.

Section 9.6 ▶ REVIEW QUESTIONS

1. In what ways does an organization benefit from providing mobile wireless devices to its sales employees?
2. Describe wireless job dispatch.
3. List some of the non-Internet intrabusiness mobile applications.

9.7 B2B M-COMMERCE AND SUPPLY CHAIN MANAGEMENT

Timely access to accurate information is critical for B2B EC success. Companies must be able to respond to business partner requirements in real time, and speedy response is especially important in managing the supply chain. Mobile computing solutions enable organizations to respond faster to supply chain disruptions by proactively adjusting plans or by shifting resources related to critical supply chain events as they occur.

The two greatest opportunities in B2B mobile commerce are to use wireless communication to share information along the supply chain and to collaborate with partners. By integrating the mobile computing device into supply chain communications, it is possible to make mobile reservations of goods, remotely check availability of a particular item in the warehouse, order a customized product from the manufacturing department, or provide secure access to confidential financial data from a management information system.

One way to share information with supply chain partners is wireless *telemetry*, which is the science of measuring physical phenomena such as temperature, volume, or an on/off condition at a remote point and transmitting the value to a distant recorder or observer. (Telemetry is described further in Section 9.9.) This technology enables automated data capture, improved timeliness and accuracy of billing, lower overheads, and increased customer satisfaction through faster and more complete service responsiveness. For example, vending machines can be kept replenished and in reliable operation if suppliers can wirelessly check inventory and service status. RFID tags (described in Section 9.11) can be used to monitor and control the flow of goods up and down the supply chain more efficiently.

Mobile devices also can facilitate collaboration among members of the supply chain. It is no longer necessary for a company to call a partner company to find its offsite employees. Instead, managers can contact these employees directly on their mobile devices.

Finally, many of the organizational benefits of sales force mobilization mentioned earlier flow up and down the supply chain, too. Direct, remote, real-time entry of sales into ERP systems can improve supply chain operations, because today's ERP systems tie into broader supply chain management solutions that extend visibility across multiple tiers in the supply chain. Mobile supply chain management (mSCM) empowers the workforce to leverage these broader systems through improved inventory management and ATP/CTP functionality that extends across multiple supply chain partners and takes into account logistics considerations.

Section 9.7 ▶ REVIEW QUESTIONS

1. Briefly describe two ways wireless communications can support B2B commerce and supply chain management.
2. What is telemetry?
3. What are the benefits of mSCM?

9.8 MOBILE CONSUMER AND PERSONAL SERVICE APPLICATIONS

A large number of applications exist that support consumers and provide personal services (see Coursaris and Hassanein 2002 and Sadeh 2002). As an example, consider the situation of a traveler taking an international flight. Before leaving home, the traveler uses his or her cell phone to query the airline's WAP-enabled Web site or SMS messaging system to see if there has been a flight delay. Upon arrival at the airport, entering the flight number into the device returns a message from the airline indicating the correct check-in desk and confirming the flight time. Singapore Airlines even allows passenger check-in via SMS at 12 international airports. Upon arrival at the airport, Singapore passengers check in luggage and pick up boarding passes from a dedicated counter, rather than wait in regular queues (*The Age* 2004a). After check-in, a GPS-enabled device could be used to determine the nearest washroom or restaurant and provide directions. Information about today's specials at a Duty Free store can be requested through an SMS number posted on advertising in the terminal's lobby. A text message from the airline alerts the traveler when boarding is about to commence. Finally, the traveler can make a taxi reservation at the destination while waiting in the airport lounge for boarding. All of these services are possible in some places and are expected to be widely available soon.

Similar scenarios can be created for hotels, a day at a theme park, conference attendance, or a night out on the town. The purpose of this section is to introduce the reader to a few of the consumer and personal service areas in which wireless devices can be used.

MOBILE GAMES

In the handheld-gaming market, Nintendo has been the longtime leader. However, Nintendo has shown minimal interest in online or mobile games. Here, Sega has capitalized on the popularity of games such as Sonic the Hedgehog to garner 2.5 million Japanese subscribers for its mobile game and entertainment services (Becker 2002). In Japan, where millions of commuters spend time during long train rides, cell phone games have become a cultural phenomenon.

With more than 1.5 billion cell phones in use by the end of 2004 (*CellularOnline* 2004), the potential audience for mobile games is substantially larger than the market for other platforms, Playstation and Gameboy included. Because of the market potential, cell phone manufacturer Nokia has decided to enter the mobile-gaming world, producing not only the phone/console but also the games that will be delivered on memory cards. It seeks to develop and market near-distance multiplayer gaming over Bluetooth and wide area gaming using cellular networks (Nokia 2002).

In July 2001, Ericsson, Motorola, Nokia, and Siemens established the Mobile Games Interoperability Forum (MGIF) (openmobilealliance.org) to define a range of technical standards that will make it possible to deploy mobile games across multigame servers, wireless networks, and over different mobile devices. Microsoft is moving into this field as well.

A topic related to games is *mobile entertainment*, discussed in Online File W9.5 at the book's Web site. Mobile gambling, a related topic, is extremely popular in some countries (e.g., horse racing in Hong Kong and racing and other events in Australia). For more on mobile gambling, see sportodds.com.

WIRELESS TELEMEDICINE

Today, two different kinds of technology are being used for telemedicine applications: (1) storage of data and transferring of digital images from one location to another and (2) videoconferencing used for real-time consultation between a patient in one location and a medical specialist in another. In most of the real-time consultations, the patient is in a rural area and the specialist is in an urban location.

Telemedicine faces a number of obstacles. Some states do not allow physicians to provide medical advice across state lines. The threat of malpractice suits is another issue, because there is no hands-on interaction between the remote physician and the patient. In addition, from a technical standpoint, many telemedicine projects are hindered by poor telecommunications support. However, those who are looking ahead to the needs of an aging population are seeing opportunities to meet some of those needs in emerging technologies. The new wireless and mobile technologies such as 3G and WiMax not only offer the possibility of overcoming the hurdles imposed by remote locations, but also open a number of new and novel application opportunities. Examples include the following:

- Typically, physicians write a prescription and the patient takes it to the pharmacy where there is typically a 15- to 30-minute wait for it to be filled. Some new mobile systems allow physicians to enter patient prescriptions into a palm-sized device. The information is transmitted by cellular modem (or Wi-Fi) to Med-i-nets (med-i-nets.com) or a similar company. There, the information is checked for insurance eligibility and conformity to insurance company and government regulations. If everything checks out, the prescription is transferred electronically to the appropriate pharmacy for a no-wait pick-up by the patient. In addition, for patients who need refills, the system tracks and notifies physicians when it is time to reorder, and the doctor can reissue a prescription with a few clicks.
- Fast response is absolutely critical in the case of a heart-attack victim. Manufacturers are developing wearable heart monitors linked to a cell phone that can automatically contact doctors or family members at the first sign of trouble.
- The Swiss Federal Institute of Technology has designed portable devices that transmit the vital signs of avalanche victims up to 80 meters (262 feet) away (Baard 2002). Not only does the device provide location information, it also provides information about body orientation that helps reduce injuries as rescuers dig for the victims.

- In-flight medical emergencies occur much more frequently than one might think. Alaskan Airlines, for example, deals with about 10 medical emergencies per day (Conrad 2002). Mobile communications already are being used to attend to medical emergencies on planes. MedLink, a service of MedAire in Phoenix, provides around-the-clock access to board-certified emergency physicians. These mobile services also can remotely control medical equipment, such as defibrillators, located onboard the plane.
- The military is involved in developing mobile telesurgery applications that enable surgeons in one location to remotely control robotic arms for surgery in another location. The technology could be particularly useful in battlefield situations.

OTHER MOBILE COMPUTING SERVICES FOR CONSUMERS

Many other mobile computer services in a variety of service categories are available to consumers. Examples include services providing news, weather, and sports reports; language translators; information about tourist attractions (hours, prices); currency, time zone, and other converters for travelers; and emergency services. CVS Pharmacy allows customers to print photos directly from their mobile phones to store kiosks (Pmai.org 2005). For more examples, see the case studies at mobileinfo.com/case_study/index.htm.

NON-INTERNET MOBILE APPLICATIONS FOR CONSUMERS

Non-Internet mobile applications for consumers have mainly been in the transportation industry. Millions of "contactless" smart cards (also called proximity cards) are used to pay bus and subway fares and road tolls. Amplified remote-sensing cards that have an RF (radio frequency) of up to 30 meters (100 feet) are used in several countries for toll collection.

Section 9.8 ▶ REVIEW QUESTIONS

1. List a few ways wireless communications can assist a traveler who is about to take a trip.
2. Describe some potential uses of mobile and wireless technologies in providing medical care.
3. How are wireless smart cards used in the transport industry?

9.9 LOCATION-BASED MOBILE COMMERCE

As briefly discussed earlier in this chapter, the use of GPS to provide location-based services (Section 9.1) enables localization of mobile services, a value-added attribute of mobile commerce (Section 9.3). Formally, **location-based m-commerce** refers to the use of GPS-enabled devices or similar technologies (e.g., triangulation of radio- or cell-based stations) to deliver products and services based on the user's location. Location-based services are attractive to both consumers and businesses alike. From a consumer or business user's viewpoint, localization offers safety (emergency services can pinpoint the mobile device owner's exact location), convenience (a user can locate what is nearby without consulting a directory, pay phone, or map), and productivity (time can be optimized by determining points of interest within close proximity). From a business supplier's point of view, location-based m-commerce offers an opportunity to provide services that more precisely meet a customer's needs.

location-based m-commerce
Delivery of m-commerce transactions to individuals in a specific location, at a specific time.

The services provided through location-based m-commerce focus on five key areas:

1. **Location.** Determining the basic position of a person or a thing (e.g., car or boat)
2. **Navigation.** Plotting a route from one location to another
3. **Tracking.** Monitoring the movement of a person or a thing (e.g., a package or vehicle)
4. **Mapping.** Creating maps of specific geographical locations
5. **Timing.** Determining the precise time at a specific location

Technologically, the ability of a location-based service to identify where a mobile consumer is located depends on the global positioning system.

Global Positioning System

As briefly discussed in Section 9.1, the global positioning system (GPS) is a worldwide satellite-based tracking system that enables users to determine their position anywhere on the earth. GPS was developed by the U.S. Defense Department for military use, but its high value for civilian use was immediately recognized, and the technology was released into the civilian domain, originally for use by commercial airlines and ships. In recent years, GPS locators have become a part of the consumer electronics market and are used widely for business and recreation (e.g., see geocaching.com).

GPS is supported by 24 U.S. government satellites. Each satellite orbits the earth once every 12 hours on a precise path at an altitude of 10,900 miles. At any point in time, the exact position of each satellite is known because the satellite broadcasts its position and a time signal from its onboard atomic clock, which is accurate to one-billionth of a second. Receivers on the ground also have accurate clocks that are synchronized with those of the satellites.

GPS locators may be stand-alone units or embedded into a mobile device. Knowing the speed of the satellite signals (186,272 miles or 299,775 kilometers per second), the GPS system can determine the location (latitude and longitude) of any locator to within 50 feet (15 meters) by triangulation, using the distance from the GPS locator to three satellites to make the computation. GPS software then computes the latitude and longitude of the receiver. More information about how the GPS system works is available in Online File W9.6 at the book's Web site. An online tutorial on GPS is available at trimble.com/gps.

Geographical Information System

The location provided by GPS is expressed in terms of latitude and longitude. To make that information useful to businesses and consumers, these measures need to be related to a specific place or address. This is done by inserting the latitude and longitude onto an electronic map, which is known as a **geographical information system (GIS)**. The GIS data visualization technology integrates GPS data into digitized map displays (see Steede-Terry 2000 for an explanation of how this is done). Companies such as mapinfo.com provide the GIS core spatial technology, maps, and other data content needed in order to deliver location-based services such as emergency assistance, restaurant locators, buddy finders, and service-call routing.

geographical information system (GIS)
An information system that integrates GPS data onto digitized map displays.

An interesting application of GPS/GIS is now available from several car manufacturers (e.g., Toyota, Cadillac) and car rental companies (e.g., Hertz, Avis). Some cars have a navigation system that indicates how far away the driver is from gas stations, restaurants, and other locations of interest. The GPS knows where the car is at any time, so the application can map the route for the driver to a particular destination. Another example of a location-based application in the transportation industry is NextBus, as described in Online File W9.7 at the book's Web site. Any GPS application can be classified as *telemetry*, a topic discussed briefly above and in more detail next.

LOCATION-BASED ADVERTISING

Imagine that you are walking near a Starbucks store, but you do not even know that one is there. Suddenly your cell phone beeps with a message: "Come inside and get a 15 percent discount." The location of your wireless device was detected, and similar to the pop-up ads on your PC, advertising was directed your way (Needleman 2002). You could use permission marketing to shield yourself from location-based advertising; if the system knows that you do not drink coffee, for example, you would not be sent a message from Starbucks.

Another use of wireless devices for advertising is described by Raskin (2003). In this case, a dynamic billboard ad could be personalized specifically for you when your car approaches a certain billboard and the system knows your preferences. Your car will be tracked by a GPS every 20 seconds. A computer scans the areas in which billboards are visible, and by cross-referencing information about your location and your preferences, a personalized ad could be placed on the billboard so you would see it as you pass.

Yet another method of location-based advertising involves putting ads on the top of taxicabs. The ad changes based on the taxi's location. For example, a taxi cruising in the theater district in New York City might show an ad for a play or a restaurant in that area; when the cab goes to another neighborhood, the ad might be for a restaurant or a business in that area of the city.

EMERGENCY RESPONSE CELL PHONE CALLS

If someone dials an emergency response number (e.g., 911 in the United States; 111, 110, or 999 in many other countries) from a regular wired phone, it is easy for the emergency response service to pinpoint the location of the phone. But what happens if someone places an emergency call from a mobile phone? How can the emergency response dispatcher locate the caller? A few years ago, the U.S. Federal Communication Commission (FCC) issued a directive to wireless carriers, requiring that they establish services to handle **wireless 911 (e-911)** calls. To offer an idea of the magnitude of this requirement, more than 156,000 wireless 911 calls are made every day, representing more than half of the 911 calls made daily in the United States (Sarkar 2003).

wireless 911 (e-911)
In the United States, emergency response calls from cellular phones.

The e-911 directive will be implemented in two phases, although the specifics of each phase vary from one wireless carrier (e.g., T-Mobile, Cingular, Sprint) to another. Phase I requires carriers, upon appropriate request by a local Public Safety Answering Point (PSAP), to report the telephone number of the wireless 911 caller and the location of the cellular antenna that received the call. Phase II, which is being rolled out over a 4-year period, from October 2002 to December 2005, requires wireless carriers to provide information that will enable the PSAP to locate a caller within 50 meters 67 percent of the time and within 150 meters 95 percent of the time. By the end of Phase II, it is expected that 95 percent of all cell phones will have these location capabilities. It is expected that many other countries will follow the example of the United States in providing this type of emergency response service.

Some expect that in the future cars will have an **automatic crash notification (ACN)** device. These still-experimental devices will automatically notify the police of an accident involving an ACN-equipped car and its location. Also, following a school bus hijacking in Pennsylvania, the Pennsylvania legislature is considering a bill to mandate satellite tracking in all school buses.

automatic crash notification (ACN)
Device that automatically sends the police the location of a vehicle that has been involved in a crash.

TELEMATICS AND TELEMETRY APPLICATIONS

Telematics refers to the integration of computers and wireless communications in order to improve information flow (see Chatterjee et al. 2002 and Zhao 2002). It uses the principles of *telemetry*, the science that measures physical phenomena at a remote point and transfers the value to a receiving station. MobileAria (mobilearia.com), for example, tracks and monitors trucks and containers for fleet management, driver communication, environmental changes, and intrusion detection, all while the vehicle or container is in motion.

telematics
The integration of computers and wireless communications to improve information flow using the principles of telemetry.

Using *mobile telemetry*, technicians can diagnose maintenance problems in equipment from a remote distance. Car manufacturers use the technology for remote vehicle diagnosis and preventive maintenance. Finally, doctors can use mobile telemetry to monitor patients and control medical equipment from a distance.

General Motors popularized automotive telematics with its OnStar system. Nokia has set up a business unit, Smart Traffic Products, that focuses solely on telematics. Nokia believes that every vehicle will be equipped with at least one Internet Protocol (IP) address by the year 2010. Smart cars are discussed in more detail in Section 9.11.

BARRIERS TO LOCATION-BASED M-COMMERCE

What is holding back the widespread use of location-based m-commerce? Several factors come into play, including the following:

- **Accuracy of devices.** Some of the location technologies are not as accurate as people expect them to be. A good GPS provides a location that is accurate up to 15 meters (50 feet). Less expensive, but less accurate, locators can be used to find an approximate location within 500 meters (1,640 feet).
- **The cost-benefit justification.** For many potential users, the benefits of location-based services do not justify the cost of the hardware or the inconvenience and time required to

utilize the service (e.g., Hamblen 2001). After all, many seem to feel that they can just as easily obtain information the old-fashioned way.

- **Limited network bandwidth.** Wireless bandwidth is currently limited; it will be improved as 3G technology spreads. As bandwidth improves, applications will improve, which will attract more customers.
- **Invasion of privacy.** When "always-on" cell phones are a reality, many people will be hesitant to have their whereabouts and movements tracked throughout the day, even if they have nothing to hide. This issue will be heightened when our cars, homes, appliances, and all sorts of other consumer goods are connected to the Internet, as discussed in Section 9.11.

Section 9.9 ▶ REVIEW QUESTIONS

1. Describe some of the potential uses of location-based m-commerce.
2. Discuss the technologies used in providing location-based services.
3. Describe GPS and GIS.
4. Discuss telematics.
5. List some of the barriers to location-based m-commerce.

9.10 SECURITY AND OTHER BARRIERS TO MOBILE COMMERCE

Despite the vast potential for mobile commerce to change the way many companies do business, several barriers are either slowing down the spread of mobile commerce or leaving many m-commerce businesses and their customers disappointed or dissatisfied (e.g., see Islam and Fayad 2003). Security of mobile communications and mobile computing systems is a major concern, and this topic is addressed first.

M-COMMERCE SECURITY ISSUES

Many m-commerce security issues mirror those of e-commerce security (see Chapter 11).

Malicious Code. In 2001, a hacker sent an e-mail message to 13 million users of the i-mode wireless data service in Japan. The message had the potential to take over the recipient's phone, causing it to dial Japan's emergency hotline (1-1-0). DoCoMo rapidly fixed the problem, so no damage was done. At the beginning of 2002, researchers in the Netherlands discovered a bug in the operating system used by many Nokia phones that would enable a hacker to send a malformed SMS message capable of crashing the system. Again, no real damage was done. In 2004, Cabir became the first known virus capable of spreading through mobile phones. Fortunately, the virus was not launched, because it was developed by a global group that creates viruses to demonstrate that no technology is reliable and safe from viruses (see *Forbes* 2004).

These three cases are indicative of the malicious code threat that may someday plague mobile computing as much as it does desktop computing. Most Internet-enabled cell phones in operation today have their operating systems and other functional software "burned" into the hardware. This makes them incapable of storing applications and, in turn, incapable of propagating a virus, worm, or other rogue program from one phone to another. However, as the capabilities of cellular phones increase and the functionality of PDAs and cell phones converge, the threat of attack from malicious code will certainly increase.

Transaction Security. Basic security goals of confidentiality, authentication, authorization, and integrity are just as important for m-commerce as they are for e-commerce but are more difficult to ensure. Specifically, m-commerce transactions almost always pass through several networks, both wireless and wired. An appropriate level of security must be maintained on each network, and this interoperability is difficult. Similarly, post-transactional security issues of auditing and nonrepudiation are more difficult because cell phones do not yet have the capability to store the digital equivalent of a receipt.

Other m-commerce security challenges are unique because of the nature of the mobile computing environment. Some of the security issues include the following.

Wireless Communication. The open-air transmission of signals opens up new opportunities through which security may be compromised. Interception of a communication in a wired network requires physical access to the wires in which the signal is being carried. Interception of a communication in a wireless network can be done with a carefully aimed, even crude, antenna (e.g., a legendary war driving tip is how to use a Pringles potato chip can to hone in on a rogue Wi-Fi signal).

Physical Security of Mobile Devices. Because of their small size, mobile devices are easily lost or stolen. Similarly, because they are mobile, cell phones, PDAs, Blackberrys, and other devices are sometimes dropped, crushed, or damaged by water and extreme temperature. A stolen device can provide the thief with valuable data and digital credentials that can be used to compromise an m-commerce network. A lost or damaged device is a security threat because of the loss of any stored data or device settings.

Ease of Use. Wireless technology lowers the temptation threshold. The very same ease-of-use factors that mobile computing users appreciate work against fulfillment of security goals. Couple this with the privacy and apparent anonymity that personal computing devices provide, and the opportunities for abuse rise dramatically (Elliott and Phillips 2004).

Many of the processes, procedures, and technologies used for e-commerce security and for general organizational computer security also apply to m-commerce security. Passwords, encryption, active tokens, and user education (all discussed in Chapter 11) apply to m-commerce security.

Special security measures for m-commerce may be required. For example, to prevent the theft of a mobile device, a user might carry a "wireless tether" that sounds a warning if a device is left behind or carried away. Wi-Fi networks have their own built-in security system known as Wired Equivalent Privacy (WEP), which is, as the name suggests, similar to encryption protocols used on wired networks. Similarly, WAP networks depend on the Wireless Transport Layer Security (WTLS), and cell phones can be protected by SIM-based authentication. These three approaches to m-commerce security are discussed in more detail in the Online File W9.8 at the book's Web site. Additional information about mobile commerce security is available in books such as Raina and Harsh (2002) and Elliott and Phillips (2004).

TECHNOLOGICAL BARRIERS TO M-COMMERCE

When mobile users want to access the Internet, the *usability* of the site is critical to achieve the purpose of the visit and increase user stickiness (the degree to which users stay at a site). However, many Web sites are not designed for viewing by mobile devices and thus are unviewable or unfriendly to mobile devices.

A related problem, referred to earlier, is the technological limitations of most mobile computing devices. Current devices have limited usability, particularly with respect to pocket-size screens or data input devices. In addition, because of the limited storage capacity and information access speed of most smartphones and PDAs, it is often difficult or impossible to download large files to these devices.

Mobile visitors to a Web site are typically paying premium rates for connections and are focused on a specific goal (e.g., conducting a stock trade). For visitors to find exactly what they are looking for easily and quickly, the navigation systems have to be fast and designed for mobile devices. Similarly, the information content needs to meet the needs of the user. For example, many WAP screens are text-based and have only simple black-and-white graphics. This means that mobile users cannot browse an online picture-based catalog, which makes mobile shopping difficult. This situation is improving as devices become more powerful and as 3G bandwidth becomes more commonplace.

Other technical barriers related to mobile computing technology include limited battery life and transmission interference with home appliances. These barriers and others are listed in Exhibit 9.9.

ETHICAL, LEGAL, AND HEALTH ISSUES IN M-COMMERCE

The increasing use of mobile devices in business and society raises new ethical, legal, and health issues that individuals, organizations, and society will have to resolve.

EXHIBIT 9.9 Technical Limitations of Mobile Computing

Limitation	Description
Insufficient bandwidth	Sufficient bandwidth is necessary for widespread mobile computing, and it must be inexpensive. It will take a few years until 3G and WiMax are available in many places. Wi-Fi solves some of the problems for short-range connections.
Security standards	Universal standards are still under development. It may take 3 or more years for sufficient standards to be in place.
Power consumption	Batteries with long life are needed for mobile computing. Color screens and Wi-Fi consume more electricity, but new chips and emerging battery technologies are solving some of the power-consumption problems.
Transmission interferences	Weather and terrain, including tall buildings, can limit reception. Microwave ovens, cordless phones, and other devices on the free, but crowded, 2.4GHz range interfere with Bluetooth and Wi-Fi 802.11b transmissions.
GPS accuracy	GPS may be inaccurate in a city with tall buildings, limiting the use of location-based m-commerce.
WAP limitations	Many mobile phone users find that WAP is expensive and difficult to access.
Potential health hazards	Potential health damage from cellular radio frequency emission is not known yet. Known health hazards include cell phone addiction, thumb-overuse syndrome, and accidents caused by people using cell phones while driving.
Human-computer interface	Screens and keyboards are too small, making mobile devices uncomfortable and difficult for many people to use.
Complexity	Too many optional add-ons are available (e.g., battery chargers, external keyboards, headsets, microphones, cradles). Storing and using the optional add-ons can be a problem.

One workplace issue is the isolation that mobile devices can impose on a workforce. The introduction of desktop computing invoked a profound change on social interaction in the workplace, illustrated by the walled cubicles featured in Dilbert cartoons. Some people had difficulty adjusting to this new environment and sought to replace face-to-face interactions with e-mail interactions, prompting organizational policies against the forwarding of non-business-related e-mail messages.

Equipping the workforce with mobile devices may have similar impacts. Field service employees dispatched remotely and who acquire replacement parts from third-party sources will visit "the office" only briefly at the start and end of each day, if at all. The result could be a reduction in organizational transparency, making it difficult for employees to know what other employees do, how the organization is evolving, and how they fit into it. These changes have powerful implications for individuals and the organization for which they work. Whether the results are good or bad depends on how the change is managed (Elliott and Phillips 2004).

The truly personal nature of the mobile device also raises ethical and legal issues in the workplace. Most employees have desktop computers both at home and at work and separate business and personal work accordingly. However, it is not so easy to separate work and personal life on a cell phone, unless one is willing to carry two phones or two PDAs. And if an organization has the right to monitor e-mail communications on its own network, does it also have the right to monitor voice communications on a company-owned cell phone?

The widespread appearance of mobile devices in society has led to the need for cell phone etiquette, the creation of "cell free" zones in airport lounges, and National Cell Phone

Courtesy Month. For an insightful essay into the impact of cell phones in work and social spaces, see Rosen (2004).

A widely publicized health issue is the potential, but not yet proven, health damage from cellular radio frequency emissions. Cell phone addiction also is a problem. A study by Seoul National University found that 30 percent of South Korean high school students reported addiction effects, such as feeling anxious when they did not have their phones with them. Many also displayed symptoms of repetitive stress injury from obsessive text messaging (Rosen 2004).

Other ethical, legal, and health issues include the ethics of monitoring staff movements based on a GPS-enabled devices or vehicles, maintaining an appropriate work–life balance when work can be conducted anywhere at anytime, and the preferred content of an organizational policy to govern use and control of personal mobile computing devices in and out of the workplace.

PROJECT FAILURES IN M-COMMERCE

As with any other technology, especially a new one, applications, as well as entire companies, have failed in their attempts to implement an m-commerce strategy. It is important to anticipate and plan for possible failures as well as to learn from them.

The case of Northeast Utilities provides some important insights. According to Hamblen (2001), Northeast Utilities, which supplies energy products and services to 1.2 million customers from Maine to Maryland, embarked on a wireless project in 1995 in which its field inspectors used wireless devices to track spills of hazardous material and report them to headquarters in real time. After 18 months and spending $1 million, the project failed. The following are some of the lessons learned from this failure:

- Do not start without appropriate infrastructure.
- Do not start a full-scale implementation; use a small pilot for experimentation.
- Pick an appropriate architecture (e.g., some users do not need to be persistently connected).
- Talk with a range of users, some experienced and some not, about usability issues.
- Users must be involved; hold biweekly meetings if possible.
- Employ wireless experts.
- Wireless is a different medium from other forms of communication. Remember that people are not used to the wireless paradigm.

Having learned from the failure, Northeast made its next wireless endeavor a success. Today, 15 field inspectors carry rugged wireless laptops that are connected to the enterprise intranet and databases. The wireless laptops are used to conduct measurements related to electricity transformers, for example. The laptops transmit the results, in real time, to chemists and people who prepare government reports about hazardous materials spills. In addition, time is saved because all the information is entered directly into proper fields of electronic forms without having to be transcribed. The new system is so successful that it has given IT workers the confidence to launch other applications, such as sending power-outage reports to executives via smartphones and wireless information to crews repairing street lights.

Section 9.10 ▶ REVIEW QUESTIONS

1. Discuss how m-commerce security is similar to e-commerce security.
2. Identify three unique security challenges for mobile devices.
3. Discuss the role that usability plays in the adoption of m-commerce.
4. List the technical limitations of m-commerce.
5. Discuss the potential impact of mobile devices on the workplace.
6. Describe the potential health hazards of mobile devices.
7. List the lessons learned in the implementation of m-commerce at Northeast Utilities.

9.11 PERVASIVE COMPUTING

Many experts believe that the next major step in the evolution of computing will be pervasive computing. In a pervasive computing environment, almost every object has processing power and a wired or wireless connection to a network. The use of RFID tags mentioned in the opening case is an example of pervasive computing. Many other initiatives already underway—smart homes, smart appliances, and sensor networks—are described in the second part of this section. The section begins with an overview of pervasive computing.

OVERVIEW OF PERVASIVE COMPUTING

pervasive computing
Invisible, everywhere computing that is embedded in the objects around us.

Pervasive computing is invisible, everywhere computing; it is computing capabilities being embedded into the objects around us. In contrast, mobile computing is usually represented by devices—handheld computers, handset phones, headsets, and so on—that users hold, carry, or wear. Even as mobile computing devices continue to mature in functionality, power, and usefulness, pervasive computing technologies are emerging.

Pervasive computing also is called *embedded computing*, *augmented computing*, or *ubiquitous computing*. However, some in this still-emerging field make a distinction between pervasive and ubiquitous computing. According to Lyytinen and Yoo (2002), pervasive computing is embedded in the environment, but typically not mobile. They define ubiquitous computing as computing that combines a high degree of mobility with a high degree of embeddedness. So, for example, most smart appliances in a smart home represent wired, pervasive computing, and mobile objects with embedded computing, such as in clothes, cars, and personal communication systems, represent ubiquitous computing. This distinction is illustrated in Online Exhibit W9.3 at the book's Web site. In this chapter, however, we define *pervasive* and *ubiquitous* as equivalent terms; pervasive computing devices are embedded in the environment around us, and they may be mobile or stationary.

The idea of pervasive computing has been around for years. Mark Weiser first articulated the current version in 1988 at Xerox's computer science laboratory, the Palo Alto Research Center (PARC). Weiser and his colleagues were attempting "to conceive a new way of thinking about computers, one that takes into account the human world and allows the computers themselves to vanish into the background" (Weiser 1991, p. 94). According to Weiser, pervasive computing is the opposite of virtual reality. In virtual reality, the user is immersed in a computer-generated environment. In pervasive computing, the user is immersed in an invisible "computing is everywhere" environment—in cars, clothes, homes, the workplace, and so on (Weiser 1991).

Invisible Computing

By invisible, Weiser did not mean to imply that pervasive computing devices would not be seen, but rather that, unlike a desktop or handheld computer, these embedded computers would not intrude on our consciousness. Think of electric motors. They exist in the devices all around us, but they are invisible to us and we do not think about using them. This is Weiser's vision for pervasive computing. The user will not think about how to use the processing power in the object; rather, the processing power automatically helps the user perform the task.

Principles of Pervasive Computing

Underlying the embeddedness of pervasive computing are four principles that will define its development (Hansmann et al. 2003):

- **Decentralization.** The decentralization of computing that began with the transition from the centralized mainframe computer to the personal computer will continue in pervasive computing. Indeed, computing devices in the future will not be computers, but tags, sensors, badges, and commonplace objects all cooperating together in a service-oriented infrastructure.
- **Diversification.** Computing devices will evolve from a fully functional one-computer-does-all paradigm to one in which specialized, diversified devices will suit the requirements

of an individual for a specific purpose. A person may own several devices that slightly overlap in functionality, but each will be the preferred tool for each specific purpose.

- **Connectivity.** The independent pervasive computing devices—tags, sensors, badges—will be seamlessly connected to the network or to each other. Open, common standards will be required to achieve this level of connectivity and interoperability.
- **Simplicity.** These devices must be designed for simplicity of use. Intuitive interfaces, speech recognition, one-handed operation, instant on, and always connected are a few of the requirements for high but simple usability.

In addition to the four principles outlined here, a list of the technical requirements for pervasive computing is provided in Online File W9.9 at the book's Web site.

Contextual Computing

As described earlier, location can be a significant differentiator when it comes to providing services. However, knowing that the user is at a particular street corner is not enough to fully anticipate and meet the user's needs. For this, we need to know information such as the weather, the time of day, what is on the user's calendar, and other relevant *contextual attributes*. Context awareness refers to capturing a broad range of contextual attributes to better understand the consumer's needs and to determine what products or services may be required to fulfill those needs.

Context awareness is part of **contextual computing**, which refers to the enhancement of a user's interactions by understanding the user, the context, and the applications and information required, typically across a wide set of user goals (see Pitkow et al. 2002 for details). Contextual computing is about actively adapting the computational environment for each user based on a variety of factors.

contextual computing The enhancement of a user's interactions by understanding the user, the context, and the applications and information required.

Many strategists working in this field view contextual computing and context awareness as the Holy Grails of m-commerce. Contextual computing offers the prospect of applications that could anticipate our every wish and provide us with the exact information and services we are looking for—and also help us filter all those annoying promotional messages that we really do not care for. Such applications are futuristic at the present time, but they become more possible in a world of pervasive computing.

PERVASIVE COMPUTING INITIATIVES

A number of pervasive computing initiatives are underway that hold substantial promise for the future of EC and m-commerce and that have the substantial financial backing that will be needed for commercial success. A few of these initiatives—RFID, smart homes, smart appliances, smart cars, smart clothes, and sensor networks—are discussed next.

Radio Frequency Identification

Radio frequency identification (RFID) technology uses radio waves to identify items. An RFID system consists of (1) an RFID tag that includes an antenna and a chip with information about the item and (2) an RFID reader that contains a radio transmitter and receiver. An RFID tag remains inactive until radio frequency energy from the radio transmitter hits its antenna, giving the chip enough power to emit a 96-bit string of information, which is read by the radio receiver. This is three times the amount of information a bar code can hold, and the tag can be read through cardboard, wood, and plastic at a range of up to 30 feet. The reader passes this information to a computer for processing, either wirelessly or through a docking station.

radio frequency identification (RFID) Technology that uses radio waves to identify items.

RFID has been around for almost 60 years, but only now has it begun to receive widespread attention. Until recently, RFID was expensive, with tags costing 50 cents or more. However, as the cost of the tags continues to decline, the use of the technology is expected to expand. RFID technology is already being used for a variety of purposes:

- **Track moving vehicles.** The E-Z Pass prepay toll system uses RFID, as does Singapore's Electronic Road Pricing system, which charges different prices to drive on different roads at different times. Online File W9.10 at the book's Web site provides an example of the use of RFID technology for toll collection on a Los Angeles highway.

- **Track people.** In some Japanese schools, tags in backpacks or clothes track students' entry and departure from school buildings. In Denmark, the Legoland amusement park offers parents a child-tracking system that combines RFID and Wi-Fi. Beginning in 2005, all U.S. passports will contain an RFID tag, scanned upon entry and departure from the United States.
- **Track individual items.** The Vatican Library is tagging 2 million items in its collection. Retail giant Marks & Spencer is using antitheft tags on clothes and is tagging employee ID cards to control entrance into secure areas. The Jacksonville, Florida, airport has a pilot test for RFID tracking of luggage. The U.S. army is tracking inventory, including weapons, with RFID tags. The Star City Casino in Sydney, Australia is using RFID to keep track of 80,000 costumes and uniforms.
- **Protect secure areas.** FedEx uses RFID-tagged wristbands to give drivers access to their vehicles, reducing theft and speeding delivery time. The New York Police Department uses RFID tags embedded in ID tags to track visitors (Ferguson 2002).
- **Record transactions.** Exxon Mobil Corp.'s Speedpass cards and key rings allow customers to speed through checkout lines. At the Baja Beach Club in Barcelona, Spain, an RFID chip embedded just under a guest's skin is used to pay for purchases, including drinks at the pool.

As suggested in the opening case and in Chapter 7, the greatest interest in this technology is to track individual items to improve inventory and supply chain management. An indication of the high interest in this was the purchase of 500 million RFID tags in early 2003 by Gillette (*RFID Journal* 2002). Gillette is using the tags in a number of trial programs, including the largest RFID trial in the world at Wal-Mart (see Real World Case in Chapter 7). Retail giants such as Albertson's, Target, and Best Buy also are supporting adoption of the technology by their suppliers (Feder 2004).

Electronic Product Code (EPC)
An RFID code that identifies the manufacturer, producer, version, and serial number of individual consumer products.

One initiative underway that could lead to widespread support for the introduction of RFID is the **Electronic Product Code (EPC)**. The EPC identifies the manufacturer, producer, version, and serial number of each item. The concept is similar to the Universal Product Code (UPC) that currently appears on almost every consumer product. The UPC is a 12-digit number that is represented by bars and spaces of varying widths, readable by a bar code scanner. The use of an EPC-enabled RFID tag instead of an UPC bar code offers several advantages. First, an RFID tag does not require line-of-sight contact to be read. Second, RFID tags are not printed on paper, so they are less likely to be ripped, soiled, or lost. Third, the RFID tag identifies the item, not just the manufacturer and product. EPC will provide the ability to track individual items as they move from factories to store shelves, considerably improving supply chain collaboration; eliminating human error from data collection; reducing inventories, loss, and waste; and improving safety and security.

Several factors will determine the speed with which RFID will take off. The first of these is how many companies will mandate that business partners use RFID. So far, only Wal-Mart and the U.S. Department of Defense have required such use. The second factor is concerns about privacy issues raised by the use of the tags (Ferguson 2002; *Wired* 2004). Finally, the cost of the tags and the needed information systems to support RFID use is still high and is likely to remain so (Spivey-Overby 2004). However, Ryan (2004) suggests that in order to be winners, manufacturers must embrace the technology. For an overview of RFID implementation issues and attempted solutions, see Kharif (2004).

Smart Homes

In a smart home, the home computer, television, lighting and heating controls, home security system, and many appliances within the home can "talk" to each other via the Internet or a home intranet. These linked systems can be controlled through various devices.

In the United States, tens of thousands of homes are already equipped with home-automation devices, and there are signs that Europe is also warming to the idea. For instance, a 2001 study by the United Kingdom's Consumers' Association found that almost half those surveyed were interested in having the functions a "smart home" could offer, if they were affordable (Edgington 2001).

Currently, home automation systems support a number of different tasks:

- **Lighting.** Users can program their lights to go on and off or dim them to match their moods and needs for comfort and security.
- **Energy management.** A home's HVAC (heat, ventilation, and air conditioning) system can be programmed for maximum energy efficiency and controlled with a touch panel or a telephone.
- **Water control.** Watercop (watercop.com) is a device that relies on a series of strategically placed moisture-detection sensors. When the moisture level rises in one of these sensors, it assumes a water leak has occurred and sends a wireless signal to the Watercop control unit, which turns off the main water supply.
- **Home security and communications.** The window blinds, garage doors, front door, smoke detectors, and home security system all can be automated from a network control panel. These can all be programmed to respond to scheduled events (e.g., when the home owner goes on vacation).
- **Home entertainment.** Users can create a multisource audio and video center around their house that can be controlled with a touch pad or remote. For example, if a person has a DVD player in the master bedroom but wants to see a movie in a child's room, with the click of a remote the signal can be directed to the child's room.

Analysts generally agree that the market opportunities for smart homes will take shape over the next 3 to 5 years. These opportunities are being driven by the increasing adoption of broadband (cable and DSL) services and the proliferation of LANs and WLANs within the home. Online File W9.11 at the book's Web site shows how pervasive computing can be used to manage the care of the elderly at an assisted-living facility.

Smart Appliances

One of the key components of the smart home initiative is the smart appliance, an Internet-ready appliance that can be controlled by a small handheld device or desktop computer via a home intranet or the Internet.

One organization that is setting standards for smart appliances is the Internet Home Alliance (internethomealliance.com). The alliance's mission is to accelerate the process of researching, developing, and testing new home products and services that require a broadband or persistent connection to the Internet. Insights and Additions 9.3 exemplifies some of the types of smart appliances being developed by members of the alliance; in this case, however, the appliances are being used for commercial purposes, not in the home.

Appliance companies also are interested in capturing more information about the service life of the appliances they manufacture. In most cases, when an appliance is purchased and taken home, the manufacturer loses touch with the appliance unless the customer registers the product for warranty purposes. A networked appliance potentially could provide the manufacturer, as well as the owner of the appliance, with information that could be used to monitor the appliance's operation, performance, and usage. In addition, the networked appliance could provide information for diagnostic purposes, such as for repairs and troubleshooting (Pinto 2002).

To date, however, consumers have shown little interest in smart appliances. As a result, manufacturers of these appliances are focusing on improving people's lives by eliminating repetitive, low-attention tasks. One example is Sunbeam's Home Linking Technology (HLT) products that communicate with one another using an embedded technology called Power Line Communication (PLC). This enables, for instance, an HLT alarm clock to coordinate an entire morning's routine. The heating system, the coffee maker, and the lights in the kids' rooms go on and the electric blanket goes off, all according to a set schedule.

Whether offerings of this sort will prove any more successful than the earlier generations of smart appliances is an open question. In the near term, one of the biggest technical barriers to widespread adoption of smart appliances will continue to be the fact that most homes lack a broadband connection to the Internet.

Insights and Additions 9.3 Washers and Dryers on the Web

Imagine hooking up your washer and dryer to the Internet. To most homeowners, this would make as much sense as networking their refrigerators or microwaves. But what about hooking up washers and dryers in a laundromat? Would the payoff or acceptance be any greater? For a few "Internet laundry" companies, the answer is yes.

USA Technologies (*usatech.com*) has teamed up with IBM to create a system called eSuds.net that eliminates a number of the hassles and tedium associated with doing laundry. The system was tested at Boston College in 2002 and is currently available at Carnegie Mellon University, Cedarville University, and others. eSuds.net provides students with the following services:

- **Coin-free transaction options.** Washing and drying can be paid for with a student ID or PIN card and charged to the student's account.
- **E-mail or pager notification.** When the washing or drying is done, the system notifies the student via e-mail or a pager.
- **A virtual view of the laundry room.** Students can access a Web site that indicates which machines are available and the status of each machine (i.e., number of minutes remaining).
- **Detergent and fabric softener injectables.** Students do not need to provide detergent or fabric softener. These can be purchased as part of the washing/drying service and injected directly from the machines into the student's wash.

The e-Suds.net system also eliminates a number of the maintenance headaches encountered by the owner and operator of a laundromat. With e-Suds.net, the laundromat operator can conduct virtually coin-free transactions (eliminating jammed machines and reducing vandalism), monitor machine usage and performance, and service machines on an as-needed basis, reducing service costs and machine down time. In addition, operators can better control costs by holding service employees accountable for cash and inventory and can boost revenue by selling injected detergent and fabric softener as part of a wash.

Washing machine manufacturers are now offering similar services. Wash Alert (marketed by Alliance Laundry Systems for Speed Queen machines) is being used at the Illinois Institute of Technology, Ohio University, and Ball State University. LaundryView (marketed by Mac-Gray for Maytag machines) is being used at two Massachusetts colleges (see a demonstration at *demo.laundryview.com*). All three companies are planning to market their systems to large apartment complexes, a much larger but not as technologically sophisticated market.

Some in the industry are skeptical about just how successful these programs can be. They wonder, for example: What real, perceivable benefits will the technology provide? Will consumers see smart washing machines as a justification for price increases? And "it has to be a benefit beyond the 'gee whiz' factor that we're seeing today" (Bonnema 2004).

Sources: Cabrera (2004) and *usatech.com* (accessed November 2004).

Smart Cars

The average automobile on the road today contains at least 20 microprocessors that are truly invisible. They are under the hood, behind the dash, in the door panels, and on the undercarriage. Microprocessors control the entertainment system, decide when the automatic transmission should shift gears, remember seat positions for different drivers, and control the inside temperature. Car computers often operate independently, but some swap data among themselves—a growing trend. They require little maintenance and operate under extreme temperature, vibration, and humidity. In the shop, the onboard microprocessors are used to diagnose problems.

Following U.S. Department of Transportation (USDOT) guidelines (U.S. Department of Transportation 2002), the automotive industry is in the process of testing a variety of experimental systems to improve auto safety in areas such as collision avoidance, computer vision for cars, vehicle stability, and driver monitoring. For example, General Motors (GM), in partnership with Delphi Automotive Systems, has developed an Automotive Collision Avoidance System that employs radar, video cameras, special sensors, and GPS to monitor traffic and driver actions in an effort to reduce collisions with other vehicles and pedestrians (Sharke 2003).

There also is a growing trend to connect car microprocessors to mobile networks and to the Internet to provide emergency assistance, driving directions, e-mail, and other services. GM's OnStar system (onstar.com), for example, uses cellular telephone and satellite technology to connect a vehicle with a 24-hour service center. Some of the services provided by OnStar include automatic air bag deployment notification, route support to guide drivers to their destinations, stolen vehicle tracking, and remote unlocking of doors.

OnStar is the forerunner of smart cars of the future. The next generation of smart cars is likely to provide even more automated services, especially in emergency situations. For instance, although OnStar automatically notifies the service center when a vehicle's air bags have been deployed and immediately contacts emergency services if the driver and passengers are incapacitated, OnStar cannot provide detailed information about a crash. Newer systems are under development that will automatically determine the impact speed, whether the car has rolled over, and whether the driver and passengers were wearing seat belts. Information of this sort might be used by emergency personnel to determine the severity of the accident and what types of services will be needed.

Ideally, smart cars eventually will be able to drive themselves. Known as *autonomous land vehicles* (ALVs), these cars follow GIS maps and use sensors in a wireless environment to identify obstacles. These vehicles are being tested on experimental roads in California, Pennsylvania, and Germany.

Smart Clothes

Wearable computer devices were discussed in Section 9.6. In those examples, mobile computing devices were attached to clothing and safety gear. But what happens when computing technology is embedded in clothing?

One technique to make clothes smarter is to use RFID. For example, RFID tags are attached to clothing items for sale at Prada's Epicenter stores in New York, San Francisco, and Los Angeles (Duan 2002). If a customer wants to know about a particular item, she can take the item toward one of the displays in the store. The RFID reader installed in the display automatically reads the ID information on the tag and provides sketches, video clips of models wearing the item, and information about the item (color, cut, fabric, materials, and availability). If a customer takes a garment into one of the dressing rooms, the tag is automatically scanned and, again, information about the item will be displayed on an interactive touch screen in the dressing room. The dressing rooms also have a video-based "Magic Mirror." When the customer tries on the garment and turns around in front of the mirror, images are captured and played back in slow motion.

A similar application of RFID technology in clothes is on display at the Microsoft Home, a demonstration home in Redmond, Washington. An RFID tag in a shirt can be read by a "smart mirror" and complementary ties and pants in the wardrobe are identified. For children, the suitability of the item for a school dress code, or a parental code can be displayed. On laundry day, the tag provides cleaning instructions (Barron 2004).

Other initiatives are embedding the technology in the clothes, rather than simply putting an RFID tag on the item. A wireless jacket from German clothier Rosner GmbH includes an MP3 player and hands-free cell phone with headphones and a microphone built into the collar and a fabric control panel on the left sleeve. Other ideas recently introduced or under development include smart socks (conductive wire in wool socks to warm up cold toes), electrotextiles (antennas sewn into soldier's vests for communication), and body-sensing fabrics (a cotton t-shirt that can monitor the wearer's heart rate, body temperature, and other vital signs) (Eisenberg 2003).

Sensor Networks

Sensor networks are an area of pervasive computing with applications in homes, workplaces, and agricultural areas. A **sensor network** consists of a series of interconnected sensors that monitor the environment in which they are placed and report collected information to a network. Typically, each sensor has (1) a device to measure temperature, humidity, vibration, sound, motion, or whatever is being measured and (2) a weak radio transmitter capable of transmitting its data to the nearest sensor in a line or grid pattern. Each sensor passes its information, bucket-brigade style, along the network to a gateway node, which transmits the information to a computer for processing or storage. Companies such as Millennial Net, Crossbow Technology, and Ember are developing sensor nets that can (Baer 2003; Feder 2004):

sensor network
A series of interconnected sensors that monitor the environment in which they are placed.

- **Protect the environment.** Sensor nets are being used to warn when oil tanker equipment is in danger of failing, when nitrates in wastewater being used for irrigation begin to exceed toxic levels, and when a forest fire has been detected. At Great Duck Island off the coast of Maine, 190 sensors form a sensor net that monitors the daily life of the Leach's storm petrel.

- **Public safety.** Sensor nets assist in air traffic control, monitor stresses on aging bridges, and look for seismic activity along earthquake faults.
- **Monitor business and agricultural areas.** Company warehouses, open storage areas, and offices can be monitored inexpensively for detrimental environmental changes and security. In North Dakota, a sensor net in a sugar beet warehouse looks for pockets of heat buildup that can start to break down the sugar in the beets. In Western Australia, a variation of a sensor net puts up a "virtual fence" to detect livestock that have wandered out of a designated area. In California, a Wi-Fi-enabled sensor net is being used to improve grape production for premium wines (see EC Application Case 9.3).

Other, far more advanced sensor networks are on the drawing boards or in the imaginations of technologists and scientists. *Smart dust* particles are sensor circuits so small and inexpensive that they can be scattered anywhere a sensor net is needed. Potential smart dust applications include fighting forest fires (to closely monitor the spread of the fire) and the tracking of enemy troop movements in military operations (Webb 2003). Advanced machine-to-machine (M2M) integration is possible with sensor networks. An embedded sensor net with actuators and activators and a hierarchy of controlling computers can control the environment of a building without human intervention (Zetie 2003).

CASE 9.3

EC Application

WI-FI SENSOR NET AIDS WINE MAKERS

Pickberry, a California vineyard, is using a sensor network to answer an age-old question: how to grow better grapes. Grapes that produce good wine sell at a premium, so getting the right conditions for good growth can mean the difference between profit and loss for small vineyards.

One problem Pickberry faces is that the Sonoma County vineyard is spread over a hill, and growing conditions vary over the different parts of the slope. In order to monitor key growing conditions, such as temperature, humidity, and soil moisture, measurements need to be taken at various points throughout the vineyard. Field monitor sensors have been available for some time, but it has been prohibitively expensive and impractical to run data cables through the vineyard.

Pickberry's viticulturists also want information that can help them work out what grape-growing conditions produce good quality grapes. In the past, they have had to retrospectively speculate why vines growing in one part of the vineyard in one year produced better grapes than vines in another part of the vineyard in another year.

The solution is a sensor net that uses Wi-Fi for data connectivity. Sensors that monitor the conditions known to be key influences on grape quality have been placed throughout the vineyard. A sensor communicates its data to a central server by hopping from one Wi-Fi access point to another. The analysis engine on the server has a series of alerts built in that tells the growers when particular levels of indicators, such as soil moisture or temperature, are reached. Then corrective action can be taken.

Wireless was a natural choice for the grape growers, according to Bill Westerman, an associate partner at Accenture who worked on the project. "We are able to get data from 30 acres back to home base without having to run cables and without having to have radio transmitters that are powerful enough to make the leap from one end of the field to the other," said Westerman.

What are the results? Obviously the data are helping the Pickberry grape growers know much more about the health of their vines in different parts of the vineyard. They better understand how water is being retained and how much water needs to be applied, promoting both healthy vines and water conservation. The analysis also has been used to reduce the application of fungicides to control mildew. Now fungicides are applied only when and where they are needed rather than blanket coverage on a regular schedule, as was done before the sensor net.

The data also are helping the viticulturists work out the conditions that produce the best grapes. According to Westerman, "They are using this data in part to verify what they did before and to get details they never had before."

Source: Adaptation of Ward, M. "Wi-Fi Sensor Net Aids Wine Makers" BBC News. July 6, 2004 *news.bbc.co.uk/go/pr/fr/1/hi/technology/3860863.stm* (accessed July 2004).

Questions

1. How is the Wi-Fi sensor net contributing to Pickberry's core competency of grape production?
2. Why is Wi-Fi such an important part of this solution?
3. What are the results for Pickberry, the environment, and for the wine industry?

BARRIERS TO PERVASIVE COMPUTING

Considering that pervasive computing is a technological area still under development, it is not surprising to find that a number of technological, legal, and ethical issues still need to be fully explored and resolved if the promise of pervasive computing is to be realized.

Invisible, everywhere computing offers an opportunity to deliver new products and services to customers, but privacy is in great danger in a world of embedded internetworked devices (Hunter 2002). For example, fashion retailer Benetton Group SpA was considering attaching RFID tags to its Sisley line of clothing to help track shipping, inventory, shoplifting, and sales in the company's 5,000 stores. The idea was to integrate the RFID tag into the clothing labels. However, privacy groups expressed concern that the tags could also be used to track buyers, and some groups even urged that the company's clothing be boycotted. As a result, Benetton backed away from the plan, at least until an impact study is completed (Rosencrance 2003). The ethics of using RFID tags to track customers in a children's clothing store is explored in a *Harvard Business Review* business case study (Fusaro 2004). Privacy also is difficult to control in context-aware systems (e.g., see Jiang and Landay 2002).

For pervasive systems to be widely deployed, it is necessary to overcome many of the technical, ethical, and legal barriers associated with mobile computing (see Section 9.10) as well as a few barriers unique to ubiquitous computing. Davies and Gellersen (2002) provide a comprehensive list of technical challenges, social and legal issues, and economic concerns (including finding appropriate business models) in deploying pervasive computing systems. They also cite research challenges, such as component interaction, adaptation and contextual sensitivity, user interface interaction, and appropriate management mechanisms.

Section 9.11 ▶ REVIEW QUESTIONS

1. Define pervasive computing.
2. List four principles of pervasive computing.
3. Define contextual computing.
4. Describe how RFID works.
5. Discuss some of the ways that pervasive computing can be used in the home.
6. Describe a sensor net.

MANAGERIAL ISSUES

Some managerial issues related to this chapter are as follows.

1. **What's our timetable?** Although there has been a great deal of hype about m-commerce in the last few years, only a small number of large-scale m-commerce applications have been deployed to date. This means that companies still have time to carefully craft an m-commerce strategy. This will reduce the number of failed initiatives and bankrupt companies.
2. **Which applications first?** Finding and prioritizing applications is part of an organization's e-strategy. Although location-based advertising is logically attractive, its effectiveness may not be known for several years. Therefore, companies should be very careful in committing resources to m-commerce. For the near term, applications that enhance the efficiency and effectiveness of mobile workers are likely to have the highest payoff.
3. **Is it real or just a buzzword?** In the short run, m-commerce and location-based m-commerce may be just buzzwords due to the many limitations they now face. However, in the long run, both concepts will fly. Management should monitor technological developments and make plans accordingly.
4. **Which system to use?** The multiplicity of standards, devices, and supporting hardware and software can confuse a company planning to implement m-commerce. An unbiased consultant can be of great help. Researching the vendors and products carefully is important. Making sure an m-commerce strategy fits into the organization's overall business strategy is most critical of all.

RESEARCH TOPICS

Here are some suggested topics related to this chapter. For details, references, and additional topics, refer to the book's "Current EC Research" in the Online Appendix.

1. **Value Chain and Business Models of M-Commerce**
   - Value chain of m-commerce in various industries
   - Framework of business models in m-commerce
   - Comparison of the performance of different m-commerce business models
   - Potential and existing inhibitors of m-commerce
   - Social issues and cross-cultural differences in mobile Internet usage
2. **Effect of M-Commerce Platforms**
   - Comparison of m-commerce platforms, such as mobile phones, PDAs, and pocket PCs
   - Comparison of mobile platforms with the wired PC platform
   - Information quality of m-commerce platforms and customers' relative preference
   - Synergistic design of wired and wireless platforms to maximize customer satisfaction
   - Potential of portable Internet using the notebook PC as a terminal
   - Pricing of portable Internet services
   - Security issues and protection schemes of m-commerce
3. **M-Payments and Mobile Banking**
   - Business models and protocols of mobile payment gateways
   - Effectiveness of mobile payment methods in comparison with other micropayment methods, such as e-cash and e-mail payment
   - Alliance and competition of mobile service providers with banks
4. **Development of Context-Aware Computing and Its Applications in M-Commerce**
   - Factors that dynamically determine mobile contexts (e.g., location and user information)
   - Applications and potentials of context-aware computing
   - Intelligence- and CRM-backed models for context-aware computing
5. **Intelligent M-Commerce Search Aids**
   - Search algorithms using collaborative filtering and contents-based search
   - Personalized search aids backed by CRM systems
6. **Applications of RFID for Pervasive Computing**
   - Design of RFID applications for supply chain management and logistics
   - Pilot and case studies of RFID applications
   - Determining the costs and benefits of RFID applications

SUMMARY

In this chapter, you learned about the following EC issues as they relate to the learning objectives.

1. **What is m-commerce?** M-commerce is any business activity conducted over a wireless telecommunications network. M-commerce is a natural extension of e-commerce.
2. **Characteristics of mobile devices.** Mobile computing devices vary in size and functionality. One limitation of m-commerce is the poor usability of mobile devices with small screens, reduced memory, limited bandwidth, and restricted input capabilities.
3. **Wireless software development is difficult.** Developing software for m-commerce applications requires that the software adapt to the device rather than the other way around. Software development also is difficult because of competing standards. It is expected that over time some of these standards will converge or clear winners will emerge.
4. **M-commerce support services.** A range of support services, principally SMS, micropayments, voice, and location-based services, at present, support implementation of m-commerce applications.
5. **Wireless telecommunications networks.** Mobile computing devices connect to networks or other devices at a personal, local, metropolitan, or wide-area level. Bluetooth (personal) and especially cellular phone networks (wide area) are known technologies and are well established in the marketplace. Wi-Fi

(local) is new but increasingly popular. WiMax (metropolitan) is still being tested.

6. **Value-added attributes of m-commerce.** M-commerce can help a business improve its value proposition to customers by utilizing its unique attributes: ubiquity, convenience, interactivity, personalization, and localization.
7. **Drivers of m-commerce.** The following are the major drivers of m-commerce: large numbers of users of mobile devices; a developing "cell phone culture" among youth; demands from service-oriented customers; vendor marketing; declining prices; a mobile workforce; improved performance for the price; and increasing bandwidth.
8. **Finance, advertising, and content-providing applications.** Many EC applications in the service industries (e.g., banking, travel, and stocks) can be conducted with wireless devices. Also, shopping can be done from mobile devices. Location-based advertising and advertising via SMSs is expected to increase. Mobile portals aggregate and provide content and services for mobile users.
9. **Intrabusiness applications.** Intrabusiness applications such as sales force mobilization, inventory management, and wireless job dispatch offer the best opportunities for high return on investment for most organizations, at least in the short term.
10. **B2B and SCM applications.** Emerging B2B applications are being integrated with the supply chain and are facilitating cooperation between business partners.
11. **Consumer applications.** M-commerce is being used to provide applications in travel, gaming, information services, and health care.
12. **Location-based commerce.** The delivery of services using the location of the device, as determined by GPS, is emerging in the advertising, emergency response, and transport industries. These applications utilize the localization attribute of m-commerce.
13. **Limitations of m-commerce.** The mobile computing environment offers special challenges for security, including the need to secure transmission over open air and through multiple connecting networks. The biggest technological changes relate to the usability of devices. Finally, ethical, legal, and health issues can arise from the use of m-commerce, especially in the workplace.
14. **Pervasive computing.** This is the world of invisible computing in which virtually every object has an embedded microprocessor that is connected in a wired or wireless fashion to the Internet. Smart homes, smart appliances, smart cars, and other applications of pervasive computing will provide a number of life-enhancing, consumer-centric, and B2B applications.

KEY TERMS

Term	Page
1G	387
2G	387
2.5G	387
3G	387
4G	387
802.11a	383
802.11b	383
802.11g	383
Automatic crash notification (ACN)	403
Blackberry	376
Bluetooth	382
Compact Hypertext Markup Language (cHTML)	380
Contextual computing	409
Electronic Product Code (EPC)	410
Enhanced Messaging Service (EMS)	381
Extensible Hypertext Markup Language (xHTML)	380
Geographical information system (GIS)	402
Global positioning system (GPS)	381
Global System for Mobile Communications (GSM)	388
Hotspot	383
Interactive voice response (IVR)	381
Location-based m-commerce	401
M-wallet (mobile wallet)	392
Microbrowser	379
Micropayments	381
Mobile commerce (m-commerce, m-business)	375
Mobile portal	394
Multimedia Messaging Service (MMS)	381
Personal area network (PAN)	382
Personal digital assistant (PDA)	376
Pervasive computing	408
Radio frequency identification (RFID)	409
Sales force mobilization	395
Sensor network	413
Short Message Service (SMS)	380
Smartphone	376
Subscriber identification module (SIM) card	386
Synchronization	377
Telematics	403
Voice portal	381
Voice XML (VXML)	380
Wearable devices	397
Wi-Fi (wireless fidelity)	383
WiMax	385
Wireless 911 (e-911)	403
Wireless access point	383
Wireless Application Protocol (WAP)	379
Wireless local area network (WLAN)	383
Wireless Markup Language (WML)	380
Wireless metropolitan area network (WMAN)	385
Wireless mobile computing (mobile computing)	377
Wireless wide area network (WWAN)	386

QUESTIONS FOR DISCUSSION

1. Discuss how m-commerce can solve some of the problems of the *digital divide* (the gap within a country or between countries with respect to people's ability to access the Internet).
2. Discuss how m-commerce can expand the reach of EC.
3. Explain the role of wireless telecommunications networks in m-commerce.
4. Discuss the impact of m-commerce on emergency medical services.
5. How are GIS and GPS related?
6. What sells best in m-commerce? Make a list of products and services that offer the best opportunity for the development of m-commerce.
7. List three to four major advantages of wireless commerce to consumers presented in this chapter and explain what benefits they provide to consumers.
8. Location-based services can help a driver find his or her car or the closest gas station. However, some people view location-based services as an invasion of privacy. Discuss the pros and cons of location-based services.
9. Discuss how wireless devices can help people with disabilities.
10. Discuss the benefits of IVR.
11. Based on what you know about Internet services and wireless technology in your own country, what success and risk factors should DoCoMo consider if it wanted to offer i-mode services in your country?
12. What is the relationship between sales force mobilization and mobile supply chain management?
13. Discuss the benefits of telemetry-based systems.
14. Discuss the ways in which Wi-Fi is being used to support m-commerce. Describe the ways in which Wi-Fi is affecting the use of cellular phones for m-commerce.
15. Which of the m-commerce limitations listed in this chapter do you think will have the biggest negative impact on m-commence? Which ones will be minimized within 5 years? Which ones will not?
16. Describe two scenarios, one personal and one professional, in which contextual computing could apply.
17. Which of the following applications of pervasive computing—smart homes, smart appliances, and smart cars—are likely to gain the greatest market acceptance over the next few years? Why?

INTERNET EXERCISES

1. Learn about PDAs by visiting vendors' sites such as Palm, Handspring, HP, IBM, Phillips, NEC, Hitachi, Compaq, Casio, Brother, Texas Instruments, and others. List the m-commerce devices manufactured by these companies.
2. Access **progressive.com**, an insurance company, from your cell phone (use the "Go to . . ." feature). If you have a Sprint PCS wireless phone, do it via the Finance menu. If you have a Palm i705, you can download the Web-clipping application from Progressive. Report on these capabilities.
3. Research the status of 3G and the future of 4G by visiting **newstrove.com** (click on 3G and 4G) and **3gnewsroom.com**. Prepare a report on the status of 3G and 4G based on your findings.
4. Explore **nokia.com**. Prepare a summary of the types of mobile services and applications Nokia currently supports and plans to support in the future.
5. Enter **kyocera-wireless.com** and view the demos. What is a smartphone? What are its capabilities? How does it differ from a regular cell phone?
6. Enter **ibm.com**. Search for *wireless e-business*. Research the resulting stories to determine the types of wireless capabilities and applications supported by IBM software and hardware. Describe some of the ways these applications have helped specific businesses and industries.
7. Go to **wi-fihotspotlist.com** and **hotspot-locations.com** to determine whether there are any Wi-Fi hotspots in your area. Enter **wardriving.com**. Based on information provided at this site, what sorts of equipment and procedures could you use to locate hotspots in your area?
8. Enter **mapinfo.com** and look for the location-based services demos. Try all the demos. Find all of the wireless services. Summarize your findings.
9. Visit **ordersup.com**, **12snap.com/uk**, and similar sites that capitalize on location-based m-commerce. What features do these sites share?
10. Enter **packetvideo.com** and **microsoft.com/mobile/pocketpc**. Examine their demos and products and list their capabilities.
11. Enter **internethomealliance.com** and review their white papers. Based on these papers, what are the major appliances that are currently in most U.S. homes?

Which of these appliances would most homeowners be likely to connect to a centrally controlled network?

12. Enter onstar.com. What types of *fleet* services does OnStar provide? Are these any different from the services OnStar provides to individual car owners?

13. Enter epcglobalinc.org. Read about the EPC and the Guidelines on EPC for Consumer Products. What is EPC? What types of technologies are needed to support it? Why is it important?

TEAM ASSIGNMENTS AND ROLE PLAYING

1. Each team should examine a major vendor of mobile devices (Nokia, Kyocera, Motorola, Palm, BlackBerry, etc.). Each team will research the capabilities and prices of the devices offered by each company and then make a class presentation, the objective of which is to convince the rest of the class why one should buy that company's products.
2. Each team should explore the commercial applications of m-commerce in one of the following areas: financial services, including banking, stocks, and insurance; marketing and advertising; manufacturing; travel and transportation; human resources management; public services; and health care. Each team will present a report to the class based on their findings. (Start at mobiforum.org.)
3. Each team will investigate a global organization involved in m-commerce, such as gsmworld.com, wimaxforum.com, and openmobilealliance.com. The teams will investigate the membership and the current projects each organization is working on and then present a report to the class based on their findings.
4. Each team will investigate a standards-setting organization and report on its procedures and progress in developing wireless standards. Start with the following: atis.org, etsi.org, and tiaonline.org.
5. Each team should take one of the following areas—homes, cars, appliances, or other consumer goods, such as clothing—and investigate how embedded microprocessors are currently being used and will be used in the future to support consumer-centric services. Each team will present a report to the class based on their findings.

Real-World Case

WASHINGTON TOWNSHIP FIRE DEPARTMENT GOES WIRELESS

The Washington Township Fire Department (WTFD) is located just north of Columbus, Ohio. WTFD responds to more than 4,500 emergency medical services (EMS) calls every year. Time is critical when WTFD is responding to emergencies, which range from heart attacks to fire injuries to highway accidents. The service is run by emergency medical technicians (EMTs).

Rushing victims to the hospital is only part of the service offered by these dedicated technicians. Providing first aid at the scene of an accident and during transport of the injured in the ambulances is the other part. When a patient arrives at the hospital, the EMTs must provide information on what treatments and medications were administered and what health-related signs they observed in the patient. Such patient-care reports are critical to the continuance of treatment in the hospital, and they become a permanent part of the medical record. The information also is used to keep EMS records for planning, budgeting, training, and reporting to the state of Ohio.

In the past, the department had problems using 8-by-14-inch, multipart, multicopy paper forms. According to Jack McCoy, using paper forms caused several problems. First, not everyone's handwriting is legible, so it often was difficult for hospital personnel as well as the WTFD office staff to decipher the information. Second, on many occasions, the information was incomplete or even inaccurate. To restore the information took considerable, valuable time. Office staff at WTFD had to spend almost 1,800 hours a year processing information after the completion of the patient-care report. In fact, 85 percent of one full-time office employee's time was required just to reenter data that were already entered on the paper reports. But the major problem was the time EMTs spent filling out the forms, because this prevented them from returning quickly to the station to respond to other emergency calls.

A solution to the paperwork problems was a mobile data collection device (MobilEMS of Clayton I.D.S. Corp. powered by SQL Anywhere Studio from Sybase Corp.). The device allows EMTs to collect patient information quickly, easily, and accurately at the scene and to deliver that information to the hospital in a printout. This is done by using a series of data entry screens with drop-down menus containing vital information such as diagnoses, treatments rendered, drugs administered, and even street names. It also includes a signature-capture feature that allows EMTs to document a patient's refusal of treatment as well as transfer of care to the hospital.

Once the incident data are entered into the system's embedded SQL database, printing reports is simple. The technician beams the information from MobilEMS to the hospital printer's infrared port, and a clear document is produced. Back at the station, the EMTs synchronize the data in their handheld computers with the department computer systems by placing the MobilEMS in a docking station.

According to McCoy, it takes about 15 seconds to move the data into the system. This is a significant improvement over manual rekeying; using MobilEMS has reduced costs by more than 90 percent. Also, by eliminating handwriting and mandating the completion of required data fields that previously could have been skipped, accuracy has increased significantly.

Finally, the system is customizable. Fields can be added and additional information can be stored. Thus, additional applications are leading to a completely paperless environment.

Source: Compiled from Sybase (2003).

Questions

1. The system uses a mobile device with a docking station for data synchronization, but no remote, wireless connection is used. Would you recommend adding wireless? What for? Why or why not?
2. What are the potential legal issues presented by this case?
3. The MobilEMS system is based on electronic forms with checkmarks. Why not use a similar set of paper forms?
4. What are the benefits of the mobile system to the patient, to the hospital, and to the employees?
5. What are the benefits of the MobilEMS system to WTFD?

REFERENCES

The Age. "Singapore Airlines Introduces SMS Check-In." *The Age*, August 3, 2004a. theage.com.au/articles/2004/08/03/1091476476848.html (accessed October 2004).

The Age. "Landlines Yield to Mobiles in India." *The Age*, October 25, 2004b. theage.com.au/articles/2004/10/25/1098667675148.html (accessed November 2004).

Asaravala, A. "Four Wireless Technologies Move Toward Starting Gate." *USA Today*, March 28, 2004. usatoday.com/tech/wireless/data/2004-03-28-coming-tech_x.htm (accessed April 2004).

Baard, M. "After the Fall: Help for Climbers." *Wired*, December 24, 2002. wired.com/news/technology/0,1282,56146,00.html (accessed November 2004).

Baer, M. "The Ultimate On-the-Fly Network." *Wired*, December 2003. wired.com/wired/archive/11.12/network.html (accessed March 2005).

Barron, J. "Speak Clearly and Carry a Manual." *New York Times*, October 21, 2004. nytimes.com/2004/10/21/garden/21SOFT.html (accessed October 2004).

Becker, D. "Sega Forms Mobile Games Division." *CNET News*, April 2002. news.zdnet.co.uk/story/0,,t269-s2108679,00.html (accessed May 2003).

Bonnema, L. "How 'Smart' Will Laundry Be?" *Appliance Magazine.com*, September 2004. appliancemagazine.com/zones/consumer/04_laundry/editorial.php?article=577&zone=4&first=1 (accessed November 2004).

Bughin, J., et al. "Mobile Portals Mobilize for Scale." *The McKinsey Quarterly* (April–June 2001).

Burkhardt, J., et al. *Pervasive Computing: Technology and Architecture of Mobile Internet Applications*. Harlow, UK: Pearson Education, 2002.

Cabrera, A. "Checking Laundry Via the Internet" *InfoTech Tuesday*, April 13, 2004. ksu.edu/InfoTech/news/tuesday/archive/2004/04-13.html#gem (accessed November 2004).

CellularOnline. "Latest Global, Handset, Base Station, & Regional Cellular Statistics." cellular.co.za/stats/statsmain.htm (accessed November 2004).

Chatterjee, A., et al. "A Road Map for Telematics." *McKinsey Quarterly*, April–June 2002.

Clarke, I. "Emerging Value Propositions for M-Commerce." *Journal of Business Strategies* 18, no. 2 (2001): 133–148.

ClickZ Stats. "Mobile Users Yearning for Micropayments." *Clickz.com*, March 21, 2002. **clickz.com/stats/sectors/wireless/article.php/995801** (accessed March 2005).

Cohen, A. "Millstone Mobilizes to Deliver Coffee." *PC Magazine*, September 17, 2002. **sybase.hu/mediahighlights/mediahiglights0830.htm** (accessed March 2005).

Conrad, D. "Medlink to the Rescue." *Alaskas World*, March 11, 2002. **alaskasworld.com/news/2002/03/11_MedLink.asp** (accessed February 2003).

Coursaris, C., and H. Hassanein. "Understanding M-Commerce: A Consumer-Centric Model." *Quarterly Journal of Electronic Commerce* 3, no. 3 (July–September 2002): 247–271.

Davidson, P. "Inventive Wireless Providers Go Rural." *USA Today*, July 14, 2004. **usatoday.com/tech/news/2004-07-14-wireless_x.htm** (accessed July 2004).

Davies, N., and H. W. Gellersen. "Beyond Prototyping: Challenges in Deploying Ubiquitous Systems." *Pervasive Computing,* January–March 2002. **ee.oulu.fi/~skidi/teaching/mobile_and_ubiquitous_multimedia_2002/beyond_prototypes_challenges.pdf** (accessed May 2004).

Dekleva, S. "Wi-Fi and WiMax: The News." Panel Presentation at the 10th Americas Conference on Information Systems, New York, New York, August 5–8, 2004.

Designerz.com. "Chinese People to Send 550 Billion Text Messages This Year." *Designerz.com News*, August 10, 2004. **technology.news.designerz.com/chinese-people-to-send-550-billion-text-messages-this-year.html** (accessed November 2004).

Diaz, S. "Sony Retreat on Handhelds Is a Blow to Palm OS." *SiliconValley.com*. **siliconvalley.com/mld/siliconvalley/8818846.htm** (accessed June 2004).

DPS-Promatic. "Innovative Pay-by-GSM Meter." DPS-Promatic, June 2002. **dpspro.com/tcs_news_park.html** (accessed January 2003).

Duan, M. "Enhancing the Shopping Experience, One $2,000 Suit at a Time." *Mpulse,* November 2002. **cooltown.hp.com/cooltown/mpulse/1102-prada.asp** (accessed March 2005).

Edgington, C. "How Internet Gateways and Smart Appliances Will Transform Our Homes." *TNTY Futures*, 2001. **tnty.com/newsletter/futures/technology.html** (accessed February 2003).

Eisenberg, A. "For the Smart Dresser, Electric Threads That Cosset You." *New York Times*, February 6, 2003. **nytimes.com/2003/02/06/technology/circuits/06next.html** (accessed March 2005).

Elliott, G., and N. Phillips. *Mobile Commerce and Wireless Computing Systems*. Harlow, England: Pearson Education, 2004.

Ellison, C. "Palm Sees Up Tick in Development of Mobile Enterprise Applications." *e-Week*, May 18, 2004, **eweek.com/article2/0,1759,1594712,00.asp** (accessed March 2005).

Estrada, M. "Bridging the Wireless Gap." *Knowledge Storm: The Upshot,* October 2002. **knowledgestorm.com/info/user_newsletter/092402/wireless.jsp** (accessed May 2004).

Feder, B. J. "Wireless Sensor Networks Spread to New Territory." *New York Times*, July 26, 2004. **nytimes.com/2004/07/26/business/26sensor.html** (accessed March 2005).

Ferguson, G. T. "Have Your Objects Call My Objects." *Harvard Business Review* (June 2002): 138–144.

Fleishman, G. "Lufthansa Says Achtzig, Bitte!" *Wi-Fi Net News*, May 28, 2003. **wifinetnews.com/archives/001686.html** (accessed October 2004).

Forbes. "Software Experts Find 'First' Mobile Virus; Not Harmful Effects Yet." *Forbes.com,* June 15, 2004. **forbes.com/technology/feeds/wireless/2004/06/16/wireless01087398037128-20040615-152500.html** (accessed November 2004).

Fusaro, R. A. "None of Our Business?" *Harvard Business Review* (December 2004): 33–46.

GSM World. "Setting the Record Straight." 2004. **gsmworld.com/technology/3g/intro.shtml** (accessed November 2004).

Hamblen, M. "Get Payback on Wireless." *Computerworld*, January 1, 2001. **computerworld.com/mobiletopics/mobile/story/0,10801,54798,00.html** (accessed May 2004).

Hansmann, U., et al. *Pervasive Computing: The Mobile World,* 2d ed. Berlin: Springer, 2003.

Henning, T. "Wireless Imaging—Overcoming the Challenges." *The Future Image Report*. 2001 **futureimage.com/sfm.cgi?sn=8LB608/t=p/WIOC** (accessed January 2003).

Hornberger, M., and C. Kehlenbeck. "Mobile Financial Services on the Rise in Europe." *Bank Systems and Technology Online,* September 19, 2002. **banktech.com/story/wireless/BNK20020919S0005** (accessed January 2003).

Hunter, R. *World Without Secrets: Business, Crime, and Privacy in the Age of Ubiquitous Computing*. New York: Wiley, 2002.

Islam, N., and M. Fayad. "Toward Ubiquitous Acceptance of Ubiquitous Computing." *Communications of the ACM* 46, no. 2 (2003).

Jiang, X., and J. A. Landay. "Modeling Privacy Control in Context-Aware Systems." *Pervasive Computing*, July–September 2002.

Kakihara, M., and C. Sorensen. "Mobility: An Extended Perspective." *Proceedings of the 35th Hawaii International Conference on System Sciences*, Big Island, Hawaii, January 7–10, 2002.

Kakihara, M., and C. Sorensen. "Mobile Urban Professionals in Tokyo: Tales of Locational, Operational, and

Interactional Mobility." Paper presented at the Stockholm Mobility Roundtable, Stockholm, Sweden, May 22–23, 2003.

Kay, R. "Quickstudy: WiMax." *Computerworld*, December 1, 2003. **computerworld.com/mobiletopics/mobile/story/0,10801,87555,00.html** (accessed September 2004).

Kharif, O. "Like It or Not, RFID Is Coming." *Business Week Online*, March 18, 2004.

Koenig, D. "7-Eleven Adopting Wireless Technology." *eWeek*, October 11, 2004. **digitalwave.co.kr/english/ir/notice_view.php?id=02&nt_id=288&page=3** (accessed March 2005).

Kontzer, T. "Top Ten Uses for SMS." *Information Week*, June 11, 2003. **informationweek.com/techcenters/networking/wireless** (accessed June 2003).

Krishnamurthy, S. *NTT DoCoMo's I-Mode Phone: A Case Study, 2001.* **http://www.swlearning.com/marketing/krishnamurthy/first_edition/case_updates/docomo_final.pdf** (accessed November 2004).

Levere, J. "Wi-Fi Service Expands Its Reach." *New York Times*, July 27, 2004. **nytimes.com/2004/07/27/business/27wifi.html** (accessed March 2005).

Lipset, V. "Bluefish and Zaryba Enable Mobile Bill Payment." January 21, 2003. **mcommercetimes.com/Solutions/309** (accessed January 2003). Note: no longer available online.

Lipset, V. "Magex Launches Mobile Payments Using SMS." December 3, 2002. **mcommercetimes.com/Solutions/299** (accessed January 2003). Note: no longer available online.

Lyytinen, K., and Y. Yoo. "Issues and Challenges in Ubiquitous Computing." *Communications of the ACM* 45, no. 12 (2002): 63–65.

McKay, J., and P. Marshall. *Strategic Management of eBusiness*. Milton, Australia: John Wiley and Sons, 2004.

Microsoft. "Taco Bell Builds a Microsoft Windows CE-Based Solution in Support of Their Mystery Shopper Program." Microsoft.com, August 27, 2002. **microsoft.com/resources/casestudies/CaseStudy.asp?CaseStudyID=13354**) (accessed March 2005).

Microsoft. "Your Mobile Work Force Needs Mobile Solutions." *MSN Tech and Gadgets*, 2003. **tech.msn.com/guides/670780.armx** (accessed October 2004).

Needleman, R. "Targeted Wi-Fi." *Business 2.0*, December 2002. **business2.com/b2/web/articles/0,17863,532732,00.html** (accessed May 2004).

Nelson, M. "Kemper Insurance Uses Wireless Digital Imaging to Lower Costs, Streamline Process." *InformationWeek*, September 25, 2000. **informationweek.com/805/photo.htm** (accessed January 2003).

Nokia. "Nokia Brings Mobility to the Games Industry by Making Rich Games Mobile." Press release, November 4, 2002.

Ojeda-Zapata, J. "Chaska Goes Wi-Fi." *Twin Cities Pioneer Press*, May 26, 2004. **twincities.com/mld/twincities/business/technology/personal_technology/8759053.htm?1c** (accessed October 2004).

Paavilainen, J. *Mobile Business Strategies: Understanding the Technologies and Opportunities*. London: Pearson Education, 2002.

Perry, R. "Wireless Fidelity." *Technology Review*, September 2003.

Pinto, J. "The Pervasive Internet and Its Effect on Industrial Automation." *AutomationTechies.com*, November 2002. **automationtechies.com/sitepages/pid1020.php** (accessed June 2003).

Pitkow, J., et al. "Personalized Search: A Contextual Computing Approach May Prove a Breakthrough in Personalized Search Efficiency." *Communications of the ACM* 45, no. 9 (2002): 50–55.

Pmai.org. "Sony Electronics' ImageStation.com Joins with CVS/Pharmacy on In-store Photo Pick-up Service." *Pmai.org*, February 19, 2005. **pma2005.pmai.org/convention_daily/dmain.asp?dt=2/19/2005** (accessed March 2005).

Poropudas, T. "ATM Connection to Boost Mobile Payments." *Mobile CommerceNet*, February 15, 2003.

Raina, K., and A. Harsh. *MCommerce Security*. New York: Osborne, 2002.

Raskin, A. "Your Ad Could Be Here! (And Now We Can Tell You Who Will See It)." *Business 2.0*, May 2003. **business2.com/b2b/web/articles/0,17863,515629,00.html** (accessed May 2004).

Republica.IT. "Busta Paga in Pensione Lo Stipendio Arriva via SMS." *Republica.IT*, March 20, 2001. **repubblica.it/online/tecnologie_internet/tim/tim/tim.html** (accessed January 2003).

RFID Journal. "Gillette to Buy 500 Million EPC Tags." *RFID Journal*, November 15, 2002. **rfidjournal.com/article/articleview/115/1/1/** (accessed May 2004).

Richtel, M. "Where Entrepreneurs Go and the Internet Is Free." *New York Times*, June 7, 2004. **nytimes.com/2004/06/07/technology/07wifi.html** (accessed June 2004).

Rosen, C. "Our Cell Phones, Ourselves." *The New Atlantis*, Summer 2004. **thenewatlantis.com/archive/6/rosen.htm** (accessed March 2005).

Rosencrance, L. "Update: Benetton Backs Away from 'Smart Tags' in Clothing Line." *ComputerWorld*, April 4, 2003. **computerworld.com/industrytopics/retail/story/0,10801,80061,00.html** (accessed May 2004).

Rupp, W. T., and A. D. Smith. "Mobile Commerce: New Revenue Machine, or a Black Hole?" *Business Horizons*, July–August 2002.

Ryan, T. "RFID in the Consumer Industries." Research Report, Aberdeen Group, March 2004.

Sadeh, N. *M-Commerce*. New York: Wiley, 2002.

Sarkar, D. "Lawmakers Form 911 Caucus." *Federal Computer Week*, February 25, 2003. **fcw.com/fcw/articles/2003/0224/web-caucus-02-25- 03.asp** (accessed May 2004).

Scanlon, J. "The Way We Work." *Wired*, May 2003. **wired.com/wired/archive/11.05/unwired** (accessed May 2004).

Schuman, E. "RFID to Be Served 7-Eleven Style" *eWeek*, September 11, 2004. eweek.com/print_article/0,17-61,a=135048,00.asp (accessed September 2004).

Scornavacca, E., and S. Barnes. "M-Banking Services in Japan: A Strategic Perspective." *International Journal of Mobile Communications* 2, no. 1 (2004): 51–66.

Sharke, P. "Smart Cars." *Mechanical Engineering*, 2003. memagazine.org/contents/current/features/smartcar/smartcar.html (accessed February 2003).

Sharma, D. "Cell Phone Shipments on the Rise" *CNET News*, May 6, 2004. news.zdnet.com/2100-9584_22-5207340.html (accessed November 2004).

Shim, R. "Wi-Fi Arrest Highlights Security Dangers." *CNET News*, November 28, 2003. znet.com.com/2100-1105-5112000.html (accessed January 2004).

SiliconValley.com. "Philadelphia Joins List of Cities Mulling Wireless Internet for All." September 1, 2004. siliconvalley.com/mid/siliconvalley/9553298.html (accessed September 2004).

Smailagic, A., et al. "CMU Wearable Computers for Real-Time Speech Translation." *IEEE Personal Communications* 8, no. 2 (April 2001).

Spivey-Overby, C. "RFID at What Cost? What Wal-Mart Compliance Really Means." ForrTel (Webcast plus telephone), *Forrester Research*, May 25, 2004.

Steede-Terry, K. *Integrating GIS and the Global Positioning System*. Redlands, CA: Environmental Systems Research Institute, 2000.

Sybase. "Clayton I.D.S and Washington/Norwich Township Fire Departments." eshop.sybase.com/detail/printthis/1,6907,1023367,00.html (accessed March 2005).

Symbol. "Symbol Fills CVS' Prescription for Wireless Communications." *Symbol.com*, 2004. symbol.com/solutions/retail/retail_food_drug_cs_cvs.html (accessed November 2004).

Synergy. "TXT-a-Park." *Synergy.com*, March 2004. synergy.co.nz/case-studies/archive/txt-a-park-casestudy.htm (accessed September 2004).

USA Technologies. "Laundry Services Overview." usatech.com/laundry_overview.php (accessed November 2004).

U.S. Department of Transportation. "Intelligent Vehicle Initiative." May 13, 2002. its.dot.gov/ivi/ivi.htm (accessed February 2003).

Ward, M. "Wi-Fi Sensor Net Aids Wine Makers." BBC News, July 6, 2004. news.bbc.co.uk/go/pr/fr/-/1/hi/technology/3860863.stm (accessed July 2004).

Webb, W. "Smart-Dust Designers Deliver Dirt-Cheap Chips." *EDN Magazine*, November 27, 2003. edn.com/article/CA336870.html (accessed March 2005).

Weiser, M. "The Computer for the Twenty-First Century." *Scientific American* 265 (1991): 94–104.

Wired. "Get Wireless." *Wired*, Special Supplement, May 2003. wired.com/wired/current.html (accessed May 2004).

Wired. "American Passports to Get Chipped." *Wired*, October 21, 2004. wired.com/news/0,1294.65412.00.html (accessed October 2004).

Yapp, E. "Connecting the Unconnected." *The Star Online*, October 21, 2004. star-techcentral.com/tech/story.asp?file=/2004/10/21/itfeature/9145077&sec=itfeature (accessed November 2004).

Zetie, C. "Machine-to-Machine Integration: The Next Big Thing?" *InformationWeek*, April 14, 2003. informationweek.com/story/showArticle.jhtml?articleID=8900042 (accessed April 2003).

Zhao, Y. "Telematics: Safe and Fun Driving." *IEEE Intelligent Systems* 17, no. 1 (2002): 10–14.

CHAPTER 10

E-AUCTIONS

Learning Objectives

Upon completion of this chapter, you will be able to:

1. Define the various types of e-auctions and list their characteristics.
2. Describe the processes involved in conducting forward and reverse e-auctions.
3. Describe the benefits and limitations of e-auctions.
4. Describe some unique e-auction models.
5. Describe the various services that support e-auctions.
6. Describe the hazards of e-auction fraud and discuss possible countermeasures.
7. Describe bartering and negotiating.
8. Describe e-auction deployment and implementation issues.
9. Analyze future directions of mobile e-auctions.

Content

EBAY—THE WORLD'S LARGEST AUCTION SITE

The Opportunity

eBay is one of the most profitable e-businesses. The successful online auction house has its roots in a 50-year-old novelty item—Pez candy dispensers. Pam Omidyar, an avid collector of Pez dispensers, came up with the idea of trading them over the Internet. When she expressed this idea to her boyfriend (now her husband), Pierre Omidyar, he was instantly struck with the soon-to-be-famous e-business auction concept.

The Solution

In 1995, the Omidyars created a company called AuctionWeb. The company was renamed eBay and has since become the premier online auction house, with millions of unique auctions in progress and over 500,000 new items added each day. Almost 120 million potential buyers use eBay. Today, eBay is much more than an auction house, but its initial success was in electronic auctions.

The initial business model of eBay was to provide an electronic infrastructure for conducting mostly C2C auctions. There is no auctioneer; technology manages the auction process.

On eBay, people can buy and sell just about anything. The company collects a submission fee upfront, plus a commission that is a percentage of the sale amount. The submission fee is based on the amount of exposure the seller wants the item to receive, with a higher fee if the seller would like the item to be among the featured auctions in a specific product category, and an even higher fee if the seller wants the item to be listed on the eBay home page under *Featured Items*. Another attention-grabbing option is to publish the product listing in a boldface font (for an additional charge).

The auction process begins when the seller fills in the appropriate registration information and posts a description of the item for sale. The seller must specify a minimum opening bid. If potential buyers feel this price is too high, the item may not receive any bids. Sellers may set the opening bid lower than the *reserve price*, a minimum acceptable bid price, to generate bidding activity.

If a successful bid is made, the seller and the buyer negotiate the payment method, shipping details, warranty, and other particulars. eBay serves as a liaison between the parties; it is the interface through which sellers and buyers can conduct business. eBay does not maintain a costly physical inventory or deal with shipping, handling, or other services that businesses such as Amazon.com and other retailers must provide. The eBay site basically serves individuals, but it also caters to small businesses.

In 2001, eBay started to auction fine art in collaboration with icollector.com (*icollector.com*) of the United Kingdom and with the art auction house Sotheby's (*sothebys.com*), whose auction page is on eBay's main menu. Due to lack of profit, as of May 2003, eBay and Sotheby's discontinued separate online auctions and began placing emphasis on promoting Sotheby's live auctions through eBay's Live Auctions technology while continuing to build eBay's highly successful arts and antiques categories. The *sothebys.com* Web site still exists, but now is focused on supporting Sotheby's live auction business.

In addition, eBay operates globally, permitting international trades to take place. Country-specific sites are located in over 31 countries, including the United States, Canada, France, Sweden, Brazil, the United Kingdom, Australia, Singapore, and Japan. eBay also has equity in or owns several country-specific sites, such as those in China, India, Korea, and Japan, that generate 46 percent of eBay's business. Buyers from more than 150 other countries participate. eBay also operates a business exchange in which SMEs can buy and sell new and used merchandise in B2B or B2C modes.

eBay has over 60 local sites in the United States that enable users to easily find items located near them, to browse through items of local interest, and to meet face-to-face to conclude transactions. In addition, some eBay sites, such as eBay Motors, concentrate on specialty items. Trading can be done anywhere, anytime. Wireless trading also is possible.

In 2002, eBay Seller Payment Protection was implemented to make it safer to sell on eBay. Now sellers are protected against bad checks and fraudulent credit card purchases. The service offers credit card chargeback protection, guaranteed electronic checks, secure processing, and privacy protection. After a few years of successful operation and tens of million of loyal members, eBay decided to leverage its large customer base and started to do e-tailing, mostly at fixed prices. This may have been in response to Amazon.com's decision to start auctions or it may have been a logical idea for a diversification. By 2003, eBay operated several specialty sites.

In addition to eBay Motors cited earlier, *half.com*, the famous discount e-tailer, is now part of eBay, and so is PayPal, the P2P payment company.

A special feature is eBay Stores. These stores are rented to individuals and companies. The renting companies can use these stores to sell from catalogs or conduct auctions. In 2002, eBay introduced the Business Marketplace, located at *ebay.com/businessmarketplace*. This site brings together all business-related listings on eBay to one destination, making it easier for small businesses to find the equipment and supplies they need.

The Results

The impact of eBay on e-business has been profound. Its founders took a limited-access off-line business model and, by using the Internet, were able to bring it to the desktops of consumers worldwide. This business model consistently generates a profit and promotes a sense of community—a near addiction that keeps traders coming back.

eBay is the world's largest auction site, with a community of close to 125 million registered users as of winter 2004, about half of them outside the U.S. According to company financial statements, in 2004, it transacted over $40 billion in sales for revenue close to $3 billion and net income of about $500 million (Schonfeld 2005).

As a matter of fact, the only place where people are doing more business online than off-line (and considerably more, at that) is auctions. For comparison, e-tailing is less than 5 percent of total retail sales (*eMarketer* 2004).

Sources: Compiled from press releases at *eBay.com* (2002, 2003a, and 2003b), Mohammadian (2004), Stroebel (2003), Coffin (2004), and Prince (2004).

WHAT WE CAN LEARN . . .

The eBay case demonstrates the success of a company that implemented an EC business model that took off very rapidly. The case presents some of the ideas of auctioning. It also demonstrates that auctions can be an online-only e-commerce channel or they can be a supplementary channel. The operations and issues of auctions, as well as their variations and economic impacts, are the subject of this chapter.

10.1 FUNDAMENTALS OF DYNAMIC PRICING AND E-AUCTIONS

auction
Market mechanism by which buyers make bids and sellers place offers; characterized by the competitive and dynamic nature by which the final price is reached.

electronic auctions (e-auctions)
Auctions conducted online.

dynamic pricing
Prices that are determined based on supply and demand relationships at any given time.

As described in Chapter 2, an **auction** is a market mechanism by which sellers place items for buyers to make bids on (forward auction) or buyers place RFPs for specific items and sellers place bids to win the jobs (reverse auction). Auctions are characterized by the competitive and dynamic nature by which a final price is reached. Auctions, an established method of commerce for generations, deal with products and services for which conventional marketing channels are ineffective or inefficient.

The Internet provides an infrastructure for executing auctions at lower administrative costs and with many more participating sellers and buyers. **Electronic auctions (e-auctions)**, which are auctions conducted online, have been in existence for several years. Individual consumers and corporations alike can participate in this rapidly growing and very convenient form of e-commerce. For an elementary introduction to auctions, see Rothkopf and Park (2001). For more on how to do auctions, see the tutorial at ebay.com.

Although many consumer goods are not suitable for auctions and are best sold through conventional sales techniques (i.e., posted-price retailing), the flexibility offered by online auction trading may offer innovative market processes. For example, instead of searching for products and vendors by visiting sellers' Web sites, a buyer may solicit offers from all potential sellers. Such a buying mechanism is so innovative that it has the potential to be used for almost all types of consumer goods (e.g., see bidville.com). By soliciting a wide range of bids from many suppliers or customers, auctions improve the chances of finding the optimal match, particularly in B2B (Carrol 2000). Charities have taken silent auctions online. For example see gobid.ca.

Many major manufacturers and e-tailers are using auctions to sell products and services (e.g., Dell, Amazon.com, Sam's Club of Wal-Mart) or to buy products and services (e.g., GE, GM, Boeing). Also, hundreds of intermediaries, ranging from ebay.com to ubid.com, are active in this fast-growing, multibillion-dollar market.

As discussed in Chapter 2, the major characteristic of an auction is that it is based on dynamic pricing. **Dynamic pricing** refers to a transaction in which the price is not fixed but fluctuates based on supply-and-demand relationships. In contrast, catalog prices are fixed, as are prices in department stores, supermarkets, and many other storefronts.

There are several types of auctions, each with its own goals and procedures. It is customary to classify dynamic pricing into four major categories depending on how many buyers and sellers are involved, as shown in Exhibit 10.1 and described here. Each of the following auction types can be done online or off-line.

EXHIBIT 10.1 **Types of Dynamic Pricing**

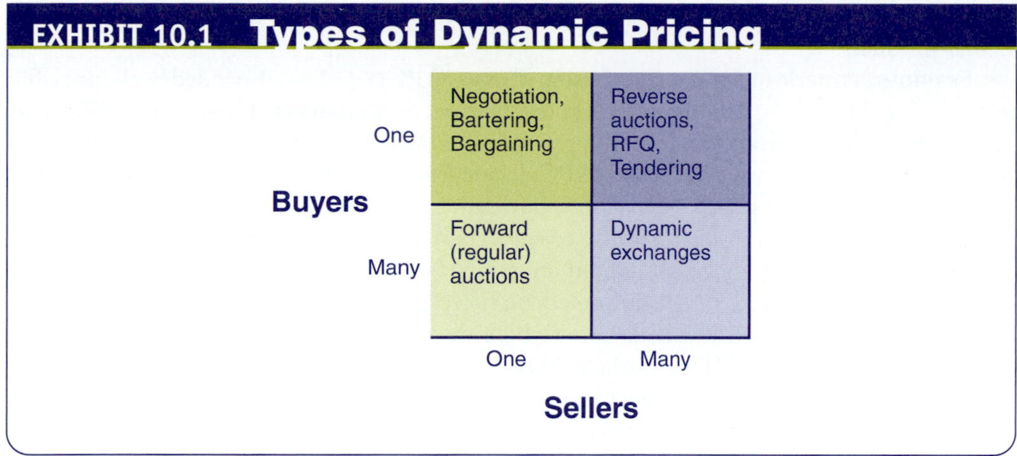

ONE BUYER, ONE SELLER

In the first configuration (pictured in the upper left-hand box in Exhibit 10.1), each party can use negotiation, bargaining, or bartering. The resulting price will be determined by bargaining power, supply and demand in the item's market, and possibly business-environment factors. This model is popular in B2B (see Chapter 5, Chapter 6, and the Real-World Case at the end of this chapter).

ONE SELLER, MANY POTENTIAL BUYERS

In the second configuration (in the bottom left-hand box of Exhibit 10.1), a seller uses a **forward auction** to offer a product to many potential bidders. There are two major types of forward auctions: liquidation and market efficiency (Exhibit 10.2). For additional details on these auctions, see Elliot (2000), Gallaugher (2002), and Kambil and van Heck (2002). Here

forward auction
An auction in which a seller offers a product to many potential buyers.

EXHIBIT 10.2 **Two Types of Forward Auctions**

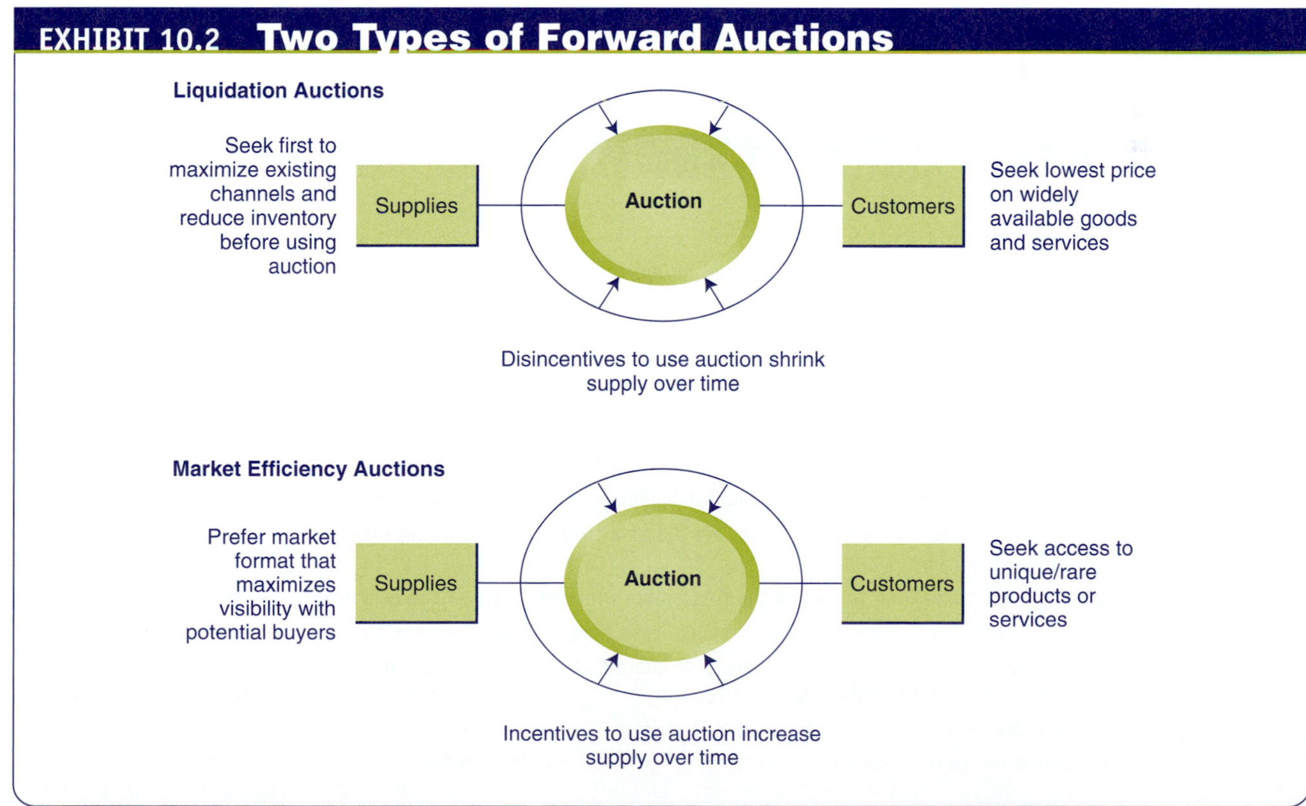

Source: Gallaugher, J. M. "E-Commerce and the Undulating Distribution Channel." *Communications of the ACM* (July 2002), Figure 3, p. 91.

is an example of a company that started auctions for liquidation but then moved to auction regular products.

Example. American Power Conversion Corp. (APC; apcc.com) needed a channel for end-of-life (old models) and refurbished power-protection products. These were difficult to sell in regular distribution channels. Before using auctions, the company used special liquidation sales that were not very successful. APC decided to use auctions to sell these items. APC turned to FreeMarkets to help it establish an online auction. Using its AuctionPlace technology, FreeMarkets deployed auction.apcc.com. (Note: *Site is no longer active.)* It also helped the company determine the best auction strategies (such as starting bid price and auction running length). The site became an immediate success. APC also started to auction some of its regular products (only merchandise for which there would be no conflict with the company's regular distributors) (FreeMarkets 2002a).

An example of B2C forward auctions is provided in Insights and Additions 10.1.

Sealed-bid auctions are another example of one seller, many potential buyers auctions. In a **sealed-bid auction**, a bidder bids only once. It is a *silent auction*, and the bidders do not know who is placing bids or what the bids are. In a *first-price* sealed-bid auction, the item is awarded to the highest bidder.

In a *second-price* sealed-bid auction (also called a **Vickrey auction**), the item is awarded to the highest bidder, *but at the second-highest price that was bid*. This is done to alleviate bidders' fears of significantly exceeding the item's true market value. (Sealed-bid auctions also can be conducted in reverse auctions.)

sealed-bid auction
Auction in which each bidder bids only once; a silent auction, in which bidders do not know who is placing bids or what the prices are.

Vickrey auction
An auction in which the highest bidder wins but pays only the second-highest bid.

reverse auction
Auction in which the buyer places an item for bid (*tender*) on a request for quote (RFQ) system, potential suppliers bid on the job, with price reducing sequentially, and the lowest bid wins; used mainly in B2B and G2B e-commerce.

ONE BUYER, MANY POTENTIAL SELLERS

Auctions in this category (pictured in the upper right-hand corner of Exhibit 10.1) are tenderings (biddings), in which one buyer solicits bids from many sellers or suppliers (see examples of GE and GM in Chapter 5). An item the buyer needs is placed on an RFQ (request for quote), and potential sellers bid on the item, *reducing the price sequentially*. (Refer back to Exhibit 2.5, page 57, for an illustration of this process.) These auctions are called **reverse auctions** because *suppliers* bid on goods or services the buyer needs. In reverse auctions, the price is reduced sequentially, and the lowest bid wins. These auctions are used mainly in B2B (both large and small businesses) or G2B; they may be combined with negotiations (see the Real-World Case at the end of this chapter).

Insights and Additions 10.1 B2C Forward Auctions: Dell Auction

Consumers who want to buy or sell used or obsolete Dell products can go to *dellauction.com*. Buyers will find lots of information on the items they are interested in. For example, a buyer can find out if the seller is Dell (B2C) or an individual (C2C). The buyer also can check product details, such as the item's warranty and condition. The site also offers general services, such as escrow. Everything on the site is organized for both buyers and sellers, from shopping carts and account management features to payment and shipping services.

The site is clearly marked with icons that denote and allow for the following:

- Reserve price, which is the lowest price at which a seller is willing to sell an item
- English auction, in which items are sold to the highest bidder at the end of auction period
- Dutch auction, in which more than one item is up for bid at a time and all winning bidders pay the same price, which is the *lowest* winning bid on the items
- QuickWin auction, in which an item is sold to the first bidder who meets the threshold price (set by the seller)
- Classified listings, in which the buyer and seller communicate off-line to decide on a price for the item
- AutoMarkdown listings, which are designed to sell large quantities of items and are posted with an initial price that declines over the course of the auction until the quantities run out
- Fixed-price listings that offer items for sale at the price listed
- "Hot" listings, indicating that an item has generated a high level of bidding interest

B2B Reverse Auctions

Most of the publicity related to auctions is around the C2C and B2C markets. However, as described in Chapters 5 through 7, B2B reverse auctions are gaining popularity as an online mechanism for buying goods and services. Sashi and O'Leary (2002) present the opportunities, advantages, and economic benefits of such B2B e-auctions. An example of a reverse auction using an intermediary is provided in EC Application Case 10.1.

C2C Reverse Auctions

Although most C2C auctions are of a forward nature (usually the English type), increasingly, individuals are conducting reverse auctions. For example, a person who wants to buy a used car may create a *request-for-bid* (RFB, for individuals) for the car of their dreams and let those who have such cars contact them. C2C auctions are provided by usanetcreations.com and by eBay.

"Name-Your-Own-Price" Model

Another type of auction in the one buyer, many potential sellers category is the **"name-your-own-price" model** pioneered by Priceline.com. In this model, a would-be buyer specifies the price (or other terms) that he or she is willing to pay to any willing and able seller. This is basically a C2B model, although it is also used by some businesses. Competitors to Priceline.com offer similar models.

"name-your-own-price" model
Auction model in which would-be buyers specify the price (and other terms) they are willing to pay to any willing seller; a C2B model, pioneered by Priceline.com.

MANY SELLERS, MANY BUYERS

In this final configuration (the bottom right-hand box in Exhibit 10.1), buyers and their bidding prices are matched with sellers and their asking prices based on the quantities on both sides and the dynamic interaction between the buyers and sellers. Stocks and commodities markets are typical examples of this type of configuration (see also Chapter 6 and the Real-World Case

CASE 10.1

EC Application

PROCUREMENT VIA AUCTIONS AT STE

Singapore Technologies Engineering (STE) (*stengg.com*), a large, integrated global engineering group specializing in the fields of aerospace, electronics, and land and marine systems, wanted to improve its e-procurement (sourcing) through the use of reverse auctions. Specifically, STE had the following goals:

- Minimize the cost of products it needed to buy, such as board parts.
- Identify a new global supply base for its multisourcing strategy.
- Maximize efficiency in the procurement process.
- Find new, quality suppliers for reliability and support.
- Consolidate existing suppliers.

These are typical goals of business purchasers. STE decided to use an intermediary. The software vendor started by training STE's corporate buyers and other staff. Then it designed an improved process that replicated the traditional negotiations with suppliers. Finally, it took a test item (printed circuit board assemblies) and prepared an RFQ, placing it for bid on the software vendor's global supply network, the database of suppliers that are exposed to the RFQs of buyers. The software vendor used a five-step process that started with the RFQ and ended with supplier management (which included supplier verification and training). At the end of the trial, STE saved 35 percent on the cost of printed circuit board assemblies.

It is interesting to note that one of STE's traditional suppliers threatened not to participate in the event. The supplier claimed that its prequoted price was so competitive that it would be impossible to beat the price through online bidding. In spite of these claims, STE followed through with the auction and subsequently awarded the business to another high-quality bidder with even better pricing.

Questions

1. Why was it necessary to restructure the purchasing process?
2. Why, in your opinion, was it beneficial for STE to use an intermediary? (Hint: See Chapter 5.)
3. Explain how STE's five goals can be achieved by using a reverse-auction process.

at the end of this chapter). Buyers and sellers may be individuals or businesses. Such auctions, which are usually done in exchanges, are called *double auctions* (see Section 10.5).

Section 10.1 ▶ REVIEW QUESTIONS

1. List the four categories of auctions.
2. List the major auction models available to one seller.
3. List the auction models available to one buyer.

10.2 BENEFITS, LIMITATIONS, AND STRATEGIC USES OF E-AUCTIONS

Electronic auctions are becoming important selling and buying channels for companies and individuals. Almost perfect market information is available to both buyers and sellers about prices, products, current supply and demand, and so on. These features provide benefits to all.

BENEFITS OF E-AUCTIONS

Electronic auctions create some economic changes that benefit both sellers and buyers. The major economic impacts of auctions are summarized in Exhibit 10.3.

Benefits to Sellers

Electronic auctions provide the following benefits to sellers.

Increased Revenues. By broadening the customer base and shortening the disposal cycle, sellers can reach the most interested buyers in the most efficient and fastest way possible and sell more at a price equal to buyer valuation of the product. This eliminates the need to predict demand and the risk of pricing items too high or too low.

Optimal Price Setting. Sellers can make use of the information about price sensitivity collected in auctions to set prices in fixed-price markets.

Removal of Expensive Intermediaries. Sellers can gain more customer dollars by offering items directly, rather than going through an expensive intermediary or by using an expen-

EXHIBIT 10.3 Economic Impacts of Auctions

Impact	Description
Market liquidity	Increases the number of buyers and sellers who can easily find each other and the auction place online and participate in the auction. This includes global participation.
Coordination mechanism for equilibrium in prices	Efficient mechanism for setting prices based on supply, demand, and participants' requirements.
Price discovery	Both buyers and sellers can easily find existing offers and bids, as well as historical price settlements. This is especially important for rare or valuable items.
Highly visible distribution mechanism	Via special offers, attention is given to certain groups of sellers (e.g., liquidators) and buyers (e.g., bargain hunters).
Price transparency	Prices are visible to all; this allows sellers to be more realistic, and buyers to be more careful in making offers.
Volume effect	The larger the auction site (e.g., eBay), the more the previous impacts are felt. Thus, transaction costs are lower, more people can find what they want, and more sellers can sell quickly at reasonable prices.

sive physical auction. Furthermore, using e-auctions via intermediaries can be more cost-effective than using a physical auction place.

Better Customer Relationships. Buyers and sellers have more chances and time to interact with each other, thus creating a sense of community and loyalty. Additionally, by making use of information gathered on customer interests, sellers can improve the overall e-commerce experiences of buyers and can deliver more personalized content, thus enhancing customer relationships.

Liquidation. Sellers can liquidate large quantities of obsolete or surplus items very quickly (see liquidation.com).

Lower Transaction Costs. Compared with manual auctions and liquidations, e-auctions offer lower transaction costs.

Lower Administrative Costs. The cost of selling via e-auctions can be much lower than the costs of selling via e-tailing or via non-Internet auctions.

Benefits of E-Auctions to Buyers

Electronic auctions provide the following benefits to buyers.

Opportunities to Find Unique Items and Collectibles. Items that are hard to find in certain areas or at certain times are auctioned regularly on the Internet. Stamps, coins, Barbie dolls, and the Pez dispensers that started the idea of eBay, are examples of popular collectible items on the Internet.

Lower Prices. Instead of buying at a fixed price, buyers can use the bidding mechanism to reduce prices.

Entertainment. Participating in e-auctions can be entertaining and exciting. The competitive environment, as well as the interaction between buyers and sellers, may create goodwill and positive feelings. Buyers can interact with sellers as much or as little as they like.

Anonymity. With the help of a third party, e-auction buyers can remain anonymous if they choose to.

Convenience. Buyers can trade from anywhere, even with a cell phone (m-commerce auctions).

Benefits to E-Auctioneers

Electronic auctions provide the following benefits to e-auctioneers.

Higher Repeat Purchases. Jupiter Communications conducted a study in 1998 that showed comparative repeat-purchase rates across some of the top e-commerce sites (Subramaniam 2000). The findings indicated that auction sites, such as eBay and uBid, tend to garner higher repeat-purchase rates than the top e-commerce B2C sites, such as Amazon.com.

A Stickier Web Site. "Stickiness" (Chapter 4) refers to the tendency of customers to stay at Web sites longer and come back more often. Auction sites are frequently stickier than fixed-priced sites. With sticky sites, more advertising revenue can be generated because of more impressions and longer viewing times.

Expansion of the Auction Business. Auctioneers easily can expand their markets (usually with the help of local partners). An example of how auctioneers can expand their business can be seen in the example of Manheim Auctions (McKeown and Watson 1999; Schermerhorn 2004; Woodham and Weill 2001).

In response to the Japanese company Aucnet's efforts to penetrate the U.S. car auction business, Manheim Auctions, the world's largest conventional auction house, created Manheim Online (MOL) in 1999 to sell program cars (cars that have been previously leased or hired). This Internet-based system has tremendous potential to change the car auction business. The United States has over 80,000 used car dealers, and Manheim auctions some 6 million cars for them each year. Trying to leverage its knowledge of the automobile market to provide services to its customers, Manheim developed two other products, Manheim Market Report and AutoConnect. It also is expanding its auction business in Europe. Manheim wants to continue to add value to Manheim Online as a way of discouraging competition and of extending sales through the Internet without cannibalizing Manheim's core business. By 2003, hundreds of car auction sites had gone online. Portals such as eBay, Yahoo!, Amazon.com, and MSN offer thousands of cars each year.

LIMITATIONS OF E-AUCTIONS

As discussed in Chapter 2, e-auctions have several limitations, including the following.

Possibility of Fraud. The fraud rate in e-auctions is very high. Auction items are in many cases unique, used, or antique. Because buyers cannot see the item, they may get a defective product. Buyers also may commit fraud. (For specific fraud techniques and how to prevent them, see Section 10.6.)

Limited Participation. Some auctions are by invitation only; others are open only to dealers.

Security. Some of the C2C auctions conducted on the Internet are not secure, and some potential participants are scared away by the lack of security.

Auction Software. Unfortunately, auction software is limited. Only a few off-the-shelf software solutions that can support the dynamic commerce functionality required for optimizing pricing strategies and that can be easily customized to a company or industry are available. However, this situation is improving with time.

Long Cycle Time. Some auctions last for days, and in some cases sellers and buyers need to meet face-to-face or with an escrow agent to complete a deal. This may take time, and buyers and sellers may not want to invest such time.

Monitoring Time. Although in some cases buyers can use intelligent agents to monitor an auction and place bids, in others they have to do this time-consuming job themselves.

Equipment for Buyers. Buyers need a PC to engage in electronic auctions, and they also need to pay for Internet access. These requirements have somewhat limited the number of potential auction participants. These requirements are changing as people are starting to use their cell phones for auctions; however, this requires an Internet-connected cell phone.

Order Fulfillment Costs. Buying at an auction site means that the buyer will pay shipment and handling costs plus any extra insurance cost.

STRATEGIC USES OF AUCTIONS AND PRICING MECHANISMS

Through dynamic pricing, buyers and sellers are able to adjust pricing strategies and optimize product inventory levels very quickly. For example, by using Web-based auctions and exchanges, suppliers can quickly flush excess inventory and liquidate idle assets. Buyers may end up with the power to procure goods and services at the prices they desire. The end game is to accurately assess and exploit market supply-and-demand requirements faster and more efficiently than the competition.

Aberdeen Group (2000) showed that e-marketplaces that are using auctions extensively are reaching liquidity ("critical mass") more rapidly than those utilizing only catalog-order-based trading environments. However, businesses are still struggling to understand how to truly implement dynamic pricing models to augment existing business practices.

One suggestion of how to do so was provided by Westland (2000), who observed that e-auctions place much more power in the hands of the consumer than does catalog-based e-tailing. He suggested that a number of lessons from stock exchange trading can be applied to e-tailing auctions; these lessons are listed in Online File W10.1.

For a summary of the impacts of electronic auctions on their participants, see Online Exhibit W10.1.

Section 10.2 ▶ REVIEW QUESTIONS

1. List the major benefits of auctions to buyers.
2. List the major benefits of auctions to sellers.
3. List the benefits of auctions to auctioneers.
4. List the limitations of auctions.

10.3 THE "NAME-YOUR-OWN-PRICE" C2B MODEL

One of the most interesting e-commerce models is the *"name-your-own-price" model.* This model, pioneered by Priceline.com (priceline.com), enables consumers to achieve significant savings by naming their own price for goods and services. Basically, the concept is that of a

C2B reverse auction, in which vendors bid on a job by submitting offers and the lowest-priced vendor or the one that meets the buyer's requirements gets the job.

Priceline.com either presents consumer offers to sellers who can fill as much of that guaranteed demand as they wish at price points requested by buyers, or, more likely, searches a Priceline.com database that contains vendors' minimum prices and tries to match supply against requests. Priceline.com asks customers to guarantee acceptance of the offer if it is at or below the requested price. Priceline.com guarantees this by having the buyer's credit card number. Priceline.com's "virtual" business model allows for rapid scaling; it uses the Internet to determine consumer demand and then tries to fill it. The approach is based on the fundamental concept of the downward-sloping demand curve in which prices vary based on demand.

However, Priceline.com and similar companies have one limitation: When a buyer names a price for an airline ticket, the buyer is *not* told the airline, how many stops are involved, or what time of the day the flight will depart until the buyer accepts the offer and pays. Then, the buyer must take the offer or lose that money that was guaranteed by a credit card. To overcome this problem, travelers can go to online travel sites such as expedia.com, orbitz.com, travelocity.com, aa.com, or others that provide price comparisons. By becoming familiar with the routes and flights, a buyer may be able to find what is available and then go to Priceline.com and bid for lower prices, knowing basically who is offering what. This way buyers will get real bargains.

Priceline.com has offered multiple products and services: travel services, personal finance services, an automotive service that offers new cars for sale, and credit cards and long-distance calling. (In 2000, Priceline.com suspended the delivery of food, gasoline, and groceries due to accumulated losses.) Some of the services are offered via partners. Priceline.com receives either a commission for referrals or royalties for use of its technology. In 2000, the company teamed up with Hutchison Whampoa Limited, one of Asia's largest owners of telecommunications and Internet infrastructure, to offer a range of services in Asia. Priceline.com also has offices in many other countries.

By 2002, the company offered products for sale in two categories: (1) A travel service that offers leisure airline tickets, hotel rooms, rental cars, vacation packages, and cruises, and (2) a personal finance service that offers home mortgages, refinancing, and home equity loans through an independent licensee. Also in 2002, Priceline.com purchased the Internet domain name and trademark of LowestFare.com, another Web-based travel site. Priceline.com licenses its business model to independent licensees.

At one point, Priceline.com initiated a service to help people get rid of old things that they no longer wanted. It was similar to an auction site, with heavy emphasis on second-hand goods, but with a different auction process. The site, named Perfect YardSale, was intended to let a user make an offer below the seller's asking price for an item, a system that is similar to the haggling that goes on at garage and yard sales. Perfect YardSale transactions were limited to local metropolitan areas, enabling the buyer and seller to meet face-to-face. Buyers and sellers would be able to swap goods in person, eliminating the expense of shipping. This service was discontinued in 2001 due to incurred losses. A variation of this service is the sale of previously owned items at fixed prices by half.com (now a subsidiary of eBay).

Section 10.3 ▶ REVIEW QUESTIONS

1. What is the logic behind the "name-your-own-price" model?
2. Describe Priceline.com's business model.
3. How does Priceline.com match supply and demand?
4. Enter priceline.com and try to book a flight. Comment on your experience.

10.4 THE E-AUCTION PROCESS AND SOFTWARE SUPPORT

A number of software products and intelligent tools are available to help buyers and sellers find an auction site, identify what is going on there, or complete a transaction. In an auction, sellers and buyers usually complete a four-phase process: Searching and comparing, getting started at an auction, bidding, and postauction activities (see Exhibit 10.4). Each phase has several support tools. Let's explore them by the auction phase in which they are used.

EXHIBIT 10.4 The E-Auction Process

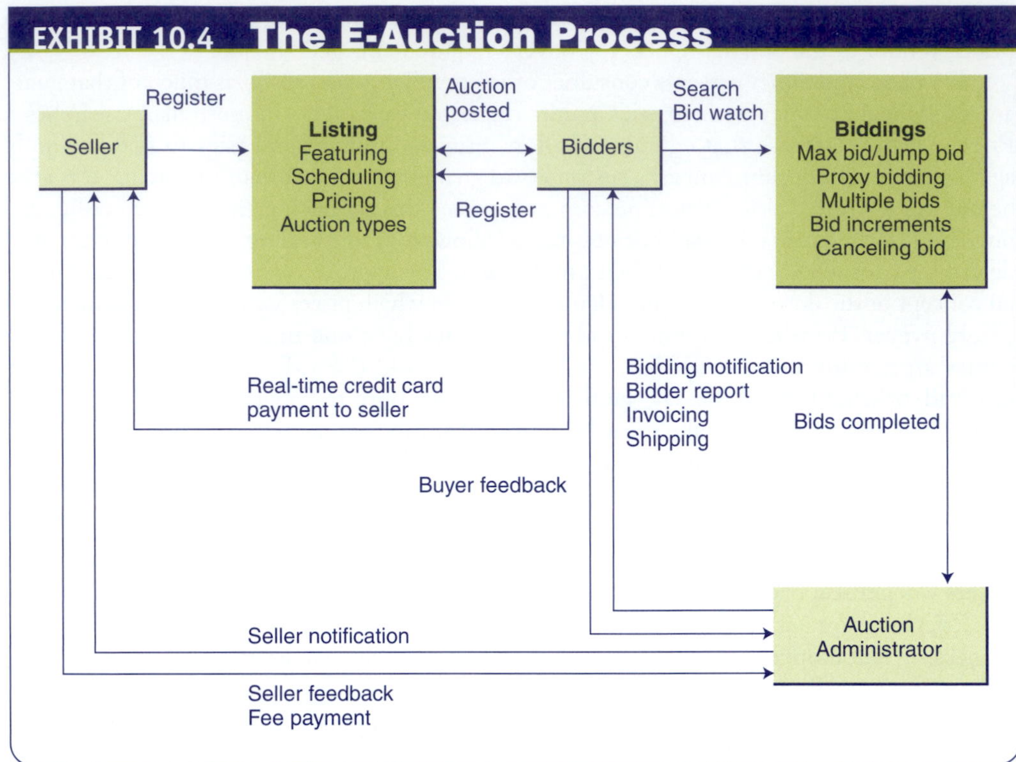

PHASE 1: SEARCHING AND COMPARING

Auctions are conducted on hundreds of sites worldwide. Therefore, sellers and buyers need to execute extensive searches and comparisons to select desirable auction locations.

Finding When and Where an Item Will Be Auctioned. Many Web sites offer links to hundreds of auction sites or provide search tools (e.g., see bidfind.com) to locate specific sites. The searching utility not only helps sellers find suitable locations to list their items, but it also enables buyers to browse available auction sites efficiently. See Insights and Additions 10.2 for an example of how to find when and where an item is being auctioned.

The following support tools may be helpful in conducting these searches and comparisons.

- Online Auctions Network (online-auctions.net) contains a directory of auction sites organized by categories, as well as auction news.
- The Internet Auction List (internetauctionlist.com) is packed with news about e-auctions worldwide and features access to innumerable specialty auctions.
- Yahoo!'s auction list (auctions.yahoo.com) contains a list of over 400 auction-related links.
- BidXS (bidxs.com) conducts searches across multiple auction houses for specific auction products and pricing information. It provides detailed historical information on previous sales.
- Turbobid (etusa.com) provides a mega-search service that helps local bidders look for items they want from a pool of e-auction sites.

Auction Aggregators and Notification. The search to find what is being auctioned and where can be difficult; there are thousands of auction sites, some of which are very specialized. **Auction aggregators** are companies that use software agents to visit Web auction sites, find information, and deliver it to users. Leading aggregators are vendio.com, bidfind.com, rubylane.com, and bidxs.com.

auction aggregators
Companies that use software agents to visit Web auction sites, find information, and deliver it to users.

At these aggregation sites, buyers fill out electronic forms specifying the item they want. Then the aggregators keep tabs on various auction sites and notify buyers by e-mail when the items they wish to bid on appear. There are two types of notification services; those that sup-

Insights and Additions 10.2 Finding a Pool Table and More

Assume a potential buyer is interested in purchasing a pool table. The following process is one example of how that buyer might use the Internet to locate the desired pool table. To find auctions that feature pool tables, the would-be buyer performs the following three steps:

1. Enter *bidfind.com*.
2. Choose "auctions".
3. Enter "pool table" as the keyword option.

The search engine claims that it searches more than 1,000 online dynamic pricing sites including auctions, shopping sites, and classified ads. The buyer's keyword search found 7 auctions, organized as shown here. BidFind links to the auction sites where the searched items are found.

Source: Courtesy of Seet Internet Ventures, Inc. © 2005.

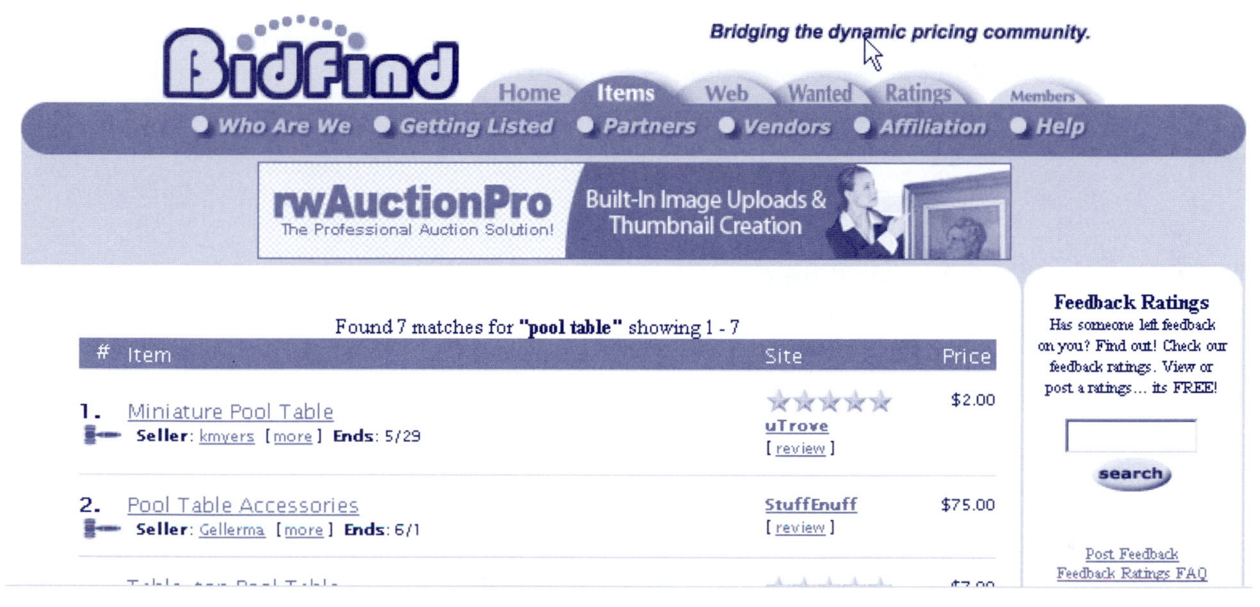

Source: Courtesy of VisionNetwork. Copyright © 1995–2005 VisionNetwork. All rights reserved. BidFind® is a registered trademark.

ply notification only for their own sites (e.g., eBay or baileyshoner.com) and those that report what is going on at many sites (e.g., bidslammer.com).

Aggregation services such as auction-portal.com are beneficial to users but may not be appreciated by the auction sites, as discussed in Online File W10.2 at the book's Web site.

The task of auction aggregation can be complex when the aggregators have to monitor several items, at several auction sites, in several auction formats. An international competition took place in 2000 called the Trading Agent Competition (TAC) to identify the best aggregators. See tac.eecs.umich.edu to read about recent TAC competitions.

Browsing Site Categories. Almost all auction homepages contain a directory of categories. Buyers can browse a category and its subcategories to narrow a search. Some sites also enable users to sort items according to the time a specific auction is being conducted.

Basic and Advanced Searching. Buyers can use search engines to look for a single term, multiple terms, or keywords. To conduct an advanced search, buyers can fill in a search form to specify search titles, item descriptions, sellers' IDs, auction item numbers, price ranges, locations, closing dates, completed auctions, and so forth.

PHASE 2: GETTING STARTED AT AN AUCTION

To participate in a third-party-managed auction, both the sellers and buyers need to register at the selected site. After registration, sellers can list, feature, schedule, and price their items on the site. Buyers can check sellers' profiles and other details, such as the minimum bid amount, the auction policy, and the payment method allowed, and then place their bids.

Registration and Participants' Profiles. Sellers and buyers must usually register their names, user IDs, and passwords before they can participate at a specific auction site. The user's page header (heading at the top of the screen) and the auction listing will display a basic description of sellers and their listings. Before submitting a bid, buyers can check a seller's profile, including the seller's membership ID and previous transactions. If the auction site provides voluntary verified-user programs such as those at winecommune.com and eBay, buyers can check whether sellers are qualified auction community members, as verified by a third-party security source.

Listing and Promoting. Several software programs are available that can help sellers list and promote their items:

- Advertisement Wizard (see illumix.com) helps users create attractive auction postings. With a simple-to-use, fill-in-the-blank interface, users can create great-looking advertisements for e-auctions or for other purposes.
- Auction Assistant (see tucows.com) and Ad Studio (adstudio.net) can be combined to create auction listings. This combination enables users to manipulate fonts, backgrounds, and themes on their listings. It also enables users to include standard details, such as shipping policy and payment terms, and to track sales, payments, and shipping.
- Auctiva Mr. Poster (auctiva.com), a software program that interacts directly with eBay, makes it simple to add pictures to a listing. The program can create up to 100 ads at a time, and it supports bulk listings.
- Auction Wizard (auctionwizard2000.com) can upload up to 100 items simultaneously. It is an auction-posting tool that saves time spent cutting and pasting. Auction Wizard also enters user ID, password, auction title, location, opening bid, category, and auction duration.
- Mister Lister (ebay.com/services/buyandsell), one of eBay's tools, enables sellers to upload the listings of many items at one time. Similarly, using Bulk Loader (see Yahoo! Auctions at auctions.yahoo.com), sellers can load several auctions into a spreadsheet program, such as Microsoft Excel.

Pricing. To post an item for bid, sellers have to decide the minimum bid amount, the bid increment, and any reserve price (i.e., the lowest price for which a seller is willing to sell an item). Sellers can search for guides for setting minimum bid amounts, the bid increments, and reserve prices for comparable auctions with Web search engines such as bidfind.com, freemerchant.com, pricescan.com, and vendio.com. If the auction site allows users to search the history of completed auctions, the transacted prices of similar items can provide a benchmark for a buyer's bidding strategy or a minimum acceptable price for a seller.

PHASE 3: BIDDING

In the bidding phase, buyers can submit bids themselves or can make use of software tools that place bids on their behalf. They also can use software tools to view the bidding status and to place bids across different sites in real time.

Bid Watching and Multiple Bids. Buyers can visit their personalized page at an e-auction Web site at any time and keep track of the status of active auctions. They can review bids and auctions they are currently winning or losing or have recently won. Tools provided in the United States by Bid Monitor (see bruceclay.com) enables bidders to view their bids across different auction sites in an organized way. Bidders also can use the tools to place bids at multiple auction sites using a single screen without switching from one window to another.

sniping
Entering a bid during the very last seconds of an auction and outbidding the highest bidder (in the case of selling items).

Sniping. The act of entering a bid during the very last seconds of an auction and outbidding the highest bidder is called **sniping**. Auto-sniping involves the use of electronic tools to perform the sniping automatically.

Occasionally, sellers use sniping in a fraudulent way: When the bidding price seems to be too low, they may enter the auction and bid for their own goods or services, pretending they are buyers. In this way, they hope to inspire other bidders to submit higher bids. (Being aware of this possible activity should help one avoid being caught up in last-minute bidding frenzy and overpaying in an online auction.)

Proxy Bids. A software system can be used for **proxy bidding**, in which the system operates as a proxy (agent) to place bids on behalf of buyers. In proxy bidding, a buyer should determine the maximum bid he or she is willing to offer and then place the first bid manually. The proxy will then execute the buyer's bids, trying to keep the bids as low as possible. When someone enters a new bid, the proxy will automatically raise the bid to the next level until it reaches the predetermined maximum price set by the bidder. This function is not applicable in a Dutch auction.

proxy bidding
Use of a software system to place bids on behalf of buyers; when another bidder places a bid, the software (the proxy) will automatically raise the bid to the next level until it reaches the predetermined maximum price.

PHASE 4: POSTAUCTION FOLLOW-UP

Postauction activities take place once an auction in completed. These activities include e-mail notifications and arrangements for payment and shipping.

Postauction Activities. Typical postauction activities include the following:

- **Bidding notifications.** Buyers receive e-mail, SMS messages, or beeper messages notifying them each time they are outbid or when they win an auction.
- **End-of-auction notices.** When an auction closes, the seller receives an e-mail (or SMS) message naming the highest bidder. End-of-auction e-mails provide seller and buyer IDs; seller and winner e-mail addresses (or cell phone numbers); a link to the auction ad, auction title, or item name; the final price; the auction ending date and time; the total number of bids; and the starting and highest bid amounts.
- **Seller notices.** After an auction ends, the seller generally contacts the buyer. The seller's notice typically provides the auction number and item name, total purchase price (winning bid plus shipping), payment preferences, mailing address, and so on.
- **Postcards and thank-you notes.** Sites such as vendio.com help sellers create a customized close-of-auction or thank-you note for winning bidders.

User Communication. User-to-user online communication provides an avenue by which auction participants can share information about goods and services being offered and about the process of online auctions. User communication appears in a number of forms:

- **Chat groups.** Areas on e-auction sites and auction-related sites where people can post messages in real time to get quick feedback from others.
- **Mailing lists.** A group of people talking about a chosen topic via e-mail messages.
- **Message boards.** Areas on e-auction and auction-related sites where people can post messages that other users can read at their convenience. Other message board participants can post replies for all to read.

Feedback and Ratings. Most e-auction sites provide a feedback and rating feature that enables auction community members to monitor each other. This feature enables users to rank sellers or bidders and to add short comments about sellers, bidders, and transactions.

Invoicing and Billing. An invoicing tool (invoicing utility) can e-mail and print one or all invoices, search and arrange invoices in a number of ways, edit invoices, and delete incorrect invoices. This utility automatically calculates shipping charges and sales tax. It also can automatically calculate and charge the seller with the listing fees and/or a percentage of the sale as commission. An example of this tool is Accounting 2002 from Billboardnet International (billboardnet.com).

Payment Methods. Sellers and winning bidders can arrange payment to be made by P2P service (e.g., paypal.com), cashier's check, C.O.D. (cash on delivery), credit card, electronic transfer, or through an escrow service (see Chapter 12). A number of online services are available for electronic transfer, escrow services, and credit card payment, including the following:

- **P2P transfer service.** Buyers can pay electronically via services at sites such as paybyweb.com, paypal.com, and bidpay.com. (See Chapter 12 for further discussion.)
- **Escrow service.** An independent third party holds a bidder's payment in trust until the buyer receives and accepts the auction item from the seller. The third party charges a fee

for the escrow service, and the service is usually reserved for high-end transactions. Examples of escrow service provider sites are moneybookers.com.com, i-escrow.com, fortis-escrow.com, and escrow.com.

- **Credit card payment.** PayPal (paypal.com) and CCNow (ccnow.com facilitate person-to-person credit card transactions (see Chapter 12).

Shipping and Postage. Finally, to complete the auction process, the purchased goods must be shipped from the seller to the buyer. Shipping providers such as iship.com help sellers by providing a one-stop integrated service for processing, shipping, and packing e-commerce goods. UPS, FedEx, the U.S. Postal Service, and other shippers move most of the purchases to their destinations (see Chapter 13 for details).

ADDITIONAL TERMS AND RULES

Each auction house has its own rules and guides. The following are some examples:

vertical auction
Auction that takes place between sellers and buyers in one industry or for one commodity.

auction vortals
Another name for a vertical auction portal.

- **Vertical auction.** A **vertical auction** is one that takes place between sellers and buyers in one industry or for one commodity (e.g., flowers, cars, or cattle). It is considered vertical because activity goes up and down the supply chain in a single industry, rather than horizontally between members of supply chains in different industries. Specialized sites for such auctions are sometimes referred to as **auction vortals**. Vertical auctions are particularly useful in B2B. At eBay "anything goes" (i.e., almost anything can be sold), but many auction sites specialize in one area. For example, policeauctions.com specializes in selling unclaimed or seized properties.
- **Bid retraction.** This is the cancellation of a bid by a bidder. It is used only in special circumstances. Usually a bid is considered to be a binding contract.
- **Featured auctions.** These are auctions that get added exposure on the auction Web site. Sellers pay extra for this service.
- **Other Services.** eBay provides many other services. For example, equipment financing is available, as are buyer tools, warranty programs, seller tools, security tools (to be discussed later), buyer and seller education, software downloads, and much more (see pages.ebay.com/services).

Section 10.4 ▶ REVIEW QUESTIONS

1. List the activities of phase 1. What software tools or agents are available to support these activities?
2. List the activities of phase 2. What software tools or agents are available to support these activities?
3. List the activities of phase 3. What software tools or agents are available to support these activities?
4. List the activities of phase 4. What software tools or agents are available to support these activities?

single auction
Auction in which at least one side of the market consists of a single entity (a single buyer or a single seller).

double auction
Auction in which multiple buyers and sellers may be making bids and offers simultaneously; buyers and their bidding prices and sellers and their asking prices are matched, considering the quantities on both sides.

10.5 DOUBLE AUCTIONS, BUNDLE TRADING, AND PRICING ISSUES

Other issues to be considered in a discussion of auctions are single versus double auctions, bundling of goods or services to attract buyers, and pricing.

DOUBLE AUCTIONS

Auctions may be single or double. In a **single auction**, an item (or several identical items) is either offered for sale by one seller and the market consists of multiple buyers making bids to buy or an item is wanted by one buyer and the market consists of multiple sellers making offers to sell. In either case, one side of the market consists of a single entity.

In a **double auction**, multiple buyers and sellers may be making bids and offers simultaneously. An example of a double auction is stock trading. In double auctions, multiple units of a product may be auctioned off at the same time. The situation becomes complicated when the quantity offered is more than one and buyers and sellers bid on varying quantities.

Although many online auctions are single, double auctions are the form used for transactions involving corporate stocks and commodities (grains, metals, livestock, etc.). In a given trading period, any seller may make an offer while any buyer makes a bid. Either a seller or a buyer may accept the offer or bid at any time. The difference between the cost and price paid is the seller's profit; the difference between the price paid and valuation is the buyer's surplus. If quantities vary, as in a stock market, a *market maker* needs to match quantities. For details, see Choi and Whinston (2000).

Prices in Double Auctions

According to Choi and Whinston (2000) and Scalas and Chincotti (2004), double-auction markets tend to generate competitive outcomes. Simply put, a double auction is an interactive market in which both buyers and sellers are competitive. In contrast, in a single auction, contract prices may be much higher or much lower than in a competitive format. This conclusion may have a significant effect on the future use of double auctions in the digital economy.

Ideally, any effort to promote competitiveness should include expanding online double auctions and similar market mechanisms, because they offer an opportunity to raise economic efficiencies that is unsurpassed by any physical market organization. For auctioneers, however, single auctions generate substantially more revenue than double auctions.

BUNDLE TRADING

One of the major characteristics of the digital economy is the ability of businesses to personalize and customize products and services. Many e-businesses do this by offering their customers a customized collection of complementary goods and services. **Bundle trading** involves selling (auctioning) several related products or services together. For example, airline tickets, hotel rooms, rental cars, meals, and amusement park admission tickets can be *bundled* as a packaged leisure product. Some bundled products that are vertically related (e.g., a software product and a hardware product) may be provided by different vendors. Although a purchase that involves multiple sellers may be carried out through a series of transactions or auctions, bundle trading offers an efficient alternative solution.

bundle trading
The selling of several related products and/or services together.

The management and operation of a bundle market is complex, and it differs considerably from those of single or double auction markets. For a discussion of the bundle market, see Choi and Whinston (2000) and Hoos and Boutilier (2001).

PRICES IN AUCTIONS: HIGHER OR LOWER?

Compared with competitive (nonauction) markets, prices in forward auctions tend to be higher, reaching monopoly level when there is only one seller or one product, such as an old painting (Choi and Whinston 2000). In general, the auction seller is in a better position to maximize revenues than is the seller in a competitive market. When the auction seller is selling a product among multiple bidders, the expected price is often higher than in the competitive market.

However, in many instances, prices in auctions are lower. This may happen in cases of liquidation, in which the seller's objective is to sell as quickly as possible. For example, truckers or airlines selling unused capacity at the last minute usually do so at a lower price. Alternatively, buyers go to online global markets where they can get products more cheaply than those imported by intermediaries. In general, buyers expect online prices to be lower, and they compare prices at aggregating auction sites. Also, considering the fact that most C2C auctions are for used merchandise and many B2B auctions may include used or obsolete products, bargain prices are likely to prevail.

Finally, a more fundamental reason for lower online auction prices is that an online auction is usually an alternative selling channel rather than an exclusive selling arrangement. Therefore, buyers can always revert to physical markets if online bids exceed prices posted in physical markets. In short, few people in online auctions are willing to pay what they are expected to pay in physical markets. However, if products are sold exclusively through online auctions (e.g., rare paintings), the average price certainly will be high.

Pricing Strategies in Online Auctions

Both sellers and buyers may develop pricing strategies for online auctions. Sellers have the option to use different auction mechanisms, such as English, Dutch, sealed-bid first price, and sealed-bid second price. Buyers need to develop a strategy regarding how much to increase a bid and when to stop bidding. These topics are relevant to off-line auctions as well and will not be dealt with here.

Section 10.5 ▶ REVIEW QUESTIONS

1. Describe double auction operations and pricing.
2. What is bundle trading?
3. Discuss the conditions under which prices in online auctions are higher or lower than prices in physical auctions.

10.6 E-AUCTION FRAUD AND ITS PREVENTION

According to the National Consumers League (nclnet.org) (McKay 2003 and NCL's National Internet Fraud Watch Information Center 2004), of all of the e-commerce activities conducted over the Internet, fraud is most prevalent and serious in e-auctions. The U.S. Fraud Complaint Center says that the median dollar loss per auction fraud was $225 in the first half of 2001, but jumped to $489 in the second half of the year, as criminals evidently focused on high-tech, big-ticket items (Lee 2002), and to $803 in 2004 (per www1.ifccfbi.gov/ 2004). In 2003, auction fraud appears to be 35 to 40 percent worse than in 2002, judging from the reported 400 frauds at any given time, as compared with 250 in 2002 (Sullivan 2003).

TYPES OF E-AUCTION FRAUD

Fraud may be conducted by sellers, buyers, or others (for a list see ftc.gov/bcp/menu-internet.htm). The following are some examples of fraud; some are unique to e-auctions, others can be found in any type of EC.

Bid Shielding. The use of phantom bidders to bid at a very high price when an auction begins is called **bid shielding**. The phantom bidders pull out at the last minute, and the bidder (friend of the phantom bidder) who bids with a very low price wins. The bogus bidders were the shields, protecting the low bid of the bidder in the stack by scaring off real bidders.

bid shielding
Having phantom bidders bid at a very high price when an auction begins; they pull out at the last minute, and the bidder who bid a much lower price wins.

Shilling. A similar type of fraud can be conducted by sellers. In this fraud, called **shilling**, sellers arrange to have fake bids placed on their items (either by associates or by using multiple user IDs) to artificially jack up high bids. If they see that the legitimate high bid does not meet their expectations as the end of an auction draws near, they might pop in to sell the item to themselves. This way they can put the item again for auction, attempting to get a higher price next time.

shilling
Placing fake bids on auction items to artificially jack up the bidding price.

Fake Photos and Misleading Descriptions. In reaching for bidders' attention, some sellers distort what they can truly sell, or fail to disclose all relevant information about the item(s). Borrowed images, ambiguous descriptions, and falsified facts are some of the tactics that sellers might employ to convey a false impression of the item.

Improper Grading Techniques. The grading of items is one of the most hotly debated issues among buyers and sellers. A seller might describe an item as 90 percent new, whereas the bidder, after receiving the item and paying the full amount, feels that it is only 70 percent new. Condition is often in the eye of the beholder. Although many grading systems have been devised and put to use, condition is still subject to interpretation.

Bid Siphoning. Luring bidders to leave a legitimate auction by offering to sell the "same" item at a lower price. The buyer then loses protections offered by the auction site, such as insurance, guarantees, quality, and so on.

Selling Reproductions as Originals. A seller sells something that the seller claims is original, but it turns out to be a reproduction.

Failure to Pay. Buyers do not pay after a deal is agreed upon.

Failure to Pay the Auction House. Sometimes sellers fail to pay the auction's listing or transaction fees.

High Shipping Costs and Handling Fees. Some sellers just want to get a little more cash out of bidders. Postage and handling rates vary from seller to seller. Some charge extra to cover "handling" costs and other overhead intangibles, whereas others charge to cover the cost of packaging supplies, even though such supplies often are available for free.

Failure to Ship Merchandise. This is the old collect-and-run routine. Money was paid out but the merchandise never arrives. A lesser problem is failure to deliver on time.

Loss and Damage Claims. Buyers claim that they did not receive an item or that they received it in damaged condition and then ask for a refund. They might be trying to get a freebie. The seller sometimes cannot prove whether the item ever arrived or whether it was in perfect condition when shipped.

Fake Escrow Services. Presenting itself as an independent trusted third party, a fake service will take the seller's items and the buyer's money and disappear

Switch and Return. The seller has successfully auctioned an item, but when the buyer receives it, the buyer is not satisfied. The seller offers a cheerful refund. However, what the seller gets back is a mess that does not much resemble the item that was originally shipped. Some buyers may attempt to swap out their junk for someone else's jewels.

Other Frauds. Many other types of fraud also are possible, including the sale of stolen goods, the use of false identities, providing false contact information, and selling the same item to several buyers.

For more about auctions see ftc.gov and scambusters.org.

PROTECTING AGAINST E-AUCTION FRAUD

The largest Internet auctioneer, eBay, has introduced several measures in an effort to reduce fraud. Some are free; others are not. The company has succeeded in its goal: less than one-tenth of 1 percent of the transactions at eBay were fraudulent in 2001 (Konrad 2002). The following are some of eBay's antifraud measures.

User Identity Verification. eBay uses the services of Equifax to verify user identities for a $5 fee. Verified eBay User, a voluntary program, encourages users to supply eBay with information for online verification. By offering their Social Security number, driver's license number, and date of birth, users can qualify for the highest level of verification on eBay.

Authentication Service. Product authentication is a way of determining whether an item is genuine and described appropriately. Authentication is very difficult to perform because it relies on the expertise of the authenticators. Because of their training and experience, experts can (for a fee) often detect counterfeits based on subtle details. However, two expert authenticators may have different opinions about the authenticity of the same item. eBay has links to companies that provide this specialized service including opinions, authentication, and grading (see the following). These companies charge a small fee.

Grading Services. Grading is a way of determining the physical condition of an item, such as "poor quality" or "mint condition." The actual grading system depends on the type of item being graded. Different items have different grading systems—for example, trading cards are graded from A1 to F1, whereas coins are graded from poor to perfect uncirculated. For a tutorial on grading diamonds, see bluenile.com.

Feedback Forum. The eBay Feedback Forum allows registered buyers and sellers to build up their online trading reputations. It provides users with the ability to comment on their experiences with other individuals.

Insurance Policy. eBay offers insurance underwritten by Lloyd's of London. Users are covered up to $200, with a $25 deductible. The program is provided at no cost to eBay users. Supplementary insurance is available from companies such as AuctionInsurance.com. At other auction sites, such as amazon.com/auctions, some insurance is provided, but extra insurance may be needed.

Escrow Services. For items valued at more than $200 or when either the buyer or seller feels the need for additional security, eBay recommends escrow services (for a fee). With an easy-to-access link to a third-party escrow service, both partners in a deal are protected. The buyer mails the payment to the escrow service, which verifies the payment and alerts the seller when everything checks out. At that point, the seller ships the goods to the buyer. After an agreed-upon inspection period, the buyer notifies the service, which then sends a check to the seller. eBay, Yahoo!, and other large online auction sites provide their own escrow services. (An example of a third-party provider of online escrow services can be found at i-escrow.com or fortis-escrow.com.) For details on how escrow services work for auctions, see auctions.yahoo.com, and ftc.gov.

Nonpayment Punishment. eBay implemented a policy against those who do not honor their winning bids. To help protect sellers, a first-time nonpayment results in a friendly warning. A sterner warning is issued for a second-time offense, a 30-day suspension for a third offense, and indefinite suspension for a fourth offense.

Appraisal Services. Appraisers use a variety of methods to appraise items, including expert assessment of authenticity and condition and reviewing what comparable items have sold for in the marketplace in recent months. An appraised value is usually accurate only at the time of appraisal. Eppraisals.com (eppraisals.com) offers users access to over 700 experts and a selection of online appraisal services that are located throughout eBay's categories of fine art, antiques, and collectibles, as well as on eBay Premier.

Physical Inspection. Providing for a physical inspection can eliminate many problems. This is especially true for collectors' items. When the seller and buyer are in the same location, it is easy to arrange for such inspections. eBay offers inspection services on a regional basis, so buyers can arrange for nearby inspections.

Item Verification. One way of confirming the identity and evaluating the condition of an item is through verification. With verification, neutral third parties will evaluate and identify an item through a variety of means. For example, some collectors have their item "DNA tagged" for identification purposes. This provides a way of tracking an item if it changes ownership in the future. In addition to the antifraud measures discussed here, one can use the general EC fraud protection measures suggested in Chapters 11 and 17, at ftc.gov/bcp/menu-internet.htm, and at infofaq.com (see online auctions).

Other Security Services. eBay has a security center that offers all the above and much more. For example, there is a dispute resolution (between a buyer and seller) center.

Section 10.6 ▶ REVIEW QUESTIONS

1. What types of fraud can be perpetuated by sellers?
2. What types of fraud can be perpetuated by buyers?
3. What kinds of protections exist for sellers?
4. What kinds of protections exist for buyers?

10.7 BARTERING AND NEGOTIATING ONLINE

In addition to the more common types of auctions, in which money is exchanged for goods, dynamic pricing can also take the form of online bartering. Also, prices in e-commerce can be arrived at through a process of negotiation.

BARTERING ONLINE

bartering
The *exchange* of goods and services.

electronic bartering (e-bartering)
Bartering conducted online, usually by a bartering exchange.

Bartering is an *exchange* of goods and services. The oldest method of trade, bartering today is usually conducted between organizations, but some individuals exchange goods and services as well. The problem with bartering is that it is often difficult to find partners. As discussed in Chapter 2, *bartering exchanges*, in which intermediaries arrange the transactions, were created to address this problem

Electronic bartering (e-bartering)—bartering conducted online, frequently in a bartering exchange—can improve the matching process by inducing more customers to take part in the exchange. Items that are frequently bartered electronically include office space, storage space, factory space, idle facilities and labor, surplus products, and banner ads. E-bartering may have tax implications that need to be considered.

Bartering Web sites include intagio.com, itex.com, irs.gov/taxtopics/tc355.html, u-exchange.com, and whosbartering.com. For more on online bartering, see fsb.com and search for "virtual bartering 101." Bartering is popular today not only between organizations, but also among individuals (e.g., see web-barter.com). A bartering matching service for professionals is available at barteryourservices.com.

NEGOTIATION AND BARGAINING

Dynamic prices also can be determined by **online negotiation**, a back-and-forth process of bargaining until buyer and seller reach a mutually agreeable price. Negotiation is a well-known process in the off-line world, especially for expensive or specialized products such as real estate, automobiles, and jewelry. Negotiations also deal with nonpricing terms, such as shipment, warranties, payment methods, and credit. E-markets allow negotiations to be used for virtually all products and services. Three factors may facilitate negotiated prices (see Choi and Whinston 2000): (1) intelligent agents that perform searches and comparisons; (2) computer technology that facilitates the negotiation process; and (3) bundling and customization of products.

online negotiation
A back-and-forth electronic process of bargaining until the buyer and seller reach a mutually agreeable price; usually done by software (intelligent) agents.

Technologies for Electronic Bargaining

According to Choi and Whinston (2000), negotiation and bargaining involve a bilateral interaction between a seller and a buyer who are engaged in the following five-step process that is necessary to complete a transaction:

1. Search. Bargaining starts with the collection of all relevant information about products and sellers or buyers. Computer-mediated markets excel in raising the search efficiency. Once information has been gathered, it is processed into a usable data set that is employed for decision making. (Search tools are described in Chapters 3 and 4.)

2. Selection. Selection filters retrieve screened information that helps the buyer and seller determine what to buy (sell) and from whom to buy (sell). This filtering process encompasses the purchasing evaluation of products and seller alternatives, based on consumer-provided criteria such as price, warranty, availability, delivery time, and reputation. The screening/selection process results in a set of names of products and partners to negotiate with in the next step. Software agents, such as Pricemix (bizrate.com), and other tools can facilitate the selection (see Chapter 4).

3. Negotiation. The negotiation stage focuses on establishing the terms of the transaction, such as price, product quality, delivery, and payment terms. Negotiation varies in duration and complexity depending on products, partners, economy, and the market. In online markets, all stages of negotiation can be carried out by automated programs or software agents (see Appendix D at the book's Web site).

Negotiation agents are software programs that make independent decisions to make bids within predetermined constraints or to accept or reject offers. The agents may be bound by negotiation rules or protocols that control how sellers and buyers interact. For example, price negotiation may start with a seller's list price as a starting point, or it may start with any bid or offer depending on the rule. For an overview of electronic negotiation and comparison, see Beam et al. (1999) and Cellich and Jain (2003).

The following are the major *benefits* of electronic negotiations:

- Buyers and sellers do not need to determine prices beforehand, and therefore do not have to engage in the difficult process of collecting relevant information. Negotiating prices transfers the burden of determining prices (i.e., market valuation) to the market itself. Insofar as the market process is efficient, the resulting negotiated prices will be fair and efficient.
- Intelligent agents can negotiate both price and nonprice attributes such as delivery time, return policy, and other transactions that add value. In addition, intelligent agents can deal with multiple partners (see Appendix D at the book's Web site). An example of such an application is negotiation among several freight dispatch centers of different companies to solve their vehicle routing problems.

Other applications include (1) a factory-floor-scheduling domain, where different companies in a subcontracting web negotiate over a joint scheduling problem, and (2) an airport resource management domain, where negotiations take place for the servicing of airplanes between flights. For further discussion, see Esmahi and Bernard (2000) and Strobel (2000).

4. Continuing Selection and Negotiation. The previous steps are repeated sequentially, if necessary, until an agreement is reached and a contract is written.

5. Transaction Completion. After product, vendor, and price are determined, the final step is to complete the transaction. This involves online payment and product delivery in accordance with the terms determined in the negotiation phase. Other characteristics, such as customer service, warranty, and refunds, also may be implemented.

Section 10.7 ▶ REVIEW QUESTIONS

1. What are the major reasons for e-bartering?
2. List the factors that may facilitate price negotiation.
3. Discuss the benefits of electronic negotiation.
4. What are the five steps of online negotiation?

10.8 ISSUES IN E-AUCTION IMPLEMENTATION

Implementing auctions may not be a simple task, and for this reason many companies use intermediaries. This section presents some issues that are relevant to auction implementation and use.

USING INTERMEDIARIES

Any seller can auction from a Web site. The question is: Will the buyers come? A similar issue was raised in Chapter 3: Should sellers sell from their own storefront, join an online mall, or use another third-party arrangement?

Large companies often choose to auction from their own Web sites. If their name is well recognized, they can feel some assurance that buyers will come. Chapter 5 presented the example of GM selling obsolete equipment from its site. Governments and large corporations also are using reverse auctions from their sites for procurement purposes. Some individuals even conduct auctions from their own Web sites.

However, most individuals, SMEs, and many large companies use third-party intermediaries whose charges are fairly low compared with the charges in physical auctions and who provide many services that are critical to the success of auctions.

The following are some of the popular third-party auction sites:

- **General sites.** Such sites include eBay (the world's largest general auction site); auctions.amazon.com, auctions.yahoo.com, bidz.com, auctions.overstock.com, and ubid.com.
- **Specialized sites.** Such sites are focused on a particular industry or product; examples include americanautobargains.com and autocastle.com (cars), baseball-cards.com, teletrad.com (coins), and oldandsold.com (antiques).
- **B2B-oriented site.** Such sites are focused on B2B transactions; examples include asset-auctions.com and liquidation.com.

USING TRADING ASSISTANTS

To encourage people to auction online, eBay and some other auction sites provide trading assistants, as described in Insights and Additions 10.3.

AUCTION RULES

The success of auctions depends on a large number of rules. These rules are intended to smooth the auction mechanism and to prevent fraud. Wurman (2001) divides the rules into three major categories: bidding rules, clearing rules, and information-revelation rules. These rules are shown in Online Exhibit W10.2. The rules provide definitions, restrictions, and timing constraints.

Insights and Additions 10.3 Using Trading Assistants at eBay

What if a person wants to sell on eBay but is not familiar with computers? What if an escrow service is needed? What if items need to be picked up? eBay provides a complete solution called Trading Assistants that helps people sell their items on eBay. To execute this service, eBay has trading assistants (or advisors) in many cities (and even countries).

What do eBay's trading assistants do? A trading assistant will pick up the items to be sold. The total of value of the items to be auctioned must be $200, and there is a minimum value of $50 per item. The trading assistant will store the items, and the items are insured. The trading assistant will prepare photos and offer the seller suggestions on how to advertise the items.

The assistant will list the items on eBay's auction site. Auctions last 7 to 10 days. If an item does not sell, it is relisted, and it is auctioned again (twice). If the item does not sell after the second auction listing, the seller can lower the minimum acceptable price or pick up the item. After successful completion of the auction, the trading assistant packs and ships the item and collects the money from buyers.

Trading assistants receive a commission of the sale price. The commission normally is 25 percent, and the seller pays only after the item sells. eBay employs tens of thousands of trading assistants. Some of them earn $100,000 to $150,000 a year in commissions. By selling an item on eBay, a seller is able to reach about 120 million potential buyers. Of course, sellers can do everything themselves and pay little commission.

Auction rules may vary from country to country due to legal considerations. They may also vary within a country due to the nature of the items auctioned, the auctioneer's policies, and the nature of competition among the auction houses.

STRATEGIC ISSUES

When a company decides to use auctions as a selling channel, it must make several important strategic decisions, such as which items (services) to auction; what type of auction to use; whether to do the auction in-house or to use an auctioneer (and which one); how long to run each auction; how to set the initial prices; how to accept a bid; what increments to allow in the bidding; and what information to disclose to the participants (e.g., the name of bidders, the current prices, etc.). For help in making such decisions, see Elliot (2000).

One of the strategic issues in B2B is the potential conflict with existing distributors and distribution channels. Therefore, some companies use auctions only to liquidate obsolete, used, refurbished, or damaged products.

AUCTIONS IN EXCHANGES

Chapter 6 mentioned that exchanges are using auctions to supplement their regular buying/selling channels. An example of such an auction is provided in EC Application Case 10.2.

INFRASTRUCTURE FOR E-AUCTIONS

Auction sites can be built as special, independent buy-side systems, integrated with sell-side or buy-side systems, or run over the Internet or private lines.

Building Auction Sites

The process of building auction applications is complex for two reasons. First, as shown in Exhibit 10.5, the number of needed features can be very large. Second, in the case of B2B auctions, auctions must be integrated with the back-end offices and with the legacy systems of participating companies. Exhibit 10.6 shows a sample integrated auction model. Because of these two complexities, even large companies typically outsource the construction of auction sites. For example, Dell used FairMarkets to build its auction site (FairMarkets is now part of eBay).

CASE 10.2

EC Application

ONLINE WINE GRAPE AUCTIONS

The wine industry is hundreds of years old, consisting of established associations between grape growers and wineries. Typically, vintners have multiyear buying contracts with growers. The adoption of the Internet to facilitate the trading grapes was slow, but in March 2001, 2,000 tons of grapes were traded in the first of many online auctions.

The WineryExchange (*wineryexchange.com*), based in Novato, California, conducted the first online grape auction. "In the past, most of the deals have been cut on the tailgate of a truck," said Doug Wilson, director of grower relations at Fetzer Vineyards, producer of 4 million cases of wine each year. His company was among some 30 buyers who intended to make $10 to $50 bottles of wine from the "super premium" grapes to be offered by 36 California coastal growers.

Unfortunately, WineyExchange had to stop auctioning grapes because it became uneconomical to manage it. It changed into an information portal for the grape-grower community. It also is a storefront for wine sellers.

Selling wines, especially antique ones, online is very popular. Although regular wines are sold via catalogs, antique, expensive wines are selling at auction much of the time. WineBid conducts auctions regularly for wine collectors (see the Auction Index at *winebid.com*). Such auctions are usually of a C2B type. If a buyer finds what he or she wants and the price is right, the buyer can track the lot (12-bottle case) or an individual bottle and see current bids before placing a new one. For instructions, see "Buying" at *winebid.com*. Several other types of wine auctions exist, including forward B2C and C2C auctions at eBay.

Sources: Compiled from Reuters (2001), *wineryexchange.com* (accessed 2002–2005), and *winebid.com* (accessed 2005).

Questions

1. What drives auctions in the winery exchange?
2. Enter *winebid.com* and find how auctions are conducted.
3. Why is the C2B model successful?
4. Find other sites that auction wines and compare them with *winebid.com*.

AUCTIONS ON PRIVATE NETWORKS

Electronic auctions that run on private networks have been in use for over 15 years. Chapter 6 introduced the flower market in the Netherlands as a B2B example of an auction on a private network. The following are additional B2B examples of auctions on private networks.

Pigs in Singapore and Taiwan

The auctioning of pigs in Singapore and Taiwan has been conducted over private networks for over 10 years (see Neo 1992). Farmers bring the pigs to one area where they are washed, weighed, and prepared for display. The pigs are auctioned (via a forward auction) one at a time while the data on each pig are displayed to approved bidders who bid by watching a displayed price. If bids are submitted, the price can be increased incrementally only by 20 cents per kilogram. The process continues until no further bids occur. The bidders' financial capability is monitored by a computer. (The computer verifies that the bidder has available funds in the prepaid account that was opened for the auction.) The process is illustrated in Exhibit 10.7.

Livestock in Australia

ComputerAided Livestock Marketing (CALM) is an online system for trading cattle and sheep that has been in operation since 1986. In contrast with the pig-auctioning system in Singapore, livestock do not have to travel to CALM, a feature that lowers stress in the animals and reduces sellers' costs. The buyers use PCs or Vt100 terminals to connect to the auction. The system also handles payments to farmers.

Section 10.8 ▶ REVIEW QUESTIONS

1. What are the reasons for using auction intermediaries?
2. What types of intermediaries exist?
3. List some of the necessary auction rules.
4. List major strategic issues in conducting B2B auctions.

EXHIBIT 10.5 Components of a Comprehensive Auction Site

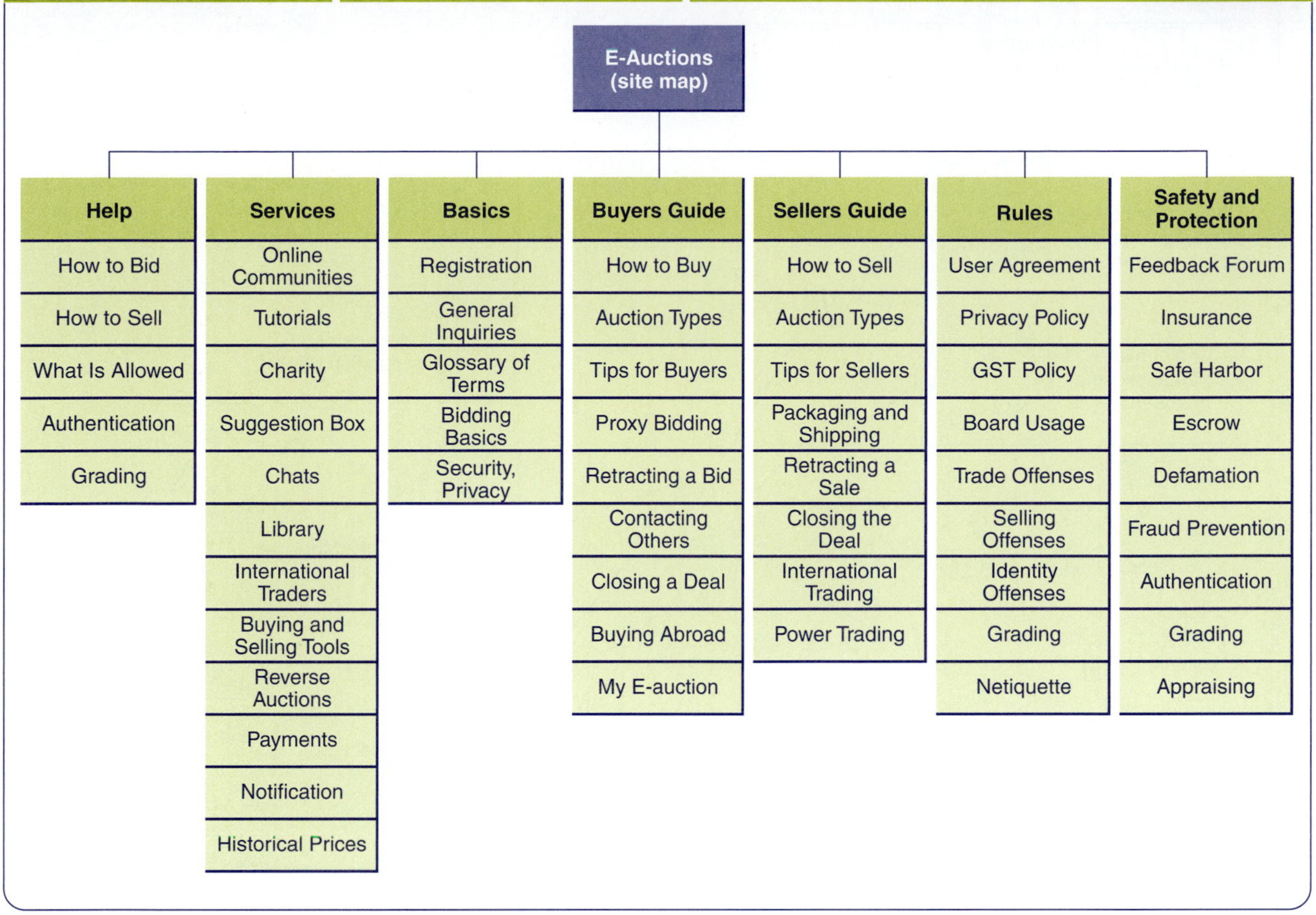

E-Auctions (site map)
Help
How to Bid
How to Sell
What Is Allowed
Authentication
Grading
Services
Online Communities
Tutorials
Charity
Suggestion Box
Chats
Library
International Traders
Buying and Selling Tools
Reverse Auctions
Payments
Notification
Historical Prices
Basics
Registration
General Inquiries
Glossary of Terms
Bidding Basics
Security, Privacy
Buyers Guide
How to Buy
Auction Types
Tips for Buyers
Proxy Bidding
Retracting a Bid
Contacting Others
Closing a Deal
Buying Abroad
My E-auction
Sellers Guide
How to Sell
Auction Types
Tips for Sellers
Packaging and Shipping
Retracting a Sale
Closing the Deal
International Trading
Power Trading
Rules
User Agreement
Privacy Policy
GST Policy
Board Usage
Trade Offenses
Selling Offenses
Identity Offenses
Grading
Netiquette
Safety and Protection
Feedback Forum
Insurance
Safe Harbor
Escrow
Defamation
Fraud Prevention
Authentication
Grading
Appraising

EXHIBIT 10.6 Integrated Auction Business Model

Business Rules
Customers
Inventory Management
Items–off-line
Items
Prices
Buying Trends
E-Commerce
Online Auction
Items
Price
Bidding Habits
Bidding Trends
Customer Data
Purchases
Accounting System

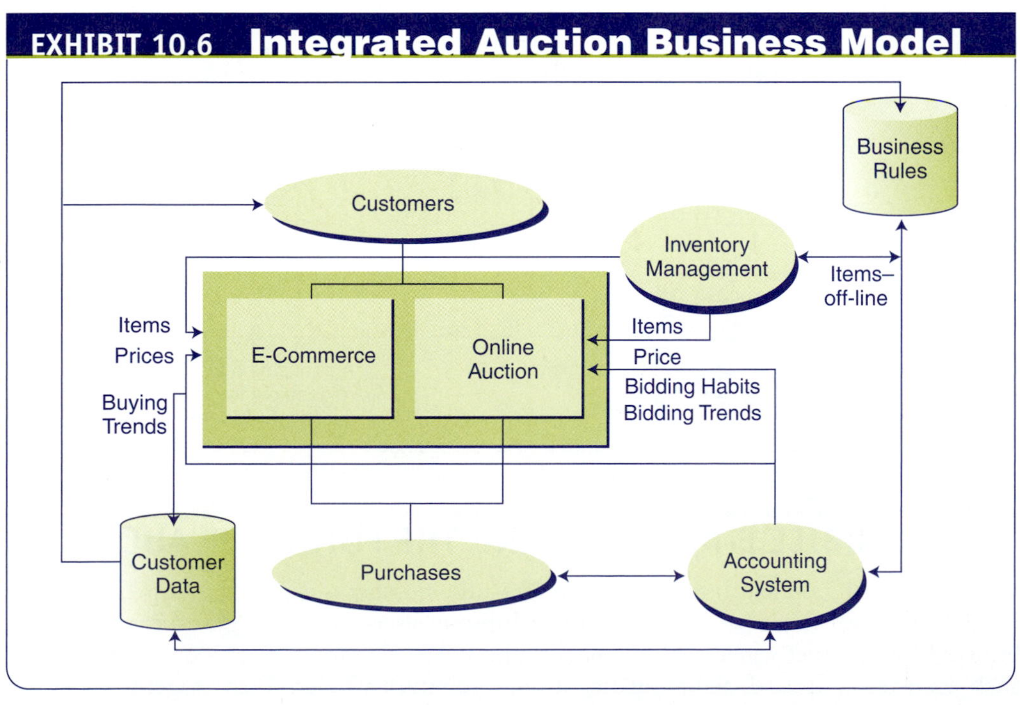

EXHIBIT 10.7 Auctioning Pigs in Singapore

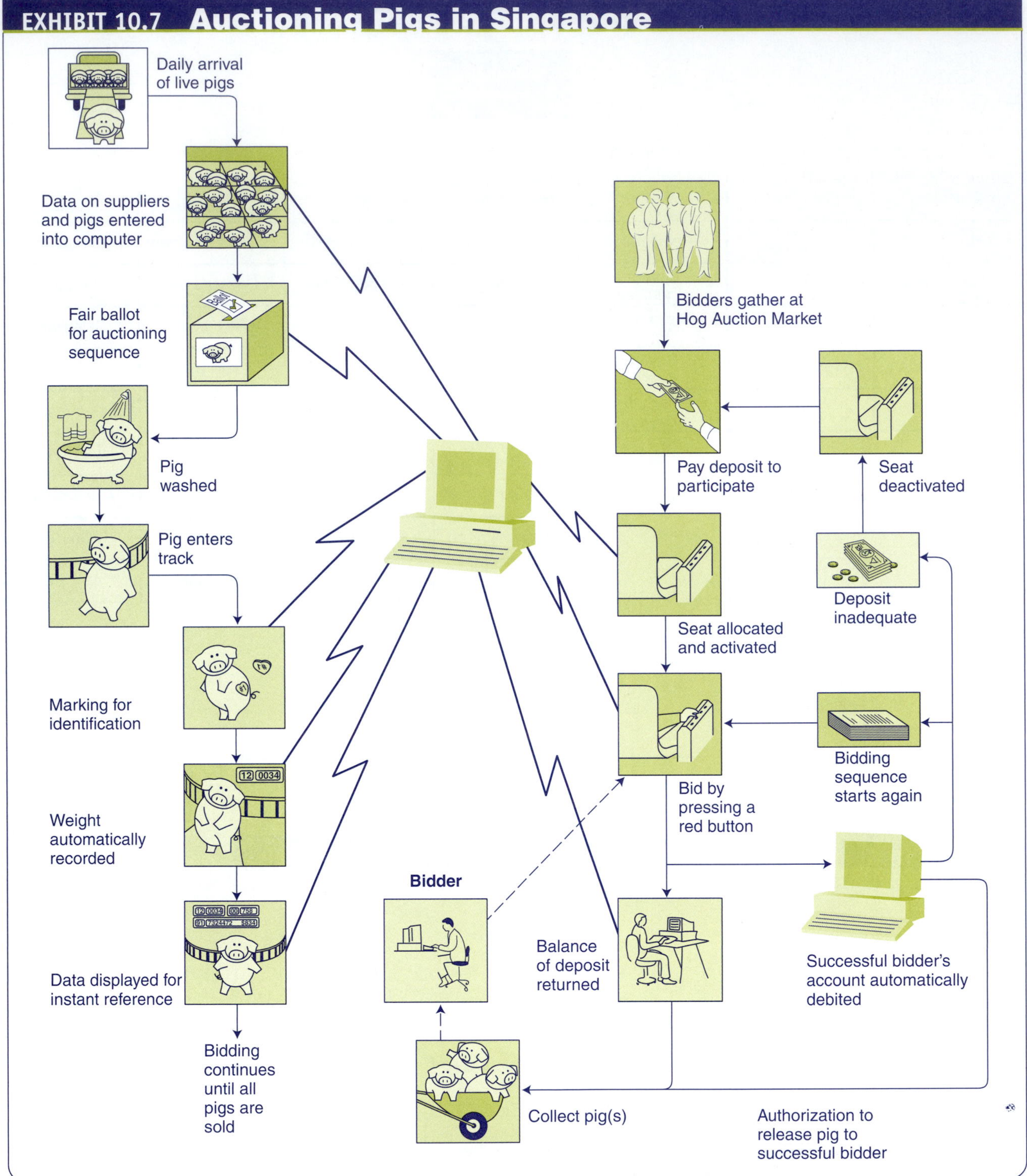

10.9 MOBILE E-AUCTIONS AND THE FUTURE OF AUCTIONS

There were 934.5 million Internet users in 2004; the number is expected to top 1.07 billion in mid-2005. Of those users, 44 percent of Internet users in 12 key global markets have browsed the Internet wirelessly in 2004 (European Travel Commission 2004). Forecasts by such agencies as Ipsos-Insights predict strong growth of wireless Web usage, because for many new Internet users, the cell phone will be their only Internet access device (reported by the European Travel Commission 2004).

Because mobile phones and other wireless devices could be the primary way that people access the Internet, large-volume m-commerce may result. In response, many auction sites are implementing m-commerce applications.

In the United States, eBay went wireless in October 1999 (E-Bay Anywhere), and uBid and FreeMarket (now part of Ariba) followed in 2000. Yahoo!, Amazon.com, and other auction sites provide wireless access to auctions. In the United Kingdom, BlueCycle (bluecycle.com), which conducts used car auctions for dealers, allows dealers to use their cell phones to bid from anywhere. Many auctions notify both buyers and sellers with SMS alerts at different stages of the bidding progress (e.g., eBay and Amazon.com).

The use of cell phones for online auctions presents a number of benefits and some limitations.

BENEFITS AND LIMITATIONS OF MOBILE AUCTIONS

The *benefits* of mobile auctions are as follows:

- **Convenience and ubiquity.** People can conduct auction business on the go and from any location via a mobile phone. One can auction anything from anywhere and search for information even in the middle of a discussion around a café table. Bids can be checked on the run.
- **Privacy.** The Internet cell phone is more private than a PC. Cell phone users can conduct business away from prying eyes; thus, participation in an auction can take place in a secure and private environment.
- **Simpler and faster.** Because online auctions require a limited amount of information, it is relatively easy to adapt Internet-enabled phones to display auction information, even if they can only handle limited bandwidth and data.

The *limitations* of mobile auctions are as follows:

- **Visual quality.** Portable devices are small and may have a problem showing auction items. One solution is provided by Sony. In 2004, the company started mass production of full-color OLED (organic light emitting diode) displays for use in a wide range of portable devices. The OLED technology provides a brighter and thinner screen that offers faster response time and better contrast. This improvement to smaller screens will enhance wireless Internet use (Kallender 2004).
- **Memory capacity.** Internet-enabled phones have limited memory capacity. In the near future, the development of new WAP services will probably press hardware producers to come up with better memory systems for mobile terminals.
- **Security.** Wireless systems are not as safe as wireline ones. These security issues, such as protecting personal data transmitted via wireless communications and avoiding computer viruses, must be addressed. New security standards, such as SIM Toolkit and WTLS, are still evolving.

See Chapter 9 for more on these and other benefits and limitations of m-commerce.

THE FUTURE OF E-AUCTIONS

The online auction industry is growing. The following are areas of potential growth.

Global Auctions

Many of the auction companies that sell products and services on the Web are extending their reach. One way to do so is by going global. However, companies that seek to serve the international market may face all the regular problems of selling online in foreign countries (see Chapter 14). Therefore, companies such as eBay are acquiring auction companies in other countries.

In December 2004, eBay announced that it auctions 30 million items each day; has 125 million registered users worldwide; and that its business volume in 2004 was almost 60 percent above that of 2003 (Maney 2004).

Selling Art Online in Real-Time Auctions

As of January 2001, collectors in the United Kingdom could bid online in live showroom auctions using an application provided by eBay and icollector.com (icollector.com). Icollector.com provides real-time access to 300 independent auction houses, such as the United Kingdom's Charter House Auctioneers and Valuers. Christie's has an online site, but as of winter 2002, it was not allowing online bidding for live showroom auctions. In the United States, Butterfields (butterfields.com) allows for real-time auction bidding and has a relationship with eBay. Butterfields.com has been purchased by Bonhams, auctioneers and valuers since 1793, but will continue to sell through eBay's Live Auctions feature, allowing online bidders to participate in auctions at traditional auction houses in real time. See Mirapaul (2001) to find out how individual artists use Internet auctions.

Strategic Alliances

Auctions may have a major impact on competition and on industry structure because they put sellers and buyers together more directly, cutting out intermediaries in a market. In addition, auctions may be used as a strategic tool by both online and off-line companies. An example of such a strategy is provided in Online File W10.3, which describes an online auction site in Australia that enables SMEs to offer heavily discounted merchandise to consumers. It appears that this type of strategic alliance will be very popular in the future due to its win-win possibilities.

Section 10.9 ▶ REVIEW QUESTIONS

1. Describe the benefits of wireless auctions.
2. Describe the limitations of wireless auctions.
3. Describe the future of global auctions.
4. Describe auctioning of art on the Internet.
5. Why are strategic alliances used in auctions?

MANAGERIAL ISSUES

Some managerial issues related to this chapter are as follows:

1. **Should we have our own auction site or use a third-party site?** This is a strategic issue, and there are pluses and minuses to each alternative. If you decide to auction from your site, you will need to advertise and attract visitors, which may be expensive. Also, you will need to install fraud-prevention mechanisms and provide services. Either way, you may need to consider connectivity to your back-office and logistics system.
2. **What are the costs and benefits of auctions?** A major strategic issue is whether you need to do auctions or not. Auctions do have risks, and in forward auctions you may create conflicts with your other distribution channels. In addition, auctions may change the manner in which companies sell their products. They also may change the nature of competition in certain industries, as well as price and margin levels. Therefore, conducting a cost-benefit analysis is essential.
3. **What auction strategies would we use?** Selecting an auction mechanism, pricing, and bidding strategy can be very complex for sellers. These strategies determine the success of the auction and the ability to attract and retain visitors on the site. Management should understand and carefully assess the options.
4. **What about support services?** Auctions require support services, such as those for escrow service, payment, and delivery. Decisions about how to provide them and to what extent to use business partners are critical to the success of repeated high-volume auctions. An efficient payment mechanism is also essential for auctions, especially when the buyers or sellers are individuals. Some innovative methods can solve the payment problem.
5. **What would we auction?** Both individuals and companies would like to auction everything. However, is it ethical or even legal to do it? Ask eBay, which is trying, for example, to clean up pornographic auctions by banning some items and directing some items into a "mature audiences" area. Another issue is pirated software, which is offered on about 2,000 auction sites worldwide. As a matter of fact, eBay was sued in 2000 by videogame manufacturers Nintendo, Sega, and Electronic Arts. eBay immediately began working with software compa-

nies and other owners of intellectual property to halt the sale of pirated items (Wolverton 2000). See Beato (2000) and Sawhney (2001) for more on this topic.

6. **What is the best bartering strategy?** Bartering can be an interesting strategy, especially for companies that need cash and have some surpluses. However, the valuation of what is bought or sold may be difficult, and the tax implications in some countries are not clear. Nevertheless, e-bartering can be rewarding and should be considered as an alternative to regular auctions.

7. **How can we promote our auction?** By monitoring what is going on in auctions (e.g., what people like, how much bidders are willing to pay, etc.), both sellers and auctioneers can foster selling strategy. Sometimes auctions bring very high prices to sellers. Auction houses such as eBay do analyses to determine advertising strategy for their business.

8. **Should we combine auctions with other models?** Consider combining auctions with other EC models. For example, group purchasing is often combined with a reverse auction once orders are aggregated.

RESEARCH TOPICS

Here are some suggested topics related to this chapter. For details, references, and additional topics, refer to the book's "Current EC Research" in the Online Appendix.

1. **E-Auctions, Negotiation, and Dynamic Pricing**
   - Types of negotiation and the contract process
   - Combined design of negotiation and auctions
   - Concepts, architectures, and protocols of negotiation
   - Effect of the seller's size in Internet auctions
   - Effect of dynamic pricing on the Internet
2. **Measurement of the Effect of E-Auctions and Applications**
   - Framework of estimating the benefits of using e-auctions
   - Social effects of online auctions
   - Importance of reputation in closing price of online auction sites
   - Relationship between products, auction rules, and trading types
   - Experimental investigation of electronic power auctions
3. **Measurement of Performance of Complex Auctions**
   - Performance of multi-attribute auctions
   - Performance of multi-item auctions
   - Performance of Vickrey second-price auctions
   - Winner determination methods for combinatorial auctions
   - Algorithms to reduce the computational complexity of winner determination
   - Combinatorial auction procedures with multiple winners
   - User understanding of the complex auction process and its adoption
4. **Bidding Behavior**
   - Bidding behavior on Internet auction sites
   - Reasons why consumers use Internet auction sites
   - Prevention of winner's curse by comparing dynamic auction prices with posted prices
5. **Design of E-Auction Systems and Software Agents**
   - Optimal design of online auction channels with analytical, empirical, and computational perspectives
   - Software agents to support real-time multiple auctions
   - Auction agents for transfer protocols
   - Importance of ordering in sequential auctions
   - Genetic algorithm to find optimal parameter values for trading agents
   - Software agents for automated negotiation
   - Multi-agent framework for automated online bargaining
   - Time-bounded negotiation for EC agents
   - Strategies for agents learning the principals' behavior patterns
6. **Security in E-Auctions**
   - Privacy preserved protocols for sealed-bid auctions
   - Security design for sealed-bid auctions
   - Cryptographic protocol with semitrusted auctioneers
   - Types of fraud in online auctions and new preventive schemes
   - Effect of feedback-posting mechanisms in preventing illegal behavior in auctions
   - Risks from the employees of auctioneer site and assurance of their ethics

SUMMARY

In this chapter, you learned about the following EC issues as they relate to the learning objectives.

1. **The various types of auctions and their characteristics.** The classification and types of auctions are based on the numbers of buyers and sellers involved. Negotiation and bartering take place between one seller and one buyer. One seller and many buyers characterize forward auctions. One buyer and many sellers typify reverse auctions. "Name-your-own-price" auctions are a form of reverse auctions. Many buyers and many sellers can participate simultaneously in auctions (called double auctions) in which prices are determined dynamically, based on supply and demand.
2. **The processes of forward and reverse auctions.** In a forward auction, the seller places the item to be sold on the auction site, specifying a starting price and closing time. Bids from buyers are placed sequentially, either increasing (English mode) or decreasing (Dutch mode). At the close, the highest bidder wins. In reverse auctions, buyers place an RFQ for a product or service, and suppliers (providers) submit offers in one or several rounds. The lowest-price bidder wins.
3. **Benefits and limitations of auctions.** The major benefits for sellers are the ability to reach many buyers and to sell quickly. Also, sellers save the high commissions they pay to off-line intermediaries. Buyers have a chance to obtain collectibles while shopping from their homes, and they can find bargains. The major limitation is the possibility of fraud.
4. **Unique auction models.** In the "name-your-own-price" reverse auction, buyers specify how much they are willing to pay for a product or service and an intermediary tries to find a supplier to fulfill the request. Also, auctions can be conducted on private networks (e.g., pigs in Singapore), can be organized as double auctions (multiple buyers and sellers bidding simultaneously), or can offer bundle trading (related products or services auctioned together).
5. **Services that support auctions.** Auction-support services exist along the entire process and include tools for (1) searching and comparing auctions for specific items; (2) registering, promoting, pricing, and so on; (3) bid watching, making multiple bids, and proxy bidding; and (4) notification, payment, and shipping.
6. **Hazards of e-auction fraud and countermeasures.** Fraud can be committed either by sellers or by buyers. Good auction sites provide protection that includes voluntary identity verification, monitoring of rule violations, escrow services, and insurance.
7. **Bartering and negotiating.** Electronic bartering can greatly facilitate the swapping of goods and services among organizations, thanks to improved search and matching capabilities.
8. **Auction deployment and implementation.** Some implementation issues are whether to use an intermediary or to run the auction oneself, various strategic issues (e.g., what rules to use and competition with regular channels), and whether to outsource construction of the auction site.
9. **Future directions and the role of mobile auctions.** B2B, C2C, G2B, and B2C auctions are all expanding rapidly. Future directions include use of wireless devices to monitor and trade at auctions, an increase in global auctioning, and strategic alliances.

KEY TERMS

Term	Page
Auction	426
Auction aggregators	434
Auction vortals	438
Bartering	442
Bid shielding	440
Bundle trading	439
Double auction	438
Dynamic pricing	426
Electronic auctions (e-auctions)	426
Electronic bartering (e-bartering)	442
Forward auction	427
"Name-your-own-price" model	429
Online negotiation	443
Proxy bidding	437
Reverse auction	428
Sealed-bid auction	428
Shilling	440
Single auction	438
Sniping	436
Vertical auction	438
Vickrey auction	428

QUESTIONS FOR DISCUSSION

1. Discuss the advantages of dynamic pricing over fixed pricing. What are the potential disadvantages?
2. The "name-your-own-price" model is considered to be a reverse auction. However, there is no consecutive bidding, so why is it called an auction? Is it an auction at all?
3. Find some material on why individuals like C2C auctions so much. Write a report.
4. Compare the "name-your-own-price" and tendering (RFQ) approaches. Under what circumstances is each advantageous?
5. Identify three fraud practices in which a seller might engage. How can buyers protect themselves? Be specific.
6. Identify three fraud practices in which a buyer might engage. How can sellers protect themselves?
7. It is said that Manheim Auction is trying to sell more online without cannibalizing its core business. Discuss this situation.
8. Discuss the need for software agents in auctions. Start by analyzing *proxy bidding* and *auction aggregators*.
9. Discuss the role of auction aggregators.
10. It is said that *individuals* prefer an English auction whereas *corporations* prefer a Dutch one. Speculate on the reasons for this.
11. When Google made its initial IPO in 2004, it used a Dutch auction. What was the logic of this?
12. Relate consumer trust to auctions.

INTERNET EXERCISES

1. Enter eBay's online partner (elance.com). Post a project and see how professionals bid on this work. Summarize your experience.
2. Enter dellauction.com and click on "site terms." Examine the policies, security and encryption statement, privacy protection statement, escrow services, payment options, and other features. Register (for free) and then bid on a computer of interest to you. If you are not interested, bid very low, so that you will not get it.

   Alternatively, try to sell a computer. If you do not have one to sell, place an asking price so high that you will not get any bids. Read the FAQs. Which of the following auction mechanisms are used on the Dell site: English, Dutch (declining), reverse, etc.

   Write a report on your experiences and describe all the features available at this site. (*Note:* If you are outside the United States, use an auction site accessible to you.)
3. Visit ebay.com and examine all of the quality assurance measures available either for a fee or for free. Prepare a list.
4. Visit vendio.com and report on the various services offered at the site. What are the site's revenue models?
5. Enter bidfind.com and report on the various services provided. Check its affiliate program. What is the site's revenue model?
6. Enter ebay.com and investigate the use of "anywhere wireless." Review the wireless devices and find out how they work.
7. Enter asset-auctions.com and liquidations.com. Compare the sites.
8. Enter escrow.com and view the tutorial on how escrow services work for both buyers and sellers in electronic commerce.
9. Enter bidxs.com and find historical prices on an item of your choice. How may this information be of help to you as a seller? As a buyer?
10. Enter priceline.com and name a price to travel from where you live to a place you would like to visit. Go through the process without actually buying the ticket (do not give your credit card number). Summarize your experience.
11. Enter icollector.com and review the process used to auction art. Find support services, such as currency conversion and shipping. Take the tour of the site. Prepare a report on buying collectibles online.
12. Enter ubid.com and examine the "auction exchange." What is unique about it? Compare this auction with those conducted on ebay.com. What are the major differences between the auctions on the two sites?
13. Enter autoparts.com and describe how auctions are being conducted there.
14. Enter web-barter.com and examine its services. Summarize them in a report.

TEAM ASSIGNMENTS AND ROLE PLAYING

1. Each team is assigned an auction method (English, Dutch, etc.). Each team should convince a (hypothetical) company that wants to liquidate items that its method is the best. Items to be liquidated include the following:
   a. Five IBM top-of-the-line mainframe systems valued at about $500,000 each
   b. 750 PCs valued at about $1,000 each
   c. A property valued at about $10 million

   Present arguments as to which auction method should be used with each item.

2. Assign teams to major third-party auction sites from your country and from two other countries. Each team should present the major functionalities of the sites and the fraud protection measures they use. Convince a user that your site is the best.

Real-World Case

DYNAMIC TRADING AT OCEANCONNECT.COM

OceanConnect.com (*oceanconnect.com*) is an e-marketplace for selling and buying marine fuels. It is a consortium backed by the major global suppliers and some large buyers of such fuels. More than 700 registered users from about 50 countries deal in this market. Marine fuels vary in quality and type, and they represent 30 to 50 percent of total operating expenses of oceangoing vessels. Traditional trading is complex, inefficient, and expensive. Trading in marine fuels is done by auctions and negotiations. Thus, an electronic solution has a potential for substantial savings if the e-commerce platform can be cost-effective and scalable. Furthermore, it must allow for negotiations on attributes other than price, and it needs to have a robust architecture.

OceanConnect.com found the proper solution in LiveExchange Enterprise (from Moai Technologies). The solution supports complex marine fuel requirements, specifically addressing the issue of different prices of different products at different ports and offering the ability to compare prices in real time and to negotiate. To do all this, OceanConnect.com uses a variety of transaction models, ranging from the more traditional sealed-bid process to reverse auctions to complex, multistage online negotiations on multiple parameters. These mechanisms allow marine fuel purchasers to invite selected participants, specify the time and place of an online transaction event, and customize product specifications and requirements. Having the ability to bid on several parameters in addition to price (such as fuel quality and delivery time and location) allows buyers and sellers to reach agreements that improve total cost of transactions, saving money for buyers and sellers alike.

OceanConnect.com supplements the auctions with features that better serve the market. For example, noticing that bidding activity peaked near the end of auction events, OceanConnect.com added an "Extension Window" feature that extends the bidding for 3 minutes if a lower bid comes in during the last 3 minutes. This feature continues as long as new bids are entered, allowing suppliers to have a "last look" at the lowest bid and affording them additional time to offer their best price.

A typical example of how OceanConnect.com brings greater efficiency to the marine fuels market is that of Neptune Orient Lines Ltd. (NOL), one of the world's largest container shipping lines, which created a transaction that generated 14 bids by 4 suppliers and closed online with one of them. NOL said that the auctions save time and money and are the best platform for bunker purchasing. Throughout the auction, NOL communicated with suppliers via OceanConnect.com's Instant Messaging feature, which allowed the buyer to request clarification on bids or answer supplier questions. The deal's closing price came in underneath the market's average low for that day.

Another feature is the "Bid Box" that allows a supplier to indicate whether there are additional charges associated with the offered price, such as barging or port charges. As a result, the total transaction cost is transparent and can be analyzed by prospective buyers when making their final purchasing decisions.

OceanConnect.com provides extra services such as access to online credit insurance. In addition, the company offers users specially developed content, including daily bunker pricing, weekly bunker market reports, top expert commentary, forward price indications, and average price charts. OceanConnect.com has added functions to the platform that allows suppliers to signal whether they plan to participate in an auction and allows participants to communicate with each other throughout the auction.

The e-commerce tools gave OceanConnect's e-marketplace the flexibility and scalability necessary to meet the rapidly changing needs of its customers. It also allowed the company to expand both its product offering and geographical reach.

Source: Compiled from Moai Technologies (2004).

Questions

1. Why is it important to consider more than the price in auctions?
2. Additional parameters, such a delivery time and location, are using negotiation techniques such as those described in Chapter 5 and facilitated by the software provided by OceanConnect.com. How do they relate to the bidding price? Why is the software support of manual negotiation so critical? Explain the value of the Instant Messaging to the negotiation process.
3. Comment on the complexity of a market such as this one.
4. Why does OceanConnect.com need several transaction modes?
5. OceanConnect.com is an exchange. Given what you learned about the successes and failures of exchanges, identify the success factors of this exchange.
6. Do you think that the negotiated parameters can be incorporated into the electronic bidding process someday? Why or why not?

REFERENCES

Aberdeen Group. "The Moment: Providing Pricing Flexibility for eMarkets." Aberdeen Group, July 27, 2000. aberdeen.com (accessed June 2001).

Beam, C., et al. "On Negotiations and Deal Making in Electronic Markets." *Information Systems Frontiers* 1, no. 3 (1999).

Beato, G. "Online Piracy's Mother Ship." *Business2.com*, December 12, 2000. business2.com/b2/web/articles/0,17863,528531,00.html (accessed March 2005).

Carrol, C. "Model E-Commerce Solutions." Boxboard.com, February 1, 2000. boxboard.com/ar/boxboard_model_ecommerce_solutions/ (accessed March 2005).

Cellich, C., and S. Jain. *Global Business Negotiations: A Practical Guide.* Cincinnati: Southwest Publishers, 2003.

Choi, S. Y., and A. B. Whinston. *The Internet Economy: Technology and Practice.* Austin, TX: SmartconPub, 2000.

Coffin, A. M. *eBay for Dummies*, 4th ed. Hoboken, NJ: John Wiley & Sons, 2004.

eBay. "eBay Launches eBay Business to Serve Its Growing Community of Business Buyers." eBay press release, January 28, 2002. investor.ebay.com/news/20030128-100772.cfm?ReleaseID=100772 (accessed April 2003).

eBay. ebay.com/help/sellerguide/safeseller.html (accessed April 2003a).

eBay. "Sotheby's and eBay Announce Change in Relationship." eBay press release, February 4, 2003b. shareholder.com/ebay/releases-2003.cfm (accessed April 2003).

Elliot, A. C. *Getting Started in Internet Auctions.* New York: John Wiley & Sons, 2000.

eMarketer. "Retail Industry Online." *eMarketer*, October 2, 2002. emarketer.com/products/report.php?retail_ind (accessed May 2003).

Esmahi, L., and J. C. Bernard. "MIAMAP: A Virtual Marketplace for Intelligent Agents." *Proceedings of the 33rd HICSS*, Maui, Hawaii, January 2000.

European Travel Commission. "New Media Review." December 3, 2004. etcnewmedia.com/review/default.asp? SectionID=10&OverviewID=6 (accessed January 2005).

fraud.org (accessed December 2004).

FreeMarkets. "American Power Conversion Corporation Case Study." FreeMarkets case study, 2002a. freemarkets.com/en/freemarkets/literature.asp#casestudy (accessed May 2002). Note: no longer available online.

FreeMarkets. "FreeMarkets and Singapore Technologies Engineering Expand Relationship." FreeMarkets press release, January 15, 2002b. ariba.com/company/press_archive.cfm?pressid=2246&selectyear=2002&archive=1 (accessed March 2005).

FreeMarkets. "Singapore Technologies Engineering Case Study." FreeMarkets case study, 2003. freemarkets.com/en/literature/CaseStudy_SingTech.pdf (accessed June 2003). Note: no longer available online.

FreeMarkets. "New Line Cinema Case Study." FreeMarkets case study, 2002c. freemarkets.com/en/freemarkets/literature.asp#case study (accessed June 2002). Note: no longer available online.

Gallaugher, J. M. "E-Commerce and the Ondulating Distribution Channels." *Communications of the ACM* (July 2002).

Hoos, H., and C. Boutilier. "Bidding Languages for Combinatorial Auctions." *Proceedings of the 17th International Joint Conference on Artificial Intelligence*, Seattle, Washington, August 2001.

Kallender, P. "Sony to Mass Produce OLEDs for Small Screens from 2005." *CIO.com*, September 17, 2004. cio.co.nz/cio.nsf/0/977FB86373ADE4EECC256F110078E5FF?OpenDocument (accessed January 2005).

Kambil, A., and E. van Heck. *Making Markets.* Boston: Harvard Business School Press, 2002.

Kewney, G. "Future of WiFi?—It's the Mobile Phone." *NewsWireless.Net*, May 22, 2003. newswireless.net/articles/030522-panel.html (accessed January 2005).

Konrad, R. "eBay Touts Anti-Fraud Software's Might." *News.com*, June 5, 2002. marketwatch-cnet.com.com/2100-1017_3-932874.html (accessed March 2005).

Lee, B. "Web's Bloom a Garden for Sophisticated Scammers." *Chicago Tribune*, March 11, 2002. chicagotribune.com/technology/local/chi-020311crime,0, 6398375.story (accessed April 2003).

Lorek, L. "Trade Ya? E-Barter Thrives." *InteractiveWeek*, August 14, 2000.

Maney, K. "The Year According to eBay." *USA Today*, December 30, 2004. usatoday.com/tech/news/2004-12-29-ebay_x.htm (accessed January 2005).

McKay, C. "Online Auctions Dominant Consumer Fraud." *National Consumers League*, March 25, 2003. nclnet.org/internetfraud02.htm (accessed May 2003).

McKeown, P. G., and R. T. Watson. "Manheim Auctions." *Communication of the AIS* 1 (1999).

Mirapaul, M. "The New Canvas: Artists Use Online Auctions for Art Projects." *New York Times*, February 5, 2001.

Moai Technologies. "Fueling Efficient Gains." moai.com (accessed November 2004).

Mohammadian, M. *Intelligent Agents for Data Mining and Information Retrieval.* Hershey, PA: The Idea Group, 2004.

Neo, B. S. "The Implementation of an Electronic Market for Pig Trading in Singapore." *Journal of Strategic Information Systems* 1, no. 5 (1992).

Prince, D. L. *How to Sell Anything on eBay. . . and Make a Fortune.* New York: McGraw-Hill, 2004.

Reuters. "Grape Auction Goes Online." *CNN.com*, March 20, 2001. cnn.com/2001/BUSINESS/03/20/wine.online.reut/ (accessed May 2003).

Rothkopf, M. H., and S. Park. "An Elementary Introduction to Auctions." *Interfaces*, November–December 2001.

Sashi, C. M., and B. O'Leary. "The Role of Internet Auctions in the Expansion of B2B Markets." *Industrial Marketing Management* 31 (2002).

Sawhney, M. *Seven Steps to Nirvana: Strategic Insights into eBusiness Transformation.* New York: McGraw-Hill, 2001.

Scalas, E., and S. Chincotti. "A Double-Auction Artificial Market." University of Connecticut Department of Economics, working paper, 2004. econpapers.hhs.se/paper/scescecf4/225.htm (accessed January 2005).

Schermerhorn, J. R. *Management,* 8th ed. New York: John Wiley & Sons, 2004.

Schonfeld, E. "The World According to eBay." *Business 2.0.*, January, 19 2005. business2.com/b2/web/articles/0,17863,1016530,00.html (accessed March 2005).

Strobel, M. "On Auctions as the Negotiation Paradigm of Electronic Markets." *Electronic Markets* 10, no. 1 (2000).

Stroebel, M. *Engineering Electronic Negotiations.* Boston, MA: Klewer Academics, 2003.

Subramaniam, R. "Experience Pricing." *Business Line*, August 31, 2000. blonnet.com/businessline/2000/08/31/stories/043101ra.htm (accessed May 2003).

Sullivan, B. "Auction Fraud on the Rise Some Say." *MSNBC*, July 29, 2003. msnbc.com/news/784132.asp (accessed April 2003).

Westland, J. C. "Ten Lessons that Internet Auction Markets Can Learn from Securities Market Automation." *Journal of Global Management* 8, no. 1 (2000).

WineBid. winebid.com (accessed 2005).

WineryExchange. wineryexchange.com (accessed January 2005).

Wolverton, T. "Survey Finds Pirates Rule Online Auctions." *CNET News*, April 11, 2000. news.com.com/2100-1017-239146.html?legacy=cnet (accessed April 2003).

Woodham, R., and P. Weill. "Manheim Interactive: Selling Cars Online." *MIT-CISB*, working paper #34. Boston: MIT Press, February 2001.

Wurman, P. "Dynamic Pricing in the Virtual Marketplace." *IEEE Internet Computing* (March–April 2001): 38–39. computer.org/internet/ (accessed August 2003).

CHAPTER 11

E-COMMERCE SECURITY

Content

Learning Objectives

Upon completion of this chapter, you will be able to:

1. Document the trends in computer and network security attacks.
2. Describe the common security practices of businesses of all sizes.
3. Understand the basic elements of EC security.
4. Explain the basic types of network security attacks.
5. Describe common mistakes that organizations make in managing security.
6. Discuss some of the major technologies for securing EC communications.
7. Detail some of the major technologies for securing EC networks components.

PHISHING

The Problem

On November 17, 2003, a number of eBay customers were notified by e-mail that their accounts had been compromised and were being restricted. The message contained a hyperlink to an eBay Web page where they could reregister. All they had to do was enter their credit card information, Social Security number, date of birth, mother's maiden name, and ATM personal identification numbers. The only problem was that eBay had not sent the e-mail, and the Web page the account holders were directed to did not really belong to eBay. Although the page looked authentic, having eBay's logo and familiar look and feel, the page was actually part of a bogus site run by Internet scammers. Those eBay customers who reregistered were victims of a **phishing attack**.

phishing attack
A high-tech scam that uses e-mail, pop-up messages, or Web pages to trick a user into disclosing sensitive information such as credit card numbers, bank account numbers, and passwords.

The Solution

Phishing attacks are not new. What *is* new is the method. In the past, scam artists relied on the telephone. Today, they rely on spoofed e-mail (spam), fraudulent pop-up messages, or fake Web pages to fool victims into thinking they are dealing with a legitimate business. The message usually links unsuspecting recipients to a Web site where they are asked to update or validate their account information. Although the Web site appears to be legitimate, it is not. At the fake site, the victims are scammed into revealing their credit card numbers, account numbers, user names, passwords, Social Security numbers, or other sensitive information. The information is then used to perpetrate credit card fraud or identity theft.

The Anti-Phishing Working Group (APWG; *antiphishing.org*) is an industry association focused on eliminating identity theft and fraud resulting from phishing and e-mail spoofing. In July 2004, 1,974 unique phishing attacks were reported to the group, up 39 percent from June 2004. The most targeted industry sector was financial services (1,649 out of 1,974 reports). The most targeted brand names were Citibank, U.S. Bank, eBay, and PayPal (1,191 out of 1,974 reports). The United States hosts the largest percentage of phishing sites (35 percent), followed by South Korea, China, and Russia. To avoid detection, most of the phishing sites have a short life span, lasting on the average about 6 days.

Computer security companies such as VeriSign (*verisign.com*) and NameProtect (*nameprotect.com*) are working to stop phishing attacks. Both companies offer services that actively search the Web (domain name servers, pages, sites, news groups, chat rooms, etc.) for signs of phishing activity. These services are used by companies such as MasterCard and other financial and retail enterprises. Once found, information about the illegal activity is passed on to the customer paying for the service and to law enforcement officials.

Although such services assist companies whose brands are being exploited, they provide little direct help to the individuals being scammed. In that case, it is really up to the individuals to avoid being hooked. As the Federal Trade Commission (FTC) (2004) suggests, individuals should:

- Avoid replying to e-mail or pop-up messages that ask for personal information.
- Avoid sending personal or financial information.
- Review credit card and bank account statements.
- Use and keep antivirus software up-to-date.
- Be cautious about opening any attachment or downloading any files received via e-mail.
- Report suspicious activity to the FTC.

The Results

The Anti-Phishing Working Group estimates that approximately 5 percent of recipients respond to phishing attacks. The overall economic impact of these attacks is uncertain. Even though there are laws on the books against e-mail spamming and identity theft, both activities are rampant. To date, there have been virtually no prosecutions against the perpetrators of phishing attacks.

Sources: APWG (2004), FTC (2004).

WHAT WE CAN LEARN . . .

Any type of EC involves a number of players who use a variety of network and application services that provide access to a variety of data sources. The sheer numbers and interconnections are what make EC security so difficult. A perpetrator needs only a single weakness in order to attack a system. Some attacks require sophisticated techniques and technologies. Many, however, are like the scams perpetrated by phishing attacks—simple techniques preying on poor security practices and human weaknesses. Because most attacks are unsophisticated, standard security risk management procedures can be used to minimize their probability and impact.

This chapter focuses on the basic security issues in EC, the major types of attacks that are perpetrated against EC networks and transactions, and the procedures and technologies that can be used to address these attacks. Because security is a multifaceted and highly technical problem, the complexities cannot be addressed in a single chapter. Those readers interested in a more comprehensive discussion should see Panko (2003) or Thomas (2004).

11.1 THE CONTINUING NEED FOR E-COMMERCE SECURITY

Computer Security Institute (CSI)
Nonprofit organization located in San Francisco, California, that is dedicated to serving and training information, computer, and network security professionals.

Evidence from a variety of security surveys provides a mixed picture of the incidence of cyber attacks and cyber crimes in EC. The best known and most widely cited survey is the one conducted by the **Computer Security Institute (CSI)** and the San Francisco Federal Bureau of Investigation's (FBI) Computer Intrusion Squad. This survey has been conducted annually since 1999. The results from the 2004 survey were based on the responses of 494 computer security practitioners in U.S. corporations, government agencies, financial institutions, medical institutions, and universities. Their responses reinforced trends that began in 2001 (see Online File W11.1 for a discussion of the 2001 and 2002 trends). Some specific trends include the following (CSI and FBI 2004):

1. For the fourth year in a row, the overall frequency of successful attacks on computer systems declined. In 2001, the percentage of respondents indicating that their organization's computer systems had experienced unauthorized use was approximately 65 percent. In 2004, the percentage was 53 percent. Among those organizations that experienced unauthorized use, the median number of incidents was between one and five incidents. Last year the median was 6 to 10 incidents.
2. The incidence of all types of attacks or misuse has declined. Of the 280 organizations that had been victimized, the percentage of companies who were successfully attacked by viruses was 78 percent. In the previous year, the percentage was 83 percent. The percentage of victimized organizations that experienced insider abuse of net access dropped from 80 percent in 2003 to 59 percent in 2004. Similarly, for these same organizations, the percentage that experienced denial-of-service attacks declined substantially, from 37 percent in 2003 to 17 percent in 2004.
3. As in the past, the majority of respondents were either unable or unwilling to estimate the dollar losses resulting from attacks or misuse. Among those who did report, there was a significant decline in the total losses reported. In 2004, total losses were approximately $140 million, down from $202 million in 2003. Virus and denial-of-service attacks accounted for approximately $81 million of those losses. This was a significant change from previous years, where the primary losses resulted from theft of proprietary information.
4. Most of the organizations in the survey conduct security audits and employ a variety of technologies and procedures to defend against cyber attacks. Virtually all of the respondents indicated that they employed antivirus software and firewalls. Between 65 and 70 percent also use access control lists, intrusion detection, and data encryption.
5. Organizations still are reticent to report computer intrusions to legal authorities. Less than 50 percent of the respondents did so in 2004. Most of the organizations indicated that they did not report the intrusion because they feared negative publicity or were worried that their competitors would use it against them.

Computer Emergency Response Team (CERT)
Group of three teams at Carnegie Mellon University that monitor the incidence of cyber attacks, analyze vulnerabilities, and provide guidance on protecting against attacks.

Contrary to the declines noted in the CSI/FBI survey, data and survey results from the **Computer Emergency Response Team (CERT)** (cert.org) at Carnegie Mellon University (CMU) indicate that cyber attacks are on the rise. CERT is a federally funded research and development center located at CMU's Software Engineering Institute. It was established in 1988 to deal with security issues on the Internet. Today, CERT works with the Department of Homeland security to coordinate responses to security compromises; identify trends in intruder activity; identify solutions to security problems; and disseminate information to the broader community.

Since its inception, CERT has received incident reports of cyber attacks from Internet sites. In 2003, the number of reported incidents was approximately 138,000, up substantially from the 82,000 incidents reported in 2002 (CERT/CC 2002). Indeed, the dramatic rise in incidents prompted CERT to discontinue collecting and reporting incident data. Instead, CERT now works with the U.S. Secret Service and *CSO Magazine* to conduct an e-crime watch survey. The 2004 survey (*CSO Magazine* 2004) was conducted in April 2004 and involved 500 security and law enforcement professionals. Seventy percent reported that their organizations experienced at least one e-crime or intrusion, and 43 percent reported that the number of incidents had increased over the previous year. The total cost of these incidents was approximately $666 million. Like the respondents in the CSI/FBI survey, the respondents to the e-crime watch survey indicated that they employed a variety of technologies to combat e-crimes, including firewalls (98 percent), physical security systems (94 percent), and manual patch management (91 percent). Firewalls were viewed by the majority of respondents as very effective, while patch management is seen as very ineffective.

Although the two surveys offer differing pictures about the trends in cyber crimes and intrusions, both provide ample evidence that e-commerce security is still a substantial problem that can result in significant financial losses for an organization. Organizations continue to take the problem seriously and exert considerable effort to thwart these unauthorized and illegal activities.

Section 11.1 ▶ REVIEW QUESTIONS

1. Are cyber crimes increasing or decreasing?
2. What types of technologies and procedures do organizations use to combat cyber attacks?
3. What is CERT?

11.2 SECURITY IS EVERYONE'S BUSINESS

As the technology underlying e-commerce has become more complex and more intertwined, the opportunities for intrusion and attack have increased. Not only are the underlying components more vulnerable, they also are harder to administer. Teenage hackers, industrial spies, corporate insiders, agents of foreign governments, and criminal elements have all taken advantage of the situation. The variety of potential perpetrators makes it difficult to deter potential attacks and detect them once they have occurred.

According to International Data Corporation (IDC), worldwide spending on corporate digital security was over $70 billion in 2003, including costs associated with people, products, and services (Market Research Summaries 2003). IDC estimates that the figure will reach $116 billion by 2007. Although spending on security has increased significantly, the average company still spends very little of its IT budget on security and very little per employee (for a discussion of the basic security spending patterns by organizational size, see Online File W11.2).

Because the Internet now serves as the control system of many of our critical infrastructures—private and public, cyber and physical, local and global—computer security can no longer rest on the efforts of individual organizations. Instead, it must also be addressed from a national and international perspective. In the United States, the coordination of cyber security efforts falls to the Department of Homeland Security (DHS). Towards this end, the DHS formulated *The National Strategy to Secure Cyberspace* (Department of Homeland Security 2004). The DHS strategy includes five national priorities:

1. A national cyberspace security response system
2. A national cyberspace security threat and vulnerability reduction program
3. A national cyberspace security awareness and training program
4. Securing governments' cyberspace
5. National security and international security cooperation

Accomplishing these priorities requires concerted effort at five levels:

- **Level 1—The Home User/Small Business.** Although not necessarily part of the critical infrastructure, unprotected home and small business computers can be used by hackers as a base of operation from which to attack key Internet nodes, important enterprises, or critical infrastructure.
- **Level 2—Large Enterprises.** These are common targets for cyber attacks. Many of these enterprises are part of the critical infrastructure. As such, these enterprises are a key element in securing cyberspace. In the future, these enterprises will need to implement information security policies and programs that comply with cyber security best practices.

- **Level 3—Critical Sectors/Infrastructure.** The security burden placed on individual enterprises can be reduced when organizations in the private sector unite with government and academic organizations to address common cyber security problems. As an example, several sectors have formed Information Sharing and Analysis Centers (ISACs) to not only monitor cyber attacks, but also to share information about trends, vulnerabilities, and best practices.
- **Level 4—National Issues and Vulnerabilities.** Some cyber security problems have national implications. Because all sectors share the Internet, any weaknesses in its underlying infrastructure (e.g., protocols) requires coordinated activities to address the problem. The same is true for weaknesses in widely used software and hardware products (e.g., the Microsoft Windows operating system).
- **Level 5—Global.** The boundaries of the Internet are global. Cyber security problems affecting one part of the world can potentially impact another part. International cooperation to share information and to prosecute cyber criminals is needed to detect, deter, and minimize the impacts of cyber attacks.

In June 2003, the DHS created the **National Cyber Security Division (NCSD)** to implement U.S. cyberspace security strategy. More specifically, the NCSD was charged with identifying, analyzing, and reducing cyber threats and vulnerabilities; disseminating threat warning information; coordinating incident response; and providing technical assistance in continuity of operations and recovery planning.

National Cyber Security Division (NCSD)
A division of the Department of Homeland Security charged with implementing U.S. cyberspace security strategy.

Section 11.2 ▶ REVIEW QUESTIONS

1. What are the major priorities of the National Strategy to Secure Cyberspace?
2. What sectors does the National Strategy to Secure Cyberspace address?
3. What is the National Cyber Security Division (NCSD)?

11.3 BASIC SECURITY ISSUES

EC security involves more than just preventing and responding to cyber attacks and intrusion. Consider, for example, the situation in which a user connects to a Web server at a marketing site to obtain some product literature. In return, the user is asked to fill out a Web form providing some demographic and other personal information in order to receive the literature. In this situation, what kinds of security questions arise?

From the user's perspective:

- How can the user be sure that the Web server is owned and operated by a legitimate company?
- How does the user know that the Web page and form do not contain some malicious or dangerous code or content?
- How does the user know that the owner of the Web site will not distribute the information the user provides to some other party?

From the company's perspective:

- How does the company know the user will not attempt to break into the Web server or alter the pages and content at the site?
- How does the company know that the user will not try to disrupt the server so that it is not available to others?

From both parties' perspectives:

- How do both parties know that the network connection is free from eavesdropping by a third party "listening" on the line?
- How do they know that the information sent back and forth between the server and the user's browser has not been altered?

These questions illustrate the types of security issues that can arise in an EC transaction. For transactions involving e-payments, additional types of security issues must be confronted. The following list summarizes some of the major security issues that can occur in EC:

- **Authentication.** When users view a Web page from a Web site, how can they be sure that the site is not fraudulent? If a person files a tax return electronically, how does the taxpayer know that it has been sent to the taxing authority? If a person receives an e-mail, how can he or she be sure that the sender is who he or she claims to be? The process by which one entity verifies that another entity is who he, she, or it claims to be is called **authentication**. Authentication requires evidence in the form of credentials, which can take a variety of forms, including something known (e.g., a password), something possessed (e.g., a smart card), or something unique (e.g., a signature).

authentication
The process by which one entity verifies that another entity is who he, she, or it claims to be.

- **Authorization.** Once authenticated, does a person or program have the right to access particular data, programs, or system resources (e.g., files, registries, directories, etc.)? **Authorization** ensures that a person or program has the right to access certain resources. It usually is determined by comparing information about the person or program with access control information associated with the resource being accessed.

authorization
The process that ensures that a person has the right to access certain resources.

- **Auditing.** If a person or program accesses a Web site, various pieces of information are noted in a log file. If a person or program queries a database, that action also is noted in a log file. The process of collecting information about accessing particular resources, using particular privileges, or performing other security actions (either successfully or unsuccessfully) is known as **auditing**. Audits provide the means to reconstruct the specific actions that were taken and often enable IT personnel to identify the person or program that performed the actions.

auditing
The process of collecting information about attempts to access particular resources, use particular privileges, or perform other security actions.

- **Confidentiality (Privacy).** The idea behind **confidentiality** is that information that is private or sensitive should not be disclosed to unauthorized individuals, entities, or computer software processes. It is intertwined with the notion of digital privacy, which is now a regulatory issue in many countries. Some examples of things that should be confidential are trade secrets, business plans, health records, credit card numbers, and even the fact that a person visited a particular Web site. Confidentiality requires that people and companies know what data or applications they want to protect and who should have access to them. Confidentiality is usually ensured by encryption.

confidentiality
Keeping private or sensitive information from being disclosed to unauthorized individuals, entities, or processes.

- **Integrity.** Data can be altered or destroyed while it is in transit or after it is stored. The ability to protect data from being altered or destroyed in an unauthorized or accidental manner is called **integrity**. Financial transactions are one example of data whose integrity needs to be secured. Again, encryption is one way of ensuring integrity of data while it is in transit.

integrity
As applied to data, the ability to protect data from being altered or destroyed in an unauthorized or accidental manner.

- **Availability.** If a person is trying to execute a stock trade through an online service, then the service needs to be available in near-real time. An online site is *available* if a person or program can gain access to the pages, data, or services provided by the site when they are needed. Technologies such as load-balancing hardware and software are aimed at ensuring availability.
- **Nonrepudiation.** If a person orders an item through a mail-order catalog and pays by check, then it is difficult to dispute the veracity of the order. If the same item is ordered through the company's "1-800" number and the person pays by credit card, then there is always room for dispute. Similarly, if a person uses the company's Web site and pays by credit card, the person can always claim that he or she did not place the order. **Nonrepudiation** is the ability to limit parties from refuting that a legitimate transaction took place. One of the keys to nonrepudiation is a "signature" that makes it difficult for a person to dispute that they were involved in an exchange.

nonrepudiation
The ability to limit parties from refuting that a legitimate transaction took place, usually by means of a signature.

Exhibit 11.1 depicts some of the major components involved in most EC applications and indicates where the above security issues come into play. It is safe to say that virtually every component in an EC application is subject to some sort of security threat.

Section 11.3 ▶ REVIEW QUESTIONS

1. If a customer purchases an item from an online store, what are some of the security concerns that might arise?
2. What are the major security issues facing EC sites?

EXHIBIT 11.1 General Security Issues at EC Sites

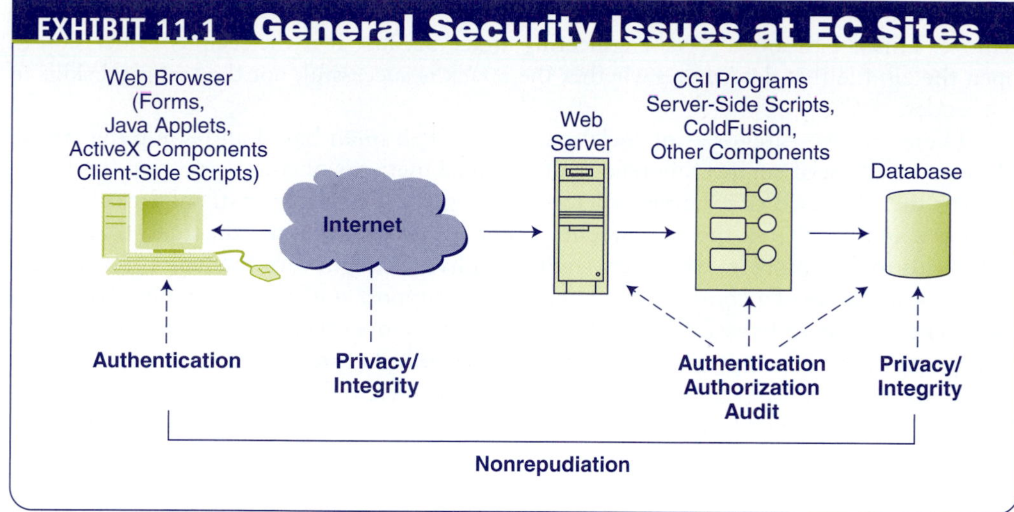

Source: Scambray, J. et al. *Hacking Exposed*, 2d ed. New York: McGraw-Hill, 2000. Copyright © The McGraw-Hill Companies.

11.4 TYPES OF THREATS AND ATTACKS

Security experts distinguish between two types of attacks—nontechnical and technical. **Nontechnical attacks** are those in which a perpetrator uses chicanery or some other form of persuasion to trick people into revealing sensitive information or performing actions that can be used to compromise the security of a network. These attacks also are called *social engineering*. The phishing attacks described earlier are of this sort. In contrast, software and systems knowledge are used to perpetrate *technical attacks*. A computer virus is an example of a technical attack. Often, attacks involve a combination of the two types. For instance, an intruder may use an automated tool to post a message to an instant messaging service. The message may offer the opportunity to download software of interest to the reader (e.g., software for downloading music or videos). When an unsuspecting reader downloads the malicious software, it automatically runs on his or her computer, enabling the intruder to take control of the machine and use it to perpetrate a technical attack.

nontechnical attack
An attack that uses chicanery to trick people into revealing sensitive information or performing actions that compromise the security of a network.

NONTECHNICAL ATTACKS: SOCIAL ENGINEERING

IT staffs tend to concentrate on the technical side of network security—firewalls, encryption, digital signatures, and the like. However, the real Achilles' heel of most networks is the humans who use them. Tricking individual users into providing information or carrying out actions that seem innocuous but are not is known as social engineering. **Social engineering** preys on an individual's desire to help, an individual's fear of getting into trouble, or the general trust among individuals.

social engineering
A type of nontechnical attack that uses social pressures to trick computer users into compromising computer networks to which those individuals have access.

Consider, for example, the following e-mail that was received by one of the authors at his place of work:

> *Dear user of xyz.com,*
>
> *We have detected that your e-mail account was used to send a large amount of spam during the recent week. Obviously, your computer had been compromised and now runs a trojan proxy server.*
>
> *We recommend you to follow the instructions in the attachment (xyz.com.zip) in order to keep your computer safe.*
>
> *Have a nice day,*
>
> *xyz.com technical support team.*

The message was sent from the e-mail PostMaster@xyz.com and appears to be a legitimate request from the company's technical support team. The sender is using the authority of the technical support team and playing on the recipient's fear that he has done something wrong and needs to comply with the request to rectify the situation. However, opening the attached zip file will install the Trojan horse proxy server the recipient is being requested to remove. This is basically a social engineering attack because it is the recipient's decision to open the zip file that determines whether the attack is successful, not the technical skills of the sender.

There are two categories of social engineering—human based and computer based. Human-based social engineering relies on traditional methods of communication (in person or over the phone). For example, a hacker posing as IT support staff might call up an employee and simply ask the employee for his or her password under the guise that the IT staff needs to fix a problem with the system. Or, a hacker might turn the tables. The hacker, posing as an officer of a company, might call the IT support staff asking for a password that the hacker claims to have forgotten. Fearing that they may seem uncooperative to upper management, the IT support staff complies. Employees also are notorious for writing their passwords on sticky notes or desk pads that easily can be viewed by people walking by or that are discarded in the trash and later retrieved by a hacker.

With computer-based social engineering, various technical ploys are used to encourage individuals to provide sensitive information. For example, a hacker may simply send an e-mail requesting sensitive information or create a Web page that surfaces a form that looks like a legitimate network log-on request for user ID and password. Over the past couple of years, Internet chat rooms and instant messaging also have been used to perpetrate social engineering attacks.

Kevin Mitnick, who spent 5 years in prison for breaking and entering into computers, and whose exploits were documented in the best-selling book *Takedown* (Shimomura 1996), was quoted as saying that more than half of his successful attacks were carried out through social engineering. From Mitnick's perspective (Mitnick and Simon 2002), the key to successful social engineering is trust: "You try to make an emotional connection with the person on the other side to create a sense of trust. That's the whole idea: to create a sense of trust and then exploit it" (quoted in Lemos 2000).

Because the key to successful social engineering rests with the victims, the key to combating social engineering attacks also rests with the victims. Certain positions within an organization are clearly more vulnerable than others. These are the individuals who have access to private and confidential information and who interact with the public on a frequent basis. Some of the positions with this sort of access and contact are secretaries and executive assistants, database and network administrators, computer operators, call-center operators, and help-desk attendants.

A multiprong approach should be used to combat social engineering (Damle 2002):

- **Education and training.** All staff, but especially those in vulnerable positions, need to be educated about the risks associated with social engineering, the social engineering techniques used by hackers, and ways and means to combat these attacks.
- **Policies and procedures.** Specific policies and procedures need to be developed for securing confidential information, guiding employee behavior with respect to confidential information, and taking the steps needed to respond to and report any social engineering breaches.
- **Penetration testing.** The policies, procedures, and responses of individual staff need to be tested on a regular basis by outside experts playing the role of a hacker. Because of the possibility of adverse effects on employee or staff morale, they should be debriefed after the penetration test, and any weaknesses should be corrected.

technical attack
An attack perpetrated using software and systems knowledge or expertise.

common (security) vulnerabilities and exposures (CVEs)
Publicly known computer security risks, which are collected, listed, and shared by a board of security-related organizations (cve.mitre.org).

TECHNICAL ATTACKS

In contrast with nontechnical attacks, software and systems knowledge are used to perpetrate **technical attacks**. In conducting a technical attack, an expert hacker often uses a methodical approach. Several software tools are readily and freely available over the Internet that enable a hacker to expose a system's vulnerabilities. Although many of these tools require expertise, novice hackers easily can use many of the existing tools.

In 1999, Mitre Corporation (cve.mitre.org) and 15 other security-related organizations began to enumerate all publicly known **common (security) vulnerabilities and exposures**

(CVEs). A *vulnerability* is a mistake in software that can be directly used by a hacker to gain access to a system or network; an *exposure* is a mistake in software that allows access to information or capabilities that can be used by a hacker as a stepping-stone into a system or network. One of the goals of the CVE list is to assign standard and unique names to each of the known security problems so that information can be collected and shared with the security community throughout the world. The number of known CVEs has grown from approximately 320 in 1999 to more than 3,000 in 2004. Additionally, there are almost 4,250 CVE *candidates*, which are those vulnerabilities or exposures under consideration for acceptance as CVEs (cve.mitre.org 1999–2005).

Since 2000, the SANS Institute, in conjunction with the FBI's **National Infrastructure Protection Center (NIPC)**, has produced a document summarizing the "Top 20 Internet Security Vulnerabilities" (SANS 2004). This year's list is actually two top 10 lists: the 10 most commonly exploited vulnerabilities in Windows and the 10 most commonly exploited vulnerabilities in UNIX and Linux. Although there are thousands of security incidents each year, the vast majority of successful attacks focus on the top 20 vulnerabilities. This list is used by organizations to prioritize their security efforts, allowing them to address the most dangerous vulnerabilities first.

National Infrastructure Protection Center (NIPC)
A joint partnership under the auspices of the FBI between government and private industry; designed to prevent vulnerabilities and protect the nation's infrastructure.

Examining the list of the top 10 or 20 CVEs, one quickly realizes that all of the CVEs are very technical in nature. For this reason, we will confine our discussion to two types of attacks that are well known and that have affected the lives of millions—distributed denial-of-service (DDoS) attacks and malicious code attacks (viruses, worms, and Trojan horses).

Distributed Denial-of-Service Attacks

At the beginning of 2004, the MyDoom.A e-mail viruses infected hundreds of thousands of PCs around the world (Fisher 2004). Like many other e-mail viruses, this virus was propagated by sending an official-looking e-mail message with a zip file attached. When the zip file was opened, the virus automatically found other e-mail addresses on the victim's computer and forwarded itself to those addresses. However, there was more to MyDoom.A than simple propagation. When the zip file was opened, the virus code also installed a program on the victim's machine that enabled the intruders to automatically launch what is known as a denial-of-service attack against a company called the SCO Group. The attack involved nothing more than having hundreds of thousands of infected machines send page requests to SCO's Web site. The site was brought to a standstill because it was overwhelmed by the large number of requests. It was first thought that SCO was a victim of irate Linux proponents who were angered by SCO's multimillion-dollar lawsuit against IBM for having allegedly included SCO's code in IBM's Linux software. Later, it was suggested that the attack was actually launched by spammers out of Russia. For another example of a brute force attack perpetrated by relatively simple means, see Online File W11.3.

denial-of-service (DoS) attack
An attack on a Web site in which an attacker uses specialized software to send a flood of data packets to the target computer with the aim of overloading its resources.

In a **denial-of-service (DoS) attack**, an attacker uses specialized software to send a flood of data packets to the target computer, with the aim of overloading its resources. Many attackers rely on software that has been created by other hackers and made available over the Internet rather than developing it themselves.

With a **distributed denial-of-service (DDoS) attack**, the attacker gains illegal administrative access to as many computers on the Internet as possible. Once an attacker has access to a large number of computers, he or she loads the specialized DDoS software onto the computers. The software lays in wait, listening for a command to begin the attack. When the command is given, the distributed network of computers begins sending out requests to the target computer. The requests may be legitimate queries for information or very specialized computer commands designed to overwhelm specific computer resources. There are different types of DDoS attacks. In the simplest case, like MyDoom.A, it is the magnitude of the requests that brings the target computer to a halt.

distributed denial-of-service (DDoS) attack
A denial-of-service attack in which the attacker gains illegal administrative access to as many computers on the Internet as possible and uses the multiple computers to send a flood of data packets to the target computer.

The machines on which the DDoS software is loaded are known as *zombies*. Zombies are often located at university and government sites and, increasingly, on home computers that are connected to the Internet through cable modems or DSL modems (see Exhibit 11.2).

Due to the widespread availability of free intrusion tools and scripts and the overall interconnectivity on the Internet, virtually anyone with minimal computer experience (often a

EXHIBIT 11.2 Using Zombies in a Distributed Denial-of-Service Attack

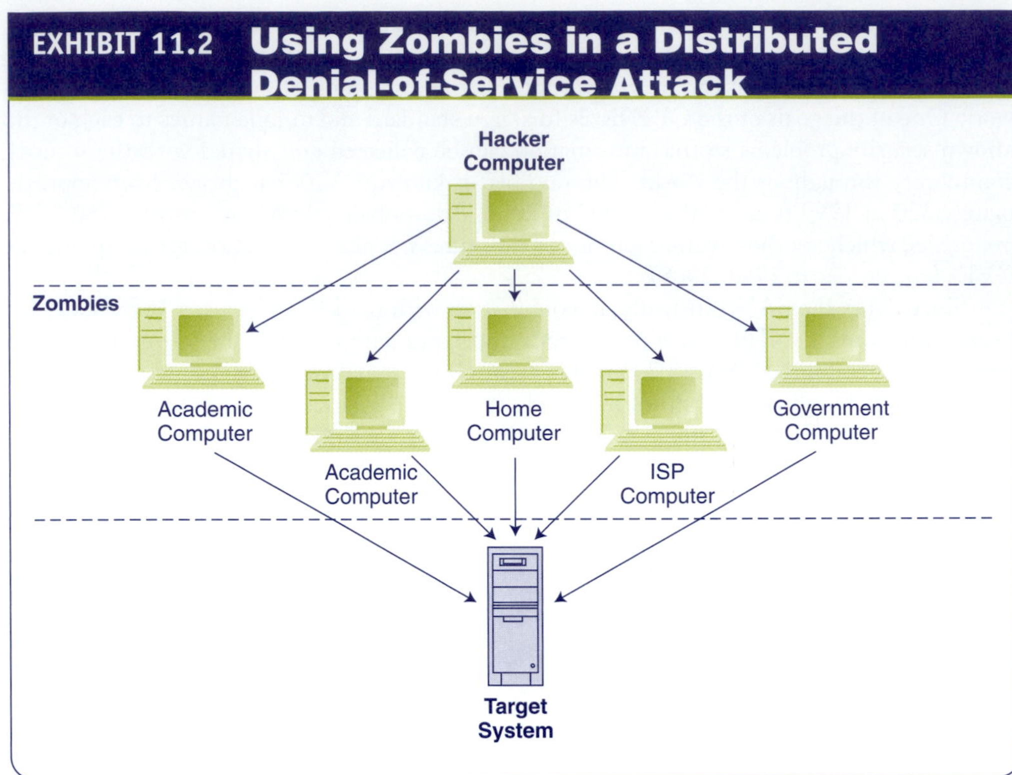

Source: Scambray, J. et al. *Hacking Exposed*, 2d ed. New York: McGraw-Hill, 2000. Copyright © The McGraw-Hill Companies.

teenager with time on his or her hands) can mount a DoS attack. EC Application Case 11.1 provides a description of one such attack.

DoS attacks can be difficult to stop. Fortunately (or unfortunately), they are so commonplace that over the past few years the security community has developed a series of steps for combating these costly attacks. In the case of SCO, the attacks were scheduled to run from February 1, 2004 to February 12, 2004. During that time, SCO shut off its original Web site sco.com and set up a new homepage at thescogroup.com. Microsoft, which was the target of MyDoom.B, redirected its Web to specialized security servers run by Akamai Technologies, Inc. (akamai.com). Depending on the type of attack, a company can sometimes thwart a DoS attack by reconfiguring its network routers and firewalls (see Section 11.7).

Malicious Code: Viruses, Worms, and Trojan Horses

malware
A generic term for malicious software.

Sometimes referred to as **malware** (for malicious software), malicious code is classified by the way in which it is propagated. Some malicious code is rather benign, but it all has the potential to do damage.

New variants of malicious code appear quite frequently. In their ninth annual survey of virus prevalence, the Computer Security Association (ICSA 2004) found that almost 90 percent of the companies surveyed felt that the problem of malicious code was "worse or much worse" than the previous year. Virtually all the respondents had been the victims of malicious code. More importantly, the number who reported that they were victims of "virus disasters"—defined as more than 25 computers infected with the same virus and suffering substantial monetary damage—was 92 out of 300 respondents, up 15 percent from the previous year. The cost of disaster recovery was also up 23 percent, to $100,000 per organization per event.

A number of factors have contributed to the overall increase in malicious code. Among these factors, the following are paramount (Skoudis and Zeltser 2003):

- **Mixing data and executable instructions.** In the past, data and executable instructions were separate. This is no longer the case. For example, all the major database programs, such as Oracle, IBM's DB2, and Microsoft's SQL Server, not only store data, but also execute database commands and have their own programming languages (e.g., PL/SQL for

CASE 11.1

EC Application

ARE HACKERS USING YOUR PC?

For Christmas 2003, Betty Carty, a 54-year-old grandmother living in southern New Jersey, purchased a Dell computer. At home, the computer was connected to the Internet through a high-speed connection from Comcast. Within a short time, her connection began to slow and her machined crashed frequently. In June 2004, Comcast curtailed her e-mail privileges. They determined that her PC was a major source of e-mail spam. However, it was not her fault. A hacker had turned her PC into a zombie, distributing up to 70,000 pieces of e-mail spam per day.

Carty's PC could have been infected in a number of ways. She could have opened an infected e-mail, visited a Web page containing malicious code, or been the victim of a network worm that worked its way onto her machine through a security hole in her computer's operating system.

Carty's machine is not alone. According to an interview study by *USA TODAY* of tech-industry and security experts (Achohido and Swartz 2004), many top-tier hackers are now focused on creating malicious code aimed at amassing networks of zombies. Once assembled, they sell access to the zombies to spammers, blackmailers, and identity thieves. Supposedly, the number of zombies has reached the millions. There is no way to determine the exact number, but one measure of the rising tide of zombies is the amount of e-mail spam. In July 2004, 94 percent of e-mail traffic was estimated to be spam. This is more than double the estimated amount from the year before. Based on another estimate, 40 percent of spam comes from zombies.

Like Carty, most home users think their PCs are safe and, as a consequence, have done little to protect against viruses, spyware, hackers, or other online threats. In October 2004, America Online (AOL) and the National Cyber Security Alliance (NCSA) released the results of a comprehensive, nationwide, in-home study of computer security. The study involved interviews with 329 participants in 22 cities and towns across the United States. In addition to being questioned, the participants' computers were examined by technicians to examine their firewall settings, antivirus software, potential virus infections, and the like. Among the key findings of the study were:

- Eighty-four percent of the participants keep sensitive information (e.g., financial records) on their computers, and over 70 percent of the participants use the Internet for sensitive transactions (e.g., online banking).
- Over 75 percent of the participants said they think their computers were very or somewhat safe from online threats.
- Over 60 percent of the participants said they had been victimized by viruses; however, a scan of their computers indicated that less than 20 percent currently had viruses.
- Over 50 percent of the participants thought that their machines had been infected by spyware, but a scan of their machines indicated the actual percentage was 80, with an average of 93 spyware components per machine.
- Eighty-five percent of the participants had antivirus software on their machines, but only one-third of the machines had been updated in the past week.
- Thirty-three percent of the participants' machines had a firewall currently running, but over 70 percent of these machines did not have the firewall properly configured.
- The majority of users were confused by the difference between a firewall and antivirus software, and a majority indicated that they did not understand how a firewall works.

In general, most users think their computers are safe from online threats but lack basic protection against viruses, spyware, hackers, and other online threats.

Sources: Achohido and Swartz (2004) and AOL/NCSA (2004).

Questions

1. What sorts of precautions do most home users employ to secure their computers?
2. What are some of the major vulnerabilities on home users' computers?

Oracle). Similarly, applications such as Microsoft Excel and Microsoft Word have their own scripting languages, which make it possible to embed programs in spreadsheets and Word documents. Likewise, Web pages combine HTML (which underlies the content and formatting of a page) with JavaScript, VBScript, and other languages. All of these combinations provide easy entry points for intruders to embed and mask malicious code.

- **Increasingly homogenous computing environments.** About 20 years ago we had minicomputers and mainframe computers, as well as PCs. They all had different kinds of computer chips and ran on a variety of operating systems and networks. Today, we are down to Windows and UNIX/Linux operating systems, Intel chips dominate the market, and virtually everything is connected via a TCP/IP network. This means that an attacker only has to develop a single piece of code in order to wreak havoc across the globe.
- **Unprecedented connectivity.** In the past, networks were basically islands of connectivity. Today, everything is connected—government computers, emergency services, financial

systems, home PCs, medical systems, retail operations, airline reservation systems, and the like. Most of it is connected by high-speed lines. This connectivity offers the opportunity for malicious code to spread at unprecedented rates.

- **Larger clueless user base.** The average computer user has minimal understanding of the complexities of his or her computer, the networks with which the computer is connected, or the risks posed by malicious code. The implication is that few users have the skills or knowledge required to install and configure the security systems (e.g., personal firewalls) and patches needed to combat malicious code. This makes home PCs and small business systems fertile ground for hackers.

As the number of attacks increases, the following trends in malicious code are emerging (Symantec 2004; Slewe 2004):

- **Increased speed and volume of attacks.** The Slammer worm exemplifies this trend. On January 25, 2003, the Slammer worm was released. The worm exploited a vulnerability in Microsoft's SQL Server database. Upon release, the worm doubled in size every 8.5 seconds, infecting approximately 75,000 machines within 10 minutes.
- **Reduced time between the discovery of a vulnerability and the release of an attack to exploit the vulnerability.** In the first half of 2004, the average time between the discovery of a vulnerability and the appearance of code exploiting the vulnerability was 5.8 days. Once the exploitive code is made available, a new vulnerability can be widely scanned for and quickly attacked, especially if the vulnerability is in a widely deployed application.
- **Remotely controlled bot networks are growing.** In the world of computer security, *bots* (short for "robots") are programs that are installed covertly on a targeted system. They allow an unauthorized user to remotely control the compromised computer for a wide variety of malicious purposes. Over the first 6 months of 2004, the number of monitored bots rose from well under 2,000 computers to more than 30,000. Bots can be upgraded easily and quickly to run malicious code designed to exploit recently discovered vulnerabilities.
- **E-commerce is the most frequently targeted industry.** During the first 6 months of 2004, e-commerce received more targeted attacks than any other industry (16 percent in 2004 versus 4 percent in 2003). This rise may indicate that the motivation of attackers may be shifting from looking for notoriety to seeking illicit financial rewards.
- **Attacks against Web application technologies are increasing.** Concomitant with the increase in e-commerce attacks is an increase in attacks on Web applications. In the first half of 2004, 39 percent of disclosed vulnerabilities were associated with Web application technologies. These attacks often provide access to confidential information without having to compromise any servers. They allow attackers to gain access to the target system simply by penetrating one end user's computer, bypassing traditional perimeter security measures.
- **A large percentage of *Fortune* 100 companies have been compromised by worms.** Over the first 6 months of 2004, Symantec observed worm traffic originating from *Fortune* 100 corporations. This data was gathered by analyzing attack data that revealed the source network (IP) addresses of attack activity. The purpose of this analysis was to determine how many of these systems were infected by worms and actively being used to propagate worms. More than 40 percent of *Fortune* 100 companies controlled network (IP) addresses from which worm-related attacks propagated. This indicates that, despite the measures taken by organizations, their systems are still becoming infected. Continued worm traffic coming from these networks indicates to potential attackers that the network is still susceptible to exploitation.

Malicious code takes a variety of forms—both pure and hybrid. The names for such codes are taken from the real-world pathogens they resemble.

virus
A piece of software code that inserts itself into a host, including the operating systems, in order to propagate; it requires that its host program be run to activate it.

Viruses. This is the best known of the malicious code categories. Although there are many definitions of a computer virus, the Request for Comment (RFC) 1135 definition is widely used: "A **virus** is a piece of code that inserts itself into a host, including the operating systems, to propagate. It cannot run independently. It requires that its host program be run to activate it." Although viruses are self-replicating, they cannot propagate automatically across a network; they require a human to move them from one computer to another.

A virus has two components. First, it has a propagation mechanism by which it spreads. Second, it has a payload that refers to what the virus does once it is executed. Sometimes the execution is triggered by a particular event. The Michelangelo virus, for instance, was triggered by Michelangelo's birth date. Some viruses simply infect and spread. Others do substantial damage (e.g., deleting files or corrupting the hard drive).

A whole industry has grown up around combating computer viruses. Companies such as Network Associates (owner of McAfee products) and Symantec (owner of Norton products) exist for the sole purpose of fighting viruses—providing antivirus software and software updates to individuals and companies. McAfee's Anti-virus and Vulnerability Response Team (AVERT) has a virus information library (vil.nai.com) and keeps a running list of the 10 biggest malicious threats, including viruses, worms, Trojan horses, and the like. A sizeable percentage of those threats include "Potentially Unwanted Programs," which give recipients the option to decide whether they want to keep software.

Worms. The major difference between a worm and a virus is that a worm propagates between systems (usually through a network), whereas a virus propagates locally. RFC 1135 defines a worm in this way: "A **worm** is a program that can run independently, will consume the resources of its host from within in order to maintain itself, and can propagate a complete working version of itself onto another machine." A worm attacks one computer, takes it over, and uses it as a staging area to scan for and attack other machines. No human intervention is required to spread a worm across a network. Code Red and SQL Slammer are examples of worms.

worm
A software program that runs independently, consuming the resources of its host in order to maintain itself, that is capable of propagating a complete working version of itself onto another machine.

Worms consist of a set of common base elements: a warhead, a propagation engine, a payload, a target-selection algorithm, and a scanning engine. The warhead is the piece of code in a worm that exploits some known vulnerability. Once a worm exploits the vulnerability, its propagation engine is used to move the rest of the worm's code across the network. The move usually is accomplished with a file transfer program. Once the entire worm is moved across, it delivers its payload and then utilizes its target-selection algorithm to look for other potential victims to attack (e.g., e-mail addresses on the victimized machine). The scanning engine determines which of the other potential victims can be exploited. When a suitable target is found, the entire process is repeated. The entire process takes seconds or less, which is why a worm can spread to thousands of machines.

Antivirus software can be used to thwart viruses as well as other forms of malware, including worms. Because worms spread much more rapidly than viruses, organizations need to proactively track new vulnerabilities and apply system patches as a defense against their spread.

Macro Viruses and Macro Worms. A **macro virus** or **macro worm** is usually executed when the application object (e.g., spreadsheet, word processing document, e-mail message) containing the macro is opened or a particular procedure is executed (e.g., a file is saved). Melissa and ILOVEYOU were both examples of macro worms that were propagated through Microsoft Outlook e-mail and whose payloads were delivered as Visual Basic for Application (VBA) programs attached to e-mail messages. When the unsuspecting recipient opened the e-mail, the VBA program looked up the entries in the recipient's Outlook address book and sent copies of itself to the contacts in the address book. If you think this is a difficult task, note that the ILOVEYOU macro was about 40 lines of code.

macro virus or **macro worm**
A virus or worm that is executed when the application object that contains the macro is opened or a particular procedure is executed.

Trojan Horses. A **Trojan horse** is a program that appears to have a useful function but contains a hidden function that presents a security risk. The name is derived from the Trojan horse in Greek mythology. Legend has it that during the Trojan War the city of Troy was presented with a large wooden horse as a gift to the goddess Athena. The Trojans hauled the horse into the city gates. During the night, Greek soldiers, who were hiding in the hollow horse, opened the gates of Troy and let in the Greek army. The army was able to take the city and win the war.

Trojan horse
A program that appears to have a useful function but that contains a hidden function that presents a security risk.

There are many types of Trojan horse programs. The programs of interest are those that make it possible for someone else to access and control a person's computer over the Internet. This type of Trojan horse has two parts: a server and a client. The server is the program that runs on the computer under attack. The client program is the program used by the person perpetrating the attack. For example, the Girlfriend Trojan is a server program that arrives in the form of a file that looks like an interesting game or program. When the unsuspecting user runs the program, the Trojan program is installed. The installed program is executed every time the attacked computer is turned on. The server simply waits for the associated client program to send a command. This particular Trojan horse enables the perpetrator to capture user IDs and passwords, to display messages on the affected computer, to delete and upload files, and so on.

One key malware trend is the rise of code that exploits and alters the user's operating system down to the kernel level. The kernel controls things such as a computer's memory, file system, hardware, and other critical components that are crucial to the operation of the machine. **Rootkits** fall into this category of code. They are special Trojan horse programs that modify the existing operating system software so that an intruder can hide the presence of the Trojan program. For example, in the UNIX operating system the "–ls" command is used to list the files on the machine. Using a rootkit, an intruder could substitute his or her own "-ls" command that would hide the Trojan program's presence by failing to list it when the "-ls" command is issued.

rootkit
A special Trojan horse program that modifies existing operating system software so that an intruder can hide the presence of the Trojan program.

The best way to defend against Trojan horses is to implement strict policies and procedures for installing new software. In an organization, end users should be forbidden from installing unauthorized programs. Administrators need to check the integrity of programs and patches that are installed. In the same vein, new programs and tools should be installed in a test environment before putting them into a production environment.

Section 11.4 ▶ REVIEW QUESTIONS

1. Describe the difference between a nontechnical and a technical cyber attack.
2. What is a CVE?
3. How are DDoS attacks perpetrated?
4. What are the major forms of malicious code?
5. What factors account for the increase in malicious code?
6. What are some of the major trends in malicious code?

11.5 MANAGING EC SECURITY

Although awareness of security issues has increased in recent years, organizations continue to make some fairly common mistakes in managing their security risks (McConnell 2002):

- **Undervalued information.** Few organizations have a clear understanding of the value of specific information assets.
- **Narrowly defined security boundaries.** Most organizations focus on securing their internal networks and fail to understand the security practices of their supply chain partners.
- **Reactive security management.** Many organizations are reactive rather than proactive, focusing on security *after* an incident or problem occurs.
- **Dated security management processes.** Organizations rarely update or change their security practices to meet changing needs. Similarly, they rarely update the knowledge and skills of their staff about best practices in information security.
- **Lack of communication about security responsibilities.** Security often is viewed as an IT problem, not an organizational one.

Given these common mistakes, it is clear that a holistic approach is required to secure an EC site. Companies must constantly evaluate and address emerging vulnerabilities and threats to their Web sites. End users must recognize that IT security is as important as physical security and must adopt responsible behavior. Senior management must articulate the need for IT security, play a key role in formulating organizational security policies, and actively support those policies. Those organizations with sound security practices rely on comprehensive risk management to determine their security needs (Kay 2003; Microsoft 2004).

SECURITY RISK MANAGEMENT

Consider an online CRM database containing confidential information about a company's customer accounts. An information asset of this sort is extremely valuable to the company, to the customers, and potentially to the company's competitors. Imagine what it would cost the company if this database were unavailable, damaged or destroyed, or fell into the hands of another party. The risks and potential threats against this asset are both physical (e.g., the machine on which the database is housed could be destroyed) and nonphysical (e.g., the data could be compromised by an irate employee or attacked by a hacker). Obviously, the asset needs to be secured in a variety of ways, including physically securing the computer on which the database is run, backing up the database to another computer, password protecting the database, putting the database on a secure network behind a firewall, and so on. For this particular asset, the costs of reducing the risks far outweigh the potential costs associated with securing the asset. The systematic process of identifying key computer, network, and information assets; assessing the risks and threats against those assets; and actually reducing those security risks and threats is known as **security risk management**.

security risk management
A systematic process for determining the likelihood of various security attacks and for identifying the actions needed to prevent or mitigate those attacks.

Security risk management consists of three phases:

- **Asset identification.** In this phase, an organization determines its key computer, network, and information assets and places a value on those assets. The valuation includes the costs of obtaining, maintaining, and replacing the asset, as well as the costs if it fell into the hands of another party. Once the assets are identified, the organization can assess the security threats, vulnerabilities, and risks against those assets.
- **Risk assessment.** Once an organization's key assets have been identified, the next step is to perform an assessment of the risks against those assets. This involves identifying threats, vulnerabilities, and risks. *Threats* include things such as natural disasters, equipment malfunction, employees, intruders, hackers, terrorist attacks, and the like. *Vulnerabilities* are those aspects of the asset that can be compromised by the potential threats. *Risks* involve the probabilities of the vulnerabilities being compromised by various threats, as well as the potential financial losses resulting from the compromises. One way to evaluate the threats and vulnerabilities facing a specific organization is to rely on the knowledge of the organization's IT personnel or to use an outside consultant, such as Granite Systems (granitesystems.net), to conduct a security assessment. Another way is to utilize software that scans for vulnerabilities, does penetration testing, or enables a firm to safely view and study attacks as they occur.
- **Implementation.** After the risks have been assessed, they need to be prioritized by probability and potential loss. A list of solutions and countermeasures should be proposed and reviewed for each of the high-priority risks. These solutions and countermeasures need to be evaluated in terms of their overall cost-benefits (e.g., a company would not spend $50,000 for a security measure when the asset is only worth $25,000) and the security measures that are currently in place. Once a set of security measures has been selected and implemented, not only does the organization need to monitor the performance and effectiveness of those measures, but it also needs to continually review its asset base and any new threats, vulnerabilities, and risks that may arise.

Section 11.5 ▶ REVIEW QUESTIONS

1. What are some common mistakes that EC sites make in managing their security?
2. Describe the basic steps in security risk management.

11.6 SECURING EC COMMUNICATIONS

As indicated by the CSI/FBI and CERT surveys cited in Section 11.1, most organizations rely on multiple technologies to secure their networks. These technologies can be divided into two major groups: those designed to secure communications *across* the network and those designed to protect the servers and clients *on* the network. This section considers the first of these technologies.

ACCESS CONTROL AND AUTHENTICATION

The simplest aspects of network security are access control and authentication. **Access control** determines who (person or machine) can legitimately use a network resource and which resources he, she, or it can use. A resource can be anything—Web pages, text files, databases, applications, servers, printers, or any other information source or network component.

access control
Mechanism that determines who can legitimately use a network resource.

Typically, access control lists (ACL) define which users have access to which resources and what rights they have with respect to those resources (i.e., read, view, write, print, copy, delete, execute, modify, or move). By default, a user's rights often are set at full access or no access. This is fine as a starting point, but each resource needs to be considered separately, and the rights of particular users need to be established individually. This process of assigning rights often is simplified by creating various roles or groups (e.g., system administrators, northwest sales reps, product marketing department, trading partners, etc.), assigning rights to those groups, and then specifying the individuals within those groups. Users often are denoted by their network login IDs, which are usually checked when the user first accesses the system.

Once a user has been identified, the user must be authenticated. As noted earlier, authentication is the process of verifying that the user is who he or she claims to be. Verification usually is based on one or more characteristics that distinguish the individual from others. The distinguishing characteristics can be based on something one knows (e.g., passwords), something one has (e.g., a token), or something one is (e.g., fingerprint). Traditionally, authentication has been based on passwords. Passwords are notoriously insecure because people have a habit of writing them down in easy-to-find places, choosing values that are guessed easily, and willingly telling people their passwords when asked.

Stronger security is achieved by combining something one knows with something one has, a technique known as *two-factor authentication*. Tokens qualify as something one has. Tokens come in various shapes, forms, and sizes. **Passive tokens** are storage devices that contain a secret code. The most common passive tokens are plastic cards with magnetic strips containing a hidden code. With passive tokens, the user swipes the token through a reader attached to a personal computer or workstation and then enters his or her password to gain access to the network.

passive tokens
Storage devices (e.g., magnetic strips) that contain a secret code used in a two-factor authentication system.

Active tokens usually are small stand-alone electronic devices (e.g., key chain tokens, smartcards, calculators, USB dongles) that generate one-time passwords. In this case, the user enters a PIN into the token, the token generates a password that is only good for a single log-on, and the user then logs on to the system using the one-time password. ActivCard (activcard.com) and CRYPTOcard (cryptocard.com) are companies that provide active token authentication devices.

active tokens
Small, stand-alone electronic devices that generate one-time passwords used in a two-factor authentication system.

Biometric Systems

Two-factor authentication also can be based on something one is. Fingerprint scanners, iris scanners, facial recognition systems, and voice recognition all are examples of **biometric systems** that recognize a person by a physical trait. Biometric systems can *identify* a person from a population of enrolled users by searching through a database for a match based on the person's biometric trait or the system can *verify* a person's claimed identity by matching the individual's biometric trait against a previously stored version. Biometric verification is much simpler than biometric identification, and it is the process used in two-factor authentication.

biometric systems
Authentication systems that identify a person by measurement of a biological characteristic, such as fingerprints, iris (eye) patterns, facial features, or voice.

To date, the uptake of biometric security has been slow. For instance, in the CSI/FBI survey cited earlier only 11 percent of the organizations indicated they were using biometric systems. A security technology adoption survey conducted by International Data Corporation showed that only 0.6 percent of North American companies use biometrics for Internet and network security (Shen 2003). In terms of overall market share, biometric security products account for around 5 percent of the security product market.

Interest in biometric security is increasing, spurred by declining prices in biometric systems, the worldwide focus on terrorism, and soaring fraud and identity theft. In a survey of 840 corporate IT directors in 21 countries conducted by Hitachi Data Systems, 65 percent said that they expected to be using biometrics sometime in the near future (Sherwood 2004). Many financial institutions, for instance, are interested in using a combination of smartcards and biometrics to authenticate customers and ensure nonrepudiation for online banking, trading, and purchasing transactions. Retail point-of-sale system vendors are looking to biometrics to supplement signature verification for credit card purchases. Biometrics also are being tested in various national security and governmental applications, including airport security, passport verification, and social service fraud prevention.

Fingerprint scanning is probably the best known and most widely used biometric. However, fingerprint scanning is only one of a number of possible biometrics that can be used to verify an individual's identity (authentication). Biometrics come in two "flavors"—physiological and behavioral. **Physiological biometrics** are based on measurements derived directly from different parts of the body. In contrast, **behavioral biometrics** are derived from various actions and indirectly from various body parts (e.g., voice scans or keystroke monitoring).

In practice, physiological biometrics are used more often than behavioral biometrics. Among the physiological biometrics, the scans of fingerprints, irises, hands, and facial characteristics are the most popular.

To implement a biometric authentication system, the physiological or behavioral characteristics of a participant must be scanned repeatedly under different settings. The scans are then averaged to produce a biometric template, or identifier. The template is stored in a database as a series of numbers that can range from a few bytes for hand geometry to several thousand bytes for facial recognition. When a person uses a biometric system, a live scan is conducted, and the scan is converted to a series of numbers, which is then compared against the template stored in the database. Examples of various types of biometric templates are detailed in the following text.

Fingerprint Scanning. Fingerprints can be distinguished by a variety of "discontinuities that interrupt the smooth flow of ridges" (Kroeker 2002) on the bottom tips of the fingers. Ridge endings, dots (small ridges), and ponds (spaces between ridges) are examples of such discontinuities. In **fingerprint scanning**, a special algorithm is used to convert the scanned discontinuities to a set of numbers stored as a template. The chance that any two people have the same template is one in a billion. Fingerprint recognition devices for desktop and laptop access are now available from a variety of vendors at low cost. Online File W11.4 describes the use of fingerprint scanning in a retail situation.

Iris Scanning. The iris is the colored part of the eye surrounding the pupil. The iris has a large number of unique spots that can be captured by a camera placed 3 to 10 inches from the eye. Within a second, a special algorithm can convert the iris scan to a set of numbers. The numbers can be used to construct an iris-scan template that can be used in **iris scanning**, in which a camera scans a person's iris, compares the scan to a template, and verifies the person's identity. The chance that any two people have identical iris templates is considerably smaller than the chance that they have the same fingerprint templates. EC Application Case 11.2 (page 474) describes the use of iris recognition for passport verification.

Voice Scanning. Differences in the physiology of speech production from one individual to the next produce different acoustical patterns that can be converted into a template that can be used in **voice scanning**. In most voice-scanning systems, the user talks into a microphone or telephone. The word that is spoken is usually the user's system ID or password. The next time a user wants to gain access to the system, the user simply repeats the spoken word. It takes about 4 to 6 seconds to verify a voice scan. Unlike fingerprint and iris scanning, the hardware needed to capture voice input (e.g., a microphone) is inexpensive and widely available.

Keystroke Monitoring. This biometric is still under development. **Keystroke monitoring** is based on the assumption that the way in which users type words at a keyboard varies from one user to the next. The pressure, speed, and rhythm with which a word is entered are converted through a special algorithm to a set of numbers to form a keystroke template. Again, the word that is employed in most of these systems is the user's system ID or password. When a user wants to gain access to a system, the user simply types in his or her system ID or password. The system checks the pressure, speed, and rhythm with which the word is typed against the templates in the database. The main problem with these systems is that there is still too much variability in the way an individual types from one session to the next.

The Biometric Consortium. The Biometric Consortium (BC) is a focal point for research and evaluation on biometric systems and applications. The consortium has over 800 government, industry, and university members and is co-chaired by the National Institute of Standards and Technology (NIST) and the National Security Agency (NSA). The BC Web site (biometrics.org) contains a variety of information on biometric technology, research results, federal and state applications, and other topics.

physiological biometrics
Measurements derived directly from different parts of the body (e.g., fingerprint, iris, hand, facial characteristics).

behavioral biometrics
Measurements derived from various actions and indirectly from various body parts (e.g., voice scans or keystroke monitoring).

fingerprint scanning
Measurement of the discontinuities of a person's fingerprint, which are then converted to a set of numbers that are stored as a template and used to authenticate identity.

iris scanning
Measurement of the unique spots in the iris (colored part of the eye), which are then converted to a set of numbers that are stored as a template and used to authenticate identity.

voice scanning
Measurement of the acoustical patterns in speech production, which are then converted to a set of numbers that are stored as a template and used to authenticate identity.

keystroke monitoring
Measurement of the pressure, speed, and rhythm with which a word is typed, which is then converted to a set of numbers that are stored as a template and used to authenticate identity; this biometric is still under development.

CASE 11.2

EC Application

THE EYES HAVE IT

With increasing concerns over terrorism, air safety, and fraud, the UK has begun testing biometric identification and authentication for both security and commercial purposes. In one pilot project, British Airways and Virgin Atlantic tested an iris-scanning system from EyeTicket Corporation at Heathrow Airport in London, JFK Airport in New York City, and Dulles Airport outside Washington D.C. The 6-month pilot, which occurred in 2002, was arranged by the UK's Simplifying Passenger Travel Project (SPT) of the International Air Transport Association (IATA). The major goal of the project was to determine whether iris scanning could be used with passports to speed the authentication process for international travelers entering the UK.

The two airlines chose participants from among their frequent flyer programs, focusing on passengers who made frequent trips between the United States and the UK. Potential participants registered for the program via e-mail. They were interviewed by the UK Immigration Service to ensure that there were no security issues. Approximately 900 people registered for the program.

The actual tests involved iris-scanning enrollment stations at Heathrow, JFK, and Dulles, as well as video cameras and a recognition station located at Heathrow. Passengers who participated in the program enrolled only once. This was done at the enrollment stations by taking a close up digital image of the passenger's iris. The image was then stored as a template in a computer file. When a passenger landed at Heathrow, the passenger's iris was scanned at the recognition station and compared to the stored template. If a match occurred, the passenger was allowed to pass through immigration. On average, the scan and match took about 12 seconds. If the match failed, the passenger had to move to the regular immigration line. The failure rate was only 7 percent. Watery eyes and long eyelashes were some of the major sources of failure.

According to the IATA's SPT regional group in charge of the project, the initial findings of the pilot project were encouraging. Not only did the biometric system simplify and speed the arrival process, but the system also successfully verified passengers, maintained border integrity, and was well received by the participants.

Despite the success of the pilot project, there are barriers to using the system for larger populations of passengers. One of the major barriers is the initial registration. According to the Immigration Service, the most difficult and time-consuming aspect of the pilot program was working through the processes and procedures for registration and risk assessment. As noted, the pilot only involved around 900 passengers. Obviously, it would be much more difficult to register thousands or millions of passengers. Likewise, it would be a much slower process to compare a scanned iris against thousands or millions of iris templates.

Another barrier to wider deployment is the lack of technical and procedural standards. On the technical front, there are no standards for iris scanning. The EyeTicket system is based on an iris-scanning algorithm originally created by Jeffrey Daugman, a professor at Cambridge University. Other iris enrollment and scanning devices use other algorithms. This makes it difficult to share templates across systems and across borders. There is also a need for standard procedures. Without common enrollment, authentication, and identification procedures, there is little basis for trust among different government agencies or different governments.

Even with standards, the prospects for using iris scanning or any other biometric at airports for identification are poor. In 2003, face-recognition systems at Boston's Logan Airport failed to recognize volunteers posing as terrorists 96 times during a 3-month period and incorrectly identified the innocent an equal number of times. Similar results were obtained in an earlier trial at Palm Beach International Airport, with more than 50 percent of those who should have been identified going undetected and two to three innocent passengers being flagged every hour. Such results in a larger population would bring airport security to its knees.

Sources: Emigh (2004) and Venes (2004).

Questions

1. What were the major components in the EyeTicket iris-scanning system?
2. What are some of the difficulties in using iris scanning to verify passengers for passport control?
3. Is it reasonable to use iris scanning or any other biometric to identify terrorists at airports?

PUBLIC KEY INFRASTRUCTURE

public key infrastructure (PKI)

A scheme for securing e-payments using public key encryption and various technical components.

The "state of the art" in authentication rests on the **public key infrastructure (PKI)**. In this case, the something one has is not a token, but a certificate. PKI has become the cornerstone for secure e-payments. It refers to the technical components, infrastructure, and practices needed to enable the use of public key encryption, digital signatures, and digital certificates with a network application. PKI also is the foundation of a number of network applications, including SCM, VPNs, secure e-mail, and intranet applications.

Private and Public Key Encryption

At the heart of PKI is **encryption**. Encryption is the process of transforming or scrambling (encrypting) data in such a way that it is difficult, expensive, or time-consuming for an unauthorized person to unscramble (decrypt) it. All encryption has four basic parts (shown in Exhibit 11.3): **plaintext**, **ciphertext**, an **encryption algorithm**, and the **key**. The simple example in the exhibit forms the basis of an actual encryption algorithm called the *Vigenère cipher*. Of course, simple algorithms and keys of this sort are useless in the networked world. More complex encryption algorithms and keys are required.

The two major classes of encryption systems are *symmetric systems*, with one secret key, and *asymmetric systems*, with two keys.

Symmetric (Private) Key System

In a **symmetric (private) key system**, the same key is used to encrypt and decrypt the plaintext (see Exhibit 11.4). The sender and receiver of the text must share the same key without revealing it to anyone else—thus making it a so-called *private* system.

For years, the **Data Encryption Standard (DES)** (itl.nist.gov/fipspubs/fip46-2.htm) was the standard symmetric encryption algorithm supported by U.S. government agencies. On October 2, 2000, the National Institute of Standards and Technology (NIST) announced that DES was being replaced by **Rijndael**, the new Advanced Encryption Standard (csrc.nist.gov/encryption/aes) used to secure U.S. government communications.

Because the algorithms used to encrypt a message are well known, the confidentiality of a message depends on the key. It is possible to guess a key simply by having a computer try all of the encryption combinations until the message is decrypted. High-speed and parallel-processing computers can try millions of guesses in a second. This is why the length of the key (in bits) is the main factor in securing a message. If a key were 4 bits long (e.g., 1011), there would be only 16 possible combinations (i.e., 2 raised to the 4th power). One would hardly need a computer to crack the key. Now, consider the time it would take to try all possible encryption keys. According to Howard (2000), there are over 1 trillion possible combinations in a 40-bit key—but even this number of combinations can be broken in 8 days (using a computer that can check 1.6 million keys per second) or in just 109 seconds (at 10 million keys per second). However, a 64-bit encryption key would take 58.5 years to be broken (at 10 million keys per second) (Howard 2000).

Public (Asymmetric) Key Encryption

Imagine trying to use one-key encryption to buy something offered on a particular Web server. If the seller's key were distributed to thousands of buyers, then the key would not remain secret for long. This is where public key (asymmetric) encryption comes into play. **Public key encryption** uses a pair of matched keys—a **public key** that is publicly available to anyone and a **private key** that is known only to its owner. If a message is encrypted with a public key, then the associated private key is required to decrypt the message. If, for example,

encryption
The process of scrambling (encrypting) a message in such a way that it is difficult, expensive, or time-consuming for an unauthorized person to unscramble (decrypt) it.

plaintext
An unencrypted message in human-readable form.

ciphertext
A plaintext message after it has been encrypted into a machine-readable form.

encryption algorithm
The mathematical formula used to encrypt the plaintext into the ciphertext, and vice versa.

key
The secret code used to encrypt and decrypt a message.

symmetric (private) key system
An encryption system that uses the same key to encrypt and decrypt the message.

EXHIBIT 11.3 Encryption Components

Component	Description	Example
Plaintext	Original message in human-readable form	Credit Card Number 5342 8765 3652 9982
Encryption algorithm	Mathematical formula or process used to encrypt/decrypt the message	Add a number (the key) to each number in the card. If the number is greater than 9, wrap around the number to the beginning (i.e., modulus arithmetic). For example, add 4 to each number so that 1 becomes 5, 9 becomes 3, etc.
Key	A special number passed to the algorithm to transform the message	Number to be added to original number (e.g., 4).
Ciphertext	Plaintext message after it has been encrypted into unreadable form	The original 5342 8765 3652 9982 becomes 9786 2109 7096 3326.

EXHIBIT 11.4 Symmetric (Private) Key Encryption

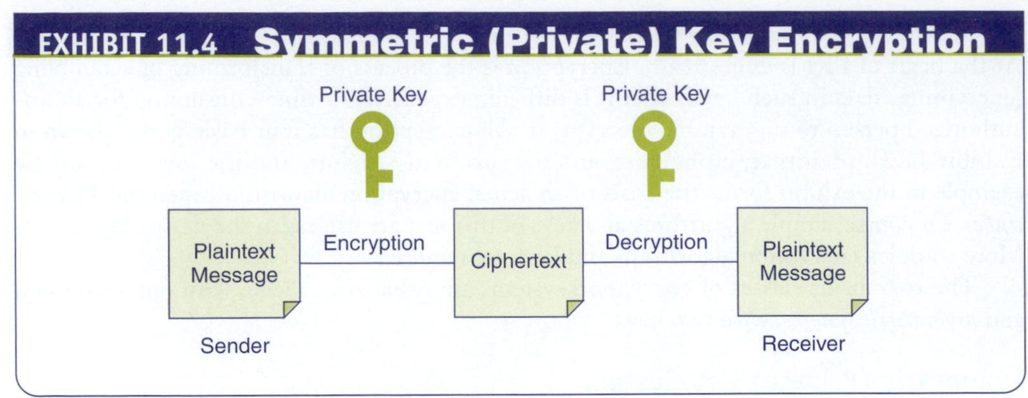

Data Encryption Standard (DES)
The standard symmetric encryption algorithm supported the NIST and used by U.S. government agencies until October 2, 2000.

Rijndael
The new Advanced Encryption Standard used to secure U.S. government communications since October 2, 2000.

public key encryption
Method of encryption that uses a pair of matched keys—a public key to encrypt a message and a private key to decrypt it, or vice versa.

public key
Encryption code that is publicly available to anyone.

private key
Encryption code that is known only to its owner.

RSA
The most common public key encryption algorithm; uses keys ranging in length from 512 bits to 1,024 bits.

digital signature
An identifying code that can be used to authenticate the identity of the sender of a document.

hash
A mathematical computation that is applied to a message, using a private key, to encrypt the message.

message digest
A summary of a message, converted into a string of digits, after the hash has been applied.

a person wanted to send a purchase order to a company and have the contents remain private, he or she would encrypt the message with the company's public key. When the company received the order, it would decrypt it with the associated private key.

The most common public key encryption algorithm is **RSA** (rsa.com). RSA uses keys ranging in length from 512 bits to 1,024 bits. The main problem with public key encryption is speed. Symmetrical algorithms are significantly faster than asymmetric key algorithms. Therefore, public key encryption cannot be used effectively to encrypt and decrypt large amounts of data. In practice, a combination of symmetric and asymmetric encryption is used to encrypt messages.

Digital Signatures

In the online world, how can one be sure that a message is actually coming from the person whom he or she thinks sent it? Similarly, how one be sure that a person cannot deny that he or she sent a particular message?

One part of the answer is a **digital signature**—the electronic equivalent of a personal signature that cannot be forged. Digital signatures are based on public keys. They can be used to authenticate the identity of the sender of a message or document. They also can be used to ensure that the original content of an electronic message or document is unchanged. Digital signatures have additional benefits in the online world. They are portable, cannot be easily repudiated or imitated, and can be time-stamped.

Exhibit 11.5 shows how a digital signature works. Suppose a person wants to send the draft of a financial contract to a company with whom he or she plans to do business as an e-mail message. The sender wants to assure the company that the content of the draft has not been changed en route and that he or she really is the sender. To do so, the sender takes the following steps:

1. The sender creates the e-mail message with the contract in it.
2. Using special software, a mathematical computation called a **hash** function is applied to the message, which results in a special summary of the message, converted into a string of digits called a **message digest**.
3. The sender uses his or her private key to encrypt the hash. This is the sender's *digital signature*. No one else can replicate the sender's digital signature because it is based on the sender's private key.
4. The sender encrypts both the original message and the digital signature using the recipient's public key. This is the **digital envelope**.
5. The sender e-mails the digital envelope to the receiver.
6. Upon receipt, the receiver uses his or her private key to decrypt the contents of the digital envelope. This produces a copy of the message and the sender's digital signature.
7. The receiver uses the sender's public key to decrypt the digital signature, resulting in a copy of the original message digest.

EXHIBIT 11.5 **Digital Signatures**

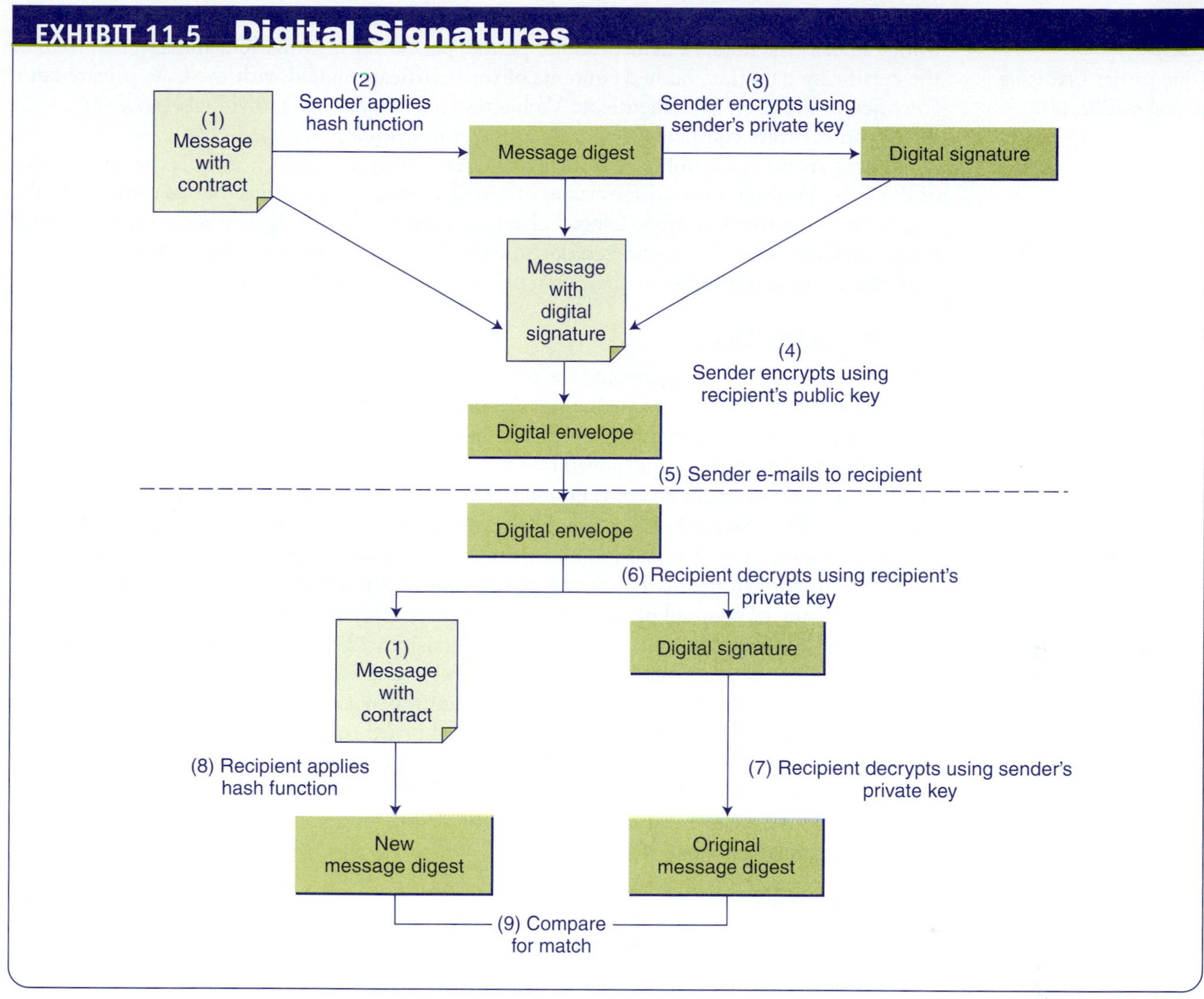

8. Using the same hash function employed in step 2, the recipient then creates a message digest from the decrypted message (as shown in Exhibit 11.5).
9. The recipient compares this digest with the original message digest.
10. If the two digests match, then the recipient concludes that the message is authentic.

digital envelope
The combination of the encrypted original message and the digital signature, using the recipient's public key.

In this scenario, the company has evidence that the sender sent the e-mail because (theoretically) the sender is the only one with access to the private key. The recipient knows that the message has not been tampered with, because if it had been the two hashes would not have matched.

According to the U.S. Federal Electronic Signatures in Global and National Commerce Act that went into effect in October 2000, digital signatures in the United States have the same legal standing as a signature written in ink on paper. Although PKI is the foundation of digital signatures, two-factor authentication is often employed to verify a person's legal identity. For example, PKI can be used with personal smart cards or biometric systems to corroborate an identity.

Digital Certificates and Certificate Authorities

digital certificate
Verification that the holder of a public or private key is who he or she claims to be.

If one has to know someone's public key to send that person a message, where does the public key come from and how can one be sure of the person's actual identity? **Digital certificates** verify that the holder of a public and/or private key is who he or she claims to be. Third

certificate authorities (CAs)
Third parties that issue digital certificates.

parties called **certificate authorities (CAs)** issue digital certificates. A certificate contains things such as the holder's name, validity period, public key information, and a signed hash of the certificate data (i.e., hashed contents of the certificate signed with the CA's private key). Certificates are used to authenticate Web sites (*site certificates*), individuals (*personal certificates*), and software companies (*software publisher certificates*).

There are a large number of third-party CAs. VeriSign (verisign.com) is the best known of the CAs. VeriSign issues three classes of certificates: Class 1 verifies that an e-mail actually comes from the user's address. Class 2 checks the user's identity against a commercial credit database. Class 3 requires notarized documents. Companies such as Microsoft offer systems that enable companies to issue their own private, in-house certificates.

Secure Socket Layer

If the average user had to figure out how to use encryption, digital certificates, digital signatures, and the like, there would be few secure transactions on the Web. Fortunately, many of these issues are handled in a transparent fashion by Web browsers and Web servers. Given that different companies, financial institutions, and governments in many countries are involved in e-commerce, it is necessary to have generally accepted protocols for securing e-commerce. One of the major protocols in use today is Secure Socket Layer (SSL), also known as Transport Layer Security (TLS).

Secure Socket Layer (SSL)
Protocol that utilizes standard certificates for authentication and data encryption to ensure privacy or confidentiality.

Transport Layer Security (TLS)
As of 1996, another name for the SSL protocol.

The **Secure Socket Layer (SSL)** was invented by Netscape to utilize standard certificates for authentication and data encryption to ensure privacy or confidentiality. SSL became a de facto standard adopted by the browsers and servers provided by Microsoft and Netscape. In 1996, SSL was renamed **Transport Layer Security (TLS)**, but many people still use the SSL name. It is the major standard used for online credit card payments.

SSL makes it possible to encrypt credit card numbers and other transmissions between a Web server and a Web browser. In the case of credit card transactions, there is more to making a purchase on the Web than simply passing an encrypted credit card number to a merchant. The number must be checked for validity, the consumer's bank must authorize the card, and the purchase must be processed. SSL is not designed to handle any of the steps beyond the transmission of the card number.

Section 11.6 ▶ REVIEW QUESTIONS

1. What are the basic elements of an authentication system?
2. What is a passive token? An active token?
3. What are the differences between physiological and behavioral biometrics?
4. Describe some of the basic types of physiological biometrics.
5. Describe the basic components of encryption.
6. What are the key elements of PKI?
7. What are the basic differences between symmetric and asymmetric encryption?
8. Describe how a digital signature is created.
9. What is a digital certificate? What role does a certificate authority play?
10. What is the SSL protocol?

11.7 SECURING EC NETWORKS

Several technologies exist that ensure that an organization's network boundaries are secure from cyber attack or intrusion and that if the organization's boundaries are compromised that the intrusion is detected. The selection and operation of these technologies should be based on certain design concepts, including (Thomas 2004):

policy of least privilege (POLP)
Policy of blocking access to network resources unless access is required to conduct business.

- **Layered security.** Relying on a single technology to thwart attacks is doomed to failure. A variety of technologies must be applied at key points in a network (see Exhibit 11.6). This is probably the most important concept in designing a secure system.
- **Controlling access.** Access to a network ought to be based on the **policy of least privilege (POLP)**. By default, access to network resources should be blocked and permitted only when required to conduct business.

EXHIBIT 11.6 **Layered Security**

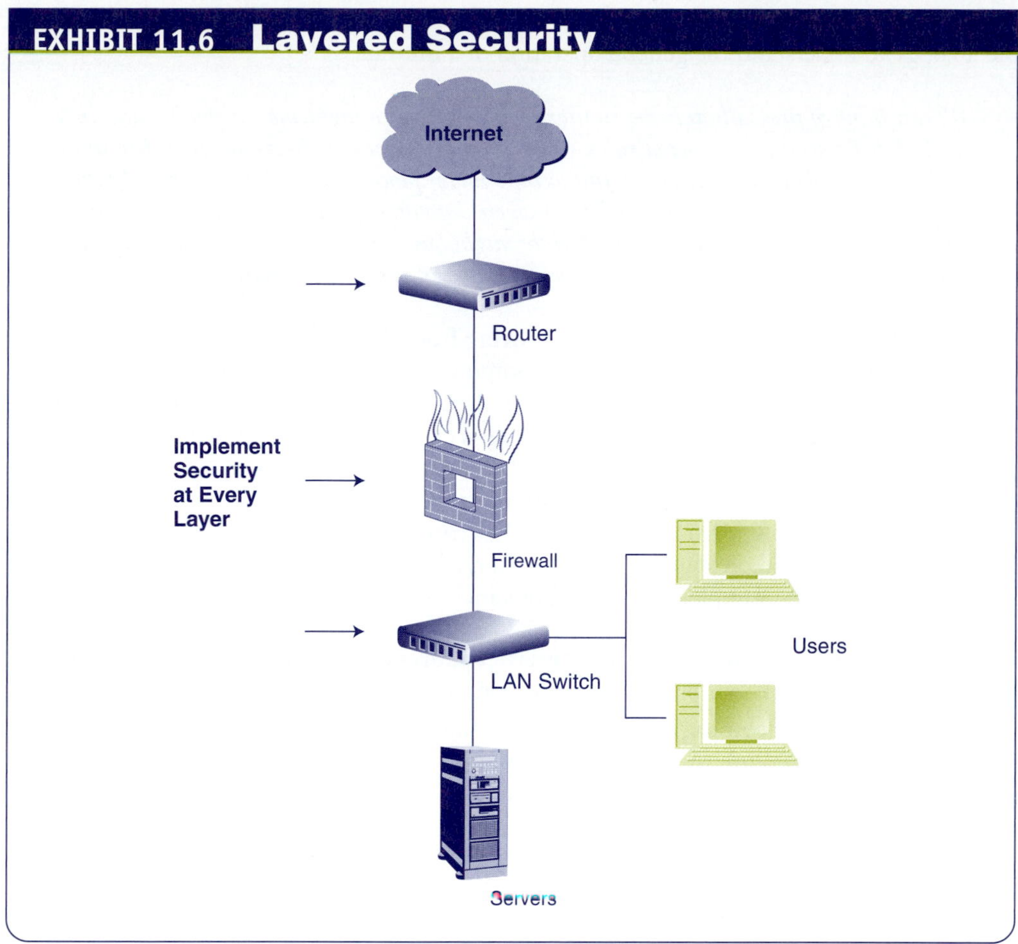

- **Role-specific security.** As noted in Section 11.5, access to particular network resources should be based on a user's role within an organization.
- **Monitoring.** As a well-known infomercial says, many organizations simply "set it and forget it." More specifically, they go through the process of establishing security plans and policies, setting up security technologies, and then fail to monitor their networks to ensure that they remain secure.
- **Keep systems patched.** Most large organizations are painfully aware that vendors (such as Microsoft) are continually patching or upgrading their software, applications, and systems to plug security holes. Obviously, the only way to take advantage of these fixes is to install the patches or upgrades. Newer versions of software (e.g., operating systems such as Windows XP) have automatic update functionality built in. This makes it easier for organizations and individuals to track fixes.
- **Response team.** Regardless of the organization's size, there is a good chance that an organization whose networks are connected to the larger Internet will be victimized by a network security attack of some sort. For this reason, organizations need to have a team in place that can respond to these attacks. The team needs to have well-established plans, processes, and resources and should practice responding when the pressure is off rather than learning during a crisis.

FIREWALLS

The term *firewall* came into use in the 1700s to describe the gaps cut into forests so that fires could be prevented from spreading to other parts of the forest (Garfinkel 2002). The term also describes a protective shield between a car engine and the interior of the car. In the world of networked computing, a **firewall** is a network node consisting of both hardware and

firewall
A network node consisting of both hardware and software that isolates a private network from a public network.

software that isolates a private network from a public network. Hazari (2000) provides a simple analogy to understand the general operation of a firewall:

> *We can think of firewalls as being similar to a bouncer in a nightclub. Like a bouncer in a nightclub, firewalls have a set of rules, similar to a guest list or a dress code, that determine if the data should be allowed entry. Just as the bouncer places himself at the door of the club, the firewall is located at the point of entry where data attempts to enter the computer from the Internet. But, just as different nightclubs might have different rules for entry, different firewalls have different methods of inspecting data for acceptance or rejection.*

Some firewalls filter data and requests moving from the public Internet to a private network based on the network addresses of the computer sending or receiving the request. These firewalls are called **packet-filtering routers**. On the Internet, the data and requests sent from one computer to another are broken into segments called **packets**. Each packet contains the Internet address of the computer sending the data, as well as the Internet address of the computer receiving the data. Packets also contain other identifying information that can be used to distinguish one packet from another. **Packet filters** are rules that can accept or reject incoming packets based on source and destination addresses and the other identifying information. Some simple examples of packet filters include the following:

- **Block all packets sent from a given Internet address.** Companies sometimes use this to block requests from computers owned by competitors.
- **Block any packet coming from the outside that has the address of a computer on the inside.** Companies use this type of rule to block requests where an intruder is using his or her computer to impersonate a computer that belongs to the company.

However, packet filters do have their disadvantages. In setting up the rules, an administrator might miss some important rules or incorrectly specify a rule, thus leaving a hole in the firewall. Additionally, because the content of a packet is irrelevant to a packet filter, once a packet is let through the firewall, the inside network is open to data-driven attacks. That is, the data may contain hidden instructions that cause the receiving computer to modify access control or security-related files.

Packet-filtering routers often are used as the first layer of network defense. Other firewalls form the second layer. These later firewalls block data and requests depending on the type of application being accessed. For instance, a firewall may permit requests for Web pages to move from the public Internet to the private network. This type of firewall is called an **application-level proxy**. In an application-level proxy, there is often a special server called a **bastion gateway**. The bastion gateway server has two network cards so that data packets reaching one card are not relayed to the other card (see Exhibit 11.7). Instead, special software programs called **proxies** run on the bastion gateway server and pass repackaged packets from one network to the other. Each Internet service that an organization wishes to support has a proxy. For instance, there is a Web (i.e., HTTP) proxy, a file transfer (FTP) proxy, and so on. Special proxies also can be established to allow business partners, for example, to access particular applications running inside the firewall. If a request is made for an unsupported proxy service, then it is blocked by the firewall.

In addition to controlling inbound traffic, the firewall and proxies control outbound traffic. All outbound traffic requests are first sent to the proxy server and then forwarded by the proxy on behalf of the computers behind the firewall. This makes all the requests look as if they were coming from a single computer rather than multiple computers. In this way, the Internet addresses of the internal computers are hidden to the outside.

One disadvantage of an application-level proxy firewall is performance degradation. It takes more processing time to tie particular packets to particular applications. Another disadvantage is that the users on the internal network must configure their machines or browsers to send their Internet requests via the proxy server.

Firewall systems can be created from scratch. However, most companies rely on commercial firewall systems. ConsumerSearch.com provides a review of a number of commercial firewall products (consumersearch.com/www/index.html).

packet-filtering routers
Firewalls that filter data and requests moving from the public Internet to a private network based on the network addresses of the computer sending or receiving the request.

packets
Segments of data and requests sent from one computer to another on the Internet; consist of the Internet addresses of the computers sending and receiving the data, plus other identifying information that distinguish one packet from another.

packet filters
Rules that can accept or reject incoming packets based on source and destination addresses and the other identifying information.

application-level proxy
A firewall that permits requests for Web pages to move from the public Internet to the private network.

bastion gateway
A special hardware server that utilizes application-level proxy software to limit the types of requests that can be passed to an organization's internal networks from the public Internet.

proxies
Special software programs that run on the gateway server and pass repackaged packets from one network to the other.

EXHIBIT 11.7 Application-Level Proxy (Bastion Gateway Host)

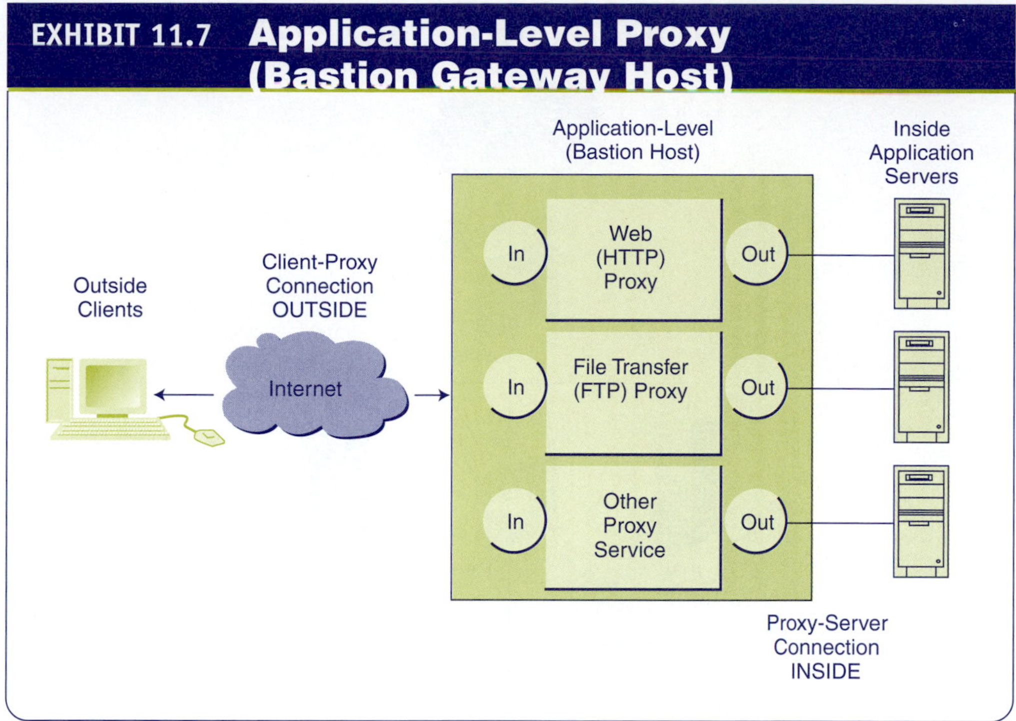

DEMILITARIZED ZONE

The term **demilitarized zone (DMZ)** often is used to describe a buffer area between two enemies, such as the DMZ between North Korea and South Korea. In computer security terms, a DMZ is a network area that sits between an organization's internal network and an external network (Internet), providing physical isolation between the two networks that is controlled by rules enforced by a firewall. For example, suppose a company wants to run its own Web site. In a DMZ setup, the company would put the Web server on a publicly accessible network and the rest of its servers on a private internal network. A firewall would then be configured to direct requests coming from the outside to the appropriate network and servers. In most cases, the internal network also is fronted by a second firewall to doubly ensure that intrusive requests do not get through to the private network (see Exhibit 11.8).

demilitarized zone (DMZ)
Network area that sits between an organization's internal network and an external network (Internet), providing physical isolation between the two networks that is controlled by rules enforced by a firewall.

PERSONAL FIREWALLS

In recent years, the number of individuals with high-speed broadband (cable modem or digital subscriber lines [DSL]) Internet connections to their homes or small businesses has increased. These "always-on" connections are much more vulnerable to attack than simple dial-up connections. With these connections, the homeowner or small business owner runs the risks of information being stolen or destroyed, of sensitive information (e.g., personal or business financial information) being accessed, and of the computer being used in a DoS attack on others.

Personal firewalls are designed to protect desktop systems by monitoring all the traffic that passes through the computer's network interface card. They operate in one of two ways. With the first method, the owner can create filtering rules (much like packet filtering) that are used by the firewall to permit or delete packets. With the other method, the firewall can learn, by asking the user questions, how particular traffic ought to be handled. A number of personal firewall products are on the market, including the highly rated Norton Personal Firewall from Symantec (symantec.com) and ZoneAlarm firewall from Check Point (checkpoint.com). For a detailed comparison of a number of these products, see firewallguide.com/software.htm.

personal firewall
A network node designed to protect an individual user's desktop system from the public network by monitoring all the traffic that passes through the computer's network interface card.

VPNs

Suppose a company wants to establish a B2B application, providing suppliers, partners, and others access not only to data residing on its internal Web site, but also to data contained in other files (e.g., Word documents) or in legacy systems (e.g., large relational databases).

EXHIBIT 11.8 **Demilitarized Zone (DMZ)**

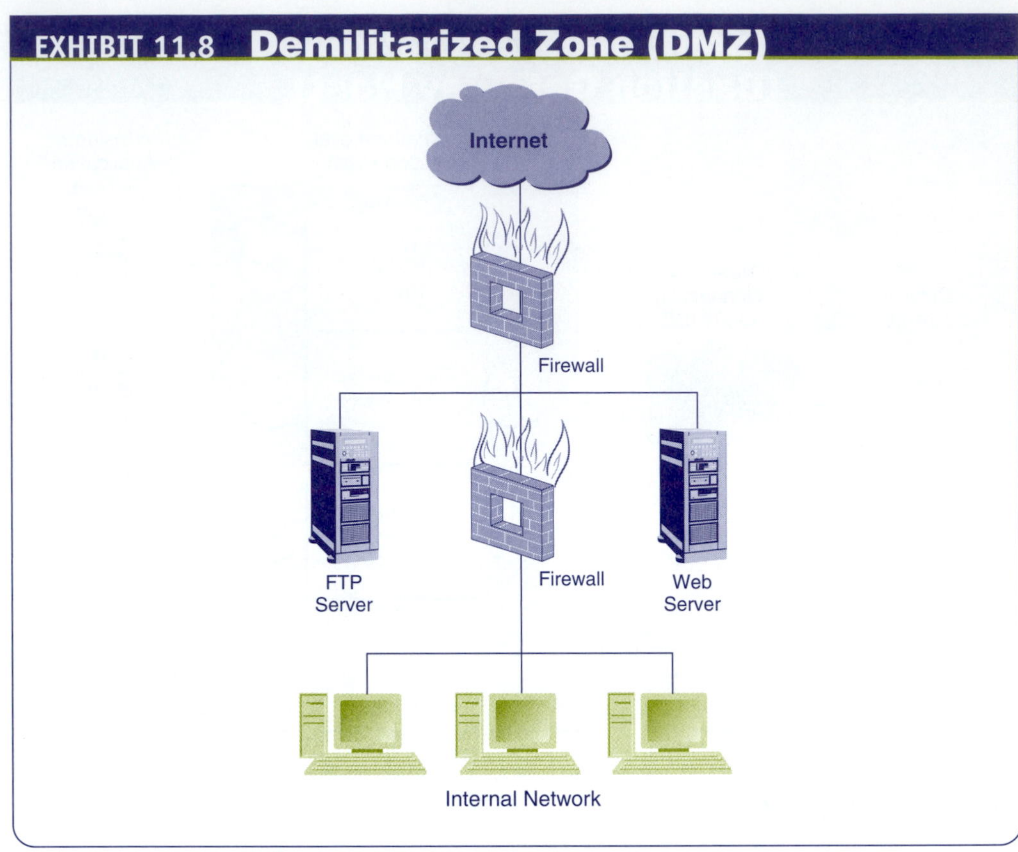

Traditionally, communications with the company would have taken place over a private leased line or through a dial-up line to a bank of modems or a remote access server (RAS) that provided direct connections to the company's LAN. With a private line, the chances of a hacker eavesdropping on the communications between the companies would be nil, but it is an expensive way to do business.

virtual private network (VPN)
A network that uses the public Internet to carry information but remains private by using encryption to scramble the communications, authentication to ensure that information has not been tampered with, and access control to verify the identity of anyone using the network.

protocol tunneling
Method used to ensure confidentiality and integrity of data transmitted over the Internet, by encrypting data packets, sending them in packets across the Internet, and decrypting them at the destination address.

A less expensive alternative would be to use a **virtual private network (VPN)**. A VPN uses the public Internet to carry information but remains private by using a combination of encryption to scramble the communications, authentication to ensure that the information has not been tampered with and comes from a legitimate source, and access control to verify the identity of anyone using the network. In addition, a VPN can also be used to support site-to-site communications between branch offices and corporate headquarters and the communications between mobile workers and their workplace.

VPNs can reduce communication costs dramatically. The reduced costs come about because VPN equipment is cheaper than other remote solutions, private leased lines are no longer needed to support remote access, remote users can place local calls or use cable or DSL lines rather than long distance or international calls to access an organization's private network, and a single access line can be used to support multiple purposes. The estimated cost savings for site-to-site networks is 20 to 40 percent for sites in the same country and 60 to 90 percent if they are in different countries (NetGear 2002). The savings for mobile and remote workers is estimated at 60 to 80 percent (Prometheum Technologies 2003).

The main technical challenge of a VPN is to ensure the confidentiality and integrity of the data transmitted over the Internet. This is where **protocol tunneling** comes into play. With protocol tunneling, data packets are first encrypted and then encapsulated into packets that can be transmitted across the Internet. The packets are decrypted at the destination address by a special host or router.

Three technologies can be used to create a VPN. First, many of the firewall packages—hardware and software—provide VPN functionality. Second, routers (i.e., special network components for controlling communications) cannot only function as firewalls, but they also can function as VPN servers. Finally, software solutions are available that can be used to handle VPN connections. The VPN Consortium (vpnc.org/vpnc-features-chart.html) provides a comparison of a number of commercial VPN products.

Many telecommunications carriers and larger ISPs offer VPN services for Internet-based dial-up and site-to-site communications. These carriers use their own private network backbones to which they have added security features, intranet connectivity, and new dial-up capabilities for remote services. Two of the carriers providing these services are AT&T VPN Services (att.com) and Cable & Wireless IP-VPN Internet (cw.com).

INTRUSION DETECTION SYSTEMS

Even if an organization has a well-formulated security policy and a number of security technologies in place, it still is vulnerable to attack. For example, most organizations have antivirus software, yet most are subjected to virus attacks. This is why an organization must continually watch for attempted, as well as actual, security breaches.

In the past, *audit logs*, which are produced by a variety of system components and applications, were manually reviewed for excessive failed log-on attempts, failed file and database access attempts, and other application and system violations. Obviously, this manual procedure had its flaws. For example, if intrusion attempts were spread out over a long period of time, they could be easily missed. Today, a special category of software exists that can monitor activity across a network or on a host computer, watch for suspicious activity, and take automated action based on what it sees. This category of software is called **intrusion detection systems (IDSs)**.

intrusion detection systems (IDSs)
A special category of software that can monitor activity across a network or on a host computer, watch for suspicious activity, and take automated action based on what it sees.

IDSs are either host based or network based. A *host-based IDS* resides on the server or other host system that is being monitored. Host-based systems are particularly good at detecting whether critical or security-related files have been tampered with or whether a user has attempted to access files that he or she is not authorized to use. The host-based system does this by computing a special signature or check-sum for each file. The IDS checks files on a regular basis to see if the current signatures match the previous signatures. If the signatures do not match, security personnel are notified immediately. Some examples of commercial host-based systems are Symantec's Intruder Alert (symantec.com), Tripwire Security's Tripwire (tripwiresecurity.com), and McAfee's Entercept Desktop and Server Agents (mcafee.com).

A *network-based IDS* uses rules to analyze suspicious activity at the perimeter of a network or at key locations in the network. It usually consists of a monitor—a software package that scans the network—and software agents that reside on various host computers and feed information back to the monitor. This type of IDS examines network traffic (i.e., packets) for known patterns of attack and automatically notifies security personnel when specific events or event thresholds occur. A network-based IDS also can perform certain actions when an attack occurs. For instance, it can terminate network connections or reconfigure network devices, such as firewalls and routers, based on security policies. Cisco Systems' NetRanger (cisco.com) and Computer Associates' eTrust Intrusion Detection (www3.ca.com/solutions/product.asp?id=163) both are examples of commercially available network-based IDSs.

HONEYNETS AND HONEYPOTS

honeynet
A way to evaluate vulnerabilities of an organization by studying the types of attacks to which a site is subjected using a network of systems called *honeypots*.

honeypots
Production systems (e.g., firewalls, routers, Web servers, database servers) designed to do real work but that are watched and studied as network intrusions occur.

Honeynets are another technology that can be used to detect and analyze intrusions. A **honeynet** is a network of honeypots designed to attract hackers like honey attracts bees. In this case, the **honeypots** are information system resources—firewalls, routers, Web servers, database servers, files, and the like—that are made to look like production systems but do no real work. The main difference between a honeypot and the real thing is that the activities on a honeypot come from intruders attempting to compromise the system. In this way, researchers watching the honeynet can gather information about why hackers attack, when they attack, how they attack, what they do after the system is compromised, and how they communicate with one another during and after the attack.

Honeynets and honeypots originated in April 1999 with the Honeynet Project (Honeynet 2004). The Honeynet Project is a worldwide, not-for-profit research group of security professionals. The group focuses on raising awareness of security risks that confront any system connected to the Internet and teaching and informing the security community about better ways to secure and defend network resources. The project runs its own honeynets, but makes no attempt to attract hackers. They simply connect the honeypots to the Internet and wait for attacks to occur.

The Honeynet Project was divided into four phases. The first three are complete. The goal of the current phase, which runs from 2004 to 2005, is to create a centralized system that can collect and correlate data from distributed honeynets.

With the Honeynet Project, honeypots are used for research. Honeypots also can be used in production systems to mitigate security risks. An organization does this simply by adding a honeypot to its existing network. Although a honeypot cannot prevent an attack, it can simplify the detection and reaction to an attack. Because the only traffic on a honeypot comes from intruders, it is easier to analyze the data produced by a honeypot (e.g., log files of system activity) to determine what is happening and how to respond. Honeypots can be built from scratch or commercial or open source versions can be used. Back Officer Friendly (nfr.com/resource/backofficer.php), Specter (specter.com/default50.htm), Honeyd (honeyd.org), and Decoy Server (enterprisesecurity.symantec.com/products/products.cfm?productid=157) are examples of commercial or open source systems.

Before a company deploys a honeynet, it needs to think about what it will do when it becomes the scene of a cyber crime or contains evidence of a crime and about the legal restrictions and ramifications of monitoring legal and illegal activity. These issues are discussed in EC Application Case 11.3.

Section 11.7 ▶ REVIEW QUESTIONS

1. List the basic types of firewalls and briefly describe each.
2. What is a personal firewall?
3. How does a VPN work?
4. Briefly describe the major types of IDSs.
5. What is a honeynet? What is a honeypot?

CASE 11.3

EC Application

HONEYNETS AND THE LAW

Millions of networks and computers are on the Internet. Given this, what is the chance that a small collection of computers connected to the Internet will be victimized by an outside intruder? In the first phase of the Honeynet Project, which ran from 1999 to 2001, the honeynet consisted of eight honeypots that were designed to mimic a typical home computer setup. Within 15 minutes of being connected to the Internet, one of the honeypots was hit. Over the course of the next few days, all of the honeypots were compromised, and over the course of the next 2 years they were attacked repeatedly.

During the first phase, many of the attacks were crude and fairly innocuous. Today, the character of both the intrusions and the intruders has changed. The proportion of hackers involved in illegal activities of all sorts has risen dramatically. If a company deploys a honeynet, there is a good chance that it will be the scene of a cyber crime or contain evidence of a crime. Some intruders may be focused solely on attacking the honeynet itself. Others may want to use it as a zombie for launching attacks, as a place to store stolen credit cards, or as a server to distribute pirated software or child pornography. Regardless, companies need to understand the types of crimes that may occur and the legal issues that may ensue if they choose to either report or ignore these crimes. Just because the activities on a honeynet are perpetrated by intruders, it does not mean that the operator has unlimited rights to monitor the users of the network.

Although many crimes can be perpetrated against or with a honeynet, the most frequent and obvious crime is network intrusion. In the United States, the federal Computer Fraud and Abuse Act, passed in 1986 and later amended in 1996, covers most computer network crimes. In addition, a number of state laws outlaw unauthorized access and damage to computers or networks. The Computer Fraud and Abuse Act makes it a crime to attack "protected computers," including computers "used in interstate or foreign commerce or communication." If a computer is on the Internet, it is used in interstate communication. All government computers and those used by banks and financial institutions also are protected. This means that most honeynets are going to be protected by the Act.

The Act also defines the types of attacks that constitute a crime. It is a felony if an attacker "knowingly causes the transmission of a program, information, code, or command,

(*continued*)

CASE 11.3 (continued)

and as a result of such conduct, intentionally causes damage without authorization, to a protected computer." Damage occurs when there is "any impairment to the integrity or availability of data, a program, a system or information." The limitations are that in order for an attack to be a felony, one or more of the following must result: aggregate damage of at least $5,000; modification or impairment to the medical examination, diagnosis, treatment, or care of one or more individuals; physical injury to a person; a threat to public health or safety; or damage to a government computer used for the administration of justice, national defense, or national security. Under these provisions, the Act covers a wide range of activities, including:

- Denial-of-service attacks, viruses, and worms
- Simple intrusions in which the attacker causes damage
- Unauthorized information gathering, especially if the information is used for commercial advantage, financial gain, in furtherance of another crime, or the information is worth more than $5,000
- Unauthorized access to nonpublic U.S. government computers
- Using computers to obtain classified information without authorization
- Computer-related espionage, which may also constitute terrorism
- Trafficking in passwords
- Threatening to damage a computer
- Attempting to commit a network crime, even though the crime was never consummated

In running a honeynet, a company needs to be careful to ensure that it is not facilitating or helping further a crime. Precautions and actions must be taken to prevent potential or actual criminal activity from harming others; to inform authorities when criminal activities or evidence comes to light; and to ensure that the data, code, programs, and systems running on the honeynet are legal (e.g., do not store contraband on the system in an effort to trap an intruder).

The primary purpose of a commercial honeynet is to monitor and analyze intrusion and attacks. Under certain circumstances, the monitoring of these activities may constitute a criminal or civil action. In the United States, the federal Wiretap Act and the Pen Register, Trap, and Trace Devices statute place legal limits on monitoring activity. The Wiretap Act makes it illegal to intercept the contents of a communication. If intruders cannot store (either directly or indirectly) data or information on a honeynet, then the Act does not apply. If they can, then there are exceptions to the rule. For instance, if the monitoring is done to prevent abuse or damage to the system, then monitoring it is not illegal. The implication is that certain honeynet purposes and configurations are illegal and others are not.

In contrast to the Wiretap Act, the federal Pen Register, Trap, and Trace Devices statute applies to the "noncontent" aspects of a communication. For example, with telephones, telephone numbers are "noncontent." Similarly, in a network communication, network addresses are "noncontent." This statute makes it illegal to capture the noncontent information of a communication, unless certain exceptions apply. The exceptions pertain primarily to actions that are taken by the communication provider (in this case the honeynet operator) to protect its rights or property. Again, certain honeynet purposes and configurations are legal and others are not.

When a company monitors the network activities of insiders and outsiders, a number of legal issues arise. Because monitoring is one of the primary activities of a honeynet, a company should consult legal counsel before a honeynet is deployed and become familiar with local law enforcement agencies that should be involved if illegal activities are observed.

Source: Honeynet Project (2004).

Questions

1. What constitutes a crime under the Computer Fraud and Abuse Act?
2. What types of activities are prohibited by the Computer Fraud and Abuse Act?
3. What types of activities are illegal under the federal Wiretap Act? The Pen Register, Trap, and Trace Devices statute?

MANAGERIAL ISSUES

Some managerial issues related to this chapter are as follows.

1. **Have we budgeted enough for security?** If one asked the senior management of the *Fortune* 500 corporations whether they take network security seriously, they would certainly answer with a resounding, "Yes." Yet, in spite of this answer, most of these organizations spend only a small percentage of their budgets on network security, have fairly small staffs working on network security issues, and generally relegate network security matters to personnel on lower rungs on the organizational ladder. Because the consequences of poor network security can be severe, it is imperative that senior management have a basic understanding of best practices in network risk management.
2. **What are the business consequences of poor security?** Ineffective security opens the door to computer and network attacks that can result in damage to technical and information assets; theft of information and

information services; temporary loss of a Web site and Internet access; loss of income; litigation brought on by dissatisfied organizational stakeholders; loss of customer confidence; and damaged reputation and credibility. In some cases, attacks literally can put a company out of business, especially if EC is its sole source of revenue.

3. **Which e-commerce sites are vulnerable to attack?** Suppose you decide to set up a B2B site in order to service your suppliers and partners. Because it is not a public site, the only ones who are likely to know of its existence are you, your suppliers, and your partners. You assume that there is no need to institute strong security measures. Wrong! Because of the prevalence of automated scanning tools, it will be only a matter of days before hackers discover your site. Once discovered, it will be only a matter of hours or minutes before the hackers have compromised your site and taken control if your system has known vulnerabilities. Regardless of how obscure, uninteresting, or unadvertised a site is, no EC site can afford to take security for granted. All sites should thoroughly review their security requirements and institute stringent measures to guard against high-priority threats.
4. **What is the key to establishing strong e-commerce security?** Most discussions about security focus on technology. One hears statements like "firewalls are mandatory" or "all transmissions should be encrypted." Although firewalls and encryption can be important technologies, no security solution is useful unless it solves a business problem. Determining your business requirements is the most important step in creating a security solution. Business requirements, in turn, determine your information requirements. Once your information requirements are known, you can begin to understand the value of those assets and the steps that should be taken to secure those that are most valuable and vulnerable.
5. **What steps should businesses follow in establishing a security plan?** Security risk management is an ongoing process involving three phases: asset identification, risk assessment, and implementation. By actively monitoring existing security policies and measures, companies can determine which are successful or unsuccessful and, in turn, which should be modified or eliminated. However, it also is important to monitor changes in business requirements, changes in technology and the way it is used, and changes in the way people can attack the systems and networks. In this way, an organization can evolve its security policies and measures, ensuring that they continue to support the critical needs of the business.
6. **Should organizations be concerned with internal security threats?** Except for viruses and worms, breaches perpetrated by insiders are much more frequent than those perpetrated by outsiders. This is true for both B2C and B2B sites. Security policies and measures for EC sites need to address these insider threats.

RESEARCH TOPICS

Here are some suggested topics related to this chapter. For details, references, and additional topics, refer to the book's "Current EC Research" in the Online Appendix.

1. **Certification Programs**
   - Limitations on the use of digital certificates
   - Certification programs that ensure trust, privacy, and safety
   - Effectiveness of certification programs in enhancing security
   - Evaluation factors for certification
   - International certification programs for secure international trades
2. **Risk Perception and the Adoption of Security Measures**
   - Customers' perceptions of risk in e-commerce and e-payment
   - Impact of consumers' perceptions of risk in conducting EC transactions
   - Inhibitors of security measure adoption
   - Relationship between a corporation's risk management system and their overall values
   - Reducing operational risk to cope with the BASEL II Accord
3. **EC Security Technologies**
   - The application of biometric technologies to authentication
   - Customer preferences for authentication schemes
   - Intelligent detection of criminal patterns on the Internet

4. **Secure Electronic Payment Protocols**
   - Protocols that avoid the disclosure of customers' bank and credit account information to merchants
   - Comparative evaluation of protocols
   - Problems with adopting the Secure Electronic Transaction (SET) protocol
5. **Design of Secure E-Commerce Sites**
   - Framework for designing secure e-commerce sites
   - Risk assessment of e-commerce sites
   - Cost and benefit of security systems for e-commerce
6. **Study Security Violation Cases and Lessons to Avoid Mistakes**
   - Cases concerning disasters caused by violated security
   - Measurements taken and studied after the violation
   - Protection schemes before the crucial violation
   - Security ethics
   - Effect of codes of conduct and certificates

SUMMARY

In this chapter, you learned about the following EC issues as they relate to the learning objectives.

1. **Trends in computer attacks.** Recent surveys of trends in computer and network attacks offer a mixed picture. Computer and network security attacks are on the rise. Data collected by the Computer Security Institute (CSI) and the FBI indicate that the number of security incidents has steadily declined over the past couple of years. In contrast, survey results from the Computer Emergency Response Team (CERT) and *CSO Magazine* indicate that there has been a substantial increase in the incidence of e-crime. Although the results of the two surveys differ substantially, both indicate that computer and network attacks are still a substantial problem that can result in sizeable economic losses.
2. **Security is everyone's business.** Because the Internet serves as the control system for many of the critical infrastructures in the United States, the coordination of efforts to secure cyberspace now falls to the Department of Homeland Security (DHS). The DHS aims to build a security response system, reduce security threats and vulnerabilities, build awareness of security issues, secure government cyberspace, and encourage international cooperation on security issues. Accomplishing these diverse aims is a complex task requiring action at multiple levels, including home users and small businesses, large enterprises, critical sectors and infrastructure, and national and international agencies.
3. **Basic security issues.** The owners of EC sites need to be concerned with a variety of security issues: authentication, verifying the identity of the participants in a transaction; authorization, ensuring that a person or process has access rights to particular systems or data; auditing, being able to determine whether particular actions have been taken and by whom; confidentiality, ensuring that information is not disclosed to unauthorized individuals, systems, or processes; integrity, protecting data from being altered or destroyed; availability, ensuring that data and services are available when needed; and nonrepudiation, the ability to limit parties from refuting that a legitimate transaction took place.
4. **Basic types of network security attacks.** EC sites are exposed to a wide range of attacks. Attacks may be nontechnical (social engineering), in which a perpetrator tricks people into revealing information or performing actions that compromise network security. Or they may be technical, whereby software and systems expertise are used to attack the network. DoS and DDoS attacks bring operations to a halt by sending floods of data to target computers or to as many computers on the Internet as possible. Malicious code attacks include viruses, worms, Trojan horses, or some combination of these. Over the past couple of years, various trends in malicious code have emerged, including an increase in the speed and volume of attacks; reduced time between the discovery of a vulnerability and the release of an attack to exploit the vulnerability; the growing use of bots to launch attacks; an increase in attacks on Web applications; and a shift in motivation behind attacks toward illicit financial gain.
5. **Managing EC security.** Even with increased awareness of security issues, organizations continue to be reactive in their security practices, with little understanding of their information assets or security needs. A systematic security risk management approach must be adopted to address these needs. This approach involves three phases: identification and valuation of key computer and network assets; assessment of the security threats, vulnerabilities and risks associated with those assets; and the selection, evaluation, and implementation of a set of security policies and measures to reduce high-priority threats, vulnerabilities, and risks.

6. **Securing EC communications.** In EC, issues of trust are paramount. Trust starts with the authentication of the parties involved in a transaction; that is, identifying the parties in a transaction along with the actions they can perform. Authentication can be established with something one knows (e.g., a password), something one has (e.g., a token), or something one is (e.g., a fingerprint). Biometric systems can be used to confirm a person's identity. Fingerprint scanners, iris scanners, facial recognition, and voice recognition are examples of biometric systems. Public key infrastructure (PKI), which is the cornerstone of secure e-payments, also can be used to authenticate the parties in a transaction. PKI uses encryption (private and public) to ensure privacy and integrity and digital signatures to ensure authenticity and nonrepudiation. Digital signatures are themselves authenticated through a system of digital certificates issued by certificate authorities (CAs). For the average consumer and merchant, PKI is simplified because it is built into Web browsers and services. Such tools are secure because security is based on SSL (TSL) communications.
7. **Technologies for securing networks.** At EC sites, firewalls, VPNs, and IDSs have proven extremely useful. Honeynets and honeypots also are being employed to detect and analyze intrusions. A firewall is a combination of hardware and software that isolates a private network from a public network. Firewalls are of two general types—packet-filtering routers or application-level proxies. A packet-filtering router uses a set of rules to determine which communication packets can move from the outside network to the inside network. An application-level proxy is a firewall that accepts requests from the outside and repackages a request before sending it to the inside network, thus ensuring the security of the request. Personal firewalls are needed by individuals with broadband access. VPNs are generally used to support secure site-to-site transmissions across the Internet between B2B partners or communications between a mobile and remote worker and a LAN at a central office. IDSs are used to monitor activity across a network or on a host. The systems watch for suspicious activity and take automated actions whenever a security breach or attack occurs. In the same vein, honeynets and honeypots are being installed at some companies in an effort to gather information on intrusions and to analyze the types and methods of attacks being perpetrated.

KEY TERMS

QUESTIONS FOR DISCUSSION

1. Survey results on the incidence of cyber attacks paint a mixed picture; some surveys show increases, others show decreases. What factors could account for the differences in the results?
2. Pretend that you are a hacker who would like to trick people into giving you their user IDs and passwords to their Amazon.com accounts. What are some of the ways that this might be accomplished?
3. B2C EC sites continue to experience DDoS attacks. How are these attacks perpetrated? Why is it so difficult to safeguard against them? What are some of the things a site can do to mitigate such attacks?
4. All EC sites share common security threats and vulnerabilities. Discuss these threats and vulnerabilities and some of the security policies that can be implemented to mitigate them. Do you think that B2C Web sites face different threats and vulnerabilities than B2B sites? Explain.
5. Based on the results of the AOL/NCSA in-home study of computer security, what advice would you give to home owners about securing their computers?
6. A business wants to share its customer account database with its trading partners and customers, while at the same time providing prospective buyers with access to marketing materials on its Web site. Assuming that the business is responsible for running all of these network components, what types of security components (e.g., firewalls, VPNs, etc.) could be used to ensure that the partners and customers have access to the account information and others do not? What type of network configuration (e.g., bastion gateway server) will provide the appropriate security?
7. A company is having problems with its password security systems and decides to implement two-factor authentication. What biometric alternatives could the company employ? What are some of the factors it should consider when deciding among the alternatives?
8. A company has decided to set up a honeynet to monitor attacks against its networks and servers. To make the honeynet more attractive, the company decides to put a customer mailing list on a Web server located on the honeynet. By doing this, what legal issues will the company encounter? What if the company did not use the customer mailing list, would the honeynet still be legal? Explain.

INTERNET EXERCISES

1. Dan Verton's book *Black Ice: The Invisible Threat of Cyber-Terrorism* argues that it is possible for terrorists to attack the U.S. infrastructure (e.g., power grid, banks, air traffic control, etc.) through the Internet. Using online reviews of Verton's book, determine the arguments for and against his claim.
2. The Computer Vulnerabilities and Exposures Board (**cve.mitre.org**) maintains a list of common network security vulnerabilities. Review the list. How many vulnerabilities are there? Based on the list, which system components appear to be most vulnerable to attack? What impact do these vulnerable components have on EC?
3. Your B2C site has just been hacked. You would like to report the incident to the Computer Emergency Response Team (**cert.org**) at Carnegie Mellon University so that they can alert other sites. How do you do this and what types of information do you have to provide?
4. McAfee's AVERT maintains a running list of the top malware threats on the Internet (**vil.nai.com**). Select one of the specific threats on the list. Using other online materials, describe the threat and the steps that can be and have been used to combat it.
5. ICSA Labs (**icsalabs.com/html/communities/firewalls/newsite/cert2.shtml**) provides a detailed list of firewall products for corporate, small business, and residential use. Select three corporate firewall products from the list. Using online materials, research and compare the benefits of each product. Based on the comparison, which product would you choose and why?
6. Select a single type of physiological biometric system. Using the Internet, identify at least two commercial vendors offering these systems. Based on the materials you have gathered, what are the major features of the systems. Which of the systems would you select and why?
7. *The National Strategy to Secure Cyberspace* (see Section 11.2) provides a series of actions and recommendations for each of its five national priorities. Obtain a copy of the strategy online. Selecting one of the priorities, discuss in detail the actions and recommendations for that priority.

8. The AOL/NCSA survey (**staysafeonline.info/news/safety_study_v04.pdf**) of in-home computer security dealt with the presence and problems of spyware and file-sharing software. Obtain a copy of the survey. Summarize their key findings with respect to these two classes of software.

9. The *Symantec Internet Security Threat Report* provides details about the trends in attacks and vulnerabilities in Internet security. Obtain a copy of the report and summarize the major findings of the report for both attacks and vulnerabilities.

TEAM ASSIGNMENTS AND ROLE PLAYING

1. At least six motives have been identified that explain why hackers do what they do. These motives are money, entertainment, ego, cause, entrance to social groups, and status. Using the Web as your primary data source, have each team member explore one or more of these motives. Each member should describe the motive in detail, determine how widespread the motive is, the types of attacks that the motive encourages, and the types of actions that can be taken to combat the associated attacks.

2. Several personal firewall products are available. A list of these products can be found at **firewallguide.com/software.htm**. Assign each team three products from the list. Each team should prepare a detailed review and comparison of each of the products they have been assigned.

3. Assign each team member a different B2C or B2B Web site. Have each team prepare a report summarizing the site's security assets, threats, and vulnerabilities. Prepare a brief security-risk-management plan for the site.

Real-World Case

DO I REALLY NEED THIS?

The Internet Security Alliance (ISAlliance; *isalliance.org*) was formed in April 2001. The ISAlliance is a collaborative endeavor of Carnegie Mellon CERT Coordination Center (CERT/CC); the Electronics Industries Alliance (EIA), a federation of trade groups; and other private and public member organizations and corporations. Its goal is to provide information sharing and leadership on information security and to represent its members and the larger security community before legislators and regulators. In the group's own words, it is not a policy shop. Instead, it is interested in practical methods to achieve pragmatic behavioral change resulting in improved security.

For the past few years, the focus of the ISAlliance has been on larger enterprises. Based on information gathered from the daily operations of CERT/CC, the ISAlliance prepared a best practices manual for top executives in July 2002—"A Common Sense Guide for Senior Managers." The advice provided in that manual is discussed in Online File W11.5. The manual became part of *The National Strategy to Secure Cyberspace* (2003), which was referenced in Section 11.2. At the end of 2003, the ISAlliance was asked by the National Cyber Security Summit to produce a similar guide for small businesses.

The ISAlliance's security guide for small businesses (ISAlliance 2004) opens with the statement, "I'm very busy; do I really need this?" Although large businesses have more to lose in absolute terms, attacks on a small business are more likely and can be devastating. For example, a survey of the spread of the MyDoom virus noted that one in three small businesses was hit by the virus, which was twice the rate for large businesses. Although the dollar value of an attack on a large business can be huge, a major attack can potentially put a small firm out of business because of the smaller margins on which it operates. It is not the size of the business that makes one organization more vulnerable than another; it is the lack of protection that makes them a target. These days, larger businesses are likely to employ risk management and other best security practices. Because of costs, lack of expertise, time constraints, and other business factors, many small businesses have virtually ignored security altogether.

In constructing the best practices guide for small businesses, the ISAlliance felt that a different approach had to be taken. Small business owners are aware of the security threats that exist. Yet, they persist in doing nothing. Given this fact, the ISAlliance utilized input from 10 focus groups, involving 100 small business owners, to construct the guidelines. The focus groups revealed that small businesses:

- Were sympathetic to national security needs, but were not going to take the time and expense to improve their network security based on common appeals
- Were not intimately familiar with computer security technology
- Had unrealistic expectations that they would not be victimized because they were too small or because they had taken elementary steps to protect their systems
- Saw security materials as too technical and hard to follow, even if they were favorably disposed to institute stricter security measures
- Needed more than information for any program to have a lasting effect on behaviors

Based on the focus group input and revelations, the ISAlliance came up with a "12 Step Program" for improving and maintaining cyber security for small businesses. The steps include:

1. Use strong passwords and change them regularly.
2. Look out for e-mail attachments and Internet download modules.
3. Install, maintain, and apply antivirus programs.
4. Install and use a firewall.
5. Remove unused software and user accounts; clean out everything on replaced equipment.
6. Establish physical access controls for all computer equipment.
7. Create backups for important files, folders, and software.
8. Keep current with software updates.
9. Implement network security with access control.
10. Limit access to sensitive and confidential data.
11. Establish and follow a security financial risk management plan; maintain adequate insurance coverage.
12. Get technical expertise and outside help when you need it.

For each of these steps, the guidelines address not only the appropriate steps to be taken, but also the costs, participants, technical skills, and consequences. A case study also is provided for each guideline. For the most part, the costs and required technical skills are minimal. For the others, the costs and skills depend on the specific approach that is selected. For example, the cost of a firewall and the skills need to install and administer it depend on the particular firewall that is chosen.

In implementing the "12 Step Program," the ISAlliance suggests that a small business address them completely rather than using a staged approach. Because most small businesses will have implemented one or more of these steps, they need to concentrate on the gaps. Once the program has been implemented, the business needs to budget for these steps on an annual basis. Like all businesses, small businesses also need to stay current on emerging threats, vulnerabilities, and security practices. Toward that end, the ISAlliance provides updated information on key security issues.

Sources: Clinton (2004), ISAlliance (2002), and ISAlliance (2004).

Questions

1. Most of the ISAlliance's recommendations seem like common sense. Why do you think that common-sense advice is required in this case? Based on what you know about information security, what other recommendations would you make for small businesses?
2. For each step, the best practices guidelines for small businesses provide the consequences for adopting the practice. Using one of the steps, explain whether this is sufficient motivation for a small business to adopt the practice. Overall, do you think these guidelines will have much impact on the behavior of small businesses? What else could be done to encourage them to adopt the practices?
3. The ISAlliance's best practice guidelines are available on its Web site. Download the guidelines for large and small businesses. What are the major differences between the two sets of guidelines?
4. Given the breadth of known vulnerabilities, what sort of impact will any set of security standards have on the rise in cyber attacks?

REFERENCES

Achohido, B., and J. Swartz. "Are Hackers Using Your PC to Spew Spam and Steal?" *USA TODAY*, September 8, 2004. **usatoday.com/tech/news/computersecurity/2004-09-08-zombieuser_x.htm** (accessed October 2004).

Anti-Phishing Working Group (APWG). "Phishing Attack Trends Report." 2004. **antiphishing.org/APWG_Phishing_Attack_Report-Jun2004.pdf** (accessed March 2005).

AOL/NCSA. "AOL/NCSA Online Safety Study." October 2004. **staysafeonline.info/news/safety_study_v04.pdf** (accessed October 2004).

CERT/CC. "CERT/CC Statistics 1988–2002." 2002. cert.org/stats/cert_stats.html (accessed April 2003).

Clinton, L. "Hearing on Protecting Our Nation's Cyber Space: Educational Awareness for the Cyber Citizen." Internet Security Alliance, April 2004. isalliance.org/testimonyLarry416.doc (accessed October 2004).

CSI and FBI. "2004 CSI/FBI Computer Crime and Security Survey." 2004. gocsi.com (accessed October 2004).

CSO Magazine. "2004 E-Crime Watch Survey Shows Significant Increase in Electronic Crimes." *CSO Magazine,* May 25, 2004. cert.org/about/ecrime.html (accessed October 2004).

cve.mitre.org (accessed 1999–2005).

Damle, P. "Social Engineering: A Tip of the Iceberg." *Information Systems Control Journal* 2 (2002).

Department of Homeland Security. *The National Strategy to Secure Cyberspace*, 2004. whitehouse.gov/pcipb (accessed October 2004).

Emigh, J. "The Eyes Have It." *Security Solutions*, March 1, 2003. securitysolutions.com/mag/security_eyes/ (accessed October 2004).

Federal Trade Commission (FTC). "How Not to Get Hooked by a 'Phishing' Scam." FTC Consumer Alert, June 2004. ftc.gov/bcp/conline/pubs/alerts/phishing alrt.htm (accessed October 2004).

Fisher, D. "MyDoom E-Mail Worm Spreading Quickly." *eWeek*, January 26, 2004. eweek.com/article2/0,1759,1460809,00.asp (accessed October 2004).

Garfinkel, S. *Web Security, Privacy and Commerce*. Sebastopol, CA: O'Reilly and Associates, 2002.

Hazari, S. "Firewalls for Beginners." *SecurityFocus.com*, November 6, 2000. securityfocus.com/infocus/1182 (accessed March 2005).

Honeynet Project. *Know Your Enemy: Learning about Security Threats,* 2d ed. Boston, MA: Addison-Wesley, 2004.

Howard, M. *Designing Secure Web-Based Applications for Microsoft Windows 2000*. Redmond, WA: Microsoft Press, 2000.

ICSA. "Malicious Code Problem Continues to Worsen, According to 9th Annual ICSA Labs Virus Prevalence Survey." TruSecure Corporation, 2004. trusecure.com/company/press/pr_20040322.shtml (accessed October 2004).

ISAlliance. "Common Sense Guide for Senior Managers." Internet Security Alliance, July 2002. isalliance.org/news/BestPractices.pdf (accessed October 2004).

ISAlliance. "Common Sense Guide to Cyber Security for Small Businesses." Internet Security Alliance, March 2004. /resources/papers/common_sense_sm_bus.pdf (accessed October 2004).

Kay, T. *Security+*. Berkeley, CA: McGraw-Hill/Osborne, 2003.

Kroeker, K. "Graphics and Security: Exploring Visual Biometrics." *IEEE Computer Society*, 2002. computer.org/cga/homepage/2002/n4/biometrics.htm (accessed April 2003).

Lemos, R. "Mitnick Teaches 'Social Engineering.'" *ZDNet News*, July 17, 2000. zdnet.com.com/2100-11-522261.html?legacy=zdnn (accessed November 2004).

Market Research Summaries. "Security, Continuity Top IT Spending Priorities." *Print on Demand.com,* September 25, 2003. printondemand.com/MT/archives/001335.html (accessed October 2004).

McConnell, M. "Information Assurance in the Twenty-First Century." *IEEE Security and Privacy*, 2002. computer.org/security/supplement1/mcc/?smsession=no (accessed November 2004).

Microsoft. "The Security Risk Management Guide," 2004. microsoft.com/technet/security/topics/policiesand procedures/secrisk/default.mspx (accessed October 2004).

Mitnick, K., and W. Simon. *The Art of Deception*. New York: Wiley, 2002.

NetGear. "Security and Savings with Virtual Private Networks." *ZDNet UK,* May 2002. whitepapers.zdnet.co.uk/0,39025945,60068895p-39000459q,00.htm (accessed October 2004).

Panko, R. *Corporate Computer and Network Security*. Upper Saddle River, NJ: Prentice Hall, 2003.

Prometheum Technologies. "How Does Virtual Private Network (VPN) Work?" April 2003. prometheum.com/m_vpn.htm (accessed November 2004).

SANS. "The SANS Top 20 Internet Security Vulnerabilities." SANS Institute, 2004. sans.org/top20/#threats (accessed October 2004).

Scambray, J. et al. *Hacking Exposed*, 2nd ed. New York: McGraw-Hill, 2000. Copyright © McGraw-Hill Companies, Inc.

Shen, M. "Trends in Biometric Security (Part 3): Buyer Behavior Analysis." *BiometriTech,* March 2003. bio metritech.com/features/shen031903.htm (accessed October 2004).

Sherwood, J. "IT Bosses Eye Up Biometric Security." *Vnunet.com,* September 2004. vnunet.com/news/1158422 (accessed October 2004).

Shimomura, T., et al. *Takedown: The Pursuit and Capture of Kevin Mitnick, America's Most Wanted Computer Outlaw, By the Man Who Did It.* New York: Warner Books, 1996.

Skoudis, E., and L. Zeltser. *Malware: Fighting Malicious Code*. Upper Saddle River, NJ: Prentice Hall, 2003.

Slewe, T., and M. Hoogenboom. "Who Will Rob You on the Digital Highway?" *Communications of the ACM* 47, no. 5 (2004): 56–60.

Symantec. "Symantec Internet Security Threat Report: Trends for January 1, 2004–June 30, 2004." Symantec, 2004. enterprisesecurity.symantec.com/content.cfm?articleid=1539 (accessed October 2004).

Thomas, T. *Network Security: First-Step*. Indianapolis, IN: Cisco Press, 2004.

Venes, R. "A Closer Look at Biometrics." *Computeractive*, June 24, 2004. infomaticsonline.co.uk/features/1156173 (accessed October 2004).

CHAPTER 12

ELECTRONIC PAYMENT SYSTEMS

Content

Learning Objectives

Upon completion of this chapter, you will be able to:

1. Understand the shifts that are occurring with regards to noncash and online payments.
2. Discuss the players and processes involved in using credit cards online.
3. Discuss the different categories and potential uses of smart cards.
4. Discuss various online alternatives to credit card payments and identify under what circumstances they are best used.
5. Describe the processes and parties involved in e-checking.
6. Describe payment methods in B2B EC, including payments for global trade.
7. Discuss electronic bill and invoice presentment and payment.
8. Understand the sales tax implications of e-payments.

FLYLADY ADOPTS PAYPAL

The Problem

A few years back, Marley Cilley created an e-mail group to provide one-on-one coaching to help subscribers with their organizational skills. Within a short time, the group grew to 60,000 members. At that point, Marley decided to offer organizational products online. The online company was called FlyLady (*flylady.net*), after her interest in fly fishing. In the beginning, FlyLady used a mail-order process to fulfill orders and a merchant account to process payments. The problem was the processing fees, which were 4.9 percent. The fees were costing her business a fortune.

In the online world, credit card payments are ubiquitous. Unfortunately, for small startups like FlyLady, the costs incurred in accepting credit card payments can make the difference between profit and loss. Not only are credit card transaction fees prohibitive, but the task and cost of setting up a full-blown, secure B2C site that accepts credit card payments can be daunting. Most small and many medium-sized businesses simply are unwilling to accept the risks. Fortunately, FlyLady's customers suggested a viable alternative—PayPal.

The Solution

Anyone who has used eBay is familiar with PayPal. eBay acquired PayPal in October 2002. Today, PayPal has a user base of over 50 million members. Member accounts are linked with bank accounts or credit cards and can be used to transfer funds to and from individuals or businesses. In 2003, PayPal processed $12.2 billion in payments. Seventy percent of those payments involved selling and buying on online auctions. Although nonauction payments are still a minor segment of its business, this segment has grown dramatically, increasing 58 percent from April to June 2004.

For small to medium-sized businesses, PayPal is easy to set up and integrate into an existing site. Even though PayPal handles credit card payments, it is not a credit card gateway. Because of this, businesses that offer PayPal as a payment alternative are not required to pass a credit check, install special equipment or software, or deal with complex banking agreements. Additionally, there is no need to gather credit card numbers from buyers or to collect sensitive financial information. Instead, an online merchant can get started by simply setting up a PayPal Business account, logging into the account, using PayPal's Merchant Tools to create a payment button (which is nothing more than an HTML form), and then copying the button to a page on the Web site. It literally can be done in minutes. PayPal charges merchants a fee of 30 cents, plus 1.9 percent to 2.9 percent of each transaction.

The Results

After deciding to adopt PayPal, the staff at FlyLady was able to implement a "Buy Now" payment button in under an hour. FlyLady's fulfillment process is based on PayPal's reporting tools. Each day the staff logs onto PayPal and downloads the company's transaction file. The contents of this file are imported into desktop software that parses and sorts the data to create orders and shipping labels, which are then handed over to the warehouse for fulfillment. FlyLady also relies on PayPal's reporting tools to monitor daily sales and business trends. Like any public Web site, FlyLady has to be concerned with security. However, it does not have to worry about securing its customers' financial information, because this is held on the PayPal site. In fact, employees never see this information. Today, FlyLady's sales are close to $5 million. As a consequence, PayPal lowered FlyLady's transaction cost from 2.9 percent to 1.9 percent.

Sources: PayPal (2004), Tsai (2004), and Sofield et al. (2004).

WHAT WE CAN LEARN . . .

The overwhelming majority of B2C purchases are paid for by credit card. For merchants, the costs of servicing card payments are high. Transaction costs, potential chargeback fees for fraudulent transactions, and the costs of creating and administering a secure EC site for handling card payments are steep. Over the years, a number of less costly e-payment alternatives to credit cards have been proposed. Digital Cash, PayMe.com, Bank One's eMoneyMail, Flooz, Beenz, Wells Fargo's and eBay's Billpoint, and Yahoo's PayDirect all are examples of alternatives that failed to gain a critical mass of users and subsequently folded (see Online File W12.1 for a short description of Beenz and Flooz). For a variety of reasons, PayPal succeeded against substantial odds (Jackson 2004). The same can be said for the world of B2B e-payments. Although a number of diverse payment methods have been proposed, few have survived.

WWW

This chapter discusses various e-payment methods for B2C and B2B and the underlying reasons why some have been adopted and others have not. It also examines related issues such as tax payments.

12.1 THE PAYMENT REVOLUTION

According to Sapsford (2004), "A currency can be anything that all members of a society agree it should be." Prior to the tenth century B.C., shells often were used in trade and barter. Metal coins appeared in Greece and India somewhere between the tenth and sixth centuries B.C. and dominated trade for 2,000 years. In the Middle Ages, checks were introduced by Italian merchants. In the United States, paper money was first issued in Massachusetts in 1690. In 1950, credit cards were introduced in the United States by Diners Club. Until recently, cash was king, at least for in-store payments; checks were the dominant form of noncash payment.

Today, we are in the midst of a payment revolution, with cards and electronic payments taking the place of cash and checks. In 2003, the combined use of credit and debit cards for in-store payments for the first time exceeded the combined use of cash and checks (Federal Reserve System 2004). Debit and credit cards accounted for 52 percent of in-store payments, with cash and checks making up the rest. The growth in the use of plastic is attributable to the substantial growth in the use of debit cards and the decline in the use of cash. From 1999 to 2003, debit cards payments went from 21 percent to 31 percent, while cash dropped from 39 percent to 32 percent (Federal Reserve System 2004).

Similar trends are occurring in noncash payments. According to a recent study by the Federal Reserve System (2004), electronic payment transactions in the United States exceeded check payments for the first time in 2003. From 2000 to 2003, the volume of electronic payment transactions grew from 30.6 billion to 44.5 billion, while the volume of checks declined from 41.9 billion to 36.7 billion over the same time period. However, in 2003 the total dollar amount of payments by check was $39.3 trillion, compared with $27 trillion by electronic payments. Again, the fastest-growing segment of electronic payments was debit cards.

For decades people have been talking about the cashless society. Although the demise of cash and checks is certainly not imminent, many individuals can live without checks and nearly without cash. In the online B2C world, they already do. In North America, for example, 90 percent of all online consumer purchases are made with general-purpose credit cards (CyberSource 2004). The same is true for the overwhelming majority of online purchases in the UK, France, and Spain. While Visa and MasterCard are certainly worldwide brands, many consumers outside these countries prefer other online payment methods. For instance, consumers in Germany, the Netherlands, and Japan prefer to pay with either direct debit or bank cards.

For online B2C merchants, the implications of these trends are straightforward. In the United States and Western Europe it is hard to run an online business without supporting credit card payments, despite the costs. It also is becoming increasingly important to support payments by debit card. Under current growth patterns, the volume of debit card payments will soon surpass credit card payments both online and off-line. For merchants who are interested in international markets, there is a need to support a variety of e-payment mechanisms, including bank transfers, COD, electronic checks, private label cards, gift cards, instant credit, and other noncard payment types such as PayPal. Merchants who offer multiple payment types have lower shopping cart abandonment rates and up to 20 percent higher order conversion on the average, resulting in increased revenues (CyberSource 2004).

As the opening case study suggests, the short history of e-payments is littered with the remains of companies that have attempted to introduce nontraditional payment systems. It takes years for any payment system to gain widespread acceptance. For example, credit cards were introduced in the 1950s but did not reach widespread use until the 1980s. A crucial element in the success of any e-payment method is the "chicken-and-egg" problem: How do you get sellers to adopt a method when there are few buyers using it? And, how do you get buyers to adopt a method when there are few sellers using it? A number of factors come into play in determining whether a particular method of e-payment achieves critical mass. Some of the crucial factors include the following (Evans and Schmalensee 2005).

Independence. Some forms of e-payment require specialized software or hardware to make the payment. Almost all forms of e-payment require the seller or merchant to install specialized software to receive and authorize a payment. Those e-payment methods that require the payer to install specialized components are less likely to succeed.

Interoperability and Portability. All forms of EC run on specialized systems that are interlinked with other enterprise systems and applications. An e-payment method must mesh with these existing systems and applications and be supported by standard computing platforms.

Security. How safe is the transfer? What are the consequences of the transfer being compromised? Again, if the risk for the payer is higher than the risk for the payee, then the method is not likely to be accepted.

Anonymity. Unlike credit cards and checks, if a buyer uses cash, there is no way to trace the cash back to the buyer. Some buyers want their identities and purchase patterns to remain anonymous. To succeed, special payment methods, such as e-cash, have to maintain anonymity.

Divisibility. Most sellers accept credit cards only for purchases within a minimum and maximum range. If the cost of the item is too small—say, only a few dollars—a credit card will not do. In addition, a credit card will not work if an item or set of items costs too much—say, an airline company purchasing a new airplane. Any method that can address the lower or higher end of the price continuum or that can span one of the extremes and the middle has a chance of being widely accepted.

Ease of Use. For B2C e-payments, credit cards are the standard due to their ease of use. For B2B payments, the question is whether the online e-payment methods can supplant the existing off-line methods of procurement.

Transaction Fees. When a credit card is used for payment, the merchant pays a transaction fee of up to 3 percent of the item's purchase price (above a minimum fixed fee). These fees make it prohibitive to support smaller purchases with credit cards, which leaves room for alternative forms of payment.

Regulations. All payment methods are governed by a number of international, federal, and state regulations. Even when a new payment method is introduced by an existing institution or association (e.g., Visa), it faces a number of stringent regulatory hurdles. PayPal, for instance, had to contend with a number of lawsuits brought by state attorneys general, which claimed that PayPal was violating state banking regulations.

Section 12.1 ▶ REVIEW QUESTIONS

1. Describe the trends that are occurring in cash and noncash payments in the United States.
2. What types of e-payments should B2C merchants support?
3. What is the "chicken-egg" problem in e-payments?
4. Describe the factors that are critical for an e-payment method to achieve critical mass.

12.2 USING PAYMENT CARDS ONLINE

payment card
Electronic card that contains information that can be used for payment purposes.

Payment cards are electronic cards that contain information that can be used for payment purposes. They come in three forms:

- **Credit cards.** A credit card provides the holder with credit to make purchases up to a limit fixed by the card issuer. Credit cards rarely have an annual fee. Instead, holders are charged high interest—the annual percentage rate—on their unpaid balances. Visa, MasterCard, and EuroPay are the predominant credit cards.
- **Charge cards.** The balance on a charge card is supposed to be paid in full upon receipt of the monthly statement. Technically, holders of a charge card receive a loan for 30 to 45 days equal to the balance of their statement. Such cards usually have annual fees. American Express's Green Card is the leading charge card, followed by the Diner's Club card.
- **Debit cards.** With a debit card, the money for a purchased item comes directly out of the holder's checking account (called a demand-deposit account). The actual transfer of funds from the holder's account to the merchant's takes place within 1 to 2 days. MasterCard, Visa, and EuroPay are the predominant debit cards.

PROCESSING CREDIT CARDS ONLINE

The processing of card payments has two major phases: authorization and settlement. **Authorization** determines whether a buyer's card is active and whether the customer has sufficient funds. **Settlement** involves the transfer of money from the buyer's to the merchant's account. The way in which these phases actually are performed varies somewhat depending on the type of payment card. They also vary by the configuration of the system used by the merchant to process payments.

authorization
Determines whether a buyer's card is active and whether the customer has sufficient funds.

settlement
Transferring money from the buyer's to the merchant's account.

There are three basic configurations for processing online payments. The EC merchant may (MasterCard 2003a):

- **Own the payment software.** A merchant can purchase a payment-processing module and integrate it with its other EC software. This module communicates with a payment gateway run by an acquiring bank or another third party.
- **Use a point of sale system (POS) operated by an acquirer.** Merchants can redirect cardholders to a POS run by an acquirer. The POS handles the complete payment process and directs the cardholder back to the merchant site once payment is complete. In this case, the merchant system only deals with order information. In this configuration, it is important to find an acquirer that handles multiple cards and payment instruments. If not, the merchant will need to connect with a multitude of acquirers.
- **Use a POS operated by a payment service provider.** Merchants can rely on servers operated by third parties known as **payment service providers (PSPs)**. In this case, the PSP connects with the appropriate acquirers. PSPs must be registered with the various card associations they support.

payment service provider (PSP)
A third-party service connecting a merchant's EC systems to the appropriate acquirers. PSPs must be registered with the various card associations they support.

For a given type of payment card and processing system, the processes and participants are essentially the same for off-line (card present) and online (card not present) purchases. Exhibit 12.1 compares, for instance, the steps involved in making a credit card purchase both online and off-line. As the exhibit demonstrates, there is very little difference between the two.

Based on the processes outlined in Exhibit 12.1, the key participants in processing credit card payments online include the following:

- **Acquiring bank.** Offers a special account called an *Internet Merchant Account* that enables card authorization and payment processing.
- **Credit card association.** The financial institution providing credit card and debit card services to banks (e.g., Visa and MasterCard).
- **Customer.** The individual possessing the payment card.
- **Issuing bank.** The financial institution that provides the customer with a payment card.
- **Merchant.** A company that sells products or services.
- **Payment processing service.** The service provides connectivity among merchants, customers, and financial networks that enables authorization and payments. Usually operated by companies such as CyberSource (cybersource.com) and VeriSign (verisign.com).
- **Processor.** The data center that processes credit card transactions and settles funds to merchants.

FRAUDULENT CREDIT CARD TRANSACTIONS

Although the processes used for authorizing and settling credit card payments off-line and online are very similar, there is one substantial difference between the two. In the online world, merchants are held liable for fraudulent transactions. In addition to the lost merchandise and shipping charges, merchants who accept fraudulent transactions can incur additional fees and penalties imposed by the credit card associations. However, these are not the only costs. There also are the costs associated with combating fraudulent transactions. These include the costs of tools and systems to review orders, the costs of manually reviewing orders, and the revenue that is lost from rejecting orders that are valid. Recent surveys by CyberSource indicate that fraudulent credit card transactions are a growing problem for online merchants in spite of their increasing efforts to combat fraud.

EXHIBIT 12.1 Credit Card Purchases: Online Versus Off-Line

Online Purchase	Off-Line Purchase
1. The *customer* decides to purchase a CD on the Web, adding it to the electronic shopping cart and going to the checkout page to enter his or her credit card information.	1. The *customer* selects a CD to purchase, takes it to the checkout counter, and hands his or her credit card to the sales clerk.
2. The *merchant* site receives the customer's information and sends the transaction information to its *payment processing service (PPS)*.	2. The *sales clerk* swipes the card and transfers transaction information to a *point-of-sale (POS)* terminal.
3. The PPS routes information to the *processor* (a large data center for processing transactions and settling funds to the merchant).	3. The POS terminal routes information to the *processor* via a dial-up connection.
4. The processor sends information to the *issuing bank* of the customer's credit card.	4. The processor sends information to the *issuing bank* of customer's credit card.
5. The issuing bank sends the transaction to the processor, either authorizing the payment or not.	5. The issuing bank sends the transaction to the processor, either authorizing the payment or not.
6. The processor routes the transaction result to the PPS.	6. The processor routes the transaction result to the POS.
7. The PPS passes the results to merchant.	7. The POS shows the merchant whether the transaction has been approved or declined.
8. The merchant accepts or rejects transaction.	8. The merchant tells the customer the outcome of the transaction.

Source: Verisign. "Business Guide to Online Payment Processing." 2004, *verisign.com/static/003190.pdf*. Used with permission of VeriSign, Inc.

For the past 6 years, CyberSource has sponsored a survey to address the detection, prevention, and management of fraud perpetrated against online merchants. CyberSource's 2004 survey of 285 merchants documented the following trends (CyberSource 2005):

- While the percentage of revenue loss per merchant was relatively flat, the total dollars lost to fraud increased substantially from $1.9 billion in 2003 to $2.6 billion in 2004. The rise was attributable to the increase in the amount of business that was being done online, which grew by 25 to 30 percent over the same time period.
- In 2004, merchants estimated that an average of 1.3 percent of their orders were fraudulent. Fifteen percent of the merchants indicated that the average was more than 2 percent of all orders. The fraudulent orders resulted in merchants crediting the real cardholder's account or a chargeback. The median value of these fraudulent orders was $150, or 50 percent above the average value of valid orders.
- Fifty-eight percent of the merchants surveyed accepted international orders outside the United States and Canada. These orders represented 16 percent of the sales for these merchants. The fraud rate for these orders was approximately 4 percent, or three times higher than the fraud rate for domestic orders.
- Certain merchants were more susceptible to fraud than others. This was due to a number of factors: the merchant's visibility on the Web, the steps the merchant had taken to combat fraud, the ease with which the merchant's products could be sold on the open market, and the merchant's size. Larger firms were less susceptible to fraud than smaller firms.
- Because of the expected increase in online sales, close to half of the merchants surveyed indicated that they expect online payment fraud to increase in the coming year. The primary reason given for this expectation is the increasing sophistication and improved methods of the fraudsters.

In addition to tracking cyber-fraud trends, the CyberSource surveys also have monitored the steps taken by merchants to combat fraud (CyberSource 2005). In 2004, merchants used more tools than in the past to combat fraud. The median number of tools was five in 2004 compared with three in 2003. Merchants also were spending more to combat fraud. The median amount was 0.4 percent of online revenues. Most of the money was spent on review staff (45 percent), followed by third-party tools and services (29 percent) and internally developed tools (26 percent). The key tools used in combating fraud were:

- **Address Verification System (AVS).** This method is used by 82 percent of all merchants. This service compares the address entered on a Web page with the address information on file with cardholder's issuing bank. This method results in a number of false positives, meaning that the merchant rejects a valid order. Cardholders often have new addresses or simply make mistakes in inputting numeric street addresses or zip codes. AVS is only available in the United States and Canada.
- **Manual review.** This method is used by 73 percent of all merchants. It relies on staff to manually review suspicious orders. For small merchants with a small volume of orders, this is a reasonable method. For larger merchants, this method does not scale well, is expensive, and impacts customer satisfaction. In spite of these limitations, the percentage of merchants using this method is increasing along with the percentage of items being reviewed. In 2004, the number of orders being reviewed was one in three versus one in four in 2003.
- **Card verification number (CVN).** This method is used by 56 percent of all merchants. It relies on comparing the verification number printed on the signature strip on the back of the card with the information on file with the cardholder's issuing bank. However, if a fraudster possesses a stolen card, the number is in plain view.
- **Fraud screens and decision models.** These methods are used by 53 percent of all merchants. These methods are based on various automated rules that determine whether a transaction should be accepted, rejected, or suspended. A key element of this method is the ability of the merchant to easily change the rules to reflect changing trends in the fraud being perpetrated against the company.
- **Negative files.** This method is used by 45 percent of all merchants. A negative file consists of the customer's information (IP address, name, shipping/billing address, contact numbers, etc.) and the status of that customer. A customer's transaction is matched against this file and flagged if the customer is a known problem.
- **Card association payer authentication services.** This method is used by 25 percent of all merchants. In the last couple of years, the card associations have developed a new set of payer identification services (e.g., Verified by Visa and MasterCard SecureCode). These services require cardholders to register with the systems and merchants to adopt and support both the existing systems and the new systems. These services are described in EC Application Case 12.1. Estimates are that by 2005 over 55 percent of the merchants will be using this method.

Address Verification System (AVS)
Detects fraud by comparing the address entered on a Web page with the address information on file with cardholder's issuing bank.

card verification number (CVN)
Detects fraud by comparing the verification number printed on the signature strip on the back of the card with the information on file with the cardholder's issuing bank.

The overall impact of these tools is that merchants are rejecting a significant number of orders due to suspicion of fraud. In 2003, merchants rejected three orders for every fraudulent order accepted. In 2004, the average number of rejected orders was four and a half for every fraudulent order accepted. In 2004, this represented a rejection rate of 6 percent of the orders. For orders outside the United States and Canada, the rejection rate was 12.5 percent. The problem with these rejection rates is that a number of the rejected orders are valid, resulting in lost revenue.

The trends in tool use uncovered by the CyberSource surveys are supported by a series of annual surveys conducted by the Merchant Risk Council (MRC) (merchantriskcouncil.org). The MRC was formed in 2002 when the Merchant Fraud Squad headed by American Express, ClearCommerce, and Expedia merged with the Internet Fraud Roundtable headed by HP and ClearCommerce. Both voluntary organizations were focused on encouraging best practices in fraud prevention. Today, MRC's membership consists of 7,500 merchants, vendors, financial institutions, and law enforcement agencies. In 2003 and 2004, the MRC surveyed its merchant members to identify and quantify their spending on fraud prevention.

The 2004 results (Merchant Risk Council 2004) indicated that fraud increased from 2003 to 2004; fraudsters are more sophisticated than in the past; merchants are using more tools to combat fraud than they did in 2003; and the most commonly used fraud prevention tools were AVS (74 percent), customer follow-up (70 percent), CVN (65 percent), and negative files (55 percent).

VIRTUAL CREDIT CARDS

Although the volume and dollar amount of online purchases are growing significantly, a number of consumers still are leery of using their credit card numbers online. Virtual credit cards were designed to address these concerns. With a **virtual credit card**, the online buyer is provided by the card company at the time of purchase with a randomly generated card number that is tied to the buyer's actual card number. The buyer enters this number rather than the actual number to complete a purchase. Generally, the number can only be used once. This is why virtual credit cards also are known as *single-use card numbers.*

virtual credit card
An e-payment system in which a credit card issuer gives a special transaction number that can be used online in place of regular credit card numbers.

Although single-use numbers combat certain types of fraud, they have their drawbacks. Purchases made with single-use numbers cannot be confirmed at a later date. For example, if a person makes an airline or hotel reservation online and needs the card number to confirm it at a later date, there is no way to obtain the number for this purpose. Similarly, if a person pre-purchases an item, there is no way to confirm the card number later, because the number will have expired. Finally, there is no way to pay recurring bills or subscriptions with a single-use number.

At one point in time, most of the major card associations and companies tried introducing virtual credit cards. American Express, for instance, had a special service called *Private Payments*. Early in 2004, it discontinued this service. Most of the card associations and companies have replaced their virtual card services with their payer authentication services based on 3-D Secure. One exception is the Discover Card. Discover Financial Services offers its customers a single-use card service called *Discover Deskshop* (discovercard.com/deskshop). Discover customers who register with the service download a small piece of software called the Deskshop. Anytime the user encounters a checkout form, the software pops up and asks the user whether he or she wants the software to automatically complete the form and enter a single-use number. Unlike earlier counterparts, the number generated by Deskshop has the same expiration date as the actual card, which means that it can be used for recurring bills, but only for the site for which the number was generated.

Section 12.2 ▶ REVIEW QUESTIONS

1. Describe the three types of payment cards.
2. What options does a merchant have in setting up an e-payment system?
3. List the major participants in processing credit cards online.
4. What costs does an online merchant incur if it submits a fraudulent credit card transaction?
5. Describe the major trends in fraudulent orders perpetrated against online merchants.
6. What steps are often taken by online merchants to combat fraudulent orders?
7. How does a virtual credit card work?

12.3 SMART CARDS

Outside North America, smart cards often are used in place of or in addition to traditional credit and debit cards. They also are used quite widely to support nonretail and nonfinancial applications. A **smart card** looks like a plastic payment card, but it is distinguished by the presence of an embedded microchip (see Exhibit 12.2). The embedded chip may be a microprocessor combined with a memory chip or just a memory chip with nonprogrammable logic. Information on a microprocessor card can be added, deleted, or otherwise manipulated; a memory-chip card is usually a "read-only" card, similar to a credit card. Although the microprocessor is capable of running programs like a computer does, it is not a stand-alone computer. The programs and data must be downloaded from and activated by some other device (such as an ATM machine).

smart card
An electronic card containing an embedded microchip that enables predefined operations or the addition, deletion, or manipulation of information on the card.

CASE 12.1

EC Application

ETRONICS TURNS TO MASTERCARD SECURECODE

eTronics is a leading EC consumer electronics retailer. It sells to consumers and small businesses, focusing on low prices, fast delivery, and nationally recognized name-brand products. Sales for the company are projected to be $75 million, accomplished with a staff of 50.

When eTronics initially opened, it confronted a classic online B2C problem: "How do you know that the online shopper is the true cardholder?" This problem also arises in the off-line world; however, with online shopping, the merchant bears responsibility for the following risks:

- **Stolen cards.** If someone steals a credit card and the valid cardholder contests the charges made by the thief, the issuer will credit the cardholder's account and chargeback the merchant.
- **Reneging by the customer.** A customer can authorize a payment and later deny it. If the denial is believable to the issuer, the merchant will bear the loss.

Within a few months of operation, eTronics' chargeback costs were over $1 million.

To combat the chargeback problem, eTronics originally relied on a rigorous multistep process involving manual inspection of billing and shipping information. Those orders that failed to meet certain criteria were evaluated with the customer and issuing bank. A substantial percentage of those orders flagged for evaluation were higher-ticket items. This manual approach proved to be too costly and time consuming for the small company. The company looked at a number of alternatives, but felt that most would be too onerous or confusing for their customers, resulting in reduced order completions and lost sales. Also, the alternatives were not widely accepted, and many were just as costly as the manual processes already in place. The company finally chose the alternative provided by CardinalCommerce.

CardinalCommerce offers an ASP hosted service enabling 3-Domain (3-D) Secure payment authentication. 3-D Secure relies on SSL encryption and a merchant server plug-in to pass information between the merchant's site and the hosted service, to query participants to authenticate the cardholder during online purchase, and to protect card information as it is transmitted via the Internet. The three domains in 3-D Secure are:

- **Issuer domain.** The issuer is responsible for managing the enrollment of its cardholders in the service, including verifying the identity of each cardholder who enrolls and authenticating cardholders during online purchases.
- **Acquirer domain.** The acquirer is responsible for defining the procedures to ensure that merchants participating in Internet transactions are operating under a merchant agreement with the acquirer and providing the transaction processing for authenticated transactions.
- **Interoperability domain.** This domain facilitates the transaction exchange between the other two domains with a common protocol and shared services.

3-D Secure authentication is supported by Verified by Visa, MasterCard SecureCode, and JCB J/Secure. Among these alternatives, eTronics decided to implement CardCommerce's MasterCard SecureCode option.

It is relatively easy to implement MasterCard SecureCode, as well as the other alternatives. Cardholders enroll in the program with their issuing bank. At that time, they select a password to be used with their online purchases. Merchants enroll in the program through their acquiring bank or a third-party supplier such as CardinalCommerce. To support 3-D authentication, the merchant or its PSP adds a plug-in to the company's payment system. When cardholders make online purchases and enter their credit card numbers, the numbers are checked against the card association's database to determine if they are enrolled. If they are, the plug-in pops up a window asking for the password. The password is then verified, and the transaction is completed or rejected.

The major benefit of 3-D Secure for merchants is the reduction in disputed transactions, handling expenses, and revenue loss. One estimate suggests that this system could eliminate 80 percent or more of these costs and losses. For example, eTronics does not bear the operational or chargeback costs for transactions conducted via MasterCard SecureCode.

Like other payment and authentication schemes, there is no guarantee that 3-D secure will gain critical mass—either among cardholders or merchants. However, it has strong backing from the card associations. For instance, MasterCard's International Operations Committee (IOC) mandated issuers to implement support for MasterCard SecureCode by November 2004. For other ways to combat the chargeback problem, see Online File W12.2.

WWW

Source: Condensed from MasterCard (2003b).

Questions

1. What type of fraud was eTronics trying to control?
2. What are the three domains in 3-D Secure payment authentication?
3. How do merchants deploy 3-D Secure?

EXHIBIT 12.2 Smart Card

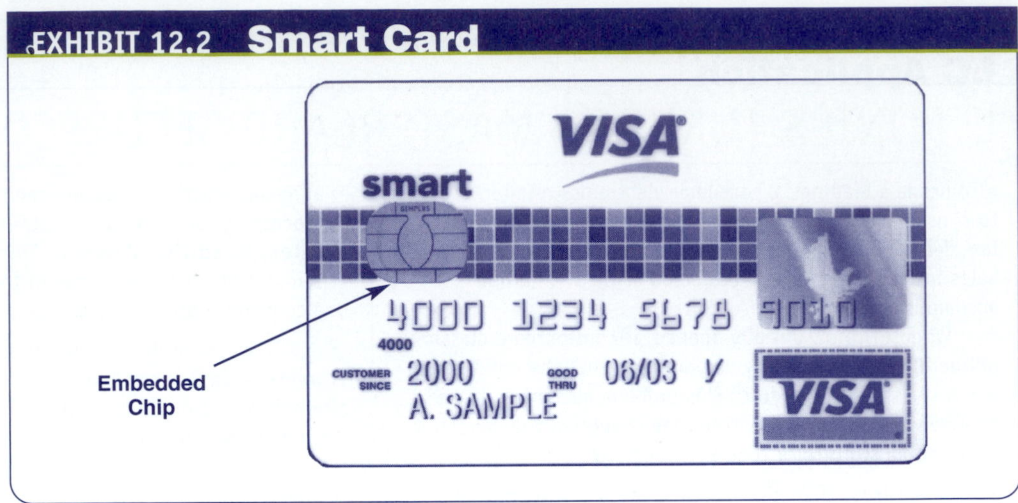

Source: Courtesy of Visa International Service Association.

TYPES OF SMART CARDS

contact card
A smart card containing a small gold plate on the face that when inserted in a smart card reader makes contact and passes data to and from the embedded microchip.

contactless (proximity) card
A smart card with an embedded antenna, by means of which data and applications are passed to and from a card reader unit or other device without contact between the card and the card reader.

There are two distinct types of smart cards. The first type is a **contact card**, which is activated when it is inserted into a smart card reader. The second type of card is a **contactless (proximity) card**, meaning that the card only has to be within a certain proximity of a smart card reader to process a transaction. *Hybrid cards* combine both types of cards into one.

Contact smart cards have a small gold plate about one-half inch in diameter on the front. When the card is inserted into the smart card reader, the plate makes electronic contact and data are passed to and from the chip. Contact cards can have electronically programmable, read-only memory (*EPROM*) or electronically erasable, programmable, read-only memory (*EEPROM*). EPROM cards can never be erased. Instead, data are written to the available space on the card. When the card is full, it is discarded. EEPROM cards are erasable and modifiable. They can be used until they wear out or malfunction. Most contact cards are EEPROM.

In addition to the chip, a contactless card has an embedded antenna. Data and applications are passed to and from the card through the card's antenna to another antenna attached to a smart card reader or other device. Contactless cards are used for those applications in which the data must be processed very quickly (e.g., mass-transit applications such as paying bus or train fares) or when contact is difficult (e.g., security-entering mechanisms to buildings). Proximity cards usually work at short range, just a few inches. For some applications, such as payments at highway toll booths, the cards can operate at considerable distances.

With *hybrid* and *dual-interface* smart cards, the two types of card interfaces are merged into one. A hybrid smart card has two separate chips embedded in the card: contact and contactless. In contrast, a dual-interface, or combi, smart card has a single chip that supports both types of interfaces. The benefit of either card is that it eliminates the need to carry multiple cards to support the various smart card readers and applications.

smart card reader
Activates and reads the contents of the chip on a smart card, usually passing the information on to a host system.

With both types of cards, smart card readers are crucial to the operation of the system. Technically speaking, a smart card reader is actually a read/write device. The primary purpose of the **smart card reader** is to act as a mediator between the card and the host system that stores application data and processes transactions. Just as there are two basic types of cards, there are two types of smart card readers—*contact* and *proximity*—which match the particular type of card. Smart card readers can be transparent, requiring a host device to operate, or stand-alone, functioning independently. Smart card readers are a key element in determining the overall cost of a smart card application. Although the cost of a single reader is usually low, the cost can be quite high when hundreds or thousands are needed to service a large population of users (e.g., all the passengers traveling on a metropolitan mass transit system).

Widespread use of smart cards for multiple applications requires standardization and interoperability among the various card and card reader technologies. Without them, end users would have to carry separate cards for every type of reader and application. Global Platform (globalplatform.org) is an international, nonprofit smart card association whose main goal is to create and advance interoperable technical specifications for smart cards, acceptance devices, and systems infrastructure. Many of the technical standards governing smart cards are set by the International Standards Organization (ISO; iso.org). ISO/IEC 7816 and ISO/IEC 14443 are the main standards pertaining to contact and contactless cards, respectively. These standards form the basis of a number of other smart card standards. For example, in 1995 Europay, MasterCard, and Visa (EMV) established a set of standards for the interoperability and security of smart credit and debit cards. EMV, whose current specification is EMV 2000 version 4, was built on ISO/IEC 7816.

Like computers, smart cards have an underlying operating system. A **smart card operating system** handles file management, security, input/output (I/O), and command execution and provides an application programming interface (API). Originally, smart card operating systems were designed to run on the specific chip embedded in the card. Today, smart cards are moving toward multiple and open application operating systems such as MULTOS (multos.com) and Java Card (java.sun.com/products/javacard). These newer operating systems enable new applications to be added during the life of the card.

smart card operating system
Special system that handles file management, security, input/output (I/O), and command execution and provides an application programming interface (API) for a smart card.

APPLICATIONS OF SMART CARDS

The growth in smart card usage is being driven by its applications. A thorough discussion of these applications can be found at the International Card Manufacturing Association Web site (icma.com/info/quick-facts.htm). The following are some of the more important applications.

Retail Purchases

The credit card associations and financial institutions are transitioning their traditional credit and debit cards to multi-application smart cards. For example, MasterCard announced in November 2004 that it had issued more than 200 million MasterCard, Maestro, and Cirrus smart cards worldwide (MasterCard International 2004). Close to half of these support the EMV card standard. These cards are accepted at over 1.5 million EMV terminals worldwide. From MasterCard's perspective, as well as that of the other card associations and card companies, smart cards have reached mass-market adoption rates in Europe, Latin America, Africa, Asia, and the Middle East.

Smart cards are more secure than credit cards and can be extended with other payment services. In the retail arena, many of these services are aimed at those establishments where payments are usually made in cash and speed and convenience are important. This includes convenience stores, gas stations, fast-food or quick-service restaurants, and cinemas. E-purses and contactless payments exemplify this sort of value-added service.

With an **e-purse** smart card application, money is loaded onto the card from the cardholder's bank account. The cardholder's account is immediately debited, and the value is transferred to a float account at the bank or the system operator. This transaction is carried out online and is PIN protected, just like a cash withdrawal from an ATM. Cardholders can use their e-purses at any POS location where e-purses are accepted. When an e-purse is used, the value is transferred from the e-purse to the terminal, and the value remaining in the e-purse is adjusted. Behind the scenes, the e-purse host system debits the float account of the issuing bank and credits the merchant's account.

e-purse
Smart card application that loads money from a card holder's bank account onto the smart card's chip.

Many of the longest running and more successful e-purse programs were initiated in 1996 in several northern European countries (STMicroelectronics 2005). One of these was *Proton*, initiated in 1996 by Banksys in Belgium. Banksys was looking for an electronic replacement for small cash purchases at stores, vending machines, parking facilities, and so on. Today, over 9 million Proton e-purses are in use. Also in 1996, Sweden implemented a national smart card e-purse system known as *CASH*. To date, close to 8 million reloadable CASH cards have been issued. The CASH cards combine e-purse functionality with credit and debit cards. There are over 35,000 CASH payment terminals at approximately 30,000 stores. The average purchase amount made with a CASH card is around US$8. Finally, also in 1996 the Dutch banks introduced the *Chipknip* e-purse, which is combined with a debit card. In 2002, over 17 million Chipknip e-purses were in use at over 5,000 locations in the Netherlands.

There are close to 75 different e-purse systems in 40 countries around the world. For the most part, an e-purse can only be used to conduct business on the terminals within its

Common Electronic Purse Specification (CEPS)
Standards governing the operation and interoperability of e-purse offerings.

own system. In some countries, multiple systems are in operation, each running in isolation from the others. The **Common Electronic Purse Specification (CEPS)** (cepsco.com) is designed to standardize and achieve global interoperability among these varied e-purse offerings (Visa International 2004). The standard, which is built on the EMV specifications, is under the control of CEPSCO LLC, an international organization supported by Europay, Visa International, CEPSCO Espanola A.I.E., EURO Kartensysteme, Groupment des Cartes Bancaires, and Proton World. Visa Cash (international.visa.com/ps/products/vcash) is an e-purse offering based on CEPS. Visa Cash comes in disposable and reloadable forms and is used in place of small cash purchases.

Although e-purses are not widely used in the United States, the card associations are piloting a number of contactless payments systems that are aimed at retail operations where speed and convenience are crucial. Mastercard's *PayPass* (mastercard.com/aboutourcards/paypass.html) smart cards and American Express's *ExpressPay* (americanexpress.com/expresspay) key fobs fall into this category. Both of these systems utilize the existing POS and magnetic stripe payment infrastructure used with traditional credit and debit cards. The only difference is that a special contactless smart card reader is required. To make a purchase, a cardholder simply waves his or her card or key fob near the terminal and the terminal reads the financial information on the card.

One company that is experimenting with contactless payments is McDonald's (Smart Card Alliance 2004a). Currently, McDonald's accepts cashless payment options at more than half of its restaurants. In August 2004, McDonald's announced a trial program with MasterCard in Dallas and New York. During the trial, selected restaurants in these states will accept MasterCard Paypass. To support the program, McDonald's will install Verifone Omni 7000 card readers to handle the contactless payments. McDonald's is interested in making the payment process more convenient. It plans to expand the program in 2005.

Transit Fares

In major U.S. cities, commuters often have to drive to a parking lot, board a train, and then change to one or more subways or buses to arrive at work. If the whole trip requires a combination of cash and multiple types of tickets, this can be a major hassle. For those commuters who have a choice, the inconvenience plays a role in discouraging the use of public transportation. To eliminate the inconvenience, most major transit operators in the United States are implementing smart card fare-ticketing systems. The U.S. federal government also is providing incentives to employers to subsidize the use of public transportation by their employees. The transit systems in Washington, D.C., San Francisco, Los Angeles, Boston, Minneapolis, Atlanta, San Diego, Orlando, and Chicago have all either instituted smart card payment systems or are currently running pilot systems (American Public Transportation Association 2003).

Metropolitan transit operators are moving away from multiple, nonintegrated fare systems to systems that require only a single contactless card regardless of how many modes of transportation or how many transportation agencies or companies are involved. The SmartTrip program run by the Washington Metropolitan Transit Authority (WMATA) in the District of Columbia exemplifies this movement (wmata.com/riding/smartrip.cfm). WMATA was the first transportation system in the United States to employ smart cards. The program started in 1999. SmarTrip is a permanent, contactless, rechargeable farecard that can hold up to $300 in fare value. The card can be used with 17 different transit systems, including Metro-operated parking lots, the Metrorail, Metrobuses, and other regional rail services. SmarTrip handles the complexities associated with the various systems, including zone-based and time-based fares, volume discounts, and bus-to-train and bus-to-bus transfers. To date, close to a half million SmarTrip cards have been issued and well over one-third of Metrorail riders use the cards regularly.

The U.S. smart card transit programs are modeled after the transit systems in Asia. One of these, the Octopus Card in Hong Kong, is described in detail in EC Application Case 12.2. Like their Asian counterparts, some U.S. transit operators are looking to partner with retailers and financial institutions to combine their transit cards with payment cards that can be used to purchase goods and services such as snacks, bridge tolls, parking fees, or food in restaurants or grocery stores located near the transit stations.

CASE 12.2

EC Application

HONG KONG'S OCTOPUS CARD

In Hong Kong, virtually everyone uses public transportation at least once in a while, and, as a consequence, close to 95 percent of the residents in Hong Kong carry a metro card. In Hong Kong, the metro card is known as the Octopus Card, named after the company—Octopus Ltd.—that issues the cards and manages the payment system. The Octopus Card is a contactless smart card that comes in many shapes and sizes. Besides its standard smart card format, the card's chip has been embedded in jewelry, watches, and mobile phones, to name just a few items. Regardless of its form, the card works the same way. The card is passed near a scanner mounted on a subway turnstile or at the front of a bus, tram, or ferry. The scanner reads the card, deducts the fare, and displays the remaining amount on the card. The scan takes about .3 seconds, compared with 1 or 2 seconds for a contact card. Altogether, the Octopus system handles over 7 million transactions per day, worth about HK$50 million.

Octopus Cards can be purchased in a number of places. They cost HK$150, of which HK$50 is a safety deposit and the remainder is the amount that can be spent on transportation fares. When the available funds on the card are exhausted, the card can be reloaded by simply inserting the card in an add-value machine along with HK$50, HK$100, or HK$500 in cash. The amount of cash is credited to the card and then it is ready to go. Physically, the card has a life span of about 10,000 transactions.

The public transportation system in Hong Kong offers a wide variety of options, including the Mass Transit Railway (MTR) subways, the Kowloon-Canton Railroad that runs to the Chinese border, the Light Rail Transit in the New Territories, the Star Ferry, the interisland ferries, the city bus system, the electric trams on Hong Kong Island, the trains to and from the airport, as well the tram to Victoria Peak. These systems are run by a number of private or quasi-government firms. Early in 1997, the various systems decided to sign with the Octopus system. In all likelihood, if they had decided to issue their own transit cards, the smart card payment system would have failed to reach critical mass.

Today, the public transportation system in Hong Kong runs on the assumption that nearly everyone has an Octopus Card. Those riders without cards often face long lines and the constant need to have coins for fares. This is especially true on the city bus system where fares must be paid with coins in the exact amount or a higher amount. The Octopus Card eliminates all of the hassle. The only downside of the card is that riders who lose their cards are out of luck. The Octopus Card is like cash, so if someone finds a card, they can use it until its value is exhausted.

Besides paying for transit fares, the Octopus Card is starting to become an all-purpose debit card. Starbucks, Circle K, 7-Eleven convenience stores, Maxim's cake shops, a number of fast-food restaurant chains, and a range of grocers now accept the card as a form of payment. Even so, over 90 percent of all transactions made with the card are for transit fares.

Sources: Bailey (2003) and Munroe (2002).

Questions

1. How does the Octopus Card work?
2. What accounts for the success of the Octopus system?

In addition to handling transit fares, smart cards and other e-payment systems are being used for other transportation applications. For instance, the city of Philadelphia has retooled all of its 14,500 parking meters to accept payment from prepaid smart cards issued by the Philadelphia Parking Authority (philapark.org). Similarly, many of the major toll roads in the United States and elsewhere accept electronic payments rendered by devices called transponders that operate much like contactless smart cards (see Online File W9.11 for an example). Readers interested in a thorough discussion of these and other smart card transportation applications should see McQueen (2001).

E-Identification

Because they have the capability to store personal information, including pictures, biometric identifiers, digital signatures, and private security keys, smart cards are being used in a variety of identification, access control, and authentication applications. As an example, several countries are in the planning or pilot stages of launching national identification smart card programs. China began the rollout of its pilot ID program in March 2004 (CardTechnology 2004). In the pilot, citizens over the age of 16 and who live in the cities of Beijing, Itanjin, Shanghai, Shenzhen, and Changsha will be issued smart cards as national identity documents. The cards are designed to reduce the widespread forging of ID papers and will enable China's citizens to move more freely within the country. The ID cards will be the size of standard bank cards and will use contactless chips. Only Chinese vendors will be allowed to supply the cards. The overall goal is to issue ID cards to 1 billion citizens by 2008.

India is another Asian country in the midst of rolling out a pilot smart card ID program (Raja 2004). The program is being run by the Indian Census with the support of the central government. Cards will be issued to the 3 million residents in 13 districts of 13 Indian states. The cards will contain personal information, such as the person's name, date of birth, and so on, as well as the resident's picture and fingerprint. The eventual goal is to link the ID with various government databases that include information on pensions, health care, rations, land, and so on.

In Europe, Belgium was the first country to adopt a standardized (e-ID) card (Smart Card Alliance 2004b). By the end of 2009, Belgium's 10 million citizens will be required to carry an e-ID card. The cards will be valid for 5 years and will contain the citizen's date of birth, family tree, civil status, current and past addresses, and military situation. The card also will contain the holder's digital signature. Unlike the Indian national ID card, the Belgium e-ID will not contain any biometric identifiers. These probably will be added at a later date.

Because of privacy concerns, the United States is not likely to implement a national ID program anytime soon. However, many federal agencies are in the process of implementing smart card IDs for employee identification and access control (Hunt and Holcombe 2004). In 2003, the U.S. Office of Management and Budget (OMB) issued a memorandum detailing the e-government initiative on authentication and identity management. In 2004, the Federal Identity Credentialing Committee (FICC) issued policy guidance on the use of smart cards in identification and credentialing systems. Its aim was to help agencies establish and implement credentialing and identification systems for government employees and their agents.

Currently, the U.S. government is sponsoring 24 smart card projects (GAO 2004). Of these, half are large-scale projects aimed providing an entire agency's employees or some other large group with smart card identification. The Department of Defense (DOD) *Common Access Card* (CAC) program is a good example of these projects. The DOD is issuing over 4 million Java-based CACs to all military and civilian employees and contractors. Eventually, it will issue over 13 million CACs in 13 different countries. The cards will be used to gain physical access to buildings and logical access to computers and will allow employees and contractors to digitally sign and encrypt electronic transactions. On a slightly smaller scale, the Department of Homeland Security (DHS) is issuing 250,000 cards to employees and contractors. These cards will store public keys and biometric identifiers (see Section 11.6) to control physical and logical access.

Like other smart card projects, many of these federal projects are combining e-identification with other functions, such as asset management and stored value for e-payments. For instance, the Marine Corps is using the DOD CACs to track weapons issued by its armories. For a complete description of these and the other U.S. federal government smart card programs, see Hunt and Holcombe (2004) and GAO (2004).

Health Care

In general, smart cards are used to store data, identify and authenticate the cardholder, and permit or limit access to physical facilities or information sources. In health care, this translates to a variety of functional possibilities, including:

- Storing vital medical information in case of emergencies
- Preventing patients from obtaining multiple prescriptions from different physicians
- Verifying a patient's identity and insurance coverage
- Speeding up the hospital or emergency room admissions process
- Providing medical practitioners with secure access to a patient's complete medical history
- Speeding up the payment and claims process
- Enabling patients to access their medical records over the Internet

Although health-care smart cards have been promoted for their data storage capabilities (e.g., storing vital medical information), in practice they are used most often to verify entitlement for health-care services. This is their primary use, for example, in Germany and France, which have two of the largest health-care smart card programs in the world. This also is the reason why health-care smart card usage in Europe is projected to grow rather dramatically over the next few years. The European Commission has mandated that existing E111 forms, which provide access to emergency health-care services to Europeans traveling throughout the European Union, will be supplanted by smart cards starting in 2004 (HBS Consulting 2004). This has the potential of expanding the smart card market to over 220 million card holders over the next 5 years.

Another trend in health care is the use of PKI to secure access to health-care data stored on networks. In this instance, smart cards contain not only the encrypted keys that are required by health-care practitioners to access patient data, but also pointers to data that may be housed in different databases on different networks. In France, the next generation of electronic social security cards (i.e., the *Vitale* card), which are used for health-care reimbursements, are incorporating cryptographic mechanisms based on PKI. Since 2001, Vitale cards have been issued to all individuals over the age of 16 who are entitled to social security coverage (European Union 2004). Approximately 60 million cards have been issued. By 2006, these cards will be upgraded to include the enhanced security feature. By doing so, the cards will be in compliance with France's new identification, authentication, and signature standards for the fields of health and welfare.

Smart card programs for health care are starting or are underway in a number of European and Asian countries, including Austria, Belgium, Czech Republic, Finland, France, German, Italy, Korea, Malaysia, Netherlands, Norway, Romania, Slovenia, Spain, Sweden, Taiwan, and the United Kingdom (HBS Consulting 2004). In all of these countries, health care is state funded or state run. For this reason, many of the countries that have implemented or are in the process of implementing multi-application ID smart cards are considering adding health-care functions to these cards. Malaysia's ID card already contains health-care information. Romania, Thailand, and Belgium are considering adding health-care functions to their ID cards in the next few years. Because of concerns about privacy and civil liberties, people are hesitant about having their personal health data mixed with other data on the same card. Most people would rather carry separate cards despite the fact that smart card operating systems can ensure the secure separation of one application from another. This is why Italy is considering launching a separate health-care card, even though it originally planned to put health-care functions on its new e-ID cards.

SECURING SMART CARDS

Smart cards store or provide access to either valuable assets (e.g., e-cash) or to sensitive information (e.g., medical records). Because of this, they must be secured against theft, fraud, or misuse. In general, smart cards are more secure than conventional payment cards. If someone steals a payment card, the number on the card is clearly visible, as is the owner's signature. Although it may be hard to forge the signature, in many situations only the number is required to make a purchase. The only protection cardholders have is that there usually are limits on how much they will be held liable for (e.g., in the United States it is $50). If someone steals a stored-value card (or the owner loses it), the original owner is out of luck.

On the other hand, if someone steals a smart card, the thief is out of luck. Some smart cards show account numbers, but others do not. Before the card can be used, the holder may be required to enter a PIN that is matched with the card. Theoretically, it is possible to "hack" into a smart card. Most cards, however, now store information in encrypted form. The smart cards can also encrypt and decrypt data that is downloaded or read from the card. Because of these factors, the possibility of hacking into a smart card is classified as a "class 3" attack, which means that the cost of compromising the card far exceeds the benefits.

Section 12.3 ▶ REVIEW QUESTIONS

1. What is a smart card? Contact card? Contactless card?
2. What is a smart card operating system?
3. What is an e-purse?
4. Describe the use of smart cards in metropolitan transportation systems.

5. Describe the smart card ID programs in China and India.
6. What is the U.S. Department of Defense CAC program?
7. What are some of the potential uses of smart cards in health care?

12.4 STORED-VALUE CARDS

stored-value card
A card that has monetary value loaded onto it and that is usually rechargeable.

What looks like a credit or debit card, acts like a credit or debit card, but isn't a credit or debit card? The answer is a **stored-value card**. As the name implies, the monetary value of a stored-value card is preloaded on the card. From a physical and technical standpoint, a stored-value card is indistinguishable from a regular credit or debit card. It is plastic and has a magnetic stripe on the back, although it may not have the cardholder's name printed on it. The monetary value of the card is stored in the magnetic stripe. This distinguishes a stored-value card from a smart card. With smart cards, the value is stored on a chip. Stored-value cards can also be used to make purchases, off-line or online, in the same way that credit and debit cards are used—relying on the same networks, encrypted communications, and electronic banking protocols. What is different about a stored-value card is that anyone can obtain one without regard to prior financial standing or having an existing bank account as collateral.

Stored-value cards come in two varieties: *closed loop* and *open loop*. Closed-loop, or single-purpose, cards are issued by a specific merchant or merchant group (e.g., a shopping mall) and can only be used to make purchases from that merchant or merchant group. Mall cards, store cards, gift cards, and prepaid telephone cards are all examples of closed-loop cards. Gift cards represent a strong growth area, especially in the United States. According to an annual survey conducted by Stored Value Systems (Ceridian 2004), over 75 percent of the population over 15 years of age said they purchased gift cards in 2004. This was a 7 percent increase from the previous year. In the 2004 survey, there also was a significant increase in the percentage of gift card users who purchased the cards for themselves in order to avoid carrying cash. In 2003, only 2 percent of the respondents used the cards for personal cash. In 2004, this figure was over 20 percent, with many gift card holders using the cards to purchase cheaper gas at large discounters.

In contrast, an open-loop, or multipurpose, card can be used to make debit transactions at a variety of retailers. Open-loop cards also can be used for other purposes, such as receiving direct deposits or withdrawing cash from ATM machines. Some open-loop cards are issued by financial institutions with card association branding, such as Visa or MasterCard. They can be used anywhere that the branded cards are accepted. Payroll cards, government benefit cards, and prepaid debit cards are all examples of open-loop cards.

Stored-value cards may be acquired in a variety of ways. Employers or government agencies may issue them as payroll cards or benefit cards in lieu of checks or direct deposits. Gift cards are purchased from and loaded by the merchant or merchant group. Prepaid debit cards can be purchased by telephone, online, or in person at various financial institutions and increasingly at nonfinancial outlets. Prepaid debit cards may be funded by cash, bank wire transfers, money orders, cashiers' checks, other credit cards, or by direct payroll or government deposits.

The stored-value card market is growing rapidly. Market analysts estimate that there are over 2,000 stored value programs with over 7 million branded cards in use today (Su and Rhine 2004). By 2006, stored-value transactions are expected to exceed $70 billion. By 2008, the number of users is expected to be around 50 million, more than doubling the current figure.

Stored-value cards are being marketed heavily to the "unbanked" and "overextended." Approximately 50 million adults in the United States do not have credit cards, and 20 million do not have bank accounts—people with low incomes, young adults, seniors, immigrants, minorities, and others (Milligan 2004). Among those with credit cards, 40 percent are running close to their credit limits. The expectation is that these groups will be major users of prepaid cards in the future. For example, individuals in the United States transferred over $12 billion to individuals in Mexico. Instead of sending money orders or cash, programs like the EasySend card from Branch Banking and Trust are being targeted to the Hispanic community as a secure alternative to transferring money to relatives and friends (BB&T 2004).

With the EasySend program, an individual establishes a banking account, deposits money in the account, and mails the EasySend card to a relative or friend, who can then withdraw the cash from an ATM machine. In a slightly different vein, Online File W12.3 describes the Splash Card, a stored-value card aimed at teenagers in the United Kingdom. The Citi Cash card and Visa Buxx program, which are described in detail in EC Application Case 12.3, are aimed at providing younger populations with a prepaid debit card alternative to credit cards or cash. Among other things, these latter alternatives provide a relatively risk-free way to teach kids fiscal responsibility. The growth in the prepaid debit card market also is being driven by employers who are using payroll cards as an extension of their direct deposit programs. Like direct deposit, payroll cards can reduce administrative overhead substantially. Payroll cards are especially useful to companies in the health-care, retail, and other industries where the workforce is part time or transient and less likely to have bank accounts.

Section 12.4 ▶ REVIEW QUESTIONS

1. What is a closed-loop stored-value card? What is an open-loop card?
2. What are the major markets for stored-value cards?

CASE 12.3

EC Application

STORED-VALUE CARDS: TAPPING THE TEEN MARKET

What do the Citi Cash Card, the Wired MasterCard, and Visa Buxx (pronounced "bucks") have in common? They are all prepaid reloadable cards. Money can be loaded onto them virtually anytime, anywhere from a credit card, debit card, or savings or checking account. These prepaid cards look like a regular plastic credit card, but the cardholder has no line of credit. Instead, the cardholder can only spend up to the amount loaded on the card.

Some of the cards are set up by parents to provide funds for their children. The Citi Cash Card is designed for students between 13 and 16 years of age. This is the same market addressed by the Visa Buxx card, although its upper limit is 18 years of age. At age 18, an individual can apply for his or her own credit card. In each of these instances, the student's name is printed on the card, and the card can be used at most locations that accept credit cards. Citi Cash can be used at any of the more than 20 million MasterCard merchants; Visa Buxx can be used at more than 20 million worldwide locations where Visa is accepted. Both can be used at ATMs around the world. One advantage of these cards over cash is that lost or stolen cards can be replaced. Visa Buxx, for instance, is protected by Visa's Zero Liability Policy.

The Visa Buxx program was started in the fall of 1999 by WildCard Systems. WildCard created the system in order to tap into the teen market. In the United States, there are more than 30 million teens between 13 and 18 years of age, and they spend more than $160 billion annually. Most of their spending involves cash provided by their parents. WildCard was looking for a way to provide a turnkey payment system that would meet the needs of both parents and teens by offering a card that would provide:

- A parent-controlled reloadable payment card that would be accepted anywhere that Visa was accepted, including online and ATM cash machines.
- Stored-value functionality, so that teens can only spend up to the amount established by their parents and loaded onto the card.
- A Web site where parents and teens could enroll for the card; add value through checking accounts, savings accounts, credit cards, or debit cards; set up recurring allowance schedules; shop online; and check balances and transaction history.
- Parental-control features so parents could maintain control over the account through the Web site.
- An educational component on the Web site so that teens could learn about financial responsibility and budgeting.

WildCard licensed the Visa Buxx product to Visa. The system was launched in 2000 by five Visa card issuers, including Bank of America, Capital One, National City, U.S. Bank, and Wachovia Bank. Today, the card is offered by a wide range of banks throughout the United States. For issuing banks, the card helps build stronger relationships with existing customers (parents) and establish relationships with new customers (the teens).

Source: Adapted from WildCard Systems. "Visa Buxx: Case Study." 2004. *corporate.wildcardsystems.com/index.cfm? pageid=p09* (accessed December 2004).

Questions

1. What is the market for the Citi Cash card and Visa Buxx?
2. How does Visa Buxx work?
3. What key characteristics underlie WildCard's Visa Buxx system?

12.5 E-MICROPAYMENTS

Consider the following online shopping scenarios:

- A customer goes to an online music store and purchases a single CD that costs $8.95.
- A person goes online to a leading newspaper or news journal (such as *Forbes* or *Business Week*) and purchases (downloads) a copy of an archived news article for $1.50.
- A person goes to an online gaming company, selects a game, and plays it for 30 minutes. The person owes the company $3 for the playing time.
- A person goes to a Web site selling digital images and clip art. The person purchases a couple of images at a cost of $0.80.

e-micropayments
Small online payments, typically under US$10.

These are all examples of **e-micropayments**, which are small online payments, usually under US$10. As noted before, credit cards do not work well for such small payments. Vendors who accept credit cards typically must pay a minimum transaction fee that ranges from 25 cents to 35 cents, plus 2 to 3 percent of the purchase price. These fees are relatively insignificant for credit card purchases above $10, but are cost-prohibitive for smaller transactions. Even if the transaction costs were less onerous, a substantial percentage of micropayment purchases are made by individuals under 18 years of age, many of whom do not have credit or debit cards.

The history of e-micropayments is one of unfulfilled promises and collapsed companies. Digicash, First Virtual, Cybercoin, Millicent, and Internet Dollar are some of the micropayment companies that went under during the dot-com crash. A number of factors played a role in their demise, including the fact that early users of the Internet thought that digital content should be free.

Today, there is some evidence that users are more willing to pay for content, music services, and applications for mobile devices such as ring tones and games (Peppercoin 2004). Market analysts point to the success of Apple's iTunes music store, which has sold about 70 million songs at 99 cents each during its first year of operation and 250 million songs by January 2005 (Cohen 2005). Forrester Research, a Massachusetts market research firm, has predicted that music downloads will reach $3.2 billion by 2008 (LeClaire 2004). The Online Publishers Association estimates that U.S. consumers spent $850 million in online content in the first half of 2004 (Online Publishers 2004). Similarly, Jupiter Research estimates that revenue from online content will reach $3.1 billion by 2009 (Marketing VOX News 2004).

In response to these market estimates, a number of companies have developed e-micropayment products. Although each enables online purchases under $10, they do it in different ways:

- **BitPass.** To use BitPass (bitpass.com), a consumer first establishes a "buyers account" and adds money to the account via PayPal or a credit card, much like one would do with a prepaid or stored-value card. For merchants or providers, BitPass can be hosted or implemented by adding BitPass gateway software to EC sites. When buyers click BitPass-enabled content, they are prompted by the BitPass software for their password. Once the buyer has been authenticated and approved, the buyer's BitPass account is debited, and the merchant is paid either by PayPal or by electronic funds transfer. BitPass has about 1,000 merchants or providers in the program.
- **Paystone.** With Paystone (paystone.com), buyers establish prepaid accounts using their bank's bill payment service or by depositing cash into any Bank of America account. Merchants or providers implement Paystone by adding special links to Paystone's e-micropayment system. When buyers click a Paystone link, they are taken to Paystone's system where they enter their password. Their accounts are debited, and they are redirected back to the content they have purchased.
- **PayLoadz.** PayLoadz (payloadz.com) works in conjunction with PayPal. Buyers actually purchase content through PayPal. In order to use PayLoadz, merchants or providers need to establish accounts at both PayPal and PayLoadz and add special PayLoadz links to their EC checkout pages. When a purchase is made, the PayLoadz site works behind the scenes with the PayPal site to complete the transaction and to notify the buyer by e-mail where they can obtain the content they have purchased.

- **Peppercoin.** With Peppercoin (peppercoin.com), there are no prepayments. Users enter their credit cards or debit card information just as they would with any other purchase. To avoid the transactions costs associated with credit and debit card purchases, the Peppercoin software works in the background, aggregating the purchases of multiple buyers and merchants into a few large transactions. In this way, the costs associated with individual transactions are avoided.

Although the market for e-micropayments may appear to be primed, all of these companies face an uphill battle. Apple has managed to sell millions of songs on iTunes using traditional payment methods, even though the songs are only 99 cents a piece. Not only are these micropayment sites struggling to gain a critical mass of buyers, they also are struggling to sign up content providers who are scattered all over the Internet and largely unaware of their offerings.

Section 12.5 ▶ REVIEW QUESTIONS

1. List some of the situations where e-micropayments can be used.
2. Describe how e-micropayment systems, such as BitPass, generally work.

12.6 E-CHECKING

As noted in Section 12.1, in the United States paper checks are the only payment instrument that is being used less frequently now than 3 years ago (Federal Reserve System 2004). In 2003, checks represented 45 percent of all noncash payments, down from 57 percent in 2000. In contrast, e-check usage is growing rapidly. In 2003, the use of online e-checks grew by 210 percent, reaching 500 million transactions. Based on a CyberSource (2004) survey of Web merchants, this percentage should continue to grow. Currently, 27 percent of Web merchants surveyed offer e-check payment. In 2005, 31 percent more Web merchants plan to offer this mode of payment, raising the total to 58 percent. Web merchants hope that e-checks will raise sales by reaching consumers who do not have credit cards or who are unwilling to provide credit card numbers online.

An **e-check** is the electronic version or representation of a paper check. E-checks contain the same information as a paper check, can be used wherever paper checks are used, and are based on the same legal framework. E-checks work essentially the same way a paper check works, but in pure electronic form, with fewer manual steps. With an online e-check purchase, the buyer simply provides the merchant with his or her account number, the nine-digit bank ABA routing number, the bank account type, the name on the bank account, and the transaction amount. The account number and routing number are found at the bottom of the check in the *magnetic ink character recognition (MICR)* numbers and characters.

e-check
A legally valid electronic version or representation of a paper check.

E-checks rely on current business and banking practices and can be used by any business that has a checking account, including small and midsize business that may not able to afford other forms of electronic payments (e.g., credit and debit cards). E-checks or their equivalents also can be used with in-person purchases. In this case, the merchant takes a paper check from the buyer at the point of purchase, uses the MICR information and the check number to complete the transaction, and then voids and returns the check to the buyer.

Most businesses rely on third-party software to handle e-check payments. CheckFree, Telecheck, AmeriNet, Paymentech, and Authorize.Net are some of the major vendors of software and systems that enable an online merchant to accept and process electronic checks directly from a Web site. For the most part, these software offerings work in the same way regardless of the vendor.

The system shown in Exhibit 12.3 is based on Authorize.Net and is typical of the underlying processes used to support e-checks. Basically, it is a seven-step process. First, the merchant receives written or electronic authorization from a customer to charge his or her bank account (step 1). Next, the merchant securely transmits the transaction information to the Authorize.Net Payment Gateway server (step 2). The transaction is accepted or rejected based on criteria defined by the Payment Gateway. If accepted, Authorize.Net formats the transaction information and sends it as an Automated Clearing House (ACH) transaction to its bank (called the Originating Depository Financial Institution, or ODFI) with the rest of the transactions received that day (step 3). The ODFI receives transaction information and passes it to the ACH Network for settlement. The ACH Network uses the bank account information provided with the transaction to determine the bank that holds the customer's account (which is known as the Receiving Depository Financial Institution, or RDFI) (step 4). The ACH Network instructs the RDFI to charge or refund the customer's account (the customer is the receiver). The RDFI passes funds from the customer's account to the ACH Network (step 5). The ACH Network relays the funds to the ODFI (Authorize.Net's bank). The ODIF passes any returns to Authorize.Net (step 6). After the funds holding period, Authorize.Net initiates a separate ACH transaction to deposit the e-check proceeds into the merchant's bank account (step 7).

Automated Clearing House (ACH) Network A nationwide batch-oriented electronic funds transfer system that provides for the interbank clearing of electronic payments for participating financial institutions.

As Exhibit 12.3 illustrates, the processing of e-checks in the United States relies quite heavily on the **Automated Clearing House (ACH) Network** (Automated Clearing House 2004). The ACH Network is a nationwide batch-oriented electronic funds transfer system that provides for the interbank clearing of electronic payments for participating financial institutions. The Federal Reserve and Electronic Payments Network act as ACH Operators, which transmit and receive ACH payment entries. ACH entries are of two sorts: credit and debit. An ACH credit entry credits a receiver's account. For example, when a consumer pays a bill sent by a company, the company is the receiver whose account is credited. On the other hand, a debit entry debits a receiver's account. For instance, if a consumer pre-authorizes a payment to a company, then the consumer is the receiver whose account is debited. In 2003, the ACH Network handled approximately 7 billion transactions worth US$21 billion (ACH 2004). The vast majority of these (close to 5 billion) were direct payment and deposit entries (e.g., direct deposit payroll). Only 500,000 of these entries were Web-based, although this represented a 200 percent increase from 2002 to 2003.

E-check processing provides a number of benefits (Electronic Check Clearing House Organization 2002):

- It reduces the merchant's administrative costs by providing faster and less paper-intensive collection of funds.
- It improves the efficiency of the deposit process for merchants and financial institutions.
- It speeds the checkout process for consumers.
- It provides consumers with more information about their purchases on their account statements.
- It reduces the float period and the number of checks that bounce because of insufficient funds (NSFs).

EXHIBIT 12.3 Processing E-Checks with Authorize.Net

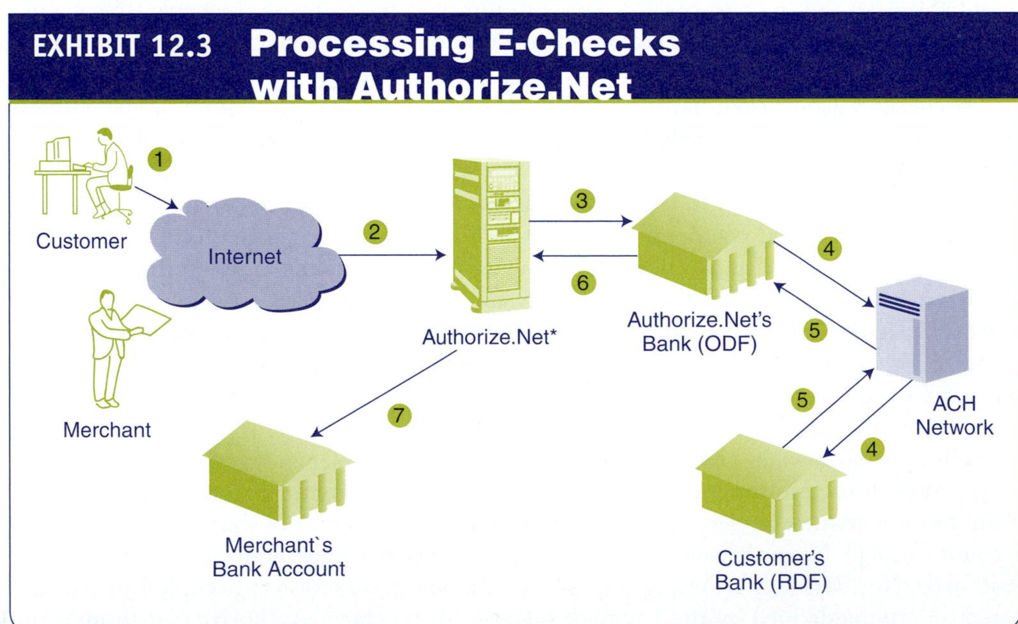

Source: Authorize.Net®. "eCheck.Net® Operating Procedures and Users Guide," October 28, 2004. *Authorize.net/files/echecknetuserguide.pdf*. Copyright 2004. Authorize.Net and eCheck.Net are registered trademarks of Lightbridge, Inc.

Section 12.6 ▶ REVIEW QUESTIONS

1. What is an e-check?
2. Briefly describe how third-party e-check payment systems work.
3. What is the ACH?
4. List the benefits of e-checking.

12.7 ELECTRONIC BILL PRESENTMENT AND PAYMENT

One area where e-checks and the ACH play a prominent role is in the area of e-billing; that is, paying recurring bills via the Internet. E-billing also is known as **electronic bill presentment and payment (EBPP)**. *Presentment* involves taking the information that is typically printed on a bill and hosting it on a bill-presentment Web server. (See Exhibit 12.4 for an example.) Once the bill is available on the Web server, a customer can access the bill with a browser, review it, and pay it electronically. After the payment is received, it must be posted against the biller's accounts receivable system. Payments generally are transferred from the customer's checking account through ACH. In e-billing, the customers may be individuals or companies.

electronic bill presentment and payment (EBPP)
Presenting and enabling payment of a bill online. Usually refers to a B2C transaction.

Although the vast majority of consumers still pay their bills the traditional way, by sending a paper check through the mail, e-billing is making some inroads. According to Jupiter Research, an Internet market analysis firm, 18.9 million households paids bills online in 2003, up from 12.2 million in 2002 (Festa 2003). They project the figure to be over 60 million by 2008. Similarly, the National Clearing House Association (NACHA) estimates that EBPP is growing 30 percent a year, and 500 million bills were paid online in 2003 (Leon 2003).

EXHIBIT 12.4 E-Bill Presentment

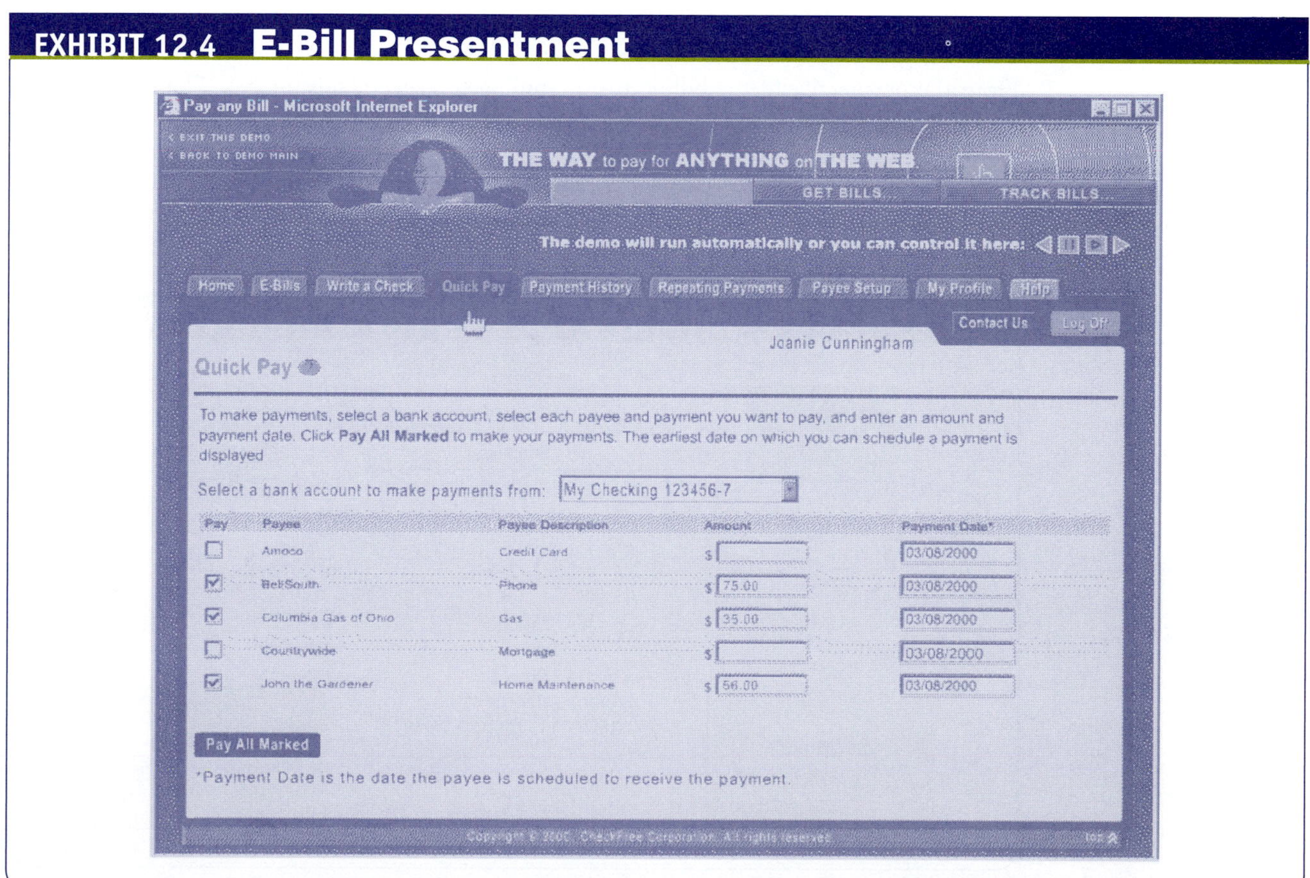

Source: Courtesy of CheckFree Corporation.

TYPES OF E-BILLING

There are three ways to pay bills over the Internet:

- **Online banking.** The consumer signs up for a bank's online bill-pay service and makes all of his or her payments from a single Web site. Some banks offer the service for free with a checking account; others offer it if the account holder maintains a minimum balance. Others charge a monthly fee of $5 to $7.
- **Biller direct.** The consumer makes payments at each biller's Web site either with a credit card or by giving the biller enough information to complete an electronic withdrawal directly from the consumer's account. Exhibit 12.5 shows the general steps in the EBPP process of a single biller. The biller makes the billing information available to the customer (presentment) on its Web site or the site of a billing hosting service (step 1). Once the customer views the bill (step 2), he or she authorizes and initiates payment at the site (step 3). The payment can be made with a credit/debit card or an ACH debit. The biller then initiates a payment transaction (step 4) that moves funds through the payment system (payment), crediting the biller and debiting the customer (step 5).
- **Bill consolidator.** Exhibit 12.6 shows the steps in the process used by bill consolidators. The customer enrolls to receive and pay bills for multiple billers (service initiation). The customer's enrollment information is forwarded to every biller that the customer wishes to activate (service initiation). For each billing cycle, the biller sends a bill summary or bill detail to the consolidator (presentment). The bill summary, which links to the bill detail stored with the biller or consolidator, is forwarded to the aggregator and made available to the customer (presentment). The customer views the bill and initiates payment instructions (payment). The customer service provider (CSP) or aggregator initiates a credit payment transaction that moves funds through the payment system to the biller (payment). Remittance data are provided to the biller, who posts this information to its own accounts receivable system (posting).

ADVANTAGES OF E-BILLING

From the perspective of the billing firm, e-billing has several advantages. The most obvious benefit is the reduction in expenses related to billing and processing payments. The estimate is that paper bills cost between $0.75 and $2.70 per bill. E-billing costs between $0.25 and $0.30 per bill. One industry source has quoted an average cost savings of $1.00 to $5.00 per e-bill (ebilling.org 2003). E-billing also enables better customer service. Not only can cus-

EXHIBIT 12.5 E-Billing Process for Single Biller

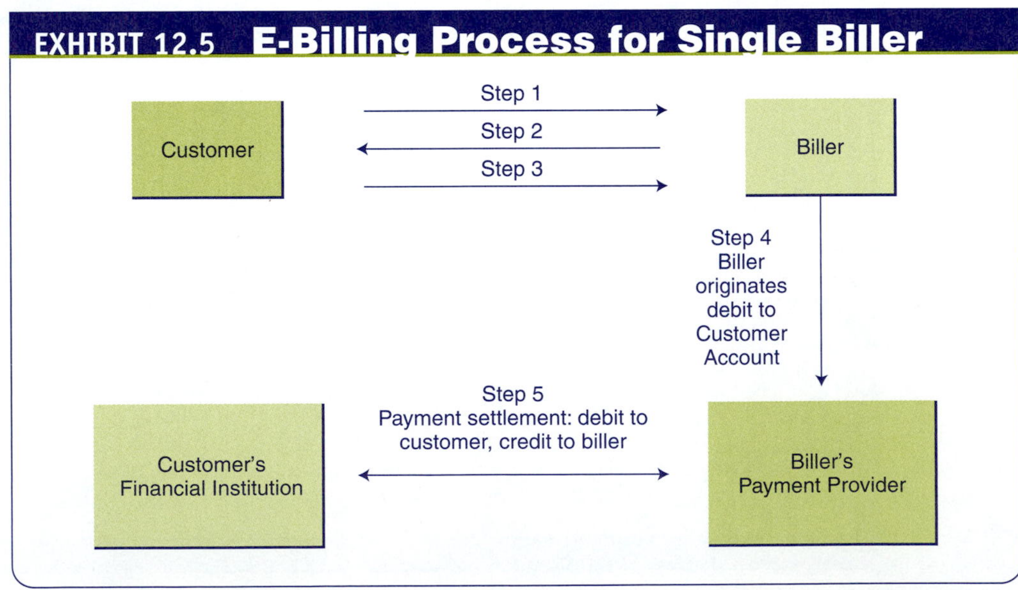

Source: ebilling.org. Courtesy of NACHA—The Electronic Payments Association, Council for Electronic Billing and Payment.

EXHIBIT 12.6 E-Billing Processes for Bill Consolidator

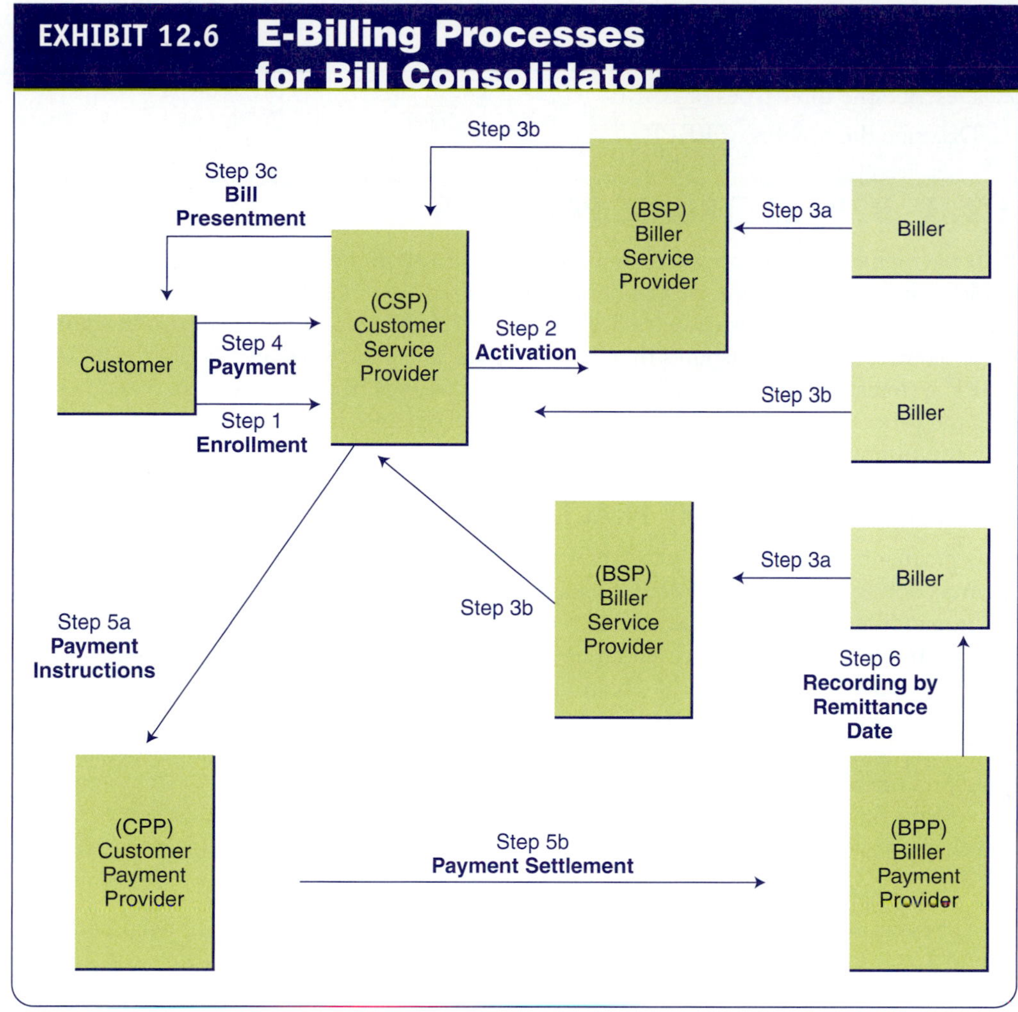

Source: ebilling.org. Courtesy of NACHA—The Electronic Payments Association, Council for Electronic Billing and Payment.

tomer service representatives see the same presentment that the customer is seeing, but the presentment also can provide access to frequently asked questions and help boxes.

Another advantage relates to advertising. A paper bill can include advertising and marketing inserts. Usually, every customer gets the same ads or materials. With e-billing, electronic inserts can be customized to the individual customer. If a customer responds to the insert, then it is much easier to trace which ads or materials are successful.

There also are advantages from the customer's perspective. E-billing reduces the customer's expenses by eliminating the cost of checks, postage, and envelopes. E-billing simplifies and centralizes payment processing and facilitates better record keeping. Customers can review and pay bills at virtually any time. In this way, the customer has direct control over the timing of the payment.

By far, CheckFree (checkfree.com) is the leading third-party e-billing vendor. CheckFree was founded in 1981 and is currently headquartered in Atlanta, Georgia. CheckFree is a consolidator, aggregating all of a customer's bills into a single presentment. It can also set up payments with companies that do not offer electronic billing. CheckFree serves about 6 million consumers in over 1,000 businesses and over 350 financial institutions (including most U.S. banks). In addition to these services, CheckFree also provides portfolio management, reconciliation products and services, check conversion, e-billing and payment and e-statement delivery, consumer e-commerce, and for years has been a leading processor of ACH payments. Today, more than two-thirds of the nation's ACH payments are processed by CheckFree. CheckFree alerts users if there is a problem with any of the payments. Users can export the transaction records to Quicken or Microsoft Money. See checkfree.com for a demo.

Section 12.7 ▸ REVIEW QUESTIONS

1. What is electronic bill presentment and payment (EBPP)?
2. Describe the three types of EBPP.
3. Describe the benefits of EBPP.

12.8 B2B ELECTRONIC PAYMENTS

B2B payments usually are much larger and significantly more complex than the payments made by individual consumers. The dollar values often are in the hundreds of thousands, the purchases and payments involve multiple items and shipments, and the exchanges are much more likely to engender disputes that require significant work to resolve. Simple e-billing or EBPP systems lack the rigor and security to handle these B2B situations. This section examines the processes by which companies present invoices and make payments to one another over the Internet.

CURRENT B2B PAYMENT PRACTICES

B2B payments are part of a much larger financial supply chain that includes procurement, contract administration, fulfillment, financing, insurance, credit ratings, shipment validation, order matching, payment authorization, remittance matching, and general ledger accounting. From a buyer's perspective, the chain encompasses the procurement-to-payment process. From the seller's perspective, the chain involves the order-to-cash cycle. Regardless of the perspective, in financial supply chain management the goal is to optimize accounts payable (A/P) and receivable (A/R), cash management, working capital, transaction costs, financial risks, and financial administration.

Unlike the larger (physical) supply chain, the financial supply chains of most companies are still characterized by inefficiencies created by a number of factors, including (Barnhart 2004):

- The time required to create, transfer, and process paper documentation
- The cost and errors associated with manual creation and reconciliation of documentation
- The lack of transparency in inventory and cash positions when goods are in the supply chain
- Disputes arising from inaccurate or missing data
- Fragmented point solutions that do not address the complete end-to-end processes of the trade cycle

These inefficiencies especially are evident with A/P and A/R processes where payments are still made with paper.

Based on a recent survey of 304 members of the Association for Financial Professionals (2004), little has changed in the world of B2B payments since the Association last conducted the survey 4 years ago in 2000. The vast majority of B2B payments are still made by check, and the barriers to electronic payments remain essentially the same. The major change is that more organizations indicated a willingness to migrate from checks to electronic payments in the future. Some of the findings of the survey are as follows:

- **Current payment practices.** Fifty-one percent of those surveyed indicated that more than 80 percent of their disbursements are made by check, whereas only 43 percent indicated that they receive more than 80 percent of their collections by check. Those companies with revenues over $1 billion make and receive significantly fewer payments by check.
- **Electronic payments.** Electronic payments are used more widely for disbursements and collections when the businesses are major suppliers or customers. However, regardless of the trading relationship between the businesses, ACH credits are the most widely used form of electronic payment, followed by wire transfers. Purchasing cards and ACH debits are used rarely.
- **Role of EDI.** There has been virtually no change in the use of EDI to send or receive remittance information associated with an electronic payment. Approximately 25 percent of the organizations use EDI to send information, and 35 percent receive informa-

tion in this format. Most remittance information is sent and received through banks and comes in the form of faxes or mail.

- **Integration of electronic payment and accounting systems.** Forty-five percent of the organizations have integrated their electronic payment systems with either their A/P systems, A/R systems, or both. In most cases, the integration has been achieved through ERP systems or via proprietary software. Those companies that have integrated their systems have done so to achieve internal operating efficiencies or to reduce costs and staff.
- **Barriers to electronic payment.** Most companies can site a long list of barriers inhibiting the move to electronic payments. The four major barriers include: a shortage of IT staff, a lack of integration of payment and accounting systems, a lack of a standard format for remittance information, and the inability of trading partners to send or receive electronic payments with sufficient remittance information.
- **Prospects for electronic payments.** Twenty-eight percent indicated that their organizations plan to convert the majority of their B2B payments from check to electronic payments over the next 3 years. In support of this move, a number of companies are planning to centralize their payment controls, use purchasing cards for capital goods and higher value items, integrate their payment and accounting systems, and image the checks they send and receive to banks for clearance and settlement.

ENTERPRISE INVOICE PRESENTMENT AND PAYMENT

The process by which companies present invoices and make payments to one another through the Internet is known as **enterprise invoice presentment and payment (EIPP)**. For many firms, presentment and payment are costly and time consuming. It can cost up to $15 to generate a paper invoice and between $25 and $50 to resolve a disputed invoice. On the payment side, it takes 3 to 5 days for a check to arrive by mail. This means that millions of dollars of B2B payments are tied up in floats. This reduces the recipients' cash flow and increases the amount they must borrow to cover the float. In the same vein, manual billing and remittance can result in errors, which in turn can result in disputes that hold up payments. Given that most firms handle thousands of invoices and payments yearly, any reduction in time, cost, or errors can result in millions of dollars of savings. According to a recent survey by Credit Research Foundation, the major reasons companies turn to EIPP solutions are improved cash flow, customer service for billing and remittance, and improved data that can be used to lower invoice processing costs (Lucas 2005).

enterprise invoice presentment and payment (EIPP)
Presenting and paying B2B invoices online.

EIPP Models

EIPP automates the workflow surrounding presentment and payment. Like EBPP, there are three EIPP models: seller direct, buyer direct, and consolidator (Council for Electronic Payment and Payment 2001).

Seller Direct. This solution links one seller to many buyers for invoice presentment. Buyers navigate to the seller's Web site to enroll in the seller's EIPP program. The seller generates invoices on the system and informs the appropriate buyers that they are ready for viewing. The buyers log into the seller's Web site to review and analyze the invoices. The buyers may authorize invoice payment or communicate any disputes. Based on predetermined rules, disputes may be accepted, rejected, or reviewed automatically. Once payment is authorized and made, the seller's financial institution processes the payment transaction.

This model typically is used when there are preestablished relationships between the seller and its buyers. If a seller issues a large number of invoices or the invoices have a high value, then there can be a substantial payoff from implementing an EIPP. For this reason, this model often is used by firms in the manufacturing, telecommunication, utilities, health care, and financial services industries.

Buyer Direct. In this model, there is one buyer for many sellers. Sellers enroll in the buyer's EIPP system at the buyer's Web site. Sellers post invoices to the buyer's EIPP, using the buyer's format. Once an invoice is posted, the buyer's staff will be notified. The buyer reviews and analyzes the invoices on the system. The buyer communicates any disputes to the appropriate seller. Based on predetermined rules, disputes may be accepted, rejected, or reviewed automatically. Once an invoice is approved, the buyer will authorize payment, which will be processed by the buyer's financial institution.

This is an emerging model that is based on the buyer's dominant position in B2B transactions. Again, it is used when the buyer's purchases result in a high volume of invoices. Companies such as Wal-Mart are in a strong position to institute buyer-direct EIPPs.

Consolidator. This is a many-to-many model with the consolidator acting as an intermediary, collecting or aggregating invoices from multiple sellers and payments from multiple buyers. Consolidators are generally third parties who not only provide EIPP services, but also offer other financial services (e.g., insurance, escrow). In this model, the sellers and buyers register with the consolidator's EIPP system. The sellers generate and transfer invoice information to the EIPP system. The consolidator notifies the appropriate buyer organization that the invoice is ready. The buyer reviews and analyzes the invoice. Disputes are communicated through the consolidator EIPP. Based on predetermined rules, disputes may be accepted, rejected, or reviewed automatically. Once the buyer has authorized the invoice payment, the consolidator initiates the payment. The payment can be processed by either the buyer's or the seller's financial institution.

The consolidator model eliminates the hassles associated with implementing and running an EIPP. The model has gained ground in those industries where multiple buyers rely on the same suppliers. The Xign Payment Services Network (XPSN; xign.com), the Global eXchange Services (GXS), TradeGrid (gxs.com), and Perfect Commerce's Open Supplier Networks (OSN; perfect.com) are all third-party consolidators linking thousands of suppliers and buyers. XPSN had more than 10,000 active suppliers in its network, generating over $20 billion in transactions. GSX's Trading Grid supports online trading among 30,000 customers in over 60 countries, exchanging 1 billion electronic transactions representing $1 trillion in goods and services. Perfect Commerce's OSN connects over 8,000 suppliers. Each of these networks eliminates the need for point-to-point connections between suppliers and buyers; automates core functions of the A/P process, including invoice receipt, validation, routing, dispute management, approval, and payment; and complements and integrates with the suppliers' and buyers' existing purchasing and procurement systems.

EIPP Options

A variety of online options are available for making payments in an EIPP system. They differ in terms of cost, speed, auditability, accessibility, and control. The selection of a particular mechanism depends on the requirements of the buyers and sellers. Some frequently used B2B payment options follow (Council for Electronic Payment and Payment 2002).

ACH Network. The ACH Network is the same network that underlies the processing of e-checks (described in Section 12.6). The difference is that B2B payments are restricted to three types, which vary by the amount of remittance information that accompanies the payments. The remittance information enables a buyer or seller to examine the details of a particular invoice or payment. The three types of ACH entries for B2B transactions are: Cash Concentration or Disbursement (CCD), which is a simple payment, usually for a single invoice, that has no accompanying remittance data and is typically initiated by the buyer who credits the seller's account; Cash Concentration or Disbursement with Addenda (CCD+), which is the same as a CCD payment except that it has a small amount of remittance data (up to 80 characters); and Corporate Trade Exchange (CTX), which generally is used to pay multiple invoices and has a large amount of accompanying remittance data (up to a maximum of 9,999 records of 80 characters each).

No special hardware is required to utilize the ACH Network. The cost of the software needed to initiate ACH transactions depends on the volume of CTX transactions. High volumes of CTX transactions require a much larger investment. In addition to hardware and software costs, the buyer's and the seller's financial institutions also charge file, maintenance, transaction, and exception handling fees for ACH transactions.

Purchasing Cards. Although credit cards are the instrument of choice for B2C payments, this is not the case in the B2B marketplace. In the B2B marketplace, the major credit card companies and associations have encouraged businesses and government agencies to rely on *purchasing cards* instead of checks for repetitive, low-value transactions.

Purchasing cards (p-cards) are special-purpose payment cards issued to a company's employees. They are to be used solely for the purpose of paying for nonstrategic materials and services (e.g., stationery, office supplies, computer supplies, repair and maintenance services, courier services, and temporary labor services) up to a limit (usually $1,000 to $2,000). These purchases often represent the majority of a company's payments but only a small percentage of the dollars spent. Purchasing cards operate essentially the same as any other charge card and are used for both off-line and online purchases. The major difference between a credit card and a purchase card is that the latter is a nonrevolving account, meaning that it needs to be paid in full each month, usually within 5 days of the end of the billing period. Exhibit 12.7 shows how a purchasing card is used.

purchasing cards (p-cards)
Special-purpose payment cards issued to a company's employees to be used solely for purchasing nonstrategic materials and services up to a preset dollar limit.

Purchasing cards enable a company or government agency to consolidate the purchases of multiple cardholders into a single account and thus issue a single invoice that can be paid through EDI, EFT, or an e-check. This has the benefit of freeing the purchasing department from day-to-day procurement activities and from the need to deal with the reconciliation of individual invoices. With a single invoice, accounts can be settled more quickly, enabling a company or agency to take advantage of discounts associated with faster payment. A single invoice also enables a company or agency to more easily analyze the spending behavior of the cardholders. Finally, the spending limits make it easier to control unplanned purchases. Some estimates suggest that efficiencies resulting from the use of purchasing cards can reduce transaction costs from 50 percent to 90 percent. To learn more about purchasing cards, see the National Association of Purchasing Card Professionals (napcp.org).

Fedwire or Wire Transfer. Among the forms of online B2B payments, Fedwire is second only to ACH in terms of frequency of use. Fedwire, also known as wire transfer, is a funds transfer system developed and maintained by the U.S. Federal Reserve system. It typically is used with larger dollar payments where time is the critical element. The settlement of real estate transactions, the purchase of securities, and the repayment of loans are all examples of situations where Fedwire is likely to be used. When Fedwire is used, a designated Federal Reserve Bank debits the buyer's bank account and sends a transfer order to the seller's Federal Reserve Bank, which credits the sellers account. All Fedwire payments are immediate and irrevocable.

EXHIBIT 12.7 Clareon Online Transaction Service

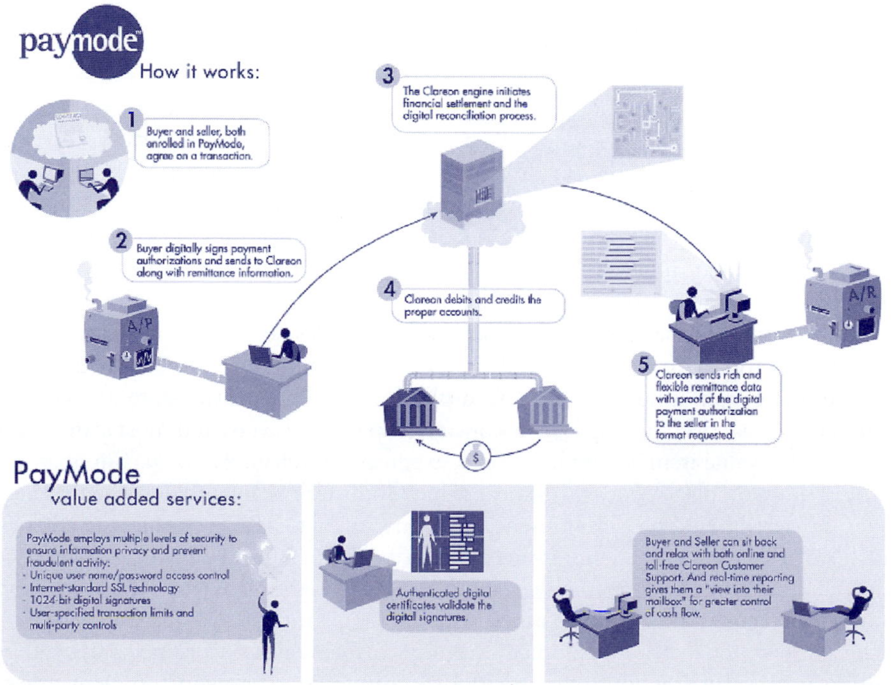

Source: Used with permission of Clareon, a division of FleetBoston.

letter of credit (LC)
A written agreement by a bank to pay the seller, on account of the buyer, a sum of money upon presentation of certain documents.

Letters of Credit for Global Payments. Letters of credit often are used when global B2B payments need to be made, especially when there is substantial risk associated with the payment. A **letter of credit**, also called an L/C or documentary credit, is issued by a bank on behalf of a buyer (importer). It guarantees a seller (exporter) that payment for goods or services will be made, provided the terms of the L/C are met. Before the credit is issued, the buyer and seller agree on all terms and conditions in a purchase and sale contract. The buying company then instructs its bank to issue a documentary credit in accordance with the contract. A credit can be payable at sight or at term. *At sight* means that payment is due upon presentation of documents after shipment of the goods or after a service is provided. Alternatively, if the seller allows the buyer an additional period, after presentation of documents, to pay the credit (30, 60, 90 days, etc.), then the credit is payable *at term.*

L/C arrangements usually involve a series of steps that can be conducted much faster online than off-line. For example, the Royal Bank of Canada offers buyers a program called TradeView (www3.royalbank.com/english/trade/WebAccess/Java/trans.html) that enables online preparation of an L/C application. Once completed, the application is transmitted to the Royal Bank for review and processing. Credit can be issued in as few as 24 hours, although online L/C can still involve substantial time and costs, as EC Application Case 12.4 and Online File W12.4 indicate.

For sellers the main benefit of an L/C is reduced risk—the bank assures the creditworthiness of the buyer. For those global situations where the buyer is resident in a country with political or financial instability, the risk can be reduced if the L/C is confirmed by a bank in the seller's country. Reduced risk also is of benefit to buyers who may use this fact to negotiate lower prices.

Section 12.8 ▶ REVIEW QUESTIONS

1. Describe the financial supply chain.
2. Describe the current state of B2B e-payments.
3. What is electronic invoice presentment and payment (EIPP)?
4. Describe the three models of EIPP.
5. Describe the basic EIPP options.
6. What is a purchasing card?

12.9 THE SALES TAX ISSUE

Suppose you buy a laptop computer online from Amazon.com. How much sales tax will you owe? Most likely, you will not owe sales tax on the purchase. What if you buy a laptop computer online from CompUSA? How much sales tax will you owe in this case? The answer is, it depends, primarily on the tax laws where you have the laptop shipped. The reason why the Amazon.com purchase is likely to be sales-tax free is because of a 1992 ruling by the U.S. Supreme Court. In that ruling, the Court held that a state cannot force out-of-state businesses to collect sales taxes unless the business has a physical presence—a store, factory, or distribution center—in the state. The court reasoned that the various sales tax systems were too complex for retailers to keep track. This ruling is still in effect. In a number of states, when a consumer makes a purchase from a business without a physical presence in the state, the consumer is required to pay a "use tax." In practice few consumers pay the use tax, and most states ignore the tax unless a high-value item is purchased (e.g., expensive jewelry). Amazon.com does not have retail stores, but CompUSA does. This means that CompUSA is required to charge sales tax in those states where it has a physical presence. The amount varies from one state to the next.

In the United States, there are over 7,500 taxing jurisdictions. Some states have consistent sales tax rates for all items in all localities. Other states charge different rates for different items. For instance, food and clothing often are exempt from sales tax. Also, in many states there is a statewide sales tax plus local (city and/or county) sales taxes that range dramatically from one jurisdiction to another. For example, sales taxes in the Denver area vary from under 4 percent to over 8 percent. When a buyer purchases an item in person, the store charges the same sales tax for the item regardless of where the buyer resides. When the same

CASE 12.4

EC Application

GOLDEN CHANG MOVES TO TRADECARD ONLINE PAYMENTS

Golden Chang is a medium-sized, Taiwanese footwear manufacturer with annual sales of over US$250 million and over 10,000 employees. The company specializes in the production of casual shoes, safety shoes, and hiking boots. It has its own trademark brand, Road Mate casuals, but it also manufactures shoes for many well-known global brands, such as Timberland, Dr. Martens, Wal-Mart, L.L.Bean, Caterpillar, and Wolverine Worldwide. Most of Golden Chang's shoes are sold overseas, with the main markets being Europe, the United States, and Canada.

Shoe manufacturing is a complex business, requiring hundreds of external suppliers to provide a range of product materials for the soles, heels, and uppers in addition to accessories such as laces, eyelets, nails, and thread. The supply of these materials has to be coordinated with peak demands in April and October, as well as a continuous stream of small deliveries aimed at replenishing retail stock on very tight delivery schedules.

Wolverine Worldwide Inc. introduced Golden Chang to the TradeCard system for automating financial processes in the supply chain. Golden Chang began using the system in 2001. One of Golden Chang's primary goals was to replace L/Cs (letters of credit) with payment-assured transactions. Assured transactions reduce bank fees and make it possible to address discrepancies online. Golden Chang estimates that assured transactions have saved about 75 percent on transaction costs, reduced the number of errors, and, as a result, substantially reduced the number of discrepancies.

TradeCard offers an "open network" that provides an online interface that can be used by all the trade partners—suppliers and buyers—across multiple supply chains. This eliminates the need to set up individual links between the partners for particular processes. The overall system enables complete processing of transactions from purchase to payment. In Golden Chang's own words, "We receive and view the online purchase order, create shipping documents, and eventually, when the consignment has been delivered to the customer, complete an invoice and submit all documents to the TradeCard engine. When any discrepancies have been resolved, we await the buyer's approval and payment." TradeCard is bank neutral and provides access to multiple financial institutions.

The TradeCard system enables Golden Chang's financial and sales staff to view all transactions online instantly; immediately check the status of any transaction; monitor and report on cash flows; negotiate discrepancies online; and approve documents regardless of whether they are in the office or on the road. This has resulted in a substantial reduction of paperwork between the company's offices in Taiwan, Macao, Hong Kong, and the United States; the elimination of errors caused by rekeying data; faster turnaround of documents and orders; cheaper document transmission; and better management of cash flows and credits.

In the future, Golden Chang plans to institute tighter integration between its trade processes and its ERP and EDI systems. Currently, its ERP system is used to manage factory operations and to link those operations to various head office functions, such as order and procurement processing. Integrating the ERP systems with TradeCard would speed the flow of documents and reduce transaction time. A key element of this integration is EDI. EDI enables the online exchange of documents between trading partners regardless of their format. EDI reduces keying errors, speeds transactions, and reduces costs. Golden Chang expects to build the integration of these systems on TradeCard.

Source: Condensed from TradeCard (2004).

Questions

1. How does Golden Chang employ the TradeCard Open Network?
2. What are the key benefits of TradeCard to Golden Chang?

item is purchased online, the merchant has to know the tax laws in the state and locale where the item is being shipped. As the 1992 Supreme Court ruling suggests, this can be a very complicated task, especially because sales tax laws change quite frequently.

Researchers at the University of Tennessee estimate that in the United States state and local governments have lost $15.5 billion in sales taxes because of online sales (Chang 2003). They project that the loss will grow to $21.5 billion by 2008 as EC continues to grow. To combat the loss, a number of states joined together a few years ago to simplify their sales tax laws, making it easier for online retailers to collect sales taxes and use taxes. Thirty-five states have signed on to a program, the Streamlined Sales Tax Project (SSTP; streamlinedsalestax.org). In 2003, state legislatures began the process of introducing legislation aimed at conforming their state sales and use taxes to the SSTP. To date, 30 states and the District of Columbia have passed the conforming legislation. However, under the legislation collection of sales taxes and use taxes by online merchants remains voluntary until the U.S. Congress or the Supreme Court makes it mandatory.

Because of the complexities, many online businesses (B2C and B2B) rely on specialized third-party software and services to calculate the taxes associated with a sale. The software and services handle the detailed computations and keep abreast of tax law changes. Some of the better known companies providing this type of software and services are:

- **Salestax.com.** This company is part of CCH Tax and Accounting (tax.cchgroup.com). It licenses a wide range of software products that are used to automatically verify shipping addresses and to calculate sales and use taxes. These products come in the form of Web Services that are incorporated into the merchants' existing EC systems. The software is updated monthly to accommodate changes in the tax laws.
- **Sales Tax Clearinghouse.** The Sales Tax Clearinghouse (STC; thestc.com) provides a variety of tools for online merchants to calculate both sales and use taxes. Merchants can utilize STC's manual online calculator; subscribe to STC's raw sales tax data, which can be incorporated in their EC systems; or license STC's TaxCalc software, which links the merchants' systems with STC tax calculation servers. For those merchants who incorporate the raw sales tax data into their systems, updates are made monthly or quarterly, depending on the merchant's preferences.
- **Taxware International.** This company (taxware.com) is part of First Data Corporation, one of the leading payment processors. Taxware provides systems that automate the calculation of sales, use, and value-added (VAT) taxes. Its systems cover all U.S. and Canadian taxes as well as calculation of VAT and other consumption taxes for over 100 countries around the world.

Section 12.9 ▶ REVIEW QUESTIONS

1. Describe the EC tax calculation problem.
2. Describe possible solutions to the tax-collection problem.

MANAGERIAL ISSUES

Some managerial issues related to this chapter are as follows.

1. **What B2C payment methods should we use?** Companies that only accept credit cards rule out a number of potential segments of buyers. Teenagers, non–U.S. customers, and customers who do not want to use credit cards online are examples of market segments that are unable or unwilling to use credit cards to make online purchases. E-checks, virtual credit cards, stored-value cards, and PayPal are some possible alternatives to credit cards. Also, when the purchase price is less than $10, credit cards are not a viable solution. In this case various e-micropayment systems can be used. Online merchants and other sellers need to be aware of the volatility and true costs of many of these alternatives. Because many of the various alternatives do not yet enjoy widespread use, it is always possible that they will not exist tomorrow.
2. **What B2B payment methods should we use?** Keep an open mind about online alternatives. When it comes to paying suppliers or accepting payments from partners, most large businesses have opted to stick with the tried-and-true methods of electronic funds transfer (EFT) or checks over other methods of electronic payment. For MROs, consider using purchasing cards. For global trade, electronic letters of credit are popular. The use of e-checks is another area where cost savings can accrue. Finally, innovative methods such as TradeCard can be very effective. With all of these methods, a key factor is determining how well they work with existing accounting and ordering systems and with business partners.
3. **Should we use an in-house payment mechanism or outsource it?** It takes time, skill, money, software, and hardware to integrate the payment systems of all the parties involved in processing any sort of e-payment. For this reason, even a business that runs its own EC site should consider outsourcing the e-payment component. Many third-party vendors provide payment gateways designed to handle the interactions among the various financial institutions that operate in the background of an e-payment system. Also, if a Web site is hosted by a third party (e.g., at Yahoo! Store), an e-payment service will be provided.
4. **How secure are e-payments?** Security and fraud continue to be a major issue in making and accepting e-payments of all kinds. This is especially true for online credit cards where fraud continues to grow. B2C merchants are employing a wide variety of tools (e.g., address verification and other authentication services) to combat fraudulent orders. These and other measures that are employed to ensure the security of e-payments have to be part of a broader security scheme that weighs risks against issues such as the ease of use and the fit within the overall business context.

RESEARCH TOPICS

Here are some suggested topics related to this chapter. For details, references, and additional topics, refer to the book's "Current EC Research" in the Online Appendix.

1. **The Payment Revolution**
   - The history of money and payments in the twentieth and twenty-first centuries
   - Patterns and trends in cash, check, and noncash payments
2. **Magnitude, Methods of Perpetration, and Preventive Measures Regarding Fraudulent Payments**
   - Patterns and trends in fraudulent payments
   - Merchant liabilities concerned with fraudulent payments
   - Categories of online orders with high fraud potential
   - Methods and tools for preventing fraudulent payments
   - Decision models and automated rules for detecting and preventing fraudulent payments
   - Role of PKI and digital signatures in preventing fraudulent payments
3. **The History and Future of Electronic Payments**
   - Economic, technological, and institutional forces shaping the credit card industry
   - History and reasons for the rapid growth and success of PayPal
   - Algorithms for producing and implementing e-payment systems
   - Global patterns and trends in the use of e-payment alternatives
   - Demographic patterns and trends in the use of e-payment alternatives
   - Cryptographic and encryption techniques underlying electronic cash and e-micropayments
   - Role of e-micropayments in the online content industry (e.g., music, video, and games)
4. **The Increasingly Important Role of Trade Networks in B2B**
   - Role of EDI in intercompany online payments
   - XML standards proposed and used for collaborative business processes and trading relationships
   - Forces determining the success or failure of online trading in various industries (e.g., auto parts)
   - Integration of e-payment systems with accounting and ERP systems
   - Issues of trust and dispute resolution in B2B e-payments
   - Network architecture in the operation of trading exchanges
5. **Smart Card Applications**
   - Components and operation of contact and contactless smart card systems
   - Operating systems and programming languages for smart cards
   - Privacy issues in e-identification and health-care applications of smart cards
   - Differences in the use and acceptance of smart cards in Europe, Asia, and North America
   - Markets for stored-value cards
   - Role of PKI and biometrics in smart card security
   - Role of smart cards in biometric security systems
   - Integration of smart cards into nationwide transportation systems

SUMMARY

In this chapter, you learned about the following EC issues as they relate to the learning objectives.

1. **Payment Revolution.** Cash and checks are no longer kings. Debit and credit cards now rule—both online and off-line. This means that online B2C businesses need to support debit and credit card purchases. In international markets outside of Western Europe, buyers favor other forms of e-payment (e.g., bank transfers). The difficulty is that many forms of e-payment other than payment cards have been tried and failed. Their failure has resulted from the confluence of a variety of factors (e.g., they required specialized hardware or setup or they failed to mesh with existing systems).
2. **Using Payment Cards Online.** The processing of online card payments is essentially the same as it is for bricks-and-mortar stores and involves essentially the same players and the same systems—banks, card associ-

ations, payment processing services, and the like. This is one of the reasons why payment cards predominate in the online world. The major difference is that the rate of fraudulent orders is much higher online. Surveys indicate that merchants have adopted a wide variety of methods to combat fraudulent orders, including address verification, manual review, card verification numbers, fraud screens and decision models, negative files, and card association authentication services.

3. **Smart Cards.** Smart cards look like credit cards but contain embedded chips for manipulating data and have large memory capacity. Cards that contain microprocessor chips can be programmed to handle a wide variety of tasks. Other cards have memory chips to which data can be written and from which data can be read. Most memory cards are disposable, but others—smart cards—can hold large amounts of data and are rechargeable. Smart cards have been and will be used for a number of purposes, including storing e-cash in e-purses for contactless payment, paying for mass transit services, identifying cardholders for government services, securing physical and network access, and verifying eligibility for health care and other government services.
4. **Stored-Value Cards.** A stored-value card is similar in appearance to a credit or debit card. The monetary value of a stored value card is housed in a magnetic strip on the back of the card. Closed-loop stored value cards are issued for a single purpose by a specific merchant (e.g., a Starbucks giftcard). In contrast, open-loop stored-value cards are more like standard credit or debit cards and can be used for multiple purposes (e.g., a payroll card). The substantial growth of stored-value cards is being spurred by those segments of the population without credit cards or bank accounts—people with low incomes, young adults, seniors, and minorities—and employers using payroll cards as an extension to their direct deposit programs.
5. **E-Micropayments.** When an item or service being sold online costs less than $10, credit cards are too costly. A number of other e-payments systems have been introduced to handle these micropayment situations. For the most part, they have failed. Many of the recent e-micropayment schemes, such as BitPass or PayLoadz, require buyers to set up prepaid accounts to handle these smaller purchases. The accounts are prepaid with a PayPal account or a credit card. Like their predecessors, most of the recent schemes have little traction among online merchants and have a small probability of success.
6. **E-Checking.** E-checks are the electronic equivalent of paper checks. They are handled in much the same way as paper checks and rely quite heavily on the Automated Clearing House (ACH) Network. E-checks offer a number of benefits, including speedier processing, reduced administrative costs, more efficient deposits, reduced float period, and fewer "bounced" checks. These factors have resulted in the rapid growth of e-check usage.
7. **Electronic bill presentment and payment.** Although most consumers still pay their bills with paper checks, the percentage paying their bills online is growing at a rapid rate. Bills can be paid one at a time (through an online banking service or directly at the biller's Web site) or several can be paid at once (through a bill consolidator). Electronic bill presentment and payment (EBPP) reduces both the billers' and customers' costs and makes it easier for customers to track and review their payment records. The leading vendor of third-party EBPP is CheckFree. CheckFree services about 6 million consumers and processes two-thirds of the nation's ACH payments.
8. **B2B Electronic Payments.** B2B payments are part of a much larger financial supply chain that encompasses the range of processes from procurement to payment and order to cash. Today, the vast majority of B2B payments are still made by check, although many organizations are moving to enterprise invoice presentment and payment (EIPP). Like EBPP, there are three models of EIPP: seller direct (buyers go to the seller's Web site), buyer direct (sellers post invoices at the buyer's Web site), and consolidator (many buyers and many sellers are linked through the consolidator's Web site). In addition to these models, there are several EIPP payment options, including the ACH Network, purchasing cards, wire transfers, and letters of credit (L/C). The move to EIPP is being inhibited by the shortage of IT staff, the lack of integration of payment and account systems, the lack of standard formats for remittance information, and the inability of trading partners to send or receive electronic payments with sufficient remittance information.
9. **Tax Issues.** The issues of sales and use taxes computation and collection for online purchases are complex. First, for any given buyer, it is difficult to determine whether sales or use taxes should be charged. Second, if taxes are charged, it is difficult to calculate how much should be charged, because the tax rate varies from one tax jurisdiction to the next. The problem is that there are thousands of taxing jurisdictions. Because of the complexities, most online B2C and B2B businesses rely on outside companies to calculate sales and use taxes.

KEY TERMS

Term	Page
Address Verification System (AVS)	499
Authorization	497
Automated Clearing House (ACH) Network	512
Card verification number (CVN)	499
Common Electronic Purse Specification (CEPS)	504
Contact card	502
Contactless (proximity) card	502
E-check	511
E-micropayment	510
E-purse	503
Electronic bill presentment and payment (EBPP)	513
Enterprise invoice presentment and payment (EIPP)	517
Letter of credit (LC)	520
Payment card	496
Payment service provider (PSP)	497
Purchasing card (p-card)	519
Settlement	497
Smart card	500
Smart card operating system	503
Smart card reader	502
Stored-value card	508
Virtual credit card	500

QUESTIONS FOR DISCUSSION

1. Suppose a company wanted to introduce a new e-micropayment method on the Web. What factors should it consider to increase the chance of success?
2. A book publisher is interested in selling books as well as individual book chapters on the Web. What e-payment methods would you recommend that the publisher use to sell the chapters?
3. Recently, a merchant who accepts online credit card payments has experienced a wave of fraudulent orders. What steps should the merchant take to combat the fraud?
4. A retail clothing manufacturer is considering e-payments for both its suppliers and its buyers. What sort of e-payment method should it use to pay for office supplies? How should it pay suppliers of raw materials? How should its customers—both domestic and international clothing retailers—pay?
5. A parent wants to provide her teenage son with the ability to make purchases online without giving him access to a credit card. What alternatives are available?
6. A metropolitan area wants to provide riders of its public transportation system with the ability to pay transit fares without using cash or credit cards. What options are available?
7. If you buy a CD online, will you owe sales taxes on the purchase? Explain.

INTERNET EXERCISES

1. This chapter listed the names of e-payment companies that failed to gain critical mass (e.g., Digital Cash, Flooz, etc.). Select two of these companies. Using information gathered from the Web, explain why you think they failed.
2. Go to checkfree.com. What sorts of EBPP services does CheckFree provide? Would you use the service? Why or why not?
3. Select one of the following companies: BitPass, Paystone, PayLoadz, or Peppercoin. Explain in detail how its e-micropayment system works. What are the key benefits and limitations of the system?
4. Select a major B2C merchant and detail the e-payment options offered. Based on CyberSource's "The Insider's Guide to e-Commerce Payment," what other types of e-payment systems could it offer?
5. Enter tradecard.com. Run the procure-to-pay demo. Summarize the processes and benefits of the service to a small exporter.
6. Go to verisign.com. Identify the services it provides for B2C e-payments. Describe the features of VeriSign's major products that provide these merchant services.
7. Go to cybersource.com. Identify the services it provides for B2B e-payments. Describe the features of CyberSource's major products that provide these merchant services.

8. Run the demo of Deskshop at the Discover Card Deskshop Web site discovercard.com/deskshop. Write a brief report describing the functions, benefits, and limitations of Discover Card's Deskshop service.

9. Download the *Government Smart Card Handbook* from smart.gov/information/smartcardhandbook.pdf. Write a report describing the major uses of smart cards in U.S. government programs.

10. Enter gxs.com. What types of companies are serviced by GXS Trading Grid? What types of products and services does the Trading Grid provide?

11. Go to nacha.org. What is NACHA? What is its role? What is the ACH? Who are the key participants in an ACH e-payment? Describe the "pilot" projects currently underway at ACH.

TEAM ASSIGNMENTS AND ROLE PLAYING

1. Select some B2C sites that cater to teens and some that cater to older consumers. Have team members visit these sites. What types of e-payment methods do they provide? Are there any differences among the methods used on different types of sites? What other types of e-payment would you recommend for the various sites and why?

2. Write a report comparing smart card applications in two or more European and/or Asian countries. In the report, discuss whether those applications would succeed in North America.

3. Have one team represent MasterCard PayPass and another represent American Express. The task of each team is to convince a company that its product is superior.

4. Have each team member interview three to five people who have made a purchase or sold an item at auction over the Internet. Find out how they paid. What security and privacy concerns did they have regarding the payment? Is there an ideal payment method?

Real-World Case

FROM PAPER TO E-PAYMENTS: THE STORY OF WELLS FARGO HOME MORTGAGE

The largest home mortgage originator in the United States is Wells Fargo Home Mortgage. It has a portfolio of more than 4.6 million loans. For most of its history, Wells Fargo's loan customers have made their payments the old fashion way—mailing their checks on a monthly basis to Wells Fargo's network of external lock boxes. A sizeable portion of its customers even drop off payments at local Wells Fargo Bank branches. For some time, it has provided a telephone payment program enabling customers, who have forgotten to mail their checks, to make payments at the last minute in order to avoid late fees.

With this large of a portfolio, the costs of handling paper collections can have a substantial impact on the bottom line. The cost to Wells Fargo of simply clearing checks is more than US$1 million annually. To address this problem, in 2000 Wells Fargo embarked on a program to increase collections efficiency and reduce the costs of processing payments.

In the first quarter of 2000, the ratio of paper to e-payments was four to one. At that time, three e-payment options were available to customers: direct payment, equity payments, and third-party processors. Of those using e-payment options, 350,000 were using direct payment, 100,000 were using equity payments, and 133,000 were utilizing third parties. By 2002, Wells Fargo Home Mortgage was offering a full suite of e-payments methods, including:

- Automatic Mortgage Payments—ACH direct payments.
- Online Payments—Internet-initiated ACH debits.
- Just in Time—Telephone-initiated ACH debits.
- EBPP—Statements are presented and bills can be paid online at a Wells Fargo hosted Web site.
- Wells Fargo Equity Enhancement Program (EEP)—Payments are debited from a customer's bank account every 2 weeks.

With the addition of these methods, customer acceptance and use of e-payments began to grow. In the first quarter of 2002, Wells Fargo processed 3.4 million e-payments. By the third quarter of 2003, the number was 4.3 million e-payments, an increase of 26 percent.

In that quarter, the ratio of paper to e-payments was 1.9 to 1. Even with the growth in e-payments, however, in 2003 lockbox payments still accounted for close to 60 percent of all payments.

For Wells Fargo, the lockboxes were by far the most expensive payment method. The cost was US$3 per loan annually. At the other end, ACH direct payments produced US$11 in cost reduction and float annually.

In 2002, the NACHA rules governing accounts receivable (check) conversion (ARC) went into effect. ARC is a service that allows consumer checks sent to a lockbox or drop box location to be converted to an ACH electronic debit. Under these rules, consumers authorize the conversion of the check payments to electronic payments when they mail their remittance and check to the biller. Before the conversion can take place, the biller must communicate its conversion intentions to the customer in the billing documentation. In essence, the conversion takes place unless the customer objects. ARC is well suited for repetitive payments, such as mortgages, utility bills, insurance payments, and the like. The challenge for the biller rests with streamlining and automating the process of converting checks to ACH debits to achieve a high acceptance rate by consumers.

In 2003, Wells Fargo Home Mortgage became the first mortgage company to implement ARC. By November 2004, four out of five of its lockbox locations were converted. Few customers opted to remain with paper check payments. Overall, the ACR program succeeded in turning the tide toward e-payments. By the end of the first quarter of 2004, e-payments comprised 88 percent of Well Fargo's loan portfolio, up from 35 percent in the pre–ARC era. At the end of the fourth quarter of 2004, the ratio of paper payments to electronic payments was one to seven.

The financial impact of the ARC program has been twofold. First, there has been close to a US$2 million savings from decreased bank fees and increased float. Second, the collection rates for checks returned due to NSF (insufficient funds) has increased significantly.

Wells Fargo Home Mortgage's experiences with ARC are not unique, although the shift from paper to e-payments is ground breaking. According to the NACHA, ARC entries went from 5.3 million in 2002 to 43.7 million in 2003 to 208 million in the second quarter of 2004. In 2004, ARC payments totaled US$60.8 billion. ARC is now the largest e-check ACH application.

Source: Condensed from Banwart (2004).

Questions

1. Like many other financial institutions Wells Fargo Home Mortgage (WFHM) has offered a number of e-payment options to its customers. Describe the options WFHM offered before ARC. Why weren't these options sufficient to move WFHM's customers from paper to e-payment?
2. Using information from the NACHA Web site, describe the basic rules underlying ARC. Why did this result in the shift from paper to e-payment for WFHM's loan customers?
3. Based on WFHM's experience, if a company wanted to convince its customers to adopt online payment, what advice would you offer?

REFERENCES

American Public Transportation Association (APTA). "Smart Cards and U.S. Public Transportation." October 2003. apta.com/research/info/briefings/briefing_6.cfm (accessed December 2004).

Association for Financial Professionals (AFP). "2004 Electronic Payments Survey." 2004. afponline.org/pub/pdf/2004_10_research_epay_report.pdf (accessed December 2004).

Authorize.Net. "ECheck.Net Operating Procedures and Users Guide." October 28, 2004. authorize.net/files/echecknetuserguide.pdf (accessed December 2004).

Automated Clearing House (ACH). "Understanding the ACH Network: An ACH Primer." 2004. onlinecheck.com/ACH_101.pdf (accessed December 2004).

Bailey, S. "Riding the Hong Kong Octopus." *ThingsAsian*, June 26, 2003. thingsasian.com/goto_article/article.2378.html (accessed December 2004).

Banwart, J. "From 81 Percent Paper to 88 Percent E-Payments in Four Years." NACHA, 2004. nacha.org/otherresources/buyers2004/BuyersGuide2004_81=88_ePay.pdf (accessed December 2004).

Barnhart, T. "The Financial Supply Chain: Could This Be the Next Corporate Paradigm After ERP?" *Darwin Magazine*, April 1, 2004. darwinmag.com/read/040104/fsc.html (accessed December 2004).

Branch Banking and Trust (BB&T). "New Money Transfer Product for Hispanic Clients." NSHP, April 12, 2004. nshp.org/?q=node/446 (accessed December 2004).

CardTechnology. "World's Largest Smart Card Project Set to Begin." *CardTechnology News Bulletin*, January 28, 2004. cardtechnology.com/cgi-bin/readstory.pl?story=20040128CTDN227.xml (accessed December 2004).

Ceridian. "Annual Gift Card Survey Reveals Anticipated Increase in Gift Card Spending." Ceridian press release,

October 27, 2004. ceridian.com/myceridian/article/printerfriendly/1,2723,11178-56271,00.html (accessed December 2004).

Chang, R. "Internet Sales Tax Looms." *PCWorld*, October 1, 2003. pcworld.com/news/article/0,aid,112723,00.asp (accessed December 2004).

Cohen, P. "iTunes Music Store tops 250 million songs sold." *MacWorld*, January 24, 2005. macworld.com/news/2005/01/24/itunes/index.php (accessed January 2005).

Council for Electronic Billing and Payment (CEBP). "Business-to-Business EIPP: Presentment Models and Payment Options, Part Two." 2002. cebp.nacha.org/b2b-payment-options-final.pdf (accessed December 2004).

Council for Electronic Billing and Payment (CEBP). "Business-to-Business EIPP: Presentment Models and Payment Options, Part One." 2001. cebp.nacha.org/documents/b2b-presentment-models.pdf (accessed December 2004).

CyberSource. "Sixth Annual Online Fraud Report." 2005. cybersource.com/resources/collateral/Resource_Center/whitepapers_and_reports/CYBS_2005_Fraud_Report.pdf (accessed January 2005).

CyberSource. "Insiders Guide to E-Commerce Payment: 20 Tools Successful Merchants Are Using to Unlock Hidden Profit." 2004. cybersource.com/cgi-bin/pages/prep.cgi?page=/promo/insidersguide/index.html (accessed December 2004).

eBilling.org. "Building the EBPP Business Case." 2002. ebilling.org/ebpp/20 (accessed December 2004).

Electronic Check Clearing House Organization. "Managing Value in the Transition to Electronic Payments: Executive Summary." April 11, 2002. eccho.com/eccho_vision.html (accessed December 2004).

European Union. "France—Identification and Authentication/eServices for Citizens." *eGovernment News*, May 4, 2004. europa.eu.int/ida/en/document/ 2519/353 (accessed December 2004).

Evans, D., and R. Schmalensee. *Paying with Plastic: The Digital Revolution in Buying and Borrowing*, 2d ed. Cambridge, MA: MIT Press, 2005.

Federal Reserve System (FRS). "2004 Federal Reserve Payments Study." 2004. frbservices.org/retail/pdf/2004paymentresearchreport.pdf (accessed December 2004).

Festa, P. "Banks Cash In as More Bills Are Paid Online." *CNET News.com*, April 21, 2003. news.com.com/banks+cash+in+as+more+bills+are+paid+online/2100-1017_3-997701.html (accessed December 2004).

Government Accounting Office (GAO). "Electronic Government: Federal Agencies Continue to Invest in Smart Card Technology." Report to the Subcommittee on Technology, Information Policy, Intergovernmental Relations, and the Census, Committee on Government Reform, House of Representatives. September 2004. gao.gov/new.items/d04948.pdf (accessed December 2004).

HBS Consulting. "Smart Cards—Current Trends, Developments, and Future Prospects in the Healthcare Industry." January 2004. mindbranch.com/catalog/product.jsp?code=R503-0011psrc=gsitemap (accessed December 2004).

Hunt, J., and B. Holcombe. *Government Smart Card Handbook.* Washington, D.C.: U.S. General Services Administration, 2004. smart.gov/information/smartcard handbook.pdf. (accessed March 2005).

Jackson, E. *The PayPal Wars.* Los Angeles, CA: World Ahead Publishing, 2004.

LeClaire, J. "Micro-Commerce Presents Mega-Opportunities." *ECT News Network,* December 10, 2004. ectnews.com/story/38734.html (accessed December 2004).

Leon, M. "Online Bill Paying Growing Up." May 27, 2003. siliconvalley.internet.com/news/article.php/2212841 (accessed December 2004).

Lucas, P. "Taming the Paper Tiger." *Collectionsworld.com,* February 2005. collectionsworld.com/cgi-bin/read story2.pl?story=20040601CCRV263.xml (accessed February 2005).

Marketing VOX News. "Micropayments Finally Fashionable." September 8, 2004. marketingvox.com/archives/2004/09/08/micropayments_finally_fashionable (accessed December 2004).

MasterCard International. "MasterCard International Surpasses 200 Million Smart Card Milestone." November 4, 2004. mastercardintl.com/cgi-bin/newsroom.cgi?id=950& (accessed December 2004).

MasterCard. "Electronic Commerce Security Architecture Best Practices." April 2003a. mastercardmerchant.com/docs/best_practices.pdf (accessed December 2004).

MasterCard. "MasterCard SecureCode Case Study: eTronics." 2003b. mastercardmerchant.com/docs/sc_case_study-etronics.pdf (accessed December 2004).

McQueen, B. *Introduction to Electronic Payments Systems and Transportation.* Washington, D.C.: Intelligent Transportation System of America, 2001.

Merchant Risk Council. "Merchants Are Using More Tools More Effectively to Combat Online Fraud, According to Annual Survey by the Merchant Risk Council." November 22, 2004. merchantriskcouncil.org/files/press_pdf/15_pr112204.pdf (accessed December 2004).

Milligan, J. "Future Threat?" *BAI Banking Strategies*, May–June 2004. bai.org/bankingstrategies/2004-may-jun/future (accessed December 2004).

Munroe, T. "Plugged In: Hong Kong Embraces the Octupus Card." *BusinessWorld Online,* June 6, 2002. itmatters.com.ph/news/news_06062002f.html (accessed December 2004).

Online Publishers. "Online Paid Content: U.S. Market Spending Report." November 2004. online-publishers.org/pdf/opa_paid_content_report_nov_04.pdf (accessed December 2004).

PayPal. "FlyLady.net Case Study." 2004. paypal.com/en_us/pdf/flyladycasestudy.pdf (accessed December 2004).

Peppercoin. "Quantifying the Small Payments Potential." 2004. **corp.peppercoin.com/marketvision/pov.shtml** (accessed December 2004).

Raja, M. "Smart Cards Make Inroads into Asia." *Asia Times Online*, October 2, 2004. **atimes.com/atimes/south_asia/fj02df03.html** (accessed December 2004).

Sapsford, J. "The Power of Plastic." *Wall Street Journal*, November 2004. **wsjclassroomedition.com/archive/04nov/econ_plasticnation.htm** (accessed January 2005).

Smart Card Alliance. "McDonald's Expands Cashless Payment Options for Customers with MasterCard Paypass." Smart Card Alliance, August 20, 2004a. **smartcardalliance.org/industry_news/industry_news_item.cfm?itemid=1327** (accessed March 2005).

Smart Card Alliance. "SCM Microsystems Delivers Smart Card Readers for Belgium's National e-ID Program." *Smart Card Alliance Industry News*, October 26, 2004b. **smartcardalliance.org/industry_news/industry_news_item.cfm?itemid=1345** (accessed December 2004).

Sofield, S., et al. *PayPal Hacks*. Sebastopol, CA: O'Reilly Media, 2004.

STMicroelectronics. "Smartcard Solutions: E-Purse References." 2005. **st.com/stonline/products/families/smartcard/sc_app_finance_epurse_ref.htm** (accessed January 2005).

Su, S., and S. Rhine. "Stored Value Cards: An Alternative for the Unbanked?" Federal Reserve Bank of New York, July 2004. **newyorkfed.org/regional/stored_value_cards.html** (accessed December 2004).

TradeCard. "Golden Change Case Study 2004." **tradecard.com/documents/goldenchangcasestudy.pdf** (accessed December 2004).

Tsai, M. "PayPal Sees Smaller Online Retailers as Next Frontier." *DowJones*, September 29, 2004. **shareholder.com/paypal/news/20040929-dowjones.html** (accessed December 2004).

VeriSign. "Business Guide to Online Payment Processing." 2004. **verisign.com/static/003190.pdf** (accessed December 2004).

Visa International. "Common Electronic Purse Specifications (CEPS)." 2004. **international.visa.com/fb/paytech/ceps** (accessed December 2004).

WildCard Systems. "Visa Buxx: Case Study." 2004. **corporate.wildcardsystems.com/index.cfm?pageid=p09** (accessed December 2004).

CHAPTER 13

ORDER FULFILLMENT, eCRM, AND OTHER SUPPORT SERVICES

Learning Objectives

Upon completion of this chapter, you will be able to:

1. Describe the role of support services in EC.
2. Define EC order fulfillment and describe the EC order fulfillment process.
3. Describe the major problems of EC order fulfillment.
4. Describe various solutions to EC order fulfillment problems.
5. Describe CRM, its methods, and its relationship with EC.
6. Describe eCRM implementation and tools.
7. Describe other EC support services.
8. Discuss the drivers of outsourcing support services and the use of ASPs.

Content

HOW AMAZON.COM FULFILLS ORDERS

The Problem

With traditional retailing, customers go to a physical store and purchase items that they then take home. With e-tailing, items are shipped to customers' homes, thus maintaining an inventory of items becomes critical. Maintaining inventory and shipping products costs money and takes time, which may negate the advantages of e-tailing. Let's see how Amazon.com, the "king" of e-tailing, handles the situation.

When Amazon.com was launched in 1995, the business model called for virtual retailing—no warehouses, no inventory, no shipments. The idea was to take orders and receive payments electronically and then let others fill the orders. It soon became clear that this model, although appropriate for a small company, would not work for a giant e-tailer.

The Solution

Amazon.com decided to change its business model and handle its own inventory. The company spent close to $2 billion to build warehouses around the country and became a world-class leader in warehouse management, warehouse automation, packaging, and inventory management. The actual shipment of products to customers is outsourced to UPS and the U.S. Postal Service.

How is Amazon.com able to efficiently fulfill millions of orders?

- **Step 1.** When a customer places an order online, a computer program checks the location of the item. It identifies the Amazon.com distribution center that will fulfill the order. Alternatively, it may identify the vendor that will fulfill the order in those cases where Amazon.com acts as an intermediary only. The order is transmitted electronically to the appropriate distribution center or vendor. Here we describe what happens in Amazon.com's distribution centers, such as the 800,000-square-foot facility in Fernley, Nevada
- **Step 2.** A "flowmeister" (see exhibit) at the distribution center receives all orders and assigns them electronically to specified employees.
- **Step 3.** The items (books, games, CDs, etc.) are stocked in bins. Each bin has a red light and a button (see exhibit). When an order for an item is assigned, the red light is turned on automatically. Pickers move along the rows of bins and pick an item from the bins with red lights; they press the button to reset the light. If the light returns, they pick another unit, until the light goes off.
- **Step 4.** The picked items are placed into a crate moving on a conveyor belt, which is part of a winding belts system more than 10 miles long in each warehouse. Each crate can reach many destinations; items in the crate are identified by bar code readers (operated automatically or manually) at 15 different points in the conveyor maze. This tracks the location of an item at any given time and reduces errors to zero.
- **Step 5.** All crates arrive at a central location where bar codes are matched with order numbers. Items are moved from the crates to chutes where they slide into cardboard boxes. Sophisticated technology allows items picked by several people in different parts of the warehouse to arrive in the same chute.
- **Step 6.** If gift wrapping was selected, this is done by hand.

Published in NYT 01/22/02: A picture caption in Business Day yesterday about Amazon.com's shipping methods misstated the job of Carrie Peters, shown at a computer keyboard in a warehouse. She is a public relations official, not what the company calls a flowmeister, an employee who directs warehouse operations.

Photographer: David Bernett/Contact Press Images

Photographer: David Bernett/Contact Press Images

- **Step 7.** Boxes are packed, taped, weighed, labeled, and routed to one of 40 truck bays in the warehouse. From there, they go to UPS or the USPS. The items are scanned continuously.

Source: Photographer: Marilyn Newton/The New York Times

The Results

Each warehouse can deliver 200,000 or more pieces a day. All five warehouses must handle close to 3 million pieces a day during the busiest part of the holiday season. However, in 2004, the warehouses were able to deliver only 1 million pieces a day, creating some delays during peak periods. Amazon.com leases space to other retailers with online businesses (e.g., such as Target and Toys"R"Us) as well as companies overseas.

The system gives Amazon the ability to offer lower prices and stay competitive, especially since the company is becoming a huge online marketplace that sells thousands of items. As of 2004, profitability is increasing steadily.

To increase efficiency, items are combined into one shipment if they are small enough. Returns of unwanted merchandise are not handled by the shipping warehouses, but by Altrec.com Warehouse in Auburn, Washington.

Sources: Compiled from news items at Heizer and Render (2004) and Kopytoff (2004).

WHAT WE CAN LEARN . . .

The Amazon.com case illustrates the complexity of order fulfillment by a large e-tailer and some of the solutions employed. Order fulfillment is a major EC support service, and it is the topic of this chapter. Other support services also are examined in this chapter, primarily customer services and CRM.

13.1 ORDER FULFILLMENT AND LOGISTICS—AN OVERVIEW

The implementation of most EC applications requires the use of support services. The most obvious support services are security (Chapter 11), payments (Chapter 12), infrastructure and technology (Online Chapter 18), and order fulfillment and logistics (this chapter). Most of the services are relevant for both B2C and B2B. The major services described in these chapters are summarized in Exhibit 13.1, which organizes services into the following categories, as suggested by the Delphi Group (delphigroup.com): e-infrastructure, e-process, e-markets, e-content, e-communities, and e-services. The exhibit shows representative topics in each category. This section of the chapter gives an overview of order fulfillment and logistics.

Taking orders over the Internet could well be the easy part of B2C. Fulfillment and delivery to customers' doors are the sticky parts (e.g., see Lee and Whang 2001; Bhise et al. 2000). As a matter of fact, many e-tailers have experienced fulfillment problems. Amazon.com, for

EXHIBIT 13.1 E-Commerce Services

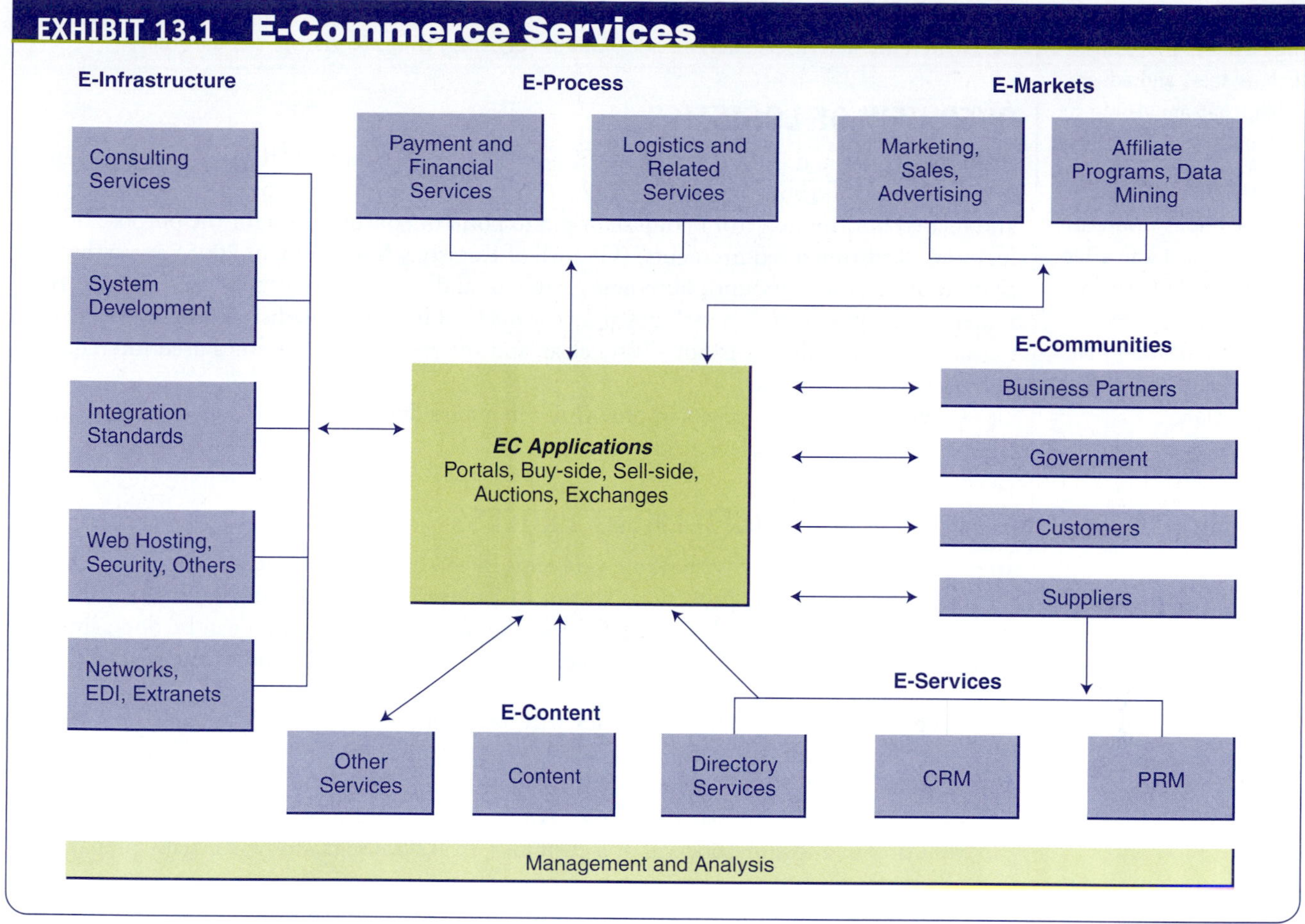

Source: Adapted from Chio (1997), p. 18.

example, which initially operated as a totally virtual company, added physical warehouses with thousands of employees in order to expedite deliveries and reduce order fulfillment costs.

Deliveries may be delayed for several reasons. They range from an inability to accurately forecast demand to ineffective e-tailing supply chains. Off-line businesses are affected by many of the same problems. One problem typical to EC is that EC is based on the concept of "pull" operations that begin with an order, frequently a customized one. This is in contrast with traditional retailing, which usually begins with a production to inventory that is then "pushed" to customers (see Exhibit 2A.1 on page 80). In the EC pull case, it is more difficult to forecast demand because of lack of experience and changing consumer tastes. Another reason for delays is that in a B2C pull model, many small orders need to be delivered to the customers' doors, whereas in brick-and-mortar retailing, the goods are shipped in large quantities to retail stores where they are picked up by customers.

Before we analyze the order fulfillment problems and describe some solutions, we need to introduce some basic order fulfillment and logistics concepts.

order fulfillment
All of the activities needed to provide customers with ordered goods and services, including related customer services.

back-office operations
The activities that support fulfillment of sales, such as accounting and logistics.

OVERVIEW OF ORDER FULFILLMENT

Order fulfillment refers not only to providing customers with what they have ordered and doing so on time, but also to providing all related customer services. For example, a customer must receive assembly and operation instructions with a new appliance. This can be done by including a paper document with the product or by providing the instructions on the Web. (A nice example of this is available at livemanuals.com.) In addition, if the customer is not happy with a product, an exchange or return must be arranged.

Order fulfillment is basically a part of the **back-office operations**, which are the activities that support the fulfillment of orders, such as accounting, inventory management, and

front-office operations
The business processes, such as sales and advertising, that are visible to customers.

logistics
The operations involved in the efficient and effective flow and storage of goods, services, and related information from point of origin to point of consumption.

shipping. It also is strongly related to the **front-office operations**, or *customer-facing activities*, which are activities, such as sales and advertising, that are visible to customers.

OVERVIEW OF LOGISTICS

Logistics is defined by the Council of Logistics Management as "the process of planning, implementing, and controlling the efficient and effective flow and storage of goods, services, and related information from point of origin to point of consumption for the purpose of conforming to customer requirements" (Council of Logistics Management 2005). Note that this definition includes inbound, outbound, internal, and external movement and the return of materials and goods. It also includes *order fulfillment*. However, the distinction between logistics and order fulfillment is not always clear, and the terms are sometimes used interchangeably, as we do in this text.

Obviously, the key aspects of order fulfillment are delivery of materials or services at the right time, to the right place, and at the right cost.

THE EC ORDER FULFILLMENT PROCESS

In order to understand why there are problems in order fulfillment, it is beneficial to look at a typical EC fulfillment process, as shown in Exhibit 13.2. The process starts on the left, when an order is received. Several activities take place, some of which can be done simultaneously; others must be done in sequence. These activities include the following steps:

- **Step 1: Making sure the customer will pay.** Depending on the payment method and prior arrangements, the validity of each payment must be determined. This activity may be done in B2B by the company's finance department or financial institution (i.e., a bank or a credit card issuer such as Visa). Any holdup may cause a shipment to be delayed, resulting in a loss of goodwill or a customer. In B2C, the customers usually prepay, usually by credit card.
- **Step 2: Checking for in-stock availability.** Regardless of whether the vendor is a manufacturer or a retailer, as soon as an order is received, an inquiry needs to be made regarding stock availability. Several scenarios are possible here that may involve the material management and production departments, as well as outside suppliers and warehouse facilities. In this step, the order information needs to be connected to the information about in-stock inventory availability.
- **Step 3: Arranging shipments.** If the product is available, it can be shipped to the customer (otherwise, go to step 5). Products can be digital or physical. If the item is physical and it is readily available, packaging and shipment arrangements need to be made. Both the packaging/shipping department and internal shippers or outside transporters may be involved. Digital items are usually available because their "inventory" is not depleted. However, a digital product, such as software, may be under revision, and thus unavailable for delivery at certain times. In either case, information needs to flow among several partners.
- **Step 4: Insurance.** Sometimes the contents of a shipment need to be insured. Both the finance department and an insurance company could be involved, and again, information needs to flow, not only inside the company, but also to and from the customer and insurance agent.
- **Step 5: Replenishment.** Customized orders will always trigger a need for some manufacturing or assembly operation. Similarly, if standard items are out of stock, they need to be produced or procured. Production can be done in-house or by contractors. The suppliers involved may have their own suppliers.
- **Step 6: In-house production.** In-house production needs to be planned. Production planning involves people, materials, components, machines, financial resources, and possibly suppliers and subcontractors. In the case of assembly and/or manufacturing, several plant services may be needed, including possible collaboration with business partners. Services may include scheduling of people and equipment, shifting other products' plans, working with engineering on modifications, getting equipment, and preparing content. The actual production facilities may be in a different country than the com-

EXHIBIT 13.2 **Order Fulfillment and the Logistics System**

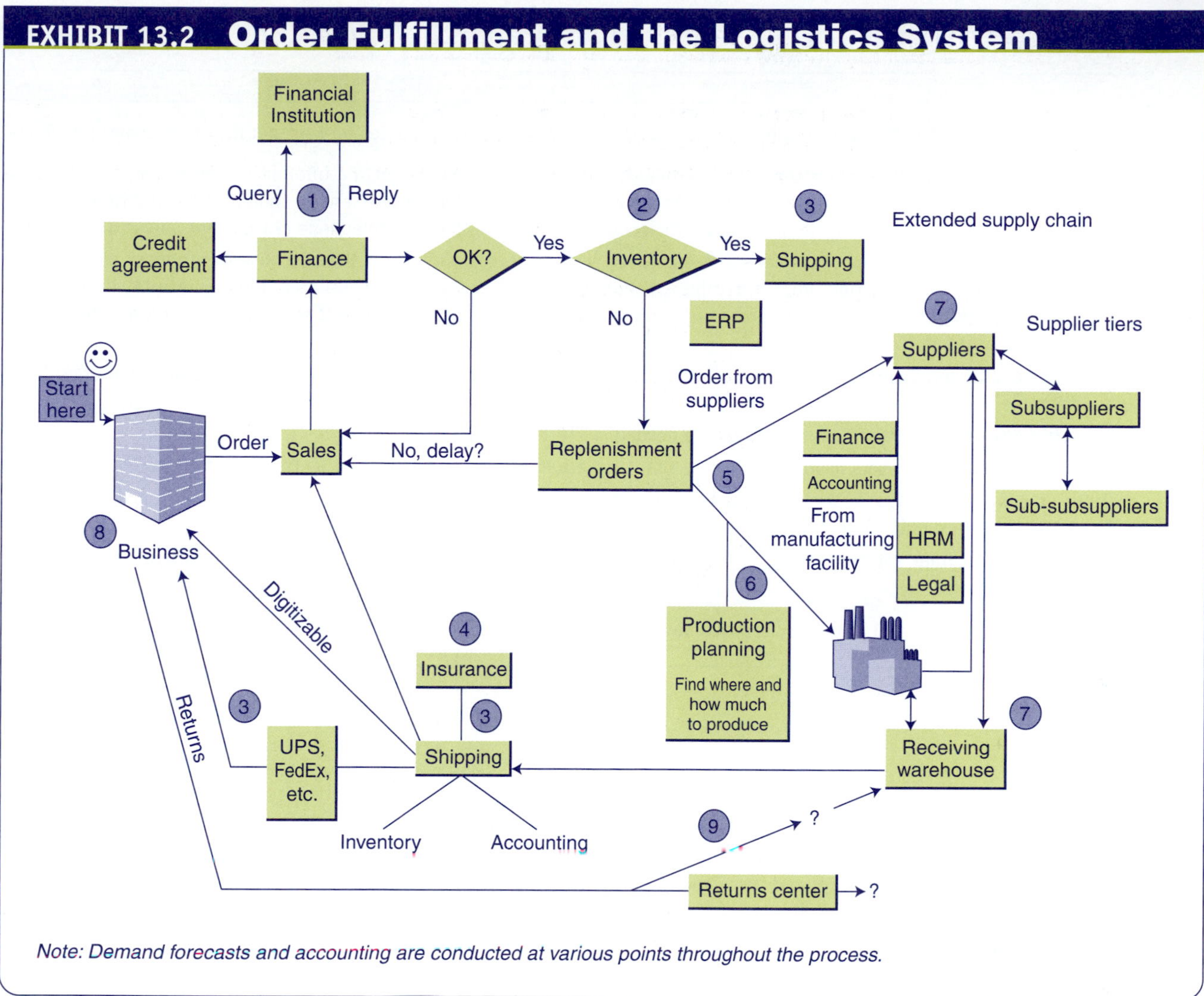

Note: Demand forecasts and accounting are conducted at various points throughout the process.

pany's headquarters or retailers. This may further complicate the flow of information and communication.

- **Step 7: Use suppliers.** A manufacturer may opt to buy products or subassemblies from suppliers. Similarly, if the seller is a retailer, such as in the case of amazon.com or walmart.com, the retailer must purchase products from its manufacturers. Several scenarios are possible. Purchased items can be stocked in warehouses, which is what Amazon.com does with its best-selling books, toys, and other commodity items. However, Amazon.com does not stock books for which only a few orders are received. In such cases, special deliveries from the publishers or intermediaries must be made. In either case, appropriate receiving and quality assurance of incoming materials and products must take place.

  Once production (step 6) or purchasing from suppliers (step 7) is completed, shipments to the customers (step 3) are arranged.

- **Step 8: Contacts with customers.** Sales representatives need to keep in constant contact with customers, especially in B2B, starting with notification of orders received and ending with notification of a shipment or a change in delivery date (see Insights and Additions 13.1). These contacts are usually done via e-mail and are frequently generated automatically.

- **Step 9: Returns.** In some cases, customers want to exchange or return items. Such returns can be a major problem, as more than $100 billion in North American goods are returned each year (Kuzeljevich 2004). Returns cost UK retailers EU$720 million a year (Boles 2004). The movement of returns from customers back to vendors is called **reverse logistics**.

reverse logistics
The movement of returns from customers to vendors.

Insights and Additions 13.1 What Services Do Customers Need?

Bayles (2001) provides the following insights on online customer services, which are based on Forrester Research studies (1999–2001):

- **Customer preferences.** Customers tend not to do much self-service in terms of getting information from companies (e.g., only 19 percent use FAQs), so they require attention. As more companies offer online self-service, though, this situation is changing. When contacting companies for information, customers use e-mail more than the telephone (71 percent versus 51 percent).
- **Types of service.** Four types of service exist, based on where the customer is in the purchase experience: *during shopping* (search products, compare, find product attributes); *during buying* (questions on warranties, billing, receipt, payment); *after the order is placed* (checking status in processing and in shipment); and *after the item is received* (checking return procedures, how to use the item).
- **Problem resolution.** Customers expect problems to be solved quickly and to their satisfaction. Easy returns and order tracking are desirable.
- **Shipping options.** Several shipping options are needed.
- **Fraud protection.** Customers need to make sure that they are not going to be cheated by the sellers or others.
- **Order status and updates.** Customers want to have some way to check on the status of their order, either by phone or online. These services are highly desired, including order notification and a clear return policy.
- **Developing customer relationships.** This includes building trust, providing security, and ensuring privacy protection (see Chapters 4, 11, and 17).

For details on these and other services, see Bayles (2001).

Order fulfillment processes may vary, depending on the product and the vendor. The order fulfillment process also differs between B2B and B2C activities, between the delivery of goods and of services, and between small and large products. Furthermore, additional steps may be required in certain circumstances, such as in the case of perishable materials or foods.

Order Fulfillment and the Supply Chain

The nine-step order fulfillment process just described, as well as order taking, are integral parts of the *supply chain.* The flows of orders, payments, information, materials, and parts need to be coordinated among all the company's internal participants, as well as with and among external partners (see Bayles 2001). The principles of SCM (Online Tutorial T2 and Handfield et al. 2002) must be considered when planning and managing the order fulfillment process.

Traditional Versus EC Logistics

e-logistics
The logistics of EC systems, typically involving small parcels sent to many customers' homes (in B2C).

EC logistics, or **e-logistics**, refers to the logistics of EC systems mainly in B2C. The major difference between e-logistics and traditional logistics is that the latter deals with movement of large amounts of materials to a few destinations (e.g., to retail stores). E-logistics shipments typically are small parcels sent to many customers' homes. Other differences are shown in Exhibit 13.3.

Section 13.1 ▶ REVIEW QUESTIONS

1. Define order fulfillment and logistics.
2. List the nine steps of the order fulfillment process.
3. Compare logistics with reverse logistics.
4. Compare traditional logistics with e-logistics.

13.2 PROBLEMS IN ORDER FULFILLMENT

During the 1999 holiday season, the B2C e-tailers, especially those that sold toys, were plagued with logistics problems. Price wars boosted demand, and neither the e-tailers nor the manufacturers were ready for it. As a result, supplies were late in coming from manufacturers.

EXHIBIT 13.3 How E-Logistics Differs from Traditional Logistics

Characteristic	Traditional Logistics	EC Logistics
Type	Bulk, large volume	Small, parcel
Destinations	Few, concentrated in one area	Large number, highly dispersed
Demand type	Push	Pull
Value of shipment	Very large, usually more than $1,000	Very small, frequently less than $100
Nature of demand	Stable, consistent	Seasonal (holiday season), fragmented
Customers	Business partners (in B2B), usually repeat customers (B2C), not many	Usually unknown B2C, many
Inventory order flow	Usually unidirectional	Usually bidirectional
Accountability	One link	Through the entire supply chain
Transporter	Frequently the company, sometimes outsourced	Usually outsourced, sometimes the company
Warehouse	Common	Only very large shippers (e.g., *amazon.com*) operate their own

Toys"R"Us, for example, had to stop taking orders around December 14. The manufacturers, warehouses, and distribution channels were not in sync with the e-tailers. As a result, many customers did not get their holiday gifts on time. (For more on the order fulfillment troubles experienced by Toys"R"Us, see Chapter 3 and Online File W13.1 at the book's Web site.)

TYPICAL SUPPLY CHAIN PROBLEMS

The inability to deliver products on time is a typical problem in both off-line and online commerce. Several other problems have been observed along the supply chain: Some companies grapple with high inventory costs; quality problems exist due to misunderstandings; shipments of wrong products, materials, and parts occur frequently; and the cost to expedite operations or shipments is high. The chance that such problems will occur in EC is even higher due to the lack of appropriate infrastructure and e-tailing experience, as well as the special characteristics of EC. For example, most manufacturers' and distributors' warehouses are designed to ship large quantities to several stores; they cannot optimally pack and ship many small packages to many customers' doors. Improper inventory levels are typical in EC, as are poor delivery scheduling and mixed-up shipments.

Another major activity related to the supply chain problem is the difficulties in *demand forecasting*. In the case of standard items, such as toys, a demand forecast must be done in order to determine appropriate inventories of finished goods at various points in the supply chain. Such a forecast is difficult in the fast-growing field of ordering online. In the case of customized products, it is necessary to forecast the demand for the components and materials required for fulfilling customized orders. Demand forecasting must be done with business partners along the supply chain, as was described in Chapter 7. Supply chain problems jeopardize order fulfillment.

WHY SUPPLY CHAIN PROBLEMS EXIST

Many problems along the EC supply chain stem from *uncertainties* and from the need to *coordinate* several activities, internal units, and business partners.

A major source of the uncertainties in EC, as noted earlier, is the demand forecast. Demand is influenced by factors such as consumer behavior, economic conditions, competition, prices, weather conditions, technological developments, consumer confidence, and more. Any one of these factors may change quickly. The demand forecast should be conducted frequently, in conjunction with collaborating business partners along the supply chain in order to correctly gauge demand and make plans to meet it. As was shown in Chapter 7, companies attempt to achieve accurate demand forecasts by methods such as information sharing in collaborative commerce.

Other uncertainties that lead to supply chain and order fulfillment problems are variable delivery times, which depend on many factors ranging from machine failures to road conditions, and quality problems of materials and parts, which may create production time delays.

This area can be improved with RFID. RFID helps locate shipments in real time so delays are minimized and customer service is enhanced.

Pure EC companies are likely to have more problems because they do not have a logistics infrastructure already in place and thus are forced to use external logistics services rather than in-house departments for these functions. These external logistics services often are called **third-party logistics suppliers (3PL)**, or *logistics service providers*. Outsourcing such services can be expensive, and it requires more coordination and dependence on outsiders who may not be reliable. For this reason, large virtual retailers such as Amazon.com are developing their own physical warehouses and logistics systems. Other virtual retailers are creating strategic alliances with logistics companies or with experienced mail-order companies that have their own logistics systems.

third-party logistics suppliers (3PL)
External, rather than in-house, providers of logistics services.

In addition to uncertainties, EC supply chain/fulfillment problems also are created by lack of coordination and inability or refusal to share information among business partners. One of the most persistent order fulfillment problems is the bullwhip effect (see Chapter 7).

EC (and IT) can provide solutions to these order fulfillment problems, as will be shown in the next section.

Section 13.2 ▶ REVIEW QUESTIONS

1. List some problems along the EC supply chain.
2. Explain how uncertainties create order fulfillment problems. List some of these problems.
3. Describe the role of 3PLs.

13.3 SOLUTIONS TO ORDER FULFILLMENT PROBLEMS

Many EC logistics problems are generic; they can be found in the non-Internet world as well. Therefore, many of the solutions that have been developed for these problems in brick-and-mortar companies also work for e-tailers. Most of these solutions are facilitated by IT and by EC technologies, as was shown in Chapter 7. In this section, we will discuss some of the specific solutions to the EC order fulfillment problems (see Rao et al. 1999).

IMPROVEMENTS IN THE ORDER-TAKING PROCESS

One way to improve order fulfillment is to improve the order-taking process and its links to fulfillment and logistics. Order taking can be done via EDI, EDI/Internet, the Internet, or an extranet, and it may be fully automated. For example, in B2B, orders can be generated and transmitted automatically to suppliers when inventory levels fall below a certain threshold. The result is a fast, inexpensive, and more accurate (no need to rekey data) order-taking process. In B2C, Web-based ordering using electronic forms expedites the process, makes the process more accurate (e.g., intelligent agents can check the input data and provide instant feedback), and reduces processing costs for sellers. When EC order taking can interface or integrate with a company's back-office system, it shortens cycle times and eliminates errors.

Order-taking improvements also can take place *within* an organization, for example, when a manufacturer orders parts from its own warehouse. Whenever delivery of such parts runs smoothly, disruptions to the manufacturing process are minimized, reducing losses from downtime. For example, as detailed in the Online File W13.2, Dell has improved the flow of parts in its PC repair operations, resulting in greater efficiency and cost savings.

Implementing linkages between order-taking and payment systems also can be helpful in improving order fulfillment. Electronic payments can expedite both the order fulfillment cycle and the payment delivery period. With such systems, payment processing can be significantly less expensive and fraud can be better controlled.

WAREHOUSING AND INVENTORY MANAGEMENT IMPROVEMENTS

A popular EC inventory management solution is a **warehouse management system (WMS)**. WMS refers to a software system that helps in managing warehouses. It has several components. For example, in the case of Amazon.com the system supports item pickers as well as packaging. Amazon.com's B2C WMS can handle hundreds of millions of packages. In EC Application Case 13.1, we describe a B2B WMS at Schurman Inc., which demonstrates several applications.

warehouse management system (WMS)
A software system that helps in managing warehouses.

CASE 13.1

EC Application

HOW WMS HELPS SCHURMAN IMPROVE ITS INTERNAL AND EXTERNAL ORDER FULFILLMENT SYSTEM

Schurman Fine Paper is a manufacturer and retailer of greeting cards and related products. It sells through its own 170 specialty stores (Papyrus), as well as through 30,000 independent retail outlets.

Using RedPrairie integrated logistics software solutions, Schurman improved its demand forecast and minimized both out-of-stocks and overstocking. The system also allows physical inventory counts to be conducted without the need to shut down the two central warehouses for a week three times a year.

The central warehouses receive shipments from about 200 suppliers worldwide (500 to 1,000 orders per day). Until 2003, all inventory and logistics management was done manually. One problem solved by the software is picking products from multiple Stock Keeping Unit (SKU) locations. Picking is faster now, with a minimum of errors.

Orders go directly from the EDI to shipping, which ignites the fulfillment and shipment process. An advanced ship notice is automatically generated (replacing the lengthy process of manual scanning). The new system also automates the task of assessing the length, width, height, and weight of each item before it goes into a box (to determine which item goes to what box). The system also improved inventory replenishment allocations. In the past, the list of items to be picked up included items not available in the primary location. Pickers wasted time looking for these items, and unfound items had to be picked up later from the reserve storage center, resulting in delays. The WMS simultaneously created two lists, expediting fulfillment. This tripled the number of orders fulfilled per picker per day. The system also generates automatic replenishment orders for items falling below a minimum level at any storage location.

In addition, special software provides Schurman's customer service department with *real-time* access to inventory and distribution processes, allowing the department to track the status of all orders. The WMS also tracks the status of all orders and sends alerts when an order problem occurs (e.g., delay in downloading). An e-mail goes to all necessary parties in the company, so they can fix the problem. Finally, information collected about problems can be analyzed so remedies can be made quickly. All of this helps to reduce both overstocks and out-of-stocks.

Source: Compiled from Parks (2004).

Questions

1. Identify what the WMS automates, both in receiving and shipping.
2. In the future, RFID tags could replace the bar codes that are currently used. What would be the advantages of using RFID?
3. How has inventory management been improved?

Other Inventory Management Improvements

WMS is useful in reducing inventory and decreasing the incidence of out-of-stocks. Such systems also are useful in maintaining an inventory of repair items so repairs can be expedited (e.g., Dell, see Online File W13.2); picking items out of inventory in the warehouse (e.g., Amazon.com and Schurman); communicating (e.g., Schurman); managing product inventory (e.g., Schurman); receiving items at the warehouse (e.g., Schurman); and automating the warehouse (e.g., Amazon.com). For example, inventories can be minimized by introducing a make-to-order (pull) production process and by providing fast and accurate demand information to suppliers. By allowing business partners to electronically track and monitor inventory levels and production activities, inventory management can be improved, and inventory levels, as well as the administrative expenses of inventory management, can be minimized. In some instances, the ultimate inventory improvement is to have no inventory at all; for products that can be digitized (e.g., software), order fulfillment can be instantaneous and the need for inventory can be eliminated. Two methods of inventory improvements are VMI and the use of RFID (Chapter 7).

Automated Warehouses

Large-volume EC fulfillment requires automated warehouses. Regular warehouses are built to deliver large quantities to a small number of stores and plants. In B2C, however, businesses need to send small quantities to a very large number of individuals. Automated warehouses can minimize the order fulfillment problems that arise from this need.

Automated warehouses may include robots and other devices that expedite the pick-up of products. An example of a company that uses such warehouses is Amazon.com (see the opening case).

The largest EC/mail-order warehouse in the United States was operated by a mail-order company, Fingerhut. This company handled its own order fulfillment process for mail orders and online orders, as well as orders for Wal-Mart, Macy's, KbKids, and many others. Other companies (e.g., fosdickfulfillment.com and efulfillmentservices.com) provide similar order fulfillment services. The keys to successful inventory management, in terms of order fulfillment, are efficiency and speed, which can be facilitated by wireless devices.

Using Wireless Technologies

Wireless technologies have been used in warehouses for over a decade (see Chapter 9). An example of how wireless supports WMS is provided in EC Application Case 13.2.

Using RFID to Improve WMS. In Chapter 7, we introduced the potential uses of RFID in the supply chain. We provided an example of how RFID can be used to track items as they are moved from the manufacturer's to the customer's warehouses. Once inside the customer's warehouse, RFID can be used to track the whereabouts of the items (see EC Application Case 13.1, question #2). This can facilitate inventory counts as well as save pickers' trips.

SPEEDING DELIVERIES

In 1973, a tiny company initiated the concept of "next-day delivery." It was a revolution in door-to-door logistics. A few years later, that company, FedEx, introduced its "next-morning delivery" service. Today, FedEx moves over 4 million packages a day, all over the globe, using several hundred airplanes and several thousand vans. Incidentally, by one report (Pickering 2000), 70 percent of these packages are the result of EC.

Same Day, Even Same Hour, Delivery

In the digital age, however, even the next morning may not fast enough. Today we talk about *same-day delivery*, and even delivery within an hour. Deliveries of urgent materials to and from hospitals are an example of such a service. Two of the newcomers to this area are eFullfillment Service (efulfillmentservice.com) and One World (owd.com). These companies have created networks for the rapid distribution of products, mostly EC-related ones. They offer national distribution systems across the United States in collaboration with shipping companies, such as FedEx and UPS.

Delivering groceries is another area where speed is important, as discussed in Chapter 3. Quick pizza deliveries have been available for a long time (e.g., Domino's Pizza). Today, many pizza orders can be placed online. Also, many restaurants deliver food to customers who order online, a service called "dine online." Examples of this service can be found at dineonline.com, gourmetdinnerservice.com.au, and letsdineonline.com. Some companies even offer aggregating services, processing orders from several restaurants and making deliveries (e.g., dialadinner.com.hk in Hong Kong).

Supermarket Deliveries

Supermarket deliveries are done same day or next day. Arranging and making such deliveries may be difficult, especially when fresh food is to be transported, as discussed in Chapter 3. Buyers need to be home at certain times to accept the deliveries. Therefore, the distribution systems for such enterprises are critical. For an example of an effective distribution system, see Online File W13.3 about Woolworths of Australia at the book's Web site.

One of the most comprehensive delivery systems is that of GroceryWorks (now a subsidiary of Safeway UK). The system is illustrated in Exhibit 13.4. Note that the delivery trucks can pick up other items (such as rented videos and dry cleaning).

Failed Delivery Companies

As described in Chapters 1 and 3, one of the most publicized dot-com failures was Webvan, an express-delivery company that lost $1.2 billion (the largest of any failed dot-com loss). Another well-publicized failure was that of Kozmo.com, described in EC Application Case 13.3.

CASE 13.2

EC Application

PEACOCKS USES WIRELESS TO SMOOTH ITS SUPPLY CHAIN

Peacocks of Wales operates approximately 250 retail stores, selling clothes and home furniture in Wales and southern England. The company had a problem with its internal supply chain: Its paper-based system of managing product distribution was prone to problems, such as incorrectly completed pick-lists, wrongly picked items, transcription errors, delays in generating and receiving data, and much more. These interfered with the company's growth strategy and reduced its profit.

In 1997, Peacocks consolidated its 6 warehouses into a single distribution center (100,000 square feet, 3 stories). Stores were ordering more than 4,000 SKUs each day. These needed to be picked and shipped to stores effectively and efficiently. Using one place instead of six solved some of Peacocks' problems; however, the paper-based communication system was still ineffective. With the paper-based pick system, it was easy to run out of product at a specific location. When this occurred, the picker had to either wait for more product to arrive or return to his or her original location. The paper-based pick system had delays built into it, and stock problems were difficult to predict.

In 1998, the company began to replace its paper-based system with a wireless system (from Symbol Technologies; *symbol.com*). The fully automated distribution center now is equipped with a hands-free, real-time put-away and picking system. It is based on a combination of 28 wearable computers and 6 truck-mounted terminals supported by a wireless LAN. The system provides real-time control. Whether an item is moved by hand or by truck, Peacocks knows precisely where it is. If at any point in the process someone is at the wrong location, handling the wrong product, or trying to send it to the wrong place, the system simply sends out an alert and prevents the action. When Peacocks receives a delivery from a manufacturer, the consignment is checked and the individual cartons from each delivery are given an identifying bar code label and scanned to report receipt. In this way, every item can be tracked through the distribution center from the minute it arrives. The system immediately knows if there is a requirement at a pick location.

Once individual cartons are labeled, Peacock uses an automated conveyor system to send cartons to either the pick face or to the pallet store, as directed by the wireless WMS.

Each member of the picking team wears a wrist-mounted terminal that receives picking instructions from Peacocks' host system via the wireless LAN. As empty trolleys arrive in the pick area, the picker scans a bar code on the empty trolley, and the terminal's LCD screen tells the picker which aisle to go to, which location to pick from, and which items to pick. When a picker arrives at the pick face, the picker scans the bar code mounted at the end of the aisle. This verifies that the picker is in the correct aisle. The picker then scans another bar code at the product location to verify that the location is correct. Finally, the picker scans each item as it is placed into the trolley.

Once each pick is complete, the conveyor system takes each trolley to the dispatch area to be loaded into crates for delivery to a Peacocks store.

Because the data are sent to the host in real-time as the picking operation proceeds, the system knows when pick-face stocks are approaching the replenishment level set by Peacocks. When an item needs to be replenished, the system sends an alert to a truck-mounted terminal in the pallet store. As with the wrist-mounted terminals, an LCD screen on the truck terminal directs the driver to a precise location in the pallet racking. On arrival at the location, the driver uses a handheld scanner to scan the location bar code. This confirms that the truck driver is at the right location and selecting the right product.

The hands-free arrangement saves time and minimizes damage to the devices. The system also is user-friendly, so training is minimal.

Source: Compiled from Symbol Technologies (2005).

Questions

1. Describe Peacocks' internal order fulfillment process.
2. Identify all segments of Peacocks' supply chain that are improved by the system and describe the improvements.
3. How has the new system corrected the previous problems?
4. What are the advantages of wireless tools?
5. Investigate how RFID may improve this system in the future.

PARTNERING EFFORTS AND OUTSOURCING LOGISTICS

An effective way to solve order fulfillment problems is for an organization to partner with other companies. For example, several EC companies partner with UPS or FedEx, which may own part of the EC company.

One such unsuccessful partnering was demonstrated by the joint venture of MailBoxes Etc. with a fulfillment services company, Innotrac Corp., and with a logistics firm, AccuShip.com. The three companies developed a comprehensive logistics system that used software that connected e-tailers and order management systems to an intelligent system. The system determined whether a customer who wanted to make a return could do so and if they were entitled to a

EXHIBIT 13.4 Order Fulfillment at GroceryWorks

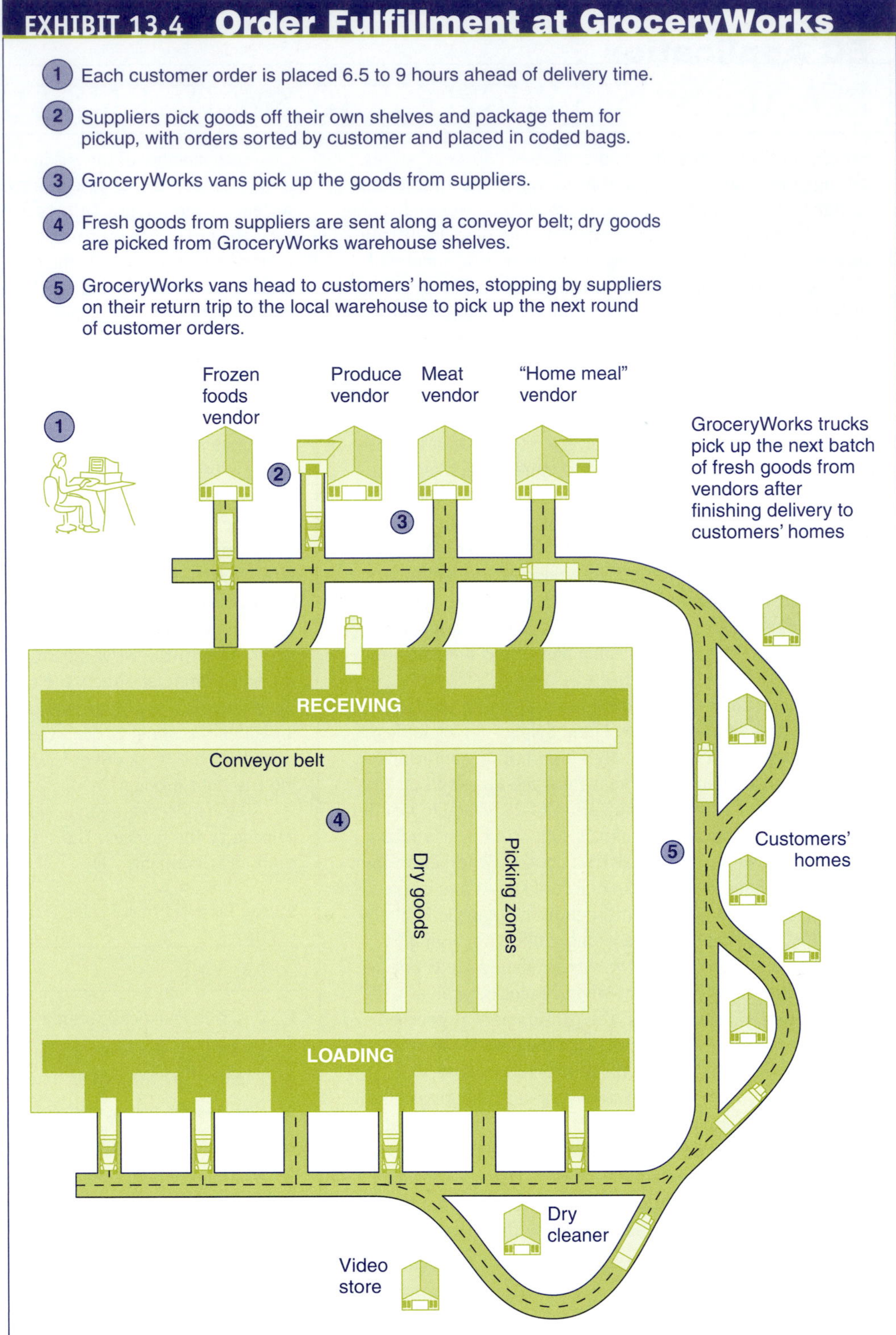

Source: As seen in *InteractiveWeek*, © 2005 by XPLANE® Corp.

CASE 13.3

EC Application

THE RISE AND FALL OF KOZMO.COM

The idea sounded logical: Create an express delivery system for online orders and deliver within an hour. The idea is not new. Domino's Pizza built its fortune on this idea, and today pizzas are delivered by many companies, door-to-door, in less than an hour.

Kozmo.com's business model was based on this idea. But instead of pizzas, Kozmo.com envisioned delivery of food items, rented videos, electronic games, and convenience products. Also, the model targeted only large cities, especially New York and Boston, where people use public transportation that may not be in operation at certain times. Items were delivered by "Kozmonauts"—employees with vans, bikes, or scooters. Orders were placed on the Internet, but telephone and fax orders also were accepted. The products were delivered from Kozmo.com's distribution centers.

The first logistics problem faced by Kozmo.com was the *return* of the rented videos. It was uneconomical to send the Kozmonauts to collect them. So Kozmo.com built drop boxes (like the FedEx boxes), initially in New York. Many of these boxes were vandalized. In an attempt to solve the problem, Kozmo.com partnered with Starbucks and moved the boxes to Starbucks cafes, some of which are open 24 hours a day. In exchange, Starbucks became an investor in Kozmo.com. Kozmo.com started to deliver coffee products to Starbucks' customers, and Starbucks printed Kozmo.com's logo on its coffee cups.

With a venture capital investment of over $250 million, the company expanded rapidly to 10 cities. During the initial period, delivery was free, and no minimum dollar amount of order was required. This strategy attracted many customers, but resulted in heavy losses, especially on small-value items. The company's growth was rapid: By the end of 2000, it had 1,100 employees, and an IPO was launched.

Soon after, problems started to surface. As with other B2C dot-coms, the more Kozmo.com sold, the larger the losses grew. In response, Kozmo.com closed operations in San Diego and Houston, imposed minimum charges, and added more expensive items (such as rented DVD players) to its offerings. This helped to generate profits in New York and San Francisco. However, with hundreds of dot-coms going out of business in late 2000 and early 2001, a major financial backer withdrew its support. Kozmo.com eventually ran out of cash and as a result had to close its doors on April 11, 2001.

Sources: Compiled from *kozmo.com* (2002) (note: site no longer available) and Blair (2000, 2001).

Questions

1. Draw the supply chains for food and rented items at Kozmo.com. What logistics problems did these supply chains present?
2. Compare Kozmo.com with Domino's Pizza. Why did Domino's do so well while Kozmo.com failed? Analyze the situation from an order fulfillment point of view.
3. The partnership with Starbucks was said to be extremely innovative, but it was cancelled by Kozmo.com when its financial problems began. (Kozmo.com had paid money to Starbucks for the permission to place the drop boxes.) Analyze this partnership.
4. Later in this chapter, you will learn about returns. After you have read that discussion, come back to this case and answer the following question: What advice could you have given Kozmo.com regarding the return of rented items?

refund. If allowed to make a return, customers had the option of doing so using the kiosks in MailBoxes Etc.'s physical franchises. This partnership failed, and many of the MailBoxes Etc. stores now have been taken over by UPS and renamed "The UPS Store."

Logistics-related partnerships can take many forms. For example, another partnering example is marketplaces managed by forwarders.com and aacb.com that help companies with goods find "forwarders"—the intermediaries that prepare goods for shipping. The company also helps forwarders find the best prices on air carriers, and the carriers bid to fill the space with forwarders' goods that need to be shipped.

SkyMall (skymall.com), now a subsidiary of Gem-Star TV Guide International, is a retailer that sells from catalogs on airplanes, over the Internet, and by mail order. It relies on its catalog partners to fill the orders. For small vendors that do not handle their own shipments and for international shipments, SkyMall contracts distribution centers owned by fulfillment outsourcer Sykes Enterprise. To coordinate the logistics of sending orders to thousands of customers, SkyMall uses an EC order management integrator called Order Trust. As orders come in, SkyMall conveys the data to Order Trust, which disseminates the data to the appropriate vendor or to a Sykes distribution center. A report is then sent to SkyMall, and SkyMall pays Order Trust a transaction fee. In the third quarter of 2004, the publishing segment of Gem-Star TV Guide International (including *TV Guide* magazine, SkyMall, and online businesses) reported revenues of $90.6 million (Fair Disclosure Wire 2004).

Comprehensive Logistics Services

Comprehensive logistic services are offered by major shippers, notably UPS and FedEx. These services are for B2C, B2B, G2B, and other types of EC. See Insights and Additions 13.2 for a description of the broad EC services offered by UPS.

Outsourcing Logistics

Instead of a joint venture or equity ownership with partners, most companies simply outsource logistics (see Bayles 2001). One advantage of this is that it is easy to change the logistics provider, as can be seen in the case of National Semiconductor Corp. described in Online File W13.4. Outsourcing is especially appealing to a small company such as BikeWorld, as illustrated in EC Application Case 13.4.

Insights and Additions 13.2 UPS Provides Broad EC Services

UPS is not only a leading transporter of goods sold on the Internet, but it also is a provider of expertise, infrastructure, and technology for managing global commerce—synchronizing the flow of goods, information, and funds for its customers.

UPS has a massive infrastructure to support these efforts. For example, it has an over 120-terabyte (10^{12}-byte) database that contains customer information and shipping records. More than 60,000 UPS customers have incorporated UPS Online Tools into their own Web sites to strengthen their customer services. In addition, UPS offers the following EC applications:

- Electronic supply chain services for corporate customers, by industry. This includes a portal page with industry-related information and statistics.
- Calculators for computing shipping fees.
- Helping customers manage their electronic supply chains (e.g., expediting billing and speeding up accounts receivable).
- Improved inventory management, warehousing, and delivery.
- A shipping management system that integrates tracking systems, address validation, service selection, and time-in-transit tools with Oracle's ERP application suite (similar integration with SAP exists).
- Notification of customers by e-mail about the status and expected arrival time of incoming packages.

Representative Tools

UPS's online tools—a set of seven transportation and logistics applications—lets customers do everything from tracking packages to analyzing their shipping history using customized criteria to calculating exact time-in-transit for shipments between any two postal codes in the continental United States.

The tools, which customers can download to their Web sites, let customers query UPS's system to get proof that specific packages were delivered on schedule. For example, if a company is buying supplies online and wants them delivered on a certain day, a UPS customer can use an optimal-routing feature to ensure delivery on that day, as well as to automatically record proof of the delivery in its accounting system.

UPS is offering logistics services tailored for certain industries. For example, UPS Logistics Group provides supply chain reengineering, transportation network management, and service parts logistics to vehicle manufacturers, suppliers, and parts distributors in the auto industry worldwide. UPS Autogistics improves automakers' vehicle delivery networks. For example, Ford reduced the time to deliver vehicles from plants to dealers in North America from an average of 14 days to about 6. UPS Logistics Group offers similar supply chain and delivery tracking services to other kinds of manufacturers.

UPS also is expanding into another area important to e-business—delivery of digital documents. The company was the first conventional package shipper to enter this market in 1998 when it launched UPS Document Exchange. This service monitors delivery of digitally delivered documents and provides instant receipt notification, encryption, and password-only access.

UPS offers many other EC-related services. These include the ability to enter the UPS system from wireless devices; helping customers configure and customize services; and providing for electronic bill presentation and payment (for B2B), EFT, and processing of COD payments.

Sources: Compiled from Violino (2000), Farber (2003), and UPS (2005).

Questions

1. Why would a shipper such as UPS expand to other logistic services?
2. Why would shippers want to handle payments?
3. Why does UPS provide software tools to customers?
4. What B2B services does UPS provide? (*Note:* Check *ups.com* to make sure that your answers are up-to-date.)

CASE 13.4

EC Application

HOW BIKEWORLD FULFILLS ORDERS

The Problem

BikeWorld, based in San Antonio, Texas, is known for its high-quality bicycles and components, expert advice, and personalized service. The company opened its Web site (*bikeworld.com*) in February 1996, hoping it would keep customers from using out-of-state mail-order houses. The Web represented a 24-hour global retail space where small companies such as BikeWorld, with its 16 employees, had the same reach and potential for success as much larger ones.

However, BikeWorld encountered one of Internet retailing's biggest problems: fulfillment and after-sale customer service. Sales of its high-value bike accessories over the Internet steadily increased, including in global markets, but the time spent processing orders, manually shipping packages, and responding to customers' order status inquiries was overwhelming for the small company.

The Solution

BikeWorld decided to outsource its order fulfillment to FedEx. FedEx offered reasonably priced quality express delivery, exceeding customer expectations while automating the fulfillment process. "To go from a complete unknown to a reputable worldwide retailer was going to require more than a fair price. We set out to absolutely amaze our customers with unprecedented customer service. FedEx gave us the blinding speed we needed," says Whit Snell, BikeWorld's founder.

The exhibit below shows the five steps in BikeWorld's order fulfillment process.

The Results

Four years after venturing online, BikeWorld's sales volume has more than quadrupled, and the company was on track to surpass $7.5 million in 2004. The company is consistently profitable. It has a fully automated and scalable fulfillment system; access to real-time order status, enhancing customer service and leading to greater customer retention; and is able to service customers around the globe.

Source: Courtesy of BikeWorld and FedEx.

Questions

1. Show the flow of parts from the company to customers.
2. Discuss the advantages of outsourcing to BikeWorld.
3. What activities are performed by FedEx?

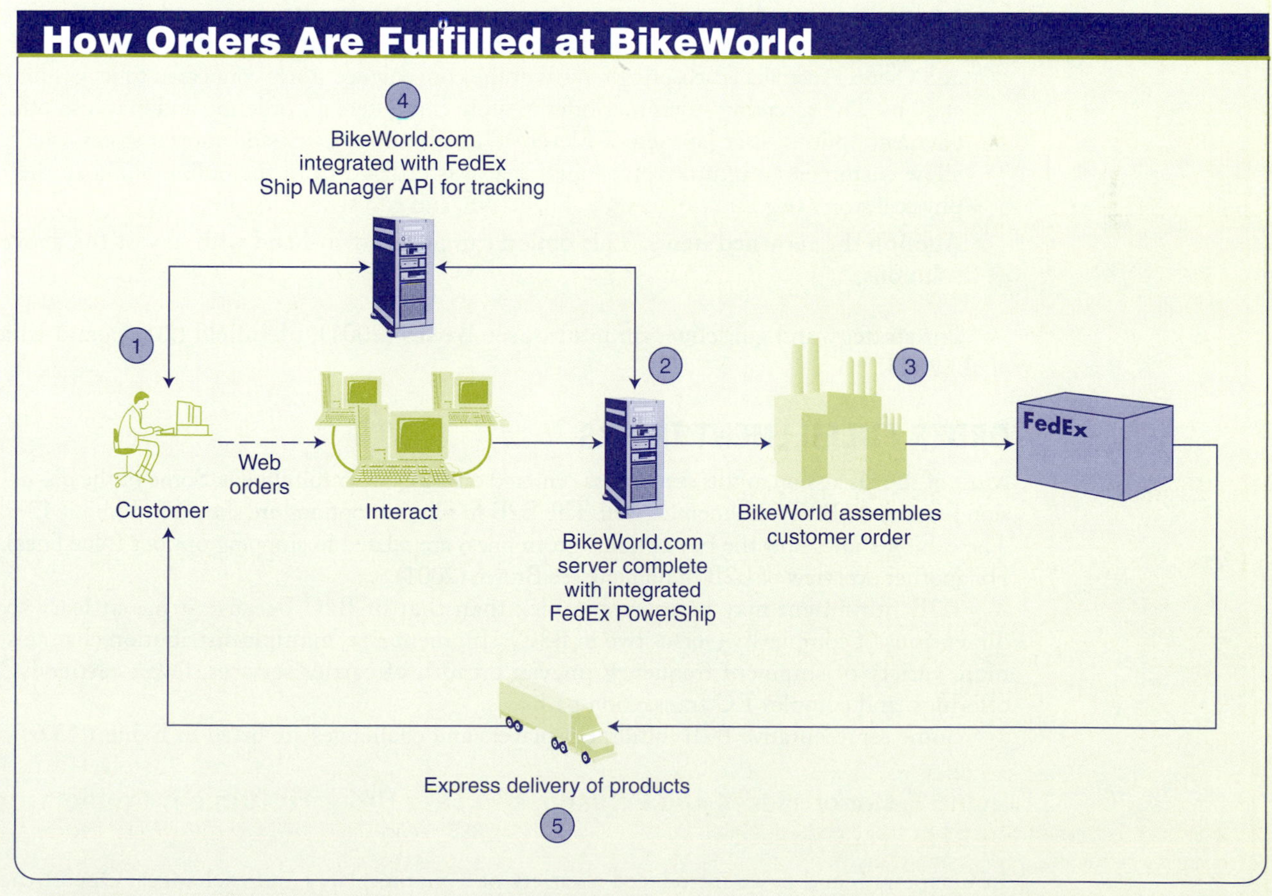

Source: Courtesy of BikeWorld and FedEx.

HANDLING RETURNS

Allowing for the return of unwanted merchandise and providing for product exchanges are necessary to maintain customers' trust and loyalty. The Boston Consulting Group (2001) found that the "absence of a good return mechanism" was the number two reason shoppers cited for refusing to buy on the Web frequently. According to Bayles (2001), a good return policy is a must in EC.

Dealing with returns is a major logistics problem for EC merchants. Several options for handling returns exist:

- **Return the item to the place where it was purchased.** This is easy to do with a purchase from a brick-and-mortar store, but not a virtual one. To return a product to a virtual store, a customer needs to get authorization, pack everything up, pay to ship it back, insure it, and wait up to two billing cycles for a credit to show up on his or her statement. The buyer is not happy, and neither is the seller, who must unpack, check the paperwork, and resell the item, usually at a loss. This solution is workable only if the number of returns is small or the merchandise is expensive (e.g., at Blue Nile, Chapter 2).
- **Separate the logistics of returns from the logistics of delivery.** With this option, returns are shipped to an independent returns unit and are handled separately. This solution may be more efficient from the seller's point of view, but it does not ease the returns process for the buyer.
- **Completely outsource returns.** Several outsourcers, including UPS and FedEx, provide logistics services for returns (as described in Bayles 2001). The services deal not only with delivery and returns, but also with the entire logistics process. FedEx, for example, offers several options for returning goods (see fedex.com).
- **Allow the customer to physically drop the returned item at a collection station.** Offer customers locations (such as a convenience store or The UPS Store) where they can drop off returns. In Asia and Australia, returns are accepted in convenience stores and at gas stations. For example, BP Australia Ltd. (gasoline service stations) teamed up with wishlist.com.au, and Caltex Australia is accepting returns at the convenience stores connected to its gasoline stations. The accepting stores may offer in-store computers for ordering and may also offer payment options, as at Japanese 7-Eleven's (7dream.com). Click-and-mortar stores usually allow customers to return merchandise that was ordered from the online outlet to their physical stores (e.g., amazon.com, walmart.com, and eddiebauer.com).
- **Auction the returned items.** This option can go hand-in-hand with any of the above solutions.

For strategy and guidelines on returns, see Bayles (2001), Steinfield (2002), and Elia et al. (2004).

ORDER FULFILLMENT IN B2B

Most of the discussion in this section has centered on B2C order fulfillment. Some of the discussion pertains to B2B fulfillment as well. The B2B fulfillment options are shown in Exhibit 13.5. The exhibit shows how the buy options (green lines) are related to shipping options (blue lines). For another overview of B2B fulfillment, see Brown (2001).

B2B fulfillment may be more complex than that of B2C because it has at least six dimensions of complexity (versus two in B2C): shipment size, multiple distribution channels, more variety of shipment frequency, uneven breadth of carrier services, fewer carrier EC offerings, and complex EC transaction paths.

Some representative B2B fulfillment players and challenges are listed in Exhibit 13.6.

Using E-Marketplaces and Exchanges to Ease Order Fulfillment Problems in B2B

In Chapters 5 and 6, we introduced a variety of e-marketplaces and exchanges. One of the major objectives of these entities is to improve the operation of the B2B supply chain. Let's see how this works with different business models.

EXHIBIT 13.5 **B2B Buy and Ship Options**

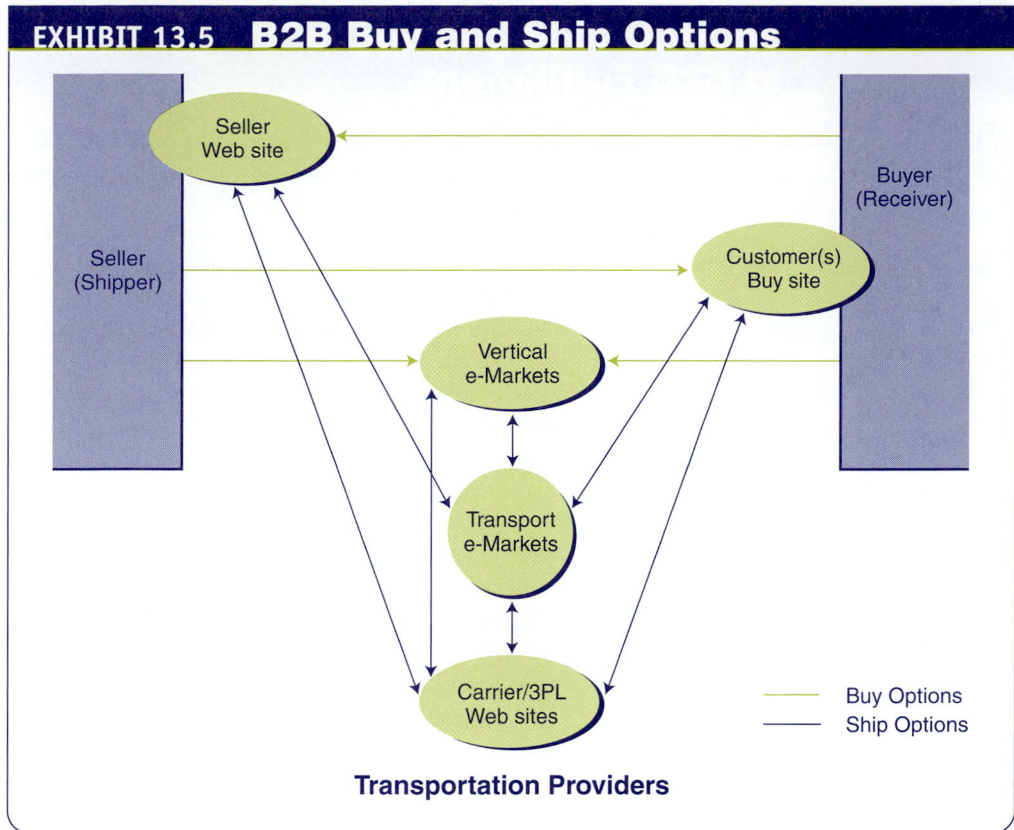

Source: Courtesy of Norbridge Inc., © 2003.

- A company-centric marketplace can solve several supply chain problems. For example, CSX Technology developed an extranet-based EC system for tracking cross-country train shipments as part of its supply chain initiative and was able to effectively identify bottlenecks and more accurately forecast demand.
- Using an extranet, Toshiba America provides an ordering system for its dealers to buy replacement parts for Toshiba's products. The system smoothes the supply chain and delivers better customer service.
- A vertical exchange, such as that of Covisint in the automotive industry, connects thousands of suppliers with automakers. Hundreds of vertical exchanges exist all over the world; many of them deal with both buying and selling. The direct contact between buyers and sellers in such exchanges reduces communication and search problems in the supply chain and helps with order fulfillment.

For additional discussion on how fulfillment is done in B2B, see fedex.com, ups.com, and Bayles (2001).

Order Fulfillment in Services

Thus far, we have concentrated on order fulfillment with physical products. Fulfilling service orders (e.g., buy or sell stocks, process insurance claims) may involve more information processing, which requires more sophisticated EC systems. One such system is described in the Real-World Case at the end of this chapter (CIGNA Corp.).

INNOVATIVE E-FULFILLMENT STRATEGIES

Lee and Whang (2001) and Brian (2002) propose several innovative e-fulfillment strategies. They call one of these innovations *logistics postponement*. Supply chain partners can move information flows and hold off shipping actual physical goods until a point at which they can make more-direct shipments. Two examples of logistics postponement are (1) merge-in-transit and (2) rolling warehouses.

EXHIBIT 13.6 Players and Challenges in B2B Fulfillment

Players	Challenges
Shippers (sellers)	Mix of channels, choice of logistics partners, go solo or use aggregation, what to outsource, integration of strategic/tactical/operational decisions
Receivers (buyers)	Solo and/or consortia buy sites, supply chain collaboration, total delivered costs, when to buy
Carriers	Self-service Web sites, links to vertical transportation e-marketplaces, institutional drag
Third-party logistics providers	Cooperation from carriers, breadth of modes/services, IT resources, customer acquisition
Warehouse companies	Location, operational intensity, capital investment, mode of automation, choice of builders
Vertical e-marketplaces	Where is the "ship-it" button? Who's behind it? What services are offered?
Transportation e-marketplaces	Moving beyond spot transactions to ASPs and value-added services, neutrality versus alignment, market mechanisms (e.g., bidding)
Logistics software application vendors	Comprehensive solutions, e-marketplace involvement, strategic partnerships, integration with existing software

merge-in-transit
Logistics model in which components for a product may come from two different physical locations and are shipped directly to customer's location.

rolling warehouse
Logistics method in which products on the delivery truck are not preassigned to a destination, but the decision about the quantity to unload at each destination is made at the time of unloading.

Merge-in-transit is a model in which components for a product may come from two different physical locations (Croxton et al. 2003). For example, in shipping a PC, the monitor may come from the East Coast of the United States and the CPU from the West Coast. Instead of shipping the components to a central location and then shipping both together to the customer, the components are shipped directly to the customer and merged into one shipment by the local deliverer (so the customer gets all the parts in one delivery), reducing unnecessary transportation.

With a **rolling warehouse**, products on the delivery truck are not preassigned to a destination, but the decision about the quantity to unload at each destination is made at the time of unloading (Knaack 2001). Thus, the latest order information can be taken into account, assisting in inventory control and lowering logistics costs (by avoiding repeat delivery trips). The rolling warehouse method also works in the ocean shipping industry, where it is called a *floating warehouse*.

Another example of innovative e-fulfillment strategies proposed by Lee and Whang (2001) is *leveraged shipments*. By this, they mean planning shipments based on a combination of size (or value) of the order and the geographic location. The size of the orders shipped by most e-tailers is small. The cost of delivery is justified only if there is a high concentration of orders from customers located in close proximity or if the value of the order is large enough. *Delivery-value density* is a decision support tool that helps determine whether it is economical to deliver goods to a neighborhood area in one trip. (The density is computed by dividing average total dollar volume of the shipment per trip by the average travel distance per trip.) The larger the density value, the better. One example of leveraging shipments is to deliver to specific geographic areas on specific days of the week and to install delivery receptacles at the destination so drivers do not have to return to or wait at the site for a customer to arrive. A second example of leveraging shipments is when a 3PL hires "dealers" that are familiar with the physical region of the delivery. The 3PL provides the dealers with the products, and the dealers deliver to the final destination.

WWW

For more discussion of the innovative e-fulfillment strategies proposed by Lee and Whang (2001), see Online File W13.5. For other innovative applications, see Online File W13.6 about Ingram Micro.

Section 13.3 ▶ REVIEW QUESTIONS

1. List the various order-taking solutions.
2. List solutions for improved delivery.
3. Describe same-day shipments.
4. Describe some innovative e-strategies for order fulfillment.
5. Describe how the return of items can be effectively managed.
6. Describe issues in B2B fulfillment.

13.4 CRM AND ITS RELATIONSHIP WITH EC

Customer relationship management (CRM) recognizes that customers are the core of a business and that a company's success depends on effectively managing its relationships with them (see Greenberg 2004). CRM focuses on building long-term and sustainable customer relationships that add value both for the customer and the company (Romano and Fjermestad 2001–2002; Kalakota and Robinson 2001). (See also insightexec.com and crmassist.com.)

Just like their off-line counterparts, online companies also must deliver *customer services.* Customer services are an integral part of CRM.

WHAT IS CRM: DEFINITIONS, TYPES, AND CLASSIFICATIONS

In Chapter 1, we provided some definitions of CRM. Greenberg (2004) provides more than 10 definitions, several made by CEOs of CRM providers or users. The Patricia Seybold Group (2002) provides several additional definitions, as do Tan et al. (2002). Why are there so many definitions? The reason is that CRM is new and still evolving. Also, it is an interdisciplinary field, so each discipline (e.g., marketing, MIS, management) defines CRM differently. We will repeat part of the definition from Chapter 1 here.

> **Customer relationship management (CRM)** *is a business strategy to select and manage customers to optimize long-term value. CRM requires a customer-centric business philosophy and culture to support effective marketing, sales, and service processes. (*crmguru.com *2005)*

customer relationship management (CRM)
A customer service approach that focuses on building long-term and sustainable customer relationships that add value both for the customer and the company.

Types of CRM

In Chapter 1, we distinguished three types of CRM activities: operational, analytical, and collaborative. Operational CRM related to typical business functions involving customer services, order management, invoice/billing, or sales and marketing automation and management. Analytical CRM involves activities that capture, store, extract, process, interpret, and report customer data to a user, who then analyzes them as needed. Collaborative CRM deals with all the necessary communication, coordination, and collaboration between vendors and customers.

Classification of CRM Programs

Tan et al. (2002) distinguish the following classifications of CRM programs:

- **Loyalty programs.** These programs are aimed at increasing customer loyalty. An example is the frequent-flyer points given by airlines.
- **Prospecting.** These promotion programs are intended to win new, first-time customers (see Chapter 4).
- **Save or win back.** These are programs that try to convince customers not to leave or, if they have left, to rejoin. When one of the authors of this book left AOL, for example, the company's representative offered many incentives to stay.
- **Cross-sell/up-sell.** By offering complementary products (cross-sell) or enhanced products (up-sell) that customers would like, companies make customers happy and increase their own revenue.

Another classification of CRM programs divides them by the service or product they offer (e.g., self-configuration, account tracking, call centers). These programs are presented in Section 13.5.

eCRM

Managing customer relationships is a business activity that has been practiced by corporations for generations. As evidenced by the many successful businesses that existed before the computer, computers are not required to manage one's customers well. However, since the mid-1990s, CRM has been enhanced by various types of information technologies. CRM technology is an evolutionary response to environmental changes, making use of new IT devices and tools. The term eCRM was coined in the mid-1990s when customers started using Web browsers, the Internet, and other electronic touch points (e-mail, POS terminals, call centers, and direct sales). eCRM also includes online process applications such as segmentation and personalization. The use of the Internet, intranets, and extranets made customer services, as well as services to partners (see partner relationship management [PRM] in Chapter 6), much more effective and efficient than before the Internet.

eCRM
Customer relationship management conducted electronically.

Through Internet technologies, data generated about customers can easily be fed into marketing, sales, and customer service databases for analysis. The success or failure of CRM efforts can now be measured and modified in real time, further elevating customer expectations. In the Internet-connected world, eCRM has become a requirement for survival, not just a competitive advantage. eCRM covers a broad range of topics, tools, and methods, ranging from the proper design of digital products and services to pricing and loyalty programs (e.g., see e-sj.org, the *Journal of Service Research*, jsr.sagepub.com, and ecrmguide.com).

Note that eCRM is sometimes referred to as *e-service* (see Rust and Lemon 2001). However, the term *e-service* has several other meanings. For example, some define e-service as EC in service industries, such as banking, hospitals, and government, whereas others confine its use to e-self-service. To avoid confusion, we prefer to use the term *eCRM* rather than *e-service.* Note that people use the terms *eCRM* and *CRM* interchangeably. Most vendors use just *CRM,* and that term also is most often used in the accounting-profession literature.

THE SCOPE OF CRM

For online transactions, CRM often provides help features. In addition, if a product is purchased off-line, customer service may be offered online. For example, if a consumer purchases a product off-line and needs expert advice on how to use it, he or she may find detailed instructions online (e.g., livemanuals.com).

According to Voss (2000), there are three levels of CRM:

1. **Foundation services.** This includes the *minimum necessary* services, such as site responsiveness (e.g., how quickly and accurately the service is provided), site effectiveness, and order fulfillment.
2. **Customer-centered services.** These services include order tracing, configuration and customization, and security/trust. These are the services that *matter the most* to customers.
3. **Value-added services.** These are *extra services,* such as dynamic brokering, online auctions, and online training and education. An example of how value-added services helped a B2C company in Italy succeed is provided in Online File W13.7.

The Extent of Service

Customer service should be provided throughout the entire product life cycle. The value chain for CRM is composed of four parts (Plant 2000):

1. **Customer acquisition (prepurchase support).** A service strategy that reflects and reinforces the company's brand and provides information to potential customers to encourage them to buy.
2. **Customer support during purchase.** This service strategy provides a shopping environment that the consumer sees as efficient, informative, and productive.
3. **Customer fulfillment (purchase dispatch).** This involves timely delivery; including keeping the customer informed about the fulfillment process, especially if there are any delays.
4. **Customer continuance support (postpurchase).** Information and support help maintain the customer relationship between purchases.

EC Application Case 13.5 provides several examples of how companies use eCRM. An additional example is provided in the Real-World Case at the end of this chapter.

BENEFITS AND LIMITATIONS OF CRM

The major benefit of CRM is the provision of superior customer care through the use of the Internet and IT technologies. In other words, CRM makes customers happy by providing choices of products and services, fast problem resolution and response, easy and quick access to information, and much more (see Section 13.5). Companies try to gain competitive advantage over their competitors by providing better CRM.

The major limitation of CRM is that it requires integration with a company's other information systems, which may not be an easy task. Also, as will be discussed later in this section, justifying the expense of CRM is not easy. It is difficult to support mobile employees with some CRM applications (e.g., those who travel). It is only in the last few years that m-commerce has encouraged the creation of exciting CRM applications.

CRM IMPLEMENTATION ISSUES

According to a *CIO Insight* study (2004), culture, commitment, and communication lead to CRM success—not technology. Seybold and Marshak (1998) highlight some important steps in building an EC strategy that is centered on the customer. These steps include a focus

CASE 13.5

EC Application

HOW COMPANIES USE eCRM

Almost all large companies have a formal CRM program (Agarwal et al. 2004). However, CRM programs may be implemented in a variety of different ways due to the large number of tools available (Section 13.5). Here are a few examples of how companies have implemented CRM:

- Continental Airlines monitors telephone calls to its data center, using software from Witness Systems (*witness.com*), which uses agents to analyze recorded conversations. The analysis tells Continental what customers really want. It also helps the company craft marketing plans and business strategy. Agents are able to serve customers better and resolve problems immediately, saving the company $1 million annually. To increase efficiency, Continental uses CallMiner, a labor-saving Witness Systems' program that automatically transcribes conversations into digitized text.
- Employees at more than 200 Sheraton Hotels owned by Starwood Hotels and Resorts are using a new eCRM system to coordinate fast responses to guests' complaints and unmet needs. When an employee does not respond to a request or complaint within a time frame predetermined by hotel management, the color of a computerized notice changes from green to yellow, and possibly to red. Red triggers management to quickly intervene and perhaps include special compensation for the guest. Starwood has reported significantly better operating results since the system was implemented. For details, see Babcock (2004).
- Boots the Chemists, a UK retailer of over 1,400 health and beauty stores, uses business intelligence and data mining (eCRM analytics) to learn about customers in its e-loyalty programs. The retailer uses data mining to acquire insights into customer behavior. Customer service agents can analyze, predict, and maximize the value of each customer relationship. This enables better one-to-one marketing efforts and reduces customer dissatisfaction.
- In a similar manner, outdoor product retailer, REI brings customer data into a single location and analyzes and manages it in real time. The results are used for various CRM initiatives. See Amato-McCoy (2003) for details.
- Harrah's Entertainment Inc. treats its customers differently: The more a customer spends in a casino—the more rewards the customer gets. The company assigns a value to each customer by using data mining.
- FedEx's CRM system enables the company to provide superb service to millions of customers using 56 call centers. Each of its 4,000 call center employees has instant access to a customer's profile. The profile tells the employee how valuable the customer is and the details of the current transaction. The more an agent knows about the customer, the better the service provided. Customers use one phone number regardless of where the company is or the destination of the package. The CRM reduced calls for help, increased customer satisfaction, and enabled better advertising and marketing strategy. For details, see Guzman (2004).

Questions

1. Identify common elements of CRM in these examples.
2. In addition to customer service, CRM systems provide managerial benefits. Identify and discuss these benefits.
3. Why is data mining becoming so important in CRM?

on the end customer; systems and business processes that are designed for ease of use and from the end customer's point of view; and efforts to foster customer loyalty (the key to profitability in EC). To successfully make these steps, businesses must take the following actions:

- Deliver personalized services (e.g., dowjones.com)
- Target the right customers (e.g., aa.com, national.com)
- Help customers do their jobs (e.g., boeing.com)
- Let customers help themselves (e.g., iprint.com)
- Streamline business processes that impact customers (e.g., ups.com, amazon.com)
- "Own" the customer's total experience by providing every possible customer contact (e.g., amazon.com, hertz.com).
- Provide a 360-degree view of the customer relationship (e.g., wellsfargo.com, verizon.com)

Many of these steps are valid both for B2C and for B2B EC. In B2B, CRM is known as PRM (see Chapter 6).

Large-scale CRM implementation is neither easy nor cheap. Tan et al. (2002) suggest five factors that are required to implement a CRM program effectively:

1. **Customer-centric strategy.** A customer-centric strategy should be established first at the corporate level. The strategy must be based on and consistent with the overall corporate strategy and must be communicated across the whole organization.
2. **Commitments from people.** The more commitments from people across the corporation to the transformation of the business strategy, the more likely the CRM implementation will succeed. Employees should be willing to learn the necessary technological skills.
3. **Improved or redesigned processes.** It is inherently difficult to identify the processes that need to be involved and frequently redesigned when implementing CRM.
4. **Software technology.** CRM software can record business transactions, create operations-focused databases, facilitate data warehousing and data mining, and provide decision-making support and marketing campaign management tools. Companies should select the appropriate CRM packages to meet specific corporate CRM needs as well as to enable integration with legacy enterprise applications such as the ERP system. Major CRM vendors are Siebel, Oracle, SAP, IBM, and Nortel/Clarify. Smaller players are Vignettee, BroadVision, Onyx, Microstrategy, E.piphany, Roundarch, and KANA. Major CRM consultants are KMPG Consultants, Deloitte Consultants, and the Patricia Seybold Groups (see Greenberg 2004).
5. **Infrastructure.** Effective CRM implementation requires a suitable corporate infrastructure. This infrastructure includes network setup, storage, and data backup, computing platforms, and Web servers. However, only effective corporate infrastructure *integration* can provide solid support for CRM implementation.

Agarwal et al. (2004) claim that many CRM projects are disappointing at the beginning and require remediation because companies do not manage them properly. They offer an extensive methodology on how to implement CRM. See Compton (2004) and Johnson (2004) for additional tips on CRM implementation.

INTEGRATING CRM INTO THE ENTERPRISE

Some CRM applications are independent of enterprise systems. However, many CRM applications must be integrated with other information systems. To understand why, let us examine Exhibit 3.3 (page 88 in Chapter 3).

As can be seen in the exhibit, CRM lies primarily between the customers and the enterprise. The communication between the two is done via the Internet, regular telephone, snail mail, and so on. However, to answer customer queries it is necessary to access files and databases. In medium and large corporations, these are usually part of a legacy system and/or ERP system. Companies may check data relevant to a customer order with their manufacturing plants, transportation vendors, suppliers, or other business partners. Therefore, CRM needs to interface with the supply chain, and do so easily, inexpensively, and quickly. In addition, CRM must be integrated with the data warehouse because, as is shown in Online

Appendix W4A, it is easier to build applications using data in the warehouse than using data residing in several internal and external databases. Finally, CRM itself collects customer and product data, including click stream data. These need to be prepared for data mining and other types of analysis.

The integration of ERP and CRM must include low-level data synchronization as well as business process integration so that the integrity of business roles can be maintained across systems and workflow tasks can pass between the systems. Such integration also ensures that organizations can perform *business intelligence* across systems.

JUSTIFYING CUSTOMER SERVICE AND CRM PROGRAMS

Two major problems arise when companies try to justify expenditures for customer service and CRM programs. The first problem is the fact that most of the benefits of CRM are intangible, and the second is that substantial benefits can usually be reaped only from loyal customers over the long run. This, of course, is true for both off-line and online organizations. In a 1990 study published in *Harvard Business Review* titled "Zero Defections: Quality Comes to Services" (see details at Reichheld and Schefter 2000), researchers demonstrated that the high cost of acquiring customers renders many customer relationship programs unprofitable during their early years. Only in later years, when the cost of retaining loyal customers falls and the volume of their purchases rises, do CRMs generate big returns (Reichheld and Schefter 2000). Therefore, companies are very careful about determining how much customer service to provide (see *CIO Insight* 2004 and Petersen 1999). For approaches for CRM justification, see Chapter 15 and Bonde (2004).

eCRM Analytics

To derive the most benefits from eCRM, it is necessary to properly collect and analyze relevant customer data. Nemati et al. (2004) provide results of a study on the integration of data in eCRM analytics. Analytics can analyze and document online customer/visitor patterns to acquire and retain users. Using data mining properly provides companies with valuable information on how to serve customers online. According to a 2004 CRM study (*CIO Insight* 2004), 75 percent of all large CRM users are using or will soon use CRM with data mining and analytics.

Metrics in Customer Service and CRM

One way to determine how much service to provide is to compare a company against a set of standards known as **metrics**. Metrics are either quantitative or qualitative. (See Jagannathan et al. 2001 and Sterne 2002.) Here are some Web-related metrics a company can use to determine the appropriate level of customer support:

metrics
Performance standards; may be quantitative or qualitative.

- **Response time.** Many companies have a target response time of 24 to 48 hours. If a company uses intelligent agents, a response can be made in real time or the system can provide an acknowledgment that the customer's message has been received and a response will be forthcoming.
- **Site availability.** Customers should be able to reach the company's Web site at any time (24 hours a day). This means that downtime should be as close to zero as possible.
- **Download time.** Users usually will not tolerate downloads that last more than 10 to 20 seconds.
- **Timeliness.** Information on the company site must be up-to-date. The company sets an interval (say, every month) at which information must be revised. If a set interval is not used, companies may have new products in stores but not on the Web or vice versa. In either case, potential sales may be lost.
- **Security and privacy.** Web sites must provide sufficient privacy statements and an explanation of security measures. (This metric is measurable as "yes" or "no"—either the statement and explanation are there or they are not.)
- **On-time order fulfillment.** Order fulfillment must be fast and comply with promised delivery dates. For example, a company can measure the time it takes to fulfill orders, and it can count the number of times it fails to meet its fulfillment promises.

- **Return policy.** In the United States and several other countries, return policies are a standard service. Having a return policy increases customer trust and loyalty. The ease by which customers can make returns is important to customer satisfaction.
- **Navigability.** A Web site must be easy to navigate. To gauge navigability, companies might measure the number of customers who get part way into an order and then "bail out."

A large number of applications can be used to provide CRM, as will be illustrated in Section 13.5.

Section 13.4 ▶ REVIEW QUESTIONS

1. Define CRM.
2. Describe the benefits and limitations of CRM.
3. List the major types of CRM.
4. Define eCRM.
5. Describe some implementation issues relating to CRM, including integration with the enterprise.
6. Discuss the issue of justifying CRM service.
7. Describe metrics related to CRM and customer service.

13.5 DELIVERING CUSTOMER SERVICE IN CYBERSPACE: CRM APPLICATIONS AND TOOLS

CRM applications are customer service tools designed to enhance customer satisfaction (the feeling that a product or service has met the customer's expectations). CRM applications improve on traditional customer service by means of easier communications and speedier resolution of customer problems, frequently by automatic responses to questions or by customer self-service. Today, in order to satisfy increased customer expectations, EC marketers must respond by providing the best, most powerful, and innovative systems and software. As a matter of fact, they must create customer-centric EC systems.

Customer service (or support) is the final link in the chain between providers and customers. It adds value to products and services and is an integral part of a successful business. Almost all medium and large companies today use the Web as a customer support channel (Chaudhury et al. 2001). CRM applications on the Web can take many forms, ranging from providing search and comparison capabilities (Chapter 3) to allowing customers to track the status of their orders.

The first step to building customer relationships is to give customers good reasons to visit and return to the Web site. In other words, the organization should create a site that is rich in information, hopefully with more content than a visitor can absorb in a single visit. The site should include not just product information, but also have value-added content from which visitors can get valuable information and services for free. Exhibit 16.10 (page 695) lists some ways in which online businesses can build customer relationships through content.

CLASSIFICATIONS OF CRM APPLICATIONS

The Patricia Seybold Group (2002) distinguishes among *customer-facing*, *customer-touching*, and *customer-centric intelligence* CRM applications. These three categories of applications are described below and are shown in Exhibit 13.7. The exhibit also shows how customers interact with these applications.

- **Customer-facing applications.** These include all the areas where customers interact with the company: call centers, including help desks; sales force automation; and field service automation. Such CRM applications basically automate information flow or support employees in these areas.
- **Customer-touching applications.** In this category, customers interact directly with the applications. Notable are self-service activities, such as FAQs; campaign management; and general-purpose EC applications.

EXHIBIT 13.7 CRM Applications

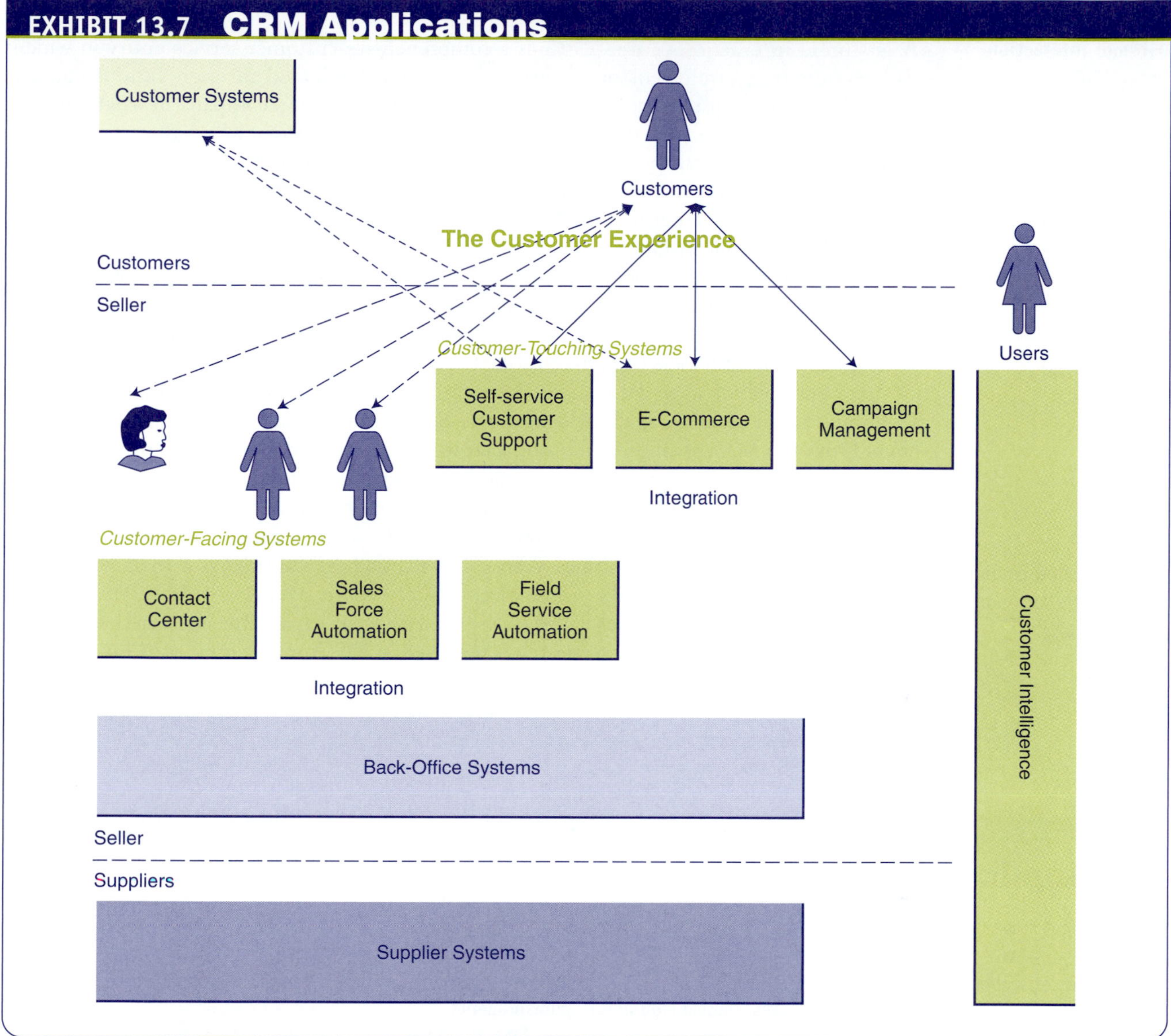

Source: *An Executive's Guide to CRM*, Patricia Seybold Group, March 21, 2002. Used with permission.

- **Customer-centric intelligence applications.** These are applications that are intended to analyze the results of operational processing and use the results of the analysis to improve CRM applications. Data reporting and warehousing and data mining are the prime topics here.

To this classification of CRM applications, we add the following fourth category:

- **Online networking and other applications.** Online networking refers to methods that provide the opportunity to build personal relationships with a wide range of people. These include chat rooms and discussion lists.

We use these four categories of applications to organize our presentation of CRM applications in the remainder of this section. (Further details on the first three categories can be found at psgroup.com, in the free download of *An Executive's Guide to CRM*.)

CUSTOMER-FACING APPLICATIONS

Customer-facing applications are those where customers interact with a company. The primary application is *Web-based call centers*, otherwise known as customer interaction centers.

Customer Interaction Centers

customer interaction center (CIC)
A comprehensive service entity in which EC vendors address customer-service issues communicated through various contact channels.

A **customer interaction center (CIC)** is a comprehensive customer service entity in which EC vendors take care of customer service issues communicated through various contact channels. It allows customers to communicate and interact with a company in whatever way they choose. Providing well-trained customer service representatives who have access to data such as customer history, purchases, and previous contacts is one way to improve customer service (see Adria and Chowdhury 2002). New products are extending the functionality of the conventional call center to e-mail, fax, voice, and Web interactivity (e.g., Web chat), integrating them into one product—the CIC.

A multichannel CIC works like this: (1) The customer makes a contact via one or more channels. (2) The system collects information and integrates it with a database, then determines a service response. (3) The customer is routed to self-service or to a human agent. (4) The service is provided to the customers (e.g., the customer's problem is resolved or question is answered).

telewebs
Call centers that combine Web channels with portal-like self-service.

An example of a well-managed integrated call center is that of Bell Advanced Communication in Canada, whose subscribers can submit customer service queries over the Web. From the Bell Advanced Web site, a customer can fill out an e-mail form with drop-down menus that help pinpoint the customer's problem. The e-mail then is picked up by the call center, which either answers the question immediately or tries to have a human response within 1 hour. Another example is a product called Customer Service Management Suite from e.epicor.com, which combines Web channels, such as automated e-mail reply, Web knowledge bases, and portal-like self-service, with call center agents or field service personnel. Such centers are sometimes called **telewebs**, and their capabilities are listed in Online Exhibit W13.1. An example of a teleweb is provided in EC Application Case 13.6.

A comprehensive description of Web-based call centers, including a tutorial, articles, and information on leading vendors is available at call-centers.org. For more examples of CICs and call centers, see callcenterops.com.

CASE 13.6

EC Application

DEVELOPING IBM'S TELEWEB CHANNEL

IBM's sales of technology to large and small businesses began in the 1960s with sales representatives, individually or in teams, calling on customers to sell their business machines. A transformation of the sales and marketing channels began in the 1990s with a decrease in the cost of electronically offered support tools.

Initially, in the early 1990s, 130 call centers provided support to customers in 150 countries, using 5,000 agents who were available to answer questions and take orders by telephone. These centers were organized into 25 specialized call centers by the mid-1990s, each specializing in areas such as multilingual support or Web responses. Concurrently, an e-commerce channel was built at *ibm.com*. However, the company discovered that online customers were seeking help from human representatives, and call-center use increased with Web usage.

This led to the integration of the telephone-based system and EC by connecting Web sites with customer-support call centers known as the TeleWeb. The TeleWeb provides seamless service, improves selling leverage and market coverage, and reduces costs. The various communication channels used by customers now are integrated to provide around-the-clock support for the programs and applications offered by IBM. Such integration has increased customer satisfaction and decreased the need for human agents.

Specific innovations that led to the success of the TeleWeb include dedicated tele-coverage representatives for specific business accounts; "e-sites" customized for individual accounts; online support, 24/7; and continual experimentation with innovative ways of handling customer needs (e.g., "click-and-connect" or "call-me-back" buttons).

By integrating TeleWeb channels, putting more services on the front and back ends of the buying process and involving humans in the middle process, IBM reaps many benefits. Two of those benefits have been the freeing up of agent time, which has saved millions of dollars, and larger order sizes (30 percent more on Web-only transactions).

Sources: Compiled from Diorio (2002), pp. 209–213, and *ibm.com* (accessed 2002).

Questions

1. What are the advantages of the multichannel TeleWeb?
2. Why is IBM so committed to the TeleWeb project?
3. What were the success factors of the project?

Intelligent Agents in Customer Service and Call Centers

To ease information overload from CRM activities, companies can use intelligent agents (see Chapter 4). Of special interest is a suite of five agents ("SmartBots") from Artificial-Life, Inc. (artificial-life.com). How intelligent agents function in a call center is shown schematically in Exhibit 13.8. As shown, an agent called Web Guide can interactively assist customers to navigate a Web site using plain English or another language. An agent called Messenger evaluates incoming e-mail and generates autoresponses. The Call Center agent provides the problem-resolution component to the conversations between the Web Guide and customers. It also refers the customer to a real person, if necessary. The EC agent executes EC-related tasks, such as providing real-time information on account status. Finally, the Sales Rep agent can create a user profile based on information collected from the other agents. For further details on agents, see agentland.com and Gateau et al. (2004).

Automated Response to E-Mail (Autoresponder)

The most popular online customer service tool is e-mail. Inexpensive and fast, e-mail is used to disseminate information and to conduct correspondence on many topics, including responses to customer inquiries.

The ease of sending e-mail messages has resulted in a flood of customer e-mails. Some companies receive tens of thousands of e-mails a week, or even a day. Answering these e-mails manually would be expensive and time-consuming. Customers want quick answers, usually within 24 hours (a policy of many organizations). Several vendors offer automated e-mail reply systems known as **autoresponders**, which provide answers to commonly asked questions. Autoresponders, also called *infobots* and *e-mail on demand*, are text files that are returned via e-mail, automatically on demand. They can relay standard information for support of customer service, marketing, and promotions. (See egain.com, aweber.com, and firepond.com.) The eGain system (egain.com), for example, looks for certain phrases or key words such as "complaint" or "information on a product" and then taps into a knowledge base to generate a canned, matching response. For messages that require human attention, the query is assigned an ID number and passed along to a customer agent for a reply.

autoresponders
Automated e-mail reply systems (text files returned via e-mail) that provide answers to commonly asked questions.

EXHIBIT 13.8 Intelligent Agents in Call Centers

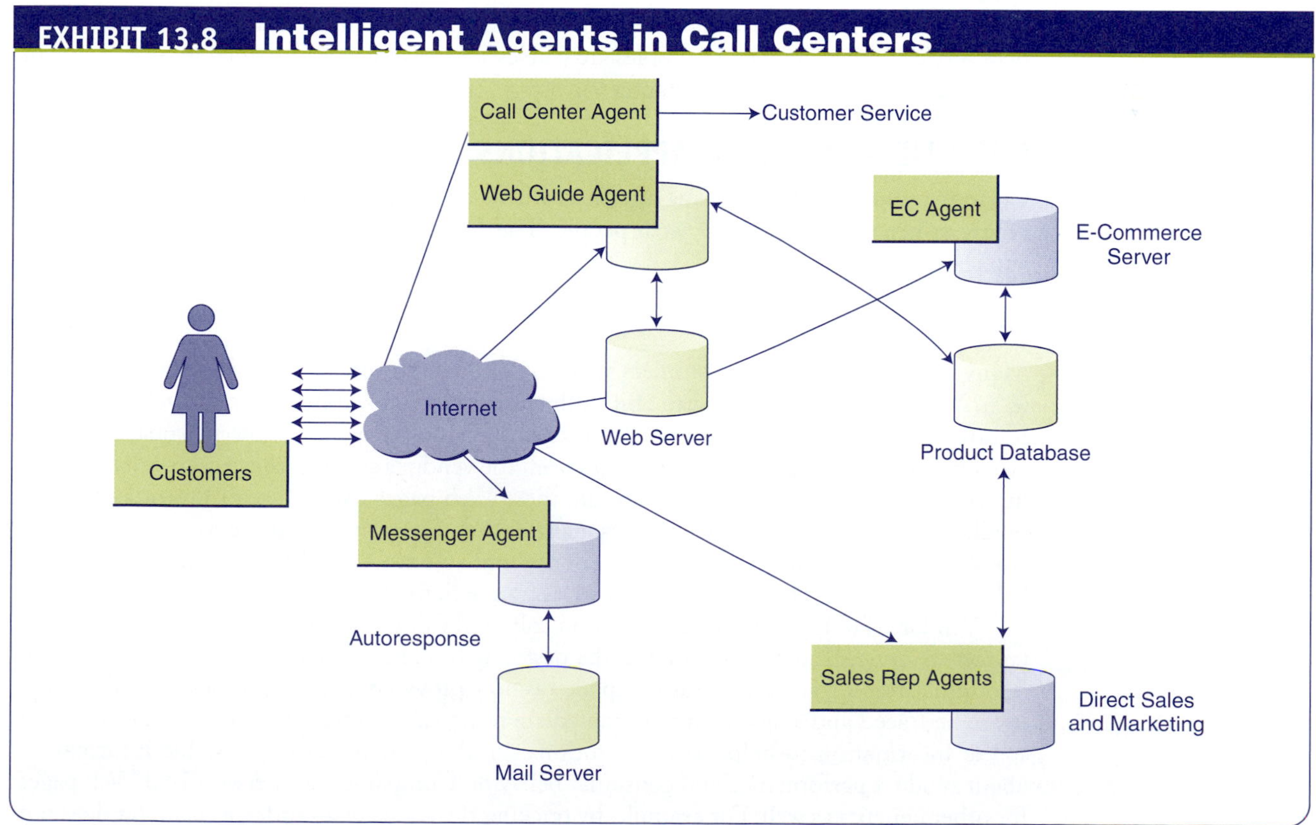

Severina Publications is a full-service Internet publishing and marketing company that offers autoresponders as a service to clients as well as a library of autoresponders as part of its Internet marketing strategy. Examples of the company's responders are:

- 12steps@severina.co.uk, which retrieves a list of 12 ways to promote a Web site off-line.
- Classified@severina.co.uk, which retrieves a list of classified ad sites on the Internet.
- Ezines@severina.co.uk, which retrieves a list of e-zines on the Web.

Many companies do not provide actual answers in their automatic responses, but only acknowledgment that a query has been received. Customer queries are classified in a decision-support repository until a human agent logs in and responds. This can be done in a call center using intelligent agents.

Sales Force Automation

sales force automation (SFA)
Software that automates the tasks performed by sales people in the field, such as data collection and its transmission.

Sales people constitute the major contact point with customers (both individuals and businesses). The more automation they have available, the better (quicker, more accurate) service they can provide to customers. **Sales force automation (SFA)** applications support the selling efforts of a company's sales force, helping salespeople manage leads, prospects, and customers through the sales pipeline. An example of such an application is a wireless device that allows quick communication with the corporate intranet. Another example was provided in the Maybelline case in Chapter 1 (pages 36–37); that company implemented a reporting system involving mobile devices. For further discussion, see information on B2E in Chapter 7; for advanced software products, see saleforce.com.

Field Service Automation

Field service employees, such as sales representatives, are on the move, and they interact directly with the customers. Field service representatives include repair people (e.g., from the telephone or electric company) who go to customers' homes. Providing service employees with automation can increase customer service. Field service automation applications support the customer service efforts of field service reps and service managers. These applications manage customer service requests, service orders, service contracts, service schedules, and service calls. They provide planning, scheduling, dispatching, and reporting features to field service representatives. Examples are wireless devices, such as provided in SFA. Some of these are *wearable devices* (see Chapter 9).

CUSTOMER-TOUCHING APPLICATIONS

Customer-touching applications are those where customers use interactive computer programs rather than interacting with people. The following are popular customer-touching applications.

Personalized Web Pages

Many companies provide customers with tools to create their own individual Web pages (e.g., MyYahoo!). Companies can efficiently deliver customized information such as product information and warranty information when the customer logs on to the personalized page. Not only can a customer pull information from the vendor's site, but the vendor can also push information to the consumer. In addition, these Web pages can be used to record customer purchases and preferences. Typical personalized Web pages include those for bank accounts, stock portfolio accounts, credit card accounts, and so on. On such sites, users can see their balances, records of all current and historical transactions, and more.

Vendors can use customer information collected from customized Web sites to facilitate customer service. Information that in the past may have been provided to the customer 1 to 3 months after a transaction was completed is now provided in real or almost-real time, and it can be traced and analyzed for an immediate response or action. Companies now use customer information to help market additional products by matching valuable information about product performance and consumer behavior. Companies use personalized Web pages for other benefits as well. For example, by tracking the status of an order, a customer does not need to call the company about it, saving the customer time, and at the same time saving the company the cost of having an employee answer the call. American Airlines is an example of one company that uses personalized Web sites to help increase the bottom line, as shown in EC Application Case 13.7.

E-Commerce Applications

As described in Chapter 1, e-commerce applications implement marketing, sales, and service functions through online touch points, most typically the Web. These applications let customers shop for products through a virtual-shopping-cart metaphor and purchase the products in their shopping carts through a virtual-check-out metaphor. Customers may also perform self-service support tasks such as checking order status, history inquiry, returns processing, and customer information management. This provides convenience to many customers and also saves them money, thus increasing their satisfaction. Details on such EC applications are provided in Chapter 3 and throughout the book.

Campaign Management

Campaign management applications automate marketing campaign activities such as online ad planning and analysis. They present offers to targeted leads, prospects, and customers on demand, on a schedule, or in response to business events through direct mail, e-mail, a contact center, field sales, and Web touch points. Ideally, these applications should be able to record responses to offers. Campaign management applications were presented in Chapter 4. For further details, see Greenberg (2004).

Web Self-Service

The Web environment provides an opportunity for customers to serve themselves. Known as **Web self-service**, this strategy provides tools for users to execute activities previously done by corporate customer service personnel. Personalized Web pages, for example, are one tool that

Web self-service
Activities conducted by users on the Web to find answers to their questions (e.g., tracking) or for product configuration.

CASE 13.7

EC Application

AMERICAN AIRLINES OFFERS PERSONALIZED WEB SITES

In late 1998, American Airlines (AA) unveiled a number of features on its Web site (*aa.com*) that some thought made the site the most advanced (at that time) for personalized, one-to-one interactions and transactions on the Web. The site's most innovative feature was its ability to generate personalized Web pages for each of more than 1 million registered, travel-planning customers. How was AA able to handle such a large amount of information and provide real-time customized Web pages for each customer? The answer—intelligent agents.

The AA site was developed by BroadVision (*broadvision.com*), a major developer of one-to-one marketing applications, using a complex software called One-to-One Application. One of the core components needed to generate personalized Web pages is intelligent agents, which dynamically match customer profiles (built on information supplied by the customer, observed by the system, or derived from existing customer databases) to the database of contents. The output of the matching process triggers the creation of a real-time customized Web page, which for AA can contain information on the consumer's home airport and preferred destinations.

By using intelligent agent technology, AA built a considerable edge over its competitors. Personalizing Web pages offered the potential to increase customer loyalty and cement relationships with customers. The Web site also fostered the community of AA frequent flyers.

In May 2002, AA launched the new and improved Web site using the flexibility of Art Technology Group's (ATG) Relationship Management platform. The new site offers more value and convenience and greater personalization with its platform upgrade, new booking engine, and improved navigation. Today, most competitors have similar systems.

Sources: Compiled from *aa.com* (accessed 2002), *broadvision.com* (accessed 2002), and Yoon (2002).

Questions

1. What are the benefits of the personalized pages to American Airlines?
2. What role do intelligent agents play in the personalization process?

may support Web self-service. Self-service applications can be used with customers (e.g., to support CRM; see rightnow.com) and with employees, suppliers, and any other business partners.

A well-known example is FedEx's *self-tracking* system. Previously, if customers wanted information about the whereabouts of a package, they had to call a representative, give the information about their shipment, and wait for an answer. Today, customers go to fedex.com, insert their airbill number, and view the status of their package shipment. Many other examples exist, ranging from checking the arrival time of an airplane to finding the balance of a checking account. Initially, self-service was done in voice-based customer response systems (known as voice-activated response [VAR]; e.g., netbytel.com). Today, these systems are integrated and complementary to Web-based systems.

Some self-service applications are done only online. Examples are using FAQs at a Web site and self-diagnosis of computers online. On the other hand, updating an address with a personnel department can be done online or via VAR.

The benefits of Web self-service for customers are quick response time; consistent, and sometimes more accurate, replies or data; the possibility of getting more details; and less frustration and more satisfaction. The benefits for organizations are lower expenses of providing service (up to 95 percent savings), the ability to scale service without adding more staff, strengthening business partnerships, and improved quality of service.

It is not easy to implement large-scale self-service systems. They require a complex blend of work processes and technology. Also, only well-defined and repeatable procedures are well-suited for such systems. For further details and implementation tips, see Cunningham (2001).

Of the various self-service tools available, three are of special interest: self-tracking, FAQs, and self-configuration.

Self-Tracking. Self-tracking refers to systems, like that of FedEx, where customers can find the status of an order or service in real (or close to real) time. Most large delivery services provide such services as do direct marketers such as Dell, Amazon.com, and Staples. Some auto manufacturers (e.g., Ford) allow customers to track the progress of the production of a customized car. Some employers, universities, and public agencies will let job applicants track the status of their job application.

Customer Self-Service Through FAQs. Every Web site needs a FAQ page that helps customers help themselves. A **FAQ page** lists questions that are frequently asked by customers and the answers to those questions. By making a FAQ page available, customers can quickly and easily find answers to their questions, saving time and effort for both the Web site owner and the customer. An effective FAQ page has the following characteristics:

FAQ page
A Web page that lists questions that are frequently asked by customers and the answers to those questions.

- **The FAQ page is easy to find.** The FAQ page should be available from a navigation bar or navigation column, even if it is on a pull-down menu. Alternatively, include a prominently placed link on the homepage and on every page offering customer service.
- **The FAQ page loads fast.** The FAQ page should deliver answers to questions a customer might have, and do so fast. Both purposes are best met with text; only rarely will diagrams, pictures, or art be justified. If the number of questions or the length of the answers increase page size enough to negatively impact loading time, then the FAQ page should be divided into a number of smaller pages by category (e.g., product FAQ, customer support FAQ, shipping FAQ). Alternatively, create a FAQ index page with all the questions and link to individual pages with answers.
- **The questions are easy to find.** Do not force visitors to page down through screens of questions and answers to find the question they want to ask. List all questions at the top of the page and use an internal hyperlink to take the visitor to the repeated question with an answer further down the page. After each answer, include a "back to top" link to assist visitors who have additional questions. Questions should be grouped by category, with headings, and in a logical order (e.g., questions about placing an order should precede questions about shipping).
- **The answers are written from a customer's perspective.** Answers should be written in a simple and straightforward manner with a focus on telling the customer what to do and how to do it. Limit the use of technical terms and clearly explain any that are used. If the

Web site serves two or more distinctive markets, more than one FAQ page may be needed to serve each type of customer.

- **The answers do not repeat information offered elsewhere.** Writing duplicate information is a waste of FAQ space and creates problems when the original information is updated and the FAQ page is not. For example, the answer to the question, "Is my credit card information safe?" should include a one-word answer—yes—with a link to the privacy policies page. Similarly, do not be afraid to refer the answers to complex questions to user manuals or technical documents, especially if they are available online. Finally, if the answer to a question is best provided by an external Web site, create a link to that page, but in a new window so that the customer can easily return to the original Web site.
- **Offer an opportunity to ask a question not on the FAQ.** Because no FAQ page can answer every question a visitor might ask, every FAQ page should also have an e-mail address, telephone number, a "search this site" box, and a prominently placed "ask your question here" box.
- **The FAQ page is never done.** Customer service representatives should always be looking for new questions customers are asking that need to be added to the FAQ page. Be open-minded in this process; many people may be asking the same question in different ways. By definition, a FAQ page is not intended to answer every question that is asked or submitted, but someone should be responsible for looking for truly frequently asked questions. Similarly, at least twice each year each question should be reviewed by relevant staff to ensure that the question is still justified and that the answer is correct. Perhaps every new staff person should be required to read the FAQ page and suggest additions, deletions, and changes.

Self-Configuration and Customization. Many build-to-order vendors, from Dell to Mattel, provide customers with tools to self-configure products or services. One of the best ways to satisfy customers is provide them with the ability to customize products and services (see Chapters 1 and 2). Holweg and Pil (2001) assert that in order to have an effective build-to-order system, companies and their suppliers must first understand what customers want. This can be done by finding the customers' requirements (e.g., via self-configuration) and then linking the configured order directly to production so that production decisions are based on real customer demand (see the Dell case in Chapter 1). In addition, customers should be linked interactively to the company and *if necessary* to product designers at the company (see Chapter 7). According to Berry (2001), the superior "new retailer" provides for customization, offers superb customer services, and saves the customer time.

CUSTOMER-CENTRIC APPLICATIONS

Customer-centric applications support customer data collection, processing, and analysis. The major applications are as follows.

Data Reporting and Warehousing

CRM data need to be collected, processed, and stored. The general business intelligence process is described in Online Appendix W4A. Here we present two elements of the process: reports and data warehouses.

Data Reports. Data reporting presents raw or processed CRM-related information, which managers and analysts can view and analyze. Reports provide a range of tabular and graphical presentation formats. Analysts can interact with the report presentation, changing its visual format, "drilling up" into summary information, or "drilling down" into additional detail.

data warehouse
A single, server-based data repository that allows centralized analysis, security, and control over the data.

Data Warehouse. Medium and large corporations organize and store data in a central repository called a **data warehouse** so that it will be easy to analyze later on, when needed. The process is described in Online Appendix W4A. Data warehouses contain both CRM and non-CRM data. According to the Patricia Seybold Group (2002), data warehouses can be effective CRM tools if they contain the following information: customer information used by all operational CRM applications and by possible analytic applications (such as customer

scores); information about the company's products and services and the channels through which it offers them; information about the company's marketing, sales, and services initiatives and customers' responses to them; information about customer requests and the company's responses; and information about customer transactions.

Data Analysis and Mining

Analytic applications automate the processing and analysis of CRM data. Many statistical, management science, and decision support tools can be used for this purpose (e.g., see Turban et al. 2005; Patricia Seybold Group 2002). Analytic applications process a warehouse's data, whereas reports merely present that information. Analytic applications are tools that can be used to analyze the performance, efficiency, and effectiveness of an operation's CRM applications. Their output should enable a company to improve the operational applications that deliver customer experience in order to achieve the CRM objectives of customer acquisition and retention. For example, analytic applications may be designed to provide insight into customer behavior, requests, and transactions, as well as into customer responses to the corporation's marketing, sales, and service initiatives. Analytic applications also create statistical models of customer behavior, values of customer relationships over time, and forecasts of customer acquisition, retention, and desertion. See SAS (2004) for additional information and examples.

Data mining is another analytic activity that involves sifting through an immense amount of data to discover previously unknown patterns. In some cases, the data are consolidated in a data warehouse and data marts; in others, they are kept on the Internet and in intranet servers. For more on data analysis and data mining, see Online Appendix W4A.

ONLINE NETWORKING AND OTHER APPLICATIONS

Online networking and other applications support communication and collaboration among customers, business partners, and company employees. Representative technologies are discussed here.

Online Networking

Representative online networking tools and methods include the following:

- **Forums.** Available from Internet portals such as Yahoo! and AOL, forums offer users the opportunity to participate in discussions as well as to lead forums on a "niche" topic.
- **Chat rooms.** Found on a variety of Web sites, they offer one-to-one or many-to-many real-time conversations.
- **Usenet groups.** These are collections of online discussions, grouped into communities. (See usenet2.org for details.)
- **E-mail newsletters.** These newsletters usually offer the opportunity for readers to write in, particularly in "Let us hear from you" sections. Users can find newsletters of interest by browsing a topic in a search engine. Many newsletter services (e.g., emarketer.com) invite you to sign in. Others (e.g., aberdeen.com) only allow access to articles to users who register. Usually registration is an opt-in option (i.e., a person can remove his or her name from the list at any time).
- **Discussion lists.** A discussion list is a redistribution tool through which an e-mail is sent to one address and then is automatically forwarded to all the people who subscribe to the list.

These last two networking tools are discussed in more detail in the following text.

E-Mail Newsletters

The goal of an e-mail newsletter, according to Kinnard (2002), is to build a relationship with the subscribers. The best beginning is to focus on service by providing valuable information about an industry, which may range from tips ("tip of the day") to a full-blown newsletter consisting of extensive text and graphics.

Because of the current bulk of e-mail advertising and marketing, customers may initially be distrustful of e-mail marketing. Therefore, newsletter articles, commentary, special offers, tips, quotes, and other pieces of information e-mailed to people must be presented in a professional and attractive manner. As customers find that they can trust the information provided, they will supply a company with more demographic and personal information that can be added to the company's customer database.

Sample resources for information on e-mail newsletters are list-universe.com and new-list.com.

Discussion Lists

Discussion lists automatically forward an e-mail to all the people who subscribe to the list so that they can react to it. Discussion lists are distributed *post-by-post* (each recipient gets each e-mail from other members individually) or as *digests* (all e-mails are compiled and sent out according to a schedule, e.g., once per day).

The three main reasons a company may use such lists are (1) to learn more about customers in a particular industry (assuming customers will react to the e-mail), (2) to market the company's products and services, and (3) to gather and share information with a community of individuals with similar interests. If a company hosts a discussion list, it can define the subject matter to be discussed, determine the frequency of the publication, and even make it a revenue-gathering tool. Sources for more information on discussion lists are title.net and everythingemail.net/email_discussion.html.

Additional information about networking online can be found at The Creative Enterprises Network at creativethought.com, About.com's chat site at chatting.miningco.com, and Usenet 2 at usenet2.org.

MOBILE CRM

Mobile CRM refers to the delivery of CRM applications to any user, whenever and wherever needed. This is done by use of the wireless infrastructure and/or mobile and wearable devices.

mobile CRM
The delivery of CRM applications to any user, whenever and wherever needed. This is done by use of the wireless infrastructure and/or mobile and wearable devices.

Many wireless and mobile m-commerce tools can be used to provide customer service. As described in Chapter 9, services such as finding a bank balance, stock trading, and checking airline arrival times are available with wireless devices. The major objective is to provide customer service faster and more conveniently. Furthermore, companies can use a "push" rather than a "pull" approach to giving customers needed information (e.g., by sending SMSs). As was shown in the 511 case in Chapter 1, the government also is going wireless with some of its public services. Finally, many employees' and partners' services are provided in a wireless environment. The advantages of mobile CRM over traditional CRM are shown in Exhibit 13.9.

Giving mobile workforces the same power to interact with customers as they have on the desktop significantly expands a company's ability to build successful customer relationships. Mobile CRM can be provided both to sales representatives and service employees (B2E, Chapters 8 and 9) and directly to customers (Chapter 9). For a comprehensive presentation, see PeopleSoft (2002).

Voice Communication

The most natural way of communicating is by voice. Given the opportunity to do so, many customers prefer to connect to the Internet via voice. During the 1990s, VAR systems became popular. Today, Web-based voice systems are taking their place. One solution for accessing the Internet by voice is provided by companies such as bevocal.com and TellMe (tellme.com). It involves converting voice to text, processing and transmitting the text message, and then converting text to voice. Such systems excel in finding information on the Internet. Even more advanced systems will be available in the near future.

Imagine the following scenario: A traveler gets stuck in traffic on the way to the airport. She calls the airport on her cell phone and hears "All agents are busy. You are important to us; please stay on the line." With Visual Text to Speech technology from AT&T, she can click on "talk to agent" on her Internet-enabled smartphone. The smiling face of a virtual agent appears on the phone screen. The traveler tells the agent her problem and asks to reschedule her flight. A voice confirmation is provided in seconds, and action is taken within a short time.

EXHIBIT 13.9 Traditional Versus Mobile CRM

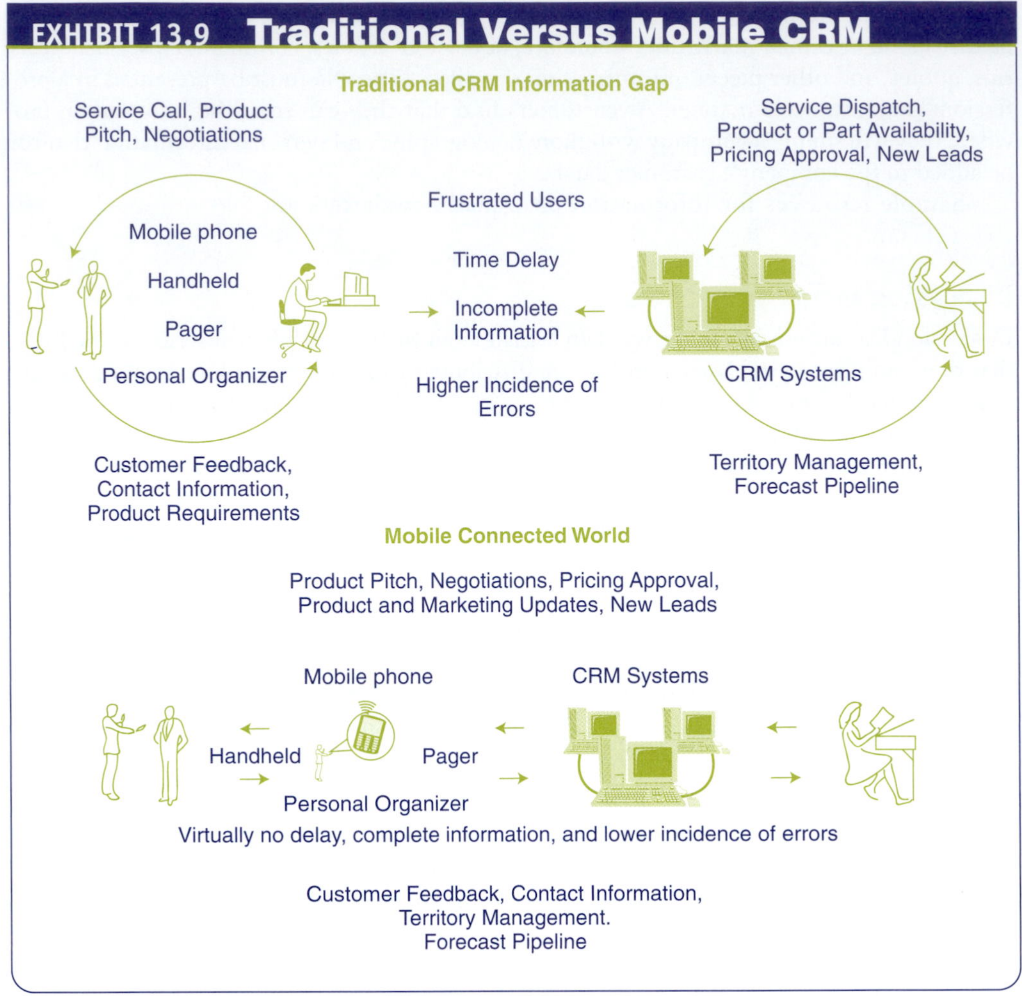

Most people are more comfortable talking with a person, even a virtual one, than they are interacting with machines. The smile and the clear pronunciation of the agent's voice increases shoppers' confidence and trust. For details, see Lohr et al. (2002).

Language Translation

Some people prefer customer service to be in their native or selected language. Web site translation is most helpful in serving tourists. A device called InfoScope (from IBM) can read signs, restaurant menus, and other text written in one language and translate them into several other languages. Currently, these translators are available only for short messages. For more on this topic, see Chapter 14.

The Role of Knowledge Management and Intelligent Agents in CRM

Automating inquiry routing and answering queries requires *knowledge,* which can be generated from historical data and from human expertise and stored in knowledge bases for use whenever needed. Examples would be the answers to FAQs or the detailed product information requested by customers. Companies need to automate the provision of such knowledge in order to contain costs. *Intelligent agents* support the mechanics of inquiry routing, autoresponders, and so on. Some autoresponders, for example, use agents that use keyword recognition to guess what the query is about. The answer may be correct in only 80 percent of the cases, but the savings to the company and the instant reply may justify such an answer. Of course, in such a case, the customer needs to be aware that this is a machine-generated response (and that it might be wrong). Smarter agents are coming that know what they can or cannot answer. In the latter case, they will refer you to a human. However, they are not 100 percent correct either. (Their accuracy increases with time.)

Kwok et al. (2001) developed a much more intelligent system that can answer less-structured and nonroutine questions. This is done via intelligent information retrieval systems, using a technology called *natural language processing*. A similar system that "understands" incoming customer e-mail queries is iPhrase Contact Classification Server from iPhrase.com. It is based on neural computing.

For more on intelligent agents in CRM, see Chapter 4. A summary of some of the applications presented in this chapter, as well as some additional applications, is provided in Online Exhibit W13.2.

Section 13.5 ▶ REVIEW QUESTIONS

1. Discuss key customer-facing CRM applications.
2. Describe customer-touching CRM applications, including Web self-service.
3. Describe customer-centric CRM applications.
4. List online networking CRM applications.

13.6 OTHER EC SUPPORT SERVICES

Depending on the magnitude of the EC project, a company may require several other support services.

CONSULTING SERVICES

How does a firm learn how to do something that it has never done before? Many firms, both startups and established companies, are turning to consultants that have established themselves as experts in guiding their clients through the maze of legal, technical, strategic, and operational problems and decisions that must be addressed in order to ensure success in this new business environment. Some of these firms have established a reputation in one area of expertise, whereas others are generalists. Some consultants even take equity (ownership) positions in the firms they advise. Some consultants will build, test, and deliver a working Web site and may even host it and maintain it for their clients. There are three broad categories of consulting firms.

The first type of consulting firm includes those that provide expertise in the area of EC, but not in traditional business. Some of the consultants that provide general EC expertise are Agency.com, Virtusa.com, Sun.com, Inforte, SBI & Company, Organic, Sapient, Verity, WebTrends, and WebMethods.

Also included in the first category of consulting firms are those that provide very specialized expertise. There are thousands of these smaller, more specialized consulting firms. Some fill a unique niche in this growing field. Matching these consultants with clients can be done via service companies such as eLance, and Sologig features a robust search system, enabling firms to showcase their services to prospective clients.

See Online File W13.8 for an overview of the EC consulting services offered by one firm, Sapient.

The second type of consulting firm is a traditional consulting company that maintains divisions that focus on EC. These include the so-called "Big 4" U.S. accounting firms and the large established U.S. national consulting firms. These firms leverage their existing relationships with their corporate clients and offer EC value-added services. Representative companies are Accenture, Computer Services Corp., Cambridge Technology Partners, Boston Consulting Group, Booz-Allen & Hamilton, Deloitte & Touche, Ernst and Young, EDS, KPMG, McKinsey, and PricewaterhouseCoopers. Also, most large technology companies have extensive management-oriented consulting services (e.g., IBM, Microsoft, Sun Microsystems, Oracle, SAP, and Intel).

The third category of consulting firms is EC hardware and software vendors that provide technology-consulting services. These include SAP, IBM, Oracle, Sun Microsystems, and many more.

It is imperative that any firm seeking help in devising a successful online strategy select not only an experienced and competent consulting firm, but also one with sufficient synergies with the client firm. For a discussion of vendor selection and management, see Online Chapter 18.

CRM SUITES

Several vendors offer CRM software suites (see Team Assignment #4). Notable are NetCRM (from NetSuite), Accpacom (from Accpac International), Sforce (from Salesforce.com) and Siebel On Demand (from Siebel). Details on the capabilities of CRM suites are available at Caton (2004). Also, adding visualization to CRM is useful (see Ganapathy et al. 2004).

DIRECTORY SERVICES, NEWSLETTERS, AND SEARCH ENGINES

The EC landscape is huge, with hundreds of thousands of companies online. How can a buyer find all suitable sellers? How can a seller find all suitable buyers? In B2B, vertical exchanges can help with this matching process, but even vertical exchanges include only a limited number of potential partners, usually located in one country. To overcome the problem of finding buyers or sellers online, a company may use directory services.

Directory Services

There are several types of directory services. Some simply list companies by categories; others provide links to companies. In many cases, the data are classified in several different ways for easy search purposes. In others, special search engines are provided. Finally, value-added services, such as matching buyers and sellers, are available. The following are some popular directories:

- B2Business.net (b2business.net) is a major resource for B2B professionals. It includes listings of business resources in about 30 functional areas, company research resources (e.g., credit checks, customs research, and financial reviews), information on startups (business plans, domain names, recruiting, patents, incubators, and even a graveyard), general EC information (e.g., books, articles, reports, events, and research), e-marketplace directories (e.g., enablers and builders, services, support services, and major markets), and infrastructure resources (e.g., security, connectivity, catalogs, content, portal builders, and ASPs).
- B2BToday.com (b2btoday.com) is a directory that contains listings of B2B services organized by type of service (e.g., Web site creation, B2B marketing, and B2B software) and product category (e.g., automotive and books). Each part of the directory highlights several companies at the start of the list that pay extra fees to be listed on the top; after the premium slots, the directory is organized in alphabetical order. The directory listings are hyperlinked to the companies' Web sites. Many of the sites are involved in B2C.
- CommunityB2B (communityb2b.com) offers many B2B community services, such as news, a library, events calendar, job market, resource directory, and more.
- A2Z of B2B (a2zofb2b.com) is a directory of B2B companies organized in alphabetical order or industry order. It specifies the type and nature of the company, the venture capital sponsor of the B2B, and the stock market ticker (if the company's stock is listed on a publicly traded stock exchange).
- i-Stores.co.uk (i-stores.co.uk) is a UK–based directory that targets online stores. The company provides validation of secure Web sites.
- Webster (websteronline.com) is a large business directory organized by location and by product or service. In addition, it provides listings by industry and subindustry (according to SIC and NAICS codes).
- The ThomasNet (thomasregister.com) provides a directory of more than 150,000 manufacturers of industrial products and services.
- Yahoo! Small Business (smallbusiness.yahoo.com/marketplace.html) provides business directories. As of 2005, over 300,000 companies are listed (dir.yahoo.com/Business_and_Economy/Directories/Companies).

Newsletters

There are many B2B newsletters to choose from. Several are e-mailed to individuals free of charge. Examples of B2B newsletters are emarketer.com/newsletters (look for *B2B Weekly*) and line56.com. Many companies (e.g., Ariba, Intel) issue corporate newsletters and e-mail them to people who request them. Also, companies can use software from onlinepressreleases.com to send online press releases to thousands of editors.

Directories and newsletters are helpful, but they may not be sufficient. Therefore, one may need specialized search engines.

Search Engines and News Aggregators

Several search engines can be used to discover B2B-related information. Some of these are embedded in the directories. Here are some examples:

- Moreover (moreover.com) is a search engine that locates information and aggregates B2B (and other business) news.
- Google offers a directory of components for B2B and B2C Web sites. These range from currency exchange calculators to server performance monitors (see directory.google.com).
- iEntry (ientry.com) provides B2B search engines, targeted "niche engines," and several industry-focused newsletters. iEntry operates a network of Web sites and e-mail newsletters that reaches over 2 million unique opt-in subscribers. Newsletters are available in each of the following categories: Web Developers, Advice, Technology, Professional, Sports & Entertainment, Leisure & Lifestyles, and Web Entrepreneurs. Click on a newsletter to get a brief description and view sample content.

SOME MORE EC SUPPORT SERVICES

Many other service providers support e-commerce in different ways. Each service provider adds a unique value-added service. This section describes representative examples.

Trust Services. Chapter 4 introduced the role of trust in B2C. Trust also is important in B2B because one cannot touch the seller's products and because buyers may not be known to sellers. Trust-support services such as TRUSTe, BBBOnline, and Ernst & Young's trust service are used both in B2C and B2B. For more discussion of these trust services, see Chapter 17.

Trademark and Domain Names. A number of domain name services are available. Examples are verisign.com, mydomain.com, register.com, easyspace.com, and whois.net.

Digital Photos. Companies such as IPIX (ipix.com) provide innovative pictures for Web sites.

Global Business Communities. The eCommerce Portal from Wiznet (wiznet.net) is a global, Web-based "business community" that supports the unique requirements of buying organizations, including cross-catalog searches, RFQ development and distribution, and decision support, while simultaneously enabling suppliers to dictate the content and presentation of their own product catalogs.

Access to Commercial Databases. Subscribers to Thomson Dialog (dialog.com) can access about 1,000 databases, including those containing patents, trademarks, government reports, and news articles.

Online Consulting. Find/SVP (findsvp.com) sells instant consulting. For an ad hoc fee starting at $500 or an annual fee of up to $10,000 (in 2005) (*Entrepreneur.com* 2003), clients can reach over 70 consultants for phone- or Web-based queries. Answers to business questions are produced within 24 hours, with backup documents. Experts give advice on product launches, market segmentation, and potential competitors' moves. A Web-only service to SMEs is available for only $400 a year (in 2002).

Knowledge Management. Lotus Domino, a major knowledge management and collaboration company, offers the capability to manage Web content with its Domino product (see Chapter 7).

Client Matching. TechRepublic (techrepublic.com) matches business clients with firms that provide a wide variety of IT services. It works like a matchmaking service. Clients define what they want, and TechRepublic performs the searching and screening, checking against some general parameters and criteria. This reduces the risk of clients making bad choices. Buyers also save time and have greater exposure to a larger number of IT service providers.

E-Business Rating Sites. A number of services are available for businesses to research rankings of potential partners and suppliers. Bizrate.com, forrester.com, gomez.com, and consumersearch.com all provide business ratings.

Security and Encryption Sites. VeriSign (verisign.com) provides valuable encryption tools for all types of EC organizations. It provides domain site registration and several security mechanisms.

Web Research Services. A number of Web research providers help companies learn more about technologies, trends, and potential business partners and suppliers. Some of these are WebTrack (webtrack.net), IDC (idc.com), ZDNet (zdnet.com), and Forrester (forrester.com).

Coupon-Generating Sites. A number of vendors help companies generate online coupons. Some of these are Q-pon.com (q-pon.com), CentsOff.com (centsoff.com), and TheFreeSite.com (thefreesite.com).

Additional services available for B2B operations are presented in Exhibit 13.10.

Section 13.6 ▶ REVIEW QUESTIONS

1. Describe the role of EC consultants and list their major types.
2. Describe the value offered by directory services. Provide three examples of what value they add.
3. Explain why specialized search engines are needed.
4. List some other EC support services.

13.7 OUTSOURCING EC SUPPORT SERVICES

Most companies do not maintain in-house support services. Instead, they outsource many of these services.

EXHIBIT 13.10 Other B2B Services

Category	Description	Examples
Marketplace concentrator (aggregator)	Aggregates information about products and services from multiple providers at one central point. Purchasers can search, compare, shop, and sometimes complete the sales transaction.	InternetMall, DealerNet, InsureMarket, Industrial Marketplace
Information brokers (infomediaries)	Provide product, pricing, and availability information. Some facilitate transactions, but their main value is the information they provide.	PartNet, Travelocity, Auto-by-Tel
Transaction brokers	Buyers can view rates and terms, but the primary business activity is to complete the transaction.	E*TRADE, Ameritrade
Digital product delivery	Sells and delivers software, multimedia, and other digital products over the Internet.	Build-a-Card, PhotoDisc, SonicNet
Content provider	Creates revenue by providing content. The customer may pay to access the content, or revenue may be generated by selling advertising space or by having advertisers pay for placement in an organized listing in a searchable database.	*Wall Street Journal* Interactive, Tripod
Online service provider	Provides service and support for hardware and software users.	CyberMedia, TuneUp.com
Specializes directories	Provide leads to a variety of B2B services categories.	Business.com Knowledgestorm.com Techlisting.com Searchedu.com

WHY OUTSOURCE EC SERVICES?

Historically, early businesses were vertically integrated—they owned or controlled their own sources of materials, manufactured components, performed final assembly, and managed the distribution and sale of their products to consumers. Later, nearly all firms began to contract with other firms to execute various activities along the supply chain, from manufacturing to distribution and sale, in order to concentrate their activities in their *core competency*. This practice is known as *outsourcing*.

When EC emerged, it became obvious that it would be necessary to outsource some of the support services involved in its deployment. The major reasons why many companies prefer to do this include the following:

- A desire to concentrate on the core business
- The need to have services up and running rapidly
- Lack of expertise (experience and resources) for many of the required support services
- The inability to have the economy of scale enjoyed by outsourcers, which often results in high costs for in-house options
- Inability to keep up with rapidly fluctuating demands if an in-house option is used
- The number of required services, which usually are simply too many for one company to handle

To show the importance of outsourcing, we will look at the typical process of developing and managing EC applications (the e-infrastructure), a topic we address in detail in Online Chapter 18. The process includes the following major steps:

1. EC strategy formulation
2. Application design
3. Building (or buying) the systems
4. Hosting, operating, and maintaining the EC site

Each of these steps may include several activities, as shown in Exhibit 13.11. A firm may execute all the activities of this process internally or it may outsource some or all of them. In

EXHIBIT 13.11 E-Commerce Application Development Process

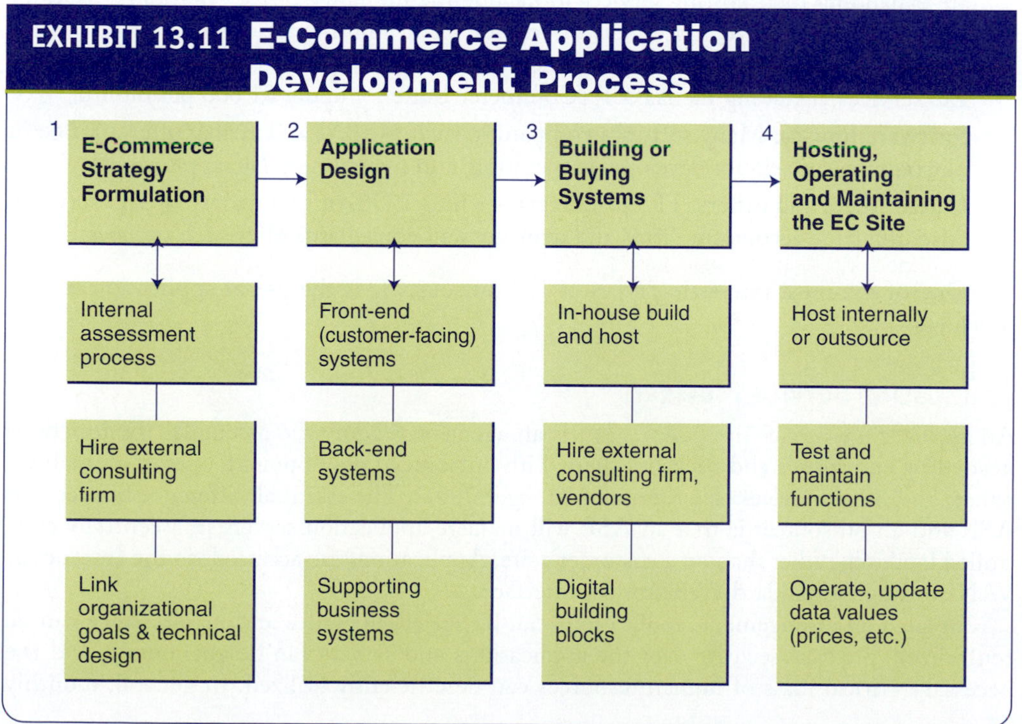

addition to design and maintenance of technical systems, many other system design issues and business functions related to using a Web site also must be addressed. For example, a firm doing EC must design and operate its order fulfillment system and outbound logistics (delivery) functions; it must provide dynamic content on the site; and it must also provide services to its customers and partners.

IT OUTSOURCING AND APPLICATION SERVICE PROVIDERS

IT is the most frequently outsourced business activity. Most enterprises engaged in EC practice a very large degree of IT outsourcing. While concentrating on core competencies, they develop strategic alliances with partner firms in order to provide activities such as payment processing, order fulfillment, outbound logistics, Web site hosting, and customer service.

SMEs with few IT staff and smaller budgets are best served by outside contractors. Outside contractors also have proven to be a good choice for large companies wanting to experiment with EC without a great deal of up-front investment. In addition, outsourcing allows them to protect their own internal networks or to rely on experts to establish sites over which they will later assume control. Some of the best-known B2C sites on the Web (e.g., eddiebauer.com and 1800flowers.com) are run by third-party vendors.

Several types of providers offer services for creating and operating electronic storefronts:

- **Internet malls.** There are several thousand malls on the Web. Like a real-world mall, an Internet mall offers a single point of entry to a collection of storefronts. A well-run Internet mall offers cross-selling from one store to another and provides a common payment structure where buyers can use a single credit card purchase to buy products from multiple stores. Theoretically, an Internet mall has wider marketing reach than a stand-alone site and, as a consequence, generates more traffic. The downside is that the online store must share income with the mall owner. For additional details, see Chapter 3.
- **ISPs.** In addition to providing Internet access to companies and individual users, a large number of ISPs offer hosting services for EC. For the most part, ISPs are focused on operating a secure transaction environment and not on store content. This means that merchants using the services of an ISP must still design their own pages. Of course, this task can be outsourced to a different third party. A listing of top site designers can be found at internetworld.com.
- **Telecommunication companies.** Increasingly, the large telecommunications companies are expanding their hosting services to include the full range of EC solutions. MCI, for example, offers Convergence Networking for a flat monthly fee. Web Commerce runs on Microsoft Commerce Server technologies. Similarly, AT&T provides a number of EC services, including the AT&T eCommerce Suite for under $1,000 per month.
- **Software houses.** Many software companies, such as IBM and Ariba, offer a range of outsourcing services for developing, operating, and maintaining EC applications.
- **Outsourcers and others.** IT outsourcers, such as EDS, offer a variety of EC services. Also, the large accounting firms and management consultants offer such services.

One of the most interesting types of EC outsourcing is the use of application service providers.

Application Service Providers

application service provider (ASP)
An agent or vendor who assembles the functions needed by enterprises and packages them with outsourced development, operation, maintenance, and other services.

An **application service provider (ASP)** is an agent or vendor who assembles the functions needed by enterprises and packages them with outsourced development, operation, maintenance, and other services (see Kern and Kreijger 2001). The essential difference between an ASP and an outsourcer is that an ASP will manage application servers in a centrally controlled location, rather than on a customer's site. Applications are accessed via the Internet or VANs through a standard Web browser interface.

In such an arrangement, applications can be scaled, upgrades and maintenance can be centralized, physical security over the applications and servers can be guaranteed, and the necessary critical mass of human resources can be efficiently utilized. In general, monthly fees, which include fees for the application software, hardware, service and support, maintenance, and upgrades, are paid by the end-user businesses. The fee may be fixed or based on use. According to Scott McNealy, Sun Microsystems CEO, by 2005, "if you're a CIO with a head for business, you won't buy software or computers anymore. You'll rent all your resources from a service provider" (Bonnerjee 2000).

Leasing from an ASP is a particularly desirable option for SMEs, for whom in-house development and operation of EC applications can be time consuming and expensive. Leasing from ASPs not only saves various expenses (such as labor costs) in the initial development stage, it also helps reduce the software maintenance and upgrading and user training costs in the long run. A company can always select another software tool from the ASP to meet its changing needs and does not have to invest further in upgrading the existing one. In this way, overall business competitiveness can be strengthened through reducing time-to-market and enhancing the ability to adapt to changing market conditions. This is particularly true of EC applications for which timing and flexibility are crucial. A detailed list of benefits and risks of using ASPs is provided in Online Exhibit W13.3.

Leasing from ASPs does have its disadvantages. Many companies are concerned with the adequacy of the protection offered by ASPs against hackers, theft of confidential information, and virus attacks. Leased software often does not provide the perfect fit for the desired application. It also is important to ensure that the speed of the Internet connection is compatible with that of the application in order to avoid distortions in its performance. For example, it is not advisable to run heavy-duty applications on a modem link below a T1 line or a high-speed DSL.

ASPs are especially active in enterprise computing and EC applications, which may be too complex to build and too cumbersome to modify and maintain (e.g., see Ward 2000). Therefore, the major providers of ERP software, such as SAP and Oracle, also offer ASP options. An example can be seen at mysap.com. IBM, Microsoft, and Computer Associates also offer ASP services. Similarly, major EC vendors, such as Ariba, offer ASP services.

For an analysis of ASPs in EC, including its advantages and pitfalls, see Segev and Gebauer (2001).

Section 13.7 ▶ REVIEW QUESTIONS

1. List the major reasons why companies outsource EC support services.
2. Which types of services are outsourced the most?
3. Describe the benefits of using ASPs.
4. Comment on the risks of using ASPs.

MANAGERIAL ISSUES

Some managerial issues related to this chapter are as follows.

1. **Have we planned for order fulfillment?** Order fulfillment is a critical task, especially for virtual EC vendors. Even for brick-and-mortar retailers with physical warehouses, delivery to customers' doors is not always easy. The problem is not just the physical shipment, but also the efficient execution of the entire order fulfillment process, which may be complex along a long supply chain.
2. **How should we handle returns?** Dealing with returns can be a complex issue. A company should estimate its percentage of returns and design and plan a process for receiving and handling them. Some companies completely separate the logistics of returns from that of order fulfillment and outsource its execution.
3. **Do we want alliances in order fulfillment?** Partnerships and alliances can improve logistics and alleviate supply chain problems. Many possibilities and models exist. Some are along the supply chain, whereas others are not related to it.
4. **What EC logistics applications would be useful?** One should think not only about how to create logistical systems for EC, but also how to use EC applications to improve the supply chain.
5. **How is our response time?** Acceptable standards or metrics for response in customer service must be set. For example, customers want acknowledgment of their query within 24 hours. Many companies seek to provide this response time and do so at a minimum cost.

6. **How do we measure and improve customer service?** The Internet provides an excellent platform for delivery of superb customer service via a variety of tools. The problem is that the returns are mostly intangible and may only be realized in the distant future.
7. **Is CRM for real?** CRM is a necessity; most companies must have some CRM in order to survive. The issue is how much to provide. However, it is difficult to justify CRM, and there are many CRM software programs from which to choose. Therefore, a careful analysis must be done (see Caton 2004).
8. **Do we have to use electronically supported CRM?** For a large company, it is a must. It is not economically feasible to provide effective CRM otherwise. Some eCRM programs, such as e-mail response, are inexpensive. However, large computerized call centers are expensive to install and operate.
9. **EC consultants are expensive. Should we use them?** It depends. If the company lacks expertise or time, consultants may be the best solution. However, first consider using publicly available information on the Internet. Some publicly available information is quite valuable.
10. **Should we outsource EC services?** Outsourcing is a viable option that must be considered. Even large IT companies outsource. Again, if a company lacks time or expertise, selective outsourcing may be the best course of action.

RESEARCH TOPICS

Here are some suggested topics related to this chapter. For details, references, and additional topics, refer to the book's "Current EC Research" in the Online Appendix.

1. **Order Fulfillment and Logistics**
   - Optimal delivery strategy and routing in the demand chain environment
   - The performance of third-party logistics with regards to the geographic topology between suppliers and buyers
   - Business models of logistic partnerships and their performance
   - Delivery time reduction by using a third-party deliverer's hub warehouse
   - Comparative country and industry studies of culture and power related to bearing the delivery cost and its influence in delivery cost reduction (e.g., USA, Japan, Korea, and China)
   - Consumer behavior regarding the charge of delivery cost—independent or included models—and its impact on the diffusion of e-commerce
   - Delivery cost comparison of portal sites and application of the XRML approach
2. **Applications of RFID in Logistics**
   - POS management with RFID
   - Optimal dynamic routing control in the RFID environment
   - Cross-docking management with RFID in an in-demand chain situation
   - Process monitoring and control with RFID
3. **Outsourcing to ASPs**
   - The available and appropriate outsourcing services from ASPs for the implementation of e-business, particularly for SMEs
   - The risks of outsourcing from ASPs and remedies to improve the management of potential risks
   - How to integrate ASPs with internal ERP and legacy systems
   - Factors that determine the company's trust of ASP, specifically the need for secure network transmissions and the importance of authenticating users.
   - Certification programs for ASPs and their effectiveness in ensuring trust
   - Users' concerns about the risk of censorship and violation of privacy by ASPs
   - Calculation of corporate tax in ASPs and government incentives for transparent tax reporting by third-party ASPs
4. **Content Management**
   - Standardization efforts and adoption by the big players
   - Reconciliation of multiple perspectives of contents categorization
   - Aggregating external content online and organizing it from the user's point of view

SUMMARY

In this chapter, you learned about the following EC issues as they relate to the learning objectives.

1. **The role of support services in EC.** Support services are essential to the success of EC. They range from order fulfillment to providing customer service. They can be done by the companies or they can be outsourced.
2. **The order fulfillment process.** Large numbers of support services are needed for EC implementation. Most important are payment mechanisms and order fulfillment. On-time delivery of products to customers may be a difficult task, especially in B2C. Fulfilling an order requires several activities ranging from credit and inventory checks to shipments. Most of these activities are part of back-office operations and are related to logistics. The order fulfillment process varies from business to business and also depends on the product. Generally speaking, however, the following steps are recognized: payment verification, inventory checking, shipping arrangement, insurance, production (or assembly), plant services, purchasing, customer contacts, and return of products.
3. **Problems in order fulfillment.** It is difficult to fulfill B2C orders due to uncertainties in demand and potential delays in supply and deliveries. Problems also result from lack of coordination and information sharing among business partners.
4. **Solutions to order fulfillment problems.** Automating order taking (e.g., by using forms over the Internet) and smoothing the supply chain are two ways to solve order fulfillment problems. Several other innovative solutions exist, most of which are supported by software that facilitates correct inventories, coordination along the supply chain, and appropriate planning and decision making.
5. **CRM, its technologies, and EC connection.** CRM is becoming a necessity for doing business, and it is facilitated by IT. Its major categories are customer-facing applications, customer-touching applications, and customer-centric intelligent applications. Using CRM methods, customers can order online more easily, check their orders and accounts, and communicate and collaborate with the company better.
6. **Implementing customer service online.** Retaining customers by satisfying their needs is the core of customer service. Customer service on the Web is provided by e-mail, on the corporate Web site, at customer interaction (call) centers, by automated responses, in personalized Web pages, by the use of data warehousing and data mining, by online networking, and by intelligent agents. Online customer service is media rich, effective, and usually less expensive than off-line services.
7. **Other support services.** EC support services include consulting services, directory services, infrastructure providers, and many more. One cannot practice EC without some of them. These support services need to be coordinated and integrated. Some of them can be done in-house, others must be outsourced.
8. **Outsourcing EC services and using ASPs.** Selective outsourcing of EC services usually is a must. Lack of time and expertise forces companies to outsource, despite the risks of doing so. Using ASPs is a viable alternative, but they are neither inexpensive nor risk-free.

KEY TERMS

Term	Page
Application service provider (ASP)	570
Autoresponders	557
Back-office operations	533
Customer interaction center (CIC)	556
Customer relationship management (CRM)	549
Data warehouse	561
E-logistics	536
eCRM	550
FAQ page	560
Front-office operations	534
Logistics	534
Merge-in-transit	548
Metrics	553
Mobile CRM	563
Order fulfillment	533
Reverse logistics	535
Rolling warehouse	548
Sales force automation (SFA)	558
Telewebs	556
Third-party logistics suppliers (3PLs)	538
Warehouse management system (WMS)	538
Web self-service	559

QUESTIONS FOR DISCUSSION

1. Discuss the problem of reverse logistics in EC. What types of companies may suffer the most?
2. Explain why UPS defines itself as a "technology company with trucks" rather than as a "trucking company with technology."
3. Chart the supply chain portion of returns to a virtual store. Check with an e-tailer to see how it handles returns. Prepare a report based on your findings.
4. Under what situations might the outsourcing of EC services not be desirable?
5. Why does it make sense to use a consultant to develop an e-strategy?
6. UPS and other logistic companies also provide financial services. Discuss the logic behind this.
7. Differentiate order fulfillment in B2C from that of B2B.
8. Discuss the pros and cons of using ASPs.
9. How do the CRM techniques discussed in Section 13.5 add value for the customer and the company?
10. Many question the short-term return on investment of CRM tools. Explain why.
11. How would you convince a CEO to invest in Web self-services? With what issues could the CEO counter your advice?

INTERNET EXERCISES

WWW

1. The U.S. Postal Service also is in the EC logistics field. Examine its services and tracking systems at usps.com/shipping. What are the potential advantages of these systems for EC shippers?
2. Enter rawmart.com and find what services the site provides that support logistics. Also find what shipment services it provides.
3. Visit ups.com and find its recent EC initiatives. Compare them with those of fedex.com. Then go to onlinestore.ups.com and simulate a purchase. Report your experiences.
4. Visit freightquote.com and the sites of one or two other online freight companies. Compare the features offered by these companies for online delivery.
5. Enter efulfillmentservice.com. Review the products you find there. How does the company organize the network? How is it related to companies such as FedEx? How does this company make money?
6. Enter categoric.com and find information about products that can facilitate order fulfillment. Write a report.
7. Enter kewill.com. Find the innovations offered there that facilitate order fulfillment. Compare it with shipsmo.com. Write a report.
8. Enter rikai.com. Find any Japanese Web site that deals with a topic of your choice and try to get the English translation. Report your results.
9. Enter b2byellowpages.com and a2zofb2b.com. Compare the information provided on each site. What features do both sites share? How do the sites differ?
10. Visit b2btoday.com. Go to the B2B Communities area and identify the major vendors there. Then select three vendors and examine the services they provide to the B2B community. Also enter communityb2b. com and examine the information provided and the usefulness of joining the site.
11. Enter ahls.com and find out what services it offers. Comment on the uniqueness of the services.
12. Enter dell.com and attempt to buy a PC online. Fill in the forms and examine all of the available options. What CRM services are provided? (You do not have to buy the computer you configured.)
13. Enter support.dell.com and examine all the services available. Examine the tracking services Dell provides to its customers. Finally, examine Dell's association with bizrate.com. Write a report about customer service at Dell.
14. Enter siebel.com. Find what it offers in its CRM OnDemand product. Why does Siebel collaborate with IBM's OnDemand program?
15. Review Insights and Additions 13.2 and enter ups.com and answer the following questions:
    a. Why would a shipper such as UPS expand to other logistic services?
    b. Why would shippers want to handle payments?
    c. Why does UPS provide software tools to customers?
    d. What B2B services does UPS provide?

TEAM ASSIGNMENTS AND ROLE PLAYING

1. Each team should investigate the order fulfillment process offered at an e-tailer's site, such as amazon.com, staples.com, or landsend.com. Contact the company, if necessary, and examine any related business partnerships. Based on the content of this chapter, prepare a report with suggestions for how the company can improve its order fulfillment process. Each group's findings will be discussed in class. Based on the class's findings, draw some conclusions about how order fulfillment can be improved.
2. FedEx, UPS, the U.S. Postal Service, DHL, and others are competing in the EC logistics market. Each team should examine one such company and investigate the services it provides. Contact the company, if necessary, and aggregate the team's findings into a report that will convince classmates or readers that the company in question is the best. (What are its best features? What are its weaknesses?)
3. Each team should select an overnight delivery service company (FedEx, DHL, UPS, U.S. Postal Service, and so on). The team will then identify all of the online customer service features offered by the company. Each team then will try to convince the class that its company provides the best customer service.
4. Each team is assigned to a CRM software company (e.g., Siebel, Salesforce, NetSuite, Accpac, or E.piphany). Find the company's leading products and prepare a presentation of their capabilities. All teams should consult Caton (2004).

Real-World Case

HOW CIGNA FULFILLS SERVICE ORDERS AND IMPROVES CRM

The Problem

CIGNA (*cigna.com*) is the fourth-largest insurance company in the United States. Increased competition in the insurance industry contributed to a $500 million net loss for CIGNA in 2002 and a 40 percent decrease in the company's stock price. CIGNA was under other business environment pressure as well.

First, the company, along with other national insurers, such as Aetna and Humana, was being sued by thousands of doctors nationwide who were furious about delays in payment for patient care. The doctors accused the insurers of deliberately delaying payments and improperly rejecting claims in order to save money.

Second, CIGNA's sales team, in order to win large employer accounts in an increasingly competitive environment, had promised that CIGNA would be implementing new EC systems to provide improved customer service. However, the systems had not yet been developed.

Third, CIGNA's management was under pressure to cut costs after posting disappointing earnings. Executives were anxious for the new system's promised cost reductions and productivity gains.

The Solution

CIGNA developed an ambitious plan to consolidate and upgrade its antiquated IT systems, some of which dated back to 1982, to a Web-based EC system. The idea was to have an integrated system for enrollment, eligibility, and claims processing so that customers would receive one bill, medical claims could be processed faster and more efficiently, and customer service representatives would have a single, unified view of customers (called "members").

To accomplish these goals, CIGNA would have had to consolidate its old systems for claims processing and billing and integrate them with new EC applications. CIGNA thus developed and integrated two systems: one for claims eligibility for use by customers and another for billing. CIGNA's IT group had to build an entire information infrastructure from scratch that could support the two main systems. To do all of this, the IT group had to completely reengineer its legacy back-end systems.

CIGNA hired Cap Gemini Ernst & Young (CGEY) to help implement the change management and business processes involved. CIGNA also worked with CGEY to develop and implement the new EC customer-facing applications that would allow members to enroll, check the status of their claims and benefits, and choose from different health-plan offerings—all online. Those applications also give customer service representatives a single unified view of members' accounts, so that when a member calls with problems or questions the representatives would have a full history of the member's interactions with the company.

The Results

In January 2002, CIGNA's $1 billion IT overhaul and CRM initiative went live in a big way, with 3.5 million members moved from 15 legacy systems to the two new platforms in a matter of minutes. The migration to the new systems did not go smoothly. In fact, there were glitches in customer service.

After 6 months of hard work, CIGNA succeeded in fixing the problems with the new systems. The company also launched myCIGNA.com, an online portal where CIGNA members can look up their benefits, choose from an array of health plans, check on the status of their claims, retrieve health-related information, and talk to nurses online.

Source: Compiled from Bass (2003).

Questions

1. Why is it sometimes necessary to restructure and automate the customer-facing systems and the back-end systems?
2. Identify the CRM activities implemented by CIGNA.
3. How do the CRM activities relate to "order fulfillment" in services? Identify who is placing orders and who fulfills them.
4. How has the system improved the order fulfillment process?

REFERENCES

Adria, M., and S. D. Chowdhury. "Making Room for the Call Center." *Information Systems Management* (2002).

Agarwal, A., et al. "Organizing for CRM." *McKinsey Quarterly, member edition* (August 2004).

Amato-McCoy, D. M. "REI Conquers Mountains of Customer Data." *Stores*, September 2003.

American Airlines. **aa.com** (accessed 2002).

Babcock, C. "Five-star Application Service." *Information Week*, March 22, 2004. **informationweek.com/story/showarticle.jhtml?articleid=18400885** (accessed March 2005).

Bass, A. "CIGNA's Self-Inflicted Wounds." *CIO Magazine*, March 15, 2003.

Bayles, D. L. *E-Commerce Logistics and Fulfillment*. Upper Saddle River, NJ: Prentice Hall, 2001.

Berry, L. L. "The Old Pillars of New Retailing." *Harvard Business Review* (April 2001).

Bhise, H., et al. "The Duel for the Doorstep." *The McKinsey Quarterly* (April–June 2000).

BikeWorld. **bikeworld.com** (accessed 2005).

Blair, J. "Behind Kozmo's Demise." *New York Times*, April 13, 2001.

Blair, J. "Online Delivery Sites Finding That Manhattan Can Be a Hard Place to Make It." *New York Times*, October 2000.

Boles, T. "Returned Goods Clog British Roads." *Knight Ridder Tribune Business News*, October 24, 2004.

Bonde, A. "The Big Payoff from Self-Service." *ROI Insider*, November 24, 2004.

Bonnerjee, A. "ASPs: Exploring the Buzzword." *Network Computing*, August 8, 2000. **zdnetindia.com/biztech/ebusiness/asp/stories/554.html** (accessed December 2004).

Boston Consulting Group. "Winning the Online Consumer: The Challenge of Raised Expectations." 2001. **bcg.com/publications/files/022101_winning_online_consumer_report_summary.pdf** (accessed March 2005).

Brian, H. "Return to Sender: How to Make Key e-fulfillment Strategies Work for You." *Materials Management and Distribution* 47, no. 4 (2002).

BroadVision. **broadvision.com** (accessed 2002).

Brown, J. "What Led to Kozmo's Final Delivery." *Business Week*, April 16, 2001. **businessweek.com/bwdaily/dnflash/apr2001/nf20010416_207.htm** (accessed December 2004).

Caton, M. "Hosted CRM Systems Mature." *eWeek*, May 31, 2004.

Chaudhury, A., et al. "Web Channels in E-Commerce." *Communications of the ACM*, January 2001.

Chio, S. Y., et al. *The Economics of Electronic Commerce.* Indianapolis, IN: Macmillan Technical Publishing, 1997.

CIO Insight. "A CRM 2004 Survey." *CIO Insight,* August 1, 2004.

Compton, J. "How to . . . Select a CRM Implementation Partner." *Customer Relationship Management* 8, no. 11 (2004).

Council of Supply Chain Management Professionals. **cscmp.org** (accessed March 2005).

CRM Guru. **crmguru.com** (accessed January 2005).

Croxton, K. L., et al. "Models and Methods for Merge-in-Transit Operations." *Transportation Science* 37, no. 1 (2003).

Cunningham, M. J. "Ten Steps to Successful Web Self-Service." *e-Business Advisor*, July–August 2001, 34–39.

Diorio, S. *Beyond "e."* New York: McGraw-Hill, 2002.

Elia, E. **informatik.uni-trier.de/~ley/db/indices/a-tree/l/lefebvre:louis_a=.html**, and **informatik.uni-trier.de/**

~ley/db/indices/a-tree/l/Lefebvre:=Eacute=lisabeth.html. "Typology of B-to-B E-Commerce Initiatives and Related Benefits in Manufacturing SMEs." *Proceedings of 37th HICSS Conference*. January 2004. Kona, Hawaii, January 5–8, 2004.

Entrepreneur.com. "Where Do I Find One?" *Entrepreuner.com*, June 1999. entrepreneur.com/mag/article/0,1539, 2303 76-3-,00.html (accessed December 2004).

Fahrenwald, B., and D. Wise. "Logistics and Fulfillment: E-Commerce Meets the Material World." *Business Week*, special advertising section, June 26, 2000. norbridgeinc.com/services/norbridge_ecommerce_bwk_june%2026%202000.pdf (accessed March 2005).

Fair Disclosure Wire. "Event Brief of Q3 2004 Gemstar-TV Guide International Earnings Conference Call—Final." November 9, 2004.

Farber, D. "UPS Takes Wireless to the Next Level." *ZDNet.com*, April 25, 2003. techupdate.zdnet.com/techupdate/stories/main/0,14179,2913461,00.html (accessed December 2004).

FedEx. "BikeWorld Goes Global Using FedEx Technologies and Shipping." FedEx case study, August 2000. fedex.com/us/ebusiness/ecommerce/bikeworld.pdf?link=4 (accessed December 2004).

Ganapathy, S., et al. "Visualization Strategies and Tools for Enhancing CRM." *Communications of the ACM* (November 2004).

Gateau, B., et al. "Contract Model for Agent Mediated Electronic Commerce." *Proceedings of the Third International Joint Conference on Autonomous Agents and Multiagent Systems,* New York, July 19–23, 2004.

Greenberg, P. *CRM at the Speed of Light: Capturing and Keeping Customers in Internet Real Time,* 3d ed. New York: McGraw-Hill, 2004.

Guzman, Y. "FedEx Delivers CRM." SearchCRM.com, April 14, 2004. searchcrm.techtarget.com/originalcontent/0,289142,sid11_gci958859,00.htm (accessed March 2005).

Handfield, R. B., et al. *Supply Chain Redesign: Transforming Supply Chains into Integrated Value Systems*. Upper Saddle River, NJ: Prentice Hall, 2002.

Heizer, J., and B. Render. *Operations Management*, 7th ed. Upper Saddle River, NJ: Prentice Hall, 2004.

Holweg, M., and F. Pil. "Successful Build-to-Order Strategies." *MIT Sloan Management Review* (Fall 2001).

IBM. ibm.com (accessed 2002).

Jagannathan, S., et al. *Internet Commerce Metrics.* Upper Saddle River, NJ: Prentice Hall, 2001.

Johnson, J. "Making CRM Technology Work." *The British Journal of Administrative Management*, 2004.

Kalakota, R., and M. Robinson. *E-Businesses: Roadmap for Success*. Reading, MA: Addison Wesley, 2001.

Kern, T., and J. Kreijger. "An Exploration of the ASP Outsourcing Option." *Proceedings of the 34th HICSS*, Maui, Hawaii, January 2001.

Kinnard, S. *Marketing with E-Mail.* Gulf Breeze, FL: Maximum Press, 2002.

Knaack, M. "Rolling Warehouse." *Reeves Journal* 81, no. 10 (2001).

Kopytoff, V. "Amazon Perfects New Process of Packaging Multiple Orders." *San Francisco Chronicle*, December 21, 2004. sfgate.com/cgi-bin/article.cgi?f=/c/a/2004/12/21/bug01aetcm1.dtl (accessed March 2005).

Kuzeljevich, J. "Targeting Reverse Logistics." *Canadian Transportation Logistics* 107, no. 9 (2004).

Kwok, C., et al. "Scaling Question Answering to the Web." *ACM Transactions on Information Systems* 19, no. 3 (2001).

Lee, H. L., and S. Whang. "Winning the Last Mile of E-Commerce." *MIT Sloan Management Review* (Summer 2001).

Lohr, S., et al. "The Future in Gear." *PC Magazine*, September 3, 2002.

Nemati, R., et al. "e-CRM Analytics: The Role of Data Integration." *PCAI*, March 2004.

Parks, L. "Schurman Fine Papers Rack Up Labor Savings." *Stores*, February 2004.

Patricia Seybold Group. *An Executive's Guide to CRM*. Boston, MA: Patricia Seybold Group, 2002. psgroup.com/vm/crm/ (accessed December 2004).

PeopleSoft. "The Business Case for Mobile CRM: Opportunities, Pitfalls, and Solutions." White Paper, February 2002. peoplesoft.com/corp/en/doc_archive/white_paper/biz_case_mobile_crm_s_13013.jsp (accessed December 2004).

Petersen, G. S. *Customer Relationship Management Systems: ROI and Results Measurement*. New York: Strategic Sales Performance, 1999.

Pickering, C. "New Power Centers—FedEx Hub." *Business 2.0*, January 2000.

Plant, R. T. *E-Commerce: Foundation of Strategy*. Upper Saddle River, NJ: Prentice Hall, 2000.

Rao, B., et al. "Building a World-Class Logistics, Distribution, and EC Infrastructure." *Electronic Markets* 9, no. 3 (1999).

Reichheld, F. F., and P. Schefter. "E-loyalty: Your Secret Weapon on the Web." *Harvard Business Review* 78, no. 4 (2000).

Romano, N. C., Jr. and J. Fjermestad (eds.). "Introduction to the Special Section: Electronic Commerce Customer Relationship Management (ECCRM)." *International Journal of Electronic Commerce* (Winter 2001–2002).

Rust, R. T., and K. N. Lemon. "E-Service and the Consumer." *International Journal of Electronic Commerce* 5, no. 3 (2001): 85–101.

SAS. sas.com (accessed December 2004).

Segev, A., and J. Gebauer. "B2B Procurement and Marketplace Transformation." *Information Technology and Management* 2, no. 3 (2001).

Seybold, P. B., and R. Marshak. *Customer.com: How to Create a Profitable Business Strategy for the Internet and Beyond.* New York: Times Books, 1998.

Steinert-Threlkeld, T. "GroceryWorks: The Low-Touch Alternative." *Interactive Week*, January 31, 2000.

Steinfield, C. "Understanding Click-and-Mortar E-Commerce Approaches: A Conceptual Framework and

Research Agenda." *Journal of Interactive Advertising* 2, no. 2, 2002. **jiad.org/vol2/no2/steinfield/** (accessed March 2005).

Sterne, J. *Web Metrics: Proven Methods for Measuring Web Site Success*. New York: Wiley, 2002.

Symbol Technologies. "Peacocks Case Study." **symbol.com/uk/solutions/case_study_peacocks.html** (accessed March 2005).

Tan, X., et al. "Internet Integrated Customer Relationship Management." *Journal of Computer Information Systems* (Spring 2002).

Tomsen, M. *Killer Content: Strategies for Web Content and E-Commerce*. Boston: Addison-Wesley, 2000.

Turban, E., et al. *Decision Support Systems and Intelligent Systems*, 7th ed. Upper Saddle River, NJ: Prentice Hall, 2005.

UPS. "E-Logistics: Your Inventory Is Worth More Than Money." **e-logistics.ups.com** (accessed March 2005).

Violino, B. "Supply Chain Management and E-Commerce." *InternetWeek*, May 4, 2000.

Voss, C. "Developing an eService Strategy." *Business Strategy Review* 11, no. 11 (2000).

Ward, L. "How ASPs Can Accelerate Your E-Business." *e-Business Advisor*, March 2000.

Yoon, S. "Brand Names Are at the Virtual Mall." *Wall Street Journal Europe*, June 13, 2002.

CHAPTER 14

E-COMMERCE STRATEGY AND GLOBAL EC

Content

Learning Objectives

Upon completion of this chapter, you will be able to:

1. Describe the strategic planning process.
2. Describe the purpose and content of a business plan.
3. Understand how e-commerce impacts the strategic planning process.
4. Understand how EC applications are formulated, justified, and prioritized.
5. Describe strategy implementation and assessment, including the use of metrics.
6. Evaluate the issues involved in global EC.
7. Analyze the impact of EC on small and medium-sized businesses.

SEARCH WARS

The Problem

One of the most spirited arenas of Internet competition is Web search engines, and never more so than in 2004. Historically, the title of "top search engine" had been held by Excite, Lycos, AltaVista, Inktomi, and others. These search engines mostly relied on keyword analysis—counting the frequency and placement of keywords in the Web page—and few ever made a profit. For example, AltaVista was developed by Digital Equipment to showcase Digital's ultrafast Alpha hardware, not to add profit to Digital's bottom line.

The Web search world changed in 1998 when Google introduced *link popularity*—counting the number of links and importance of those links—in its search algorithm (see *The Economist* [2004] for an explanation of this search algorithm). Soon, Google was the top search engine, and now it has become part of our everyday language (e.g., *to google* is now a verb and *google bombing* is a page-ranking strategy). Google also is the Internet's first lucrative search engine, earning substantial profits from sponsored ads and achieving a highly successful IPO launch in mid-2004.

Google's success has not gone unnoticed. Nothing attracts competition like success, and in 2004 other companies, large and small, began to enter this competitive arena. The biggest battles in the search wars are likely to be between Google and some of the giants of electronic commerce.

In February 2004, Yahoo!, an innovative and profitable company that had changed from a Web directory into an Internet portal, launched Yahoo! Search. It is based on Yahoo!'s 2002 and 2003 acquisitions of search engine technology from Inktomi, AltaVista, and AllTheWeb; all of which were significant search engines in their own right (Sullivan 2004).

In September 2004, Amazon.com introduced A9 (*a9.com*), a "search engine with memory." A9 allows users to store and edit bookmarks, revisit links clicked on previous visits, and make personal notes on Web pages for later viewing. Commentators describe Amazon.com's competitive advantage as follows: "The ability to search through your own history of Web searches is insanely powerful" and "It's not just about search, it's about managing your information" (Markoff 2004b).

In November 2004, Microsoft released its test version of MSN Search, its primary artillery in the search wars (MSN stands for Microsoft Network). MSN Search seeks to fulfill the battle cry Chairman Bill Gates had issued earlier in 2004: "We took an approach [ignoring the Web search market] that I now realize was wrong, [but] we will catch them" (Markoff 2004a). Perhaps more significantly, Microsoft plans to include comprehensive Web and desktop search capabilities in Longhorn, the code name for its next major Windows operating system, due for release in 2006.

Google also is facing competition from smaller companies that are trying to create the next "great leap forward" in Web search technology (Roush 2004):

- Teoma (*teoma.com*) uses an authority-based ranking algorithm that ranks Web page results according to their standing among recognized authorities on a topic (*teoma* is Gaelic for "expert").
- Mooter (*mooter.com*) makes searches more personal by recording which links get clicked and adjusting the ranking of Web sites in subsequent searches based on these preferences.
- Dipsie's (*dipsie.com*) claim to fame is its ability to search the so-called *deep Web*, pages that are protected behind sign-up forms or assembled on the fly from data stored in databases, such as product catalogs. These pages compose perhaps nearly 500 times the volume of the surface Web.
- Clusty (*clusty.com*) organizes search results into folders, or "clusters," by grouping similar items together based on textual and linguistic similarity. For example, a search on "George Bush" produces clusters such as "White House," "election," "quotes," and "Iraq," and each cluster contains a number of search results.
- Snap (*snap.com*) uses click-stream information (e.g., what sites Web users visit, how long they stay) to rank Web search results as well as sort the results based on various criteria.

Why this intense interest in Web search technology and winning the search wars? All of these companies want to be the next Google, obtaining the profits and fame that Google has acquired. However, winning in this arena also is about power. Brewster Kahle, the founder of the Internet Archive, notes that 20 percent of all Web traffic goes to only 10 Web sites, and that list is dominated by search engines. He observes: "The level of mind space that provides is enormous. If you want to control the world, it's essential that you be there" (Markoff 2004c).

The Solution

Google is meeting the competitive challenges it faces head on. Google offers an expanding repertoire of tools in line with its core competency in search technology. Some of these tools were still in beta testing as this was being written at the end of 2004:

- Froogle (*froogle.google.com*) is a product-comparison search engine for online shopping. A similar search tool is Google Catalogs (*catalogs.google.com*), which searches a database of mail-order catalogs.
- Google News (*news.google.com*) searches news-oriented Web sites and displays stories according to a computer algorithm that rates stories based on how many news sites are publishing the stories, how recently the articles were published, and, for searches, keyword occurrence.

- Google Scholar (*scholar.google.com*) searches the scholarly literature, including peer-reviewed papers, theses, books, preprints, abstracts, and technical reports. Many hits are abstracts or citations, not full articles, and some are "cloaked" behind subscription-only journal subscriptions. The Google Scholar algorithm replaces link popularity with citation analysis (i.e., the most frequently cited articles are ranked the highest), presumably putting the best papers at the top of the search results.
- Google also has introduced Google Wireless (*google.com/options/wireless.html*); Google Groups (*groups.google.com*); Google Answers (*google.com/answers*), which is an ask-an-expert site; and more (see *google.com/options/index.html*).

Strategically, Google is leveraging its widely recognized brand name and search technology expertise into areas beyond Web searching. Sometimes these projects bring Google into direct competition with the EC giants mentioned earlier.

- Google Print (*print.google.com*) is similar to Amazon.com's "search inside the book" feature. Users can search by keyword (e.g., "books about Nelson Mandela") and then search for keywords or phrases within the books.
- GMail (*gmail.google.com*) is Google's offering in the huge Web-based e-mail market that is currently dominated by Microsoft's Hotmail and Yahoo! Mail. In beta testing and only available by invitation as of late 2004, GMail offers new services, such as grouping related messages together and keyword searching through e-mail messages.
- Google Desktop (*desktop.google.com*) searches the contents of computer files, e-mail messages, and even recently viewed Web pages. This is a dramatic improvement on the Windows "Find" feature, which only searches computer files and then mostly by file name. Google Desktop preempts technology that Microsoft is intending to put into Longhorn.
- Orkut (*orkut.com*) is a social-networking service that competes in one of the fastest-growing Internet markets—Web sites that connect people through networks of friends or business contacts to find new friends or contacts. Competitors include Friendster and Linkedin.

The Results

The new services Google is launching utilize its expertise in search technology beyond "searching the Web" to searching e-mail messages, books, and computer files. The strategic moves Google is making are all in line with its mission statement: "to organize the world's information and make it universally useful and accessible."

Financially, Google also is proving to be very successful, reporting revenues of almost $806 million in the second quarter of 2004. As of November 2004, its market capitalization is $52 billion, more than Ford and General Motors combined (Fallows 2004).

What is ahead for Google? Financial observers have noted that while its roots are in search engine technology, its revenues and profits are in sponsored advertising, the same as portals such as MSN and Yahoo! (Munarriz 2004). Will further expansion by Google into new territory dilute its search engine reputation, brand name, and profits? Or, are these moves necessary to assist in its inevitable evolution into a portal? What business is Google really in? The answers to these questions will determine Google's next moves in the Internet marketspace.

Sources: *The Economist* (2004), Fallows (2004), Markoff (2004a, 2004b, 2004c), Munarriz (2004), Roush (2004), and Sullivan (2004).

WHAT WE CAN LEARN . . .

The opening case raises some compelling issues related to strategic planning for EC. First, the moves Google is making are consistent with its core competencies in search technology and the value proposition it offers to its customers, as stated in its mission statement "to organize the world's information."

Google was not a first mover in Web search engines, but it has been a best mover, innovating the Web search technology market and becoming phenomenally successful. It hopes the same best-mover strategy will be successful with GMail and Google Print. Google also is looking to be a first-mover with products such as Google Desktop. First-mover and best-mover strategies are discussed in Section 14.4.

Google is naming most of its new products with the Google brand name or variations of it (e.g., Google News, Froogle, GMail). As discussed in this chapter, this is a good approach when a firm has a strong, positive, and well-recognized brand name in the marketplace.

In summary, Google's innovative approach to its strategic placement in the marketplace exemplifies many of the key points about EC strategy made in this chapter. EC strategy is the main subject of this chapter. The chapter also presents the related topics of global EC and EC in small and medium-sized enterprises (SMEs).

14.1 ORGANIZATIONAL STRATEGY: CONCEPTS AND OVERVIEW

Strategy happens all the time. At a personal level, a university student decides on a career as a long-term strategy and then puts into place certain goals (e.g., a degree in the chosen field) and objectives (e.g., timely competition of courses at a desired level of achievement) in order to implement that strategy. Nationally and internationally, world leaders set economic, political, and social strategies, which are implemented through legislation, regulations, policies, and projects.

Organizational leaders strategize, too—in goal setting, business planning, resource allocation, and project management activities. An organizational **strategy** is a broad-based formula for how a business is going to compete, what its goals should be, and what plans and policies will need to be implemented to accomplish these goals (Porter 1980). An organization's strategy addresses fundamental questions about the current position of a company and its future directions, such as (Jelassi and Enders 2005):

strategy
A broad-based formula for how a business is going to compete, what its goals should be, and what plans and policies will be needed to carry out those goals.

- What is the long-term direction of our organization?
- What is the overall plan for deploying our organization's resources?
- What trade-offs are necessary?
- What is our unique positioning vis-à-vis competitors?
- How do we achieve sustainable competitive advantage over rivals in order to ensure lasting profitability?

As the third question in the list emphasizes, strategy is more than deciding what a company should do next. Strategy also is about making tough decisions about what *not* to do. Strategic positioning is about making decisions about trade-offs, recognizing that a company must abandon or not pursue some products, services, and activities in order to excel at others. How are these trade-offs determined? Not merely with a focus on growth and increases in revenue, but also on profitability and increases in shareholder value over the long run. How is this profitability and economic value determined? By establishing a unique *value proposition* and the configuration of a tailored *value chain* that enables a company to offer unique value to its customers. Therefore, strategy has been, and remains, focused on questions about organizational fit, trade-offs, profitability, and value (Porter 1996; 2001).

Any contemporary strategy-setting process must include the Internet. Strategy guru Michael Porter (2001) argues that a coherent organizational strategy that includes the Internet is more important than ever before: "Many have argued that the Internet renders strategy obsolete. In reality, the opposite is true . . . it is more important than ever for companies to distinguish themselves through strategy. The winners will be those that view the Internet as a complement to, not a cannibal of, traditional ways of competing" (p. 63).

To illustrate this point, Porter (2001) has identified several ways that the Internet impacts each of the five forces of competitiveness—bargaining power of consumers and suppliers, threats from substitutes and new entrants, and rivalry among existing competitors—that were originally described in one of his seminal works on strategy (Porter 1980). These five forces and associated Internet impacts are shown in Exhibit 14.1. In this figure, a negative sign (-) implies a negative impact on the long-term profitability of firms operating in the industry and a positive sign (+) represents a positive impact. The majority of impacts are negative, reflecting Porter's view that "The great paradox of the Internet is that its very benefits—making information widely available; reducing the difficulty of purchasing, marketing, and distribution; allowing buyers and sellers to find and transact business with one another more easily—also make it more difficult for companies to capture those benefits as profits" (Porter 2001, p. 66).

e-commerce strategy (e-strategy)
The formulation and execution of a vision of how a new or existing company intends to do business electronically.

Of course, Exhibit 14.1 is a generalization, and the impact of the Internet on strategic competitiveness and long-term profitability will differ from industry to industry. Accordingly, many businesses are taking a focused look at the impact of the Internet and EC on their future. For these firms, an **e-commerce strategy**, or **e-strategy**, is the formulation and execution of a vision of how a new or existing company intends to do business electronically. The process of building an e-strategy is explained in detail later in this chapter. First, though, we continue our overview of organizational strategy.

EXHIBIT 14.1 How the Internet Influences Industry Structure

Threat of substitute products or services

(+) By making the overall industry more efficient, the Internet can expand the size of the market

(-) The proliferation of Internet approaches creates new substitution threats

Bargaining power of suppliers

(+) Procurement using the Internet tends to raise buyers' bargaining power over suppliers, though it can also give suppliers access to more customers

(-) The Internet provides a channel for suppliers to reach end users, reducing the leverage of intervening companies

(-) Internet procurement and digital markets tend to give all companies equal access to suppliers, and gravitate procurement to standardized products that reduce differentiation

(-) Reduced barriers to entry and the proliferation of competitors downstream shifts power to suppliers

Rivalry among existing competitors

(-) Reduces differences among competitors as offerings are difficult to keep proprietary

(-) Migrates competition to price

(-) Widens the geographic market, increasing the number of competitors

(-) Lowers variable cost relative to fixed cost, increasing pressures for price discounting

Buyers

Bargaining power of channels

(+) Eliminates powerful channels or improves bargaining power over traditional channels

Bargaining power of end users

(-) Shifts bargaining power to end consumers

(-) Reduces switching costs

Barriers to entry

(-) Reduces barriers to entry such as the need for a sales force, access to channels, and physical assets—anything that Internet technology eliminates or makes easier to do reduces barriers to entry

(-) Internet applications are difficult to keep proprietary from new entrants

(-) A flood of new entrants has come into many industries

Source: Porter, M.E. "Strategy and the Internet." *Harvard Business Review*, March 2001, p. 67.

THE STRATEGIC PLANNING PROCESS

A strategy is important, but the *process* of developing a strategy is even more important. (See Online Exhibit W14.1 on the book's Web site for what some famous people have said about the planning process.) No matter how large or how small the organization, the strategic planning process forces corporate executives, a company's general manager, or a small business owner to assess the current position of the firm, where it should be, and how to get from here to there. The process also involves primary stakeholders, including the board of directors, employees, and strategic partners. This involvement ensures that stakeholders buy into the strategy and reinforces stakeholder commitment to the future of the organization.

Strategy development will differ depending on the type of strategy, the implementation method, the size of the firm, and the approach that is taken. Nevertheless, any strategic planning process has four major phases, as shown in Exhibit 14.2. (Note that the phases in Exhibit 14.2 correspond to section numbers in this chapter.) The major phases of the strategic planning process, and some identifiable activities and outcomes associated with each phase, are discussed briefly in the following text. The phases are then discussed more extensively as part of the e-commerce strategic planning process in Sections 14.4 through 14.7.

Strategy Initiation

strategy initiation The initial phase of strategic planning in which the organization examines itself and its environment.

In the **strategy initiation** phase, the organization examines itself and its environment. The principal activities include setting the organization's mission and goals, examining organizational strengths and weaknesses, assessing environmental factors impacting the business, and

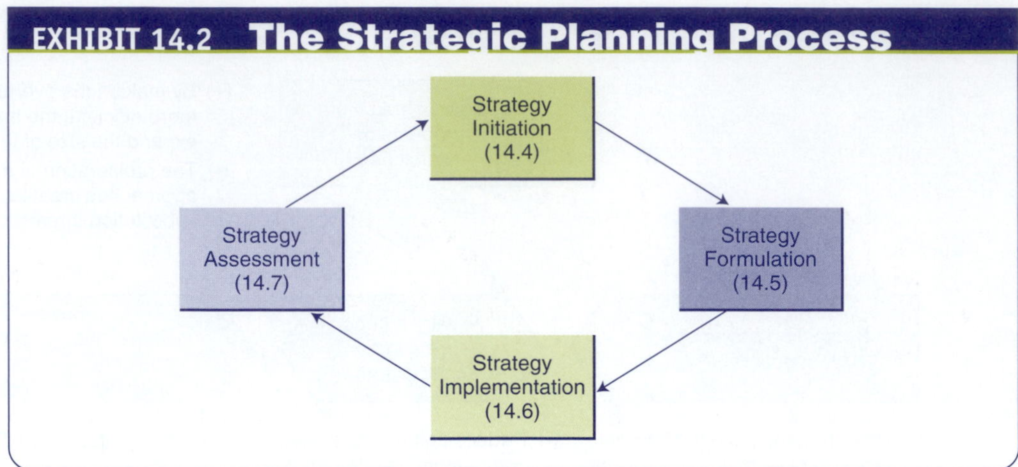

conducting a competitor analysis. As emphasized throughout this chapter, this includes an examination of the potential contribution that the Internet and other emerging technologies can make to the business.

Specific outcomes from this phase include:

- **Company analysis.** The company analysis includes the vision, mission, value proposition, goals, capabilities, constraints, strengths, and weaknesses of the company. Questions typically asked in a company analysis are: What business are we really in? Who are our future customers? Do our mission statement and our goals adequately describe our intended future? What opportunities, and threats, do our business and our industry face? One key outcome from this analysis should be a clear statement of the company's **value proposition**—the benefit that a company's products or services provide to customers or the consumer need that is being fulfilled. It is only by knowing what benefits a business is providing to customers that chief-level executives can truly understand "what business they are in" and who their potential competitors are (Harmon et al. 2001). For example, Amazon.com recognizes that it is not just in the book-selling business, but that it also is in the information-about-books business. Amazon.com's strategists know this is where customers find value in shopping at Amazon.com and where a great deal of Amazon's competitive advantage lies. So Amazon.com has introduced new services such as "search inside the book" to deliver on that value proposition to its customers.

value proposition
The benefit that a company's products or services provide to customers; the consumer need that is being fulfilled.

- **Core competencies.** A core competency refers to the unique combination of the resources and experiences of a particular firm. It takes time to build these core competencies, and they can be difficult to imitate (Rowe et al. 1994). For example, Google's core competency is its expertise in information search technology, as emphasized in the opening case.
- **Forecasts.** Forecasting means identifying business, technological, political, economic, and other relevant trends that are currently affecting the business or that have the potential to do so.
- **Competitor (industry) analysis.** Competitor analysis involves scanning the business environment to collect and interpret relevant information about direct competitors, indirect competitors, and potential competitors. Several methodologies are available to conduct such an analysis, including a SWOT analysis and competitor analysis grid.

Strategy Formulation

Strategy formulation is the development of strategies to exploit opportunities and manage threats in the business environment in light of corporate strengths and weaknesses. In an EC strategy, the end result is likely to be a list of EC applications or projects to be implemented.

strategy formulation
The development of strategies to exploit opportunities and manage threats in the business environment in light of corporate strengths and weaknesses.

Specific activities and outcomes from this phase include:

- **Business opportunities.** If the strategy initiation has been done well, a number of scenarios for future development of the business will be obvious. How well these scenarios fit with the future direction of the company are assessed. Similarly, the first phase may also have identified some current activities that are no longer relevant to the company's future and are candidates for divestiture, outsourcing, or elimination.

- **Cost-benefit analysis.** Each proposed opportunity must be assessed in terms of the potential costs and benefits to the company in light of its mission and goals. These costs and benefits may be financial or nonfinancial, tangible or intangible, or short-term or long-term. More information about conducting a cost-benefit analysis is included in Chapter 15.
- **Risk analysis, assessment, and management.** The risks of each proposed opportunity must be analyzed and assessed. If a significant risk is evident, then a risk management plan is required. Of particular importance in an EC strategy are business risk factors such as transition risk and partner risk, which are discussed in Section 14.5.
- **Business plan.** Many of the outcomes from these first two phases—goals, competitor analysis, strategic opportunities, risk analysis, and more—come together in a business plan. As described in Section 14.2, every business—large or small, new or old, successful or not—needs a business plan to acquire funding and to ensure that a realistic approach is being taken to implementation of the business strategy.

Strategy Implementation

In this phase, the emphasis shifts from "what do we do?" to "how do we do it?" In the **strategy implementation** phase, detailed, short-term plans are developed for carrying out the projects agreed on in strategy formulation. Specifically, decision makers evaluate options, establish specific milestones, allocate resources, and manage the projects.

strategy implementation The development of detailed, short-term plans for carrying out the projects agreed on in strategy formulation.

Specific activities and outcomes from this phase include:

- **Project planning.** Inevitably, strategy implementation is executed through a project or a series of projects. Project planning includes setting specific project objectives, creating a project schedule with milestones, and setting measurable performance targets. Normally, a project plan would be set for each project and application.
- **Resource allocation.** Organizational resources are those owned, available to, or controlled by a company. They can be human, financial, technological, managerial, or knowledge based.
- **Project management.** This is the process of making the selected applications and projects a reality—staff are hired; equipment is purchased; software is licensed, purchased, or written, and so on.

Strategy Assessment

Just as soon as implementation is complete, assessment begins. **Strategy assessment** is the continuous evaluation of progress toward the organization's strategic goals, resulting in corrective action and, if necessary, strategy reformulation. In strategy assessment, specific measures called *metrics* (discussed in Section 14.7) are used to assess the progress of the strategy. In some cases, data gathered in the first phase can be used as baseline data to assess the strategy's effectiveness. If not, this information will have to be gathered.

strategy assessment The continuous evaluation of progress toward the organization's strategic goals, resulting in corrective action and, if necessary, strategy reformulation.

What happens with the results from strategy assessment? As shown in Exhibit 14.2, the strategic planning process starts over again, immediately. Early descriptions of the strategic planning process described strategy development as a linear process that terminated at implementation. However, a linear approach simply is not viable in the modern, fast-paced world of competitive business activity. Instead, a cyclical approach is required—a strategic planning process that requires constant reassessment of today's strategy while preparing a new strategy for tomorrow.

A major organizational restructuring and transformation was the reason for the development of a new strategic plan for InternetNZ, as described in EC Application Case 14.1.

STRATEGIC PLANNING TOOLS

Strategists have devised a number of strategic planning tools and techniques that can be used in strategic planning. A partial list of these tools is shown in Exhibit 14.3. A few of the most popular tools are described briefly in this section. A strategic management textbook or handbook can provide more information about these and other strategic planning tools.

CASE 14.1

EC Application

STRATEGIC PLANNING AT INTERNETNZ

InternetNZ is not only an Internet-based business, its business is the Internet. An incorporated, nonprofit organization, InternetNZ describes itself as "the guardian of the Internet for New Zealand," and its primary business activity is management of the .nz ccTLD (Country Code Top-Level Domain).

After a somewhat turbulent transition from its predecessor organization, the Internet Society of New Zealand, in early 2004 InternetNZ embarked on a comprehensive strategic planning exercise. The result of that exercise, *InternetNZ Strategic Plan: 2004–2007,* is a model of content that should be in every strategic plan.

Environment Analysis. In addition to describing trends that affect the global Internet and the Internet in New Zealand, a PEST analysis lists factors in the political, economic, and social environment that affect the conduct of InternetNZ's business, for example: "No large pro-censorship lobby in NZ" (political), "Increasing dependence on the Internet for information" (social), and "The Internet bridges NZ's geographical disadvantage" (economic).

Vision Statement. A vision statement for 2007 ("The Internet, open and uncapturable, offering high performance and unfettered access for all") is followed by 16 visionary goals (e.g., "Benefits of the Internet have been extended to all New Zealanders").

Mission Statement. "To protect and promote the Internet in New Zealand" captures many of the characteristics—visionary, realistic, easily understood, short and concise—of a good mission statement.

SWOT Analysis. A SWOT analysis lists 13 strengths (e.g., "Committed, involved, clever volunteers," "Has created a best practice model for .nz ccTLD"), 13 weaknesses (e.g., "Perception of InternetNZ as mainly 'geeks' or 'techies,'" "Lack of internal resources to respond to rapidly changing environment"), 14 opportunities (e.g., "A leader in the fight against spam," "Help insure widespread broadband access"), and 11 threats (e.g., "Unnecessary government intervention or regulation," "Low level of membership, hence providing little funding and vulnerable to take over").

Core Values. Six core values—openness, transparency, ethical behavior, neutrality, supportive, commitment—are identified and described briefly.

Goal Statements. Eight strategies (e.g., management of .nz ccTLD, advocacy and representation to government, promote the Internet, support Internet innovation and technical leadership) are listed. For each strategy, one to eight goals are listed and the InternetNZ committee held accountable for achievement of the strategy is clearly identified. For each goal, a goal statement of purpose, projected outcomes, and specific examples for execution of the goal are identified from the 2004–2007 InternetNZ business plan.

Business Plan. Separate from, but an integral part of the *InternetNZ Strategic Plan: 2004–2007,* is the *InternetNZ Business Plan: 2004–2007*. This document lists, describes, and prioritizes the specific activities that are expected to be necessary to achieve the goals, with associated income and expenses.

The InternetNZ Council adopted the strategic plan and the business plan at its April 2004 meeting, and both plans are in the process of being implemented.

Source: InternetNZ. *InternetNZ Strategic Plan: 2004–2007*. April, 2004. Available from *internetnz.net.nz/public/planning040424strat-plan-v3.2.pdf* (accessed December 2004). Adapted with permission.

Questions

1. Why would a nonprofit organization such as InternetNZ need a strategic plan or a business plan?
2. What is the difference between a vision statement and a mission statement?

SWOT analysis
A methodology that surveys external opportunities and threats and relates them to internal strengths and weaknesses.

competitor analysis grid
A strategic planning tool that highlights points of differentiation between competitors and the target firm.

SWOT analysis is a methodology that surveys the opportunities (O) and threats (T) in the external environment and relates them to the organization's internal strengths (S) and weaknesses (W).

A **competitor analysis grid** is a strategic planning tool that highlights points of differentiation between competitors and the target firm. The grid is a table with the company's most significant competitors entered in the columns and the key factors for comparison entered in the rows. Factors might include mission statements, strategic partners, sources of competitive advantage (e.g., cost leadership, global reach), customer relationship strategies, and financial resources. An additional column includes the company's data on each factor so that significant similarities and differences (i.e., points of differentiation) will be obvious. A competitor analysis grid template is available in Online Tutorial T1 (An E-Business Plan Tutorial) on the book's Web site.

Scenario planning offers an alternative to traditional planning approaches that rely on straight-line projections of current trends. These approaches fail when low-probability events occur that radically alter current trends. The aim of scenario analysis is to generate several plausible alternative futures, giving decision makers the opportunity to identify actions that can be taken today to ensure success under varying future conditions (see Levinson 1999–2000).

EXHIBIT 14.3 Strategic Planning Tools

Tools Used in Strategy Initiation	
SWOT analysis	Analyze external opportunities and threats and relate them to internal strengths and weaknesses (discussed in text).
Competitor analysis grid	Seek points of differentiation between competitors and the target firm (discussed in text).
Strategy canvas	Plot a strategic profile based on competition factors (see Kim and Mauborgne 2002).
PEST analysis	Assess political, environmental, socio-cultural, and technological (PEST) factors for their impact on the organization (see Johnson and Scholes 1999).
Tools Used in Strategy Formulation	
Scenario planning	Generate, and prepare for, several plausible alternative futures (discussed in text).
Return on investment (ROI)	A quantitative financial measure of costs and benefits (discussed in text).
BCG growth-share matrix	Compare projects on potential market growth and market share to determine the best projects to adopt, sell, redesign, or abandon (discussed in Section 14.5).
Tools Used in Strategy Implementation	
Project management	A planned effort to accomplish a specific effort of defined scope, resources, and duration.
Business process reengineering (BPR)	Redesign an enterprise's processes to accommodate a new application (discussed in Section 14.6).
Tools Used in Strategy Assessment	
Balanced scorecard	A tool that measures organizational performance in finance, customer assessment, business processes, and other areas (discussed in text).
Web analytics	Tracking Web site visitor behavior to discover interactions between a site's content and design and visitors' activities (discussed in Section 14.7).

Return on investment (ROI) is a ratio of required costs and perceived benefits of a project or application. Because it is a quantitative financial tool, all costs and benefits must be expressed in financial numbers. The tricky part of ROI is expressing in financial terms costs such as short-term business disruptions and financial benefits such as streamlined business processes. More information about ROI is available in Chapter 15.

Balanced scorecard is an adaptive tool that assesses organizational progress toward strategic goals by measuring performance in a number of different areas. Originally proposed by Kaplan and Norton (1996) as an alternative to narrowly focused financial assessments, the balanced scorecard seeks more balance by measuring organizational performance in four areas: finance, customers' assessments, internal business processes, and learning and growth. More information about the balanced scorecard is available in Chapter 15.

scenario planning
A strategic planning methodology that generates plausible alternative futures to help decision makers identify actions that can be taken today to ensure success in the future.

return on investment (ROI)
A ratio of required costs and perceived benefits of a project or an application.

balanced scorecard
An adaptive tool that assesses organizational progress toward strategic goals by measuring performance in a number of different areas.

Section 14.1 ▶ REVIEW QUESTIONS

1. What is strategy?
2. Which is more important, a plan or the planning process? Why?
3. Describe the four phases of strategic planning.
4. Why is a cyclic approach to strategic planning required?
5. Describe five tools that can be used for strategic planning.

14.2 BUSINESS PLANNING

business plan
A written document that identifies the company's goals and outlines how the company intends to achieve those goals.

One almost inevitable outcome of strategy setting is a business plan. A **business plan** is a written document that identifies the company's goals and outlines how the company intends to achieve the goals. An outline of a business plan is shown in Exhibit 14.4. This outline follows the Online Tutorial T1 (An E-Business Plan Tutorial) at the book's Web site, where detailed information about each section is available.

BUSINESS PLAN FUNDAMENTALS

Business plans are written for a variety of purposes. The customary reason why a business needs a business plan is to acquire funding. Entrepreneurs in start-up companies use business plans to get funding from investors, such as a *venture capitalist* or a bank. An existing company may write a business plan to get funding from a bank, the financial markets (e.g., an initial public offering), or a prospective business partner.

A second reason to write a business plan is to acquire nonfinancial resources. A prospective landlord, equipment supplier, or ASP may want to see a viable business plan before entering into a contract. Similarly, a business plan can be useful for recruiting senior management. Any person truly capable of leading a medium-sized or large business will want to see an organization's business plan before accepting the position.

Another purpose for writing a business plan is to obtain a realistic approach to the business. The process of writing the plan forces the business owner to think ahead, set achievable goals, seek out and analyze competitors, figure out how to reach target markets, anticipate problems, and compare projected revenue streams against realistic expense statements. As with strategy setting, the process, not the plan itself, increases the likelihood that the business will be a success.

A realistic approach also means that sometimes the most successful outcome of writing a business plan is a decision not to proceed. Researching and writing a plan can reveal the reali-

EXHIBIT 14.4 Outline of a Business Plan

Executive Summary: The executive summary is a synopsis of the key points of the entire business plan. Its purpose is to explain the fundamentals of the business in a way that both informs and excites the reader.

Business Description: The business description describes the nature and purpose of the business and includes the firm's mission statement, goals, value proposition, and a description of the products and services it provides. The purpose of the business description is to objectively explain and justify the business idea in a positive and enthusiastic manner.

Marketing Plan: The central part of the marketing plan is the market analysis, which defines the firm's target markets and analyzes how the organization will position its products or services to arouse and fulfill the needs of the target markets in order to maximize sales. Other aspects of the marketing plan include pricing strategy, promotion plan, distribution plan, and a demand forecast.

Competitor Analysis: The competitor analysis (a) outlines the competitive strengths and weaknesses of rivals in the industry and (b) reveals the firm's competitive position in the marketspace.

Operations Plan: The operations section of the business plan describes the inputs, processes, procedures, and activities required to create what products the business will sell or what services it will deliver.

Financial Plan: The financial plan estimates the monetary resources and flows that will be required to carry out the business plan. The financial plan also indicates when and by how much the business intends to be profitable. Finally, the financial statements (e.g., balance sheet, cash flow statement) tell a lot about the entrepreneur in terms of business commitment and financial wherewithal to make the business a profitable success.

ties of tough competition, a too-small target market, or an income and expense statement that is awash in red ink. Many owners of failed start-ups would have saved considerable time, money, and heartbreak if a proper business plan had been done.

When do a business plan? The most obvious time is when a new business is seeking start-up funds and other resources. However, a business plan may also be required if an existing company is planning to create a separate company, reengineer or restructure the existing company, or launch the company in a new direction. Of course, a plan also is required when the existing plan is reaching its use-by date. If the original plan set forth a 3-year plan and the business just celebrated its second birthday, it is time to write a new plan.

Several software packages are available for the creation of business plans (e.g., see bplans.com and planware.org). Insights and Additions 14.1 highlights the differences between a traditional business plan and an e-business plan.

BUSINESS CASE

A distinctive type of business plan is the *business case.* As emphasized in the previous section, a business plan often is used when launching a new business. A **business case** is a business plan for a new initiative or project *inside an existing organization.* Its purpose is the same as with a business plan—to justify a specific investment of funds—but the audience is the company's board of directors and senior management, not an external funding agency. The business case helps clarify how the organization will use its resources by identifying the strategic justification ("Where are we going?"), operational justification ("How will we get there?"), technical justification ("When will we get there?"), and financial justification ("Why will we win?") (Kalakota and Robinson 2001). Examples of EC initiatives that may require a business

business case
A business plan for a new initiative or project inside an existing organization.

Insights and Additions 14.1 Putting the "E" in E-Business Planning

How is an e-business plan different from any other business plan? First, it must be said that there are far more similarities than differences. A business is a business and a plan is a plan, so most of what one would expect to see in a business plan also will be in an e-business plan. Beyond adding an "e" to the title, what are some of the differences that make writing an e-business plan different from writing a business plan?

- The Internet is unlike any other sales channel (Walsh 2004). The Internet allows companies to distribute information at the speed of light and at almost zero cost, reach out to customers with both reach and range, introduce new and innovative business models, and reduce costs and generate savings. There are many, many more differences, as discussed elsewhere in this book. On the other hand, the Internet also creates more bargaining power for the customer, creates a more perfect information market to the customer's benefit, and makes it easier for competitors to invade a company's marketplace, as also discussed in this textbook. So the first, and biggest, difference in e-business planning is the need for the entrepreneur to recognize the different and unique capabilities of the Internet and to begin to think differently, and creatively, about the opportunities and problems the Internet presents.
- The Internet is global. Being on the Web means a business will be visible to an international audience. This introduces complexity for payment options (e.g., show prices in U.S. dollars or local currency?), distribution channels, Web site design, and the logistics of product returns.
- Web storefronts never close. Being on the Web means a store will be open 24/7. The e-business plan must account for this difference in Web hosting and customer service requirements.
- E-commerce is conducted at Internet speed. This means Web site deployment must be planned in months, or even weeks, not years. First-mover advantage will be lost if companies are unable to move at Internet speed, and e-business plan readers know that.
- The Web allows greater opportunities for personalization of content, one-to-one marketing, and customer self-service. A company must incorporate these into its e-commerce strategy, because its competitors certainly will.
- The Internet intensifies customer relationship management. Business has always been about "getting close to the customer," but that was in a world without the potential of personalization, one-on-one marketing, data mining, concurrent reach and range, and customer relationship management. The Internet, and the customer-oriented applications that the Internet makes possible, means that every e-business must be totally focused on the customer.

In all of these ways, and more, writing a business plan for an e-business is different, new, exciting, and difficult.

case include the launch or major revision of a Web site, implementation of an e-procurement project, or purchase of CRM software.

As a special case of a business plan, the content of a business case is similar to that of a business plan. One difference is that the business plan concentrates on the viability of a company, whereas a business case assesses both viability of the project and the fit of the initiative with the firm's mission and goals. A business case also will almost certainly have more operational detail and a justification that it is the best way for the organization to use its resources to accomplish the desired strategy. Other differences between a business plan and a business case are highlighted throughout Online Tutorial T1 (An E-Business Plan Tutorial) on the book's Web site.

With a firm foundation of organizational strategy and business planning in place, we now turn our attention to e-commerce strategy.

Section 14.2 ◗ REVIEW QUESTIONS

1. What is a business plan?
2. List three situations in which a business plan is recommended or required.
3. How is an e-business plan different from a traditional business plan?
4. What is a business case? How is it different from a business plan?

14.3 EC STRATEGY: CONCEPTS AND OVERVIEW

What is the role of the Internet in organizational strategy? According to Ward and Peppard (2002), strategy setting begins with the business strategy—determining an organization's vision, mission statement, and overall goals (see Exhibit 14.5). Then the information systems (IS) strategy is set, primarily by determining *what* information and associated information systems are required to carry out the business strategy. The information and communications technology (ICT) strategy is decided based on *how* to deliver the information and information systems via technology. The solid downward pointing arrows in Exhibit 14.5 depict this process.

The Internet impacts all levels of organizational strategy setting, as shown by the shaded boxes in Exhibit 14.5. Business strategists need to consider the Internet's role in creating or innovating products, in product and service delivery, in supplier and customer relationships, and its impact on competition in the marketplace. Generally, strategic planners need to view the Internet as a complement to traditional ways of competing, not as a source of competitive advantage in and of itself (Porter 2001). Information systems strategists need to consider the Internet as a tool for collecting information and distributing to where it is required. ICT planners will need to plan the integration of the Internet-based technologies into the existing ICT infrastructure. Thinking about and planning for the Internet should be subsumed into each of the three strategy levels (McKay and Marshall 2004).

EXHIBIT 14.5 The Role of the Internet in Strategy

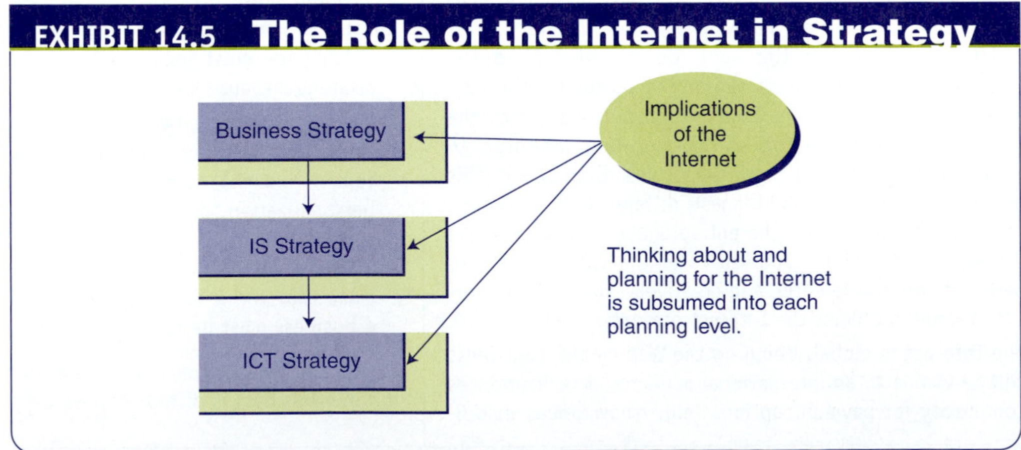

Source: *Strategic Planning for Information Systems* (2002). Ward, J. and Peppard J., p. 41 fig. 1. Copyright 2006. Copyright John Wiley & Sons Ltd. Reproduced with permission.

Many businesses are taking a broad, multilevel look at the impact of the Internet and EC on their future. Companies are being urged to seek competitive differentiation in the marketplace through value-added activities such as Internet-based search, evaluation, problem-solving, and transaction processes (Lumpkin and Dess 2004). Brick-and-mortar firms are looking for "e-commercializing" business operations (Shi and Wright 2003). In these ways and more, businesses continue to evolve their own e-commerce strategies, defined earlier as the formulation and execution of a vision of how a new or existing company intends to do business electronically. The process of building an e-strategy is explained in detail in the following sections.

Section 14.3 ▶ REVIEW QUESTIONS

1. Describe the role of the Internet in setting organizational strategy.
2. How should the Internet and EC be considered by business strategic planners? By IS strategists? By ICT planners?

14.4 E-STRATEGY INITIATION

In the *strategy initiation* phase, the organization prepares information about itself, its competitors, and its environment. Information that describes the contribution that EC can make to the business is of special importance here. The steps in strategy initiation are to review the organization's vision and mission; to analyze its industry, company, and competitive position; and to consider various initiation issues.

ISSUES IN E-STRATEGY INITIATION

With company, competitor, and trend data in hand, the company faces a number of questions about its approach to and operation of its EC strategy, as discussed next.

Be a First Mover or a Follower?

Is there a real advantage to being the first mover in an industry or market segment? In e-commerce, does "the early bird get the worm"? Or does the old saying about pioneers—"they are the ones with arrows in their backs"—apply to EC? The answers to these questions are far from clear.

The business, IT, and e-commerce worlds all have examples of companies that succeeded with first-mover advantage, companies that failed despite first-mover advantage, and late movers that are now success stories. Generally, the advantages of being first include an opportunity to make a first and lasting impression on customers, to establish strong brand recognition, to lock in strategic partners, and to create switching costs for customers. The risks of being a first-mover include the high cost of developing EC initiatives, making mistakes followers into the market can avoid, the chance that a second wave of competitors will eliminate a first-mover's lead through innovation, and the risk that the move will be too early, before the market is ready (e.g., home banking systems in the early 1990s). Although the importance of a speedy market entry cannot be dismissed, some research suggests that over the long run first movers are substantially less profitable than followers (Boulding and Christen 2001) and that switching costs and network effects are not as substantial as claimed (Porter 2001).

So what determines whether a first mover succeeds or fails? In their examination of "the first-mover advantage misconception," Rangan and Adner (2001) suggest that the following factors are important determinants of EC marketplace success: (1) the size of the opportunity (i.e., the first-mover company must be big enough for the opportunity and the opportunity must be big enough for just one company); (2) the nature of the product (i.e., first-mover advantage is easier to maintain in commodity products in which later entrants have a hard time differentiating their product); and (3) whether the company can be the best in the market. This last point is emphasized in Insights and Additions 14.2. Time and time again, first-mover advantage has been lost because the company failed to capitalize on its first-mover position or, more precisely, a late mover offered a better and more innovative product or service. Usually it is *best*-mover advantage, not first-mover advantage, that will determine the market leader.

Insights and Additions 14.2 First-Mover and Best-Mover Success Stories

Companies that "got there first" and leveraged their first-mover advantage for success	
eBay	eBay was a first mover into the online auction market. Listening to customers and constantly adding new features and services has kept eBay on top.
Blogger	Blogger.com was the first Web site to provide Weblog (blog) hosting services to blog authors; it is still the dominant provider.
Yahoo!	The world's first Internet directory remains the world's most popular Internet directory. Innovations such as MyYahoo! (*my.yahoo.com*), Yahoo! Groups (*groups.yahoo.com*), and Web-page hosting (*geocities.yahoo.com*) have helped Yahoo! morph into a profitable Internet portal.
Apple Computer	Being first with a Windows desktop, mouse, hard floppy disk, floppyless laptops, and wireless technology has given Apple a frontier-pushing reputation that keeps it in the personal computer operating system market, while others (e.g., IBM's OS/2) have floundered in the face of the Microsoft Windows juggernaut.
Companies that had first-mover advantage, but lost the marketplace battle to late movers	
Citibank	The company that invented automatic teller machines has lost the ATM protocol race to Cirrus.
Sony	Being first and having the technically superior Betamax videotape format did not prevent Sony from being beaten by Matsushiata's VHS format.
Chemdex	The original B2B digital exchange closed down when revenue growth slowed and the owners decided to change to a different business model.
Netscape	The world's first Internet browser company saw its dominance of the browser market diminish as Microsoft bundled Internet Explorer into the Windows operating system.
Companies that were late movers, but gained success over first movers by being best movers	
Intel	Intel did not invent the microchip, but its alliance with Microsoft ("Wintel") and its world-best research and development efforts have made Intel the world's leading microchip manufacturer.
America Online	Innovative marketing (e.g., mass distribution of free installation disks) and provision of online information people could use moved AOL to the top of the ISP market, while first movers (e.g., CompuServe, Prodigy) failed.
Google	While other search engines battled for supremacy in the "keyword ranking" battleground, Google invented "link popularity" and soared to the top of the search engine market.

Born-on-the-Net or Move-to-the-Net?

Another key distinction in EC strategy at the initiation phase is whether the company is a *born-on-the-Net* or a *move-to-the-Net* business (also called *brick-and-click* or *click-and-mortar*). Born-on-the-Net and move-to-the-Net firms both start with substantial assets and liabilities that influence their ability to formulate and execute an e-commerce strategy (see Exhibit 14.6). However, the difference between success and failure is rarely the assets and liabilities on the company's strategy balance sheet, but in the company's ability to utilize its strengths effectively. For example, the customer, product, and market knowledge in the move-to-the-Net firm is worthless unless processes and systems are in place to acquire, store, and distribute this knowledge to where it is needed, and innovative management direction is required to recognize its use for competitive advantage in the marketplace. Similarly, whereas the lack of a logistics channel and value chain partnerships is a born-on-the-Net liability, it is easier to build a brand-new, Web-based value chain than to change an established one with flawed practices and processes.

Lonely Planet is a move-to-the-Net firm that is using its strengths—a superb reputation, a community of independent travelers, an immense database of maps and travel information—to find new opportunities on the Internet (see Online File W14.1 on the book's Web site). Sears,

EXHIBIT 14.6 An EC Strategy Balance Sheet for Born-on-the-Net and Move-to-the-Net Firms

Assets of the Born-on-the-Net Firm	Liabilities of the Born-on-the-Net Firm
• Executive management tends to be young and entrepreneurial and is willing to take risks and make commitments for the long-term. • The organizational structure is flat and flexible, with wide spans of control, so the organization can respond rapidly to change. • Information systems are new, allowing rapid implementation of fast, Web-based services that customers demand. • The company as a whole is agile, flexible, hungry for success, and looking to topple the market leader from its perch.	• Executive management tends to be focused on the short-term, looking after satisfactory next quarter results rather than the long-term viability of the company. • Product knowledge, logistics channels, and value chain partnerships must be built from scratch. • The lack of a brand, reputation, and physical presence raises issues of quality uncertainty among customers. Assets such as brand and reputation must be built, at considerable cost. • The born-on-the-Net business must be built from scratch, using limited venture capital funds or bank loans. If results, and revenues, do not appear fast, the company will go under.
Assets of the Move-to-the-Net Firm	**Liabilities of the Move-to-the-Net Firm**
• A customer base and decades of knowledge about customers and their requirements is available. This knowledge base can be mined to anticipate customer needs and demands. • Years of experience in the product marketplace are available to the company, which knows what its customers buy, how they buy, and why they buy. • An established brand, a marketplace reputation, and a physical presence gives customers reassurance in terms of trust, long-term viability, and convenience (e.g., for returns). • The initiation of an EC application or project can be funded from existing or redirected resources. A long-term commitment to funding an EC application is possible.	• The customer base on day one is zero, and each new customer must be acquired from an existing firm within a competitive marketplace. • The organizational infrastructure is old and lethargic, with layers of management that make responding to change difficult. • Legacy information systems make implementation of strategic EC applications difficult. • The company as a whole is rigid, satisfied with the established way of doing things, and, if it is an industry leader, complacent in its market prominence.

Source: Adapted from Plant (2000), pp. 13, 38, 78–79.

Roebuck and Company also is attempting to leverage its physical presence and iconic brand name into a powerful move-to-the-Net strategy, as described in EC Application Case 14.2.

Determining Scope

Inevitably, most e-strategy efforts are intended to grow the business. This can be done in a variety of ways, primarily by expanding the firm's appeal to a new set of customers, by increasing the size or scale of the business, or by broadening the scope through a wider range of products and services. Expanding the customer base is discussed in market segmentation in Chapter 4, and economies of scale is discussed in Chapter 15. This section offers a few comments on the proper determination of scope.

When determining scope, the organization considers the number of products or services it sells. The most efficient way to expand an organization's scope is to introduce new products or services into new or existing markets without increasing production facilities or staff. This way revenues and profits grow while production costs increase only slightly. This strategy is usually most effective when the expanded scope is consistent with the firm's existing core competencies and value proposition to its customers. For example, almost all of Google's expanding scope is based on its core competency in search technology (see the opening case).

Expanding scope as an e-strategy usually is less effective when it requires large investment and when it threatens the existing value proposition. Sears discovered this when it expanded from a retail store into financial services and real estate. Neither strategy

CASE 14.2

EC Application

BRICK-AND-CLICK STRATEGY AT SEARS, ROEBUCK AND COMPANY

Sears, Roebuck and Company began in 1888 as a mail-order catalog business, the first of its kind in the United States. In its initial years, Sears faced many of the same challenges that contemporary born-on-the-Net businesses face, such as shoppers skeptical of a new way of shopping and the lack of a physical presence. In 1925, Sears opened its first retail store, and the company rapidly became an icon in the U.S. retail industry.

By the early 1990s, competition from discount stores such as K-Mart and Wal-Mart had severely eroded Sears' market share. Diversification into financial services and real estate did little for the bottom line, and the company was approaching bankruptcy. In response, Sears initiated a number of cost-cutting initiatives, some of which were, in hindsight, counterintuitive to the creation of an e-commerce presence. For example, in 1993 Sears closed its catalog operations, shedding the distribution, fulfillment, and direct-marketing capabilities that are fundamental building blocks of a successful e-tail business. In 1996, Sears sold its stake in Prodigy, one of the first online Internet services.

Also in 1996, Sears launched its online presence with an information-only Web site. By the following year, Sears had become convinced that there was potential in online shopping and piloted a program to sell Craftsman tools online. Following a classic move-to-the-Net strategy, Sears chose Craftsman tools because the product line had a widely recognized, high-quality brand name. Selling apparel and appliances, more dominant offerings in its retail product mix, was considered too problematic.

Despite initial success in hard goods and gift items, classic move-to-the-Net problems began to appear in Sears' strategy. Skeptics pointed out that catalog and home shopping had been popular at first, too, but then faltered. There also was considerable concern about cannibalization. Some executives saw the Internet as a threat that would draw customers away from the retail stores.

In 1999, CEO Arthur C. Martinez made an organizational commitment to Sears becoming a brick-and-click organization. A senior manager in charge of online ventures was appointed and an internal Web team was created. PartsDirect, with 4.2 million parts and accessories, was added to the Web site, followed by major appliances, in which Sears had a huge market share. Here Sears' physical retail experience worked to its advantage, because it had the logistics, delivery, installation, and repair capabilities already in place.

Sears launched a number of initiatives to advance its move-to-the-Net strategy. Strategic partnerships were made with Sun Microsystems to promote the Internet-connected home, with IBM to launch a Web site promoting home decorating, with home improvement guru Bob Vila to create a Web site for home improvement solutions, and with America Online for joint promotion activities. A new Web site was launched, and new features such as online delivery scheduling and online bill payment were added.

Sears began to see its Web site as a way to encourage customers to make in-store purchases. It introduced in-store pick-up of products sold online and installed in-store kiosks that enabled customers to do product research online. In the B2B area, Sears joined with others to launch an e-marketplace named GlobalNetXchange. Finally, to relieve concerns about cannibalization, Sears began offering a commission to its retail stores on all online sales, based on the zip code of the online order. In May 2002, Sears bought Lands' End, effectively reentering the mail-order catalog business via one of America's largest and most successful online apparel companies.

Despite Sears' best efforts, its move-to-the-Net strategy has not had a significantly positive impact on the bottom line. All of Sears' competitors have made the same moves to online retailing. The global e-marketplace, GlobalNetXchange, has produced mixed results. Finally, rapid technological growth has produced a somewhat fragmented set of information systems.

Sears' EC strategy continues to evolve as it faces questions such as: What is the best way to attract customers and sell a mixed product line over the Internet? How should B2B EC initiatives be extended or enhanced? How can Lands' End's capabilities be used for Sears' continuing evolution into an e-business?

Source: Ranganathan, C., et al. "E-Business Transformation at the Crossroads: Sears' Dilemma." *Journal of Information Technology*, June 2004, 19, no. 2, pp. 117+. Copyright © 2005 Palgrave Macmillan Ltd. Adapted with permission of Blackwell Publishing.

Questions

1. What decisions favored Sears' move-to-the-Net strategy? What decisions did not support the strategy?
2. How is Sears' EC strategy in line with its bricks-and-mortar history?
3. What solution did Sears implement to reduce employees' fear of cannibalization of the retail store channel?

was profitable, and Sears eventually withdrew from these markets (see EC Application Case 14.2). In summary, the critical question that businesses contemplating an EC strategy that involves expanding products and services should ask is: What else do our customers want to buy in addition to the products and services we currently offer (Jelassi and Enders 2005)?

Have a Separate Online Company?

Separating a company's online operations into a new company makes sense when: (1) the volume of anticipated e-business is large, (2) a new business model needs to be developed apart from the constraints of current operations, (3) the subsidiary can be created without dependence on current operations and legacy systems, and (4) the online company is given the freedom to form new alliances, attract new talent, and raise additional funding (Venkatraman 2000). Barnes & Noble, Nordstrom Shoes, Halifax in the United Kingdom, and the ASB Bank in New Zealand (see Online File W14.2) are a few examples of companies that have established separate companies or subsidiaries for online operations.

The advantages of creating a separate company include reduction or elimination of internal conflicts; more freedom for the online company's management in pricing, advertising, and other decisions; the ability to create a new brand quickly (see next section); the opportunity to build new, efficient information systems that are not burdened by the legacy systems of the old company; and an influx of outside funding if the market likes the e-business idea and buys the company's stock. The disadvantages of creating an independent division are that it may be very costly and/or risky; expertise vital to the existing company may be lost to the new firm; and the new company will not benefit from the expertise and spare capacity in the business functions (marketing, finance, distribution) unless it gets superb collaboration from the parent company.

Creating a separate company versus in-house development are not the only two approaches that are available to a brick-and-mortar firm looking to enhance its EC future. These are two options at the ends of a continuum that also includes strategic partnerships (e.g., Rite Aid bought an equity stake in Drugstore.com) and joint ventures (e.g., KB Toys joined forces with BrainPlay.com to create Kbkids.com). These options, and other permutations along the integration continuum, enable an aspiring click-and-mortar company to strike an effective balance between the freedom and flexibility that come with separation and the marketing leverage and access to organizational knowledge that is inherent with in-house development (Gulati and Garino 2000).

Have a Separate Online Brand?

A company faces a similar decision when deciding whether to create a separate brand for its online offerings. Generally, companies with strong, mature, international brands will want to retain and promote those brands online. As noted in the opening case, Google has chosen extensions or variations of its strong brand name—Google Desktop, Google Print, GMail, Froogle—in introducing new products and services.

However, existing firms with a weak brand or a brand that does not reflect the intent of the online effort may decide to create a new brand. For example, Axon Computertime (axon.co.nz) had a high-value, low-cost reputation in the highly competitive computer sales, configuration, and service market. An analysis from an e-commerce strategic planning effort identified an opportunity to deliver an integrated e-commerce solution in the marketplace (see also EC Application Case 14.3, p. 605). To capitalize on this opportunity and retain its reputation, the company created a new division and launched a new brand, Quality Direct, to distinguish this effort within the parent company.

Section 14.4 ▶ REVIEW QUESTIONS

1. Describe the advantages, risks, and success factors that first movers face.
2. What are the advantages and disadvantages of creating a separate online company?
3. Why would an existing company want to create a new brand for its e-commerce initiative?

14.5 E-STRATEGY FORMULATION

Based on the results of the company and competitive analyses, the company is ready to evaluate potential EC strategies and select a small number for implementation. *Strategy formulation* activities include evaluating specific EC opportunities and conducting cost-benefit and risk analyses associated with those opportunities. Specific outcomes include a list of approved EC projects or applications, risk management plans, pricing strategies, and a business plan that will be used in the next phase of strategy implementation.

SELECTING EC OPPORTUNITIES

The outcome of the strategy initiation phase should have been a number of potential EC initiatives that exploit opportunities and manage threats in the business environment in light of corporate strengths and weaknesses. In the strategy formulation phase, the firm must decide which initiatives to implement and in what order.

As with many other business decisions, there are correct approaches to EC strategy selection and incorrect ones. According to Tjan (2001), incorrect approaches include indiscriminately funding many projects and hoping for a few winners (this wastes scare resources); betting it all in a single, high-stakes initiative; and "trend-surfing," which means following the crowd to the newest and most fashionable idea.

More productive strategy selection approaches can be used when compelling internal or external forces drive the strategy selection process. A *problem-driven strategy* may be best when an organization has a specific problem that can be solved with an EC application. For example, disposing of excess equipment was the motivation behind the implementation of forward e-auctions at General Motors. A *technology-driven strategy* can occur when a company owns technology that it needs to be put to use, as IBM has done with much of its proprietary technology. A *market-driven strategy* can occur when a company waits to see what competitors in the industry do. As noted earlier, this late-mover strategy can be effective if the company can use its brand, technology, superior customer service, or innovative products and strategies to overcome any lost first-mover advantage.

Consulting company PricewaterhouseCoopers (PWC) has developed, with Carnegie Mellon University, an *e-business maturity model* (known by the acronym emm@). The model evaluates online initiatives within the context of established business criteria. Described as both a diagnostic and a prescriptive tool for assessing a company's e-business capability, the model is designed to help companies think of what's necessary to implement an e-business.

Most times, however, businesses are best served by a systematic methodology to determine an appropriate EC application profile that determines which initiatives to pursue and when. Such an approach is described in the next section.

DETERMINING AN APPROPRIATE EC APPLICATION PORTFOLIO

For years, companies have tried to find the most appropriate portfolio (group) of projects among which an organization should share its limited resources. The classic portfolio strategy attempts to balance investments with different characteristics. For example, the company would combine long-term speculative investments in new, potentially high-growth businesses with short-term investments in existing, profit-making businesses.

One well-known framework of this strategy is Boston Consulting Group's *growth-share matrix* with its "star," "cash cow," "wild card," and "dog" opportunities (Stern and Stalk 1998).

An Internet Portfolio Map for Selecting Applications

Tjan (2001) adapted the Boston Consulting Group's approach to create what he calls an "Internet portfolio map." Instead of trading off market potential and market share, the Internet portfolio map is based on *company fit* and *project viability*, both of which can be either low or high. *Viability* can be assessed by various criteria such as market value potential, time to positive cash flow, time to implementation, and funding requirements. Similarly, *fit* can be evaluated by metrics such as alignment with core capabilities, alignment with other company initiatives, fit with organizational structure, and ease of technical implementation. Together, these create an *Internet portfolio map* (see Exhibit 14.7).

EXHIBIT 14.7 Internet Portfolio Map

Viability of Project	Company Fit (low)	Company Fit (high)
High	Sell project	Adopt project
Low	Reject project	Redesign project

Source: Reprinted by permission of *Harvard Business Review*. From "Finally, a Way to Put Your Internet Portfolio in Order," by A. K. Tjan, *Harvard Business Review*, 2001.

Each company will want to determine for itself the criteria used to assess viability and fit. Each proposed EC initiative (e.g., a B2B procurement site, a B2C store, an enterprise portal) is evaluated by senior managers and outside experts on each of these criteria, typically on a quantitative (e.g., 1 to 100) or qualitative (e.g., high, medium, low) scale. If some criteria are more important than others, these can be weighted appropriately. The scores are combined, and average fit and viability scores are calculated for each initiative. Initiatives in which there is high agreement on rankings can be considered with more confidence.

The various initiatives are then mapped onto the Internet portfolio map. If both viability and fit are low, the project is *rejected*. If both are high, the project is *adopted*. If fit is high but viability is low, the project is *redesigned*. Finally, if the fit is low but the viability is high, the project is *sold*. (An example of this process is shown in Online File W14.3 on the book's Web site.) Senior management must also consider factors such as cost-benefit (discussed in Chapter 15) and risk (discussed below) in making the final decision about what initiatives get funded and in what order. However, the Internet portfolio map can be an invaluable guide for navigating an e-commerce strategy through uncharted waters.

RISK ANALYSIS AND MANAGEMENT

Risk is inherent in all business activities, and especially when organizations are moving into new territory, as an e-commerce strategy inevitably implies. Managing that risk is a process of analyzing the risk factors and then taking the steps necessary to reduce the threat to the business from that risk. Adapting a definition of IT risk from Markus (2000), **e-commerce (EC) risk** is the likelihood that a negative outcome will occur in the course of developing and operating an e-commerce strategy.

e-commerce (EC) risk
The likelihood that a negative outcome will occur in the course of developing and operating an electronic commerce strategy.

Mention e-commerce risk and most business professionals think of information security—the threat posed by hackers and negligent loss of data. This is the most obvious, but not the most threatening, aspect of EC risk. *The most dangerous risk to a company engaged in e-commerce is business risk*—the possibility that developing and operating an e-commerce strategy could negatively impact the well-being of the organization itself. Chapter 12 focuses on information security; the emphasis here is on business risk.

The first step in any risk assessment is risk analysis—identifying and evaluating the sources of risk. Deise et al. (2000), for example, list 15 sources of e-business risk: dependence on partners, competitive environment, operations, human resources, legal and regulatory, reputation, strategic direction, technology, security, culture, project management, governance, business process controls, tax, and currency. Similarly, Viehland (2001) identifies four sources of business risk: *competitive risk* (i.e., Can a strategy intended to introduce competitive advantage have negative, unanticipated consequences?); *transition risk* (i.e., What are the consequences for current customers, distribution channels, and business processes if an organization adopts e-commerce as a new growth strategy?); *customer-induced risk* (i.e., How can an organization manage customer relations in an online world that is different from the traditional marketplace?); and *business partner risk* (i.e., How can increasing dependence on business partnerships be managed?).

Once sources of risk have been identified, the next step is *risk management*—to put in place a plan that reduces the threat posed by the risk. Risk management involves taking steps to reduce the probability that the threat will occur, minimizing the consequences if it occurs anyway, or both. Many risk management strategies in the off-line world of business apply to e-commerce risk management. For example, commonly used control systems can mitigate risk factors in e-commerce sourcing (Saeed and Leitch 2003). In other risk areas, new and innovative risk management strategies are necessary. For example, putting trust-generating policies and procedures in place can minimize customer-induced risk.

Various methods can be used to conduct risk assessment (e.g., see Wheelen and Hunger 2003; Vose 2000). A number of sources offer specific advice about analyzing and managing e-commerce risk (e.g., Deise et al. 2000; Hiles 2001; Suh and Han 2003; Viehland 2001).

ISSUES IN STRATEGY FORMULATION

A variety of issues exist in strategy formulation, depending on the company, industry, nature of the applications, and so forth. Some representative issues are discussed in this section.

How to Handle Channel Conflict

As discussed in Chapters 2 and 3, channel conflict may arise when an existing company creates an additional distribution channel online. Several options exist for handling channel conflict. These include the following:

- Let the established distributors handle e-business fulfillment, as the auto industry is doing. Ordering can be done online or directions to distributors can be provided online.
- Provide online services to intermediaries (e.g., by building portals for them) and encourage them to reintermediate themselves in other ways.
- Sell some products only online, such as Lego (lego.com) is doing. Other products may be advertised online but sold exclusively off-line.
- Avoid channel conflict entirely by not selling online. Of course, in such a case, a company could still have an EC presence by offering promotion and customer service online, as BMW (bmw.com) is doing.

How to Handle Conflict Between the Off-Line and Online Businesses

In a click-and-mortar business, the allocation of resources between off-line and online activities can create difficulties. Especially in sell-side projects, the two activities can come to be viewed as competitors. In this case, personnel in charge of off-line and online activities may behave as competitors. This conflict may cause problems when the off-line side needs to handle the logistics of the online side or when prices need to be determined. As noted in EC Application Case 14.2, Sears lessened this conflict by offering a sales commission to its retail stores on all online sales, based on the zip code of the online order.

Corporate culture, the ability of top management to introduce change properly, and the use of innovative processes that support collaboration will all determine the degree of collaboration between off-line and online activities in a business. Clear support by top management for both the off-line and online operations and a clear strategy of "what and how" each unit will operate are essential.

Pricing Strategy

Traditional methods for determining price are the cost-plus and competitor models. *Cost-plus* means adding up all the costs involved—material, labor, rent, overhead, and so forth—and adding a percentage mark-up as profit. The *competitor model* determines price based on what competitors are charging for similar products in the marketplace.

Pricing products and services for online sales changes these pricing strategies in subtle ways:

- **Price comparison is easier.** In traditional markets, either the buyer or, more often, the seller has more information than the other party, and this situation is exploited in determining a product's price. By facilitating price comparison, the Internet helps create what economists call a *perfect market*—one in which both the buyer and the seller have ubiquitous and equal access to information, usually in the buyer's favor. On the Internet, search engines, price comparison sites (e.g., mysimon.com, comparenet.com), infomediaries, and intelligent agents make it easy for customers to find who offers the product at the best price.

- **Buyers sometimes set the price.** Name-your-own-price models such as Priceline.com and auction sites such as marketplace.onsale.com mean that buyers do not necessarily just take the price; sometimes they *make* the price.
- **Online and off-line goods are priced differently.** Pricing strategy may be especially difficult for a click-and-mortar company. Setting prices lower than those offered by the off-line business may lead to internal conflict, whereas setting prices at the same level will hurt competitiveness.
- **Differentiated pricing can be a pricing strategy.** For decades, airline companies have maximized revenues with yield management—charging different prices for the same product. In the B2C EC marketplace, one-on-one marketing can extend yield management from a class of customer (e.g., buying an airline seat early or later) to individual customers. In the B2B EC marketplace, extranets with customized pricing pages present different prices to different customers based on purchasing contracts, the customer's buying history, and other factors. **Versioning**, which is selling the same good but with different selection and delivery characteristics (Shapiro and Varian 1999), is especially effective in selling digitized goods. For example, time-critical information such as stock market prices can be sold at a higher price if delivered immediately. As with all forms of differentiated pricing, versioning information is based on the fact that some buyers are willing to pay more to receive some additional advantage.

versioning
Selling the same good, but with different selection and delivery characteristics.

The overall impact of these changes is good news for the consumer. Internet technologies tend to provide consumers with easier access to pricing information, which increases their bargaining power. To remain competitive and profitable, sellers will have to adopt smarter pricing strategies. Specifically, businesses will have to look at ways of using the Internet to optimize prices, primarily through greater precision in setting prices, more adaptability in changing prices, and new ways of customer segmentation for differentiated pricing (see Exhibit 14.8).

EXHIBIT 14.8 Three Strategies for Smarter Pricing on the Internet

Pricing Strategy	Source of Value from the Internet	B2C Examples	B2B Examples
Precision: Determine the highest price that has little or no impact on purchase decisions (i.e., price at the top of the zone of price indifference).	Prices can be tested continually in real time, leading to better understanding of the zone of price indifference.	Commodity products, such as toys, books, and CDs.	Maintenance, repair, and operation (MRO) products.
Adaptability: Change prices frequently in response to market conditions, inventory levels, or competitor pricing.	Prices can be changed fast and frequently and in response to Internet-monitored conditions.	Consumer goods with short product life cycles (e.g., electronics); goods with fluctuating demand (e.g., luxury cars).	Perishable goods (e.g., chemicals) or goods with fluctuating demand and availability (e.g., raw materials).
Segmentation: Divide customers into different classes and offer different prices based on customer segments.	Easily identify which segment a buyer belongs to and create barriers between segments.	Products in which customer profitability varies widely (e.g., credit cards, mortgages) or goods purchased in response to special offers (e.g., automobiles).	"Fill-in" customers (purchasing in emergency) will pay more than regular customers (e.g., industrial components, business services).

Source: Reprinted by permission of *Harvard Business Review*. From "Price Smarter on the Net" by Baker et al., *Harvard Business Review*, 2001.

Dewan et al. (2000) and Prasad and Harker (2000) have developed quantitative economic models for making pricing decisions. Watson et al. (2000) discuss pricing-setting strategy in conjunction with marketing strategy.

Section 14.5 ▶ REVIEW QUESTIONS

1. Describe how a company should *not* select EC applications.
2. Explain Tjan's Internet portfolio map.
3. List four sources of business risk in EC. What questions exemplify each source of risk?
4. Discuss three strategies for smarter pricing online.

14.6 E-STRATEGY IMPLEMENTATION

The execution of the strategic plan takes place in the *strategy implementation* phase, in which detailed, short-term plans are developed for carrying out the projects agreed on in strategy formulation. Decision makers evaluate options, establish specific milestones, allocate resources, and manage the projects.

Typically, the first step in strategy implementation is to establish a Web team, which then initiates the execution of the plan. As EC implementation continues, the team is likely to introduce changes in the organization. During the implementation phase, it also becomes necessary to develop an effective change management program, including the possibility of business process reengineering.

In this section, we deal with some of the topics related to this implementation process. Chapter 16 continues the implementation discussion with an overview of many of the practical considerations involved in launching an online business.

Create a Web Team

In creating a Web (project) team, the organization should carefully define the roles and responsibilities of the team leader, team members, Web master, and technical staff. The purpose of the Web team is to align business goals and technology goals to implement a sound EC plan with available resources. A Web team needs individuals who are knowledgeable about the technology that is required, as well as employees who are familiar with business information and data and how they should be structured and delivered.

Every Web project, and every Web team, also requires a project champion. In his study of EC strategy in 43 companies, Plant (2000) found, "In every successful e-commerce project studied for this book, a strong project champion was present in the form of a senior executive or someone in a position to demonstrate to a senior executive the potential added value such a project could bring to the organization" (pp. 34–35). Similarly, "top management championship" was identified as a critical factor for organizational assimilation of Web technologies (Chatterjee et al. 2002). The **project champion** is the person who ensures that the project gets the time, attention, and resources required and defends the project from detractors at all times. The project champion may be the Web team leader or a senior executive.

project champion
The person who ensures the EC project gets the time, attention, and resources required and defends the project from detractors at all times.

Start with a Pilot Project

Implementing EC often requires significant investments in infrastructure. Therefore, a good way to start is to undertake one or a few small EC pilot projects. Pilot projects help uncover problems early, when the plan can easily be modified before significant investments are made.

General Motors' pilot program (GM BuyPower) is an example of the successful use of a pilot project. On its Web site, gmbuypower.com, shoppers can choose car options, check local dealer inventory, schedule test drives, and get best-price quotes by e-mail or telephone. GM BuyPower started as a pilot project in four western U.S. states before expanding to all states. Similarly, when Home Depot decided to go online in 2000, it started in six stores in Las Vegas, then moved to four other cities in the western United States, and eventually went nationwide.

Allocate Resources

The resources required for EC projects depend on the information requirements and the capabilities of each project. Some resources—software, computers, warehouse capacity, staff—will be new and unique to the project or application. Even more critical for the project's success is effective allocation of infrastructure resources that are shared by many applications, such as databases, the intranet, and possibly an extranet.

Manage the Project

A variety of tools can assist in resource allocation. Project management tools such as Microsoft Project assist with determining project tasks, milestones, and resource requirements. Standard system design tools (e.g., data flow diagrams) can help in executing the resource-requirement plan.

STRATEGY IMPLEMENTATION ISSUES

There are many strategy implementation issues, depending on the circumstances. Here we describe some common ones.

Application Development

Implementation of an EC application requires access to the Web, construction of the Web site, and integration of the site with the existing corporate information systems (e.g., front end for order taking, back end for order processing). At this point, the company is faced with a number of decisions of whether to build, buy, or outsource various construction aspects of the application implementation process. Some of these decisions include the following:

- Should site development be done internally, externally, or by a combination of internal and external development?
- Should the software application be built or will commercially available software be satisfactory?
- If a commercial package will suit, should it be purchased from the vendor or rented from an ASP?
- Will the company or an external ISP host the Web site?
- If hosted externally, who will be responsible for monitoring and maintaining the information and system?

Each option has its strengths and weaknesses, and the correct decisions will depend on factors such as the strategic nature of the application, the skills of the company's technology group, and the need to move fast or not. Many of these options—build or buy, in-house or outsource, host externally or internally—are discussed in more detail in Chapter 16 and especially in Online Chapter 18.

Partners' Strategy

Another important issue is that many EC applications involve business partners—ASPs, ERP vendors and consultants, and ISPs—with different organizational cultures and their own EC strategies and profit motives. A key criterion in choosing an EC partner is finding one whose strategy aligns with or complements the company's own.

When negotiating a partnership, one must recognize that the partner's goal is to make a profit, and it is the negotiator's responsibility to make sure that is not being done at the expense of the company's bottom line. One popular EC partner strategy is **outsourcing**, which is the use of an external vendor to provide all or part of the products and services that could be provided internally. For example, many firms in the United States have found it advantageous to outsource call center functions offshore. Outsourcing critical functions such as customer support has served many firms well, but caution needs to be exercised. An outsourcer's promise to manage any critical function with world-class service at lower long-term, stable costs has great appeal to a CEO and CFO. However, one must question how an outsourcer can do this and still make a profit. If it sounds too good to be true, it probably is not true.

outsourcing
The use of an external vendor to provide all or part of the products and services that could be provided internally.

As discussed in Chapter 13 and Online Chapter 18, a new and Internet-savvy case of outsourcing is the *application service provider (ASP)*, an outsourcer that sells access to software applications. By distributing the cost to purchase, operate, and maintain expensive applications, such as an ERP system, the savings offered by an ASP can be very real. The bottom line here is that partnerships can be an effective way to develop and implement an EC strategy, but they require a realistic evaluation of the potential risks and rewards.

Business Alliances

At a higher level of cooperation and trust than a partnership is a business alliance. Specifically, the EC strategic planning process may identify a strategic opportunity that is larger than the organization itself. It may be a large-scale EC application, an initiative that is too difficult or complex for one company to undertake alone, an idea that works best across the industry rather than within a single firm, or a strategy that requires a variety of competencies to implement. In these cases, an alliance may be formed with other businesses, perhaps even competitors.

One type of business alliance is a B2B e-marketplace. As noted in EC Application Case 14.2, Sears was one of the founding members of GlobalNetXchange (GNX). The purpose of GNX was to reduce procurement costs and product prices for its members while making the purchase process more efficient. Eventually Sears, Carrefour (a European and Latin American retailer), Kroger (U.S.), Metro AG (Europe), Coles Myer (Australia), and others joined GNX (Ranganathan et al. 2003). Similarly, General Motors, Ford, and others in the automotive industry created a huge B2B e-marketplace called Covisint (see Chapter 6).

virtual corporation (VC)
An organization composed of several business partners sharing costs and resources for the production or utilization of a product or service.

Another form of business alliance is a **virtual corporation (VC)**, an organization composed of several business partners sharing costs and resources for the production or utilization of a product or service. A virtual corporation typically includes several companies, each creating a portion of the product or service in an area in which it has a core competency (e.g., product development, manufacturing, marketing) or special advantage (e.g., exclusive license, low cost). VCs may be *permanent* (designed to create or assemble a broad range of productive resources on an ongoing basis) or *temporary* (created for a specific purpose and existing for only a short time).

co-opetition
Two or more companies cooperate together on some activities for their mutual benefit, even while competing against each other in the marketplace.

A particularly interesting type of business alliance is co-opetition. **Co-opetition** is a combination of the words *cooperate* and *competition*. It describes when two or more companies cooperate together on some activities for mutual benefit, even while competing against each other in the marketplace. A global airline alliance such as OneWorld or Star Alliance is an example of co-opetition. Individually, the airlines compete against each other for passengers. However, when flights can be combined to save costs without compromising customer service, the airlines cooperate through the alliance. The most visible aspect of this is code-share flights in which passengers who bought tickets from a number of different airlines fly together on the same flight. Through co-opetition, the airlines are reducing inefficiencies in their competing supply chains, and the result is an excellent example of strategic supply chain alignment. Brandenburger and Nalebuff (1996) describe various aspects of co-opetition in the business market.

There are several other types of business alliances, such as resource-sharing partnerships, permanent supplier-company relationships, and joint research efforts. Ernest et al. (2001) examined the viability of e-alliances in light of the dot-com failures of 2000–2001. Their conclusion is that e-alliances are more essential now than ever because EC implementation requires a diversity of support services, which a single organization can seldom provide by itself. An e-alliance provides synergy when companies bring complementary contributions.

Working with partners may not be a simple task; partnerships can be risky and difficult to manage. Adobor and McMullen (2002) offer guidelines on how to make strategic alliances work; Xie and Johnston (2004) offer a typology of e-business alliances.

Redesigning Business Processes

An internal issue many firms face at the implementation stage is the need to change business processes to accommodate the changes an EC strategy brings. Sometimes these changes are incremental and can be managed as part of the project implementation process. Sometimes the changes are so dramatic that they affect the manner in which the organization operates. In this instance, business process reengineering is usually necessary.

Business process reengineering (BPR) is a methodology for conducting a comprehensive redesign of an enterprise's processes. BPR may be needed for the following reasons:

business process reengineering (BPR) A methodology for conducting a comprehensive redesign of an enterprise's processes.

- To fix poorly designed processes (e.g., processes are not flexible or scalable)
- To change processes so that they will fit commercially available software (e.g., ERP, e-procurement)
- To produce a fit between systems and processes of different companies that are partnering in e-commerce (e.g., e-marketplaces, ASPs)
- To align procedures and processes with e-services such as logistics, payments, or security

On its way to becoming an e-business, IBM instituted a comprehensive BPR initiative for several of the reasons cited above. The results were dramatic improvements in IBM's global operations, as described in Online File W14.4.

BPR may be very complex and expensive, especially when many business partners are involved. A major tool used in conjunction with redesign is workflow technology (see Chapter 7). For more on BRP for e-business, see El Sawy (2001) and Kim and Ramkaran (2004).

Section 14.6 ▸ REVIEW QUESTIONS

1. Describe a Web (project) team and its purpose.
2. What is the role of a project champion?
3. What is the purpose of a pilot project?
4. Discuss the major strategy implementation issues of application development, partners' strategy, business alliances, and BPR.

14.7 E-STRATEGY AND PROJECT ASSESSMENT

The last phase of e-strategy begins as soon as the implementation of the EC application or project is complete. *Strategy assessment* includes both the continual assessment of EC metrics and the periodic formal evaluation of progress toward the organization's strategic goals. Based on the results, corrective actions are taken and, if necessary, the strategy is reformulated.

THE OBJECTIVES OF ASSESSMENT

Strategic assessment has several objectives. The most important ones are:

- Measure the extent to which the EC strategy and ensuing projects are delivering what they were supposed to deliver. If they are not delivering, apply corrective actions to ensure that the projects are able to meet their objectives.
- Determine if the EC strategy and projects are still viable in the current environment.
- Reassess the initial strategy in order to learn from mistakes and improve future planning.
- Identify failing projects as soon as possible and determine why they failed to avoid the same problems on subsequent projects.

Web applications grow in unexpected ways, often expanding beyond their initial plan. For example, Genentec Inc., a biotechnology giant, wanted merely to replace a homegrown bulletin-board system. It started the project with a small budget, but soon found that the intranet had grown rapidly and had become very popular in a short span of time, encompassing many applications. Another example is Lockheed Martin, which initially planned to put its corporate phone directory and information about training programs on the intranet. Within a short time, many of its human resources documents were placed on the intranet as well, and, soon thereafter, the use of the Web for internal information expanded from administrative purposes to collaborative commerce and PRM applications.

MEASURING RESULTS AND USING METRICS

Each company measures success or failure by a different set of standards. Some companies may find that their goals were unrealistic, that their Web server was inadequate to handle demand, or that expected cost savings were not realized. Others may experience so much success that they have to respond to numerous application requests from various functional areas in the company.

Assessing EC is difficult because of the many configurations and impact variables involved and the sometimes intangible nature of what is being measured. However, a review of the requirements and design documents should help answer many of the questions raised during the assessment. It is important that the Web team develop a thorough checklist to address both the evaluation of project performance and the assessment of a changing environment. One way to measure a project's performance is to use metrics.

EC Metrics

metric
A specific, measurable standard against which actual performance is compared.

A **metric** is a specific, measurable standard against which actual performance is compared. Metrics assist managers in assessing progress toward goals, communicating the strategy to the workforce through performance targets (Rayport and Jaworski 2002), and identifying where corrective action is required. Exhibit 15.3 in Chapter 15 lists a number of tangible and intangible metrics for various EC users, and a number of financial metrics are suggested by Barua et al. (2001). An example of a company that has implemented a comprehensive EC metrics approach is Axon Computertime, as shown in EC Application Case 14.3.

Some of the metrics in EC Application Case 14.3 highlight the importance of including nonfinancial measures in the measurement of strategy performance. As discussed earlier, the *balanced scorecard* approach is a popular strategy assessment methodology that encourages measuring organizational performance in a number of areas. Taking a balanced scorecard approach, Plant (2000) suggests seven areas for assessment of an e-commerce strategy: financial impact, competitive leadership, brand, service, market, technology, and internal site metrics. Similarly, Zhu and Kraemer (2002) suggest four metric areas—information, transaction, interaction and customization, and supplier connection—that manufacturing firms should use for assessing performance of their e-commerce strategy. Finally, Rayport and Jaworski (2002, 2004) propose five categories of financial and nonfinancial metrics to assess strategy in a five-step process they call the *performance dashboard* (see Exhibit 14.9).

For an extensive discussion on metrics and management, see Straub et al. (2002a, 2002b).

Web Analytics

Web analytics
The analysis of click-stream data to understand visitor behavior on a Web site.

One large and growing area of EC strategy assessment is **Web analytics**, the analysis of click-stream data to understand visitor behavior on a Web site. Web analytics begins by identifying data that can assess the effectiveness of the site's goals and objectives (e.g., frequent visits to a site map may indicate site navigation problems). Next, analytics data are collected, such as where site visitors are coming from, what pages they look at and for how long while visiting the site, and how they interact with the site's information. The data can reveal the impact of search engine optimization or an advertising campaign, the effectiveness of Web site design and navigation, and, most important, visitor conversion. Because the goal of most EC Web sites is to sell product, the most valuable Web analytics are those related to step-by-step conversion of a visitor to a customer down the so-called purchase funnel (Burby 2004).

Information about Web analytics is available from Palmer (2002), Sterne (2002), Watchfire (2001), emetrics.org, and jimnovo.com. Two of many Web analytics tools include WebTrends (webtrends.com) and ClickTracks (clicktracks.com).

Section 14.7 ▶ REVIEW QUESTIONS

1. Describe the need for assessment.
2. Define metrics and their contribution to strategic planning.
3. Describe the performance dashboard approach to strategy assessment.
4. Define Web analytics.

14.8 GLOBAL E-COMMERCE

Global electronic activities have existed for more than 25 years, mainly EFT and EDI in support of B2B and other repetitive, standardized financial transactions. However, these activities required expensive and inflexible private telecommunications lines and, therefore, were

CASE 14.3

EC Application

MEASURING PROFIT ON THE WEB

Axon Computertime is an IT solutions company with locations in New Zealand's four largest cities. Axon's goal is "to be New Zealand's most recommended IT Services Company."

In 2002, as part of an examination of the success of its Quality Direct service, Axon issued a white paper that examined business profitability on the Web. Specifically the white paper listed four areas of potential profits from Web activities and metrics that were being used at Axon to assess the impact of the Web on business profit. This EC Application Case provides a real example of a small business that is profiting from its Web-based delivery of services and has collected some quantitative data to demonstrate its EC success.

Metrics were applied in four areas. Each of the four areas are described briefly below, followed by some of the metrics (a partial list) Axon used to assess goal achievement.

Cost Avoidance and Reduction

Web technologies can enhance profitability by reducing or eliminating transaction costs (e.g., product purchase) or interaction costs (e.g., a meeting, a phone call). Cost avoidance and reduction happens through activities such as improved access to information, customer self-help, and error reduction.

The following metrics demonstrated cost avoidance and reduction by Axon:

- Selling costs were reduced by 40 percent for each dollar of margin generated.
- Call volume to sales support increased at less than 50 percent of the traditional rate.
- Warehouse space was reduced by 40 percent, while volume increased by 40 percent.
- Obsolete stock write-offs as percentage of revenue were reduced by 93 percent.

Customer Service Enhancements

Delivering information to customers on all aspects of their transactions helps make the product or service more visible. Increased visibility generates increased value from a customer's perspective.

The following metrics demonstrated customer service enhancements by Axon:

- Average days to delivery were reduced by 20 percent over 2 years.
- Satisfaction with the delivery process is consistently greater than 80 percent.

New Market Opportunities

New market opportunities include new services to existing clients, changing the value proposition for existing clients, and targeting new markets.

The following metrics demonstrated new market opportunities by Axon:

- Product revenue increased over 40 percent in first 12 months of full operation.
- New customers were added at twice the rate that previously was being achieved.

New Media Options

"New media" includes improved communication, advertising, and marketing efforts through lower collateral costs, improved target marketing, subscriber lists, and sold advertising space.

The following metrics demonstrated the use of new media options by Axon:

- Cost per item for e-mail is less than 1 percent of the cost per item for postal mail.
- Response rate to e-mail is five times the response rate to postal mail.
- Expenditures on brochure design and production were reduced by 45 percent.

Sources: Green (2002) and *axon.co.nz* (accessed March 2005).

Questions

1. List four areas in which Axon is demonstrating increased profitability through the use of the Web.
2. Describe the characteristics of the metrics listed here (e.g., financial, customer service, quantitative, time based).
3. Based on Exhibit 15.3 in Chapter 15, what other metrics might apply?

limited mostly to large corporations. The emergence of the Internet and technologies such as extranets and XML have resulted in an inexpensive and flexible infrastructure that can greatly facilitate global trade.

A global electronic marketplace is an attractive thrust for an EC strategy. "Going global" means access to larger markets, mobility (e.g., to minimize taxes), and flexibility to employ workers anywhere. However, going global is a complex and strategic decision process due to a multiplicity of issues. Geographic distance is the most obvious dimension of conducting business globally, but frequently, it is not the most important dimension. Instead cultural, administrative, and economic dimensions of distance are equally likely to threaten a firm's

EXHIBIT 14.9 **Blueprint of the Performance Dashboard**

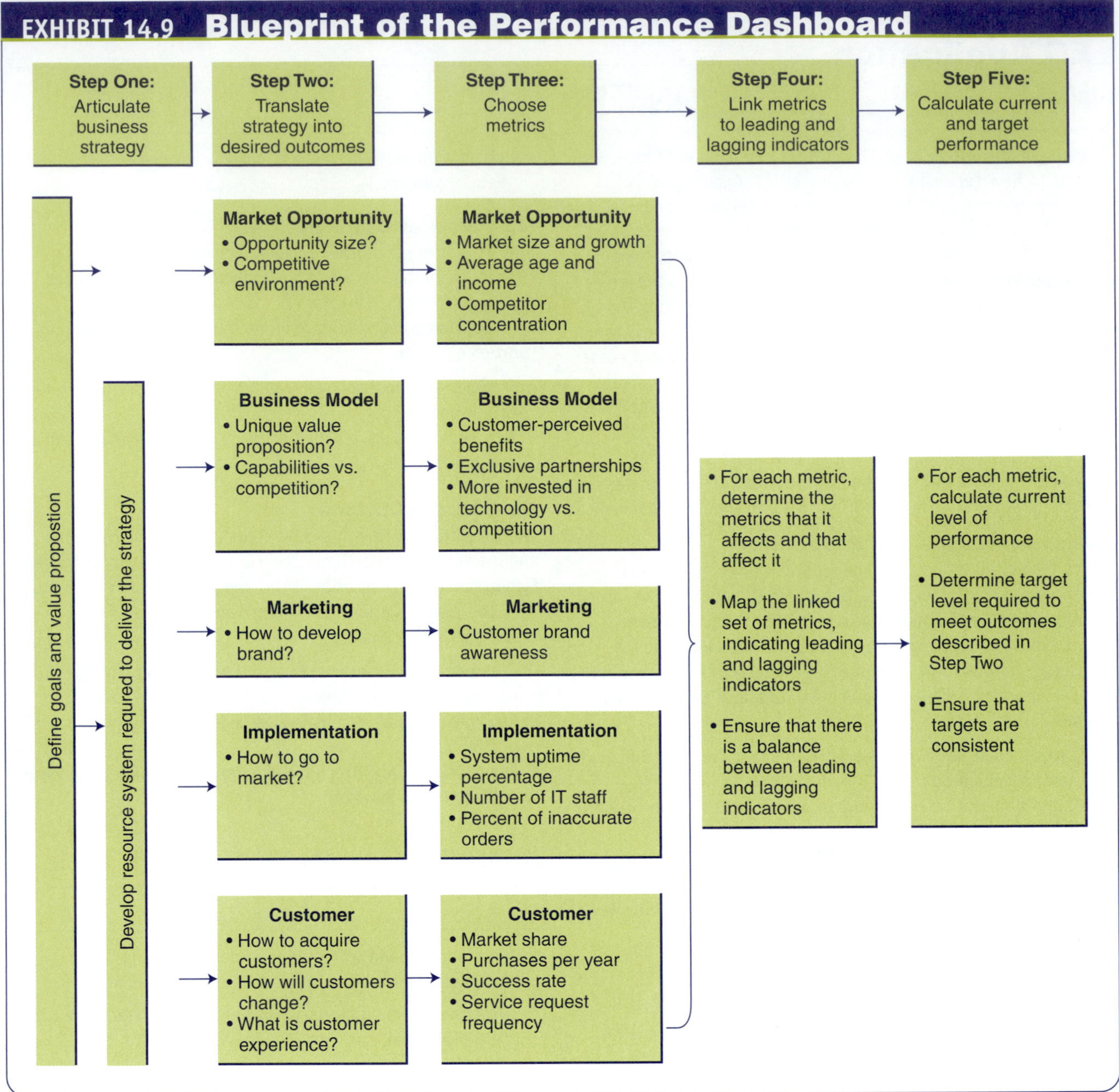

Source: Rayport, J., and B. J. Jaworski. *Introduction to E-Commerce,* 2d ed. Boston: McGraw-Hill, 2004. Copyright © McGraw-Hill Companies, Inc.

international ambitions (Ghemawat 2001). This section briefly examines the opportunities, problems, and solutions for companies using e-commerce to go global.

BENEFITS AND EXTENT OF OPERATIONS

The major advantage of EC is the ability to do business at any time, from anywhere, and at a reasonable cost. These are the drivers behind global EC, and there have been some incredible success stories in this area. For example:

- One can use E*TRADE or boom.com to buy and sell stocks in several countries.
- Exchanges such as e-Steel and ChemConnect have members in dozens of countries.
- Amazon.com sells books to individuals and organizations in over 190 countries.
- Small companies, such as ZD Wines (zdwines.com), sell to hundreds of customers worldwide. Hothothot (hothothot.com) reported its first international trade only after it went online; within 2 years global sales accounted for 25 percent of its total sales.

- Major corporations, such as GE and Boeing, have reported an increasing number of out-of-the-country vendors participating in their electronic RFQs. These electronic bids have resulted in a 10 to 15 percent cost reduction and an over 50 percent reduction in cycle time.
- Many international corporations considerably increased their success in recruiting employees for foreign locations when online recruiting was utilized.
- Several global trading exchanges have been created in the past few years.

BARRIERS TO GLOBAL EC

Despite the benefits and opportunities offered by globalization, there are many barriers to global EC. Some of these barriers face any EC venture but become more difficult when international impacts are considered. These barriers include authentication of buyers and sellers (Chapter 11), generating and retaining trust (Chapters 4 and 7), order fulfillment and delivery (Chapter 13), security (Chapter 11), and domain names (Chapter 16). Others are unique to global EC. We will use the CAGE (culture, administration, geography, economics) distance framework proposed by Ghemawat (2001) to identify areas in which natural or man-made barriers hinder global EC. Each of the four factors represents a different type of distance (difference) between two companies.

Cultural Issues

The Internet is a multifaceted marketplace made up of users from many cultures. The multicultural nature of global EC is important, because cultural attributes determine how people interact with companies, agencies, and each other based on social norms, local standards, religious beliefs, and language (Ghemawat 2001). Doing business globally requires *cultural marketing*, a strategy for meeting the needs of a culturally diverse population (DePalma 2000).

Cultural and related differences include language (e.g., English versus other languages), spelling differences (e.g., American versus British spelling), information formatting (e.g., dates can be mm/dd/yy or dd/mm/yy), graphics and icons (e.g., mailbox shapes differ from country to country), measurement standards (e.g., metric versus imperial system), the use of color (e.g., white is a funeral color in some countries), protection of intellectual property (e.g., Chinese tolerance of copyright infringement has Confucian roots), time standards (e.g., local time zones versus Greenwich Mean Time), and information requests (e.g., requiring a zip code in an order form can lead to abandoned shopping carts in countries without postal codes). Even the way individuals access the Web—at home, work, or an Internet cafe—varies from country to country, with implications for the use of graphics and personalization strategies.

Solutions for overcoming cultural barriers begin with an awareness of the cultural identities and differences in the target markets. Different sites may need to be created for different cultural groups, taking into account site design elements, pricing and payment infrastructures, currency conversion, customer support, and language translation. Language translation is one of the most obvious and most important aspects of maintaining global Web sites. The primary problems with language translation are speed and cost. It may take a human translator a week to translate a medium-sized Web site into another language. For large sites, the cost can be up to $500,000, depending on the complexity of the site and languages of translation. Some companies address these problems by translating their Web pages into different languages through so-called machine translators (a list of these translator programs is available in Online File W14.5 on the book's Web site). However, machine translation is considered only about 60 percent accurate, which is why many companies use native-language, in-country translators to review and revise the results from automatic translation software (Dubie 2003).

At a more subtle level is the need for business practices to be changed and reflected in both the Web site and the interactions with international customers. A study of EC cultural issues in China found that the socializing effects of commerce, transactional and institutional trust, and attitudes toward debt were major impediments to e-commerce in China (Efendioglu and Yip 2004). Overcoming barriers such as these are not dependent on a customized Web site, but on factors such as the need to partner with a respected local firm.

Administrative Issues

One of the most contentious areas of global EC is the resolution of international legal issues. A number of national governments and international organizations are working together to find ways to avoid uncoordinated actions and encourage uniform legal standards.

An ambitious effort to reduce differences in international law governing EC is the United Nations Commission on International Trade Law (UNCITRAL) Model Law on Electronic Commerce. Its purpose is to "offer national legislators a set of internationally acceptable rules which detail how a number of legal obstacles to the development of e-commerce may be removed, and how a more secure legal environment may be created" (*e-Business World* 2000). The Model Law has been adopted in some form in many countries and legal jurisdictions, including Singapore, Australia, Canada, Hong Kong, and some American states.

International trade organizations such as the World Trade Organization (WTO) and the Asia-Pacific Economic Cooperation (APEC) forum have working groups that are attempting to reduce EC trade barriers in areas such as pricing regulations, customs, import/export restrictions, tax issues, and product specification regulations.

Geographic Issues

The geographic issues of shipping goods and services across international borders are well known. Barriers posed by geography differ based on the transportation infrastructure between and within countries and the type of product or service being delivered. For example, geographic distance is almost irrelevant with online software sales.

Companies launching a worldwide EC strategy need to evaluate bandwidth requirements and availability in the main target countries. A country's market-access infrastructure is key to accommodating all users and all types of data. Monitoring and complying with technical standards will also minimize the possibility of incompatible technologies between the company and the international user.

Economic Issues

Economic and financial issues encompassing global EC include government tariffs, customs, and taxation. In areas subject to government regulation, tax and regulatory agencies have attempted to apply the rules used in traditional commerce to electronic commerce, with considerable success. Exceptions include areas such as international tariff duties and taxation. Software shipped in a box would be taxed for duties and tariffs when it arrives in the country. However, software downloaded online relies on self-reporting and voluntary payment of tax by the purchaser, something that does not happen very often.

The key financial barrier to global EC is electronic payment systems. To sell effectively online, EC firms must have flexible payment methods that match the ways different groups of people pay for their online purchases. Although credit cards are used widely in the United States, many European and Asian customers prefer to complete online transactions with off-line payments. Even within the category of off-line payments, companies must offer different options depending on the country. For example, French consumers prefer to pay with a check, Swiss consumers expect an invoice by mail, Germans commonly pay for products upon delivery, and Swedes are accustomed to paying online with debit cards.

Pricing is another economic issue. A vendor may want to price the same product at different prices in different countries in consideration of local prices and competition. However, if a company has one Web site, differential pricing will be difficult or impossible. Similarly, what currency will be used for pricing? What currency will be used for payment?

BREAKING DOWN THE BARRIERS TO GLOBAL EC

A number of international organizations (e.g., OECD 2001) and experts (e.g., Josephson 2001; Sheldon and Strader 2002) have offered suggestions on how to break down the barriers to global EC. Some of these suggestions include the following:

- **Be strategic.** Identify a starting point and lay out a globalization strategy. Remember that Web globalization is a business-building process. Consider what languages and countries it makes sense for the company to target and how the company will support the site for each target audience.

- **Know your audience.** Carefully consider the target audience. Be fully informed of the cultural preferences and legal issues that matter to customers in a particular part of the world.
- **Localize.** As much as practical and necessary, offer Web sites in national languages; offer different sites in different countries (e.g., "Yahoo! Japan" is at yahoo.co.jp); price products in local currencies; and base terms, conditions, and business practices on local laws and cultural practices. Chapter 4 includes a brief discussion of localization in advertising.
- **Think globally, act consistently.** An international company with country Web sites managed by local offices must make sure that areas such as brand management, pricing, corporate information, and content management are consistent with company strategy (DePalma 2001).
- **Value the human touch.** Trust the translation of the Web site content only to human translators, not automatic translation programs (Dubie 2003). Involve language and technical editors in the quality assurance process. One slight mistranslation or one out-of-place graphic may turn off customers forever.
- **Clarify, document, explain.** Pricing, privacy policies, shipping restrictions, contact information, and business practices should be well documented and located on the Web site and visible to the customer. To help protect against foreign litigation, identify where the company is located and the jurisdiction for all contract or sales disputes.
- **Offer services that reduce barriers.** It is not feasible to offer prices and payments in all currencies, so link to a currency exchange service (e.g., xe.com) for the customer's convenience. In B2B e-commerce, be prepared to integrate the EC transaction with the accounting/finance internal information system of the buyer.

We close our discussion of global e-commerce with a reference to the Real-World Case that concludes this chapter. Briefly, Pierre Lang Europe is a jewelry design and manufacturing company with a strong customer base in Western Europe. When Pierre Lang became interested in expanding into Eastern Europe, the firm realized it would have to change its information systems. Like other companies expanding internationally, it needed to be able to handle the multiple legal and language requirements of doing business in many different countries. The Real-World Case details the challenges Pierre Lang faced in "going global" and how it met those challenges.

Section 14.8 ▸ REVIEW QUESTIONS

1. Describe globalization in EC and the advantages it presents.
2. Describe the major barriers to global EC in each dimension of the CAGE framework.
3. What can companies do to overcome the barriers to global EC?

14.9 EC IN SMALL AND MEDIUM-SIZED ENTERPRISES

Some of the first companies to take advantage of Web-based electronic commerce were small and medium-sized enterprises (SMEs). While larger, established, tradition-bound companies hesitated, SMEs moved onto the Web because they realized there were opportunities in marketing, business expansion, business launches, cost cutting, and tighter partner alliances. Some examples are virtualvine.com, hothothot.com, and philaprintshop.com.

SMEs still consider the Internet to be a valuable business tool. According to a 2004 survey by Interland (eMarketer 2004), 28 percent of small businesses expect more than three-quarters of their annual sales to come from the Internet. And it isn't only online sales that are being used to measure success. Although one-third of respondents measure site success by sales, almost half (47 percent) measure site success based on measures such as customer comments about the site and the volume of site traffic.

However, many SMEs have found it difficult to formulate or implement an EC strategy, mainly because of low use of EC and IT by customers and suppliers, lack of knowledge or IT expertise in the SME, and limited awareness of the opportunities and risks (OECD 2001). A more complete list of major advantages and disadvantages of EC for SMEs is provided in Exhibit 14.10.

EXHIBIT 14.10 Advantages and Disadvantages of EC for Small and Medium-Sized Businesses

Advantages/Benefits	Disadvantages/Risks
• Inexpensive sources of information. A Scandinavian study found that over 90 percent of SMEs use the Internet for information search (OECD 2001). • Inexpensive ways of advertising and conducting market research. Banner exchanges, newsletters, chat rooms, and so on are nearly zero-cost ways to reach customers. • Competitor analysis is easier. The Scandinavian study found that Finnish firms rated competitor analysis third in their use of the Internet, after information search and marketing. • Inexpensive ways to build (or rent) a storefront. Creating and maintaining a Web site is relatively easy and cheap (see Chapter 16). • SMEs are less locked into legacy technologies and existing relationships with traditional retail channels. • Image and public recognition can be generated quickly. A Web presence makes it easier for a small business to compete against larger firms. • An opportunity to reach worldwide customers. No other medium is as efficient at global marketing, sales, and customer support. • Other advantages for SMEs include increased speed of customer payments, closer ties with business partners, reduced errors in information transfer, lower operating costs, and other benefits that apply to all businesses.	• Lack of financial resources to fully exploit the Web. A transactional Web site may entail relatively high up-front, fixed costs in terms of cash flow for an SME. • Lack of technical staff or insufficient expertise in legal issues, advertising, etc. These human resources may be unavailable or prohibitively expensive to an SME. • Less risk tolerance than a large company. If initial sales are low or the unexpected happens, the typical SME does not have a large reserve of resources to fall back on. • When the product is not suitable or difficult for online sales (e.g., experiential products such as clothes or beauty products; perishable products, such as certain foods) the Web opportunity is not as great. • Reduced personal contact with customers represents the dilution of what is normally a strong point for a small business. • Inability to afford entry to or purchase enough volume to take advantage of digital exchanges.

CRITICAL SUCCESS FACTORS FOR SMEs

EC success for small businesses is not a just matter of chance. Considerable research has been done to identify the critical success factors that help determine whether a small business will succeed in EC. Many of the small businesses that have succeeded on the Internet, either as click-and-mortar or virtual businesses, have the following strategies in common:

- **Product is critical.** The most effective product strategy for SMEs has been niche or specialty items. It is difficult to compete against online bookstores such as Amazon.com unless one specializes, as lindsaybks.com does in the technical book market. Other strategies are to sell a wide variety of low-volume products that regular stores do not stock (e.g., dogtoys.com), international products not readily available in neighborhood stores (e.g., russianfoods.com), goods that appeal to hobbyists or a community's special interests (e.g., diecastmodelcars.com), regional products (e.g., newyorkartworld.com), or local information (e.g., baliadventuretours.com).
- **Payment methods must be flexible.** Some customers prefer to mail or fax in a form or talk to a person rather than transmit a credit card number over the Internet.
- **Electronic payments must be secure.** Fortunately, ISPs and banks can easily provide this security.
- **Capital investment should be kept to a minimum.** Doing so enables the company to keep its overhead and risk low. For example, SMEs typically outsource Web hosting.
- **Inventory control is crucial.** Carrying too much stock ties up valuable capital. Too little stock on hand results in unfilled orders and disappointed customers. Contingency plans for scaling up inventory fast are recommended.

- **Logistics services must be quick and reliable.** Many small businesses have successfully subcontracted out their logistical services to shipping firms such as UPS, FedEx, or DHL.
- **Owner support.** The higher the owner's level of familiarity with the Internet, the more likely the firm will adopt the Internet and its applications (Karakaya and Khalil, 2004).
- **High visibility on the Internet.** The Web site should be submitted to directories such as Yahoo! and search engines such as Google, MSN Search, and Lycos and optimized for prominent search engine placement, as described in Chapter 16.
- **Join an online community.** The company may want to become a member of an online service or mall, such as AOL or ViaWeb's Viamall. Other partnership strategies that bring in customers include affiliate programs (see affiliatematch.com) and Web rings (see webring.com).
- **A Web site should provide all of the services needed by consumers.** In addition, the Web site should look professional enough to compete with larger competitors and be updated on a continual basis to maintain consumer interest. Chapter 16 covers this topic in more detail.

SUPPORTING SMEs

SMEs have a variety of support options. Almost every country in the world has a government agency devoted to helping SMEs become more aware of and able to participate in electronic commerce (e.g., sba.gov, business.gov.au).

Vendors realized the opportunity represented by thousands of business going online, and many have set up a variety of service centers that typically offer a combination of free information and fee-based support. Examples are IBM's Small Business Center (ibm.com/businesscenter) and Microsoft's bCentral (bcentral.com). Other small business support centers are sponsored by professional associations, Web resource services (e.g., smallbusiness.yahoo.com, workz.com), and small businesses that are in the business of helping other small businesses go online (e.g., bellzinc.ca).

Section 14.9 ▶ REVIEW QUESTIONS

1. What are the advantages/benefits of EC for small businesses?
2. What are the disadvantages/risks of EC for small businesses?
3. What are the CSFs for small businesses online?

MANAGERIAL ISSUES

Some managerial issues related to this chapter are as follows.

1. **What is the strategic value of EC to the organization?** Management needs to understand how EC can improve marketing and promotions, customer service, and sales. More significantly, the greatest potential of EC is realized when management views EC from a strategic perspective, not merely as a technological advancement.
2. **Who determines EC strategy?** Strategy is, of course, ultimately the responsibility of senior management. But participation in setting an e-commerce strategy is something that should happen at all levels and in all areas of the organization. It frequently is said that "soon all business will be e-business." If this is true, then planning this evolutionary process must include marketing, operations, information technology, and all other areas of the business.
3. **What are the benefits and risks of EC?** Strategic moves have to be carefully weighed against potential risks. Identifying CSFs for EC and doing a cost-benefit analysis should not be neglected. Benefits often are hard to quantify, especially because gains tend to be strategic. In such an analysis, risks should be addressed with contingency planning (deciding what to do if problems arise).
4. **Why do we need a plan?** A strategic plan is both a document and a process. Dwight D. Eisenhower, former U.S. army general and U.S. president, once said "Plans are nothing, planning is everything." A planning process that includes management, employees, business partners, and other stakeholders not only produces a planning document that will guide the business into the future, but also achieves buy-in among the

participants about where the company is going and how it intends to get there. The same can be said for business planning—the process is as important as the plan itself.

5. **What metrics should we use?** The use of metrics is very popular, but the problem is that one must compare "apples with apples." Companies first must choose appropriate metrics for the situation and then exercise caution in deriving conclusions whenever gaps between the metrics and actual performance are seen.
6. **What staffing is required?** Forming a Web team is critical for EC project success. The team's leadership, the balance between technical and business staff, getting the best staff representation on the team, and having a project champion are essential for success.
7. **How can we go global?** Going global is a very appealing proposition, but it may be difficult to do, especially on a large scale. In B2B, one may create collaborative projects with partners in other countries. Once such partners are discovered, exchanges and third-party marketplaces that promote global trade may lose business.
8. **Can we learn to love smallness?** Small can be beautiful to some; to others it may be ugly. Competing on commodity-type products with the big guys is very difficult, and even more so in cyberspace. Finding a niche market is advisable, but it will usually be limited in scope. More opportunity exists in providing specialized support services than in selling goods and services.
9. **Is e-business always beneficial?** According to Coltman et al. (2002), e-business may not fit some businesses. It may be too expensive to justify the benefits or it may result in internal conflicts. Many businesses simply do not need e-business. Therefore, a careful analysis of fitness must be conducted (see Wilson and Abel 2002).

RESEARCH TOPICS

Here are some suggested topics related to this chapter. For details, references, and additional topics, refer to the book's "Current EC Research" in the Online Appendix.

1. **Critical Success Factors for EC Within the EC Life Cycle**
   - The CSFs for EC from corporate, industry, and country perspectives
   - CSFs in the development of B2B EC strategy (see also Chapter 5)
   - CSFs in the development of e-tailing strategy (see also Chapter 3)
   - The relationship between CSFs and the balanced scorecard approach
   - Predict the future of EC with a Delphi study
2. **Strategies for E-Business Transformation**
   - Alignment of a corporation's business strategy with its e-business strategy
   - Framework of market mix models in EC
   - Challenges for EC strategies
   - Strategic readiness for EC by company, industry, and country
   - B2C and Web marketing strategies (see also Chapter 3)
   - Strategies for B2B EC (see also Chapter 5)
   - Strategies for transforming traditional businesses to e-businesses, including synergistic combination and substitution of strategies
   - Relationship of project champions to e-business project success
3. **Performance Assessment of EC Using the Balanced Scorecard**
   - Impact of EC on business performance
   - Performance measures for the planning and control of EC strategies
   - Association of balanced scorecard with the functional areas of e-business (e.g., marketing, CRM, procurement, SCM, and c-commerce)
   - How to design the balanced scorecard—top-down and bottom-up approaches
4. **The Dynamics of EC Technology Adoption**
   - Reconciliation of the cost-benefit model with the technology-acceptance model (TAM)
   - What makes people believe that EC can be adopted easily
   - Dynamic changes in EC adoption
   - Industry and case studies of the various circumstances of EC adoption
5. **Localization in Global EC**
   - Challenges of global EC: culture, laws, and languages
   - Comparative country study of international policies for global EC

- Transformation of international trade brokers in EC
- The role of brands in international EC
- Implementation of the letter of credit in the EC context
- Custom services for the international trade of digital products and services
- Procedures to handle sales tax for cross-border/interstate B2C and B2B transactions

6. **The Connectivity of SMEs in EC**
   - Readiness of SMEs for EC at industry and country levels
   - Role of buying corporations in the readiness of SMEs
   - Benefit to SMEs of accommodating the buying organization's standards
   - How to harmonize the heterogeneous protocols of multiple buying organizations
   - Survival strategy of SMEs in Internet marketing and e-tailing
   - Adoption of ASPs by SMEs to implement e-business—executive perception and organization learning
   - Reconciliation of MIS strategy with e-business strategy in SMEs

SUMMARY

In this chapter, you learned about the following EC issues as they relate to the learning objectives.

1. **The strategic planning process.** This process is composed of four major phases: initiation, formulation, implementation, and assessment. A variety of tools are available to carry out this process.
2. **Writing a business plan.** A business plan is an essential outcome of a strategic planning process. Writing the business plan may produce more significant outcomes than the plan itself.
3. **The EC strategic process.** Considering e-commerce in strategy development does not radically change the process, but it does impact the outcome. Move-to-the-Net firms must approach the process differently than born-on-the-Net firms, but both types of firms must recognize the way electronic technologies such as the Internet make an e-difference. Because of the comprehensiveness of EC, formal strategic planning is a must.
4. **E-strategy initiation and formulation.** The strategy initiation phase involves understanding the company, the industry, and the competition. Companies must consider questions such as "Should we be a first mover?" "Should we go global?" "Should we create a separate company or brand?" In strategy formulation, specific opportunities are selected for implementation based on project viability, company fit, cost-benefit, risk, and pricing.
5. **E-strategy implementation and assessment.** Creating an effective Web team and ensuring that sufficient resources are available initiate the implementation phase. Other important implementation issues are whether to outsource various aspects of development and the need to redesign existing business processes. Immediately after implementation, assessment begins. Metrics provide feedback, and management acts by taking corrective action and reformulating strategy, if necessary.
6. **Issues in global EC.** Going global with EC can be done quickly and with a relatively small investment. However, businesses must deal with a number of different issues in the cultural, administrative, geographic, and economic dimensions of global trading.
7. **Small businesses and EC.** Depending on the circumstances, innovative small companies have a tremendous opportunity to adopt EC with little cost and to expand rapidly. Being in a niche market provides the best chance for small business success, and a variety of Web-based resources are available that small business owners can use to help ensure success.

KEY TERMS

Strategy	582	**Strategy initiation**	583	**Versioning**	599
Strategy assessment	585	**SWOT analysis**	586	**Virtual corporation (VC)**	602
Strategy formulation	584	**Value proposition**	584	**Web analytics**	604
Strategy implementation	585				

QUESTIONS FOR DISCUSSION

1. How would you identify competitors for a small business that wants to launch an EC project?
2. How would you apply the five forces and Internet impacts in Exhibit 14.1 to the Internet search industry, as described in the opening case?
3. Why must e-businesses consider strategic planning to be a cyclical process?
4. How would you apply the SWOT approach to a small, local bank that is evaluating its e-banking services?
5. Discuss how writing an e-business plan differs from writing a traditional business plan.
6. Offer some practical suggestions as to how a company can include the impact of the Internet in all levels of planning.
7. Explain the logic of Tjan's Internet portfolio map.
8. Amazon.com decided not to open physical stores, whereas First Network Security Bank (FNSB), which was the first online bank, opened its first physical bank in 1999. Compare and discuss the two strategies.
9. Discuss the pros and cons of going global with a physical product.
10. For each part of the CAGE framework, briefly discuss one barrier that may negatively impact e-commerce companies doing business globally.
11. Find some SME EC success stories and identify the common elements in them.

INTERNET EXERCISES

1. Survey several online travel agencies (e.g., **travelocity.com**, **orbitz.com**, **cheaptickets.com**, **priceline.com**, **expedia.com**, **bestfares.com**, and so on) and compare their business strategies. How do they compete against physical travel agencies?
2. Enter **digitalenterprise.org** and go to Web analytics. Read the material on Web analytics and prepare a report on the use of Web analytics for measuring advertising success.
3. Check the music CD companies on the Internet (e.g., **cduniverse.com**, **musica.co.uk**, **venusrecords.com**). Do any focus on specialized niche markets as a strategy?
4. Enter **ibm.com/procurement** and go to the e-procurement section. Prepare a report on how IBM's Supplier Integration Strategy can assist companies in implementing an EC strategy.
5. Compare the following search engines: **google.com**, **search.yahoo.com**, **teoma.com**, **mooter.com**, and **dipsie.com**. Conduct a comparative search (i.e., search for the same term at each site), learn more about how each search engine works (e.g., click on "about us" or similar link), and look for comparative articles at Web sites such as **searchenginewatch.com**. Consider the strengths and weaknesses of each site, when would one be more useful than another, and what special features distinguish it in the search engine marketspace. Prepare a report based on your findings.
6. One of the most global companies is Amazon.com (**amazon.com**). Find stories about its global strategies and activities (try **fortune.com**, **forbes.com**, and **google.com**). What are the most important lessons you learned?
7. Visit **abcsmallbiz.com** and find some of the EC opportunities available to small businesses. Also, visit the Web site of the SBA (Small Business Administration) office in your area. Summarize recent EC-related topics for SMEs.
8. In 2004, K-Mart acquired Sears. Enter **sears.com**, **kmart.com**, **walmart.com**, and **target.com**. Compare the sites on functionality, ease of use, product offerings, homepage layout, and so on. Prepare a report based on your findings.
9. Enter **alloy.com** and **bolt.com**. Compare the sites on functionality, ease of use, message boards, homepage layout, and so on. Prepare a report based on your findings.

10. Find out how Web sites such as **tradecard.com** facilitate the conduct of international trade over the Internet. Prepare a report based on your findings.
11. Use a currency conversion table (e.g., **xe.com/ucc**) to find out the exchange rate of $100 (U.S.) with the currencies of Brazil, Canada, China, India, Sweden, the European Union, and South Africa.
12. Conduct research on small businesses and their use of the Internet for EC. Visit sites such as **bcentral.com** and **uschamber.org**. Also, enter **google.com** or **yahoo.com** and type "small businesses + electronic commerce." Use your findings to write a report on current small business EC issues.

TEAM ASSIGNMENTS AND ROLE PLAYING

1. Have three teams represent the following units of one click-and-mortar company: (1) an off-line division, (2) an online division, and (3) top management. Each team member represents a different functional area within the division. The teams will develop a strategy in a specific industry (a group of three teams will represent a company in one industry). Teams will present their strategies to the class.
2. The relationship between manufacturers and their distributors regarding sales on the Web can be very strained. Direct sales may cut into the distributors' business. Review some of the strategies available to handle such channel conflicts. Each team member should be assigned to a company in a different industry. Study the strategies, compare and contrast them, and derive a proposed generic strategy.
3. Each team must find the latest information on one global EC issue (e.g., cultural, administrative, geographic, economic). Each team will offer a report based on their findings.
4. Survey **google.com**, **electronicmarkets.org**, and **isworld.org** to find out about EC efforts in different countries. Assign a country or two to each team. Relate the developments to each country's level of economic development and to its culture.

Real-World Case

PIERRE LANG EXPANDS INTO EASTERN EUROPE

Pierre Lang Europe (*pierrelang.com*) sells designer jewelry throughout Western Europe. Its traditional business model was to sell earrings, pendants, necklaces, and other jewelry through the firm's 5,500 sales representatives. When Pierre Lang decided to expand into Eastern Europe, the firm decided it needed to change this business model and the underlying information systems and business processes.

The company knew it was losing business because it was unable to keep track of customers and it did not have direct contact with them. If sales representatives left the company for any reason, they would take their customers with them. Pierre Lang Europe wanted more than sales from its customers, it wanted customer relationships for follow-on sales and customer support.

Like many companies expanding globally, Pierre Lang also anticipated that this expansion could double its revenues and order volume. The company needed better information about its finances, improved control of its order process, and a system that could handle the multiple legal and language requirements of doing business in many different countries.

Pierre Lang selected mySAP after evaluating several competing solutions. Installation began in July 2003, early rollout projects were in place by November, and financial and controlling capabilities went live in all company locations in January 2004.

Today, Pierre Lang uses country-specific versions of mySAP to handle invoicing, tax, language, and fiscal issues. France, for example, has unique requirements for tracking the import and export of gold and silver. "Lots of small things like that have to be considered because they're vital for Pierre Lang. It has to work perfectly in every country, so they have to know whom they will charge what, and do that automatically," says Rudolf Windisch, one of Pierre Lang's consulting partners on this project. "They also have to deal with all the tax issues, which vary considerably from one country to another. There are no homogeneous tax systems in Europe."

Pierre Lang expects to increase the accuracy of its information and eliminate the need for manual transfers of tax data to develop reports. Executives also anticipate decreased inventory costs through improved material disposition as well as better information about sales efforts and costs that will lead to improved forecasting and planning.

As noted in this chapter, expanding regionally or globally can have a dramatic impact on a company's bottom line, but only if it is prepared to deal with the heterogeneous legal and financial systems in different countries. Pierre Lang knew this and met the challenge.

Source: SAP AG. "Pierre Lang Europe." Available from *sap.com/solutions/business-suite/erp/pdf/CS_Pierre_Lang.pdf* (accessed December 2004). Adapted with permission.

Questions

1. Why was it necessary for Pierre Lang to look at fundamental changes in its business model and information systems?
2. Relate the facts of this case to the CAGE framework discussed in Section 14.8.
3. What have been the results of implementing mySAP at Pierre Lang?

REFERENCES

Adobor, H., and R. McMullen. "Strategic Partnering in E-Commerce: Guidelines for Managing Alliances." *Business Horizons* 45, no. 2 (2002): 67–76.

axon.co.nz (accessed March 2005).

Baker, W., et al. "Price Smarter on the Net." *Harvard Business Review* (February 2001): 122–127.

Barua, A., et al. "Measures for E-Business Value Assessment." *IT Pro*, January–February 2001, 47–51.

Boulding, W., and M. Christen. "First-Mover Disadvantage." *Harvard Business Review* (October 2001): 20–21.

Brandenburger, A. M., and B. J. Nalebuff. *Co-Opetition: A Revolution Mindset That Combines Competition and Cooperation*. New York: Currency, 1996.

Burby, J. "Meaningful Metrics: Collect What Counts." *ClickZ Experts*, May 25, 2004. clickz.com/experts/crm/analyze_data/article.php/3358121 (accessed May 2004).

Chatterjee, D., et al. "Shaping Up for E-Commerce: Institutional Enablers for the Organizational Assimilation of Web Technologies." *MIS Quarterly* (June 2002).

Coltman, T., et al. "Keeping E-Business in Perspective." *Communications of the ACM* 45, no. 8 (August 2002): 69.

Deise, M. V., et al. *Executive's Guide to E-Business—From Tactics to Strategy*. New York: Wiley, 2000.

DePalma, D. "Meet Your Customers' Needs Through Cultural Marketing." *e-Business Advisor*, August 2000.

DePalma, D. "Think Globally, Act Consistently." *e-Business Advisor*, June 2001, 24–26.

Dewan, R., et al. "Adoption of Internet-Based Product Customization and Pricing Strategies." *Proceedings of the 33rd HICSS*, Maui, Hawaii, January 2000.

Dubie, D. "Going Global" *eBusinessIQ*, March 13, 2003. knowledgeiq.com/news/208-knowledgeiq_news.html (accessed April 2004).

e-Business World. "Global Imperative . . . and the Pitfalls of Regionalism." *e-Business World*, January–February 2000, 8–10.

The Economist. "How Google Works." *The Economist Technology Quarterly*, September 16, 2004. economist.com/science/tq/displaystory.cfm?story_id=3171440 (accessed January 5, 2005).

Efendioglu, A. M., and V. F. Yip. "Chinese Culture and E-Commerce: An Exploratory Study." *Interacting with Computers* 16, no. 1 (2004): 45–62.

El Sawy, O. *Redesigning Enterprise Processes for E-Business*. New York: McGraw-Hill, 2001.

eMarketer. *Small Businesses Expecting E-Sales. eMarketer*, December 14, 2004. emarketer.com/article.aspx?1003177 (accessed January 2005).

Ernest, D., et al. "A Future for E-Alliances." *The McKinsey Quarterly* (April–June 2001).

Fallows, J. "The Stock? Whatever. Google Keeps On Innovating." *New York Times*, October, 31, 2004. nytimes.com/2004/10/31/business/yourmoney/31tech.html (accessed November 2004).

Ghemawat, P. "Distance Still Matters: The Hard Reality of Global Expansion." *Harvard Business Review* (September 2001): 137–147.

Green, S. *Profit on the Web*. Auckland, New Zealand: Axon Computertime, 2002.

Gulati, R., and J. Garino. "Get the Right Mix of Bricks and Clicks." *Harvard Business Review* (May–June 2000): 107–114.

Harmon, P., et al. *Developing E-Business Systems and Architectures: A Manager's Guide*. San Francisco: Morgan Kaufmann Publishers, 2001.

Hiles, A. "E-Commerce: Managing the Risks." *MyITAdvisor*, Winter 2001.

InternetNZ. *InternetNZ Strategic Plan: 2004-2007*. April 2004. internetnz.net.nz/public/planning040424strat-plan-v3.2.pdf (accessed December 2004).

Jelassi, I., and A. Enders. *Strategies for e-Business*. Harlow, England: FT Prentice Hall, 2005.

Johnson, G., and K. Scholes. *Exploring Corporate Strategy: Text and Cases,* 5th ed. London: Pearson Education, 2002.

Josephson, M. *Why a Content Management System Won't Take You Global.* September 2001. Available from **idiomtech.com/solutions/globalization-leadership.asp** (accessed April 2003).

Kalakota, R., and M. Robinson. *E-Business 2.0—Roadmap for Success.* Reading, MA: Addison-Wesley, 2001.

Kaplan, R. S., and D. P. Norton. *The Balanced Scorecard: Translating Strategy into Action.* Boston: Harvard Business School Press, 1996.

Karakaya, F., and O. Khalil. "Determinants of Internet Adoption in Small and Medium-sized Enterprises." *International Journal of Internet and Enterprise Management* 2, no 4 (2004): 341–365.

Kim, H., and R. Ramkaran. "Best Practices in e-Business Process Management: Extending a Reengineering Framework." *Business Process Management Journal* 10, no 1 (2004): 27–43.

Kim, W. C., and R. Mauborgne. "Charting Your Company's Future." *Harvard Business Review* (June 2002): 77–83.

Levinson, M. "Don't Stop Thinking About Tomorrow." *CIO Magazine*, December 1999–January 2000.

Lumpkin, G. T., and G. G. Dess. "How the Internet Adds Value." *Organizational Dynamics* (April–June 2004): 161–171.

Markoff, J. "The Coming Search Wars." *New York Times*, February 2, 2004a. **news.com.com/2100-1032-5151934.html** (accessed February 2004).

Markoff, J. "Amazon to Take Searches on Web to a New Depth." *New York Times*, September 15, 2004b. **nytimes.com/2004/09/15/technology/15search.html** (accessed September 2004).

Markoff, J. "Microsoft Unveils Its Internet Search Engine, Quietly." *New York Times*, November 11, 2004c. **nytimes.com/2004/11/11/technology/11search.html** (accessed November 2004).

Markus, L. "Toward an Integrated Theory of IT-Related Risk Control." In Baskerville, R., et al. (eds.), *The Social and Organizational Perspective on Information Technology,* pp. 11–27. London: Chapman & Hall, 2000.

McKay, J., and P. Marshall. *Strategic Management of eBusiness.* Milton, Australia: John Wiley & Sons. 2004.

Munarriz, R. A. "What's Google's Growth Strategy?" *The Motley Fool Take*, August 31, 2004. **fool.com/news/take/2004/take040831.htm** (accessed September 2004).

OECD (Organization for Economic Cooperation and Development). *Enhancing SME Competitiveness: The OECD Bologna, Italy, Ministerial Conference.* 2001.

Palmer, J. "Web Site Usability, Design, and Performance Metrics." *Information Systems Research* (June 2002): 151–167.

Plant, R. T. *E-Commerce: Formulation of Strategy*. Upper Saddle River, NJ: Prentice Hall, 2000.

Porter, M. E. *Competitive Strategy: Techniques for Analyzing Industries and Competitors.* New York: The Free Press, 1980.

Porter, M. E. "What Is Strategy?" *Harvard Business Review* (November–December 1996): 61–78.

Porter, M. E. "Strategy and the Internet." *Harvard Business Review* (March 2001): 63–78.

Prasad, B., and P. Harker. "Pricing Online Banking Services Amid Network Externalities." *Proceedings 33rd HICSS*, Maui, Hawaii, January 2000.

Rangan, S., and R. Adner. "Profits and the Internet: Seven Misconceptions." *Sloan Management Review* (Summer 2001): 44–53.

Ranganathan, C., et al. "E-Business Transformation at the Crossroads: Sears' Dilemma." *Proceedings of the 24th International Conference on Information Systems*, Seattle, Washington, December 14–17, 2003, pp. 1048–1065.

Rayport, J., and B. J. Jaworski. *Introduction to E-Commerce.* Boston: McGraw-Hill, 2002.

Rayport, J., and B. J. Jaworski. *Introduction to E-Commerce,* 2d ed. Boston: McGraw-Hill, 2004.

Roush, W. "Search Beyond Google." *Technology Review*, March 2004. **technologyreview.com/articles/04/03/roush0304.asp** (accessed March 2005).

Rowe, A. J., et al. *Strategic Management: A Methodological Approach.* Boston: Addison-Wesley, 1994.

Saeed, K. A., and R. A. Leitch. "Controlling Sourcing Risk in Electronic Marketplaces." *Electronic Markets* 13, no. 2 (June 2003): 163–172.

SAP AG. "Pierre Lang Europe." **sap.com/solutions/business-suite/erp/pdf/cs_pierre_lang.pdf** (accessed December 2004).

Shapiro, C., and H. Varian. *Information Rules: A Strategic Guide to the Network Economy.* Boston: Harvard Business School Press, 1999.

Sheldon, L. A., and T. J. Strader. "Managerial Issues for Expanding into International Web-Based Electronic Commerce." *SAM Advanced Management Journal* (Summer 2002): 22–30.

Shi, X., and P. C. Wright. "E-Commercializing Business Operations." *Communications of the ACM* (February 2003): 83–87.

Stern, C. W., and G. Stalk. *Perspectives on Strategy from the Boston Consulting Group.* New York: John Wiley & Sons, 1998.

Sterne, J. *Web Metrics: Proven Methods for Measuring Web Site Success.* New York: John Wiley & Sons, 2002.

Straub, D. W., et al. "Measuring E-Commerce in Net-Enabled Organizations: An Introduction to the Special Issue." *Information Systems Research* (June 2002a): 115–124.

Straub, D. W., et al. "Toward New Metrics for Net-Enhanced Organizations." *Information Systems Research* (September 2002b): 227–238.

Suh, B., and I. Han. "The IS Risk Analysis Based on a Business Model." *Information and Management* 41, no. 2 (December 2003): 149–158.

Sullivan, D. "Search Wars: Battle of the Superpowers." April 29, 2004. **searchenginewatch.com/searchday/article.php/3347181** (accessed November 2004).

Tjan, A. K. "Finally, a Way to Put Your Internet Portfolio in Order." *Harvard Business Review* (February 2001): 76–85.

Venkatraman, N. "Five Steps to a Dot-Com Strategy: How to Find Your Footing on the Web." *Sloan Management Review* (Spring 2000): 15–28.

Viehland, D. "Managing Business Risk in Electronic Commerce." *Proceedings of the 2001 Americas Conference on Information Systems*, Boston, Massachusetts, August 3, 2001.

Vose, D. *Risk Analysis: A Quantitative Guide,* 2d ed. New York: John Wiley and Sons, 2000.

Walsh, B. "Building a Business Plan for An E-Commerce Project." **nwc.com/917/917f2.html** (accessed March 2005).

Ward, J., and J. Peppard. *Strategic Planning for Information Systems*, 3d ed. Chichester, UK: John Wiley & Sons, 2002.

Watchfire. *You Can't Manage What You Don't Measure: Improving Website ROI Through E-Metrics and Website Management.* Kanata, Ontario: Watchfire Corporation, 2001.

Watson, R. P., et al. *Electronic Commerce: The Strategic Perspective.* Fort Worth, TX: Dryden Press, 2000.

Wheelen, T., and J. Hunger. *Cases in Strategic Management and Business Policy*, 9th ed. Upper Saddle River, NJ: Prentice Hall, 2003.

Wilson S. G., and I. Abel. "So You Want to Get Involved in E-Commerce." *Industrial Marketing Management* 31 (January–February 2002).

Xie, F. T., and W. J. Johnston. "Strategic Alliances: Incorporating the Impact of e-Business Technological Innovations." *Journal of Business and Industrial Marketing* 19, no. 2 (March 2004): 208–255.

Zhu, K., and K. Kraemer. "E-Commerce Metrics for Net-Enhanced Organizations: Assessing the Value of E-Commerce to Firm Performance in the Manufacturing Sector." *Information Systems Research* (September 2002): 275–295.

CHAPTER 15

ECONOMICS AND JUSTIFICATION OF ELECTRONIC COMMERCE

Content

Learning Objectives

Upon completion of this chapter, you will be able to:

1. Describe the need for justifying EC investments, how it is done, and how metrics are used to determine justification.
2. Understand the difficulties in measuring and justifying EC investments.
3. Recognize the difficulties in establishing intangible metrics and describe how to overcome them.
4. List and briefly describe traditional and advanced methods of justifying IT investments.
5. Understand how e-CRM, e-learning, and other EC projects are justified.
6. Describe some economic principles of EC.
7. Understand how product, industry, seller, and buyer characteristics impact the economics of EC.
8. Recognize key factors to the success of EC projects and the major reasons for failures.

JUSTIFYING EC AND IT INVESTMENT IN THE STATE OF IOWA

The Problem

For years, there was little planning or justification for EC and IT projects by the government of the state of Iowa. Any state agency that needed money for an EC or IT project slipped it into its budget request. State agencies requested many projects, knowing that only a few would be funded. Bargaining, political favors, pressures, and other outside influences determined which agencies' requests were. As a result, some important projects were not funded, and unimportant ones were. In addition, there was very little incentive to save money. This was the situation in Iowa until 1999, and it still exists in many other states, countries, cities, and other public institutions. However, in Iowa, everything changed in 1999 when a request for $22.5 million to resolve the Y2K problem was made.

The Solution

Iowa's solution to its IT planning and spending program, the Iowa Return on Investment Program (ROI Program), is an *IT value model*. The basic idea is to promote **performance-based government**, an approach that measures the results of government programs. The state of Iowa developed the ROI Program to justify investment in the Y2K solution. The basic principles of the model follow.

performance-based government
An approach that measures the results of government programs.

First, new investments are funded primarily from a pot of money called the Pooled Technology Account, which is appropriated by the legislature and controlled by the state's IT department. Pooling of funds makes budget oversight easier and prevents duplications. Second, agencies submit requests for funding future EC and IT projects from the pooled account. To support their requests, agency managers must document the expected costs and benefits of the project based on a set of factors. The maximum score for each factor ranges from 5 to 15 points, for a maximum total score of 100 points. In addition, they must specify metrics related to those factors in order to determine the project's success. The scores are based on 10 criteria that are used to determine value (for details on these criteria, see Varon 2003).

The ROI Program requires agencies to detail their technology requirements and functional needs. This enforces standards, and it also helps officials identify duplicate projects and expenditures. For example, in 2001 several agencies proposed building pieces of an ERP system that would handle e-procurement and human resources management. The IT department suggested that the state deploy a single, more cost-effective ERP system that could be shared by several agencies. The project, which had an estimated cost of $9.6 million, could easily have cost many times that amount if agencies were allowed to go it alone. Once a project is funded, the state saves money by scrutinizing expenses. Agencies must submit their purchase orders and invoices to the Enterprise Quality Assurance Office for approval before they can be reimbursed. This IT value model is universal and fits EC projects as well. The IT department reimburses agencies for expenses from the Pooled Technology Account only after verifying that the expenses were necessary. If an agency's expenditures are not in line with the project schedule, it presents a red flag for auditors that the project could be in trouble.

The Results

Iowa's ROI Program became a national model for documenting value and prioritizing IT and EC investments in the public sector. In 2002, the program was named the "Best State IT Management Initiative" by the National Association of State Chief Information Officers (NASCIO). It saved taxpayers more than $5 million in less than 4 years (about 16 percent of the spending on new IT projects).

The process also changed users' behavior. For example, during fiscal year 2003, 17 EC and IT projects were requested through the budget approval process, and only 6 were approved. For the year 2004, four projects were requested, all of which were approved. Also, there is considerable collaboration and use of cross-functional teams to write applications. State agencies are now thinking through their IT and EC investments more carefully. Another improvement is collaboration among agencies that submit joint proposals, thereby eliminating duplicate projects. Finally, the methodology minimizes political pressure. The success of Iowa's ROI Program led to the Iowa Accountable Government Act of 2001, which requires establishing a similar methodology for all state investments, not just EC or IT projects.

Source: Compiled from Varon (2003).

WHAT WE CAN LEARN . . .

Today, one of the most important decisions a company must make is whether an EC project is economically justified. The unique aspects of EC make its justification and economics different in many respects from the economics of other aspects of business, or even IT.

The opening case demonstrates that by conducting a formal analysis, organizations can improve their ROI in IT as well as eliminate politics from fund allocation decisions. This chapter examines the difficulties in justifying EC projects and identifies methods that can be used to overcome these difficulties. In addition, the economics of EC will be discussed, with an explanation of why EC can be very advantageous. The chapter concludes with an examination of EC successes and failures.

15.1 WHY JUSTIFY EC INVESTMENTS? HOW CAN THEY BE JUSTIFIED?

Companies need to justify their EC investments for a number of different reasons.

INCREASED DEMAND FOR FINANCIAL JUSTIFICATION

Once upon a time, or so the story goes, the beggars of New York City decided to conduct a competition as to who could collect the most money in one day. Many innovative ideas were employed, and several beggars collected almost a thousand dollars each. The winner, however, collected $5 million. When asked how he did it, the beggar replied: "I made a sign that said 'EC experts need funding for an innovative electronic marketplace' and put the sign in front of the New York Stock Exchange."

This story symbolizes what happened from 1995 through 2000, when EC projects and start-up companies were funded with little analysis of their business cases or finances. The result of the rush to invest was the 2001–2003 "dot-com bust," when hundreds of EC start-ups went out of business and the stock market crashed. Some companies and individual investors lost over 90 to 100 percent of their investments! Furthermore, many companies, such as Disney, Merrill Lynch, and Sears (see the Chapter 16 Real-World Case), terminated EC projects after losing considerable amounts of money and realizing few benefits from huge investments. The positive result of the crash was the "back-to-basics" movement, namely, a return to carefully checking and scrutinizing any request for EC funding.

Today, companies are holding the line on IT and EC budgets. According to Pisello (2004), IT executives feel the demand for financial justification and planning from executives, but most face an uphill battle to address this new accountability, as demonstrated by the following statistics:

- Sixty-five percent lack the knowledge or tools to do ROI calculations.
- Seventy-five percent have no formal processes or budgets in place for measuring ROI.
- Sixty-eight percent do not measure how projects coincide with promised benefits 6 months after completion.

At the same time, demand for expanding or initiating e-business projects remains strong. In order to achieve the optimal level of investment, CIOs will need to effectively communicate the value of proposed EC projects in order to gain approval.

OTHER REASONS WHY EC JUSTIFICATION IS NEEDED

The following are some additional reasons for conducting EC justification:

- Companies now realize that EC is not necessarily the solution to all problems. Therefore, EC projects *compete for funding and resources* with other internal and external projects, as described in Chapter 14. Analysis is needed to determine when funding of an EC project is appropriate.
- In some large companies, and in many public organizations, a formal evaluation of requests for funding is mandated.
- Companies need to assess the success of EC projects after they have been completed and then on a periodic basis (see Chapter 14).
- The success of EC projects may be assessed in order to pay bonuses to those involved with the project.

According to a study by *CIO Insight* (2004), the major reasons that companies conduct IT and EC justification are pressure from top management, internal competition for funding, the large amount of money involved, and weak business conditions. The same study found that justification forces EC and IT into better alignment with the corporate business strategy. Finally, justification increases the credibility of an EC project.

EC INVESTMENT CATEGORIES AND BENEFITS

Before we look at how to justify EC investments, let's examine the nature of such investments. One basic way to categorize different EC investments is to distinguish between investment in infrastructure and investment in specific EC applications.

The *IT infrastructure* provides the foundation for EC applications in the enterprise. The IT infrastructure includes intranets, extranets, data centers, data warehouses, and knowledge bases, and the infrastructure is shared by many applications throughout the enterprise (see Broadbent and Weill 1997). Infrastructure investments are made for the long-term.

EC applications are specific systems and programs for achieving certain objectives; for example, taking a customer order online or providing e-CRM. The number of EC applications is large. They may be in one functional department or they may be shared by several departments, which makes evaluation of their costs and benefits more complex.

Another way to look at EC and investment categories is proposed by Ross and Beath (2002). Their categories are based on the *purpose of the investment*. They also suggest a cost justification (funding) approach as well as the probable owner of each application (e.g., specific department or corporate ownership). Still other investment categories are offered by Devaraj and Kohli (2002), who divide EC investments into operational, managerial, and strategic types. The variety of EC investment categories demonstrates the complex nature of IT investment.

Specific Benefits

According to a *CIO Insight* (2004) survey, companies want to get the following benefits from an IT investment: cost reduction (84 percent); productivity improvement (77 percent); improved customer satisfaction (66 percent); improved staffing levels (57 percent); higher revenues (45 percent); higher earnings (43 percent); better customer retention (42 percent); more return of equity (33 percent); and faster time-to-market (31 percent). (*Note:* Separate data for EC are not available.)

HOW IS AN EC INVESTMENT JUSTIFIED?

cost-benefit analysis
A comparison of the costs of a project against the benefits.

Justifying an EC investment means comparing the costs of the project against its benefits in what is known as a **cost-benefit analysis**. To conduct such an analysis, it is necessary to define and measure the relevant EC benefits and costs. Cost-benefit analysis is frequently referred to as *return of investment (ROI),* which is also the name of a specific method for evaluating investments (see Paton and Troppito 2004).

A number of different methods are used to measure the business value of EC and IT investments. Traditional methods that support such analyses are net present value (NPV) and return on investment (ROI) (see Online File W15.1). More advanced methods also can be used to justify these investments. Traditional and more advanced justification methods are discussed in Section 15.3.

Our discussion here is limited mostly to individual EC projects or initiatives. EC projects deal mostly with the automation of business processes, and as such, they are *capital investment* decisions. Investment in a start-up company is discussed in Chapter 16.

WHAT NEEDS TO BE JUSTIFIED? WHEN SHOULD JUSTIFICATION TAKE PLACE?

Not all EC investments need to be formally justified. In some cases, a simple one-page justification will do. The following are cases where formal evaluation may not be needed:

- When the value of the investment is relatively small for the organization
- When the relevant data are not available, inaccurate, or too volatile
- When the EC project is mandated—it must be done regardless of the costs and benefits involved

However, even when formal analysis is not required, an organization should have some qualitative analysis to explain the logic of investing in the EC project. For more details, see Seddon et al. (2002) and Sawhney (2002a).

USING METRICS IN EC JUSTIFICATION

A **metric** is a specific, measurable standard against which actual performance is compared. Metrics are used to describe costs, benefits, or the ratio between them. They are used not only for justification, but also for other economic activities (e.g., to compare employee performance in order to reward specific employees). Metrics can produce very positive results in organizations by driving behavior in a number of ways. According to Rayport and Jaworski (2002), metrics can:

metric
A specific, measurable standard against which actual performance is compared.

- Define the value proposition of business models
- Communicate a business strategy to the workforce through performance targets
- Increase accountability when metrics are linked with performance-appraisal programs
- Align the objectives of individuals, departments, and divisions to the enterprise's strategic objectives
- Track the performance of EC systems, including usage, types of visitors, page visits, conversion rate, etc.
- Assess the health of companies by using tools such as balanced scorecards and performance dashboards

An example of IT metrics implementation can be found in a white paper on the impact of a new online service on the profitability of Axon Computertime, a small computer services business in New Zealand (Green 2002). Axon used the following metrics: *revenue growth*, *cost reduction*, *cost avoidance*, *customer fulfillment*, *customer service*, and *customer communications*. The last few metrics in this list highlight the importance of including nonfinancial measures in the measurement of organizational performance.

In many cases, such measures involve intangible benefits, a topic we will discuss later. Also, note that metrics require the definition of a particular measure.

Metrics, Measurements, and Key Performance Indicators

Metrics need to be defined properly with a clear way to measure them. For example, *revenue growth* can be measured in total dollars, in percentage change over time, or in percentage growth as compared to the larger industry. *Cost avoidance,* for example, can be achieved in many ways, one of which may be "decrease obsolete stock write-offs as percentage of revenue." Defining the specific measures is critical; otherwise, what the metrics actually measure may be open to interpretation.

The balanced scorecard method uses customer metrics, financial metrics, internal business processes metrics, and learning and growth metrics. Metrics are related to the goals, objectives, vision, and plans of the organization. Metrics that deal directly with performance (e.g., sales, profits) are frequently measured by **key performance indicators (KPI)**, which are the quantitative expression of critically important metrics (known as *critical success factors*). Frequently, one metric has several KPIs.

key performance indicators (KPI)
The quantitative expression of critically important metrics.

Metrics can be used in any organization, private or public. Let's look at an example. In Australia, the government of Victoria (vic.gov.au) is one of the leaders in exploiting the Internet to provide a one-stop service center called "Do It Online." In the United States, MyCalifornia (my.ca.gov) offers many services for the citizens of California. In either case, the service of renewing drivers' licenses is justified by the metric of "wait time" for the citizens who would otherwise have to visit a physical office.

Now that we understand the need for conducting EC justification and the use of metrics, let's see why EC justification is so difficult to accomplish.

Section 15.1 ▶ REVIEW QUESTIONS

1. List some of the reasons for justifying an EC investment.
2. Describe the risks of not conducting an EC justification study.
3. Describe how an EC investment is justified.
4. List the major EC investment categories.
5. When is justification of EC investments unnecessary?
6. What are metrics? What benefits do they offer?

15.2 DIFFICULTIES IN MEASURING AND JUSTIFYING EC INVESTMENTS

Justifying EC (and IT) projects can be a complex, and therefore difficult, process. Let's see why.

THE EC JUSTIFICATION PROCESS

The EC justification process varies depending on the situation and the methods used. However, in its extreme, it can be very complex, as shown by Gunasekaran et al. (2001). They identified five areas that must be considered in the justification of IT projects, as shown in Exhibit 15.1. In this section, we will discuss intangibles and tangibles. In Chapter 14, we discussed some strategic and tactical considerations.

We will see later in this section that one major difficulty with EC justification is measuring intangible benefits and costs, which are a major component in the model just presented. Other difficulties in conducting justifications are provided next.

DIFFICULTIES IN MEASURING PRODUCTIVITY AND PERFORMANCE GAINS

One of the major benefits of using EC is increased productivity. However, productivity increases may be difficult to measure for a number of different reasons, which are discussed below.

Data and Analysis Issues

Data, or the analysis of the data, may hide productivity gains. Why is this? For manufacturing, it is fairly easy to measure outputs and inputs. For example, General Motors produces motor vehicles—relatively well-defined products—that show gradual quality changes over time. It is not difficult to identify the inputs used to produce these vehicles with reasonable

EXHIBIT 15.1 A Model for IT Project Justification

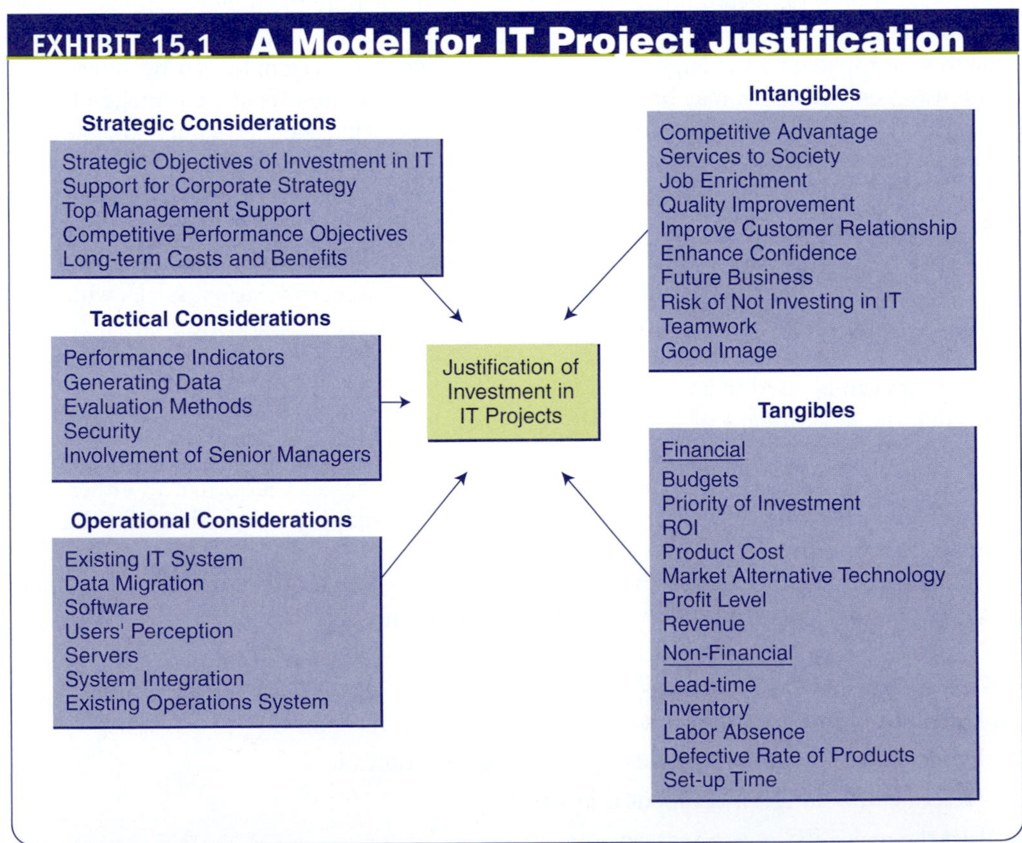

Source: Reprinted from *International Journal of Information Management* March 2001, Gunasekaran A. P. Love, F. Rahimi, and R. Miele. "A Model for Investment Justification in Information Technology Projects," copyright (2006), with permission from Elsevier.

accuracy. However, in service industries, such as finance or health-care delivery, it is more difficult to define what the products are, how they change in quality, and how they may be related to corresponding benefits and costs.

For example, banks now use EC to handle a large portion of deposits and withdrawal transactions through ATMs. The ability to withdraw cash from ATMs 24/7 is a substantial benefit for customers compared with the limited hours of the business day if they wish to use live tellers. But, what is the value of this to the bank in comparison with the associated costs? If the incremental value exceeds the incremental costs, then it represents a productivity gain; otherwise the productivity impact is negative.

EC Productivity Gains May Be Offset By Losses in Other Areas

Another possible difficulty is that EC gains in certain areas of the company may be offset by losses in other areas. For example, increased online sales may decrease off-line sales, a situation known as *cannibalism*. Or, consider the situation where an organization installs a new EC system that makes it possible to increase output per employee; if the organization reduces its production staff but has to increase its IT staff, the productivity gains from EC could be small, or even negative.

Incorrectly Defining What Is Measured

The results of any investment justification depend on what is actually measured. For example, to assess the benefits of EC investment, one should usually look at productivity improvement in the area where the EC project was installed. However, productivity increase may not necessarily be a profitable improvement (e.g., due to losses in other areas). The problem of definitions can be overcome by using appropriate metrics and key performance indicators.

Other Difficulties

Other performance measurement difficulties also have been noted. A number of researchers have pointed out, for example, that time lags may throw off productivity measurements (Reichheld and Schefter 2000; Qing and Plant 2001). Many EC investments, especially those in e-CRM, take 5 to 6 years to show results, but many studies do not wait that long to measure productivity changes. Another possible problem was suggested by Devaraj and Kohli (2003), who tried to relate the actual rather than the potential uses of a system with IT expenditures. For a list of other factors that impact performance, see Devaraj and Kohli (2002).

RELATING IT EXPENDITURES TO ORGANIZATIONAL PERFORMANCE

Some of the difficulties in finding the relationship between EC investment and organizational performance can be seen in Exhibit 15.2. The exhibit shows that the relationship between investment and performance is indirect; factors such as shared IT assets and how they are used can impact organizational performance and make it difficult to assess the value of an IT (or EC) investment.

Furthermore, changes in organizational performance may occur years after an EC application is installed. Thus, proper evaluation must be done over the entire life cycle of the system. This requires forecasting, which may be difficult. In EC, it is even more difficult, because investors often require that risky and fast-changing EC systems pay for themselves within 3 years.

DIFFICULTIES IN MEASURING COSTS AND BENEFITS

Broadly speaking, EC costs and benefits can be classified into two categories: tangible and intangible. *Tangible* costs and benefits are easier to measure once metrics, such as the cost of software (cost) and the amount of labor saved (benefit), are determined. *Intangible* costs and benefits may be more difficult to measure.

Tangible Costs and Benefits

Tangible costs are those that are easy to measure and quantify and that relate directly to a specific investment. The costs involved in purchasing hardware, software, consulting, and support services usually are tangible, as are the costs of telecommunication services, maintenance,

EXHIBIT 15.2 Process Approach to IT Organizational Investment and Impact

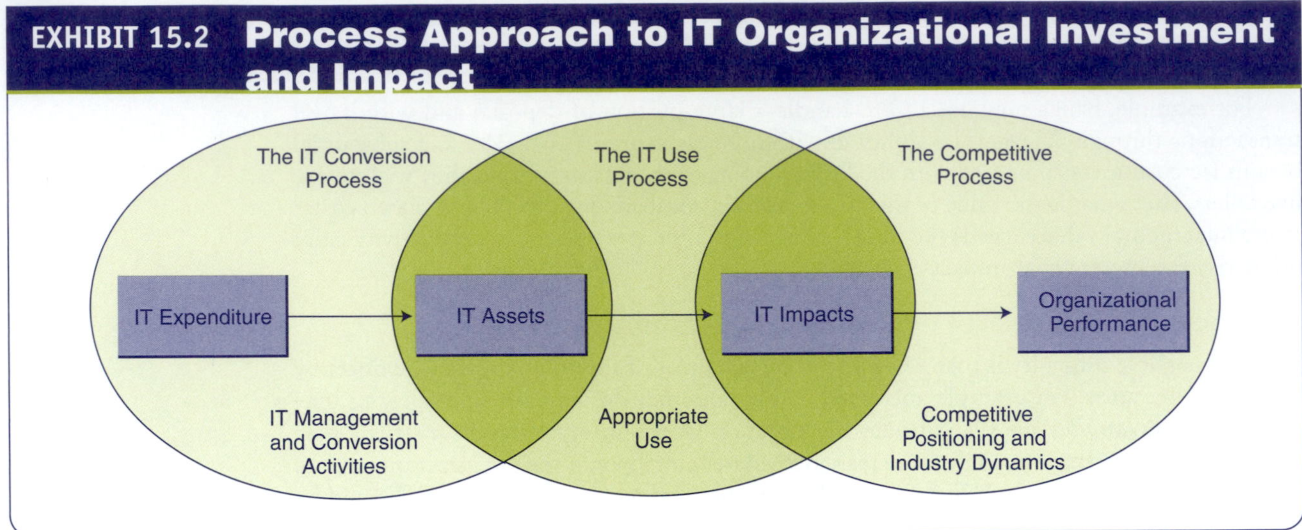

Source: Soh, C., and L. M. Markus, "How IT Creates Business Value: A Process Theory Synthesis," *Proceedings of the 16th International Conference on Information Systems*, Amsterdam, Netherlands, December 1995. Used with permission of the authors.

and labor. These costs can be measured through accounting information (e.g., from the general ledger). Similarly, tangible benefits, including increased profitability, improved productivity, and greater market share, can be measured with relative ease.

Intangible Costs and Benefits

When it comes to *intangible* costs and benefits, organizations must develop innovative metrics to track them as accurately as possible. Intangible costs may include the learning curve of the firm's customer service employees to incorporate an EC system to respond to customer inquiries. Another intangible cost may involve having to change or adapt other business processes or information systems, such as processing items returned by customers or building and operating an inventory tracking system. An additional difficulty is separating EC costs from the costs of routine maintenance of inventory and other relevant systems.

In many cases, EC projects generate intangible benefits, such as faster time-to-market, increased employee and customer satisfaction, easier distribution, greater organizational agility, and improved control. These are very desirable benefits, but it is difficult to place an accurate monetary value on them. For example, many people would agree that e-mail improves communications, but it is not at all clear how to measure the value of this improvement. Managers are very conscious of the bottom line, but no manager can prove that e-mail is responsible for so many cents per share of the organization's total profits.

Let's consider the case of Web-based portals that are used to consolidate information across the organization so that employees and customers can quickly access information and services from a single point. A large part of the ROI of a portal lies in the efficiency gained by internal users. Portals enable employees to access customer information quickly, accurately, and efficiently in order to better respond to the customer's needs. Such benefits are intangible.

One EC application may generate multiple intangible benefits, some of which will materialize only after a year or two. Another example of multiple intangible benefits, provided in the Real-World Case at the end of this chapter, is Citigroup's Global Corporate and Investment Banking division's Web portal—Mystic—which was implemented to increase productivity and quality performance and to improve project control. The benefits resulting from Mystic are both tangible and intangible.

Intangible benefits can be complex, yet substantial. For example, according to Arno Penzias, a Nobel Laureate in physics, the New York Metropolitan Transit Authority (MTA) had not found the need to open another airport for almost two decades, even though air traffic had tripled. According to Penzias' study, the existing airports were able to meet increased air traffic needs due to productivity gains derived from improved IT systems (quoted by Devaraj and Kohli 2002). IT systems added by the MTA played critical roles in ticket reservations, passenger and luggage check-in, crew assignment and scheduling, runway maintenance and management, and gate assignments. These improvements enabled MTA to cope with increased traffic without adding new facilities, saving hundreds of millions of dollars. Many similar examples of increased capacity exist. Intangible benefits are especially common in service and government applications (see Steyaert 2004).

One class of intangible benefits, according to Ryan and Gates (2004), is *social subsystem issues* that include comfort to employees, impact on environment, changes to the power distribution in an organization, and preventing invasion of the privacy of employees and customers.

An analyst could ignore intangible benefits, but doing so implies that their value is zero, which may lead the organization to reject EC investments that could substantially increase revenues and profitability. Therefore, it is necessary to consider intangible benefits in a way that reflects their potential impact. The question is how to do it.

Handling Intangible Benefits

The first step in dealing with intangible benefits is to define them and specify how they are going to be measured by attaching metrics to them. An example of intangible and tangible metrics as they relate to EC users is provided in Exhibit 15.3.

EXHIBIT 15.3 Sample EC Metrics for Various Entities of Users

EC User	Tangible Metrics	Intangible Metrics
Buyer (B2C)	• Cost/price of the product • Time in executing the transaction	• Ease of use of EC • Convenience in purchasing • Reliability of the transaction • Privacy of personal data
Seller (B2C)	• Profit per customer • Conversion rate of visitors • Inventory costs • Profit per item sold	• Customer satisfaction • Customer loyalty • Market share • Transaction security
Net-enhanced organization (B2B)	• Design-to-market (time) • Cash-to-cash cycle • Percentage of orders delivered on time or early • Profit per item sold	• Flexibility in changing purchase orders • Agility to sustain unplanned production increase • Risk reduction
Government (G2C)	• Reduction in cost of transactions • Reduction in licensing fees • Increase in participation in government programs • Lower tax rates	• Citizen satisfaction • Reelection of candidates • Choice of interacting with elected officials • Promoting democratic principles

Additional Examples of Metrics

- More than one-third of consumers use the same password for online banking as they do for other online activities.
- More than 50 brands were targeted by phishing scams in November 2004.
- More than half of consumers say they are less likely to respond to an e-mail from their bank because of phishing threats.
- Experts say that the infrastructures of large industries are likely to be hit by cyber attacks.
- Some consumers of financial products say phishing has turned them away from Web transactions.
- Consumers are slightly more likely to receive permission-based e-mails from online merchants than other retail businesses.
- Two-thirds of computers have spyware on them.
- Spam messages are considerably shorter than legitimate e-mails.
- eBay tops the list of online destinations on Black Friday (the day after Thanksgiving).
- More than 10 percent of all U.S. Web traffic went to shopping or classified ad sites
- Spam takes up volume, but not bandwidth.

Source: Compiled from *cio.com/metrics/index.cfm* (accessed December 2004–January 2005).

The most straightforward solution to the problem of evaluating intangible benefits in cost-benefit analysis is to make *rough estimates* of the monetary values of all of the intangible benefits and then conduct a ROI or similar financial analysis. The simplicity of this approach is attractive, but in many cases the assumptions used in these estimates are debatable. If the technology is acquired because decision makers assigned too high a value to intangible benefits, the organization could find that it has wasted some valuable resources. On the other hand, if the valuation of intangible benefits is too low, the organization may reject the investment and later find itself losing market share to competitors who did implement the technology. See Plumtree Corp. (2001) for a study on translating intangible benefits to dollar amounts.

Intangible costs and benefits may be approached in a number of different ways (e.g., see Sawhney 2002a). Several of the methods presented in Section 15.3 also can be used to evaluate intangible benefits. For more on intangible costs and benefits, see Online File W15.2.

The problems of measuring intangible costs and benefits become more complex as companies try to justify large investments in EC because of the special characteristics of EC. Intuitively, we know that EC provides significant benefits of flexibility, ease of use, and low transaction costs. However, how can these intangible benefits be quantified? Nucleus Research (2002) suggests that ROI justification metrics should provide management with a consistent, reliable, and repeatable process that can compare the relative impact of investment opportunities on the company's bottom line.

Section 15.2 ▶ REVIEW QUESTIONS

1. How do organizations measure performance and productivity? What are the difficulties in measuring performance and productivity?
2. Why is it difficult to relate EC (IT) investments to organizational performance? List the major reasons.
3. Define tangible costs and benefits.
4. Define intangible costs and benefits and explain why they must be considered when justifying an IT investment.
5. Why is it difficult to measure the value of intangible benefits?
6. Describe a simple approach to the intangibles problem.

15.3 METHODS AND TOOLS FOR EVALUATING AND JUSTIFYING EC INVESTMENTS

Now that we have an understanding of the difficulties of EC justification and how organizations evaluate EC investments, let's examine the methods and tools used for such evaluation and justification. Companies use commercially available tools or develop in-house tools through the use of spreadsheets (e.g., Excel spreadsheets). And as with the economic justification of non-EC investments, a number of different methods can be applied to EC investments.

Devaraj and Kohli (2002) discuss a number of different justification methods, such as *cost-benefit analysis*, *break-even point*, *net present value (NPV)*, *economic value added*, and *real options* for traditional IT investment. At their core, all economic justification approaches attempt to account for the costs and benefits of investments. They differ in their ability to account for the tangible and intangible and the present and future costs and benefits of IT, particularly when compared to other corporate investments.

METHODOLOGICAL ASPECTS OF JUSTIFYING EC INVESTMENTS

Before presenting the specific methods for EC justification, let's examine the methodological issues that are common to most of these methods.

Types of Costs

Although costs may appear to be the simple side of a cost-benefit analysis, they may not be so simple. Here are a few things to consider:

- **Distinguish between initial (up-front) costs and operating costs.** The initial costs may be a one-time investment or they may spread over several months or a year.
- **Direct and indirect costs.** *Direct costs* can be related directly to a specific project. *Indirect costs* usually are infrastructure-related costs. In addition, the costs may be related to several projects. Therefore, one needs to *allocate* these costs to the specific projects. Such allocation may not be easy to perform; a number of approaches to cost allocation are available (consult an accountant).
- **In-kind costs.** Although monetary payments are easily tracked, costs also may be *in kind*; for example, contributions of labor, machine time, and so on. These frequently are indirect costs, which complicates their calculation.

Break-Even Analyses

A *break-even point* is a special case of cost-benefit analysis. It is the point at which the benefits of a project are equal to the costs. Firms use this type of analysis to determine the point at which the EC investment will pay for itself.

The Total Cost of Ownership

The costs of an IT system may accumulate over many years. An interesting approach for IT cost evaluation is the **total cost of ownership (TCO)**. TCO is a formula for calculating the cost of owning, operating, and controlling an IT system, even one as simple as a PC. The cost includes acquisition costs (hardware and software), operations costs (maintenance, training, operations, evaluation, technical support, installation, downtime, auditing, virus damage, and power consumption), and control costs (standardization, security, central services). The TCO may be 100 percent higher than the cost of the hardware, especially for PCs.

total cost of ownership (TCO)
A formula for calculating the cost of owning, operating, and controlling an IT system.

By identifying these various costs, organizations can make more accurate cost-benefit analyses. A methodology for calculating TCO is offered by David et al. (2002). They also provide a detailed example of the items to be included in TCO calculations. For further discussion, see Vijayan (2001) and Blum (2001). For a comprehensive study of TCO, see Ferrin and Plank (2002).

A similar concept is **total benefits of ownership (TBO)**. This method includes both tangible and intangible benefits. By calculating and comparing TCO and TBO, one can compute the payoff of an IT investment (i.e., *Payoff = TBO – TCO*). For details on TBO calculations, see Devaraj and Kohli (2002).

total benefits of ownership (TBO)
Benefits of ownership that include both tangible and the intangible benefits.

Business ROI

When conducting cost-benefit analyses, it is advisable to distinguish between *business ROI* and *technology ROI.*

Business ROI relates to the EC investment benefits incurred for the improvement of the business and its operations, such as:

- Improved user ability to access all of the resources to deliver key business processes
- Streamlined and lower costs of business processes both inside and outside the organization
- Enablement of people to collaborate across locations to gain operational efficiencies
- Embedded training within the EC application to ensure organizational compliance
- Increased satisfaction among users as well as partners
- Transformation of the organization by streamlining access to information and automating processes such as online filing of expense statements, ordering office supplies, and making travel arrangements

Technology ROI

Technology ROI relates to the EC investment benefits incurred by improvements in the integration of technology and its deployment, such as:

- Architecture that supports continued growth and proliferation of an EC project throughout the organization
- Simplified purchase, use, and deployment of technology

- Establishment of an open development environment to ensure seamless integration and access to information
- Embedded collaboration across all of an organization's applications
- Reduced complexity of managing content, applications, infrastructure, and stand-alone tools

Technology ROI usually is shared by several EC and IT projects, so it is difficult to allocate costs to specific EC projects. Technology ROI often is ignored in traditional ROI analysis, where the focus generally is only on the business ROI. Although the business case and ROI must drive the decision-making process, the technology ROI constitutes the evaluation of soft costs, which, if ignored, can bias the business ROI. Without the rigor of analysis offered by ad-hoc ROI calculators, EC projects may not live up to the scrutiny of financial experts.

ROI Calculators

ROI calculator
Calculator that uses metrics and formulas to compute ROI.

Vendors and consulting companies have accumulated quite a bit of experience in developing metrics and tools called **ROI calculators** to evaluate investments. Recently, companies specializing in ROI also have developed ROI calculators, some of which are in the public domain.

Nucleus Research, Inc. (NRI; nucleusresearch.com), a research and advisory company, uses several ROI calculators in helping businesses evaluate IT investments. Online File W15.1 presents one of NRI's tools that can be used to calculate ROI in a real-world EC investment setting. NRI argues that if a company must make frequent justifications for EC and has unique intangible costs and benefits, it may be necessary to custom build an ROI evaluation tool.

ROI calculators for e-services also are available. For instance, Streaming Media, Inc. (streamingmedia.com) provides an ROI calculator to measure the costs and benefits of telecommunication bandwidth for videoconferencing, streaming video, and video file servers.

Few organizations have attempted to assess the ROI on e-learning, perhaps because it is so difficult to calculate and justify. However, Learnativity.com (learnativity.com) provides resources such as ROI calculators, methodologies, a bibliography, and online communities to support the assessment of e-learning (see learnativity.com/roi-learning.html).

ROI calculators also are available from various other companies, such as Phoenix Technologies (phoenix.com) and Alinean, Inc. (alinean.com). For more examples of ROI calculators, see roi-calc.com, gantrygroup.com, and phormion.com.

Economic Value Added

Economic value added (EVA) attempts to quantify the net value added by an investment. It is the return on invested capital (i.e., after-tax cash flow) generated by a company minus the cost of the capital used in creating the cash flow. If the earnings per share are 10 percent and the cost of capital is 12 percent, the investment reduces rather than adds economic value.

TRADITIONAL (GENERIC) METHODS FOR EVALUATING IT INVESTMENTS

The following are the most popular methods for evaluating IT investments.

Rate of ROI Method

The rate of ROI method uses a formula that divides the net benefits (revenues less costs, for each year) by the initial cost. The result is a ration that measures the ROI for each year, or for an entire period. The formula and an example are provided in Online File W15.1.

Payback Period

With the payback period method, the company calculates how long it will take for the net benefits to pay back the initial investment. The details of this method are provided in Online File W15.1.

Net Present Value

Organizations often use net present value (NPV) calculations for cost-benefit analyses. In an NPV analysis, analysts convert future values of benefits to their present-value equivalents by discounting them at the organization's cost of funds. This requires the analyst to determine a discount rate, which can be the average or the marginal interest rate paid by a company to obtain loans. Then the analyst can compare the present value of the future benefits with the costs required to achieve those benefits to determine whether the benefits exceed the costs. For more specific guidelines and decision criteria on how NPV analysis works, consult a financial management textbook.

ADVANCED METHODS FOR EVALUATING IT AND EC INVESTMENTS

A comprehensive list of over 60 different appraisal and justification methods for IT investments can be found in Renkema (2000). For details of some of these and other methods, see McKay and Marshall (2004). Most justification methods can be categorized into the following four types:

- **Financial approaches.** These appraisal methods consider only those impacts that can be valued monetarily. They focus on incoming and outgoing cash flows as a result of the investment made. NPV and ROI are examples of financial-approach methods.
- **Multicriteria approaches.** These appraisal methods consider both financial impacts and nonfinancial impacts that cannot be (or cannot easily be) expressed in monetary terms. These methods employ quantitative and qualitative decision-making techniques. Examples include information economics, balanced scorecard, and value analysis (see Online File W15.3).

- **Ratio approaches.** These methods use several ratios to assist in IT investment evaluation (e.g., IT expenditures versus total turnover). The metrics used usually are financial in nature, but other types of metrics can be used as well. An example of this would be IT expenditures divided by annual sales or IT expenditures as a percentage of the operating budget.
- **Portfolio approaches.** These methods apply portfolios (or grids) to plot several investment proposals against decision-making criteria. Portfolio methods are more informative than multicriteria methods and generally use fewer evaluation criteria. These are very complex; for more information see Hovenden et al. (2005).

The following representative methods are particularly useful in evaluating EC investment: value analysis, information economics, benchmarks, management by maxim, real-option valuation, activity-based costing, and economic value added:

- **Value analysis.** With the **value analysis** method, the organization evaluates intangible benefits using a low-cost, trial EC system before deciding whether to commit a larger investment in a complete system.
- **Information economics.** Using the idea of critical success factors, this method focuses on key organizational objectives and the potential impacts of the proposed EC project on each of them.
- **Scoring methodology.** This method assigns weights and scores to various aspects of the evaluated project (e.g., weights to each metric) and then calculates a total score. Information economics methods are used to determine the aspects to include in the scoring.
- **Benchmarks.** This method is appropriate for evaluating EC infrastructure. Using industry standards, for example, the organization can determine what the industry is spending on e-CRM. Then the organization can decide how much it should spend. Benchmarks may be industry metrics or best practices recommended by professional associations or consultants.
- **Management by maxim.** An organization may use this method to determine how much it should invest in large EC (and IT) infrastructures. It is basically a combination of brainstorming and consensus-reaching methodologies.
- **Real-options valuation.** This is a fairly complex assessment method, and it is used only infrequently. It can be fairly accurate in certain situations. The idea behind this method is to look at future opportunities that may result from the EC investment and then place monetary values on them.

value analysis
Method where a company evaluates intangible benefits using a low-cost, trial EC system before deciding whether to commit a larger investment to a complete system.

EXHIBIT 15.4 Methods of Evaluating EC and IT Investments

Method	Advantages	Disadvantages
Internal rate of return (IRR)	Brings all projects to common footing. Conceptually familiar.	Assumes reinvestment at same rate. Can have multiple roots. No assumed discount rate.
Net present value (NPV) or net worth (NW)	Very common. Maximizes value for unconstrained project selection.	Difficult to compare projects of unequal lives or sizes.
Payback period	May be discounted or nondiscounted. Measure of exposure.	Ignores flows after payback is reached. Assumes standard project cash flow profile.
Benefit-to-cost analysis or ratio	Conceptually familiar. Brings all projects to common footing.	May be difficult to classify outlays as expenses or investments.
Economic value added	Measures net value created for the stakeholder.	The true benefits can be difficult to measure.
Real options	Measures cascading opportunities beyond primary benefits (e.g., flexibility and agility to respond to market changes).	The competitive conditions may change, but the business must still bear the cost of the option.

- **Balanced scorecard.** This method evaluates the health or performance of the organization by looking at a broad set of factors, not just financial ones. It is becoming a popular tool for assessing EC projects.
- **Performance dashboard.** This is a variant of the balanced scorecard that is used widely in e-business situations. A **dashboard** is a single view that provides the status of multiple metrics.
- **Activity-based costing.** This managerial accounting concept was adapted for assessing EC investments in recent years and has been proven to be fairly successful.

dashboard
A single view that provides the status of multiple metrics.

More information on these methods is provided in Online File W15.3.

Unfortunately, none of these methods is perfect or universal. Therefore, one needs to look at the advantages and disadvantages of each. Exhibit 15.4 provides a summary of the major methods of evaluating EC and their advantages and disadvantages. Exhibit 15.5 shows the popularity (or use) of the major methods.

EXHIBIT 15.5 Popularity of the Various Justification Methods

Technique	Percentage Who Use It
ROI	44
Internal ROI	40
Activity-based costing	37
Company-specific measure	36
Net present value	35
Economic value added	29
Balanced scorecard	24
Return on assets	24
Return on equity	18
Portfolio management	16
Applied information economics	9
Real options	6

Source: Compiled from *CIO Insight* (2004).

Section 15.3 ▶ REVIEW QUESTIONS

1. List the items that constitute the business ROI and the technical ROI for an EC portal application.
2. What are the components of the balanced scorecard?
3. What are ROI calculators?
4. Define the economic value added method.
5. Describe the real-options method.

15.4 EXAMPLES OF EC PROJECT JUSTIFICATION

The methods and tools described in the previous section can be used alone, in combination, or with modifications to justify different EC projects. Here we provide a few examples of how these methods and tools can be used to justify different types of EC projects.

E-PROCUREMENT

E-procurement (see Chapter 5) is not limited to just buying and selling; it also encompasses the various processes involved in buying and selling: selecting suppliers, submitting formal requests for goods and services to suppliers, getting approval from buyers, processing purchase orders, fulfilling orders, delivering and receiving items, and processing payments.

Given the diversity of activities involved in e-procurement, the metrics used to measure the value of e-procurement must reflect how well each process is accomplished. However, the focus on the metrics used will differ for buyers and sellers. For example, *buyers* will be interested in metrics such as how quickly they can locate a seller; *sellers* will be most interested in click-to-release time, (i.e., the time that elapsed from when the customer clicked to buy an item online until the warehouse staff had a ticket to pick and pack the order). For examples of e-procurement metrics, see Insights and Additions 15.1. Setting metrics for e-procurement is especially difficult when procurement is done in exchanges (see Online File W15.4). One solution to ease such problems is the use of Web Services (see Online File W15.5).

CUSTOMER SERVICE AND E-CRM

Customer service and e-CRM (Chapter 13) can be provided in a number of different ways. For example, Lowe's seeks to improve customer service on its Web site (lowes.com) by providing a "do it yourself" information portal (e.g., offering information about how to install a ceiling fan or fix paint problems). Such information may already be available online and used by the company to train service personnel. EC-based banking sites often add customer value by lowering risks and providing information relating to the last successful log on and the number of unsuccessful log-on attempts. Online prescription drug companies such as Medco Health Solutions (medcohealth.com) proactively provide information via e-mail on prescription refills and warn consumers of drug recalls.

Recent surveys of e-CRM applications have continued to show mixed payoffs. Only a fraction of companies have been able to demonstrate positive ROI for their e-CRM investments. What can we learn from those companies that have successfully deployed e-CRM and have extracted significant business value? For answers, look at Insights and Additions 15.2.

The issues in assessing the ROI of e-CRM also are echoed in a report from a survey of small- and medium-sized enterprises (SMEs) conducted by the Yankee Group, an IT consulting company. The Yankee Group found that CRM-based EC applications are effective only when they are part of a company's overall business plan and not just an EC investment (Kingston 2004). The Yankee Group report outlines key e-CRM metrics in three areas: sales, marketing, and service, as shown in Exhibit 15.6. These CRM success metrics can also be viewed as tangible, intangible, and risk-related measures. For instance, financial tangible metrics are represented by revenue per salesperson; marketing dollars and efficiency metrics are captured in the average time to close and average response time. Intangible metrics are captured as customer satisfaction and call quality. Although financial and efficiency measures can also be classified as risk measures, risk metrics in the Yankee Group report are captured through the

Insights and Additions 15.1 E-Procurement Metrics

Measuring the success of e-procurement is in many ways similar to measuring the success of the purchasing department. Some direct measures involve the company's ability to secure quality, cost-effective materials and supplies that are delivered on time. The following metrics indicate progress in e-procurement:

- Increased order fulfillment rate
- Increased on-time deliveries
- Decreased number of rejects received from suppliers
- Decreased purchase order processing time
- Decreased prices due to increased supplier visibility and order aggregation
- Decreased ratio of freight costs to purchases

Indirect metrics include minimized costs, including:

- Reduced inventory costs
- Reduced raw material costs
- Reduced rework costs
- Reduced operating costs
- Reduced freight costs

E-procurement can directly or indirectly affect these metrics. Measuring and monitoring e-procurement activities is crucial to identifying both problematic and successful areas. It provides insight into what an organization is doing right and wrong so that it can pinpoint which activities it needs to investigate and adjust.

The University of Pennsylvania measures e-procurement performance through several metrics, as shown here.

E-Procurement Performance Metrics and KPIs at the University of Pennsylvania

Performance Metric	Description	Sample Metrics
Customer satisfaction	Customer satisfaction and performance surveys	• Ease of ordering • Ability to find items
Spend management	Utilization of University-authorized buying methods	• Dollars spent • Percent of purchases
Strategic contracting	Specific and group purchasing contracting activity	• Total purchasing contracts
Contract utilization	Preferred contract supplier purchase activity	• Percent of total purchase order dollars with preferred contract suppliers
Group purchasing	Group purchasing organization supplier	• Total group purchase order dollars purchase activity
E-procurement enablement	Penn Marketplace supplier purchase activity	• Total number of marketplace-participating suppliers
Diversity inclusion	Diversity and local community supplier purchase activity	• Number of diversity suppliers
Electronic invoicing	EDI purchase order invoice transaction activity	• Percent of invoices processed via EDI
Cost savings	Formal cost containment activity	• Total cost containment program savings • Year-to-date savings
Electronic sourcing	Online formal competitive bidding initiatives	• Annual savings by major product category
Supplier rationalization	Strategic supplier rationalization activities	• Number of deactivated suppliers and dollar amounts
Transaction audits	Purchasing card utilization audits for e-procurement suppliers	• Transaction leakage (amount purchased from participating suppliers outside of e-procurement)
Electronic marketing	Showcase electronic marketing activity	• Number of visitors

Table source: Modified from a table on the University of Pennsylvania Web site (*purchasing.upenn.edu/about/performance.php*).

Sources: Compiled from Minahan (2004) and Cisco Systems (2005).

Insights and Additions 15.2 Assessing E-CRM ROI

Pisello (2004) argues that the biggest problem in CRM evaluation is a failure to define and measure success. Additionally, most companies say that when it comes to determining value, intangible benefits are more significant than tangible cost savings. Yet companies often fail to establish KPIs in order to judge these intangible benefits. A formal business plan must be in place before the e-CRM project begins—one that quantifies the expected costs, tangible financial benefits, and intangible strategic benefits, as well as the risks. The plan should include an assessment of the following:

- **Tangible net benefits.** The plan must include a clear and precise cost-benefit analysis that lists all of the planned project costs and tangible benefits. This portion of the plan should also contain a strategy for assessing key financial metrics, such as ROI, NPV, and internal rate of return (IRR) an accounting measure of interest (discount) rate that makes the NPV of an investment zero; this makes the present value of a future cash flow equal the invested amount (i.e., NPV = 0). It should specify a payback period.
- **Intangible benefits.** The plan should detail the expected intangible benefits, and it should list the KPIs that will be used to measure successes and shortfalls. Often, an improvement in customer satisfaction is the primary goal of the e-CRM solution, but in many cases this key value is not measured before and after the project.
- **Risk assessment.** The risk assessment is a list of all of the potential pitfalls related to the people, processes, and technology that are involved in the e-CRM project. Having such a list helps to lessen the probability that problems will occur. And, if they do occur, a company may find that, by having listed and considered the problems in advance, the problems are more manageable than they would have been otherwise.

Assessing the issues in implementation costs, benefits, and risks helps establish a business case for the project and helps in postproject success measurement.

Implementation Costs

Implementation costs often are split between EC and IT costs and business-unit costs.

EC and IT costs include the following:

- E-CRM software licensing and support contracts
- Licensing and support contracts for EDI tools, databases, operating systems, and other software
- Hardware purchases and support contracts, specifically server-, storage-, and network-related expenses.
- Software integration and customization, including design, development, testing, and maintenance
- Implementation labor
- Ongoing administration and support labor

Business-unit costs include the following:

- Planning and requirements meetings
- User training and learning time
- Process change management

Tangible and Intangible Benefits

Benefits typically include increases in staff productivity, cost avoidance, revenues, and margins, and reduced inventory costs (due to the elimination of errors). The following are some of the objectives that should be considered:

- Reduce the cost of sales.
- Reduce sales administration overhead.
- Improve the lead-to-sale closure ratio.
- Increase customer retention.
- Improve customer satisfaction and loyalty.

Potential Pitfalls and Risks

Some potential pitfalls of e-CRM include the following:

- Taking on more than can be delivered. The e-CRM solution should target specific sales or service business functions or specific groups of users. Additionally, it is essential to manage the project's scope, goals, and objectives throughout the project-development phase and deployment.
- Getting over budget and behind schedule.
- Poor user adoption. Ease of use and adequate training are essential.
- Expensive maintenance and support.
- Isolation. The effectiveness of a project may suffer if the CRM data are not used throughout the company.
- Garbage in–garbage out. Because e-CRM systems require so much data entry, users often put in placeholders, misguided estimates, or inaccurate information, which leads to poor analytical results and decision-making errors.
- Failure to measure success. Measurement of preproject status and postproject achievements is essential for a company to show success.

Teradata Corp. (*teradata.com*) offers an approach for measuring the ROI for CRM that begins with setting ROI objectives and ends with tracking CRM performance over time, analyzing it, and revising and refining CRM efforts accordingly (*teradata.com* 2004).

Sources: Pisello, T. "CRM ROI: Facts or Fiction?" *CIO.com* February 3, 2004. Adapted with permission.

EXHIBIT 15.6 Key Metrics for Measuring CRM Success

Sales	Marketing	Service
Revenue per sales person	Marketing dollars as a percentage of revenue	First-call resolution rate
Average sale cycle; average deal size	Average return on marketing	Call quality (as measured by quality monitoring)
Sales representative turnover rate	Total leads generated	Voice service level (by type of call)
New rep ramp time	Average response rate	E-mail service level (by type of e-mail)
Average administrative time/rep	Lead qualification rate	Average speed of answer
Percentage of representatives that achieve quota	Lead close rate	Abandon rate
Average time to close	Percent of marketing collateral used by sales representatives	Average handle time
Average price discount	Change in market penetration	Cost per contact (calls, e-mail)
Percentage of accurate forecasted opportunities	Improved time-to-market	Average call value
Average number of calls to close deal	Number of feedback points	Average close rate
Average number of presentations necessary to close deal	Marketing execution time	Agent turnover
Average number of proposals needed to close the deal	Message close rate	Customer satisfaction
Average win rate	Marketing dollars as a percentage of revenue	Accuracy of data entered (e.g., trouble tickets)

Source: Kingstone, S. "The Financial Realities of CRM: A Guide to Best Practices, TCO and ROI," Boston, MA: The Yankee Group, 2004. page 7. Exhibit 6.

first-call resolution rate and the accuracy of the data entered (listed under the "Service" column of Exhibit 15.6). These metrics constitute what is of value to the EC sellers and buyers.

JUSTIFYING A PORTAL

In making the case for investing in a Web portal, Bisconti (2004) suggests that the fundamental business case should be made from the internal and external perspectives of the business. The internal payoff must result in productivity improvements, whereas the external value is determined by revenue generation. In the Welch's example (Online File W15.6), we consider the benefits that Welch's extracted from its corporate portal, such as reduced customer complaint calls and/or cross-selling of products. Although several commercial portal development environments are available, large companies may consider building theirs in-house. Bisconti argues that metrics and ROI analysis can serve as a prerequisite to the build-versus-buy decision.

Large companies often have an array of intranet and other information systems; the integration of these systems becomes key to the success of the portal. Thus, the compatibility and flexibility of the portal technology becomes paramount. Bisconti asserts that justification for a portal must focus on business ROI as well as technology ROI. For examples of ROI of portals, see Plumtree Corp. (2001).

JUSTIFYING E-TRAINING PROJECTS

The pervasive use of IT means that knowledge of and the ability to use IT is essential, no matter what kind of work is being done. Whether in a government agency or a multinational corporation, inadequate employee IT skills will undermine the day-to-day functioning of any organization.

End-user training that helps employees acquire or improve their IT skills plays a key role in ensuring the smooth operation of organizations in the information economy. However, such training and retraining can be expensive, slow, and ineffective. Therefore, a large number of organizations are considering e-training (Chapter 8) to supplement or substitute traditional classroom training.

When comparing e-training and traditional training methods, several factors, most of which are intangible, must be evaluated. Mahaptra and Lai (2005) developed a framework

EXHIBIT 15.7 Factors to Consider in Evaluating E-Training

Evaluation Level	Evaluator	Factors to Evaluate
Technology	Training provider	• Effectiveness of IT in supporting training-related tasks • Ease of use and usefulness of IT-based tools used by training providers
	Trainee	• Delivery and presentation of training materials • Ease of use and usefulness of communication tools
Reaction	Trainee	• Relevance of the course to the trainee's job • Satisfaction with course content and presentation • Quality of instruction • Effectiveness of instructor • Overall satisfaction with the training experience
Skill acquisition	Trainee	• Knowledge and skill learned
Skill transfer	Trainee	• Ability to apply the skill learned at work
	Manager	• Effect of the training on the trainee's performance
Organizational effect	Manager	• Effect of the training on organizational goal achievement

Source: Mahapatra, R., and Vincent S. Lai. "Evaluating End-User Training Programs." *Communications of the ACM*, January 2005. © 2005 ACM, Inc. Used with permission.

for evaluating end-user training. Exhibit 15.7 shows some of the metrics that may be included in such an evaluation. In executing such a justification, the organization also needs to consider the financial factors of e-training versus traditional training methods.

JUSTIFYING AN INVESTMENT IN RFID

Many medium and large corporations are considering implementing RFID systems to improve their supply chain operations (see Chapter 7). Although such systems offer many tangible benefits that can be defined, many measures cannot be developed due to the fact that the technology is new and that legal requirements (for privacy protection) are still evolving. For a discussion of RFID justification, see Online File W15.7.

JUSTIFYING SECURITY PROJECTS

More than 85 percent of viruses enter business networks via e-mail. Cleaning up infections is labor intensive, but antivirus scanning is not. ROI calculators are available to judge the cost of using an expert to decontaminate a system versus the use of software to keep the system virus free (Keepmedia.com 2005).

Employee security training is usually poorly done. Employees told what to do, with little or no time devoted to why specific security rules are in place. ROI calculators are available to estimate the cost for training sessions with enough time to explain "why," allowing workers to understand the consequences of ignoring or misusing security procedures. (Ross 2005).

Section 15.4 ▸ REVIEW QUESTIONS

1. List five success factors for e-procurement.
2. List five performance metrics for e-procurement.
3. List three tangible and three intangible benefits of e-CRM.
4. List some metrics that can be used to justify e-training.

15.5 THE ECONOMICS OF EC

EC business models and applications have capabilities that may change several economic factors and trade-off relationships. These, in turn, provide the advantages of EC over traditional commerce. For example, with online purchases the incremental or variable costs of delivering digital content to individual customers or of processing transactions are very low and, therefore, the market for EC is large and growing rapidly.

The economic environment of e-commerce is broad and diversified. In this section, we present only representative topics that are related to the traditional economic profit formula:

Profit = Revenues − Production costs − Transaction costs

E-commerce helps to decrease costs and increase revenues, resulting in increased profits.

PRODUCTION COSTS

Production costs are the costs to produce the product or service a company is selling. E-commerce makes a major contribution to lower production costs. For example, e-procurement may result in cost reductions. Much of intrabusiness EC deals with cost reductions. These reductions are expressed in the following economic principles.

Increasing Returns to Scale

Economist Brian Arthur (1996) describes the economic theory of increasing returns by starting with the familiar concept that the economy is divided into different sectors: one that produces physical products and another that focuses on information. Producers of physical products (e.g., foodstuffs, petroleum, automobiles) are subject to *decreasing returns*. Although producers may have initial increasing economies of scale, they eventually reach a point where costs increase faster than revenues when they produce more of the product, and additional production becomes less and less profitable (Exhibit 15.8).

network effects
Effects created when leading products in an industry attract a base of users, which leads to the development of complementary products, further strengthening the position of the dominant product.

lock-in effect
Effect created when users do not switch to another site because of barriers posed by having to learn new site navigation systems and transaction processes.

Arthur (1996) notes that in the information economy, the situation is very different. For example, initial costs to develop new software are very high, but the cost of producing additional copies is very low. The result is *increasing returns*, where profitability rises more rapidly when production increases (Exhibit 15.8). This enables a company to command high market share. A firm with a high market share can use its additional profits to improve the product or to enhance marketing in order to strengthen its leading position.

In addition to higher profitability, two other factors favor firms with higher market share. The first is **network effects**. The leading products in an industry attract a base of users, and this base leads to the development of complementary products, further strengthening the position of the dominant product. For instance, eBay and Amazon.com both have used their large market share to increase product variety and offer new services.

The second factor is the **lock-in effect**. Moving to a new Web site usually requires the user to understand the manner in which transactions are conducted and to learn to navigate the new

EXHIBIT 15.8 Increasing Versus Decreasing Returns

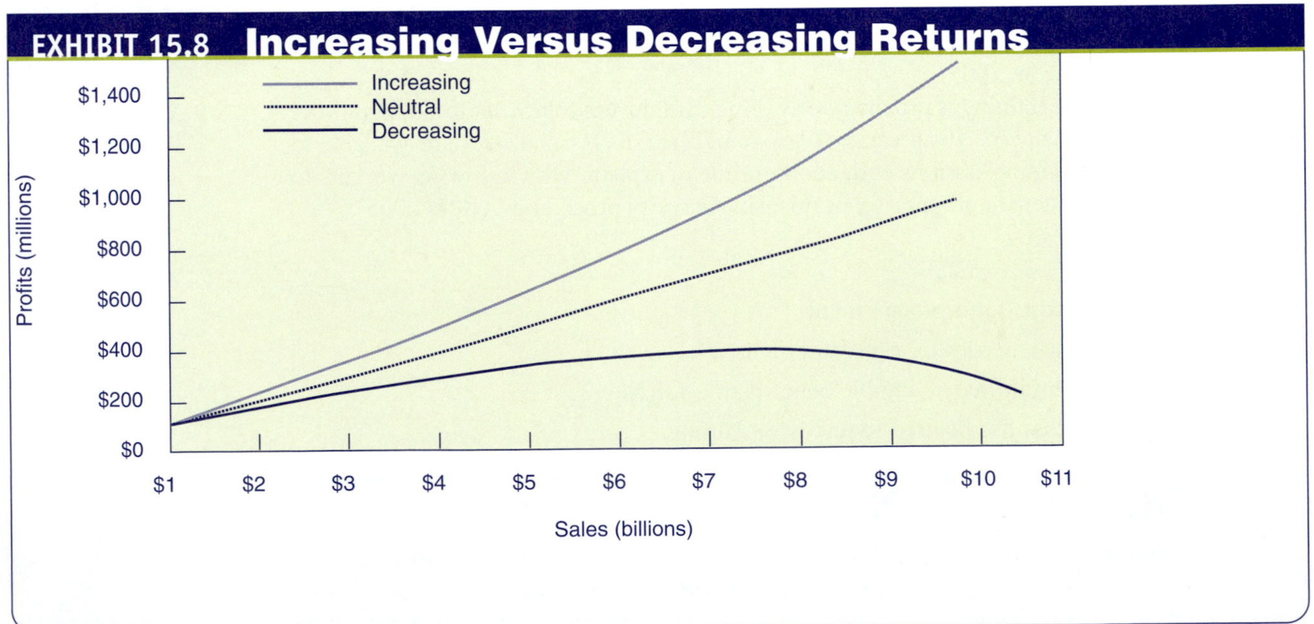

site, so users typically will not switch to a different Web site unless it is much more powerful or they are forced into making the change. For instance, when customers input their credit card information, shipping address, preferences, and other personal details into a form on a Web site, switching to another vendor will require reentry of that data. Amazon.com provides customers with its 1-click technology so that they do not have to reenter data with every new order.

Product Cost Curves

The **average-cost curve (AVC)** represents the behavior of average costs as quantity changes. The AVC of many physical products and services is U shaped (see Exhibit 15.9a). This curve indicates that, at first, as quantity increases, the average cost declines. As quantity increases still more, the cost goes back up due to increasing variable costs (especially administrative and marketing costs) and fixed costs (more management is needed) in the short run. However, the variable cost per unit of digital products is very low (in most cases) and almost fixed (once the initial investment is recovered), regardless of the quantity. Therefore, as shown in Exhibit 15.9b, with digital products the average cost per unit declines as quantity increases, because the fixed costs are spread (prorated) over more units. This relationship results in increasing returns with increased sales.

average-cost curve (AVC)
Behavior of average costs as quantity changes; generally, as quantity increases, average costs decline.

Production Function

The **production function**, shown in Exhibit 15.10a, represents a mathematical formula that indicates that for the same quantity of production, Q, companies either can use a certain amount of labor or invest in more automation (e.g., they can substitute IT capital for labor). For example, for a quantity $Q = 1{,}000$, the lower the amount of labor needed, the higher the required IT investment (capital costs). When EC enters the picture, it shifts the function inward (from L_1 to L_2), lowering the amount of labor and/or capital needed to produce the same $Q = 1{,}000$.

Kleist (2003) points to the importance of production function outcomes in evaluating whether EC really leads to greater production output or if results are simply increased page views and "eyeballs," as has been the case with many Web-based technologies. Hahn and Kauffman (2004) applied the production function to EC by treating the functionalities of a Web site as inputs and the completed Web transactions as the outputs to arrive at the effectiveness of EC applications. Such a value-driven approach is a simple as well as goal-oriented way to measure the effectiveness of EC investments.

production function
An equation indicating that for the same quantity of production, Q, companies either can use a certain amount of labor or invest in more automation.

Agency Costs

Exhibit 15.10b shows the economics of the firm's **agency costs** (or *administrative costs*). These are the costs incurred in ensuring that certain support and administrative tasks related to production are performed as intended (e.g., by an agent). In the "old economy," agency

agency costs
Costs incurred in ensuring that the agent performs tasks as expected (also called *administrative costs*).

EXHIBIT 15.9 Cost Curve of (a) Regular and (b) Digital Products

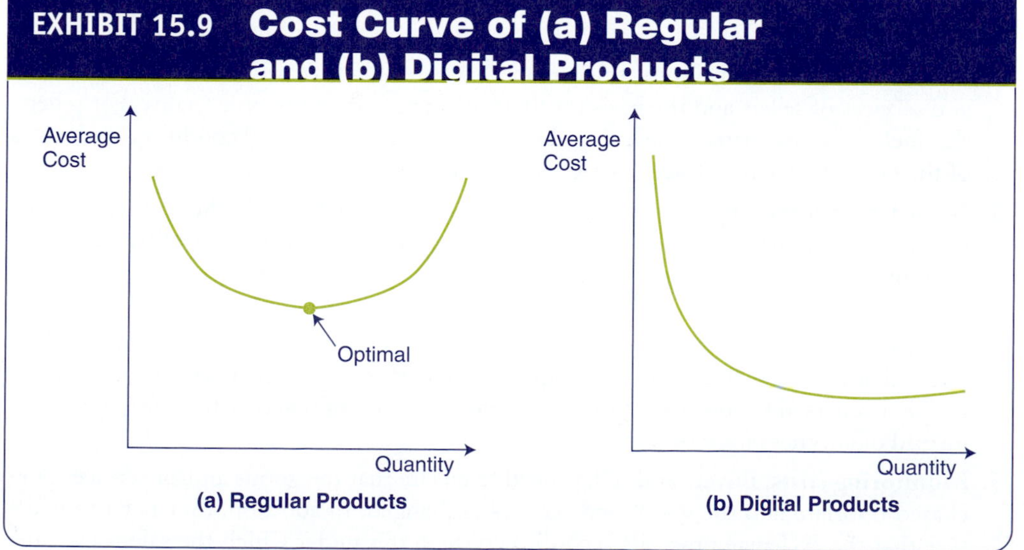

EXHIBIT 15.10 **The Economic Effects of EC: The Production Function and Agency Costs**

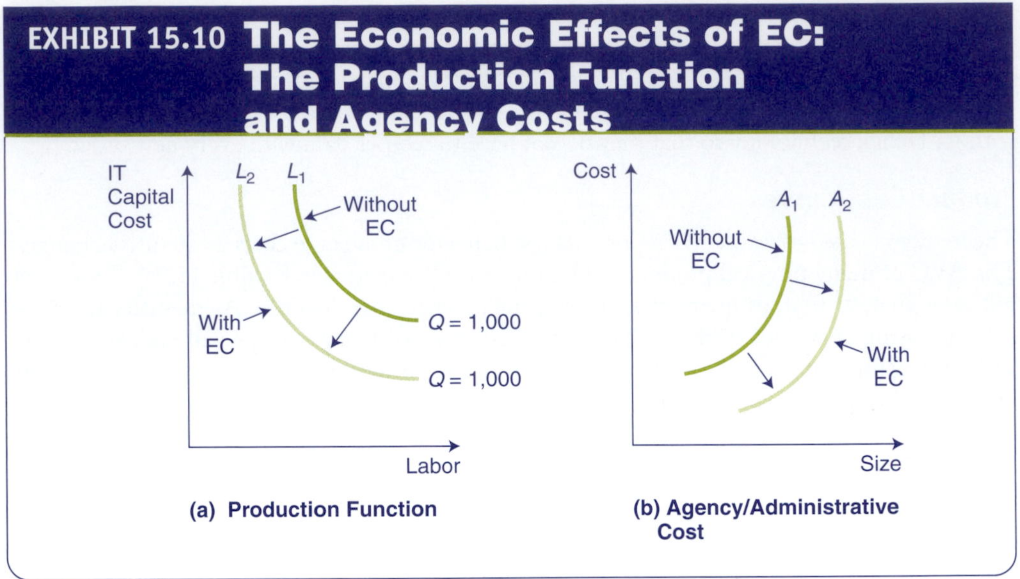

costs (A_1) grew with the size (and complexity) of the firm, reaching a high level of cost quickly, and frequently preventing companies from growing to a very large size. In the digital economy, the agency costs curve is shifted outward, to A_2. This means that as a result of EC, companies can significantly expand their business without too much of an increase in administrative costs before a high level of cost is reached.

Balance between EC investments and administrative and other infrastructure costs must be achieved. Kleist (2003) cautions that returns on EC investments may peak at a certain point, and upon reaching that point businesses may not see many additional benefits, especially when compared with other types of investments, such as those in warehouses, machinery, and the sales force. The key, according to Kleist, is that businesses should identify a mix of optimal EC administrative and infrastructure investments to maximize production from total investments. When computing agency cost, only production-related cost should be considered and transaction cost should be disregarded.

Transaction Costs

transaction costs
Costs that are associated with the distribution (sale) and/or exchange of products and services including the cost of searching for buyers and sellers, gathering information, negotiating, decision making, monitoring the exchange of goods, and legal fees.

Transaction costs cover a wide range of costs that are associated with the distribution (sale) and/or exchange of products and services. Most economists (e.g., Chen 2005) divide these costs into the following six categories:

1. **Search costs.** Buyers and sellers incur costs in locating each other and in locating specific products and services.
2. **Information costs.** For buyers, this includes costs related to learning about the products and services of sellers and the basis for their cost, profit margins, and quality. For sellers, this includes costs related to learning about the legitimacy, financial condition, and needs of the buyer, which may lead to a higher or lower price.
3. **Negotiation costs.** Buyers and sellers need to agree on the terms of the sale (e.g., quantity, quality, shipments, financing, etc.) Negotiation costs result from meetings, communication-related expenses, exchanges of technical data and/or brochures, entertainment, and legal costs.
4. **Decision costs.** For buyers, decision costs result from the evaluation of sellers and their internal processes, such as purchasing approval, to ensure that they meet the buyers' policies. For sellers, decision costs arise in the determination of whether to sell to one buyer instead of another buyer, or not at all.
5. **Monitoring costs.** Buyers and sellers need to ensure that the goods and/or services purchased translate into the goods and services exchanged. In addition, they need to make sure that the exchange proceeds according to the terms under which the sale was made.

This may require transaction monitoring, inspection of goods, and negotiations over late or inadequate deliveries or payments.

6. **Legal-related costs.** Buyers and sellers need to ensure that unsatisfied terms are remedied. Legal-related costs include costs that arise from fixing defects and providing substitutions and agreeing on discounts and other penalties. They also include litigation costs in the event of a legal dispute.

As we have seen throughout the book, e-commerce can reduce all of these costs. For example, search engines and comparison bots can be used to reduce search costs and information costs. EC also can drastically reduce the costs of monitoring, collaborating, and negotiating.

One aspect of transaction cost is reflected in Exhibit 15.11. As can be seen in the exhibit, there is a trade-off between transaction cost and size (volume of business). Traditionally, in order to reduce transaction costs, firms had to grow in size (as depicted in curve T_1). In the digital economy, the transaction cost curve is shifted downward, to position T_2. This means that EC makes it possible to have low transaction costs even with smaller firm size and to enjoy much lower transaction costs as firm size increases.

INCREASED REVENUES

Throughout the text, we have demonstrated how an organization can use EC to increase revenues through online storefronts, auctions, cross-selling opportunities, multichannel distribution arrangements, and so on. EC can also be used to improve reach and richness.

Reach Versus Richness

Another economic impact of EC is the trade-off between the number of customers a company can reach (called *reach*) and the amount of interactions and information services it can provide to them (*richness*). According to Evans and Wurster (2000), for a given level of cost (resources), there is a trade-off between reach and richness. The more customers a company wants to reach, the fewer services it can provide to them. This economic relationship is depicted in Exhibit 15.12a. With EC, the curve can be shifted outward.

Exhibit 15.12b shows the implementation of the reach versus richness trade-off at Charles Schwab. Initially, Schwab attempted to increase its reach. To do so, the company went downward along the curve, reducing its richness. However, with its Web site (schwab.com) (depicted by the upward arrow in Exhibit 15.12b), Schwab was able to drastically increase its reach and at the same time provide richness in terms of customer service and financial information to customers. For example, Schwab's *Mutual Fund Screener* allows customers to design their own investment portfolios by selecting from an array of mutual funds. Providing such services (richness) allows Schwab to increase the number of customers (reach), as well as charge higher fees than competitors that provide few value-added services. In summary, the Internet pushes the curve outward

EXHIBIT 15.11 The Economic Effects of EC: Transaction Costs

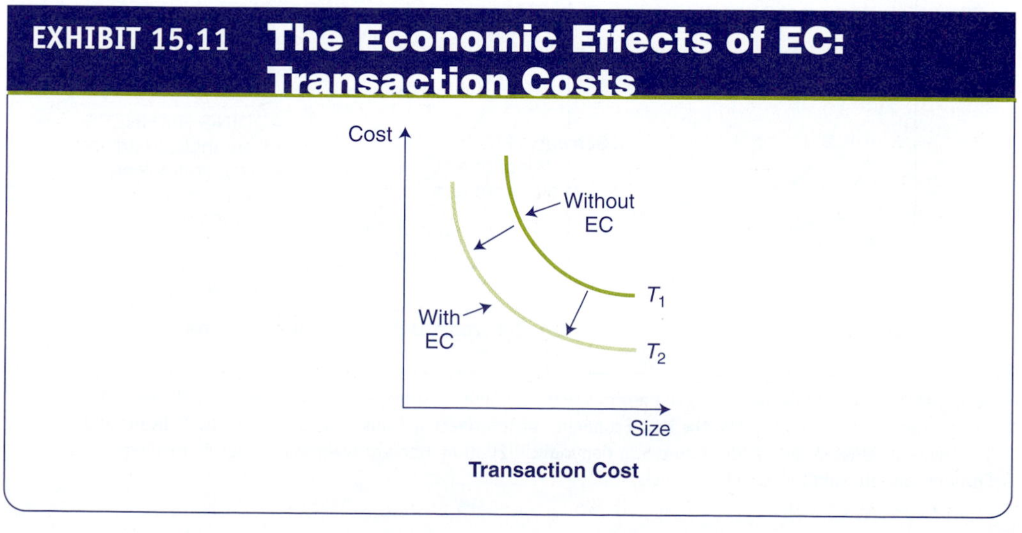

toward the upper right-hand corner of the chart, allowing more reach with the same cost. For additional details, see Slywotzkty and Morrison (2001) and Jelassi and Enders (2005).

Other Ways to Increase Revenues

Straub (2004) suggests other ways that EC can be used to increase revenues:

- Increased revenues via products or services from a larger global market because of more effective product marketing on the Web
- Increased margins attained by using processes with lower internal cost (e.g., using lower-cost computers) and from higher prices because of value-added services to the customer (e.g., information attached to product)
- Increased revenues as a consequence of becoming an online portal
- Value-added content sold from selling searches, access to data, and electronic documents

The remainder of this section deals with some other issues related to the economics of EC.

REDUCING TRANSACTION FRICTION OR RISK

Kambil (2001) suggests that organizations can increase the value of their products or services by using the unique capabilities of EC to reduce risks to consumers, such as those involving psychological relationships, quality concerns, delays, and financial transactions.

Psychological risks can be reduced by allowing the customer to utilize an EC-based calculator and avoid potentially embarrassing situations. For example, online tracking tools reduce psychological risk by allowing customers to check the status of a package. By publishing specifications and providing product comparison engines, EC can help reduce a customer's risk of purchasing an unwanted product or one of poor quality. EC also has been instrumental in providing customers with an accurate picture of product availability, helping them to avoid the risk of unexpected delays. EC also can mitigate customer concerns over the security of EC transactions. Finally, customer concerns over privacy and security can be addressed by linking the transaction to third-party security providers such as the Better Business Bureau or VeriSign. In this way, EC can provide value by lowering the transaction friction or risk and providing the customer with *economic value.*

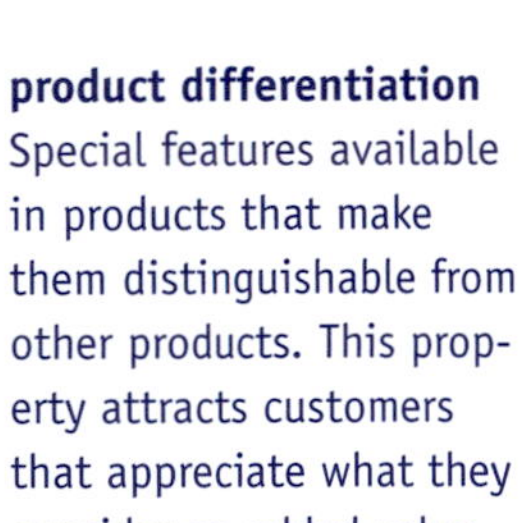
product differentiation Special features available in products that make them distinguishable from other products. This property attracts customers that appreciate what they consider an added value.

PRODUCT DIFFERENTIATION

EC can be exploited to provide greater value to customers by enabling product differentiation. Organizations can use EC to provide **product differentiation**—products with special features. For example, McAfee allows users of its VirusScan virus-detection software to

EXHIBIT 15.12 Reach Versus Richness

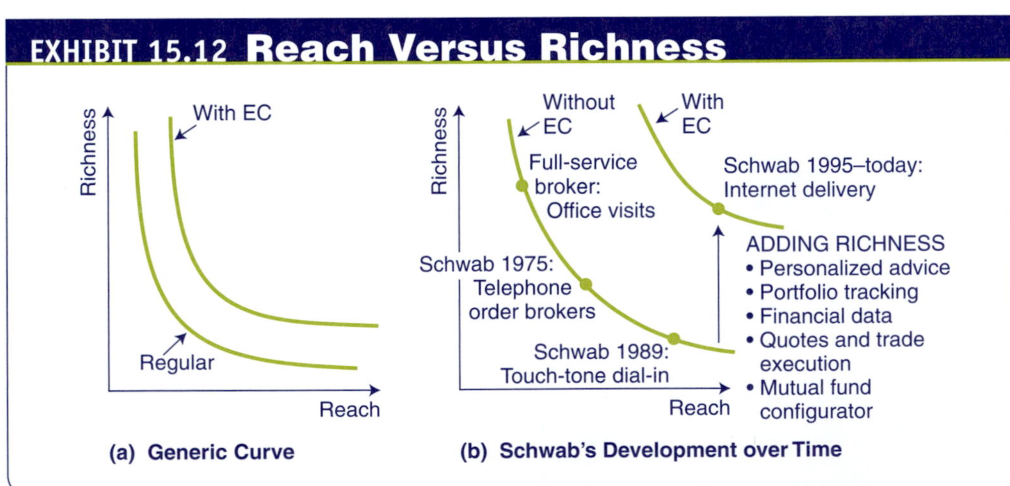

Sources: Part (a) was developed by the authors. Part (b) Reprinted by permission of Harvard Business School Press. From "Blown to Bits: How the New Economics of Information Transforms Strategy," by P. Evans and T. S. Wurster. Boston, MA: 2000, figure 5.2. Copyright © 2000 by Harvard Business School Publishing Corporation, all rights reserved.

update the latest security patches online, differentiating itself from those that require manual upgrades. Differentiation does not necessarily require a physical product; services also can be differentiated. EC can provide differentiation through better product information, informing users on how to use the product, how to replenish it, and how to supply feedback.

AGILITY

EC can provide firms with the **agility** to monitor, report, and quickly respond to changes in the marketplace. Companies with agile systems can respond to customer requests quickly, improving customer service. FedEx, UPS, and other delivery companies can provide location information because they use EC to connect with customers and make available package tracking information. EC systems enable companies to learn more about customers and understand their buying habits. This enables a company to better predict trends for better planning and quickly introducing changes when needed. Similarly, e-procurement has given firms the ability to quickly locate sellers and place orders. Sellers, in turn, use e-fulfillment to quickly locate products in their warehouses and fill customer orders.

agility
An EC firm's ability to capture, report and quickly respond to changes happening in the marketplace.

MARKETS AND E-MARKETS

As described in Chapter 2, a *market* is a medium for the exchange of goods, services, and information between many potential buyers and many potential sellers. Electronic markets are markets in which the exchanges are conducted electronically among buyers, sellers, market employees, and support services, (e.g., financial institutions) in an *efficient* and *effective* manner (see Malone et al. 1989). E-markets are more efficient because they increase the amount of information, the speed at which it is sent, and its accuracy. At the same time, they may reduce the flow of physical goods. For example, as described in Online File W6.1, in a B2B flower exchange, it is not necessary to bring the flowers to the auction place. The flowers can go directly from a seller to a buyer. The same is true for many other goods, such as used cars.

WWW

Even if the flow of physical goods is not decreased, the information provided in e-markets makes participants more informed, and therefore better able to make decisions. This helps in reducing market friction, which benefits the entire economy by making it more efficient. This is the primary reason why many governments provide incentives for e-commerce (see Davis and Benamati 2003).

VALUATION

Valuation is the process of trying to determine the value or worth of a company. It is done for the purpose of selling a company or determining its value for a proposed merger. In the EC context, valuation often is conducted to determine a reasonable IPO price when a company goes public.

valuation
The fair market value of a business or the price at which a property would change hands between a willing buyer and a willing seller who are both informed and under no compulsion to act. For a publicly traded company, the value can be readily obtained by the price the stock is selling over the exchange.

Many valuation methods exist. The three most common ones, according to Rayport and Jaworski (2002), are the comparable method, the financial performance method, and the venture capital method:

- **The comparable method.** With this method, analysts compare the company with similar companies on as many factors as possible (e.g., size, industry, customer base, products, growth rate, book value, debt, sales, financial performance). In addition, they may look at performance trends, management teams, and other features. A major difficulty with this method is finding such information for privately held companies.
- **The financial performance method.** This method uses projections of future earnings (usually 5 years), cash flows, and so on to find the NPV of a company. With this method, the analyst needs to discount future cash flows using a discount or interest rate. The major problem with this method is in determining the discount rate, which is based on future interest rates. Analysts may use pro forma income statements, free cash flow values, and the company's terminal value (the value of the company, if sold, 3 to 5 years in the future) to generate a valuation.

- **The venture capital method.** Venture capital (VC) firms (Chapter 16) invest in start-ups and usually take them through to their IPOs. They may use combinations of the first two methods, concentrating on terminal value. The VC firm then discounts the terminal value of the company, using a very high discount rate (e.g., 30 to 70 percent). When companies pay using their stocks, they themselves have high valuation, so they can afford to buy a high valuation EC company. An example is IAC/Interactive Corp. that purchased AskJeeves in March 2005 in an all-stock acquisition.This compensates them for the high risk they assume.

Let's look at one of the most successful IPOs of an EC company—Google. Google floated its IPO in Fall 2004, targeting it at $85 per share. Within a few weeks, the share price more than doubled, giving Google a market capitalization of $55 billion (GM's market capitalization is $21 billion, and its profit are $4 billion a year, versus Google's $400 million).

The increase in share price indicated that investors were willing to pay huge premiums for anticipated future performance and valuation. Many acquisitions and mergers from 1996 through 2001 involved unrealistically high valuations. Note that when EC companies acquire other EC companies, they frequently pay in the form of stock, not cash, so such high valuations are more appropriate. Google uses this same strategy to acquire other companies.

In summary, the economics of EC enable companies to be more competitive and more profitable. It also enables them to grow faster, collaborate better, provide superb customer service, and innovate more quickly. As in any economic environment, here, too, those that capitalize on these opportunities will excel; the rest are doomed to mediocrity or failure.

Section 15.5 ▶ REVIEW QUESTIONS

1. How can EC enhance increasing returns in a business? (Hint: Consult roi-calc.com.)
2. How does EC impact the production cost curve?
3. Define transaction costs. List some examples and explain how EC can reduce such costs.
4. How can EC be used to increase revenues?
5. What are the benefits of increasing reach? How can EC help?
6. How can psychological risk be reduced?
7. Explain the impact of EC on product differentiation and agility.
8. Define valuation. Why is it so high for some EC start-ups?

15.6 FACTORS THAT DETERMINE EC SUCCESS

The economic capabilities of EC described in Section 15.5 influence some industries more than others. The success factors of EC depend on the industry, the sellers and buyers, and the products being sold. Furthermore, the ability of sellers to create economic value for consumers will determine the EC success. When deciding to sell online, the potential for success can be evaluated by looking at the major factors that determine the impact of EC. Strader and Shaw (1997) have identified four categories of e-market success factors: product, industry, seller, and consumer characteristics.

Product Characteristics

Digitizable products, such as software, documents, music, and videos, are particularly well suited for e-markets because they can be distributed to customers electronically, resulting in instant delivery and very low distribution costs. Digitization also decreases the amount of time involved in the order-taking cycle, because automation can be introduced to help customers search for, select, and pay for a product, anyplace and anytime, without the intervention of a sales or technical person. Finally, product updates can be communicated to customers rapidly.

A product's *price* may also be an important determinant of its success. The higher the product price, the greater the level of risk involved in the market transaction between buyers and sellers who are geographically separated and who may have never dealt with each other before. Therefore, some of the most common items currently sold through e-markets are low-priced items such as CDs and books. Riquelme (2001) found that the price of low-price products depends on the customer's benefits of information search in the e-marketplace (i.e.,

Riquelme (2001) found that for more expensive products, such as fine wines, diamonds, and perfumes, or service-based products, such as hotel and vacation bookings, customers often rely on the e-marketplace's *reputation* or information availability rather than just on price. In either case, EC can play a significant role in facilitating business.

Another product characteristic is the cost and speed of *product customization*. Millions of consumers configure computers, cars, toys, clothes, and services to their liking, and if sellers can fulfill such requests at a reasonable cost and in a short amount of time, success is assured (e.g., Dell). Finally, computers, electronic products, consumer products, and even cars can be sold online, because consumers know exactly what they are buying. The more product information that is available, the better it is for the customer. The use of multimedia and product tutorials (e.g., see bluenile.com) can dramatically facilitate product description.

Another aspect of a product's characteristics is *cross-selling* and *up-selling*. As will be shown in Chapter 16, EC enables efficient and effective cross-selling and up-selling of many (but not all) products and services.

Industry Characteristics

Electronic markets are most useful when they are able to match buyers and sellers directly. However, some industries require transaction brokers. These industries may be affected less by e-markets than those that do not require brokers. Stockbrokers, insurance agents, and travel agents may provide needed services, but in some cases, software may reduce the need for these brokers. This is particularly true as intelligent systems become more available to assist consumers.

These findings are supported by Zhu (2001), who argues that in B2B it is desirable to make a vast amount of data about prices and costs available on the Internet, which makes e-marketplace information more transparent.

Other important industry characteristics include the following: Who are the major players (corporations) in the industry? How many companies in the industry are well managed? How strong is the competition, including foreign companies?

Seller Characteristics

Electronic markets reduce *search costs*, allowing consumers to find sellers that offer lower prices and/or better service. As in the case of the motion picture industry, this may reduce profit margins for sellers that compete in e-markets, but it may increase the number of transactions that take place (i.e., people watching more movies). However, if sellers are unwilling to participate in this environment, then the impact of e-markets may be reduced. In highly competitive industries with low *barriers to entry*, sellers may not have a choice but to join in; otherwise, online customers' searches will lead them to an online competitor's distribution channel.

Consumer Characteristics

Consumers can be classified as impulse, patient, or analytical. Electronic markets may have little impact on industries in which a sizable percentage of purchases are made by impulse buyers. Because e-markets require a certain degree of effort and preparation on the part of the consumer, e-markets are more conducive to consumers who do some comparisons before buying (i.e., the patient and analytical buyers).

Analytical buyers can use the Internet to evaluate a wide range of information before deciding where to buy. On the other hand, *m-commerce,* and especially *l-commerce*, which provides and even customizes services based on a customer's location, are banking on impulse buyers—on the customer being in the right place at the right time. However, m-commerce also offers indirect benefits to consumers through improved location services. Team Assignment #2 presents a case where you can identify costs and benefits of a mobile computing system.

THE LEVELS OF EC MEASUREMENT

An issue related to establishing EC metrics is the *level of measurement* at which the EC value is being calculated. Metrics vary based on whether the level of measurement is an individual EC customer, an EC firm, an EC-enabled process, or the EC value chain. For an individual, EC metrics will include product variety, price savings, and satisfaction. For an EC firm, the metrics of interest will be converting site visitors to customers, inventory turns, and cross-selling. At the process level, firms may be interested in the speed of the order-taking process or in a change in the routing of a product. The EC value chain involves firms and their suppliers and customers on either side of a transaction. EC value chain metrics may involve cost reductions in acquiring raw materials, producing the product, and delivering it to the customer.

Ultimately, the level of measurement relates to *what is of value* to the various constituents at each level. Value manifests itself in various forms. In Chapter 2, we examine how the real value of EC can be extracted by exploiting product characteristics with an EC strategy. This value of EC may be economic (e.g., cost savings), or it may be from reduced transaction friction or risk, product differentiation, or increased agility. For further discussion, see Rayport and Jaworski (2002).

Section 15.6 ▶ REVIEW QUESTIONS

1. Describe product characteristics in EC.
2. Describe pricing issues in EC.
3. What are industry characteristics in EC?
4. What are seller characteristics in EC?
5. What are consumer characteristics in EC?
6. List the four levels of metric measurement.

15.7 OPPORTUNITIES FOR SUCCESS IN EC AND AVOIDING FAILURE

Now that EC has been around for several years, it is possible to observe certain patterns that contribute to its success or failure. By examining EC patterns, one can find indications of the opportunities that lie ahead and avoid pitfalls along the way. This section examines EC failures, the key factors to EC success, how EC is creating digital options, and the complementary investments that are needed to enable EC success.

E-COMMERCE FAILURES

By examining the economic history of previous innovations, the failure of EC initiatives and EC companies (see discussions in Chapters 1 through 3 and 6) should come as no surprise. Three economic phenomena suggest why this is the case:

1. At a macroeconomic level, technological revolutions, such as the railroad and the automobile industries, have had a boom–bust–consolidation cycle. For example, between 1904 and 1908, more than 240 companies entered the then-new automobile manufacturing business in the United States. In 1910, the shakeout began. Today, there are only three U.S. automakers, but the size of the auto industry has grown by several hundred times.

   Arthur (1996) compared the Internet revolution with the railroad revolution and found that both followed a similar pattern. First there was the excitement over the emerging technology, then irrational euphoria followed by inflated market values of anything related to the new technology, and then the bust. However, Arthur notes that following the bust, the railroads saw their golden period, in which railroad activities in England grew tenfold. Why was this the case? Arthur believes that the real benefits of a technology come when organizations structure their activities around the cluster of technologies (e.g., after railroads emerged, steel rails, track safety systems, traffic control systems, and so on were needed). Similarly, businesses relocated to where the cost and availability of raw material were favorable along the railroad lines.

   Similar to the railroads, we are now seeing a reemergence in EC activity. For example, early B2B online businesses involved simple transactions; today, B2B involves electronic integration and synchronization with supply chain partners.

2. At a mid-economic level, the bursting of the dot-com bubble in 2000–2003 is consistent with periodic economic downturns that have occurred in real estate, precious metals, currency, and stock markets.
3. At a microeconomic level, the "Web rush" reflected an overallocation of scarce resources—venture capital and technical personnel—and too many advertising-driven business models. This is analogous to the influx of people and resources to specific places during a "gold rush."

Some of the specific reasons for failure in B2C EC are provided in Chapter 3: lack of profitability, excessive risk exposure, the high cost of customer acquisition, poor performance, and static Web site design. Two additional financial reasons are lack of funding and incorrect revenue models (discussed in Chapter 2).

With EC, B2B businesses have been trying to improve interfirm operations and customer service by allowing customers and partners to interact directly with the Web sites to do self-service. However, Schultze and Orlikowski (2004) found that in click and mortar EC applications, the use of the self-serve technology made it more difficult for sales reps to build and maintain customer relationships. The use of IT altered the nature and quality of information shared by the participants, undermined the ability of sales reps to provide consulting services to customers, reduced the frequency of their interaction, and prompted sales reps to expend social capital to promote the customers' technology adoption. These changes produced intended and unintended shifts in the network relations and raised serious challenges to the viability of their business model.

In both the B2C and B2B markets, other anecdotal reasons for failure include misdirected energies; a lack of understanding of market needs; poor business planning; greed; and a mismatch of innovative youth, inexperience, and overeager sponsors (Yap 2002). The reasons for past failures are important in that they provide insight for avoiding such failures in the future.

E-COMMERCE SUCCESSES

Despite the failure of hundreds of start-ups and thousands of EC projects, EC is alive and well and has continued to grow rapidly after a short pause in 2001–2002 as discussed throughout the text.

EC success stories abound, primarily in specialty and niche markets. One example is puritan.com, a successful vitamin and natural health-care product store. Another is campusfood.com, which allows college students to order take-out food online (Chapter 1). Also doing very well are employment sites, such as monster.com. Alloy.com is a successful shopping and entertainment portal for young adults. As pointed out in Chapter 3, online services such as stock trading, travel reservations, online banking, and more are commanding a major part of the business in their industries. For a comparison of how these and other thriving online businesses have translated CSFs from the old economy into EC success, see Exhibit 15.13.

EXHIBIT 15.13 Critical Success Factors: Old Economy and EC

Old Economy CSFs	EC CSFs
Vertically integrate or do it yourself	Create new partnerships and alliances, stay with core competency
Deliver high-value products	Deliver high-value service offerings that encompass products
Build market share to establish economies of scale	Optimize natural scale and scope of business, look at mass customization
Analyze carefully to avoid missteps	Approach with urgency to avoid being locked out; use proactive strategies
Leverage physical assets	Leverage intangible assets, capabilities, and relationships—unleash dormant assets
Compete to sell product	Compete to control access and relationships with customers; compete with Web sites

The following are some of the reasons for EC success and suggestions from EC experts and consultants on how to succeed in EC.

Strategies for EC Success

Thousands of brick-and-mortar companies are adding online channels, with great success. Examples are uniglobe.com, staples.com, homedepot.com, clearcommerce.com, 800flowers.com, and Southwest Airlines (iflyswa.com). Weill and Vitale (2001) suggest that existing firms can use organizational knowledge, brand, infrastructure, and other "morphing strategies" to migrate from the off-line marketplace to the online marketspace (see also Chapter 16). Weill and Vitale (2001) forecast that in the post-dot-com-bust EC world, a few dot-coms will exist in each major business sector; most will evolve with a combination of online and physical business models, and traditional businesses will need to make substantial investments in EC to succeed. Other experts and researchers have blended a variety of factors into their own recipes for EC success. Following is a partial list of these strategies and critical success factors that aid the achievement of these strategies.

- Kauffman et al. (2002) assert strategies that include moving to higher-quality customers, changing products or services in their existing market, and establishing an off-line presence (e.g., moving from pure-play dot-com to click-and-mortar).
- Pavlou and Gefen (2004) found that institutional-based trust, which is derived from buyers' perceptions that effective third-party institutional mechanisms are in place, is critical to EC success. These mechanisms include (1) feedback mechanisms, (2) third-party escrow services, and (3) credit card guarantees. This helps explain why, despite the inherent uncertainty that arises when buyers and sellers are separated in time and in space, online marketplaces are proliferating.
- A group of Asian CEOs recommend the following EC CSFs: select robust business models, anticipate the dot-com future, foster e-innovation, carefully evaluate a spin-off strategy, co-brand, employ ex-dot-com staffers, and focus on the e-generation, as alloy.com and bolt.com have done (Phillips 2000).
- Agrawal (2001) suggests that companies should match a value proposition with customer segments, control extensions of product lines and business models, and avoid expensive technology.
- Huff and Wade (2000) suggest the following EC CSFs: add value, focus on a niche and then extend that niche, maintain flexibility, get the technology right, manage critical perceptions, provide excellent customer service, create effective connectedness, and understand Internet culture.
- Barua et al. provide a systematic approach for driving EC excellence, including guidelines for selecting appropriate business models and assuring sufficient ROI.
- Kambil and van Heck (2002) found that for an EC exchange to be successful, it has to create value for *all* participants, not just the sellers, the market maker, or the buyers. The issue of value in an online exchange is the subject of debate among the many suppliers in the electronic marketplace. In Team Assignment #3, you will learn more about electronic hubs and have the opportunity to participate in identifying collaborative opportunities. These authors also recommend that for EC to be successful it should support and enrich human interactions through technologies such as virtual reality (i.e., increase richness).
- Pricing in EC has continued to be a challenge for sellers because of handling and shipping costs. Often the seller and market maker will see the potential for profits and ignore the fact the buyers will subscribe to EC only if they see the benefit in price or product variety. For example, in January 2005, Amazon.com decided to absorb such costs for orders above a certain level (e.g., $25).
- New technologies can boost the success of EC. For example, RFID has great potential for improving the supply chain (Chapter 7); however, it will take a large investment in EC infrastructure and applications to realize its full potential (see Section 15.4).

Many more keys to success have been proposed by a number of experts and consultants (e.g., Paul and Franco 2001; Yap 2002).

Additional Guidelines for EC Success. A research study of 30 organizations identified the following factors that contributed to the successful implementation of B2C and B2B EC projects (Esichaikul and Chavananon 2001):

- The top three factors for successful B2C e-commerce were effective marketing management, an attractive Web site, and building strong connections with the customers.
- The top three factors for successful B2B e-commerce were the readiness of trading partners, information integration inside the company and in the supply chain, and the completeness of the EC system.
- The top three factors for the overall success of an e-business were a proper business model, readiness of the firm to become an e-business, and internal enterprise integration.

At this still-early stage of the EC revolution, success cannot be assured, and failure rates will remain high. However, if companies learn from the mistakes of the past and follow the guidelines offered by experts and researchers, the chances for success are greatly enhanced.

In the remaining parts of this section, we will discuss important strategies and factors that should be considered to assure EC success. The first one is the creation of digital options.

CREATING DIGITAL OPTIONS

The EC project evaluation process, including the tools of economic justification (Section 15.3), has been welcomed by firms, because it allows them to justify an investment, compare it with other potential investments, and evaluate the potential risk or payoff. However, EC and information technologies play an innate role in supporting business projects that may not be well suited for the types of economic justification that work well for other types of investments. Researchers and practitioners are rethinking the extent to which ROI and related financial measures should play a role in the decision to invest in EC.

Sawhney (2002a) argues that increased focus on ROI in evaluating e-business initiatives can lead to the bias of looking inward only and forcing out initiatives with little immediate and tangible ROI but with significant long-term value to the company. He suggests that firms should think broadly and follow the unanticipated benefits of EC projects, as in the example of Eli Lilly & Co., which created a Web site called InnoCentive (innocentive.com) to attract scientists to solve chemistry problems in exchange for financial rewards. In doing so, Eli Lilly has established contact with over 8,000 scientists that the human resources department can tap into for future hiring and consulting needs.

Sambamurthy et al. (2003) refer to such opportunities from EC applications as **digital options**, a set of IT-enabled capabilities in the form of digitized enterprise work processes and knowledge systems. They refer to these capabilities as *options* because, as in the case of Eli Lilly, the firm has an option to exploit the project for other purposes. They suggest that exploiting such options increases agility. Had Eli Lilly only used the ROI justification approach, it might not have invested in the EC-based Web site. However, the "value" it provides in identifying and establishing contact with over 8,000 scientists may be significant and last for the long-term.

digital options
A set of IT-enabled capabilities in the form of digitized enterprise work processes and knowledge systems.

EC Applications Case 15.1 describes how GE Aircraft Engines has created digital options from a data collection system created to improve manufacturing operations.

COMPLEMENTARY INVESTMENTS

The returns from EC investments can be maximized to make **complementary investments**. Complementary investments are cases in which a smaller project is added that requires different capabilities; the projects are then jointly funded. Ignoring complementary investments can lead to less-than-optimal payoffs, and even contribute to failure. Zhu (2004) found that complementary investment in information technology infrastructure can play a critical role in the use of EC for improved performance. He found that when the complementary investments are made in infrastructure, such as personal computers or LANs, improved firm performance is realized through increased returns on assets, sales per employee, costs of goods sold per employee and reduced inventory turnover.

complementary investments
Additional investments, such as training, made to maximize the returns from EC investments.

Sherer et al. (2003) studied Cisco's upgrade of the operating system on 34,000 employee PCs and found that the firm's complementary investment in change management led to a

CASE 15.1

EC Application

GE AIRCRAFT ENGINES' DIGITAL OPTIONS

Over 25 years ago, GE Aircraft Engines (GEAE) created a system that enables the remote monitoring of aircraft engines. Each aircraft engine has hundreds of sensors that relay information to an onboard computer while the aircraft is in flight. The data are then transmitted via a satellite to a ground-based computer system. Over the years, this data collection system has blossomed into an entire operations system for engine control. GEAE has used this information technology to create digital options.

GEAE uses the collected information to inform and educate its engineers and maintenance workers. This enables the company to continually improve its engines, and thereby improve customer service. GEAE created a revenue-generating digital option by selling some of the information it collects back to the airlines. It sells information such as guidelines on how and when to service engines, which engines perform better under what flying conditions, and the costs of maintaining fleets in-house versus outsourcing their the maintenance.

Further, GEAE has improved customer relationships through its ability to predict and identify when an engine part needs to be replaced, notifying customers so that parts are ready and available when the plane lands. This has enabled the airlines to minimize maintenance time and keep their airplanes in the air. Thus, GEAE's digital option has led to improved product designs, improved customer service, and additional revenue.

Source: Compiled from Sviokla and Wong (2003).

Questions

1. What digital option did GEAE create?
2. List some other options that GEAE might be able to create.
3. What metrics can GEAE use to calculate ROI of the EC project (the electronic feedback information system)?

smooth transition, which was reflected in the higher client satisfaction ratings. Other complementary investments include training programs for customers, linking of internal systems, creating customer support teams, and establishing links with suppliers and service providers.

CULTURAL DIFFERENCES

Chapter 1 mentions culture as a barrier to the use of EC. In Chapter 14, we discuss the need to understand cultural issues such as differences in social norms, measurement standards, and nomenclature. Here we raise the issue of cultural differences so that appropriate metrics can be developed.

One of the strengths of EC is the ease with which its adopters can reach a global population of consumers. However, EC-driven businesses must consider the cultural differences in this diverse global consumer base, because without the broad acceptance of the EC channel, consumers may choose not to participate in online transactions. Critical elements that can affect the value of EC across cultures are perceived trust, consumer loyalty, regulation, and political influences. Even the content of online ads can mean different things in different cultures. Due to these differences, the transaction costs, including coordination costs, may vary among the consumer base.

A 2005 research study by Sung (2005) found that security, privacy, and technical expertise are the most explanatory EC CSFs in South Korea; in contrast, ease of use is the most important success factor in the United States. Firms must address EC issues arising from cultural differences. For instance, to deal with issues such as transactional trust, in which consumers may not trust foreign firms, EC sellers can partner with respectable local firms, banks, or chambers of commerce and build trust among their prospective clientele. Further, online testimonials from local customers can positively influence transactional trust. EC metrics from other countries should not be applied automatically.

EC IN DEVELOPING ECONOMIES

Similar to cultural differences, developed and developing economies vary in how EC is used and whether the economics favor this channel of commerce. Developing economies struggle with various issues taken for granted in developed economies, such as the United States or Singapore.

Developing economies often face power blackouts, unreliable telecommunications infrastructure, undependable delivery mechanisms, and the fact that only a few customers own credit cards. Such limitations make it difficult for firms to predict whether EC investments will pay off, and when. However, developing economies such as China and India represent a significant opportunity for EC to connect businesses to customers, as well as other businesses. The potential volume of transactions in developed countries can make EC investments more attractive for established firms. This is because much of the cost of EC systems development would have already been recovered because existing IT infrastructures can frequently be used for EC initiatives. However, to be successful, firms must rethink their assumptions about computing in developed and developing countries.

The traditional EC assumption is that every computer user has the investment capacity to own a computer and maintain a dedicated connection, as is the case in developed economies. In developing economies, the assumption will have to be revised to incorporate low cost access, pay for use, a community of users, and mass coverage. The payoffs from EC use in developing countries are likely to go beyond financial returns. Enabling people to take advantage of EC technology without disrupting their traditions may be the most valuable, yet intangible, return. An example of such a situation is presented in EC Application Case 15.2.

CASE 15.2

EC Application

THE SUCCESS STORY OF *E-CHOUPAL*

In the remote villages of southern India, most farmers are illiterate and have never used a computer. They grow soybeans, wheat, and coffee on small plots of land. After the crop is harvested, it generally takes them up to two days to transport it to the local auction. Due to a lack of information, they have been unaware of current market prices.

ITC, one of India's leading agribusiness companies, set up an e-market called *e-choupal* (*echoupal.com*), the Hindi word for "gathering place." Run by a *sanchalak* (an operator, usually a male) and accessed by a PC at the operator's home or at kiosks in public places, e-choupals act as community meeting places as well as e-commerce hubs.

The e-choupal model required ITC to make relatively large investments in creating and maintaining its own IT network in rural India. It also had to identify and train local farmers to manage each e-choupal. The e-choupal computer or kiosk is linked to the Internet via phone lines or, increasingly, by a VSAT connection. Each e-choupal serves an average of 600 farmers in 10 surrounding villages within a 5-km radius. Each e-choupal costs between US$3,000 and US$6,000 to set up and about US$100 per year to maintain. The farmers can use the system for free. The sanchalak is obligated by a public oath to serve the entire community; the sanchalak benefits from increased prestige and a commission paid for each e-choupal transaction.

Farmers benefit from more accurate pricing information, improvements in the product-weighing process, faster processing time, prompt payment, and access to a wide range of information, including accurate market prices and market trends, which help them decide when, where, and at what price to sell. Farmers also are able to access information on soils and planting improvements, crop planning, and building relationships that ensure the flow of supplies. Farmers use the e-choupal system to purchase seed and fertilizer, order soil-testing kits, share best practices, and check grain prices, including those at the Chicago Board of Trade.

The e-choupal system has had a measurable impact on what the farmers choose to plant and where they sell their products. In areas covered by e-choupals, the percentage of farmers planting soy, for example, has increased dramatically, from 50 to 90 percent in some regions. The volume of soy marketed through "mandis" (open-air markets) has dropped by as much as half.

Further, by selling through the e-choupal, farmers take their crops directly to ITC collection points, saving on the cost of packing and transportation that would be involved in going to the auction market. By reintermediation (as discussed in Chapter 2), instead of disintermediation, ITC saves $5 per ton as well.

The e-choupal system has decreased ITC's net procurement costs by about 2.5 percent (it saves on commission fees and on transportation costs it would otherwise pay to traders who serve as its buying agents at the mandi), and it has more direct control over the quality of what it buys. The company reports that it recovered its equipment costs in the first year of operation and that the venture as a whole is profitable. By 2004, the e-choupal system had grown to 1,000 kiosks. The farmers have been able to save money without changing their lifestyle.

Sources: Compiled from Sawhney (2002b), Hammond, and Prahalad (2004), and *digitaldividend.org/case/case_echoupal.htm* (accessed January 2005).

Questions

1. List the metrics that can be used to measure the EC success of the e-choupal system.
2. How does e-choupal differ from a regular electronic meeting place?

Section 15.7 ▶ REVIEW QUESTIONS

1. List three reasons why EC failure should not come as a surprise.
2. What are some reasons for EC success?
3. Define digital options.
4. What are complementary investments?

MANAGERIAL ISSUES

Some managerial issues related to this chapter are as follows:

1. **How do we measure the value of EC investment?** EC investments must be measured against their contribution to business objectives. Such investments will involve direct and indirect costs as well as benefits. The impact of EC on integrating existing processes and systems must not be ignored. Furthermore, EC must create value for all participants, support or improve existing processes, and supplement rather than replace the human element of transactions. The measurement of EC value should occur against the backdrop of metrics that define business performance and success.
2. **What complementary investments will be needed?** Companies should expect to make complementary investments in other functional areas to ensure EC success. Procurement is done differently in many organizations; introducing models such as forward auctions and affiliate programs may have a major impact on marketing and sales.
3. **Shift from tangible to intangible benefits.** Few opportunities remain for automation projects that simply replace manual labor with IT on a one-for-one basis. Therefore, the economic justification of EC applications will increasingly depend on intangible benefits, such as increased quality or improved customer service. It is much more difficult to accurately estimate the value of intangible benefits prior to the actual implementation. Managers need to understand and use tools that bring intangible benefits into the decision-making processes for IT investments.
4. **Who should conduct a justification?** For small projects, the finance department can do the analysis. For a large or complex project, an outside consultant may be advisable.
5. **Should we use the ROI calculator provided by a vendor who wants to sell us an EC system?** It is always safer to use a calculator from an unbiased source. However, some vendors may provide calculators that better fit with your application.

RESEARCH TOPICS

Here are some suggested topics related to this chapter. For details, references, and additional topics, refer to the book's "Current EC Research" in the Online Appendix.

1. **Technology-Level Economic Analysis**
   - Internet access pricing
   - Impact of the technical transparency of software agents in Internet markets
   - Cost-effectiveness of the Internet for buyers and sellers
   - Impact of XML standards in expanding the network externality
2. **Product-Level Economic Analysis**
   - Pricing of digital products and services
   - Ability to search for a product on the Internet and its impact on product purchase
   - Value of digital–physical bundles
   - Effect of network externality on EC
3. **Business-Process-Level Economic Analysis**
   - Governance theories for the EC business environment
   - Value propositions of governance for buyers and suppliers, large and small firms
   - Optimal selection of buyers by suppliers as well as the optimal selection of sellers by buyers

- Effect of EC on a firm's internal structure
- Benefits and risks of virtual alliances in EC
- EC business models that can offer sustainable competitive advantage
- EC competitive advantage versus competitive necessity

4. **Market-Level Economic Analysis**
   - Theories that explain the boundary conditions for effective digital intermediation or explain the dynamics of disintermediation in the presence of software agents
   - Theories that characterize efficiency problems in electronic markets
   - Understanding how multi-item and multi-unit auctions operate on the Internet
   - The human decision-making processes in EC, such as in Internet-based auctions
   - New models to determine what constitutes value of Internet-related network effects from the user/customer perspective
   - Understanding the value and performance of B2B e-markets
   - Normative models for the adoption of B2B market services
   - New theories and empirical results on the efficacy of trust mechanisms for Internet commerce
5. **Macroeconomic-Level Economic Analysis**
   - Measurement of the digital economy
   - EC proliferation in developing nations
   - Design of optimal EC taxation and assessment of the performance of the design
   - Economic antecedents of EC
   - Social effects of EC in the international setting

SUMMARY

In this chapter, you learned about the following EC issues as they relate to the learning objectives.

1. **The need for EC justification.** Like any other investment, EC investment (unless it is small) needs to be justified. Many start-up companies have crashed because of no or incorrect justification. In its simplest form, justification looks at revenue minus all relevant costs. Analysis is done by defining metrics that are related to organizational goals.
2. **The difficulties in justifying EC investment.** The nature of EC makes it difficult to justify due to the presence of many intangible costs and benefits. In addition, the relationship between investment and results may be complex, extending over several years. Also, both costs and benefits may be shared among several projects, and impacts (sometimes negative) may be felt in several areas.
3. **Difficulties in established intangible metrics.** Intangible metrics may be difficult to define. Some of these benefits change rapidly; others have different values to different people or organizational units. Intangible metrics have qualitative measures that are difficult to compare. One solution is to quantify the qualitative measures. This can be done with scoring methodology, value analysis, and other advanced methods, as described in Online File W15.3. WWW
4. **Traditional methods for evaluating EC investments.** Evaluating EC involves a financial analysis, usually an ROI analysis (profit = revenue − cost), as well as an assessment of the technology and its architecture. This may be discounted, using the NPV method, if the costs and benefits will extend over several years. A payback period describes how long it will take to recover the initial investment. However, financial ROI alone can lead to an incomplete and misleading evaluation. Tools to integrate the various ROI aspects of EC investment include the balanced scorecard (BSC), which also focuses on the internal business processes and learning and growth perspective of the business. EC ROI should take into account the risk of reducing possible failures or adverse events that can drain the financial ROI. Other advanced methods (e.g., real options, value analysis, benchmarks, and management by maxim) look at future benefits. No method is universal or perfect, so selecting a method (or a mix of methods) is critical.
5. **Understand how specific EC projects are justified.** All EC projects include intangible and tangible benefits and costs that must be identified. Then a method(s) must be selected to match the particular characteristics of the EC application.
6. **EC investment evaluation.** Economic fundamentals must be kept in mind when evaluating an EC investment. With traditional products, the cost curve shows that average per unit costs decline as quantity increases. However, with digital products, the variable cost per unit usually is low, and thus the evaluation will

differ. Similar differences are evident in EC's ability to lower transaction costs, agency costs, and transaction risks. EC can also enable the firm to be agile in responding faster to changing market conditions and ensure increasing returns to scale regardless of the volume involved. Finally, EC enables increased reach with multimedia richness at a reasonable cost.

7. **E-marketplace economics.** Products, industry, seller, and consumer characteristics require different metrics of EC value. With the growing worldwide connectivity to the Internet, EC economics will play a major role in supporting buyers and sellers. As compared with traditional commerce, EC can quickly succeed due to its ability to create network effects, lock-in effects, and disintermediation, especially in case of digital products.

8. **Reasons for EC success and failure.** Like other innovations, EC is expected to go through the cycle of enormous success, followed by speculation, and then disaster before the reality of the new situation sets in. Some EC failures were the result of problematic Web site design, lack of sustained funding, and weak revenue models. Success in EC has come through automating and enhancing familiar strategies, such as branding, morphing, trust building, and creating value for all trading partners by enriching the human experience with integrated and timely information. EC investments can go beyond the traditional business models by creating digital options. To ensure success, complementary investments must be made in managing change and responding to cultural differences among EC users.

KEY TERMS

Term	Page
Agency costs	639
Agility	643
Average-cost curve (AVC)	639
Complementary investments	649
Cost-benefit analysis	622
Dashboard	632
Digital options	649
Key performance indicators (KPIs)	623
Lock-in effect	638
Metric	623
Network effects	638
Performance-based government	620
Product differentiation	642
Production function	639
ROI calculator	630
Total benefits of ownership (TBO)	629
Total cost of ownership (TCO)	629
Transaction costs	640
Valuation	643
Value analysis	631

QUESTIONS FOR DISCUSSION

1. You have been hired by a mail-order catalog company that is adding online selling. Develop EC success metrics for the company. Develop a set of metrics for the company's customers.
2. Your state government is considering an online vehicle registration system. Develop a set of EC metrics and discuss how these metrics differ from those of an online catalog company (see the previous question).
3. Consider the various economic justification methods. Are there conditions under which one may be more useful than the others?
4. Provide an example of when you or someone you know has experienced the lock-in effect with regard to an online business.
5. How has Amazon.com caused disintermediation? Name two other companies or industries where EC has resulted in disintemediation.
6. A local grocery chain is considering building portals for its employees, its business partners, and its customers. List the types of information it should provide for each constituency.
7. A craftsperson operates a small business making wooden musical instruments in a small U.S. town. The business owner is considering using EC to increase the business's reach to the nation and the world. How can the business owner use EC to increase richness to make the products more attractive to consumers?
8. You are considering moving your bank account to an online bank. What features and services can the bank provide to reduce your psychological risk in making EC transactions?
9. How does EC facilitate the creation of digital options?
10. The balanced scorecard approach can be adapted for various applications. Develop a balanced scorecard and a set of metrics for your college bookstore.
11. Discuss how a company can increase its market share by using EC and explain the benefits of doing so.

12. A company is planning a wireless-based CRM system. Almost all of the benefits are intangible. How can the project be justified to top management?
13. The valuation of Google is more than twice that of GM even though its profits are about 10 percent of GM's. This means that people are willing to pay 20 times more for a share of Google. Given people's experiences in the dot-com bust, is there any logic to this behavior? Discuss.
14. Discuss the value of TCO and TBO concepts for EC investment evaluation.
15. Enter businesscase.com and find material on ROI analysis. Discuss how ROI is related to a business case.

INTERNET EXERCISES

1. Enter alinean.com/AlineanPress_ROITWhitepaper.asp. Find information that explains Alinean's approach to measuring return on IT. You can download two free e-books from the site that are related to this chapter. Summarize your findings in a report.
2. Enter doubleclick.com. Go to "Knowledge Central" and then "Research." Examine research on the value of consumer responses to online advertising. Summarize the issues considered by researchers.
3. Enter nucleusresearch.com. Go to "Research," "Latest Research," and then click "View ROI Scorecards." Open the PDF file entitled "Market Scorecard: Hosted CRM" for a review of hosted CRM vendors. Summarize your findings in a report.
4. Enter schwab.com. Examine the list of online services available for "Trading and Investing." Relate them to richness and reach.
5. Go to computerweekly.com and search for articles dealing with the ROI of RFID. List the key issues in measuring the ROI of RFID.
6. Go to plumtree.com and click "What's your ROI?" (or go directly to resultsimperative.com/secure/plumtreeROI_024.asp). Follow the directions and insert your assumptions about a company and an EC investment in order to assess its ROI.
7. Go to acecostanalyzer.com and register. Review the ACE Demo Training Video. Find the capabilities of the calculators. Calculate the ROI of a project of your choice as well as the TCO.
8. Enter sas.com, corvu.com, balancedscorecard.com, and cio.com. Find demos and examples of how the various tools and methods can be used to evaluate EC projects. Write a report.
9. Enter solutionmatrix.com and find information about ROI, metrics, and cost-benefit tools. Write a report based on your findings.
10. Enter roi-calc.com. View the demos. What investment analysis services does the company provide?
11. Enter retail.zebra.com and phormion.com and find their ROI calculators. What analysis is provided by the calculators?
12. Enter advisorzones.com and baseline.com. Find information related to EC investment evaluation. Summarize your findings in a report.

TEAM ASSIGNMENTS AND ROLE PLAYING

1. Download the ROI case study "Venda Xerox Document Supplies (Case Study E11)" from the Nucleus Research Web site. Read the Venda Xerox case study. While you are connected to the Internet, click "ROI Help Tutorial" in the NR_Standard_ROI_Tool.xls file and read modules 1 through 4. Enter your assumptions of costs and benefits into the calculator and examine how they impact the overall ROI, payback period, NPV, and average yearly cost of ownership (under the Summary tab).

   Answer the following questions based on the Venda Xerox Document Supplies ROI case study.

   a. What were the key reasons why Xerox developed an EC system?
   b. What were the areas in which Xerox could benefit from EC?
   c. How did Xerox calculate the ROI of the EC system?
2. In this activity, you will measure the business value of a mobile computing system for the field service representatives at Alliance Insurance Company (AIC), a fictitious company based on some actual companies.

   AIC is a national insurance company that provides B2B automobile, property, and industrial insurance in major U.S. metropolitan areas. It has 16 field offices that support 450 field inspectors who visit insured sites to conduct inspections and settle insurance claims. Transactions are overseen by 250 auditors who ensure that the business is running smoothly.

With the current system, inspectors get preliminary property or damage information over the phone. After collecting the information, they make site visits to assess the nature of the customer's needs, return to the office to run the numbers and prepare the paperwork, and then make another on-site appointment to finish the transaction. Inspectors fill out weekly activity logs and audit their transactions to ensure accuracy and high quality of service. Oftentimes, the field inspectors come back to the office only to find out that their next visit is in the same general location that they just returned from.

One major limitation of the current system is that field inspectors must frequently return to the office to consult the volumes of manuals to accurately insure clients or settle claims. Frequent updates of insurance rates and risk estimates and a constant flow of new products has made it impossible for the inspectors to carry these manuals with them.

AIC is considering a mobile computing infrastructure that will enable field inspectors to access online manuals as well as other information necessary to conduct business. The system will also enable the central office make appointments for the field inspectors as well as conduct mailings and other official business. In other words, the field inspectors will work from a virtual mobile office.

a. Divide the class into two teams. One team will identify the *costs metrics*—tangible as well as intangible—of the mobile computing system. In determining costs, consider hardware, software, application development, integration with back-office applications, and other implementation costs. The second team will identify the *benefit metrics* of the mobile computing system. Productivity, cost reduction, reduced duplication, and so on should be considered when determining benefit metrics.

b. Use a spreadsheet program to create a spreadsheet and assign your team's costs and benefits estimates. Share these with the other team for their comments.

c. Each group should identify specific metrics to recommend to AIC so that a postimplementation ROI can be conducted.

3. As the speed of change in the global e-marketplace increases, collaboration and coordination costs along the supply chain will increase (Lewis and Byrd 2003). Further, meeting increased demands for the introduction of new products and services will be a challenge. Form teams to study the role and status of RosettaNet. Each member will be assigned to one area of activity performed at RosettaNet. Prepare a report on the potential value of e-hub partnerships.

Cisco Systems' leadership role in the creation and expansion of RosettaNet standards and eHub are visionary initiatives that will reduce friction in e-marketplaces through the collaboration of partners across the supply chain. Evidence from industrywide initiatives by Proctor & Gamble and Baxter with similar visions indicates that such collaboration can lead to cost reductions for all partners through improved forecasting and planning and waste reduction.

The success of such EC initiatives depends on the number of partners that join. Many potential partners are sitting on the fence and waiting for reassurance that their investment in eHub will indeed lead to some business value. After all, implementation of each eHub PIP (Partner Interface Process) is estimated to cost the partner up to $500,000 (Rayner 2001). However, the supply chain only becomes a "value chain" after internal processes are integrated via ERP systems. In addition, suppliers and customers also must be integrated into the supply chain, which requires further expense and effort on the part of the partners to integrate their internal systems with eHub.

For additional information on eHub and Rosetta Net, see the eHub collaboration report from IBM Business Consulting Services, which is available at **www-1.ibm.com/industries/cpe/download7/17843/ehubs_electr.pdf**, and Mark Schenecker's article, "Inside RosettaNet's Automated Enablement," which is available at **ebizq.net/topics/dev_tools/features/5487.html**.

a. What metrics can Cisco use to demonstrate the potential opportunities resulting from the eHub partnership to current and prospective partners?

b. How will prospective partners weigh the benefits against their concerns over sharing pricing and inventory information with everyone on eHub?

(Note: This assignment is based on material compiled from Twentyman (2001), Lewis (2001), and Rayner (2001). The students are encouraged to review these sources and explore recents sources in regard to RosettaNet.)

Real-World Case

HOW CITIGROUP MEASURES ITSELF

Global Corporate and Investment Banking (GCIB) is one of five major business divisions within Citigroup, the giant financial services company. Following several mergers and acquisitions, GCIB is now a global organization of 6,000 employees, with an annual budget of more than $1 billion. GCIB's IT department faced a challenge in implementing consistent productivity control processes and standards for all of the organizations that were brought together to form GCIB.

In response to this challenge, GCIB developed Mystic (My Systems and Technology Information Center), an internal performance monitoring and asset management Web portal used by all the IT employees along with their business partners. The system provides corporate-wide access so that projects' sponsors from the business side can check the status of their projects. The system presents a comprehensive set of metrics and a multifaceted view of all IT and EC projects, tracking them by project owner, delivery date, budget, and numerous other factors. High-level results indicate that the investment in Mystic has added value to Citigroup GCIB. Since its initial rollout, there has been an across-the-board 15 percent improvement in on-time delivery, while the project load has increased by nearly 50 percent. Implementation of large EC initiatives that touch almost everyone in the organization are not without complications. How did Citigroup achieve such a success?

Citigroup GCIB found that rolling out such a visible, enterprisewide method of monitoring performance and other metrics represented a major cultural shift, which generated some anxiety. Citigroup responded to such concerns by first launching Mystic as a pilot. Then, as the pilot was deployed, Citigroup encouraged continuous communication and allowed employees to air their concerns and suggest refinements to the metrics that reflect the appropriate level of complexity of certain projects and situations.

Mystic's primary function is monitoring the performance of Citigroup GCIB's IT staff. Mystic tracks performance in three categories: productivity, quality, and controls. The productivity metrics quantify how much a developer is getting done by measuring the average completion time of projects, the status of late projects, cost per project, cost variance, the extent and value of application component reuse (usability), support costs, and other factors. The quality metrics measure both project sponsor and developer satisfaction with the project. Controls measure project risk, budgeted versus actual spending per project, and data quality.

Mystic tracks these metrics for every employee, project, and manager, all the way up to the CIO, indicating compliance with the schedule with a green or yellow light for projects that are on-track or running late as well as highlighting cost concerns. The first set of metrics included with the initial deployment came close to measuring what the CIO needed to know. After watching the effectiveness of those metrics over time, the metrics were refined as needed. Citigroup has found that maintaining flexibility and a willingness to modify the metrics is essential. Therefore, as the Mystic system has matured, so, too, has its measurement framework.

Following the completion of each project, Mystic sends customer satisfaction surveys to the project sponsors, who rate the developers' performance throughout the project. In a novel approach, project developers also rate business sponsors on their participation in the projects, thus stressing the partnership between IT and the business sponsors. One advantage of the survey process is that it results in a greater emphasis up front to ensure that project specifications are complete and fully understood by both parties.

Managers can keep tabs on their individual expenditures and performance, monitor their groups' performance, and maintain a departmental-level view. The level of detail available is scaled to each person's view, according to job title and managerial status, but everyone is looking at the same data. The performance data gathered and stored within Mystic serve as a component of employee evaluations. Managers conducting reviews still apply their own subjective analysis, but project scores tracked through Mystic do play a part.

Besides monitoring employee performance, Mystic also manages Citigroup's technology assets—both those from external vendors and applications developed in-house. The Citigroup Technology Catalog (CTC) tracks all technologies in use, such as servers, network routers, and packaged applications, indicating performance levels for those technologies, where and how they are being used, and when they will near the end of their life cycles. On the applications side, the Citigroup Systems Inventory, which is part of the CTC, tracks technical specifications for applications developed in-house, including deployment details, how they were built, and how they are working.

Another part of Mystic, the Reusable Asset Manager (RAM), tracks reusable code components based on who developed them, what they are, what they do, and where they are being used. This provides developers with an inventory of code components they can reuse to expedite future development projects. In 2003, RAM helped the IT staff identify reusable software components worth a total of $117 million, resulting in a significant savings to the business and improved quality and time-to-market.

The nature of the data tracked within Mystic and the manner in which it is organized helps Citigroup GCIB's IT managers keep a close eye on the top projects in their portfolio of more than 15,000 projects a year. The business and IT managers focus on the top 100 projects for each business by configuring Mystic to display specific views of those top-tier projects. This also helps with project prioritization.

Because it holds large sets of data, metrics, and performance figures, Mystic also serves as a knowledge management repository. The Knowledge Centers built into

Mystic provide a centralized library of in-house development expertise. When an expert in a particular technology is identified, part of the expert's job is to document his or her particular knowledge on the system and to serve as an internal consultant to other Citigroup developers. The Knowledge Centers also serve a knowledge-retention function. The online archive of development expertise and best practices within Mystic preserves that technological knowledge recorded by the in-house experts in the event that an expert leaves the company.

The constant availability and visibility of performance metrics makes communicating the value of IT services to the business unit leaders and senior management of Citigroup GCIB easier, and it makes the entire process transparent.

The Citigroup GCIB governance framework embodied in Mystic also impacts outside technology purchases. When a piece of software needs to be purchased, employees must first consult the standard technology catalog built into Mystic that lists approved, supported software.

Source: Compiled from Low (2004).

Questions

1. List the productivity benefits resulting from the Mystic portal.
2. What intangible benefits were created?
3. List the specific performance metrics that can be measured.
4. Assume that a department is requesting funding for an EC project from top management at GCIB. Explain the logic of performance tracking at such high detail.

REFERENCES

Agrawal, V. L. "E-Performance: The Path to Rational Exuberance." *The McKinsey Quarterly* 1 (2001).

Arthur, W. B. "Increasing Returns and the New World of Business." *Harvard Business Review* 74, no. 4 (1996).

Barua, A., et al. "Driving E-business Excellence." *MIT Sloan Management Review* 43, no. 1 (2001).

Benaroch, M. "Managing Information Technology Investment Risk: A Real Options Perspective." *Journal of Management Information Systems* 19, no. 2 (2002).

Bisconti, K. "Determining the Value and ROI of an Enterprise Portal, Part 2." *Enterprise Systems,* November 16, 2004. **esj.com/enterprise/article.aspx?EditorialsID=1197** (accessed January 2005).

Blum, R. *Network and System TCO.* Murray Hill, NJ: Lucent Technology, 2001.

Broadbent, M., and P. Weill. "Management by Maxim: How Business and IT Managers Can Create IT Infrastructures." *Sloan Management Review* (Spring 1997).

Chen, S. *Strategic Management of E-Business,* 2d ed. West Sussex, England: John Wiley & Sons, Ltd., 2005.

CIO.com. **cio.com/metrics/index.cfm** (accessed December 2004–January 2005).

CIO Insight. "Top Trends for 2005." *CIO Insight,* December 2004.

Cisco Systems. "What You Need to Implement an E-Procurement Solution." *Cisco.com.* **cisco.com/en/US/netsol/ns339/ns444/ns448/networking_solutions_white_paper0900aecd800eb908.shtml** (accessed February 2005).

David, J. S., et al. "Managing Your IT Total Cost of Ownership." *Communications of the ACM* 45, no. 1 (2002).

Davis, W. S., and J. Benamati. *E-Commerce Basics.* Boston: Addison Wesley, 2003.

Devaraj, S., and R. Kohli. "Information Technology Payoff Paradox and System Use: Is Actual Usage the Missing Link?" *Management Science* 49, no. 3 (2003).

Devaraj, S., and R. Kohli. *The IT Payoff: Measuring Business Value of Information Technology Investment.* Upper Saddle River, NJ: Financial Times Prentice-Hall, 2002.

Digital Dividend. **digitaldividend.org/case/case_echoupal.htm** (accessed January 2005).

Esichaikul, V., and S. Chavananon. "Electronic Commerce and Electronic Business Implementation Success Factors." *Proceedings of the 14th Bled Electronic Commerce Conference,* Bled, Slovenia, June 25–26, 2001.

Evans, P., and T. S. Wurster. *Blown to Bits: How the New Economics of Information Transforms Strategy.* Boston, MA: Harvard Business School Press, 2000.

Ferrin, B. G., and R. E. Plank. "Total Cost of Ownership Models: An Exploratory Study." *Journal of Supply Chain Management,* Summer 2002.

Green, S. *Profit on the Web.* Auckland, New Zealand: Axon Computertime, 2002.

Gunasekaran, A., et al. "A Model for Investment Justification in Information Technology Projects." *International Journal of Information Management* (March 2001).

Hahn, J., and R. Kauffman. "A Methodology for Business Value-Driven Web Site Evaluation: A Data Envelopment Analysis Approach." University of Minnesota, Minneapolis, MN Working Paper 04-25, 2004. **misrc.umn.edu/workingpapers/fullpapers/2004/0425_090304.pdf** (accessed January 2005).

Hammond, A. L., and C. K. Prahalad."Selling to the Poor." *Foreign Policy* 142 (2004).

Hovenden, D., D. St. Clair, and M. Potter. "From Projects to Portfolios: A Strategic Approach to IT Investment." *ATKearney Executive Agenda*, 6, no. 1, March 2005. **atkearney.com/main.taf?p=5,1,1,61** (accessed March 2005).

Huff, S., and M. Wade. *Critical Success Factors for Electronic Commerce.* New York: Irwin/McGraw-Hill, 2000.

Jelassi, T., and A. Enders. *Strategies for E-Business.* Harlow, England: FT/Prentice Hall, 2005.

Kambil, A. "Reduce Customer Risks with eCommerce." Accenture, 2001. **accenture.com/xd/xd.asp?it=enweb&xd=ideas\outlook\pov\pov_reduce.xml** (accessed January 2005).

Kambil, A., and E. van Heck. *Making Markets: How Firms Can Design and Profit from Online Auctions and Exchanges.* Boston, MA: Harvard Business School Press, 2002.

Kauffman, R. J., et al. "When Internet Companies Morph: Understanding Organizational Strategy Changes in the 'New' New Economy." *First Monday* 7, no. 7 (2002). **firstmonday.dk/issues/issue7_7/kauffman** (accessed January 2005).

Keen, P. G. W. *The Process Edge: Creating Value Where It Counts.* Boston, MA: Harvard Business School Press, 1997.

Keepmedia.com. "Tool: The Return on Stopping Viruses." Keepmedia.com, February 7, 2005. **keepmedia.com/pubs/baseline/2005/02/07/721943** (accessed April 2005).

Kingstone, S. "The Financial Realities of CRM: A Guide to Best Practices, TCO, and ROI." The Yankee Group, 2004.

Kleist, V. F. "An Approach to Evaluating E-Business Information Systems Projects." *Information Systems Frontiers* 5, no. 3 (2003).

Lewis, B. C., and T. A. Byrd. "Development of a Measure for IT Infrastructure Construct." *European Journal of Information Systems*, June 2003.

Lewis, N. "Cisco Closes the Gap with eHub." *EBN,* February 16, 2001. **my-esm.com/showarticle.jhtml?articleid=2910958** (accessed January 2005).

Low, L. "How Citigroup Measures Up." *CIO Magazine,* April 15, 2004. **cio.com/archive/041504/citigroup.html** (accessed January 2005).

Mahapatra, R., and V. S. Lai. "Evaluating End-User Training Programs." *Communications of the ACM* (January 2005).

Malone, T. W., et al. "The Logic of Electronic Markets." *Harvard Business Review* 67, no 3 (1989).

McKay, J., and P. Marshall. *Strategic Management of E-Business.* Milton, Australia: Wiley, 2004.

Minahan, T. "The E-procurement Benchmark Report: Less Hype, More Results." Aberdeen Group, September 29, 2004. **aberdeen.com/summary/report/benchmark/eProcurement122904b_tm.asp** (accessed January 2005).

Nucleus Research. "Manifesto: Separating ROI Fact from Fiction." Research Note C51, 2002. **nucleusresearch.com/research/c51.pdf** (accessed March 2005).

Paton, D., and D. Troppito. "Eye on ROI: ROI Review." *DM Review,* March 25, 2004. **dmreview.com/article_sub.cfm?articleId=1000671** (accessed March 2005).

Paul, L., and A. Franco. "Twelve Rules to Avoid." *Business Online,* August 2001.

Pavlou, P. A., and D. Gefen. "Building Effective Online Marketplaces with Institution-Based Trust." *Information Systems Research* 15, no. 1 (2004).

Phillips, M. "Seven Steps to Your New E-Business." *Business Online,* August 2000.

Pisello, T. "CRM ROI: Fact or Fiction?" *Alinean.com,* April 27, 2004. **webpronews.com/enterprise/crmanderp/wpn-15-20040427crmroifactorfiction.html** (accessed March 2005).

Plumtree. "MyAPlus.com: A Return-on-Investment Study of Portals." A Meta Group White Paper, November 12, 2001.

Qing, H. U., and R. Plant. "An Empirical Study of the Casual Relationship between IT Investment and Firm Performance." *Information Resources Management Journal*, July–September 2001.

Rayner, B. "The Power of the Hub." *EBN,* June 27, 2001. **my-esm.com/showarticle.jhtml?articleid=2912371** (accessed February 2005).

Rayport, J., and B. J. Jaworski. *Introduction to E-Commerce.* New York: McGraw-Hill, 2002.

Reichheld, F., and P. Schefter. "E-loyalty—Your Secret Weapon on the Web." *Harvard Business Review* (July–August 2000).

Renkema, T. J. W. *The IT Value Quest: How to Capture the Business Value of IT-Based Infrastructure.* Chichester (UK) and New York: John Wiley & Sons. (2000)

Riquelme, H. "An Empirical Review of Price Behaviour on the Internet." *Electronic Markets* 11, no. 4 (2001).

Ross, J. W., and C. M. Beath. "Beyond the Business Case: New Approaches to IT Investment." *MIT Sloan Management Review* (Winter 2002).

Ross, S. S. "Computer Security: The First Step." Baseline.com, February 1, 2005. **baselinemag.com/article2/0,1397,1766043,00.asp** (accessed April 2005).

Ryan, S. D., and M. S. Gates. "Inclusion of Social Subsystem Issues in IT Investment Decisions: An Empirical Assessment." *Information Resources Management Journal* (January–March 2004).

Sambamurthy, V., et al. "Shaping Agility Through Digital Options: Reconceptualizing the Role of Information Technology in Contemporary Firms." *MIS Quarterly* 27, no. 2 (2003).

Sawhney, M. "Damn the ROI, Full Speed Ahead: 'Show Me the Money' May Not Be Right Demand for E-Business Projects." *CIO Magazine* 15, no. 19 (2002a).

Sawhney, M. "Fields of Online Dreams: E-commerce Can Flourish Anywhere If You Build the Right Business Model." *CIO Magazine* 16, no. 2 (2002b).

Schultze, U., and W. J. Orlikowski. "A Practice Perspective on Technology-Mediated Network Relations: The Use of Internet-Based Self-Serve Technologies." *Information Systems Research* 15, no. 1 (2004).

Seddon, P., et al. "Measuring Organizational IS Effectiveness." *DataBase* (Spring 2002).

Sherer, S. A., R. Kohli, and A. Baron. "Complementary Investment in Change Management and IT Investment Payoff." *Information Systems Frontiers* 5, no. 3 (2003).

Slywotzkty, A. J., and D. J. Morrison. *How Digital Is Your Business?* London: Nicholas Brealy Publishing, 2001.

Soh, C., and L. M. Markus. "How IT Creates Business Value: A Process Theory Synthesis." *Proceedings of the 16th International Conference on Information Systems*, Amsterdam, Netherlands, December 1995.

Steyaert, J. C. "Measuring the Performance of Electronic Government Services." *Information and Management* (January–February 2004).

Strader, T. J., and M. J. Shaw. "Characteristics of Electronic Markets." *Decision Support Systems* 21, no. 3 (1997).

Straub, D. *Foundations of Net-Enhanced Organizations.* Hoboken, NJ: Wiley, 2004.

Sung, T. K. "E-commerce Critical Success Factors: East Versus West." *Technological Forecasting and Social Change* (forthcoming 2005).

Sviokla, J., and A. Wong. "CRM Is Not for Micromanagers: Get Value from CRM, Use IT to Empower People—Not Keep Tabs on Them." *CIO Magazine* 16, no. 12 (2003). **cio.com/archive/040103/reality.html** (accessed January 2005).

Twentyman, J. "Private Members' Club." *Infoeconomy.com*, December 16, 2001. **infoconomy.com/pages/information-age/group45945.adp** (accessed January 2005).

University of Pennsylvania. **purchasing.upenn.edu/about/performance.php** (accessed January 2005).

Varon, E. "R.O.Iowa: By Centralizing Its State IT budget Process, Establishing a Scoring Method and Instituting Value Metrics, Iowa Has Become a National Model for Gauging Project ROI." *CIO Magazine* 16, no. 16 (2003).

Vijayan, J. "The New TCO Matrix." *Computerworld*, June 18, 2001.

Weill, P., and M. Vitale. *Place to Space: Migrating to E-business Models.* Boston, MA: Harvard Business School Press, 2001.

Weill, P., and M. Vitale. "What IT Infrastructure Capabilities Are Needed to Implement E- Business Models?" *MIS Quarterly Executive* 1, no. 1 (2002).

Yap, E. "Seven Keys to Successful e-Business." *MIS Asia*, March 1, 2002.

Zhu, K. "Information Transparency in Electronic Marketplaces: Why Data Transparency May Hinder the Adoption of B2B Exchanges." *Electronic Markets* 12, no. 2 (2001).

Zhu, K. "The Complementarity of Information Technology Infrastructure and E-Commerce Capability: A Resource-Based Assessment of Their Business Value." *Journal of Management Information Systems* 21, no. 1 (2004).

CHAPTER 16

LAUNCHING A SUCCESSFUL ONLINE BUSINESS AND EC PROJECT

Content

Learning Objectives

Upon completion of this chapter, you will be able to:

1. Understand the fundamental requirements for initiating an online business.
2. Describe the process of initiating and funding a start-up e-business or large e-project.
3. Understand the process of adding EC initiatives to an existing business.
4. Describe the issues and methods of transforming an organization into an e-business.
5. Describe the process of acquiring Web sites and evaluating building and hosting options.
6. Understand the importance of providing and managing content and describe how it is accomplished.
7. Evaluate Web sites on design criteria such as appearance, navigation, consistency, and performance.
8. Understand how search engine optimization may help a Web site obtain high placement in search engines.
9. Understand how some major support e-services are provided.
10. Understand the process of building an online storefront.
11. Be able to build an online storefront with templates.

OBO SETS ITS GOALS FOR SUCCESS

The Problem

OBO of New Zealand sells protective gear for field hockey goalkeepers. The leg guards, helmets, gloves, and other products are designed to protect goalies from the hard hockey ball without inhibiting the goalie's need to move quickly and easily. OBO's protective foam has a tighter and more consistent cell structure than competitors' products to provide maximum, long-wearing protection, and OBO's unique three-dimensional thermo-bonding manufacturing process produces equipment that is shaped to reflect the way the body moves. By manufacturing a quality product and listening to its customers, OBO has become the market leader in most of the 20 countries in which its products are sold. In the 2000 Olympics, all of the medal-winning teams wore OBO gear.

OBO is based in Palmerston North, a small provincial town in New Zealand that is a very long way from its principal markets in Europe and the Americas. OBO sells a niche product that is best sold through agents or stores to ensure a proper fit. How does OBO use its Web site to market an experiential product to a global market from New Zealand?

The Solution

The goals of the *obo.co.nz* Web site are community building, product sales, and research and development. As the "About OBO" page proudly boasts, "OBO loves the Web because it lets us have contact with the people we exist to serve."

Community building happens through online discussion forums, sponsored players, and an image gallery. OBO's company director Simon Barnett says: "We sponsor goalkeepers. We e-mail out to 900–1,000 people biweekly and give them the opportunity to ask an expert about the game and the equipment, join a database, link to other hockey sites, and seek readers' opinions. We try to get people involved by having their photo on the Web site. If we can get people involved, they'll love the brand name and the image and the feelings that go with it" (New Zealand Ministry of Economic Development [MED] 2000, p. 12).

OBO also sells goalie equipment through the Web site. However, the main marketing and sales goal of the Web site is to convince the visitor of the value of the product and direct the customer to a store or agent to make the purchase. Barnett calls the Web site "a support mechanism for the brand and the sale of equipment through the agents, and we will pick up the odd sale here and there" (New Zealand MED 2000, p. 12).

The research and development goal is met through online surveys, solicitation of players' opinions of the products, and focus groups. According to Barnett: "We use the Web site for research and development through focus groups. We give a topic such as goalkeeping shoes—Is there a need for them? What features should they have? What pricing? The focus group is carefully selected off the database, given the brief (the purpose of the questions), and asked to respond by the end of the week with their opinions" (New Zealand MED 2000, p. 12).

The Results

The OBO Web site is most successful at community building. In 2000, over 100,000 people visited the Web site, many of them first-time OBO equipment buyers who must register their product warranty online. Many become registered "team players" and contribute to discussion forums as well as create their own "favorites" section and online address book. The site also builds community by promoting a goalie-friendly approach to OBO's customers. Simon Barnett signs his introduction letter as "Team Captain" and says, "the most special thing about OBO are its people. The people who bring you the OBO product are dedicated, honest, and earnest about our work" (*obo.co.nz* 2005).

Online product sales are modest and growing slowly. This is in line with the company's expectation that the Web site should support, not compete with, OBO's agent network. For example, prices at the Web site are slightly higher than in retail stores. However, online sales are expected to grow because OBO has introduced a new line of clothes designed specifically for goalies that is sold exclusively through the Web site.

The focus groups deliver high-value feedback at almost no cost, and the discussion forums contribute to both community building and a constant stream of feedback about OBO's product in the marketplace.

Sources: Compiled from New Zealand Ministry of Economic Development (2000) and OBO (2005).

WHAT WE CAN LEARN . . .

OBO's use of the Web matches many of the expectations that online business owners have for their own Web sites. A small company with a great product is using its Web site to reach its target markets in distant countries. Like many successful online businesses, OBO uses its site to support business goals and to meet the needs and expectations of its target audience. The Web site is simple and well designed: It includes "attractors" that encourage customer interaction and keep customers coming back, it contains content that promotes cross-selling, and it effectively promotes sustainable customer relationships. OBO is one of tens of thousands of small businesses successfully using the Web for e-commerce. The purpose of this chapter is to describe the requirements for creating and maintaining a successful e-business or EC initiative. This chapter builds on the conceptual material offered in previous chapters to provide a practical understanding of what it takes to be successful in the competitive world of electronic commerce. Finally, it teaches you how to build a storefront quickly.

16.1 GETTING INTO E-COMMERCE

Now that you are familiar with EC and its potential, you may want to know how to get into EC yourself. An e-commerce venture can be started in any number of ways; your only limit is your imagination. In this chapter, we will discuss some of the most common ways of starting an e-business. Specifically, this chapter presents the following topics:

- Starting a new online business (a *startup*; see Section 16.2)
- Adding e-commerce initiative(s) to an existing business (i.e., becoming a click-and-mortar organization; see Section 16.3)
- Transforming to an e-business (Section 16.3)
- Opening a storefront on the Web (Section 16.9)

Almost any e-commerce initiative will require support activities and services as well as plans for attracting visitors to a Web site (see Kavassalis et al. 2004). This chapter presents the following with regards to these types of activities:

- Developing a Web site (Section 16.4)
- Hosting the Web site and selecting and registering a domain name (Section 16.5)
- Developing, updating, and managing the content of a Web site (Section 16.6)
- Designing a Web site for maximum usability (Section 16.7)
- Providing support services (Section 16.8)

16.2 STARTING A NEW ONLINE BUSINESS

Success in the online marketplace is never an assured outcome. As in the brick-and-mortar marketplace, the failure rate for online companies is high (Kauffman et al. 2002; Saracevic 2000). Why do a few online companies succeed while many others fail? What does the *ontrepreneur*—the online entrepreneur—need to know to launch a profitable online business?

Online businesses may be *pure play* companies (online only) or *click-and-mortar* companies that add online projects, such as e-procurement or selling online, as additional marketing channels.

CREATING A NEW COMPANY OR ADDING AN ONLINE PROJECT

Most new businesses—brick-and-mortar, pure play, or click-and-mortar—begin in a similar manner. The process can be described by the following three steps:

- **Step 1: Identify a consumer or business need in the marketplace.** Many businesses simply begin with a good idea. A magazine article, a personal observation, an unsolved problem, a small irritation, or a friend's suggestion may trigger an idea, and the prospective business owner sees a gap between what people want and what is available. For example, both Amazon.com (see EC Application Case 16.1) and eBay began this way.
- **Step 2: Investigate the opportunity.** Just because a person perceives that an opportunity exists does not mean that it is real. Perhaps the number of individuals interested in purchasing the product or service is too small. Perhaps the cost of manufacturing, marketing, and distributing the product or providing the service is too large. The revenue model may be wrong, others may have tried already and failed, satisfactory substitute products may be available, and so on. For example, online grocery shopping would seem to be a wonderful opportunity—relieving busy professionals of the time-consuming and tiresome task of regular visits to a grocery store. Many large- and small-scale online grocery ventures have been tried (e.g., NetGrocer, Peapod, HomeGrocer, Webvan), but most have failed or continue to lose money because they misjudged the logistical problems associated with grocery warehousing and delivery (Bakshi and Deighton 1999; Kurnia et al. 2005). This is why it is so important to develop a business plan. One of the purposes of a business plan is to determine the feasibility of a business opportunity in the marketplace.
- **Step 3: Determine the business owner's ability to meet the need.** Assuming that a realistic business opportunity exists, does the prospective business owner have the ability to convert the opportunity into success? Some personal qualities are important: Is the business

CASE 16.1

EC Application

A BRILLIANT IDEA

Call it fate or call it the right person having the right idea at the right time. Whatever you call it, the idea behind Amazon.com and its founder, Jeff Bezos, seemed destined for each other.

Jeff Bezos was born in January 1964 in Albuquerque, New Mexico. Even as a boy his cleverness, intelligence, and entrepreneurial skills were obvious. At the age of 12, Bezos built a motorized mirrored Infinity Cube because he couldn't afford the $20 to buy one. A few years later, he graduated as valedictorian of his Florida high school. As a young entrepreneur, he created a summer camp for middle school students and promoted it by saying that it "emphasizes the use of new ways of thinking in old areas," which was in many ways a prediction of his future success.

Bezos graduated from Princeton University with a degree in computer science, and his first employment was in electronic commerce, building an EDI network for settling cross-border equity transactions. A few jobs later, he was a senior vice president at the hedge fund firm D. E. Shaw, responsible for exploring new business opportunities on the Internet. It was then that his intelligence, entrepreneurial talents, computing education, and e-commerce experience all came together in a brilliant idea: The most logical thing to sell over the Internet was books! Several years later he added dozens of other products.

Why books? Behind the thousands of brick-and-mortar bookstores are just two large book distributors, with an extensive list of books already online in the distributors' databases. Bezos was willing to bet that book buyers would be willing to give up the cozy, coffee-shop, browsing environment of the local bookstore if he could offer them the "earth's biggest bookstore," fantastic customer service, and features that no physical bookstore could match—customer book reviews, author interviews, personalized book recommendations, and more.

The other driving force behind his idea was what Bezos calls his "regret-minimization framework." "When I am 80," he asked himself, "am I going to regret leaving Wall Street? No. Will I regret missing a chance to be there at the start of the Internet? Yes" (Bayers 1999).

The rest of the story is the stuff of legend. Bezos left his six-figure Wall Street salary and wrote the Amazon.com business plan during a cross-country move to Seattle, Washington. The Amazon.com Web site was built in a cramped, poorly insulated garage. When Amazon.com launched in July 1995, a bell would ring every time the server recorded a sale. Within a few weeks the constant bell ringing became unbearable, and they turned it off. Today, on a busy day, Amazon.com sells to about 3 million customers.

In the late 1990s and early 2000s, Amazon.com invested $2 billion in physical warehouses (see the opening case to Chapter 13) and expansion opportunities. This was in line with Bezos' vision for Amazon.com as "broader than books and music." After years of large losses, Amazon.com announced its first small profit in the fourth quarter of 2001. By 2005, the company had become even more profitable. It all began with a smart entrepreneur whose life experiences gave him a brilliant idea that led to the founding of a legendary e-tailing company.

During its first decade of operation, Amazon.com changed its business model several times, adding innovative ideas. It also acquired other companies or stakes in companies in several countries (e.g., *joyo.com*—the largest e-tailer of books, music, and videos in China). Amazon Services, Inc., a subsidiary of Amazon.com, has projects with a number of different partners (e.g., American Express). Amazon Theater offers film viewing from its Web site as well as many more innovations. However, Bezos' most original idea is his vision of Blue Origin, a futuristic center for suborbital spaceships (Klotz 2005). Perhaps it will only be a matter of time before customers can purchase tickets for space trips from Amazon.com.

Sources: Compiled from Spector (2000), Business Wire (2004a and 2004b), and Klotz (2005).

Questions

1. What was the gap in the consumer market that inspired Bezos to create Amazon.com?
2. What factors, at both personal and business levels, led Bezos to his brilliant idea?

in an industry the prospective business owner knows well? Is it something the entrepreneur loves doing? Are family and friends supportive? Business skills in staff recruitment, management, negotiation, marketing, and financial management are required, as well as entrepreneurial attitudes such as innovation, risk taking, and being proactive. Many good ideas and realistic initiatives have failed in the execution stage because the owners or principals of the business lacked sufficient business skills to make it a reality. Boo.com, for example, seemingly had a great concept (retailing ultramodern, designer clothing) and superior software, but it failed because of the inability of management to organize the business and manage the projects necessary to bring Boo.com online before it burned through $120 million of start-up capital (Cukier 2000).

The process for developing EC projects in existing companies is similar, except that step 3 is changed to: "Determine the organization's ability to meet the need."

Beyond these general platitudes about what it takes to start a prosperous business, the owner of an online business must consider some requirements that reflect the online nature of the business. The first of these is the need to understand Internet culture. Activities such as spam, extensive use of graphics, forced visitor registration, and intrusive pop-up browser windows are counter to the accepted norms of behavior on the Internet (Huff et al. 2001). Similarly, business owners new to the Net need to realize that, contrary to expectations, textual exchanges of information are "media rich" (Markus 1994; Huang et al. 1996; Stam 2005); customers are active in how they absorb and use information; and the Internet is a personal, helping, and sharing place for most users. Businesses that ignore the cultural and behavioral norms of the Internet do so at their peril.

A second requirement that the owner of an online business must consider is the nature of appropriate products and services. Although virtually anything is available for sale on the Internet, the degree of sales success is somewhat dependent on the type of item or service being offered. For example, products that can be digitized (e.g., information, music, software) sell well and can be delivered easily. Similarly, services (e.g., stock brokering, ticket sales) and commodities (e.g., books, CDs) also have been quite successful. In contrast, experiential products, such as expensive clothes, do not sell well. However, one of the greatest opportunities the Internet offers is in niche marketing. Rare and quirky sales ideas, such as antique Coke bottles (antiquebottles.com), gadgets for left-handed individuals (anythingleft-handed.co.uk), Swedish gourmet food (wikstromsgourmet.com), toys for cats and dogs (cattoys.com), and gift items from Belize (belizenet.com), would rarely succeed in a physical storefront, but the Internet offers the owners of these sites an opportunity to pursue their business idea and be successful. The Internet's worldwide reach makes it easy for people with a common interest to find each other and conduct business together.

ONLINE BUSINESS PLANNING

Every new online business needs at least an informal business plan. As defined in Chapter 14, a **business plan** is a written document that identifies a company's goals and outlines how the company intends to achieve those goals and at what cost. A business plan includes both *strategic* elements (e.g., mission statement, value proposition, and competitive positioning statement) and *operational* elements (e.g., operations plan, financial statements) of how a new business intends to do business. Medium and large businesses, or those seeking external funding, must have a formal business plan.

business plan
A written document that identifies a company's goals and outlines how the company intends to achieve the goals and at what cost.

The primary reason an entrepreneur writes a business plan is to acquire funding from a bank, an angel investor, a venture capitalist, or the financial markets. Similarly, in an existing business a *business case* needs to be written for any new large EC project, so management can decide whether to fund it (see the Iowa ROI opening case in Chapter 15). A business plan also is important for a new venture as a tool to recruit senior management and to convince business partners to make a commitment to the business. A business plan helps ensure a thriving business by encouraging an entrepreneur to set goals, anticipate problems, set measures for success, and keep the business on track after it is started. A business plan forces the entrepreneur to be realistic about the business's prospects. Indeed, sometimes the most successful outcome of a business plan is a decision not to proceed.

The Nature of a Business Plan

A business plan for an online business—an *e-business plan*—differs only subtly from a traditional, off-line business plan. After all, a business is a business and a plan is a plan, so most of what one finds in a business plan is also in an e-business plan. Many of the differences between the two types of plans are obvious and can readily be accounted for—an online business never closes, the market may be global instead of local, and e-commerce is conducted at "Internet speed."

The biggest difference in e-business planning is for the ontrepreneur to recognize that the Internet is unlike any other sales channel. As discussed in previous chapters, the Internet allows companies to interact with consumers with both reach and richness (Evans and

Wurster 2000), to introduce new and innovative business models, and to distribute information at the speed of light at almost zero cost. The Internet also changes business assumptions, such as creating more bargaining power for the customer and less bargaining power for the supplier (see Chapter 15 and Porter 2001), creating a more perfect information market to the customer's benefit, and making it easier for competitors to invade a company's marketplace and vice versa. Finally, the Internet creates greater opportunities for focusing on the customer through personalization of content, one-to-one marketing, and customer self-service. Because the Web allows these and other customer service features, online businesses must make them part of their business plan before their competitors do. These differences, and more, make the "e-difference" in e-business planning.

Online Tutorial T1 (An E-Business Plan Tutorial) on the book's Web site explores this topic in further depth and offers a detailed explanation of how to prepare a business plan.

business case
A document that is used to justify the investment of internal, organizational resources in a specific application or project.

The Business Case

An existing brick-and-mortar business looking to move online also needs a **business case**—a document that is used to justify the investment of internal, organizational resources in a specific application or project. A business case for a large, resource-intensive EC project resembles a business plan. The similarities and differences in writing such a business case are included in Online Tutorial T1 (An E-Business Plan Tutorial) on the book's Web site. To some extent, the business case can be viewed as the part of a business plan that justifies the EC company's existence. For a small or medium-size project, the business case can be much simpler. Insights and Additions 16.1 presents a business case template that can be used to justify an online application or project, such as a new Web site, the addition of transactional processing to an existing Web site, an e-newsletter, an extranet, or participation in a digital exchange.

FUNDING A NEW ONLINE BUSINESS

Launching an online business can be expensive. The brave entrepreneur is usually willing to invest personal funds from savings, personal lines of credit, or a house mortgage, but these sources of "bootstrap funding" are unlikely to be enough. The new venture involves significant risk, so some traditional sources of debt financing, such as a bank loan, are difficult or impossible to get. What are other sources of funding for a start-up business?

Initial Funding: Angel Investors and Incubators

angel investor
A wealthy individual who contributes personal funds and possibly expertise at the earliest stage of business development.

Usually, the entrepreneur's personal funds are insufficient. The entrepreneur will then go to friends, family members, or to angel investors. An **angel investor** is a wealthy individual who contributes personal funds and possibly expertise at the earliest stage of business development.

A typical angel investor scenario begins with a young software developer who has identified a niche in the market for a new software application and has used his own money to get started but has insufficient funding to continue. An angel investor may provide the developer with an office, hardware, software, salary, and access to the human and financial resources required to write the software application. In most cases, the angel investor also provides guidance and/or access to management expertise. In addition to sometimes-altruistic goals, the angel investor is looking for a reasonable return on the investment once the business is ready to launch. In other words, the angel investor is almost always a pre-venture-capital (VC) funding source and may be paid later from the infusion of venture capital funds. An angel investor is an excellent source of funding for the ontrepreneur; however, angel funding is scarce and difficult to find.

incubator
A company, university, or nonprofit organization that supports businesses in their initial stages of development.

Another important source of support, if not funding, for pre-VC firms is an incubator. An **incubator** is a company, university, or nonprofit organization that supports promising businesses in their initial stages of development. Although some incubators offer start-up funding, the primary purpose of most incubators is to offer a variety of support services—office space, accounting services, group purchasing schemes, reception services, coaching, and information technology consulting—at little or no cost. In return, the incubator receives a modest fee, start-up equity in the company, or both (Phan et al. 2005; Conway 2004).

Insights and Additions 16.1 A Business Case Template

This template is best used to justify the expenditure of resources on a specific online project or initiative in an existing business. If the business is considering a number of different initiatives, a separate business case should be prepared for each one. If the initiative is for a new business, a more comprehensive business plan will be required.

- **Goals.** Begin with a specific description of what the business intends to achieve through the initiative—increased sales, reinforcement of the brand or corporate image, improved customer support, reduction in communications and marketing costs, and so forth. A useful approach is to define the problem, propose a solution, and describe the expected outcomes or impacts. Conclude this section with *goals*—one or more statements that succinctly describe a desired future condition toward which efforts will be directed.
- **Cost savings.** If one or more goals include reduction of existing expenditures, then calculate the following: (1) an itemized and quantified list of existing costs that will be affected by the project and (2) the estimated levels of savings that the project will generate (e.g., reduce long-distance telephone costs by 45 percent). When costs and saving levels are multiplied together, the expected reduction of expenditures will be known. These savings should be estimated for a short-term time frame, perhaps the first 3 years of the project's operation.
- **New revenue.** If one or more of the goals suggests an increased revenue stream, then calculate: (1) an itemized and quantified list of existing net income (revenue from sales minus cost of sales) that will be affected by the application or project and (2) the estimated levels of new sales that are expected (e.g., increase product sales by 12 percent). When net income and increased sales levels are multiplied together, the expected amount of increased revenue will be revealed. Do this for the same multiyear time frame as used in the cost-savings calculation.
- **Extra benefits.** List and, if possible, quantify any additional fiscal benefits that are associated with the project (e.g., improved staff productivity, faster collection of outstanding debts). If these are difficult to estimate accurately, it is best to list them but not quantify them nor add them to the benefits identified previously. This approach will produce an overall more conservative estimate of benefits, building in an extra cushion for project success in the event that not all quantified benefits are realized.
- **Cost of the solution.** This is an itemized and quantified list of costs associated with the online project. Both direct costs (e.g., amortized costs of Web site development and Web site hosting) and indirect costs (e.g., staff training) should be estimated for the period.
- **Net benefits.** Add together all benefits (i.e., cost savings, new revenue, extra benefits) and subtract the costs. The result should be a specific amount of expected monetary gains (or losses) resulting from successful implementation of the project in each year of the period being examined.
- **Recommendation.** Summarize the decision that is being recommended in light of the foregoing analysis. If the net benefit result is strongly positive, then a decision to proceed is likely, and the next steps (e.g., a risk analysis, customer survey, staff hiring) can be started. If the results are slightly positive or negative in one or all years of operation, the decision to proceed may still be justified on the basis of seeing the online initiative as a long-term strategy, a competitive imperative, or simply the cost of staying in business. If the bottom line is strongly negative, then the most likely outcome will be a decision that there is no justification for the project, saving the business a lot of time and money. Even that can be viewed as a positive outcome of a business case.

Secondary Financing: Venture Capital

One major source of funding during the dot-com boom was venture capital. **Venture capital (VC)** is money invested in a business by an individual or a group of individuals (venture capitalists) in exchange for equity in the business. Venture capitalists tend to invest in companies that have identified what seems to be an outstanding business opportunity, have taken some action to make the opportunity happen (e.g., written a new software application, secured a patent, built a Web site, conducted some experiments, and recruited key personnel), and need an infusion of funds and management expertise to expand and launch the business. Venture capitalists usually invest large sums of money and expect, in return, some management control and a profit on their investment within 3 to 5 years when the successful startup goes public (an IPO) or is merged with or acquired by a larger company. The start-up company receives the funds and experienced management guidance it needs during its launch and expansion stages.

venture capital (VC)
Money invested in a business by an individual or a group of individuals (venture capitalists) in exchange for equity in the business.

The downside for the start-up business to acquire a VC is minimal; it loses some control over the business in return for funds it is unlikely to acquire from any other source. The more difficult problem is *finding* venture capital. Due to the many dot-com failures in 2000 and onward, many VC sources have disappeared, and competition for venture capital is fierce.

The downside for the venture capitalist is that if the business fails, or even if it is a mediocre success, then the promised return on equity from going public, merging, or being bought out does not happen. This occurrence is common, and venture capitalists plan on one wildly successful investment to make up the losses from other less-than-successful ventures.

Some well-known venture capital companies are vFinance Capital (vfinance.com), the Capital Network (thecapitalnetwork.com), and Garage Technology Ventures (garage.com), which was founded by personal-computing guru Guy Kawasaki. VCs themselves may be startups. Most of them lost large amounts of money for their investors during the dot-com bust. Rayport and Jaworski (2003) offer a more comprehensive discussion of venture capital markets and other sources of equity financing, such as holding companies and corporate ventures. For more information, see the National Venture Capital Association (nvca.org), the Venture Capital Marketplace (v-capital.com.au/), Mobius Venture Capital (mobiusvc.com), and Vcapital (vcapital.com).

Additional Funding: A Large Partner

As part of a VC investment or after the VC money is depleted, one or more large companies may step into the process. For example, Yahoo!, IBM, Microsoft, Motorola, AOL (Time Warner), and Oracle have invested in hundreds of EC start-up companies. Eventually, they may acquire the startup completely. Such investments are frequently done in complementary or competing areas. For example, Yahoo! is a major investor in Google.

The IPO

Once the company is well known and successful, it will go to a stock exchange to raise money via an *initial public offer* (IPO). In such offerings, investors will pay a much larger amount of money per share than that paid by the initial and secondary funders, sometimes 5 or 10 times more per share.

Section 16.2 ▶ REVIEW QUESTIONS

1. Describe the formation process of a typical online business.
2. What special requirements must an online business consider in its formation? In e-business planning?
3. What is a business plan and how does it contribute to business success? What is a business case and how does it contribute to business success?
4. Describe initial, secondary, and IPO funding options available to a startup.

16.3 ADDING EC INITIATIVES AND TRANSFORMING TO AN E-BUSINESS

Creating an e-business startup certainly is exciting, but it also is very risky. As with any other business, the failure rate is very high. However, in cyberspace the risks and uncertainties, plus lack of experience, result in an even higher rate of failure. Nevertheless, tens of thousands of new online businesses have been created since 1995, mostly small ones (see Section 16.9 and Chapter 14). A much more common option is adding one or several EC initiatives to an existing business.

ADDING EC INITIATIVES TO AN EXISTING BUSINESS

Almost all medium-to-large organizations have added or plan to add EC initiatives to the existing business. The most common additions are:

- **A storefront.** Adding an online sales channel is common in both B2C (e.g., godiva.com, walmart.com) and B2B (e.g., ibm.com). The required investment is fairly low, because storefront hosting is available from many vendors (see Sections 16.5 and 16.9). Customers like the option of buying online, and gradually more and more of them will use the storefront. A storefront can be built fairly quickly, and the damage in case of failure may not be too large. Because the required investment is not large, it may not be necessary to expend the time and money in developing a formal business case. This is a practical strategy for an SME (Chapter 14). For a large-scale storefront, a company will need to follow the steps suggested in Section 16.2, especially the preparation of a business case, in order to secure internal funding and the blessing of top management. For further details on developing storefronts, see Online Chapter 18 and the "Getting Started Guide" at smallbusiness.yahoo.com. A major issue in developing a storefront is deciding what support services to offer and how to provide them.

- **A portal.** As discussed in Chapter 7, there are many types of corporate portals. Almost all companies today have one or several portals that they use for external and/or internal collaboration and communication. A storefront for employees or for external customers may be a part of a portal. Adding a portal (or several portals) may be a necessity, and it may not be preceded by a formal business case. Issues of content and design, as well as security, are of utmost importance. Because many vendors offer portal-building services, vendor selection may be an important issue (see Online Chapter 18).

- **E-procurement.** This EC initiative is popular with large companies and was described in Chapter 5. The development of an e-procurement initiative is described in Online Chapter 18. E-procurement usually requires significant investment; therefore, a business case is needed. E-procurement also requires extensive integration (both internally and externally), so an EC architecture must be in place.

- **Auctions and reverse auctions.** Large corporations need to consider building their own auction and/or reverse auction (for e-procurement) sites. Although forward auctions can be added to a storefront at a reasonable cost, a reverse auction usually requires more integration with business partners and, consequently, a larger investment and a business case.
- **Other initiatives.** Organizations may consider many other EC initiatives, following the business models presented in Chapter 1. For example, Qantas Airways (qantas.com.au) sells tickets online directly from its Web site and from a B2B exchange; it buys supplies and services from its e-procurement site as well as from several exchanges; it provides e-training for its employees; operates several corporate portals; offers online banking services to its employees; provides e-CRM and e-PRM; manages its frequent flyers program; supports a wireless notification system to customers; and so on. Large companies such as GE and IBM have hundreds of active EC projects. Other initiatives are illustrated in the Real-World Case at the end of this chapter.

TRANSFORMATION TO AN E-BUSINESS

As the brick-and-mortar organization implements more and more EC projects, it becomes a click-and-mortar organization, and eventually an e-business. Being an e-business does not imply that the organization is a pure online company, it just means that as many processes as possible are conducted online (see the Siemans case in Online File W16.1).

What Is Organizational Transformation?

Organizational transformation is a comprehensive concept that implies a major organizational change. According to McKay and Marshall (2004), a *transformation* is not only a major change, but also a sharp break from the past. The key points in understanding organizational transformation are as follows:

- The organization's ways of thinking and vision will fundamentally change.
- There will be revolutionary changes to the process and context involved in creating a new organizational vision and rethinking business models and business strategy.
- The change must involve a substantial break from previous ways of acting. It will likely involve discovering and developing new opportunities and new ways of doing things.
- The change must permeate through and impact on the behavior of a majority of organizational members.
- The change will involve creating new systems, procedures, and structures that not only enable and dictate how new processes function, but will also impact on the deeply embedded business models and understandings that drive the organization.

According to Hendon (2003), an e-business transformation is not solely about technology. Technologies must be integrated with business strategy, processes, organizational culture, and infrastructure.

How an Organization Can Be Transformed into an E-Business

Transforming an organization, especially a large company, into an e-business can be a very complex endeavor (see the Real-World Case at the end of this chapter and Online File W16.1). For an organization to transform itself into an e-business, it must transform several major processes, such as procurement, sales, CRM, and manufacturing, as well as deal with *change management*.

Such a transformation involves several strategic issues. Lasry (2002) raised several of these issues in an investigation of the rate at which brick-and-mortar retail firms adopt the Web as an additional sales channel. He examined organizational strategies such as internal restructuring, the formation of joint ventures, and outsourcing. He concluded that implementing EC requires a disruptive and potentially hazardous change in core features. He suggests that companies spin off EC activities as part of the transformation process (see the discussion in Chapter 14).

Ginige et al. (2001) provide a comprehensive description of the transformation to e-business, describing both the internal and external processes supported by IT, as shown in Exhibit 16.1. They then show the support of IT at each stage. Finally, they describe the necessary change management activities.

Several other studies have examined transformation to e-business. For example, Chen and Ching (2002) explored the relationship of BPR and e-business and investigated the change process both for individuals and organizations. They proposed a process of redesigning an organization for e-business, providing several research propositions. Bosilj-Vuksic et al. (2002) explored the use of simulation modeling for enabling transformation to e-business. They examined the process of BPR and suggested using simulation and process maps to support the process. Lee (2003) described the use of business intelligence and intelligent systems. Finally, Jackson and Harris (2003) explored organizational change issues in transformation to e-business.

Software Tools for Facilitating Transformation to E-Business

Several vendors offer methodologies and tools that can be used to facilitate transformation to e-business (e.g., see El Sawy 2001 and Ould 2003). A methodology developed by Integic Corp. (integic.com/solutions/methodology.cfm) includes a framework for e-strategy, solution development and deployment, a guide for organizational change, a framework for project management, and a systematic approach to quality management. Using this methodology, organizations in the public sector, such as the Federal Aviation Administration, the Office of the Comptroller in New York City, as well as public utilities, have achieved dramatic cost and cycle time reductions (see "Case Studies" at integic.com).

Section 16.3 ▶ REVIEW QUESTIONS

1. Which EC initiatives are most likely to be added to brick-and-mortar organizations?
2. Describe the major characteristics (key points) of organizational transformation.
3. Describe the stages in becoming an e-business (per Ginige et al. 2001).
4. List some of the issues involved in transforming to an e-business.

16.4 BUILDING OR ACQUIRING A WEB SITE

Every online business needs a Web site. A Web site is the primary way any firm doing business on the Internet advertises its products or services and attracts customers. Many Web sites also sell products and services, and businesses with digital products usually deliver their products via the Web site as well. The Web site may be a storefront, a portal, an auction site, and so on. How can an organization build or acquire such a site? First, let's examine the different types of Web sites that exist.

EXHIBIT 16.1 **Roadmap to Becoming an E-Business**

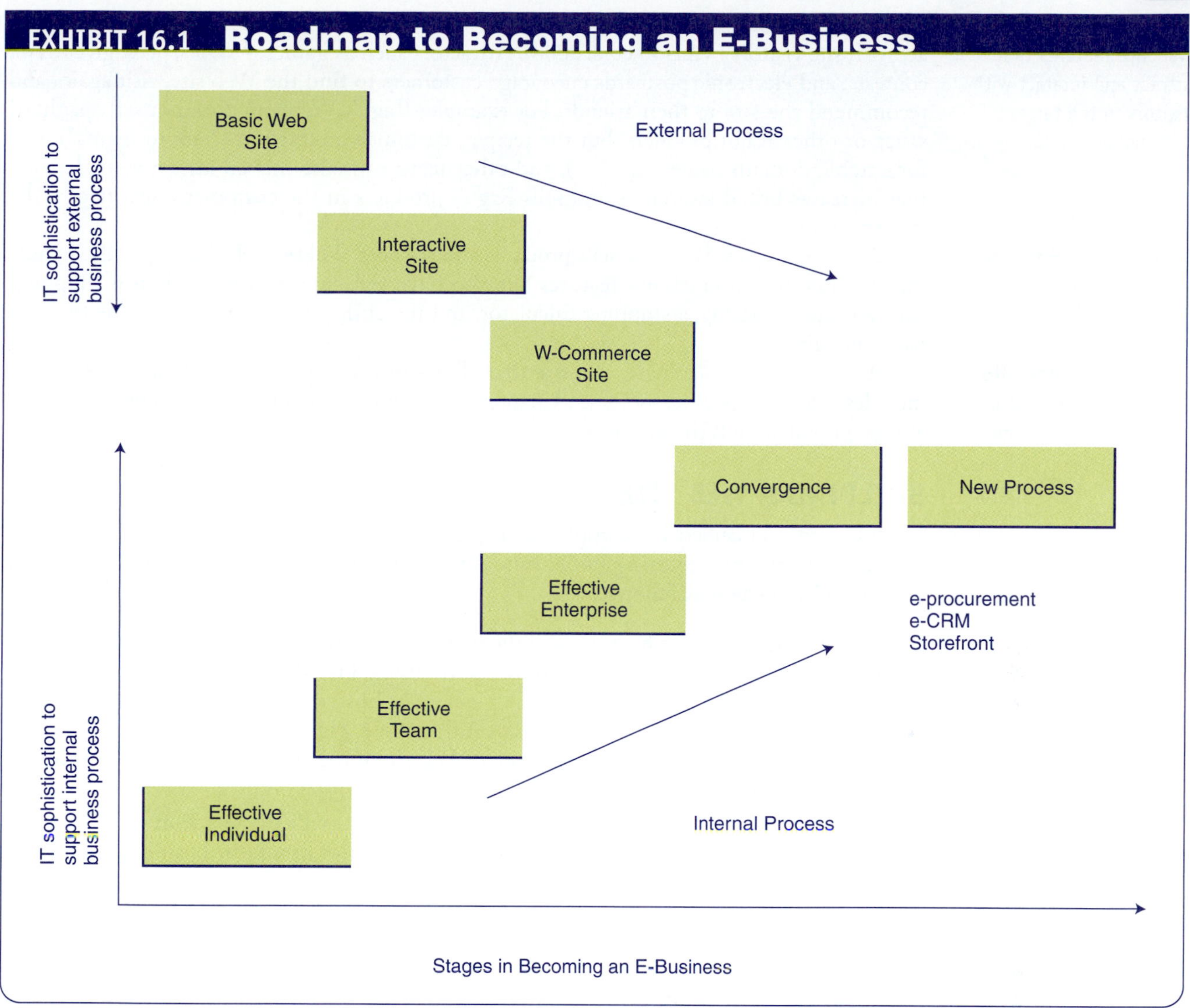

Source: Ginige, A. et al. "A Road Map for Successfully Transforming SMEs into E-Business." *Cutter IT Journal*, May 2001. Used with permission of the author.

CLASSIFICATION OF WEB SITES

Web sites come in all kinds, shapes, and sizes. One of the major distinctions made in Web site classification is the level of functionality inherent in the site. An **informational Web site** does little more than provide information about the business and its products and services. For many brick-and-mortar businesses, such as a New England weathervane shop (vtweatherworks.com), a Cook Islands beach house (varas.co.ck), or a B2B secure storage facility (safestoreusa.com), an informational "brochureware" Web site is perfectly satisfactory.

informational Web site
A Web site that does little more than provide information about the business and its products and services.

An **interactive Web site** provides opportunities for the customers and the business to communicate and share information. An interactive site will contain all of the information about products and services that an informational site does, but it also will deliver informational features intended to encourage interaction between the business and customers or between customers, such as an e-newsletter, product demonstrations, and customer discussion forums. An interactive Web site will strongly encourage feedback by including contact e-mail addresses, providing feedback forms, and encouraging completion of online surveys. Navigation can be made more interactive with features such as the ability to search the site, a well-designed site map, and mouseovers (clickable buttons that change shape or color when a visitor passes a mouse cursor over the button). Interactivity can be enhanced with value-added tools such as currency converters, price comparisons, calendars, and various types of calculators (e.g., a mortgage calculator on a bank's Web site).

interactive Web site
A Web site that provides opportunities for the customers and the business to communicate and share information.

attractors
Web site features that attract and interact with visitors in the target stakeholder group.

At a higher level of interactivity are **attractors**—Web site features that attract and interact with site visitors (Watson et al. 2000). Attractors such as games, puzzles, prize giveaways, contests, and electronic postcards encourage customers to find the Web site, visit again, and recommend the site to their friends. For example, Ragu's Web site does not sell spaghetti sauce or other Ragu products, but the recipes, customer interaction ("talk to mama"), unforgettable domain name (eat.com), and other features make this an attractor-loaded site that increases brand awareness and sells Ragu's products in the customer's next trip to the grocery store.

transactional Web site
A Web site that sells products and services.

A **transactional Web site** sells products and services. These Web sites typically include information and interactivity features but also have sell-side features such as a shopping cart, a product catalog, a shipping calculator, and the ability to accept credit cards to complete the sale.

collaborative Web site
A site that allows business partners to collaborate

A **collaborative Web site** is a site that allows business partners to collaborate (i.e., it includes many supportive tools; see Chapters 6, 7, and 13). Collaboration capabilities may also be provided by B2B exchanges.

BUILDING A WEB SITE

Assuming that a business has completed the preparatory work of business formation, writing a business plan, and acquiring initial funding, as outlined in Section 16.2, the process of building a Web site is as follows:

- **Step 1—Select a Web host.** One of the first decisions that an online business will face is where the Web site will be located on the Internet. The Web site may be included in a virtual shopping mall, such as activeplaza.com, or hosted in a collection of independent storefronts, as at Yahoo! (smallbusiness.yahoo.com). However, many medium-size and large businesses will build a stand-alone Web site either with an independent hosting service or through self-hosting arrangements.
- **Step 2—Register a domain name.** Nearly concurrent with the selection of a Web host will be the domain name decision. In a mall or Web storefront, the business's name may be an extension of the host's name (e.g., *smallbusiness.yahoo.com/mybusiness*). A stand-alone Web site will have a stand-alone domain name (e.g., *mybusiness.com*), and decisions will have to be made about which top-level domain name to use and whether the domain name includes the business name or some aspect of branding.
- **Step 3—Create and manage content.** The Web site also needs content—the text, images, sound, and video that deliver the information that site visitors need and expect. Content can come from a variety of sources, but getting the right content in place, making it easy for viewers to find, delivering it effectively, and managing content so it remains accurate and up-to-date are crucial to the success of the online business (see discussion in Section 16.6). Exhibit 16.2 lists the primary criteria Web site visitors use to evaluate the content of a Web site.
- **Step 4—Design the Web site.** This is the critically important and creative part of the process that determines what the site will look like (e.g., color schemes, graphics, typography) and how visitors will use it (e.g., information architecture, navigation design). Mall or storefront businesses may have limited options, but the design choices for the stand-alone Web site are nearly unlimited. Exhibit 16.2 also lists the primary criteria that Web site visitors use to evaluate the design of a Web site. Details are provided in Section 16.7 and in Online Technical Appendix B.

- **Step 5—Construct the Web site and test.** Businesses must also decide whether to design and construct the Web site internally, contract it out to a Web design firm, or some combination of both. When the business owners are satisfied with the Web site, it is transferred to the Web site host. At this point, the Web site is open for business, but final testing is required to ensure that all of the links work and that the processes function as expected (e.g., acceptance of credit cards). For details, see Section 16.8 and Online Chapter 18.

- **Step 6—Market and promote the Web site.** At this stage, the location or URL of the Web site is widely promoted by the business on products, business cards, letters, and promotional materials. Many of the advertising strategies discussed in Chapter 4—banner

EXHIBIT 16.2 Web Site Evaluation Criteria

How Web Site Visitors Evaluate Content	
Criteria (and related "subcriteria")	**Explanation**
Relevance (applicable, related, clear)	Concerned with issues such as relevancy, clearness, and "goodness" of the information.
Timeliness (current, continuously updated)	Concerned with the currency of the information.
Reliability (believable, accurate, consistent)	Concerned with the degree of accuracy, dependability, and consistency of the information.
Scope (sufficient, complete, covers a wide range, detailed)	Evaluates the extent of information, range of information, and level of detail provided by the Web site.
Perceived usefulness (informative, valuable, instrumental)	Visitors' assessment of the likelihood that the information will enhance their purchasing decision.
How Web Site Visitors Evaluate Web Site Design	
Criteria (and related "subcriteria")	**Explanation**
Access (responsive, loads quickly)	Refers to the speed of access and the availability of the Web site at all times.
Usability (simple layout, easy to use, well organized, visually attractive, fun, clear design)	Concerned with the extent to which the Web site is visually appealing, consistent, fun, and easy to use.
Navigation	Evaluates the links to needed information.
Interactivity (customized product; search engine; ability to create list of items, change list of items, and find related items)	Evaluates the search engine and the personal features (e.g., shopping cart) of the Web site.

Source: McKinney et al., "The Measurement of Web-Customer Satisfaction: An Expectation and Disconfirmation Approach." *Information Systems Research* 13, no. 3, September 2002, pp. 296–315. Courtesy of Blackwell Publishing.

exchanges, chat rooms, viral marketing—can be used. Another key strategy for attracting customers is increased visibility via search engine optimization, which is discussed in Section 16.8.

Each of these steps and processes is discussed in the forthcoming sections.

Section 16.4 ▶ REVIEW QUESTIONS

1. Distinguish between informational, interactive, transactional, and collaborative Web sites.
2. List the six steps in building a Web site.
3. Describe five criteria that Web site visitors use to evaluate Web site content. Describe four criteria that visitors use to evaluate Web site design.

16.5 WEB SITE HOSTING AND OBTAINING A DOMAIN NAME

Every brick-and-mortar business has a storefront from which it sells goods and services. The business either owns or rents the storefront in a mall or independent location. Every online business usually has a storefront. The decisions about whether to own (self-host) or rent, where to host the Web site (store builder service, ISP, pure Web hosting service, or self-hosting), and the site's domain name are some of the first important decisions an online business owner has to make. This section discusses the considerations in making these decisions.

WEB HOSTING OPTIONS

The following are the major Web hosting options.

Storebuilder Service

A **storebuilder service** (also called a design-and-host service) provides Web hosting as well as disk space, templates, and other services to help small businesses build a Web site quickly and cheaply.

storebuilder service
A hosting service that provides disk space and services to help small and micro businesses build a Web site quickly and cheaply.

An example of a company that offers comprehensive storebuilding hosting services and software is Yahoo! Web Hosting. Yahoo!'s base service offers Web hosting as well as customized templates and other support for $11.95 per month; the next plan up, which is offered for $19.95 a month, offers additional services; a package for professionals that includes security features is available for $39.95 a month. All levels of Yahoo! Web Hosting include access to template-based software, SiteBuilder, which offers more than 330 customizable templates. The software can be used to build a storefront quickly and easily (see Section 16.9 and Team Assignment #6). Yahoo!'s Web Hosting package also provides marketing tools, domain name selection assistance, a payment gate, disk space, and shipment services. The package also works with the Yahoo! Merchant Solutions, which is described in Section 16.9. Yahoo! Web Hosting usually offers a Web site address (e.g., a URL such as smallbusiness.yahoo.com/mybusiness), management tools, security features, and Internet connection maintenance. Yahoo! combines Web hosting and store building, but other vendors may separate the two functions, as will be shown later in this section.

The advantage of a storebuilder service is that it is a quick, easy, and inexpensive way to build a Web site. The disadvantages are the lack of a strong online identity, limited functionality (e.g., accepting credit cards may not be possible), dependence on the service for proper management of connectivity to the site, and some lack of differentiation (the Web site tends to look like other sites because everyone is using the same set of templates). Despite the disadvantages, storebuilder services are the prime choice of small and sometimes medium-size businesses (see EC Application Case 16.2). Other businesses use the following alternatives.

ISP Hosting

ISP hosting service
A hosting service that provides an independent, stand-alone Web site for small and medium-sized businesses.

The same company that delivers e-mail and Web access to a business also is likely to be able to host the company's Web site. An **ISP hosting service** provides an independent, stand-alone Web site for small and medium-sized businesses. The ISP is likely to provide additional hosting services (e.g., more storage space, simple site statistics, credit card gateway software) at the same or slightly higher cost than the storebuilder services.

The major difference between a storebuilder and an ISP hosting service is that with the ISP service, the time-consuming and sometimes expensive task of designing and constructing the Web site becomes the responsibility of the business. The business owners, usually with the help of a contracted Web designer, must use a Web site construction tool to create the Web site (e.g., ibuilt.net at ibuilt.net) or a Web page editor (e.g., Dreamweaver at macromedia.com or FrontPage at microsoft.com). This is not necessarily a bad thing. Compared with a storebuilder template, the combination of an ISP hosting service and a Web designer or builder offers the business increased flexibility as to what it can do with the site, so the site can be distinctive and stand out from the competition. Sites hosted by an ISP also will have a branded domain name. However, one disadvantage of using an ISP is that most providers have limited functionality (e.g., an ISP may be unwilling to host a back-end database). Another consideration is the commitment of the ISP to maintaining quality service and keeping its hosting services up-to-date. In many cases, the main business of an ISP is providing Internet access, not hosting Web sites.

Typically, the search for an ISP host begins by contacting local ISPs for information, asking others in the business community for recommendations, and consulting with local telecommunications and computer user groups. Most businesses will want to use a local ISP, because face-to-face contact is helpful if there are problems with customer access to the Web site or the business's ability to update it. However, a business may decide to host the site in another location for cost-saving or customer-location purposes. If so, lists of ISPs and providers of commercial Internet access can be found at The List of ISPs (thelist.com).

A Pure Hosting Service

Web hosting service
A dedicated Web site hosting company that offers a wide range of hosting services and functionality to businesses of all sizes.

A **Web hosting service** is a dedicated Web site hosting company that offers a wide range of hosting services and functionality to businesses of all sizes. Companies such as Hostway (hostway.com) and DellHost (appsitehosting.com/index.aspx) offer more and better services

CASE 16.2

EC Application

HOW SMALL COMPANIES USE A STOREBUILDER

The following are illustrative examples of how small companies build e-stores using store-building services.

- Laura Modrell was looking for the best price for the Thomas the Tank Engine character adored by her son. Searching the Web, she discovered that people were buying these toy trains and reselling them online at a huge profit. So she built a simple storefront in 1999 using free templates and selling unique educational toys including Thomas the Tank Engine and Friends. The business grew rapidly, and in 2000 she switched to Yahoo! Store. She needed not only the professional look, but also the support services. By using Yahoo! Store, Modrell has complete control over her site (*trains4tots.com*) with regards to product descriptions, prices, orders, and so on at a minimal cost and with limited computer knowledge. Revenues grew from $100,000 in 2000 to about $2,000,000 in 2005.
- Kristine Wylie started writing ads and Web content in 2002. As a freelance writer, she needed to promote her writing and copyediting services. She selected Yahoo's Web Hosting and its e-mail service. Using SiteBuilder, she constructed a site (*mswrite.com*) in 2003, and within a year, she obtained clients in several countries around the world. Income tripled in a year, enabling Wylie to hire helpers and expand the business further.
- Ken and Pat Gates retired in 2001. While surfing the Internet, they discovered how easy it was to go into e-commerce. The couple decided to sell online products related to their favorite collegiate sports teams. Using Yahoo's Web Hosting service and templates, in 2003 they built their store, College Sports Stuff (*collegesportsstuff.com*), and generated $35,000 in sales. By 2005, they covered 62 teams, including noncollege ones, tripling their sales. Customers' orders are shipped within an hour.
- Using Yahoo!'s SiteBuilder software, Springwater Woodcraft, an established Canadian furniture manufacturer, was able to add a new sales channel (*springwaterwoodcraft.com*). The software helped not only with sales, but also with accounting. It also led the company into the international market.
- TailorMade-adidas Golf (TMaG) is the world's leading manufacturer of metal and wood golf clubs. When they launched the revolutionary 7 Quad Driver, they had to make sure that their customers (golf retailers) would understand the new product and its benefits in order to transform those benefits into customer sales. To do that, they created courses that they offered online to educate the golf retailers. Using Yahoo! Merchant Solutions, this e-training B2B project was launched rapidly (*tmagconnection.com*). Participation in the course was high, and when the store opened online, it attracted 15 percent of all TMaG customers who placed $600,000 in orders in the first 3 months. The company created several other storefronts (e.g., one for selling its products to employees of TMaG's parent company).

Source: Compiled from Yahoo! (2005).

Questions

1. What benefits did the owners of these businesses derive from using Yahoo!'s services?
2. Identify the common elements in all of these cases.
3. Why would a large company such as TMaG use templates to create a B2B site?

than an ISP because Web site hosting is their core business. Almost all Web hosting companies have internal Web design departments, so the cooperation between the designer and host is assured. Also, functionality such as database integration, shipping and tax calculators, sufficient bandwidth to support multimedia files, shopping carts, site search engines, and comprehensive site statistics are likely to be readily available.

A Web hosting service can be the best option for an online business that needs one or more mirror sites. A **mirror site** is an exact duplicate of the original Web site, but it is physically located on a Web server on another continent. A business may decide that a mirror site is needed when large numbers of customers are a long distance from the original site. A mirror site reduces telecommunications costs and improves speed of customer access because the distance between the Web server and the customer's browser is reduced. Typically, customers do not know, or care, that they are accessing a mirror site.

A variation of the Web hosting service is **co-location**. In this arrangement, a Web server owned and maintained by the business is placed in a Web hosting service that manages the server's connection to the Internet. This allows the business maximum control over site content and functionality, as with self-hosting (described next), but without the need for specialized staff or other requirements for 24/7 network management.

mirror site
An exact duplicate of an original Web site that is physically located on a Web server on another continent.

co-location
A Web server owned and maintained by the business is placed in the hands of a Web hosting service that manages the server's connection to the Internet.

Self-Hosting

self-hosting
When a business acquires the hardware, software, staff, and dedicated telecommunications services necessary to set up and manage its own Web site.

The highest level hosting option is **self-hosting**. With this option, the business acquires the hardware, software, staff, and dedicated telecommunications services necessary to set up and manage its own Web site. Self-hosting is considered beneficial when a business has special requirements such as maximum data security, protection of intellectual property, or, most likely, when the business intends to have a large and complex site.

The disadvantages of self-hosting are the cost and the speed of construction. The other Web-hosting options allow the hosting company to amortize the costs of site hosting across hundreds or thousands of customers. A business that hosts its own Web site will have to bear these costs alone, not to mention concerns about security and full-time Web site management. These costs must be weighed against the benefits of better control over site performance and increased flexibility in site design, improvement, and functionalities.

REGISTERING A DOMAIN NAME

Selecting a domain name is an important marketing and branding consideration for any business. The domain name will be the business's online address, and it provides an opportunity to create an identity for the business.

domain name
A name-based address that identifies an Internet-connected server.

A **domain name** is a name-based address that identifies an Internet-connected server. The domain name should be an easy-to-remember name (e.g., congress.gov) that the *domain name system (DNS)* maps to a corresponding IP (Internet Protocol) address (e.g., 140.147.248.209). Each domain name starts with a *top-level domain (TLD)* at the far right. This is either a general top-level domain (e.g., .com or .biz for commercial businesses, .org for nonprofit organizations, .name for individuals), or it is a country-code top-level domain (ccTLD) (e.g., .au for Australia, .jp for Japan). Most ccTLDs also have a *second-level domain name* that indicates the type of organization (e.g., redcross.org.au, yahoo.co.jp). At the left side of the domain name is the organization's name (e.g., dell.com), a brand name (e.g., coke.com for Coca-Cola), or a generic name (e.g., plumber.com). For legal issues related to domain names, see Chapter 17.

Domain name assignment is under the authority of the Internet Corporation for Assigned Names and Numbers (ICANN; icann.org). ICANN has delegated responsibility for domain name registration procedures and database administration in the general TLDs to top-level domain administrators such as Afilias (for .info), Public Interest Registry (for .org), and VeriSign Global Registry Services (for .com and .net). Similarly, regional Internet registries administer the ccTLDs (e.g., Nominet for the .uk domain, Japan Registry Service for .jp).

domain name registrar
A business that assists prospective Web site owners with finding and registering the domain name of their choice.

Actual registration of domain names is carried out by hundreds of ICANN-accredited registrars. These are located in various countries, but most are in the United States. A list of these registrars is available at icann.org/registrars/accredited-list.html. A **domain name registrar** is a business that assists prospective Web site owners with finding and registering a domain name of their choice.

The first step for a prospective Web site owner is to visit a domain name registrar such as AllDomains (alldomains.com) or directNIC (directnic.com). Typically, the owner will use the domain name lookup service at the registrar's Web site to determine if the desired domain name is available. If it is, the visitor is invited to register it through the registrar for a small fee. The registrar submits the domain name and the owner's details to the appropriate domain name database, and the name then becomes unavailable to anyone else. If the domain name is not available, most registrars automatically offer a list of available alternatives.

If the desired domain name has already been taken, it sometimes can be purchased from the current owner. The Better Whois database of registered domain names (betterwhois.com) contains the name, postal address, e-mail address, and telephone number of the domain name owner. A business with an established Web site will be reluctant to give up a domain name, but if the domain name is reserved but not in use, the owner may be willing to sell it for a reasonable price.

Once the name is registered with a registrar it can be held by the registrar until the hosting service is in place. Then management of the domain name can be transferred from the registrar or previous owner to the host for establishment of the Web site.

Some suggestions for selecting a good domain name are provided in Online File W16.2.

A useful resource for learning more about domain names and the registration process is About Domains (aboutdomains.com), which offers "guides and resources for successful Internet presence," including a domain name glossary, a registration FAQ file, and "horror stories" from domain name owners who have had bad experiences with registrars.

Section 16.5 ▶ REVIEW QUESTIONS

1. What are the advantages and disadvantages of the different Web hosting options?
2. What is a mirror site? Why would a company use a mirror site?
3. What criteria should an online business consider in choosing a Web hosting service?
4. What is a domain name? Why is selecting a domain name an important step for going online?

16.6 CONTENT CREATION, DELIVERY, AND MANAGEMENT

Content is the text, images, sound, and video that make up a Web page. Creating and managing content is critical to Web site success, because content is what a visitor comes looking for at a Web site, and content is what the Web site owners use to sell the site, the product or service, and the company that stands behind the site. A successful Internet presence has always been about effective delivery of the information the visitor wants—"Content is king!" (Agarwal and Venkatesh 2002). This section describes the role content plays in successful online business operations and the key aspects of creating, delivering, and managing Web site content.

content
The text, images, sound, and video that make up a Web page.

Providing content to EC sites may be a complex job because of the variety and quantity of sources from which content is acquired and the fact that the content must frequently be updated (see Chapter 10 in Coupey 2001). Also, B2B content, especially in online catalogs, must include pictures, diagrams, and even sound.

The major content categories are information about the company, products, services, customers, investor relations, press releases, and so on; detailed product information provided in electronic catalogs, which are sometimes personalized for major customers; customers' personalized Web pages; and information provided to the B2B community, such as industry news. One of the difficulties in Web content management is that some content needs to be kept up-to-the-minute (e.g., news, stock prices, weather). This is referred to as **dynamic Web content**, as distinguished from *static Web content*, which is updated infrequently.

dynamic Web content
Content that must be kept up-to-date.

For each type of content, companies may use a different approach for content creation and delivery. Exhibit 16.3 shows the content life cycle. As shown in the exhibit, once content is created, it may appear in different sources (e.g., text, video, music). Then, it is moved to a content syndicator. A syndicator (to be described later in this section) moves the content to a

EXHIBIT 16.3 Digital Content Delivery Life Cycle

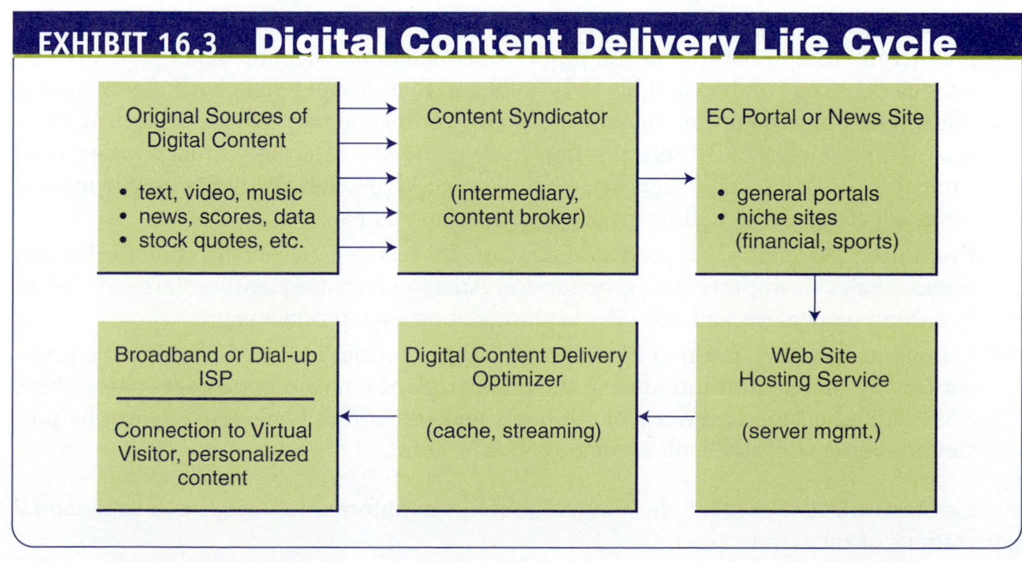

portal or news site. From there, a hosting service moves the content, possibly via an optimizer (such as akamai.com). The optimizer delivers the content to the final consumer. We will discuss this process and its elements in more detail a bit later.

Content may be in the public domain or it may be proprietary in nature (e.g., information about the company and its products and services). The sites at which content is offered may be general-purpose consumer portals, such as Yahoo! or Lycos, or they may be specialized portals designed to appeal to a specific audience, such as espn.com or ski.com.

Up-to-the-minute dynamic content is what attracts new and returning customers ("eyeballs") and makes them stay longer ("stickiness"). Therefore, dynamic content contributes to customer loyalty.

commodity content
Information that is widely available and generally free to access on the Web.

Although every Web site has content, Web sites differ according to the criticality of the content to the company's business goals. Some sites offer **commodity content**, which is information that is widely available and generally free (Tomsen 2000). Portals such as MSN.com and content aggregators such as Nua Internet Surveys (nua.ie) collect information published elsewhere on the Net and make it available to visitors. The value added is the *aggregation* of the content.

Web sites such as Amazon.com are content rich because they offer unique content, such as book reviews and author interviews. At most Web sites, publishing quality content is a strategy to achieve the real purpose of the site, which is to sell the product or service.

CONTENT CREATION AND ACQUISITION

Effective content creation begins with examining business and marketing goals. The primary purpose of content is to contribute to the Web site's goals of product sales, company promotion, branding, and customer service. For example, content is one of the most effective ways for a Web site to differentiate itself from its competitors, and content can create an identity that is consistent with the branding strategy. To fulfill these goals, the content should be complete, accurate, and timely and should project the image that a business intends to portray in its online presence.

Content pages should contain more than information about the product itself (the *primary content*). A Web site also should include *secondary content* that offers marketing opportunities, such as the following:

cross-selling
Offering similar or related products and services to increase sales.

up-selling
Offering an upgraded version of the product in order to boost sales and profit.

- **Cross-selling.** Using content for **cross-selling** means offering similar or related products and services to increase sales. In the off-line world, cross-selling is exemplified by the McDonald's question, "Would you like fries with that?" In the online world, Amazon.com offers book buyers options such as "customers who bought this book also bought . . ." and "look for similar books by subject." Accessories, add-on products, extended warranties, and gift-wrapping are other examples of cross-selling opportunities that can be offered to buyers on the product pages or in the purchase process.
- **Up-selling.** Creating content for **up-selling** means offering an upgraded version of the product in order to boost sales and profit. McDonald's practices up-selling every time a sales clerk asks a combo-meal buyer "Would you like to super-size that?" Amazon.com offers "great buy" book combinations (buy two complementary books for slightly more than the price of one). (It also practices *down-selling* by offering visitors cheaper, used copies of a book directly under the new book price.) Up-selling activities usually include offering products with a different design, color, fabric, or size.
- **Promotion.** A coupon, rebate, discount, or special service is secondary content that can increase sales or improve customer service. Amazon.com frequently offers reduced or free shipping charges, and this offer is promoted on each product page.
- **Comment.** Reviews, testimonials, expert advice, or further explanation about the product can be offered after introducing the product. Amazon.com book pages always have editorial and customer reviews of the book, and sometimes book contents can be previewed online with the "look inside this book" feature.

Creating effective content also means fulfilling the information needs and experiential expectations of the visitor.

Creating Content

Where does content come from? Content on most sites is created by the site's owners and developers. Typically, it begins by collecting all the content that is currently available (e.g., product information, company information, logos). Then the value of additional content—e-newsletters, discussion forums, customer personalization features, FAQ pages, and external links—is assessed for inclusion in the Web site. This assessment determines what is critical, important, or merely desirable by carefully considering how each bit of content will serve the site's goals and whether customers will want it or expect it. The assessment leads to a content development plan that may, for example, call for launching the site with all of the critical information and the most affordable important content (e.g., external links, a FAQ page) in place. As time and resources permit, the rest of the important content (e.g., personalization) can be added.

Content also can be generated by customers—through product reviews, testimonials, discussion forums, and other ways. Content can be provided by companies downstream in the supply chain (e.g., a chemical industry digital exchange would not need to duplicate product information but could simply source it from the chemical manufacturers). Original content can also be created by freelance researchers, compilers, and writers.

Buying Content

Content can be purchased or licensed. Lonely Planet, the Australian travel guide company, and the popular Mobile Travel Guide both sell travel information to Web sites such as Travelocity. *Content syndicators* such as Content Outfitter (contentoutfitter.com), NewsEdge (dialog.com/newsedge), and Content Finder (electroniccontent.com/conFinder.cfm) serve as intermediaries that link content creators with businesses interested in acquiring content. Finally, some individuals and businesses, such as Mike Valentine's WebSite 101 (website101.com/freecontent.html), provide free content and ask only for proper attribution in return.

Content that is acquired from outside sources should be supplemental content, not primary content. If primary content is purchased that does not add any additional value, visitors will go to the originating site and not return. A major source for a secondary content is syndicators.

Buying from a Syndicator

According to Werbach (2000), **syndication** involves the sale of the same good to many customers, who then integrate it with other offerings and resell it or give it away for free. Syndication has long been extremely popular in the world of entertainment and publishing, but was rare elsewhere until the arrival of the Internet. The digitization of products and services, and the resulting ease with which information can flow, makes syndication a popular business model (e.g., see yellowbrix.com). Let's look at a few examples.

syndication
The sale of the same good (e.g., digital content) to many customers, who then integrate it with other offerings and resell it or give it away free.

Virtual stockbrokers, such as E*TRADE, offer considerable information on their portals (e.g., financial news, stock quotes, research, etc.). Yahoo! and other portals offer other types of information. These brokers and portals buy the information from information creators or originators, such as Reuters, who sell *the same information* to many other portals or users. Customers may buy directly from the information creators, but in many cases creators use a supply chain of syndicators and distributors, as shown on Exhibit 16.4, to move news and information to the end consumers. Content creators, such as Inktomi (see Carr 2000) and Reuters, make their money by selling the same information to many syndicators and/or dis-

EXHIBIT 16.4 **The Syndication Supply Chain**

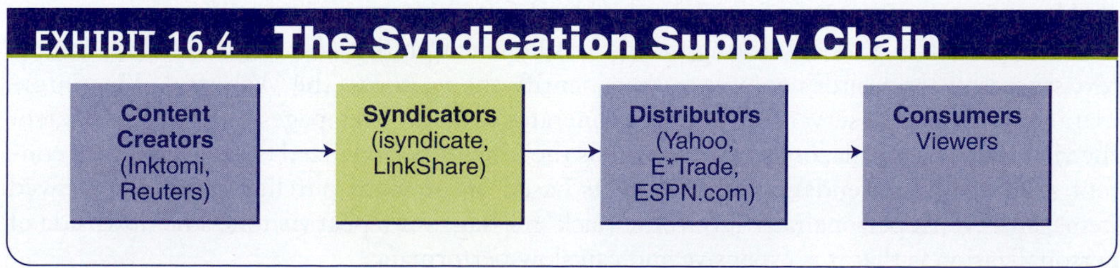

tributors (e.g., yellowbrix.com). The information distributors, such as E*TRADE, then distribute free information to the public (customers).

Syndication is an especially popular way to distribute content, but it also is used with software and other digitizable items. For example, companies syndicate EC services such as payments and shopping-cart ordering systems used by e-tailers. Logistics, security, and systems integration tools often are syndicated.

RSS. RSS (short for "Rich Site Summary," "RDF site summary," or "Really Simple Syndication") is an XML format for syndicating Web content. A Web site that wants to allow other sites to publish some of its content creates an RSS document and registers the document with an RSS publisher. A user that can read RSS-distributed content can use the content on a different site. This enables the sharing of Web content. It can be viewed as a distributable "What's New" on a site, and it is popular with bloggers. Major sites such as CNET, BBC, CNN, Disney, ZDNet, Red Herring, and Wired use RSS to share content among themselves. This technology solves problems such as long traffic delays caused by increased site traffic and expediting the gathering and distributing of news. For a tutorial, see mnot.net/rss/tutorial. According to eMarketer (2005), RSS is listed as one of the "top 10 E-Business trends for 2005." RSS is included in Mozilla's Firefox Web browser, making it very popular. Several advertisers have begun to use it as platform for targeted advertisements.

Content Providers and Networks

Content providers and distributors provide and distribute content online. These services are offered by several specialized companies (e.g., akamai.com, sandpiper.net, and mirror-image.com), as well as by news services such as the Associated Press and ABC News.

Web sites such as nytimes.com and cnn.com sit at the top of the content ladder. These sites are content driven because delivering **premium content**—content not available elsewhere on the Web—is their mission. Many content-driven sites are successful enough at delivering premium content that they can charge for it (e.g., thestreet.com).

premium content
Content not available elsewhere on the Web.

Representative Content-Related Vendors

A large number of vendors support content creation and management that facilitates the sharing of an organization's digital assets. Representative vendors are described in Online File W16.3.

Thus far, we have discussed the role of intermediaries and other third-party B2B providers in channeling digital content to the sites that display the content to consumers. Discussion will now turn to the next step in the content delivery chain, the task of optimizing and delivering digital content to customers.

Content Delivery Networks. Content delivery is a service that is sometimes offered by hosting companies to help customers manage their content. Using *content delivery networks (CDNs)*, companies can update content, improve the quality of the site, increase consistency, control content, and decrease the time needed to create or maintain a site. CDNs are provided by Mediasurface (mediasurface.com) and Akamai (akamai.com). The case of Akamai is discussed later in this section.

In B2B, the information contained in electronic catalogs is of extreme importance. Companies can create and maintain the content in-house or they can outsource such tasks.

Personalizing Content

Personalized content is of high value to site visitors. **Personalized content** is Web content that is prepared to match the needs and expectations of the individual visitor. Such content enables visitors to find the information they need faster than at traditional sites.

personalized content
Web content that is prepared to match the needs and expectations of the individual visitor.

The process begins by tracking the visitor's behavior on the Web site via cookies (bits of text stored on the visitor's computer that identify the visitor to the Web site). This information is provided to server software that generates dynamic Web pages that contain content the visitor can use. Amazon.com's Web site is the king of personalized content, offering content such as recommendations for products based on previous purchases, recently viewed items, and even a personalized "Welcome Back" message for repeat visitors. The downside of personalization is that it is expensive and can slow performance.

Delivering Content By E-Newsletter

One of the most effective strategies for delivering content of interest to potential customers is an e-mail newsletter. An **e-newsletter** is a collection of short, informative articles sent at regular intervals by e-mail to individuals who have an interest in the newsletter's topic. An e-newsletter can be used to support the business and the product. For details see Chapter 4 and Online File W16.4.

e-newsletter
A collection of short, informative articles sent at regular intervals by e-mail to individuals who have an interest in the newsletter's topic.

Writing Effective Content

Delivering effective content involves not only what is said, but how it is said. Some of the rules Web wordsmiths use when creating Web content are provided in Online File W16.5.

CONTENT MANAGEMENT

Content management is the process of collecting, publishing, revising, and removing content from a Web site to keep content fresh, accurate, compelling, and credible. Almost all sites begin with a high level of relevant content, but over time material becomes dated, irrelevant, or incorrect. Content management makes sure a site remains relevant and accurate long after the initial push to launch the site is over. Content management applies quality assurance processes and content development to promote the reliability and integrity of the site (Awad 2002). *Web content* management differs from *Web site* management, which focuses on ease of navigation, availability, performance, scalability, and security (see Online Chapter 18). Web content management makes sure that a site eliminates clutter and does not waste visitors' time. For an overview of Web content management, see Gupta et al. (2001); for a list of content management vendors, see Clyman (2002).

content management
The process of adding, revising, and removing content from a Web site to keep content fresh, accurate, compelling, and credible.

Content Testing

The most obvious task in content management is testing the content. Web managers need to make extensive and frequent checks of material for accuracy, clarity, typos, poor punctuation, misspelled words, and inconsistencies. Employees knowledgeable about the content should read site material to test it for accuracy; customer focus groups and professional editors should read it to check for clarity; and everyone should read new content to find mistakes. For ongoing testing, new employees may be asked to read the Web site content to learn about the company and to look for improvements with a "fresh eye."

Measuring Content Quality

How does a company know if the content on its Web site is meeting its e-commerce goals? How does a company know if it is delivering what its customers need? According to Barnes (2001b), companies need metrics to control the quality of their online content. In addition, content must meet privacy requirements, copyright and other legal requirements, language translation needs, and much more. Guidelines for knowledge management may be used as well. Metrics are available from W3C (w3c.org/PICS) and periodically at e-businessadvisor.com. Measuring the quality of content also requires appropriate Web traffic measurement tools (see Online Chapter 18). For specific suggestions on how to effectively use metrics to measure content quality, see Barnes (2001a), Radoff (2000), and Sterne (2002).

Pitfalls of Content Management

According to Byrne (2002), companies face various content management pitfalls. The top six content management pitfalls, and the best practices for avoiding them, are presented in Online File W16.6.

Content Removal

An important task within content management is removing old, out-of-date pages from the Web server. Even if all references to the page in the Web site have been removed, the page is still visible to search engines, searches on the site itself, and links from other Web pages. Expired pages should be deleted or moved to an off-line location that can serve as an archive.

Content Management Software

Content management software allows nontechnical staff to create, edit, and delete content on the company's Web site. The driving forces behind *content management software (CMS)* include the desire for companies to empower content owners to manage their own content and the inability of the computing services staff to keep up with demands for new or changed content on the Web site.

Content management systems generally include workflow systems for monitoring content creation, review, approval, distribution, posting, and evaluation processes. Most contain tools that allow nontechnical personnel to publish content without specialized training. Other features include content expiration schedules, backup and archive management, security features, and enterprise application integration functions.

Despite the strong driving forces and the promise of CMS to create and maintain content with great efficiency, most systems have failed to live up to expectations. A 2003 Jupiter Research study reported that "over-complicated, end-to-end packages can as much as quintuple Web site operational costs over human alternatives. In fact, 61 percent of companies who have already deployed Web content management software still rely on manual processes to update their sites" (Jupiter Media 2003). Companies embarking on a CMS purchase should do the following (Arnold 2003):

- Conduct a thorough needs analysis.
- Document requirements and discuss them with at least two other companies that have purchased a CMS.
- Start small and with content management software that has a trial version or low entry cost.
- Assess the system after 30 days to determine what is right, wrong, needed, and unnecessary.
- Repeat the assessment process regularly, increasing functionality as requirements and resources permit.

For information about and a comparison of the most popular CMS packages, see Rapoza (2004).

CATALOG CONTENT AND ITS MANAGEMENT

Much of the content in B2B and B2C sites is catalog based. Chapter 2 discussed the benefits of electronic catalogs. Although there are many positive aspects of electronic catalogs, poorly organized ones may deter buyers (e.g., see Kapp 2001). Companies need to make sure that their catalog content is well managed.

For buyers who aggregate suppliers' catalogs on their own Web sites, content management begins with engaging suppliers and then collecting, standardizing, classifying, hosting, and continually updating their catalog data. That is no small task, considering that most large buying organizations have hundreds of suppliers, each using different data formats and nomenclature to describe their catalog items. An example of a successful e-catalog is that of Bloomsburg Carpet (see Online File W16.7). The management of catalog content has some unique aspects and options, as shown in Online File W16.8.

TRANSLATION OF CONTENT TO OTHER LANGUAGES

In the global marketplace, content created in one language often needs to be translated to another in order to reach customers in other countries. Furthermore, in some cases an effective Web site may need to be specifically designed and targeted to the market that it is trying to reach. Language translation is less of a problem in B2B, due to the ability of many business people to speak English. It is a big problem in B2C, though, especially in countries such as China, Japan, and Korea, where relatively few people understand English well enough to use it online. The language barrier between countries and regions presents an interesting and complicated challenge (see worldlingo.com).

The primary problems with language customization are cost and speed. It currently takes a human translator about a week to translate a medium-size Web site into just one language. For larger sites, the cost ranges from $30,000 to $500,000, depending on the complexity of the site and languages of translation.

WorldPoint (worldpoint.com) presents a creative solution to these translation issues with its WorldPoint Passport multilingual software tool. The WorldPoint Passport solution allows Web developers to create a Web site in one language and to deploy it in several other languages. However, automatic translation may be inaccurate. Therefore, many experts advocate manual translation with the help of the computer as a productivity booster. As time passes, though, automatic translation is improving (see Sullivan 2001).

According to Sullivan (2001), the best way to assess machine translation is to use the following criteria: (1) intelligibility (i.e., How well can a reader get the gist of a translated document?); (2) accuracy (i.e., How many errors occur during a translation?); and (3) speed (i.e., How many words per second are translated?).

For more on automatic language translation, including some translation tools, see Online File W14.5 in Chapter 14.

CONTENT MAXIMIZATION AND STREAMING SERVICES

Many companies provide media-rich content, such as video clips, music, or Flash media, in an effort to reach their target audience with an appealing marketing message. For example, automakers want to provide a virtual driving experience as seen from the car's interior, realtors want to provide 360-degree views of their properties, and music sellers want to provide easily downloadable samples of their songs. Public portals and others are using considerable amounts of media-rich information as well. Finally, B2B e-catalogs may include thousands of photos.

These and other content providers are concerned about the download time from the user's perspective. Impatient or fickle Web surfers may click "Stop" before the multimedia has had a chance to be fully downloaded. Remember that B2C and B2B customers not only want their news stories, music, video clips, reference information, financial information, and sports scores delivered to them over the Web, but they also want them to be delivered quickly and effortlessly. Therefore, it is important that content providers and marketers use technical delivery solutions that will not cause "traffic jams" during the download process. Several technical solutions are available from vendors who are referred to as *content maximizers* or *streaming services*. One such vendor is Akamai, described in EC Application Case 16.3.

Section 16.6 ▶ REVIEW QUESTIONS

1. What is content? Commodity content? Premium content? Dynamic content? Personalized content?
2. How can content be used for cross-selling? For up-selling? For promotion?
3. Where does content come from? Identify four sources of Web site content. What is content creation?
4. What is syndication? How does it relate to content?
5. What e-newsletter content does a subscriber value most? (Hint: see Online File W16.4.)

6. What is the purpose of content management?
7. Describe content maximization.

16.7 WEB SITE DESIGN

The goal of any Web site is to deliver quality content to its intended audience and to do so with an elegant design (Taylor et al. 2002; Zhang and Cao 2003). With the Web site's content in hand, the Web site owner's next task is Web site design, including information architecture, navigation design, colors and graphics, and maximizing site performance. The purpose of this section is to enable you to contribute to the design of a Web site when working with professionals.

Successful Web site design is about meeting customer expectations. Design starts with identifying customer needs, expectations, and problems. Then a site is designed that meets those needs and expectations or that solves the customers' problems. A list of important Web site design criteria, with relevant questions, is shown in Exhibit 16.5. Some of these criteria, such as interactivity, scalability, and security, are discussed elsewhere in this and other

CASE 16.3

EC Application

AKAMAI CORPORATION

An Internet company decided to name itself after a Hawaiian word that means "intelligent, clever, or cool"—*Akamai* (AH-kuh-my). And indeed, the company has created a clever product. Let's explain.

As user interest in high-speed Internet connections has grown, demand for bandwidth-heavy applications and media also has begun to surge. Paul Kagen Associates estimated that revenues from streaming media services will total $1.5 billion by 2002 and $21 billion by 2008 (as reported at Three Squared Inc. 2000). In addition, the interactive broadcast video market will reach $4.2 billion by 2005 (Internetnews Staff 1999). Finally, according to a DFC Intelligence study (reported in Saunders 2001), the streaming video market is estimated to grow to over $1 billion by 2005. (These estimates were proven to be correct through 2004.)

However, user connection speeds are only part of the streaming media picture. How will the networks themselves handle the influx of bandwidth-chewing material? With a growing number of users and an abundance of rich media, the Internet is becoming extremely congested. Network traffic control is needed. Akamai and its competitors (Digital Island, Ibeam, and Mirror Image) are stepping in to manage Internet traffic.

Akamai products act as Internet traffic cops by using complicated mathematical algorithms to speed Web pages from the closest Akamai-owned server to a customer's location, thereby passing through fewer router hops. This process also helps to eliminate Internet gridlock. Today, caching and content distribution are the only practical ways to reduce network delay.

How does it work? To provide the service, Akamai maintains a global network of thousands of servers and leases space on them to giant portals such as Yahoo! and CNN. These sites use the servers to store graphic-rich information closer to Internet users' computers in order to circumvent Web traffic jams and enable faster page loads; delivery time to the users is reduced by 20 to 30 percent. If a company's Web server is located in Germany and a user in the United States visits the Web site, the multimedia content of the site has to be transmitted halfway around the globe. Akamai's FreeFlow technology speeds the delivery of images, multimedia, and other Web content by placing that content on servers worldwide. Using the FreeFlow Launcher, Web site designers "Akamaize" their sites by marking content to be delivered using the Akamai network. FreeFlow takes this content and stores it on Akamai Web servers around the world. When a user visits a Web site that has been "Akamaized," the images and multimedia content are downloaded from an Akamai server near the user for faster content delivery. Akamai allows customer data to move to and from big Web sites through its global network for a fee. (In 2004, the fee was $2,500 for setup and $5,500/month per data center.)

Unfortunately, the service is not 100 percent reliable. The speed for the end user depends on how many people are using the user's LAN at any given point in time and also on the speed of the server downloading any given Web site. A number of competing technologies are trying to provide the same solutions, and only a limited number of large companies that use lots of rich media are willing to pay for the service.

In 2001, Akamai started to diversify, offering a comprehensive suite of content delivery, streaming audio and video, traffic management, and other services, such as dynamic page view, bundled in a package called EdgeAdvantage. Akamai and its competitors were losing money in early 2001, but their revenues were increasing rapidly. By January 2005, the company had 14,000 servers in 65 countries, storing data for its worldwide clientele (Junnarkar 2003; *akamai.com* 2005).

One advantage of using Akamai or a similar service is the added security. For example, on June 15, 2004, a cybercriminal attacked some of Akamai's major clients including Microsoft, Google, and Apple using a DoS attack (see Chapter 11). Within minutes, Akamai deleted the attacks and solved the problem (Fogarty 2005).

Sources: Compiled from Mulqueen (2001), Korzeniowski (2002), *Business 2.0* (2002), Junnarkar (2003), and *akamai.com* (accessed 2003).

Questions

1. What services are provided by Akamai?
2. What is the company's revenue model?
3. What are the service's limitations?

chapters. The focus of this section is on the fundamental design criteria of navigation, consistency, performance, appearance, and quality assurance.

INFORMATION ARCHITECTURE

information architecture
How the site and its Web pages are organized, labeled, and navigated to support browsing and searching throughout the Web site.

A Web site's **information architecture** determines how the site and its Web pages are organized, labeled, and navigated to support browsing and searching (Rosenfeld and Morville 2002). Information architecture begins with designing the site's structure. The most common site structure is hierarchical. A typical hierarchical structure for an online store is shown in Exhibit 16.6. Most hierarchical Web sites are built wide and shallow, putting 3 to 10 sections in the second level and limiting most sections to two or three levels. If the hierarchy is narrow

EXHIBIT 16.5 Web Site Design Criteria

Navigation	Is it easy for visitors to find their way around the site? Does the site comply with the three-click rule?
Consistency	Are design elements, especially look and feel, consistent from page to page? Will the Web site and contents appear the same on all visitors' screens?
Performance	How long does it take for the page to appear? Does the site comply with the 12-second rule? With the 4-second rule?
Appearance	Is the site aesthetically pleasing? Does the site's look and feel express the company's desired image? Is the site easy to read, easy to navigate, and easy to understand?
Quality assurance	Do the site's calculators, navigation links, visitor registration processes, search tools, etc., work properly? Are all dead links fixed promptly? Is the site available for full service 24 hours a day, 7 days a week?
Interactivity	Does the site encourage the visitor to play an active role in learning about the business's products or services? Are all appropriate contact details available on the Web site so that visitors can submit feedback and ask questions?
Security	Is customer information protected? Does the customer feel safe in actions such as submitting credit card information?
Scalability	Does the site design provide a seamless path for enhancements or upgrades in the future? Will site growth and increased usage protect the initial investment in site construction?

Source: Adapted from Awad (2002), pp. 145–146.

EXHIBIT 16.6 A Simple Hierarchical Web Site Structure

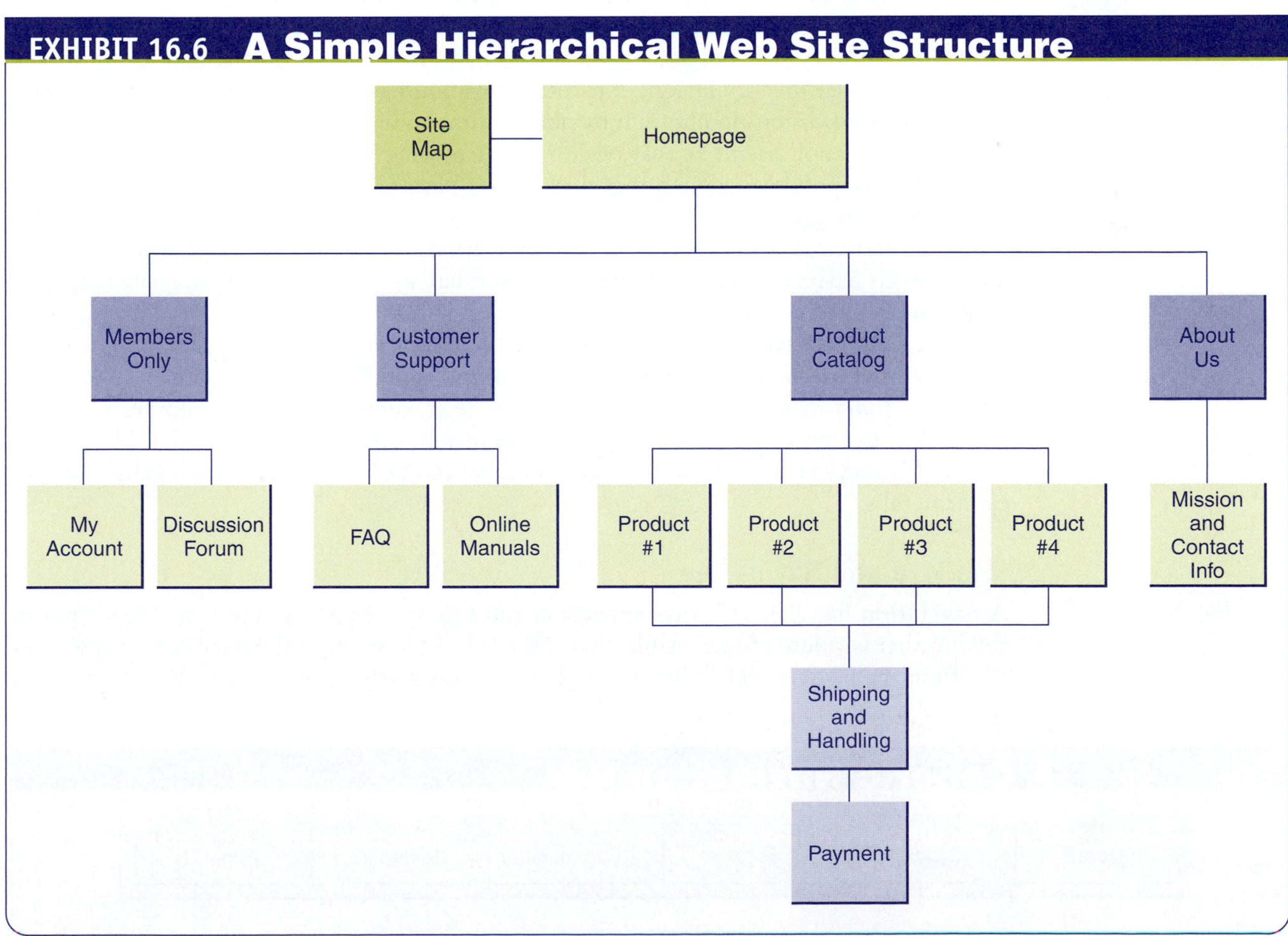

(few second-level sections) and deep (many levels), visitors become frustrated by being forced to click through numerous levels to find the information they need.

Other, less-frequently-used structures are circular and linear ones. A circular structure is useful when presenting training materials. A linear structure is useful when telling a story or presenting a tutorial. For example, Online Exhibit W16.1 presents an abbreviated version of the linear structure of the Online E-Business Plan Tutorial (T1).

A Web site typically includes a *homepage* that welcomes a visitor and introduces the site; *help* pages that assist the visitor to use or navigate through the site; *company* pages that inform the visitor about the online business; *transaction* pages that lead the customer through the purchase process; and *content* pages that deliver information about products and services at all stages of the purchase process, from information search to postpurchase service and evaluation.

Getting the homepage right is especially critical because it is the Web site's front door; it is the first page that visitors see if they enter the company's URL (e.g., www.company.com) into a Web browser. The purpose of the homepage is not to sell products or the business, but to sell the Web site. It does so by describing what is available or new at the site, helping the visitor to move around the site, and establishing a look and feel—the site's "personality"—that reflects the branding strategy and that is continued throughout the site. All pages within the site should link back to the homepage. Search engines or external links may bring visitors into the Web site's interior pages—an action known as **deep linking**—but the site owner will want the new visitor to be able to easily find the homepage.

deep linking
Entry into a Web site via the site's interior pages, not the homepage, typically through search engines or external links.

Some suggestions for organizing and labeling the site and its Web pages to support browsing and searching are provided in Online File W16.9.

SITE NAVIGATION

The purpose of **site navigation** is to help visitors quickly and easily find the information they need on a Web site. Among the questions to be considered in site navigation are: How will visitors enter a site? How will visitors use the site? How will they find what is available at the site? How will they get from one page to another and from one section to another? How will visitors find what they are looking for? Site navigation has to help visitors find information quickly, because visitors do not want to take the time to figure out how to move around on a site. Site navigation has to be easy; visitors want moving around the site to be predictable, consistent, and intuitive enough that they do not have to think about it (Cheung and Lee 2005; Iwaarden et al. 2003).

site navigation
Aids that help visitors find the information they need quickly and easily.

Web designers execute successful site navigation through consistency (described later) and through navigation aids such as a navigation bar, a navigation column, a site map, and search tools.

The simplest navigation aid is a *navigation bar* (see example in Exhibit 16.7). A navigation bar provides the visitor an opportunity to link to likely destinations (e.g., homepage, "about us") and major sections of the Web site (e.g., product catalog, customer support). Generally, the items in the bar should decrease in importance from left to right, beginning with the homepage at the far left. A navigation bar can be built using text, clickable buttons, or menu tabs.

Site Map and Navigation

A navigation bar almost always appears at the top of the page where it will load first in the browser window and be visible "above the fold." However, if the page contains banner ads, then the navigation bar should be placed prominently below the ads. Why? Frequent

EXHIBIT 16.7 A Generic Navigation Bar

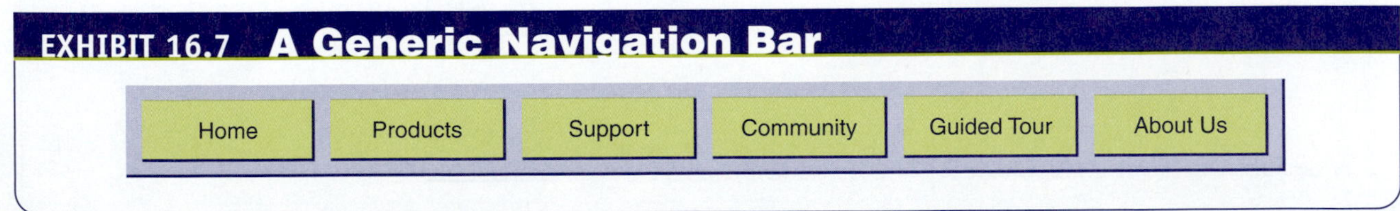

Web users develop "banner ad blindness" in which they ignore banner ads and everything above them.

A second navigation bar should appear at the bottom of every page. Then visitors who have read the page and have not found what they are looking for can easily be guided to where they need to go next. An effective navigation scheme is to offer a simple, attractive, graphical navigation bar at the top of the page and a longer, text navigation bar at the bottom of each page.

If the site's contents need more options than what can fit on a navigation bar, subsections can be placed in each section of the navigation bar (e.g., customer support might include subsections such as customer service FAQ, product information, order status). The subsections can appear on the navigation bar via a pull-down menu or a mouseover (when a visitor passes a mouse cursor over the button a submenu will pop up).

A Web site that has a lot to offer needs a navigation column on the left side of the browser window. This concept arose with the introduction of browser frames in the mid-1990s. A **frame** is an HTML element that divides the browser window into two or more separate windows. For the most part, frames are no longer used, but the idea of a navigation column as a site's "table of contents" remains as a familiar, comfortable, and easy navigation aid.

frame
An HTML element that divides the browser window into two or more separate windows.

Large and medium-size sites should include a *site map* page so that the visitor who is unsure of where to go can be presented with all of the available options. The site map should be easily accessible, reflect the information structure of the Web site, and be simply presented with easy-to-understand text links.

A large or medium-size site also should be searchable. A "search this site" box should appear near the top of the homepage and on navigation-oriented pages such as the site map. The Web site hosting service can assist with implementing this feature, which involves computer scripts and indexing tools.

Many of the information architecture and navigation concepts discussed here are illustrated in Exhibit 16.8.

Other suggestions for designing successful Web site navigation are provided in Online File W16.10.

CONSISTENCY

Closely linked to both information architecture and site navigation is consistency in a Web site's design. First and foremost, consistency means that there is a common look and feel to the Web site's pages. A site's **look and feel** consists of the elements, such as layout, typeface, colors, graphics, and navigation aids, that visually distinguish the site from others. Visitors will become confused if different layouts, colors, and navigation bars are used on different pages. Web page construction aids such as cascading style sheets help ensure a consistent look and feel on a Web site.

look and feel
The elements, including layout, typeface, colors, graphics, and navigation aids, that visually distinguish a site from any other.

EXHIBIT 16.8 A Web Page Layout Grid

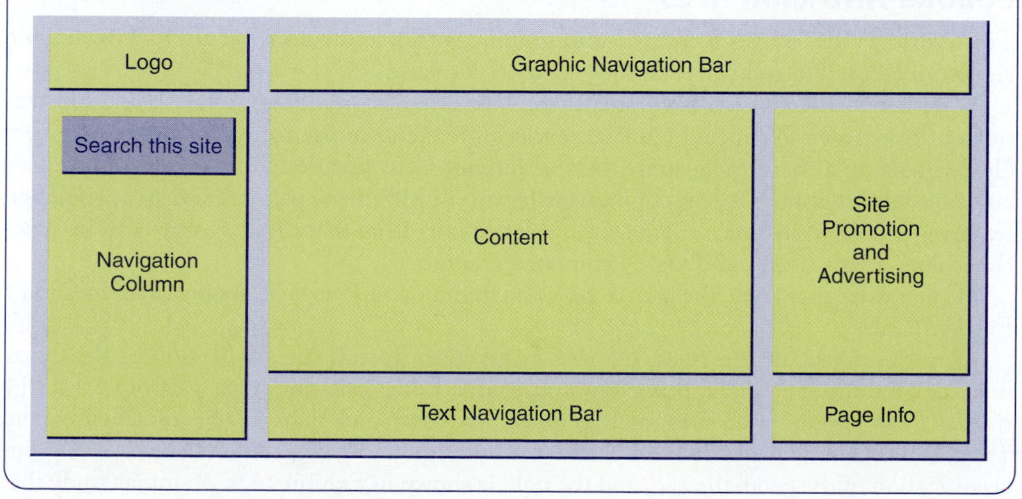

Consistency begins with clear and uniform navigation. Every page should have navigation aids, and the aids should be of the same format, style, and in approximately the same location on each page. For more on consistency, see Online File W16.11.

PERFORMANCE

Speed ranks at or near the top of every list of essential design considerations, for good reason. Visitors who have to wait more than a few seconds for a Web page to load are likely to hit the "stop" or "back" button and go somewhere else.

A number of factors affect the speed at which the page is transferred from the Web server to the client's browser. Factors out of the control of the Web designer and site owner are the visitor's modem speed, the bandwidth available at the customer's ISP, and, to some degree, the current bandwidth available at the Web host where the server is located. The critical factor that is under the control of the Web designer is the content and design of the page. A competent Web designer will know what can be done to improve a page's download speed or at least give it the appearance of loading fast.

The most widely recognized cause of long download times is a large graphic or a large number of small graphics on a single page. Graphics should be created at the lowest possible resolution so that the visitor can clearly see the picture, art, or icon but so that the graphic file is only a few kilobytes in size. If a large, high-resolution graphic image is important, thumbnail images can be put on the page and linked to full-size, higher-resolution images available at the visitor's discretion.

Other design traps that affect a page's loading time are page personalization features that require information from a back-end database for dynamic page creation, Java applets, sound files, animated banner ads, and complex table structures, especially the page-in-a-table that requires the entire table/page to load before any of it displays. To decrease page download time, these features should be avoided or used sparingly.

A good benchmark by which to judge speed and responsiveness of the Web site is the 12-second rule: Every page on the Web site should appear within 12 seconds; if visitors have to wait longer than that for a page to appear, they will likely stop the transfer and move on to the competition. The 12-second rule should be speed-tested for the lowest common denominator in the site's target audience. A site that appeals to young gamers with fast connectivity can have a higher level of graphic content than one designed for rural farmers who are unlikely to have high bandwidth connections. Again, the fundamental rule of Web design is to design the site for the intended audience.

A variation of the 12-second rule is the 4-second rule, which says that something should appear in the visitor's browser in 4 seconds or less. Even if downloading the whole page takes slightly longer than 12 seconds, if visitors can see that something is happening they will be unlikely to halt the download and move on. So, for example, a large graphic or image map can be divided into composite smaller images that begin to appear immediately.

COLORS AND GRAPHICS

The World Wide Web is a colorful and graphic world, and colors, pictures, artwork, and video can be used to good effect if they are used correctly.

The key to effective use of color and graphics is to design the site to match the expectations of the target audience. Financial services sites tend to use formal colors (e.g., green, blue) with simple charts to illustrate the text, but not many pictures. Sites directed at a female audience tend to feature lighter colors, usually pastels, with many pictures and an open design featuring lots of white space. Game sites are one type of site that can get away with in-your-face colors, Flash effects, and highly animated graphics.

Other rules that guide the use of color and graphics on Web sites are provided in Online File W16.12.

Are these Web design rules followed in practice? To test the application of theory on practice, usability gurus Jakob Nielsen and Marie Tahir tested homepages from 50 of the world's most popular Web sites, such as eBay, Microsoft, and Victoria's Secret (Nielsen and Tahir 2002). Their analysis of compliance with design and navigation standards, using our classification of the good, the bad, and the ugly, is shown in Exhibit 16.9. A similar study that

EXHIBIT 16.9 Homepage Usability: Lessons from Practice

The Good

- The median homepage was 1,018 pixels high, or about two full screens. This is consistent with recommended design practice.
- All homepages had a logo, and 84 percent placed the logo in the upper-left corner. This is very nearly a standard, and all Web sites should adopt this practice.
- All sites had navigation aids, frequently more than one. At the top of the page, 30 percent used a left-hand navigation column, 30 percent used a navigation bar with tabs, and 18 percent used a navigation bar with links. At the bottom of the page, 80 percent included a navigation bar with a median of 7.5 links.
- Only 4 percent of homepages used frames, consistent with most designers' recommendations to avoid this design element.
- Nine out of 10 homepages provided a way for visitors to easily find contact information, 60 percent of the time through a "Contact Us" link on the homepage and 22 percent of the time through the "About Us" page.
- Only three of the sites had a splash page, a site feature that Nielsen and Tahir (2002) call "a curse on the Web."
- Only two of the pages offered music automatically, another practice criticized by most Web designers.
- The median number of graphics on the homepage was three, and only 8 percent had a significant portion of the page devoted to graphics. The lesson is clear: Top sites use few or no graphics.
- None of the sites had a mandatory registration procedure for visitors to browse the site. Fifty-two percent offered registered users a sign-in box on the homepage to access special features, personalized information, or user-supplied content.
- White was the set background color on 84 percent of the sites. Black text was used by 72 percent of the sites (8 percent used blue text and 8 percent used gray text).
- When a text font was set, 96 percent used a sans-serif font such as Helvetica or Arial. These contemporary fonts look good on low-resolution computer screens.

The Bad

- Average download time was 26 seconds. Only 28 percent of the homepages downloaded in 10 seconds, and 26 percent took more than 30 seconds.
- Only 48 percent of these top sites provided a site map.
- Fourteen percent of the homepages did not have a "search this site" feature, a percentage Neilson and Tahir called "unbelievable." Nielsen and Tahir recommend a white (97 percent) search box (81 percent) that is 25 to 30 characters wide in the upper-left (31 percent) or upper-right (35 percent) corner with a "search" (42 percent) or "go" (40 percent) button. (These percentages indicate the proportion of homepages that follow this recommendation.)
- Eighty-four percent of the homepages had an "About Us" link. Nielsen and Tahir think that this should be 100 percent.
- Eighty-six percent of the top homepages had a link to the company's privacy policy. Again, Neilsen and Tahir believe that this should be at or near 100 percent for sites that collect information from visitors or customers.
- The median number of ads from external companies was three, the "absolute upper limit from a usability perspective" according to Nielsen and Tahir. Almost half (46 percent) carried advertising promoting products from other companies.

The Ugly

- Only 18 percent of the homepages used a liquid layout that automatically adapts the page's content to fill the browser window. The other 82 percent of pages used a frozen layout that risked having text cut off or a large amount of white space on the right side of the screen.
- Only 42 percent of the pages with graphics used the ALT text tag that benefits visually impaired users and those users who browse with graphics turned off. The authors call this "a disgrace" because it makes pages inaccessible to visually impaired users.

Source: Compiled from Nielson and Tahir (2002).

tested 62 Web sites in the United Kingdom on 12 design tests found that most companies are committing fundamental errors when presenting themselves online (BBC Training and Development 2002).

QUALITY ASSURANCE

Quality assurance is about making sure the Web site design is properly tested before it is launched and ensuring that it continues to perform up to expectations after launch. This is a critically important part of Web design because the Web is constantly changing—content goes out-of-date, external links go dead or become meaningless, new browsers and Web standards come out.

A lesson most Web designers can learn from total quality management (TQM) principles is to design the site for easy maintenance. Keeping the page layout neat and simple not only makes it easier for the visitor to find the information, but also makes ongoing maintenance simpler. Using text instead of graphics also increases flexibility in maintenance because it is much easier to change a bit of text than a graphical icon.

Quality Web sites have responsible owners who test all features of the site personally and do not leave maintenance to the technical staff. Quality Web sites also have responsive owners who know that successful sites are never done. It is a never-ending task to weed out dead links, identify and fix broken graphics, add new pages, update old pages, and constantly review the site's look and feel for improvements.

Quality Web sites are tested regularly. Take a tip from fire departments that encourage the testing of fire alarms when clocks are set forward or backward for daylight savings time. Set a similar time (e.g., when first and third quarter reports are due or just before the peak selling season and 6 months later) for a comprehensive "site test" to review all current content, eliminate or consolidate infrequently accessed pages, check the content development plan for new content that may be required, update the FAQ file, and test all links to be sure they are working and still reflect the intended purpose.

Web site performance also is an ongoing concern. The 12-second rule should continue to be tested under a number of different scenarios, including a typical customer using a dial-up modem in another country at the Web host's peak traffic period. The look, speed, and feel of the site should be tested on a number of hardware and software options. Services such as Net Mechanic (netmechanic.com) and Trimak (trimak.com) offer tools and services that speed up download time, identify dead links, optimize graphics, and assess browser compatibility.

Section 16.7 ▶ REVIEW QUESTIONS

1. Describe eight criteria used to judge Web site design.
2. What is deep linking? Why is it a problem for site designers? What should they do about it?
3. Describe four site navigation aids.
4. Why is performance a key design criterion? What causes slow performance? What can be done to decrease download time?
5. Describe some issues for proper use of color and graphics on a Web site. (Hint: See Online File W16.12.)
6. What are some actions Web site owners should take to ensure a quality Web site?

WWW

16.8 PROVIDING EC SUPPORT SERVICES

Creating content and designing the Web site are the creative aspects of building a Web site. Determining how the Web site actually will be built and by whom are the business parts of Web site construction. Web site construction is usually about three options—internal development, outsourcing, and partnering—spread over two time periods—start-up construction and ongoing maintenance.

WHO BUILDS THE WEB SITE?

Early in the Web site development process, the online business owner has to decide whether to build the Web site with internal staff, an outside contractor, or a combination of these two options. This involves managerial considerations such as control, speed, and desired organizational competencies, as generally described in information technology textbooks (e.g., Turban et al. 2006; Post and Anderson 2003; especially McNurlin and Sprague 2002). This section will cover some of the most important of these managerial considerations as they apply specifically to Web site construction.

Do It Yourself

Internal Web site development is the do-it-yourself option of building and maintaining the Web site with company staff. Factors that lead companies to develop their own Web sites include the following:

internal Web site development
The process of building and/or maintaining the Web site with company staff.

- **Use of existing in-house expertise.** Having an experienced Web designer or Webmaster on the company's payroll is a good first reason for internal development.
- **Desire to build in-house expertise.** A closely related reason is that a company may not have existing expertise on the staff, but wishes to add Web site development to the company's skill set. In this case, new employees are hired or existing staff members are trained in order to build and maintain the site.
- **Protection of proprietary technologies.** If new software or an internally developed Web-based application is critical to the company's EC value proposition, then a business is likely to use its own staff to protect that intellectual property and advance its ongoing development.
- **Tighter control and responsiveness.** Especially in the maintenance stage, a company is likely to find that problem resolution, content management, and ongoing development of the site will be faster, less expensive, and more responsive if internal staff members are responsible for the Web site.

Outsource

External Web site development, or outsourcing, takes place when the business hires another firm to build and/or maintain the Web site. Factors that tend to favor external development include the following:

external Web site development
When the business hires another firm to build and/or maintain the Web site.

- **Speed to market.** If getting online fast is critical to the company's start-up success, an outside firm that specializes in Web site construction will have the resources necessary to build the site quickly. Generally, but not always, internal development takes more time.
- **Not a core competency.** Frequently, companies decide that Web site development and maintenance should not be one of their core competencies. Outsourcing Web site development allows an online business to focus more on promoting the product, increasing sales, building business relationships, and other business activities.
- **Access to special expertise.** Especially with initial site construction, a Web design firm is more likely to have access to all the expertise and development tools that site construction requires. For example, a business may have competent HTML writers, but database integration or specialized programming expertise may be missing. This expertise could be hired in on an individual contract basis, but it will be expensive and time consuming.

Hybrid

This last point suggests that the internal-or-external decision does not need to be all one way or the other. Instead, some form of **partnering Web site development** may be the best option. Depending on the nature of the Web site and the skills required, a mixture of internal and external development to build or maintain the site is possible and may be desirable. The principal downside to partnering is the additional overhead of contract and relationship management—managing a partnership can sometimes be more difficult than doing it all internally or externally. For a generic discussion of internal versus external development, see Online Chapter 18.

partnering Web site development
When a mixture of internal and external development is used to build and/or maintain a Web site.

Web Site Construction and Maintenance

Developing a Web site occurs over two time periods, and each period imposes different considerations on Web site development.

Web site construction consists of the initial content creation, design, programming, and installation phases of a Web site's development. As suggested earlier, this is likely to require a variety of expert skills that only rarely are available inside the company (e.g., information architects, Web page designers, database integration expertise, and programmers). Unless the

Web site construction
The initial content creation, design, programming, and installation phases of a Web site's development.

Web site is small and offers limited functionality or one of the factors favoring internal development is especially compelling, most businesses decide on external development or partnering as the best option for Web site construction.

Web site maintenance
The ongoing process of keeping the Web site open for business, managing content, fixing problems, and making incremental additions to the site.

Web site maintenance begins when construction ends. This period consists of the ongoing process of keeping the Web site open for business, managing content, fixing problems, and making incremental additions to the site. Building a Web site is one process, maintaining it is another. Once the initial Web site has been constructed, the ongoing development and maintenance usually can be managed internally or externally.

Managing Web Site Construction

The Web site construction team and online business owner are in a partnership to achieve the same goal: a well-designed, functional Web site that works. However, each partner also comes into the construction process with different incentives, especially in keeping the cost of a Web site reasonable. Some suggestions for the business owner to successfully manage this partnership include the following:

- **Start with a plan.** Before interviewing Web designers, know what the goals of the site are, prepare a list of prioritized content, visit some Web sites to acquire some preferences for the overall design, and have a budget figure in mind. Having a plan will make it easier for the designer to quickly learn what is expected and give an accurate bid.
- **Set goals early and stick to them.** What the site intends to accomplish is the driving force behind the design. If the Web designer begins by talking about page layout, interesting graphics, and site architecture, go find a designer who starts with a discussion of goals and content. Then stick those goals in a prominent place and justify every feature and every page by the contribution they make to achieving those goals.
- **Use a fixed-price contract.** A Web designer may want to be paid by the hour because then the designer is assured payment for each hour worked. However, the buyer does not have any certainty about what the final cost will be, and there is little incentive for the designer to keep the hours to a minimum. The result is likely to be higher costs and delayed implementation. Using fixed pricing, either for the entire site or per page, requires more preproduction planning, but Web sites should be designed and constructed with plenty of advance planning.
- **Justify graphics and features.** Pictures, art, sound, and video all represent escalating costs in terms of production, page design, disk space, and bandwidth. Some graphics (e.g., a logo, products), features (e.g., shopping cart), and visual effects (e.g., mouseovers) are required or desirable for functionality or aesthetics. However, each of these should be justified in the context of the site's goals, not at the whim of the designer. In other words, avoid "feature creep"—the adding of features that were not in the original plan.

PAYMENTS: ACCEPTING CREDIT CARDS

You can't do business if you can't get paid! This truism means that every online business has to face decisions about electronic payment systems. The dominant form of B2C payment is accepting credit cards over the Internet.

The process for accepting credit card payments was described briefly in Chapter 13. As noted there, processing credit card payments on the Internet differs only slightly from the process in traditional, face-to-face transactions. What are these differences from a merchant's perspective? What are the basic requirements for an online business to be able to accept credit cards for payment?

First, in the online process, the credit card reader in the store is replaced with credit card processing software (a credit card gateway) that is capable of accepting input from a Web page and submitting it into the credit card system (the merchant's bank, the customer's bank, and the credit card interchange, such as Visa or MasterCard).

card-not-present (CNP) transaction
A credit card transaction in which the merchant does not verify the customer's signature.

Second, with online transactions, a signature and verification of the signature by the merchant is not required, resulting in what is known as a **card-not-present (CNP) transaction**. This situation removes a considerable amount of certainty and security from the process. In response to this increased risk, banks are more selective about who gets an online merchant account, and they require that the entire process be as secure as possible (e.g., checking that the shipping address provided by the customer matches the billing address on file at the customer's bank). In addition, banks charge higher transaction fees for CNP transactions to offset the increased risks.

An online business that wants to accept credit cards for payment generally has to do the following (Kienan 2001):

- **Open a merchant account.** It is likely that the business's current bank will be happy to extend banking privileges for the business to accept credit cards online. However, some small, regional banks may not offer this service; other banks may establish thresholds that are too high for the business to qualify (i.e., banks are more selective about CNP merchant accounts). Opening a merchant account means acquiring bank approval, making an application, signing a contract with one or more credit card companies, and paying the bank and card companies a set-up fee. Ongoing costs for a merchant account include a percentage-based transaction fee and additional charges for other services, such as when a customer credit is issued.
- **Purchase credit card processing software.** Credit card gateway companies such as CyberCash and CyberSource provide credit card processing software and services that accept credit card numbers and manage their transfer into and back from the credit card system. Factors to consider in deciding which gateway company to use include companies that the site developer has worked with before and what software the organization hosting the Web site will accept. A business typically pays the credit card gateway a set-up fee and a per-transaction fee.
- **Integrate the credit card processing software into the transaction system.** To work effectively, the software must be able to manage the flow of data between the transaction and customer databases and the credit card systems. The site developer writes scripts that enable the different components in the credit card transaction to share data they require.

For best practices regarding merchants' protection against fraud, see Chapter 17 and Merchantrates.com (2005).

WEB SITE PROMOTION

Every successful online business needs a highly visible Web site (see Kavassalis et al. 2004). External Web site promotion through advertising (e.g., banner ads, pop-up ads) and marketing strategies (e.g., banner swapping, chat room sponsorship) was discussed in Chapter 4. This section focuses on internal Web site promotion (selling the Web site on the site) and search engine optimization (getting the Web site to the top of the search engine listings).

Internal Web Site Promotion

Internal Web site promotion begins by including content that establishes the site as a useful site for customers so that they remember the site and return and make a purchase. To do this, the Web site should become not only a place to buy something, but also an indispensable resource with compelling content, useful links to other Web sites, and features that will make customers want to return.

Promoting the Web site internally often includes a page of testimonials from satisfied customers. If the site or the business has received any awards, those should be drawn to the attention of the visitor. If the business owner's background or credentials are related to the business, then any degrees, professional affiliations, and awards that relate to the online business should be listed.

Site promotion continues with a marketing plan that includes the URL on every product, business card, letterhead, package, and e-mail message that leaves the business. A **signature file** is a simple text message that an e-mail program adds automatically to outgoing messages. A typical signature file includes the person's name, title, contact details, and name and URL of the business. A promotional signature file also includes something that encourages the reader to visit the Web site. For example, a diet center includes this teaser on all

signature file
A simple text message an e-mail program automatically adds to outgoing messages.

outgoing messages: "Are you the right weight for your shape? The answer might surprise you. Take our body shape quiz and find out for yourself."

Search Engine Optimization

How is a Web site found in the vast world of cyberspace? How does a new online business get noticed ahead of its more well-established competitors? In addition to promotional and advertising strategies discussed in this and other chapters, perhaps the most important and cost-effective way to attract new customers is search engine optimization. **Search engine optimization (SEO)** is the application of strategies intended to position a Web site at the top of Web search engines such as Google, AllTheWeb, and Teoma. Search engines are the primary way many Web users find relevant Web sites; an online business cannot ignore SEO strategies.

search engine optimization (SEO)
The application of strategies intended to position a Web site at the top of Web search engines.

The strategies to maximize a Web site's ranking in search engines should be part of content creation, Web site design, and site construction. Optimizing search engine rankings through keyword placement and link building is much easier, less time consuming, and less expensive if it is integrated into the Web site development process. Online File W16.13 provides a comprehensive guide to SEO.

Several SEO services (e.g., webposition.com, searchsummit.com) are available that will supervise the entire SEO process for a Web site. However, SEO requires constant monitoring to be effective, and decisions such as which companies are acceptable linking partners are management decisions that should not be left to neutral parties. SEO services can assist, but successful SEO requires supervision and involvement by the site owner.

CUSTOMER RELATIONSHIP MANAGEMENT

As defined in Chapter 13, *customer relationship management (CRM)* is a customer service approach that focuses on building long-term and sustainable customer relationships that add value for the customer and the company. Entire books have been written about delivering effective CRM (e.g., Brown and Gulycz 2002; Cunningham 2002; Dyche 2001), and that material cannot be duplicated or even summarized here. This section focuses on what every start-up online business needs to know in order to initiate an effective CRM program. After getting these fundamentals right, successful online firms will be ready to move into more advanced CRM techniques, such as contact management, data mining, and personalization.

Using Content to Build Customer Relationships

The first step to building customer relationships is to give customers good reasons to visit and return to the Web site. In other words, the site should be rich in information and have more content than a visitor can absorb in a single visit. The site should include not just product information, but also value-added content from which visitors can get valuable information and services for free. Exhibit 16.10 lists some ways in which online businesses can build customer relationships through content.

Listening to Customers

Web sites that practice successful CRM listen to customers through a variety of methods. Customers may provide information overtly through surveys or contests in which they indicate customer preferences. Customers also provide valuable business information through the e-mail messages they send. A business can listen to customers by following these suggestions:

- **Mine e-mail for information.** E-mail messages should not be deleted until they have been mined for valuable information about product performance, frequently asked questions, and necessary improvements in the business's processes and operations.
- **Survey customers quickly and frequently.** Customer surveys are an easy feedback tool for an online business. A survey form can easily be created online and results can be imported into a spreadsheet or database for analysis. Unsolicited surveys can provide rich feedback, but the results can be skewed because only individuals who have time or a complaint may complete an online survey. One successful strategy to get more complete and accurate results is to invite a certain proportion (e.g., every tenth customer) to com-

EXHIBIT 16.10 Building CRM Through Content

Content Strategy	Description	CRM Benefits
Provide membership	Offer registration at the site to gain access to premium content and services	Community building, targeted marketing, paid subscription opportunity
Personalize the user experience	Present content that the site visitor has indicated an interest in through previous browsing or member profiles	Community building, targeted commerce offers, customer and site loyalty
Support users	Provide responsive and convenient customer service	Community building, customer and site loyalty, repeat purchases
Communicate via the community	Allow visitors to communicate with each other and the publisher through the site	Community building, customer and site loyalty
Reward visitors	Provide visitors with rewards for visiting and using the Web site	Customer and site loyalty, promotional product up-sell and cross-sell opportunities
Market effectively	Promote the site's content and products without alienating current and potential customers	Customer and site loyalty, promotional product up-sell and cross-sell opportunity
Set up smart affiliate relationships	Establish affiliate relationships with both private (consumer) and commercial Web publishers	Customer and site loyalty, new revenue stream

Source: *Killer Content Strategies for Web Content and E-Commerce* by Tomsen. © Reprinted by permission of Pearson Education, Inc., Upper Saddle River, NJ.

plete a survey, perhaps with a small incentive (e.g., $3 off their next purchase). All surveys, solicited or not, should be short, requiring, at most, 5 minutes of the customer's time. Surveys should include easy-to-answer and easy-to-analyze multiple choice and Likert scale (e.g., a five-point scale ranging from very satisfied to very unsatisfied) questions. Such surveys should include only a few open-ended questions, but offer numerous opportunities for respondents to make comments. The most important questions should be asked first, just in case the survey is submitted incomplete. The amount of personal information that is asked should be kept to a minimum.

- **Create an e-mail list.** An **e-mail discussion list** is a group of people who share a common interest and who communicate with each other via e-mail messages managed by e-mail list software. Basically, visitors to the Web site sign up for an e-mail list sponsored by the site. Then a list member with a question or a comment sends an e-mail message to the e-mail list software, which sends it to all members on the list. The list should be moderated by an individual who reads and approves all messages before they are sent to the group. The moderator should not censor communications, but inappropriate or off-topic messages should be intercepted and discarded before being forwarded to the e-mail list.

e-mail discussion list
A group of people who share a common interest and who communicate with each other via e-mail messages managed by e-mail list software.

- **Create a discussion forum.** An **electronic discussion (e-forum)** is a portion of the Web site where visitors can post questions, comments, and answers. An e-forum has a similar purpose as an e-mail list, except that the messages are posted on the business's Web site, not distributed through e-mail. Most message boards are moderated. The main disadvantage of a message board is that the participants must make an effort to visit the site and read the messages, whereas messages from an e-mail discussion group are delivered directly to the recipient's mailbox.

electronic discussion (e-forum)
A portion of the Web site where visitors can post questions, comments, and answers.

- **Create a chat group.** A **chat group** is a portion of the Web site where visitors can communicate synchronously. Basically, participants read and respond to messages in real time as they are typed. Few online businesses have enough Web site traffic to support chat groups, not to mention the cost and staffing requirements to maintain them.

chat group
A portion of the Web site where visitors can communicate synchronously.

From the business's perspective, all three types of electronic discussion groups—e-mail lists, discussion forums, and chat groups—offer an opportunity for the business to keep track of industry news and customer concerns, to implicitly promote the firm's products, and to gain visibility among people who are in some way interested in what the business is selling. However, these positive benefits can be undermined if the business promotes its products too blatantly, if the discussion gets off track or is spammed (thus the need for a moderator), or if there is only a small amount of significant discussion. This last point is an important one. There should be evidence of a sizable audience, willingness to participate, and compelling topics to talk about before launching an electronic discussion group. If a business sets up an e-mail list or discussion forum and only a few customers join and even fewer participate, it may be viewed as an embarrassment for the business.

Section 16.8 ▶ REVIEW QUESTIONS

1. Define the three options for Web site construction.
2. What factors favor internal development of a Web site? What factors favor external development?
3. How is site construction best managed?
4. Describe the process required for an online business to accept credit cards over the Internet.
5. List four types of Web site content that can promote the Web site internally.
6. What is search engine optimization? Why is it important?
7. List ways Web sites can use content to manage customer relationships.
8. Describe three electronic discussion groups, with an emphasis on their similarities and differences.

16.9 OPENING A WEB STOREFRONT

The most common EC project on the Internet is the *storefront*. Millions of storefronts exist on the Internet, mostly those of small businesses. However, large corporations as well as many individuals, including students and even children, have storefronts as well. As we have seen throughout the book, most online entrepreneurs, such as the initiators of campusfood.com, amazon.com, cattoys.com, and thaigem.com, started with a storefront. Storefronts appear in all different shapes, and their construction and operating expenses vary greatly. Storefronts are designed primarily to sell products or services, yet their functionalities differ considerably (for a list of functionalities, see Online Chapter 18).

OPTIONS FOR ACQUIRING STOREFRONTS

Storefronts can be acquired in several ways:

- **Build them from scratch.** Pioneering storefronts such as hothothot.com, wine.com, and amazon.com built their stores from scratch. Specifically, they designed them and then hired programmers to program all of the necessary software. The major advantage of this approach is that the site owner can customize the site to his or her liking. The disadvantages are that the process is slow, expensive, and error prone and requires constant maintenance. Consequently, only large corporations build their storefronts from scratch today. See Online Chapter 18 for more on how to build a storefront from scratch.

- **Build them from components.** This option is faster and less expensive than the first one. The site owner purchases off-the-shelf components, such as a shopping cart, an e-catalog, and a payment gate, and then assembles them. The components can be replaced if they become obsolete, so the site owner can save on maintenance. The downside is that the resulting site may not fit the online business owner's needs very well. See Online Chapter 18 for information on how to build a site from components. This approach allows for adapting the application design to the specific needs of the business and for differentiating the storefront from those of the competitors. An example of this type of solution is Microsoft's Site Server Commerce Edition, which has a built-in wizard that helps users model their own online business processes graphically. This ap-

proach, however, is usually more costly than building from templates and may take longer. In addition, it usually requires some in-house technical expertise for installation of the required hardware and software as well as for continued operation and maintenance.

- **Build with templates.** Several vendors provide storebuilding templates. Some provide them free, free for 30 days, or for a nominal monthly fee that includes hosting the site on their servers. Using this approach is especially attractive to small businesses, because the cost is relatively low (usually $10 to $99 per month), the store can be constructed in one or a few days, and extensive programming skills are not required. The site owner basically fills out forms and attaches pictures. Another major benefit of this approach is that hosting is usually provided, as well as support services such as payment collection, shipments, and security. Furthermore, the vendor will take care of all software maintenance. Many vendors also offer store and inventory management as well as other features, as described later in this section. Finally, and perhaps most important, if the site owner uses a vendor such as Yahoo!, the site will be included in Yahoo!'s e-marketplace, which provides a great deal of exposure. The downside of this approach is that the site owner is limited to the available templates and tools. However, some vendors provide a professional version that allows customization. Representative vendors that provide templates are:
    - Yahoo! Small Business (see next section)
    - Bigstep (bigstep.com)
    - StoreFront (storefront.net)
    - 1and1.com and shopping.com
    - ShoppingCartsPlus.com (shoppingcartsplus.com)
    - MonsterCommerce (monstercommerce.com)
- **Use someone else's storefront.** Another option is to place products on someone else's storefront. The most notable example of this is amazon.com. People can sell used items on Amazon.com. The easiest things to sell are items that are already in Amazon.com's catalog (e.g., items that a person purchased at Amazon.com in the past that are no longer needed). Amazon.com even tells sellers how much they can expect to receive for the items. To sell an item that is not in Amazon.com's catalog, a seller can add it to the catalog by adding a product detail page using the Pro Merchant feature (available only to those with a Seller Account). Amazon.com also provides payment and shipping services.

Selecting a Development Option

Before choosing the appropriate development option, a number of issues need to be considered in order to generate a list of requirements and capabilities (Online Chapter 18). The following is a list of representative questions that need to be addressed when defining requirements:

- **Customers.** Who are the target customers? What are their needs? What kind of marketing tactics should be used to promote the store and attract customers? How can customer loyalty be enhanced?
- **Merchandising.** What kinds of products or services will be sold online? Are soft (digitizable) goods or hard goods being sold? Are soft goods downloadable?
- **Sales service.** Can customers order online? How? Can they pay online? Can they check the status of their order online? How are customer inquiries handled? Are warranties, service agreements, and guarantees available for the products? What are the refund procedures?
- **Promotion.** How are the products and services promoted? How will the site attract customers? Are coupons, manufacturer's rebates, or quantity discounts offered? Is cross-selling possible?
- **Transaction processing.** Is transaction processing in real time? How are taxes, shipping and handling fees, and payments processed? Are all items taxable? What kinds of

shipping methods will be offered? What kinds of payment methods, such as checks, credit cards, or cyber cash, will be accepted? How will order fulfillment be handled?

- **Marketing data and analysis.** What information, such as sales, customer data, and advertising trends, will be collected? How would such information be utilized for future marketing?
- **Branding.** What image should the storefront reinforce? How is the storefront different from those of the competition?

The initial list of requirements should be as comprehensive as possible. It is preferable to validate the identified requirements through focus-group discussions or surveys with potential customers. The requirements can then be prioritized based on the customers' preferences. The final list of prioritized requirements serves as the basis for selecting/customizing the appropriate package or designing a storefront from scratch.

In the remainder of this section, we will introduce the Yahoo! Store package.

YAHOO! SMALL BUSINESS

One of the most popular storefront packages is offered by Yahoo! at smallbusiness.yahoo.com. Yahoo! offers three levels of merchant solutions: *starter, standard, and professional.* The capabilities and fees of each plan are available on Yahoo's Web site. Yahoo offers an 11-step guide that explains how Yahoo! Merchant Solutions works and how it can be used to build, manage, and market an online business. Read on to gain valuable tips and guidance that will help you succeed in developing your own online storefront.

Getting Started

Read the online Getting Started Overview or download the full step-by-step Getting Started Guide (380 pages). A summary of the 11-step guide (as of January 2005) is provided in Online File W16.14 and at smallbusiness.yahoo.com/merchant/gstart.php.

Take a Tour

To see all of the features that come with Yahoo! Merchant Solutions, take a tour (click "Tour"). Once welcomed, you will be shown a slide show that lists all of its capabilities. Notable features include the following: Web hosting and domain name registration; e-mail; EC tools (shopping cart, payment processing, inventory management); business tools and services (site design, marketing, site management); order processing tools; site development tools (site editor, templates, uploading content, for example, with Yahoo! SiteBuilder); finding and keeping customers (per Chapter 4; from e-mail campaigns to cross-selling suggestions); payment acceptance tools; tax calculators; order notification and confirmations; and performance-tracking tools (statistics, drill-downs, measuring the effectiveness of marketing campaigns).

Using the Templates

You can build your store in several ways. Your primary tool is an easy-to-use online Store Editor. You can create a front page, and you can set up various store sections and add to them. You can upload content developed in Microsoft FrontPage, Macromedia Dreamweaver, or Yahoo! SiteBuilder (discussed in Section 16.5). See Online File W16.15 for how to create "sections" and "items" with the editor.

Section 16.9 ▶ REVIEW QUESTIONS

1. List the various options for acquiring a storefront.
2. What are the advantages of building with templates? What are the disadvantages?
3. List the typical features of a storefront.
4. What are some of the selection criteria for a software option?

MANAGERIAL ISSUES

Some managerial issues related to this chapter are as follows.

1. **What does it take to create a successful online business?** The ability of a business to survive, and thrive, in the marketplace depends on the strength of the business concept, the capabilities of the entrepreneur, and successful execution of the business plan. Creativity, entrepreneurial attitudes, and management skills represent a human capital investment that every potentially successful business needs.
2. **Is creating a Web site a technical task or a management task?** It is both. Although somewhat expensive, the technical skills required to build a Web site are readily available in the marketplace. The prerequisite managerial skills are somewhat more difficult to find. Online business owners need to possess traditional business skills as well as understand the technical aspects of building a Web site in order to be able to hire and work with information architects, Web designers, and Web site hosting services.
3. **How do we attract visitors to the Web site?** Search engine optimization is important, but the key to attracting visitors, getting them to return, and encouraging them to tell others about the site is to offer credible content that fulfills a value exchange proposition. That is, both the site owner and the customer must receive value from the visit. What the site says (content) is important, but so is *how* it is said. Web design delivers content in a compelling manner that enhances the readability of the content and the quality of the customer experience.
4. **How do we turn visitors into buyers?** Getting people to come to the Web site is only half the battle. Visitors become buyers when a Web site offers products and services that customers need, with promotions and a price that entice visitors to buy there rather than go somewhere else, in an environment that promotes trust.
5. **Are best practices useful?** For an inexperienced EC person or company, the best practices of others can be extremely useful (see Maguire 2005). The experiences of vendors, companies, academicians, and others are most useful. E-Business Advisor and E-Commerce Advisor (at advisorzones.com) provide many resources, and you can get advice for a fee. Free advice is available from many sources (e.g., ecommercepartners.net).
6. **How much of my new business should we give to funders?** It all depends. The important thing is to maintain control by keeping at least 51 percent of the shares (at least up to the IPO).
7. **How do we save on Web hosting expenses?** If you use templates and a storebuilder, you will pay very little for hosting. If you need a more complicated site, you can use a tendering system with an RFQ (see example in Online File W16.16).

RESEARCH TOPICS

Here are some suggested topics related to this chapter. For details, references, and additional topics, refer to the book's "Current EC Research" in the Online Appendix.

1. **Common Web Site Design Features**
   - Important design features
   - Benchmarking design features
   - Opportunities for enhancing a commercial Web site
   - Factors that require a specific configuration for a Web site
2. **Factors That Influence Web Site Design**
   - Curiosity as a design factor
   - Cultural differences in perceptions of Web site design characteristics
   - Models for small-scale Web sites
   - Effects of country, industry, and market on Web site design
3. **Web Site Implementation**
   - Web site implementation by small businesses
   - The determinants of success of Web site development and how they vary in different countries
   - The effect of consumer shopping orientation on the creation of a retail Web site
   - Development of Web sites for impaired users
   - Empirical studies on the key elements of B2C and B2B Web sites
4. **Factors for Web Site Evaluation**
   - Criteria for Web site evaluation, including business function, corporate credibility, content reliability, Web site attractiveness, systematic structure, and navigation

- Factors associated with Web site success for EC (e.g., information and service quality, system use, playfulness, and system design quality)
- Factors such as download delay, navigation, content, interactivity, and responsiveness on the success of Web sites
- Dimensions of Web quality, including content, content quality, appearance, and technical adequacy
- Ability to attract and inform visitors to Web sites
- Special-interest content versus general-interest content in generating Web site traffic

5. **Web Site Evaluation Methods and Tools**
   - Industry-specific Web site evaluation methods and tools
   - The use of benchmarking in the evaluation of Web sites
   - Tools that assess Web-based EC applications
   - Tools that measure a site's ease of use and effectiveness
6. **Adoption and Value of Web Sites**
   - Consumer preferences on commercial Web sites
   - Impact of Web site value and advertising on the firm's performance in the context of EC
   - Effect of cultural differences in adopting Web sites
   - Motivations and reasons why users choose to use particular Web sites
   - Effect of Web sites on the flow of human interaction
   - How Web sites have evolved and changed over time
7. **Factors That Influence User's Attitude Toward Web Sites**
   - User expectations and the ranking of quality factors
   - Domain name and site hosting preferences
   - Effects of adaptive Web sites
   - Effects of personalization on the use of Web sites
   - Effects of culture and context on perception and interaction with multilingual EC Web sites

SUMMARY

In this chapter, you learned about the following EC issues as they relate to the learning objectives.

1. **Fundamental requirements for initiating an online business.** A good idea becomes a successful online business when owners with the required skills, attitudes, and understanding of Internet culture execute a powerful business plan.
2. **Funding options for a start-up online business.** Incubators usually provide support services, whereas angel investors and venture capitalists provide funds for a prospective online business. The business and business owners usually benefit greatly from these arrangements, but the funding sources are scarce and competition for funds is stiff.
3. **Adding e-initiatives.** Adding e-initiatives (or projects) is common. A large project requires a business case. Additions are made gradually that eventually make the business a click-and-mortar one. Common projects are e-procurement, e-CRM, and a storefront.
4. **Transformation to e-business.** In an e-business, all possible processes are conducted online. Achieving such a state in a large organization is a complex process involving change management.
5. **Web site hosting options for an online business.** Storebuilder services, ISPs, dedicated Web site hosting services, and self-hosting give online business owners a range of options in deciding how and where to host the Web site. A well-chosen domain name is an "address for success," a way of making the site easy to find and remember. Choosing a domain name is an important step in setting up the hosting site.
6. **Web site construction options for an online business.** Internal development, external contracting, and partnerships give business owners a range of options in deciding who builds the Web site.
7. **Provide content that attracts and keeps Web site visitors.** Content is king! Content can be created, purchased, or acquired for free and used for site promotion, sales, and building customer relationships. Successful Web sites offer content that the site's target audience wants and expects.
8. **Design a visitor-friendly site.** Although text is content rich and inexpensive, a text-only site is a barren and unmemorable site. Graphics and colors should be selected with the site's business goals and visitors' needs in mind. Web site owners and designers should never overestimate the attention span of the site visitor, so it is best to include small graphics that are few in number so that the end result is an attractive page but one that also will load fast. The key to visitor-friendly navigation is to project a visitor's mental map on the Web site: where they are, where they have been, where they should go next, and how to get to where they want to be.
9. **High placement in search engines is key.** Keyword occurrence and placement on a merchants' site and promoting link popularity are the fundamental strategies for search engine optimization. High placement on search engine keyword searches will guarantee visitors, the essential first step toward online business success.

KEY TERMS

Term	Page	Term	Page	Term	Page
Angel investor	666	Dynamic Web content	677	Personalized content	680
Attractors	672	E-mail discussion list	695	Premium content	680
Business case	666	E-newsletter	681	Search engine optimization (SEO)	694
Business plan	665	Electronic discussion (e-forum)	695	Self-hosting	676
Card-not-present (CNP) transaction	692	External Web site development	691	Signature file	693
Chat group	695	Frame	687	Site navigation	686
Collaborative Web site	672	Incubator	666	Storebuilder service	673
Co-location	675	Information architecture	684	Syndication	679
Commodity content	678	Informational Web site	671	Transactional Web site	672
Content	677	Interactive Web site	671	Up-selling	678
Content management	681	Internal Web site development	691	Venture capital (VC)	667
Cross-selling	678	ISP hosting service	674	Web hosting service	674
Deep linking	686	Look and feel	687	Web site construction	691
Domain name	676	Mirror site	675	Web site maintenance	692
Domain name registrar	676	Partnering Web site development	691		

QUESTIONS FOR DISCUSSION

1. Compare and contrast setting up a traditional, brick-and-mortar business and an online business. Consider factors such as entrepreneurial skills, facilities and equipment, and business processes.
2. Compare and contrast the creation of a new online business and the establishment of an online initiative in an existing company. Consider factors such as resource acquisition, start-up processes, and competitor analysis.
3. How is an e-business plan different from a traditional business plan?
4. Discuss the logic of adding an e-storefront versus making all sales off-line.
5. Define organizational transformation and discuss some of the difficulties involved.
6. Discuss the logic of outsourcing the combined Web hosting and site construction. What are some of the disadvantages?
7. How would you decide which Web site hosting option an online business should use? List and briefly explain factors to consider in your decision.
8. What are the trade-offs in giving the customer everything possible (e.g., personalized content, high-resolution graphics, a feature-full site) and the fundamental rules of Web design?
9. Who should be on a Web site development team for a small business? For a large business?
10. Should a small business build its own Web site? Why or why not? Should a large business build its own Web site? Why or why not?
11. Should a small business maintain its own Web site? Why or why not? Should a large business maintain its own Web site? Why or why not?
12. Several times in this chapter online business owners are advised to gather competitive intelligence from competitors (e.g., in SEO, what sites link to competitor sites). Is this ethical? Why or why not?
13. Why is a store such as **cattoys.com** not economically feasible off-line?
14. What are the advantages and disadvantages of using templates to build a storefront?
15. Yahoo! provides many services, including Web site hosting, storebuilding tools, and an online mall. List the benefits of these services. What are the drawbacks, if any?

INTERNET EXERCISES

1. Go to the vFinance Capital (**vfinance.com**) and the National Venture Capital Association (**nvca.com**) Web sites and identify any trends or opportunities in acquiring start-up funding.
2. Go to a Yahoo! category, such as tourist agencies or insurance companies, and pick 10 sites. Classify them as informational, interactive, or transactional Web sites. Make a list of any informational, interactive, or transactional features.
3. Many individuals try to make a living simply by buying and selling goods on eBay. Visit **ebay.com** and

make a list of the ways in which these entrepreneurs use cross-selling and up-selling in their sales activities.

4. Visit The Webmaster Forums (webmaster-forums.net). Register (for free) and visit the Web site critique area. Compare the design rules offered in this chapter with some of the Web sites being offered for critique at the site. Offer at least one design suggestion to a Webmaster who is soliciting feedback.
5. Visit "Seven Point Checklist" (waller.co.uk/eval.htm), the "Web Site Scorecard" (hurolinan.com), or other sites that provide design tips. Then go to two Web sites you visit regularly and critique their design.
6. Visit "Safe Web Colors for Color-Deficient Vision" (more.btexact.com/people/rigdence/colours) to learn what colors work and do not work for people with color blindness. Visit at least five Web sites and rate them on their use of color for Web users with color blindness.
7. Explore the Web to find five dedicated Web site hosting services. Compare them using the criteria listed in this chapter. Write a report based on your findings.
8. Select five firms from an industry, such as banking, stock trading, or ISPs. Go to google.com and enter *link:URL* for each of the five firms where URL is the firm's homepage. Which firms have higher numbers of incoming links? Examine their Web sites and try to determine why this is so.
9. Go to integic.com and examine its services and methodology. In what way can it help in the transformation of a brick-and-mortar bank, hospital, or toy manufacturer?
10. Enter monstercommerce.com. View the demo. What features impress you the most and why?
11. Compare the shopping malls of Yahoo! and amazon.com and internetmall.com.
12. Go to godaddy.com. Examine their Traffic Blazer. How can it help you with SEO?
13. Enter 1and1.com. Examine their hosting, development, and other tools. Take the Test Drive. Write a report.
14. Enter bontragerconnection.com. View their tutorials and comment on their usefulness to EC site builders.

TEAM ASSIGNMENTS AND ROLE PLAYING

1. Pretend your team has been asked to make a 20-minute presentation to a local business group about how to launch an online business. Prepare the presentation by highlighting the most important considerations you learned in this chapter.
2. Write an RFQ for a fictitious company following the example provided in Online File W16.16. Submit the RFQ to several local ISPs. (Be honest and tell them this is a student assignment; most ISPs will be happy to assist if you volunteer to send them a copy of your report.) Write a report that compares the responses, selects a winning ISP, and justifies your decision.
3. The students should form teams. Assume that a commercial or nonprofit organization in your community has asked for your assistance in selecting and registering a domain name. Write a report that identifies several appropriate available domain names, explain the pros and cons of each name, make a recommendation, and justify your recommendation.
4. Form two teams, a client team and a Web design team. After suitable preparation, both teams meet for their first Web site planning meeting. Afterwards, both teams critique their own and the other team's performance in the meeting.
5. Form two debating teams. One team supports the proposition that using a number of images and colors on a Web site is okay because "soon everyone will have a high-speed connection to the Internet." The other team disagrees with this statement and its justification.
6. Enter webhosting.yahoo.com/ps/sb/ and download the SiteBuilder. As a team, build a storefront for your dream business. You can try it for free for 30 days. Use the design features available. Have visitors check out the site. Rewards will be given to the best stores.

Real-World Case

SEARS' TRANSFORMATION TO CLICK-AND-MORTAR

The fierce competition in retailing and the added competition from e-tailing drove Sears to transform itself into a click-and-mortar company. This transformation has included Sears' acquisition of Lands' End, a mail-order clothier company that sells more than 35 percent of its volume online. The various initiatives related to the transformation are shown in the following exhibit.

Key E-Business Initiatives at Sears

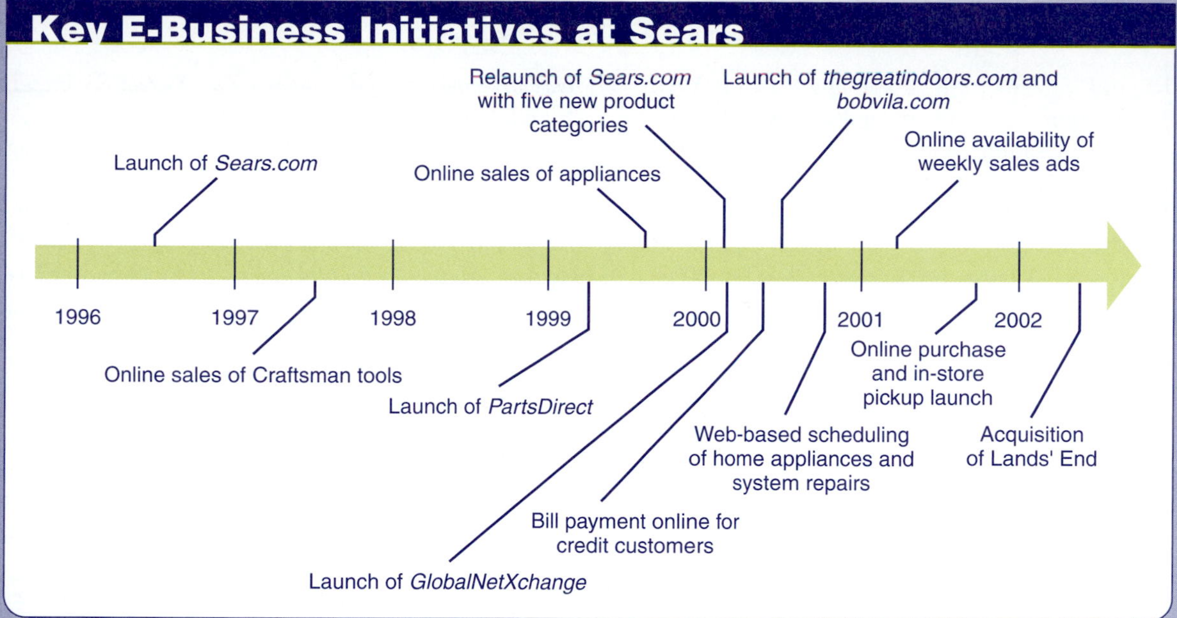

Source: Ranganathan, C., et al. "E-business Transformation at a Crossroads: Sears' Dilemma." *Journal of Information Technology,* 19, no. 2, 2004. Copyright © 2005 Palgrave Macmillan Ltd. Used with permission.

Although Sears invested heavily in e-business initiatives from 1996 through 2002, the ROI from these investments was very poor. For example, Sears was a founding member of GlobalNetXchange, a global B2B exchange that featured 50,000 suppliers. The ROI of this venture was low. In January 2003, a newly appointed CIO, Garry Kelly, sought to expedite Sears' e-transformation as well as concentrate on improving returns from current EC projects. The purchase of Lands' End provided opportunities for multichannel sales across stores, Web sites, and catalogs, as well as combining back-end operations. Some of the issues faced by Sears were:

- Which products should be sold online? Which products should not be offered online?
- How many storefronts should it support? For what product categories?
- Should sale and return policies for all sites be the same?
- How could it merge with the successful and profitable Lands' End site? How could it take advantage of Lands' End strengths to improve Sears' e-business efforts?

Kelly's objective was to make Sears a profitable click-and-mortar company—a multichannel retailer that would attract many more customers. To fulfill this goal, Kelly had to reorient his technology organization, reexamine and improve on the e-business initiatives, and move forward. The IT and EC infrastructure was fragmented; there were too many point-of-sale systems, too many inventory systems, and so on. Kelly needed to standardize and integrate many information systems. However, three strategic questions first needed to be answered:

1. What is the best way to utilize the Web to attract and sell a varied range of products?
2. How should Sears extend and enhance its B2B EC initiatives?
3. How can it use Lands' End technologies and operations to turn around its e-business?

Other issues regarding the transformation were:

- How could relevant strategic alliances be used to boost e-business?
- What e-business capabilities are required to make the successful transformation? How should such capabilities be built?
- How can the firm's business strategy be aligned with an e-business strategy?
- Should online and off-line prices differ?

Kelly started to address all these issues. However, in the summer of 2004, Sears was acquired by K-Mart, and the e-business transformation is now part of a much larger company's strategy.

Source: Compiled from Ranganathan et al. (2004).

Questions

1. Given what you learned in Section 16.3 and on additional searches you conduct, in your opinion what were the major reasons why the e-business initiatives were problematic and unsuccessful?
2. If you were in Kelly's situation would you have outlined the same issues to be resolved first? Why or why not? Are there any other issues you would suggest for consideration?
3. What would you advise Kelly to do (disregard K-Mart)?
4. What actions would you suggest the K-Mart/Sears Company to take?
5. Should the successful Lands' End operate as an independent e-business unit? Why or why not?

REFERENCES

Agarwal, R., and V. Venkatesh. "Assessing a Firm's Web Presence: A Heuristic Evaluation Procedure for the Measurement of Usability." *Information Systems Research* 13, no. 2 (2002): 168–186.

Akamai. "Thomson Financial Contracts Akamai's Industry-Leading EdgeSuite Service for Guaranteed Uptime of Web Operations." Akamai press release, April 8, 2003. **akamai.com/en/html/about/press/press391.html** (accessed April 2003).

Arnold, S. E. "Content Management's New Realities." *OnLine Magazine* 27, no. 1 (2003). **infotoday.com/online/jan03/arnold.shtml** (accessed March 2005).

Awad, E. M. *Electronic Commerce: From Vision to Fulfillment*. Upper Saddle River, NJ: Prentice Hall, 2002.

Bakshi, K., and J. Deighton. *Webvan: Groceries on the Internet*. Boston: Harvard Business School Press, 1999.

Barnes, H. "Implement Strategic Content Management." *e-Business Advisor*, April 2001a.

Barnes, H. "Three Steps to Effective Web Content Measurement." *e-Business Advisor*, June 2001b.

Bayers, C. "The Inner Bezos." *Wired* 7, no. 3 (1999): 115–121, 172–187.

BBC Training and Development. *The 12 Deadly Sins of Site Design*. October 2002. (Note: no longer available online.)

Bosilj-Vuksic, V., et al. "Assessment of E-Business Transformation Using Simulation Modeling." *Simulation*, December 2002.

Brown, S. A., and M. Gulycz. *Performance-Driven CRM: How to Make Your Customer Relationship Management Vision a Reality*. New York: John Wiley & Sons, 2002.

Business 2.0 staff. "The Who's Who of E-Business." *Business 2.0*, January 2002. **business2.com/b2/web/articles/0,17863,514258,00.html** (accessed January 2005; must be a subscriber to access).

Business Wire. "Amazon Services to Provide American Express Merchants with Special Offer for Selling through Amazon.com." July 24, 2004A. **findarticles.com/p/articles/mi_m0ein/is_2004_July_29/ai_n6132981** (accessed January 2005).

Business Wire. "Amazon.com to Acquire Joyo.com Limited." August 19, 2004b. **findarticles.com/p/articles/mi_m0ein/is_2004_August_19/ai_n6161725** (accessed January 2005).

Byrne, T. "Top Six Content Management Pitfalls." *PC Magazine*, September 17, 2002.

Carr, N. G. "On the Edge." *Harvard Business Review*, May–June 2000.

Chen, J. S., and R. K. H. Ching. "A Proposed Framework for Transition to an e-Business Model." *Quarterly Journal of E-Commerce*, October–December 2002.

Cheung, C. M. K., and M. K. O. Lee. "The Asymmetric Impact of Web Site Attribute Performance on User Satisfaction: An Empirical Study." *Proceedings of the Hawaii International Conference on System Sciences*, Big Island, Hawaii, January 3–6, 2005.

Clyman, J. "From Chaos to Control (Content Management)." *PC Magazine*, September 17, 2002.

Conway, C. "Incubators and Hatcheries." *International Journal of Entrepreneurship and Innovation* 5, no. 4 (2004).

Coupey, E. *Marketing and the Internet*. Upper Saddle River, NJ: Prentice Hall, 2001.

Cukier, K. N. "Boo's Blues." *Red Herring*, May 4, 2000. **redherring.com/vc/2000/0504/vc-boo050400.html** (accessed March 2005; members only).

Cunningham, M. J. *Customer Relationship Management*. New York: Capstone Publishing/John Wiley, 2002.

Dyche, J. *The CRM Handbook: A Business Guide to Customer Relationship Management*. Reading, MA: Addison-Wesley Information Technology, 2001.

El Sawy, O. A. *Redesigning Enterprise Process for e-Business*. New York: McGraw-Hill, 2001.

eMarketer. "Top Ten E-Business Trends for 2005." *eMarketer.com*, January 5, 2005. **emarketer.com/article.aspx?1003202** (accessed January 2005).

Evans, P., and T. Wurster. *Blown to Bits: How the New Economics of Information Transforms Strategy*. Boston: Harvard Business School Press, 2000.

Fogarty, K. "Your Money or Your Network." *Baseline*, February 2005.

Ginige, A., et al. "A Road Map for Successfully Transforming SMEs into E-Business." *Cutter IT Journal*, May 2001.

Gupta, V. K., et al. "Overview of Content Management Approaches and Strategies." *Electronic Markets* 11, no. 4 (2001).

Hendon, I. M. "E-Business: Think Big, Start Small, Act Quickly." *Aviation Now*, December 18, 2003.

Huang, W., et al. "Transforming a Lean CMC Medium into a Rich One: An Empirical Investigation in Small Groups." *Proceedings of the 17th International Conference on Information Systems*, Cleveland, Ohio, December 1996, pp. 265–277.

Huff, S., et al. *Cases in Electronic Commerce*, 2d ed. Boston: Irwin McGraw-Hill, 2001.

Internetnews Staff. "Interactive Video to Reach $4.2 Billion by 2005." Internetnews.com, December 1, 1999. **internetnews.com/bus-news/article.php/8161_252461** (accessed March 2005).

Iwaarden, J. V., et al. "Applying SERVQUAL to Web Sites: An Exploratory Study." *The International Journal of Quality & Reliability Management* 20, no. 8/9 (2003).

Jackson, P., and L. Harris. "E-business and Organizational Change: Reconciling Traditional Values with Business Transformation." *Journal of Organizational Change Management* 16, no. 5 (2003).

Junnarkar, S. "Akamai Ends Al-Jazeera Server Support." *CNET News*, April 4, 2003. **news.com.com/1200-1035-995546.html** (accessed May 2003).

Jupiter Media. "New Research on Web Content Management from Jupiter Research Released Today at Jupiter Content Management Conference and Expo." Jupitermedia.com, February 26, 2003. **jupitermedia.com/corporate/releases/03.02.26-jupresearch.html** (accessed March 2005).

Kapp, K. M. "A Framework for Successful E-Technology Implementation." *Journal of Organizational Excellence*, October–December 2001.

Kauffman, R. J., et al. "When Internet Companies Morph: Understanding Organizational Strategy Changes in the 'New' New Economy." *First Monday*, July 2002. **firstmonday.dk/issues/issue7_7/kauffman** (Note: no longer available online.)

Kavassalis, P., et al. "What Makes a Web Site Popular?" *Communications of the ACM*, February 2004.

Kienan, B. *Managing Your E-Commerce Business.* Redmond, WA: Microsoft Press, 2001.

Klotz, I. "Space Race 2: Bezos and Life Beyond Amazon." *Washingtontimes.com.* January 18, 2005. **washingtontimes.com/upi-breaking/20050117-073812-8136r.htm** (accessed March 2005).

Korzenionwski, P. "ESI Does It." *eWeek*, April 1, 2002.

Kurnia, S., et al. "An Evaluation of Australian on Swiss E-whops in the Grocery Sector." *Proceedings of the 38th Hawaii International Conference on System Sciences*, Big Island, Hawaii, January 3–6, 2005.

Lasry, E. M. "Inertia.com: Rates and Processes of Organizational Transformation in the Retail Industry." *Quarterly Journal of E-Commerce* (July–September 2002).

Lee, J. "Smart Products and Services for E-Business Transformation." *International Journal of Technology Management* (January–March 2003).

Maguire, J. "E-Commerce Best Practices: Ten Rules of the Road." *Ecommercepartners.net,* January 11, 2005. **ecommerce-guide.com/solutions/advertising/article.php/3457431** (accessed March 2005).

Markus, L. "Electronic Mail as the Medium of Managerial Choice." *Organizational Science* 5 (1994): 502–527.

McKay, J., and P. Marshall. *Strategic Management of e-Business.* Milton, Australia: John Wiley and Sons, Australia, 2004.

McKinney, V., et al. "The Measurement of Web-Customer Satisfaction: An Expectation and Disconfirmation Approach." *Information Systems Research* 13, no. 3 (2002): 296–315.

McNurlin, B. C., and P. Sprague. *Information Systems: Management in Practice,* 5th ed. Upper Saddle River, NJ: Prentice Hall, 2002.

Merchantrates.com. "ECommerce Best Practices and Fraud Control Programs." 2005. **merchantrates.com/MOTO/default.asp** (accessed January 2005).

Mulqueen, J. T. "Fast 50: #1 Akamai." Eweek.com, July 9, 2001. **eweek.com/article2/0,1759,1247037,00.asp** (accessed March 2005).

New Zealand Ministry of Economic Development (MED). *E-Commerce: A Guide for New Zealand Business.* Wellington, New Zealand: New Zealand Ministry of Economic Development, 2000.

Nielsen, J., and M. Tahir. *Homepage Usability: 50 Web Sites Deconstructed.* Indianapolis, IN: New Riders Publishing, 2002.

OBO. **obo.co.nz** (accessed January 2005).

Ould, M. A. *Business Process.* Chichester, UK: John Wiley & Sons, 2003.

Phan, P. H., et al. "Science Parks and Incubators: Observations, Synthesis, and Future Research." *Journal of Business Venturing* 20, no. 2 (2005).

Porter, M. E. "Strategy and the Internet." *Harvard Business Review* (March 2001): 63–78.

Post, G. V., and D. L. Anderson. *Management Information Systems: Solving Business Problems with Information Technology.* Boston: McGraw-Hill, 2003.

Radoff, J. "Smart Content Management." *e-Business Advisor*, June 2000.

Ranganathan, C., et al. "E-business Transformation at a Crossroads: Sears' Dilemma." *Journal of Information Technology* 19, no. 2 (2004).

Rapoza, J. "Web Content Management Face-off." *eWeek*, August 7, 2004.

Rayport, J., and B. J. Jaworski. *Introduction to E-Commerce,* 2d ed. Boston: McGraw-Hill, 2003.

Rosenfeld, L., and P. Morville. *Information Architecture for the World Wide Web*, 2d ed. Cambridge, MA: O'Reilly, 2002.

Saracevic, A. T. "Vulture Capitalists." *Business 2.0* (November 2000): 158–169.

Saunders, C. "Study: Streaming Media Marketing to Rake in $3.1 Billion in 2005." *Internetnews.com*, June 18, 2001. **internetnews.com/iar/article.php/12_786611** (accessed April 2003).

Spector, R. *Amazon.com—Get Big Fast: Inside the Revolutionary Business Model That Changed the World.* New York: HarperBusiness, 2000.

Stam, N. "Media Here, Media There, Media Everywhere!" *PC Magazine,* January 2005. **findarticles.com/p/articles/mi_zdpcm/is_200501/ai_n8671118** (accessed January 2005).

Sterne, J. *Web Metrics.* New York: John Wiley & Sons, 2002.

Sullivan, D. "Machine Translation: Is It Good Enough?" *e-Business Advisor*, June 2001.

Taylor, M. J., et al. "Methodologies and Web Site Development: A Survey of Practice." *Information and Software Technology* 44, no. 6 (2002).

Three Squared Inc. "Three Squared First to Market as One-Stop-Shop for Streaming Media Services." *Three Squared* Press Release, April 2000. **threesquared.com/download/market.pdf** (accessed March 2005).

Tomsen, M. *Killer Content: Strategies for Web Content and E-Commerce*. Boston: Addison-Wesley, 2000.

Turban, E., et al. *Information Technology for Management*, 5th ed. New York: John Wiley & Sons, 2006.

Watson, R. T., et al. *Electronic Commerce: The Strategic Perspective*. Fort Worth, TX: Dryden Press, 2000.

Werbach, K. "Syndication—The Emerging Model for Business in the Internet Era." *Harvard Business Review* (May–June 2000).

Yahoo! "Merchant Success Stories." **smallbusiness.yahoo.com** (accessed January 21, 2005).

Zhang, Q. Y., and M. Cao. "Human–Machine Web Interface Design for Electronic Commerce: A Review and Design Perspectives, Objectives, Dimensions, and Techniques." *International Journal of Services Technology and Management* 4, no. 4–6 (2003).

CHAPTER 17

LEGAL, ETHICAL, AND SOCIETAL IMPACTS OF EC

Content

Learning Objectives

Upon completion of this chapter, you will be able to:

1. Describe the differences between legal and ethical issues in EC.
2. Understand the difficulties of protecting privacy in EC.
3. Discuss issues of intellectual property rights in EC.
4. Describe unsolicited ad problems and remedies.
5. Understand the conflict between free speech and censorship on the Internet.
6. Describe major legal issues in EC.
7. Describe the types of fraud on the Internet and how to protect against them.
8. Describe representative societal issues in EC.
9. Describe the role and impact of virtual communities on EC.
10. Describe the future of EC.

FILE SHARING ON THE WEB AND INTELLECTUAL PROPERTY RIGHTS

The Problem

Before the advent of the Web, people made audiotape copies of music. They either gave these tapes to friends and family or used them for their own personal enjoyment. Few individuals had either the interest or the means to create and distribute copies to larger populations. For the most part, these activities were ignored by the producers, distributors, and artists who had the legal rights to the content (Spaulding 2000).

Then came the Web and a variety of enterprising sites such as MP3.com, Napster (now Roxio), and Kazaa. MP3.com enabled users to listen to music from any computer with an Internet connection without paying royalties. Using peer-to-peer (P2P) technology, Napster supported the distribution of music and other digitized content among millions of users. When asked whether they were doing anything illegal, MP3.com and Napster claimed that they were simply supporting what had been done for years and, like private individuals, were not charging for their services. Other companies extended the concept to other digitizable media, such as videos and movies. The popularity of MP3.com and P2P services was too great for the content creators and owners to ignore. Music sales declined through 2003. However, in 2004 U.S. album sales were up for the first time in four years in a 52-week comparison with 2003, according to Nielsen SoundScan (Christman 2005). This is possibly the result of the legal action taken by the music industry. To the creators and owners, the Web was becoming a vast copying machine for pirated software, CDs, movies, and the like. Losses from pirated software alone were estimated at $29 billion for 2003 (Weiss 2004). If left undeterred, MP3.com and online file sharing services would cause the destruction of many thousands of jobs and millions of dollars in revenue.

The Solution

In December 2000, eMusic (*emusic.com*) filed a copyright infringement lawsuit against MP3.com. It claimed ownership of the digital rights to some of the music made available at MP3.com. Warner Brothers Music Group, EMI Group PLC, BMG Entertainment, and Sony Music Entertainment followed suit. A year later, Napster faced similar legal claims, lost the legal battle, and was forced to pay royalties for each piece of music it supported. This resulted in its collapse. As described in previous chapters, some P2P companies, such as Kazaa, have moved to other countries, but the legal problems follow them.

Copyright laws have been in existence for decades, and copyright infringement cases are nothing new. By the year 2000, the EC laws should have been clear. However, the legal system can be picky and slow to resolve legal difficulties and close loopholes. First, existing copyright laws were written for physical, not digital, content. Second, the U.S. Copyright Infringement Act states, "the defendant must have willfully infringed the copyright and gained financially." With respect to the second point, a MIT student named David LaMacchia was sued for offering free copies of Excel, Word, and other software titles on the Internet. The suit was settled in his favor because there was no financial gain. This loophole in the Act was later closed.

The Results

In 1997, the U.S. No Electronic Theft (NET) Act was passed, making it a crime for anyone, including individuals, to reproduce and distribute copyrighted works. The Act further clarified that it applied to reproduction or distribution accomplished by electronic means. It also stated that even if copyrighted products are distributed without charge, financial harm is experienced by the authors or creators of a copyrighted work.

Given the precedents and laws, MP3.com and Napster had little recourse but to capitulate. MP3.com suspended operations in April 2000 and settled the lawsuit, paying the litigants $20 million each. Napster suspended service and settled its lawsuits for $26 million. With the backing of Bertelsmann AG's record company, BMG, Napster tried—with little success—to resurrect itself as an online music subscription service. Napster eventually filed for bankruptcy in June 2002. Its assets were purchased by Roxio (*roxio.com*). Roxio revived Napster in early 2004 as a royalty-paying service.

Sources: Olavsrud (2000), Spaulding (2000), *roxio.com* (accessed 2002–2004), Weiss (2004), and Christman (2005).

WHAT WE CAN LEARN . . .

Every type of commerce involves a number of legal, ethical, and regulatory issues. Copyright, trademark, and patent infringement, freedom of thought and speech, theft of property, and fraud are not new issues in the world of commerce. However, as this opening case illustrates, EC adds to the scope and scale of these issues. It also raises a number of questions about what constitutes illegal behavior versus unethical, intrusive, or undesirable behavior. This chapter examines some of the major legal and ethical issues arising from EC and the various legal and technical remedies and safeguards. The chapter also examines some social impacts of EC and, finally, assesses the future of EC.

17.1 LEGAL ISSUES VERSUS ETHICAL ISSUES

Using the Internet in general and EC in particular raises a number of legal and ethical issues, some of which will be explored in this chapter. First, let's distinguish between legal issues and ethical ones.

In theory, one can quickly distinguish between legal issues and ethical issues. Laws are enacted by governments and developed through case precedents (common law). Laws are strict legal rules governing the acts of all citizens within a particular jurisdiction. If a person breaks the law, that person has done something illegal and can be held liable for punishment by the legal system.

In contrast, **ethics** is a branch of philosophy that deals with what is considered to be right and wrong. Over the years, philosophers have proposed many ethical guidelines, yet what is unethical is not necessarily illegal. Ethics are supported by common agreement in a society as to what is right and wrong, but they are not subject to legal sanctions (except when they overlap with activities that also are illegal). A framework for ethical issues is shown in Online Exhibit W17.1 at the book's Web site.

ethics
The branch of philosophy that deals with what is considered to be right and wrong.

EC opens up a new spectrum of unregulated activity, where the definitions of right and wrong are not always clear (e.g., see Hamelink 2001). Business people engaging in e-commerce need guidelines as to what behaviors are reasonable under any given set of circumstances. Consider the following scenarios:

- A Web site collects information from potential customers and sells it to its advertisers. Some of the profiles are inaccurate; consequently, people receive numerous pieces of inappropriate and intrusive e-mail. Take, for example, the case of when a company provides customers with free credit reports According to Morris (2004), a friend of hers applied for a free credit report. In addition to the report, she received a stream of e-mails from all kind of vendors, as many as 1,800 a day, and had to change her e-mail account. Should junk e-mail of this sort be allowed? Should it come with a warning label?
- A company allows its employees to use the Web for limited personal use. However, the employees do not know that the IT staff not only monitors the volume of their e-mail messages, but also examines their content. If the staff finds objectionable content, should the company be allowed to fire the offending employees?

Whether these actions are considered unethical (or even illegal) depends on the regulatory and value systems of the country in which they occur. What is unethical in one culture may be perfectly acceptable in another. Many Western countries, for example, have a much higher concern for individuals and their rights to privacy than do some Asian countries. In Asia, more emphasis is placed on the benefits to society rather than on the rights of individuals. Some countries, such as Sweden and Canada, have very strict privacy laws; others have none. This situation may obstruct the flow of information among countries. Indeed, the European Community Commission issued guidelines in 1998 to all member countries regarding the rights of individuals to access information about them and to correct errors. These guidelines may cause problems for companies outside Europe that do business there.

THE MAJOR ETHICAL AND LEGAL ISSUES DISCUSSED IN THIS CHAPTER

Of the many ethical and legal issues related to e-commerce, the following will be discussed in this chapter:

- **Privacy.** Internet users in many countries rate privacy as their first or second top concern.
- **Intellectual property rights and online piracy.** Rights to intellectual property are easy to violate on the Internet, resulting in billions of dollars of losses to the owners of the rights.
- **Unsolicited electronic ads and spamming.** This issue became uncontrollable. Legal, technological, and administrative measures are finally helping.
- **Free speech versus censorship.** The issue of attempting to control offensive, illegal, and potentially dangerous information on the Net is controversial. This collides with rights of free speech.
- **Consumer and merchant protection against fraud.** It is easy to reach millions on the Internet and to conduct different types of EC-related fraud. The success of EC depends on the protection provided to consumers and merchants.

EC ETHICAL ISSUES

There are many EC- and Internet-related ethical issues (Kracher and Corritore 2004; Murphy 2003; Petrovic-Lazarevic and Sohal 2004). Examples of ethical issues discussed elsewhere in this book are channel conflict (Chapter 3), pricing conflict (Chapter 3), disintermediation (Chapters 2, 3, and 7), and trust (Chapter 4). Two additional EC-related ethical issues are non-work-related use of the Internet and codes of ethics.

Non-Work-Related Use of the Internet

Employees are tempted to use e-mail and the Web for non-work-related purposes. In some companies, this use is tremendously out of proportion with its work-related use (see Anandarajan 2002). The problem has several dimensions. For example, e-mail can be used to harass other employees or pose a legal threat to a company. It also can be used for illegal gambling activity (e.g., betting on results of a football game). Some employees may use the company e-mail to advertise their own businesses. Using other corporate computing facilities for private purposes may be a problem, too. For example, in some universities 50 to 70 percent of all Internet use is related to entertainment, clogging the systems at times. Last, but not least, is the amount of time employees waste surfing non-work-related Web sites during working hours.

Urbaczewski and Jessup (2002) explored the utility of monitoring employee usage, calling it "one of the most controversial EC issues" (see Team Assignment #4).

Codes of Ethics

A practical approach to limiting non-work-related Internet surfing is to develop an Internet usage policy and make it known to all employees (Siau et al. 2002). Without a formal policy, it is much more difficult to enforce desired behavior and deal with violators. Some companies send monthly reminders on the intranet about the usage policy. Others tell employees that their movement may be monitored and that their e-mail may even be read. Such notification can be a part of a code of ethics.

Corporate *codes of ethics* express the formalization of rules and expected behavior and action. Typically, the ethics code should address offensive content and graphics, as well as proprietary information. It should encourage employees to think about who should and who should not have access to information before they post it on the Web site. The code should specify whether the company allows employees to set up their own Web pages on the company intranet and about private e-mail usage and non-work-related surfing during working hours. A company should formulate a general idea of the role it wants Web sites to play in the work place. This should guide the company in developing a policy and providing employees with a rationale for that policy. Finally, do not be surprised if the code of ethics looks a lot like simple rules of etiquette; it should.

The following are some useful guidelines for a corporate Web policy:

- Issue written policy guidelines about employee use of the Internet.
- Make it clear to employees that they cannot use copyrighted trademarked material without permission.
- Post disclaimers concerning content, such as sample code, that the company does not support.
- Post disclaimers of responsibility concerning content of online forums and chat sessions.
- Make sure that Web content and activity comply with the laws in other countries, such as those governing contests.
- Make sure that the company's Web content policy is consistent with other company policies.
- Appoint someone to monitor Internet legal and liability issues.
- Have attorneys review Web content to make sure that there is nothing unethical, or illegal, on the company's Web site.

Section 17.1 ▶ REVIEW QUESTIONS

1. Define ethics and distinguish it from the law.
2. Give an example of an EC activity that is unethical but legal.

3. List major EC ethical issues (consult Online Exhibit W17.1).
4. List the major EC ethical/legal issues presented in this chapter.

17.2 PRIVACY

Privacy means different things to different people. In general, **privacy** is the right to be left alone and the right to be free of unreasonable personal intrusions. (For other definitions of privacy and for its relationships to EC, see Rykere et al. 2002.) Privacy has long been a legal, ethical, and social issue in many countries.

privacy
The right to be left alone and the right to be free of unreasonable personal intrusions.

The right to privacy is recognized today in virtually all U.S. states and by the federal government, either by statute or by common law. The definition of privacy can be interpreted quite broadly. However, the following two rules have been followed fairly closely in past U.S. court decisions: (1) The right of privacy is not absolute. Privacy must be balanced against the needs of society. (2) The public's right to know is superior to the individual's right of privacy. These two rules show why it is difficult, in some cases, to determine and enforce privacy regulations (see Buchholz and Rosenthal 2002).

COLLECTING INFORMATION ABOUT INDIVIDUALS

In the past, the complexity of collecting, sorting, filing, and accessing information manually from several different government agencies was, in many cases, a built-in protection against misuse of private information. It was simply too expensive, cumbersome, and complex to invade a person's privacy. The Internet, in combination with large-scale databases, has created an entirely new dimension of accessing and using data. The inherent power in systems that can access vast amounts of data can be used for the good of society. For example, by matching records with the aid of a computer, it is possible to eliminate or reduce fraud, crime, government mismanagement, tax evasion, welfare fraud, family support filchers, employment of illegal aliens, and so on. The question is: What price must every individual pay in terms of loss of privacy so that the government can better apprehend these types of criminals?

The Internet offers a number of opportunities to collect private information about individuals. Here are some of the ways that the Internet can be used to find information about an individual:

- By reading an individual's newsgroup postings
- By looking up an individual's name and identity in an Internet directory
- By reading an individual's e-mail
- By conducting surveillance on employees (Steinberg 2001)
- By wiretapping wireline and wireless communication lines and listening to employees (Ghosh and Swaminatha 2001)
- By asking an individual to complete a registration form on a Web site
- By recording an individual's actions as they navigate the Web with a browser, usually using cookies
- By using spyware and similar methods

Of these, the last three are the most common ways of gathering information on the Internet.

Web Site Registration

Americans are a little schizophrenic when it comes to privacy and the Internet. A 2002 poll conducted by Jupiter Media Metrix (American City Business Journals Inc. 2002) indicated that 70 percent of U.S. consumers worried about their privacy. A joint study by TNS and TRUSTe (2004) found that Internet users were skeptical of the necessity of giving personal information to online businesses. Among the 1,068 participants, 71 percent dislike registering at Web sites they visit, 15 percent refuse to register at all, and 43 percent do not trust companies not to share their personal information. Another survey conducted by ReleMail (2004) found that 96 percent of respondents said that e-mail privacy is important to them.

Virtually all B2C and marketing Web sites ask visitors to fill out registration forms. During the process, customers voluntarily provide their names, addresses, phone numbers, e-mail addresses, sometimes their hobbies and likes or dislikes, and so forth in return for information, for the chance to win a lottery, or for some other item of exchange. There are few restraints on the ways in which the site can use this information. The site might use it to improve customer service. Or, the site could just as easily sell the information to another company, which could use it in an inappropriate or intrusive manner.

Cookies

Another way that a Web site can gather information about an individual is by using cookies. As described in Chapter 4, in Internet terminology, a *cookie* is a small piece of data that is passed back and forth between a Web site and an end user's browser as the user navigates the site. Cookies enable sites to keep track of users without having to constantly ask the users to identify themselves. Web bugs and spyware, described in Section 4.4, are similar to cookies. Spyware is the greatest threat to networks in 2005 (69 percent versus 23 percent for viruses and 10 percent for phishing) (Broida 2005).

Originally, cookies were designed to help with personalization and market research, as described in Chapter 4. However, cookies also can be used to invade an individual's privacy. Cookies allow Web sites to collect detailed information about a user's preferences, interests, and surfing patterns. The personal profiles created by cookies often are more accurate than self-registration, because users have a tendency to falsify information in a registration form.

The personal information collected via cookies has the potential to be used in illegal and unethical ways. EC Application Case 17.1 details the resistance faced by online advertiser, DoubleClick, when it attempted to use cookies to better target its advertising. Although the ethics of the use of cookies are still being debated, concerns about cookies reached a pinnacle in 1997 at the U.S. Federal Trade Commission (FTC) hearings on online privacy. Following those hearings, Netscape and Microsoft introduced options enabling users to block the use of cookies. Since that time, the furor has abated, and most users willingly accept cookies.

Users can protect themselves against cookies: They can delete them from their computers or they can use anticookie software such as Pretty Good Privacy's (pgp.com) Cookie Cutter or Luckman's Anonymous Cookie. Anticookie software disables all cookies and allows the user to surf the Web anonymously. The problem with deleting or disabling cookies is that the user will have to keep reentering information and in some instances may be blocked from viewing particular pages.

Today, a Microsoft product called *Passport* raises some of the same concerns as cookies. Passport is an Internet technology that lets consumers create a permanent information profile and a password that can be used repeatedly to access services at multiple sites. (See the discussion on e-purses in Chapter 12 for details.) Critics say that Passport affords the same opportunities as cookies to invade an individual's privacy. Critics also feel that the product gives Microsoft an unfair competitive edge in EC.

Spyware and Similar Methods

In Chapter 4, we briefly introduced *spyware* as a tool that some merchants use to spy on users without their knowledge. Spyware (also known as *spybots* or *tracking software*) is a software program that secretly collects information about the user and relays it to advertisers. It may enter the user's computer as a virus or as a result of the user clicking an option in a deceptive pop-up window. Sometimes when users download and install legitimate programs, they get spyware as well. Spyware is very effective in tracking users' Web surfing habits. It can scan computer hard drives for sensitive files and send the results to hackers or spammers. Spyware is clearly a violation of the computer user's privacy. It can also slow down computer performance. Spyware writers are getting more innovative and are trying to avoid detection. For example, *Keystroke Logger* runs in the background of the user's computer and records every keystroke the user makes. A hacker can then steal the user's social security number, bank account number, and password!

Protecting Against Spyware. Antivirus software and Internet firewalls cannot "see" spyware; special protection is needed. Many antispyware software packages are on the market. Many are free. Representative free programs are Ad-Aware, Spybot, Spykiller, and PestPatrol.

CASE 17.1

EC Application

PRIVACY ADVOCATES TAKE ON DOUBLECLICK

DoubleClick is one of the leading providers of online advertising. Like other online advertisers, DoubleClick uses cookies to personalize ads based on consumers' interests (see EC Application Case 4.2 in Chapter 4). Although privacy advocates have long criticized the use of cookies, they generally tolerated the practice because there was no way to tie the data collected by a cookie with a consumer's identity. All of this changed in January 1999 when DoubleClick bought catalog marketer Abacus Direct and announced plans to merge Abacus's off-line database with DoubleClick's online data.

Following the announcement, several class-action lawsuits were brought against DoubleClick that claimed that the company was "tracking Internet users and obtaining personal and financial information such as names, ages, addresses, and shopping patterns, without their knowledge" (Dembeck and Conlin 2000). Many of these suits were consolidated into a single suit brought in DoubleClick's home state of New York. A short time later, the Electronic Privacy Information Center (EPIC) filed a complaint with the FTC, alleging that DoubleClick was using unfair and deceptive trading practices. The attorney general of Michigan claimed that DoubleClick was in violation of the state's Consumer Protection Act and asked it to stop placing cookies on consumers' computers without their permission.

In January 2001, the FTC ruled that DoubleClick had not violated FTC policies. In March 2002, DoubleClick reached a preliminary settlement, clearing up a number of the class-action suits brought by the states. DoubleClick agreed to enhance its privacy measures and to pay legal fees and costs of up to $18 million. One of the key provisions of the settlement requires DoubleClick to "obtain permission from consumers before combining any personally identifiable data with Web surfing history" (Olsen 2002).

Prior to the settlement, DoubleClick had already appointed a chief privacy officer and substantially strengthened its privacy policies. (For a detailed listing of the policies, see *doubleclick.com/us/corporate/privacy*.) Despite these changes and the proposed settlement, EPIC was still not satisfied. As Marc Rotenberg, EPIC's executive director, stated, "You have to keep in mind DoubleClick's unique position—its consumer profiles are collected from Web sites it supplies advertising to. For this reason, we should expect a much higher standard for privacy protection" (Olsen 2002). DoubleClick, which provides advertising services for hundreds of commercial sites using cookies and similar technologies, was attacked in April 2004 by angry hackers who used zombies to orchestrate a DoS attack (UPI 2004), causing delays and frustration for the company and its customers.

Sources: Compiled from Dembeck and Conlin (2000), Olsen (2002), UPI (2004), and *doubleclick.com* (accessed 2004).

Questions

1. What are some of the ways in which DoubleClick's use of cookies might infringe on an individual's privacy rights?
2. What are some of the key elements in DoubleClick's new privacy policies?
3. Enter *doubleclick.com* and *google.com* and find recent issues relating to privacy.

For-fee programs include SpySubstract, SpySweeper, Ad-Aware Plus, and SpyWasher. For information and an evaluation of the various products, see Germain (2004). Luber (2004) offers an overview of spyware and detection and removal solutions. According to Germain (2004), in addition to blocking spyware, users also can use proactive scanning (see the Real-World Case at the end of the chapter).

The danger of spyware has resulted in quick legislation in the United States. The U.S. House of Representatives passed the Spy Act (H.R. 2929) in October 2004 (399 to 1). The Act prohibits outside entities from installing or modifying any software or disabling antivirus software without the user's permission or authorization. The California Anti-Spyware Bill (September 2004) bans the unauthorized installation of spyware and allows consumers to sue spyware developers for damages (SB 1436). A major objective of the federal and state legislation is to combat *identity theft* (see later discussion). Several other U.S. states are working on similar legislation (e.g., Utah's Spyware Control Act).

RFID's Threat to Privacy

As mentioned in earlier chapters, privacy advocates fear that the information stored on RFID tags or collected with them may be used to violate an individual's privacy. To protect the individual, RSA Security and others are developing locking technologies that will protect consumers from being tracked after buying products with RFID tags. Several states (e.g., California) are considering legislation to protect customers from a loss of privacy due to the tags.

Privacy of Employees

In addition to customers' privacy, there is the issue of the privacy of employees. Many employers monitor their employees' e-mail and Web activities. In addition to wasting time online, employees may disclose trade secrets and possibly make employers liable for defamation based on what they do on the corporate Web site. In response to these concerns, 77 percent of companies monitor their employees' communications (Lewis 2002).

Privacy of Patients

The privacy of patients is an extremely important issue for health-care providers due to the sensitive information they collect. EC Application Case 17.2 offers an example of how one health-care company guards patient confidentiality.

PROTECTION OF PRIVACY

The ethical principles commonly used when it comes to the collection and use of personal information also apply to information collected in e-commerce. These principles include the following:

opt-out clause
Agreement that requires computer users to take specific steps to *prevent* the collection of personal information.

opt-in clause
Agreement that requires computer users to take specific steps to *allow* the collection of personal information.

- **Notice/awareness.** Consumers must be given notice of an entity's information practices prior to the collection of personal information. Consumers must be able to make informed decisions about the type and extent of their disclosures based on the intentions of the party collecting the information.
- **Choice/consent.** Consumers must be made aware of their options as to how their personal information may be used, as well as any potential secondary uses of the information. Consent may be granted through **opt-out clauses**, which require steps to *prevent* collection of information. In other words, no action equals consent. Or, consumers may grant consent through **opt-in clauses**, which require steps to *allow* the collection of information.

CASE 17.2

EC Application

HOW CLEARCUBE'S PC BLADES GUARD PATIENT CONFIDENTIALITY

In the United States, work space in hospitals is limited. Computers can be found on the floor and underneath desks. This may not only result in damage to the computers, but it also raises concerns about the hospitals' ability to keep patient information private. The Health Insurance Portability and Accountability Act of 1996 (HIPAA) mandates patient privacy standards.

In 2003, the Medical Center of Central Georgia (MCCG) decided to ease its PC storage problems with PC blades from ClearCube Technology, Inc. In the PC blade environment, the monitor, keyboard, and mouse are at the employee's desk and are connected to a server located in a data center or other secure area. The server includes the hard drive, processor, and memory. Patient information is stored on these secure servers, and unauthorized employees are unable to view or download the information.

MCCG has more than 4,000 employees and more than 2,400 PCs, about a third of which are PC blades, with the rest being traditional desktops, mostly from Dell. MCCG uses ClearCube's C/Port, a device that sits on the desktop and connects the monitor and keyboard to a chassis in a back room via a Category 5 Ethernet cable. C/Port devices cannot sit more than 200 feet from the PC blade, and each user has a dedicated blade. Another ClearCube device, I/Port, uses a fiber-optic connection, and thus is not distance limited, that allows for multiple users on a single PC blade.

In addition to the security benefits, work spaces at MCCG are now less crowded, PC repair time has been reduced, and IT administrators do not have to travel to an employee's desk if there is a problem with a computer.

Source: Reprinted from Burt J. "Vertical Slice: Health Care, Privacy Therapy." *eWEEK*, July 26, 2004, with permission.

Questions

1. How does MCGG use PC blade technology to enhance privacy protection?
2. How has the space-shortage problem been solved?

- **Access/participation.** Consumers must be able to access their personal information and challenge the validity of the data.
- **Integrity/security.** Consumers must be assured that their personal data are secure and accurate. It is necessary for those collecting the data to take whatever precautions are required to ensure that data are protected from loss, unauthorized access, destruction, and fraudulent use, and to take reasonable steps to gain information from reputable and reliable sources.
- **Enforcement/redress.** A method of enforcement and remedy must be available. Otherwise, there is no real deterrent or enforceability for privacy issues.

In the United States, these principles are supported by specific pieces of legislation (see Nickell 2001). For example, the Federal Internet Privacy Protection Act of 1997 prohibits federal agencies from disclosing personal records or making available identifying records about an individual's medical, financial, or employment history. Probably the broadest in scope is the Communications Privacy and Consumer Empowerment Act (1997), which requires (among other things) that the FTC enforce online privacy rights in EC, including the collection and use of personal data.

For existing U.S. federal privacy legislation, see Online Exhibit W17.2. In addition to existing legislation, there are several pending laws, both in the United States and in other countries. Numerous privacy legislation bills are in various committees and subcommittees of the U.S. House and Senate, as they have been since 2001, including H.R. 237, the Consumer Internet Privacy Enhancement Act of 2001; H.R. 48, the Global Internet Freedom Act; H.R. 69, the Online Privacy Protection Act of 2003; and H.R. 71, the Wireless Privacy Protection Act of 2003 (see epic.org/privacy/bill_track.html). For the status of pending legislation in the United States, visit cdt.org.

THE USA PATRIOT ACT

The USA PATRIOT Act (officially, Uniting and Strengthening America by Providing Appropriate Tools to Intercept and Obstruct Terrorism) was introduced October 2, 2001, and passed October 4, 2001, in the aftermath of the September 11 terrorist attacks of that year. Its intent is to give law enforcement agencies broader range in their efforts to protect U.S. citizens. The American Civil Liberties Union, the Electronic Freedom Foundation, and other organizations have grave concerns, including (1) expanded surveillance with reduced checks and balances, (2) overbreadth with a lack of focus on terrorism, and (3) rules that would allow Americans to be more easily spied upon by U.S. foreign intelligence agencies. Between October 2001 and September 2002, federal agencies used this Act for many federal cases not directly pertaining to terrorist activities (see house.gov/judiciary/patriotlet051303.pdf). For more information, see eff.org/privacy/surveillance/terrorism/hr3162.html and infowars.com.

Parts of the Act allow expanded surveillance in the following areas:

- E-mail and Internet searches
- Nationwide roving wiretaps
- Requirement that ISPs hand over more user information
- Expanded scope of surveillance based on new definitions of terrorism
- Government spying on suspected computer trespassers with no need for court order
- Wiretaps for suspected violations of the Computer Fraud and Abuse Act
- Dramatic increases in the scope and penalties of the Computer Fraud and Abuse Act
- General expansion of Foreign Intelligence Surveillance Act (FISA) authority
- Increased information sharing between domestic law enforcement and intelligence
- FISA detours around federal domestic surveillance limitations; domestic surveillance detours around FISA limitations

PRIVACY PROTECTION IN OTHER COUNTRIES

In 1998, the European Union passed a privacy directive (EU Data Protection Directive) reaffirming the principles of personal data protection in the Internet age. Member countries are required to put this directive into effect by introducing new laws or modifying existing laws in their respective countries. The directive aims to regulate the activities of any person or company that controls the collection, storage, processing, or use of personal data on the Internet.

In many countries, the debate continues about the rights of the individual versus the rights of society (see Buchholz and Rosenthal 2002). Some feel that the ISPs should be the regulators; others feel that self-regulation is the best alternative. However, some empirical data suggest that self-regulation does not work. For instance, in 1998 the U.S. FTC audited 1,400 commercial Web sites in the United States to measure the effectiveness of self-regulation (Federal Trade Commission 1998). They found that privacy protection at these sites was poor. Additionally, few sites provided end users with the following privacy protections: details about the site's information-gathering and dissemination policies; choices over how their personal information is used; control over personal information; verification and oversight of claims made by the site; and recourse for resolving user complaints.

Fortunately, users can take steps to improve their online privacy. Tynan (2002) provides 34 tips for how to do so. See pcworld.com/26702 for more suggestions.

Section 17.2 ▶ REVIEW QUESTIONS

1. Define privacy.
2. List some of the ways that the Internet can be used to collect information about individuals.
3. What are cookies and what do they have to do with online privacy?
4. List four common ethical principles related to the gathering of personal information.
5. How does the USA PATRIOT Act expand the government's reach?

17.3 INTELLECTUAL PROPERTY RIGHTS

intellectual property Creations of the mind, such as inventions, literary and artistic works, and symbols, names, images, and designs, used in commerce.

According to the World Intellectual Property Organization (WIPO; wipo.org), **intellectual property** refers to "creations of the mind: inventions, literary and artistic works, and symbols, names, images, and designs used in commerce." Whereas privacy protection is the major concern for individuals, intellectual property protection is the major concern of those who own intellectual property. Intellectual property rights are one of the foundations of modern society (Kwok et al. 2004). Without these rights, the movie, music, software, publishing, pharmaceutical, and biotech industries would collapse (Schmidt 2004). There are four main types of intellectual property in EC: copyrights, trademarks, domain names, and patents.

COPYRIGHTS

copyright An exclusive grant from the government that allows the owner to reproduce a work, in whole or in part, and to distribute, perform, or display it to the public in any form or manner, including over Internet.

A **copyright** is an exclusive grant from the government that confers on its owner an essentially exclusive right to: (1) reproduce a work, in whole or in part, and (2) distribute, perform, or display it to the public in any form or manner, including the Internet. In general, the owner also has an exclusive right to export the copyrighted work to another country (Delgado-Martinez 2005).

The following types of works usually have copyrights:

- Literary works (e.g., books and computer software)
- Musical works (e.g., compositions)
- Dramatic works (e.g., plays)
- Artistic works (e.g., drawings, paintings)
- Sound recordings, films, broadcasts, cable programs

On the Web, copyrights also can be used to protect images, photos, logos, text, HTML, JavaScript, and other materials.

The greatest threat to intellectual property is wide-scale individual theft. Tens of millions of individuals are using the Internet to illegally download music, videos, games, software, movies, and other digital products (see discussion on P2P in Chapter 8). However, the theft of even an obscure piece of research in which only a few are interested is still theft.

Various international treaties provide global copyright protection. Of these, the Berne Union for the Protection of Literary and Artistic Property (Berne Convention) is one of the most important. The Berne Convention dates to 1886. It is administered by the WIPO and is supported by over 90 percent of the world's countries.

A copyright owner may seek a court injunction to prevent or stop any infringement and to claim damages. Certain kinds of copyright infringements also incur *criminal liabilities*. These include: commercial production of infringing works, selling or dealing in infringing works, possessing infringing works for trade or business, and manufacturing and selling technology for defeating copyright protection systems.

A copyright does not last forever; it is good for a fixed number of years after the death of the author or creator (e.g., 50 in the United Kingdom). In the United States, copyright was extended to 70 years after the death of the author by the 1998 Sonny Bono Copyright Extension Act. After the copyright expires, the work reverts to the public domain.

Piracy of Software, Music, and Other Digitizable Material

Global piracy of digitizable material is threatening the software, music, and movie industries. According to Weiss (2004), global software piracy losses alone totaled $29 billion in 2003 (36 percent of all software sold!). The U.S. piracy rate was 22 percent of the total amount of software sold, while in China and Vietnam it was 92 percent.

According to Kontzer (2004), more and more movies are being downloaded illegally. In South Korea, for example, 60 percent of Internet users admitted to downloading movies (versus 20 percent in Australia).

The magnitude of the piracy is so large that the U.S. Congress is considering the Inducing Infringement of Copyright Act of 2004, which would hold technology companies liable for enabling copyright infringement whether or not there is intent to do so. (This bill is still under consideration as of early 2005.) According to Motion Picture Association of America's (MPAA) figures, movie studios are losing more than $3 billion each year.

Legal actions have not been very successful. In August 2004, a federal appeals court ruled that makers of two leading file sharing programs are not legally liable for songs, movies, and other copyrighted work their users swap online (Napster lost its case in court because the company maintained shared file indexes on central servers that could be regulated by a P2P company).

Frustrated with its limited success in courts against Kazaa and other P2P companies, MPAA and other associations are launching civil suits against individuals for "stealing movies or songs," seeking damages of up to $30,000 per download. The Recording Industry Association of America (RIAA) has tried to use the Digital Millennium Copyright Act (DMCA) to get ISPs to reveal the identity of customers who illegally swap pirated files. Some feel that the DMCA provides too much power to copyright holders. Nevertheless, in late 2003 and early 2004, the RIAA obtained names from some ISPs and sued 3,400 users; at least 600 of the cases were settled for about $3,000 each (Kravets 2004).

Copyright Protection Approaches

In 2004, the U.S. Congress failed to act on a number of copyright bills. Among the bills that did not pass was one that would have allowed entertainment companies and artists to sue those who induce copyright violations. Another bill that did not pass would have established prison sentences for the electronic distribution of copyrighted works (Gross 2004).

It is possible to use software to produce digital content that cannot be copied. The following are two approaches that are being used to design effective electronic copyright management systems (see Piva et al. 2001):

- The use of cryptography to prevent copyright violations (e.g., IBM's Cryptolope at domino.research.ibm.com/comm/wwwr_thinkresearch.nsf/pages/packinginfo396.html)
- The tracking of copyright violations (e.g., see baytsp.com)

digital watermarks
Unique identifiers embedded in digital content that make it possible to identify pirated works.

Another successful method is digital watermarks (Mulligan 2003). Similar to watermarks on fine paper, which indicate the maker of the paper, **digital watermarks** are unique identifiers that are imbedded in the digital content. Although they do not prevent an individual from making illegal copies, they do make it possible to track and identify pirated works. If a pirated copy is placed on the Internet, sophisticated search programs, such as

Digimarc's MarSpider, can be used to locate the illegal copies and notify the rightful owner. For more on copyright protection methods, see Kwok (2003) and Kwok et al. (2004).

Digital Rights Management

Digital rights management (DRM) is an umbrella term for any of several arrangements that allow a vendor of content in electronic form to control the material and restrict its usage in various ways that can be specified by the vendor. Typically, the content is a copyrighted digital work to which the vendor holds rights. The actual arrangements are called *technical protection measures.*

In the past, when content was analog in nature, it was easier to buy a new copy of a copyrighted work on a physical medium (e.g., paper, film, tape) then to produce such a copy independently. The quality of most copies often was inferior, thus making the copy process less attractive, and in some cases, less effective. The situation changed with the introduction of digital technologies. It is now possible to produce an essentially perfect copy of any digital recording with minimal effort. The Internet has virtually eliminated the need for a physical medium to transfer a work—thus the need for effective DRM systems. However, DRM systems may restrict the *fair use* of material by individuals (use for noncommercial purposes). This controversy was the subject of a special *Communications of the ACM* issue (see Mulligan 2003).

TRADEMARKS

trademark
A symbol used by businesses to identify their goods and services; government registration of the trademark confers exclusive legal right to its use.

A **trademark** is a symbol used by businesses to identify their goods and services. The symbol can be composed of words, designs, letters, numbers, shapes, a combination of colors, or other such identifiers. Trademarks need to be registered in a country in order to be protected by law. To be eligible for registration, a trademark must be distinctive, original, and not deceptive. Once registered, a trademark can last forever, as long as a periodic registration fee is paid.

The owner of a registered trademark has exclusive rights to:

- Use the trademark on goods and services for which the trademark is registered
- Take legal action to prevent anyone else from using the trademark without consent on goods and services that are identical or similar to those for which the trademark is registered

On the Internet, fake brand names and products can be sold or auctioned from anywhere. In the United States, the Federal Dilution Act of 1995 protects famous trademarks from dilution (trademarks preempt domain names). Trademark infringement carries criminal liabilities. In particular, it is a crime for anyone to fraudulently use a registered trademark, including the selling and importing of goods bearing an infringing trademark, and to use or possess equipment for forging registered trademarks. For example, in 1998, Playboy was able to shut down an adult Web site that was using the Playboy trademark.

Domain Names

A variation of a trademark is a domain name. As explained in Chapter 16, a *domain name* refers to the upper category of an Internet address (URL), such as prenhall.com or oecd.org. Two controversies surround domain names. One is whether additional (new) top-level domain names (similar to .com, .org, and .gov) should be added. The other is the use of trademarked names that belong to other companies as domain names. In 2003 and 2004, the Internet's governing body on domain names approved the following top-level names: .biz, .info, .name, .pro, .museum, .aero, and .coop. Country-code top-level domain names exist for most countries (e.g., .uk, .ca). For an overview, see the FAQs at iccann.org.

Network Solutions, Inc. At the heart of the controversies is Network Solutions, Inc. (NSI), a subsidiary of VeriSign, which has been contracted by the U.S. government to assign domain addresses. Until 1998, NSI exclusively assigned domain names for several top levels: .com, .net, .gov, .edu, and .org. The United States, as well as the rest of the world, had been subject to NSI for domain names, and critics in Europe and elsewhere were ready to relieve the United States of that responsibility. Europe was weary of the United States assuming the right to direct Internet governance, effectively subjecting the Internet to U.S. law.

On June 1, 1998, the monopoly of NSI over domain names ended. NSI created a registration system that it shares with several other competing companies. The new registration system is handled by Internet Corporation for Assigned Names and Numbers (ICANN), an international nonprofit corporation. Instilling competition in the registration system has caused the price of registration to drop.

Domain Name Disputes and Resolutions. The Council of Registrars (CORE), a European private-sector group, and the Global Internet Project, a U.S. private-sector group, want to increase the number of top-level names. One of the objectives is to create an adults-only top-level name that will prevent pornographic material from getting into the hands of children.

Both CORE and the Global Internet Project also want to repair disputes over domain names. Companies are using the trade names of other companies as their domain addresses to help attract traffic to their Web sites. For example, DC Comics is suing Brainiac Services, Inc., for using one of its comic book names, Brainiac. Private-sector groups will have to resolve this issue in the future before more lawsuits begin to surface. Major disputes are international in scope, because the same corporate name may be used in different countries by different corporations. (The U.S. Patent and Trademark Office offers a guide to domain names, which is available at uspto.gov/web/offices/tac/notices/guide299.htm.)

In order to avoid legal battles, the Internet community created a speedy way to resolve domain name disputes using *arbitration*. A new domain name dispute-resolution procedure was adopted on January 1, 2000, for domain name addresses ending in .com, .net, and .org. Three arbitration organizations have been given the authority to make determinations regarding domain name disputes. They are the Disputes.org Consortium, the National Arbitration Forum, and the WIPO. If one of these organizations makes a determination regarding a domain name dispute, NSI/ICANN will respect the decision and will transfer the registration of the disputed domain name in accordance with the arbitration determination. One advantage of this new procedure is its speed; it takes less than 45 days, compared to the months it used to take to resolve disputes through legal actions. A core set of policies, rules, and procedures for dispute resolution under the three organizations is set forth in a document entitled "Rules for Uniform Domain Name Dispute Resolution Policy," which can be found through ICANN at icann.org/dndr/udrp/uniform-rules.htm.

The following are two interesting arbitration rulings:

- The World Wrestling Federation won the first ever arbitration ruling, which was against a California resident who filed for the name worldwreslingfederation.com.
- Penguin Books was denied the name penguin.org. The name (which is not currently in use) was instead given to a person who was known by the nickname "Mr. Penguin."

In addition to the resolution of disputes by arbitration, legal action can also be initiated in various jurisdictions. Legal action provides a more potent protection, because in addition to an organization's winning the right to use a certain domain name, courts can also grant monetary damages and enforce specific *anticybersquatting* legislation, discussed next. For more on domain names and resolutions, visit verisign.com.

cybersquatting
The practice of registering domain names in order to sell them later at a higher price.

Cybersquatting. Cybersquatting refers to the practice of registering domain names in order to sell them later at a higher price. The Consumer Protection Act of 1999 is aimed at cybersquatters who register Internet domain names of famous companies or people and hold them hostage for "ransom" payments from the person or company. Companies such as Christian Dior, Nike, Deutsche Bank, and even Microsoft have had to fight or pay to get the domain name that corresponds with their company's name. In the case of tom.com, the original owner of the tom.com domain name received about $8 million for the name from a large media company in Hong Kong that changed its name to Tom.com to correspond with the URL. In this case, the sale was judged both ethical and legal. However, in other cases, cybersquatting can be illegal, or at least unethical (e.g., see Stead and Gilbert 2001). For an overview of cybersquatting, see Moringiello (2004).

In the past, the governing bodies of the Internet gave several private individuals the right to use domain names that involved trademarked names. For example, in 1998 a New Jersey dealer named Russell Boyd applied for and was given the rights to 50 domain names, including juliaroberts.com and alpacino.com. He then proceeded to auction the names on eBay. In that same year, Julia Roberts complained to WIPO. In the summer of 2000, WIPO's

Complaint and Arbitration Center, which coordinates international patents, copyrights, and trademarks, upheld the actress's claim. It ruled that Boyd had no rights to the domain name juliaroberts.com even though the actress by that name was not using it at that time. The Anticybersquatting Consumer Protection Act of 1999 lets trademark owners sue for statutory damages.

PATENTS

patent
A document that grants the holder exclusive rights to an invention for a fixed number of years.

A **patent** is a document that grants the holder exclusive rights to an invention for a fixed number of years (e.g., 17 years in the United States and 20 years in the United Kingdom). Patents serve to protect tangible technological inventions, especially in traditional industrial areas. They are not designed to protect artistic or literary creativity. Patents confer monopoly rights to an idea or an invention, regardless of how it may be expressed. An invention may be in the form of a physical device or a method or process for making a physical device.

Thousands of IT-related patents have been granted over the years. Examples of EC patents given to Open Market Corp., for example, are Internet Server Access Control and Monitoring (patent 5708780), Network Sales Systems (5715314), and Digital Active Advertising (5724424). Juno Online Services received an interactive ad patent (5809242). IBM has many patents, including 5870717, a system for ordering from electronic catalogs, and 5926798, a system for using intelligent agents to perform online commerce. Finally, Google has patent 6269361 for its GoTo.com advertisement method. Technology patents are traded at delphion.com.

Certain patents granted in the United States deviate from established practices in Europe. For example, Amazon.com successfully obtained a U.S. patent on its 1-Click ordering procedure. Using this patent, Amazon.com sued Barnes & Noble in 1999 and in 2000, alleging that its rival had copied its patented technology. Barnes & Noble was enjoined by the courts from using the procedure. Similarly, in 1999, Priceline.com filed a suit against Expedia.com alleging that Expedia was using Priceline's patented reverse auction business model. The suit was settled on January 9, 2001, when Expedia.com agreed to pay Priceline.com royalties for use of the model. However, in Europe and many Asian, African, and South American countries, it is almost impossible to obtain patents on business methods or computer processes. For more on the relationship between copyrights and patents, see Burk (2001).

FAN AND HATE SITES

Fan and hate Web sites are part of the Internet self-publishing phenomena that includes *blogging* (see Chapter 8). Fan sites may interfere with intellectual property. For example, some people get advanced copies of new movies or TV programs and create sites that compete with the formal sites of the movie or TV producer. Although the producers can get a court order to close such sites, new sites can appear the next day. Although the intention of the fans may be good, they may cause damage to the creators of the intellectual property.

cyberbashing
The registration of a domain name that criticizes an organization or person.

Hate Web sites can cause problems for corporations as well. Many hate sites are directed against large corporations (e.g., Wal-Mart, Microsoft, Nike). Associated with hate sites is the idea of **cyberbashing**, or *cybergriping*, which is the registration of a domain name that criticizes an organization or person (e.g., paypalsucks.com, kbhomessucks.com, walmartblows.com, or even ms-eradication.org). As long as the sites contain only legitimate gripes that are not libelous, defaming, or threatening, they are allowed to operate (see Rupp and Parrish 2002 for details). (Note that the freedom of expression guaranteed in the U.S. Constitution has, thus far, allowed sites such as those cited here.)

According to Kopp and Suter (2001), material published on fan sites, hate sites, and newsgroups may violate the copyrights of the creators or distributors of intellectual property. This issue shows the potential collision between protection of intellectual property and free speech, the topic of our next section.

Section 17.3 ▶ REVIEW QUESTIONS

1. List three types of intellectual property.
2. List the legal rights covered by a copyright.
3. What is the purpose of a digital watermark?

4. List the legal rights of a trademark owner.
5. Describe domain name issues and solutions.
6. Define patents.
7. Distinguish between cybersquatting and cyberbashing.

17.4 UNSOLICITED ELECTRONIC ADS: PROBLEMS AND SOLUTIONS

As the diversity and innovation of Internet advertising increases, so does the quantity of *unsolicited ads* (see Reda 2003). Such ads are not only an invasion of privacy, they also are an aggravating interference when surfing the Internet. The flood of unsolicited ads clogs the networks of ISPs, sometimes to the point of paralysis, and may prevent legitimate messages from getting through. The problem is reaching epidemic proportion in two areas: e-mail spamming and pop-up ads.

As discussed elsewhere in this book, *spamming* refers to the practice of indiscriminately broadcasting messages over the Internet (e.g., junk mail and pop-up screens). At some of the largest ISPs, spam now comprises 25 to 50 percent of all e-mail (Black 2002). This volume significantly impairs an already-limited bandwidth, slowing down the Internet in general and, in some cases, shutting down ISPs completely. In the United States, the Electronic Mailbox Protection Act requires those sending spam to identify it as advertising, to indicate the name of the sender prominently, and to include valid routing information. Recipients may waive the right to receive such information. Also, ISPs are required to offer spam-blocking software, and recipients of spam have the right to request termination of future spam from the same sender and to bring civil action if necessary. The cost of spamming to a company of 10,000 employees is $15.75 per employee in 2005 (Spanger 2005).

E-MAIL SPAMMING

E-mail spamming, also known as **unsolicited commercial e-mail (UCE)**, involves using e-mail to send unwanted ads or correspondence. It has been part of the Internet for years. Unfortunately, the situation is getting worse with time. IDC (2004) reported that spam will continue to be a major problem, accounting for 12 billion daily e-mails. The Pew Internet and American Life Project (2003) found that 60 percent of e-mail users reduced their e-mail use because of spam, and 52 percent said spam has made them less trusting of e-mail in general (for more statistics, see Reda 2003). Let's look at some of the drivers of spamming and then at some of the potential solutions.

unsolicited commercial e-mail (UCE)
The use of e-mail to send unwanted ads or correspondence.

What Drives UCE?

Although many people think that spamming is mostly the result of legitimate commercial activities, this is not the case. According to the Coalition Against Unsolicited Commercial E-mail (CAUCE; cauce.org 2004), many spammers are just trying to get people's financial information—credit card or bank account numbers—in order to defraud them. The pornography industry is another major source of spamming.

The major drivers of increased UCEs are that the "postage" is free, the time and energy entailed in mass mailings is minimal, and it is easy to get a mailing list. Because the entry hurdles are relatively low compared with the potential payoff, spammers have an incentive to find new ways to circumvent protective software, and they are succeeding: The total number of spammers and/or the quantity of e-mails delivered by each spammer is increasing. For example, Bill Gates, Microsoft's chairman, gets 4 million e-mails a day, making him the world's most spammed person (CNN 2004).

Why It Is Difficult to Control Spamming

Let's look at one of the most well-known spammers, Al Ralsky. According to Stone and Lin (2002), Ralsky sends out more than 30 million e-mails each day using 120 servers. Verizon is suing Ralsky, alleging that he crashed its servers. Ralsky (and others) buy bulk mailing lists, which can be purchased for as little as $2,000 for a list of 100 million addresses. Ralsky works with content providers that craft "pitches." He claims that he helps millions of people buy cars, earn money, and so on, and that he helps small businesses advertise. By some estimates, spam generates about 25 sales for every 1 million e-mails (Stone and Lin 2002).

Spammers send millions of e-mails, shifting Internet accounts to avoid detection. Using cloaking, they strip away clues (name and address) about where the spam originates, and the server substitutes fake addresses. Many spam messages are sent through unregulated Asian e-mail routes and then back to the United States.

Spammers use different methods to find their victims. For example, they scour Web sites and chat rooms for addresses and they send e-mails to common names at mail servers, hoping to find a match. They also use computer programs that randomly generate thousands of addresses. In addition to regular commercial spammers that push products (e.g., ink for your printer) and services (e.g., home loans and insurance), pornography spamming is increasing rapidly. Spammers also steal e-mail lists from other databases.

For more information, see the CAUCE's Web site (cauce.org). An example of how a spam blocker works is shown in Exhibit 17.1.

Solutions to Spamming

Although antispam legislation is being considered in many countries, its implementation may not be simple (see Piazza 2004). Therefore, others must take action. ISPs and e-mail providers, such as Yahoo!, Google, MSN, and AOL, provide several options, ranging from junk-mail filters and automatic junk-mail deleters to the blocking of certain URLs and e-mail addresses (e.g., see hotmail.com). AOL, Verizon, and others are especially keen on fighting the problem in their most recent editions (e.g., AOL version 8 and higher have built-in spam control).

An effective solution may be found in the 2004 SP2 edition of Microsoft Windows. In addition, many software packages are available to help users deal with the problem. For example, mailwasher.net can eliminate spam by reviewing e-mails before they are downloaded. Junkbusters.com offers users free information and ideas for fighting spam. A free tool called 602LAN offers antispam capabilities combined with antivirus and firewall protection (software602.com). Other antispam tools are available from junkspy.com, spamex.com, fbmsoftware.com, mailshell.com, surfcontrol.com, mymailoasis.com, contactplus.com, mcafee.com, and many others. Spam prevention tips are offered by Cournane and Hunt (2004). Tips include instructions on the use of Outlook Express and Netscape Mail filters, how to opt out of permission-based e-mails, as well as how to surf smart, block cookies, deal with viruses, block hackers, use encryption, and more (see find.pcworld.com/26702). The problem with spam-blocking software is that spammers find ways to circumvent the programs.

EXHIBIT 17.1 How Spam Blockers Work

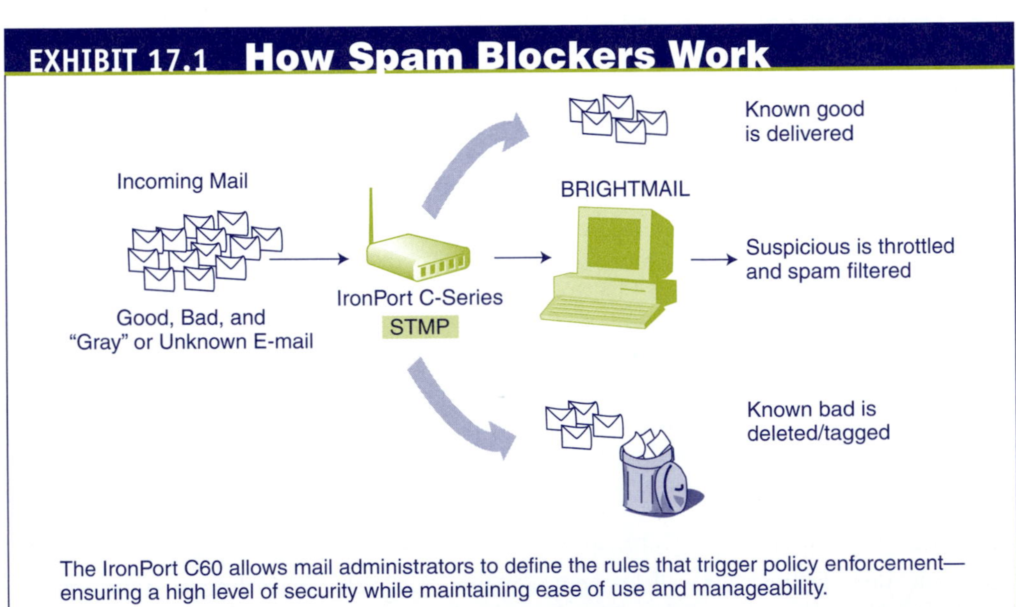

Source: Ironport.com. "Charter Get Hooked: Ironport Understands ISPs." Ironport.com 2004. *ironport.com/pdf/ironport_charter_communications_case_study.pdf* (accessed January 2005).

Antispam Legislation

One major piece of U.S. legislation addressing marketing practices in EC is the Electronic Mailbox Protection Act, passed in 1997. The primary thrust of this law is that commercial speech is subject to government regulation, and secondly, that spamming, which can cause significant harm, expense, and annoyance, should be controlled.

On January 1, 2004, the Controlling the Assault of Non-Solicited Pornography and Marketing Act, also known as CAN-SPAM, became U.S. law. The following are some of the specifics of this law (Peppers and Rogers Group 2004):

- It prohibits the use of misleading "from" or "subject" e-mail message headers.
- It requires marketers to identify their physical location by including their postal address in the text of the e-mail messages.
- It requires an opt-out link in each message, which must also give recipients the option of telling senders to stop all segments of their marketing campaigns.
- It allows for suits to be brought by ISPs, state attorneys generals, and the federal government.
- It carries penalties of up to $250 per spammed e-mail message, with a cap of $2 million, which can be tripled for aggravated violations. There is no cap on penalties for e-mail sent with false or deceptive headers.
- Those found guilty of violating the law may face up to 5 years in prison.

Additional information on electronic marketing and the antispam regulations can be found in Nettleton (2004).

Spam also affects Internet-based wireless devices, and the problem is exploding. DoCoMo, which operates the mobile portal i-mode, is taking several defensive measures, including imposing a fee on calls returned by unsuspecting users who return calls to the spammers (Asahi Shimbun News Service 2002).

Users can complain about spam at abuse.com, which will transfer the complaint to the appropriate authority. Users can also contact mail-abuse.com.

Do-Not-Spam Lists. According to Ki-Tae (2002), in South Korea people can effectively block unsolicited e-mail by registering their e-mail addresses and telephone numbers on a government-run Web site. The service frees them from receiving unwanted commercial e-messages on regular computers and to smart phones connected to the Internet. In addition, it reduces the regular telemarketing UCE calls to regulary telephones. To register, people enter nospam.go.kr or antispam.go.kr. Vendors are banned from sending unsolicited messages to the registered individuals. Offenders may lose their business license for up to a year or may be subject to criminal punishment.

Unfortunately, the South Korean system only covers registered businesses. Small, unregistered businesses can easily evade regulatory monitoring. However, the South Korean government plans to make it compulsory for all businesses to refer to the antispam list. The government also plans to require all senders of promotional materials to identify them as commercials. Monitoring is done in collaboration with consumer protection groups.

A similar do-not-call list to stop unwanted phone calls from telemarketers went into effect October 1, 2003 in the United States. The list was opposed by marketers who felt it violated their constitutional rights to advertise freely (Ackman 2003). Proposed legislation in both Canada (CAN. ACT S.630) and the United States (H.R. 3888) may address and curb e-mail spam.

Protecting Employees. With up to 75 percent of all e-mail being UCEs, companies are trying to minimize UCEs by using different kinds of blockers. The Real-World Case at the end of the chapter shows how four companies are trying to reduce the amount of spam that reaches their employees.

PROTECTING AGAINST POP-UP ADS

As discussed in Chapter 4, use of pop-ups and similar advertising programs is exploding. Sometimes it is even difficult to close these ads when they appear on the screen. Some of these ads may be part of a consumer's permission marketing agreement, but most are unsolicited. What can a user do about unsolicited pop-up ads? Tips for curbing pop-up ads are offered in Cournane and Hunt (2004). In addition, the following tools are useful in stopping pop-ups.

Tools for Stopping Pop Ups

Several software packages offer pop-up stoppers. Some are free (e.g., panicware.com); others are available for a fee. For tips and other products, see find.pcworld.com/27401 (as well as articles *28221, 27424,* and *27426*). According to Luhn and Spanbauer (2002), users should consider the following ad blockers: Adsubtract Pro (intermute.com), Guidescope (guidescope.com), Norton Internet Security (symantec.com), and Webwasher (webwasher.com). These programs block banners, flash ads, and cookies. Also, some cookie tools (e.g., Cookie Cop) are adding pop-up window killers. Finally, as with e-mail blocking, all major ISPs are providing pop-up protection.

CONCLUDING REMARKS

The spam situation has not yet been resolved. However, it seems that both e-mail spamming and pop-ups are not increasing, and according to Marketingvox.com (2005), they may even be declining. Here are some facts:

- An antispam bill passed by the U.S. Senate on October 22, 2003, requires spammers to clearly identify themselves and the product they are selling.
- Microsoft, Yahoo!, AOL, and EarthLink continuously file legal actions against spammers worldwide. For example, in December 2004, Microsoft filed 11 lawsuits against alleged senders of pornographic spam. The suits charged the defendants with violating the federal CAN-SPAM Act of 2004 and Washington State's Commercial Electronic Mail Act (Claburn 2004).
- PW Marketing LLC was fined $2 million for sending UCEs, violating California's anti-spam law.
- The Interactive Advertising Bureau (IAB) issued guidelines that state that "Each user should be exposed to no more than one pop up ad for each visit to an online site." According to an eMarketer Survey (reported at Noticiasdot.com 2004), 83 percent of Web publishers said that they comply with the guidelines; 20 percent said they have completely banned pop-ups on their sites.
- Most North American companies (eMarketer 2004) favor spam filtering over "blacklists" of spamming e-mailers.
- Jeremy Jaynes, a top U.S. spammer, was sentenced in November 2004 to 9 years in prison for illegal spam under Virginia's anti-spam law.
- ITU, an agency in the United Nations system, is promoting a global initiative to rid the world of spam by 2006. It works with 60 regulatory bodies across the globe (United Nations 2001).
- The U.S. Justice Department shut down a network of about 7,000 spammers in August 2004 (Anderson 2004). In November 2004, a cyber sweep operation netted over 100 people charged with Internet fraud.
- A student at the University of Texas and his partner were sued by the State of Texas and Microsoft, which alleged that the pair was running one of the largest spam operations in the world. The lawsuits claim the two violated the federal CAN-SPAM Act and the Texas Electronic Mail and Solicitation Act (Porter 2005).

Hopefully, all of these actions will help, and all of us will be happier while working online.

Section 17.4 ▶ REVIEW QUESTIONS

1. Why did e-mail spam spread so rapidly?
2. Why is it difficult to control spamming?
3. How can users fight e-mail spamming?
4. Describe the South Korean solution to spamming.
5. Describe the various pop-up solutions.

17.5 FREE SPEECH VERSUS CENSORSHIP AND OTHER LEGAL ISSUES

Several surveys indicate that the issue of censorship is one of the most important to Web surfers. Censorship usually ranks as the number one or two concern in Europe and the United States; privacy is the other main issue (e.g., see the GVU User Surveys at gvu.gatech.edu/user_surveys/). On the Internet, *censorship* refers to government's attempt to control, in one way or another, the material that is presented.

At a symposium on free speech in the information age, Parker Donham (1994) defined his own edict, entitled "Donham's First Law of Censorship." This semiserious precept states: "Most citizens are implacably opposed to censorship in any form—except censorship of whatever they personally happen to find offensive" (see efc.ca/pages/donham2.html).

Take, for example, the question, "How much access should children have to Web sites, newsgroups, and chat rooms containing 'inappropriate' or 'offensive' materials, and who should control this access?" This is one of the most hotly debated issues between advocates of censorship and proponents of free speech. Free speech proponents contend that there should be no government restrictions on Internet content and that parents should be responsible for monitoring and controlling their children's travels on the Web. The advocates of censorship feel that government legislation is required to protect children from offensive material.

The Children's Online Protection Act (COPA) exemplifies the protective approach. Passed in 1998, this law required, among other things, that companies verify a viewer's age before showing online material that is deemed "harmful to minors" and that parental consent be obtained before personal information can be collected from a minor. The fact that the Act was ruled unconstitutional illustrates how difficult it is to craft legislation that abridges freedom of speech in the United States. In June 2004, the Supreme Court ruled that the lower court was correct and the Act likely violates the First Amendment.

In addition to concern for children, many also are concerned about hate sites (e.g., see Kopp and Suter 2001), defamatory sites, and other offensive materials. On December 10, 2002, in a landmark case, Australia's highest court gave a businessman the right to sue for defamation in Australia over an article published in the United States and posted on the Internet. This reasoning basically equates the Net with any other published material. The publisher, Dow Jones & Co., said that it will defend those sued in a jurisdiction (Australia) that is far removed from the country in which the article was prepared (the United States).

Advocates of censorship also believe that it is the responsibility of ISPs to control the content of the data and information that flows across their networks and computers. The difficulty is that ISPs have no easy way of monitoring the content or determining the age of the person viewing the content. The only way to control "offensive" content is to block it from children and adults alike. This is the approach that AOL has taken, for instance, in blocking sites pandering to hate groups and serial killer enthusiasts.

OTHER LEGAL ISSUES

Privacy, intellectual property, and censorship receive a great deal of publicity because consumers easily understand them. However, there are numerous other legal issues related to EC and the Internet. These usually arise as new situations come up, and they must be worked out in courts of law and in legislatures—a time-consuming process. One such issue, for example, is whether a company can link to a Web site without permission. See the story of Ticketmaster versus Microsoft provided in Online File W17.1.

Some of these EC legal issues are summarized in Exhibit 17.2. For an overview of legal issues, see Matsuura (2004). A few of these will be discussed in more detail here.

Electronic Contracts

A legally binding contract requires a few basic elements: an offer, acceptance, and consideration. However, these requirements are difficult to establish when the human element in the processing of the transaction is removed and the contracting is performed electronically. For example, Web site development agreements can be very complex. For software-supported B2B trading contracts, see Chapter 5.

EXHIBIT 17.2 Other EC Legal Issues

Issue	Description
E-filings in court	Litigation means a large quantity of paper. Electronic filing of such documents is allowed in some courts (e.g., Manhattan Bankruptcy Court, New York).
Evidence	Some electronic documents can be used as evidence in court. The State of New York, for example, allows e-mails to be used as evidence. For an overview of digital evidence, see Schwerha (2004).
Jurisdiction	Ability to sue in other states or countries: Whose jurisdiction prevails when litigants are in different states or countries? Who can sue for Internet postings done in other countries?
Liability	The use of multiple networks and trading partners makes the documentation of responsibility difficult. How can liability for errors, malfunctions, or fraudulent use of data be determined?
Defamation	Is the ISP liable for material published on the Internet because of services they provide or support? (Usually not.) Who else is liable for defamation? What if the publisher is in another country? (See Heydary 2004).
Identity fraud	The Identity, Theft, and Assumption Deference Act of 1998 makes identity fraud a federal felony carrying a 3- to 25-year prison sentence.
Computer crime	The Information Infrastructure Protection Act (IIP Act, 1996) protects information in all computers.
Digital signature	Digital signatures are now recognized as legal in the United States and some other countries, but not in all countries (see Chapter 11).
Regulation of consumer databases	The United States allows the compilation and sale of customer databases; the European Union Directive on Data Protection prohibits this practice.
Encryption technology	Export of U.S. encryption technology was made legal in 1999. (Countries still restricted from export are Iran, Syria, Sudan, North Korea, and Cuba.)
Time and place	An electronic document signed in Japan on January 5 may have the date January 4 in Los Angeles. Which date is considered legal if disputes arise?
Location of files and data	Much of the law hinges on the physical location of files and data. With distributed and replicated databases, it is difficult to say exactly where data are stored at any given time.
Electronic contracts	If all of the elements to establish a contract are present, an electronic contract is valid and enforceable.
E-communications privacy	The Electronic Communications Privacy Act (ECPA) of 1986 makes it illegal to access stored e-mail as well as e-mail in transmission.
IPOs online	Web sites with the necessary information on securities offerings are considered a legal channel for selling stock in a corporation.
Antitrust	*U.S. v. Microsoft* found that (1) Microsoft used predatory and anticompetitive conduct to illegally maintain the monopoly in Windows OS; (2) Microsoft illegally attempted to monopolize the market for Internet browsing software; and (3) Microsoft illegally bundled its Web browser with Windows OS, engaging in a tying arrangement in violation of the Sherman Act.
Taxation	Taxation of sales transactions by states is on hold in the United States and some (not all) countries, but the issue will be revived. An additional issue is whether (and how) taxes can be collected from online gambling winnings.
Money laundering	How can money laundering be prevented when the value of the money is in the form of a smart card? (Japan limits the value of money on a smart card to about $5,000; other countries, such as Singapore and Hong Kong, set even lower limits.)
Corporate reporting	Online corporate reports are difficult to audit because they can be changed frequently, and auditors may not have time to perform due diligence. How should auditing of online reports be conducted? What legal value does it have?

Sources: Compiled from Alberts et al. (1998), Burnett (2001), Cheeseman (2004), Guernsey (2001), and Mykytyn (2002).

In the United States, the Uniform Electronic Transactions Act of 1999 seeks to extend existing provisions for contract law to cyberlaw by establishing uniform and consistent definitions for electronic records, digital signatures, and other electronic communications. This Act is a procedural one that provides the means to effect transactions accomplished through an electronic medium. The language purposefully refrains from addressing questions of substantive law, leaving this to the scope of the Uniform Commercial Code (UCC).

The UCC is a comprehensive body of law regarding business conduct. An amendment to the UCC is Article 2B, which is designed to build upon existing law by providing a government code that supports existing and future electronic technologies in the exchange of goods or services. This law was approved in 1999 and enacted in 2000. It is one of the more significant EC legal developments.

Shrink-wrap agreements or *box-top licenses* (part of the UCC code) appear in or on a package that contains software. The user is bound to the license by opening the package, even though the user has not yet used the product or even read the agreement. This has been a point of contention for some time. The U.S. Court of Appeals for the Seventh Circuit (in ruling No. 96-1139) felt that providing information such as warranties or handling instructions *inside* the package would provide more benefit to the consumer, given the limited space available on the exterior of the package. The *ProCD v. Zeidenberg* case (June 1996) supported the validity of shrink-wrap agreements when the court ruled in favor of the plaintiff, ProCD.

Click-wrap contracts are an extension of this ruling. These are contracts derived entirely over the Internet. The software vendor offers to sell or license the use of the software according to the terms accompanying the software. The buyer agrees to be bound by the terms based on certain conduct; usually that conduct is retaining the product for a sufficient time to review the terms and return of the software if unacceptable.

In Fall 2000, the Electronic Signatures in Global and National Commerce Act was approved. This federal law gives contracts signed online the same legal status as a contract signed with pen on paper. Similar laws have been enacted in several European and Asian countries.

Intelligent Agents and Contracts. Article 2B of the Uniform Computer Information Transactions Act, passed in October 2000, makes it clear that contracts can be formed even when a human is not directly involved. It states that a contract is formed if the interaction of electronic agents results in operations that confirm the existence of a contract or indicate agreement. Further, such a contract can be made by interaction between an individual and an electronic agent, or even between two electronic agents, even if an individual was unaware of or did not review the actions. The Act recognizes that counteroffers are ineffectual against electronic agents (which is one limitation of e-commerce), and so it provides that a contract is formed if an individual takes action that causes an electronic agent to perform or promise benefits to the individual. The basic idea is that if an individual sets electronic agents to work, the contract is valid and that individual is responsible for the outcome.

The Uniform Electronic Transactions Act (UETA) includes the following two provisions: (1) electronic records satisfy the requirement for a contract and (2) an electronic signature is equal to a written signature on a paper contract.

Gambling

Examples of betting sites can be found all over the Internet. For example, the World Sports Exchange (wsex.com) advertises, "If you can use a mouse, you can place a wager." Ostensibly located in Antigua, where gaming is legal, not only has this site shown the ease of wagering, it has made it its slogan. At the site, a user can establish an account by wiring or electronically transferring funds. The user can even send a check to establish an electronic gaming account. This account is used to fund wagers on all types of sporting events that can be viewed and transacted online. The issue is that anyone who travels physically to Antigua can play there legally. But what about electronic travel from places where gambling is illegal?

In the United Sates, gaming commissions have had a tough time regulating gambling laws in Nevada, on Indian reservations, in offshore casinos, in sports bars, and other places where gambling is legal. Technology makes this effort all the more difficult to monitor and enforce because the individuals abusing the rules have at least the same level of sophistication available as law enforcement officials; in many cases, they are even better equipped. The ease and risk of online wagering is evidenced by many recent cases of individuals losing their life savings without understanding the implications of what they are doing on their home PCs.

Online casinos have all of the inherent dangers of physical gaming houses, with the added risk of accessibility by minors or individuals of diminished capacity who may financially injure themselves without the constraints otherwise found in a physical environment. As is the case with most issues in cyberspace, self-regulation may be the best policy. However, given the sometimes-addictive nature of gambling, legal steps have been taken.

The U.S. Internet Gambling Prohibition Act of 1999 was established to make online wagering illegal except for minimal amounts. The Act provides criminal and civil remedies against individuals making online bets or wagers and those in the business of offering online betting or wagering venues. Additionally, it gives U.S. district courts original and exclusive jurisdiction to prevent and restrain violations, and it subjects ISPs to the duties of common carriers (telecommunications carriers such as AT&T, Verizon, etc.). The impact of this legislation is to make ISPs "somewhat" liable for illegal currency movements and for reportable transactions requiring documentation by the carriers.

According to the Australian Internet Industry Association (AIIA 2001), the Communication Ministry is looking favorably on imposing a total ban on interactive gambling in Australia through the use of filtering technology. The attempt is to block Australian Internet users from accessing gaming sites. In 2003, there was a moratorium on *new* interactive gaming. Although the AIIA campaigns against the ban, many politicians support it. Civil liberties groups in Australia, as in many other countries, oppose any Internet filtering.

Related to the control of gambling is the tax on winners' profits. Because it is currently illegal to charge sales tax on Internet transactions, should sales taxes (or VAT taxes) be paid on electronic winnings? If so, to whom would they be paid? How would they be collected? Despite all of these legal issues, online gambling is mushrooming (King 2003).

TAXING BUSINESS ON THE INTERNET

As just noted, EC taxation is another controversial issue. This issue is extremely important because it is related to global EC, as well as to fairness in competition when EC competes with off-line marketing channels, which require the collection of taxes. It also is an important issue due to the large volume of online trade that is forecast for the next decade. EC transactions are multiplying at an exponential rate, and the $2.64 trillion in sales forecasted for 2004 (Keenan 2000) means lots of potential sales tax. Cities, states, and countries all want a piece of the pie. For an overview of Internet taxation, see Vijayasarathy (2001).

THE TAX-EXEMPTION DEBATE

The Internet Tax Freedom Act passed the U.S. Senate on October 8, 1998. This Act sought to promote e-commerce through tax incentives, by barring any new state or local sales taxes on Internet transactions until October 2001. (Note that this law dealt only with *sales* tax, *not* with federal or state *income* taxes that Internet companies must pay.) Similar acts exist in several other countries, including Hong Kong. This Act also carried an amendment known as the Children's Online Privacy Protection Act, which was added in an effort to prevent extension of tax benefits to pornographers. The Act also created a special commission to study Internet taxation issues and recommend new policies. In April 2000, the special commission recommended the following to the U.S. Congress:

- Eliminate the 3 percent federal excise tax on telecommunications services.
- Extend the current moratorium on multiple or discriminatory taxation of EC through 2006.
- Prohibit taxation of digitized goods sold over the Internet.
- Make permanent the current moratorium on Internet access taxes.
- Establish nexus standards for U.S. businesses engaged in interstate commerce—rules that would spell out whether the use of a Web server in Indiana, for example, gives an Internet company based in New Jersey "nexus" in Indiana, where residents are subject to sales taxes.
- Place the burden on states to simplify their own telecommunications, sales, and use tax systems.
- Clarify state authority to use federal welfare money to give poor people more Internet access.

- Provide tax incentives and federal matching funds to states to encourage public–private partnerships to get low-income families online.
- Respect and protect consumer privacy.
- Continue to press for a moratorium on international tariffs on electronic transmissions over the Internet.

The U.S. Congress extended the tax moratorium until 2006, giving it time to digest the contents of the report and hash out contentious tax issues. State and local governments (which depend on sales tax revenues) and traditional brick-and-mortar retailers (which compete against e-tailers) generally want to tax EC. Internet companies, antitax advocates, and many politicians champion keeping the Internet tax free.

The taxation issue, which involves 30,000 state and local jurisdictions in the United States, in addition to the innumerable international jurisdictions, will add numerous volumes to an already complex tax code. Applying existing law to this new medium of exchange is far more difficult than ever imagined. The global nature of business today suggests that cyberspace be considered a *distinct tax zone* unto itself, with unique rules and considerations befitting the stature of the online environment.

This is, in fact, what has occurred. The moratorium on taxation of Internet transactions is a fine temporary solution where no precedent exists; however, longer-range strategies must be developed quickly. Some complicating factors must be considered. For example, several tax jurisdictions may be involved in a single transaction, not only on a domestic level but also internationally. The implications of such involvement are tremendous; the identity of the parties involved and transaction verification is frequently a problem. The probabilities for tax evasion also are potentially large. Tax havens and offshore banking facilities will become more accessible. Singapore has passed a law to establish itself as a legal and financial safe haven for the rest of the world for the EC industry, similar to Swiss banks' role in the off-line financial industry.

Arguments continue to rage over tax-free policies. Some say that tax-free policies give online businesses an unfair advantage. For instance, some argue that Internet phone services should be exempt from paying access charges to local telephone companies for use of their networks. In their effort to avoid sales taxes, Internet merchants like to point to the difficulty of tracking who should be paid what. The opposition argues that the same is true for telephone transactions, so existing laws should suffice. The same opposition asks, "Should EC business be allowed to operate without taxing consumers, while regular telephone companies cannot?"

Non-EC industries feel that Internet businesses must pay their fair share of the tax bill for the nation's social and physical infrastructure. They feel that the Internet industries are not pulling their own weight. These companies are screaming that the same situation exists in the mail-order business, for which some sales tax laws *have* been established, and that there are sufficient parallels to warrant similar legal considerations. In fact, in many states, EC has already been treated the same as mail-order businesses. Others suggest simply applying the established sales tax laws. "You've got a tax structure in place—it's called sales tax," said Bill McKiernan, chairman and CEO of Cybersource.com, "Just apply that to Internet transactions" (Nelson 1998).

Proposed Taxation in the United States

The National Governors' Association, the National League of Cities, and the U.S. Conference of Mayors fought the Tax Free Bill for the Internet. The National Governors' Association estimates that in 2004 state and local governments lost more than $35 billion in tax revenues on difficult-to-control mail-order sales to out-of-state merchants and customers (Associated Press 2004). They figure that more is lost through EC sales and are suggesting that the IRS "come to the rescue" with a single and simplified national sales tax. This would reduce 30,000 different tax codes to "no more than 50." Internet sales would be taxed at the same rate as mail-order or Main Street transactions. Although states could set their own rate, each sale could be taxed only once. The details of Internet taxation would be settled by a panel of industry and government officials.

In November 2004, the U.S. Congress blocked state and local governments from taxing connections that link consumers to the Internet, at least until November 2007. The bill also blocks multiple states and local taxes from being imposed on merchandise purchased over the Internet.

For discussion of services that compute sales tax, see Chapter 12. To calculate international tax levies on European Union sales, see europa.eu.int.

Section 17.5 ▶ REVIEW QUESTIONS

1. Describe the conflict between free speech and the right to present offensive material on the Internet.
2. Describe the Electronic Mailbox Protection Act.
3. Describe the issues related to electronic contracting.
4. Why is it difficult to control online gambling?
5. Discuss the issues relating to Internet taxation.

17.6 EC FRAUD AND CONSUMER AND SELLER PROTECTION

When buyers and sellers cannot see each other, and may even be in different countries, chances are high that dishonest people will commit all types of fraud and other crimes over the Internet. According to the FTC (ftc.gov), more than 50 percent of all fraud complaints received are Internet related (see CBS News 2004). An eMarketer report showed that in 2004, merchant losses from online payment fraud amounted to $2.6 billion (1.8 percent of total sales). The threat of online crime has alarmed customers (reported by shop.org 2005). During the first few years of EC, many types of crime came to light, ranging from the online manipulation of stock prices to the creation of a virtual bank that disappeared together with the investors' deposits. This section is divided into the following parts: Internet fraud, consumer protection (including automatic authentication), and seller protection.

FRAUD ON THE INTERNET

Internet fraud has grown even faster than the Internet itself (see CyberSource Corporation 2005). Some examples of fraud are presented in Insights and Additions 17.1. The following examples demonstrate the scope of the problem.

Online Auction Fraud. Internet auction fraud accounts for 87 percent of all incidents of online crime, according to eMarketer (reported by Saliba 2001). See Online Chapter 18 for a discussion of the problem and some remedies.

Insights and Additions 17.1 Typical Fraud Schemes

The following are several typical online fraud attempts; some were experienced by the authors and their friends:

- When one of the authors advertised online that he had a house to rent, several "doctors" and "nurses" from the UK and South America applied. They agreed to pay a premium for a short-term lease and said they would pay with a cashier's check. They asked if the author would accept checks for $6,000 to $10,000 and send them back the balance of $4,000 to $8,000. When advised that this would be fine, and the difference returned upon clearance of the checks, they all disappeared.
- Similarly, an acquaintance of one of the authors sold an expensive dog for which he received a large cashier's check with a request to return the balance. When the check arrived, he contacted the bank and found that the check had already been cashed.
- Extortion rings in the UK and Russia pried hundreds of thousands of dollars from online sports betting Web sites. Any site refusing to pay protection fees was threatened with Zombie computers using DoS attacks (see Chapter 11).
- In July 2004, criminals in Florida were sentenced to jail, fined $2.2 million, and their eight Web sites shut down, after pleading guilty to operating an illegal green card lottery immigration scam. Consumers paid $40 to $70 for a 1-year service, and $150 to $250 for a 10-year service.
- Fake escrow sites take advantage of the inherent trust of escrow sites, stealing buyers' deposits. Dozens of fake escrow sites on the Internet have convincing names like Honest-Escrow.net and use ads such as: "Worried about getting scammed in an Internet auction? Just use an escrow service like us."

Internet Stock Fraud. In fall 1998, the U.S. Securities and Exchange Commission (SEC) brought charges against 44 companies and individuals who illegally promoted stocks on computer bulletin boards, online newsletters, and investment Web sites. Details on both settled and pending cases can be found at sec.gov. In most cases, stock promoters spread false positive rumors about the prospects of the companies they touted. In other cases, the information provided may have been true, but the promoters did not disclose that they were paid to talk up the companies. Stock promoters specifically target small investors who are lured by the promise of fast profit.

The following is a typical example. In November 1996, a federal judge agreed to freeze the assets of the chairman of a small company called Systems of Excellence (SEXI) and the proprietors of an Internet electronic newsletter called SGA Goldstar. The latter illegally received SEXI stocks in exchange for promoting the stock to unwary investors. As a result, SEXI stock jumped from $0.25 to $4.75, at which time the proprietors dumped the shares (called a "pump-and-dump" scheme). Six people were convicted of criminal violations; two were sentenced to federal prison. As of 2004, the SEC has recovered approximately $11 million in illegal profits from the various defendants (Stocks-investing.com 2005).

Cases like this, as well as ones involving nonregistered securities, are likely to increase because of the popularity of the Internet.

Other Financial Fraud. Stocks are only one of many areas where swindlers are active. Other areas include the sale of bogus investments, phantom business opportunities, and other schemes (see CyberSource Corporation 2005). With the use of the Internet, financial criminals now have access to far more people, mainly due to the availability of e-mail. An example of a multibillion-dollar international financial fraud is provided in EC Application Case 17.3. In addition, foreign-currency-trading scams are increasing on the Internet because most online currency-exchange shops are not licensed (see Commodity Futures Trading Commission 2001).

Identity Theft and Phishing. Over the past few years, the problem of *identity theft* has increased. It is frequently done by soliciting information from the victims via the Internet (Gage 2004). **Identity theft** refers to a criminal act in which someone presents himself (or herself) as another person, using that person's social security number, bank account numbers, and other identifying information to obtain loans, purchase items, make obligations, sell stocks, and so on.

identity theft
A criminal act in which someone presents himself (herself) as another person and uses that person's social security number, bank account numbers, and so on, to obtain loans, purchase items, make obligations, sell stocks, etc.

The criminals obtain such information in different ways. For example, they may use spyware. Or, as discussed in Chapter 11, they may use *phishing* techniques. A popular method of phishing is to collect information through fake Web sites. For example, a person may get an e-mail from someone posing as a bank or telephone company representative that asks the person to update his or her personal information on a fake Web site that looks exactly like the real one. The URL of the fake site is included in the e-mail. The e-mail may threaten that the person must enter this information or their service will be stopped. To safeguard against this type of fraud, users should always go to the Web site directly, and not through the link (see EC Application Case 17.3).

Microsoft and Amazon.com filed a lawsuit against a Canadian company, claiming that it sent fake e-mails posing as representatives of Microsoft and Amazon.com. On July 15, 2004, the Identity Theft Penalty Enhancement Act was signed into law, creating tough punishments for stealing IDs in conjunction with committing another crime (such as stealing money). Critics claim that the law is incomplete because it does not make the process of phishing itself a crime and it does not establish new safeguards for online transactions (Hines 2004).

Other Type of EC Fraud

Many nonfinancial types of fraud also exist on the Internet. For example, customers may receive poor-quality products and services, may not get products in time, may be asked to pay for things they assume will be paid for by sellers, and much more. For typical schemes, see ftc.gov.

Buyers can protect against EC fraud in several ways. The major methods are described next.

CONSUMER PROTECTION

Consumer protection is critical to the success of any commerce, especially electronic, where buyers do not see sellers. The FTC enforces consumer protection laws in the United States (see ftc.gov). The FTC provides a list of 12 scams labeled the "dirty dozen" (the name of a

CASE 17.3

EC Application

HOW A FRAUDULENT INVESTMENT SCHEME WORKS

David Lee, a 41-year-old Hong Kong resident, replied to an advertisement in a respected business magazine that offered free investment advice. When he replied to the ad, he received impressive brochures and a telephone sales pitch. Then he was directed to the Web site of Equity Mutual Trust (Equity), from which he was able to track the impressive daily performance of a fund that listed offices in London, Switzerland, and Belize. From that Web site, he was linked to sister funds and business partners. He monitored what he believed were independent Web sites that provided high ratings on the funds (he reached these sites by clicking on a banner of Equity). Finally, he was directed to read about Equity and its funds in the respected *International Herald Tribune*'s Internet edition; the article appeared to be a news item, but was actually a paid advertisement.

Convinced that he would receive good short-term gains, Lee mailed US$16,000, instructing Equity to invest in the Grand Financial Fund. Soon he grew suspicious when letters from Equity came from different countries, telephone calls and e-mails were not answered on time, and the daily Internet listings dried up.

When Lee wanted to sell, he was advised to increase his investment and shift to a Canadian company, Mit-Tec, allegedly a Y2K-bug troubleshooter. The Web site he was directed to looked fantastic. However, this time Lee was more careful. He contacted the financial authorities in the Turks and Caicos Islands—where Equity was based at that time—and was referred to the British police.

Soon he learned that chances were slim that he would ever see his money again. Furthermore, he learned that several thousand victims had paid billions of dollars to Equity. Most of the victims live in Hong Kong, Singapore, and other Asian countries. Several said that the most convincing information came from the Web sites, including the seemingly "independent" Web sites that rated Equity and its funds.

Source: *South China Morning Post* (1999).

Questions

1. How could such a large-scale crime go undetected for months? Speculate on the reasons.
2. What advice would you give to people looking for investment opportunities on the Internet?

famous movie) that are most likely to arrive by bulk e-mail (see ftc.gov/bcp/conline/pubs/alerts/doznalrt.htm). In addition, the European Union and the United States are attempting to develop joint consumer protection policies. For details, see tacd.org/about/about.htm. For more about the FTC and Internet scams, see Teodoro (2001).

Tips for safe electronic shopping include the following:

- Users should make sure that they enter the real Web site of well-known companies, such as Wal-Mart, Disney, and Amazon.com, by going directly to the site, rather than through a link, and shop for reliable brand names at those sites.
- Check any unfamiliar site for an address and telephone and fax numbers. Call and quiz a salesperson about the seller.
- Check out the seller with the local chamber of commerce, Better Business Bureau (bbbonline.org), or TRUSTe (described later).
- Investigate how secure the seller's site is and how well it is organized.
- Examine the money-back guarantees, warranties, and service agreements before making a purchase.
- Compare prices online with those in regular stores—too-low prices may be too good to be true.
- Ask friends what they know. Find testimonials and endorsements.
- Find out what redress is available in case of a dispute.
- Consult the National Fraud Information Center (fraud.org).
- Check the resources available at consumerworld.org.

In addition to these tips, consumers also have shopper's rights on the Internet, as described in Insights and Additions 17.2.

Insights and Additions 17.2 Internet Shopping Rights

Although the Web offers new ways to shop, users can still benefit from legal protections developed for shopping by telephone, mail, and other similar means. The two most important consumer protection laws for online shopping come from the U.S. government: the Mail/Telephone Order Rule and the Fair Credit Billing Act.

Mail/Telephone (E-Mail) Order Rule

According to the Mail/Telephone (E-Mail) Order Rule (2003), sellers must deliver goods within a certain time period or face penalties from the FTC. If the seller advertises or tells a buyer a delivery date before the buyer makes a purchase, the item must be delivered by that date. If the seller does not give the buyer a delivery date, the seller must deliver the item within 30 days after receiving the order.

If the seller cannot deliver by the required date, it must give the buyer notice before that date, so that the buyer can either choose to cancel the order and receive a full and prompt refund or permit the seller to deliver at a later date. If delivery problems continue, consumers should see the resources at the end of this feature for additional rights and how to make a complaint.

Fair Credit Billing Act

Using a credit card on the Web is like using it at a store. The Fair Credit Billing Act (2003) gives buyers certain rights if there is an error or dispute relating to a bill. If there is an error on a consumer's statement, the consumer can withhold payment for the disputed amount while they notify the creditor. The consumer also can withhold payment when a bill contains a charge for the wrong amount, for items that were returned or not accepted, or for items not delivered as agreed.

Creditors should be notified of errors promptly, no later than 60 days after the first bill on which the error appeared. All correspondence should be in writing. The consumer should describe the error clearly and include his or her name, address, and credit card number. After receiving the notice, the creditor must give written acknowledgment within 30 days and must resolve the error within 90 days.

New Payment Methods

Although consumer protections for traditional credit cards are well established, protections for those who use new forms of "digital payment"—such as digital cash and the like—are unclear. Some of the forms of payment resemble credit cards; others resemble debit cards; still others are brand-new forms of payment. Check the resources at the end of this feature for the latest information on new regulations that may help protect consumers using these payment methods.

Resources for Further Information

The following are useful sources of information on the rights of Internet shoppers:

- The FTC (*ftc.gov*): abusive e-mail should be forwarded to *uce@ftc.gov*, tips for online shopping and Internet auctions are provided at *ftc.gov/bcp/menu-internet.htm*
- National Fraud Information Center (*fraud.org*)
- Consumer Information Center (*pueblo.gsa.gov*)
- U.S. Department of Justice (*usdoj.gov*)
- The FBI's Internet Fraud Complaint Center (*ifccfbi.gov*)
- The American Bar Association provides online shopping tips at *safeshopping.org*
- The Better Business Bureau (*bbb.org* and *bbbonline.org*)
- The U.S. Food and Drug Administration (*fda.gov/oc/buyonline*)
- The Direct Marketing Association (*shopthenet.org*)

For information on consumer protection in the European Union, see McDonald (2000).

Disclaimer: This is general information on consumer rights. It is not legal advice on how any particular individual should proceed. If you require specific legal advice, consult an attorney.

Source: Based on Rose (1997), p. 104, and Privacy Rights Clearinghouse (2005).

Third-Party Assurance Services

Several public organizations and private companies attempt to protect consumers. The following are just a few examples.

TRUSTe's "Trustmark." TRUSTe (truste.org) is a nonprofit group whose mission is to build users' trust and confidence in the Internet by promoting the policies of disclosure and informed consent. Sellers who become members of TRUSTe can add value and increase consumer confidence in online transactions by displaying the TRUSTe Advertising Affiliate "Trustmark" (a seal of quality). This mark identifies sites that have agreed to comply with responsible information-gathering guidelines. In addition, the TRUSTe Web site provides its members with a "privacy policy wizard," which is aimed at helping companies create their own privacy policies. The site offers seven types of seals: privacy, children, e-health, safe harbor, wireless, e-mail services, and international services (in January 2005).

The TRUSTe program is voluntary. The licensing fee for use of the Trustmark ranges from $500 to $5,000, depending on the size of the online organization and the sensitivity of the information it is collecting. By the end of 2002, more than 1,500 Web sites were certified as TRUSTe participants, including AT&T, CyberCash, Excite, IBM, Buena Vista Internet Group, CNET, GeoCities, Infoseek, Lycos, Netscape, the *New York Times*, and Yahoo! (TRUSTe 2005). However, there still seems to be fear that signing with TRUSTe could expose firms to litigation from third parties if they fail to live up to the letter of the TRUSTe pact, and that fear is likely to deter some companies from signing up.

How well can TRUSTe and others protect your privacy? According to Rafter (2000), there are continuous violations of privacy by companies carrying the TRUSTe seal.

Better Business Bureau. The Better Business Bureau (BBB), a private nonprofit organization supported largely by membership, provides reports on businesses that consumers can review before making a purchase. The BBB responds to millions of inquiries each year. Its BBBOnLine program (bbbonline.com) is similar to TRUSTe's Trustmark. The goal of the program is to promote confidence on the Internet through two different seals. Companies that meet the BBBOnLine standards for the Reliability Seal are members of the local BBB and have good truth-in-advertising and consumer service practices. Those that exhibit the BBBOnLine Privacy Seal on their Web sites have an online privacy protection policy and standards for handling consumers' personal information. In addition, consumers are able to click on the BBBOnLine seals and instantly get a BBB report on the participating company.

WHICHonline. Supported by the European Union, WHICHonline (which.net) gives consumers protection by ensuring that online traders under its Which?Web Trader Scheme abide by a code of proactive guidelines. These guidelines outline issues such as product information, advertising, ordering methods, prices, delivery of goods, consumer privacy, receipting, dispute resolution, and security.

Web Trust Seal and Others. The Web Trust seal program is similar to TRUSTe. It is sponsored by the American Institute of Certified Public Accountants (cpawebtrust.org). Another program, Gomez.com (gomez.com), monitors customer complaints and provides merchant certification.

Online Privacy Alliance. The Online Privacy Alliance is a diverse group of corporations and associations that lead and support self-regulatory initiatives that create an environment of trust and foster the protection of individuals' privacy online. They have guidelines for privacy policies, enforcement of self-regulation, and children's online activities. Major members are AT&T, Bell Atlantic, Dell, IBM, Microsoft, NETCOM, AOL Time Warner, and Yahoo! The Online Privacy Alliance supports third-party enforcement programs, such as the TRUSTe and BBB programs, because the symbol awarded by these programs signifies to consumers the use of a privacy policy that includes the elements articulated by the Online Privacy Alliance.

Evaluation by Consumers A large number of sites include product and vendor evaluations offered by consumers. For example, Deja.com, now part of Google, is home to many communities of interest whose members trade comments about products at groups.google.com/. In addition, epubliceye.com allows consumers to give feedback on reliability, privacy, and customer satisfaction. It makes available a company profile that measures a number of elements, including payment options.

Authentication and Biometric Controls

In cyberspace, buyers and sellers do not see each other. Even when videoconferencing is used, the authenticity of the person on the other end must be verified, unless the person has been dealt with before. However, if one can be assured of the identity of the person on the other end of the line, one can imagine improved and new EC applications: Students will be able to take exams online from any place, at any time, without the need for proctors. Fraud among recipients of government entitlements and transfer payments will be reduced to a bare minimum. Buyers will be assured who the sellers are, and sellers will know who the buyers are, with a very high degree of confidence. Arrangements can be made so that only authorized people in companies can place (or receive) purchasing orders. Interviews for employment and other matching applications will be accurate, because it will be almost impossible for imposters to represent other people. Overall, trust in online transactions and in EC in general will increase significantly.

As discussed in Chapter 11, the solution for such *authentication* is provided by information technologies known as *biometric controls*. Biometric controls provide access procedures that match every valid user with a *unique user identifier (UID)*. They also provide an authentication method that verifies that users requesting access to the computer system are really who they claim to be. Authentication and biometric controls are valid for both consumer and merchant protection.

For more information on protection against fraud online, see fraud.org, cfenet.com, and asisonline.org.

SELLER PROTECTION

The Internet makes fraud by customers or others easier because of the ease of anonymity. Sellers must be protected against:

- Customers who deny that they placed an order
- Customers who download copyrighted software and/or knowledge and sell it to others
- Customers who give false payment (credit card or bad checks) information in payment for products and services provided
- Use of their name by others (e.g., imposter sellers)
- Use of their unique words and phrases, names, and slogans and their Web addresses by others (trademark protection)

What Can Sellers Do?

The Web site cardcops.com provides a database of credit card numbers that have had chargeback orders recorded against them. Sellers who have access to the database can use this information to decide whether to proceed with a sale. In the future, the credit card industry is planning to use biometrics to deal with electronic shoplifting. Also, sellers can use PKI and digital certificates, especially the SET protocol, to help prevent fraud (see Chapter 11).

Other possible solutions include the following:

- Use intelligent software to identify possibly questionable customers (or do this identification manually in small companies). One technique, for example, involves comparing credit card billing and requested shipping addresses.
- Identify warning signals for possibly fraudulent transactions. After writing off $4.1 million of uncollectible accounts receivable in May 2000, Expedia developed a list of such warning signals for its own use (Angwin 2000).
- Ask customers whose billing address is different from the shipping address to call their bank and have the alternate address added to their bank account. Retailers agree to ship the goods to the alternate address only if this is done.

For further discussion of what merchants can do to protect themselves from fraud, see Adams (2000), Chua and Wareham (2004), and combatfraud.org. Also, third-party escrow and trust companies help to prevent fraud against both buyers and sellers. Finally, Cybersource Corporation (2005) provides lists of fraud management tools for fraud detection, including intelligent systems.

Section 17.6 ▶ REVIEW QUESTIONS

1. Why is there so much fraud on the Internet?
2. What types of fraud are most common?
3. Describe identity theft and phishing.
4. Describe consumer protection measures.
5. Describe assurance services.
6. What must a company do to protect itself against fraud? How can this be accomplished?

17.7 SOCIETAL ISSUES

At this point in the chapter, our attention turns to societal issues of EC. The first topic is one of concern to many—the digital divide.

THE DIGITAL DIVIDE

digital divide
The gap between those who have and those who do not have the ability to access electronic technology in general, and the Internet and EC in particular.

Despite the factors and trends that contribute to future EC growth, since the inception of the Internet, and e-commerce in particular, a gap has emerged between those who have and those who do not have the ability to use the technology (Sipior et al. 2004). This gap is referred to as the **digital divide**.

The gap exists both *within* and *between* countries. The U.S. federal and state governments are attempting to close this gap (see egovmonitor.com 2005) within the country by encouraging training and supporting education and infrastructure. The gap among countries, however, may be widening rather than narrowing. For statistics see Cherry et al. (2004). Many government and international organizations are trying to close the digital divide (Mandal 2004; Papazafeiropoulou 2004). For strategies on how to close the divide, see Law (2004) and Vigna et al. (2003).

OTHER SOCIETAL ISSUES

Many other societal issues can be related to EC. Three in which EC has had a generally positive impact are mentioned here: education, public safety, and health. For more details on societal issues, see Akhter (2003), Lubbe and Van Heerden (2003), and Wresch (2003).

Education

E-commerce has had a major impact on education and learning, as described in Chapter 8. Virtual universities are helping to reduce the digital divide. Companies can use the Internet to retrain employees much more easily, enabling them to defer retirement if they so choose. Home-bound individuals can get degrees from good institutions, and many vocational professions can be learned from home.

Public Safety, Criminal Justice, and Homeland Security

With increased concerns about public safety after September 11, many organizations and individuals have started to look at technologies that will help to deter, prevent, or detect criminal activities of various types. Various e-commerce tools can help increase our safety at home and in public. These include the e-911 systems (described in Chapter 9 and by McGinity 2004); global collaborative commerce technologies (for collaboration among national and international law enforcement units); e-procurement (of unique equipment to fight crime); e-government efforts at coordinating, information sharing, and expediting legal work and cases; intelligent homes, offices, and public buildings; and e-training of law enforcement officers.

Health Aspects

Is EC a health risk? Generally speaking, it is probably safer and healthier to shop from home than in a physical store. However, some believe that exposure to cellular mobile communication radiation may cause health problems (e.g., Lin 2001). It may take years before the truth of this claim is known. Even if communication radiation does cause health problems, the damage could be insignificant due to the small amount of time most people spend on wireless shopping and other wireless activities. However, given the concern of some about this issue, protective devices may soon be available that will solve this problem.

EC technologies such as collaborative commerce can help improve health care. For example, using the Internet, the approval process of new drugs has been shortened, saving lives and reducing suffering. Pervasive computing helps in the delivery of health care. Intelligent systems facilitate medical diagnoses. Health-care advice can be provided from a distance. Finally, intelligent hospitals (Weiss 2002), doctors (Landro 2002), and other health-care facilities use EC tools (see Flower 2004 and Hendrickson 2004).

Section 17.7 ▶ REVIEW QUESTIONS

1. Define the digital divide.
2. Describe how EC can improve education.
3. Describe how EC can improve safety and security.
4. Describe the impact of EC on health services.

17.8 VIRTUAL (INTERNET) COMMUNITIES

A topic somewhat related to the societal impact of EC is Internet communities. A *community* is a group of people with some interest in common who interact with one another. A **virtual (Internet) community** is one in which the interaction takes place by using the Internet. Virtual communities parallel typical physical communities such as neighborhoods, clubs, or associations, but people do not meet face-to-face. Instead, they meet online. Virtual communities offer several ways for members to interact, collaborate, and trade (see Exhibit 17.3 and Blanchard and Markus 2004). Similar to the click-and-mortar model, many *physical communities* have a Web site for Internet-related activities.

virtual (Internet) community
A group of people with similar interests who interact with one another using the Internet.

CHARACTERISTICS OF COMMUNITIES

Pure-play Internet communities may have thousands or even millions of members. This is one major difference from purely physical communities, which usually are smaller. Another difference is that off-line communities frequently are confined to one geographic location, whereas only a few online communities are geographically confined.

EXHIBIT 17.3 Elements of Interaction in a Virtual Community

Category	Element
Communication	Bulletin boards (discussion groups)
	Chat rooms/threaded discussions (string Q&A)
	E-mail and instant messaging
	Private mailboxes
	Newsletters, "netzines" (electronic magazines)
	Blogging
	Web postings
	Voting
Information	Directories and yellow pages
	Search engine
	Member-generated content
	Links to information sources
	Expert advice
EC element	Electronic catalogs and shopping carts
	Advertisements
	Auctions of all types
	Classified ads
	Bartering online

Insights and Additions 17.3 Examples of Communities

The following are examples of online communities.

- **Associations.** Many associations have a Web presence. These range from PTAs (parent–teacher associations) to professional associations. An example of this type of community is the Australian Record Industry Association (*aria.com.au*).
- **Ethnic communities.** Many communities are country or language specific. An example of such a site is *elsitio.com*, which provides content for the Spanish- and Portuguese-speaking audiences mainly in Latin America and the United States. A number of sites, including *china.com*, *hongkong.com*, *sina.com*, and *sohu.com*, cater to the world's large Chinese-speaking community.
- **Gender communities.** *Women.com* and *ivillage.com*, the two largest female-oriented community sites, merged in 2001 in an effort to cut losses and become profitable.
- **Affinity portals.** These are communities organized by interest, such as hobbies, vocations, political parties, unions (*workingfamilies.com*), and many, many more. Many communities are organized around a technical topic (e.g., a database), a product (e.g., Lotus Notes), or a company (e.g., Oracle Technology news at *oracle.com/technology*).
- **Catering to young people (teens and people in their early 20s).** Many companies see unusual opportunities here. Three community sites of particular interest are *alloy.com*, *bolt.com*, and *blueskyfrog.com*. Alloy.com is based in the United Kingdom and claims to have over 10 million members. Bolt.com claims to have 4.5 million members and operates from the United States. Blueskyfrog.com operates from Australia, concentrating on cell phone users, and claims to have more than 2.5 million devoted members.
- **Mega communities.** Megacommunities combine numerous smaller communities under one "umbrella" (under one name). GeoCities is one example of a mega community with many subcommunities. Owned by Yahoo!, it is by far the largest online community.
- **B2B online communities.** Chapter 6 introduced many-to-many B2B exchanges. These are referred to by some as *communities* (e.g., Raisch 2000 and Commerce One 2005). B2B exchanges support community programs such as technical discussion forums, interactive Webcasts, user-created product reviews, virtual conferences and meetings, experts' seminars, and user-managed profile pages. Classified ads can help members to find jobs or employers to find employees. Many also include industry news, directories, links to government and professional associations, and more.

Many thousands of communities exist on the Internet. Several communities are independent and are growing rapidly. For instance, GeoCities grew to 10 million members in less than 2 years and had over 50 million members in 2004 (Geocities 2005). GeoCities members can set up personal homepages on the site, and advertisers buy ad space targeted to community members. A number of examples of online communities are presented in Insights and Additions 17.3.

Virtual communities can be classified in several ways. One possibility is to classify members as *traders*, *players*, *just friends*, *enthusiasts*, or *friends in need*. A more common classification is the one proposed by Hagel and Armstrong (1997). This classification recognizes the four types of Internet communities shown in Exhibit 17.4. For a different, more complete classification, see that proposed by Schubert and Ginsburg (2000).

COMMERCIAL ASPECTS OF COMMUNITIES

Another classification of communities has been proposed by Cashel (2004), who identified 10 specific niches within the online community space that are bucking the trend and demonstrating strong revenues. These 10 important trends include: (1) search communities; (2) trading communities; (3) education communities; (4) scheduled events communities; (5) subscriber-based communities; (6) community consulting firms; (7) e-mail-based communities; (8) advocacy communities; (9) CRM communities; and (10) mergers and acquisitions activities. See Cashel (2004) for details.

A logical step as a community site grows in members and influence may be to turn it into a commercial site. Examples of such community–commercial sites include ivillage.com and geocities.yahoo.com. The following are suggestions on how to make the transformation from a community site to a commercial one:

EXHIBIT 17.4 Types of Virtual Communities

Community Type	Description
Transaction	Facilitates buying and selling (e.g., *ausfish.com.au*; see Online File W17.2). Combines information portal with infrastructure for trading. Members are buyers, sellers, intermediaries, etc. focused on a specific commercial area (e.g., fishing).
Purpose or interest	No trading, just exchange of information on a topic of mutual interest. Examples: Investors consult The Motley Fool (*fool.com*) for investment advice; rugby fans congregate at the Fans Room at *nrl.com.au*; music lovers go to *mp3.com*;. *Geocities.yahoo.com* is a collection of several areas of interest in one place.
Relations or practice	Members are organized around certain life experiences. Examples: *ivillage.com* caters to women, *seniornet.com* to senior citizens. Professional communities also belong to this category. Examples: *isworld.org* for information systems faculty, students, and professionals.
Fantasy	Members share imaginary environments. Examples: sport fantasy teams at *espn.com;* GeoCities members can pretend to be medieval barons at *dir.yahoo.com/Recreation/Games/Role_Playing_Games/Titles/*. See *games.yahoo.com* for many more fantasy communities.

Source: Compiled from Hagel and Armstrong (1997).

- Understand a particular niche industry, its information needs, and the step-by-step process by which it does the research needed to do business, and try to match the industry with a potential or existing community.
- Build a site that provides that information, either through partnerships with existing information providers or by gathering it independently, or identify a community that can be sponsored.
- Set up the site to mirror the steps a user goes through in the information-gathering and decision-making process (e.g., how a chip designer whittles down the list of possible chips that will fit a particular product).
- Build a community that relies on the site for decision support (or modify an existing one).
- Start selling products and services that fit into the decision-support process (such as selling sample chips to engineers who are members of the community).

Electronic communities can create value in several ways. This value-creation process is summarized in Exhibit 17.5. Members input useful information to the community in the form of comments and feedback, elaborating on their attitudes and beliefs and information needs. This information can then be retrieved and used by other members or by marketers. The community organizers may also supply their own content to communities, as AOL does.

Rheingold (1993) thinks that the Web is being transformed from just a communication and information-transfer tool into a social Web of communities. He thinks that every Web site should incorporate a place for people to chat. A community site should be an interesting place to visit, a kind of virtual community center. He believes that it should be a place where discussions may range over many controversial topics. Many issues are related to the operation of communities. For example, Mowbray (2001) raised the issue of freedom of speech and its control in a community. Malhotra (2002) raised the issue of knowledge exchange among community members. Sanguan (2005) discusses perspectives on the success of virtual communities.

Virtual communities also are closely related to EC. For example, Zetlin and Pfleging (2002) describe online, consumer-driven markets in which most of the consumers' needs, ranging from finding a mortgage to job hunting, are arranged from a community Web site. This gathering of needs in one place enables vendors to sell more and community members to get discounts. Internet communities will eventually have a massive impact on almost every company that produces consumer goods or services, and they could change the nature of

EXHIBIT 17.5 Value Creation in Electronic Communities

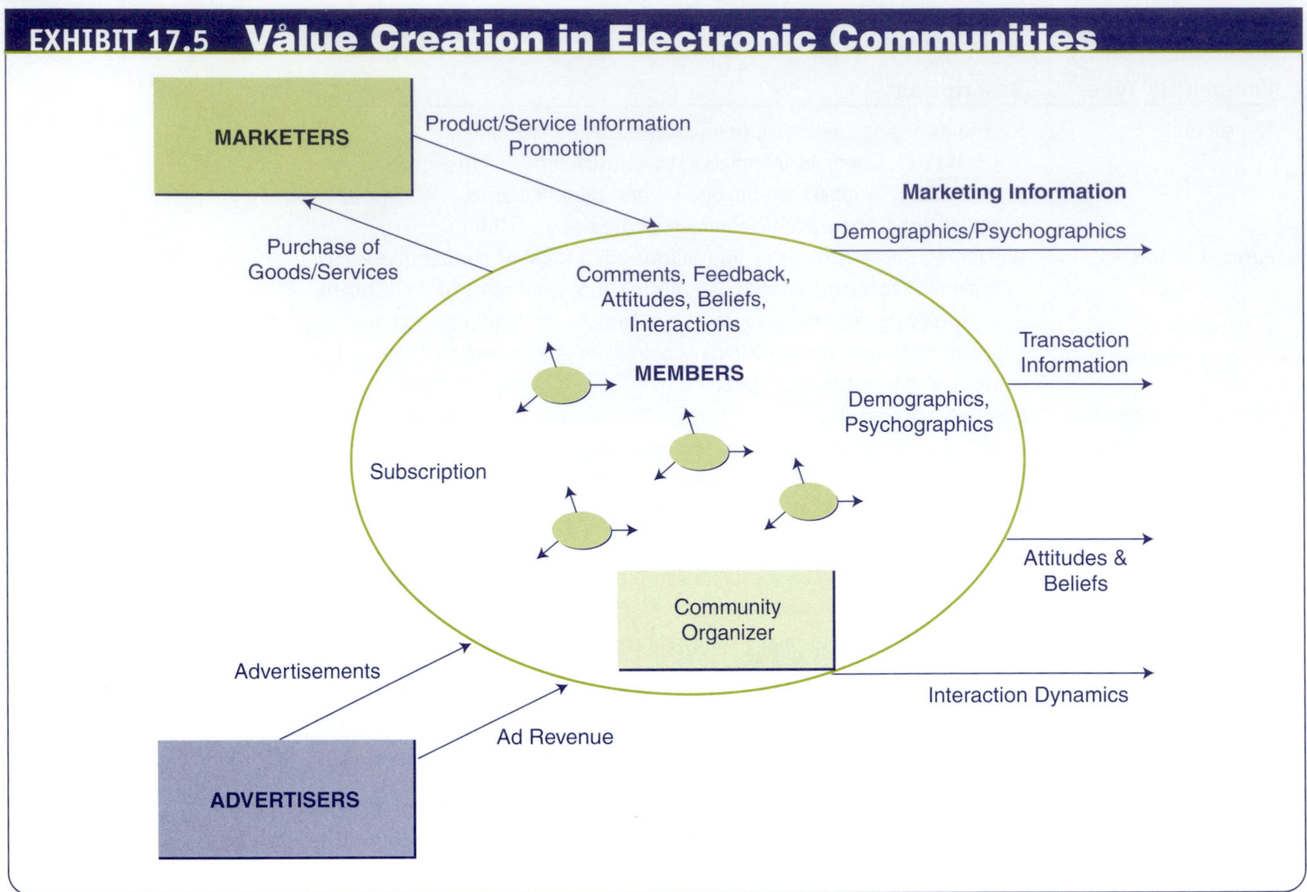

Source: Kannen, P. K., et al., "Marketing Information on the I-Way," *Communications of the ACM*. © 1998, ACM, Inc. Used with permission.

corporate advertising and community sponsorship strategies and the manner in which business is done. Although this process of change is slow, some of the initial commercial development changes can be observed. Finally, blogging (Chapter 8) is related to online communities (Stauffer 2002).

Also, some communities charge members content fees for downloading certain articles, music, or pictures, thus producing sales revenue for the site. Finally, because many community members create their own homepages, it is easy to learn about them and reach them with targeted advertising and marketing. For more on this topic, see Lee et al. (2003).

Financial Viability of Communities

The revenue model of communities can be based on sponsorship, membership fees, sales commissions, and advertising, or some combination of these. The operating expenses for communities are very high due to the need to provide fresh content and free services. In addition, most communities initially provide free membership. The objective is to have as many registered members as possible and to build a strong brand in order to attract advertisers (see McWilliam 2000 and Zetlin and Pfleging 2002).

The model of self-financing communities (i.e., those without a sponsor) has not worked very well. Several communities that were organized for profit sustained heavy losses. Examples include ivillage.com, china.com, and elsitio.com. Several other communities ceased operations in 2000 and 2001 (e.g., esociety.com and renren.com). The trend toward mergers and acquisitions among communities, started in 2001, is expected to improve the financial viability of some communities.

KEY STRATEGIES FOR SUCCESSFUL ONLINE COMMUNITIES

The management consulting company Accenture outlined the following eight critical factors for community success (see details in Duffy 1999):

1. Increase traffic and participation in the community.
2. Focus on the needs of the members; use facilitators and coordinators.
3. Encourage free sharing of opinions and information—no controls.
4. Obtain financial sponsorship. This factor is a must. Significant investment is required.
5. Consider the cultural environment.
6. Provide several tools and activities for member use; communities are not just discussion groups.
7. Involve community members in activities and recruiting.
8. Guide discussions, provoke controversy, and raise sticky issues. This keeps interest high.

Leimeister and Krcmar (2004) add the following top five success factors based on their own 2004 survey:

1. Handle member data sensitively.
2. Maintain stability of the Web site with respect to the consistency of content, services, and types of information offered.
3. Provide fast reaction time of the Web site.
4. Offer up-to-date content.
5. Offer continuous community control with regard to member satisfaction.
6. Establish codes of behavior (netiquette/guidelines) to contain conflict potential.

Examples of some communities that use one or more of these principles of success include the following: earthweb.com, icollector.com, webmd.com, terra.es, eslcafe.com, ivillage.com, icq.com, letsbuyit.com, paltalk.com, radiolinja.fi, and projectconnections.com. For more details and discussion of communities, see Dholakia et al. (2004), Porter (2004), and Tedeschi (2004).

Section 17.8 ▶ REVIEW QUESTIONS

1. Define virtual (Internet) communities and describe their characteristics.
2. List the major categories of virtual communities.
3. Describe the commercial aspects of virtual communities.
4. Describe the CSFs for virtual communities.

17.9 THE FUTURE OF EC

Generally speaking, the consensus is that the future of EC is bright. EC will become an increasingly important method of reaching customers, providing services, and improving operations of organizations. Analysts differ in their predictions about the anticipated growth rate of EC and how long it will take for it to be a substantial portion of the economy, as well as in the identification of industry segments that will grow the fastest. However, based on the following factors and trends, there is general optimism about the future of EC.

NONTECHNOLOGICAL SUCCESS FACTORS

The rosy scenario for the future of EC is based partially on the following nontechnological factors and trends.

Internet Usage. The number of Internet users is increasing rapidly. With the integration of computers and television, Internet access via mobile devices, increased availability of access kiosks, increased publicity about the Internet, and availability of inexpensive computers (such as the *simputer*, short for "simple computer"), the number of Internet surfers will continue to increase. As younger people (who have grown up with computers) grow older, usage will increase even faster. There is no question that sooner or later there will be a billion people who surf the Internet. Estimates are that by 2020, the number of worldwide Internet users will be 800 million, including more than half of the U.S. population.

Opportunities for Buying. The number of products and services available online is increasing rapidly with improved trading mechanisms, search engines, online shopping aids, intermediary services, presentations in multiple languages, and the willingness of more sellers and buyers to give EC a try. It is logical to expect significantly more purchasing opportunities. U.S. annual sales increased an average of 41 percent in 2001 (Boston Consulting Group 2002).

M-Commerce. With over 1.2 billion people using cell phones in 2003 (Charny 2003), the ease with which one can connect from them to the Internet, and the introduction of 3G capabilities, it is clear that m-commerce will play a major role in EC. Forrester Research predicts that as many as 50 percent of these wireless users will be online by 2007 (Golvin 2002). The fact that one does not need a computer to go online will bring more and more people to the Web. M-commerce, as discussed in Chapter 9, has special capabilities that will result in new applications, as well as in more people using traditional applications.

Purchasing Incentives. The buyers' advantages described in Chapter 1 are likely to increase. Prices will go down, and the purchasing process will be streamlined. Many innovative options will be available, and electronic shopping may even become a social trend. Also, for many organizations, e-procurement is becoming an attractive EC initiative.

Increased Security and Trust. One of the major inhibitors of growth of B2C and B2B EC is the perception of poor security and privacy and a lack of trust. As time passes, significant improvements in these areas are expected. For more information on augmenting trust, see Patton and Josang (2004).

Efficient Information Handling. More information will become accessible from anywhere, at any time. Using data warehouses, data mining, and intelligent agents, companies can constantly learn about their customers, steering marketing and service activities accordingly. The notion of *real-time marketing* might not be so far away. This will facilitate the use of EC.

Innovative Organizations. Organizations are being restructured and reengineered with the help of IT (Turban et al. 2006; El Sawy 2001; Ahadi 2004). Using different types of empowered teams, some of which are virtual, organizations become innovative, flexible, and responsive. The trend for process reengineering is increasing, as is organizational creativity. Innovative organizations will probably be more inclined to use EC.

Virtual Communities. Virtual communities of all kinds are spreading rapidly, with some already reaching several million members. Virtual communities can enhance commercial activities online. Also, some communities are organized around professional areas of interest and can facilitate B2B and B2C EC.

Payment Systems. The ability to use e-cash or person-to-person (P2P) payments and to make micropayments online is spreading quickly. When these systems are implemented on a large scale, many EC activities will flourish. B2B payment systems also have matured, and attractive options are available. As international standards become the norm, electronic payments will extend globally, facilitating global EC.

B2B EC. Figures about the growth of B2B are revised frequently. In some cases, industry-type extranets are forcing many buyers and sellers to participate in B2B EC (e.g., Covisint, see Chapter 6). B2B will continue to dominate the EC field (in terms of volume traded) for the intermediate future. More sellers, more buyers, and more services will continue to appear; the rapid growth of B2B will continue. The success of B2B will depend on the success of integrating EC technology with business processes and with conventional information systems.

B2B Exchanges. In 2000, the number of B2B exchanges exploded, but many subsequently collapsed in 2001 and 2002. The few that have remained are maturing, providing the infrastructure for $12.8 trillion of B2B trade forecasted by 2006 (Sharrard et al. 2001). However, company-centric (private) marketplaces will account for the majority of the B2B trade.

Auctions. The popularity of auctions and reverse auctions is increasing rapidly in B2B, B2C, G2B, and C2C. This is an effective and efficient EC business model. eBay is probably the most successful large dot-com. On December 30, 2004, eBay reported that in one year the number of registered users increased from 86 to 125 million, the value of goods sold increased from $20 billion to $32 billion, and the number of items available at any time increased from 19 to 30 million (Maney 2004).

Going Global. One of the most appealing benefits of EC is the ability to go global. However, many barriers exist to global EC. With time, these are expected to be reduced, but at a fairly slow pace.

E-Government. Starting in 1999, many governments launched comprehensive G2C, G2B, G2G, and G2E projects. By 2005, more than 160 countries had established some form of e-government program.

Intrabusiness EC. Many companies are starting to discover opportunities for using EC in-house, particularly in improving the internal supply chain and communications with and among employees.

E-Learning. One of the fastest-growing areas in EC in 2005 was e-learning. Large numbers of companies have installed e-learning programs, and many universities are experimenting with distance-learning programs. E-learning should grow even faster in the near future.

EC Legislation. The legislative process is slow, especially when multiple countries are involved. However, with passage of time, the necessary EC framework will be in place.

EC TECHNOLOGY TRENDS

The trend in EC technologies generally points toward significant cost reduction coupled with improvements in capabilities, ease of use, increased availability of software, ease of site development, and improved security and accessibility. Specific technology trends include the following.

Clients. PCs of all types are getting cheaper, smaller, and more capable. The concept of a network computer (NC), also known as a *thin client*, which moves processing and storage off the desktop and onto centrally located servers running Java-based software on UNIX (Windows on Microsoft's version), and the simputer could bring the price of a PC to that of a television (e.g., Wal-Mart was selling laptops for less than $500 in 2004).

Embedded Clients. Another major trend is the movement toward *embedded clients*. In such a case, a client can be a car or a washing machine with an embedded microchip. In many cases, an expert system is embedded with rules that make the client "smarter" or more responsive to changes in the environment. It is a typical device in pervasive computing.

Wireless Communications and M-Commerce. For countries without fiber-optic cables, wireless communication can save considerable installation time and money. In 1998, wireless access reached T1 speed (about 1.5 mbps), with cost savings of over 80 percent. However, wireless networks may be too slow for some futuristic digitized products (see Chapter 9). An exception is Wi-Fi WLANs, which are growing rapidly. According to Rogers and Edwards (2003), wireless communications is expected to change the nature of e-commerce from content to context, reaching customers whenever and wherever they are ready to buy.

Pervasive Computing. The Gartner Group calls pervasive computing "the next big thing" in IT (Fenn and Linden 2001). Pervasive computing (Chapter 9) is starting to impact EC positively. Pervasive computing is facilitated by improvements in wireless communication and wearable devices.

Wearable Devices. With advances in pervasive computing and artificial intelligence, the number of wearable computing devices (Chapter 9) will increase. Wearable devices will enhance collaborative commerce, B2E, and intrabusiness EC.

RFID. This experimental application of pervasive computing will have a great impact on e-supply chains. Wal-Mart's completion of its pilot implementation should cut costs and settle privacy issues. In addition to inventory monitoring, there will be many other areas of application, ranging from security to e-CRM.

Servers and Operating Systems. A major trend is to use Windows XP and NT as the enterprise operating system. Among NT's capabilities is *clustering*. Clustering servers can add processing power in much smaller increments than was previously possible. Clustering servers also is very economical, resulting in cost reductions. Special EC servers are offered by Microsoft and others (see Online Chapter 18).

Networks. The use of EC frequently requires rich multimedia (such as color catalogs or samples of movies or music). A large bandwidth is required to deliver this rich multimedia. Several broadband technologies (such as XDSL) will increase bandwidth many-fold. This could help in replacing expensive WANs or VANs with the inexpensive Internet. Security on the Internet can be enhanced by the use of VPNs.

EC Software and Services. The availability of all types of EC software will make it easier to establish stores on the Internet and to conduct all types of trade. Already, hundreds of sites rent inexpensive pages for a variety of activities, ranging from conducting auctions to selling in a foreign language. Other support services, such as escrow companies that support auctions and multiple types of certifications, also are developing rapidly. In addition, a large number of consultants are being trained to assist in specialty areas.

Search Engines. Search engines are getting smarter and better. Use of this improved technology will enable consumers and organizational buyers to find and compare products and services easier and faster.

Peer-to-Peer Technology. P2P technology is developing rapidly and is expected to have a major impact on knowledge sharing, communication, and collaboration by making these activities better, faster, less expensive, and more convenient.

Integration. The forthcoming integration of the computer and the TV and of the computer and the telephone will increase Internet accessibility (e.g., see Silberman 1999). Web Services (see next item) also will facilitate integration.

Web Services. Web Services (see Chapter 7 and Online Chapter 18) are being developed rapidly, solving major problems in EC systems development and integration, especially in complex B2B systems and exchanges. Web Services will enable companies to build EC applications more quickly, efficiently, and cheaply.

Software Agents. Users will be able to dispatch intelligent software agents to search, match, negotiate, and conduct many other tasks that will facilitate EC activities.

Interactive TV. Although it has shown few signs of success, some believe that in the future interactive TV may outshine the Net for e-commerce (see Williamson 2001). According to a research report by eMarketer (2002), 51.9 percent of U.S. households are predicted to use iTV by 2005. This is a dramatic increase from only 3 percent in 2000.

Universities are using interactive TV to teach classes in multiple locations. Eastern Illinois University in Charleston, Illinois, offers MBA classes concurrently on both the Charleston campus and at Parkland Community College in Champaign, Illinois.

Tomorrow's Internet. Many research institutions around the world are working on tomorrow's Internet. Although projects such as Internet2 are slow to progress, sooner or later these efforts will greatly advance EC applications (Boyles 2000 and internet2.org).

utility computing
Computing resources that flow like electricity on demand from virtual utilities around the globe—always on and highly available, secure, efficiently metered, priced on a pay-as-you-use basis, dynamically scaled, self-healing, and easy to manage.

Utility Computing. According to Bill Gates, **utility computing** is computing that is as available, reliable, and secure as electricity, water services, and telephony (CNET News.com Staff 2002). The vision behind utility computing is to have computing resources flow like electricity on demand from virtual utilities around the globe—always on and highly available, secure, efficiently metered, priced on a pay-as-you-use basis, dynamically scaled, self-healing, and easy to manage.

An example of using utility computing in EC is the case of Mobile Travel Guide, which rates over 25,000 restaurants and hotels in the United States and publishes travel guides for various regions. To accommodate the ever-increasing traffic of Web servers that are looking for its ratings, the company is using IBM's on-demand hosting services. With this service, the company not only solved all its capacity problems but also increased security at a 30 percent cost reduction compared to having its own servers.

Grid Computing. Conventional networks, including the Internet, are designed to provide communication among devices. The same networks can be used to support the concept of *grid computing,* in which the unused processing cycles of all computers in a given network can be harnessed to create powerful computing capabilities. Grid computing coordinates the use of a large number of servers and storage, acting as one computer. Thus problems of spikes in demand are solved without the cost of maintaining reserve capacity (see oracle.com/grid).

Grid computing is already in limited use, and many of the current grid applications are in areas that formerly would have required supercomputers. An example of using grid computing in EC is the case of J.P. Morgan Chase Investment Bank supporting electronic trading in real time using the computing power of thousands of employees (see Hamblen 2004).

INTEGRATING THE MARKETPLACE WITH THE MARKETSPACE

Throughout this book, we have commented on the relationship between the physical marketplace and the marketspace. We have pointed out conflicts in certain areas, as well as successful applications and cooperation. The fact is that from the point of view of the consumer, as well as of most organizations, these two entities exist, and will continue to exist, together.

Probably the most noticeable integration of the two concepts is in the click-and-mortar organization. For the foreseeable future, the click-and-mortar organization will be the most prevalent model (e.g., see Otto and Chung 2000), though it may take different shapes and formats. Some organizations will use EC as just another selling channel, as most large retailers do today. Others will use EC for only some products and services, while they sell other products and services the conventional way (e.g., Lego and GM). As experience is gained on how to excel at such a strategy, more and more organizations, private and public, will move to this dual mode of operation.

A major problem with the click-and-mortar approach is how the two outlets can cooperate in planning, advertising, logistics, resource allocation, and so on and how the strategic plans of the marketspace and marketplace can be aligned. Another major issue is conflict with existing distribution channels (i.e., wholesalers, retailers).

Another area of coexistence is in many B2C ordering systems, where customers have the option to order the new way or the old way. For example, consumers can do their banking both online and off-line. People can trade stocks via the computer, by placing a call to their broker, or just by walking into a brokerage firm and talking to a trader. In the areas of B2B and G2B, the option to choose the old way or the new way may not be available much longer; some organizations may discontinue the old-economy option as the number of off-line users declines below a certain threshold. However, in most B2C activities, the option will remain, at least for the foreseeable future.

In conclusion, many people believe that the impact of EC on our lives will be as much as, and possibly more profound than, that of the Industrial Revolution. No other phenomenon since the Industrial Revolution has been classified in this category. It is our hope that this book will help you move successfully into this exciting and challenging digital revolution.

Section 17.9 ▶ REVIEW QUESTIONS

1. Describe nontechnological EC trends.
2. Describe technological trends for EC.
3. Discuss the integration of marketplaces and marketspaces.

MANAGERIAL ISSUES

Some managerial issues related to this chapter are as follows.

1. **What sorts of legal and ethical issues should be of major concern to an EC enterprise?** There is no set list of ethical and legal issues that are paramount in EC. However, some of the key issues to consider include the following: (1) What type of proprietary information should we allow on our site? (2) Who will have access to information that is posted by visitors to our site? (3) Do the content and activities on our site comply with the laws in other countries? (4) Do we need to post disclaimers concerning the content of our Web site? (5) Are we inadvertently using trademarked or copyrighted materials without permission? Regardless of the specific issues, an attorney should periodically review the content on the site, and someone should be responsible for monitoring legal and liability issues.
2. **What are the most critical ethical issues?** Issues of privacy, ethics, and so on may seem tangential to running a business, but ignoring them may hinder the operation of an organization. Privacy protection can cut into profits, especially in B2C in which sellers need to learn more about customers and their behaviors but cannot do so (Hildebrand 1996).
3. **Should we obtain patents?** Some people claim that patents should not be awarded to business or computer processes related to EC (as is the case in Europe). Therefore, investing large amounts of money in developing or buying patents may be financially unwise in cases where patents may not hold.
4. **What impacts on business is EC expected to make?** The impacts of EC and the Internet can be so strong that the entire manner in which companies do business will be changed, with significant impacts on procedures, people, organizational structure, management, and business processes. (Read "The Economic and Social Impact of Electronic Commerce" at oecd.org/subject/e_commerce.)
5. **Do we have a community?** Although sponsoring a community may sound like a good idea, it may not be simple to execute. Community members need services, and these cost money to provide. The most difficult task is to find a community that matches your business.

RESEARCH TOPICS

Here are some suggested topics related to this chapter. For details, references, and additional topics, refer to the book's "Current EC Research" in the Online Appendix.

1. **Fraud on the Internet**
   - Areas of significant potential for misleading and fraudulent practices
   - Consumers' perceptions of online credit card theft
   - Trusted e-mail
   - Remedies and tools to prevent fraud
   - Intelligent systems for fraud detection
2. **Intellectual Property Rights**
   - Reasons why the Digital Millennium Copyright Act is a failure
   - The promise and problems of the No Electronic Theft (NET) Act
   - Risks of digital rights management
   - Protection strategies for online software and digital content distribution
   - Watermarking of electronic text documents to prevent their illegal copy and redistribution
   - Influence of institutional prestige on the licensing of university inventions
3. **E-Taxation**
   - Pros and cons of taxing electronic commerce
   - Taxation systems of state and local governments in the United States
   - Issues of the neutral sales tax between online and traditional channels
   - Sales tax protocol for international taxation
   - Taxation policy and appropriate electronic payment methods
   - Tax jurisdiction for cross-border trades
   - Optimal methods to register foreign supplies in the countries where the B2C customers are located
   - Buyer's self-assessment principle for cross-border B2B taxation
   - IT architecture system design for the cross-border tax clearance
4. **Freedom of Speech**
   - The effect of the Child Online Protection Act on the civil liberties of Americans
   - Legal basis for monitoring pornography and sexual harassment online
5. **Anonymity**
   - Legal issues of anonymity and pseudonymity
   - Technical solutions for producing anonymous communication
   - Software for secure, consistent, and pseudonymous aliases for Web users
6. **Privacy**
   - Users' concerns, technologies, and implications of privacy on the Web for businesses and individuals
   - Antecedents and consequences of consumer privacy concerns
   - Typology of Internet users and online privacy concerns
   - Necessity of balancing privacy and digital rights management
   - Conflict between personalization and privacy
   - Tools for Internet privacy protection
   - Privacy seal programs
   - Framework of relationship marketing and social exchange theory to explain trust and privacy
   - Managing the cost of information privacy
   - The legal environment on direct marketers' use of public records
   - Privacy disclosures and consumer database information
   - Cross-cultural studies on privacy

SUMMARY

In this chapter, you learned about the following EC issues as they relate to the learning objectives.

1. **Differences between legal and ethical issues.** The legal framework for EC—both statutory and common law—is just beginning to solidify. To date, the major legal issues in EC have involved rights of privacy, intellectual property, freedom of speech and censorship, and fraud. In the absence of legal constraints, ethical codes help to fill the gap. The problem is that ethics are subjective and vary widely from one culture to the next.
2. **Protecting privacy in EC.** B2C companies require customer information in order to improve products and services and sell them via one-to-one marketing. Registration and cookies are two of the ways used to collect this information. The key privacy issues are who controls this information and how private it should remain. Although legal measures are being developed to protect the privacy of individuals, it is basically up to the EC companies to regulate themselves. If they fail to do so to the satisfaction of consumers, they may face bad publicity from consumer- and privacy-oriented organizations.
3. **Intellectual property rights in EC.** It is extremely easy and inexpensive to copy or steal intellectual works on the Internet (e.g., music, photos, graphics, movies, and the like) and to distribute or sell them without the permission of the owners—violating or infringing on copyrights, trademarks, and patents. Although the legal aspects are now fairly clear, monitoring and catching violators is sometimes difficult.
4. **Unsolicited ads and spamming.** Unsolicited ads and spamming are a major problem on the Internet, interfering with surfing as well as e-commerce. Efforts by governments, ISPs, commercial portals, and others, along with tough legal action, are finally starting to ease the problem.
5. **Conflict between free speech and censorship.** There is ongoing debate about censorship on the Internet. The proponents of censorship feel that it is up to the government and various ISPs and Web sites to control inappropriate or offensive content. Others oppose any form of censorship; they believe that control is up to the individual. In the United States, most legal attempts to censor content on the Internet have been found unconstitutional. The debate is not likely to subside in the near term.
6. **Legal issues.** Doing business electronically requires a supportive legal environment. Of special importance are electronic contracts (including digital signatures), the control of offshore gambling, and what taxes should be paid to whom on interstate and international transactions. Although the trend is not to have a sales tax or a value-added tax, this may not be the case for too much longer.
7. **Protecting buyers and sellers online.** Protection is needed because there is no face-to-face contact, because there is a great possibility for fraud, because there are insufficient legal constraints, and because new issues and scams appear constantly. Several organizations, private and public, are attempting to provide the protection that is needed to build the trust that is essential for the success of widespread EC.
8. **Societal issues and EC.** EC has impacted society in several different ways. Some of these impacts are very positive, such as improvements in education, public safety and criminal justice, and health care. On the negative side is the creation of the digital divide.
9. **The role of virtual communities.** Virtual communities create new types of business opportunities—people with similar interests that are congregated in one Web site are a natural target for advertisers and marketers. Using chat rooms, members can exchange opinions about certain products and services. Of special interest are communities of transactions, whose interest is the promotion of commercial buying and selling. Virtual communities can foster customer loyalty, increase sales of related vendors that sponsor communities, and facilitate customer feedback for improved service and business.
10. **The future of EC.** EC will continue to expand fairly rapidly for a number of reasons. To begin with, its infrastructure is becoming better and less expensive with time. Consumers will become more experienced and will try different products and services and tell their friends about them. Security, privacy protection, and trust will be much higher, and more support services will simplify the transaction process. Legal issues will be formally legislated and clarified, and more and more products and services will be online at reduced prices. The fastest growing area is B2B EC. Company-centric systems (especially e-procurement) and auctions will also continue to spread rapidly. The development of exchanges and other many-to-many e-marketplaces will be much slower. The most promising technology for facilitating integration is Web Services. Finally, wireless technologies (especially Wi-Fi) will facilitate EC.

KEY TERMS

Copyright	**716**	**Identity theft**	**731**	**Trademark**	**718**
Cyberbashing	**720**	**Intellectual property**	**716**	**Unsolicited commercial e-mail (UCE)**	**721**
Cybersquatting	**719**	**Opt-in clause**	**714**	**Utility computing**	**744**
Digital divide	**736**	**Opt-out clause**	**714**	**Virtual (Internet) community**	**737**
Digital watermarks	**717**	**Patent**	**720**		
Ethics	**709**	**Privacy**	**711**		

QUESTIONS FOR DISCUSSION

1. Provide two privacy examples in EC in which the situation is legal but unethical.

2. Distinguish between self-registration and cookies in EC. Why do you think Internet users are concerned about cookies?

3. What are some of the things that EC Web sites can do to ensure that personal information is safeguarded?

4. On the Internet, why is it difficult to protect intellectual property? Do you think that sites such as MP3.com and Kazaa should be able to operate without restriction? Justify your answer.

5. Who should control minors' access to "offensive" material on the Internet—parents, the government, or ISPs? Why?

6. Should spamming be illegal? Explain why or why not.

7. Discuss the relationship between virtual communities and doing business on the Internet.

8. Discuss the issue of the digital divide and how to deal with the problem. (Search at **egovmonitor.com** and **google.com**.)

9. Discuss the conflict between freedom of speech and the control of offensive Web sites.

10. Discuss the insufficient protection of opt-in and opt-out options. What would you be happy with?

11. The IRS buys demographic market research data from private companies. These data contain income statistics that could be compared with tax returns. Many U.S. citizens feel that their rights within the realm of the Electronic Communications Privacy Act (ECPA) are being violated; others say that this is an unethical behavior on the part of the government. Discuss.

12. Clerks at 7-Eleven stores enter data regarding customers (gender, approximate age, and so on) into the computer. These data are then processed for improved decision making. Customers are not informed about this, nor are they being asked for permission. (Names are not keyed in.) Are the clerks' actions ethical? Compare this with the case of cookies.

13. Many hospitals, health maintenance organizations, and federal agencies are converting, or plan to convert, all patient medical records from paper to electronic storage (using imaging technology). Once completed, electronic storage will enable quick access to most records. However, the availability of these records in a database and on networks or smart cards may allow people, some of whom are unauthorized, to view another person's private medical data. To protect privacy fully may cost too much money or may considerably slow the speed of access to the records. What policies could health-care administrators use to prevent unauthorized access? Discuss.

14. Why do many companies and professional organizations develop their own codes of ethics?

15. Cyber Promotions Inc. attempted to use the First Amendment in defense of its flooding of AOL subscribers with junk e-mail. AOL tried to block the junk e-mail. A federal judge agreed with AOL that unsolicited e-mail is annoying, a costly waste of Internet time, and often inappropriate, and therefore should not be sent. Discuss some of the issues involved, such as freedom of speech, how to distinguish between junk and nonjunk e-mail, and the analogy with regular mail.

16. Digital Equipment paid over $3 million for the AltaVista name and Tom.com paid $8 million for its domain name. Why are companies willing to pay millions of dollars for domain names?

17. The Communication Decency Act, which was intended to protect children and others from pornography and other offensive material online, was approved by the U.S. Congress but then was ruled unconstitutional by the courts. Discuss the importance and implications of this incident.

18. Why does the government warn customers to be careful with their payments for EC products and services?

19. Some say that it is much easier to commit fraud online than off-line. Do you agree?

20. This book includes many innovative ideas. Why can't they be patented? How are the rights of the authors and publisher protected?

INTERNET EXERCISES

1. Two commonly used Internet terms are *flaming* and *spamming*. Surf the Web to find out more about these terms. How are they similar? How are they different?
2. You want to set up a personal Web site. Using legal sites such as **cyberlaw.com**, prepare a report summarizing the types of materials you can and cannot use (e.g., logos, graphics, etc.) without breaking copyright law.
3. Use **google.com** to prepare a list of industry and trade organizations involved in various computer privacy initiatives. One of these groups is the World Wide Web Consortium (W3C). Describe its Privacy Preferences Project (**w3.org/tr/2001/wd-p3p-20010928**).
4. Enter the Web site of an Internet community (e.g., **tripod.com** or **geocities.yahoo.com**). Build a homepage free of charge. You can add a chat room and a message board to your site using the free tools provided.
5. Investigate the community services provided by Yahoo! to its members (**groups.yahoo.com**). List all the services available and assess their potential commercial benefits to Yahoo!
6. Enter **pgp.com**. Review the services offered. Use the free software to encrypt a message.
7. Enter **calastrology.com**. What kind of community is this? Check the revenue model. Then enter **astrocenter.com**. What kind of site is this? Compare and comment on the two sites.
8. Enter **nolo.com**. Try to find information about various EC legal issues. Find information about international EC issues. Then go to **legalcompliance.com** or **webtriallawyer.com**. Try to find information about international legal aspects of EC. Locate additional information on EC legal issues with a visit to **google.com** or a search on Yahoo! Prepare a report on the international legal aspects of EC.
9. Find the status of the latest copyright legislation. Try **fairuse.stanford.edu**. Is there anything regarding the international aspects of copyright legislation?
10. Enter **ftc.gov** and identify some of the typical types of fraud and scams on the Internet.
11. Enter **usispa.org** and **ispa.org.uk**, two organizations that represent the ISP industry. Identify the various initiatives they have undertaken regarding topics discussed in this chapter.
12. Check the latest on domain names by visiting sites such as **internic.net**. Prepare a report.
13. Private companies such as **thepubliceye.com** and **investigator.com** can act as third parties to investigate the honesty of a business. What do these companies do? Why are the services of these companies necessary given the services of TRUSTe and BBBOnLine? (That is, are the services of TRUSTe and BBBOnLine somehow insufficient?)
14. Visit **consumers.com**. What protection can this group give that is not provided by BBBOnLine?
15. Find the status of fingerprint identification systems. Try **bergdata.com** and **morpho.com**. Prepare a report based on your findings.
16. Download freeware from **junkbuster.com** and learn how to prohibit unsolicited e-mail. Describe how your privacy is protected.
17. Enter **scambusters.com** and identify and list its antifraud and antiscam activities.
18. Enter **ironport.com** and see how it protects e-mail. List all of the product's capabilities.

TEAM ASSIGNMENTS AND ROLE PLAYING

1. Over the past few years, the number of lawsuits in the United States and elsewhere involving EC has been increasing. Have each team prepare a list of five or more such cases on each topic in this chapter (e.g., privacy, defamation, domain names). What have been the outcomes of these cases? If there has not yet been an outcome in certain cases, what is likely to happen and why?
2. Each team member is assigned to a different type of community, per Exhibit 17.4. Identify the services offered by that type of community. Have each team compare the services offered by each type of community. Prepare a report.
3. Have a debate between two teams. One team is for complete freedom of speech on the Internet, the other team advocates the censoring of offensive and pornographic material. Other class members will act as judges.
4. It is legal to monitor employees' movements on the Internet and read their e-mail. But is it ethical? Should it be practiced? Have two teams debate this issue.
5. Enter **whatis.techtarget.com**. Read all about spam. Find how spam filters work (also see **ironport.com** and other vendors). Finally, take the self-assessment quiz at **searchcrm.techtarget.com** or **networkcomputing.com**. Prepare a report and class presentation.

Real-World Case

HOW COMPANIES FIGHT SPAMMING

The following are case studies of four companies that are successfully fighting spam.

Pier 1 Imports

Employees of the Pier 1 chain (1,100 stores) were spending too much time clearing huge amounts of spam from their e-mail boxes on a daily basis. The entire e-mail system became more trouble than help when spam accounted for 80 percent of all e-mails. Employee productivity suffered drastically. At first, Pier 1 used a keyword filter to block messages containing words the company deemed inappropriate. This system failed; IT blocked legitimate messages with words that had dual meanings. Also, spammers became more innovative, using creative misspellings to evade the filter.

Pier 1 found a suitable solution, MailFrontier Enterprise Gateway, which works well with Microsoft's e-mail software. MailFrontier is placed in front of Microsoft Exchange in order to inspect all incoming e-mail. It then accepts good e-mail and rejects spam. The software uses 17 predictive techniques to filter spam, stopping 98 percent of all spam at Pier 1. Pier 1 is collaborating with MailFrontier to add antivirus and antifraud capabilities. For further details, see Korolishin (2004).

Charter Communications

Charter Communications, the fourth-largest U.S. television and Internet cable company, provides e-mail accounts to over 1.7 million users and handles 150 million messages a day. The company suffered from spammers who abused Charter's network infrastructure. Spam comprised well over 50 percent of inbound e-mail. It also created a nuisance for customers. Charter needed to minimize the spam (as well as viruses) reaching customers' inboxes. Initially, Charter used open source filters, which were not very effective.

Today, Charter is using two unique tools from IronPort: The IronPort C60 e-mail security appliance (described in Exhibit 17.1) allows Charter to divide e-mail senders into unique categories (e.g., by IP address, domain name, sender reputation). For each sender, the tool provides specific thresholds for the acceptance or rejection of e-mail messages. The second tool, Reputation Filtering, complements the first one. It allows e-mail administrators to sort e-mail senders based on the importance of the mail they send. Poor quality messages are rejected. For details, see the Charter Case Study at *ironport.com* (2004).

The Catholic Diocese of Richmond

Managers of the information system at the Catholic Diocese of Richmond, Virginia, needed to stop the flow of spam to about 200 employees at three locations. The organization now is using PowerTools from Nemx (Canada). The tool achieves quality spam blocking by using the combination of five modules including Content Manager, Concept Manager, Spam Manager. For details, see Piazza (2004).

First Banking Services of Florida

First Banking Services' 250 employees use desktops to provide core data processing services to banks in the southeastern United States. The company is connected with many business partners, and its e-mail messages have different characteristics; many have large attachments. Spam was becoming a major problem. After careful evaluation, the company selected a spam-fighting solution called Mail Warden Pro (from Wareford Technologies, Ireland).

Mail Warden Pro allows users to set rules that distinguish spam from nonspam in a very flexible manner. The software also provides generic rules that have been found to be excellent in stopping spam and protecting against attachments with viruses. The volume of spam has been reduced from 65 percent of all e-mails to less than 5 percent. For details, see Piazza (2004).

Sources: Korolishin (2004), *ironport.com* (accessed 2004), and Piazza (2004).

Questions

1. The four companies use different blockers, each with a proprietary method. Why do each of the companies use different products from different vendors?
2. Regular spam stoppers from e-mail providers (e.g., Microsoft Exchange) were insufficient. However, such spam stoppers are getting better with time. Research the issues involved. Do you think that in the future the need for blockers such as those described here will wane?
3. In all cases, the companies felt that the investment in spam-fighting software was justifiable, but no formal ROI was done. Is this a reasonable approach? Why or why not?
4. What is the logic of combining antispam, antivirus, and antifraud software?

REFERENCES

Ackman, D. "Do-Not-Call List Likely to Call Back." *Forbes.com,* September 25, 2003. forbes.com/2003/09/25/cx_da_0925topnews.html (accessed January 2005).

Adams, J. "Inoculating the Internet for Fraud." *USBanker,* 2000.

Ahadi, H. R. "An Examination of the Role of Organizational Enablers in Business Process Reengineering and the Impact of Information Technology." *Information Resources Management Journal* 17, no. 4 (2004).

Akhter, S. H. "Digital Divide and Purchase Intention: Why Demographic Psychology Matters." *Journal of Economic Psychology* 24, no. 3 (2003).

Alberts, R. J., et al. "The Threat of Long-Arm Jurisdiction to Electronic Commerce." *Communications of the ACM* 41, no. 12 (1998).

American City Business Journals, Inc. "Consumers Fret About Online Privacy—But Do Little." *Sacramento Business Journal,* June 3, 2002. bizjournals.com/sacramento/stories/2002/06/03/daily8.html (accessed January 2005).

Anandarajan, M. "Internet Abuse in the Workplace." *Communications of the ACM* 45, no. 1 (2002).

Anderson, C. "Government Cracks Down on Peer-to-Peer Network and Spam." *InformationWeek,* August 25, 2004. informationweek.com/showarticle.jhtml?articleid=31700003 (accessed January 2005).

Angwin, J. "Credit-Card Fraud Has Become a Nightmare for E-Merchants." *Wall Street Journal Interactive Edition,* September 19, 2000. mcnees.org/mainpages/misc/security/sec_subpages/wsj_cc_fraud_919.htm (accessed January 2005).

Asahi Shimbun News Service. News item, August 30, 2002.

Associated Press. "States Push for Net Sales Taxes." *Wired.com,* March 3, 2004. wired.com/news/business/ 0,1367,62526,00.html (accessed January 2005).

Australian Internet Industry Association (AIIA). Interactive Gambling Bill 2001. Submission to the Environment, Communications, Information, Technology and the Arts Legislation Committee, April 24, 2001. iia.net.au/news/senate_submission2.html (accessed January 2005).

Black, J. "The High Price of Spam." *BusinessWeek Online,* March 1, 2002. businessweek.com/technology/content/mar2002/tc2002031_8613.htm (accessed January 2005).

Blanchard, A. L., and M. L. Markus. "The Experienced 'Sense' of a Virtual Community: Characteristics and Processes." *The DATA BASE for Advances in Information Systems* 35, no. 4 (2004).

Boston Consulting Group. "Online Sales in 2001 Generated Profits for More Than Half of All U.S. Retailers Selling Online." June 12, 2002.

Boyles, H. "Internet2: Fostering Tomorrow's Internet." *Global Electronic Commerce,* 2000.

Broida, R. "Spyware: IT's Public Enemy No. 1." ZDNet News, January 20, 2005. news.zdnet.com/2100-1009-5541802.html (accessed April 2005).

Buchholz, R. A., and S. B. Rosenthal. "Internet Privacy: Individual Rights and the Common Good." *SAM Advanced Management Journal* 67, no. 1, Winter 2002.

Burk, D. L. "Copyrightable Functions and Patentable Speech." *Communications of the ACM* 44, no. 2 (2001).

Burnett, R. "Legal Aspects of E-commerce." *Computing & Control Engineering Journal* 79, no. 3 (2000).

Burt, J. "Vertical Slice: Health Care, Privacy Therapy." *eWeek,* July 26, 2004.

Cashel, J. "Top Ten Trends for Online Communities." *Online Community Report.* onlinecommunityreport.com/features/10 (accessed October 2004).

CBS News. "Web Deceit Complaints Dominate." *CBS News.com,* January, 22, 2004. cbsnews.com/stories/2004/01/22/tech/main595128.shtml (accessed January 2005).

Charny, B. "Microsoft: Security Fix Due for Phone OS." *CNET News.com,* January 17, 2003. news.com.com/2100-1033-981244.html?tag=fd_top (accessed January 2005).

Cheeseman, H. R. *Business Law,* 5th ed. Upper Saddle River, NJ: Prentice Hall, 2004.

Cherry, S. M., et al. "A World Divided by a Common Internet." *IEEE Spectrum,* February 2004.

Christman, E. "U.S. Music Sales Break Losing Streak in 2004." Reuters, January 7, 2005. entertainment-news.org/breaking/17116/music-sales-break-losing-streak-in-2004.html (accessed April 2005).

Chua, C. E. H., and J. Wareham. "Fighting Internet Auction Fraud: An Assessment and Proposal." *IEEE Computer* 37, no. 10 (2004).

Claburn, T. "Microsoft Files Seven Lawsuits Against Spammers." *InformationWeek.com,* December 2, 2004. informationweek.com/showarticle.jhtml?articleid=54201964 (accessed January 2005).

CNET News.com Staff. "Gates memo: 'We can and must do better.'" CNETNews.com, January 17, 2002. news.com.com/2009-1001-817210.html (accessed April 2005).

CNN. "Bill Gates Drowning in Spam." *CNN.com,* November 18, 2004. hacktivismo.com/news/index.php?p=138 (accessed April 2005).

Coalition Against Unsolicited Commercial E-mail (CAUCE). cauce.org (accessed January 2005).

Commerce One. commerceone.com (accessed January 2005).

Commodity Futures Trading Commission (CFTC). "CFTC Issues Two Advisories Addressing the Offering of Foreign Currency (FOREX) Trading Opportunities to the Retail Public." CFTC News Release 4489-01, February 8, 2001. cftc.gov/opa/enf01/opa4489-01.htm (accessed January 2005).

Cournane, A., and R. Hunt. "An Analysis of the Tools Used for the Generation and Prevention of Spam." *Computer & Security* 23, no. 2 (2004).

CyberSource Corporation. *Sixth Annual Online Fraud Report: Online Payment Fraud Trends and Merchants' Response*. 2005. **cybersource.com/resources/collateral/resource_center/whitepapers_and_reports/cybs_2005_fraud_report.pdf** (accessed April 2005).

Delgado-Martinez, R. "What Is Copyright Protection?" **whatiscopyright.org** (accessed January 2005).

Dembeck, C., and R. Conlin. "Beleaguered DoubleClick Appoints Privacy Board." *E-Commerce Times*, May 17, 2000. **ecommercetimes.com/story/3348.html** (accessed April 2005).

Dholakia, U. M., et al. "A Social Influence Model of Consumer Participation in Network- and Small-Group-based Virtual Communities." *International Journal of Research in Marketing* 21, no. 3 (2004).

Donham, P. "An Unshackled Internet: If Joe Howe Were Designing Cyberspace." *Proceedings of the Symposium on Free Speech and Privacy in the Information Age*, University of Waterloo, November 26, 1994. **efc.ca/pages/donham2.html** (accessed January 2005).

DoubleClick. **doubleclick.com** (accessed January 2005).

Duffy, D. "It Takes an E-Village." *CIO Magazine*, October 25, 1999.

eGovmonitor.com. "Government announces new plans to close Digital Divide." eGovmonitor.com, April 1, 2005. **egovmonitor.com/node/343** (accessed April 2005).

El Sawy, O. *Redesigning Enterprise Processes for E-Business*. New York: McGraw-Hill, 2001.

eMarketer. Interactive TV: Reality and Opportunity." *eMarketer.com*, March 2002. **emarketer.com/report.aspx?itv_reality** (accessed January 2005).

eMarketer. "Stopping the Spam but Losing the Ham?" *eMarketer.com*, July 23, 2004. **emarketer.com/article.aspx?1002952** (accessed January 2005).

Federal Trade Commission. "FTC Names Its Dirty Dozen: 12 Scams Most Likely to Arrive Via Bulk E-mail." **ftc.gov/bcp/conline/pubs/alerts/doznalrt.htm** (accessed January 2005).

Federal Trade Commission. "Privacy Online: A Report to the Congress." June 1998. **ftc.gov/reports/privacy3** (accessed January 2005).

Fenn, J., and A. Linden. "Wearing It Out: The Growth of the Wireless Wearable World." Gartner Group, April 17, 2001.

Flower, J. "American Health Care, Internet Style." *Physician Executive* 30, no. 3 (2004).

Gage, D. "AGIA: Identity Crisis." *Baseline*, October 1, 2004.

Geocities. **geocities.yahoo.com** (accessed January 2005).

Georgia Institute of Technology, Graphics, Visualization, and Usability (GVU) Center. *Tenth WWW User Survey*, 1998. **cc.gatech.edu/gvu/user_surveys/survey-1998-10/** (accessed December 2004).

Germain, J. M. "Special Report: New Era of Deadly Spyware Approaches." *Technewsworld*, August 14, 2004. **technewsworld.com/story/35748.html** (accessed April 2005).

Ghosh, A. K., and T. M. Swaminatha. "Software Security and Privacy Risks in Mobile E-Commerce." *Communications of the ACM* 44, no. 2 (2001).

Golvin, C. S., et al. "Mobile Applications That Drive Revenue." Forrester Research, October 2002. **forrester.com/er/research/report/summary/0,1338,15068,00.html** (accessed January 2005).

Gross, G. "Congress Fails to Act on Copyright Bills." IDG News Service, December 13, 2004. **pcworld.com/news/article/0,aid,118915,00.asp** (accessed April 2005).

Guernsey, L. "Welcome to the World Wide Web. Passport, Please?" *New York Times*, March 15, 2001.

Hagel, J., and A. Armstrong. *Net Gain*. Boston: Harvard Business School Press, 1997.

Hamblen, M. "J.P. Morgan Harnesses Power with Grid Computing System." *ComputerWorld*, March 15, 2004.

Hamelink, C. J. *The Ethics of Cyberspace*. Thousand Oaks, CA: Sage Publishers, 2001.

Hendrickson, D. "E-health Movement Gains Momentum with Doctors." *Mass High Tech* 22, no. 9 (2004).

Heydary, J. "Troubling Global Trends Emerging in Online Defamation." *E-Commerce Times*, August 5, 2004.

Hildebrand, C. "Privacy vs. Profit." *CIO Magazine*, February 15, 1996.

Hines, M. "Amazon, Microsoft Team for Spam Suits." *News.com*, September 28, 2004. **news.com.com/2100-1030_3-5385956.html** (accessed January 2005).

ICANN. **iccann.org** (accessed January 2005).

IDC. "Worldwide E-mail Usage 2004-2008 Forecast: Spam Today, Other Content Tomorrow." August 26, 2004.

IronPort. "Charter Get Hooked: Ironport Understands ISPs." *Ironport.com*, 2004. **ironport.com/pdf/ironport_charter_communications_case_study.pdf** (accessed January 2005).

Kannen, P. K., et al. "Marketing Information on the I-Way." *Communications of the ACM* 41, no. 3 (1998): 35–40.

Keenan, V. "Internet Exchange 2000: B2X Emerges as New Industry to Service Exchange Transactions." Keenan Vision Inc., April 24, 2000. **eyefortransport.com/archive/keenanvision17.pdf** (accessed January 2005).

Kenny, D., and J. F. Marshall. "Contextual Marketing: The Real Business of the Internet." *Harvard Business Review* (November–December 2000).

Ki-tae, Kim. "Spam-Filtering Site to Open Today." *Korean Times*, August 22, 2002.

King, R. "Online Gambling's Mr. Big." *Business 2.0*, April 2003.

Kontzer, T. "Illegal Movie Downloads Are Growing, Hollywood Says." *InformationWeek*, July 9, 2004.

Kopp, S. W., and T. A. Suter. "Fan Sites and Hate Sites on the World Wide Web." *Quarterly Journal of Electronic Commerce* 2, no. 4 (2001).

Korolishin, J. "Taking a Bite Out of Spam: Pier 1 Imports Blocks Unwanted E-Mail with the Help of Mailfrontier." *Stores*, August 2004.

Kracher, B., and C. L. Corritore. "Is there a Special E-Commerce Ethics?" *Business Ethics Quarterly* 14, no. 1 (2004).

Kravets, D. "Movie Studios Lose in Case against File Sharing Applications." *InformationWeek*, August 20, 2004.

Kwok, S. H. "Watermark-Based Copyright Protection System Security." *Communications of the ACM* 46, no. 10 (2003).

Kwok, S. H., et al. "Intellectual Property Protection for Electronic Commerce Applications." *Journal of Electronic Commerce Research* 5, no. 1 (2004).

Landro, L. "Is There a Doctor in the House?" *Wall Street Journal Europe*, June 14–16, 2002.

Law, D. "Bridging the Digital Divide: A Review of Current Progress." *Library Management* 25, nos. 1 & 2 (2004).

Lechner, U., et al. (eds.). "Communities and Platforms." Special issue of *Electronic Markets* 10, no. 4 (2001).

Lee, M., et al. "Virtual Communities Informatics: A Review and Research Agenda." *Information Technology Theory and Applications* 5, no. 1 (2003).

Leimeister, J. M., and H. Krcmar. "Success Factors of Virtual Communities from the Perspective of Members and Operators: An Empirical Study." *Proceedings of the 37th Annual HICCS Conference*, Kauai, Hawaii, January 4–7, 2004.

Lewis, J. B. "I Know What You E-Mailed Last Summer." *Security Management* (January 2002).

Lin, J. C. "Specific Absorption Rates Induced in Head Tissues by Microwave Radiation from Cell Phones." *IEEE Microwave Magazine* 2, no. 1 (2001).

Lubbe, S., and J. M. Van Heerden (eds.). *The Economic and Social Impacts of E-Commerce*. Hershey, PA: The Idea Group, 2003.

Luber, A. "Beware of Spyware, Adware, & Sneakware." *Smart Computing*, August 2004.

Luhn, R., and S. Spanbauer. "AdSubtract 2.5." *PCWorld*, September 27, 2002. **pcworld.com/downloads/file_description/0,fid,21340,00.asp** (accessed January 2005).

Malhotra, Y. "Enabling Knowledge Exchanges for E-Business Communities." *Information Strategy: The Executive's Journal* 18, no. 3, Spring (2002).

Mandal, P. "Inter-Country Analysis of E-Business." *Journal of Global Information Technology Management* 7, no. 2 (2004).

Maney, K. "The Year According to eBay." *USA Today*, December 30, 2004.

Marketingvox.com. "Pop-Ups Decline in Number, Effectiveness." *Marketingvox.com*, March 3, 2005. **marketingvox.com/archives/2005/03/03/popups_decline_in_number_effectiveness/** (accessed April 2005).

Matsuura, J. H. "An Overview of Leading Current Legal Issues Affecting Information Technology Professionals." *Information Systems Frontiers* 6, no. 2 (2004).

McDonald, F. "Consumer Protection Policy in the European Union." *European Business Journal* 12 (2000).

McGinity, M. "Weaving a Wireless Safety Net." *Communications of the ACM* 47, no. 9 (2004).

McWilliam, G. "Building Stronger Brands Through Online Communities." *Sloan Management Review*, Spring 2000.

Moringiello, J. M. "Grasping Intangibles: Domain Names and Creditors' Rights." *Journal of Internet Law* 8, no. 3 (2004).

Morris, T. "Protecting Your Privacy in the Electronic Mortgage Process." *The Maui News*, December 18, 2004.

Mowbray, M. "Philosophically Based Limitations to Freedom of Speech in Virtual Communities." *Information Systems Frontiers* 3, no. 1 (2001).

Mulligan, D. K. "Digital Rights Management and Fair Use by Design." *Communications of the ACM* 46, no. 4 (2003).

Murphy, J. W. "Internet Ethics." *Social Science Computer Review* 21, no. 3 (2003).

Mykytyn, P. P., Jr. "Some Internet and E-Commerce Legal Perspectives Impacting the End User." *Journal of End User Computing* 14, no. 1 (2002).

Nelson, M. "U.S. Governors Support Tax on Internet Commerce." *InfoWorld Electric*, February 26, 1998.

Nettleton, E. "Electronic Marketing and the New Anti-Spam Regulations." *Database Marketing & Customer Strategy Management* 11, no. 3 (2004).

Nickell, J. "Legislation: Privacy, Telecom, Copyrights, and Taxes." *Smart Business*, December 1, 2001.

Noticiasdot.com. "Are Pop-Ups On The Way Out?" **banners.noticiasdot.com/termometro/boletines/docs/consultoras/emarketer/2004/0704/emarketer_020704-3.pdf** (accessed April 2005).

OECD. **oecd.org/subject/e_commerce** (accessed January 2005).

Olavsrud, T. "Bertelsmann, Napster Create Membership-based Service." *Internetnews.com*, October 31, 2000. **internetnews.com/ec-news/article.php/499541** (accessed January 2005).

Olsen, S. "DoubleClick Nearing Privacy Settlements." *CNET News.com*, March 29, 2002. **news.com.com/2100-1023-871654.html** (accessed January 2005).

Otto, J. R., and O. B. Chung. "A Framework for Cyber-Enhanced Retailing: Integrating EC Retailing with Brick-and-Mortar Retailing." *Electronic Markets* 10, no. 3 (2000).

Papazafeiropoulou, A. "Inter-Country Analysis of Electronic Commerce Adoption in South Eastern Europe: Policy Recommendations for the Region." *Journal of Global Information Technology Management* 7, no. 2 (2004).

Patton, M. A., and A. Josang. "Technologies for Trust in Electronic Commerce." *Electronic Commerce Research*, April 2004.

Peppers and Rogers Group. "E-mail Marketing as a Relationship Strategy: The Four Steps to High Impact E-mail Marketing." White paper, 2004.

Petrovic-Lazarevic, S., and A. S. Sohal. "Nature of E-Business Ethical Dilemmas." *Information Management & Computer Security* 12, no. 2/3 (2004).

Pew Internet & American Life Project. "Spam: How It Is Hurting E-Mail and Degrading Life on the Internet." October 22, 2003. **pewinternet.org/report_display.asp?r=102** (accessed April 2005).

Piazza, P. "Had Your Fill of Spam?" *Security Management*, April 2004.

Piva, A., et al. "A New Decoder for the Optimum Recovery of Non-Additive Watermarks." *IEEE Transactions on Image Processing* 10, no. 5 (2001).

Porter, C. E. "A Typology of Virtual Communities: A Multi-Disciplinary Foundation for Future Research." *Journal of Computer-Mediated Communication* 10, no. 1 (2004).

Porter, D. "Texas Spammer Sued by State and Microsoft." *Axcess News*, January 15, 2005. **axcessnews.com/technology_011505a.shtml** (accessed January 2005).

Privacy Rights Clearinghouse. **privacyrights.org/fs/fs23-shopping.htm** (accessed January 2005).

Rafter, M. V. "Trust or Bust?" *The Standard*, March 6, 2000.

Raisch, W. D. *The eMarketplace: Strategies for Succeeding in B2B E-Commerce*. New York: McGraw-Hill, 2000.

Reda, S. "You've Got Spam." *Stores*, September 2003.

ReleMail. "ReleMail E-mail Privacy Survey." *Sacramento Business Journal,* November 2004. **bizjournals.com/sacramento/stories/2002/06/03/daily8.html** (accessed January 2005).

Rheingold, H. *The Virtual Community: Homesteading on the Electronic Frontier*. Reading, MA: Addison-Wesley, 1993.

Rogers, G. S., and J. S. Edwards. *Introduction to Wireless Technology*. Upper Saddle River, NJ: Prentice Hall, 2003.

Rose, L. "Know Your Online Shopping Rights." *Internet Shopper* 1, no. 1 (1997): 104.

Roxio. "Roxio to Acquire Assets of Napster." November 15, 2002. **roxio.com/en/company/news/archive/prelease021115.jhtml** (accessed January 2005).

Rupp, W. T., and N. J. Parrish. "Help! I've Been Cybersquatted On!" *Business Horizons*, March–April 2002.

Rykere, R., et al. "Online Privacy Policies: An Assessment." *Journal of Computer Information Systems*, Summer 2002.

Saliba, C. "Study: Auction Fraud Still Top Cybercrime." *E-Commerce Times*, January 10, 2001. **ecommercetimes.com/perl/story/6590.html** (accessed January 2005).

Sanguan, S. "Virtual Community Success: A Uses and Gratification Perspective." *Proceedings of the 38th HICSS Conference*, Big Island, Hawaii, January 3–6, 2005.

Schmidt, D. P. "Intellectual Property Battles in a Technological Global Economy: A Just War Analysis." *Business Ethics Quarterly* 14, no. 4 (2004).

Schubert, P., and M. Ginsburg. "Virtual Communities of Transaction: The Role of Personalization in E-Commerce." *Electronic Markets* 10, no. 1 (2000).

Schwerha, J. J., IV. "Cybercrime: Legal Standards Governing the Collection of Digital Evidence." *Information Systems Frontiers* 6, No. 2 (2004).

SEC. "SEC Charges 44 Stock Promoters in First Internet Securities Fraud Sweep." SEC news release, October 28, 1998. **sec.gov/news/headlines/netfraud.htm** (accessed January 2005).

Sharrard, J., et al. "Global Online Trading Will Climb to 18 Percent of Sales." Forrester Research, December 26, 2001. **forrester.com/er/research/brief/excerpt/0,1317,13720,00.html** (accessed January 2005).

Shop.org. "E-Business Trends." March 2005. **shop.org/learn/stats_ebizz_security.asp** (accessed April 2005).

Siau, K., et al. "Acceptable Internet Use Policy." *Communications of the ACM* 45, no. 1 (2002).

Silberman, S. "Just Say Nokia Wired." *Wired,* September 1999.

Sipior, J. C., et al. "A Community Initiative That Diminished the Digital Divide." *Communications of the Associations of Information Systems* 13, no. 5 (2004).

South China Morning Post (1999).

Spanger, T. "How to Beat Back the Digital Horde: Five Steps to Protecting Your Computers from Viruses, Spam, and Other e-Garbage. *Baseline*, February 2005.

Spaulding, M. "The ABC's of MP3: A Crash Course in the Digital Music Phenomenon." In *Signal or Noise? The Future of Music on the Net*. Berkman Center for Internet & Society at Harvard Law School and the Electronic Frontier Foundation, August 23, 2000. **cyber.law.harvard.edu/events/netmusic_brbook.html#_Toc475699191** (accessed January 2005).

Stauffer, T. *Blog On: Building Online Communities with Web Logs*. New York: McGraw-Hill 2002.

Stead, B. A., and J. Gilbert. "Ethical Issues in Electronic Commerce." *Journal of Business Ethics* no. 34 (November 2001).

Steinberg, D. "Privacy: Surveillance vs. Freedom." *Smart Business*, December 1, 2001.

Stocks-investing.com. "The SEC Is Tracking Internet Investment Fraud." **stocks-investing.com** (accessed March 2005).

Stone, B., and J. Lin. "Spamming the World." *Newsweek,* August 19, 2002.

Tedeschi, B. "More E-Commerce Sites Aim to Add 'Sticky' Content." *New York Times*, August 9, 2004.

Teodoro, B. "Internet Scams 101: How You Can Protect Yourself." *CNNFN*, June 6, 2001. **money.cnn.com/2001/06/06/news/q_scams/** (accessed January 2005).

TNS and TRUSTe. "Consumer Behaviors and Attitudes about Privacy." TNS-TRUSTe Consumer Privacy Index Q4, 2004.

TRUSTe. "TRUSTe 2002 Annual Report." TRUSTe, March 2003.

Turban, E., et al. *Information Technology for Management*, 5th ed. New York: John Wiley & Sons, 2006.

Tynan, D. "How to Take Back Your Privacy: Keep Spammers and Online Snoops at Bay." *PCWorld,* June 2002.

United Nations. "In Interconnected World All People Must Have Access to Internet Says Secretary-General, in World Telecommunication Day Message." UN press release, May 17, 2001.

UPI. "Hackers Go After DoubleClick." *The Washington Times*, July 28, 2004.

Urbaczewski, A., and L. M. Jessup. "Does Electronic Monitoring of Employee Internet Usage Work?" *Communications of the ACM*, January 2002.

Vigna, D. C., et al. "4-H Cyber Fair: Bridging the Digital Divide." *Journal of Family and Consumer Sciences* 95, no. 4 (2003).

Vijayasarathy, L. R. "Internet Taxation, Privacy and Security." *Quarterly Journal of Electronic Commerce*, March 2001.

Weiss, G. "Welcome to the (Almost) Digital Hospital." *IEEE*, March 2002.

Weiss, T. T. "Study: Global Software Piracy Losses Totaled $29B in 2003." *Computerworld,* July 7, 2004. **computerworld.com/softwaretopics/software/story/0,10801,94364,00.html** (accessed January 2005).

Williamson, R. "Changing Channels." *Interactive Week*, April 2, 2001.

WIPO. **wipo.org/about-ip/en/overview.html** (accessed January 2005).

Wresch, W. "Initial E-commerce Efforts in Nine Least Developed Countries: A Review of National Infrastructure, Business Approaches and Product Selection." *Journal of Global Information Management* 11, no. 2 (2003).

Zetlin, M., and B. Pfleging. "The Cult of Community." *Smart Business Magazine*, June 2002.

GLOSSARY

1G The first generation of wireless technology, which was analog based.

2G The second generation of digital wireless technology; accommodates voice and text.

2.5G An interim wireless technology that can accommodate voice, text, and limited graphics.

3G The third generation of digital wireless technology; supports rich media such as video.

4G The expected next generation of wireless technology that will provide faster display of multimedia.

802.11a This Wi-Fi standard is faster than 802.11b but has a smaller range.

802.11b The most popular Wi-Fi standard; it is inexpensive and offers sufficient speed for most devices. However, interference can be a problem.

802.11g This fast but expensive Wi-Fi standard is mostly used in businesses.

access control Mechanism that determines who can legitimately use a network resource.

active tokens Small, stand-alone electronic devices that generate one-time passwords used in a two-factor authentication system.

ad management Methodology and software that enable organizations to perform a variety of activities involved in Web advertising (e.g., tracking viewers, rotating ads).

ad views The number of times users call up a page that has a banner on it during a specific time period; known as *impressions* or *page views*.

Address Verification System (AVS) Detects fraud by comparing the address entered on a Web page with the address information on file with cardholder's issuing bank.

admediaries Third-party vendors that conduct promotions, especially large-scale ones.

advanced planning and scheduling (APS) systems Programs that use algorithms to identify optimal solutions to complex planning problems that are bound by constraints.

advertising networks Specialized firms that offer customized Web advertising, such as brokering ads and targeting ads to select groups of consumers.

advertorial An advertisement "disguised" to look like editorial content or general information.

affiliate marketing An arrangement whereby a marketing partner (a business, an organization, or even an individual) refers consumers to the selling company's Web site.

agency costs Costs incurred in ensuring that the agent performs tasks as expected (also called *administrative costs*).

agility An EC firm's ability to capture, report, and quickly respond to changes happening in the marketplace.

angel investor A wealthy individual who contributes personal funds and possibly expertise at the earliest stage of business development.

application service provider (ASP) An agent or vendor who assembles the functions needed by enterprises and packages them with outsourced development, operation, maintenance, and other services.

application-level proxy A firewall that permits requests for Web pages to move from the public Internet to the private network.

associated ad display (text links) An advertising strategy that displays a banner ad related to a term entered in a search engine.

attractors Web site features that attract and interact with visitors in the target stakeholder group.

auction A competitive process in which a seller solicits consecutive bids from buyers (forward auctions) or a buyer solicits bids from sellers (backward auctions). Prices are determined dynamically by the bids.

auction aggregators Companies that use software agents to visit Web auction sites, find information, and deliver it to users.

auction vortals Another name for a vertical auction portal.

auditing The process of collecting information about attempts to access particular resources, use particular privileges, or perform other security actions.

authentication The process by which one entity verifies that another entity is who he, she, or it claims to be.

authorization The process that ensures that a person has the right to access certain resources. With regards to credit or debit cards, the process of determining whether a buyer's card is active and whether the customer has sufficient funds.

Automated Clearing House (ACH) Network A nationwide batch-oriented electronic funds transfer system that provides for the interbank clearing of electronic payments for participating financial institutions.

automatic crash notification (ACN) Device that automatically sends the police the location of a vehicle that has been involved in a crash.

autoresponders Automated e-mail reply systems (text files returned via e-mail) that provide answers to commonly asked questions.

avatars Animated computer characters that exhibit human-like movements and behaviors.

average-cost curve (AVC) Behavior of average costs as quantity changes; generally, as quantity increases, average costs decline.

B2B portals Information portals for businesses.

back end The activities that support online order-taking. It includes fulfillment, inventory management, purchasing from suppliers, payment processing, packaging, and delivery.

back-office operations The activities that support fulfillment of sales, such as accounting and logistics.

balanced scorecard method Analysis of a variety of matrices (finance, internal operations, agility, customer opinions) for evaluating the overall health of an organization or for assessing organizational progress toward strategic goals.

bandwidth The speed at which content can be delivered across a network; it is rated in bits per second (bps).

banner On a Web page, a graphic advertising display linked to the advertiser's Web page.

banner exchanges Markets in which companies can trade or exchange placement of banner ads on each other's Web sites.

banner swapping An agreement between two companies to each display the other's banner ad on its Web site.

bartering The exchange of goods or services.

bartering exchange An intermediary that links parties in a barter; a company submits its surplus to the exchange and receives points of credit, which can be used to buy the items that the company needs from other exchange participants.

bastion gateway A special hardware server that utilizes application-level proxy software to limit the types of requests that can be passed to an organization's internal networks from the public Internet.

behavioral biometrics Measurements derived from various actions and indirectly from various body parts (e.g., voice scans or keystroke monitoring).

bid shielding Having phantom bidders bid at a very high price when an auction begins; they pull out at the last minute, and the bidder who bid a much lower price wins.

biometric systems Authentication systems that identify a person by measurement of a biological characteristic, such as fingerprints, iris (eye) patterns, facial features, or voice.

Blackberry A handheld device principally used for e-mail.

blog A personal Web site that is open to the public to read and to interact with; dedicated to specific topics or issues.

Bluetooth A set of telecommunications standards that enables wireless devices to communication with each other over short distances.

brick-and-mortar organizations Old-economy organizations (corporations) that perform most of their business off-line, selling physical products by means of physical agents.

brick-and-mortar retailers Retailers who do business in the non-Internet, physical world in traditional brick-and-mortar stores.

build-to-order (pull system) A manufacturing process that starts with an order (usually customized). Once the order is paid for, the vendor starts to fulfill it.

bullwhip effect Erratic shifts in orders up and down supply chains.

bundle trading The selling of several related products and/or services together.

business case A document that is used to justify the investment of internal, organizational resources in a new initiative or project inside an existing organization.

business model A method of doing business by which a company can generate revenue to sustain itself.

business plan A written document that identifies the company's goals and outlines how the company intends to achieve those goals and at what cost.

business process reengineering (BPR) A methodology for conducting a comprehensive redesign of an enterprise's processes.

business-to-business (B2B) E-commerce model in which all of the participants are businesses or other organizations.

business-to-business e-commerce (B2B EC) Transactions between businesses conducted electronically over the Internet, extranets, intranets, or private networks; also known as *eB2B* (*electronic B2B*) or just *B2B*.

business-to-business-to-consumer (B2B2C) E-commerce model in which a business provides some product or service to a client business that maintains its own customers.

business-to-consumer (B2C) E-commerce model in which businesses sell to individual shoppers.

business-to-employee (B2E) E-commerce model in which an organization delivers services, information, or products to its individual employees.

buy-side e-marketplace A corporate-based acquisition site that uses reverse auctions, negotiations, group purchasing, or any other e-procurement method.

card verification number (CVN) Detects fraud by comparing the verification number printed on the signature strip on the back of the credit or debit card with the information on file with the cardholder's issuing bank.

card-not-present (CNP) transaction A credit card transaction in which the merchant does not verify the customer's signature.

certificate authorities (CAs) Third parties that issue digital certificates.

channel conflict Situation in which an online marketing channel upsets the traditional channels due to real or perceived damage from competition.

chat group A portion of the Web site where visitors can communicate synchronously.

chatterbots Animation characters that can talk (chat).

ciphertext A plaintext message after it has been encrypted into a machine-readable form.

click (click-through or ad click) A count made each time a visitor clicks on an advertising banner to access the advertiser 's Web site.

click-and-mortar (click-and-brick) organizations Organizations that conduct some e-commerce activities, but do their primary business in the physical world.

click-and-mortar retailers Brick-and-mortar retailers that offer a transactional Web site from which to conduct business.

click-through rate (or ratio) The ratio between the number of clicks on a banner ad and the number of times it is seen by viewers; measures the success of a banner in attracting visitors to click on the ad.

clickstream behavior Customer movements on the Internet.

clickstream data Data that occur inside the Web environment; they provide a trail of the user's activities (the user's clickstream behavior) in the Web site.

codecs The compression algorithms that are used to encode audio and video streams; short for *compression and decompression*.

collaboration hub The central point of control for an e-market. A single c-hub, representing one e-market owner, can host multiple collaboration spaces (c-spaces) in which trading partners use c-enablers to exchange data with the c-hub.

collaborative commerce (c-commerce) E-commerce model in which individuals or groups communicate or collaborate online through the use of digital technologies that enable companies to collaboratively plan, design, develop, manage, and research products, services, and innovative EC applications.

collaborative filtering A personalization method that uses customer data to predict, based on formulas derived from behavioral sciences, what other products or services a customer may enjoy; predictions can be extended to other customers with similar profiles.

collaborative planning, forecasting, and replenishment (CPFR) Project in which suppliers and retailers collaborate in their planning and demand forecasting to optimize flow of materials along the supply chain.

collaborative portals Portals that enable collaboration.

collaborative Web site A site that allows business partners to collaborate.

co-location A Web server owned and maintained by the business is placed in the hands of a Web hosting service that manages the server's connection to the Internet.

commodity content Information that is widely available and generally free to access on the Web.

common (security) vulnerabilities and exposures (CVEs) Publicly known computer security risks, which are collected, listed, and shared by a board of security-related organizations (*cve.mitre.org*).

co-opetition Two or more companies cooperate together on some activities for their mutual benefit, even while competing against each other in the marketplace.

Common Electronic Purse Specification (CEPS) Standards governing the operation and interoperability of e-purse offerings.

Compact Hypertext Markup Language (cHTML) A scripting language used to create content in i-mode.

company-centric EC E-commerce that focuses on a single company's buying needs (many-to-one, or buy-side) or selling needs (one-to-many, or sell-side).

competitive forces model Model, devised by Porter, that says that five major forces of competition determine industry structure and how economic value is divided among the industry players in an industry; analysis of these forces helps companies develop their competitive strategy.

competitor analysis grid A strategic planning tool that highlights points of differentiation between competitors and the target firm.

complementary investments Additional investments, such as training, made to maximize the returns from EC investments.

Computer Emergency Response Team (CERT) Group of three teams at Carnegie Mellon University that monitor the incidence of cyber attacks, analyze vulnerabilities, and provide guidance on protecting against attacks.

Computer Security Institute (CSI) Nonprofit organization located in San Francisco, California, that is dedicated to serving and training information, computer, and network security professionals.

confidentiality Keeping private or sensitive information from being disclosed to unauthorized individuals, entities, or processes.

consortium trading exchange (CTE) An exchange formed and operated by a group of major companies to provide industrywide transaction services.

consumer-to-business (C2B) E-commerce model in which individuals use the Internet to sell products or services to organizations or individuals seek sellers to bid on products or services they need.

consumer-to-consumer (C2C) E-commerce model in which consumers sell directly to other consumers.

contact card A smart card containing a small gold plate on the face that when inserted in a smart card reader makes contact and passes data to and from the embedded microchip.

contactless (proximity) card A smart card with an embedded antenna, by means of which data and applications are passed to and from a card reader unit or other device without contact between the card and the card reader.

content The text, images, sound, and video that make up a Web page.

content management The process of adding, revising, and removing content from a Web site to keep content fresh, accurate, compelling, and credible.

contextual computing The enhancement of a user's interactions by understanding the user, the context, and the applications and information required.

conversion rate The percentage of site visitors who actually make a purchase.

cookie A data file that is placed on a user's hard drive by a Web server, frequently without disclosure or the user's consent, that collects information about the user's activities at a site.

copyright An exclusive grant from the government that allows the owner to reproduce a work, in whole or in part, and to distribute, perform, or display it to the public in any form or manner, including over the Internet.

corporate (enterprise) portal A major gateway through which employees, business partners, and the public can enter a corporate Web site.

cost-benefit analysis A comparison of the costs of a project against the benefits.

CPM (cost per thousand impressions) The fee an advertiser pays for each 1,000 times a page with a banner ad is shown.

cross-selling Offering similar or related products and services to increase sales.

customer interaction center (CIC) A comprehensive service entity in which EC vendors address customer-service issues communicated through various contact channels.

customer relationship management (CRM) A customer service approach that focuses on building long-term and sustainable customer relationships that add value both for the customer and the company.

customer-to-customer (C2C) E-commerce in which both the buyer and the seller are individuals, not businesses; involves activities such as auctions and classified ads.

customization Creation of a product or service according to the buyer's specifications.

cyberbashing The registration of a domain name that criticizes an organization or person.

cybermediation (electronic intermediation) The use of software (intelligent) agents to facilitate intermediation.

cybersquatting The practice of registering domain names in order to sell them later at a higher price.

cycle time reduction Shortening the time it takes for a business to complete a productive activity from its beginning to end.

dashboard A single view that provides the status of multiple metrics.

data conferencing Virtual meeting in which geographically dispersed groups work on documents together and exchange computer files during videoconferences.

Data Encryption Standard (DES) The standard symmetric encryption algorithm supported by the NIST and used by U.S. government agencies until October 2, 2000.

data warehouse A single, server-based data repository that allows centralized analysis, security, and control over the data.

deep linking Entry into a Web site via the site's interior pages, not the homepage, typically through search engines or external links.

demilitarized zone (DMZ) Network area that sits between an organization's internal network and an external network (Internet), providing physical isolation between the two networks that is controlled by rules enforced by a firewall.

denial-of-service (DoS) attack An attack on a Web site in which an attacker uses specialized software to send a flood of data packets to the target computer with the aim of overloading its resources.

desktop purchasing Direct purchasing from internal marketplaces without the approval of supervisors and without the intervention of a procurement department.

differentiation Providing a product or service that is unique.

digital certificate Verification that the holder of a public or private key is who he or she claims to be.

digital divide The gap between those who have and those who do not have the ability to access electronic technology in general, and the Internet and EC in particular.

digital economy An economy that is based on digital technologies, including digital communication networks, computers, software, and other related information technologies; also called the *Internet economy*, the *new economy*, or the *Web economy*.

digital envelope The combination of the encrypted original message and the digital signature, using the recipient's public key.

digital options A set of IT-enabled capabilities in the form of digitized enterprise work processes and knowledge systems.

digital products Goods that can be transformed to digital format and delivered over the Internet.

digital signature An identifying code that can be used to authenticate the identity of the sender of a document.

digital watermarks Unique identifiers embedded in digital content that make it possible to identify pirated works.

direct marketing Broadly, marketing that takes place without intermediaries between manufacturers and buyers; in the context of this book, marketing done online between any seller and buyer.

direct materials Materials used in the production of a product (e.g., steel in a car or paper in a book).

disintermediation The removal of organizations or business process layers responsible for certain intermediary steps in a given supply chain.

distance learning Formal education that takes place off campus, usually, but not always, through online resources.

distributed denial-of-service (DDoS) attack A denial-of-service attack in which the attacker gains illegal administrative access to as many computers on the Internet as possible and uses the multiple computers to send a flood of data packets to the target computer.

domain name The name used to reference particular computers on the Internet; the name is divided into segments separated by periods.

domain name registrar A business that assists prospective Web site owners with finding and registering the domain name of their choice.

dotted-quad addressing The format in which Internet addresses are written as four sets of numbers separated by periods.

double auction Auction in which multiple buyers and sellers may be making bids and offers simultaneously; buyers and their bidding prices and sellers and their asking prices are matched, considering the quantities on both sides.

dynamic pricing A rapid movement of prices over time, and possibly across customers, as a result of supply and demand.

dynamic trading Exchange trading that occurs in situations when prices are being determined by supply and demand (e.g., in auctions).

dynamic Web content Content that is updated infrequently.

e-bartering Bartering conducted online, usually by a bartering exchange.

e-book A book in digital form that can be read on a computer screen or on a special device.

e-business A broader definition of EC that includes not just the buying and selling of goods and services, but also servicing customers, collaborating with business partners, and conducting electronic transactions within an organization.

e-check A legally valid electronic version or representation of a paper check.

e-commerce (EC) risk The likelihood that a negative outcome will occur in the course of developing and operating an electronic commerce strategy.

e-commerce strategy (e-strategy) The formulation and execution of a vision of how a new or existing company intends to do business electronically.

e-co-ops Another name for online group purchasing organizations.

e-distributor An e-commerce intermediary that connects manufacturers (suppliers) with business buyers by aggregating the catalogs of many suppliers in one place—the intermediary's Web site.

e-government E-commerce model in which a government entity buys or provides goods, services, or information to businesses or individual citizens.

e-grocer A grocer that takes orders online and provides deliveries on a daily or other regular schedule or within a very short period of time.

e-learning The online delivery of information for purposes of education, training, or knowledge management.

e-logistics The logistics of EC systems, typically involving small parcels sent to many customers' homes (in B2C).

e-loyalty Customer loyalty to an e-tailer.

e-mail discussion list A group of people who share a common interest and who communicate with each other via e-mail messages managed by e-mail list software.

e-mall (online mall) An online shopping center where many online stores are located.

e-marketplace An online market, usually B2B, in which buyers and sellers exchange goods or services; the three types of e-marketplaces are private, public, and consortia.

e-micropayments Small online payments, typically under US$10.

e-newsletter A collection of short, informative articles sent at regular intervals by e-mail to individuals who have an interest in the newsletter's topic.

e-procurement The electronic acquisition of goods and services for organizations.

e-purse Smart card application that loads money from a card holder's bank account onto the smart card's chip.

e-sourcing The process and tools that electronically enable any activity in the sourcing process, such as quotation/tender submittance and response, e-auctions, online negotiations, and spending analyses.

e-supply chain A supply chain that is managed electronically, usually with Web technologies.

e-supply chain management (e-SCM) The collaborative use of technology to improve the operations of supply chain activities as well as the management of supply chains.

e-tailers Retailers who sell over the Internet.

e-tailing Online retailing, usually B2C.

e-zines Electronic magazine or newsletter delivered over the Internet via e-mail.

eCRM Customer relationship management conducted electronically.

edutainment The combination of education and entertainment, often through games.

elasticity The measure of the incremental spending by buyers as a result of the savings generated.

electronic auctions (e-auctions) Auctions conducted online.

electronic banking (e-banking) Various banking activities conducted from home or the road using an Internet connection; also known as *cyberbanking, virtual banking, online banking*, and *home banking*.

electronic bill presentment and payment (EBPP) Presenting and enabling payment of a bill online. Usually refers to a B2C transaction.

electronic catalogs The presentation of product information in an electronic form; the backbone of most e-selling sites.

electronic commerce (EC) The process of buying, selling, or exchanging products, services, or information via computer networks.

electronic data interchange (EDI) The electronic transfer of specially formatted standard business documents, such as bills, orders, and confirmations, sent between business partners.

electronic discussion (e-forum) A portion of the Web site where visitors can post questions, comments, and answers.

electronic market (e-marketplace) An online marketplace where buyers and sellers meet to exchange goods, services, money, or information.

Electronic Product Code (EPC) An RFID code that identifies the manufacturer, producer, version, and serial number of individual consumer products.

electronic retailing (e-tailing) Retailing conducted online, over the Internet.

electronic shopping cart An order-processing technology that allows customers to accumulate items they wish to buy while they continue to shop.

electronic voting Voting process that involves many steps ranging from registering, preparing, voting, and counting (voting and counting are all done electronically).

encryption The process of scrambling (encrypting) a message in such a way that it is difficult, expensive, or time-consuming for an unauthorized person to unscramble (decrypt) it.

encryption algorithm The mathematical formula used to encrypt the plaintext into the ciphertext, and vice versa.

Enhanced Messaging Service (EMS) An extension of SMS that can send simple animation, tiny pictures, sounds, and formatted text.

enterprise invoice presentment and payment (EIPP) Presenting and paying B2B invoices online.

ethics The branch of philosophy that deals with what is considered to be right and wrong.

exchanges (electronic) Many-to-many e-marketplaces, usually owned and run by a third party or a consortium, in which many buyers and many sellers meet electronically to trade with each other; also called *trading communities,* or *trading exchanges.*

exchange-to-exchange (E2E) E-commerce model in which electronic exchanges formally connect to one another for the purpose of exchanging information.

expert location systems Interactive computerized systems that help employees find and connect with colleagues who have expertise required for specific problems—whether they are across the country or across the room—in order to solve specific, critical business problems in seconds.

Extensible Hypertext Markup Language (xHTML) A general scripting language; compatible with HTML; set by W3 Consortium.

Extensible Markup Language (XML) Standard (and its variants) used to improve compatibility between the disparate systems of business partners by defining the meaning of data in business documents.

external Web site development When the business hires another firm to build and/or maintain the Web site.

extranet A network that uses a virtual private network (VPN) to link intranets in different locations over the Internet; an "extended intranet."

FAQ page A Web page that lists questions that are frequently asked by customers and the answers to those questions.

fingerprint scanning Measurement of the discontinuities of a person's fingerprint, which are then converted to a set of numbers that are stored as a template and used to authenticate identity.

firewall A network node consisting of both hardware and software that isolates a private network from a public network.

forward auction An auction in which a seller offers a product to many potential buyers.

frame An HTML element that divides the browser window into two or more separate windows.

front end The portion of an e-seller's business processes through which customers interact, including the seller's portal, electronic catalogs, a shopping cart, a search engine, and a payment gateway.

front-office operations The business processes, such as sales and advertising, that are visible to customers.

geographical information system (GIS) An information system that integrates GPS data onto digitized map displays.

global positioning system (GPS) A worldwide satellite-based tracking system that enables users to determine their position anywhere on the earth.

Global System for Mobile Communications (GSM) An open, nonproprietary standard for mobile voice and data communications.

government-to-business (G2B) E-government category that includes interactions between governments and businesses (government selling to businesses and providing them with services and businesses selling products and services to government).

government-to-citizens (G2C) E-government category that includes all the interactions between a government and its citizens.

government-to-employees (G2E) E-government category that includes activities and services between government units and their employees.

government-to-government (G2G) E-government category that includes activities within government units and those between governments.

grid computing A form of distributed computing that involves coordinating and sharing computing, application, data, storage, or network resources across dynamic and geographically dispersed organizations.

group decision support system (GDSS) An interactive computer-based system that facilitates the solution of semistructured and unstructured problems by a group of decision makers.

group purchasing Quantity purchasing that enables groups of purchasers to obtain a discount price on the products purchased.

groupware Software products that use networks to support collaboration among groups of people who share a common task or goal.

hash A mathematical computation that is applied to a message, using a private key, to encrypt the message.

hit A request for data from a Web page or file.

honeynet A way to evaluate vulnerabilities of an organization by studying the types of attacks to which a site is subjected using a network of systems called *honeypots.*

honeypots Production systems (e.g., firewalls, routers, Web servers, database servers) designed to do real work but that are watched and studied as network intrusions occur.

horizontal exchange An exchange that handles materials used by companies in different industries.

horizontal marketplaces Markets that concentrate on a service, materials, or a product that is used in all types of industries (e.g., office supplies, PCs).

hotspot An area or point where a wireless laptop or PDA can make a connection to a wireless local area network.

hypermediation Extensive use of both human and electronic intermediation to provide assistance in all phases of an e-commerce venture.

hypertext transport protocol (HTTP) A lightweight communication protocol that enables Web browsers and Web servers to converse with one another; of its seven commands, GET and POST make up the majority of requests issued by browsers.

identity theft A criminal act in which someone presents himself (herself) as another person and uses that person's social security number, bank account numbers, and so on, to obtain loans, purchase items, make obligations, sell stocks, etc.

incubator A company, university, or nonprofit organization that supports businesses in their initial stages of development.

indirect materials Materials used to support production (e.g., office supplies or light bulbs).

infomediaries Electronic intermediaries that control information flow in cyberspace, often aggregating information and selling it to others.

information architecture How the site and its Web pages are organized, labeled, and navigated to support browsing and searching throughout the Web site.

information economics An approach similar to the concept of critical success factors in that it focuses on key organizational objectives, including intangible financial benefits, impacts on the business domain, and impacts on IT itself.

information intelligence Information, data, knowledge, and semantic infrastructure that enable organizations to create more business applications.

information portal A single point of access through a Web browser to business information inside and/or outside an organization.

informational Web site A Web site that does little more than provide information about the business and its products and services.

integrity As applied to data, the ability to protect data from being altered or destroyed in an unauthorized or accidental manner.

intellectual property Creations of the mind, such as inventions, literary and artistic works, and symbols, names, images, and designs, used in commerce.

interactive marketing Online marketing, enabled by the Internet, in which advertisers can interact directly with customers and consumers can interact with advertisers/vendors.

interactive voice response (IVR) A computer voice system that enables users to request and receive information and to enter and change data through a telephone.

interactive Web site A Web site that provides opportunities for the customers and the business to communicate and share information.

intermediary A third party that operates between sellers and buyers.

internal procurement marketplace The aggregated catalogs of all approved suppliers combined into a single *internal* electronic catalog.

internal Web site development The process of building and/or maintaining the Web site with company staff.

Internet A public, global communications network that provides direct connectivity to anyone over a LAN via an ISP or directly via an ISP.

Internet Corporation for Assigned Names and Numbers (ICANN) Nonprofit organization that manages various technical and policy issues relating to the Internet that require central coordination; it has no regulatory or statutory power.

Internet ecosystem The business model of the Internet economy.

Internet radio A Web site that provides music, talk, and other entertainment, both live and stored, from a variety of radio stations.

Internet service providers (ISPs) Companies that provide Internet delivery subnetworks at the local and regional level.

Internet2 The next generation of the Internet; it will create a network for the national research community, enable revolutionary Internet applications, and ensure the rapid transfer of new network services and applications to the broader Internet community.

Internet-based (Web) EDI EDI that runs on the Internet and is widely accessible to most companies, including SMEs.

interorganizational information systems (IOSs) Communications system that allows routine transaction processing and information flow between two or more organizations.

interstitial An initial Web page or a portion of it that is used to capture the user's attention for a short time while other content is loading.

intrabusiness EC E-commerce category that includes all internal organizational activities that involve the exchange of goods, services, or information among various units and individuals in an organization.

intranet A corporate LAN or WAN that uses Internet technology and is secured behind a company's firewalls.

intraorganizational information systems Communication systems that enable e-commerce activities to go on *within* individual organizations.

intrusion detection systems (IDSs) A special category of software that can monitor activity across a network or on a host computer, watch for suspicious activity, and take automated action based on what it sees.

IP version 4 (IPv4) The current version of Internet Protocol, under which Internet addresses are 32 bits long and written as four sets of numbers separated by periods.

IP version 6 (IPv6) Version of the Internet Protocol, still in the planning stage, that will replace IPv4 and improve network management.

iris scanning Measurement of the unique spots in the iris (colored part of the eye), which are then converted to a set of numbers that are stored as a template and used to authenticate identity.

ISP hosting service A hosting service that provides an independent, stand-alone Web site for small and medium-sized businesses.

key The secret code used to encrypt and decrypt a message.

key performance indicators (KPI) The quantitative expression of critically important metrics.

keystroke monitoring Measurement of the pressure, speed, and rhythm with which a word is typed, which is then converted to a set of numbers that are stored as a template and used to authenticate identity; this biometric is still under development.

keyword banners Banner ads that appear when a predetermined word is queried from a search engine.

knowledge management (KM) The process of capturing or creating knowledge, storing it, updating it constantly, interpreting it, and using it whenever necessary.

knowledge portal A single point of access software system intended to provide timely access to information and to support communities of knowledge workers.

learning agents Software agents that have the capacity to adapt or modify their behavior (to learn).

letter of credit (LC) A written agreement by a bank to pay the seller, on account of the buyer, a sum of money upon presentation of certain documents.

localization The process of converting media products developed in one environment (e.g., country) to a form culturally and linguistically acceptable in countries outside the original target market.

location-based commerce (l-commerce) M-commerce transactions targeted to individuals in specific locations, at specific times.

lock-in effect Effect created when users do not switch to another site because of barriers posed by having to learn new site navigation systems and transaction processes.

logistics The operations involved in the efficient and effective flow and storage of goods, services, and related information from point of origin to point of consumption.

look and feel The elements, including layout, typeface, colors, graphics, and navigation aids, that visually distinguish a site from any other.

m-business The broadest definition of m-commerce, in which e-business is conducted in a wireless environment.

m-wallet (mobile wallet) Technologies that enable cardholders to make purchases with a single click from their wireless device.

macro virus or macro worm A virus or worm that is executed when the application object that contains the macro is opened or a particular procedure is executed.

malware A generic term for malicious software.

management by maxim A five-step process that brings together corporate executives, business-unit managers, and IT executives in planning sessions to determine appropriate infrastructure investments.

market liquidity The degree to which something can be bought or sold in a marketplace without affecting its price. It is measured by the number of buyers and sellers in the market and the transaction volume.

market maker The third-party that operates an exchange (and in many cases, also owns the exchange).

market segmentation The process of dividing a consumer market into logical groups for conducting marketing research, advertising, and sales.

marketspace A marketplace in which sellers and buyers exchange goods and services for money (or for other goods and services), but do so electronically.

mass customization Production of large quantities of customized items.

maverick buying Unplanned purchases of items needed quickly, often at non-pre-negotiated higher prices.

merchant brokering Deciding from whom (from what merchant) to buy a product.

merge-in-transit Logistics model in which components for a product may come from two different physical locations and are shipped directly to customer's location.

message digest A summary of a message, converted into a string of digits, after the hash has been applied.

meta tag An HTML element that describes the contents of a Web page.

metric A specific, measurable standard against which actual performance is compared; may be quantitative or qualitative.

metric benchmark A method that provides numeric measures of performance.

microbrowser Wireless Web browser designed to operate with small screens and limited bandwidth and memory requirements.

micropayments Electronic payments for small-purchase amounts (generally less than US$10).

mirror site An exact duplicate of an original Web site that is physically located on a Web server on another continent.

mobile agents Software agents that can transport themselves across different system architectures and platforms in order to perform their tasks.

mobile commerce (m-commerce) E-commerce conducted via wireless devices.

mobile computing Permits real-time access to information, applications, and tools that, until recently, were accessible only from a desktop computer.

mobile CRM The delivery of CRM applications to any user, whenever and wherever needed. This is done by use of the wireless infrastructure and/or mobile and wearable devices.

mobile portal A customer interaction channel that aggregates content and services for mobile users that is accessible via a mobile device, especially cell phones and PDAs.

mobility The degree to which the agents themselves travel through the network.

MRO (maintenance, repair, and operation) Indirect materials used in activities that support production.

multiagent systems Computer systems in which there is no single designer who stands behind all the agents; each agent in the system can be working toward different, even contradictory, goals.

multichannel business model A business model where a company sells in multiple marketing channels simultaneously (e.g., both physical and online stores).

Multimedia Messaging Service (MMS) The next generation of wireless messaging; MMS will be able to deliver rich media.

name-your-own-price model Auction model in which a would-be buyer specifies the price (and other terms) he or she is willing to pay to any willing and able seller. It is a C2B model that was pioneered by Priceline.com.

National Cyber Security Division (NCSD) A division of the Department of Homeland Security charged with implementing U.S. cyberspace security strategy.

National Infrastructure Protection Center (NIPC) A joint partnership under the auspices of the FBI between governmental and private industry; designed to prevent and protect the nation's infrastructure.

Netizen A citizen surfing the Internet.

network access point (NAP) An intermediate network exchange point that connects ISPs to NSPs.

network effects Effects created when leading products in an industry attract a base of users, which leads to the development of complementary products, further strengthening the position of the dominant product.

network service providers (NSPs) Major telecommunication companies, such as MCI and Sprint, that maintain and service the Internet's high-speed backbones.

Next Generation Internet (NGI) Consortium initiated and sponsored by the U.S. government to link government research agencies, universities, and national labs over high-speed networks, promote experimentation with the next generation of networking technologies, and demonstrate new public policy applications requiring high-speed networks.

Next Generation Internet Protocol (IPng) Protocol that, when implemented, will improve upon IPv4's scalability, security, ease of configuration, and network management.

nonrepudiation The ability to limit parties from refuting that a legitimate transaction took place, usually by means of a signature.

nontechnical attack An attack that uses chicanery to trick people into revealing sensitive information or performing actions that compromise the security of a network.

on-demand delivery service Express delivery made fairly quickly after an online order is received.

one-to-one marketing Marketing that treats each customer in a unique way.

online intermediary An online third party that brokers a transaction online between a buyer and a seller; may be virtual or click-and-mortar.

online negotiation A back-and-forth electronic process of bargaining until the buyer and seller reach a mutually agreeable price; usually done by software (intelligent) agents.

online publishing The electronic delivery of newspapers, magazines, books, news, music, videos, and other digitizable information over the Internet.

ontology A type of hierarchical thesaurus in which each subheading inherits all the characteristics of the headings above it.

Open Profiling Standard (OPS) Standard that provides Internet site developers with a uniform architecture for using Personal Profile information to match personal preferences with tailored content, goods, and services while protecting users' privacy.

opt-in clause Agreement that requires computer users to take specific steps to *allow* the collection of personal information.

opt-out clause Agreement that requires computer users to take specific steps to *prevent* the collection of personal information.

order fulfillment All of the activities needed to provide customers with ordered goods and services, including related customer services.

organizational knowledge base The repository for an enterprise's accumulated knowledge.

outsourcing The use of an external vendor to provide all or part of the products and services that could be provided internally.

P2P distributed computation Computer architecture that uses P2P resource sharing to combine idle computer resources over a network, forming a *virtual computer* across which large computational jobs can be distributed.

packet filters Rules that can accept or reject incoming packets based on source and destination addresses and the other identifying information.

packet-filtering routers Firewalls that filter data and requests moving from the public Internet to a private network based on the network addresses of the computer sending or receiving the request.

packets Segments of data and requests sent from one computer to another on the Internet; consist of the Internet addresses of the computers sending and receiving the data, plus other identifying information that distinguish one packet from another.

partner relationship management (PRM) Business strategy that focuses on providing comprehensive quality service to business partners.

partnering Web site development When a mixture of internal and external development is used to build and/or maintain a Web site.

passive tokens Storage devices (e.g., magnetic strips) that contain a secret code used in a two-factor authentication system.

patent A document that grants the holder exclusive rights to an invention for a fixed number of years.

payment card Electronic card that contains information that can be used for payment purposes.

payment service provider (PSP) A third-party service connecting a merchant's EC systems to the appropriate acquirers. PSPs must be registered with the various card associations they support.

peer-to-peer (P2P) A network architecture in which workstations (or PCs) share data and processing with each other directly rather than through a central server; can be used in C2C, B2B, and B2C e-commerce.

performance-based government An approach that measures the results of government programs.

permission advertising (permission marketing) Advertising (marketing) strategy in which customers agree to accept advertising and marketing materials.

personal area network A wireless telecommunications network for device-to-device connections within a small range.

personal digital assistant (PDA) A handheld computer principally used for personal information management.

personal firewall A network node designed to protect an individual user's desktop system from the public network by monitoring all the traffic that passes through the computer's network interface card.

personalization The ability to tailor a product, service, or Web content to specific user preferences.

personalized content Web content that is prepared to match the needs and expectations of the individual visitor.

pervasive computing Invisible, everywhere computing that is embedded in the objects around us.

phishing attack A high-tech scam that uses e-mail, pop-up messages, or Web pages to trick a user into disclosing sensitive information such as credit card numbers, bank account numbers, and passwords.

physiological biometrics Measurements derived directly from different parts of the body (e.g., fingerprint, iris, hand, facial characteristics).

plaintext An unencrypted message in human-readable form.

policy of least privilege (POLP) Policy of blocking access to network resources unless access is required to conduct business.

pop-under ad An ad that appears underneath the current browser window, so when the user closes the active window, he or she sees the ad.

pop-up ad An ad that appears in a separate window before, after, or during Internet surfing or when reading e-mail.

premium content Content not available elsewhere on the Web.

privacy The right to be left alone and the right to be free of unreasonable personal intrusions.

private e-marketplaces Online markets owned by a single company; may be either sell-side or buy-side e-marketplaces. Also known as *company-centric marketplaces.*

private key Encryption code that is known only to its owner.

procurement management The coordination of all the activities relating to purchasing goods and services needed to accomplish the mission of an organization.

product brokering Deciding what product to buy.

product differentiation Exploiting EC to provide products with special features to add greater value to customers.

product lifecycle management (PLM) Business strategy that enables manufacturers to control and share product-related data as part of product design and development efforts.

production function An equation indicating that for the same quantity of production, *Q*, companies either can use a certain amount of labor or invest in more automation.

project champion The person who ensures the EC project gets the time, attention, and resources required and defends the project from detractors at all times.

protocol A set of rules that determine how two computers communicate with one another over a network.

protocol tunneling Method used to ensure confidentiality and integrity of data transmitted over the Internet, by encrypting data packets, sending them in packets across the Internet, and decrypting them at the destination address.

proxies Special software programs that run on the gateway server and pass repackaged packets from one network to the other.

proxy bidding Use of a software system to place bids on behalf of buyers; when another bidder places a bid, the software (the proxy) will automatically raise the bid to the next level until it reaches the predetermined maximum price.

public e-marketplaces (public exchanges) B2B marketplaces, usually owned and/or managed by an independent third party, that include many sellers and many buyers; also known as *exchanges.*

public key Encryption code that is publicly available to anyone.

public key encryption Method of encryption that uses a pair of matched keys—a public key to encrypt a message and a private key to decrypt it, or vice versa.

public key infrastructure (PKI) A scheme for securing e-payments using public key encryption and various technical components.

purchasing cards (p-cards) Special-purpose payment cards issued to a company's employees to be used solely for purchasing nonstrategic materials and services up to a preset dollar limit.

radio frequency identification (RFID) Technology that uses radio waves to identify items.

random banners Banner ads that appear at random, not as the result of the user's action.

Real-Time Protocol (RTP) Streaming protocol that adds header information to the UDP packets, thus enabling the synchronized timing, sequencing, and decoding of the packets at the destination.

Real-Time Streaming Protocol (RTSP) Streaming protocol that adds controls for stopping, pausing, rewinding, and fast-forwarding the media stream; it also provides security and enables usage measurement and rights management.

recommendation systems Intelligent agents that provide recommendation services.

reintermediation Establishment of new intermediary roles for traditional intermediaries that have been disintermediated.

request for quote (RFQ) The "invitation" to participate in a tendering (bidding) system.

resident agents Software agents that stay in the computer or system and perform their tasks there.

return on investment (ROI) A ratio of required costs and perceived benefits of a project or an application.

revenue model Description of how the company or an EC project will earn revenue.

reverse auction (bidding or tendering system) Auction in which the buyer places an item for bid (*tender*) on a request for quote (RFQ) system, potential suppliers bid on the job, with the price reducing sequentially, and the lowest bid wins; primarily a B2B or G2B mechanism.

reverse logistics The movement of returns from customers to vendors.

Rijndael The new Advanced Encryption Standard used to secure U.S. government communications since October 2, 2000.

ROI calculator Calculator that uses metrics and formulas to compute return-on-investment (ROI).

rolling warehouse Logistics method in which products on the delivery truck are not preassigned to a destination, but the decision about the quantity to unload at each destination is made at the time of unloading.

rootkit A special Trojan horse program that modifies existing operating system software so that an intruder can hide the presence of the Trojan program.

routers Special computers that determine the paths traversed by data packets across the Internet.

RSA The most common public key encryption algorithm; uses keys ranging in length from 512 bits to 1,024 bits.

sales force automation (SFA) Software that automates the tasks performed by sales people in the field, such as data collection and its transmission.

sales force mobilization The process of equipping sales force employees with wireless computing devices.

scenario planning A strategic planning methodology that generates plausible alternative futures to help decision makers identify actions that can be taken today to ensure success in the future.

scoring methodology A method that evaluates alternatives by assigning weights and scores to various aspects and then calculating the weighted totals.

screen sharing Software that enables group members, even in different locations, to work on the same document, which is shown on the PC screen of each participant.

sealed-bid auction Auction in which each bidder bids only once; a silent auction, in which bidders do not know who is placing bids or what the prices are.

search engine A computer program that can access a database of Internet resources, search for specific information or keywords, and report the results.

search engine optimization (SEO) The application of strategies intended to position a Web site at the top of Web search engines.

Secure Socket Layer (SSL) Protocol that utilizes standard certificates for authentication and data encryption to ensure privacy or confidentiality.

security risk management A systematic process for determining the likelihood of various security attacks and for identifying the actions needed to prevent or mitigate those attacks.

self-hosting When a business acquires the hardware, software, staff, and dedicated telecommunications services necessary to set up and manage its own Web site.

sell-side e-marketplace A Web-based marketplace in which one company sells to many business buyers from e-catalogs or auctions, frequently over an extranet.

sensor network A series of interconnected sensors that monitor the environment in which they are placed.

settlement Transferring money from the buyer's to the merchant's account.

shilling Placing fake bids on auction items to artificially jack up the bidding price.

shopping portals Gateways to e-storefronts and e-malls; may be comprehensive or niche oriented.

shopping robots (shopping agents or shopbots) Tools that scout the Web on behalf of consumers who specify search criteria.

Short Message Service (SMS) A service that supports the sending and receiving of short text messages on mobile phones.

signature file A simple text message an e-mail program automatically adds to outgoing messages.

simple agents Software agents that work within the context of a single application and focus on a single set of tasks with a circumscribed set of outcomes.

single auction Auction in which at least one side of the market consists of a single entity (a single buyer or a single seller).

site navigation Aids that help visitors find the information they need quickly and easily.

smart card An electronic card containing an embedded microchip that enables predefined operations or the addition, deletion, or manipulation of information on the card.

smart card operating system Special system that handles file management, security, input/output (I/O), and command execution and provides an application programming interface (API) for a smart card.

smart card reader Activates and reads the contents of the chip on a smart card, usually passing the information on to a host system.

smartphone Internet-enabled cell phones that can support mobile applications.

SMEs Small to medium enterprises.

sniping Entering a bid during the very last seconds of an auction and outbidding the highest bidder (in the case of selling items).

social computing An approach aimed at making the human–computer interface more natural.

social engineering A type of nontechnical attack that uses social pressures to trick computer users into compromising computer networks to which those individuals have access.

software (intelligent) agents Software agents that continuously perform three functions: they perceive of dynamic conditions in the environment, they take action to affect conditions in the environment, and they use reasoning to interpret perceptions, solve problems, draw inferences, and determine actions.

spamming Using e-mail to send unwanted ads (sometimes floods of ads).

spot buying The purchase of goods and services as they are needed, usually at prevailing market prices.

spyware Software that gathers user information over an Internet connection without the user's knowledge.

stickiness Characteristic that influences the average length of time a visitor stays in a site.

storebuilder service A hosting service that provides disk space and services to help small and micro businesses build a Web site quickly and cheaply.

stored-value card A card that has monetary value loaded onto it and that is usually rechargeable.

storefront A single company's Web site where products or services are sold.

strategic sourcing Purchases involving long-term contracts that usually are based on private negotiations between sellers and buyers.

strategy A broad-based formula for how a business is going to compete, what its goals should be, and what plans and policies will be needed to carry out those goals.

strategy assessment The continuous evaluation of progress toward the organization's strategic goals, resulting in corrective action and, if necessary, strategy reformulation.

strategy formulation The development of strategies to exploit opportunities and manage threats in the business environment in light of corporate strengths and weaknesses.

strategy implementation The development of detailed, short-term plans for carrying out the projects agreed on in strategy formulation.

strategy initiation The initial phase of strategic planning in which the organization examines itself and its environment.

streaming The delivery of content in real time; consists of two types, *on demand* (HTTP streaming) and *live* (true streaming).

subscriber identification module (SIM) card An extractable storage card used for identification, customer location information, transaction processing, secure communications, and the like.

supplier relationship management (SRM) A comprehensive approach to managing an enterprise's interactions with the organizations that supply the goods and services it uses.

supply chain The flow of materials, information, money, and services from raw material suppliers through factories and warehouses to the end customers.

SWOT analysis A methodology that surveys external opportunities and threats and relates them to internal strengths and weaknesses.

symmetric (private) key system An encryption system that uses the same key to encrypt and decrypt the message.

synchronization The exchange of updated information with other computing devices.

syndication The sale of the same good (e.g., digital content) to many customers, who then integrate it with other offerings and resell it or give it away free.

technical attack An attack perpetrated using software and systems knowledge or expertise.

teleconferencing The use of electronic communication that allows two or more people at different locations to have a simultaneous conference.

telematics The integration of computers and wireless communications to improve information flow using the principles of telemetry.

telewebs Call centers that combine Web channels with portal-like self-service.

tendering (reverse auction) Model in which a buyer requests would-be sellers to submit bids; the lowest bidder wins.

third-party logistics (3PL) suppliers External, rather than in-house, providers of logistics services.

total benefits of ownership (TBO) Benefits of ownership that include both tangible and the intangible benefits.

total cost of ownership (TCO) A formula for calculating the cost of owning, operating, and controlling an IT system.

trademark A symbol used by businesses to identify their goods and services; government registration of the trademark confers exclusive legal right to its use.

transaction costs Costs that are associated with the distribution (sale) and/or exchange of products and services including the cost of searching for buyers and sellers, gathering information, negotiating, decision making, monitoring the exchange of goods, and legal fees.

transaction log A record of user activities at a company's Web site.

transactional Web site A Web site that sells products and services.

Transmission Control Protocol/Internet Protocol (TCP/IP) Two combined protocols that together solve the problem of global internetworking by ensuring that two computers can communicate with each other reliably; each TCP communication must be acknowledged as received or the sending computer will retransmit the message.

Transport Layer Security (TLS) As of 1996, another name for the SSL protocol.

Trojan horse A program that appears to have a useful function but that contains a hidden function that presents a security risk.

trust The psychological status of involved parties who are willing to pursue further interaction to achieve a planned goal.

Uniform Resource Locator (URL) The addressing scheme used to locate documents on the Web.

unique visit A count of the number of visitors to a site, regardless of how many pages are viewed per visit.

unsolicited commercial e-mail (UCE) The use of e-mail to send unwanted ads or correspondence.

up-selling Offering an upgraded version of the product in order to boost sales and profit.

User Datagram Protocol (UDP) Transport protocol used in place of TCP by streaming servers.

user profile The requirements, preferences, behaviors, and demographic traits of a particular customer.

utility computing Computing resources that flow like electricity on demand from virtual utilities around the globe—always on and highly available, secure, efficiently metered, priced on a pay-as-you-use basis, dynamically scaled, self-healing, and easy to manage.

valuation The fair market value of a business or the price at which a property would change hands between a willing buyer and a willing seller who are both informed and under no compulsion to act. For a publicly traded company, the value can be readily obtained by the price the stock is selling over the exchange.

value analysis Method where a company evaluates intangible benefits using a low-cost, trial EC system before deciding whether to commit a larger investment to a complete system.

value proposition The benefit that a company's products or services provide to customers; the consumer need that is being fulfilled. Also, the benefits a company can derive from using EC.

value-added networks (VANs) Private, third-party-managed networks that add communications services and security to existing common carriers; used to implement traditional EDI systems.

vendor managed inventory The practice of retailers making suppliers responsible for determining when to order and how much to order.

venture capital (VC) Money invested in a business by an individual or a group of individuals (venture capitalists) in exchange for equity in the business.

versioning Selling the same good, but with different selection and delivery characteristics.

vertical auction Auction that takes place between sellers and buyers in one industry or for one commodity.

vertical exchange An exchange whose members are in one industry or industry segment.

vertical marketplaces Markets that deal with one industry or industry segment (e.g., steel, chemicals).

Vickrey auction An auction in which the highest bidder wins but pays only the second-highest bid.

video teleconference Virtual meeting in which participants in one location can see participants at other locations on a large screen or a desktop computer.

viral marketing Word-of-mouth marketing in which customers promote a product or service to friends or other people.

virtual (Internet) community A group of people with similar interests who interact with one another using the Internet.

virtual corporation (VC) An organization composed of several business partners sharing costs and resources for the production or utilization of a product or service.

virtual credit card An e-payment system in which a credit card issuer gives a special transaction number that can be used online in place of regular credit card numbers.

virtual (pure-play) e-tailers Firms that sell directly to consumers over the Internet without maintaining a physical sales channel.

virtual meetings Online meetings whose members are in different locations, even in different countries.

virtual private network (VPN) A network that uses the public Internet to carry information but remains private by using encryption to scramble the communications, authentication to ensure that information has not been tampered with, and access control to verify the identity of anyone using the network.

virtual (pure-play) organizations Organizations that conduct their business activities solely online.

virtual reality (VR) System that delivers interactive computer-generated 3D graphics to a user through a head-mounted display.

virtual university An online university from which students take classes from home or other off-site locations, usually via the Internet.

virus A piece of software code that inserts itself into a host, including the operating systems, in order to propagate; it requires that its host program be run to activate it.

visit A series of requests during one navigation of a Web site; a pause of a certain length of time ends a visit.

voice portal A Web site with an audio interface that can be accessed through a telephone call.

voice scanning Measurement of the acoustical patterns in speech production, which are then converted to a set of numbers that are stored as a template and used to authenticate identity.

voice XML (VXML) An extension of XML designed to accommodate voice.

Voice-over-IP Communication systems that transmit voice calls over Internet Protocol–based networks.

vortals B2B portals that focus on a single industry or industry segment; "vertical portals."

warehouse management system (WMS) A software system that helps in managing warehouses.

wearable devices Mobile wireless computing devices for employees who work on buildings and other climbable workplaces.

Web analytics The analysis of clickstream data to understand visitor behavior on a Web site.

Web bugs Tiny graphics files embedded on e-mail messages and in Web sites that transmit information about the user and their movements to a Web server.

Web hosting service A dedicated Web site hosting company that offers a wide range of hosting services and functionality to businesses of all sizes.

Web self-service Activities conducted by users on the Web to find answers to their questions (e.g., tracking) or for product configuration.

Web Services An architecture enabling assembly of distributed applications from software services and tying them together.

Web site construction The initial content creation, design, programming, and installation phases of a Web site's development.

Web site maintenance The ongoing process of keeping the Web site open for business, managing content, fixing problems, and making incremental additions to the site.

Webcasting A free Internet news service that broadcasts personalized news and information, including seminars, in categories selected by the user.

Webinars Seminars on the Web (Web-based seminars).

Weblogging (blogging) Technology for personal publishing on the Internet.

Wi-Fi (wireless fidelity) The common name used to describe the IEEE 802.11 standard used on most WLANs.

wikiLog (wikiblog) A blog that allows everyone to participate as a peer; anyone may add, delete, or change content.

WiMax A wireless standard (IEEE 802.16) for making broadband network connections over a large area.

wireless 911 (e-911) In the United States, emergency response calls from cellular phones.

wireless access point An antenna that connects a mobile device to a wired LAN.

Wireless Application Protocol (WAP) A suite of network protocols designed to enable different kinds of wireless devices to access WAP-readable files on an Internet-connected Web server.

wireless local area network (WLAN) A telecommunications network that enables users to make medium-range wireless connections to the Internet or another network.

Wireless Markup Language (WML) A scripting language used to create content in the WAP environment; based on XML, minus unnecessary content to increase speed.

wireless metropolitan area network (WMAN) A telecommunications network that enables users to make long-range wireless connections to the Internet or another network.

wireless mobile computing (mobile computing) Computing that connects a mobile device to a network or another computing device, anytime, anywhere.

wireless wide area network (WWAN) A telecommunications network that offers wireless coverage over a large geographical area, typically over a cellular phone network.

workflow The movement of information as it flows through the sequence of steps that make up an organization's work procedures.

workflow management The automation of workflows, so that documents, information, and tasks are passed from one participant to the next in the steps of an organization's business process.

workflow systems Business process automation tools that place system controls in the hands of user departments to automate information-processing tasks.

worm A software program that runs independently, consuming the resources of its host in order to maintain itself, that is capable of propagating a complete working version of itself onto another machine.

Index

A

B

C

D

E

F

G

H

I

J

K

L

M

N

O

P

Q

R

S

T

U

V

W

X

Y

Z